THE EARTH TRANSFORMED

The Silk Roads: A New History of the World
The New Silk Roads: The Present and Future of the World
The First Crusade: The Call From the East

THE EARTH TRANSFORMED

An Untold History

PETER FRANKOPAN

BLOOMSBURY PUBLISHING
LONDON · OXFORD · NEW YORK · NEW DELHI · SYDNEY

BLOOMSBURY PUBLISHING
Bloomsbury Publishing Plc
50 Bedford Square, London, WC1B 3DP, UK
29 Earlsfort Terrace, Dublin 2, Ireland

BLOOMSBURY, BLOOMSBURY PUBLISHING and the Diana logo are trademarks of
Bloomsbury Publishing Plc

First published in Great Britain 2023

A catalogue record for this book is available from the British Library

ISBN: HB: 978-1-5266-2256-3; TPB: 978-1-5266-2257-0; EBOOK: 978-1-5266-2258-7

2 4 6 8 10 9 7 5 3 1

Maps and charts created by Mike Athanson
Plate section designed by Phil Beresford
Typeset by Newgen KnowledgeWorks Pvt. Ltd., Chennai, India
Printed and bound in Great Britain by CPI Group (UK) Ltd, Croydon CR0 4YY

To find out more about our authors and books visit www.bloomsbury.com
and sign up for our newsletters

To Jessica

When God created the first human, He took him and led him round all the trees of the Garden of Eden and said to him … 'Pay attention that you do not corrupt and destroy My world; if you corrupt it, there is no one to repair it after you.'

Midrash Ecclesiastes Rabbah, 7:13

The drought is so excessive,
And we are tormented by the heat.
I have not stopped offering sacrifices …
To the powers above and below I have made sacrifices and buried offerings.
There are no spirits I have not honoured.

King Xuan of Zhou (r. 827–782 BC), 'Yunhan' (雲漢)
from Shijing (詩經, Classic of Poetry)

[God] has raised the heavens and set up everything in balance,
Therefore do not transgress the balance that has been established.

Qur'ān, 55:7–8

A change in our climate … is taking place … Both heats and colds are become much more moderate.

Thomas Jefferson, Notes on the State of Virginia (1785)

The poorest nations, already beset by man-made disasters, have been threatened by a natural one: the possibility of climatic changes.

Henry Kissinger, Address to the Sixth Special Session of
the United Nations General Assembly (April 1974)

I've seen it, I've read some of it … I don't believe it.

Donald Trump, 45th President of the
United States of America, on the
US National Climate Assessment 2018

Contents

Note on Transliteration

Historians can tie themselves in knots trying to work out the best way to transliterate names of peoples, places and individuals. I have tried to use my judgement as best I can to make the text readable and, in doing so, to recognise that some readers may on occasion prefer a more faithful rendition, most notably when transliterating non-European languages. Nevertheless, I ask for forbearance from the reader who demands consistency. In return, I hope to inform, enlighten and help provide new perspectives on how we might look at the world we live in.

Maps

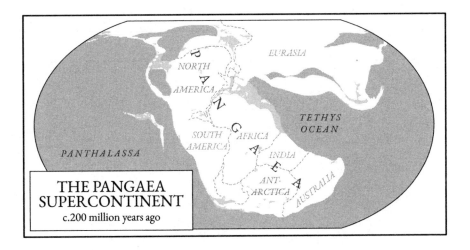

**THE PANGAEA
SUPERCONTINENT**
c.200 million years ago

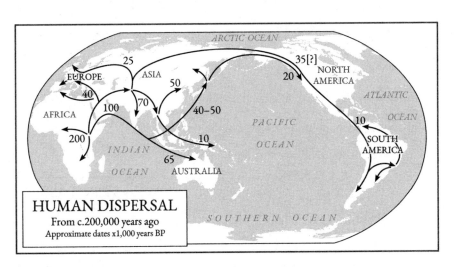

HUMAN DISPERSAL
From c.200,000 years ago
Approximate dates x1,000 years BP

EASTERN ASIA
Civilisations and settlements

0   500   1,000 km

LAOHUSHAN–DAKOU

GOBI DESERT

QIJIA

Shimao

Xinzhai Kaifeng

SHAN-TUNG

QINLING MTS

ERLITOU

Taxila

TIBETAN PLATEAU

Yufucun

Harappa

Judeirjo-daro Banawali

Mohenjo-daro

Chanhu-daro

Dholavira

Surkotada

HIMALAYAS

Ganges

Brahmaputra

Narmada

Indus

Mekong

Yangtze

Yellow

BAODUN

LIANGZHU

Hattusa

Çatalhöyük

Çayönu

Euphrates

Uffa Göbekli Tepe

Tell Halula

Emar

Ebla

Tell Leilan

Dur-Šarrukin

Qermez Dere

Nineveh

Assur

M E S O P O T A M I A

Z A G R O S   M T S

Ectabana

Palmyra

Mari

Caspian Sea

Mediterranean Sea

Tyre

Jericho 'Ain Ghazal

Jerusalem

Tall el-Hammam

SYRIAN DESERT

Sippar

Babylon

Akkad(?)

Nippur

Uruk

Lagash

Ur

Susa

Giza

Memphis

'Ain Jammam

AN-NAFUD

The Gulf

Nile

Naqada

Thebes

Nekhen

E G Y P T

Red Sea

NUBIA

KUSH

WESTERN ASIA
Civilisations and settlements

0   250   500 km

WEST AFRICA

Civilisations and settlements

0   250   500 km

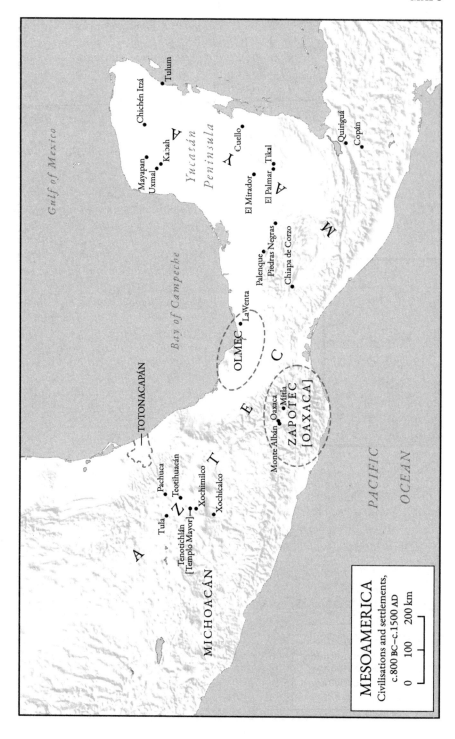

Gulf of Mexico

Tulum

Chichén Itzá

Yucatán Peninsula

Kazah
Mayapan
Uxmal

Cuello

El Mirador
El Palmar Tikal

Quiriguá
Copán

M

Palenque
Piedras Negras
Chiapa de Corzo

Bay of Campeche

La Venta
OLMEC

C

E

TOTONACAPÁN

ZAPOTEC
[OAXACA]
Monte Albán Oaxaca
Mitla

T

Pachuca
Teotihuacán
Tula
Xochimilco
Xochicalco

Z

Tenotichlán
[Templo Mayor]

A

PACIFIC

OCEAN

MICHOACÁN

MESOAMERICA
Civilisations and settlements,
c.800 BC–c.1500 AD

0   100   200 km

Loma Negra
Chacapoyas
Sipán
San Jose de Moro
Farfán
Cajamarca
El Brujo
Huanchaquito-Las Llamas
Chen Chen
Huacas del Sol y la Luna
Pañamarca
Manchan
Caral

0   100   200 km

Palmitopamba

Chacapoyas
Farfán
Cajamarca
Chen Chen
Manchan
Caral
SEE INSET

Hatun Xauxa
Pachacamac
Huari
Ollantaytambo
Cuzco
Jincamocco
Cahuachi
Nasca

PACIFIC

OCEAN

Cerro Baúl
Moquegua
Tiwanaku
Cochabamba

TIWANAKU

Potosí

THE ANDES
Civilisations and settlements,
Antiquity–c.1500 AD

0   100 200   300 km

GOBI DESERT

YOUZHOU

Liadong

Sogyong
[Pyongyang]

Songdu

Taiyuan

XIHAI

SONG DYNASTY (c.1100)

•Lanzhou

•Yan'an

•Jinan

*Yellow
Sea*

Yellow

•Kaifeng

•Chang'an

C H I N A

•Yangzhou

•Xiangfan

Chang Jiang

•Suzhou

•Chengdu

Yangzi

•Ya'an

•Hangzhou

*East
China
Sea*

•Dali

•Tanzhou

•Nanchang

•Ganzhou

•Fuzhou

•Quanzhou

•Guangzhou

Lancang

Đai La

DAI VIET

*Philippine
Sea*

Vien Chan [Vientiane]

SUKHOTHAI

•Sukhothai

•Kamphaeng Phet

AYUT-

Mekong

Indrapura

*South
China
Sea*

U
Thong

•Ayutthaya

•Champassak

Vijaya

THAYA

•Angkor

•Vat Nokor

Phnom Penh

—PANDURANGAL

Chaiya

Maha
Rosei

*Gulf
of
Thailand*

—KADARAM

S R I V I J A Y A

A N N A M

C H A M P A

K H M E R

Panai

THE RISE OF SOUTH
AND SOUTH-EAST
ASIAN EMPIRES, c.1000 AD

0   250   500 km

1. Thanjavur
2. Nagapattinam
3. Gaṅgaikoṇḍa Chōlapuram

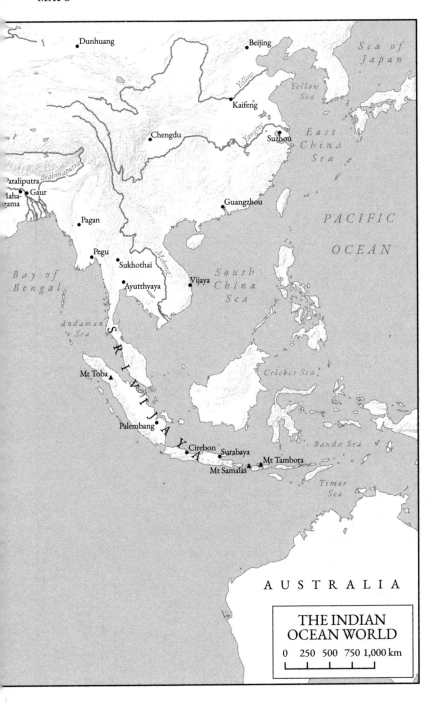

THE INDIAN
OCEAN WORLD

0   250   500   750 1,000 km

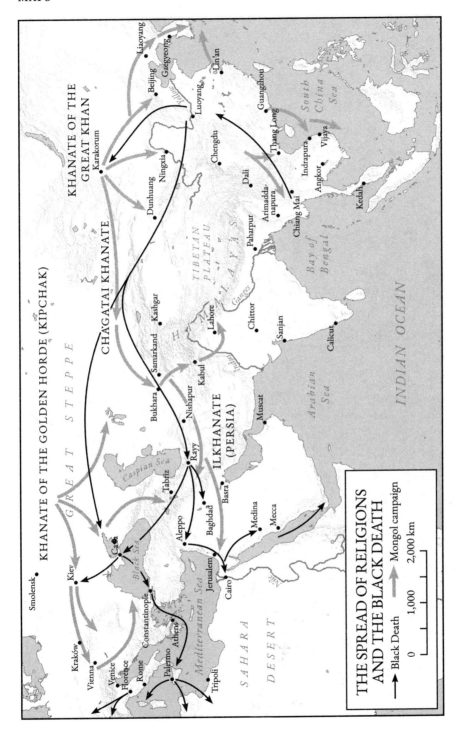

THE SPREAD OF RELIGIONS
AND THE BLACK DEATH

→ Black Death
➜ Mongol campaign

0   1,000   2,000 km

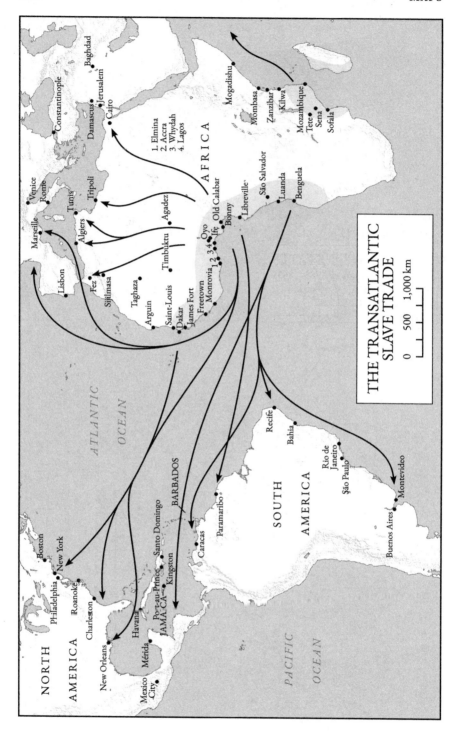

THE TRANSATLANTIC
SLAVE TRADE

0   500   1,000 km

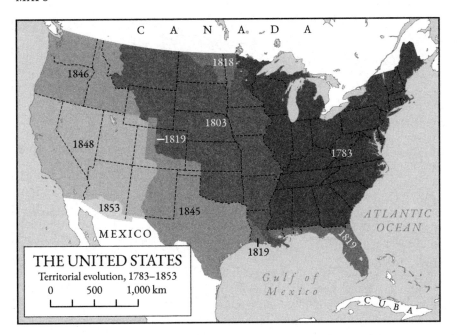

THE UNITED STATES
Territorial evolution, 1783–1853
0   500   1,000 km

Introduction

Three things exercise a constant influence over the minds of men: climate, government and religion.

Voltaire, *Essai sur les mœurs et l'esprit des nations* (1756)

'Man's first disobedience', wrote John Milton at the start of *Paradise Lost*, was to eat the fruit 'of that forbidden tree' in the Garden of Eden. The decision 'brought death into the World, and all our woe'. The loss of paradise turned the earth from a place of beauty and plenty into one of sorrow and sadness, where 'peace and rest can never dwell, hope never come' and where life was turned into 'torture without end'.[1]

Milton's epic poem, first published in the second half of the seventeenth century, was a retelling of the story that appears at the start of the Book of Genesis explaining how humans came to be the architects of their own demise. By allowing themselves to be tempted by the 'infernal Serpent', Adam and Eve condemned all future generations to lives of ecological challenge, ones where the environment was no longer always benign, where food was not always easy to come by and where humans had to work, rather than receive benefits from God. Paradise had been lost.

In today's world, the ways that our species works the land, exploits natural resources and treats sustainability are topics of vehement discussion – not least since many believe human activities to be so extensive and so damaging that they are changing the climate. This book sets out to look at how our planet, our enclosed garden (the literal meaning of the word 'paradise'), has changed since the beginning of time, sometimes as a result of human endeavours, calculation and miscalculation, but also thanks to a host of other actors, factors, influences and impulses that have shaped the world we live in – often in ways we do not think about or understand. This book will explain how our world has always been one of transformation, transition and change because, outside the Garden of Eden, time does not stand still.

My first encounter with the human impact on the environment and climate change came with a children's current affairs programme called *John Craven's Newsround* which was shown every day in the UK when I was a young boy. *Newsround* was a flagship BBC project that was a lifeline, connecting younger viewers to the world beyond the British Isles. One of the few programmes my parents allowed my siblings and me to watch when we were growing up, it introduced me to the suffering of people at the hands of the Khmer Rouge, to the complexities of the Middle East and to the realities of the Cold War.

One of the themes that came up regularly in the late 1970s and early 1980s was the subject of acid rain. I remember being transfixed by the horror of trees without leaves and by the thought that human activity was responsible for the degradation of nature. The idea that the factories belched emissions that devastated forests, killed animals and contaminated the ground came as a shock to me. Even as a young boy, it seemed obvious that the choices we made to produce goods and products had impacts that had long-term effects on us all.

These misgivings were compounded by a fear of devastation that was a hallmark of my childhood. I am part of a generation that was brought up to believe that the world might see global nuclear war between the United States and the Soviet Union that would result in large-scale death not only from the detonation of countless intercontinental ballistic missiles (ICBMs) but from the nuclear winter that would result from mushroom clouds released by warheads on impact. One film, *When the Wind Blows*, which came out in the mid-1980s, painted a poignant and awful picture of what lay ahead: sadness, suffering, hunger and death – all because of humanity's ability to invent weapons of mass destruction that would not only kill millions through firestorms and explosions, but would change the earth's climate so drastically that survival alone would be a miracle.

The detonation of scores of nuclear weapons promised to throw so much debris into the atmosphere that we would have to learn to live in sub-zero temperatures. Sunlight would be blocked by blankets of dust and particles with the result that plants would die. Animals would succumb as a result too – leaving those who survived the blasts not only freezing cold but hungry. Fallout from radiation would contaminate flora and fauna, poisoning all forms of life. The aim was to get through the apocalypse and to hope to be one of the survivors. In due course, we hoped, the climate would reset. Then it would be a case of seeing how many people were left alive and where, and starting again.

The fears of my generation were swelled by disaster, the most dramatic of which was the explosion in 1986 of the reactor at Chernobyl in what is now Ukraine. The reports of the catastrophic failure – strenuously denied for days by the Soviet authorities – were a reminder that miscalculations, misjudgements and incompetence could affect the world we lived in. In the months that followed, I studied maps of the fallout, was careful about what I ate and became acutely aware of the dangers posed by the potential for climatic change.

We used to spend our summers by a lake in the middle of Sweden. We said that we would flee there if there was ever a chance of a nuclear war breaking out. As most people know, Sweden is not the warmest country in the winter as it is; but I was reassured by the idea that being out of the way of soldiers, tanks and missiles would be a benefit. I was also comforted by the knowledge that blueberries (still my favourite fruit) were resilient to the cold. So I had a little bag packed by the side of my bed that I would update each year with my necessities for when (not if) changes to the world's climate would demand adaptation: a bar of chocolate; a Swiss Army penknife so I could make bows and arrows; some woollen gloves; a deck of cards and three balls; two pens (in case one ran out of ink); and some paper.

As it happened, my preparations were never needed – although it turns out that this was often because of luck rather than skill. As we now know, missile launches almost took place because of bears breaking down wire fences in search of food; because of misunderstandings about military exercises that made one side believe an attack was imminent; and because of weather balloons being misidentified as ballistic weapons systems. I grew up in a world of close shaves, near disasters and human error.

To be sure, there were many other things that scared me growing up: the 1970s and 1980s were a time of injustice, hatred, instability, terrorism, famine and genocide. But ecological devastation, climate and climate change were constantly in the background as current problems that would get worse in the future. Few things were certain for my generation. One thing was clear: we were all but guaranteed to live on a planet that was more hostile, more unstable and more dangerous than the one we had grown up in. I assumed that that would be because of the catastrophe of global war or large-scale accidents.

It did not cross my mind that the end of the Cold War would lead to an age of ecologies being placed under ever greater stress, or that increased global economic co-operation would result in massive rises in levels of carbon emissions and a warming world. I was brought up to believe that disaster stemmed from the horrors of war; after all, that was what I was taught in the classroom. Peace and harmony, on the other hand, were supposed to be the solution – not part of the problem. And so, a journey that began many years ago watching *Newsround* has led me to think about human interventions in the landscape, about how the climate might have changed in the past, and above all about the role that climate has played in shaping the history of the world.

We live in a world teetering on the brink of disaster because of climate change. 'Every week brings new climate-related devastation,' said António Guterres, Secretary General of the United Nations in 2019. 'Floods. Drought. Heat waves. Wildfires. Superstorms.' This was no apocalyptic prediction, he said, for 'climate disruption is happening now, and it is happening to all of us'. As to what the future has in store, he went on, there is little hope. Lying in wait is nothing less than 'catastrophe for life as we know it'.[2]

There are many problems facing humanity, said Barack Obama in his penultimate address as President of the United States of America; 'and no challenge – no challenge – poses a greater threat to future generations than climate change'.[3] 'Today's ecological crisis, especially climate change,' said Pope Francis in 2019, 'threatens the very future of the human family.' The situation looks bleak. 'Future generations stand to inherit a greatly spoiled world,' he added. 'Our children and grandchildren should not have to pay the cost of our generation's irresponsibility.'[4]

Agreements reached by governments to deal with carbon emissions and global warming represent 'the minimum steps to be taken to protect the Earth, our shared homeland', noted President Xi of the People's Republic of China in 2020. 'Humankind can no longer afford to ignore the repeated warnings of nature.' It is vital, therefore, to 'launch a green revolution and move faster to create a green way of development and life, preserve the environment and make Mother Earth a better place for all'.[5]

Others have put the threat personally as well as forcefully. 'You have stolen my dreams and my childhood with your empty words. And yet I'm one of the lucky ones,' said Greta Thunberg at the UN Climate Action Summit in September 2019. 'People are suffering. People are dying. Entire ecosystems are collapsing. We are in the beginning of a mass extinction, and all you can talk about is money and fairy tales of eternal economic growth. How dare you!'[6]

If climate change is going to be – or already is – the theme that will dominate the twenty-first century, sparking water shortages, famines, large-scale migrations, military conflict and mass extinction, then understanding what the future holds should be essential not just for politicians, scientists and activists, but for everyone. As a historian, I know that the best way to address complex problems is to look back in time, as this helps provide context and perspective for current and future challenges. And history can also teach valuable lessons that help formulate questions and sometimes even answers relating to some of the big issues that lie ahead of us.

This is particularly true when it comes to the relationship between human activities, the environment and the natural world in the regions and places that I have spent decades researching. In many if not all, availability and use of water, the expansion of food production and the geographic challenges and opportunities of local as well as long-distance trade are not just important factors but fundamental elements that underpin the broad sweep of history. As Fernand Braudel put it, the study of the past does not just involve the competition between humans and nature; it *is* the competition between humans and nature.[7]

When I first studied the Sasanian and 'Abbāsid empires, I quickly learned that the success and stability of the state were closely linked to the irrigation of fields that enabled a rise in agricultural yields and supported larger populations.[8] Looking at the histories of China led me to research which argues that the rises, falls and replacement of imperial dynasties stretching back more than a millennium are closely correlated with changes in temperature, with colder phases serving as periods of demographic decline, conflict and the replacement of imperial rulers with new regimes.[9]

Likewise, reading poetry such as *Meghadūtam* ('The Cloud Messenger') by the famous fifth-century Sanskrit poet Kālidāsa made clear how the monsoons and the rains, as well as the seasons, play a fundamental role in the literature, culture and histories of South Asia.[10] I learned long ago too that in the more recent past, Soviet policy in Central Asia in the 1950s was not only environmentally disastrous but had a significant impact on the Cold War and plays a role in the use of coerced labour in the region today.[11] I also know from experience how pollution in places I visit regularly is acrid, damaging and dangerous – with cities like New Delhi, Bishkek and Lahore ranked among the worst in the world for air quality. In Tashkent, the capital of Uzbekistan, the air was classified as dangerous 80 per cent of the time in the course of 2020.[12]

So I have set out to examine environmental history and to understand more clearly what the past tells us about human behaviour, about anthropogenic change in the natural world and about how extreme weather events, long-term weather patterns and climatic change have influenced and impacted history. I have wanted to assess why we seem to have arrived at the edge of a precipice where the future of our species – as well as those of a significant part of the animal and plant worlds – is at risk. Rather as a doctor should have full knowledge of an illness before trying to devise a cure, so too is investigating the causes of the current problems essential if we are to suggest a way to deal with the crises now confronting us all.

Historians are living in something of a golden age thanks to a rash of new evidence and new types of materials that help improve understanding of the past. Machine learning, computer models and data analysis are not just providing new lenses to look at other periods in history but revealing a plethora of information that was unknown and unseen. For example, networks of villages in the Amazon rainforest dating back many centuries and which were set out to mirror the cosmos have been identified thanks to Light Detection and Ranging (LIDAR) technology.[13] Advances in cost-effective laboratory visible-near infrared/shortwave infrared spectroscopy data have enabled groundbreaking work to reach conclusions about the social change in the Mapungubwe landscape at the confluence of the Shashi and Limpopo rivers during the twelfth century.[14] Isotope data from human burials and from pig teeth in what is now Papua New Guinea help shed light not only on settlement patterns but on proportions of marine foods that people were eating more than 2,000 years ago.[15] And new technology has helped identify the mineralisation process of seeds preserved in refuse pits and cesspits in ʿAbbāsid-era Jerusalem, providing support for hypotheses about the westward diffusion of crops in the early Islamic period.[16]

Some of the most exciting advances have come in the way we understand the climate. These include inventive ways of using written sources that have been ignored or poorly utilised in the past. For example, clam shells from the coast of Peru enable climate reconstructions through changes in the chemistry of shells that allow researchers to identify yearly, monthly and even weekly ocean temperatures.[17] Records of cherry blossom festivals in Japan that go back to the start of the ninth century and note the date of the flowering of cherry trees help establish when spring arrived each year over the course of many centuries.[18] Registers kept by the harbour authorities in Tallinn in Estonia covering the last 500 years show the arrivals of the first ships each year, and consequently not only reveal when the sea became ice-free, but indicate patterns in longer and warmer springs.[19] Driftwood from the Svalbard archipelago in the Arctic shows considerable variability of sea ice between 1600 and 1850 which in turn points to unusual climatic patterns in this period.[20]

Above all, new and exciting 'climate archives' are being added to all the time. Many will feature in this book. We will consider information from growth rings in trees from the Altai mountains in Central Asia and from the build-up of mineral deposits from caves in Spain that show changes in temperature and rainfall; we will look at air bubbles trapped in ice cores in Greenland and in glaciers in the European Alps that provide evidence of volcanic eruptions as well as of human activities such as metallurgy and the burning of crops, forests or fossil fuels; we will encounter fossilised pollen from Oman and pollen deposits in lake valves in Anatolia that provide insights into changes of vegetation, both through natural causes and because of human intervention; we will come across carbonised and desiccated seeds in South-East Asia, dried nutshells from northern Australia and digested and partly digested foods from Palestine that provide evidence of diets as well as disease. We will look at climate conditions conducive to the spread of parasitic pathogens in the Americas and at evidence for crop cycles in West Africa – as well as at phylogenetic trees of plague in Ethiopia, Kyrgyzstan and Cambridgeshire.

Many new sources of climate data are becoming available that allow us better to understand the natural world deep into the past. For example, a team of researchers are working on an eighty-metre-deep sedimentary layer in south-east Kazakhstan that provides a record of soil moisture – as well as offering insights into the role that Central Asia plays in global climate evolution in general and into the land–atmosphere–ocean water cycle in the northern hemisphere in particular. This is of considerable significance not only for studies of the past but also for future long-term global climate analysis.[21] So too is new research on the Tibetan plateau, where modelling based on findings from high, treeless areas – which are home to far more species than mountain forests – suggests a major decrease in plant diversity in alpine habitats in the coming centuries.[22]

Such new sources of evidence have led to revolutionary new ideas being developed about the past. New climate data provides insights into a tumultuous period in the middle of the third century in the Roman empire, with some scholars seeking to link reduced levels of solar activity, increases of sea ice and several major volcanic eruptions with rapid cooling, disrupted food production and a series of political, military and monetary crises precisely in this period.[23] Data about the persecution of Jews in Europe drawn from almost a thousand cities between 1100 and 1800 shows that a decrease in the average growing-season temperature of about one-third of 1 degree Celsius is correlated with a rise in the probability of Jews being attacked in the subsequent five-year period – with those living in and near locations with poor soil quality and weaker institutions more likely still to be the victims of violence during times of food shortages and higher prices.[24]

And a comparison of cold temperatures and wheat prices in Europe has led to new models being proposed about which cities were more resilient than others to price shocks; this has in turn spurred hypotheses that cooler weather in England in the early modern period led to agricultural revolution, which in turn prompted and rewarded the development of new technologies that led to an energy transition and ultimately gave rise to an age of European global empires.[25]

Not surprisingly, eye-catching arguments like these are a matter of lively discussion and sometimes heated debate among historians, with particular concerns voiced about historical and environmental determinism and about the problems of distinguishing between correlation and causation.[26] There are other challenges of interpretation. A case in point comes from the Indian subcontinent, a region that is ecologically and culturally diverse and home to a wide array of 'settled villages, hunter-gatherers, swidden cultivators, nomadic pastoralists and fisherfolk', as well as possessing astonishing species diversity and great climatic and ecological variety; as such, some scholars argue not only that are there dangers in making generalisations about the subcontinent as a whole, but that comparisons with other parts of the world are simply not appropriate.[27]

Another related issue is that those who write about climate and its impact often focus heavily on societal collapse, usually with a narrow band of signature examples – most notably the Maya, Easter Island and the 'fall' of the Roman empire – which have all been attributed to climate change in recent bestselling books.[28] Apart from the problems of oversimplifying complex narratives into narrow explanations (which authors are sometimes at pains to note), some believe that the urge to impart lessons – about the exhaustion of natural resources, about the failures to adapt to changing environmental conditions and to the consequences of not living sustainably – is a case of the tail wagging the dog, which is to say viewing the past through the prism of contemporary concerns.[29]

Much depends therefore on lightness of touch when dealing with new kinds of materials – just as good history requires sound judgement when dealing with written sources and with material culture. The problem then is not that climate science, data or new approaches are themselves flawed or misleading; rather they need to be handled carefully and put in contexts that are balanced, persuasive and appropriate.[30]

By and large, the weather, climate and environmental factors have rarely been seen as a backdrop to human history, let alone as an important lens through which to view the past. There are a handful of cases where climate features prominently, though usually not always plausibly. The famous story of King Xerxes ordering the waters of the Hellespont to be given 300 lashes after a storm brought down bridges that slowed his invasion of Greece in 480 BC would seem to be an apocryphal tale told to highlight the illogical rage of a barbaric, tyrannical ruler rather than a reliable statement of fact.[31]

That two attacks ordered by Kublai Khan, the grandson of the great Činggis (or Genghis) Khan, on Japan in the late thirteenth century were thwarted by 'divine winds' or 'kamikaze', sent by the gods to frustrate the invaders, says more about how these events came to be seen in Japanese history than about the reason for the failure of Yuan dynasty which controlled most of what is now China to conquer Japan.[32] Most celebrated of all, though, is the onset of a hard Russian winter, which in popular imagination played a decisive role both in derailing Napoleon's ill-fated attack on Moscow in 1812 and in grinding German forces to a standstill and then to disaster after Hitler's attack on the Soviet Union in 1941. Both popular tropes obscure the fact that overambitious objectives, inefficient supply lines, poor strategic decisions and worse execution of plans on the ground were what doomed both invasions as much as, if not more than, the snow.[33]

In the main, though, we ignore climate and long-run climate patterns or changes altogether when we look at history. Most people can name the great leaders and major battles in the past, but few can name the biggest storms, the most significant floods, the worst winters, the most severe droughts, or the ways that these influenced harvest failures, provoked political pressures or were catalysts in the spread of disease. Reintegrating human and natural history is not just a worthwhile exercise; it is fundamentally important if we are to understand the world around us properly.[34]

Assessing the role of weather, extreme events, long-run climate patterns and changes in climate requires a detailed understanding of how the global climate system and subsystems are connected. The earth's climate is shaped by several closely related factors. First is the global weather system, which is constantly modulating because of changing atmospheric conditions, ocean currents and ice-sheet behaviour, as well as because of geological and plate tectonics and oscillations in the flow of liquid iron in earth's outer core. The tilt of the planet's axis, the mild eccentricity of the earth's orbit around the sun and the uneven distribution of energy between the equator and the poles also affect weather and climate patterns – as do the interactions between all these factors.[35]

The main source of seasonal climate anomalies is the El Niño–Southern Oscillation (ENSO), which describes the relationship between the atmospheric and oceanic conditions in the equatorial Pacific, including the direction and strength of trade winds, surface water temperature and air pressure. The ENSO cycle of alternating warm El Niño and cold La Niña events is the dominant year-to-year climate signal on earth.[36] It affects volumes of rainfall in South America, but also affects conditions in South Asia, East Africa and Australia – although the Indian monsoon can also be influenced by episodic climatic shifts in the North Atlantic.[37]

Other subsystems also play a significant role in temperature and climate conditions and variations spanning years or even decades. For example, the North Atlantic Oscillation (NAO), which describes the balance of sea-level pressure between the Azores and Iceland, creates periods of cyclonic and anti-cyclonic patterns which affect western Europe. It also plays a role in dictating winter precipitation in the Mediterranean and Black Sea, as well as driving cold air from Siberia and polar regions into central and western Europe.[38] Antarctica and Greenland produce meltwater that increases subsurface ocean warming – although recent research indicates that the impact on the Southern Ocean is much more significant for global temperature and sea level than the impact on the Arctic.[39]

Solar activity has an important function in global climatic conditions of orbitally induced changes because of the variability in the behaviour of the sun, and in particular because of its magnetic activities. The most prominent of these are sunspots and aurora which follow cycles typically lasting eleven years.[40] Solar activity is also modulated by long-term variations which result in more active and more settled patterns, known as grand maxima and grand minima.[41] The most recent example of the latter is known as the Maunder Minimum, which took place between around 1645 and 1715 when sunspot activity was extremely rare.[42]

Volcanic activity is also an important factor in forcing alterations in climate. In 1991, for example, a major eruption of Mount Pinatubo in the Philippines injected twenty megatons of sulphur dioxide into the atmosphere which was then oxidised to form stratospheric particles of sulphate aerosols; these then propagated, increasing the opacity of the stratosphere. Among the startling results was a reduction of direct sunlight by 21 per cent and a reduction in insulation that led to an averaged global temperature cooling of about 0.5 °C.[43]

These figures mask important regional patterns. While the North Atlantic dipped to 5 °C cooler than average, the following winter in Siberia, Scandinavia and central North America was significantly warmer than normal; the year after the eruption saw extensive flooding in the south of the United States and significant water shortages and droughts in sub-Saharan Africa, South and South-East Asia as well as many parts of central and southern Europe. Nevertheless, taken as a whole, the impact was dramatic. The reduction of shortwave solar radiation resulted in a globally averaged sea surface temperature reduction of 0.4 °C – or around one hundred times the total annual worldwide energy consumption.[44]

Volcanic eruptions bring other wide-ranging consequences for the natural world. These include producing phytoplankton blooms through the input of lava into the ocean and localised warming up of deep waters that rise to supply the sunlit layer with nutrients.[45] As we shall see, eruptions can lead to sharp reductions in agricultural production which in turn can result in economic, social and political disruption. We shall also look at the impact that eruptions have by changing habitats for disease-carrying species, or by being catalysts for different enzootic cycles for pathogens or by opening up what one scholar has called 'epidemic highways'.[46]

One crucial element in volcanic eruptions is that their timing can matter as much as their magnitude and scale. New research using supercomputers and thousands of simulations has shown that eruptions that take place during the summer produce a much higher impact on global climate than those that occur during the winter and spring.[47] The locations of large-scale eruptions are also important, with models now showing that volcanoes outside tropical regions have produced stronger hemispheric cooling than tropical volcanoes over the last thirteen centuries.[48] Studies of volcanoes and volcanic areas have also shown a substantial increase in recent years of CO_2 flux, with emissions of degassing volcanoes far greater than those produced by relatively short-lived eruptions.[49]

There are other phenomena where the climate has a significant impact on the natural world. Heavy rains on the Indo-Gangetic Plain to the north of the Indian subcontinent can increase stress loads on the earth's crust, leading to a decrease in micro-seismicity (or minor tremors) in the adjacent Himalaya region.[50] Evidence linking strong typhoons in east Taiwan with seismic activity beneath the island suggests not only that weather conditions may trigger geological responses but that they might do so in small, modest and regular ways that prevent single, large and devastating earthquakes.[51]

Climate and temperature shape biodiversity too: the number of species decreases drastically from the equator to the poles – with some estimating that tropical forests contain more than half the species of flora and land-based fauna on earth. However, it now emerges that while tropical forests are astonishing in the range of animals and plant that they host, this is the result of gradual changes over extended periods of time; in fact, new species form faster in cold, dry, unstable and extreme environments.[52]

Historians have long noted that solar activity, long-term weather cycles and the impact of volcanic activity seem to form patterns that span decades and even centuries. Some of these periods have been given names to encapsulate a sense of uniformity, mainly based on the behaviour of the sun and the resultant impact on the complex global climate subsystems. The Roman Optimum (c.100 BC–AD c.200) and the Medieval Climate Anomaly (c.900– c.1250) are two such examples, purportedly times of favourable, warmer-than-average but above all stable conditions, while the Little Ice Age (c.1550–c.1800) was a time of distinctly cooler temperatures, lower solar irradiance and global crisis.[53]

That, at least, is the theory. One of the challenges posed by climate science is that new evidence from other areas and increasing levels of accuracy can show that what holds in one part of the world does not hold in another. While the central and eastern Pacific Ocean appears to have been unusually cold in the fifteenth century, for example, the same does not seem to have been the case elsewhere, much as north-western Europe and the south-eastern parts of North America appear to have endured harsher conditions in the cooler seventeenth century than other regions. In fact, there is no evidence for globally coherent warm or cold periods over the two millennia before the industrial revolution.[54]

Just how much care needs to be taken can be shown by looking at the period c.1220–50. During this relatively narrow window, the hydroclimatic situation was rather favourable for cereal production in the eastern Mediterranean and the southern Levant (roughly modern

Israel, Palestine, Jordan) but was much less so just a few hundred kilometres away in the central Mediterranean, Sicily and southern Italy.[55] It is important, in other words, not to extrapolate too much from site-specific information and apply it to other locations where evidence has not been gathered either because they have not been so intensively studied or because they do not offer suitable corroborative material.

Synoptic frequency of extreme marine heat across ocean basins from 1900–2019

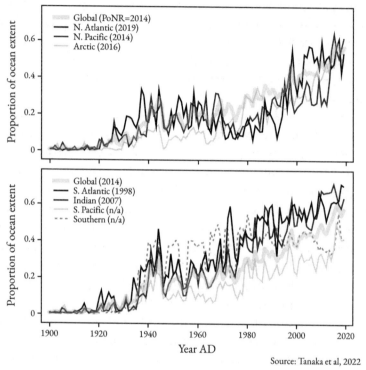

Source: Tanaka et al, 2022

The question of regional climate coherence is an issue too in today's world where global warming is affecting 98 per cent of its surface area, apart from the Antarctic, where warming has not yet been observed over the entire continent.[56] Warming patterns do not affect all parts of the earth the same way nor do they do so at the same rate. Indeed, as a recent report noted, while the majority of countries around the world will experience the 'pernicious effects' of climate change, a small number may actually benefit.[57]

Nevertheless, even before considering the accuracy and margins of error of future climate models, analyses of the here and now makes for a sobering read. The Atlantic Meridional Overturning Circulation (AMOC) – a system of interconnected surface and deep currents in the Atlantic Ocean that is largely responsible for the relative warmth of the northern hemisphere – is at its weakest in almost 2,000 years.[58] Early-warning indicators from multiple sea surface temperature and salinity data from across the Atlantic Ocean basin suggest that currents may be nearing a shutdown, something that would cause severe disruption to the global climate system and increase the chances of a cascade of further transitions – including the distribution of rain in tropical monsoons and the melting of the Antarctic ice sheet.[59] Some scientists argue that these risks represent nothing less than 'an existential threat to civilization'.[60]

These current and major changes to global climate are almost entirely due to human impact on the environment. Anthropogenic impacts began to have a radical effect from the second half of the eighteenth century, following the invention of the steam engine and the energy and industrial revolutions that transformed production and societies and marked the start of a fundamentally different human relationship with the natural world. The era that began with the Industrial Revolution has been named the 'Anthropocene', following the suggestion of the Nobel-prize-winning chemist Paul J. Crutzen in 2002 to describe a period that has seen levels of carbon dioxide and methane emissions rise sharply and consistently.[61] More recently, a panel of distinguished international scientists agreed to treat the Anthropocene as a formal gatepost in history – and voted to consider this as starting in the middle of the 20th century, a point when carbon emissions from human activities began to rise extremely quickly.[62]

Burning fossil fuels like coal and oil releases water vapour, carbon dioxide (CO_2), methane (CH_4), ozone and nitrous oxide (N_2O), which trap heat and are therefore known as greenhouse gases. Rising populations, increased energy demand, falling production prices and massive investment in infrastructure have seen dramatic surges in fossil-fuel use, leading to substantial rises in emissions and to sharp temperature rises. For 800,000 years until the start of the industrial revolution, there were around 250 parts of CO_2 for every million air molecules. In 2018, this had risen to over 408 parts per million – levels that have not been so high since the Pliocene era, over 3 million years ago, when sea levels were almost twenty-five metres higher than today and when average temperatures were 2–3 °C warmer than today.[63] By the summer of 2022, levels were higher still, measured by the Mauna Loa Atmospheric Baseline Observatory in Hawai'i at a monthly average of 421 parts per million.[64]

There are multiple knock-on effects. Global warming leads to melting of the ice caps, which in turn raises sea levels. A single iceberg, known as A68, that broke free from the Larsen-C ice shelf in Antarctica in 2017 was dumping 1.5 billion tonnes of fresh water into the ocean every single day before it disappeared in 2021.[65] This has obvious implications for the world's largest cities, many of which are located on the coast. Modelling using artificial intelligence and highly accurate readings of elevations suggests that land that is currently home to 300 million people will flood at least once a year by 2050, with Asian populations most heavily affected. As it is, around 1 billion people already live on land less than ten metres above high-tide levels, and 230 million live in coastal communities at less than one metre's elevation above water.[66]

The UK's energy infrastructure is highly exposed to even modest rises in sea level, with all nineteen of the country's nuclear reactors situated in coastal locations, as are all the major fossil-fuel power stations in Scotland, Wales and Northern Ireland.[67] Some estimates suggest that $3–11 trillion worth of assets in the United States are at risk from flooding, depending on the amount and speed of rising sea levels.[68]

There could be 'catastrophic outcomes', notes the International Monetary Fund (IMF), if steps are not taken to reduce emissions, including lower agricultural yields, frequent disruption of economic activity, destruction of infrastructure, deterioration of health and increased prevalence of infectious diseases.[69] According to UNICEF, 1 billion children – almost half the world's children – are already at 'extremely high risk' of the impacts of the climate crisis.[70]

The scale of the challenge in minimising the consequences of the rapid warming in the coming decades is hard to exaggerate. Recent modelling has suggested oil and gas production must decline globally by 3 per cent each year until 2050 – and that 60 per cent of oil and fossil methane gas and 90 per cent of coal must remain unextracted to keep within a 1.5 °C carbon budget.[71] The fact that not a single one of the world's major economies, including the entire G20, had climate plans in 2021 that met their own commitments under the Paris Agreements of 2015 indicates that we should be preparing for the worst rather than the best case – even though some commentators stress that doomsday scenarios provide little or no scope for adaptation, technological innovation or successful mitigation of some or all of the worst potential problems.[72]

There is of course much to be said about the dangers of over-relying on the twin temptations of crystal-ball gazing and catastrophising. However, recent models suggest an even bleaker future than many have predicted with temperature rises of around 4 °C by 2100. In fact, a report by the US National Highway Traffic Safety Administration in 2018 said that there was little point in enforcing fuel-efficiency standards in cars because this would have little practical impact in the long run, since moving away from fossil fuels would require 'the economy and the vehicle fleet' to operate in ways that were 'not currently technologically feasible or economically practicable'.[73] This was taken by many as a statement that the planet's fate is considered sealed – at least in some parts of the US government.[74]

Less hard to argue with are the problems that are already very much part of the present and not of the near or distant future. The energy revolution has had a disastrous impact on human health, with air-pollution levels in some cities at levels ten times higher than World Health Organisation minimum standards: indeed, 92 per cent of the world's population live in places which exceed these limits.[75] Dirty air is not simply the result of fossil fuels being burned for energy; it also comes from open-air burning of rubbish. An estimated 40 per cent of global waste is burned in the open air, resulting in substantial injections of particulate matter and polycyclic hydrocarbons into the atmosphere.[76]

Air pollution is lethal. In 2015, it resulted in approximately 9 million premature deaths worldwide.[77] The latest figures put the number of annual deaths attributable to air pollution in India at more than 1.6 million, with the highest number of fatalities in states with low per capita incomes.[78] Indeed, in 2017, the death toll from air pollution in war-torn Afghanistan was almost eight times higher than the number of civilian casualties.[79]

While chronic levels of pollution affect large parts of the developing world, those living in wealthy countries also pay the price for the failure of governments to understand fully or deal with the dangers posed. In Europe as a whole, 8 per cent of mortalities can be attributed to exposure to particulate matter with a diameter of less than or equal to 2.5 μm ($PM_{2.5}$) and to exposure to nitrogen dioxide (NO_2) – almost 500,000 deaths per year, in other words.[80] Recent research goes further still, suggesting that 18 per cent of total global deaths in 2018 were caused by the effects of fossil-fuel pollution.[81]

As with so many other issues, air pollution is also closely connected to socio-economic status and to income levels – including in wealthy, developed countries. Businesses that produce pollutants are more likely to be located in communities that are home to populations with high numbers of minorities and lower incomes.[82] The damage goes much further too: particulate matter has a strong and highly detrimental impact on cognitive function, reducing memory, orientation, verbal fluency and visual-spatial ability.[83] Breathing in nitrogen oxides and fine particulate matter as a child or an adolescent is a risk factor for mental illness in adulthood and for dementia, as well as for an elevated risk of self-harm.[84] Exposure to pollution for even a single day in childhood can profoundly affect the cardiovascular and immune systems in later life, resulting in gene regulation and a detrimental impact on long-term health.[85]

According to a recent study by the World Bank, the cost of health damages associated with exposure to air pollution is $8.1 trillion – or more than 6 per cent of global GDP.[86] Human behaviour, lifestyles and impact on the environment do not just end up killing people; these factors also affect how they behave, how they think and how they communicate with each other.

Human impact on the natural environment has been devastating almost everywhere, in almost every way, from water contamination to erosion, from plastics entering the food chain to pressure on animal and plant life that has reached such a high level that the most recent United Nations report talks of declines in biodiversity at rates that are unprecedented in human history, and that threaten an erosion of 'the very foundations of our economies, livelihoods, food security, health and quality of life worldwide'.[87]

Human activities compromise the world's rivers, seas and oceans with plastic debris present in every major ocean basin over a decade ago – impacting wildlife because of contamination, intestinal blockage, internal injury and entanglement.[88] The scale of pollutants is mind-boggling, with an estimated nine trillion microplastic fibres shed from synthetic clothing being discharged from washing machines every week in the UK alone.[89] These can be now found in astonishing volumes all around the planet, with one survey of the Arctic finding forty microplastic particles on average for every cubic metre of seawater.[90] Studies in the US suggest that people consume and inhale 74,000–121,000 pieces of microplastics per year, while separate research shows the presence of microplastics in the placentas of pregnant mothers, and in high concentrations in the stools of infant children, as well as in all human blood.[91]

Pressure on the environment is now so great that 40 per cent of the world's plants are considered endangered.[92] This is partly the result of the collapse of insect populations, which in turn stems from deforestation, heavy use of pesticides, urbanisation and climate change, developments that now not only threaten animal and plant food chains but have potentially catastrophic implications for agriculture and food production.[93] Some estimate that almost $600 billion worth of global crops are already at risk annually because of pollinator loss.[94]

With millions of hectares of tropical forests being cleared every year and chronic overfishing in the world's oceans, animals are responding to climate change by changing their habitats – and their shapes and sizes. Some animals are responding to warmer climates by altering the ways that they thermoregulate, or cool themselves down, with limbs, ears, beaks and other appendages changing shape and size as a result of increased temperatures.[95] Maternal heat stress reduces growth in calves, especially of organs linked to the immune system – which has obvious implications for both dairy and meat production.[96]

Land-based species on mountainsides are moving upslope to avoid warming lowlands, while fish have been driven deeper by warming sea surfaces. Terrestrial taxa are moving towards the poles by seventeen kilometres per decade and marine species are moving more than four times as far.[97] Many species of butterflies and moths in the Himalayas have moved a thousand metres higher – or more – in search of better habitats.[98] Marine animals such as fish, crustaceans and cephalopods (including octopus, squid and cuttlefish) are moving an average of fifty-five metres deeper in the Mediterranean in search of cooler waters.[99]

As it is, the average population sizes of vertebrate species that have been monitored closely have fallen by almost 70 per cent in the last fifty years.[100] Bird numbers in North America have declined by nearly 3 billion since 1970, while more than 40 per cent of amphibian species are at risk.[101] Models that estimate potential extinction rates not only show dramatic collapses, but likely underestimate falls in species abundance and distribution.[102]

Declines are not uniform – and in fact, although some species and ecosystems are collapsing, others are not doing so badly and, in some cases, are thriving, as the case of tree species in boreal forests in eastern Canada shows.[103] Moreover, declines in some species open up opportunities for others.[104] Some scientists also point out the importance of evaluating at the local rather than the global level, and suggest that catastrophic falls in some species populations should be assessed as clusters of extreme decline (or increase) rather than taken to illustrate general, widespread and potentially misleading patterns.[105]

Nevertheless, there is a wide consensus among scientists about an ongoing 'biological annihilation' taking place in front of our eyes that is now regularly referred to as a 'mass extinction event'.[106] Research on polar oceans suggests that changes to food webs are already under way with profound implications not only for marine but for global ecosystems.[107] Many warn of a 'cascading erosion of biodiversity' and 'co-extinctions' affecting all levels of flora and fauna.[108] The 'sixth mass extinction' is different to those that have gone before because this time an animal species is responsible – humans.[109] One recent report spelt things out bluntly: 'The scale of the threats to the biosphere and all its lifeforms – including humanity – is in fact so great that it is difficult to grasp, even for well-informed experts.'[110]

This book is not about what will happen in the future. Nor is its aim to challenge the overwhelmingly uniform voices of the scientific community, either on the basis of the current global conditions or through examining what steps might be taken to mitigate some or even many of the worst problems posed by climate change, whether through adaptation or the introduction of new technologies. Its aim, rather, is to look at the past and to understand and explain how our species has transformed the earth to the point that we now face such a perilous future.

Originally, I had thought I would write only about the history of how the climate shaped the world around us and about the ways in which modulations in global temperatures, rainfall and sea level – along with extreme events, such as major storms, volcanic eruptions and meteor strikes – have influenced the past, setting out moments, periods and themes that explain what an important role climate has played in global history.

However, it became clear very early on when I started thinking about this book that opening the door to climate, to changes in weather patterns and to human intervention in the natural world led on to a much bigger set of questions and challenges about the relationship between agricultural surplus and the origins of the bureaucratic state; about the connection between pastoralists and nomads on the one hand and sedentary societies in villages, towns and cities on the other; about the role and development of religions and belief systems as a function of climate, environment and geography; about race and slavery and their part in the process of extraction of resources; about the spread of foods, pathogens and disease; about demographics, poverty and consumption patterns in the centuries since the industrial revolution; about globalisation, the standardisation of industry, agriculture, food and fashion in the last century; about why the twenty-first century is at a moment of crisis.

So this book has three goals. The first is to reinsert climate back into the story of the past as an underlying, crucial and much overlooked theme in global history and to show where, when and how weather, long-run climate patterns and changes in climate – anthropogenic and otherwise – have had an important impact on the world. The second is to set out the story of human interaction with the natural world over millennia and to look at how our species exploited, moulded and bent the environment to its will, both for good and for ill.

And the third is to expand the horizons of how we look at history. Study of the past has been dominated by the attention paid to the 'global north', that is the wealthy societies of Europe and North America, with the history of other continents and other regions often relegated to secondary significance or ignored entirely. That same pattern applies to climate science and research into climate history, where there are vast regions, periods and peoples that receive little attention, investment and investigation – something that speaks volumes about long-accepted perspectives of the past as well as about how academic funding (and intellectual silos) develop and deepen in practice.

If that points to one fundamental reason to reassess history, so too does the heavy overemphasis by historians on towns and cities and on states that resemble each other in terms of leadership, bureaucracy and behaviour. Indeed, 'civilisation' itself literally refers to the life of cities, of those who lived in them and who projected power and ruled from them. This is reflected in most written historical materials – narrative accounts, records of land sales, tax receipts and so on – that served to reinforce the administration of hierarchies. Much of history has been written by people living in cities, for people living in cities, and has focused on the lives of those who lived in cities. This skews the way we look at the past and at the world around us.[111]

And yet 'civilisation' is by far the single greatest factor in environmental degradation and the most important cause of anthropogenic climate change – because of the demands that the populations of cities place on energy and on the consumption of natural resources, including food and water. Although cities occupy only 3 per cent of the earth's land surface, urban areas accommodate more than half the world's population. Cities are not only responsible for a substantial proportion of global warming, but they will also be greatly affected by it in coming decades.[112]

It is no coincidence, then, that the last century, which has seen a rapid expansion in the number, size and populations of cities, has also seen the most serious depletions of the environment and the most rapid growth in the rates of consumption. As cities rise, so too do pressures on nature, biodiversity and sustainability through changes in land use and cover, because of the modification of hydrologic systems and as a result of the impact of altered and compromised biogeochemical cycles.[113] In the years 2001–18 alone, built-up areas in China expanded by 47.5 per cent, while in the US they increased by 9 per cent. Indeed, the world's population living in cities is forecast to rise by some 3 billion to around 7 billion by 2050 based on current demographic trends.[114] To put that in historical perspective, just over 15 per cent of the global population lived in towns and cities in 1900; by 2050, more than 70 per cent will do so.[115]

New technologies speeding up and driving down costs of production have spurred radical shifts in manufacturing, transportation and consumption patterns. More than 75 per cent of all the virgin plastics ever created are estimated to have become waste, of which about 9 per cent has been recycled, 12 per cent incinerated and the remainder – about 5 billion metric tons, or around 60 per cent of all plastics ever produced – has accumulated in landfill or in the natural environment.[116]

By some measures, while human-made mass – such as concrete, construction materials and metals – was equal to about 3 per cent of global biomass a century or so ago, today it exceeds it. On average today, further human-made mass that is more than the equivalent of the body weight of every person on earth is produced every single week, a phenomenon closely linked to the rise of cities and megacities, and to high levels of consumption of food, water, energy and non-perishable goods.[117] This in turn is connected to globalisation and to supply chains and networks that form both a virtuous circle of hyperconnectivity, standardisation, high velocities of exchange and low prices, and a vicious circle of extraction, resource depletion and environmental damage.

Throughout history, on the other hand, peasants, pastoralists and nomads, indigenous peoples and hunter-gatherers, who have had to understand the limitations of the land and adapt to even modest changes, have been either written out of the story of the past or typified as barbaric, erratic and primitive. One who has no need for the city, wrote Aristotle, 'is either an animal or a god'.[118] Nomads in Central Asia had been 'abandoned by heaven', stated a Chinese author a few centuries later; Ibn Faḍlān, writing in the tenth century, agreed after meeting mobile pastoralists: they 'live in poverty, like wandering asses', he wrote. 'They do not worship God, nor do they have any recourse to reason.'[119]

These attitudes persist today in many parts of the world, often manifested in the creation and funding of wildlife reserves that evict local populations to create what look to city inhabitants like natural paradises since they are devoid of humans. One good example of this comes from the Grand Canyon, 'a natural wonder which ... is absolutely unparalleled throughout the rest of the world', according to President Theodore Roosevelt after his visit in 1903. 'Man can only mar it,' he added in a telling statement of how the 'natural' can be seen as pure and unblemished only if kept free of human intervention. Just over a decade later, the Grand Canyon became a national park, imposing restrictions and controls over lands that had been lived on by the Havasupai and other indigenous peoples for more than 700 years.[120]

In today's world, we see regular, aggressive, overtly racist campaigns against indigenous peoples, hunter-gatherers and foragers such as Bushmen in Botswana, the Baka in West Africa, Adivasi peoples in India or traditional nomads in large parts of Central Asia, invariably laced with insults about supposedly 'primitive' ways of life. This is ironic given that indigenous populations maintain forest levels well, storing more carbon as a result, as well as developing strategies that support biodiversity conservation and good long-term stewardship of the environment.[121]

One of the difficulties of writing history is that there are inevitably major gaps in coverage. It is true that scholars are using new and increasingly sophisticated ways to interpret the oral histories of societies which did not produce literary forms, such as in the American south-west or in the Mount Saint Elias region in what is now northern Canada and Alaska.[122] However, the lack of written materials from many parts of the world, such as Australia or southern Africa, means that inevitably a book like this cannot be fully balanced in terms of its geographic focus. The fact that most climate research by scientists is focused on and based in countries that are well explored and well resourced compounds the problem of imbalance. This is particularly ironic given that the greatest impact of climate change will be felt in the poorest regions and countries, precisely those whose voices have been silent or ignored by history for decades, centuries and millennia.[123]

Such problems cannot be solved by one book. But what a book can do is provide a broader perspective, and introduce themes, regions and questions that can help push the boundaries of history and of historical research in the future. Perhaps, too, it can offer some grounds for optimism, as well as constructive suggestions for how to best navigate a time not only of profound climatic but also of technological, political and economic change.

Writing this book has taught me a great many lessons about how we conceptualise the world around us. But it has also made me realise that the reason we are at such a dangerous intersection is the result of trends that have deep roots in the past. As far back as written records go, people worried about human interaction with nature and warned of the dangers of overexploitation of resources and of long-term damage to the environment. It may well be that we are now on the verge of finally becoming victims of our own success as a species, and that the stresses and strains that our behaviour has put on ecosystems has pushed us close to or even beyond a tipping point that has catastrophic consequences. We cannot say, however, that we were not warned.

I

The World from the Dawn of Time
(c.4.5bn–c.7m BC)

In the beginning when God created the heavens and the earth, the earth was a formless void …

Book of Genesis, 1:1

We should all be grateful for dramatic changes to global climate. Were it not for billions of years of intense celestial and solar activity, repeated asteroid strikes, epic volcanic eruptions, extraordinary atmospheric change, spectacular tectonic shifts and constant biotic adaptation, we would not be alive today. Astrophysicists talk of habitable regions around stars that are not too hot and not too cold as being in the 'goldilocks zone'. The earth is one of many such examples. But conditions have changed constantly and sometimes catastrophically since the creation of our planet around 4.6 billion years ago.[1] For almost all the time that the earth has existed, our species would not and could not have survived. In today's world, we think of humans as architects of dangerous environmental and climate change; but we are prime beneficiaries of such transformations in the past.

Our role on this planet has been an exceptionally modest one. The first hominins appeared only a few million years ago, and the first anatomically modern humans (including Neanderthals) around 500,000 years ago.[2] What we know of the period since then is patchy, difficult to interpret and often highly speculative. As we get closer to the modern day, archaeology helps us understand more reliably how people lived; but to know what they did, thought and believed we have to wait till the development of full-writing systems around 5,000 years ago. To put that into context, accounts, documents and texts that allow us to reconstruct the past with nuance and detail cover around 0.000001 per cent of the world's past. We are not just fortunate to exist as a species, but in the grand scheme of history we are new and very late arrivals.

Like rude guests who arrive at the last minute, cause havoc and set about destroying the house to which they have been invited, human impact on the natural environment has been substantial and is accelerating to the point that many scientists question the long-term viability of human life. That in itself is not unusual, however. For one thing, our species is not alone in transforming the world around us, for other species of biota – that is to say, flora, fauna and microorganisms – are not passive participants in or simple bystanders to a relationship that exists solely or even primarily between humans and nature. Each is actively involved in processes of change, adaptation and evolution – sometimes with devastating consequences.

This is one reason why some scholars have criticised the idea and the name of the 'Anthropocene', which prioritises humans into 'a distinguished species' that has claimed the right to identify what is and is not wild, to classify 'resources' as ones that can be used – sustainably or otherwise. Such, argue some, is the 'arrogance that greatly overestimates human contributions while downplaying those of other life forms almost to the point of nonexistence'.[3]

For around half the earth's existence, there was little or no oxygen in the atmosphere. Our planet was formed through a long period of accretion, or gradual accumulation of layers, followed by a major collision with a Mars-sized impactor – which released enough energy to melt the earth's mantle and create the earliest atmosphere from the resultant exchange between a magma ocean and vapour that was anoxic, that is to say, lacking in oxygen.[4]

The earth's biogeochemical cycles eventually resulted in a radical transformation. Although there is considerable debate about how, when and why oxygenic photosynthesis occurred, evidence from organic biomarkers, fossils and genome-scale data suggests that cyanobacteria evolved to absorb and take energy from sunlight, using it to make sugars out of water and carbon dioxide, releasing oxygen as a by-product. New models suggest that 1 to 5 billion lightning flashes that occurred per year on early earth may have been the source of large volumes of prebiotic reactive phosphorus that played an important role in the emergence of terrestrial life.[5]

Around 3 billion years ago – if not earlier – enough oxygen was being produced to create 'oases' in protected nutrient-rich shallow marine habitats.[6] Whether because of chemical reaction, evolutionary development, sudden superabundance of cyanobacteria, volcanic eruptions or a slowdown in the earth's rotation (or a combination of all five), atmospheric oxygen levels accumulated rapidly around 2.5–2.3 billion years ago, resulting in an episode known as the Great Oxidation Event. This was a key moment that paved the way for the emergence of complex life as we know it.[7]

It also led to dramatic changes in climate, as rapidly increasing oxygen reacted with methane, producing water vapour and carbon dioxide. Alongside the effects of a supercontinent being formed from the collisions of landmasses, the earth's greenhouse was weakened, leading to the planet being covered completely in ice and snow.[8] Changes in the earth's orbit around the sun, known as the Milankovitch cycle, may also have played a role in this process.[9] So too might giant meteorite impacts which not only threw up debris into the atmosphere that blocked the sun's light and heat but also played an important role in the formation of the continents.[10] The glacial episodes may have been weaker or stronger over the course of several hundred million years, but in general the effect of 'Snowball Earth' was so dramatic that some scientists refer to this period as a whole as a 'climate disaster'.[11]

This process was precarious and complex, and is the subject of considerable advances in current research.[12] As with later glaciations, however, it resulted in profound changes for the planet's plant and animal life.[13] One outcome appears to have been the evolution of small organisms into larger sizes, capable of moving at faster speeds to compensate for the high viscosity of cold seawater.[14] It has recently been suggested that the formation of 8,000-kilometre long belts of 'supermountains' may have played a role in the rise of atmospheric oxygen and in stimulating biological evolution as a result of phosphorus, iron and nutrients being deposited into oceans as mountains eroded over the course of hundreds of millions of years.[15]

The fossil record of complex, macroscopic organisms begins with the Ediacara Biota period which started 570 million years ago and which saw at least forty recognised species developing into multicellular animals that were symmetrical – presumably helpful for functions such as mobility.[16] It marked a period of extraordinary diversification in the variety of animals living in the oceans and in their evolution, development and adaptation, with some creatures like trilobites developing respiratory organs on their upper limbs.[17]

Near the end of the Ordovician period, around 444 million years ago, a sudden cooling, perhaps triggered by tectonic shifts that produced the Appalachian mountains, led to sharp falls in temperature and initiated shifts in deep ocean currents, as well as declines in sea level that shrank habitats for marine planktonic and nektonic species. That cooling produced one pulse of extinction; another came when temperatures moderated, sea levels rose and ocean current patterns stagnated, with a resultant sharp fall in oxygen levels.[18] Traces of mercury and indications of significant acidification suggest that volcanic activity was a key factor in the second stage of a process that ultimately brought about the extinction of 85 per cent of all species.[19]

This was just one of several spectacular episodes that wiped out life for all but a small proportion of living organisms. The moon may have played a part in the changes in the millions of years that followed. Formed from debris thrown into space at the time of the impact that created the earth, the moon has a gravitational pull that plays a major role in ocean tides; as such, it is responsible for the flows that help transport heat away from the equator and towards the poles, fundamentally shaping earth's climate.[20]

As the moon used to be much closer to the earth – perhaps half the distance away that it is today – these forces were considerably stronger and therefore had a greater impact on the earth's climate and also perhaps on its wildlife: recent modelling suggests that big tidal ranges may have been responsible for forcing bony fish into shallow pools on land, thereby prompting the evolution of weight-bearing limbs and air-breathing organs.[21] The moon played a role not only in the transformation of the earth, in other words, but also in the development of life on this planet.

It still exerts an important influence. The reproductive cycles of many marine creatures are closely synchronised with lunar phases, with migration and spawning in fish, crab and plankton species triggered by the moon's glow.[22] Coral genes change their activity level according to the waxing and waning phases of the moon.[23] Lunar phases seem to influence the timing of the mating season of wildebeest in the Serengeti, and have been linked to spontaneous delivery in cows.[24] Many primates become more active at night during a full moon – perhaps because higher light levels offer greater chances of predator evasion.[25] It has been noted too that albatrosses are more active on moonlit nights.[26] Though little studied, lunar phases and moonlight seem to be closely connected to the annual migrations of billions of seasonal animal species, especially birds, whose fuelling opportunities are heavily light-dependent.[27]

Indeed, there seem to be important links between human behaviour, activity and even fertility and lunar rhythms. Studies of indigenous communities in Argentina that do not have access to electricity (and therefore offer helpful control conditions) show that sleep starts later and is shorter on nights before the full moon, when moonlight is available in the hours following dusk. This suggests too that pre-industrial communities that did not have access to artificial light may likewise have had sleep patterns strongly influenced by lunar activity.[28] Long-term data from women's menstrual cycles shows a correlation with lunar light and lunar gravity, with some scholars arguing that human reproductive behaviour was originally synchronous with the moon, but has been modified more recently by modern lifestyles.[29]

While the role of the moon in influencing and disturbing human behaviour is often reflected in popular culture and even in language – with the word 'lunatic' suggestive of a relationship between mental illness and the moon – any causal links are usually downplayed by scientists.[30] However, some researchers have emphasised that manic episodes in patients with bipolar disorders have a remarkable synchrony with three distinct lunar phases.[31] The moon, in other words, plays an important role in ocean currents, global temperatures and climate, as well as in reproductive cycles, and life on earth in general.

More work needs to be done to assess the role that lunar tides play in the ionosphere–thermosphere weather system, as well as in past evolutionary processes or during extinction events.[32] The latter were not uncommon. The most deadly was the so-called Great Dying, which took place 252 million years ago. The primary cause was an epic volcanic episode in what is now Siberia that produced enormous volumes of magma.[33] It is possible that a key moment came when lava stopped erupting above ground and began to form as sheets of magma that trapped gases underground until pressure was released in a series of gigantic, violent eruptions.[34] Whatever the precise circumstances, the ultimate result was the injection of enormous amounts of greenhouse gases into the atmosphere that destabilised the biosphere. Soil and seawater temperatures may have risen initially by 8–10 °C and then later by an additional 6–8 °C, with temperatures at the equator perhaps as high as 40 °C. The result was the extinction of 96 per cent of marine life, three quarters of land animals and all the earth's forests.[35]

Other massive volcanic events brought about significant transformation, such as at the end of the Triassic era, around 200 million years ago, when a period of changing marine conditions led to sharp drops in sea levels and water-column freshening, which in turn resulted in less saline, shallow-water complex communities of microorganisms.[36] This was accompanied by huge wildfires and abrupt injections of volcanogenic gases into the atmosphere that quadrupled carbon dioxide levels, acidified the oceans and prompted another wave of mass extinction of plant and animal life.[37]

Such events produced major ecosystem remodelling, as flora and fauna responded to change and diversified rapidly.[38] New kinds of plant assemblages and food demanded adaptation, one of which, in the case of the Triassic, was the evolution of more powerful jaws which generated the strength for shearing bites that enabled efficient feeding. This was especially important in the context of harder, tougher plant materials that became more common – and a key factor in dictating which herbivores thrived and which died out.[39]

The single most famous moment of large-scale transformation in the past, however, was caused by an asteroid strike that impacted the earth 66 million years ago on the Yucatan peninsula, near what is now the town of Chicxulub in Mexico, and led to the demise of the dinosaurs.[40] This was just one of many major extraterrestrial impacts since the formation of the earth, one of the earliest identified examples of which dates to around 3 billion years ago and has an impact crater near Maniitsoq in west Greenland.[41]

While the local devastation of the strike near Chicxulub must have been dramatic – including high levels of thermal radiation from the impact plume, hurricane-force winds and likely giant tsunamis and landslides that scoured the ocean floor – the consequences of this particular strike were global: around 325 gigatons of sulphur and 425 gigatons of CO_2 were forced into the atmosphere at speeds of more than 1 kilometre per second. The result would have included firestorms caused by ejecta heating on re-entry to the earth's atmosphere, short-term cooling from the dust blocking the sun's light, long-term warming from the release of enormous volumes of CO_2 and high levels of ocean acidification.[42]

What made this strike so deadly was the size of the impactor – likely part of a comet from the Oort cloud at the edge of the solar system that was around twelve kilometres in diameter – but also how and where it hit the earth. Astrophysicists were able to understand how catastrophic the effect of the size of an object could be in 1994 when the Shoemaker–Levy 9 comet hit Jupiter. On that occasion, parts of the comet disintegrated into smaller pieces before impact, with the largest final fragment only a kilometre or so in size. It was enough to produce impact scars of some 100,000 kilometres – almost eight times the diameter of the earth – and to leave watching scientists visibly shocked by the scale of the strike and its after-effects.[43]

This has obvious implications for the Chicxulub strike, for other similar impacts in the past and for those that will take place in the future – especially given that new research has suggested that estimates of the chances of similar long-period comets hitting earth should be raised by a factor of ten.[44] The specific angle of entry likewise mattered, with new simulations showing that a steeply inclined trajectory amounted to a worst-case scenario that produced maximum lethality for life on earth thanks to the catastrophic volumes of debris pushed up into the atmosphere.[45] The timing was significant too: because the Chicxulub impact occurred during the boreal spring/summer and soon after the spawning season for fish and most continental taxa, follow-on implications for flora and fauna were particularly acute.[46]

That the impact occurred at about the same time as enormous volcanic eruptions may have made matters even worse; and indeed some scientists have argued that volcanic activity was more significant than the extra-terrestrial impact.[47] Either way, the outcomes included 10–16 °C cooling in mean surface air temperature on land and sharp drops in seawater temperatures, especially at shallower depths – and mass extinction of plant and animal life.[48]

Such events were spectacular and devastating. They also each played a part in the extraordinary series of flukes, coincidences, long shots and

serendipities that ultimately brought about the rise of humankind, as well
as the many species of flora, fauna and biota that exist today. All life on earth
today descends from animals, plants and organisms that survived not one
but multiple mass extinction events, as well as a near inexhaustible series
of smaller-scale episodes of major changes in climatic and atmospheric
conditions that created the world that we think of as familiar.

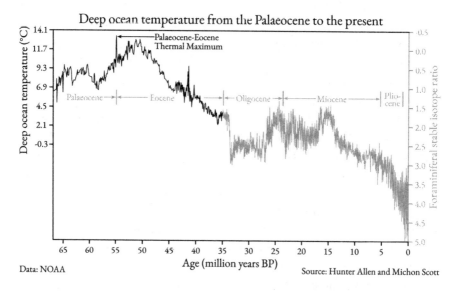

Deep ocean temperature from the Palaeocene to the present

Data: NOAA

Source: Hunter Allen and Michon Scott

Even the most cataclysmic event that brought such large-scale change had
consequences that we think of as fundamental hallmarks of contemporary
global ecosystems, although their roots lie tens of millions of years in
the past. For example, pollen-grain analysis from South America shows
that the Chicxulub strike helped create tropical rainforests as we now
know them. Before the impact, tropical forest trees were spaced far apart,
allowing light to reach the forest floor. After it, they grew much more
densely, perhaps as a result of the extinction of large herbivores, with
greater shading and enabling the flourishing of legumes and pods that
take nitrogen from the air thanks to interactions with bacteria. Ashfall
from the impact added weatherable phosphorus minerals to terrestrial
ecosystems, which in turn were crucial in stimulating soil fertility and
forest productivity. This would also have enhanced the relative advantage
for flowering plants over conifers and ferns, thereby creating a springboard
for a surge in biodiversity and the conditions for the enormous rainforests
that are such an important part of the carbon cycle today.[49]

There were other, more modest events of climatic change that produced substantial results without causing mass extinction. A good example is the Palaeocene–Eocene Thermal Maximum, a period of significant warming around 56 million years ago that followed the release of massive amounts of carbon into the ocean-atmosphere system, leading to a rise in global temperatures of at least 4–5 °C lasting around 200,000 years.[50] Some have suggested that tropical temperatures rose to as high as 40 °C.[51] So large were the carbon dioxide volumes that studies have speculated that concentrations were sixteen times the levels of CO_2 during the pre-industrial period.[52]

Although the source of the carbon is a matter of debate, volcanic eruptions would again seem to be the most likely cause of the destabilisation that brought about large shifts in geographic ranges of marine and terrestrial organisms, spurred rapid evolutionary processes and affected food chains.[53] It also brought about a boom in diversity of flora – at least in tropical regions – as well as increasing levels of precipitation around the world, including in North America, South Asia, North Africa and Antarctica.[54] The latter became home to lush forests until thick continental ice sheets began to form, a process that has been linked to a substantial decline in the concentration of atmospheric carbon dioxide levels that affected much of the terrestrial southern hemisphere.[55]

Other shifts in regional and global climates occurred following forty-two enormous eruptions since the demise of the dinosaurs, each of which was more than 150 times more powerful than the Mount Pinatubo eruption of 1991. The most notable was at Fish Canyon Tuff in what is now Colorado around 28 million years ago, the single largest volcanic eruption in the last 500 million years.[56] Asteroid and meteorite strikes also transformed the natural environment, such as one caused by an object 2 kilometres in diameter whose impact 800,000 years ago threw debris across the eastern hemisphere, including much of Asia, Australia and Antarctica and whose crater has only recently been identified in what is now Laos, partly because it was hidden under a volcanic lava field created by later eruptions.[57] And change was also brought about by periods of long-term warming such as during the Piacenzian phase of the Pliocene (around 3 million years ago), which saw temperatures more than 3 °C warmer and sea levels twenty metres higher than today, when more carbon dioxide was present in the atmosphere than at any time until the twentieth century thanks to a large-scale reorganisation of global weather patterns.[58]

Geology and movement of tectonic plates also played a significant role in shaping and reshaping the earth, and in creating the geographic distribution of water, land and life as we know it. Over the course of millions of years, a single giant supercontinent broke up, perhaps because of mantle plumes at the core–mantle boundary causing motion, perhaps because of the negative buoyancy of oceanic plates exerting pressure from above, or perhaps a combination of the two.[59] In some cases, surges of hot material from a supervolcano caused plates to split and rotate – as happened with the Indian plate that broke away from Africa just over a million years ago.[60]

Ultimately, of course, these movements led to the distribution of the world's continents in the positions they occupy today. However, the process of their formation and relocation was one that had important implications. For one thing, not all landmasses remained above sea level. Indeed, an elevated area surrounding what is now New Zealand and New Caledonia was part of a single continuous body of land of which almost 95 per cent became submerged and was so vast that some have called it the earth's 'eighth continent'.[61]

In this instance, the disappearance of a large landmass beneath the waves was the result of stretching and thinning. It was a different story when a piece of continental plate around the size of Greenland broke off from what later became North Africa, crashed into southern Europe and was eventually forced underneath it.[62] Impacts like this resulted in enormous forces being created and in land becoming crumpled, creating the great mountain ranges of the world. These include the Andes in South America and the Himalayas, formed when the Indian subcontinent smashed into Eurasia around 50 million years ago, pushing land that had been at sea level upwards – with the result that marine fossils can be found at or near the summits of some of the highest peaks on earth.[63]

The formation of these extensive mountain ranges has in turn played a part in changing and shaping local, regional and even global climate patterns. It is widely assumed, for example, that the location and size of the Rockies affects precipitation patterns and storm-track development on the east coast of North America, in the North Atlantic and perhaps as far away as Norway.[64] It has long been argued too that the uplift of the Himalaya and Tibetan plateau determines rainfall distribution over Africa, although recent sensitivity modelling suggests that the influence is a weak and modest one.[65] Rather, changes in land cover and dust emission both appear to play a much more important role in the strength of monsoon precipitation in Asia, at least over the course of the last few thousand years.[66]

The reconfiguration of global landmasses has had important implications for flora and fauna, and also specific consequences for the development of human societies. For example, evolutionary change over the course of millions of years led to very sharp differences in the numbers and distribution of large mammal species in Eurasia compared with the Americas. Of particular significance was the lack of animals suitable for domestication in the latter by the time of early human settlements around 25,000 years ago: this had a profound impact not only on how societies understood and interacted with the natural world, but also on farming techniques, the capacity to generate food surplus, the emergence of social hierarchies and even the immunological response to disease – one of the key by-products of close interaction with domesticated animals.[67]

The break-up of the supercontinent and the creation of the continents that began around 250 million years ago did more, however, than create maps that are familiar to us today. For example, one outcome was the closing off of a huge body of water called the Tethys Sea just over 20 million years ago causing it to shrink and eventually diminish into the Mediterranean. This led to a reorganisation of global climate patterns that included the aridification of large parts of Africa and the onset of the long-term glaciation of Antarctica.[68] Changing conditions brought about the 'Messinian salinity crisis' around 5.6 million years ago, which resulted in the desiccation by evaporation of the Mediterranean and created plant and animal pathways between Europe, Africa and the Middle East that lasted until Atlantic waters forced their way through the Straits of Gibraltar about 300,000 years later and rapidly refilled the Mediterranean basin in an event known as the Zanclean flood.[69]

From the perspective of the twenty-first century, however, what was even more significant was the fact that the continental rifts, collisions and changes to major ocean basins resulted in the creation of giant hydrocarbon deposits worldwide: almost all the world's 877 giant oil and gas fields (namely those containing 500 million barrels or more) cluster in just twenty-seven key regions around the world.[70] The location of these fields underpins a fossil-fuel economy worth trillions of dollars a year – but it is also the main driver of climate change in the modern era: the energy revolution that began with the burning of fossil fuels accelerated rapidly with the development of motors, engines and power stations that are fired by oil and gas. Contemporary anthropogenic climate change, global warming and pollution are all fuelled, in other words, by shifts that took place over the course of hundreds of millions of years.

Indeed, these long-term developments are not only linked to current environmental problems; they are also central to the story of global economic, social and political powershifts in the modern age. For example, the bulk of the coal that powered the industrial revolution was formed from plant debris in the Carboniferous and early Permian period around 300 million years ago caused by a massive fall in atmospheric CO_2 levels.[71]

The location of these deposits was therefore of crucial significance once coal-powered mechanisation offered new and extraordinary opportunities to boost production and productivity. Indeed, some scholars have argued that one of the reasons for the Great Divergence – the point where Europe leapfrogged past states such as Qing dynasty China and elsewhere in Asia – was because coal fields in the former were closer to potential manufacturing centres, had access to more labour pools to extract them and could therefore be exploited both more quickly and more cheaply.[72] As we shall see, there were many other factors involved in the rise of European powers, but luck of the geological draw was profoundly important once the energy revolution opened up new possibilities at a time of intensifying globalisation.

It helped open up new ecological frontiers too. For example, the rise of cities and railways across the midwest in the United States and beyond was facilitated by vast fossil-fuel deposits of coal, oil and gas in states like Illinois, Iowa and Nebraska, and then in a further giant belt stretching south from the Dakotas and Wyoming and through Colorado down into New Mexico.[73] In the second half of the nineteenth century, 'instant cities' began to pop up in the American heartlands, with industrialisation and urbanisation rising hand in hand. This helped create a manufacturing powerhouse, but it also resulted in an important redistribution of population from the coast to the interior.[74]

Conversely, more recently pressure on jobs in the coal-mining industry, driven by government incentives for cleaner energy production and by sharply reducing costs of renewable energy, has influenced responses at the ballot box during presidential elections, with a strong surge in support for pro-coal Republican party candidates. The location of coal reserves and of the populations who have been involved in its extraction, historically and today, influences who does – and who does not – get into the White House every four years.[75]

That geological chance plays an important role in the modern world can be underlined by many other parallels. For example, during the Cretaceous period, 139–65 million years ago, the world was much warmer and sea levels were much higher than they are today. Billions of marine microorganisms that died formed sedimentary levels that ultimately created oil reservoirs. But their demise produced other outcomes. In the southern part of the United States, massive chalk formations grew up from plankton and sea life that died out as the world cooled and sea levels dropped. This led to swathes of extremely fertile land, especially after rainfall dissolved nutrient-poor carbonate minerals.

The arc of lands that marks a swoosh across the south-eastern states, known as the Black Belt thanks to its rich, dark soils, proved to be ideal for intensive crop production, especially of cotton. Following the arrival of Europeans in the Americas and the establishment of the transatlantic slave trade, these lands became heavily populated by Africans who were shipped in enormous volumes and grotesque conditions to do work that was labour-intensive. Despite the abolition of slavery in 1865, large numbers of black Americans were excluded from voting until the Voting Rights Act that outlawed discriminatory voting practices was passed a century later. Americans with African ancestry make up a majority of the population in many counties in the Black Belt region today, especially those with high unemployment levels and poor education and healthcare provision. Votes cast not just in this part of the United States but in specific counties have an important role in determining the outcomes of presidential elections.[76] Climatic change is not just a topic for the present and the future; it is also a fundamental part of the past.

It is a similar story with the distribution of resources in other parts of the world. The story of oil and gas is one that has played a central role in global geopolitics for the last century. Massive reserves in Saudi Arabia,

Iran, the Gulf and elsewhere in the Middle East and North Africa are closely linked to the story of military intervention, to the imposition of autocratic and theocratic regimes and to a host of wider issues. American engagement with this region may not define US presidencies over the last fifty years; but it is no coincidence that hostage crises, weapons sales, invasions, terrorism and nuclear deals have been essential elements to US foreign policy since the 1970s, if not before. Had there been no oil and gas in the Middle East, things would have been very different.[77]

The same is true for Britain, Germany and Japan in the nineteenth and first half of the twentieth centuries. One of the curious serendipities of the creation of the British empire was that while it famously covered almost a quarter of the world's surface area by the time of the First World War, the vast imperial landmass contained few significant oil deposits. So it was necessary to find reliable sources and to establish control over them in order to nourish the sinews of empire. The resultant decisions about military and political interventions reshaped the Middle East after the First World War and produced consequences that resonate to this day.[78] Likewise, the lack of oil resources available to both Germany and Japan influenced strategic decisions during the Second World War, not least the major military pushes towards the Caucasus and into South-East Asia respectively that ultimately overstretched supply lines and capabilities.[79]

Similarly the distribution of other resources, natural and otherwise, has played a fundamental role in human history and will continue to do so. The world's accessible reserves of precious metals, including gold, are the result of the earth being bombarded by a flux of meteorites after its formation.[80] This has shaped the fortunes of those living in locations – for good and for bad – where gold has been abundant and where costs of extraction have been low, leading to forced and free population movements and in some cases to military confrontation.

Heavy metals, including rare earths – minerals that are in fact not scarce but are rarely found in concentrations that make their extraction practicable – likely originate as by-products of explosions of supernovas typically thirty times the weight of the sun.[81] Many of these can be subsequently associated with alkaline igneous activity and magmatic systems on earth.[82] Here too geology and chance have dictated how easily these can be mined, and helped determine political developments, military rivalries and the evolution of societies and states: some predict that the twenty-first century will be shaped by a scramble for a new set of elements like beryllium, dysprosium and yttrium which had little value or use a few decades ago but are now essential components in many hi-tech devices. New technologies will enhance competition in the future – one reason for the renewed interest in lunar and planetary missions, and in particular for mineral prospecting and extraction on extraterrestrial objects.[83]

Nor is the distribution of the earth's resources a matter only of energy or precious metals – for the environmental lottery applies to a host of other materials and substances, including flora and fauna. The importance of spices, most notably from South and South-East Asia, helped stimulate trading networks that brought these regions into intensive contact with the Middle East, Africa and the Mediterranean, as well as with China, Japan and beyond. The habitat of the silk worm, likewise, was instrumental in the manufacture of textiles that were light, tough and expensive and prompted high demand from thousands of kilometres away. As we shall see, the spread of animals and plants as a result of short-, medium- and long-distance trade – both deliberately and inadvertently – is a central part of the world's ecological history and one in which humans have played a disproportionately significant role.

One challenge, then, is determining how our species understands the natural world and perhaps, most importantly, conceptualises our own place within it. Conservationists sometimes imply that there is a way in which time can be made to stand still, that the rainforests should remain untouched, that grasslands should be left intact, that 'nature' should be spared human intervention. Yet plants and animals have their own methods of causing change and even degradation and destruction. Nature is not a harmonious, benign and complementary concept that preserves balance, for ecosystems have always been transformed and reshaped by many non-human forces.

What humans do, on the other hand, is to bring about change through conscious modification of landscapes, deliberate interventions into ecosystems and intentional, ill-conceived decisions that lead to overexploitation. These can bring about inadvertent outcomes too, including chain reactions after the introduction of species into new environments, or the spread of pathogens and disease that have dramatic effects not only on human life but on flora and fauna too.

In that sense, the evolution of our species has been the single most important development in the history of this planet. Extinction events in the past have been caused by volcanoes and by comets, but humans have managed to develop technologies to bring about mass extinction independently. Some would argue that the unsustainable way that we live in the twenty-first century and the impact of global warming is putting the existence of humanity at risk, and of countless animals and plants. Our interactions with each other are partly responsible for this, in the form of travel and transportation, as well as the globalisation of goods, produce and ideas.

However, we have also developed the capabilities to ensure our own destruction by other means. Accidents like the failure of the reactor at the Chernobyl nuclear power plant, the *Exxon Valdez* oil spill and the leak at the Union Carbide plant in Bhopal, India, provide warnings that our new technologies can lead to large-scale environmental disasters. The development of nuclear weapons has shown likewise, both at Hiroshima and Nagasaki at the end of the Second World War and at test sites in the former Soviet Union, in North America and in the Pacific.[84]

The power of nuclear arsenals means that we could achieve the same outcome as an extra-terrestrial strike ourselves – including by accident.[85] False alarms happen worryingly often, as in 2018 when a ballistic-missile alert was sent to television, radio and mobile phones in Hawai'i.[86] The laws of probability suggest that it is matter of when, and not if, a catastrophic accident resulting from human error, escalation of political rivalries or geopolitical miscalculation takes place.

It is perhaps ironic that the greatest threat following a major nuclear confrontation, triggered intentionally or otherwise, would not be from the massive missile-delivered payloads but from the rapid global cooling that would follow in a so-called nuclear winter. Soviet and US modelling of precisely this scenario played an important role in encouraging arms-control agreements in the 1980s and efforts to control proliferation of nuclear weapons and technology.[87]

These are areas that have become important once again in the contemporary world – meaning that risk levels of human-induced disaster are greater than at any point in history since the emergence of our species. So how is it, then, that humans have become so central to the present and future of a planet where we have only been present for what amounts to the batting of an eyelid in the billions of years of history since the earth was formed?

2

On the Origins of Our Species
(c.7m–c.12,000 BC)

I will here attempt to give a brief, but I fear imperfect, sketch of the progress of opinion on the Origin of Species.

Charles Darwin, *On the Origin of Species by Means of Natural Selection* (1870)

The origin of *Homo sapiens* is something of a mystery, as well as a matter of considerable debate. The human lineage diverged from that of apes around 7 million years ago and likely much earlier, if recent estimates on mutation rates in chimpanzees are correct.[1] The fossil record strongly suggests that all human ancestors lived in Africa, although identifying the location is neither easy nor a matter of agreement. Early hominins included several species of *Australopithecus*, the most famous of whom was christened Lucy after her discovery in Ethiopia in 1974, and an even more complete specimen nicknamed Little Foot that was excavated at the Sterkfontein Caves near Johannesburg and dates back to about 3.67 million years.[2] Recent analysis of Little Foot's shoulder blades, joints and collarbones shows a spine configuration well suited for tree climbing and hanging from branches, in turn providing insights into likely habitat.[3]

The genus of *Homo*, from which our own species descends, emerged perhaps around 3 million years ago, with the first possible example found in 2013 of a jawbone with teeth still in place dating back about 2.8 million years.[4] While the appearance of the first members of the

Homo genus is sometimes seen as a momentous transformation, the transition and emergence were neither sudden nor profound, with many features shared with australopithecines.[5] Indeed, some scholars have argued that some early *Homo* species should be reclassified as *Australopithecus*.[6]

Recent research suggests that there was considerable diversity within the *Homo* genus – and as a result there is little consensus about how to describe or explain variations and differences and even about what constitutes a species.[7] How *Homo rudolfensis*, *Homo habilis* and *Homo erectus* developed and how they were different is a source of considerable conjecture, as is the question of how they relate to later *Homo heidelbergensis*, from which both *Homo neanderthalensis* and *Homo sapiens* may have evolved. Nevertheless, all seem to have shared characteristics that distinguished them from other primates, including bipedal locomotion, erect posture, larger brains and perhaps the use of specialised tools.[8]

It has long been argued that the evolution of hominins was accelerated by shifting climate patterns that brought about a change from forests to drier conditions, resulting in evolutionary pressures that favoured an upright posture, larger brains and changes in tooth size and either necessitated or rewarded the ability to cover longer distances – or both.[9] These changes were not uniform; nevertheless, key factors in the resilience, success and expansion of the genus as a whole were dietary flexibility during times of environmental unpredictability and an ability to reduce mortality risks.[10]

Certainly, stone and bone tools from a unique cave site in southern Africa point to adaptation in the face of substantial changes in ecosystems for multiple species of hominins.[11] These echo findings from East Africa where volcanism has left stratigraphic sequences of fossil and archaeological remains which are possible to date with some accuracy, and which demonstrate cases of problem solving through social co-operation.[12] Examples include the use of core–flake–hammerstone technology from the Oldupai Gorge site in modern Tanzania, and evidence of the use of tools for hunting and butchering, defleshing and demarrowing animals such as the *Parmularius*, a now extinct member of the bovid family that includes the wildebeest, as well as aquatic species such as fish, crocodiles and turtles that were also incorporated in the hominin diet.[13]

This was important because such food sources provide specific nutrients needed for human brain growth, in particular polyunsaturated fatty acids and docosahexaenoic acid and as such were vital in the evolution of greater and new capabilities.[14] Indeed, some scholars have argued that changes in neurochemistry of the basal ganglia in the brain were the critical factor in the emergence of hominins from apes, as well as in subsequent developments of the cerebral cortex that help explain social behaviour, including communication, empathy and altruism.[15]

Some have also argued that the increase in brain size is correlated with rising population levels and reflects the need to adapt to growing group size (the 'social brain hypothesis'). Others however stress that the pressures of new or changing ecological environments were crucial, requiring intelligence for adaptation in order to ensure survival. A pivotal genetic mutation in *Homo sapiens* that dramatically increased the number of brain cells may also have brought cognitive advantages that had far-reaching consequences. While this is a lively area of scholarly discussion, there is wide agreement that ecological and social competition were 'motors' of evolution, driving biological, neurological and behavioural changes.[16]

Key to this too was the human ability to use and control fire, whose benefits include cooking, warmth and protection from predators and the encroachment of wildlife. Natural fire occurs primarily as a result of the hundreds of millions of lightning flashes that occur annually over the earth.[17] Changes to the human body, to teeth and brain size, and in the development of language and of more complex cognitive skills have been linked to the introduction of the cooking of foods – although each was part of steady progression spread over long periods of time.[18] Evidence of burned wood, bone, grasses and other material from cave sites in southern Africa, the Levant and eastern China suggest that at least some *Homo* populations had learned to control fire by between 1 million and 500,000 years ago, with traces becoming common at many sites in Europe, Africa, Asia and elsewhere by around 400,000 years ago.[19]

One of the most challenging problems facing early *Homo* was fluctuating climate patterns with stratigraphic, lake, faunal and other data suggesting regular dynamic shifts between aridity and moisture across hundreds of thousands of years. These were driven by tectonic and volcanic impacts, by the eccentricity of the earth's orbital cycle, by solar activity and by changes in moisture availability linked to the strength of monsoon intensity, the size of large lakes and the El Niño–Southern Oscillation (ENSO). Taken together, these required versatility, and played important roles in shaping dietary, cognitive and social adaptability in early *Homo*.[20]

Africa was the melting pot for different species – so much so that the genetic diversity in African groups and individuals for the most recent human species is greater than in any other part of the world.[21] By around 2 million years ago, some *Homo* species and populations had migrated to other continents, likely in two dispersal events.[22] The earliest attested example – of *Homo erectus* – can be found in the Caucasus.[23] There is evidence of *Homo erectus* in China and Java around 1.7 million years ago and then of the colonisation of western Europe over a million years ago.[24]

The context, nature and timing of these processes are unclear, as are the differences within as well as between different *Homo* populations. While a range of explanations seek to explain these divergences, our own species may have started to emerge as distinct from *Homo neanderthalensis* as much as 800,000 years ago – considerably earlier than the first fossil records from sites in North-West Africa and Ethiopia that are usually dated to 315,000–195,000 years old, though this is a matter of fierce debate.[25]

What is not contested is that recent research has underlined that the story of hominin population is more complicated and more varied than has long been thought. New hominin populations have recently been identified, some of which must have mixed with modern humans.[26] Scholars have argued that specific haplotypes (sets of genetic variants that can be inherited) in Native American populations reflect the fact that the descendants of some of these were among the first settlers of the Americas, while it has also been suggested that some passed on genes that helped modern humans survive at high altitude.[27]

Neanderthals inhabited western Eurasia over many millennia, and later evidently reproduced with our own species – though not everywhere: Neanderthal ancestry is found in human genomes today, and in ancient populations as far apart as northern Europe, Siberia and China, with little present in sub-Saharan Africa.[28] Admixture between Neanderthals and *Homo sapiens* introduced groups of genes into modern humans which, for example, affect the immune systems – some have been linked with resistance to COVID-19 infection, and others to increased susceptibility.[29]

Neanderthal population distribution appears to have been heavily impacted by climatic stress, more so than our own species was (at least by around 45,000 years ago), because larger bodies, bigger brains and consequently high energy and food requirements perhaps resulted in lower levels of resilience, especially during periods of rapid cooling.[30] This might explain long-term patterns where large parts of Europe were colonised, then abandoned and then recolonised by Neanderthals, depending on weather conditions being more or less favourable.[31] This might also explain separate radiations of Neanderthals attested by mitochondrial DNA (mtDNA) from cave sediments in western Europe and southern Siberia.[32] Indeed, it has been argued that cold episodes provided crucial triggers for major divergences within Neanderthal populations, as well as prompting variations in mtDNA of other hominin groups living in Europe and Asia.[33]

Coping mechanisms for extremely challenging climate spells, such as around 450,000 years ago when ice-cap and permafrost advances in Europe made much of the continent uninhabitable, may have included drastic adaptations for *Homo* groups including Neanderthals: it has even been suggested that surprisingly high levels of serum parathyroid hormone in skeletal finds in Atapuerca, northern Spain, provide indications of bodies entering a hypometabolic state. Some of our ancestors, in other words, appear to have hibernated during cold winters. This hypothesis is highly speculative; but if the findings are accurate, it may be that adults were able to do so successfully on occasion, while adolescents appear to have found the process more difficult.[34]

Neanderthals and *Homo sapiens* shared many characteristics and abilities including similar auditory and speech capacities.[35] Nevertheless, *Homo sapiens* is a relatively homogeneous species, with mtDNA and Y-chromosome genealogy pointing to the fact that all modern humans descend from a small or even a very small population size, followed by a highly effective and successful expansion.[36] Changes in climate over the last 200,000 years seem to have been crucial in demographic dispersals as well as in repeated redistributions of genes – as geographic sinks formed that were peopled by groups like the Hadza in Tanzania, the Baka/Biaka and Mbuti/Efe Pygmies in western and eastern Central

Africa respectively, that are comparatively unmixed descendants of an early, modern human population.[37] More favourable climatic conditions in specific regions and pockets brought about genetic, cultural and behavioural change, while those living in more challenging locations in Africa found that survival was difficult or even impossible.[38]

The ability to adapt, learn and pass on information was important – and was acquired successfully: as one recent study based on a site in southern France shows, early humans 170,000 years ago understood how to position a hearth in caves in the optimal location for smoke dispersal (and therefore to lower exposure to smoke levels) but ideal for their social, heating and cooking needs.[39]

One key point in the history of our species came around 130,000 years ago with a sudden and dramatic reorganisation of global temperatures, sea level and weather which were modulated by changes in ocean circulation and deep-water ocean CO_2 storage.[40] This was likely caused by a so-called Heinrich event, in which large numbers of icebergs are discharged from the Laurentide Ice Sheet through the Hudson Strait into the North Atlantic Ocean, leaving layers of debris in the ocean sediment.[41] This would have significantly reduced North Atlantic Deep Water formation and interfered with ocean circulation, leading to heat accumulation in the southern hemisphere. In any event, the result was a rapid rise in polar temperatures, which led to the 'greening' of the Arctic as plants expanded their habitats northwards.[42] In due course, seawater melt led to global sea levels going up by several metres, and perhaps to as much nine metres above present-day levels.[43]

Evidence from chironomids (non-biting midges) trapped in sediment layers in Denmark has helped with temperature reconstructions which suggest that this period was one of sustained warming for a period lasting several thousand years.[44] It also corresponds to changes to vegetation and drainage networks across the Sahara that opened up a network of corridors linking East Africa to the Mediterranean and led to the first *Homo sapiens* settlements in the Levant.[45] The identification of six phases of lake formation, each with distinct sedimentary markers which can be detected using luminescence dating, and which mirror stone-tool usage by early humans, suggests that this process took place not in one go but in a series of pulses.[46]

There is still considerable uncertainty about the timings, routes and nature of dispersal of modern humans from Africa – although pioneering work in whole-genome sequencing technology is providing new insights into genetic and regional variation, into mixing with Neanderthals and Denisovans and into the existence of other human populations that disappeared but are known through skeletal records.[47]

Human expansion and settlement were shaped above all by finding areas that were ecologically benign. These included a wide variety of habitats, ranging from warm wooded environments to savannah grasslands, as well as coastal areas rich in marine life – although it seems that very open environments were deliberately avoided.[48] One particularly attractive location was the narrow strip of woodland between the Mediterranean coast and the flanks of Jordan's Rift Valley, a location with stable water supplies and wildlife that could be exploited with relative ease. There is evidence that this region was inhabited concurrently with a Neanderthal population that had moved southwards from Eurasia, as evidenced by burials and skeletal and dental remains, as well as by signs of interbreeding with the modern humans who had also established themselves there.[49]

Existence could be precarious, as this case proves: around 73,000 years ago, a period of extreme aridity and glaciation brought about such difficult times that the populations in the Levant appear to have failed and died out. The cause may have been a massive eruption at Mount Toba in what is now Indonesia, the largest on earth in the last 2 million years. The injection into the stratosphere of volcanic fine-particle sulphate aerosols was so great that a volcanic winter resulted that lasted for several years, leading to a sharp drop in temperatures in many locations around the world. Deposits were left across millions of square kilometres, with more than 1 per cent of the earth's surface being covered with at least ten centimetres of ash.[50] More than two and a half metres fell on southern India, with the subcontinent as a whole subjected to large-scale deforestation and the transformation of woodland into grasslands.[51] It has been argued that pressures on food supplies and survival were so great as to drive a major reduction in the human gene pool globally.[52]

Although devastating, the impact of the Mount Toba eruption was not uniform. Global climate model simulations suggest that the effects in Europe, North America and Central Asia were pronounced, but were much more modest in the southern hemisphere.[53] This would explain why sediment from Lake Malawi does not indicate any significant temperature change through this period.[54] Archaeological sites in South Africa meanwhile show that humans thrived through the Toba eruption and the glacial conditions that followed. There are signs too from a valley in central India – which was covered with 1 million cubic metres of tephra (pyroclastic material ejected by volcanoes during eruptions) – that the human population was able either to overcome the challenging conditions or, if not, to reoccupy sites not long afterwards that had been previously lived in.[55] Recent research has proposed that the eruption was so powerful that it ejected sulphates in concentrations of such large particle size that the cooling effect was both shorter and less dramatic than previous models have suggested, thanks to heavy particles falling to earth relatively quickly.[56] Ironically, the human survivors of this episode were fortunate, in other words, that the eruption was as powerful as it was.

Even before the Toba eruption, a more successful series of dispersals of *Homo sapiens* from Africa had already begun, again either provoked or influenced by environmental pressures. One speculative hypothesis suggests migration across the Red Sea from what is now Eritrea to the coast of Yemen was linked to all-time low marine-life and sea levels around 85,000 years ago, leading to shortages in seafood and protein sources which prompted a search for more favourable habitats. In due course, humans spread out into South-East Asia, China and beyond, reaching Australia by around 65,000 years ago.[57]

By this time, humans had already long been working on how to manage ecosystems, for example developing forest-management techniques that included deliberate use of fire to clear areas, influencing vegetation composition and in some cases causing soil erosion.[58] These became increasingly important not only because of the effects of the eruption but also because of a new period of cooling lasting several millennia that was under way in the northern hemisphere in response to a warming of the South Atlantic Ocean.

This also brought about more humid conditions and higher levels of rainfall in southern Africa and consequently a platform for increases in population size, density and increased socialisation. Linking cultural patterns to rapid changes in climate is a problematic exercise. It is striking, nonetheless, that what must have been challenging conditions coincided with the emergence of symbolic expression through engraved ochres, tools and jewellery that bear testimony to important innovations not only in behaviour but also in the development of new technologies.[59] Beads found at Blombos Cave in Western Cape in South Africa were made of estuarine molluscs around 70,000 years ago, with use-wear patterns consistent with friction from rubbing against thread, skin or other beads.[60] These were broadly contemporaneous with the earliest paintings, chunks of ochre engraved with complex geometric patterns that were found in the same location.[61]

It was a similar story with other shifting behaviours and innovations, for example with practical tools, including the emergence of projectiles and weapons such as the bow and arrow that create greater acceleration than hand-cast spears, enhancing wounding capacity while also improving personal security by enabling the ability to wound or kill at greater distances.[62] Such devices had the further benefit of increasing the size of potential targets, which in turn had further effects on social organisation for human populations.[63]

All such transformations were gradual, not uniform, and are not always easy to interpret or understand. For example, it has been suggested that the expansion and then collapse of social networks across eastern and southern Africa around 50,000–33,000 years ago, which can be attested by ostrich eggshell beads, was influenced by global and regional climatic change, and moreover that a later improvement in conditions led to a renewal of contact between communities, including the spread of standardised cultural behaviour.[64] Such hypotheses are compelling, but they depend on relying on wisps of evidence that can be interpreted in many different ways.

Clearly, however, the social world of hunter-gatherers became more complex, with rituals starting to develop that helped manage and regulate relationships, alongside an emerging context for symbolic expression. By around 50,000 BC, Neanderthals had been experimenting with artistic forms, including creating ornamental works – perhaps as jewellery – as well as undertaking cave paintings such as at Cueva de Ardales in Spain.[65]

By around 40,000 years ago, geometric and iconographic representations were becoming common and are well documented in the Near East and North Africa.[66] Different kinds of artistic forms also began to be used. The earliest cave art attributed to *Homo sapiens* comes in the form of two cave paintings depicting two warty pigs from the limestone karsts of South Sulawesi, in modern Indonesia, which were created around 45,000 years ago according to uranium-series dating.[67]

In Europe, where the first *Homo sapiens* are first attested by that time, early cave art depicts humans and animals interacting with each other.[68] Some rare examples can also be found of therianthropes – that is, mythical figures – that are half human and half animal; these hint at the development of narrative fiction, religion, folklore and ideas about the supernatural.[69]

It has recently been argued that the blossoming of cave art that took place 42,000 years ago was linked to an abrupt period of dramatic climate change. An episode known as the Laschamps Excursion saw simultaneous shifts of precipitation and wind patterns in the Pacific and Southern Ocean, a sharp decline in the strength of earth's magnetic field and a spell of unstable solar activity that included multiple massive flares that also affected global weather patterns. The results included glacial expansions in the Andes and aridification in Australia that were so profound that they led to the wholesale extinction of large animals. The expansion of the Laurentide Ice Sheet and the cooling of North America and Europe, combined with electrical storms and auroras that produced spectacular light shows in the skies, forced modern humans to seek protection in caves for longer periods and perhaps provided inspiration for more creative forms of social engagement and artistic expression. That, at least, is one intriguing hypothesis – which has not convinced many specialists.[70] Another is that early artists looking for inspiration might have been inspired, intentionally or otherwise, by low concentrations of oxygen levels at the back of deep, dark caves that caused altered states of consciousness, resulting in hallucinations and out-of-body experiences.[71]

The period around 40,000 years ago also marked the disappearance of the Neanderthal population in Europe, with the sudden harsh subarctic conditions appearing to be a contributing factor, and perhaps even a decisive one.[72] The Neanderthals had already begun to experience a rapid demise across Eurasia, with a range of explanations advanced to explain the demographic collapse – including changes to vegetation, rising levels of disease and interbreeding. While each may have played a role, it may be that their fate was sealed by the fact that *Homo sapiens* proved better at exploiting food resources that became scarce as temperatures become colder – although recent research suggests that Neanderthals and *Homo sapiens* coexisted for far longer than had previously been assumed in at least some locations.[73] The tenfold expansion of the modern human population in Europe around this time also meant that there were not only better competitors but many more of them. It seems that the Neanderthals had died out entirely around 35,000 years ago.[74]

Neanderthals were not the only ones who suffered as a result of shifting climatic patterns and, perhaps just as importantly, of the resultant changes in ecosystems. It is no coincidence, for example, that the expansion of savannahs from Indo-China across South-East Asia to what is now Indonesia had corresponded with maximum hominin diversity.[75] As conditions changed, almost all hominin species failed to survive – even though the transitions were gradual and spread across thousands of years. Nevertheless, what is most striking about *Homo Sapiens* was the ability to cope with and even flourish in different conditions across rainforest and marine habitats.[76] The fact that modern humans set off for new pastures around this time, settling remote parts of Oceania like Vanuatu and Polynesia, shows both resourcefulness and remarkable initiative.[77]

Of course, it is all very well to suggest that modern humans' adaptability, versatility and durability were key ingredients for success, but it is clear that these alone were not enough. So while it is tempting to focus on the fact that a community at the Madjedbebe rock shelter in the Kakadu region of northern Australia was able to thrive and expand during a long period of cold weather that brought about major water shortages to most of the continent around 30,000 years ago, it is more revealing that most of Australia was abandoned at the same time.[78]

It was a similar story in other parts of the world during the Last Glacial Maximum which started at roughly the same time and led to an expansion of ice sheets in the northern hemisphere, a decrease in Pacific sea temperatures and a decline in atmospheric CO_2 levels.[79] Population levels in central Europe collapsed as human populations either died out or relocated in search of more hospitable conditions.[80] Refuges like the Grotta del Romito in southern Italy became extremely important settlements and provide invaluable case studies in helping show how people lived, coped and managed through difficult times.[81]

The western Mediterranean was particularly affected through this cold period, which lasted for several thousand years, with the formation of clay dune and pollen records indicating significant falls in precipitation levels. Archaeological evidence, meanwhile, shows repeated migration from unstable 'high-risk' parts of what is now southern Spain to the north, as well as presenting a picture of substantial demographic decline.[82] While much of the period of the Last Glacial Maximum (c.26,500–19,000 years ago) was dry, it was punctuated by a 3,000-year phase of massive autumnal and early-winter snowfall in the European Alps that resulted in the expansion of glaciers – and to conditions that were unforgiving if not unsurvivable.[83]

Evidence from marine cores from North Africa throughout the Last Glacial Maximum show collapsed rainfall levels but also very sharp cooling, with temperatures 15 °C – and perhaps as much as 21 °C – lower than today.[84] Land temperatures fell by around 6 °C based on studies of noble gases dissolved in groundwater measured across six continents.[85] Sea levels in the South China Sea dropped by 100–120 metres and by even more in the East China Sea.[86] The winter monsoons became considerably stronger and also changed distribution of rainfall patterns – resulting in marked shifts in vegetation, including increased desertification in the north of what is now China and an expansion of deciduous forests in the south.[87]

It was not just humans who struggled in these cold conditions. Sites in Morocco reveal that Aleppo pine and evergreen oaks benefited at the cost of cedar trees, which found it all but impossible to grow because of the cold and the lack of rainfall.[88] Further south, in what is now the Democratic Republic of Congo, forest cover was reduced – although assessing how and when is more complex than adopting a story of simple contraction and expansion.[89] Changing ecosystems and vegetation in South-East Asia, meanwhile, brought about losses of grazing lands for elephants, rhinos and tapirs and the extinction of hyenas in this region and perhaps for the *Gigantopithecus blacki*, the largest ape ever to have existed, which stood at around three metres (double the height of an orang-utan) and weighed as much as 270 kilos – considerably more, in other words, than the largest modern mountain gorilla.[90]

These were just the latest in a series of massive losses of animal life. Between 50,000 and 10,000 years ago, there were spectacular declines of megafauna – that is, large mammals such as woolly rhinoceroses and sabre-toothed cats. Over this period, at least 97 of the 150 known genera weighing more than 44 kilos became extinct. The causes of these losses have been much debated, with the main explanations being that they were precipitated by human expansion principally through hunting, by anthropogenic change of habitats, by environmental and climatic change, by the lack of access to freshwater sources or by a combination of all four.[91] The result was a set of animal extinctions that were of a speed and scale that had been unprecedented for millions of years.[92]

The fact that disappearance rates of large animals in South America were high despite evidence of stable environmental conditions and that they appear mainly to have taken place after the arrival of the first humans around 15,000 years ago provides a telling pointer to the conclusion that our ancestors played an important role in large-scale losses in this continent and perhaps in others too.[93] Some scholars have suggested that the decline in large animals forced humans to hunt smaller prey and to develop new technologies better suited to doing so; indeed the lack of availability of large game in the southern Levant has been linked to foragers broadening their dietary range and even to the beginnings of agriculture.[94] It is worth stressing, however, that this is a complicated picture and that the regions that suffered the most significant climatic disruption across this period also experienced the greatest losses.[95]

The extinctions of such large numbers of species and in such high volumes naturally had an impact on terrestrial ecosystems. There were striking changes in flora distribution, including declines in large-seeded tree species as well as fruit dispersal, as a result of the disappearance of large herbivores. These changes had an effect on carbon storage in Amazonian forests, leading to a significant reduction in capacity.[96] Evidence from Australia also suggests that megafauna disappearance, whether because of hunting and expansion or environmental change, brought about relaxed herbivore pressure on vegetation that helped transform ecosystems – as did increased and deliberate use of fire in the landscape by the human population.[97]

Deglaciation around 19,000 years ago began a new set of modifications to landscapes. Ice sheets across North America began to melt, resulting in megafloods that were among the largest flood events in the world's history and whose courses were shaped by the deformation and tilting of the earth's crust – changing the elevation of topography by hundreds of metres in the process.[98] The retreat of ice sheets in the northern hemisphere and of glaciers over several thousand years resulted in the addition of enormous volumes of freshwater into the oceans. The results included major sea-level rises around the world that averaged eighty metres, the disturbance of terrestrial and marine ecosystems and a net release of carbon dioxide and methane into the atmosphere.[99]

To give just one example of the scale of change, around 2 million square kilometres of Australia became submerged between around 15,000 and 8,000 years ago, eventually reducing the land mass by a third. New research using predictive models, satellite imagery, acoustic surveys and topographic and bathymetric LIDAR reveals multiple human settlements 160 kilometres from the current coastline which had to be abandoned as sea levels rose. Assessing what socio-economic and cultural consequences these had is difficult, but they must have been substantial.[100] Even though population concentrations appear to have been relatively small, the fact that the coastline receded by an average of more than twenty metres per year shows that changes must have seemed both never ending and ominous as the sea kept advancing and land kept disappearing.[101]

The impacts elsewhere in the world were also substantial. Most scholars date the arrival of the first modern humans in the Americas to around 22,000 years ago, with genomic data showing that ancestral Native Americans diverged from Siberians and East Asians before crossing the Bering Straits into what is now Alaska, helped by lower sea levels which revealed an archipelago of islands that turned the straits into a series of stepping stones.[102] Subsequent genetic divergences split those who reached the Americas into two further distinct groups.[103]

The nature, causes and migration routes of the dispersals are currently the subject of major re-evaluation, partly thanks to new discoveries, but also thanks to better and more accurate techniques used for interpreting materials.[104] For example, radiocarbon and luminescence dates for a high-altitude cave in the Astillero mountains in the state of Zacatecas in Mexico, as well as cut marks on rabbit and deer bones from the Tehuacán Valley, have recently pushed the date for the earliest settlers in the Americas back by some 10,000 years, to around 30,000 BC, while recent research on the Colorado plateau suggests an earlier date still, to around 37,000 years ago.[105] Forest sanctuaries along the Pacific coast of North America seem to have played vital roles in ensuring the survival of the first peoples to reach the Americas by providing refuges that offered shelter, food and other resources.[106] What is most striking, however, is not just the dates of expansion of populations, but the fact that sparse examples above all show how precarious life was for the first settlers. Waves of groups may have arrived and simply have died out time and time again, until conditions improved to enable more successful, long-term settlement.

If this was the most likely scenario, then it is perhaps no coincidence that a marked improvement in environmental and climatic conditions corresponds to much greater evidence of successful migration and permanent settlement across North America and the Caribbean, as well as in Central and South America.[107] One attraction for the expansion of groups southwards may well have been that post-glacial warming began first in parts of the southern hemisphere, making such regions more hospitable and attractive.[108]

Between 16,000 and 10,000 years ago, there were considerable rises in global temperature, with estimates suggesting a likely range of 4–7 °C for the increase in surface air heat and lesser but still significant rises in the warmth of oceans.[109] An abrupt warming in the northern hemisphere around 14,700 years ago seems to have been caused by the release of heat from warm waters in the deep North Atlantic Ocean which in turn was linked to increased salinity at depths that had previously preserved the static stability of the water column.[110]

Records from speleothems and from marine and lake pollen cores in the Levant reveal that there was a rise in precipitation around 10,000–7,000 years ago – something that has been linked with prompting an expansion of foragers, who fanned out into new locations across this region, bringing with them lithic tools.[111] Indeed, some have suggested that improving ecological conditions played a role not only in encouraging wider dispersal patterns of the existing population, but in attracting new settlers, including from North Africa.[112]

Macrofossil and pollen records taken from hundreds of sites around the world show that changes to vegetation as the Last Glacial Maximum subsided were substantial – especially at mid- to high latitudes in the northern hemisphere, in South America and in tropical and temperate southern Africa, as well as across the Indo-Pacific region and Oceania. This warming phase saw significant uplifts in atmospheric CO_2 concentrations, rising from 190 to 280 parts per million during the period of deglaciation. However, temperature increases did not lead to uniform ecological change and in some cases even produced counter-intuitive outcomes.[113] For example, studies on plants in the contemporary world which show that some species respond to warming through adaptation remind us how important it is to think not just about human reactions when faced with changing conditions – and also to bear in mind the nuances and complexities of understanding climate change as a whole.[114] This is significant given that the rate of global warming in the coming decades is projected to be in the order of sixty-five times as high as it was during the last major deglaciation.[115] Understanding how, where, when and why plant – as well as human and animal – life reacts to change is fundamental to making sense of what the future is likely to hold in store locally, regionally and globally.

A new climate shock that occurred around 12,900 years ago brought about an abrupt reversal of the long-term warming process. The causes of this event, known as the Younger Dryas, remain controversial. The prevailing view is that the cooling was the result of large ice-sheet discharge of freshwater into the North Atlantic.[116] However, some scholars have proposed that a supernova explosion in the Vela constellation depleted the ozone layer, prompting atmospheric and surface changes that led to cooling.[117] A remarkable platinum spike at the aptly named Wonderkrater site in Limpopo province, South Africa, has persuaded some that a meteor or asteroid strike was responsible.[118] The presence of volcanic gas aerosols in well-dated sediment at a site in Texas, however, suggests a large-scale eruption as the most likely cause of change – with the Laacher See volcano in Germany a particular suspect.[119] There certainly were comet strikes elsewhere around this time, such as in the Atacama desert in northern Chile, where one impact generated so much heat that sandy soil was turned into glass.[120] It is not impossible, of course, that multiple events may have been responsible for the rapidly changing climate – and that they combined to produce effects that, although not as dramatic as major extinction events, were nevertheless substantial.

Temperatures fell rapidly, producing substantial drops within as little as three years.[121] They fell so steeply that some studies of the nitrogen-isotope signal suggest they eventually settled at 15 °C (+/– 3 °C) colder than temperatures today.[122] Carbonate geochemistry from lake sediments in northern China provides evidence of abrupt cooling during a thousand-year-long period that altered the atmospheric coupling of the North Atlantic and East Asian weather patterns.[123] So does the pollen record from New Zealand, although this also suggests that parts of the southern hemisphere were getting colder before the Younger Dryas event.[124]

One obvious result was an increase in the variability of sea-ice cover and unstable global climatic conditions generally.[125] Another was a change in monsoon rainfall, although there were significant spatial differences, with the calcium carbonate record from Lake Qinghai on the Tibetan plateau suggestive of a decline in precipitation, while palaeohydrological records from the middle reaches of the Yangtze indicate higher rainfall levels following the Younger Dryas event.[126] High-resolution studies from Lakes Malawi, Tanganyika and Bosumtwi indicate abrupt shifts in the wind-driven circulation of these lakes, while a range of other evidence suggests an abrupt northward translation of the African monsoon system that resulted in marked increases in precipitation in the northern tropics and drought conditions in the south.[127]

Naturally, the impacts on flora and fauna were profound. There was a new wave of large-scale animal extinctions – once again as a result of hunting, climate stress or a combination of the two.[128] There were substantial changes to vegetation distribution in Europe, Canada, Africa and elsewhere.[129] Not surprisingly, there are also clear indications of contractions in the human populations, for example in North America.[130] DNA evidence suggests genetic substitutions in Europe and elsewhere that are indicative of major demographic reductions around this period.[131] A marked decrease in the number of sites occupied by humans in Japan also provide a telling signature of population collapse.[132]

In the Levant, a response to more hostile conditions was the establishment of small settlements inhabited by permanent or semi-permanent populations. Such developments may have enabled a pooling of resources and skills, but also served as a collaborative solution for security and defence needs against other groups at a time of rising food shortages and pressures. Staying put may also have been an effective way of protecting land that yielded wild cereals and of ensuring that the best sites were not taken over opportunistically by others.[133]

After around a thousand years of these cold conditions came a reset some 11,900 years ago. Climate archives show that the first signs of a warming process began in the western tropical Pacific and the southern hemisphere, which then spread into the North Atlantic over the course of around two centuries.[134] Ice-core records from Greenland suggest that, once temperatures started to rise, they did so extremely quickly, going up by more than 10 °C in sixty years.[135] The scale of warming, as well as the acceleration over such a short period, again has implications for understanding the potential consequences of climate change in the contemporary world, not least since many current projections assume global warming will be gradual and constant, rather than sudden and dramatic.

The end of the Younger Dryas marked the start of a new period, first named the Holocene – literally 'an entirely new era' – in the 1860s by the French palaeontologist Paul Gervais, who was struck by the changes to the sediment layer following the deglaciation that marked the end of the Ice Age. Scholars today now typically pinpoint the start of the Holocene by stable isotope data from Greenland ice cores that measure the ratio of stable oxygen isotopes to 11,700 years ago.[136]

Since that time, there have been fluctuations and changes, including ones that have seemed and have even been substantial. Seen in the long run, the end of the Younger Dryas is little more than a staging post in history, just another moment in the fluctuations between cooling and warming phases marked by the expansion or retreat of ice sheets, by alterations of monsoon and precipitation patterns and by changes to air surface and ocean temperatures that, while not uniform, brought challenges and in many cases resulted in adaptive changes for vegetation, animal and marine life. One good example comes from the sudden appearance of Pacific nitrogen in the Arctic basin as the land bridge linking what is now Russia and Alaska flooded with the rise in sea levels, changing ecosystems for plankton and the food chains that build upwards from them.[137]

From a human perspective, however, it marked a watershed. The onset of a long period of warmer, stable conditions corresponded with some profound changes in demographic expansion, settlement patterns and innovations – the most significant of which was the emergence of agriculture. Even before the onset of the Holocene, there is evidence that rising levels of complexity were producing innovations in technology and in cultural behaviour. In North Africa, for example, new lithic and bladelet technologies start to appear around the time of the deglaciation.[138] This was also the case across many parts of Asia, such as in northern Mongolia, where rock art in the form of petroglyphs, often depicting ibex, began to appear in the early Holocene.[139]

The earliest examples of human cemeteries are suggestive of changing ideas about the body, about life and about identity – as is the fact that burials provide evidence of the deliberate removal of healthy teeth, likely at an early age and above all but not only among women; this may have been part of an attempt at enabling group identification within relatively restricted geographic zones, and as such reflects the adoption of ideas about the distinction between kinship and social groups.[140] The transition from mobile hunter-gatherer societies into more sedentary economies required new ways not only of acting, but also of thinking.[141]

There is abundant evidence too from the Levant from before the Younger Dryas of some communities adopting either semi- or even fully sedentary lifestyles, and building structures with stone foundations, including storage buildings. The presence of grinding stones at several locations has been interpreted by some scholars as indicating not only the collection of wild cereals but also their cultivation.[142]

Many scholars have sought to associate behavioural change with environmental factors during the Younger Dryas itself, arguing for example that the earliest experimentations with plant cultivation were responses to the need to increase food production during periods of declining resource abundance.[143] These were translated into more systematic and successful efforts to grow food once climate conditions became more favourable. These in turn prompted innovations in tool manufacture as well as the generation of surpluses which enabled human groups to select and establish themselves in environmentally favourable locations that did not require seasonal mobility and allowed ever larger communities to live together.

Over time, this laid the basis for villages, towns and cities and as such spurred the development of writing systems, religions, complex economies, new social and political structures – indeed for 'civilisation' in its literal meaning of urbanised settlements. Such transitions, as we shall see, were not straightforward or without their costs. And, as we shall also see, other forms of engagement with flora and fauna, including pastoral nomadism – that is to say, the domestication of livestock – developed and were often both complementary to and in competition with sedentary societies.

Nevertheless, looking at the period up to the start of the Holocene in the round, it is hard not to be both surprised and impressed by how modern humans defied the odds time and again, managing to survive volcanic eruptions, intense or reduced solar activity and meteorite strikes – as well as dramatic changes in climate induced by tectonic, geological or axial movements that brought about sharp swings in habitats. Many species were unable to navigate these challenges – including all other hominins, who became extinct one by one.

Not all our ancestors made it, of course, with doomed expansions and settlements a part of the human story of trying and failing, as well as succeeding and surviving. And yet enough pockets flourished by adapting, by innovating and perhaps most importantly by being lucky enough to avoid being in the wrong place at the wrong time. By around 11,000 years ago, modern humans had managed to spread out across all the world's continents, except for Antarctica: some estimate three-quarters of terrestrial nature was inhabited, used and changed by this time, meaning that lands that were untouched were as rare then as they are today.[144] Striking as that is, what was more significant was that this meant that species risk was diversified, significantly raising the long-term chances of survival.

Even more fortuitously, then, while the last eleven millennia have not been uniformly clement or favourable, they have been less unstable and variable than at many times in the past.[145] While contending with potentially catastrophic global warming in the course of the twenty-first century should not be downplayed, current projected rises of 1.5–2 °C are modest in the grand scheme of climatic change, not only in the history of the earth but in that of humans too, and look paltry indeed compared to the very many and regular double-digit rises and falls that have occurred in the past.

Fortunately, our own limited sense of time is helpful in avoiding too many sleepless nights. When we think of history, we conceptualise time with reference to human achievements and to events we choose to relate to. By necessity this makes our frames of reference both highly self- and species-centred and laughably narrow. Casting our minds back to the age of the Victorians is to imagine another world – inviting us to investigate how people thought and behaved, to wonder what they wore, wrote and listened to, and to marvel at their lives. Thinking back four millennia to the time of kingdoms in Mesopotamia and Egypt, to the cities like Harappa or Mohenjo-daro, to communities in the Niger Delta or Middle Yangtze, or to sites like Kotosh in the Andes or Tlapacoya in central Mexico seems almost impossibly exotic and difficult, a challenge for historians, archaeologists, anthropologists and others to imagine how societies in the past were structured and functioned.

However, periods spanning decades, centuries and even millennia are the briefest of blinks of an eye in terms of the history of this planet; and in that sense they are perhaps not even important ones either: the earth has been spinning around the sun for billions of years, and will continue to do so for billions of years more. In one way, then, the Holocene is the perfect tag for the modern age – a time that is geologically and climatically distinct, but which also corresponds to the era of modern humans, an era we invariably fail to place within the bigger picture.

Since its beginnings – whenever or wherever those may be – our species has expanded, colonised, reproduced, created and dominated, but it has also destroyed, devastated and exterminated. It has done so better than almost any other organism that has lived in the last 4.5 billion years. It is no coincidence that a more benign climate provided the springboard for all that to happen.

3

Human Interactions with Ecologies
(c.12,000–c.3500 BC)

Those who are too lazy to plough in the right season will have no food at the harvest.

Book of Proverbs, 20:4

The Holocene marked the start of much more favourable climate conditions in many locations around the world. For one thing, the shift from around 10,000 years ago began a long period of stable weather patterns, which in itself was significant, reducing the number and frequency of shocks – although there were of course significant spatial differences between and within continents. Generally, however, temperatures rose, as did levels of rainfall. Crucially, CO_2 content in the atmosphere also increased sharply from levels during the Last Glacial Maximum that were so low that photosynthesis would have been limited and would therefore have affected the capacity, durability and reliability of plants as food resources. As one influential research paper has put it, agriculture may not have been impossible before the Holocene, but it suited conditions perfectly after its onset.[1]

Sedimentary sequences and pollen spectra from Guxu Lake in eastern China show clear evidence of warmer and more humid conditions, as does the expansion of evergreen–deciduous broadleaf mixed forests, starting around 8000 BC.[2] Radiocarbon-dated sediment cores from eastern Guatemala indicate progressive increases in precipitation and erosion levels spanning a period of 5,000 years after c.7500 BC.[3] North

Africa experienced profound changes that were closely correlated to and perhaps explained by increased summer insolation and Arctic sea-ice loss – which seems to have driven strong solar heating in the northern hemisphere generally.[4] Much of the Sahara was transformed into grass savannah, opening up new areas for human occupation and transforming plant and animal ecosystems in the process.[5] This has often been attributed to the rotation of tilt of the earth's axis that occurs roughly every 25,000 years, which enhanced the summer monsoon, although some now propose that the so-called Green Sahara was the result of a southward shift of the Mediterranean winter precipitation system.[6]

The effects of these changes were particularly important in the Levant, above all in the Fertile Crescent where population levels rose during the Younger Dryas – probably a reflection of migrations from less hospitable locations as conditions elsewhere became harsher.[7] Higher levels of competition presumably put pressure on flora and fauna food resources, something that would have been made worse by the apparent declining availability of wild cereals and pulses before environmental conditions began to improve at the start of the Holocene.[8] One response was for settlers to pay more attention to harvesting wild plants; another was the systematic exploitation of wild herds of sheep, goat and gazelle.[9]

Many scholars today stress the importance of gender in the development of agriculture, in terms both of crop cultivation and of food storage and preparation.[10] Women played crucial roles in rituals of gathering, preparation, display and use of plants, while burials of women inside houses can also be understood not as reflecting domestic roles, but as evidence of their role as primary intercessors with ancestors and the spiritual world.[11] The sheer number of figurines depicting women as deities across multiple cultures in Mesopotamia and elsewhere underlines the fact that gender roles were enormously significant in the development of ideas about fertility and sustenance as well as about life and death.[12]

The centrality of women to early agriculture is also evident from the osteological analysis that reveals upper-body strength at levels that would have surpassed today's elite female athletes.[13] Musculoskeletal stress levels in both men and women suggest that there was a sharing of labour when it came to early sowing and reaping of crops leading some to suggest that separate gender roles did not emerge until around 3000 BC.[14]

Across the Fertile Crescent and the Zagros mountains in Iran, evidence of rising domestication of crops and animals from around 8000 BC suggests that knowledge was being spread as coping skills became the bedrock of new ways of living.[15] Domestic cereals like single-grained einkorn wheat, emmer wheat and hulled barley, as well as lentils, peas and bitter vetch, became established parts of human diets and spread first across the Fertile Crescent itself and then into Anatolia, Egypt and beyond.[16] Around the same time, the first signs of herding appear in South-West Asia, suggesting that sheep and goats were domesticated first, with cattle and pigs being brought under human control soon afterwards.[17]

These processes were slow and likely haphazard. It took time for new skills to be learned and refined, and when they were, they took time to be taught and to spread. And while it can be tempting to think of a 'transition' from hunter-gathering and foraging to agriculture and domestication, the reality was much more opaque – so much so that the value of the labels that describe apparent lifestyles is itself questionable. Development and adoption of new skills did not replace existing knowledge or make it redundant: in other words, the question is not so much where one draws lines between concepts like collection of food, cultivation, domestication and agriculture but why it is necessary to do so in the first place.[18]

What is clearer is that the start of the Holocene saw the emergence and expansion of new ways of dealing with food and with animals, and of seeking to optimise their benefits. That climatic and environmental change played a catalytic role in stimulating these developments would help explain why it is possible to identify similar patterns emerging in several parts of the world more or less concurrently. For example, despite reaching the Americas long after arriving in other continents, the human population also began to exploit the land more intensively around this time, with scholars arguing that reductions in numbers of large animals through hunting and because of climate impact were closely linked to efforts to secure more sedentary sources of food. Indeed, some have even argued that the extinction of large herbivores (weighing 200 kilos or more) may have been helpful to early crop domestication because their removal meant lower levels of disruption to plant habitats – and therefore lower risk and better reward for cultivators.[19]

In China, the evidence for the dating of more intensive engagement with crops is much debated and remains controversial. It is possible, for example, that early rice cultivation took place at Shangshan in the lower Yangtze River region around 8000 BC, though there is more certainty from other sites in central China, such as at Jiahu on the upper Huai River a thousand years later.[20] Nevertheless, the emergence of new settlement patterns, especially in the form of villages in both north and south China, point to fundamental socio-economic and ideological changes as populations shifted from the exploitation of wild plants to their management and cultivation and then to their domestication.[21]

The availability of reliable wild and domesticated food supplies not only facilitated the rise of sedentary life and of villages, but also enabled the concentrations of people that they could support. During earlier periods, groups living together in the Levant occupied sites that were small and were inhabited seasonally. Now, however, the size and number of settlements started to grow steadily over time – with communities numbering in the hundreds and sometimes even in the thousands by around 7000 BC. Naturally, this spurred a series of revolutions in social behaviour and in the adoption of new ideas, for example about the treatment of the dead – as attested by more elaborate burial practices, which included painting, retrieval and circulation of bones and skeletal parts, and of skulls in particular.[22] In at least some locations, it seems that vibrancy was injected by migration patterns, with new arrivals not only bringing new ideas and technologies with them, but also boosting gene pools. Diverse populations helped spur cultural dynamism, even if the ways in which they did so varied: in Upper Mesopotamia and some parts Asia Minor, for example, early sedentary communities were arranged around biological family lines, while others were marked by different kinship and social structures.[23]

Objects, totems and idols from multiple locations indicate rising interest in asking and answering cosmological questions about the human relationship with nature, the divine and unseen forces. These included stone stelae at Göbekli Tepe in south-eastern Anatolia, as well as sculptures of birds, snakes and anthropomorphic figures found at other sites in the same region.[24] Some were in human form, such as a stone carving of a man wearing a necklace, clasping his hands, found at Urfa in what is now Turkey, or a remarkable, very striking human-shaped idol, carved from wood and standing more than five metres in height, that was discovered by gold miners in the Shigir peat bog near Sverdlovsk more than a century ago.[25] Monumental buildings in north-western Arabia in which animal horns and cranial elements were arranged deliberately meanwhile provide evidence for an early cattle cult that should be understood alongside the rock art of this region.[26] A cemetery by Lake Onega in the largest-known burial ground in north-east Europe that has yielded large numbers of ornaments and pendants made of elk teeth – likely used to create rattling sounds for drumming, ceremonial dances and shamanic and other rituals – has been linked with changes in cultural and socio-economic practices that were driven by climatic shifts around 8,000 years ago.[27]

It has been argued that the advent of farming demanded the development of concepts of possession and of private property that had previously not been necessary – which is both logical and plausible, but for which it is difficult to provide hard evidence.[28] Rather more easy to demonstrate is the introduction of new skills and technologies, not least in architecture, with the construction of different types, sizes and uses of buildings.[29] Again, none of this was quick: the changes here were spread not just over decades and centuries, but over millennia.

In North Africa, the Sahara and the Nile Valley, settled communities also became more common as a result of more plentiful resources – in this case, fish life in particular, which was abundant in the vast chains of lakes and river networks that once criss-crossed the heart of the continent. Large volumes and variety of fish and molluscs are attested in the archaeological record, such as in the Takakrori rock shelter in south-west Libya in what is now the heart of the Sahara desert, as are remains of amphibian, reptile and bird species normally associated with aquatic environments.[30]

Changing ecosystems and shifts to a more sedentary way of life brought about new habits and lifestyles, with goods that were not easily transportable like grindstones becoming more common as people stayed in or close to fixed locations.[31] It is perhaps no coincidence, then, that the changing settlement patterns saw growing experimentation with new technologies. In north-west China, for example, new types of microlithic tools, blades and arrowheads were introduced and became increasingly common from around 8000 BC.[32] It was a similar story in the Americas, where assemblages of distinct and new tools that emerged at the start of the Holocene are linked by most scholars to changing ecologies and ways of living.[33]

The rapid diffusion of ceramics in many different regions around the same time suggests too that this was a time of innovation and rising complexity. What had previously been very limited production of pottery in Japan now expanded dramatically, perhaps as a result of new strategies of storage, perhaps because of rising sedentism, perhaps because of population growth – or a combination of all three. The spread of pottery technology across northern Eurasia and to Alaska suggests that a new era demanded new solutions.[34]

Some of the oldest examples of ceramics come from Niger and the Dogon plateau in Mali in West Africa and date to c.8000 BC.[35] In their earliest phase, ceramics were very rare in African settings. One explanation for this is that while the introduction of ceramics in general is sometimes seen as a moment of pivotal technological importance, the reality is that many low-tech containers had done a perfectly good job for the transportation and storage of food and water in the past. Reed baskets may not have been as durable as ceramic vessels, for example, but they required lower levels of investment of time, energy and competence. Likewise, ostrich eggshells had not only been widely used for decorative purposes for tens of thousands of years in Africa but had served effectively as water containers. The introduction of ceramics did not therefore represent a breakthrough in capabilities nor open new opportunities. Indeed, this is precisely why some scholars suggest that the earliest ceramics were primarily devised for social and ritualistic use.[36]

Ceramics were being produced in other parts of the continent by 7000 BC, most notably across a broad arc stretching from central Sahara to the Upper Nile.[37] By this time, ceramics were also widely attested across settled communities in much of the Levant, south-east Anatolia and in what is now the Nefud desert in Saudi Arabia but which at that time was studded with lakes and rivers and was an attractive habitat for human activity.[38] Curiously, the use of pottery for aquatic products in particular seems to be a recurrent theme across many global settings, as indicated by chemical and isotopic residue analysis from Korea, for example.[39]

Shifts to more sedentary ways of living were not instantaneous, and nor were they uniform geographically. And of course, while some communities formed in small settled clusters and others were more substantial, the distinctions between those who lived in permanent settlements and foragers or hunter-gatherers were often blurred. Certainly, there were wide ranges of different lifestyles, resource-gathering techniques and energy-expenditure decisions, as well as competition and co-operation that was dependent on location, season and population size. In other words, there was no 'one size fits all', but rather considerable nuance and difference depending on time, place and habitat.

Nor were settlements always successful. While attention is usually paid to groups and locations that settled and flourished, the reality is that in many cases attempts to live from the fruits of the land ended in failure.[40] Even in the Levant, where it has long been thought that the rise of village settlements was both inexorable and rarely punctuated by disruptions, recent research has revealed that abandonment of sites happened often, reflecting the fragilities and realities of efforts to build sustainable communities.[41] It is likely too that competition for resources and for the best locations brought about intergroup rivalry, conflict and violence – which in turn led to innovations in defensive fortification measures, as more contemporary examples from New Guinea in the south-western Pacific show.[42]

Nevertheless, perhaps the most important result of the improving climate conditions that marked the onset of the Holocene was a sharp rise in human population.[43] Certainly, the reliability and diversity of cereals reduced the risk of hunger, as did the construction and management of storage pits in which surplus could be kept for winter months and mitigate seasonal shocks. New tools and more durable storage vessels evidently helped with productivity jumps too, enabling larger communities to support themselves, especially in ecologically favourable locations.

The increase in calorie availability and the reduction in energy expenditure that resulted from being able to live on the produce of dependable and abundant resources in close proximity – from cereals or marine stocks – would seem in itself to go a long way to explaining rising population sizes.[44] So too does rising sedentism: modern ethnographies indicate that women in hunter-gatherer and forager societies such as the Agta in the Philippines typically have fewer children and longer gaps between childbirths than those in sedentary communities.[45] The fact that shorter interbirth intervals and higher levels of fertility are associated with increased carbohydrate consumption which in turn is linked to higher body mass index is also significant.[46] In other words, changes to living patterns as well as new engagement with plant-food sources may have influenced gender relationships and in particular maternal roles and expectations. This fits neatly with skeletal data from burial sites in Iberia from the early Holocene onwards that supports the hypothesis that changes to settlement and nutrition patterns were instrumental in driving higher numbers of births – and therefore in boosting population sizes.[47]

There were trade-offs to the rise in reliance on cereals and to rising densities of habitation – not least the impact on health. For one thing, work involving heavier tools for grinding and processing grain placed greater demands on the human body, resulting in cases of osteoarthritis rising as crop cultivation became more widespread; for another, the sugars in cereal carbohydrates brought about degradations in tooth enamel, with resulting high incidence of dental cavities.[48] The decline in dental health seems to have had a greater impact on women, perhaps because of higher fertility levels and resultant hormonal fluctuations, immunological competence during pregnancy and concurrent and subsequent variations in saliva composition.[49]

The harnessing of oxen around 6000 BC, initially for threshing, was significant therefore, helping relieve pressure on human labour forces thanks to time and energy boosts that helped provide the basis for a major uplift in food consumption.[50] The use of large animals in agriculture in turn spurred innovations such as carts and ploughs that helped further increase production, allowed more land to be cultivated more quickly and therefore supported larger populations. These developments had societal consequences too. For one thing, they brought about another change in gender roles as women shifted into domestic household tasks while men increasingly took over horticultural and agricultural activities.[51] For another, the construction and ownership of ploughs and carts produced rewards and surpluses for those who owned them. As one leading scholar has put it, in these intensifications 'lay the seed of social inequality'.[52] So did those of gender inequality.[53]

An even bigger biological price to pay came from the costs of living close together. These included faecal pollution and poor sanitation that could cause bacterial disease, and conditions that favoured the spread of viruses and parasites from person to person.[54] Stored food resources attracted rodents, which were important vectors for zoonotic disease – that is to say, illnesses that jumped from animals to humans – as were cattle, goats and sheep, as they became domesticated and used as sources of food, milk, clothing and textiles.[55] These included diseases such as mumps, chicken pox, rubella and whooping cough, which all jumped from animal species and spread easily from person to person thanks to higher population densities.[56]

Set in this context, population increases were all the more remarkable, with reproductive increases more than setting off the negative drag of morbidity and mortality caused by disease. There were silver linings too for communities where infectious pathogens thrived: while they were often ravaged in the short run, repeated outbreaks eventually resulted in populations becoming 'disease-experienced', with partial immunity being built up thanks to frequent exposure.[57]

Ironically, this provided long-term advantages when climatic conditions opened up new regions, or when population sizes necessitated outward migrations. Pathogen exposure and lack thereof could have significant impacts in terms of competition for land, power and resources. One obvious example is the arrival of the Spanish in the Americas after Columbus' Atlantic crossing in 1492 when the immunological naivety of the indigenous peoples to smallpox is often cited as the cause of catastrophic demographic and political collapse.[58] Another comes from the way that Bantu peoples spread out into much of west and central West Africa around 3,000 years ago, when built-up resistance to malaria was a key factor in the expansion of culture, language, identity and genetics.[59] As we shall see, this immunity was to play a crucial role in the re-shaping of the world in later periods.[60]

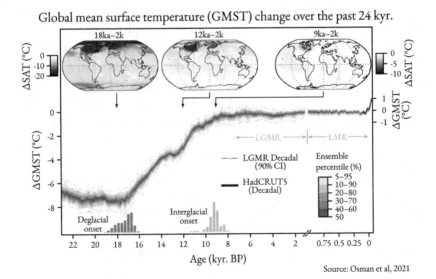

Global mean surface temperature (GMST) change over the past 24 kyr.

Source: Osman et al, 2021

As the Holocene progressed, further waves of migration kept opening up new ecological zones. Those who moved brought not just abstract concepts about farming with them or even new tools, but crops too. New corridors opened up into Central Asia, the Mediterranean basin, the Nile Valley and Europe that disseminated wheat and barley, as well as other crops from south-west Asia. By around 7000 BC, agriculture had appeared in Crete and Greece, and not long afterwards as far afield as Andorra and Spain, Bosnia and Sicily. Calcified tissue on the teeth roots of sheep and goats, as well as cut marks to bone remains, shows that they were being farmed in the Fergana Valley in Central Asia by 6000 BC.[61] By 5500 BC, farming culture was established across much of central Europe, as well as in northern France, with villages studding the landscape from southern Spain to the Nile Valley to the Caucasus.[62] Such movements of ideas and of people are best understood not as single, large waves but as many cases of small-scale mobility that together add up to a large-scale signal – a hypothesis that is convincingly supported by DNA evidence.[63]

Those who brought crops and new concepts to Europe also made their own genetic impact. Advances in genomics allow us to identify separate and distinct groups of early farmers and others who moved west, with farmers from Anatolia and the Levant beginning to arrive around 7000 BC, while populations from the Caucasus reached eastern Europe around the same time. They introduced gene variants responsible for the evolution of light skin pigmentation in modern Europeans.[64]

In fact, genetic variants associated with light skin arose in Africa, which is home to a vast range of skin colours. Darker skin provides UV protection in equatorial zones, while at higher latitudes lighter skin maximises vitamin D production. As early human populations had moved out of Africa, responses to different intensities of sunlight had triggered mutations that were then passed along to subsequent generations. As the incidence of the SLC24A5 gene was particularly common with west Eurasian populations, when these groups moved into Europe there was a slow but substantial replacement of the relatively dark skin pigmentation of earlier arrivals who had been poorly adapted to high-altitude conditions.[65] The genetic signal of lighter skin also helps track population movements into Central Asia, north India and East Africa – where haplogroup data demonstrates important migrations back from Asia to what is now Ethiopia and Tanzania, in the period from around 7000 BC onwards.[66]

The ecological lottery again played a role in differences in other parts of the world. Although California has many climatic, topographic and ecological parallels with the Fertile Crescent, its plant domesticates had much lower rates of self-fertilisation, as well as no large-seeded grasses. Taken alongside the difficulties of controlling pollination in maize to achieve optimal outcomes and maintain genetic purity, it is perhaps not surprising that plant-intensive subsistence only developed much later in the western flank of North America.[67]

Agricultural revolutions took place at different times in different places and with different effects. In most parts of Africa, for example, unlike other continents, herding of goats, sheep and cattle preceded crop farming, with the domestication of indigenous plants occurring only in the last 5,000 years – starting with wild pearl millet, groundnut, yams, sorghum and other crops, with distribution varied and dependent on suitable climatic conditions.[68] South Asia and eastern North America present pictures that are dissimilar to the Near East, with archaeobotanical evidence pointing to food production being undertaken by mobile and small population groups, rather than by larger farming communities.[69] In China, although there is evidence of sedentary villages around 7000 BC, plant and animal domesticates do not become common until around two millennia later.[70] By that point, intensive agricultural practice known as Banpo had begun to spread throughout the Yellow and Wei River systems.[71]

Around 6200 BC, however, a large-scale shock event took place that prompted a new series of challenges and changes. In what is sometimes referred to as a 'Goldilocks abrupt climate change event' because of its importance in helping model future disaster planning, an ice dam over Hudson Bay collapsed, resulting in the catastrophic drainage of Lakes Agassiz and Ojibway.[72] The results included an acceleration of melt of the Laurentide Ice Sheet that contributed to the weakening of Atlantic circulation patterns, cooling across large parts of the northern hemisphere of 1–3 °C that lasted 160 years and releases of freshwater into the oceans in pulses that caused global sea-level rises of up to one metre.[73]

In the grand scheme, such changes hardly seem dramatic enough to require major -adaptation. However, the consequences did prove momentous. Sediment data from the central Sahara shows significant falls in lake levels and increasing aridity around this time, presumably because of changes to the monsoon system that resulted from interruption to Atlantic circulation patterns.[74] These changes appear to have affected South Asia too, where severe and sudden desiccation at precisely this time underlines the relationship of the Indian summer monsoon with the North Atlantic in general but also with the climate event of 6200 BC specifically.[75] Pollen and stalagmite records from Bigeum Island, South Korea, at this time that reveal substantial changes to vegetation bear witness to the global impact and also demonstrate the fragility of ecosystems when subject to what seem to be relatively modest changes.[76]

Survival was dependent on adaptation – and good fortune. Adaptation was more achievable in some locations than others, but much must also have depended on the ability to devise coping mechanisms in the face of sudden change. It might be, for example, that climate shock provided the context for the move of livestock herders from the Levant into Africa – with mobility to be understood as a response to uncertainties of resource supply and to perceptions of increased competition and risk, perhaps from other humans, from predators or even from the environment itself.[77] This was also broadly when new genetic markers appear in East Africa, including lighter skin pigmentations as populations with historic ancestry in Africa returned and brought subsequent mutations back with them.[78]

Sharp decreases in human activity in places like western Scotland, north-eastern Spain and some parts of the Danube are substantial enough to have led scholars to ask whether they were abandoned in the aftermath of the event or whether the populations in each simply could not and did not survive.[79] Some studies have sought to link the event with an impetus towards further expansion by early farmers from Anatolia and parts of Greece to new pastures in Macedonia, Thessaly and the Balkans, although the dating, circumstances and nature of these dispersals is not clear.[80]

The effects were also felt in South-West Asia, where this was a time of stress with disruptions at multiple sites in southern Turkey, northern Mesopotamia, Syria and even Cyprus – although how this was influenced by or connected to new climate conditions is not clear. Those living at Çatalhöyük, one of the best-known and most intensively studied sites in Turkey, shifted settlement from its east to its west mound, and also seem to have moved habitations further apart.[81] Changes in hydrogen isotopic composition of animal fats preserved in pottery vessels found at the site show that there were also major shifts in food production at this time.[82] It was a period of cultural change too, not least in terms of evolving ideas about cosmology, religion and the divine.[83]

At Tell Sabi Abyad in northern Syria this was also a time of transition, with the introduction of new architectural and pottery styles, and evidence of a more diversified population that included mobile pastoralists as well as sedentary farmers. The discovery of stamp seals and abstract tokens used to control access to goods or services points to changing ideas about personal property – and presumably to the need for higher levels of identification and protection during a challenging period.[84] While many speculative theories about societal collapse have been associated with the climatic shift around 6200 BC, more sober assessment shows that the most useful conclusions to draw are ones about the human propensity for resilience and adaptation.[85]

The same cannot be said for a major natural disaster that took place at about the same time as the sudden cooling of the northern hemisphere that reshaped the geography of Europe. In around 6150 BC, a 190-kilometre shelf of sediment off the coast of Norway was dislodged, likely by an earthquake, creating a giant tsunami that swept south through the North Sea.[86] The scale of the wave and the devastation it inflicted can be shown by models which estimate that it would have reached twenty-one kilometres inland – twice as far as the Fukushima tsunami in 2011.[87] It swamped and submerged an area known as Doggerland that connected Britain with the European continent, although the most recent research suggests that the tsunami may have created an archipelago of islands that only later disappeared as sea levels rose around 5000 BC.[88] Nevertheless, whether or not the geographical detachment was completed in stages, the consequences not only for European but for global politics in the early and modern eras were substantial: Britain's separation from continental Europe was crucial in everything ranging from the development and dominance of British sea power to the military outcome of the Second World War to the exceptionalism that helped drive the Brexit vote to leave the European Union in 2016.[89]

At the time, the wave would have killed everything and everyone in its path. Moss-stem analysis shows that the slippage of the sediment shelf and the tsunami took place late enough in the year to sweep away peoples on the North Sea coast of Norway who typically spent the warmer months on high ground hunting reindeer but wintered close to the coast. Those who managed to survive would have struggled to make it through the winter because of the loss of their dwellings, boats, equipment and supplies.[90]

In due course, things slowly improved into what is sometimes called a climatic optimum, with warm and humid conditions favouring the development of agricultural economies. Archaeobotanical evidence shows the spread of domesticated breeds of plants such as maize varieties across South America from around 6000 BC into many areas of the continent including Colombia and north-western Ecuador, coastal and then highland areas of Peru and eventually the central Andes.[91] As in other parts of the world, shifts to farming brought about changes in dental health there and over time even to tooth shape.[92] And as elsewhere, the return of more benign circumstances, combined with stable food production – themselves supplemented by terracing and irrigation canals – brought about rising population sizes, although these were not uniform geographically or chronologically across the continent.[93]

The period up to c.3000 BC was one marked by considerable ecological and demographic change. One reason for this was an unusually high level of volcanic activity, attested by the volumes and concentrations of sulphur traces in the ice-core record.[94] The effects of solar minima and in particular the ≈2,400-year Hallstatt cycle – a time when the sun's reduced activity was connected with cooling, with the expansion of glaciers and with the release of iceberg rafts from the Arctic into the Atlantic Ocean – also played a role in impacting global climates.[95]

The widespread adjustment of complex and mutually dependent global weather patterns was influenced by other factors too. It seems that a warming phase in the southern hemisphere had resulted in glacial melt, decreasing Pacific Ocean surface temperatures; this in turn had an effect on the El Niño–Southern Oscillation (ENSO), which reduced in both intensity and variability up until around 3000 BC.[96] This may have been more significant than the cyclical changes in earth's orbital geometry, which is usually assumed to have played a key role in the strength of the ENSO, and therefore in global climate patterns.[97]

Evidence from Central Asia shows the retreat of the monsoon from c.4000 BC, from which point Indian proxies suggest greatly reduced rainfall as well.[98] The concurrent weakening of the West African monsoon system, followed by a dramatic decline around three centuries later, turned the period up to c.3000 BC into one of rising and consistent aridity.[99] This brought about a major population shift as lakes and rivers in the Sahara started to dry up – rapidly in East and North-East Africa, and more gradually in places like northern Chad, to judge from pollen and sedimentological records from Lake Yoa.[100] Oases that had reliable water and pasture sources evidently offered attractive solutions, as did the Nile Valley which in time also drew in significant numbers of migrants presumably searching for more hospitable locations.[101] Other adaptations seem to have included increased reliance on sheep and goats, and seasonal use of shelter.[102]

Some parts of North-West Africa, including coastal areas of what is now Mauritania, continued to experience considerable rainfall.[103] However, the effect was such that the Sahara began to desertify, expanding as it did so to create new environmental conditions – and becoming the increasingly impregnable barrier for human movements that we know today. This led to genetic divergences that resulted in strong differentiation in Y-chromosome haplogroup compositions in the respective populations in northern and sub-Saharan Africa that do not much persist in the modern world but define and reinforce the realities of the peoples of Africa as representing the highest levels of diversity anywhere on the planet.[104] In other words, climate change divided Africa not only geographically and environmentally but genetically.

These sharp changes brought about what have been called 'cascades of adjustments' in vegetation, fauna, humans and pathogens. Among these were new cultural practices such as cattle burials and livestock bone deposits set within built structures at sites in eastern Egypt and south-western Libya that evidently had a ritualistic context – though whether these are related to religious beliefs or to emerging ideas about protection from disease at a time when pathogen environments were changing rapidly is not clear. The fact that aridity negatively affects the availability of fodder and water and is closely related to increased susceptibility to disease, for both humans and livestock, would logically appear to be important.[105]

When the ENSO started to kick back in around 5,000 years ago, it brought a new set of effects as it did so that were not globally uniform. North America experienced droughts and severe water shortage, with lakes either falling in water levels or drying up completely.[106] Pollen and tree records provide evidence of aridity and changes to vegetation as atmospheric circulation patterns shifted.[107] Precipitation levels in the Mediterranean changed too, leading to the 'Mediterraneanisation' of landscape ecologies – that is to say, transforming them into how we think of them today – dominated by evergreen shrubs and trees that are adapted to summer drought and cold, wet winters.[108]

It was a different story in South and South-East Asia, where northern India and northern Indo-China seem to have been particular beneficiaries of higher precipitation, although mapping out likely patterns elsewhere is subject to considerable uncertainty because of the limited study of potential proxies that might help – such as lake sediment, pollen, stalagmite data and more.[109]

Abundant evidence from elsewhere however helps show that parts of East Asia saw wetter conditions as Africa became drier. The Inner Mongolian plateau became warmer and experienced higher levels of rainfall from around 4000 BC in a new climate pattern that lasted for over two millennia. Temperature and precipitation levels in the Tibetan plateau remained stable, however, as they did in Xinjiang.[110] Analysis of fossilised single-cell organisms and coral off the coasts of Indonesia, Papua New Guinea and the Great Barrier Reef suggests cooling sea surface temperatures – which together with evidence for lower sea levels around 3500–3200 BC provide further indications that this was a period of considerable climate shift in some parts of the world, if not in all.[111]

How human populations reacted and responded to the challenges is not immediately clear, and nor should it be. As we shall see, extreme events could have catastrophic consequences and sear the experiences into collective memories. However, on a day-to-day, month-to-month and year-to-year basis, even very substantial alterations to weather patterns can hardly have been discernible. Decisions to move or migrate, to adopt new habits and to engage differently with each other and with the environment would not have been instantaneous or immediate, but reached or developed in the face of continual incremental change.

Likewise, ecological shifts brought about by changing rainfall, by temperature differences, by transformations of habitats for flora and fauna were not rapid either, but spread over decades and centuries. As such, then, it is more productive to think about how societies started to conceive of the world around them, of how people thought about the human relationship with nature, with animal and plant life, and how they conceptualised the roles of our species relative not only to changing climatic circumstances but to the wider question of resource exploitation.

Our ability to make sense of such questions becomes a lot easier from c.3500 BC because of the growing complexity of human societies that in turn demanded new ideas, new solutions and new tools. Changing climates did not create the need for political systems, pave the way for the rise of towns, cities or states or lead to the development of writing systems. All were the product of rising population numbers, greater demands on water and food resources in particular and the need for social organisation. And yet the role of the environment was central to all. If societies were going to survive and flourish, humans would need not only to dominate nature, but to bend it to their will.

4

The First Cities and Trade Networks
(c.3500–c.2500 BC)

He is the man who built Uruk.

Sumerian King List (c. 2100 BC)

By around 3500 BC, the human impact on the environment was not just changing but was becoming so significant that it had itself become a factor in changing ecological habitats of flora and fauna. Spatial modelling suggests that more and more land that was suitable for agriculture was being exploited around the world, with pastoralism also spreading further into more arid regions. For some scholars, this level of activity represents nothing less than the start of the anthropogenic transformation of the earth.[1]

Indeed, some have gone further, arguing that human activities had an impact on the climate itself. For one thing, recent studies have suggested that population levels in China and Europe were much higher around 5,000 years ago than is usually assumed, raising questions about how much land was needed to support such substantial numbers of people, as well as about the ways in which land was used.[2] Climate records show that this was a time of significant additions of heat-trapping CO_2 to the atmosphere, which some scholars have also linked to deforestation.[3] The signature of high levels of methane found in ice cores in Greenland dating back to c.3000 BC meanwhile has likewise been associated with intensifications in wet-rice farming that lead to a complex soil process involving plant–microbe interactions and an increase in emissions.[4]

This has led to the formulation of what has become known as the early anthropogenic hypothesis, which posits that by around 5,000 years ago human activities and behaviour had so great an impact on global climate as fundamentally to change it.[5] Recent modelling has been used to support this argument, with the authors suggesting that a new glacial period was averted because of the warming generated by higher than expected greenhouse-gas concentrations in the atmosphere, with farming considered the most likely cause of these emissions.[6]

The problem with such hypotheses is that differentiating between correlation and causation is not straightforward – that is to say, identifying broadly simultaneous warming patterns on the one hand and demographic and behavioural changes on the other is not the same as proving that the latter was responsible for the former. Linking the two can be tempting, but it is fiendishly difficult to prove that the association was anything more than coincidental.

For example, changing climate has been suggested as a major factor (if not the prime cause) in the downturn of settlements of Trypillia culture that were spread out over the region between the Carpathians and the Dniepr in eastern Europe and which had become both more numerous and larger from around 5000 BC. Some of these became so substantial in size that they have been described as megasites, and deserving of the title the 'earliest known cities'. Often regarded as the largest sites in Eurasia and the world, settlements were typically centred on large buildings that were used for ritual activities and for the storage and consumption of surplus. Each site was part of a major trading network that involved exchanges of flint, manganese, copper and salt, sometimes over long distances.[7] Day-to-day needs were satisfied by a combination of cereals, domesticated and wild animals and dairy products.[8]

By around 3500 BC, these sites showed signs of stress, with buildings not being maintained, lower levels of occupation and the emergence of social hierarchies that have been interpreted as signs of social inequality that stemmed from diminishing availability of resources.[9] As it happens, these pressures are attested not only by lower levels of pollen – which indicate lower levels of agricultural productivity – but also by colder temperatures, which some have identified as a key factor in forcing population dispersal.[10]

It may be that demographic decline was precipitated not by climatic change, however, but by other factors, including the exhaustion of the soil through overexploitation.[11] Or perhaps the explanation lies in disease, with high population densities, combined with the large-scale presence of animals, providing ideal conditions for the emergence and spread of infectious disease.[12] It is perhaps no coincidence, therefore, that new research has found unambiguous evidence of *Yersinia pestis*, the aetiological agent of plague, in the Eurasian steppe around this time – as well as multiple lineages branching out between c.4000 and c.3000 BC.[13]

The possibility of multiple causes of demographic decline, depopulation and societal change would go some way to explaining why most large settlements in central Europe disappeared around 3300 BC, with evidence pointing to a compressed timeframe for catastrophic change.[14] The fact that this was a time of growing uncertainty would also help explain an intensification of ritual practices at many locations in Europe, particularly since the changes in social behaviour are widely thought to be reflections of increasingly challenging circumstances.[15]

These were hardly the only places in the world that were going through rapid and major societal transitions. The first signals of growing links between populations, material cultures and languages in southern China, Taiwan, what is now the Philippines, Indonesia, Melanesia and the Pacific begin around 3000 BC. This is often seen as a process of expansion from north to south, albeit one that should be measured across many centuries, often involving indigenous peoples adopting and spreading customs, ideas and technologies, rather than a sudden and rapid surge.[16]

It was a similar story on the Atlantic and Gulf coasts of North America, where around 3000 BC communities began to create circular middens known as shell rings from faunal and floral remains, centred on a plaza.[17] While many interpretations have been offered for these structures, they were evidently central features in settlements, and, as recent evidence suggests, focal points for local trade and within networks that stretched for hundreds of kilometres.[18] Surveys using remote sensing and machine learning have now revealed more such rings in coastal forests and marshes that suggest the existence of a larger number of communities, as well as even more intensive patterns of exchange starting to build up around this time than had previously been thought.[19]

Although questions about the early dispersal of Transeurasian languages, including Japanese, Korean, Tungusic, Mongolic and Turkic, are contested, the triangulation of genetics, linguistics and archaeology points convincingly to the conclusion that common agropastoral and basic vocabularies were spread by farmers and the associated expansion of farming across north-east and eastern Eurasia in this period.[20]

Europe also saw waves of mass movement of the peoples of the Yamnaya culture from the forest-steppe region above the Black Sea to the west. This had a profound demographic impact but also brought about sharp cultural change, again including the spread of languages.[21] Those coming from the Pontic–Caspian steppe in relatively small numbers settled on islands in the Aegean and in what is now Greece, where they built the first monumental palaces and urban centres in Europe.[22]

The expansion of new pottery styles identified as belonging to peoples of the Corded Ware and Bell Beaker cultures spread rapidly from c.2750 BC, covering much of Europe and North-West Africa in a matter of two centuries. What was even more striking, however, was the population turnover that also took place: in what amounts to one of the most comprehensive movements of people ever recorded, mitochondrial genome data shows the almost complete replacement of the gene pool of Europe.[23] In the case of Britain alone, it is estimated that the population turnover was a minimum 90 per cent.[24] In parts of central Europe, it was 100 per cent.[25] Emulation of culture was important, but migration much more so.[26]

In Mesopotamia, the Nile Valley, the Yellow and Yangtze River regions in China, the Indus Valley in South Asia and the valleys of Andes, however, the story was one not of population dispersal but of accretion. Although it is true that the period c.3500–3000 BC saw demographic growth generally, more significant was the expansion of the numbers of villages as well as the rising numbers of those who lived in them. While people were being pushed out of permanent and semi-permanent settlements north of the Black Sea, in other places they were being pushed together. The fact that this happened in many locations at around the same time suggests that similar impulses drove similar trends. So too does the speed of a process that gave rise not only to large numbers of villages, but to the rapid expansion in size of some of these into substantial urban centres.[27]

As one scholar has observed, while it is important to note where cities emerged, it is also worth paying attention to where they did *not* do so – above all in western Europe, the Amazon basin and eastern North America. That the locations where large conurbations did start had different soil types, drainage, rainfall, temperature and even altitude means that it was not coincidental that they all had one thing in common: these early cities rose in 'circumscribed land', that is to say locations that were locally bountiful but hemmed in by hostile geographic features such as deserts, mountains and the sea.[28] As such, the motors that drove the rise of cities – and therefore of 'civilisation' – were powered by pressures that forced populations into narrow bands of environmentally hospitable and productive land, where the ability to expand ecological footprints were limited. Early cities rose, in other words, as products of necessity where co-operation was essential to prospects of survival.

Increasing levels of local and regional trade within and between these hotspots paved the way for the consolidation of social interaction and for the centralisation of political authority. From around 4000 BC, the homogenisation of styles across the Fertile Crescent, such as in pottery and settlement plans, provides a strong indication that commercial and cultural exchanges were rising steadily – a process that finds a parallel in the regions of the Black Sea, Mediterranean, Aegean and Anatolian plateau at the same time.[29] This was accompanied and perhaps even spurred on by the development of sophisticated metallurgical industries that had already spread from Anatolia to Mesopotamia, Iran, Pakistan and south-east Europe and to the Black Sea – and later to Sicily and the Iberian peninsula. Along with the introduction of new crops that diversified diets, the emergence of new commodities and materials that could themselves be traded, either as staple foods or as luxury, exotic items, opened up possibilities for new ways of life and also for the expression of status.[30]

These trends can also be found in East Asia, South Asia, North Africa and South America – in the Hongshou cultures along the River Liao, the Dawenkou cultures of the Lower Yellow River valley and groups in the Indus Valley, along the Nile and in the Norte Chico ('Little North') of coastal Peru. All also saw similar patterns of demographic growth, agricultural improvements, greater crop diffusion and the creation of long-distance trade networks and the spread of ideas and technologies such as those related to metallurgy – following similar trajectories to Mesopotamia, albeit at a later date.[31]

The establishment of permanent settlements required that ideas take shape about personal possessions, including movable and non-movable goods, and about access to and control over land and the resources it could yield. The development and existence of social hierarchies in the ancient as well as the contemporary world are often associated with urban settings and above all with property ownership – whether of fields, crops, animals or goods – whose relevance is enhanced by higher population densities: wealth accumulation and transmission enable the creation of social elites and therefore shape political structures and decision-making. Wealth disparities became a signature of the populations that urbanised earliest and most intensively.[32]

That is not to say that equality is a hallmark of non-urban societies. Indeed, recent research on four present-day pastoral groups in East Africa, West Africa and South-West Asia found substantial levels of intergenerational transmission of assets as well as status.[33] Even though the effect is more modest, life chances are measurably influenced by intergenerational wealth transmission in hunter-gatherer populations too.[34] Nevertheless, and taking into account substantial differences between the pre-modern and modern worlds, the rise of cities spurred a series of dramatic changes, involving a range of issues from kingship to religion, from the rise of bureaucracies to ideas about slavery. The rise of cities also went hand in hand with ideas about civic identity and with the emergence of 'states', a term that needs to be understood in very broad terms because of the obvious problems of over-simplification.[35]

In northern parts of Mesopotamia, curiously, some of the largest settlements had grown up around 3000 BC not in better-watered areas but mostly away from the major rivers in a series of alluvial plains and basins. These communities appear to have been egalitarian and communally oriented, with no centralised leadership and little evidence of the marking of status.[36] Some of these settlements were large, such as at Brak in what is now Syria, which grew to cover as much as 130 hectares, although how people lived, how many the town and land supported and how these changed over time is unclear.[37]

It was a different story in southern Mesopotamia where larger, more complex and more hierarchical settlements began to build up. The earliest and most significant of these was Uruk, although stories written later in Sumerian, as well as in the Old Testament, offered competing, retrospective claims for locations ranging from Nippur to Eridu to Babylon.[38] Much later accounts identify Uruk's founder as Enmerkar, who was said to be the son of the sun god Utu and of the good cow Ninsumuna; he was 'the man who built Uruk' according to the *Sumerian King List*.[39] Above all, however, Enmerkar's achievements were not architectural but political – revolving around his success in taking up a leadership role and being able to direct others and also to take credit for the outcomes. Enmerkar and his wife Enmerkar-zi, reads a text written around 3,000 years ago, 'know how to build towns, make bricks and brick pavements'. They knew too how to make wooden ploughs and yokes, cables and threshing sledges. And they knew how to make 'irrigation canals and all kinds of irrigation ditches'.[40]

Whether Enmerkar's skill set was quite as wide as this source claims is open to question. But that they are attributed to him – and also, strikingly, to his wife – is revealing for what it says about the emergence of elites in places like Uruk and other major urban centres. Some scholars see the role played by those able to acquire high status and wealth for themselves as crucial in the process of cities becoming larger and more efficient. The ruling class who dominated land ownership, owned herds and controlled production were able to provide incentives as well as to use coercion to accumulate more for themselves, producing ambitions and efficiencies that shaped the physical setting of cities and determined socio-political structures.[41] The results can be seen in the first instance in the construction of temples and in lavishly decorated buildings that are sometimes referred to as palaces.[42] It is significant that these temples were controlled by priestly hierarchies who concentrated power in their own hands while also regulating, monitoring and even controlling trade.[43]

Again, this finds obvious echoes elsewhere, not least in Egypt, where the same dual principles of secular and priestly authority evolved and likewise built up monopolies of power by a ruling class that dominated land ownership and affirmed their status through the erection of temples, stone buildings and elaborate burial monuments – most famously, the pyramids. In the case of Egypt and the Nile Valley, by 3500 BC ideas about kingship emerged in tandem with urban centres at Naqada, Hierakonpolis, Abydos and elsewhere, which in due course became consolidated with one ruler overseeing multiple regions and cities.[44] The process of centralisation may have been helped by demographic growth and perhaps also by environmental factors: either way, pressure on available land supply led to intensification in its exploitation, which helps explain the evolution of a more unified state structure.[45]

A parallel process took place across multiple chronologically overlapping cultures in what is now China, where dispersed, politically decentralised cultures such as the Yangshao faded and were replaced by the Liangzhu, Longshan and Hongshan in what is now respectively south-east, central and north-east China, that were dominated by theocratic elites operating from increasingly large urban centres. A prime example was Liangzhu city itself, centred on a palace complex and protected by large walls, where burial tombs show social differentiation and rising levels of stratification, with the wealthy being buried alongside rare, exotic and valuable objects that were connected with ritual and hence imply that their owners had a status that was not based simply on wealth.[46] In Liangzhu, as well as in the many other cultures in East Asia at this time, jade played a uniquely important role as a rare and valuable material that served as a marker of wealth and status.[47]

The East Asian examples were unusual too, as the belief systems that developed were very different to those that dominated in Egypt, Mesopotamia and (later) South Asia. At the apex of the social pyramid in all these cases were rulers who enforced their position by claiming a connection with a supernatural world that often gave them unique genealogical pedigrees that cemented their authority as well as being a source of divine powers. Mesopotamian kings derived power from being outsiders and found advantages in being 'strangers in their own lands,' for example, while the rulers of the Chu state in what is now northern Jiangsu and Anhui province in China traced their lineage to a deity, the god of fire, Zhurong (祝融), who was said to control the water spirit and ensure fertile soils and good harvests.[48] This was part of a cycle that is familiar in other regions and periods and one that some anthropologists argue is linked to the growing complexity of societies on the one hand and the origins of religion on the other.[49]

In this model, as societies become larger in size and more specialised in their work, rulers and priests become the interpreters of everything from natural disaster to environmental challenges, from resource surpluses to shortfalls, from military defeats to premature deaths, helping explain punishments or bounties that were being administered by unseen gods. Environmental and natural calamities in particular were closely linked to 'moralising gods' who, out of anger or simply from boredom, handed out punishments for transgressions and apparent lack of respect. It is striking, though perhaps not surprising, that regions that were vulnerable to changes in weather conditions – above all droughts, but also floods and storms – developed cosmological systems based on 'moralising gods' who used such events to punish, show their displeasure and teach lessons.[50]

As we shall see, deities who were prone to infighting or unleashing disasters on humans played an important role in Babylonian and Egyptian literature and theology, as they did later in post-Harappan India and in the Mediterranean: it was claimed that Greek gods had provoked wars, had petty vendettas with each other (and with individual humans) and rained down misfortune on those who dishonoured them while showering others with rewards. In East Asia, however, things were rather different, as is clear from both literature and religious practice, where the primary themes are not of destruction and punishment, but altogether more abstract and pacific. Perhaps one reason why the early Chinese did not quarrel with their gods as others did elsewhere, one scholar has argued, was 'because there was less to quarrel about, ecologically and environmentally', thanks to climate conditions being more benevolent and predictable. And perhaps even distinctive ideas about ancestral status were shaped by the cold climates of north China, where the long period required for the decay of the body enabled extended pre-burial rituals – and more opportunities for priests and those connected to curating ideas about belief systems to emphasise their own importance.[51]

The use of temples, sacred spaces and special treatment in death for those of high status to affirm links with the divine and to assert a relationship between elites and supernatural beings evidently served as a tool of control and as a marker of social stratification. Such barriers were reinforced, not only in Mesopotamia, Egypt, the Indus, East Asia and Mesoamerica but all over the world (albeit in different time periods that corresponded to locally arising complexity) by the use of human sacrifice. The deliberate and ritual killing of an individual to placate supernatural beings is known from early Arab, Turkic, Inuit, American, Austronesian, Chinese and Japanese cultures, as well as from Mesopotamia. While many suggestions have been offered to explain the purpose and aims of human sacrifice, perhaps the most compelling is that such acts legitimise the authority of rulers by demonstrating their power over the population and also their exclusive ability to please the gods.[52]

This was emphasised not only in life but also in death. Dead rulers were often presented with offerings, such as Uranamma, who received daily offerings in Nippur.[53] Elite funerals also played an important role, with lavish ceremonies accompanied by music and feasting accentuating the status of those of high social class and wealth.[54] The Royal Tombs at Ur in southern Mesopotamia that were first excavated in the 1920s and 1930s yielded thousands of skeletons, including some of young retainers who had been buried with their prestigious kings and queens around the middle of the third millennium BC. They had been struck with an instrument with a small acute end that must have been hit with enough force to penetrate the skull. CT scans show that the attendants' bodies had been preserved so that they could 'continue' their service in the next world – as does the fact that they had been dressed and arranged around the corpses of their masters and mistresses.[55]

While there are ambiguities about how far we can generalise about social hierarchies from one place to the next and also across different periods, what is clearer is that the scale and positioning of public buildings testify not only to central planning but to the effective mobilisation of mass labour.[56] The most celebrated example is undoubtedly the construction of the Great Pyramid at Giza, which involved at least 10,000 men working for thirty years – something that presented considerable logistical challenges, not least that of feeding the workforce every day.[57]

Elite control of the infrastructure of new cities was such that workers neither owned nor had rights over agricultural lands that supported the populations. Instead, as later Mesopotamian texts attest, they depended on institutions, temples and the wealthy for compensation in the form of rations, or by way of a share of the produce they were responsible for.[58] Cuneiform texts from cities like Lagash, Nippur, Ur and elsewhere record distributions of barley and other cereals to workers of all kinds – including shepherds and weavers, agricultural workers and brewers.[59]

The scale of landholdings of powerful institutions and individuals grew to astonishing proportions. By around 2300 BC, some temples are attested as controlling thousands and even tens of thousands of hectares of land, with the crown overseeing many times that size in multiple regions across Mesopotamia.[60] In this respect, what mattered was control of workforces and the ability to direct and monopolise their labour. That perhaps explains why food production, distribution and even cooking were centralised, with ovens and hearths located not in houses but in temples.[61] It might also help explain why there are few signs of settled rural populations living near the city: it would seem that if the workforce lived on the land, they did so on a temporary basis.[62]

One way to maintain control therefore may have been to build walls around cities. It has been suggested that at least in some cases early city walls were built to protect against environmental factors and above all water and flooding, though they later assumed the role of serving as defensive fortifications.[63] As has been pointed out recently, the scale of city walls at locations like Uruk was far greater than any conceivable military needs might have required, raising the question of whether they were built not as fortifications against attacks but as symbolic expressions of power in their own right.[64] This has a natural parallel in Egypt, where investment in and expenditure on military forces appear to be a reflection of royal prestige rather than related to defence at a time when external threats were limited.[65]

Another suggestion, which might not be mutually exclusive, is that walls served to curtail freedom of movement to ensure the labour supply was constant: this, after all, was one way to guarantee that there were enough people to maintain the grain supply and therefore to secure the long-term future of the city itself. Cities depended on food supply; as such, therefore, the availability of a large enough workforce to exploit the land was not just crucial to their short-, mid- and long-term success but essential to their basic viability.[66] Ancient cities in Mesopotamia, and presumably elsewhere, were likely characterised by more deaths than births because of disease prevalence and lack of sanitation. As such, constant streams of new arrivals were needed for urban populations to stay stable, let alone grow.[67]

In practice, this meant attracting inflows of migrants, as these were important to the maintenance of urban populations, and essential for their expansion.[68] Extensive evidence of slavery in southern Mesopotamia suggests that not everything was left to chance, with forced labour being used to support irrigation systems and, in the case of women, to work on textile production.[69] All this meant that by around 3000 BC cities like Nippur, Adab, Kish, Ur and Umma were all home to substantial populations – although none was as large as Uruk, which covered 250 hectares and was home to somewhere between 20,000 and 40,000 people.[70]

Higher levels of regional exchange, coupled with demographic increases and rising levels of production that were facilitated by new tools, new techniques and the development of irrigation canals, demanded higher levels of administrative oversight and competence by emerging cities and states. This created a model of the city or the state as a parasite, where growth was powered by the labour force and the benefits harvested by an elite who set up and maintained barriers to cement their own positions and restrict access at the same time.

The purpose of an emergent bureaucracy was to standardise, homogenise and harmonise – and, in doing so, drive ever greater rewards to the centre. This required institutions and tools that would make it possible to measure and account for productivity and to monitor goods and labour in ways that prevented leakage from the system. One obvious example was the standardisation of weights and measures; another was the expansion of administrative norms into neighbouring towns and settlements. But the most obvious and important innovation was in the development of writing systems that emerged around this time in the Fertile Crescent.

Clay tokens representing units of goods had begun to be used at the start of the Holocene in Mesopotamia for basic accounting purposes. By around 3500 BC, cylinder seals were being used to mark bales of goods as well as other produce.[71] Two centuries or so later, these were being replaced by two-dimensional pictographic signs, inscribed by a stylus on clay tablets, that recorded numerals and goods; the signs developed over a few centuries into a writing system of phonetic signs that started with the transcription of the names of individuals before expanding further.[72] These were stages in a process that led not only to the creation of alphabets but to the opening of new horizons in which uses of language and communication widened dramatically.[73]

Events, stories, thoughts and myths could now be written down, allowing them to be disseminated widely and passed on in a standardised form. But these breakthroughs all traced back to needs that were much more mundane and unromantic: the desire to record goods and trade; the drive to charge and collect tax; and the efforts by elites to monopolise exchange networks and their hold over power. We have the needs of tax collectors 5,000 years ago to thank for the great works of literature that have been produced since: without accountants there would perhaps have been no Torah, Bible or Qur'ān, no Shakespeare, no *Bābur-Nāma* and no Tolstoy.

Nor would there have been any Babylonian epics – combinations of myths, stories and histories that relate to this early period of history in Mesopotamia – or indeed literatures from other parts of the world where the same processes of urbanisation along with the emergence of hierarchies and priesthoods, of political leadership and of bureaucracies took place. Societies in Mesoamerica and in the Nile, Indus Valley and Yellow and Yangtze River regions in China – and in other regions too – did not pass the same staging posts at the same time as southern Mesopotamia or as each other when it came to developing writing systems; but the pathways were similar in each case, even if the Indus scripts have yet to be interpreted or fully understood.[74]

Elites elsewhere also developed in much the same way as in Mesopotamia, with the ruling class in Egypt, for example, monopolising the labour of the rural peasantry and retaining power within a self-selecting priestly class.[75] Bureaucracies emerged that became obsessive compilers of information, with endless lists recording the names of towns, peoples, foods and cereals – just as they did in Mesopotamia.[76] The desire to tie the labour force to the land to ensure high levels of agricultural production was a core focus of officials in Qin dynasty China, with registers being maintained to prevent peasant mobility and to tie workers to the land.[77]

By c.2500 BC, cities in southern Mesopotamia like Uruk, Eridu, Umma, Uqair and Ur had blossomed and grown, as had urban centres like Naqada and Nekhen in Egypt, Mohenjo-daro and Harappa in the Indus Valley, and Liangzhu as well as Baodun and Yufucun in what is now Sichuan province, China. Urbanisation seems to have spurred change in neighbouring regions, leading to higher population densities and social stratification among nearby peoples – presumably as a reaction to opportunities presented by bigger markets with growing demands.

A good example is Nubia, where pastoralists began to settle around what became the city of Kerma in what is now Sudan and within a few centuries formed the centre of the powerful kingdom of Kush, which was a rival to the Middle Kingdom of Egypt.[78]

This was important, for higher population densities are also closely connected with the emergence of social stratification. This explains why things looked rather different in the Indus Valley, where there is less evidence of the consolidation of political power into the hands of a single ruler, dynasty or elite. In this region, there is also less evidence of the elaborate tombs and monumental architecture celebrating individuals and specific families, and generally a considerably lower footprint of temples and religious buildings – suggesting a different spiritual and social arc for the people of this region.[79] It seems, therefore, that the communities living in the alluvial plains of the Indus and its tributaries were more egalitarian than those living further west between the Tigris and Euphrates or along the Nile.[80]

This also appears to have been the case in the Norte Chico region in South America in what is now Peru. A rapid transformation around 3000 BC led to the first large, permanent settlements that were characterised by monumental public architecture and large ceremonial buildings.[81] Although it has been argued that coastal locations, supplied by bountiful marine resources, formed the catalyst for change and also the basis of expansion, it is now clear that the largest and most important towns were situated in valleys in the interior and in the highlands, with access to arable farmland.[82] The most significant of these was Caral, which may have served as an administrative centre controlling a wider region.[83] Similarities of layouts, storage areas and ritual structures across locations which in some cases were situated at considerable distances from each other suggest local exchange networks that began to create a common culture between villages and regions from c.3000 BC onwards.[84] New developments in irrigation and soil management and an expansion in production, processing and consumption of crops – especially maize – helped support larger settlements and spectacular demographic growth.[85] Some believe the population rose by a factor of thirty in the course of three centuries.[86]

Many urban settlements were centred on mounds that were important for celebrating ceremonials and sacred rites. Although only a small number of people appear to have been allowed on to these mounds (which might point to elite power and status), other evidence suggests that social stratification was weak.[87] What is most striking, however, is that there are no signs of warfare or violence in the regions that made up the Norte Chico: all the sites that have been identified in a mosaic of settlements are not only situated in 'distinctly non-defensive locations', but also lack fortifications, walls and other pointers to suggest that conflict and confrontation were significant or regular occurrences.[88] One obvious explanation for this is that links between communities were weak, especially between different geographic and climatic settings, with limited exchange between those living on the coast, those in the lower valleys of the interior and those in the highlands.[89]

A key differential, however, also seems to lie in the population size as a whole and, more importantly, in settlement densities: as in the Indus Valley, Andean civilisations were spread out over much greater distances than Mesopotamia and Egypt. Even within villages and cities, space was at less of a premium than in other more ecologically pressed niches. As with the Trypillia megasites, then, the fact that a ruling class does not seem to have emerged in the same way in the Indus and the Andes as it did elsewhere may reflect a culture of plenty of production: greater quantities and qualities of land, and the absence of anxieties about food shortage, in turn meant that the need to protect assets and demonstrate status was simply not so acute.[90]

The correlation of status and hierarchy on the one hand and competition for resources and space on the other goes a long way to explaining competition between cities. This was especially the case in Mesopotamia, where cities were clustered closely together. Rivalries were sometimes fierce and protracted – with Lagash and Umma engaging in a border conflict that started around 2500 BC and lasted for 150 years.[91] The problem was not so much land as water. Unlike the Nile, whose floods were regular (even if not always constant), or northern Mesopotamia, where annual rainfall supported farming, agricultural production in southern Mesopotamia relied on the flows of the Tigris and Euphrates and on irrigation and canal construction. Access to prime land and water was what mattered.[92]

Also in short supply, however, were materials for tools, weapons and jewellery and luxury materials for temples, palaces and homes. Metals like copper and tin were rare, while even basic resources such as stone and timber were in short supply and hard to come by. Perhaps not surprisingly, sources of new minerals and other materials were usually 'revealed' by the gods to kings, who used such messages from the divine to send out expeditions to look for, exploit and bring back much needed supplies.[93] This sharpened animosities towards and rivalry with other cities, who had their own shortages to confront, with the result that struggles for control of locations which were rich in minerals and resources could be acute. That spurred socio-economic development and innovation.

It also led to the creation of networks of satellite settlements and colonies that controlled access to regions where metal and stone were abundant, where wool and raw materials for textiles could be acquired (or taken); these evidently also served as strategic outposts to protect the commercial interests of the mother cities and as gateways to long-distance trade networks that by 2500 BC extended not only to include the Nile, Anatolia and the Indus region but into the Caucasus and Mediterranean as well. Needless to say, these networks were not one-way, but instead enabled the spread of goods, ideas and technologies to join North Africa, the Middle East and at least some parts of South Asia into an interlinked system of exchange.[94]

They also helped shape ideas about kingship, partly because rulers sponsored trading expeditions (and therefore benefited most from their outcomes) and partly because the acquisition of exotic, rare and unusual materials, goods and objects allowed them to boost their own status – visually and otherwise – as well as providing rewards for retainers. Additionally, because gift exchange between rulers was an important part of an expression of power and of diplomatic alliance-building, what one scholar has called a 'brotherhood of kings' arose, helping expand rituals, develop new ceremonials and even elaborate the nature of kingship itself.[95] These contacts played an important role in driving higher levels of social stratification both at an abstract level and practically, with oversight and the benefits of trade in luxury items enabling the rise of elites in South-West Asia, in many parts of China and elsewhere.[96]

These processes helped fuel the rise of elites and therefore of states: locations such as southern Mesopotamia, which were well-suited for crops and pasturelands, offered opportunities for the production of surplus food and goods. This set a premium on controlling the labour force and on extracting profits, as this embedded and deepened hierarchies, rewarding those at the top of social pyramids. Additionally, these were protected and enhanced by writing systems and by the creation of import and export markets for luxury goods.[97]

Men were prime beneficiaries, for patriarchy was a core feature of states and empires in all periods of history. The realities and the glamourisation of violence, of warfare, all helped fuel what one scholar has called 'the triumph of aggressive cultures'. Group violence increased as societies became more complex, while rewards and prestige flowed to those who were proficient at combat or at leading others in battle. As states rose, violence, patriarchy and centralisation were hand-in-hand: and all had impacts on the environment - and on the role of women.[98]

The development of trading networks, acquisition of raw materials, tools and technologies and the increasing competence of central bureaucracies all produced remarkable efficiency gains which allowed cities to attract and support larger and larger populations. So too did improvements in agriculture and irrigation which opened up new lands for production in what must have seemed like a never-ending cycle of expansion that funded spectacular monuments ranging from ziggurats in Mesopotamia to pyramids in Egypt to bathhouses in the Indus Valley.

The trouble was that scale creates pressure. More people required more food, meaning either that land had to be worked harder, that marginal areas needed to be exploited or that the footprint of land being sown became larger and therefore further away from where its produce was consumed. Naturally, this created competition for the best lands not only between cities but also from within them. As social differentiation widened, so must consumption have changed, with the wealthy demanding greater qualities, quantities and ranges of goods and food – putting further pressure on ecological resources.

These were ideal conditions for political opportunism. But they were also the ideal conditions for environmental and ecological stress. It did not take much to expose the vulnerability of densely populated communities to episodes of fragility. These could be anthropogenic and result from expensive confrontations that depleted resources, took workers from the fields and reduced food supplies as fewer crops were sown or harvested. But they could also come as a result of climate events or environmental degradation. Agrarian economies were particularly dependent on rainfall and water availability – which are of course closely linked to climate patterns. When abundant, the great rivers such as the Tigris and Euphrates, the Yellow River, the Yangtze and the Indus and their tributaries meant that land could be cultivated easily. Scarcity on the other hand meant shortages, crop failure and famine, alongside associated risk of disease.[99]

It is perhaps no surprise, then, that some of the earliest ideas that were set down in writing were stories about the origins of the earth – and about the perfect conditions that had been created for humans. In the Sumerian creation story 'Enki and the World Order', the god Enki 'stood up full of lust like a rampant bull, lifted his penis, ejaculated and filled the Tigris with flowing water'.[100] The Babylonians had a similar if less vivid version. *Enūma Eliš*, often known as *The Epic of Creation*, discovered in the ruined library of Ashurbanipal at Nineveh in the nineteenth century, explains that at the start of time all that existed was water swirling in chaos. This divided into fresh, sweet water and bitter, salty water which ultimately turned into the source of the rivers Tigris and Euphrates.[101] Eventually, the gods decided to create the first man, Lullu, who was directed to serve them by maintaining order on earth. Nevertheless, it was the gods who were responsible for 'pasturage and watering places', ensuring there was 'pure ploughland in the countryside' and enough grain for all. It was the god Enibulu, in the end, 'who heaps up a surplus for people, who brings rain of abundance over the broad earth, and makes vegetation grow profusely'.[102]

It was a similar story in South Asia, where four great collections of hymns, incantations and ritual formulas known as the Vedas record the early histories and beliefs of the Aryan people in the sacred language of Sanskrit. The earliest and most famous are the *Rig Veda* – or 'Verses of Knowledge' – that were written down around 2,500 years ago, but record songs and poems dating perhaps a millennium further back in time. Among the collection is the story of how Indra, one of three main deities, released rains that had been held captive in clouds by Vritra, the demon of drought, and forced them to pour down on to the scorched earth. No longer bound by evil spells, 'the clouds discharge their liquid', leading rivers to swell and those working the land to rise with 'deep delight and thankful heart' that their leafless fields would soon be home to crops waving in the wind and that 'Mother Earth' would transform from a state of being 'brown and bare' to being clothed with 'a robe of brilliant green'.[103]

The story that is best known, however, is that of the Abrahamic tradition that is set out in the Book of Genesis. 'In the beginning when

God created heaven and the earth, the earth was a formless void and darkness covered the face of the deep.' After creating land, sea, vegetation and 'swarms of living creatures', God created humans, ordering that they should 'have dominion over the fish of the sea, and over the birds of the air, and over the cattle and over all the wild animals of the earth, and over every creeping thing that creeps upon the earth'.[104]

Man and woman were told to 'be fruitful and multiply, and fill the earth and subdue it'. Behold, said God, I have provided plants, fruit and food for you, and made sure that every beast on earth, every bird in the air and 'everything that has the breath of life' give you all you need in terms of food and nourishment. Things did not work out quite as intended, and rather than having a life where all was provided for, Adam and Eve and their descendants were cast out of the Garden of Eden, forced to sweat and to work the land, struggling against thorns and thistles.[105] The world, in its original form, was benign and generous. After the fall, it was difficult and dangerous. In Jewish, Christian and Muslim teaching, the earth was created by God for humans to enjoy; but their disobedience led to punishment – and ejection from a world of perfection in paradise to one of labour and of climatic and environmental risk.

Shifting weather patterns were one of a number of potential triggers that could have serious consequences for societies operating at the fringes of their ecological and agricultural sustainability. Moreover, the bigger the state, city or society, the greater the vulnerability at a time of unexpected risk, as they became dangerously exposed to even relatively modest pressure or confluence of pressures. The idea of corporations or states being 'too big to fail' is one that entered public consciousness during the financial crisis in the first decade of the twenty-first century. But, as history shows only too well, the past has been shaped by precisely the opposite happening: empires forming and then collapsing – usually at speed. Rather than being too big to fail, increasing size and complexity create their own momentum that can lead to a house of cards tumbling down, chaotically, quickly and decisively.

On the Risks of Living Beyond One's Means
(c.2500–c.2200 BC)

May your holy walls, to their highest point, resound with mourning!

'The Curse of Akkad' (c.2100 BC)

Around 2300 BC, the ruler of the city of Akkad (in Mesopotamia in modern Iraq), Sargon, embarked on a campaign of conquest, bringing a host of cities across Mesopotamia under his control and establishing what is usually referred to as an empire.[1] He was not modest in celebrating his achievements, leaving triumphant inscriptions recording the names of those he had defeated and proclaiming him as 'king of the world'.[2] 'I cut through mighty mountains with copper pickaxes,' he boasted, climbed high mountains and sailed around the seas three times.[3] He had 'neither rival nor equal', according to the *Chronicle of the Early Kings*, a history written much later, and succeeded in dominating all his enemies and destroying places that defied him 'so that there was not even a perch for a bird left' standing.[4]

Sargon's conquests were not universally welcomed, as the accounts of the many revolts that he faced during his reign make clear. As usually happens with the expansion of states, the centralisation of power as well as of resources inevitably involved consolidation of trade routes that stimulated and facilitated exchange between locations but also led to dislocations of supply, with Sargon's relentless pulling down of city walls attesting to a deliberate policy of ensuring that potential rivals remained weak and also that goods, materials and labour were diverted to the centre of the empire. These funded new temple constructions that further validated the authority of the ruler and the elite – who also benefited from control over the distribution of agricultural production that saw millions of litres of crops like barley and emmer being dispatched by barge to regional centres favoured by the Akkadian leadership.[5]

By the time Sargon's grandson, Naram-Sin, took power two and a half decades after Sargon's death in 2253 BC, some cracks were already starting to show. One account talks of a major rebellion taking place when 'all four corners of the world together revolted against me', while another talks of the ruler losing divine favour, defying the gods and insulting them by attacking sacred sites.[6] He was also the subject of one of the famous texts of the ancient world which associated his reign with catastrophe.

Known as 'The Curse of Akkad', the account explains the punishment meted out by the deities because of Naram-Sin's insulting behaviour: for the first time since cities were built and founded, it says, 'the large arable tracts yielded no grain, the inundated tracts yielded no fish, the irrigated orchards yielded no syrup or wine, the thick clouds did not rain'. Crop failure led to price inflation in the markets of all the cities of the empire. Death was everywhere, leading to people not being buried. 'People were flailing at themselves from hunger.'[7]

Climate data seems to offer firm support for a hypothesis of an 'evaporation event' that resulted in drought that would have had a dramatic effect on areas that were ecologically sensitive. Sediments from the northern Red Sea, for example, indicate environmental changes around 2200 BC that have been connected to shifts in the North Atlantic Oscillation, solar variability or perhaps both.[8] Fossilised corals off the coast of Oman show prolonged winter dust-storm seasons which have been linked to likely agricultural failure in Mesopotamia.[9] A spike in magnesium concentrations in the stalagmite record of the Gol-e-Zard Cave in Iran, dateable very precisely using uranium-thorium chronology, testifies to the start of a long and difficult period of aridity that lasted for several centuries.[10]

Places like Tell Leilan in what is now north-eastern Syria that had previously been home to a prosperous and lively population saw a rapid decline in activity – which reflected dramatic upheaval elsewhere.[11] Increasingly difficult conditions resulted in land degradation, plummeting cereal yields and desertification that was closely linked to a process of rapid deurbanisation and abandonment of towns and large settlements as precipitation fell by 30–50 per cent. Building projects were stopped mid-construction, while there are signs that some locations were abandoned suddenly.[12]

The results were catastrophic, prompting the start of what one scholar has called a 'Dark Age'. Famine and economic breakdown were everywhere. Refugees fled from their homes and flooded into southern lowlands before the empire was overrun by fierce nomadic peoples known as the Gutians, described by one near contemporary source as 'an unbridled people with human intelligence but canine instincts and monkeys' features: like small birds they swooped on the ground in great flocks. Nothing escaped their clutches.'[13] Political disintegration and chaos followed swiftly. Changes in climate had brought about nothing less than the collapse of the Akkadian empire.[14]

For some, the collapse of the Akkadian empire has become an important and salutary example for the modern age. Living in the shadow of impending environmental catastrophe, it serves as a stark warning of how mighty civilisations can fold in on themselves quickly and comprehensively. Indeed, it has become so embedded in public and scholarly consciousness that geologists have chosen 2200 BC to serve as a boundary moment between distinct geological periods: pollen, diatom, testate amoebae assemblages and other indicators from all seven continents point to aridity and drought conditions setting in around this time.[15]

This moment has even been named as the start of the Meghalayan Age, named after a cave in north-eastern India where the change in oxygen atom isotopes is particularly revealing of a decrease in monsoon rainfall. According to the International Commission on Stratigraphy, climatic changes around 2200 BC provoked a megadrought that caused the collapse of civilisations not only in Mesopotamia but in many other places too, such as in Egypt, Greece, Syria, Palestine, the Indus Valley and the Yangtze River Valley. As such, the Commission stated, 2200 BC was a defining moment not only in geological history but in history itself.[16]

In fact, however, there is considerable uncertainty about global climate uniformity, its potential causes and its effects. While multiple studies of North and South America, as well as of Europe, Egypt,

East Africa, Mesopotamia, the Indus Valley and several regions in what is now China, suggest that conditions became unusually dry in many parts of the world around the same time, the process of aridity was not uniform either geographically or chronologically.[17] Its causes too are disputed and by no means clear. While many studies have linked declining precipitation to polar ice-raft release and subsequent falling sea surface temperatures in the North Atlantic, recent research suggests that the relationship was minimal, if it existed at all.[18] Another explanation might be provided by a model of amplified feedbacks caused by vegetation changes and atmospheric dust loads, caused above all by the transition from a green to a drying Sahara: this appears to have driven a redistribution of moisture away from northern Africa, the Middle East and northern China and even had an impact on the El Niño–Southern Oscillation.[19]

Establishing a single date as a significant boundary and talking of it as an 'event' can be a useful short cut inviting consideration of wider conclusions. Doing so hides the complexity of changes, and it also obscures the fact that shifts in climate patterns took place over decades and centuries, rather than in a sudden, dramatic moment – as did the consequences. As a result, some have warned that the desire to identify patterns of 'collapse' around 2200 BC may influence both the choice and interpretation of data, including cases where evidence is limited, absent or contradictory.[20] That the archaeological sources are not conclusive nor emphatic in many locations presents obvious similar problems – with some cautioning that, if there really was a new era, it is attested by a whimper rather than a bang.[21]

Ideas of societal or civilisational 'collapse' can easily oversimplify the timing, nature and reality of what actually took place. In the southern half of the Iberian peninsula, for example, rather than being a time of decline, it was one of social and economic transformation, driven by high levels of genomic turnover that are indicative of migration, as well as being a period of sharp rises in mobility and regional connectivity that saw increases in exchange with Sicily and with Africa.[22]

In the Indus Valley, meanwhile, the archaeological evidence suggests that cities continued to function and even grow with little or no problem for some 300 years after their predesignated catastrophic collapse. The longevity of cities like Harappa and Mohenjo-daro from 2200 to 1900 BC have puzzled some scholars who expected to see higher levels of stress, economic and social pressure and civic breakdown long before the first clear signs of these began to become apparent.[23]

Despite the widespread assumption that Indus urban settlements had developed in tandem with a glacial-fed Himalayan river (often identified as the mythical Sarasvati), in fact they had blossomed in an abandoned river valley and were sustained by monsoonal rains.[24] The weakening of the monsoon substantially changed the dynamics of agriculture and of population distributions, as rivers gradually dried or became seasonal.[25] Changing weather patterns were nuanced, producing more erratic and less extensive precipitation during the summer, but higher levels of winter rain. This led to a series of adaptations, including settlement downsizing as well as crop diversification and a shift towards traditional winter crops like wheat and barley.[26] Far from collapsing, then, challenging climatic conditions resulted in the development of coping strategies and adaptation.

Another response that took place over time was a significant relocation from flood-deficient valleys to the more reliable plains of the Himalayan foothills – where the result was population growth and higher urban densities. Demographic expansion was both rapid and unplanned, resulting in increasingly disorganised settlement plans. One outcome was a marked deterioration in sanitation conditions, which in turn provided a perfect context for infectious diseases to spread. These included mycobacterial tuberculosis, which had been circulating in South Asia populations for millennia, as well as leprosy, which is attested to by skeletal records from this period. Strikingly, though perhaps not surprisingly, disease prevalence was highest in communities that were socially and economically marginalised.[27]

The pressures of changing demographics, of closer and dirtier living conditions and of the spread of infectious disease and declining health proved a heady cocktail – perhaps made worse by a second wave of rainfall reduction.[28] By around 2000 BC, evidence of mangrove shells and other archaeological indicators at the well-excavated site of Dholavira in India suggest much thinner habitation levels, including signs pointing to a lack of new buildings and of maintenance, as well as a noticeable deterioration in the quality of craftsmanship.[29] Within a century, rising levels of interpersonal violence can be detected, alongside population dispersal to the south and the collapse of Indus Valley civilisations.[30] Climate certainly played a role in this process, and perhaps was even a catalyst to change; but it was one of many factors in a complex picture that requires a carefully balanced explanation.

In the case of the different Chinese cultures, again much is in the eye of the beholder as we try to judge what the effects might have been of climate variations. There are significant regional imbalances in the work that has been done in recent years to assess what these variations might have been – to say nothing of gauging their potential impacts. It seems, for example, that there were very different circumstances to the north and to the south of a boundary broadly stretching from the Qinling mountains to the lower reaches of the Yangtze River.[31]

If assessing regional variations is problematic, so too is linking real or imagined change across and within different regions in East Asia. One recent hypothesis has used speleothem and other palaeoclimatic and archaeological data to show that a two-decade period around 2300 BC brought about such high levels of rain that the Liangzhu culture of the Yangtze River Delta was engulfed by floods, and that extensive hydraulic complexes such as large earthen dams that had offered effective defences for flood mitigation and/or irrigation were overwhelmed. The result was the inundation of low-lying land, thus impeding rice farming especially on the Taihu Plain region of the Lower Yangtze Delta, and causing Liangzhu city to fail and its population to disperse.[32]

According to traditional Chinese chronologies, the rise of the Xia dynasty is often dated to c.2070 BC and linked to a devastating flood which later historians state resulted in the Yellow River being dredged by the dynasty's founder, Yu 'the Great', thereby protecting the people from being affected in the same way in the future. Recent research suggests at least one major flood around 1920 BC, likely caused by the collapse of a dam following an earthquake.[33] Several studies have sought to associate the rise of the Xia with management of river flooding and with a transition towards drier conditions that are apparent from stable isotope records from caves across precisely the regions where a new power centre emerged in this period.[34]

Whether this really provided the context for consolidation of lands and peoples into a single entity, and if it did, why it did so, is not clear. Likewise, while the Xia dynasty – likely associated with the Erlitou culture and centred on a newly founded city at Xinzhai (新砦) – seems to have brought an end to regional competition and constant warfare, correlating this process with changing climate conditions is controversial, not least since most scholars reckon the earliest date for Erlitou to be c.1750 BC.[35]

While there is evidence of contractions within advanced agricultural societies such as the Qijia culture of the Gansu–Qinghai region and the Laohushan–Dakou culture of central Inner Mongolia around 2000 BC, it is by no means clear that there were major changes across many parts of what is now China as a result of changing climate. Indeed, there is little to suggest that c.2200 BC marked a watershed moment or period in East Asia.[36]

In this sense, it might then be asked why other previous and lengthy periods of drought had not brought about similarly damaging effects – and whether it is right to ascribe so fundamental a role to drought on this occasion. It is important to note that the same climate records attest to a similarly arid spell lasting many decades around three centuries earlier, and that the cities and polities of Mesopotamia and elsewhere were able somehow to navigate the challenges more successfully at that time: indeed, one of the studies that identified a spike in magnesium concentrations around 2200 BC found a similar surge 250 years earlier which did not spark socio-economic or political chaos.[37] Rather than marking a climatic or geological boundary, in other words, the significance of a date of c.2200 BC seems to have become magnified by apparent and supposed societal and social consequences, rather than by a more sober analysis of realities on the ground.

In any event, it is not clear what 'collapse' at that date means: while it can be tempting to focus on large-scale architecture, symbols of royal power and the powers of the bureaucracy and to correlate their disappearance and reduction with societal failure, it is perhaps more useful to question how life changed in practice for agricultural workers, women, children and families if this really was a time of profound change. Poorly maintained buildings or dispersal from cities may have been bad news for those at the political centre, whose power, authority and wealth lay in the ability to control trade, religion, status and labour, but it is less obvious that there were negative outcomes for everyone. Indeed, for many, being freed from obligations may even have represented a liberation of sorts. Lower availability of different textiles, or of rare and tastier foods, for example, that meant a narrowing of dietary habits may have been disappointing, but that did not spell the end of the world.

That the implosion of a central administration, the disappearance of elites and of the symbols of their authority, had different consequences for different parts of society of course says much about how commentators and historians think about the world around them, both today and 4,000 years ago – and about the way that structures are so often looked at from the top down rather than the bottom up. In fact, as some have argued, even declines and contractions (to say nothing of purported collapses) are more interesting as examples of resilience and resistance than as signs of cataclysmic disaster for which there is often little evidence.[38] So while deurbanisation and population resettlement might at first glance appear to be negative indicators of fortunes, they can be more productively seen as logical and effective solutions to problems of under-supply and over-demand – and to the failure of centralised governments to overcome bumps in the road.

This is a moot point when it comes to the Akkadian empire specifically. Although Naram-Sin's reign is linked with catastrophe because of 'The Curse of Akkad', in fact it was also a time of territorial expansion resulting in the conquests of Armanum and Ebla, an achievement commemorated in an inscription on a monument set up in the city of Ur which proclaimed that Naram-Sin had done something that no other king had been able to do 'since the creation of mankind'.[39] Naram-Sin took to calling himself the King of the Four Corners of the World, hardly an immodest title to choose for someone who was supposed to have presided over disaster and societal failure.[40] In fact, modern scholars of Mesopotamian history now argue that military and administrative reforms under Naram-Sin were what transformed Akkad from a successful kingdom into an empire.[41] Far from overseeing collapse, in other words, the subject of the Curse of Akkad oversaw a strengthening of the imperial centre.

The attribution to Naram-Sin of disaster and the motivation behind the conception of the Curse reflect later Sumerian desires to draw lessons that were less about environmental stress and sudden climate change than about the nature of kingship and above all about the relationship between rulers and the gods. What was important to those who read or heard this story in later centuries was that dishonouring the gods – as Naram-Sin was alleged to have done when he desecrated the Ekur temple in Nippur and had himself declared a living god – had consequences: gods could choose to be benevolent, but they needed to be kept happy. If not, there was trouble.[42]

Moreover, while it is tempting to see the causes of later political instability as linked to climate factors, there had been frequent rebellions against Sargon's successors long before rainfall patterns changed, including a major uprising in 2276 BC and the Great Revolt in 2236 BC in which simultaneous coalitions of northern and southern cities rose up against Naram-Sin.[43] Food shortages had also been common, to judge from the *Chronicle of the Early Kings*, which not only mentions famine but connects it to immoral behaviour – for example when the god Marduk punished Sargon for disturbing the soil of Babylon by causing food shortages to take place and misery to follow.[44]

These dangers were familiar in the world of antiquity, which was why particularly prominent episodes were passed on from generation to generation. A notable example is a giant flood that is discussed at length in Babylonian texts such as *The Sumerian Flood Story*, *The Epic of Atrahasis* and *The Epic of Gilgamesh* as well as in the Egyptian *Book of the Heavenly Cow* and, perhaps most famously, in the Book of Genesis. All these accounts relate similar versions of a great flood that was unleashed on humans as divine punishment for their wickedness and impiety, with the aim of wiping them out altogether.

Many versions single out sympathy for an individual who was warned in advance of the impending deluge: in the case of the *Atrahasis*, the eponymous hero was advised to build an ark for his safety, and told to load a pair of every kind of animal before 'the flood roared like a bull, like a wild ass screaming', as the winds howled and darkness fell, blocking out the sun.[45] The Book of Genesis tells a strikingly similar story. God had turned to Noah and declared, 'I am going to put an end to all people, for the earth is filled with violence because of them. I am surely going to destroy both them and the earth. So make yourself an ark of cypress wood.' Noah had done so, enabling him, his family and the animals to remain safe as rains kept coming, causing floodwaters that rose to cover 'all the high mountains under the entire heavens'.[46] There was a long tradition, then, that the gods – or God – rewarded those who lived well and obediently with environmental stability; those who did not, had to contend with environmental disaster.

The fact that a single, devastating event played such a central role in collective memory across a wide region and for such a long period of time says much about the shock of sudden catastrophic events. The same was true of the destruction of Sodom and Gomorrah, towns that God decided to punish because they were permeated with sin. 'Burning sulphur' was rained down from heaven, leaving the cities with 'dense smoke rising from the land, like smoke from a furnace' – and Lot's wife turned into a pillar of salt.[47]

This too may be based on a real event, in this case a cosmic airburst or multiple airbursts caused by a comet or meteorite dating to around 1650 BC, which flattened the city of Tall el-Hammam in the southern Jordan valley: the city's massive four-metre-thick walls were destroyed, as was much of the palace complex. Heating reconstructions suggest that temperatures exceeded 2000 °C, with all settlements within a twenty-five-kilometre radius being abandoned for centuries, partly because of the effect of the hypersalinity of the soil following an airburst-related influx of salt. The transformation of Lot's wife in the Book of Genesis into a pillar of salt may not be coincidental; skeletal remains at the site indicate extreme fragmentation suggests that the idea of people being turned into ash may have a basis in fact, rather than being conjured up by an active imagination or by poetic licence.[48] Whether Tall el-Hammam and Sodom were one and the same is a matter of conjecture; however, the close similarities – and the fact that the story was not only part of the Book of Genesis but features prominently in the Qur'ān – shows that in the milieu of the Levant and the Middle East memories of catastrophic events lived long in the mind, and were closely associated with divine punishment for sinfulness and, in the case of the Qur'ān, for homosexuality in particular.[49]

Famine and disease, however, were both more common and more devastating than spectacular natural disaster and – despite contemporary belief to the contrary – were usually the result of human miscalculation. In the case of the Akkadian empire, the problems owed much to the realities of an expanding and extractive imperial realm and to the way relentless centralisation led to political fragmentation and fracture as well as to acute supply problems.

It was not for nothing, therefore, that 'The Curse of Akkad' specifically mentions that vast amounts of agricultural produce, as well as cattle, goats and exotic goods, were shipped to the imperial capital – so much, indeed, that the city's most prominent deity, Innana, 'did not know how to receive these deliveries of food'.[50] It is not hard to see that those who were obliged to transmit resources to the political centre would seek ways to challenge and mount effective resistance for local political opportunistic ends or because the diversion of food put regional populations under pressure – or both.

It did not take much, then, for a precarious balance to be upset. A single bad harvest could cause problems that included not only famine but political turbulence and social upheaval. And in that sense the crucial question should not be what were the effects of a substantial change in climate around 2200 BC, but rather what steps were taken to mitigate the challenges that this posed. What mattered, in other words, was whether rulers, elites, priests, bureaucrats and workers could adapt, not least to rising environmental pressures, and whether those choices and steps were appropriate and effective. It was not so much that climate brought down the Akkadian empire as that the Akkadian empire collapsed under its own weight, splintering into a new constellation of city states that in many ways were a reversion to the time before Sargon's unification. That might have been bad news for Sargon's descendants and their retainers, but it was good news for others, as local powers were restored to local hands.

In Egypt, too, this was a time of tumult, as a rock-cut tomb belonging to a southern provincial governor named Ankhtifi makes clear. No one could have accused Ankhtifi of being shy. 'I am a brave man who does not have an equal,' declare several inscriptions in his tomb. 'I have done more than my ancestors did, and my successors will never equal me, not for a million years, in all that I have done,' says another. However, the inscriptions also paint a devastating picture of life in the period that followed the reign of Pepi II (d. c.2184 BC). We learn that Egypt had descended into chaos, with rival factions fighting bitter battles. Famine was everywhere, affecting the whole of Upper Egypt so badly that many starved to death. Others were so hungry that they turned to cannibalism and ate their own children. People everywhere roamed about naked and without footwear. Anarchy was all around.[51]

This seems to be confirmed by another source, *The Admonitions of Ipuwer*, which talks of crop failure, and refers to all luxuries – from spices to clothes – as being in short supply. 'The storehouse is empty,' while scribes were being 'killed and their writings taken away'. Stray cattle wandered about with no one to look after them, and foreign soldiers were rampaging everywhere.[52]

It is tempting to attribute the breakdown in Egypt to drier conditions and to the diminution or even failure of the Nile floods: geological and archaeological evidence shows a sharp decrease in summer precipitation in the Ethiopian Highlands that resulted in catastrophically low discharges into the Blue Nile drainage basin as well as occasional intensive rainfall that produced dangerous flood conditions.[53]

While water shortage (and occasional excess) may well have produced problems, pressure also came from the breakdown in long-distance trade that accompanied Akkadian collapse, cutting off important sources of revenue. It is perhaps no coincidence, then, that one of Ankhtifi's inscriptions also mentions that elites had been targeted by the wider population and had goods and assets taken from them by force: the wealthy and well-connected had been extremely successful in winning privileges, tax exemptions and land grants from the crown in the centuries and decades before.[54] Those who had been rich now gasped for water, says *The Admonitions of Ipuwer*, while those who had begged for dregs now had overflowing bowls. Those who had had no food now owned barns filled with goods; enslaved people had now become enslavers. The old order, in other words, had been overthrown.[55]

That is what these sources seem to suggest anyway. Whether they are reliable, however, is another matter. While the archaeological evidence points to a time of economic contraction, it does not suggest a time of upheaval, tumult and dislocation.[56] The purpose of the inscriptions in Ankhtifi's tomb is to underline that he was a saviour, bringing hope, comfort and relief to the people, as well as restoring stability to his own province.

And in fact the key question is precisely how what seemed to be robust and durable states could be so unstable and precarious. One cause of weakness was failure of adaptation; but another was the domino effect that made bad situations worse. That failure to respond was a crucial element in the centralised political systems that were built on the demands of entrenched elites which not only lacked the necessary skills to respond to changed circumstances, but actively resisted doing so – for fear of losing power, wealth and status. The cascades of dislocation spilled far beyond the local: one of the key factors in the rise of cultures and civilisations in the Nile, Mesopotamia and the Indus in particular had been their interconnectivity. Exchanges across and between these well-populated complex societies had stimulated trade as well as sparking cultural rivalry and assimilation. Something similar had happened in East Asia, where models of rulership, settlement and trade had drawn geographically separate cultures into frequent and even intensive contact.

Indeed, it might even be argued that the opportunities and ambitions within these clusters and competition between and within them were decisive features in their development and evolution: for example, wheat and barley had spread eastwards across Eurasia in the fourth millennium BC, with rice and millet being introduced in the opposite direction in the centuries that followed.[57] Crops from Africa such as sorghum and finger millet were being planted in north-west India by around 2000 BC, while melons and citron, fruits of South and South-East Asian origin, were being planted in the Levant, Egypt and eastern Mediterranean perhaps earlier still.[58] There was also significant contact between India and Australia around this time, to judge from substantial genetic evidence, as well as from changes in tool technology and the way food was collected and cooked; the appearance in the fossil record of the dingo – one of the animals most closely associated with Australia in the modern era but which came from Asia – was another product of regular if not intensive contact.[59]

Key to the expansion and interlocking of these networks was the uneven distribution of valuable raw materials, such as copper, tin, carnelian and lapis lazuli, but also of technologies such as metallurgy. The need for copper for body ornaments, weaponry and tools made metals highly desirable for social differentiation and rituals as well as for more practical purposes. Some scholars even go so far as to talk of an age of 'Bronzisation' as a shorthand to describe the ways in which closer interactions brought peoples, cultures and regions together in a process that mirrors many understandings of globalisation.[60]

These mechanisms that had enabled the spread of goods, foods and ideas now broke down as environmental, social and economic pressures took their toll. By around 2000 BC, trade between Mesopotamia and the Indus Valley which had been based on ivory, copper, textiles and perishables declined sharply, to judge from the written and archaeological evidence.[61] The drying up of markets must have had an impact on the social and economic landscape too, just as rising aridity did on the physical environment.

Such compressions and collapses are a recurrent part of human history. Often, climatic and environmental change were factors that played a role in unfolding crises. As the economist and Nobel laureate Amartya Sen has argued so persuasively, famines are caused by poor decision-making, by weak leadership or by intentional suppression of measures that might have mitigated or even prevented food shortages. Famines, he suggests, are the result not of lack of availability but of pricing problems, in particular affecting those who cannot afford food at times of sharply rising prices. Such prices, furthermore, are made worse not only by inflationary pressure in the face of poor harvests or supply shocks, but by hoarding practices, either for profit or from fear.[62]

While Sen's work is concerned with the twentieth century, the same principles can be applied when we consider dislocations in the more distant past. Certainly, weather conditions and extreme events could create problems, not only in the ancient world but in history more broadly. Most of the time, however, these were navigated or solved successfully – by adjustments, by coping strategies that included migration, resettlement and the development of new ways of living. In the case of the events of 2200 BC, then, we should be looking at the wider question of why societies struggled, rather than being tempted by the convenience of a simple and even a seemingly logical answer that starts and finishes with climate. And one of the most interesting things to look at is how problems could be contagious, and how troubles in one location could produce vulnerabilities in others.

6

The First Age of Connectivity
(c.2200–c.800 BC)

If you do not quickly arrive here, we ourselves will die of hunger.

Ugaritic tablet (c.1200 BC)

The breakdowns that took place around 2200 BC onwards are illustrative of the fact that interlocking regional networks could telegraph shocks as well as facilitate the transport of goods and ideas. The contraction of these trading systems was not permanent, with old connections eventually being re-formed or new ones being made.

In the period that followed the crises of c.2200 BC, a new set of nodes and links began to emerge and expand, resulting in the recreation of an interconnected geographic region that in due course spread from the eastern Mediterranean to the Indian Ocean and beyond. To start with at least, fragmentation had resulted in a series of city states blossoming, the most notable of which was the kingdom of Ur in Mesopotamia, whose rulers sought to connect the city and themselves to the great kings of Uruk, namely Enmerkar, Lugalbanda and Gilgamesh, and to position themselves as their heirs.[1]

One of the most significant trends of the centuries which followed the crises, however, was the movement towards political centralisation and of imperial dynasties establishing themselves across substantial areas. These were characterised by bureaucratic administrations that produced efficiencies through streamlining behaviour and practices and devising rules and laws that set out the responsibility of rulers, as well as of their subjects. A good example comes from the code of Ur-Nammu, ruler of Ur around 2050 BC, which stipulates the punishment for anyone bearing false witness when testifying during disputes.[2]

The best-known set of laws, however, was laid down by Hammurabi, ruler of the first Babylonian empire, which grew from around c.1900 BC to become economically and militarily dominant across much of Mesopotamia. These laws are known from several sources, the most striking of which is a diorite stele originally set up in the temple of Marduk in the capital city of Babylon and which is now in the Louvre in Paris. 'I have inscribed my precious pronouncements', reads Hammurabi's inscription, 'in order that the strong [do] not wrong the weak [and] to provide justice for the hungry and the widowed.' The code consists of 282 rules concerned with subjects ranging from trade and tariffs to marriage and divorce, from theft to non-payment of debt. They also detail the punishment for those who deliberately cause environmental damage, such as cutting down another man's orchard without the owner's permission.[3]

New states sprang up elsewhere too in ecological and environmental niches that supported rising populations, were located along trade routes, or had access to raw materials that were in wide demand elsewhere – or all three. The Assyrians established a series of merchant colonies in eastern Anatolia, for example, trading tin and textiles in return for silver and gold with local kingdoms, the most powerful of which, Hatti, grew to absorb others and form what today is often confusingly called the Hittite state, a term derived from Old Testament references to an entirely different people from Palestine. The Assyrians were themselves architects of a state in their own right that was centred on the cities of Nineveh and Assur and on what is now northern Iraq, north-eastern Syria and south-east Turkey, which was simultaneously a peer, ally, rival and competitor with the other great kingdoms of the Near Eastern world such as those of the Mitanni, the Ebla and the Kassites – the latter controlled Babylonia following the fall of the Old Babylonian empire around 1600 BC.[4]

New technologies opened up opportunities for exchange networks to blossom and expand further. Crucial to this was the development of Crete in the first instance and then of myriad towns scattered across the Aegean, mainland Greece and Asia Minor which spurred the evolution of sailing ships and (of course) the nautical skills required to navigate as well as to handle them in difficult conditions.[5] While there is considerable discussion among scholars about the nature of social and political structures on Crete in particular, the fact that substantial building complexes were being constructed by c.1900 BC suggests at the very least a widening of horizons of all kinds at a time when contacts between the island and other locations were increasing.[6] As elsewhere, the creation of writing scripts in Crete (Linear A) and then Mycenae (Linear B) and the evolution of increasingly elaborate burials again attest to institutions and elites forming as societies became more populous, more stratified and more closely connected to other worlds through the trade in rare, exotic and expensive commodities – above all metals, but also foods as shown by new research on traces of starch grain found on ceramic vessels.[7]

Much the same happened in Lower Nubia where the weakening of Egypt produced a vacuum that others were able to fill. By far the most successful were the kings of Kush who became so powerful that, once the pharaonic rulers in Egypt had stabilised their authority to the north c.1850 BC, they had to resort to building massive chains of fortresses to protect themselves from attack – as well as erecting abusive inscriptions about their new rivals. So successful was the Kush state that it grew to cover large parts of the Nile Valley and had an influence as far as the Horn of Africa. The 'empire of Kush', notes one historian, grew to become the 'largest political entity in Africa at the time'.[8]

States create hierarchies, but they also create stability and therefore usually help galvanise favourable conditions for trade by providing the security required to protect merchants able and willing to move produce to more distant markets. One Assyrian ruler in a typical inscription dating to around 1900 BC boasted that he had established freedom for his people and protected them from attacks and disruption.[9] This was an achievement in itself and clearly one that affirmed the role of the king as a saviour and protector. But it was also an essential prerequisite for the development of exchange – and was closely connected to the creation of social structures.

Indeed, it was precisely the expansion of closer trading networks that served as a catalyst for complex, hierarchical societies in West Africa and also for what subsequently became the heartlands of the Kush state.[10]

Together with the development of early metallurgical traditions in the Akjoujt region of what is now Mauritania and the Eghazzer basin in Niger, these changes to social organisation provided a similar backdrop that was essential for peoples, communities, goods and ideas to become linked over increasingly wide geographic areas.[11] Taken together, this paved the way for the consolidation of the power and resources of mobile pastoral elites in the central Libyan Sahara.[12]

In the Indian subcontinent, on the other hand, one of the key drivers of change was large-scale population movement. The centuries following the decline of the Indus Valley civilisations c.1900 BC were a period of profound demographic upheaval as a result of the arrival of new peoples migrating from the steppes. While the causes, nature and precise timing of the waves of migration are questions of considerable sensitivity and frequently a source of controversy, it is now clear that these arrivals largely postdate the dispersal of populations from Harappa and elsewhere, rather than being either coterminous or a cause of downfall.[13]

The genomic data leaves little scope for doubt about the extent of the mixing of the existing population with new waves of arrivals, and leads to the emphatic conclusion that the overwhelming majority of the migrants were men. So substantial were the migrations that almost 18 per cent of men in India today belong to haplogroup R1a which is widely represented across populations in Scandinavia, central Europe and Siberia.[14] Languages spread too, with Proto-Indo-European tongues providing another marker of the realities of an interconnected world more than 3,500 years ago.[15] Linguistic similarities between Balto-Slavic and Indo-Iran subfamilies of Indo-European languages are reflections of the movement of people and also of common pasts that lead to the steppe lands of Eurasia.[16] As recent pioneering research has shown, however, expansions of people and languages were complex and there are often surprises when genetic and linguistic data is assessed independently of long-held assumptions, with entirely different patterns identifiable in Europe and South Asia, not to mention Anatolia and the Near East.[17]

The arrival of these new populations in the Indian subcontinent in a series of waves is often associated with the introduction or rapid evolution of new ideas.[18] Chief among these is the caste system, which has long been associated with the rise of Vedic religion, its beliefs system and social practices.[19] However, the fact that genetic lineages point to the gradual merging of immigrants and indigenous populations suggests that new concepts were not imposed or adopted decisively, but adapted and developed over time.[20]

These ideas were set out in a language known as Sanskrit (from *saṃskṛta*, meaning 'perfectly formed' or 'pure and perfected'), with the oldest documents – the Vedas – written down around 1500 BC. Establishing the precise origin and nature of these ideas and charting how they had evolved is not straightforward, not least because the Vedic texts – consisting of the *Rig Veda*, *Sama Veda*, *Yajur Veda* and *Atharva Veda* – are the religious foundational texts of Hinduism. They are held to set out *sanatana dharma* – an eternal order that adherents believe is subject to neither influence nor change. Sanskrit accounts of the three Vedic worlds of earth (*bhūrloka*), heaven (*svarloka*) and 'mid-space' (*bhuvarloka* or *antarikṣa*) which contained air and light suggest calm and serenity, as do hymns in the *Atharva Veda* saying 'the earth is our mother and we are its children'; the constant warnings about respecting forests, animals and water sources speak of harm and damage being regularly done to these – they are not paeans to careful attention being paid to each and to all.[21] The revelation of the Vedas (literally 'knowledge') was made possible only when Indian sages who were suitably sensitive spiritually were finally able to hear and record vibrations that had resounded through the universe since the beginning of time.[22]

As we shall see, alongside the ideals, duties and responsibilities that these texts set out as virtues are detailed instructions on how to engage with the natural environment and how to understand the relationship between the human world and that of animals and plants – as well as that of the divine. This spread of ideas, customs and behaviour is echoed in other parts of the world around the same time. In Egypt, for example, a dynasty known as the Hyskos rose to power c.1640 BC and dominated the country, ruling from a capital city at Avaris over territory that stretched from the Nile Delta south as far as Cusae, and controlling western trade routes linked by oases to Nubia.[23] Although the main written account of this period by the Ptolemaic priest Manetho describes the Hyskos rulers as outsiders who attacked from the Levant and took control by force, strontium isotope analysis of skeletal remains and tooth enamel reveals that, while the Hyskos did indeed originate from outside Egypt, their seizure of power was a local uprising by members of a community who had first moved to the region around 2000 BC, rather than the result of a contemporary foreign invasion.[24]

As with migrants to the Indian subcontinent, they were a source of innovations, ranging from clothing to ceramics, from weaponry to burial practices, which did not involve traditional amulets or scarabs that originated in western Asia.[25] Here again there seems to have been a gender imbalance, in this case with a sex bias towards women, with considerably more evidence for men with Egyptian names marrying women with non-Egyptian names than the other way around.[26] Although the Hyskos were eventually overthrown by a dynasty from Thebes in Upper Egypt, innovations they introduced had a lasting impact, locally as well as beyond. These may have included the alphabet, perhaps spread to Egypt by miners who had initially developed or at least adopted alphabetic script by c.1800 BC.[27] Other technologies that were likely introduced from the Levant and South-West Asia included the composite bow and the horse-drawn chariot, all of which proved to have very significant implications, paving the way for expansions of political, social and economic authority.[28]

Something similar may have happened in the Mitanni kingdom in what is now northern Syria. Scholars have noted that, unusually, despite the language of the kingdom being Hurrian – a non-Indo-European language – rulers took Old Indic throne names and, when drawing up treaties with their Hittite neighbours and rivals, invoked some of the most prominent and important deities known from Vedic texts, including Indra, Varuna and the Nāsatya twins.[29] One hypothesis is that the Mitanni kingdom was founded by mercenaries, perhaps charioteers or horsemen, who were part of the same movement of peoples that led to Indo-European settlement in the Indian peninsula in broadly the same period.[30] It is more likely, however, that linguistic and theological ideas were spread by contact and by absorption, rather than by large-scale migrations – for which evidence is very limited indeed in the case of Anatolia and the surrounding region.[31] This certainly seems the most logical explanation for the transmission of ideas about astronomy and cosmology, and for similarities of Mesopotamian ideas about the three paths of heaven (to the north, middle and south) to those that appear in Vedic literature.[32]

This was the case too in the Andean civilisations from around 1800 BC onwards, with rising levels of cultural and economic exchange between communities on the coast, in the valleys of the interior and in the highlands. Over time, ceremonials, temple design, ceramic styles and foodstuffs grew increasingly standardised as interactions between regions became more frequent and more intensive.[33] Again, these contacts resulted in the expansion of languages – in this case Aymara and Quechua – with some scholars linking these processes specifically to the adoption and spread of agricultural practices.[34]

As had been the case in the Near East, increasing contact, higher levels of exchange and the adoption of new ideas, methods and technologies all played important roles in the creation of large states that incorporated peoples of different origins and developed cultures that drew them together, with a single focal point, their elites having simultaneous roles as spiritual interpreters and beneficiaries of status, power and wealth. In the Andean world, this had happened by around 1000 BC, with Chavín de Huántar starting to emerge as the ceremonial centre for most of what is now north and central Peru, as well as extending its influence deep into the south, bringing peoples, communities and topographies together within a unified cultural, religious and political envelope.[35]

This paralleled what happened in East Asia. By 2000 BC, an enormous walled settlement had become established at Shimao in the Central Plains area of China which was one of the largest in the world at the time. At its heart was a pyramid palace complex that was at least seventy metres tall, dominating the city and surrounding area. Thousands of jade artefacts reveal that Shimao was the centre point of a vast local and long-distance trade network – while human sacrifices on a massive scale provide evidence of elite control and show that the city was a place of power.[36]

Recent excavations have shown the importance of Shimao, in the process turning long-accepted ideas about early Chinese civilisations on their head. The picture in East Asia starts to become a little clearer first with the vast city of Erligang and then, from c.1200 BC, when a state emerged under the Shang dynasty that extended its authority across what is now north and central China – although the precise dating remains uncertain because of contradictions in the literary and archaeological records.[37] Once more, the result of an overarching political structure was a homogenisation and standardisation of cultural styles, as well as of religious practices and social structures.[38] The expansion of agriculture was fuelled by labour gangs supporting a royal household that was strongly incentivised to maximise crop yields as its source of wealth, largesse and authority. As elsewhere, an emerging bureaucracy and administrative elite developed writing scripts – in this case inscriptions carved into bones – enabling instructions and decisions to be recorded and driving a familiar process of cementing and centralising power.[39]

Curiously, then, while historians are often quick to discuss the role of climate in the collapse or decline of empires, kingdoms and states, they are rather more reluctant to do so when it comes to patterns of consolidation, expansion or efflorescence, such as in the long period that followed the crises of c.2200 BC. In some ways, of course, this is not surprising: the principal regions that saw large-scale permanent settlements were environmentally and ecologically well suited to supporting populations and, crucially, to facilitating their growth – either through increasing the size of cultivated land or through more intensive interventions such as irrigation and canalisation.

The benign disease environment was also an important factor in enabling demographic expansion and conversely in explaining why other regions did not blossom in the way that Mesopotamia, the Nile, parts of China and the north-western flank of South America did in the millennium after 2200 BC. In South-East Asia and in many areas of West Africa, malaria acted as a brake on population size, as did the lack of availability of seeds, grains and foods that were so important elsewhere.[40] In the case of equatorial Africa, a vicious cycle developed with the Bantu migrations that started c.1500 BC: although the adoption of banana and plantain allowed larger permanent settlements and both geographic and demographic expansion, these became centres for malarial infection, producing the same effect as the so-called 'white man's grave' 2,000 years later when Europeans involved in the slave trade died in droves. Populations which had no resistance to malaria were replaced by those whose ancestors had developed Duffy Negativity, the genetic variation that provided immunity from *vivax* malaria; but this took many centuries to occur, and meanwhile prevented the rise of towns and cities in the same way as in some other parts of the world.[41]

In other cases, climatic changes, extreme weather events or natural disasters could have devastating implications in the emergence of diseases. The enormous eruption of the Thera/Santorini volcano c.1600 BC, one of the largest in the last 5,000 years (it had the power of 2 million atomic bombs of the type dropped on Hiroshima), is an obvious example of the latter. In fact, the most important impact of the event was not the catastrophic and famous tsunami that engulfed the island of Crete, nor even the reorientation of the Mediterranean civilisations that essentially occurred as a direct result.[42] Rather it was that it may have played a role in pathogen emergence, and specifically of the variola virus, which appeared in the Nile region, perhaps as a consequence of the evolutionary forces resulting from the eruption, its fallout and ejection of gases and acids.[43]

If this was indeed the case, it is hard to overstate the importance of looking at the bigger picture of how events in the world's natural history have had major long-term impacts that affected the world not just of the past but of the present too – or, in this case, of the near present: variola virus, better known as smallpox, claimed the lives of 300 million people in the twentieth century alone, and perhaps as many as half a billion between 1850 and the eradication of the disease in 1977.[44] Among its first victims were members of the ruling dynasty of Egypt, including Pharaoh Ramses V, whose mummified body bears clear traces of the virus's unmistakable pustules, especially on his cheeks.[45]

Such one-off events as major volcanic eruptions could produce dramatic and unexpected results. More broadly, however, the real problem was not flooding, or long periods of drought that lasted decades, although these could act as triggers. What presented the greatest risk was population load. Harvests that failed repeatedly became an issue if there were too many mouths to feed; crops that were washed away by unexpected and unusual amounts of rain could mean disaster for communities that had to make adjustments in consequence; hoarding as a result of panic or in order to take advantage of inflated prices could make a disaster out of a precarious situation.

The demand for authority and wealth, driven by the centre, encouraged the exploitation of resources – and often brought about their exhaustion. What little timber had existed in Mesopotamia, for example, had been quickly used up, leading by 2000 BC to the need to import wood from as far away as Oman and the western coast of India.[46] Demand for metals such as copper, tin and lead in Shang dynasty China for the production of ritual vessels as well as weapons and tools caused limited local deposits to become depleted quickly and gave rise to a dependence on long-distance sourcing networks, although claims that these reached as far as Africa appear to be misguided.[47]

The weakness of course lay primarily in the size of individual cities, as this was where risks were greatest in times of shortage. Urban settlements were also centres for potential crisis because they were where uprisings could start as citizens who were disaffected, hungry or worse sought to take matters into their own hands. However, the size of the territory under the control of a single ruler and administration was an obvious source of weakness too, for it did not require much for newly or recently incorporated peoples to rise up, especially if they had been conquered militarily. Locations that were peripheral had most to lose from domination by faraway centres and provided the greatest opportunities for old or new elites to offer alternative visions and solutions that could generate their own steam.

In today's world, we refer to systems that link peoples and places together as globalisation. As has become clear in recent years, as well as having significant environmental costs, the processes that enable goods and produce to be made or grown, fuels to be extracted and resources tapped at the lowest possible prices and shipped at the optimum speed relative to outlay create positives and negatives. There are winners and losers in equations that involve threats and competition as well as efficiencies and benefits.

As we have also learned, however, these globalised forces create another more specific and difficult challenge, namely that close connections can suddenly tip from being part of a solution to the cause of problems. Interdependence means fragilities can easily be magnified – and can spread quickly and seemingly out of control.

A case in point are the widespread calamities that took hold c.1200 BC and brought about concurrent crises in Egypt, the eastern Mediterranean, the Near East and Mesopotamia. These included chronic food shortages which we learn were relieved, at least to start with, by shipments of grain from Egypt following the order given by the pharaoh, Merneptah, to keep the people of these regions alive.[48] Send food urgently, begged one Hittite King; 'it is a matter of life or death'.[49]

Records from Emar in what is now Syria are short and simple, begging for help: 'If you do not quickly arrive here,' they urged, 'we ourselves will die of hunger. You will not see another living soul from your land.'[50] Other clay tablets from the city state that families were so desperate that they were forced to sell their children in order to survive.[51] Sources from Babylon and Assyria also describe challenging times, with references to crop failure, food shortage and outbreak of disease. In time, Egypt too was affected by poor harvests – and by repeated strikes by workers at the royal tomb in the Valley of the Kings primarily as a result of inadequate or overdue rations.[52] By around 1170 BC, shortages had resulted in rampant inflation as grain prices rose eightfold, and on occasion even more steeply.[53]

This was a time of considerable disruption thanks to a group or perhaps groups who were identified at the time as coming from 'islands in the midst of the sea' and are usually referred to today as the Sea Peoples, a name coined by the French scholar Emmanuel de Rougé in the late nineteenth century. These included those who are referred to in the Hebrew Bible as Philistines, who migrated from southern Europe to the Middle East.[54] They are reported to have brought chaos to a wide area in the eastern Mediterranean. 'Now the ships of the enemy have come,' reads one cuneiform tablet purporting to relate the words of the King of Ugarit. 'They have been setting fire to my cities and have done harm to the land.'[55]

Egypt suffered the same way, to judge from texts engraved in the mortuary temple of the pharaoh Ramses III at Medinet Habu and in papyrus accounts from this period. 'Those who came together on the sea, the full flame was in front of them at the river-mouths, while a stockade of lances surrounded them on the shore,' says the inscription on the wall of Ramses' tomb. 'They were dragged in, enclosed, and prostrated on the beach, killed and made into heaps from tail to head. Their ships and their goods were as if fallen into the water.'[56] The Sea Peoples devastated one community after another as they laid their hands upon all the lands of the earth, mourned one contemporary account.[57]

These events took place during a challenging period of lower rainfall, attested by multiple proxies across these regions, including pollen data, charred plant remains, low lake levels in the Dead Sea and the Sea of Galilee, a drop in discharges in the Nile and drops in sea surface temperatures in the Mediterranean which are often associated with reduced precipitation levels.[58] However, once again, the time horizon for these changes was an extensive one. All were part of long-term trends that dated back centuries – perhaps even some 400 years earlier to the volcano on Thera/Santorini and the modifications that such a large eruption can produce in local and global weather patterns.[59]

Lower rainfall may have made life more and more difficult, and have pushed the margin of error to become ever narrower and more precarious, but other factors may have been much more important in bringing about the end of the Bronze Age.[60] For example, divisions and disputes among the social elite have been suggested as a leading cause of upheaval in the Hittite empire around this time.[61] As another scholar has noted, citing Claudius in Shakespeare's *Hamlet*, 'When sorrows come, they come not single spies / But in battalions,' the fifty-year period between 1225 and 1175 BC saw an 'earthquake storm' along the geological fault lines in the Aegean and eastern Mediterranean, with multiple destructive quakes measuring 6.5 or higher on the Richter scale.[62]

More significant than identifying a single, primary cause of multiple collapses, therefore, is the principle of contagion: the failure of one part of a network, whether because of poor harvest, earthquake damage or infighting between blood relatives, could cascade into the interruption, dislocation and even the system breakdown of the network as a whole. Elaborate long-distance exchange networks that facilitated trade and underpinned the status of the wealthy and powerful were also mutually dependent: the upside of hypercoherence was increased availability of luxury goods; the downside was infectious hyperfragility.[63]

It did not take much for networks to fall apart, in other words; and when they did, social structures, states and empires could wobble and even collapse. This was recognisable across many regions and periods of history. One example is the fall of the Roman empire in western Europe many centuries later, when modest pressure led to a downward spiral into what historians used to refer to as the Dark Ages; another is the collapse of the Soviet bloc at the end of the twentieth century, when what had looked like an impregnable empire dissolved almost overnight. Economists too are interested in models showing how minor shocks can create ripples that lead to failure and breakdown in supply chains – a principle known as the bullwhip effect.[64]

Seemingly all-powerful, well-structured empires and networks could unravel and fall apart rapidly under relatively little pressure – because of the availability of new commodities, for example, or, in the opposite case, because of resource shortage. Climate and weather were often aggravating factors rather than the direct cause of cataclysmic change. Moreover, while single shocks could occasionally have profound effects, what was more usual was that shifts that were spread out over the long term slowly eroded the ability and willingness of peoples to co-operate, leading to dispersals of population in waves rather than in one go.

A good example of this is the breakdown of the Poverty Point culture in the lower Mississippi Valley around 1300 BC. The central point of the communities in this region, which were socially, politically and ethnically diverse and likely spoke a range of different languages, was a massive earthen mound marked by concentric half-circle ridges that had been built with impressive skill, starting around three centuries earlier.[65] Stratigraphic analysis from Jaketown indicates that exceptional rainfall caused flooding that breached a levee in a particularly dramatic single incident c.1310 BC.[66]

However, what was more decisive in triggering large-scale population movements was the fact that flooding occurred regularly and unpredictably for several hundred years.[67] Ironically, communities could survive single traumas better than persistent threats that undermined cohesion and encouraged dispersal to new locations. Once environmental challenges had stabilised or disappeared, sites were often reoccupied and repurposed – as was the case in the lower Mississippi Valley as Early Woodland peoples recolonised settlement spots that had become benign, as they had been in the past.[68]

It was certainly true that difficult times which arose from poor harvests were not easy for ruling regimes to negotiate, for under the right circumstances these offered opportunities that were ripe for exploitation by opportunistic rivals. The trick, then, for rulers was to make sure no such rivals existed, or if they did, that they were either kept under control or managed well. When that did not happen, the outcome could be dramatic, as was the case in central and northern China in 1046 BC, when the Shang dynasty was overthrown by the Western Zhou. Later accounts attributed the fall of the last Shang Emperor Di Shin (商帝辛)

to his personal shortcomings, blaming his indolence, cruelty and love of luxury, principally in order to serve as a mirror for princes and to offer warnings that had a contemporary resonance.[69] But the point was clear: a single bad apple could rot the entire crop.

Although the fall of the Shang marked a new chapter in Chinese history, it effectively amounted to a management change that adapted, added to and introduced new strategies and cultural practices. Further west, however, the picture was rather more muted. It took time for exchange networks to recover. Some places, like Egypt, did better than others, because they were less dependent on outside imports, were better organised or simply proved more resilient under pressure – or perhaps a combination of all three. There were other beneficiaries too, with a handful of locations that were propitiously located emerging as pockets that survived intact and eventually wove new tapestries of connections (and rivalries) – the rise of kingdoms and city states in the Aegean such as Mycenae, Athens, Sparta and others that became the backbone of the ancient Greek world offering a case in point. Groups of cities and states rose and fell together, stimulating and spurring each other on through exchange and competition – creating a mutual dependence that could also result in failure, as well as success.

The period around 1200 BC was also one of population movements, colonisations and change in Near and Remote Oceania in the Pacific, where archaeological sites with large numbers of shellfish as well as bones of giant tortoises, land crocodiles and bird species attest to waves of migration of the Lapita culture first to Vanuatu, New Caledonia and Fiji and later to Tonga and then Samoa.[70] It has been suggested that these movements may have been responses to changing and reversing wind patterns that made sailing west to east both easier and quicker – meaning that less time was needed at sea, which in turn meant reduced food and water requirements.[71]

It is striking, then, that 3,000 years ago – if not earlier still – questions about the threats of overpopulation, of fragility and of the risks posed by interdependence had already started to concern thinkers, priests, administrators and rulers. There was already not only awareness but acute concern about unforeseen problems that could suddenly appear and threaten disaster. Learning how to identify, anticipate and deal with these challenges became a fundamental concern for those living millennia ago. At the heart of the question of how to conceptualise the world was the problem of how to understand the human relationship with the divine – and with nature – in order to anticipate challenges, be ready to deal with them and, better still, prevent them from appearing in the first place.

7

Regarding Nature and the Divine
(c.1700–c.300 BC)

The Lord is my shepherd, I shall not want; he makes me lie down
in green pastures.

Psalm 23

The dangers of environmental degradation, overconsumption of
resources and unsustainable population load were not lost on people
living thousands of years ago. For example, *The Epic of Atrahasis*, an
Old Babylonian text of which the earliest clay tablets date to around
1700 BC, reveals an acute awareness of the vulnerabilities that came
from pushing ecological boundaries beyond their limits. The gods had
created humans, says the narrator of the text, because they realised that
they had too much work to do themselves: 'mortal man' was created
therefore, with the specific instruction that he should 'bear the load
of the gods'.[1] The trouble was that the gods had not accounted for the
length of a natural lifespan, which soon resulted in overpopulation. It
was not long before the number of people became 'too numerous' and
'the country was as noisy as a bellowing bull'.[2]

This annoyed the god Ellil, who 'had to listen their noise' and soon
complained that he was 'losing sleep over the racket'. This happened
on several occasions, leading to the gods taking matters into their
own hands and deciding to kill off most of the population in order to
achieve some peace and quiet. As a result, they sent terrible droughts
that brought famine as well as other 'solutions' to the problem of the

excessive noise and the excessive number of people, including disease and pestilence.[3]

The most dramatic attempt was a great flood, an episode attested by archaeological evidence and presumably the basis for later Egyptian accounts and for those that feature in biblical versions.[4] As well as speaking of the inundation as divine punishment, implicit in each version of the flood is the theme of population loss and population control. In the case of *The Epic of Atrahasis*, the issue is specific and explicit: there had been too many people living on the earth, so steps needed to be taken to reduce numbers and to stop the same thing from happening again.

The mother goddess Nintu, says that account, had been particularly upset by the flood and the deaths of so many people because it deprived her of the regular offerings of beer that she had much enjoyed receiving from humans keen to maintain her goodwill. Once it became clear that Atrahasis and his ark had been saved, however, the gods came up with a new way of dealing with overpopulation: they tweaked the design of humans, to create a new, updated race who were not as fertile as the last. Their scheme included women who were unable to have children, higher levels of miscarriage and the consecration of virgins to serve the deities. All the tweaks were intended to reduce reproductive levels and to allow the population to be smaller, more sustainable – and quieter.[5]

While the flood story was a dramatic one, the connection between overpopulation and fragility is a powerful one that fits within the wider picture of concern about resource depletion, environmental degradation and the detrimental impact of human intervention within and on the physical landscape. Such concerns were well founded, for prolonged periods of reduced agricultural production, whether because of lower rainfall or as a result of soil depletion that came from land being overworked, presented acute problems, particularly in ecologically sensitive regions like southern Mesopotamia.

Both the nature and the scale of the problem are clear from a study of crop yields, which shows that these declined precipitously and consistently as greater demands were made of the land. For much of the third millennium BC, good agricultural land had produced around 2,000 litres per hectare per year; by around the time of Naram-Sin's reign in c.2200 BC, they were producing only just over half of that amount. Things got worse in the centuries that followed as the Akkadian empire was replaced by a smattering of new states that rose in its place, the most brilliant of which was the Third Dynasty of Ur. By 1700 BC, yields had fallen to around 700 litres per hectare per year, although a significant proportion was producing less than 400 litres per hectare.[6] Overexploitation meant that land was producing just 20 per cent of what it had been able to achieve a few centuries earlier.

For some scholars, collapse in production was the direct result not only of rising population levels but of a rapacious central bureaucracy, whose own need and aspirations placed demands that forced farmers to push their lands to their ecological limits. In particular, the problem was caused by excessive irrigation that ruined soils by causing salinity levels to rise. The search for short-term gain resulted in outcomes that were not only unsustainable but damaging. As we have seen in the cases of implosions of states and the breakdown of trade networks, rising complexity produces diminishing returns as well as magnifying vulnerability. Far from success breeding success, in other words, what seemed like never-ending success as states expanded and land under cultivation increased in extent was often an exercise in the seeds of ruin being sown inadvertently.[7]

There is considerable evidence in the sources too of the awareness of the dangers posed by overexploitation of nature. The writer of *The Epic of Gilgamesh*, for example, counsels that drought followed deforestation.[8] Perhaps most striking is the moment when Gilgamesh kills Humbaba, the forest god, whose murder stands as a metaphor for the deforestation of Mesopotamia and humans' simultaneous encroachment on and lack of respect for the natural world.[9] Sensitivity to the natural environment and to the delicacy of ecological equilibrium is also implied in the personalisation of flora and fauna, which have the power of speech as well as a capacity for feeling, with trees, rivers and wild animals weeping with sorrow when Gilgamesh later kills his friend and companion Enkidu.[10]

Gilgamesh's exploits stand as a metaphor for struggles against natural disasters that were caused by the gods. The eponymous hero was revered by the people of Uruk, we are told, because he restored order by rebuilding holy places that had been destroyed by flooding; his was the task of fighting against a devastating drought, sent down from the heavens, that 'dried up the groves, reedbeds and marshes' and lowered the river by seven cubits – around three and a half metres.[11] Man was in a struggle not only against nature, in other words, but against hostile forces that sought to challenge, reduce and even destroy humanity. Other Mesopotamian texts, like the *Enūma Anu Enlil*, contain multiple references to celestial and atmospheric signs, which show a sharp interest in trying to make sense of meteorological conditions and even in trying to influence them.[12]

The rise of the Neo-Assyrian empire in the centuries that followed the collapse of the Bronze Age brought about profound changes to the environmental, socio-economic and political landscapes of northern Mesopotamia in particular. Urban centres began to grow to astonishing sizes, with some new cities founded – like Dur-Šarrukin – and others expanded dramatically, such as Nineveh, which grew to some 750 hectares during the reign of Sennacherib (705–681 BC).[13]

This required different thinking about and engagement with the land. One change was the introduction of massive investments in irrigation systems that completely transformed the physical and natural environments as webs of canals were built that transported snowmelt from the mountains and rivers to where it was most needed – namely, the major cities that were few in number but vast in size (and therefore vulnerable to both food and water shortages) and the fields that surrounded them.[14] It was not only the succession of imperial capitals that became home to the Assyrian rulers that benefited; so too did more rural areas that were home to lower population densities.[15]

These interventions were an important part of an ideological transformation of the landscape that emphasised the power of the Assyrian kings, who were able to tame rivers, redirect their supply, enable cultivation of new lands and ensure enough food for all. Not surprisingly, then, these achievements were the subject of boastful inscriptions that praised the king and the works he had overseen. '[I] Sennacherib, great king, strong king, king of the world', reads one, transformed fields that were wasteland into ones that bore abundant fruit. People had used to turn their eyes to the skies in hope of rain; he dug wells, created irrigation channels, built canals and constructed sluices and dams to control the water supply. These works were so glorious and effective, it adds, that 'I had a royal image of myself expressing humility' set up at the mouth of the canal. The inscription ends with an entreaty from its royal author: if any of his descendants dismantles or does not maintain these works in the future, 'may the great gods overthrow his dynasty'.[16]

Domination over nature was supplemented by the creation of networks of roads, tracks and way stations that can be identified today from satellite photos. All these were maintained by the crown, as well as by those taken prisoner during Assyrian wars of expansion.[17] Perhaps as many as 1.5 million people were forcibly resettled by the authorities in the two centuries after 800 BC, to reduce the risk of local rebellions, to exploit the empire's resources systematically and to live within ecological limits.[18]

Those who were dispersed travelled in comfort. Letters such as that addressed to Tiglath-Pileser III (r. 745–727 BC) recorded that the King had instructed deportees to be given 'provisions, sackcloth, leather bags, sandals and oil'. If the King's donkeys had been available, it notes, these would have been provided, as would carts for them to pull. Assyrian royal art shows men, women and children often travelling on animals or on wagons – and never tied up.[19] In their dealings with those who were resettled and deported, kings were frequently compared to gardeners, uprooting precious trees and replanting them in the best possible environment for them to flourish.[20]

As we have seen before and shall see again, in pre-industrial societies exploitation of the land was dependent on human labour. As such, a key driver in territorial expansion was not only the earning of prestige or the acquisition of good land, but the boosting of manpower. This was not always done by force: when the Assyrian army besieged Jerusalem in 701 BC, envoys were sent on behalf of King Sennacherib to appeal to the city's inhabitants: 'Make your peace and come out to me!' If they did, they were told, they would be taken away to a land just like their own, 'a land of grain and wine, a land of bread and vineyards, a land of olive trees and honey', where they would be looked after and cherished.[21]

The elision of royal power and control over nature extended into other areas too, notably in the form of the king hunting wild and dangerous beasts which represented his mastery over the animal kingdom and the metaphorical protection he gave in defending his people from threats. Reliefs that show the great Ashurbanipal (r. 669–631 BC) wrestling with a lion with his bare hands were intended to show the ruler's superhuman bravery and skill, setting him apart from normal men and thereby affirming his authority.[22]

Presiding over giant feasts was another way that the king could show his wealth both literally and through the range and quantity of food at his disposal. A stele found in 1951 at Kalḫu (known today as Nimrud, near Mosul) records a spectacular event that demonstrates this perfectly. We learn from the inscription that King Ashurnasirpal II held a ten-day celebration for precisely 69,574 guests, laying on '1000 barley-fed oxen, 1000 young cattle ... 14,000 common sheep ... 1000 lambs, 500 deer, 500 gazelles, 1000 large birds, 500 geese, 500 fowls, 1000 suki-birds, 10,000 fish and 10,000 locusts', as well as 10,000 earthenware jars of beer and the same number of goatskins filled with wine.[23]

The creation of non-native ecosystems within capital cities that included elements such as simulated marshes and imported flora were likewise intended to demonstrate dominance over the natural world.[24] Perhaps the best example was the astonishing garden made by Sennacherib at Nineveh, near modern Mosul, one of the wonders of the ancient world; associated thanks to a series of later manipulations, misunderstandings and confusions with an entirely different city, it seems to have become known as the Hanging Gardens of Babylon.[25]

Despite many changes across hundreds and indeed thousands of years in the Middle East, there were continuities too, for example in agriculture, architecture, political structure and the economy. Empires rose and fell; regions were sometimes more and sometimes less intensively linked with each other over short and long distances. Even languages came and went – with Assyrian cuneiform and language largely disappearing following the sack of Nineveh in 612 BC at the hands of a powerful Babylonian state that rose in its place, until it too was supplanted, this time by the Achaemenids of Persia.[26]

One of these continuities lay however, in cosmology. Societies differed in their allegiances to individual gods, in the specifics of how to win their favour and of how to interpret advice and admonitions. But the approaches were very similar when it came to trying to make sense of the world and to interpret and intervene – particularly in relation to climate and its vagaries. Astronomical diaries recorded astrological phenomena, as a way both of tabulating knowledge and of creating a framework to identify and then try to understand anomalies.[27] The job of interpreting was taken up by seers and priests in the Mesopotamian world, who claimed responsibility for explaining signs and omens to help humans understand the whim and will of the gods.

Animals were offered in sacrifice in order to win the favour of the deities and to ensure smooth channels of communication. Sometimes questions were whispered to sheep as they were being slaughtered so that messages could be delivered quickly and directly to the gods.[28] If animals had birth defects, such as no bladder, it was inferred that 'the flood in the river will be cut off, the rain in the sky will be scarce'.[29]

Not all of these omens were linked to weather and climate. Will an enemy army gather, get organised, march and fight with us? asked one powerful ruler of the Neo-Assyrian empire that rose from the ashes of the Bronze Age collapse. No, came the reply. Would a young man be likely to recover from epilepsy? came another question. Yes, was the response. Often, however, there were warnings that the price of goods would rise or that there would be shortages. If the moon seemed to have a halo, for example, grain supplies would fall. If Mars was erratic, barley would become more expensive. Many omens were concerned with the harvest, with rainfall, with starvation or with locust swarms that could devastate crops. Predictions therefore could give warnings to the ruler, to tell him he should be cautious and prepare accordingly.[30] Naturally, this was textbook forward planning by seers – who could always say that their admonitions had not been heeded if disaster struck, but that they had been if it did not.

It was a similar equation for those interpreting the natural world in Shang dynasty China, where the power of elites was closely connected to the ability to control and explain reality and to commune with a complex pantheon of gods that included Di (帝),the high god, and nature powers like the river, mountain and sun, as well as mythical and semi-mythical beings and ancestors. Oracle bones made mainly from ox scapulae and turtle shells were used as divination tools with the king or his diviners applying a hot rod to produce a series of heat cracks and then interpreting the 'answers' accordingly. 'Auspicious', reads one example. 'We will receive harvest.'[31]

The relationship with the supernatural world was administered by the Shang ruler, who had a shamanistic role in undertaking rituals and ceremonies and acting as an intermediary with the deities as well as with royal ancestors.[32] This required suitable gifts to be given up in offerings to ensure rain, good harvests and other benign conditions, and to appease hostile or malevolent spirits. The offerings could be substantial, as is clear from a set of oracle bones that record '100 cups of wine, 100 Qiang prisoners, 300 cattle, 300 sheep and 300 pigs' being given up by one ruler on a single occasion.[33] Human sacrifice of prisoners, usually in groups of ten but sometimes numbering hundreds, followed by interment of their decapitated, dismembered bodies in royal burials alongside retainers and relatives, was an important part of creating a dynamic that underlined the king's unique political, social, cultural and spiritual position.[34]

As in Mesopotamian cultures, a wide range of topics were investigated, including whether those who were ill would be cured, what the outcomes might be of conflict with neighbouring peoples, what the gender of offspring would be and what the status was of the king's health. Many questions were concerned with the weather and in particular with rain, for which Di was primarily responsible. Di was feared for his ability to 'send down' disasters on humans and for his power to control the winds, to order rain or to send thunder.[35] 'From today', reads one bone oracle, 'Di will order rain.' If the king goes hunting on a given day, reads another, 'he will have no disasters and it will not rain'.[36]

The Shang rulers' concern with avoiding disaster, overseeing sufficient rainfall and ensuring good harvests was shared by the Zhou dynasty, which took power in 1046 BC, and which celebrated new or perhaps existing rituals that demonstrated royal patronage over the land and the fruits it yielded. These included the ploughing of the sacred field at the start of the agricultural year.[37] 'Be attentive in your tasks,' warned one classic poem, and 'prepare your spades and hoes'. The king 'has himself come to scrutinize you' as you work; as a result of his involvement and thanks to heaven, there will be a plentiful harvest.[38]

Assuming responsibility for good outcomes in the natural world served as a powerful claim to be the conduit between heaven and earth, something that the Zhou rulers emphasised with gusto as they shuffled the cosmological deck of cards to introduce a new concept of Tian (天) – broadly equating to heaven or nature, a universalised concept which blended a supreme deity with a cosmic moral force that ruled the world and took an interest in the affairs of human beings. One reason for doing so may have been the need for political propaganda to assert the legitimacy of their rule, while pacifying those whose loyalties lay with the Shang – a substantial challenge made clear by a major rebellion that broke out soon after the Zhou took power.[39]

Crucial in this revised model was an even greater emphasis on the role of the ruler maintaining a bilateral bond, under which authority was vested by heaven and maintained by the king. According to the *Classic of Poetry*, the 'Zhou is an old people / but its Mandate is new'. The Shang had fallen, says the author of the poem, because they had neither understood nor fulfilled their commitment to protect the will of heaven. Luckily, the Zhou had arrived to protect everyone, in the first instance under its founder, King Wen. Although it would not be easy, Wen and his descendants would protect the 'Mandate of Heaven' and, in doing so, bring peace, prosperity and harmony to all.[40]

Careful attention was needed, therefore, in times of adverse conditions. Lack of rain was a particular concern. The poem 'Yunhan' (雲漢) from the celebrated *Shijing* (詩經, *Classic of Poetry*) records the anguish of King Xuan at a time of drought around 800 BC.

> The drought is so excessive,
> And we are tormented by the heat.
> I have not stopped offering sacrifices.
> From the suburban altar I have gone to the temple hall.
> To the powers above and below I have made sacrifices and buried offerings.
> There are no spirits I have not honoured …
> The drought is so excessive,
> And it cannot be alleviated.
> It is terrifying and perilous,
> Like lightning and thunder.
> Of the dark masses that still remain in Zhou
> There will not be a single one left.[41]

The ruler was at pains to ensure that he had made the appropriate offerings and had followed the right rituals in order to demonstrate not only that the drought was not his fault but also that he had done, and was continuing to do, all he could to alleviate the challenging circumstances.

Excessive rain could also cause problems, as another poem written almost 3,000 years ago during the period of the Western Zhou dynasty notes: heaven was 'sending down rain' after being 'arrayed in anger', leading to widespread famine and to people having to leave their homes and become 'wandering fugitives'.[42] Such events could easily undermine the authority of rulers, both because of the practical problems that pressure on food production posed for social stability and because of questions about the competence, efficacy and suitability of those entrusted with ensuring smooth relations with gods, spirits and the divine.

This was one reason why efforts were made to understand and record natural phenomena. The legendary Emperor Yao, one of the first figures recorded by Chinese sources, was said to have instructed 'astronomical officers to observe sunrise and sunset, and the stars and the planets, and to make a solar and lunar calendar with 366 days and also calculate the leap month'.[43] Weather observations and celestial occurrences, such as eclipses, were avidly recorded in Mesopotamia in the form of astronomical diaries dating at least to the mid-seventh century BC if not earlier, to help anticipate and explain unusual celestial and environmental occurrences.[44]

Efforts were also made to interpret signs for guidance to what the future might hold, with predictions based on the combined positions of various stars relative to the sun being taken as a warning that 'cities will start vying with each other, city walls will be destroyed [and] the people will be dispersed'.[45] Some hedged their bets, such as Akkullanu, royal astrologer to King Ashurbanipal, who wrote to the ruler in the middle of the seventh century BC 'about this year's rains that were diminished and no harvest was reaped'. In fact, he claimed, 'this is a good omen for the life and wellbeing of the king my lord'. Moreover, it was an omen of opportunity: if the King 'takes the road against the enemy, he will conquer whatever [land] he will go to and his days will become long'.[46]

If that was a case of fancy footwork and trying to avoid blame for agricultural failure, others were more careful not to leave things to chance. 'I brought the Nile to the upland in your fields,' boasted one pharaoh in Egypt, 'so that plots were watered that had never known water before.'[47] The rewards of investing in infrastructure like irrigation channels were for the general population, but the credit was taken by the ruler.

The fusion of benign climate, divine favour and reward for good leadership was one with deep roots in many parts of the world. Writing in the eighth century BC, for example, the Greek author Hesiod argued that when people 'deal in justice straight and fair' and observe the law, 'their city flourishes, their people bloom'. In particular, 'famine and folly pass the righteous by' and 'the just feast on what well-worked fields supply. The earth abounds for them.' Hesiod did not just recommend moral qualities but extolled the benefits of hard work: 'It's work that prospers men, and makes them rich … it's working which endears you to the immortals.' In contrast, those who commit evil deeds are not just punished personally; 'often a whole city pays the price'.[48]

The elision of natural order and power would become a fundamental part of Chinese political and religious philosophy and of imperial political ideology in particular over the course of three millennia. It effectively fused the role of emperor with good outcomes – environmental and otherwise. To justify the mandate, rulers had to rule well. This equation worked both ways: credit could be taken for periods of plenty, prosperity and peace; but, equally, disequilibrium could be interpreted as a sign of celestial order being disturbed and therefore a justification for punishment and hardship. Shrewd leaders could of course use this opportunistically, taking advantage of challenging circumstances to blame others and remove rivals, real or imaginary. Nevertheless, ideas about balance – and the need to maintain order – were hugely important and influential, and could be applied to the state, the ruler and each individual.

Many offered suggestions for how best to do this – so many, in fact, that the period from the sixth century BC onwards, a period when the number of cities and their populations rose sharply in Eastern Zhou dynasty China, became known as the time of the Hundred Schools of Thought.[49] Among figures prominent in this period was Kong Qiu (better known in the west as Confucius), who counselled that people should aspire to live moral lives and show filial devotion, respect for ritual and benevolence towards others. Just as a society as a whole should reflect the celestial order, so too should rulers protect it, while all should live in a way that defended stability and harmony.[50]

Others, like Laozi ('Old master') and Zhuangzi, reacted to this, attacking the vanity of those who claimed to know and practise virtue. In fact, they argued, what governed the universe was an abstract theory based on the concept of Dao ('the Way'), a force that unified existence in a state of harmony. 'Man takes his law from the Earth; the Earth takes its law from Heaven; Heaven takes its law from the Dao. The law of the Dao is its being what it is.'[51] Being virtuous required more than being humane. It demanded the abandonment of luxurious living, renunciation of war and a life of simplicity and innocence. The best three 'treasures' were compassion, frugality and 'daring not to be first in the world'.[52]

This all sounded very nice, argued Mozi, but examples needed to be set by those in positions of authority. 'When the state is well ordered, the laws and punishments will be justly administered.' Those of poor moral character should be weeded out, while 'no special consideration' should be shown to those 'of their own kin, no partiality for the eminent and rich, no favouritism for the good-looking and attractive'. It was the duty of the ruler to provide and maintain a structure. Balance did not just happen on its own, in other words.[53]

Such discussions and debates were not entirely dissimilar in India, where the earliest hymns of the Vedic Aryans articulated notions of heaven and earth and of *ṛta* (ऋत – a fixed or settled order) and explained how the universal laws that governed *ṛta* were sustained by the guardian deity Varuna. Early Indian literature took the form of *sruti* (श्रुति – sayings that were later written down) that could be understood only by a *rishi* (ऋषि – a sage or a wise man) who had acquired the requisite skills through a process of contemplation and revelation. Such texts included the Vedas and the *Bhagavad Gita*, a 700-verse scripture that is preserved as part of the epic *Mahābhārata*.[54]

The collections of hymns that make up the four Vedas (*Rig, Yajur, Sama* and *Atharva*), conventionally thought to have been composed c.1500–1000 BC, explore the relationship between the terrestrial and the celestial, extolling the way the combination of heaven and earth can 'shower down honey for us' as well as 'great glory, reward and heroic strength'. Verses in the *Rig Veda* bid heaven and earth to 'bring unto us gain, reward and riches'.[55]

Advice in the Vedas was practical as well as existential and spiritual, and included prayers to keep serpents away alongside guidance on how to use plants such as the *apāmārga* (*Achyranthes aspera*) to overcome disease, and how to ward off curses, avoid bad dreams, remove the threat of hunger and thirst and stop losing at dice.[56] Some herbs could help keep the air free of foul smells and pollutants, an important quality given that fresh air was important for human health.[57]

These texts make frequent references to wider conceptualisations about the human relationship with the natural environment. 'The oceans are the treasure of wealth, so you should protect them,' says the *Yajur Veda*, which also warns that water should be kept clear, clean and fresh and not be polluted. Do not pollute the water, it adjures, and do not harm or cut the trees.[58] Animal welfare was important, not least because some creatures were useful: 'No person should kill animals that are helpful to all.' This advice was expanded for the sake of rulers, along with an explanation: 'O King, you should never kill animals like bullocks that are useful in agriculture, or like cows which give us milk, and all other helpful animals – and you must punish those who kill or do harm to such animals.'[59]

Many of the verses are concerned with the idea of deities as beneficent beings choosing to hand out riches and rewards, a theme that recurs repeatedly in the Vedas. One hymn sings of Dawn, personified as a beautiful woman, appearing each morning in her chariot to usher in a new day as she rides across the skies. 'Without fail she continually creates wealth. Making her path toward prosperity, the much praised goddess, bringing all desirable things, becomes radiant.'[60]

Such ideas were elaborated on in a series of later works that built on the teachings of the Vedas and the early Upaniṣads; these were composed around 600 BC and set out norms for ideal ways of living.[61] In one, we learn of the story of King Bṛhadratha, who gave up the throne to his son and went to live in the forest to ponder the purpose of his existence and the 'essence of the self'. He came to understand that life was transient, and that 'flies, gnats and other insects, as well as herbs and trees', would first grow and then die. But what truly concerned him was 'the drying up of great oceans', the 'submergence of the earth' and constant change that meant things were not in their right place. Seeing the world in this way, he said, 'what is the use of the enjoyment and pleasures in a world such as this?' Life was barely worth living, he told a famous holy man he met living in the forest: 'I am like a frog in a dry well.'[62]

Taken as a whole, scriptural texts, historical narratives, law codes, myths and legends and philosophical tracts that are collectively known as *smriti* (स्मृति – or recollections) set out frameworks for making sense of the universe, as well as advising on the most appropriate ritual practices and pushing at the boundaries of philosophy, ethics and epistemology. When it came to the natural world, much of the advice was again practical and prescriptive: the planting of trees was to be praised, while the polluting of water was to be condemned. Being surrounded by animals and by fresh, green trees and away from other humans was an effective way of being at peace – enabling, as the great *Rāmāyana* epic suggests, all living beings to exist in a state of blissful harmony.[63]

These texts set out complex theological explanations and vested authority in those who were trusted to understand, relate and interpret them. In South Asia, this privileging of information concentrated spiritual authority in the hands of a priestly class who were able to engage with the wishes of Brahmanaspati (the Lord of Prayer) and Vāch (the goddess of speech). *Brāhmans* (holy men or priests) controlled rituals, techniques and knowledge that enabled intercessions with and even control over the supernatural – including control over favourable climatic conditions. Some would ask which god should be honoured and thanked for creating all humans and all animals, for the 'snow-covered mountains' (the Himalayas), the great river (the Rasā that marks the boundary of the earth) and the shining deep waters of the seas. Only those who knew the hymn would be able to provide the answer: Prajāpati.[64]

That such views were written down, survived and were disseminated and added to naturally attests to their significance as the basis of what later became known as Hinduism.[65] What is rather harder to determine, however, is how they were perceived and understood beyond the elites who clearly invested time, energy and resources preserving teachings that contained universal truths about the earth, the gods and how to win the favour of the latter.

Challengers emerged who set out rival cosmologies, and many of them placed a premium on how people lived and behaved. In some cases, there were reactions against the idea that knowledge and wisdom lay in the hands of others rather than in the self. Among the most prominent and successful of these were the teachings of the Buddha, the son of a nobleman who spurned a life of luxury to search for enlightenment, which he discovered under a sacred peepal tree at Gayā in what is now Bihar, northern India.

Many of the sermons and views attributed to the Buddha are best understood as being formulated by his followers and successors, *bhikkhus* (भिक्षु), who were instructed to wear yellow robes and to continue his preaching after his death, which modern scholars now usually date to around 400 BC.[66] One central element of Buddhist philosophy was that the path to enlightenment was a highly personal one, centred on the doctrine of the 'Four Noble Truths'. These truths held that life was a journey of suffering; that this suffering was the result of desire and craving; that suppressing such desires removed sorrow; and that suppression could be achieved only through strict discipline resulting from intense concentration and meditation.[67]

While some scholars caution that treating Buddhism as a reaction to Vedic Brahmanism can be misleading, the fact that the journey towards enlightenment was a highly personal one which involved each individual discovering truths for themselves – rather than relying on others to intervene on their behalf – was significant.[68] The theoretical stance of Buddhism was one that did not require *brāhmans*, in other words; as the *Sutta Nipāta* pointedly notes, claims by others of moral superiority were ill placed:

> No *brāhman* is such by his birth
> No outcast is such by his birth
> An outcast is such by his deeds.
> A *brāhman* is such by his deeds.

What mattered, therefore, were personal actions rather than deep understanding of the workings of the universe that could be revealed by ancient Sanskrit texts.[69]

It was not for nothing, then, that many of the teachings set out by the Buddha and his followers were practical rather than theological. A husband should treat his wife by honouring her; treating her with respect; remaining faithful to her; giving her charge of the home; and regularly giving her gifts and adornments. A master should not overwork his servants; should ensure they are well fed and well paid; should look after them through illness; should share 'especially tasty luxuries' with them; and should let them take holidays at appropriate intervals.[70] Being charitable, kind, restrained and reserved was the source of personal treasure – treasure, furthermore, that could not be stolen by thieves or given to others.[71]

While Buddhism is often co-opted today and celebrated for its supposed ideas about ecological awareness and environmental sustainability, these are modern constructs rather than reflections of reality. In fact, for early Buddhists, the natural world was a place that was transitory; far from being a place of wonder, the physical world, like human life, was primarily about 'suffering, decay, death and impermanence'.[72]

That a canon of Buddhist texts was curated, preserved and disseminated provides a clear indication, of course, that not everything was left to the individual. Guidance could be sought to help steer one towards the goal of enlightenment, meaning that even within a notionally egalitarian world special status was reserved for monks and holy men. These texts contain warnings too of the dangerous and devious teachings of the 'Six Tirthakas' (false teachers), contemporaries of the Buddha whose views ranged from dismissing efforts to identify reason and order in the universe to denunciations of ideas about moral goodness. There was no benefit or reward in giving alms, performing sacrifices or giving offerings, said Ajita Kesakambala, for example: those who believed that doing 'good deeds' would result in future rewards were fools. 'There is no passing from this world to the next,' and anyone who taught that there were connections between the material and supernatural world were talking nonsense, indeed lying.[73]

Some sages advocated more stark re-thinking about the world, about life in general and about nature in particular. According to Vardhamāna Mahāvīra ('Great Hero'), the inspiration behind the Jain religion, the lover of possessions is deluded and falls into great pain – an idea that finds an echo in Buddhism. Jainism went further, however, by arguing that all organisms including plants were alive, as were the elements themselves. 'Injury to the earth is like striking, cutting, maiming or killing a blind man,' states one of the canonical texts of Jain scripture, the *Ācārāṅga Sūtra*. 'Knowing this, a man should not sin against earth, or cause or permit others to do so.'[74]

Jain ecological cosmology was extensive and demanded an asceticism that presented human beings as participants in a rich panoply of living entities that included 'earth and water, fire and wind, grass, trees and plants and all creatures that move'. In hurting any of these, 'men hurt themselves'.[75] As such, it was not enough to be mindful and to seek enlightenment and detachment. What was required was an unlimited awareness and heightened consciousness which revealed that trees felt pain as they were cut, stripped and sawn, that iron anvils trembled in pain and suffering when struck by the hammer and tongs of a blacksmith.[76]

It was essential, according to Jain teaching, to understand that humans are part of a living, connected environment and ecosystem and that they could be affected, hurt and damaged by human actions. 'A man who lights a fire kills living things,' states one text, for insects could hop into a fire inadvertently, worms living in wood that was used as fuel could be burned, and cutting down plants not only killed them but disrupted habitats for other plants and animals. So anyone who possessed wisdom and understood the meaning of life 'should never light a fire'.[77]

Some modern scholars have often associated the efflorescence of new ideas in India, which also extended into grammar, law, literature and drama, with wider social and political change driven by agricultural surplus in the first instance and by a new wave of urbanisation starting in the sixth century BC.[78] This was accompanied by a period of centralisation and consolidation as a succession of small kingdoms sprang up and then coalesced into sixteen large kingdoms (*mahājanapadas*), before these too expanded and merged.[79]

This presented new challenges and resulted in substantial shifts in thinking, and it was striking that some of the new ideas involved challenging traditional brahmanic teaching – in particular, those to do with animal sacrifice. Buddhist texts, for example, disdained the slaughter of animals, with the Buddha warning that animal offerings achieve no great results. Indeed, animal sacrifices are said to have produced negative outcomes, including longing, hunger and decrepitude, that themselves quickly multiplied to create ninety-eight further ailments.[80]

Conversely, notes the *Dīgha Nikāya*, offerings could be given where no animals and plants were hurt. Behold, it says, 'no cows were killed, no goats were killed, no cocks and pigs were killed, nor were the diverse living creatures subjected to slaughter, trees were not cut down for sacrificial posts nor were grasses mown …The sacrifice was pursued with clarified butter, fresh butter, curds, honey and molasses.'[81]

This was a provocative and revolutionary approach that effectively called into question the rights of the Vedic priesthood to control ritual and access to the divine, while asserting, if only implicitly, that their methods of doing so were unnecessary and suspect. In turn, efforts were made to articulate a model that explained the roles of the different members of society. The most prominent were centred on *varṇadharma*, a sacred set of laws that held that four hierarchical classes (*varṇas*) had been created, each of which was subject to their own *dharma* and order. Dividing society into *brāhmans* (priests and teachers), *kṣatriyas* (nobles and warriors), *vaiśyas* (merchants and agriculturalists) and *śūdras* (servants and menial labourers) amounted to a detailed political philosophy that not only dealt with abstract concepts about engagement with the natural world, but also offered formal explanations and guidance about the workings of secular society that went hand in hand with laws setting out the responsibilities of rulers (*rājadharma*).[82]

It may be that ideas about reincarnation developed in response to increasing spiritual competition, although both the timing and context are hard to pinpoint. Most scholars agree that there is no concept of rebirth in the Vedas and that the earliest expression comes in one of the early Upaniṣads. 'When people depart from this world,' it says, 'it is to the moon that they all go,' since the moon is 'the door to the heavenly world'. Those who are unable to pass through to the other side are turned into rain, which then falls on the earth and 'they are born again in these various conditions – as a worm, an insect, a fish, a bird, a lion, a boar, a rhinoceros, a tiger, a man, or some other creature – each in accordance with his actions and his knowledge'.[83]

This can be interpreted as humans trying to make sense of their fortunes and misfortunes in life, and seeking explanations for the events outside their control that took place in an earlier manifestation.[84] It is notable that similar hypotheses were being posited in the eastern Mediterranean around the same time. Herodotus, writing in the fifth century BC, observed that Egyptians and then Greeks had adopted the belief 'that the soul of a human being is immortal, and that each time the body dies the soul enters another creature just as it is being born'.[85] Some, like Pythagoras, were said not only to have lived previous lives, but even to have known who they had been – with the great mathematician apparently able to offer 'indisputable proofs that he had been Euphorbos son of Panthoos, the opponent of Patroklos', who had featured in *The Iliad*.[86] Another, Empedokles, had a wider set of experiences, noting that 'in the past, I have been a boy and a girl, a bush, a bird and a mute fish swimming in the sea'.[87]

Ideas about the immortality of the soul, about reincarnation and about goodness were bound up with wider questions of how one's actions should be judged both in this life and after death; this was a time when philosophers like Plato held that one would be rewarded or punished accordingly.[88] Such questions were part of broad and vibrant philosophical reconfigurations, many of which reflected on interaction between humans, their interaction with the divine, with the natural world or all three. Among the cosmological views adopted in ancient Greece were the beliefs that the universe was animate, sentient and intelligent, held together by harmonious forces.[89]

This inevitably informed ideas about all living things, which according to Plato, were all 'endowed with soul and reason'.[90] Those with ascetic beliefs took this further, arguing that eating animals and plants was wrong as this usually involved killing them. Food 'that has had life' was scorned, therefore, in favour of milk, cheese, honey, wine, oil and leafy vegetables which could be consumed without harming a living animal and therefore guilt-free.[91]

Such lifestyle choices seem remarkably up to date, even fashionable in the world of today where decisions about food in particular are often influenced by opinions of animal and plant welfare – which are themselves sometimes set within a wider context of resource availability and sustainability. As today, however, it would be wrong to think that such attitudes were mainstream. Not only did many other philosophers not equate animals and plants with human beings, some suggested an entirely different hierarchical model. For Aristotle, plants existed for the benefit of animals; animals existed for the sake of people; and inferior people served as slaves to those who were superior.[92] Socrates was even blunter, at least according to Plato: there was nothing to be learned from trees, nature and the countryside; the only place one could gain knowledge was in the city, from other men.[93]

Nevertheless, anxieties about environmental degradation and pollution had their champions both on an individual basis and, in some places, institutionally. As early as c.700 BC, Hesiod was warning about the dangers of urinating or defecating in springs or rivers, stressing that doing so could lead to disease and suffering. Xenophon was one of many who advocated the benefits of good treatment of ecological habitats: the earth rewarded those who treated it well, he wrote, 'for the better she is served, the greater the benefits she gives in return'.[94] Others, like Theophrastus, took to observing which habitat suited which plants best, and devised and recorded typologies in order to systematise knowledge so that it could be useful for future generations.[95]

Further east, what started as a local revolt by the Persian leader Cyrus in the mid-sixth century BC eventually ended with him overthrowing Neo-Babylonian rulers and expanding the frontiers into an enormous empire that stretched from the Mediterranean to the Indus Valley. The new masters championed a set of beliefs centred on a supreme deity, Ahura Mazda (literally 'Lord Wisdom'), and on a reverence of nature so profound that some scholars have even referred to the faith – known to its followers as Mazdaism or the Good Religion, but to most as Zoroastrianism – as the world's 'first environmentalist religion'.[96]

Zoroastrians sought to focus on goodness and purity, especially articulated in the form of fire, water and soil. The insistence on avoiding pollution was commented on by others. Because they greatly revere rivers, wrote Herodotus; 'they do not urinate, or spit into them, nor do they wash their hands there, or allow anyone else to either,' while the later Roman writer Strabo noted that Persians did not bathe in water, nor 'throw anything unclean into it'.[97]

The inspirational figure behind the religion was one Zarathustra (or Zoroaster to Europeans), a figure about whom little is known, with speculation about the dates when he was alive ranging from c.1800 to c.600 BC.[98] Many of the teachings attributed to him were recorded in a set of texts, the earliest of which is a collection of seventeen hymns known as Gathas. The oldest of these in turn contains an appeal to Ahura Mazda to look after cattle and pastures:

> What help shall my soul expect from anyone,
> In whom am I to put my trust as a protector of my cattle ...
> How is he to obtain the cattle which brings prosperity, O
> Wise One,
> He who desires it, together with the pastures?

Only those who behold the sun, live their lives well and with righteousness, would deserve such benefits, says the hymn.[99]

Another hymn offers thanks to Ahura Mazda, 'who created water and good plants', as well as order, light, earth 'and all good things'.[100] In yet another hymn, the soul of an ox offers a lament to the Wise Lord, pondering the 'cruelty and tyranny' imposed by humans who seek to kill it. 'Humans do not understand how to treat the lowly,' laments the ox, who goes on to note that even Zarathustra's appointment as his protector left him at the mercy of 'the powerless word of a powerless man'.[101] Nature should be a source of joy, says another hymn.[102] However, as these texts make clear both implicitly and explicitly, the relationship between people and the natural world was an imperfect one, not least because of the destructive habits and tendencies that shaped human behaviour.[103]

The championing of the teachings of Zarathustra was a feature of Persian kingship and of a new ruling class that reserved authority and status in the hands of the few and, as in other periods and regions, provided the elites with a powerful tool for the concentration of cosmological interpretation and spiritual intercession. The emergence of new hierarchies, as well as debates and arguments, discussions and competitions for prominence, took place in many different places in Asia, North Africa and the Mediterranean concurrently in a way that makes it tempting to see not only patterns of development but also ideas, influences and reactions within and between peoples, cultures and civilisations.

This included Judaism, which had been heavily influenced by contemporary accounts of the Jewish experience at the hands of the Assyrian and Neo-Babylonian empires in the seventh and sixth centuries BC. The extent of these influences can be shown on the one hand by the fact that the Assyrians are mentioned 150 times in the Bible, always negatively, and on the other by the sack of Jerusalem and the destruction of the Temple by King Nebuchadnezzar in the 580s BC, and by the resulting Babylonian captivity which lasted for decades.[104] The release from bondage following the rise of the Persians and the fall of the Neo-Babylonian empire, and the edict permitting the rebuilding of the Temple in Jerusalem, resulted in the Persian leader, Cyrus, being deemed by the Prophet Isaiah to have been 'anointed by God'.[105]

These experiences had a profound impact on how Jewish scholars thought about the natural world around them and about the past. As many scholars have pointed out, the narrative portions of the Torah were written following the destruction of the Temple and the exile of the Jews. These include the discussion of the relationship between God, nature and mankind in the Book of Genesis, the causes and meaning of the enslavement and departure of the people of Israel from Egypt recounted in the Book of Exodus, and the consequences of breaking the Covenant that God had agreed with Moses outlined in the Book of Deuteronomy. Jewish experiences had resulted in texts which were first set down around this time and which emphasised the importance of devotion, of obedience and of following the priestly teaching.[106]

Jewish writers drew on a rich set of stories, stretching deep into the past. These include the accounts of Noah and the flood that derived from events that had happened many centuries, millennia even, earlier, as we have already seen, and of the Tower of Babel, which has many similarities with a tale that appears in the Sumerian *Enmerkar and the Lord of Aratta*.[107] Other events from the distant and not-so-distant past were woven into texts that were written down and went on to form the basis of scriptural texts as we know them today. One was the story of Joseph, who rose to become the right-hand man of the Pharaoh and one of the most powerful men in Egypt; this likewise would appear to draw on the life of a high-ranking official, likely a chancellor named Baya who lived around 1200 BC.[108] The way in which the expulsion of the Hyskos rulers from Egypt influenced Jewish thinking has been a subject of lively scholarly discussion in recent years.[109]

Perhaps the most interesting element in Jewish thought, however, was the antipathy that was displayed towards urban space – one element in a wider rejection of the high culture of the Near East.[110] The desert, not the city, was the place where the faithful could get to know God directly and also be tested by Him – both in Judaism but in the other Abrahamic faiths too, namely Christianity and Islam. Another important part of the evolution of Judaism was the rejection of polytheism in favour of a monotheistic faith, while the condemnation of animal sacrifice and the worship of idols likewise reflect a strident formulation of a set of beliefs that stood in sharp contrast to the attitudes of those who had oppressed the Israelites from imperial capitals.[111]

The equation of Jewish engagement with the natural world thus diverged in important ways from traditional views of the environmental framework of the Levant. Although the Garden of Eden had served as an idyll of plenty, it was a paradise lost with the fall of Adam and Eve. Humans had been created to work or serve in this garden, in the same way that priests serve God in the Temple. This relationship continued, nevertheless, with God being served through the cultivation of the earth and the careful stewardship of its resources.[112]

This was typified by evocations of idealised rural rather than urban settings, and with God himself as a pastoralist, looking after his flock – most obviously in Psalm 23: 'The Lord is my shepherd, I shall not want; he makes me lie down in green pastures. He leads me beside still water; he restores my soul.'[113] Key figures in scriptural narratives are regularly portrayed as farmers and shepherds, including Abraham, David and all the patriarchs.[114]

Indeed, the Covenant made between God and his people following the redemption from slavery in Egypt and settlement in Canaan is specifically related to the divine bestowal of an ecological agreement: in return for their following the commandments, including disavowing the worship of idols and other deities, God agreed to make the land fertile and productive, and to ensure peace for Israel. The terms of the Covenant also involved environmental punishment: as Moses reminded his people, the Promised Land was not like Egypt, where 'you planted your seed and watered it with your foot like a vegetable garden'; rather it was a place 'watered by the rains of heaven'. As such, any breach of the agreement with God would result in rains being withheld, with obvious consequences for food, health and happiness.[115] The elision between God and nature was such that the Almighty appeared in the guise of a cloud so that Moses and others could hear what he had to say, having previously marked the 'sign of the covenant' in the form of a rainbow.[116]

Conversely, those who see themselves – rather than God – as masters of the earth and its resources were to be punished. Annoyed by Pharaoh's bragging about how he controlled the River Nile and had improved it, God threatened that 'Egypt will become a desolate wasteland' and so be taught a lesson. 'I will make the land of Egypt a ruin,' came the warning in the Book of Ezekiel, and ensure that 'The foot of neither man nor beast will pass through it; no one will live there for forty years.' Cities would be ruined and become depopulated, and Egypt would turn into a 'lowly kingdom' that was 'so weak that it will never again rule over the nations'. Not only could God bend nature to his will, in other words; but in doing so he would instil the virtue of humility among men who thought too much of their own powers and too little of those of the Lord.[117]

The extent and vibrancy of the formulations and reformulations of philosophy, religion and behaviours from the eighth to the third centuries BC in the Yellow and Yangtze River valleys, the eastern Mediterranean, the Levant and the Ganges Valley have been much remarked on, most notably by the German philosopher Karl Jaspers who in an influential book published soon after the Second World War characterised this period as an 'Axial age'. This was a time, suggested Jaspers, when humanity was taking 'a deep breath' and pondering profound questions that stimulated new levels of consciousness, which Jaspers contended had happened independently across these five 'islands of light', namely in India, China, Persia, Palestine and the eastern Mediterranean.[118]

Other scholars have followed suit, arguing that this was a period of 'cultural crystallisation', an 'Age of Transcendence', marked by a new ability described as 'standing back and looking beyond'.[119] It was a revolutionary era 'in the realm of ideas and their institutional bases which had irreversible effects' not only in many regions but 'on human history in general', leading to an 'extensive re-ordering of the internal contours of societies as well as their internal relations' and changing 'the dynamics of history' as a result.[120]

Not all are convinced by the argument of multiple simultaneous watersheds during which archaic values were abandoned or modernised, dismissing the hypothesis as too simplistic and noting that some of the apparent transformations took place hundreds, or even thousands of years before the supposed 'age' of change.[121] What does appear to have been significant, however, was not a notional cognitive shift in ways of thinking as much as a change in the mechanics of how knowledge was codified and disseminated.

It was the proliferation of texts and, no less importantly, their preservation, transmission and copying that was crucial. Lists, narratives and scriptures as well as other written materials established corpuses of information that could be learned, discussed, added to and interpreted. While religion was clearly important, it was by no means the only branch of knowledge that benefited from the boost in more people writing, as is clear from seminal works of philosophy, mathematics and sciences being produced notably but not only in the eastern Mediterranean.[122]

An additional factor seems to have been rising levels of urbanisation and of affluence which fuelled a counter-intuitive shift away from material rewards towards self-discipline and selflessness – a common feature across many of the belief systems that blossomed around the sixth century BC, including Buddhism and Jainism in South Asia, Stoic philosophy in ancient Greece and the teachings of Confucius, Laozi and others in East Asia. The emphasis is on moderation and on the suppression of desires through fasting, abstinence, suffering and compassion at the expense of greed, indulgence and consumption. These ideas may in turn have stemmed from the emergence of a new class of scholars and thinkers who had the resources and influence to spend time contemplating questions existential – and thus represent the interests, as well as lifestyles, of elites expanding their spheres of authority beyond economic power and into more ethereal domains.[123]

Perhaps not surprisingly, this then spilled over not only into giving advice to rulers but into castigating them for adverse natural phenomena. In one chapter of the *Shangshu* (尚書), the Book of Documents compiled around the fifth century BC (though sometimes drawing on older materials), an explicit link is drawn between good harvests and the stability provided by a conscientious ruler, by an 'enlightened administration' and by the reliance on 'talented men'.[124] The connection is forcefully made between the shortcomings of a king's character and weather conditions: excessive rains were a reflection of a lack of discipline, excessive wind a sign of foolishness, excessive cold an indicator of poor judgement, excessive heat the result of laziness and drought the result of arrogance. This was one reason why for many centuries kings led ritual ceremonies to mark the start of the agricultural years.[125] Weather was therefore connected to morality, giving precious little climatic room to manoeuvre; anything meteorologically unexpected or harmful was the fault of a single person – the ruler. This equation proved remarkably durable in Chinese cultures over the centuries.[126]

Conversely, this opened up opportunities for intermediaries, such as official rainmakers who had devised elaborate rituals to encourage rain, through dances, offerings and prayers. Stories of extraordinary personal suffering became more common in accounts written from around the third century BC about the sacrifices made by Chinese kings as they tried to protect others. Presumably intended to create idealised images of previous rulers for contemporary audiences, these tales often spoke of deprivation so acute that it led to organ failure, to bodies shrivelling and to physical deformities that took away the ability to walk. Many involved exposure to the sun, fervent prayer and threats of self-immolation, including by leading officials, whose willingness to suffer was intended both as a cipher for their own selflessness and as oblique criticism of their masters.[127]

This was part of a familiar pattern of elite acquisition and guarding of political powers through control of ritual in general, but also through control of water and climate in particular across regions and indeed periods. The royal bath ceremony of late nineteenth-century Madagascar provides one compelling example; another is provided by pre-colonial Balinese society, where water and ritual were used to dramatise status and authority, as a central element of what one influential scholar memorably described as a 'theatre state'.[128] Pre-Buddhist ascetics undertook retreats in preparation for monsoon rains in a practice that was then adopted as a requirement of Buddhist monastic discipline and developed into a series of rituals known as the *varṣāvāsa*.[129]

Ideas about rains evolved over time, with beliefs in serpent deities in northern India, particularly in the Mahāyāna tradition, finding echoes in East Asia, where it was held that dragons controlled the rains and that these powers could be appropriated by suitably qualified intermediaries. Such intermediaries not only used rituals to showcase their skills, but produced literatures attesting to these abilities that shrewdly also emphasised aristocratic and royal patronage and eminence as well as drawing putative connections with Buddhist 'dragon kings'.[130]

In Central America, population density and colonisation levels had remained low until the start of the 'Classic period', which scholars usually date to AD c.250. As they rose, the importance of control over water became increasingly important, both because the thin karstic soils of the Maya lowlands were dependent on seasonal rainfall that could be erratic and because of an absence of natural water sources.[131] Rain petitioning became an important element in religious thinking, social hierarchy and climatic engagement. Archaeological evidence suggests that rain-related ceremonies took place in caves, with finds of whistles, flutes, bone rasps and turtle shells used as drums.[132] In some cases, children were offered as human sacrifices to the rain deity, part of a tradition that stretched back to c.1500 BC.[133]

Fertility rituals connected to the land and to clement weather and climate conditions were widespread, if not as ubiquitous, as ceremonials based on elaborate cosmological explanations were devised to demonstrate human agency in influencing the weather via engagement with the divine. Those who controlled the knowledge protected their privileged positions jealously: in the case of the Eleusinian Mysteries in ancient Greece, divulgence of secrets was punished by sentence of death.[134]

While there were wide variations in interpretations and in attempts to ensure benign climate conditions, the principles were the same: take the credit for plentiful harvests and assign blame for extreme weather events that led to food shortages. It was hardly a surprise, therefore, that this equation was accompanied in many locations by a growing awareness that resources were finite and that overexploitation could lead to depletion and exhaustion that not even the gods could resolve – let alone their intercessors on earth.

In 524 BC, Duke Mu of Shan, a senior official at the court of the Zhou King, warned of the dangers of unsustainable cutting down of 'the forests of the mountains'. It would not just be bad for the environment if trees disappeared and 'thickets and marshes have come to the last days of their existence'; if these things happened, 'the forces of the people will be weakened, the farmland where cereals and hemp grow will be uncultivated and they will lack resources'. This was not simply a question of caring about those who would suffer as a result. Any right-minded individual 'should be concerned about this problem' and furthermore should do so 'without relaxation'. After all, it was not hard to understand that this would create problems for all in society, not just for those who worked the land.[135]

In some cases, laws were passed to prevent access to and exploitation of natural resources. In 243 BC, for example, the Emperor Ashoka, grandson of Chandragupta Maurya who had founded an empire that covered much of northern India, issued an edict that forbade setting fire to forests.[136] This was partly about establishing imperial control over resources and over locations that had gained (and retained) reputations of teeming with lawbreakers, robbers and ascetics: indeed, the Buddha himself had been involved in a celebrated altercation with Aṅgulimāla, a violent brigand whom he met as he passed through the forests, persuading the latter to give up his ways and follow the Buddhist path.[137]

However, Ashoka's motivations seem to have been intertwined with a wider philosophical attitude towards animals and plants. Rock edicts set up across his territories announced that 'no living beings are to be slaughtered or offered in sacrifice'. For centuries, these inscriptions add, 'killing or harming of living beings' (including humans) had increased. It was vital that all should practise 'self-control and purity of heart' rather than being ruled by 'various desires and passions'. To support compassionate behaviour, the Emperor declared that he had 'made provision for two types of medical treatment: medical treatment for humans and medical treatment for animals. 'Wherever medical herbs suitable for humans or animals are not available, I have had them imported and grown. Wherever medical roots or fruits are not available I have had them imported and grown. Along roads I have had wells dug and trees planted for the benefit of humans and animals.'[138]

This remarkable investment in welfare, assuming it is a reflection of reality, was furthered by the announcement that the royal household would become vegetarian. 'Formerly, in the kitchen,' stated Ashoka, 'hundreds of thousands of animals were killed every day to make curry.' From now on, however, 'only three creatures, two peacocks and a deer, are [to be] killed, and the deer not always. And in time, not even these three creatures will be killed.'[139]

Ashoka took other steps to protect wildlife, issuing proclamations protecting 'parrots, mynas, aruna, ruddy geese, wild ducks, bats, queen ants, terrapins, boneless fish, tortoises, porcupines', along with many other animals – including 'all four-footed creatures that are neither useful nor edible'. The sale of fish was forbidden on designated days, as was the castration of 'billy goats, rams, boars and other animals' and the branding of horses and bulls.[140]

How these orders were enforced, by whom, where and when is not clear. Nor is the line between Ashoka's religious and spiritual beliefs and his royal powers entirely distinct, for an important element of such commands was plainly that of asserting rights not only over animals and plants, but also over behaviour, customs and standards. Nevertheless, the fact that they were carved into rocks across Ashoka's lands is itself significant in so far as it demonstrates rulers claiming a mandate not only over their human subjects, but also over the environment, its animals and plants as well as its natural resources.

Another example of this comes from the *Arthaśāstra* of Kauṭilya, a text written in the first century AD which drew on sources at least a hundred years older.[141] A lengthy section sets out the role and responsibilities of judicious leaders. The advice proffered includes recommendations to grant land exempt from taxes and fines to scholars and holy men, as well as gifts that could not be sold or mortgaged to officials with important functions – among them revenue officers, supervisors, elephant and horse trainers and courtiers. Land that was not being cultivated should be confiscated and redistributed, and all help should be given to those working it to ensure that revenues were generated, 'for a king with a depleted treasury devours' and preys on his own subjects.'[142]

Among the recommendations for a functioning bureaucracy was the appointment of a 'Superintendent of Agriculture', 'who must be either proficient in agricultural science, geometry and plant science, or assisted by experts in these'. The fact that special prayers were to be offered using a set formula – praising Prajāpati, Kāśyapa, Deva and Goddess Sītā, 'at the first sowing of any kind of seed', with the first fistful prepared by being immersed beforehand 'in water containing gold' – suggests that while Ashoka's own devotion to Buddhism had been extensive, the invocations either existed alongside Vedic beliefs or were displaced by them in the decades after his death and the fall of his empire.'[143]

In any event, the point here is that Kautilya – one of the most important thinkers and authors writing in classical India two millennia ago – declared that rulers should protect and manage all the key resources of the state. To this end, careful attention needed to be paid to domesticated animals, human crafts, agriculture, mining and commerce, as well as to wildlife, forests, forest produce and water. Those who damaged or overexploited these resources should be punished with death.[144] The subtext was clear: good governance led to optimal outcomes. And underpinning this was the virtue of social, economic and environmental sustainability.

It was a message that echoed what some had been writing thousands of kilometres away around the same time. Expressions of idealised nature, in which names of plants serve as implicit and explicit metaphors for moral qualities, do not so much occur regularly in the poetry of the Han dynasty in China that took power in 206 BC as define collections such as *The Songs of the South* (楚辭).[145] To put it another way, wrote Xenophon in the *Oikonomikos* a few centuries earlier, 'the earth willingly teaches righteousness to those who can learn; for the better she is treated, the more good things she gives in return.'[146] He did not need to say what this also meant: that those who extracted too much and overexploited resources did not just damage the earth, they demonstrated their failings as humans too.

8

The Steppe Frontier and Formation of Empires
(c.1700–c.300 BC)

History has become an organic whole.

Polybius (second century BC)

As we have seen, human settlement and social patterns had changed sharply with the cultivation of crops. The domestication of goats, sheep and then cattle had likewise brought a series of mini-revolutions as a result of the availability of stable sources of protein, sources of materials such as wool and leather hides that could be used for clothing, storage and new technologies. New sources of energy were also released as animals were put to work, enabling greater agricultural returns for lower human input – which in turn opened up ways to invest this additional time.

No less important than these developments was the domestication of the horse. As one scholar has put it, horses – which can travel at around ten times the speed of humans – were 'essential to the creation of large empires in the classical age'.[1] Indeed, their central role in global history extends far beyond antiquity, not least in the Americas, where the impact of the introduction of horses on indigenous peoples is difficult to overestimate.[2] Above all, the domestication of horses transformed human engagement with, use of and treatment of the environment.

Although both Europe and Asia were home to large horse populations at the start of the Holocene, ecosystem change brought about a sharp decline in the former regions, where the demise of steppe-tundra landscape and the return of forests as a result of warming climate patterns offered less suitable habitats for horses and perhaps even caused an increase in the frequency of genetic variants coding for darker coat colour as a result of lower exposure to sunlight in dense forest environments.[3]

While horse populations in most parts of Europe seem to have become fragmented and genetically isolated, it was a different story on the steppes of Central Asia where conditions were much more climatically favourable.[4] Although dating and location are matters of considerable scholarly debate, among the first to tame and breed horses were the Botai people who lived in what is now Kazakhstan around 3500–3000 BC. Hundreds of thousands of horse bone fragments attest to widespread dependence on the creatures, with tests on pottery showing fatty deposits that suggest horses were prized for their milk.[5] At least some peoples mastered horseback riding in this period, as well as training horses to pull chariots and wagons, although heavy, rugged cheekpieces, as well as scrape marks on horse teeth, show that harnessing and controlling horses was not easy at all.[6]

It did not take long for horses to be introduced to other regions, such as Mesopotamia, where at least initially they were regarded as more of a curiosity than a widely utilised animal, and where accounts record them as often having been fed to lions that were kept in captivity as entertainment for local rulers.[7] In general, across western Asia from the time they first start to appear in written and archaeological sources, horses were considered unreliable and dangerous.[8]

Horse-drawn chariots nevertheless became crucial in enabling an expansion of control of territory under Egyptian pharaohs in the New Kingdom (c.1550–c.1050 BC), while accounts like the *Annals of Thutmose III* include booty lists that show how highly prized chariots were as markers of elite status and as tools of political control.[9] This can be shown too by the fact that six complete 'high-performance machines' were discovered as prized possessions buried alongside Tutankhamun.[10]

Poems written under the Zhou dynasty celebrated heroes driving their obedient dappled grey horses in large red painted chariots charging against enemies, rumbling and crashing 'like a roll of thunder'.[11] Horses and chariots were also high-status gifts, conferred to show favours and honour, with one-third of bronze inscriptions that record appointments to office or grants from the crown after c.900 BC recording chariot paraphernalia.[12]

'I confer on you a chariot with bronze fittings, trappings of soft leather painted red for the horses,' one ruler announced, with 'a canopy of tiger skin with red lining, bronze bells for the yoke bar, gilded bow holder and fish-scale quiver, a team of four horses with their bits and bridles and bronze ornaments, gilt girth straps and a scarlet banner with two bells'.[13]

Across Eurasia, horses were given an important ritual status. The Hittite *Code of the Nesilim*, for example, a legal text written around 1600 BC, held that while anyone found having sex with pigs, dogs or cows should be tried and sentenced to death, bestiality with horses should not be considered a punishable act.[14] Horses were also revered further east, appearing in the *Rig Veda* in India as offerings in ritual sacrifice to the gods, as an animal mastered and ridden by deities, or transporting gods by pulling them in chariots.[15]

What is most striking about the expansion of horse culture, however, is both how far and how fast it spread. By around 1200 BC, horse sacrifice was being practised across large swathes of Eurasia, from Kazakhstan to north-western China and Mongolia.[16] In South Asia, horse immolation was also a key means of reinforcing the authority and power of the priesthood in general and of the ruler in particular. The *Śatapatha Brāhmaṇa*, a text compiled c.900–700 BC, sets out in detail the practice of *aśvamedha*, the sacrificial killing of a horse, that was one of the most important rites in Vedic ritual. As the text makes clear, horses were of particular significance and value – so that while Prajāpati, the lord of creation, treated by the author as the supreme deity, assigned other sacrifices to other gods, he claimed horse sacrifice for himself.[17]

By c.1200 BC, it seems that horse-handling, training and herding techniques had become increasingly sophisticated, resulting in both higher levels of dietary reliance and economic exploitation. Perhaps most significantly, however, zooarchaeological evidence points to large increases in the numbers of horses being reared, alongside the emergence of widespread horseback riding in Mongolia and across Central Asia.[18] Human skeletal remains from this period also show substantial increases to the muscle, tendon and ligaments connected to foot, hip and elbow joints that are most logically connected with horseback riding – providing an indication of the extensive and rapidly growing practice of riding.[19]

Although the causes of this transition are not clear, that it took place around the same time as a climatic reorganisation that affected large parts of the Levant and beyond may not be coincidental. As stable nitrogen isotope values taken from bone collagen show, before the emergence of horse riding, meat and milk products consumed on the steppes were primarily from sheep, goats and cattle.[20] The fact that the domestication of horses took place and expanded dramatically at a time when the open steppe regions stretching from the Black Sea across Central Asia into Mongolia were particularly dry has been noted by scholars, who have suggested that pastoral subsistence and a turn to horses as a source of food, protein and milk and as a labour supplement were responses to changing climate conditions. High aridity levels in central and western Mongolia in particular would have produced dryland grasses and steppe plants on which horses thrive, while the long grazing ranges and resilience of horses faced with water shortages explains why more time and effort went into horse herding.[21]

Moreover, while linking the adoption of new equine strategies and techniques with a period of rising aridity seems both plausible and logical, identifying cause and effect is an altogether more complex and difficult exercise. In any event, what mattered more were the ecological impacts that horse riding brought with it: a transition to a more diverse pastoral economy from one which had previously been primarily based on sheep; larger and larger herds of horses, which in turn had implications for the amount of pasture required; and major shifts in settlement patterns from semi-sedentary to more dispersed levels of living, and higher levels of mobility.[22] Isotopic data suggests that while ruminants were intensively grazed close to settlements, horses were moved over extensive areas across the steppe.[23]

These changes were instrumental in creating networks of long-distance contacts that enabled and encouraged the spread of ideas, beliefs and rituals, as well as exchanges of goods and technologies.[24] Mobile pastoralists had already played an important part in the transmission of crops across Eurasia over the course of many centuries – millennia even. That the earliest evidence comes from carbonised seeds of barley, wheat and broomcorn millet found in mortuary contexts (often human cremations) suggests that trade may initially have been linked to rituals rather than driven by the importance of foodstuffs to diet or calorie consumption.[25]

By c.1500 BC, domesticated grains such as millet, wheat and barley had been spread from South-West Asia to the east of the continent, including into the mountain regions of Inner Asia.[26] Millet seems to have been particularly important, likely thanks to its short growing season and resilience, especially when faced with hot conditions.[27] Foodstuffs were not the only thing moved along the networks of herders and nomads, for so were commodities such as copper and tin, and technologies such as ceramics and metallurgy which saw the appearance of bronze knives, axes and other artefacts produced in similar ways and in similar styles across the steppe as part of a 'Transeurasian exchange' mechanism.[28]

The introduction of horse riding must have played a part in the intensification of contacts between diverse ecological zones, partly as a result of herders fanning out in search of greater spaces for grazing, which led to competition for the best pasture lands and water sources, and partly because it brought peoples into closer and more regular contact with each other. One effect can be seen in substantial genetic turnovers and genetic admixtures across Central Asia around this time.[29] Another is apparent from a phase of rapid socio-economic transformation, including widening of social hierarchies in mobile populations shown by increasingly elaborate burial rituals in the steppe lands, as well as by evidence that points towards rising levels of craft specialisation.[30]

As some scholars have pointed out, there were significant variations that were closely linked to local ecological conditions and constraints. Different settlement patterns developed in locations where summer rainfall was abundant or where soils were richer; in such instances, agriculture could be intensified and in some cases expanded through the development of irrigation systems.[31] There were significant regional differences too, with plentiful evidence for farming in the eastern steppe contrasting sharply with limited and even minimal evidence further west.[32]

Nevertheless, as analysis of tooth enamel and skeletal remains shows, nomadic peoples developed a highly diversified range of economic strategies, rather than relying on uniform models of pastoralism.[33] As well as showing that agriculture was an important part of pastoralist lifeways, the production of the food sources that could and presumably did generate surpluses played a vital role in rethinking uses of the land and engagement with the environment by peoples living on the steppes; it was no less important in helping scholars understand the rise of nomadic empires – which provides one of the great themes of Eurasian and global history.[34]

In antiquity, nomads came on to the radar of writers based in cities intrigued by their way of living but also by their resilience. Herodotus explains how 'Scythian' horse riders were able not only to hold off the mighty Persian armies, but also to harass them effectively and to melt away to fight another day. When asked why he kept retreating and refusing to fight in open battle, the Scythian ruler purportedly replied, 'What I am doing now is not far removed from my usual way of life during peacetime. I'm not going to fight you and I'll tell you why. If we had towns we might worry about the possibility of them being captured, and if we had farmland we might worry about it being laid to waste; but we don't have either.' While this exchange clearly reflects artistic licence, the articulation of the idea that nomads could benefit from an indefinite margin of retreat when in conflict with sedentary rivals captures the reality of the relationship between the peoples of the steppes and those within striking distance.[35]

It was not quite true that nomadic peoples did not have permanent settlements. Groupings like the Xiongnu, Uighur and Liao that rose to prominence over later centuries and established control over vast territories all created or expanded large urban areas that included monumental structures, gardens, orchards and irrigation systems.[36] Drone surveys at Mohuchahangoukou in what is now Xinjiang in China have revealed hundreds of fields, canals, dams, cisterns and houses that show how mobile pastoralist communities combined complex and varied lifestyles that were sensitive to small environmental and ecological change and adopted strategies both to try to take advantage of these and to reduce risks as appropriate.[37]

Those who wrote about mobile pastoralists in whatever period and whatever region or continent invariably described them as barbaric and chaotic. Nomads look like monkeys, do not revere the gods, dig up truffle in the foothills and eat raw flesh, wrote one Sumerian author. They had 'the heart of wild birds and beasts', were 'unbridled people without human intelligence', 'abandoned by heaven' and 'the seedbed of evil', interested only in stealing from other people, just like wolves – to cite just a handful of examples across almost three millennia.[38] Such accounts were written by people living in towns and cities for the benefit of those living in towns and cities and represent the views of metropolitan intellectuals revelling as much in their own self-importance as in their derision of the ways that others lived.

There is some evidence that nomads were unimpressed by haughty city-dwellers who used sweet words and offered fine treasures – but always because they had ulterior motives. Do not be tempted to go to live with these people who inhabit fortresses which 'rub shoulders with the sky' and where souls get snatched, one son was told by his father. Much better, the father said, to stay away from them.[39]

Crass characterisations of nomads by urban elites do not just obscure but ignore the fact that hybrid, flexible and adaptable lifestyles required sophisticated processes of administration which combined decision-making with effective policies that ensured common purpose as well as social cohesion for groups living together. Far from being ignorant, impulsive and lacking reason, steppe societies were efficient, structured and highly successful. Indeed, even Herodotus says as much: the Scythians – a catch-all for all nomadic peoples on the steppes – could hardly be considered admirable; however, they 'have managed one thing, and that is the most important in human affairs, better than anyone else on the face of the earth: I mean their own preservation'.[40] These societies did not resemble those of city-based states, controlled by bureaucratic elites, but instead ones shaped at a local level rather than by a centralised authority, where the interests of powerful aristocrats were instrumental in processes of decision-making.[41]

What is of course most striking about the relationship between sedentary and mobile societies was their interdependence. Those who herded animals had to be located close to consumers who needed or wanted products – ranging from dairy to meat, from wool to leather, from pack animals to horses. These needs were not uniform and themselves reflected local demands, tastes and climates. For example, milk and vegetables are more important in diets across the Middle East relative to Central Asia, where meat consumption is notably higher.[42]

Nevertheless, the patterns of exchange worked in similar ways. Pastoralists provided sources of food, materials and goods, and in return could tap into sources for luxury goods and objects that were key elements helping to underpin social stratification and the authority of tribal leaders both in the exhibition of their own status and in the way they could reward their own family, kinship groups and wider networks.[43] While pasture was owned by groups collectively, animals were owned by individuals; as a result, prestige was also derived from the composition of herds, as well as from their size.[44]

***

One area of intensive interaction was in the northern and western regions of what is now China, where regular and vibrant exchanges saw animal products and animals being sold in one direction, and silks, gold and bronze ornaments, ceramics and other materials specifically designed in 'nomadic style' for nomadic markets going in the other.[45] Interaction with western Asia is also attested by trade in carnelian beads that were almost certainly finished in Mesopotamia and that feature prominently in graves in the Wei and Yellow River basins around this period.[46] These exchanges not only brought materials across long distances but also introduced ideas and designs – such as griffin motifs which spread from the Aegean, eastern Mediterranean and Persia across to East and South Asia.[47]

The discovery of large numbers of cowrie shells, perhaps from the south coast of China and possibly from the Indian Ocean, shows that this was a time of growing movement of goods and people in general and not only along land corridors. That such shells are found in graves belonging to people of modest means points to extensive circulation networks and also to widening socio-economic expansion.[48] While it has been often argued that cowrie shells were used as a form of currency, their value would seem to be more naturally associated with ornamental, ritual and funerary functions.[49]

Geography, environment and climate nevertheless played a crucial role in creating ecological as well as cultural boundaries, especially in the relationship between mobile and sedentary societies in East Asia. While Chinese sources regularly describe nomadic peoples and cultures in negative and even derogatory terms, the expansion of animal husbandry into zones that were within reasonable distance of cities and towns clearly played a role in the ability of urban populations to feed themselves and have access to materials for textiles and leather – which were of more practical and immediate importance than the movement of luxury goods and the transmission of artistic styles.

Although scholars have long noted the role played by nomads in the creation and flourishing of long-distance trade networks that spanned hundreds of kilometres, some have recently sought to emphasise that forms of mobile pastoralism were varied and that ideas about behavioural continuity over long periods (and still more between or within regions) are oversimplistic.[50] Indeed, some scholars have gone further still, seeking to emphasise that nomads did not so much offer an alternative way of life to those in settled communities as form part of an integrated world that was mutually beneficial. Rather than being the antithesis of city living, nomads in many cases galvanised their rise through the twin motors of supplying much needed goods and materials on the one hand and of presenting a threat on the other that encouraged social, political and military consolidation.[51]

The fundamental role that nomads played in the context of the Warring States period in China, and particularly during the fourth and third centuries BC, has been persuasively and eloquently put by one leading scholar who has underlined the accelerating importance in this period of steppe populations in general and of horses in particular. This was a time when rivalries and hostilities between rulers across a range of Chinese states produced a near-endless appetite for resources, starting with horses but including other animals too, such as pack animals for moving military equipment, as well as grooms, trainers, saddles, clothing and leather which had many uses, not least as armour.[52]

These demands, which can only have been increased further still by cavalry reforms and almost constant competition between states, are reflected in sources whose mounting interest in the peoples of the steppe provides a telling clue to their military and strategic importance, as well as to the increasing scale of transactions around 2,500 years ago.[53] Another pointer lies in changes in tactics and in military planning, of which the construction of massive walls was perhaps the most important: it may be that the intention was not to keep barbarian invaders out, as is usually thought, but to extend territories under the control of the state, in order to protect sources of supply.[54]

This was crucial in other settings too. Writing in the fifth century BC about the origins of Greece and how some cities had become powerful, Thucydides had observed that being able to protect fertile land was key, as was the ability and need to build up agricultural surpluses. The construction of walls was vitally important, he notes, and enabled the powerful to dominate and subjugate others, growing wealthier and stronger still in the process.[55]

As was true of Mesopotamia, investment in fortifications was centred not only on defensive motivations but also on control over the best land and over labour forces. In practice, cities, states and polities could increase capacity in one of only two ways: improvements in productivity or the annexation of additional agricultural land.[56] The dynamics of competition drove technological advances as well as a process of political centralisation. This was because, first, threats from neighbours and near neighbours demanded suitable defensive and offensive strategies that strengthened the position of those whose status derived from their ability to solve problems. Challenges from rivals inevitably prompted those at the centre to demand greater control over resources in order to support policies of expansion or resistance. Secondly, as cities, states and settlements became larger and more complex, they developed institutions that united, harmonised and homogenised to create distinct identities and encouraged integration, sociability and incentives for co-operation. These ranged from bureaucracies to writing systems, from education to religion. Perhaps counter-intuitively, though, military threats and war played important roles: both could be traumatic, expensive and further privilege elites; but they were extremely helpful in bonding people together and propelling the development and evolution of norms and what some scholars call 'ultrasociability'.[57] External threats concentrated the mind; but they also provided reasons to co-operate, and, as such, were vital in the formation and intensification of common identities.

These rhythms were common in many parts of the world. Strikingly, however, they were at their most vibrant and noisy in locations that were close to the steppes. The domestication of horses, benign ecological conditions and the intensification of exchange between peoples of the steppes and those living in cities suggests that the catalyst for rapid transformation across many parts of Asia was the interplay between agrarian states and 'mirror' nomadic confederations. This was shaped by the introduction of sophisticated cavalry tactics as well as by innovations such as saddles, stirrups and compound bows that enabled pastoral peoples to raid and exploit nearby states – in turn resulting in the latter adopting and adapting horse tactics themselves in a competition that almost resembled an arms race. This increased the effectiveness of the state but also provided greater incentives for nomads to improve their capabilities, as well as increasing the size of their potential rewards.[58]

The competition within and between the two resulted in centripetal forces that drove dramatic expansion in each: in the course of the first millennium BC a succession of weaker states and pastoral groups were eliminated in a process that saw the largest agrarian states quadruple in size in this period. The same impulses led to the agglomeration of nomadic groups into broad groupings whose identification in the sources often belie complex and diverse identities that are simplified by referring to the name of the dominant groupings – such as the Xiongnu on the Eurasian steppe, or, in later periods, the Puyŏ in Manchuria or Chosŏn in the Korean peninsula. These confederations all became significantly more powerful, overseeing more and more territory, just as agrarian states did so.[59]

One reason for this was that large confederations were all the more important as suppliers of horses, meat, dairy, textiles, leather and other materials as towns, cities and sedentary populations that were naturally constrained by the limits of the productivity of the land grew; another was that rising demand for and control of prime grazing land and substantial flocks and herds gave steppe leaders greater leverage with their own followers just as it did when it came to bargaining with those who wanted or needed produce. And of course these enhanced resources and manpower also boosted their ability to raid and to threaten to raid other tribes and neighbouring states – all of which could prove both lucrative and a source of prestige. The benefits of war as a tool for cohesion applied to all.[60]

The result was a balance that was both ambiguous and precarious – and not only in the context of antiquity, but right into the modern era. It is no coincidence, for example, that the first empires in history grew up in regions close to the steppe belt. One study has observed that even if quantification and classification can be fraught with problems, the approximation that some 85 per cent of large empires over more than three thousands years developed in or close to the Eurasian steppe tells its own story of how important were geography and the interactions between peoples who used different kinds of land in different ways.[61] Far from being a desolate wasteland that was home to wandering nomads, the steppes consistently proved to be the catalyst for imperial expansion.

New approaches to understanding the past, such as predictive models and statistical analysis, underline the importance of ecological and geographical factors in the formation of large, complex human societies. In particular, close correlations become evident: empires arise more commonly in regions where agriculture has been practised for longer and where warfare was more intense, creating pressures for societies to respond. The steppe belt played an important role in creating the opportunities and processes that generated momentum for centralisation and growth.[62]

Indeed, it is not hard to make the case that the engine of the steppes was not just a significant factor but the single most important factor in Chinese history. As one eminent historian has noted, the source of empire in Chinese history almost exclusively came from the northern frontier, which provided the source of all but one of the major 'unification events' over the course of more than 3,500 years. The only exception was that of the Ming dynasty, which had its genesis in central China – although in that case, too, context was important, as we shall see.[63]

The key factor was that of terrain. The outsize role played by the northern lands in Chinese history is explained by their flatness. The lack of natural barriers facilitated military conquest and political consolidation, both of states and of nomad confederations: indeed, before AD 1800, all major invasions came from the north. In other words, the geographical characteristics of these flat lands meant not only that there was a persistent vulnerability to nomad incursions (or worse), but also that geography played a crucial role in the emergence of a single, centralised state. Certainly, there were moments of disunity in Chinese history. But the overwhelming momentum was towards unification and a political centre that sought to defend, control and expand its periphery.[64]

This drive towards centralisation in turn produced a 'hub-and-spoke system', based on a ruler and their court that devolved limited power beyond the core, whose strengths lay in the efficient distribution of information, standardised bureaucracy and (rather unusually) a single language and writing system. Its weaknesses, however, were high levels of volatility in population levels and economic output, as well as limited resilience in the face of internal pressures. This meant frequent domestic upheavals, the overthrowing of dynasties and regular depositions of individual rulers.[65] Nevertheless, this marked a sharp difference with Europe, for example, where large states were rare and short-lived. As recent simulations have demonstrated, the location of mountains in East Asia in general and in what is now China in particular was also a factor in a relentless process of unification that intrigued contemporaries too: Lü Buwei, the chancellor of the Qin kingdom in the third century BC, noted with interest that while tens of thousands of states had once existed, now only a handful survived. His explanation – that those that had been swallowed up had failed because of 'the ineffective use of reward and punishment' – was not entirely convincing. More revealing was the fact that after his death these were reduced further still as the Qin themselves overwhelmed neighbours and rivals to establish what is often described as the first imperial state in Chinese history.[66]

It was not just that the relationship between the steppe lands that stretch from the northern lip of the Black Sea across Central Asia as far as the Pacific Ocean and regions that bordered or were close to them provides insights into the evolution of empires; it also helps explain where large states did *not* develop. Herding of livestock – including horses – was perfectly suited to arid grasslands, but it was difficult and even unviable in tropical climates, because of poor pasture and food sources and also because of the prevalence of livestock diseases.[67]

This helps explain why empires struggled to take hold in India, a location once described by the French historian Georges Duby as 'le lieu de non-Empire'. There were some obvious, fleeting exceptions in certain periods, such as under the great Ashoka in the third century BC, or under the Guptas 500 years later. For the most part, however, the motors of consolidation, expansion and centralisation that were so important in East and South-West Asia, and that were accelerated by the domestication of horses and by political competition, were either weak or non-existent in the Indian subcontinent.[68]

Ecological factors played a key role in this: in South and South-East Asia, river instability in the face of variable climate patterns could be challenging, with rivers frequently silting up, deep-water channels becoming blocked and unpredictable formations of river deltas: the Mekong and Irrawaddy expand across more than fifty metres of land a year at their river mouths, while the Solo River in Java carries around six times as much sediment as the Rhine – despite being being 60 per cent shorter.[69] This made city living precarious, with major urban settlements across South-East Asia regularly failing and being abandoned even up to the early modern period – including major locations such as Melaka, Baruas and Palembang.[70] In South Asia, even major commercial centres and political capitals failed because of their inability to adapt to environmental changes such as insufficient water supplies, riverine shifts and other hydrological challenges. Cities like Cambay, Kanauj, Debal, Kayal and Gaur were just some of the large conurbations that were effectively abandoned as a result. 'Inevitably,' as one leading commentator has put it, 'India became a graveyard of cities' – a cipher for much of South and South-East Asia.[71]

The uncertainty of climate conditions made the task of choosing where and how to create irrigation channels difficult, which helps explain why agricultural surpluses seem to have been rare – and further emphasises how difficult it was for cities to flourish.[72] Experiences such as those of Ibn Baṭṭūṭa, the great fourteenth-century explorer, were instructive. Visiting Delhi in the 1330s, he described it as the 'capital of the country of India, a very illustrious city, large, combining beauty and power'. It was 'greatest of the cities of India [*mudun al-hind*] and even of all the cities of the Islamic East'. Passing through Delhi six years later, however, he found it 'entirely abandoned ... without fire, smoke, or torch'. Once an 'immense city', now it was desolate 'and its population completely scattered'.[73]

While this may be exaggerated – he is describing Delhi after an attack by the Mongols – the idea of cities suddenly collapsing or being abandoned was one that finds echoes in many other accounts from different periods – as Bābur, the founder of the Mughal dynasty in the sixteenth century, explains in the *Bābur-Nāma*. 'In Hindustan the destruction and building of villages and hamlets, even of cities, can be accomplished in an instant. Such large cities in which people have lived for years, if they are going to be abandoned, can be abandoned in a day, even half a day, such that no sign or trace remains.' Naturally this had an impact on the location of cities and on the infrastructure that was built (or not built) accordingly. 'If they have a mind to build a city,' wrote Bābur, 'there is no necessity for digging irrigation canals or building dams ... There is no making of houses or raising of walls. They simply make huts from the plentiful straw and innumerable trees, and instantly there is a village or city.'[74]

This was a similar picture to that painted by one traveller who visited India in the 1560s and whose work was widely read in England. 'Every yeere at Buttor they make and unmake a Village,' he wrote, 'with houses and shoppes made of strawe, and with all things necessarie to their uses, and this village standeth as long as the ships ride there, and till they depart for the Indies, and when they are departed, every man goeth to his plot of houses, and there setteth fire on them, which thing made me to marvaile.'[75]

The wet monsoon climate had other consequences in South and South-East Asia, not least the existence of large tropical forests that were labour-intensive and time-consuming to clear. The lack of grasslands meant that horse breeding, rearing and herding were difficult, especially on a large scale. Horse procurement was a matter of enormous interest to the authorities, therefore, above all to support the military, where horses played a major role both as cavalry and in the chariot corps. Special attention was paid to where to acquire horses, with the finest imported from the north-west, from what is now Iran, Afghanistan and Pakistan. 'Of those fit for battle,' notes Kauṭilya in the *Arthaśāstra*, 'the best are those bred' in Gandhāra, Sindh, Punjab and Vanāyu (likely Persia); those from other regions were either of middling quality or worse.[76] Put another way, the potential of rulers in India was linked to their ability to source horses, and in turn to their geographic proximity to regions where they could do so.

Not surprisingly, therefore, one of the central stories in the development of trade links between India and its neighbours at least until the industrial age was that of the import of horses, principally from Central Asia.[77] Not only that: just as Chinese history was shaped by the activities of steppe nomads in the north, India's fate was greatly affected by similar influences. When peoples of the steppe expanded south, the impact was emphatic. One obvious example comes with the creation of the Kushan empire around 2,000 years ago, which peaked under Kanishka (r. AD c.127–50). Another was that of Bābur and the Mughals themselves – a dynasty whose roots and gaze were firmly linked to Central Asia.[78]

This did not mean that there was no centralisation or territorial expansion, as was the case in the complex relationship between those living in the steppe lands and those nearby; it simply meant that these processes were less intense and less wide-ranging. If this marked one difference, the disease environment marked another, with tropical climates proving a crucible in which infectious diseases could flourish. Demographic trends took on distinctive forms depending on region, on pathogen habitat and on the zoonotic jumps that play such an important role in the transmission of disease from animals to humans. Our understanding of the history of pathogens in general in Asia is hampered by the very limited academic research into this subject – in sharp contrast to the studies in Europe and the Americas – and also because most works on palaeogenetics have to rely on European samples.[79]

This leaves many questions about how and where different strains of malaria, tuberculosis, leprosy, smallpox and plague developed, and how these affected different regions and subregions, why and when.[80] Likewise assessing actual, likely or possible mortality levels is difficult to do with accuracy or certainty, meaning that hypotheses about what kind of brake disease applies to population growth must by necessity be both vague and cautious. Nevertheless, differing geography, ecology and climate provide a backdrop and a context to help explain wide regional variations in how societies developed in antiquity and later.

This was true in the Americas too, where there was considerable variation between structures that emerged more than two millennia ago. In South America some early entities that emerged in Andean cultures, such as the Moche, Wari and Tiwanku, seem to have been driven by competition and rivalry for control of resources, which helped elite groups assert their authority and use warfare, religion and other social norms to create overarching identities in much the same way as had been done in Mesopotamia and elsewhere in the past.[81]

As trade built up across the Gulf of Mexico around 2,500 years ago, regional chiefdoms sprang up. Not all of these expanded into states, or entities resembling states, through competition and conquest absorption; but all the states that did emerge rose from chiefdoms that became better at delegating authority, more effective at developing administrative capabilities – or both.[82]

One such case was a culture that blossomed c.800–500 BC, today known as Olmec – a name that refers to an artistic style rather than to the social, ethnic or linguistic identities of the inhabitants of parts of what is now Central America and Mexico. The most important city was La Venta, centred on a main plaza adorned with a thirty-metre-tall pyramid, a 300-metre-long platform used for rituals that demonstrated elite power, and burial chambers known as Massive Offerings that were designed and adorned to represent the model of the cosmos and the centrality of the Maize God – the begetter of food.[83] As at other sites, such as Cuello and Chiapa de Corzo, particular importance was attached to greenstones, such as jade, serpentine and gneiss.[84]

Maize was the magic ingredient in many parts of Central America over a long period of time. According to the *Popul Vuh*, the creation story of the Maya peoples, the gods had transformed the world from a place of silent, calm dark water into a place that could provide for their own needs. The efforts of the gods to create animals to provide for them proved frustrating; first they made animals such as deer, birds and pumas who were unable to speak properly; then they embarked on a botched attempt to use mud and earth to make a person, which also did not end well. 'It was still not good. It merely came undone and crumbled. It merely became sodden and mushy.' This early human could say a few words 'but without knowledge. Straightaway it would merely dissolve in water, for it was not strong.'[85]

A third effort was also in vain, with beings made from wood; but although they multiplied and had daughters and sons, they were ignorant and incapable of understanding, and crawled around 'on their hands and knees'. Fortunately, the final effort proved successful, when the gods used the marvellous ingredient of maize to make the first humans. These beings 'were able to walk and converse. They were able to listen. They were able to walk and hold things in their hands. They were excellent and chosen people.' They had consciousness and were able to become knowledgeable. Finally, here were creatures who could cultivate the earth not only for their own benefit but to satisfy the aims and needs of the gods.[86] Maize was not just a valuable food, in other words, but the very secret of intelligent life.

In West Africa too, the rhythms of the evolution of urbanism, co-operation and ideas about social systems beat in their own fashion rather than mirroring others. Like most of the rest of the continent, West Africa has been all but excluded from the mainstream of academic research on early cities.[87] Indeed, current scholarship on the Sahel – the belt of transition between the Sahara to the north and savannah lands to the south that spans the continent – emphasises that societies in this region were distinctive polities, which functioned in very different ways to those in other parts of the world at the same time.[88]

Evidence of political centralisation, social hierarchies and states absorbing each other in sub-Saharan Africa is rare. Capital cities, elite dwellings and administrative machinery designed to consolidate centralised power and co-opt people into solving problems posed by external threats are conspicuous by their absence.[89] The Tichitt Tradition, which is probably the best example of early complex society in West Africa, is attested by dozens of major settlements with drystone architecture along the Tichitt and Oualata escarpments of southern Mauritania, extending into the inland Niger Delta by c.1000 BC. Although it has long been thought that increasing population and decreasing amounts of arable land drove centralisation, excavations at Dhar Nema, one of the easternmost settlements, suggest that this was not the case, with little sign of pressure on land availability. Likewise, the range of different lifestyles attested to both here and in the Mema to the south provides a reminder that categorising populations as 'sedentary', 'mobile' or 'semi-mobile' brings with it the danger of oversimplification.[90] The relationship between large settlements and the regions that surrounded them was complex, not only in antiquity but in later periods too.[91]

The same is true of social change, which naturally was fluid over time and regularly if not constantly adjusting – often as a result of climatic change. One of the key elements in the crystallisation of Tichitt culture seems to have been the drying Sahara, which prompted population accretion in humid locations and resultant adaptations that included the domestication of bulrush millet. An acute phase of aridity c.500 BC precipitated the gradual dispersal of families, groups and individuals, who left in search of less precarious environmental conditions.[92] It has been persuasively argued that this diaspora later provided the core of a Ghanaian empire that rose and flourished from AD c.300 to c.1100, a period that was climatically benign in West Africa.[93]

The primary differences between these regional centres lay in the way in which they were – or were not – linked together. In the Americas, vibrant networks were too far removed from each other to interact in a meaningful way or even at all, until the arrival of Europeans in the late fifteenth and early sixteenth centuries, meaning that cultures in Central and South America developed independently of each other. In West Africa, in contrast, there were intensive interactions locally and regionally – with luxury goods brought over long distances playing a role in shaping tastes and styles.[94] But the intensity of these connections, the tapestry of interconnected regions, the challenges and opportunities they created and the effects that they produced were of an entirely different magnitude elsewhere.

The Greek historian Herodotus put it well when he noted that, leaving aside the obscure reasons why women's names had been given to Europe, Africa and Asia, it was folly that each had been given separate designations in the first place – since in reality, this is all one single landmass.[95] His interest was not in geography, but in the mosaic of peoples who lived in these regions and who fought, traded and jostled with each other, and in the connections, borrowings and habits of each. His aptitude was praised by the Roman orator and author Cicero, who called him 'the father of history', although others, such as Plutarch, took a rather different view, saying that his inaccuracies and prejudices meant he should be known as 'the father of lies'.[96]

What is perhaps more important here is the range of the vision of scholars and writers in the ancient world – even if the information they provide often proves to be suspect, as in the case of the Chinese chronicler who stated that in the Roman empire, 'when wind and rain are not harmonious', the emperor would abdicate 'and a worthy man rules in his stead'.[97] Such comments betray creative and even wishful thinking, and are particularly interesting in light of concern about the problems that adverse climate conditions could produce. But they attest to overlapping and interlocking networks that ultimately linked the Mediterranean through the Gulf and Red Sea to Central, South and East Asia.

This brought about the spread of ideas and beliefs as well as the exchange of goods and the movements of people. We know that ritual horse sacrifices took place in ancient Rome, for example, that were very similar to those that took place in India: this included the selection of a race-winning stallion as the offering, the symbolic division of the horse's body and the connection of the event to spiritual and material wellbeing.[98] Such resemblances revealed much about consumption patterns and demand for similar products in different parts of the world. The point struck the historian Polybius during the second century BC when he considered the age that he lived in. The past, he wrote, had once 'consisted, so to speak, of a series of unrelated episodes'. This had changed in a new chapter of increasing globalisation. Now 'history has become an organic whole: the affairs of Italy and Africa are connected with those of Asia and Greece, and all events bear a relationship and contribute to a single end'.[99] In the distant past, as well as today, globalisation had consequences for production, for ecological exploitation and for treatment of the environment.

These links are not exclusively concerned with wildlife, ecology and beliefs, but those all provide an important thread that runs for more than two millennia into the past. For example, while many centuries of scholarship have led to a traditional view that early Jewish writings were essentially framed by Mediterranean contexts, it is striking to find that elephants, peacocks, monkeys, pomegranates, textiles, ivory and other flora, fauna and produce from Asia feature prominently in them. Thus the wealth of Asia and its rulers is repeatedly referenced in the Hebrew scriptures – and so too, it seems, are Indian wisdom and folktales.[100]

Ideas about heaven and hell, the apocalypse, the last judgement, angels, a universal god and resurrection of the body owe natural and obvious debts to Zoroastrianism which itself drew on earlier traditions.[101] Seminal stories, such as the tale of King Solomon trying to resolve a dispute between two women about the parentage of a child, bear an uncanny similarity to a story that appears in the Tibetan translation of the Buddhist *Tripitaka*. Studies of Tamil *aham* poetry meanwhile point to striking parallels with the Song of Songs – including loan words from South Asia that seem to have found their way into the Hebrew versions of this story.[102] Influences from Asia are of fundamental importance in Judaism, in Christianity and later in Islam; these are usually overlooked by scholars, whose reference point is almost invariably focused on the Mediterranean – and no further east.[103]

Ironically, this narrowness of vision was not how those writing millennia ago saw things. 'The Chaldaians and the Indian wizards are the first people to my knowledge who ever said the soul of man is immortal, and one of the most important Greeks they convinced was Plato,' wrote the author Pausanias in the second century AD.[104] They might also have provided food for thought for scholars like Empedokles, who argued that living things should not be killed as their souls were later reincarnated, sometimes as lions, sometimes as 'laurel leaves with goodly foliage'.[105]

Such exchanges ran in both directions, with concepts about planetary models established by Greek astrologers being adopted in India around the time Pausanias was writing, while astronomical texts based on Hipparchus and others not only proved influential but were clearly in circulation in the centuries that followed.[106]

Common ideas evolved about beliefs and practices too. For example, tattooing has long been practised in human history, with cases in the Tyrolean Alps and the Chinchorro culture in South America and references in Chinese texts such as the *Shang Shu* revealing that tattooing on bodies was not only known across continents but dates back thousands of years.[107] Over time, however, tattoos became indicators of something different. In Chinese societies, tattooing was thought of as something done by barbarians and not by 'civilised' people.[108] Further west, however, it became synonymous with slavery specifically. Prisoners of war, captives and enslaved peoples in Egypt and Mesopotamia were branded with the name of the religious sect of their owner. This association may be why the Torah banned the practice as 'the symbol of servitude', and although a reference in the Book of Isaiah sanctions body markings, it was only as a sign of submission to God.[109] Greeks who were captured during the wars against the Persians in the fifth century BC were tattooed by their captors, something that Athenians and others did to those they vanquished in the Aegean and as far away as Sicily.[110]

Regions that were closely connected by trade networks experienced dislocation, shortage and price shocks when supply and demand in one location rose or fell. A vast archive of cuneiform tablets from Babylon provides price data for commodities including barley, wheat and wool prices, as well as for the prices that enslaved people paid for their freedom. Study of this material reveals that the campaigns of Alexander the Great across swathes of the Middle East and Central Asia led to dramatic inflation and prices that stayed high for more than two decades – perhaps because of Alexander's fiscal policies and his liberal distribution of silver to his followers, or more likely perhaps because of the large-scale handouts that were given to those competing to take power after his death in 323 BC.[111]

An interwoven maritime world also took shape, with Buddhist *Jātaka* tales describing large ships up of to 75 tons, with merchants and their goods criss-crossing the Bay of Bengal as early as 300 BC. It was the Austronesians of maritime South-East Asia and Oceania, however, who achieved 'mastery of the monsoons', learning from their experiences of sailing to and colonising islands across the Pacific as far as Easter Island, and eventually building 400- to 500-ton vessels that were fifty metres in length and capable of handling difficult sailing conditions. As one Chinese source in the third century AD put it, the ships' design and the seamanship of their crews meant that 'they do not avoid strong winds and violent waves, and therefore can travel very swiftly'.[112] What the author did not say was why this was so significant: not being at the mercy of the winds, the currents and the weather did not just open up seasons; it opened up new parts of the world.

This had happened in regions of the Pacific where large population expansion in places like Fiji resulted in major transformations of landscape and of the natural environment from around 1000 BC. New research has shown that this was a time of deliberate land clearance and of the introduction of new plant species intentionally or inadvertently brought by new arrivals from overseas. There were local beneficiaries too, such as a common native bee species that flourished as a result of new landscapes and stimuli.[113]

Perhaps the best example of the radical impact of advances in maritime technology was the settlement of populations from Borneo and what is now Indonesia in Madagascar – some 4,000 miles away – around 2,000 years ago. The imprint of paternally inherited Y-chromosomal lineages and maternally inherited mtDNA lineages was substantial, producing an admixture that is uniquely helpful in understanding wider questions about movements of people, genetics and anthropology alike.[114] It was not just genetics that flowed along these connections, for so too did language: while Malagasy – the principal language of Madagascar – borrows from Bantu languages of Africa, its predominant ancestry is from South-East Asia: 90 per cent of its basic vocabulary is shared with Maanyan, a language spoken in southern Borneo and around the Barito River specifically.[115]

The link between human migration, languages and changes to ecosystems was an important and profound one. Recent work on comparisons of linguistics and archaeobotany has resulted in new models being put forward that explain expansions of vegeculture from the Sahel to southern Africa by populations that spread the Bantu languages along savannah corridors.[116] Likewise, research on walnuts shows how the spine of Asia had become criss-crossed with routes for anthropogenic plant dispersal and changes to ecosystems as landscapes were modified, forests planted and settlements established or expanded either by trade, migration or conquest. Tracking of the dispersal of a species native to Iran and Trans-Caucasus to Central Asia, to western and eastern China and to the Mediterranean also reveals the correlation between the population structure of the common walnut and human linguistic diversity: the overlap between the spread of walnut genes and the evolution of languages helps show how plants and human agency changed biodiversity and ecosystems over thousands of years – and had linguistic consequences too.[117]

Of course, humans were not the only agents for the dispersal of seeds and plants, for this role was played by animals of all kinds whose movements, lifestyles and response to climatic conditions likewise had a major impact on global natural history.[118] The difference was that such redistributions were haphazard; this was often the case when it came to human activities and the spread of pathogens, microbes, insects and rodents that was typically both inadvertent and invisible. But the search for more resilient crops, richer sources of carbohydrates and protein, tastier foods, materials with medicinal properties and stronger or more versatile pack animals to provide energy boosts led to constant changes to ecosystems and to proliferation: hundreds of millions of people today rely on the cultivation of tubers, corn and fruit crops that originated in South-East Asia, Near Oceania and South America. These not only became parts of staple diets but came to dominate tropical agriculture around the world because of their resilience in varied and challenging climatic and ecological conditions, and because they deliver reliable food outputs with low labour inputs.[119]

It was not just political systems and human society that centralised, simplified and consolidated, in other words. Plants, crops, vegetables, fruits, spices and flowers – as well as animals like camels, horses, buffalo and donkeys – were not just part of trade and exchange networks that linked many regions of Asia, Europe and Africa; they were also part of widespread and constant reconfigurations of the environment, flora and fauna.[120] These were primarily driven by one motor: the desires and needs of human beings.

9

The Roman Warm Period
(c.300 BC–AD c.500)

You can imagine how much stronger I felt after reaching my vineyards.

Seneca (first century AD)

One of the greatest challenges that humans face is the problem of water shortage. Hydrological stress is of course closely linked to consumption demands, and is in turn magnified by population concentration. Communities whose sources of water fail as a result of lower than normal rainfall, the deviation of river courses or exhaustion or overexploitation of resources can be quickly exposed to hunger, disease and death. One way of coping with this was to anticipate problems through social reforms around resource ownership and allocation; another was to create reserves, of both water and food, to mitigate risks of catastrophe.

Those at the top of social hierarchies had the most to lose from periods of upheaval that could often follow times of unexpected climatic shifts – and the most to gain from planning ahead. The Ptolemaic rulers of Egypt were a case in point. Descendants of Alexander the Great's generals who had taken power after his death, the Ptolemies were careful to reach accommodations with the priestly classes that enabled them to retain and reaffirm control during crises.[1]

What is striking about the decrees set up around the kingdom, such as on the famous Rosetta stone, is not just that they provide evidence of how this relationship functioned, but also that the erection of inscriptions shows a statistically significant correlation to major volcanic eruptions: large eruptions in the tropics could have consequences for the annual Nile flood that is evidenced not only by accounts such as a papyrus from the early third century BC which lamented that 'most of the farmers were killed and the land has gone dry' but also by a raft of land sales that are suggestive of panicked attempts to raise money to meet tax and other obligations and of socio-economic stress more broadly.[2] On this occasion, the rulers of Egypt were not able to convince elites to side with them as they had managed to do in the past, having to contend instead with a major revolt, centred on the city of Thebes, in which the priesthood played a leading role. It took several decades before order was finally restored.[3]

While volcanic eruptions could have dramatic consequences for the Nile and for those who relied on its annual floods, it is also important to stress there were many occasions when water levels fell well below average and yet disasters were averted, food stocks proved plentiful enough to avert large-scale famine or emergency measures proved effective – as had happened around thirty years earlier when Ptolemy III had been able to secure 'the salvation of the population' by importing food 'at great expense'. What mattered, in other words, was how regimes coped with unforeseen difficulties, and how decisions were made – financial, social and political – that enabled challenges to be risen to, instead of allowing them to spark a descent into chaos.

Of course, not all climate events were equal. When it came to volcanoes, for example, there were specific and even substantial differences depending on where the eruption took place, its magnitude and also, as we have seen, what time of year it occurred, with events that take place during the summer months of the northern hemisphere having greater consequences. Nor were impacts uniform even within relatively narrow geographic regions. As scholars of the Mediterranean have shown so eloquently and forcefully, ecological differences varied not so much from one part of the sea to another as from one bay to the next.[4] As such, generalising about the impact of shifts, changes and modifications of climate variations – still less assuming that conditions exist that can be termed 'normal' – is fraught with problems.

Nevertheless, very major eruptions could produce major effects. In 43 BC, two years after a powerful but short-lived eruption, the

Okmok volcano in Alaska exploded with massive force over a period lasting many months and perhaps as long as two years. The impact was recorded in the Mediterranean, with many authors remarking that the sun's light became weak and feeble, that there seemed to be three suns in the sky – presumably because of the amount of particles in the sky – and that fruit shrivelled rather than ripened because of the cold.[5]

Data from Arctic ice cores, from carbonate deposits in north-eastern China and from tree rings in Scandinavia, Austria and California shows a sudden, sharp and severe change of climatic conditions. Simulations suggest that some areas of southern Europe and northern Africa saw falls in temperature of perhaps as much as 7 °C, which would help explain reports of sharp declines in crop yields in Egypt, the traditional breadbasket of the Mediterranean, as a result of the failure of the Nile flood in both 43 and 42 BC. Water shortage, famine, plague, inflation, migration, land abandonment and depopulation weakened the state significantly.[6] As such, social and political pressure built up steadily on Queen Cleopatra, Egypt's ruler at the time; these factors are crucial to understanding the fall of the Ptolemies, the annexation of Egypt by the Romans and the moment that marked the transition of Rome into an empire.[7]

Some contemporary scholars note that descriptions about unusual climatic conditions are generic and are often borrowed by one writer from another, sometimes long after the events in question. Moreover, and perhaps more importantly, they have warned of the obvious dangers of historical determinism that suggests a neat line between a seismic activity in one part of the world and political change in another.[8] Certainly, the fact that there were no similar upheavals in other parts of the world means that recent excitable news headlines that a volcano brought about the demise of Cleopatra need to be tempered and given context.

While the fallout of Okmok must certainly have added to the challenges facing Cleopatra, other factors explain the sequence of events that ended with the Queen's death in 30 BC. Ruling Egypt was difficult at the best of times – which explains incestuous and consanguineous marriages: Egyptian rulers would often marry their sisters, mothers, brothers, fathers or close relatives in order to concentrate power within the family and prevent other elites gaining access to power, thereby becoming a threat.[9] The Ptolemies faced the additional hurdle of being perceived as outsiders, something that could offer advantages at times but could also act as an Achilles heel at others – which meant that Egypt was particularly vulnerable to dislocation and to crises.[10]

Most important, however, was the timing of the Okmok eruption. Just a few months earlier, Julius Caesar had been assassinated on the steps of the Senate in Rome. His death had plunged the city – and the Roman Republic – into a bitter civil war, as factions wrestled for control. As they did so, they looked to all quarters for allies and for support. In such circumstances, backing the right horse could bring great benefits; backing the wrong one could spell disaster. Weakened by the situation at home, Cleopatra threw her lot in with Mark Antony, judging that his military track record and popularity would make him the likeliest of those involved to emerge on top in the struggle for power – a decision that looked eminently sensible, at least to start with. The problem came when the hunting down of Julius Caesar's assassins did not bring matters to a close, but instead triggered a further period of intense struggle between the most powerful figures in Rome, which this time saw Mark Anthony being isolated and picked off by the ambitious young Octavian, bringing Cleopatra and Egypt down with him.[11]

In many ways, Octavian's advance was a classic piece of Roman political opportunism: the domination of the Mediterranean basin by a small city on the shin of Italy was an anomaly. Tying together so many disparate regions, geographies, cultures and peoples was an extraordinary achievement and – as the last 1,500 years have shown – unique not least in its durability. Many have sought to explain the Roman achievement in social, economic, military or cultural terms, noting for example the looseness of Roman identity that allowed so many different languages to be spoken, such a wide range of religious beliefs to be practised, such diverse customs to be followed. But the most convincing is that Rome and its citizens excelled in one thing above all else: they were better organised and quicker out of the blocks than their rivals, more able to take advantage of favourable circumstances than others, more capable of translating openings into tangible gains. Put simply, Rome built an empire because it was able to outmanoeuvre all its competitors and potential competitors.[12]

The Romans were also lucky. For one thing, the fact that the Mediterranean is calmer and less treacherous to cross than other major seas and bodies of water meant that taking control of the entire littoral was cheaper and less risky than in other regions – and moreover offered opportunities for networks to be expanded or added too that boosted trade, widened intellectual horizons and enabled the spread of common cultural values.[13] For another, climatic conditions were exceptionally favourable precisely as Rome was taking on its neighbours, near neighbours and those further afield. This included a long cool and humid period starting from c.200 BC that coincided with the expansion of Greek and Phoenician colonies as well as with the rise of Rome and its principal competitor in the Mediterranean, Carthage.[14]

This period has become known as the Roman Warm Period (or Roman Climatic Optimum), which lasted for over three and a half centuries – precisely the time that Rome emerged supreme in the Mediterranean, Europe, North Africa and the Near East. It was not only easily the most humid time of the last 4,000 years but, as organic evidence from pollen, marine and lacustrine sources shows, also by far the most intensively productive in the history of the Mediterranean during the last four millennia.[15] Among other things, this helped boost agricultural outputs in southern Europe and North Africa which in turn improved demographic growth, manpower for conquest and the stability that helped political authorities legitimise and cement their own powers in the process.[16]

Set in this context, the Okmok eruption was not only extraordinarily well timed from the point of view of the Roman conquest of Egypt that followed just over a decade later, but it was also a rare exception during a period of more than 300 years of unusually low levels of volcanic activity, few extreme weather events and predictable climate patterns. As well as consistent rainfall in regions such as north-eastern France, the fact that the Nile flood occurred with almost metronomic regularity, producing particularly good outcomes every five years on average, was of considerable importance given Egypt's role as a breadbasket for the Mediterranean and the empire that emerged under Octavian – now renamed Augustus by the grateful Romans.[17]

δ¹⁸O isotopic ratio profiles at three sites in Italy from 1000 BC–1000 AD

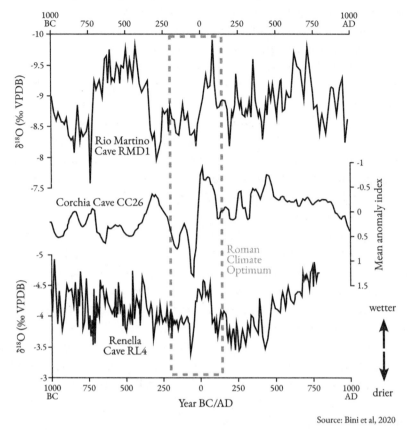

Source: Bini et al, 2020

Although proxy data from other parts of the world have been subject to considerably less assessment and analysis, it is notable that Rome's apogee was paralleled by similar developments elsewhere. The Han dynasty in China followed a comparable trajectory of rising demographics, increasing centralisation and agricultural expansion. Officials in the Red River Delta and in Jiuzhao in what is now Tranh Hoa province in northern Vietnam set about trying to teach 'correct betrothal and marriage procedures' (as well as how to wear hats and sandals) and to encourage those previously outside Han domains to learn about 'feelings of respect and morality'. But they also introduced land-reclamation techniques and new tools that helped make crop production quicker, easier and more abundant.[18]

In the Mississippi Valley, farmers began to develop more intensive techniques to support extended agriculture around 2,000 years ago, including water management, crop selection and food-storage facilities. The uplift in production, combined with greater food security, has been linked with the rise of Mississippian chiefdoms and a series of social revolutions that started a long transformation of the American south-west.[19]

In Central America, meanwhile, interventions in river courses led to the consolidation of farming villages in the Teotihuacan Valley and to the astonishing growth of the city of Teotihuacan from the first century AD into one of the biggest cities on earth – similar in the size of urban footprint to Rome itself.[20] One of the causes of the city's spectacular growth seems to have been an influx of people from the Basin of Mexico and the Puebla–Tlaxcala Valley who were migrating in search of hospitable and ecologically sustainable locations.[21] Strontium isotope analysis of bones reveals new settlement by people who had not been born in the Teotihuacan Valley, and who brought with them ideas, artefacts and building styles from Oaxaca, west Mexico and the Maya heartlands of Central America.[22] Ironically, the trigger for these movements may have been the eruption of the Xitle volcano, which archaeomagnetic dating suggests took place around the time of Rome's annexation of Egypt.[23] The boom that followed saw lavish new ceremonial structures being built or enlarged, including the enormous Sun Pyramid, with some scholars suggesting that a master plan was devised for the city's development that was then followed over the course of decades and even centuries.[24]

This was a time of empire, in other words, in multiple, disconnected parts of the world. That alone is significant, for empires often rise in tandem as neighbouring blocs form in competition, emulation and under threat from each other. It is instructive that similar processes of expansion took place during a period of propitious climate conditions generally and perhaps more importantly during a long period of stability.

Tempting though it is to attribute the rise of disparate empires to climate, more significant was the fact that each entity was able to develop the required administrative and logistical skills for maintaining social, economic and political equilibrium. Each had its own responses in doing so. In Han dynasty China, a single writing system and limited linguistic diversity served as a propeller to drive harmonisation and the strengthening of the imperial core. In Roman territories, things were rather different, with several alphabets in use, sometimes alongside each other, as well as a plethora of languages being employed not only by the population at large but also in literature – including Aramaic, Celtic, Punic and a veritable galaxy of languages in Asia Minor.[25]

In Rome's case, the achievement of uniting different peoples into a single entity was all the more impressive given the difficulties posed by geographies beyond the littoral of the Mediterranean itself. Dominating the Italian peninsula was one thing, but succeeding in taking and maintaining control of the Iberian and Balkan peninsulas, Asia Minor and North Africa, as well as large parts of the northern European plain that today comprises much of Germany, France and the Low Countries, points not only to strategic acumen but also to an extraordinary capability for keeping regions together that were so climatically, ecologically, socially and culturally different. This feat of consolidation was one that remains unrivalled in the many centuries that have followed the fall of the Roman empire.

Rome's success fostered ideas of civic service, as well as personal ambition and conspicuous consumption, particularly by members of the elites. Those with the right qualities for public affairs, urged Cicero, 'should cast aside all hesitation, strive for election to magistracies and take part in government'.[26] You should not seek glory just for yourself, the same author told his brother, even though you would be able to 'immortalise the memory of your name'; it helped that the glory would also be shared 'with me' and the next generation of the family.[27]

Cicero was full of such advice that put a gloss on idealised views of the world, not least of nature. Nothing could beat agriculture, he wrote; it was not possible to think of anything 'more fruitful, more enjoyable, more worthy of a free man', referring those who were interested to his writing where he discussed this in detail. He did not mention, however, that there was a difference between tending nature as a hobby and doing so for a livelihood, or that deriving enjoyment from backbreaking work was dependent on being able to choose to do so rather than being obliged to do so.[28]

Booty captured in war, tribute from vassals and the benefits of prosperity that came with intensifications of local exchange on the one hand and an acceleration of long-distance trade in luxury goods – including foods – on the other led to a surge in spending power.[29] According to Pliny the Elder, the finest house in Rome in the first century BC was not even one of the best hundred just over a century later.[30] Lavish banquets became a common way for the wealthy to show off and enhance their status, just one of many competitive displays that supported social and political positioning – as it has been in other cultures, regions and periods, with the Babylonian Talmud providing one example among many.[31] Indeed, as Rome had expanded, legislation had been introduced that targeted extravagant expenditure on entertaining.[32] Intellectuals regularly complained about heavy spending on domestic art and architecture, usually arguing that it showed moral failings as well as poor judgement.[33] But benefits cascaded downwards too, albeit unevenly. Juvenal put it pithily when he commented that where Romans had once chosen their own destiny and their own leaders, 'they now hoped for just two things: bread and circuses'. Rome's rulers just needed to keep food flowing in and entertainment on tap and all would be well.[34]

Rome serves as a useful case study, for, as with all empires, states and cities, political, military and economic success – along with urbanisation – came at a high ecological cost. As goods, people and ideas were drawn to the centre, strains were put on natural resources which had to be brought from a distance to supply consumers and industries that needed or demanded them. The Stoic philosopher Seneca might have marvelled at human ingenuity in being able to detect and extract metals and minerals that were 'hidden' in the earth; but, as he made clear elsewhere, there was a price to pay for the relentless industrial progress. Leaving Rome with its 'oppressive atmosphere', along with the stench of 'smoking cookers', clouds of ash and 'poisonous fumes', he wrote to a friend, led to an immediate boost not just to his health but to his mood. 'You can imagine how much stronger I felt', he noted, 'after reaching my vineyards.'[35]

As ice-core data from Greenland and northern Russia shows, the first two centuries of the Roman empire saw a quadrupling of lead pollution, perhaps linked to the exploitation of mines in northern Spain and in Germany along the Rhine following successful military campaigns. While some historians have termed this a 'peace dividend' which provides a strong indication of rising prosperity and production (especially of coins), what is more striking is that both created pressures as far as environmental sustainability was concerned.[36]

This was not lost on many commentators, who noted that deforestation had seriously depleted wood supplies in many regions. The forests in what is now Tuscany had been cut down and exhausted, wrote Strabo around 2,000 years ago, to provide wood both for ships and for houses in and around Rome, including over-the-top villas that were of 'Persian magnificence' – a nod to opulence, excess and bad taste.[37] Pliny the Elder, writing not long afterwards, noted sadly that too many people undermine nature with the sole purpose of self-enrichment; it should hardly come as a surprise, therefore, that the earth should occasionally show its displeasure, through disasters such as earthquakes. Rather than content themselves with the bounteous food and natural wealth that the world provides, humans were too busy being overwhelmed by avarice to stop overexploiting its resources.[38]

Such concerns built on a long tradition in the Mediterranean. Centuries earlier, Plato had noted that 'many great convulsions' had taken place over the course of thousands of years, changing landscapes in the process. Overwork of the land combined with these changes meant that 'what now remains compared to what then existed is like the skeleton of a sick man, all the fat and the soft soil having wasted away, and only the bare framework of the land being left'.[39] Others went further, drawing explicit links between changes to the environment caused by human activity and alteration to the climate itself. Writing in the fourth century BC, Theophrastus observed that by the city of Larissa in Thessaly 'Formerly, when there was much standing water and the plain was a lake, the air was thick and the country warmer; but now that the water has been drained away and prevented from collecting, the land has become colder and freezing is more common.' Once there had been fine tall olive trees not only in the surrounding countryside but in Larissa itself, 'whereas now they are found nowhere'. Moreover, whereas vines had never frozen before, now they did so regularly.[40]

The question of sustainability was one that concerned Roman authors too, with Lucretius Carus comparing the earth to a mother who begat the human race, but now was 'like an ageing woman' whose 'child-bearing years' have come to an end; in other words, the earth had finite resources that had to be carefully looked after.[41] 'Our poor earth', says Lucretius, 'is worn out, exhausted [and] gives birth to no more great ages.' Fields no longer produce plentiful crops, but only 'mean and stingy' returns. The farmer goes about his business with a sigh, often finding his labour yields nothing. 'When he compares the present to the past, the past was better, infinitely so.'

This had nothing to do with a changing climate, and everything to do with human incompetence – at least according to the Roman author Columella. 'Again and again, I hear leading men of our state blaming the problems of harvests first on the soil, and then on the weather in recent years.' It was preposterous, he went on, that anyone should blame this on the natural environment which was 'endowed with perennial fertility by the creator of the universe'. Crop failures happened not because of the 'fury of the elements, but rather because of our own fault'. The land had been badly looked after. Romans had only themselves to blame. Rather than working it with the greatest care, as had been done in the past, it had been handed over to those unable and unqualified to care for it properly and uninterested in doing so: coerced labourers – and hopeless ones at that.[42]

It was not only Greek and Roman authors who were anxious about overexploitation. 'Live in complete harmony with nature,' advises the *Yajur Veda*, a Vedic Sanskrit text dating back 3,000 years.[43] 'The world is beautiful and verdant and God has appointed you as His stewards over it,' says a ḥadīth, one of the collection of sayings attributed to Muḥammad, the founder of the Islamic faith, who died in the first half of the seventh century. God had created the Garden of Eden and shown it to the first human with the words 'Look at My works, how beautiful and praiseworthy they are! And all that I have created, it was for you that I created it!' – so states a passage in the *Kohelet Rabbah*, a collection of commentaries on the books of the Torah that was written around the ninth century. 'Pay attention that you do not corrupt and destroy My world,' God warned, because 'if you corrupt it, there is no one to repair it after you.'[44] 'No living creatures like birds, beasts, insects and fish should be killed wantonly,' wrote Kaibara Ekken, the leading Japanese neo-Confucian scholar of the early modern period, and 'not even grass or trees should be cut down out of season. All are objects of nature's love, having been created and nurtured by it.' Cherishing and protecting flora and fauna was 'the way to serve nature' and to protect the relationship between heaven and earth. It was wrong, he added, to love birds or beasts 'to the neglect of human beings'. Doing so was 'inhumane'.[45] Conservation, ecological stewardship and concern for the natural environment has deep roots, in other words.

It is not easy to judge how seriously to take complaints about ecological degradation in the Roman world, not least because of the plentiful evidence about the concern of landowners with arboriculture in general and tree planting in particular, which speaks to consideration for the environment, widespread knowledge of techniques such as coppicing and high levels of awareness of the value of biodiversity as well as of balancing self-sufficiency with keeping the markets supplied with firewood. Piecing together pollen research and literary evidence from multiple locations around the empire suggests serious depletion of woodland, at least in some places in some periods of the Roman empire; but more and better evidence would be needed to make the case strongly and convincingly that deforestation took place in uncontrolled and damaging ways.[46]

Although making precise calculations is not easy, there were obvious practical and logistical challenges in supplying all that was required to heat, feed and supply populations in megacities like Rome that ran into the hundreds of thousands, even if commonly cited estimates as high as 800,000–1,000,000 are implausible.[47] While the stories of emperors and their intrigues preoccupied historians at the time and have continued to do so since, the ins and outs of how mouths were fed and homes were heated were important, as was the issue of how reliable – and sustainable – such supplies were over time.[48]

As some scholars have pointed out, 'every brick, coin, tile, glass object and iron tool dating to the Roman period' can be interpreted as the product of wood fuel. Such was the scale of energy production at Rome's peak that more lead particulates were trapped in the ice of Greenland than in any other era before the start of the industrial revolution.[49] All empires leave an ecological footprint; Rome's was substantial.[50]

In addition to regional variations in the needs of people living in different climatic regions, there would have been variations in diets, personal preferences and availability of particular crops and foodstuffs. Meat consumption not only shows a wide diversity between different parts of the Mediterranean, but also varies in quantity, the result presumably of rising and falling availability, as well as of changes in appetites and broader social trends.[51]

Nevertheless, taking as a base case the assumption that adults need to consume 2,000–3,000 calories per day to be healthy, it is possible to reach some rough approximation about consumption requirements. In addition, it is reasonable to assume per capita quantities of wood that would be needed each day – not for house, temple or ship building (as contemporary commentators complained), but for basic heating and cooking. Energy was also required for animal fodder, as well as for industries such as pottery, glass, tile production and metallurgy. Taken together, these suggest a plausible estimate of 1.5 hectares required per capita, split between food production, forest and pasture. Clearly, with an empire whose population size was somewhere in the order of seventy million in the middle of the second century AD, these requirements not only presented logistical challenges when it came to delivering supplies to where they were needed, but also placed significant pressures on short-term solutions to meet demand.[52]

Long before this time, soil erosion had become a problem in some parts of the Roman Mediterranean.[53] Deficiencies in food supply have also been linked with the high incidence of malaria in the Tiber around Rome, although some have suggested this was a result of overfishing and the depletion of mosquito-eating fish in the same area.[54] Studies of dental caries and tooth wear from skeletal remains in different parts of the empire reveal differences in the eating habits – or rather differences in available foods – for those living in cities and towns compared with those in the countryside, with considerable variation suggesting that some populations were better fed and healthier than others.[55]

Demand for exotic animals for food, to be killed in the arena for entertainment or as curiosities was enormous. Cassius Dio claims that 11,000 animals were killed during a set of games lasting ten days that were laid on by the Emperor Trajan.[56] Animals were routinely hunted to the brink of extinction and sometimes beyond for the amusement of the citizens of Rome and other cities in the empire.[57] Likewise whales and other marine animals were fished to the point where stocks appear to have fallen precipitously low.[58]

There were ways to increase food and energy supplies. Improvements to tools could make some difference, although the gains delivered by such uplifts tended to be minimal. Shifts to other fuel sources – such as coal, which was widely used in Roman Britain – could have a greater impact, though much depended on the location of coal deposits and the ease of extraction.[59] A few foods could be preserved through salting, smoking and drying, one reason why fish-salting factories sprang up in the Mediterranean.[60] Most other food had to be consumed soon after slaughter, harvest or collection to prevent it spoiling, which presented challenges of supply, delivery and price. At times of crisis, such as during the reign of Diocletian (284–305), the authorities sometimes even stepped in to try to cap prices; as was usual in other periods and regions, interventions by the state made little difference and are more useful as a sign of panic among the political elite, which often had limited understanding of how markets work, rather than as actions that had meaningful (let alone positive) outcomes.[61]

Yields are not just a function of factors such as soil types, agricultural competence and weather, for much is also dependent on societal factors, such as land ownership, the size of holdings and the location relative to market and supply networks. These could be improved – and could certainly be affected – by political decisions.[62] There were clearly incentives to open up new lands, through either conquest or cultivation. This too offered obvious problems. Territorial expansion effectively delivered resources from one set of mouths to another, sometimes displacing populations in the process and sometimes not. Either way, this did not increase production, but rather amounted to re-distribution to a new set of beneficiaries.

Developing new regions for cultivation sounded simple in theory; in practice, it was usually more complicated. The major determinant of production in all contexts was the availability of labour, rather than of land itself. Control of the former was far more significant. In the case of Sudanic kingdoms in the Middle Nile, for example, the absence of animal traction, the limited use of the plough, abundant land (albeit of varying quality) and low population levels meant that there were a series of caps on how far intensification of agriculture could reasonably be taken.[63]

Where such problems could be solved, it could often be a case of diminishing returns, not only since the best land tended to have been developed first, but also because clearing and settling land took time and persuasion. Moreover, such lands were by definition likely to be peripheral to existing territories – so were either difficult to exploit or likely to be frontier zones that might require protection. Additionally, since new regions were logically and by necessity set at a distance from large urban settlements, the practicalities of getting goods to where they were wanted and needed were not simple – and not cheap.

Officials of the Northern Wei dynasty that ruled northern China for a century and a half after AD 386 took deliberate steps to 'extend the cultivated acreage, and to accumulate a stockpile of cereals' – while careful to deploy military forces to protect newly transformed fields. Around the same time, plans were made by rulers to the south to reclaim pastures that currently serviced pigs, sheep and horses, as well as to drain marshlands that had not yet been 'opened up for agriculture' but which promised to be productive. Wealthy families presented an obvious obstacle to development, being unlikely to want to give up the abundant fish stocks that they controlled. Nevertheless, it was essential that they be made to do so, for food inequality was a source of considerable problems, not least the 'many who wander hither and thither in search of food'.[64]

States could and did intervene by passing legislation and punishing transgressors severely. One law mentioned by sources from the Liu Song dynasty stated that developing land without authorisation was 'tantamount to robbery with violence', and that 'Those who steal more than ten feet of land are to be beheaded in public.' This had clearly not worked, for people had simply ignored edicts, causing untold environmental damage by cutting down vegetation on mountains and building dams across rivers. It had to stop, wrote a senior official: 'These incursions are serious abuses that damage good government.'[65]

One obvious way to mitigate risks of overconsumption was to invest in infrastructure that expanded capacity, provided a safety cushion or both. Good examples come from elaborate water-management systems that were particularly important for supplying cities, towns and even pastoralist populations. Hundreds of water-storage buildings, wells and water tanks in the kingdom of Kush (centred in what is now Sudan) on the one hand point to the extension and enhancement of royal power and to attention being paid to guaranteeing and improving taxable revenues; on the other, however, the construction, which would have required substantial co-ordination and mobilisation of labour, also demonstrates that such interventions were required to protect not only the livelihood of the population but also that of the state, its administrative apparatus and its leadership by providing insurance against shortfalls or changes in water availability.[66]

The same equation could be found in big cities, such as Constantinople, which was founded by the Emperor Constantine on a well-established site on the European banks of the Bosporus in AD 330. The major investment in a massive building campaign coupled with the arrival of a sizeable new urban population required a substantial upgrade to the existing forty-seven-kilometre aqueduct system that already fed water into the city. This was extended dramatically in the fourth and fifth centuries, covering more than ninety bridges and tunnels that fed water into giant cisterns and reservoirs. The network was around 500 kilometres in length, and possibly more, in what was the longest water-supply system of any city in the ancient world.[67] This network did not just have to be built; it had to be maintained – regularly – to prevent the build-up of calcium carbonate and contamination by clay deposits.[68]

If this provides one example of how much advance planning and investment went into supporting large populations in order to create solutions to overcome the ecological challenges of resource shortage, then the case of Tikal in northern Guatemala provides another. Sited in a location that was essentially dependent on seasonal rainfall, Tikal would not have been sustainable without human interventions to protect its citizens from considerable environmental shortcomings. While the monumental architecture was designed to emphasise the wealth and power of those who built and maintained the structures (and impresses visitors to this day), the viability of the city was based on a sophisticated series of hydrological networks that were designed to trap water. Plazas and courtyards were linked by a convex microshed water system that directed rainfall to large storage tanks lined with stones and imported clays that could hold almost a million cubic metres of water and were controlled by sluice gates that released water into causeways as needed.[69]

This proved important not only for the ecological stability of the city but also as a tool of social, political and economic control. Perhaps most important of all, however, was that it cemented Tikal's primacy relative to other urban and non-urban centres: household water-catchment tanks could hold enough water to get through one dry season; but they proved no use if rains failed for more than one year – because of regional variation or because of more fundamental changes to climate patterns.

The thought and investment that had gone into Tikal's sophisticated hydrological plan meant that the city, its inhabitants and elites could navigate short-term problems and could do so better than others. This naturally offered additional and obvious advantages, at least for those who stood to benefit from larger markets, higher tax takes and expansions of the workforce.[70]

In many ways, the primary story of the intensification of land usage, the greater extent of exploitation and the increasing degrees of social complexity lay in the fact that levels of environmental stress remained surprisingly low. There were times of shortage, certainly; but by and large the world of around 2,000 years ago was remarkably resilient, at least in terms of avoiding large-scale famine and high levels of mortality as a result of food shortages. Of course, that did not mean that there was not a price to pay for ecological expansion. Some scholars have sought to use statistical data to argue that the biological standards of living were at their lowest when population densities were at their highest. Rome's political and military ascent came not only at the price of life expectancy but even at the cost of falls in average height, if data that is geographically and chronologically uneven is to be believed.[71]

Indeed, cities were far more lethal than changes to climate patterns. While the rich grumbled about the stench and the hustle and bustle of metropolitan life, it was far more worrying that people who lived close together, often in unsanitary conditions, provided the ideal conditions for diseases to take hold and spread quickly.[72] Two examples might be provided by the Antonine plague that took hold in AD 165 and the so-called plague of Cyprian a century later: according to some modern historians, these wreaked devastation, leading to demographic collapses that triggered price and wage shocks and severely depressed agricultural yields, land values and industrial production – and perhaps even helped the spread of Christianity.[73] Others, however, are more sceptical about the impacts of these pandemics, about which even basic epidemiological details are vague.[74]

What is clearer is that the outbreaks of disease took place immediately after changes in oxygen isotope levels and spikes in sulphur contents in ice cores – which point to falls in temperature as a result of substantial volcanic eruptions, multiple ones in the case of the plague of Cyprian in the second half of the third century.[75] This was seemingly exacerbated by highly erratic precipitation (at least in north-eastern France and central

Europe), expansion both of Arctic sea ice and of European glaciers and reduced levels of solar activity.[76] The period that began shortly before the Antonine plague was one of 'climate disorganisation covering three centuries', notes a leading scholar, and one marked by climate instability which strained the Roman empire's 'reserves of strength and intervened dramatically in the course of events'. Taken as a whole, the spell from AD c.150 to c.650 'witnessed one of the most dramatic sequences of climate change in the entire Holocene'.[77]

The timing of climatic and pathogenic challenges was broadly contemporaneous with dramatic societal change – and not only in the Roman empire, which went into a tailspin in the 230s: over the next five decades twenty-six emperors came to the throne, and around double that number of would-be usurpers sought to seize power. In East Asia, the Han dynasty of China came to an end with the abdication of the Emperor Xian in AD 220 and was followed by a turbulent period known as the Three Kingdoms, which was in turn followed by that of the Sixteen Kingdoms as the state that the Han had united kept on disintegrating into smaller units. In Persia, in AD 224, Ardashir I pushed all rivals to one side and established himself as the founder of a new dynasty before expanding his territories, above all into oasis towns located along the Silk Roads. Not long afterwards, in north-eastern India, a similar process of political, economic and territorial consolidation took place that would eventually create the Gupta empire, the pre-eminent state in South Asia and an intellectual powerhouse that produced great scholars, scientists and mathematicians such as Kālidāsa, Āryabhaṭa and Varāhamihira.

The question, however, is not so much about whether climate change was a factor in these dramatic upheavals but rather about identifying the precise role that it played in some or all of these cases. While the overarching picture of shocks to weather patterns might seem to be both consistent and compelling, it is worth re-emphasising that the Mediterranean alone is composed of a wide variety of geographies, environments and climate systems; although it can be tempting to extrapolate universal models from one set of data, doing so can be both simplistic and misleading.[78] To give one example, assemblages of ceramics from across Egypt show increases in both the production and the consumption of wine – which suggests temperatures that were not cold and did not place agricultural production under extreme threat.[79]

The tumultuous social and political changes also need to be set into wider chronological and causal contexts. In Persia, the usurpation of Ardashir was a crucial moment and understandably a watershed for conceptualisations about change. As in Rome and elsewhere, the game of imperial musical chairs was primarily of interest to those who had vested interests in who won, or lost, power. Just what and how much this meant at the time – and to whom – was another matter. The family connections of whoever sat on the throne of Persia were of course significant, but they were perhaps not as important to much of the population as commentators made them out to be at the time – and often have done since.

The same was true of the success of the Gupta empire, which according to an inscription from Kaushambi covered the ancient Aryan homelands (Āryāvarta) across northern India. So extensive were Gupta-controlled territories that by the fourth-century ruler Samudra, Gupta was being acknowledged as master of regions as far away as Sri Lanka, Nepal and Gandhara, and being referred to as 'a god dwelling on earth'.[80] Rather than being persuaded by climatic factors and the patterns we are tempted to see, it is more useful to see how political opportunism, astute leadership and logistical reforms combined to stimulate exchange and to fuel the rise of a new ruling class – and a new ruling family.'[81]

Similarly, while the spectacular splintering of lands that had been consolidated under the Han dynasty is one of the features of the two centuries that followed the abdication of Emperor Xian, the reality was that the forces that destabilised the empire had been building for many decades. Underpinning these were the familiar problems of rising complexity and diminishing returns as stagnation set in, coupled with the failure of the state to adapt and adjust; the incompetence, inefficiency and corruption that were hallmarks of a bureaucratic class which became part of the problem rather than the solution; and an imbalance between revenues and expenditure that not only led to fiscal pressure and disillusion but also incentivised challengers to chance their arm in taking advantage personally, stopping the rot or both.

It was much the same in the Roman empire, where almost constant civil wars from the late third century AD onwards exacerbated existing strains. These included a collapse in public building and changes in the attitude of local elites towards civic-mindedness, perhaps because of a move away from wanting or needing to legitimise their social and political status, or perhaps because of depleting resources that enabled them to do so. Either way, a substantial slowdown in economic and cultural activity cannot be explained only through the prism of climate: even though agricultural production was closely linked to reliable weather patterns, much also depended on availability of labour, on direct and heritable control over land and on demand for non-agricultural crafts, skills and goods, as well as on the resilience of urban markets and of the spending power of consumers.[82]

Large states could prove to be surprisingly brittle therefore, and could break down under relatively modest pressures and imbalances, with cascading consequences. For example, in the Roman empire, the provisioning of supplies from the Mediterranean to the Rhine by imperial agents largely reflected military deployments as well as requirements for maintaining control of the frontier. This meant that not only was the location of markets closely correlated to army centres but consumption patterns were linked to the spending of soldiers individually and collectively. Most important of all was the fact that, as the state began to implode, these supply and trade networks broke down entirely: when grain stopped reaching the army, regional economies went into freefall, urban centres contracted and the empire's defences weakened.[83]

Pressures that built up from the periphery flowed back towards the centre, aggravating and accelerating the process of collapse. Such problems could not be remedied by simple fixes, largely because their creation in the first place was the result of direction and oversight by the political centre. Structures that had been built by state intervention were dependent on the smooth functioning of bureaucratic and logistical functions, and when these were strained or failed, it was difficult if not impossible to stem the tide. It was no coincidence, therefore, that in due course it was the western half of the Roman empire that collapsed, as this was where the arm of the state was at its longest and most active. In the eastern half, on the other hand, where cities and markets built up organically, there was much greater capacity to deal with difficulties.[84]

In other words, while it may well be that worsening climate affected agricultural yields at least in some locations, and perhaps even disrupted food supplies, there were other, more significant forces that better explain some of the concurrent turmoil and reconfigurations that began to unfurl in different parts of the world around the end of the second and start of the third centuries. Climatic changes were more decisive and important, however, in the case of events on the steppes of Central Asia from c.350 onwards.

Records of juniper tree rings from what is now Qinhai province in north-western China attest to three periods of intense drought from around 350–550 that together represent the most challenging conditions of the last 2,000 years.[85] These are usually associated with large-scale migration of constellations of nomads, with the Huns considered the prime motor that drove tribes westwards across the steppes north of the Caspian and Black seas towards the Roman frontier and also southwards through the Caucasus towards Persia. These waves carved their way through Rome's western provinces, overrunning what is now Germany, France and Spain and reaching into North Africa – and even sacking Rome in AD 410.[86]

The results included urban decline, wholesale collapse of long-distance trade and supply networks, large-scale dispersals of populations and impoverishment not only in locations that were attacked: in fact, the effects were felt from Egypt to Britain.[87] Indeed, they may even have been felt beyond the Roman world itself, with the disappearance of the Meroitic kingdom in what is now Sudan perhaps best explained in the context of the world that it abutted experiencing a long phase of social, economic and political cardiac arrest.[88] Certainly, decline did not have to be spectacular or dramatic: as multi-isotope studies on skeletal remains from cemeteries in the Carpathian basin show, many changes following the invasions by Huns and others in the fifth century were characterised not by violence but by adaptation of diet, lifestyle and farming techniques.[89] So many converted to Hunnic lifestyles, and so many Huns adopted local practices, that some wags have labelled these the effects of 'Tiller the Hun'.[90]

It did not take much for towns to suffer from dislocation, falling into disrepair and becoming depopulated not because of violent attacks but because of the steady pressure on resources. Urban centres were suffocated rather than battered to death. The descent into what scholars used to refer to as the Dark Ages resulted not from chaos and indiscriminate bloodshed but from the splintering of the state and the disappearance of centralised authority that previously glued the western provinces together.

While barbarian invasions have long enjoyed a particular, gruesome role in public imagination (as well as in modern scholarship), some historians are now seeking to argue that in addition to serving as a catalyst to migrations from the steppes, challenging climate conditions may have played a role in the deterioration in the Roman empire too – not only in the Levant and Asia Minor, where lower rainfall would clearly have affected agricultural output, but also in the western provinces.[91] The cocktail of adverse climate conditions, reduced levels of local, regional and long-distance trade and rising demand from the centre for money and manpower proved to be lethal.[92]

Of course, evaluating precisely how aridity was linked to movements of peoples, to invasions and to military conquests is not straightforward. Nor is it clear that a detailed set of climate data from one part of East Asia can be applied to the entirety of Central Asia and beyond to support a putative hypothesis that lower-than-average rainfalls lay behind decisions to move to different locations. After all, nomads were just as likely to try to adapt to changing conditions as they were to migrate or move over long distances; and in any event, if the same climatic stress was uniform across large areas, then migration did not necessarily solve the problem anyway. The explanation may lie in the fact that the southern winter pasture in the western part of the steppe was significantly more benign than that in the east and therefore able to support far greater populations of animals and their owners.[93] The shunting of tribes towards the Roman and Persian frontiers was not about the efforts of peoples of the steppes to reach let alone conquer these empires; rather, it was part of a process of competition for the best land and locations to ensure survival at a time of harsh climatic conditions.

Evidence from New Mexico and from New Zealand suggests that this period as a whole was one of considerable variation in the El Niño–Southern Oscillation (ENSO) in the equatorial Pacific and that it is plausible that this had an effect on moisture availability on the steppes. Ironically, what might have been most important, however, was not the periods of aridity and drought, but rather a long 'pluvial' period of above-average rains that interrupted the waves of dryness: this would have produced better conditions for nomads, greater levels of pasture for their livestock and a rapid build-up in numbers of horses at the disposal of a leadership structure that had already been moulded by crisis. In other words, it was not the drought or rains that was important but the relationship between the two.[94]

Where climate could also have a significant impact was in decisions that rural populations made when faced with short-term pressures. *The*

Book of Wei, a history of the Northern Wei dynasty that ruled northern China for a century and a half from AD 386, alongside other histories of this period, records when harvests were poor as well as extreme weather events, such as severe droughts and floods. These caused authorities considerable concern – primarily because they provoked rural populations to seek refuge in cities, above all Pingcheng (modern Datong in Shanxi province), whose population may have been as high as 1 million by the middle of the fifth century. Located on the Haihe River at a transitional point between semi-arid pastoral grasslands and the humid zone that favoured intensive cultivation, Pingcheng was well suited as a point of exchange with the steppes, as well as being able to benefit from a substantial agricultural hinterland.

It was not impossible and not even necessarily difficult to support a large and growing population as long as needs were predictable. For example, in AD 469 and then again six years later, imperial orders were issued instructing that grain be sent to the city from elsewhere in Wei territories. While some take this as an indication of worrying shortages at a time of an 'extraordinary cooling phase in northern China', the bigger problem was that uncertainty made forward planning difficult. It was not the drop of temperature by just over 1 °C that is attested to in the late fifth century that presented a challenge, but being sure of having food supplies where they were needed at the right time and at affordable prices. The pressures of trying to calculate what this meant are clear from the shortages of 486, when, according to some estimates, more than half of the inhabitants of Pingcheng left the city in a panic.[95]

As such, while the decision by the Xiaowen Emperor to move the capital to Luoyang in 493 was partly driven by political motivations – taking advantage of the collapse of the Liu Song state to the south – the fact that this relocation enabled the imperial court to make a fresh start in a location that was more ecologically sustainable was important: relocating in lands to the south whose economic and calorific value had been magnified by pressure on food availability not only made sense but was an obvious way to try to cope with changing circumstances. The move was no mean feat given that Pingcheng was home to more than 6,000 temples and almost 80,000 monks and nuns. Heavy investment went into Luoyang and the Longmen complex of caves, grottoes and shrines dedicated to Buddha, Buddhism and Buddhist teaching as a statement of intent that this was a site that was the subject of imperial benefaction and attention. The Longmen caves were later added to and expanded by craftsmen during the Tang dynasty (618–907). Still, the scale of the transformation of this site – and of Luoyang as a major centre – is made clear from the fact that later commentators, such as Peng Gang, an official of the Ming dynasty (1368–1644), claimed that the subsequent 'breakup of the Northern Wei state was the result of its excessively large number of stone buddhas'.[96]

That was meant, of course, as a warning to contemporary rulers who spent money on vanity projects that drained finances and also served as distractions for the population. Balancing the need to protect the power of elites with the need to administer the state, to gather taxation and to administer justice involved striking compromises. The difficulties of doing so could be aggravated by any number of challenges, including uprisings, war with neighbours, weather shocks that led to crop failure and also deeper shifts in climate patterns that brought about deeper change.

In that sense, therefore, much depended on how risks were evaluated in advance, and how threats were responded to in real time: in all disasters, the burden of calamity falls disproportionately on the poor – with modern research underlining that the decisive factor in vulnerability to socio-economic stress and famine is specifically the proportion of the population who have no assets. Put simply, the greater the number of poor people, the greater the risk of food shortage, famine and state breakdown.[97] Not surprisingly, then, it did not take much to upset the equilibrium. The consequences could not just be dramatic; in some cases, they could fundamentally transform the earth.

10

The Crisis of Late Antiquity
(AD c.500–c.600)

What avails a thousand boxes of pearls to him who is starving of cold?

King Senka (AD c.530)

Changes to climate conditions that affected humans of course drew the most attention from commentators. However, the impact on flora and fauna could be both significant and dramatic in the short and the long term. Locust migrations are closely connected with weather patterns. Studies of outbreaks of oriental migratory locusts (*Locusta migratoria manilensis*) over almost two millennia in China have revealed that locust abundance peaks in cold and dry periods, with separate research suggesting links between above-average frequencies of floods and droughts – at least in the lower Yangtze River.[1] Work on swarms in the twentieth century in the Huang Ho and Huai Ho regions meanwhile points to a strong correlation with El Niño episodes, and outbreaks in the first or second year that follows.[2]

Hormonal changes take place in locusts in response to rises in their population density, prompting morphological changes, for example to colour, body and wing size. As these occur, the locusts gather in swarms numbering in their millions, tens of millions, reaching as much as two billion, devastating crops, green plants and tree bark – they can double their weight in a single day.[3] Not surprisingly, locusts and the damage they could do feature prominently in ancient texts, ranging from the

Upaniṣads to the records of Mesopotamian, ancient Egyptian and Chinese civilisations – and beyond.[4] Biblical texts made much of the threats posed by swarms, often correlating the damage they did to food supplies with divine punishment – perhaps not surprisingly since the insects even appeared to come from the heavens. The Romans worried about locusts that were periodically swept across from Africa to Italy; their arrival forced the population to 'look for remedies in the Sybilline books', the collection of oracular sayings held in the capital, to see how best to survive the famine and the troubles that they could cause.[5]

Changes in climate patterns could trigger more frequent outbreaks of vector-borne disease following abnormally high levels of rainfall. Indeed, three of the most lethal pandemics of the last two millennia – the Justinianic plague of the sixth century, the Black Death of the 1340s and the plague of the seventeenth century – were heavily influenced by climate variation. In each case, warmer springs and wetter summers produced the sharp spikes in the prevalence of the bacterium that caused bubonic plague, although this was not enough on its own to lead to mass human fatalities: for that to happen, routes transmitting the disease from plague foci needed to exist – alongside hosts who lived close enough to infect each other.[6]

This was true for a range of other diseases, including malaria – although, as with other pathogens, this needs to be understood through microanalysis at a local level, given the significant variables of geography, hydrology, climate and human activities, as well as competition for breeding sites between mosquito species, many of which are incapable of transmitting malaria to humans.[7] Awareness of the risks of disease and the threats to health haunted people in the past, with reports and enquiries about health a standard part of the formula of letter writing across cultures – although writers were much more likely to present themselves as poorly and suffering from ailments than admit to being in robust spirits. Still, as one letter written in what is now China in AD c.400 notes, alongside an unusually upbeat report that 'Mother is blessed with good health, and everybody else here is in good health,' no one could take this for granted: 'we are constantly worried about another outbreak of malaria'.[8]

It was not always easy for humans to stay ahead of change. For example, a shift in the favourable conditions in the Andes that had facilitated intensive farming in the Patacancha Valley in southern

Peru led to significant falls in pollen levels from pasture grasses and quinoa, an important food crop, as well as from ambrosia – a plant that flourishes in disturbed soil and therefore provides a useful indication of human cultivation and intervention in the landscape. The contraction of agriculture, likely the result of sustained falls in temperature that can be detected from glacial evidence as well as from the Huascarán ice core, prompted moves towards pastoralist lifeways in order to cope with more challenging environmental circumstances.[9]

Adapting to circumstance was not easy, especially in locations where the ecological profile was precariously balanced. In the south-west United States, for example, water availability was one of the key factors in determining settlement and subsistence strategies and demographic trends (including migration), as well as shaping agricultural capabilities.[10] As such, a period of severe aridity known as the Second-Century Drought, attested to by tree-ring records, placed severe stress on animal and plant life: changes in climate that influence plant growth impact the animals that rely on them – and on humans that rely on both.[11] The pressures were so great that in order to survive, the human population had to use firewood to melt cave ice for water.[12]

The cause seems to have been connected to unusually high levels of solar irradiance that were also responsible for the Roman Climate Optimum, and for warm temperature anomalies across the northern hemisphere.[13] Other regions saw higher-than-average rainfall – such as the Basin of Mexico, where an abrupt rise of some 60 per cent was followed by a period lasting for some three centuries that featured the largest and most sustained levels of precipitation of the past 2,000 years.[14] In this case, the increase in water availability helped fuel a rise in irrigation agriculture as well as in population size – which in turn underpinned a boom in construction of monumental architecture both in Teotihuacan and at Cholula in the Puebla Valley. This was not a process of unfettered growth and prosperity, as is clear from the cessation in building around AD 250 and the near contemporaneous desecration of the Feathered Serpent Pyramid in Teotihuacan: while the cause of this turmoil is not entirely clear, it is naturally best understood as a case of an important recalibration in the city's political system, as a sign of uneasiness in the relationship between the elites and others and as a crisis of expectations, perhaps in the face of pressure on resources.[15]

In the case of the Basin of Mexico, additional water supplies resulting from higher rainfall patterns brought considerable benefits and opportunities. Elsewhere, however, this presented major problems. While it is true that vegetational growth is closely linked to climate patterns, with higher agricultural productivity accompanying warm, wet summers, the problem arose when such growth was too rapid.[16] This was especially the case in tropical regions, which required clearing and maintenance in order to support human settlement.

The present-day Congo rainforest area offers a good example of the difficulties that can be caused by a change in climate in general and in precipitation in particular. Initial migration into these regions by Bantu-speaking populations was facilitated by a reduction of forest cover in the centuries starting around 400 BC that enabled settlers to expand rapidly over a vast area, attested by pottery finds at numerous sites and in several distinctive styles.[17] Four centuries later, starting around AD 1, however, a marked trend of wetter climatic patterns led to extremely fast growth of prolific trees which transformed the forest into an increasingly damp and humid space that must have impeded food productivity, resulted in deteriorating living conditions and created substantial resource difficulties for settlers. This was at least part of the cause of a chronic decline in population density, although recent scholarship has also pointed to epidemic disease as playing a role in demographic collapse in this region around AD 400.[18] Increases in rainfall and temperature made life easier in some locations, in other words, but harder – if not impossible – in others.

As we have seen, the rise of empires could reshape landscapes owing to the demands made by rising demographics, urbanisation and consumption patterns. The fall of empires could do the same: as Rome's western provinces went into a prolonged period of decline, their botanical footprint was transformed too. Fields that had once been given over to alfalfa to supply the imperial armies' horses and livestock gave way to new crops, or even to none. From the point of view of vegetation, Rome's loss was rye's gain, as cultivation expanded rapidly in Europe between the fourth and eighth centuries. A series of 'outlaw plants' spread naturally on a south-to-north axis and curiously did not seem to accompany the great tribal shifts from east to west. So while most commentators understandably focus on the human aspects that accompanied the decline and fall of the Roman empire, such as the collapse of trade networks, lower mobility and reduced literacy levels, it is also important to note that ecological change was another important outcome.[19]

It was not surprising, then, that authors, poets, musicians and others created works that presented nature in an idealised form – invariably one that was stable, benign and under human control and agency, even if that was not always made entirely clear. This involved some sleight of hand: take 'Rhapsody on Dwelling in the Mountains' by Xie Lingyun (385–433), which describes the joys of living in seclusion alongside animals and plants in various idyllic settings; the fact that he was in the process of undertaking a massive project of expansion and renovation of a family estate – and was able to afford to do so – meant that the scenes he described were the product of human intervention in the landscape, not the result of man finding peace in an existing, natural setting.[20] Creating gardens that were seen as mirrors of the heavenly paradise, as in Constantinople, the capital of the Byzantine empire, in Syria, Jordan and Iraq following the Arab conquests, in Agra in northern India in the Mughal period or in contemporary Gloucestershire, was all very well. As one leading scholar has put it, formal, cultivated gardens were greatly admired and much in demand, but they needed people to cultivate them, and thus reflected the wealth and status of those able to afford such luxuries.[21]

The ambiguity about idealised presentations of the natural world is apparent too from Buddhist texts. Many Buddhist texts are hostile to nature, such as the *Vessantara Jātaka*, whose message was not one of respecting nature but rather of taming it. Moreover, later romanticisations of nature were often reflections of its loss as a result of human activities and overexploitation; in the case of Japan, focus on plants was closely connected with monastic control over natural resources that could be monetised, namely fields and forests.[22]

Attitudes were similarly double-sided in relation to deserts and barren spaces, especially in theological thought. Remote, desolate locations were idealised as places to commune with the divine across multiple religions – places where God's voice could be heard in the Abrahamic faiths (Judaism, Christianity and Islam). Caves, secluded and isolated sites set far away from cities and towns, were also important in Hinduism, Buddhism and Jainism. Across many faiths, communing with the divine or with higher spiritual planes was connected with getting away from other humans – often by seeking out places that were not verdant, green and offering fruits of nature but the opposite; arid, harsh and punishing. Ironically, the fame of individuals who moved to caves and deserts attracted followers and imitators, with the result that monasteries and complexes of cells turned these places of self-isolation into bustling communities in their own right, such as in Sinai, at Dunhuang or at Ellora off the coast of Mumbai. This did not defeat the point of escapism or the belief in finding spiritual fulfilment, but it certainly made it harder.

Indic literatures written fifteen hundred years ago contained a wide variety of poetic expression about the seasons, with genres focusing on the six seasons (*sadritu*) and the four rainy months (*chaumasa*), or on the twelve-month cycle of changing weather conditions and the different seasons (*barahmasa*).[23] Texts like the *Viṣṇudharmottarapurāṇa*, likely written around the sixth century AD, that bring together information from separate treatises about poetry, music and astronomy present the seasons as part of a predictable cycle that returns and can be anticipated by human actors – without allowing for the fact that there were considerable variations over the short and the long term: summers tormented and springs bloomed.[24]

Many good examples abound from this period of efforts to influence and control the weather to ensure clement conditions and plentiful agricultural yields. For example, the *Mahāpratisarā-Mahāvidyārājñī* recommends attaching a particular spell to the top of a flagstaff, promising that doing so 'calms all types of winds, cold-spells, untimely clouds, lightning and thunderbolts', as well as offering protection from 'crop destroyers' such as 'hosts of stinging insects, flies, locusts and worms'.[25] This is just one of a host of texts that focuses on rain-making rituals and protection from adverse weather and its consequences that can be found in Sanskrit, Chinese and Tibetan sources spread across multiple centuries.[26]

The idea that nature could be understood, controlled and shaped by humans belied the reality of unusual and severe weather conditions – or of other dramatic interventions such as natural disasters. Tsunamis were regular occurrences in the Mediterranean, for example, including ones of extraordinary force and violence. The port of Caesarea in the eastern Mediterranean in what is now Israel had been home to a mega-harbour built using fast-drying hydraulic cement made from ash from

Mount Vesuvius imported from Italy, while cobble and rubble that were laid down as foundations for piers had been brought from Asia Minor, Cyprus and Greece. The harbour was hit four times by major tidal waves – in AD 115, 551, 749 and 1202 – with each doing substantial damage.[27]

Other earthquakes and tsunamis were devastating, as an account of an episode in AD 365 makes clear. 'Shortly after dawn,' wrote one late Roman author, 'the solidity of the whole earth was made to shake and shudder, and the sea was driven away, its waves were rolled back and it disappeared,' stranding many ships on dry land and enabling people to walk about and pick up fish with their hands. 'As if insulted', the sea then roared back through the 'teeming shoals and dashed itself violently' on to islands and the mainland, flattening buildings, killing thousands and changing the face of the earth.[28] While some have questioned whether this description involves considerable dramatic licence on the part of an author representing a localised disaster as a universal cataclysm, it is true that the coastline of Crete was raised by as much as nine metres, likely as a result of multiple seismic events rather than a single episode.[29]

Volcanic eruptions could be devastating too, as the eruption of the Ilopango Tierra Blanca Joven volcano in what is now El Salvador shows. The force of the eruption, dated to AD c.431, was astonishing, with modelling of deposits suggesting the ejection of fifty-eight cubic kilometres of bulk rock to a column height of almost thirty kilometres.[30] The ash from the eruption would have altered ocean chemistry in the Pacific, generating a significant increase in marine productivity and bringing about changes to atmospheric carbon dioxide and oxygen levels in the years that followed. It is likely that the eruption resulted in a global cooling of around 0.5 °C, with evidence from Antarctic ice cores implying that the effects were more pronounced in the southern hemisphere. Everything within eighty kilometres of the vent would have been destroyed, including vegetation, which would have taken decades to recover.[31]

It is not easy to establish the effect on the climate of Central America because of the current paucity of high-resolution sampling – something that may be resolved in the future. Tree-ring data from central China point to this period as one of drought, raising the questions of whether this was linked to the volcanic eruption, to a cooling episode related to solar activity or both; there is the question too of what role, if any, climate pressure played in a new wave of consolidation and migration by pastoralist groups in this period, with some scholars proposing that the pressure on vegetation on the steppes served as a catalyst to movements westwards.[32] The most notable of these were the Huns, who surged into the Europe under a formidable new leader, Attila, in the decade after the eruption.[33]

In such circumstances, taking the long view was important. 'From time to time,' wrote the Greek historian Polybius, 'as a result of floods, plagues, failures of crops or similar causes, there occurs a catastrophic destruction of the human race, in which all knowledge of art and social institutions is lost.' This was to be expected, for 'such disasters, tradition tells us, have often befallen mankind and must reasonably be expected to recur'. No matter how bad things seemed, however, the human population would recover and renew 'as if from seeds'.[34]

This perspective was admirable and, on balance, was broadly correct. However, some disasters were worse than others, and could on occasion seem apocalyptic in the scale of the devastation they inflicted. In the first half of the sixth century, a sequence of climate-related phenomena brought about change on a profound scale around the world. Crucial to this was a series of large eruptions that took place in the 530s and 540s. Tree-ring data from the Altai mountains, the Austrian Alps and bipolar ice cores point to precipitous falls in temperatures in this period, which were amplified by reduced solar activity and oceans that were already cooling.[35]

Rather than starting with a single, massive explosion, the signal that can be detected from ice-core data may relate to at least two major and possibly multiple eruptions of North American, Icelandic or Kamchatkan volcanoes in c.536 and around 540.[36] This was then followed by tropical eruptions in the decade that followed which produced long-lasting effects, especially in terms of sulphate deposition.[37] Despite the assertions of many scholars to the contrary, this did not include Ilopango, whose eruption a century earlier was one of the ten largest of the last 7,000 years but whose dating has long relied on inaccurate reading of radiocarbon data.[38] The clusters of eruptions in a 'machine-gun' effect may have been part of the reason why the after-effects were so severe – with the timings and latitudes of the explosions being of particular significance.[39] Some scholars have suggested that at least one of the tropical eruptions was of an undersea volcano, which would explain the presence of warm-water marine microorganisms dating to this period that have been found in ice cores.[40] Taken together, volcanic activity produced a dramatic and substantial drop in temperature: one scholar has argued that 'the 530s and 540s were not just frosty. They were the coldest decades in the Holocene.'[41]

The ejections threw enormous quantities of debris into the atmosphere that formed a 'dust veil' around the earth and were much remarked on by contemporary commentators. Writing about the years 536–7, the Byzantine author Procopius noted that this was a time of terrible portents, with the sun giving out so little light and heat that it resembled the moon. John of Lydus recorded that the sun was all but obscured by clouds which dimmed its light to the extent that it could barely be seen for almost a year. The *Nan Shi*, written in Tang dynasty China, meanwhile reported that in the mid-530s 'yellow dust' fell 'like snow', presumably a reference to sulphuric deposits and ash falling back to earth after being ejected into the atmosphere.[42]

In fact, though, the cooling effect may not have been the most important result of the volcanic activity. It is certainly the case that crop yields are sensitive to temperature change, especially at high altitudes and latitudes.[43] But what mattered more was not so much the onset of cold conditions as the effect of the dust veil. Terrestrial photosynthesis and agricultural production are closely linked to solar radiation, with the result that blocks on the sun's light and warmth inevitably present major challenges for plant life, including that grown as human food sources.[44]

Some estimate a population decline of 70 per cent or more in some areas north of the Yellow River, although the evidence for such claims is not enormously robust.[45] More striking is the emphasis placed by some accounts of this period on famine and food shortage, from the *Annals of Ulster* noting the 'failure of bread' to the author of an early Japanese chronicle which reports King Senka in the mid-530s lamenting that 'food is the basis of the empire. Yellow gold and ten thousand strings of cash cannot cure hunger. What avails a thousand boxes of pearls to him who is starving of cold?'[46] Nevertheless, the point here is obvious: material wealth was all very well, but it did not put food in people's mouths.

Data from San Francisco bristlecone pines and from precipitation reconstructions in New Mexico show that the 540s was a period of extreme cold in the North American south-west. It has recently been argued that this was the cause of the rapid population dispersal that took place at precisely this time, and moreover that the warm and wet conditions that returned later in the sixth century drove a process of major socio-economic reorganisation on the Colorado plateau. A generation-long crisis that affected a vast area brought about a sophisticated response that saw agricultural knowledge and technology spread across communities which adopted similar patterns of sedentary lifestyles, including the widespread domestication of turkeys. It also catalysed the evolution of complex societies, spurred the emergence of villages and ultimately led to the development of hierarchies that served as foundational elements of Ancestral Pueblo culture.[47]

The dramatic change in conditions also had a major impact in Scandinavia, where this period saw the greatest change in settlement patterns in Sweden for 6,000 years as villages were abandoned in their scores. In Denmark, a sharp rise in the number of prestige objects at sacrificial sites has been linked to expressions of desperation and appeals to the divine during the traumatic downturn of the mid-sixth century.[48] Indeed, the cold weather, and specifically the diminution of the sun's strength, was such that it transformed ideas, influenced beliefs and set down models that were warnings for the future. As some leading scholars have argued, the dust veil provided the model of the *fimbulvetr*, a great winter in which Norse myths held that 'snow will drift from all directions', great frosts and keen winds will be everywhere and 'the sun will do no good'.[49] This was the prelude to the Ragnarök, the final battle at the end of the world.[50] Cinemagoers who have helped make *Thor: Ragnarok* one of the highest-grossing films of all time, taking almost 1 billion dollars at the box office, may not realise that they have a set of volcanic eruptions a millennium and a half ago to thank for their thrills.

The century of change that followed the eruptions has been the focus of considerable attention from scholars, who have often taken the volcanic explosions and associated climate impact to be the start of a sequence that includes the 'transformation of the eastern Roman Empire and collapse of the Sasanian Empire, movements out of the Asian steppe and Arabian peninsula, spread of Slavic-speaking peoples and political upheavals in China'.[51] As we shall see, they also had a bearing on major transformations in the Americas, in Africa and across South Asia, as well as paving the way for the rise of Islam and the creation of a vast Arab empire in the wake of the death of the Prophet Muḥammad.

The hundred years that followed the eruptions of the mid-sixth century certainly saw socio-economic, political and cultural transformations of extraordinary magnitude. However, it is more useful to assess the volcanic activity and its impacts not as being the cause of a series of epic social, political and economic revolutions, but rather as having aggravated existing problems, and exposed fractures that then produced radical change. For example, food shortages were a product of pressures of demographics as much as of low yields. Had King Senka's realm had a smaller population, feeding it would not have been as difficult as he claimed.

The vulnerability of cities was not just linked to climate, as we have already seen, for they could also collapse quickly as a result of flooding, the shift of trade routes, external pressure or a combination of all three – as the case of Pātaliputra shows. Pātaliputra had once been described as the greatest city in India, with buildings of such beauty that 'no human hands of this world could accomplish'; it was a city that was not only gorgeous, but would 'endure for 5,000 years'; by AD 600, however, it was in ruins, likely the result of catastrophic flooding in the wake of sustained rainfall that affected the flow of the Ganges, although precisely when this happened is not clear.[52]

Certainly, by the start of the seventh century, all the trading cities of north-west India had fallen into decline. They remained that way 200 years later when the entire region was described as being short of water, filled with bandits and a likely graveyard for invading armies that would 'die of starvation and hunger'. While such testimonies pose important questions about their aims and audience, the fact that the ties that had held the Gupta empire together dissolved quickly in the course of the late sixth century tells its own story about the fragility of states that seemed to be well organised, stratified and resourceful.[53]

It was perhaps no coincidence, therefore, that the beneficiaries of this age of upheaval were societies, peoples and cultures that were better able to adapt or take advantage of opportunities – such as Angles and Saxons, who translated roles as mercenaries in Roman Britain into political dominance, much as Slavs in the Balkans, Langobards in Italy, Berbers in North Africa, Arabs on desert fringes in Palestine, Syria and Iraq, Avars in the Pontic steppe and Huns in South Asia found their bargaining positions improved to the point that they too transitioned from being marginalised groups to becoming significant and even dominant in their own right.[54]

Naturally, there were different trends in different regions, but the general picture showed the vulnerability of hierarchical, urbanised societies. In some parts of Europe, for example, notably the north-west, the impact of the downturn of conditions was mitigated by the fact that the climate had become steadily colder and wetter in the previous decades: this had led to innovations in plough types better able to cope with heavier soils and also to the adoption of more diverse forms of food production that depended less on agricultural cultivation and more on pastoralism. As some scholars have also pointed out, recurrent barbarian invasions and attacks had broken down extended supply networks and encouraged communities to become both more localised and more self-sufficient. This provided obvious buffers against the kinds of difficulties faced by urban populations that were poorly placed to develop coping strategies in the face of pressure on food supplies.[55]

Dealing with shortages was a source of concern in many parts of a world that went through a seismic set of shocks in the mid-sixth century. In Gupta-era India, for example, scholars like Varāhamihira wrote about the dangers that accompanied dust veils in the sky, warning that if these lasted for three or four days, 'food grains and liquids [and] juicy substances will be destroyed'; if it lasted for longer, 'there will be mutinies in the armies of kings'.[56] Jain texts like the *Titthogālī*, produced around the same time, provide apocalyptic visions of a world dominated by floods, drought, famine and persecution and offer insights into this tumultuous period, even though, as some scholars note, it is not entirely clear how much we can rely on such accounts as historical testimonies and to what extent they are echoes and responses to other works in circulation at the time – in this case, the *Mahābhārata* in particular.[57]

The anxieties about food shortages and political dislocation were topics of great interest to Chinese historians and especially to those seeking to influence the decisions of emperors. Wu Jing, a court official in the Tang dynasty writing in the early eighth century, was scathing about how the Emperor Wen (r. 581–604) oversaw famine following a great drought and 'did not permit the distribution of supplies to relieve the people'. This was madness, wrote Wu Jing: when he died, Emperor Wen had enough granary supplies to last 'for fifty or sixty years'.[58] The fact that Emperor Wen was the founder of the Sui dynasty – from whom the Tang seized power – means that we should take Wu's comments with a pinch of salt. But his aim here was plain: in times of environmental catastrophe, the role of the ruler was to plan for shortages and to distribute emergency aid when needed. There was no point stockpiling too much; but, equally, enough should be set aside for when problems arose. If this advice was not taken, it was inevitable that there would be 'peril and ruin'. Needless to say, those who could help the Emperor 'preserve the realm' had vitally important roles to play. What mattered more was the lesson that had been learned: the stability of empires depended on their resilience through times of climate stress. Famine did not just kill the poor or drive anger towards the ruler; it brought regimes down.[59]

The effects of turbulence were also severe in Teotihuacan in the Valley of Mexico, which went through a period of intense social, political and religious upheaval in the middle of the sixth century that included the desecration and smashing of idols and artefacts of the deities related to rainfall, as well as systematic destruction of temples and palace complexes. This is usually interpreted as a case of popular dissatisfaction with the response of the elite to solving problems and in particular with the pressures of declining rainfall levels – and furthermore is usually correlated with the volcanic eruptions of the mid-sixth century.[60] Certainly, the fact that building work stopped elsewhere in Central America, most notably across the territories controlled by the Maya around 540, suggests that the scale of disruption caused by volcanic eruptions was both immediate and spectacular.[61]

By c.600, Teotihuacan had become a shadow of its former self, while parallel state structures elsewhere like Monte Albán and Río Viejo entered periods of decline too, as populations drifted away from large cities to smaller urban settlements, and thus to local elites with lower ambitions, less expansive geographic connections and more limited resources. The archaeological record attests to a major diminution in distribution networks of goods like obsidian, a volcanic glass that was prized for its utility and rarity and for its role in ritual. New valley centres emerged at locations like Lambityeco, Jalieza and El Palmillo, but none came close to the scale of the large cities that had dominated Mesoamerican cultures in the past.[62]

In South America, the eruptions marked a new phase in a devastating series of environmental and climatic changes made all the more difficult by increasingly frequent and severe El Niño events in the sixth century characterised by alternating patterns of severe flooding followed by long periods of drought. There are indications that an El Niño event had begun to cause problems of aridity and depletion of marine supplies as warm, nutrient-poor water displaced the rich cold waters off the coast of South America, with radiocarbon dating of clamshells suggesting that this had begun even before the eruptions – although dating of marine data needs to be handled with caution.[63]

Across the regions usually described as part of the Moche culture, the results during the sixth century were dramatic, as irrigation systems were overwhelmed, soil damaged and food production underwent precipitous decline.[64] Windblown sands proved almost impossible to deal with in some locations on the north coast and in the Cerro Blanco complex, where the city was overwhelmed – and further affected by one or more major pluvial events.[65] Competition for water and food was such that communities took steps to protect themselves by building fortifications, for example in the Jequetepeque and Zaña valleys.[66] As in Teotihuacan, reactions against the elites shaped artistic and religious responses, with the reversion to archaic iconographic motifs best understood as a turn to ancestors for help at a time of turmoil.[67] Some cultures, however, adapted better than others, with Wari and Tiwanku expanding from the central highlands of the Andes around the end of the sixth century and building empires – or at least establishing cultural supremacy – that covered much of the coastal region and interior of what is now Peru, Bolivia and northern Chile.[68]

This was a time of change in many parts of the world. For example, the Christian Aksumite kingdom that dominated the Horn of Africa and what is now Ethiopia, Eritrea and eastern Sudan had intensified contact with the state of Ḥimyar across the Red Sea at the start of the sixth century, sponsoring an expansion of Christian churches in the Arabian peninsula and interfering in politics across the region by installing rulers who were sympathetic to if not directly controlled by Aksum.[69]

By the 550s, however, things in Aksum looked bleak: grand buildings fell into disrepair and in so far as they were used at all seem to have become ad hoc shelters for what one scholar has called 'squatters'.[70]

Quarries were abruptly abandoned, pointing to the cessation of major construction projects, while the reduction in the quality of the coinage, both in metallic terms and those of production, provides another indicator of a state that had been vibrant, expansive and ambitious entering a state of terminal decline.[71]

Scholars have long noted the depopulation of Aksum in the middle part of the sixth century, often linking it to problems of oversettlement and the unsustainable depletion of resources, in particular of ivory, timber and water.[72] Some have also underlined the precipitous collapse in trade across the Red Sea following the capture of Ḥimyar first by the Persians and not long afterwards by the Arabs, thus depriving Aksum of its crucial overseas markets and depressing the economy further still.[73] Aksum began to fall into a state of decay, with non-ecclesiastical buildings and monuments no longer maintained, and the political centre – to the extent that it still existed – either moving to Kubar, a town whose location remains unknown, or possibly to a mobile capital that moved as the ruler progressed through his territories.[74]

Climate conditions may have played a decisive role in the depressed circumstances in which Aksum found itself, and indeed may explain many of the extraordinary changes that took place in this period in Africa, Europe and Asia. As we have seen, the dust veil of the volcanic eruptions put pressure on food production and in many cases contributed to environmental, material and social stress. It had another effect that was perhaps even more fundamental in shaping the revolutions of the sixth century: exceptionally cool weather created unusual opportunities for rat survival and flea reproduction, which in turn resulted in an outbreak of plague. The need to support crop failures with greater shipments of food across the Mediterranean may also have provided a surge in connectivity that resulted in an intensification of networks that enabled the rapid spread of disease. And finally the suppression of sunlight may have played an important role too, namely inducing a deficiency in vitamin D which is crucial to the human immune system and especially to its ability to respond to bacterial infections. These factors now dovetailed to create the perfect conditions for a major pandemic.[75]

The first written reports of plague come from the Egyptian port of Pelusium, a key node linking the Mediterranean with the Red Sea and

Indian Ocean. From the summer of 541, disease took hold, spreading to Gaza and across North Africa, before reaching Constantinople a few months later and then spreading 'over the whole world', according to the Byzantine author Procopius. The disease came close to annihilating the entire human race, noted the author, who claimed that at its peak plague was killing 10,000 people a day in the imperial capital. Bodies were left in heaps, as there were not enough people to bury them.[76] The Justinianic plague, as it has become known, is purported to have killed millions – tens of millions in fact, if not more, with mortality rates of perhaps 50 per cent of the population of the Mediterranean as a whole.[77]

As more recent experience has shown, even small rises in mortality levels can create major economic compression and in some cases can overwhelm governments. Disruption does not only come from large numbers of deaths, in other words, but also from dislocation of trade, transport and communication networks.[78] Nevertheless, estimates about the extent of the Justinianic plague have come under sustained attack in recent years, with scholars arguing that a range of evidence including pollen data, papyri, inscriptions and coin minting do not point to major social, demographic or economic change. According to these scholars, the impact of the disease was simply 'inconsequential'.[79]

Others have pointed out that even if there were high levels of mortality, population losses were not universal, but rather were highly localised and of marginal consequence.[80] Such highly sceptical assessments are certainly eye-catching. More sanguine assessment suggests that while it is certainly true that estimates of mortality levels involve guesswork and leaps of faith, there are good reasons to suspect that the plague did enormous damage. One of the most compelling is that multiple related but distinct plague strains from this period can be identified in France, Spain, Bavaria and even in Cambridgeshire: the fact that the disease took hold in isolated, rural locations is telling – and suggests that if plague spread in marginal, lightly populated settings, then it must have been immensely damaging in densely inhabited cities and towns.[81] Furthermore, the imperial authorities in Constantinople issued laws in the early 540s that sought to impose controls on wages, with some workers 'demanding prices double or triple what was formerly customary', which fits naturally alongside what we know about later effects of high-mortality pandemics on the labour force – namely a sharp contraction in the number of workers following large numbers of deaths. Other emergency measures taken in Constantinople likewise point strongly to a state desperately trying to shore up its finances at a time of sudden and extreme pressure.[82]

Furthermore, there are several indicators of panic and breakdown. One comes from the ending of public services such as organised rubbish collection in Roman provinces in the Levant.[83] It has been suggested too that in the Negev Highlands, the decline of viticulture and of luxury 'Gaza wine' which provided the economic basis for settlement in this region resulted not from later Islamic conquests, but from challenging climate conditions and more importantly from population contraction caused by plague and from shortages of the manpower required to plant, harvest and process the wine.[84]

A similar problem seems to have been responsible for the collapse of the Marib dam in what is now Yemen towards the end of the sixth century, which caused a flood that 'overwhelmed the lands, gardens, edifices and homes until the inhabitants of the country had perished and its citizens been wiped out'. According to one later author, the dam's failure resulted from the lack of maintenance in general and from the reduction in the size of the workforce needed to prevent its deterioration.[85]

Genetic studies of populations in the eastern Mediterranean and the Near East reveal mutations that make them more susceptible to autoinflammatory disease and as a result offer heightened resistance to *Yersinia pestis*, the bacterium that causes plague. That genomic reconstructions are consistent with the Justinianic plague, with the Black Death of the 1340s and regular occurrences thereafter, not only suggests that the outbreak of the sixth century left a genetic imprint but that this was conferred as a result of widespread exposure to infection by those who survived the pandemic.[86]

A very dramatic decline in the black rat population of Europe around this time may be the result of the pandemic, although it may also be that cooling temperatures or the breakdown of communication and trade networks in western Europe and later in the Balkans influenced the population size of these and other pests; or, of course, a combination of some or all of these factors may explain the dominant genetic impact of a second wave of rat introduction to temperate Europe starting in the eighth to tenth centuries.[87] Either way, plague did only affect humans

– but changed the distribution and size of rat colonies across many parts of Europe too.

The devastation that the pandemic wreaked may have spread to the Congo rainforest in West Africa, which saw catastrophic population collapse that was broadly coincidental with the Justinianic plague. Communities that had been present for many centuries disappeared both rapidly and entirely, save for a few scattered communities.[88] Although genomic evidence points to a Central Asian origin for the plague pathogen, groundbreaking new research is showing that there were deaths from plague in multiple locations in Europe years and perhaps even decades before the pandemic took hold in the 540s.[89] It may be that plague spread in Africa before it did so in the Mediterranean and elsewhere, though more research will be needed to determine if that was the case, or if plague was indeed a cause of catastrophic demographic decline in Congo or elsewhere in Africa.[90]

What matters more, then, than the original source of the plague strain are the routes it took and the timing of the transition from small clusters of plague victims to a pandemic that produced mass casualties. It may be no coincidence, for example, that the disease was first tracked in North Africa near the mouth of the Nile and that evidence from the Aksumite kingdom also shows significant demographic contraction in precisely this period. Some sources talk of plague arriving 'from the land of Kush' as well as from Ḥimyar, which suggests transmission through the Red Sea from sources in Central Asia or China via maritime or land trade routes. That plague outbreaks took place in Persia only after it had struck further west, and that epidemic disease in Chinese societies only struck decades later, suggests that it was the disease climate and wider climate conditions in the Mediterranean and Red Sea that provided the ideal incubator for the disease to establish itself.[91]

As one recent commentator has noted, however devastating the 'twin catastrophes' of severe climatic change and plague were, they did not lead to the collapse of the Roman empire. Indeed, they did not even bring down Justinian's regime – or topple the Emperor himself, though he may well have caught the disease and survived it, according to an ingenious reading of coins issued in this period showing the ruler with a classic boil on his neck filled with infected pus.[92]

While it is important to note that there is considerable evidence for continuity in many regions in the Mediterranean economy and notably in the Sasanian empire, which seems to have been unequivocally expanding throughout the sixth century, most indicators suggest major transformations resulted from the pandemic.[93] Of course, significant population decline would have had implications for centralised governments, resulting in lower productivity, reduced tax receipts and diminished ability to fund large-scale projects.[94] This of course affected the operation of the state; but ironically, as the evidence of Justinian's attempts to curb wage inflation implies, many do better in a shrinking economy as they are able to negotiate or acquire better rewards and status for themselves.[95] As we have seen before, 'decline and fall' means different things for different people.

The question marks about the effects of plague are part of a broad and sometimes bad-tempered debate between contemporary scholars – especially in the case of the Roman economy.[96] What is perhaps clearer is that the middle decades of the sixth century saw a series of major social and political changes in many parts of the world in which climate and disease environments were factors that in some cases aggravated or catalysed existing socio-economic trends.

For example, detailed work on resettlement patterns in sixth-century Scandinavia and the Baltic reveals widespread instances of land being abandoned and of shifts from grain production to animal husbandry. These were responses to a complex set of circumstances that included adaptation to a colder climate which began with the eruptions of the 530s and persisted for more than a century in the northern hemisphere. They were also responses to the impact of plague and the stagnation and collapse of trading networks that accompanied the waning of Roman authority in northern Europe – circumstances that fundamentally changed the dynamics of markets, altered economic and cultural horizons and transformed land ownership and labour relations.[97] Over time, this brought about a rise of large-scale land ownership and the creation of substantial estates that led to the emergence of a new 'super elite'. If this did not provide the basis for the Viking Age, it was certainly a precondition of its emergence.[98]

According to some scholars, the traumas of the mid-sixth century also help explain psychological, emotional and religious changes in Europe and beyond. For example, it has been noted that the conceptual development of the Virgin Mary as the protector of Constantinople evolved from this period, with some questioning if this was connected, directly or indirectly, with plague.[99] Others have noted that disease, bad weather, military setbacks and earthquakes in the mid-sixth century prompted heightened concern about the imminent end of the world – which continued and even strengthened in later decades even as it was patently obvious that such fears remained unfulfilled and unfounded.[100]

Gregory of Tours wrote of floods that were so bad that it was impossible to sow grain, and recounts earthquakes, possible meteorite strikes, hailstorms and fires that were 'stirred up by God'. His warnings that 'There will be plagues, famines and earthquakes in various places, and false Christs and false prophets will rise up and they will make signs and prodigies in the sky' reflect an obvious interest not only in severe climate events but in how to interpret them.[101] For Gregory, it seemed clear: these events marked 'the beginnings of the pains' that Christ warned would presage the end of time.[102]

Apocalyptic prophecies that foretold the end of time were not just a fundamental part of the Judaic and Christian tradition but a recurring one, too. Even before the challenges of the mid-sixth century, fears about the end of the world seem to have been rising with some intensity. Gloomy ideas transmitted along trade routes, particularly within the eastern Roman empire. As we shall see, they fell on particularly fertile ground in Arabia and the Middle East. But it was perhaps no coincidence that pagan communities as far away as Scandinavia began to offer precious metals such as gold and silver as part of sacrificial offerings in desperate efforts to ward off what seemed to be imminent and final catastrophe.[103]

Such cases can seem highly persuasive at first glance, but it is worth stressing that this source material is complex and needs to be placed within the context of many other works with varied and different conceptual formulations at this time which do not talk of the impending apocalypse.[104] Nevertheless, there is compelling evidence from many periods and regions that bouts of existential angst and crisis could be important in recalibrating, re-evaluating or strengthening ideas about the divine.[105] Some have noted that Buddhism made inroads in Korea and Japan precisely when the dust veil created by volcanic eruptions was at its height.[106] The expansion of Christianity into Central Asia and the conversion of steppe peoples, meanwhile, was specifically linked by contemporary accounts to the time of plague and to remedies that had proved effective: nomads who had had 'the symbol of the cross tattooed in black on their foreheads' were asked by envoys from Constantinople sent to form an alliance why this had been done; there had been a plague, they replied, 'and some Christians among them had suggested doing this [to bring divine protection] and from that time their country had been safe'.[107]

Recent work on palaeoclimatological proxies and historical records from central Italy in the sixth century reveal not only a period of very wet conditions in the later sixth century that result from a negative phase of the North Atlantic Oscillation, but also a sharp increase in reports of water miracles in accounts of saints' lives. As well as showing how climate events were reflected and interpreted by contemporary authors, these also represent – intentionally or otherwise – a means of increasing the already growing authority of bishops, monks and the Church more broadly.[108]

Traumatic single events and periods of climate shock not only shaped beliefs; in other words, they also delivered opportunities for the expansion of institutions – such as the Christian Church – and for the consolidation of authority and power for those who could offer explanations for, and protection against, future catastrophe. That proved to be significant in the early part of the seventh century when another sharp, swift downturn in temperatures across the steppes of Central Asia played a part in another set of revolutions that once again had far-reaching consequences.

II

The Golden Age of Empire
(c.600–c.900)

The orderly government of kingdoms is based upon religious beliefs, good manners, law and order.

al-Iṣṭakhrī, *Kitāb Masālik al-mamālik* (tenth century)

The first twenty-five years of the seventh century were a period of extraordinary political instability across Europe, Africa and much of Asia. The Roman and Persian empires engaged in a phase of almost continuous warfare that saw many of the greatest cities across the Middle East and North Africa change hands – and both empires embarking on military campaigns that not only brought their rival to their knees but threatened to destroy them. The swings in fortune were not just rapid but momentous: in 626, the Persian army was massed by the walls of Constantinople, with many citizens cowering inside the great city fearing the worst; just a few months later, after mounting one of the most spectacular rearguard actions in history, the Emperor Heraclius had advanced eastwards at lightning speed and crushed a large Persian force at Nineveh in what is now Iraq.[1]

Within a few weeks, the Roman army reached Dastagerd, home of the favourite palace of the Persian shah Khusro II, capturing an enormous quantity of booty that included textiles and fabrics, sugar, spices, silver and all sorts of valuable equipment, and recovering 300 military standards that had been taken in battles in the past. The confrontation between Rome and Persia had been couched on both sides in ominous, apocalyptic terms as a fight between light and darkness.² News of the advance and the overthrow of Shah Khusro by factions at his court reached Constantinople and was framed in biblical terms: 'the arrogant Khusro, opponent of God' had fallen and had been 'cast down to the depths of the earth, and his memory is utterly exterminated from the earth'. Such was the lot of the man who had spoken unjustly, arrogantly and with contempt 'against our Lord Jesus Christ the true God and his undefiled Mother, our blessed Lady, Mother of God and our ever-Virgin Mary'.³

It was no coincidence, then, that before returning to the imperial capital, Heraclius went to Jerusalem to stage a victory procession and the solemn restoration of the True Cross that had been looted by Shah Khusro. It was a day of great celebration, accompanied by 'the sound of weeping and wailing'; tears of joy 'flowed from the awesome fervour of the emotion' of onlookers who were so overcome that they were not able to sing hymns of thanks.⁴

The key to the Roman triumph had been an alliance made with the powerful ruler of the Türk empire which in the mid-sixth century had established itself across much of the steppe that ran from the northern lip of the Black Sea in the west through to the plains of Mongolia in the east. In 626, Heraclius had reached a comprehensive agreement with Ton Yabghu, *qaghan* of the western half of the lands controlled by the Türks at the time. Heraclius had been compelled to concede astonishing terms to cement this agreement. These were confirmed in an extraordinary meeting between the Emperor and the Qaghan during which the former removed a crown from his own head and placed it on that of the Türk ruler, who was then presented with elaborate gifts for him and his retinue, and shown a picture of the Emperor's daughter who was offered up in marriage.⁵ A marriage tie between a member of the imperial family and a barbarian nomad ruler was unprecedented; it demonstrated both the weakness and desperation of the Emperor's position and the importance of the support of the Türks against the Persians.⁶

Winning over the Türks as allies was crucial in turning the tide in favour of the Romans and against the Persians. The nomad grouping had risen in prominence and power around the same time as the climate crisis of the mid-sixth century. Quite how and why it did so is not entirely clear, although to judge from other expansions of nomadic states, the correlation of higher-than-normal levels of rainfall and a consequential improvement in the carrying capacity of pastureland on the one hand and an increase in the sizes of flocks and herds on the other may have been significant.[7] This seems to have been the case on this occasion – but it also mattered that the Türks had been able to reinforce their superiority through the extraction of tribute from sedentary states, through control of trade routes and networks and through the sale of animals, particularly horses.[8]

By around 550, the Türks had been able to establish a dominant position on the steppes, either absorbing their nomad rivals or displacing them eastwards into the Korean peninsula, westwards towards and beyond the Danube or southwards into India.[9] These included the Avars, who had streamed into the Balkans and were later sought out by Khusro II in the 620s as partners for the assault on Constantinople in a sign of the military capabilities of nomadic forces, their organisational ability and the important role they played in the politics of this period.[10]

Something similar was happening in East Asia at precisely the same time as the dramatic events in Persia and beyond were playing out. In 618, an aristocrat named Li Yuan led an uprising capitalising on antagonism towards the Sui dynasty, whose expensive infrastructure projects, such as the extension of what ultimately became the Grand Canal that links Beijing with Hangzhou, along with poorly thought through campaigns against Goguryeo in Korea, absorbed financial resources, demanded significant manpower and proved highly unpopular. The period of uncertainty that followed presented an opportunity for Illig, the Türk *qaghan* in the east, and notionally the supreme leader of the entire Türk confederation, who was keen to take steps against the Sui, whose wall-building efforts (which became part of the Great Wall system) closed off the best pasture and agricultural lands to the nomads.

In the 620s, the Türks were plundering northern China with abandon. In 626, the *qaghan* and his forces reached the Wei River, threatening to strike at Chang'an (modern Xian), the capital city of the newly established Tang dynasty under the Emperor Gaozu – Li's chosen regnal name. Perhaps the Türks considered an all-out assault on the city, one of the largest in the world at the time. More likely, the invading force were seeking to extract a hefty ransom in exchange for withdrawing; this was duly paid and the invaders retreated.[11]

This was the high point for the Türks in the east. Within four years, the vast confederation had disintegrated, crushed by a huge Tang army that advanced into the grasslands of the steppe and inflicted a devastating defeat.[12] Having played a crucial part in the defeat of the Persians, the Türks in the west also experienced a rapid decline, falling into difficulties in the 630s before disintegrating and paving the way for a reorganisation of peoples on the steppes north of the Black and Caspian seas. The suddenness of the collapse of the western Türk empire, mirroring that of the east, was astounding. One moment, both had been receiving tributes by the cartload; the next, they had disappeared into irrelevance.[13]

The dramatic changes in fortunes have often been ascribed to internal divisions within the Türk world. In the west, the murder of Ton Yabghu, the dominant figure on the steppes, is usually seen as instrumental in prompting a period of instability, internal competition and decline.[14] In the east too, friction within the leadership was seen as a factor in the precipitous reversal on the steppes, as contemporaries noted. A report produced for the Tang Emperor in 629 by Zhang Gongjin, the ambitious commander of the northern city of Daizhou, specifically drew attention to the rivalries as a source of opportunity. In this report, Zhang argued that the nomads were unusually vulnerable to a counter-attack and urged the Emperor to take advantage of favourable circumstances. These included their rivals' over-reliance on non-Türks, disaffection among subordinate tribes and opposition to Türk overlordship by some local populations. Another reason for their weakness, said Zhang, was a sudden period of harsh climate conditions – and the fragilities that were likely to arise as a result.[15]

New research on the tree rings from Asia, Europe, the Americas and Tasmania as well as on ice-core evidence from the Arctic and Antarctic suggests that a major eruption took place in 626, with the lack of Antarctic signal being highly suggestive of a volcano located in northern latitudes. The fact that the eruption's sulphate anomaly in the record in northern Greenland was the largest of any in the last 2,000 years (with the exception of Laki in the later eighteenth century, which we will assess later) suggests that it was responsible for a sudden drop in temperatures in the Altai mountains in Central Asia (as well as elsewhere) in the years that followed, with reconstructions indicating a cooling of as much as -3.4 °C at its peak.[16]

As well as cooling temperatures, dust veils had an impact on vegetation growth. The effects would not have been uniform: regions and locations with finely balanced ecosystems or ones near the limits of their exploitation only need small modifications to produce a cascading effect. The steppe belts were a perfect example, especially following benign climatic periods that had enabled increases in flock and herd sizes. Moreover, the effects could be exacerbated by changes to sea surface temperature in the tropical Pacific and the North Atlantic that shaped rainfall patterns in Central Asia and may have been a further aggravating factor.[17]

This helps explain the many references in the Chinese sources to unusually harsh weather, including heavy snowfall and droughts that caused food shortages and famine across large areas of central and even southern China. While it is not possible to quantify precisely what this meant for agricultural production, perhaps more important here was the impact on the steppes and on livestock in particular: modest increases in snowfall can impact mortality levels as a result of greater difficulties in finding suitable food sources.[18] These problems are made dramatically worse when they follow drought, partly because animals have been weakened by malnutrition.[19] In the first century AD, for example, the Book of the Later Han states that 'two thirds of the people and domestic animals' of the Xiongnu nomads – predecessors of the Türks – died following a short but sustained period of drought.[20]

It was not just sedentary states, therefore, that could prove to be fragile when faced with a set of circumstances that ratcheted up pressure and risk. In modern times, unusually cold periods have resulted in precipitous losses of livestock, numbering in their millions.[21] Such disasters have often triggered social consequences stemming from economic distress, including increased poverty and mass migration.[22] In the case of the Türks, it is not hard to see how the build-up of challenges identified by Zhang Gongjin combined to create a cocktail of crises. Livestock mortality, food shortages and harsh climate conditions helped unweave the ties that bound tribal groupings together – undermining the authority of the leader and causing the confederation to splinter.

The breakdown of this system could happen rapidly, in other words. As one contemporary report put it, 'the Türks rise and fall solely according to their sheep and horses'. A decline in livestock numbers, especially if sudden and dramatic, could have very serious consequences for the fortunes of individual nomad groups within the wider confederation, with the impact felt most keenly by those of the lowest status and means.[23] As such, shocks, climatic or otherwise, could suddenly make what seemed to be resilient and powerful structures brittle, providing opportunities for subordinate groups and ambitious individuals to undermine what has been aptly described as an 'inherent instability of the system of alliances and hierarchies that made a centralized leadership relatively weak'.[24]

When a massive Tang army marched to exploit the situation in the winter of 629–30, the Türks fell back into the grasslands but were caught off guard by a surprise attack that led to heavy casualties, many prisoners being taken including the *qaghan*, who spent his last years in captivity before reportedly dying of a broken heart. Just as this served as the breaking of the Türk empire in East Asia, it was the making of the Tang emperors, who were to rule much of what is now China for the next three centuries. After seizing the throne in 626, Emperor Taizong had taken the traditional titles of 'Son of Heaven' and 'August Emperor'. The dramatic change on the steppes significantly enhanced his legitimacy and strengthened his hold on power. It also emboldened the emperor to add to his titles. 'I am the Son of Heaven of the Great Tang,' he announced in a ceremony in front of the imperial palace in Chang'an. From now on, he announced, '[I] will also attend to the affairs of the Heavenly Qaghan.' New seals were created to stamp all correspondence with rulers and peoples to the north and the west of territories directly under his control. He had not just defeated the nomads, in other words; he now claimed to be their overlord.[25]

To the west too, the western Türks experienced a time of turbulence, characterised by uprisings, revolts and assassinations of senior figures, including the supreme leader, Ton Yabghu.[26] Local rulers in locations like Turfan, Kucha and Samarkand refused to pay tribute as they had done in the past, and opted to look instead to the Tang court for protection. The scale of this upheaval was remarkable. But so too was its speed; when the famous Chinese monk and traveller Xuanzang visited the western Türks in 630 and described the *qaghan* as wearing green silk robes and being surrounded by an entourage dressed in embroidered finery and lavish textiles, he would have assumed he was witnessing an empire at its apogee; in fact, he was present months before its collapse.[27]

Xuanzang was in fact surprised by his reception, not because of how alien and strange it seemed to him, but because the ordered and structured ceremonial element that he witnessed was similar to that of the world he came from. Symbolic displays of power, paying obeisance to the ruler while kneeling, the grasping of feet and touching the ground with one's head were all customs that were widely practised not only on the steppes but at courts from one end of Eurasia to the other, linking the Mediterranean to the Middle East, East Asia and the steppes of Central Asia. This was an interconnected world, in other words, far removed from crude formulations put forward by writers at the time (and in the modern world) of sedentary states and a chaotic nomadic world. Rituals and symbols were not uniform, of course, but the boundaries of these worlds were porous, flexible and adaptive.[28]

The upheavals in the steppe world opened doors for the Tang, who expanded into Korea as well as westwards, and deftly cemented their gains by reshaping ceremonies to include foreigners and honour their status; this served to incorporate and celebrate new members of the empire rather than treating them as subordinates. As it happens, this aped how nomads themselves often dealt with the absorption of new peoples (and stands in stark contrast to the European age of empire in Africa and the Americas in particular, as well as in Asia).[29]

This was important too at the other end of the Eurasian land mass where the tumultuous changes on the steppe, combined with the epic confrontation between Rome and Persia, opened the door for the dawn of a new age. Extraordinary resources of time, manpower and money had been poured into a war that had gone on for some two decades. The fighting not only had an impact on cities and markets in the Mediterranean, Levant and Persia, but depressed the economies of networks and regions that were connected to them, such as in southern Arabia.[30] The effects were felt further afield too, with some scholars linking a sudden and sharp decline in much coveted garnet in Europe at this time, which came from South Asian sources, with the dislocation of trade in general and in the Red Sea in particular.[31]

One of those to offer explanations for the seismic changes was a young merchant named Muḥammad, who had gathered a small but loyal following around himself. His warnings of imminent doomsday struck an obvious chord in the context of more challenging economic conditions along trade routes in the Ḥijāz, the continuous and ominous fighting to the north and apocalyptic propaganda in both Rome and Persia – although it is clear that there was substantial resistance to his radical message of the need for the purity, unity and loyalty that would win God's favour, as well as to the deviation from other religions that were well established in Arabia.

The decisive moment for the Prophet Muḥammad and his companions came in 628, when in a masterstroke of political accommodation he reached agreement with the ruling elite in Mecca, in which he decreed that the direction of prayer should not be towards Jerusalem but towards Mecca itself, while the Ka'ba, previously a pagan shrine, was designated the focal point within the city.[32] This paved the way for reconciliation between different factions in Arabia and laid the basis for a common identity that would provide an umbrella under which all the different peoples of the region could gather. The agreement, enshrined in the Treaty of al-Ḥudaybiya, proved to be turning point not only for Mecca, the surrounding region and Muḥammad himself; it was one of the major turning points in world history.

As it happened, the timing could not have been better. For one thing, in addition to the military setbacks, Persia was also experiencing a virulent outbreak of plague, with many being killed in the capital city, Ctesiphon – with the re-emergence of the disease perhaps linked to the eruption of 626 and the associated ecological and pathogenic conditions that followed.[33]

Muḥammad, his movement and followers emerged into a world that had been scarred by warfare and disease, by economic contraction and by a collapsing global order of sedentary states that were exhausted, and of nomadic confederations whose ties were dissolving. His own thinking had been apocalyptic too, as he warned that the time was fast approaching when the sun would be extinguished, the stars would fall, the seas would boil, the skies would be torn in two and graves would spill open, throwing out their cadavers. The Final Judgement was nigh, warned Muḥammad: the virtuous would go to paradise; the wicked to hell.[34]

As it happened, Muḥammad and his followers emerged to be the prime beneficiaries, creating a vast new empire in the process. But it might not have turned out that way. Around 630, with Rome and Persia teetering, economically and militarily exhausted, the scene was set for the nomads to expand their dominance from the steppes to create one of the greatest empires in history. The Türks held the fate of the Roman empire in their hands; Persia was teetering on the brink from their crushing defeat and the ravages of disease; in East Asia, the Tang were vassals in all but name.

The timing, then, of the collapse of the Türks stalled what might have been the creation of an empire even greater in extent than that of the Mongols, who were able to do what the Türks did not in the thirteenth century. With a different set of climatological and ecological developments precisely in the late 620s and early 630s, it might have been the Altaic languages of the steppes and the devout Buddhism of Ton Yabghu that spread quickly in all directions across the whole of Asia, and perhaps even across Europe and North Africa. The bulk of those prizes now went instead to Muḥammad and his followers – and to the Arabic language and to Islam.

The 630s and the decades that followed saw the explosive expansion of Arab armies from the Ḥijāz across the Middle East through North Africa into southern Europe and deep into Central Asia. The result was a wide spread not only of Muslim beliefs and teachings but of Arabic culture. This included the Arabic language, of course; but ideas about music, poetry and fashion spread too, as well as about art and architecture.

Arab elites in the Iberian peninsula harked back to homelands, building palaces and monuments, and commissioned historical accounts and complex genealogies of early Arab leaders with the result that Spain became 'more Arab than Arabia'.[35] One poet spoke to the single palm tree in his garden, lamenting that both were a 'stranger in the west, far from our Orient home' – recognition that ecosystems and people alike did not find it easy to adapt to new locations.[36]

The creation of an enormous new world that bonded together the core territories of the Persian empire stretching from the Caucasus and Asia Minor in the west as far as the Himalayas in the east along with some of the richest and most important parts of the Roman empire – including the breadbasket of Egypt, the harbours of the Levant and a heavy influence in the Mediterranean – also underpinned environmental and ecological changes that had far-reaching consequences.

This was partly the result of the spread of irrigation techniques and agricultural technologies across lands conquered and controlled by the Arabs; but the diffusion of crops and cultivars was no less important in knitting together a world that was not only culturally joined together but also linked through tastes for specific foods, flavours and recipes.[37] Hypotheses about the extent, nature and footprint of this 'Islamic Green Revolution' are hotly contested, with some pointing out that foods and crop species that are often linked with the spread of Islam had been grown long beforehand in other parts of the world.[38] Evidently, a measured evaluation is dependent on assessing archaeobotanical evidence, a discipline which is still an emerging area of scholarly research.[39]

What was perhaps more important than the availability of new crops was the fact that the new Arab empire provided two things that had been in short supply in preceding decades: peace and manpower. While the politics of succession at the core of the Arab leadership were bloody and brutal affairs, with three of the first four successors of Muḥammad being assassinated, elsewhere the new masters were careful to leave communities and populations largely alone and unscathed – as long as they paid their taxes. Some complained, stating that financial obligations trebled under the new overlords, although it is not clear whether such claims can be taken at face value.[40] For the most part, however, transitions appear to have been smooth and uncontested.

Relying on officials and administrators who were familiar with market practices, agricultural yields and financial expectations was a key part of this success. In Roman and Persian territories, provincial bureaucrats were retained, something that presumably left the local population sanguine as long as their property, rights and beliefs were left untouched.[41] In Central Asia, the Arabs inherited a system which had been developed to good effect by the Türks and which relied on local urban elites who used their positions to protect their own interests.[42] This too was largely left intact by the new masters.[43]

Remarkably, although there was regular internal friction within the world that was built by Muḥammad, his heirs and successors – who held the title of caliph – competition and threats from beyond were minimal for centuries. While the battle of Talas in 751 soon came to be regarded by commentators as marking the end of Muslim expansion following a heavy defeat by Tang forces, it was the mountain ranges of the Pamirs and Himalayas that acted as the most effective insulation to keep the state (the caliphate) from any serious pressure from the east. In the west, likewise, there was little by way of challenge. Expeditionary forces that moved north from Spain into France found limited fruits worth picking; the only place where there was pushback and rivalry was in Asia Minor, where the eastern Roman – or Byzantine – empire hung on for dear life and occasionally mounted a show of bravado. However, as archaeological evidence from Anatolia shows, from the middle of the seventh century onwards, regular raiding, coupled with the rising costs of military defences, led not only to long-term economic decline but to lowered living standards and falling life expectancy which created a vicious circle downwards that took centuries to correct.[44]

In contrast, in the lands under the control of the Arabs, a boom time followed, with cities expanding, swelled by rural workers migrating from the countryside. This did not just enhance civic life; it also fuelled greater economic and demographic growth both within cities but also between them as old and new networks began to throng with people, goods and ideas. These developments sparked change in other regions as new connections and opportunities emerged.

For example, the lands to the north – steppe belts fanning out across thousands of kilometres – flourished in parallel, with the Khazars thriving as a result of growing demand for animals and their by-products as well as from trade across the territories they controlled directly or indirectly through networks of subordinate tribes. To the south-east, meanwhile, Indian Ocean trade networks began to blossom too in conjunction with stable and prosperous regimes both in the Middle East and in East Asia. One prime beneficiary was the Śrīvijaya state which grew from Palembang on the island of Sumatra to control the Melaka Straits – a key artery for east–west trade.

By the seventh century, Śrīvijaya was a leading centre for Buddhist scholars and scholarship, and purportedly home to a thousand monks.[45] Its political and economic ambitions now grew rapidly, as attested by inscriptions in Old Malay that talk of conquest of other coastal towns, often at the cost of considerable bloodshed.[46] Scholars debate the nature of the Śrīvijaya and whether it is best understood as an empire, a kingdom or a chiefdom, partly because of the complexity of the relationship between the ruler (the *datu*) and the *orang laut* – the coastal peoples who were co-opted and incentivised to expand the reach of the state.[47]

What is less in doubt is that levels of exchange across the Indonesian archipelago, South and South-East Asia began to intensify as horizons narrowed, contacts rose and goods moved in increasing volumes through local, regional and long-distance maritime connections linking the coastlines and peoples of the Mediterranean, Red Sea, Indian Ocean, South China Sea and Pacific. From the eighth and ninth centuries, new states mushroomed across this whole region, such as at Pagan in what is now Burma, Angkor (Cambodia), Đại Việt and Champa (Vietnam) and the Chola (India), which shared similar characteristics of bureaucratic centralisation, cultural integration, theocratic kingship and territorial expansion at the expense of smaller, less robust polities as a result of forest clearing and the extension of ecological frontiers or both. The simultaneous trajectories of so many complex states were 'strange parallels', to use the term coined by one modern historian, interdependent regional powerhouses whose successes fuelled each other's continued expansion and success.[48]

The Arab conquests opened up new geographic, ecological and cultural frontiers. Drawing heavily on Greek scholars like Hippocrates and Aristotle who wrote about how the environment affected personal character, Arab writers considered the peoples that they now came into contact with thanks to their widened horizons. Slavs and Franks in western Europe, wrote al-Mas'ūdī, 'have large bodies, grotesque natures, difficult characters, limited intelligence and heavy tongues'. This was because they lived in damp and cold regions which saw near endless rain and snow, and which also explained why their skin colour was so white that it sometimes passed for blue. The lack of warmth made clear why their religious beliefs could be considered limp and wishy-washy. People living further north were even more stupid, grotesque and brutish – and because of the cold were so fat that their faces were round, making their eyes look small. Black people, meanwhile, had the 'bravery of lions and the slyness of foxes', but because of the heat had short concentration spans, although they were also very taken with dance and rhythm. It was simple, said al-Jāḥiẓ: climate shaped 'character, personal qualities, manners, speech, desires, ambitions and appearances'.[49]

The conquest of North Africa also opened up new links beyond the Sahara desert, the final frontier faced by the great Muslim empire. A key reason for this was the development of the trans-Saharan gold trade and access to the rich deposits located at the headwaters of the

Niger and Senegal rivers. Although the first written records of this trade come from Arabic texts, this region's integration into intercontinental exchange networks had occurred well before the expansion of the caliphate, with gold from West Africa underpinning Roman minting of coins in Carthage at least a century earlier.[50]

Interest in West Africa was partly shaped by reports of large reserves of resources, manpower and gold, which encouraged travellers, scholars and writers to find out more, with the results sometimes blending myth with reality. For example, many Arab authors believed that the populations of the world descended from the three sons of Noah – including those descended from the youngest, Ham, who had been cursed by his father for seeing him naked. As punishment, wrote Ibn Qutayba, God 'changed his colour and the colour of his descendants'.[51] Ham's progeny, who had been turned black, had then crossed into Africa where some settled in the east, some in the west.[52]

In fact, the story of the 'Curse of Ham' that appears in the Book of Genesis says nothing about skin colour, nor about population migrations or dispersals in Africa. Arab authors were adopting long-established Jewish and Christian tropes about blackness that became the subject of considerable discussion and speculation that extended into hypotheses about reproductive sciences.[53] The idea that black skin colour was connected to divine punishment caught hold. It did not just prove toxic, but became what one scholar has called the 'single greatest justification for Black slavery' that was to have profound consequences in later centuries.[54]

Arab geographers were nevertheless intrigued by the peoples living in sub-Saharan Africa, by their customs and behaviour – though many also paid attention to the wealth and the gold mines in the kingdoms of West Africa, and especially of Ghana, 'whose king is very powerful'.[55] Locations which were home to gold mines were strictly patrolled and access was forbidden; once extracted, gold was made into bricks and sold in towns like Sijilmāsa, on the northern edge of the Sahara, a city so rich as a result of its role as emporium that it was home to four enormous mosques and a main street so long that it took half a day to walk from one end to the other.[56]

Commentators were both curious and dismissive of religious and cultural practices – evidently in order to justify their own superiority, to emphasise the 'civilising' influence of Islam and also because development of the slave trade went hand in hand with demeaning racial caricatures. Many peoples in Africa, wrote al-Iṣṭakhrī, did not deserve lengthy descriptions: 'the orderly government of kingdoms is based upon religious beliefs, good manners, law and order, and the organisation of settled life directed by sound policy. These people lack all these qualities.'[57] It was hardly surprising, therefore, that many learned to be cautious when dealing with Arab traders: some insisted on negotiating at a distance and in using signs to reach agreements – the result, wrote one author, of 'their extreme wariness', which he equated to the 'wariness of domestic animals faced by beasts of prey'.[58] It was not hard to conclude that this trepidation was well judged given unbalanced views about race and the threat of enslavement.

By the ninth century, Muslim Arab and Berber merchants were active in the city of Gao, situated on the banks of the Niger River, involved in the trade not only of gold but of textiles and ivory too.[59] Gao's location as a crossroads was important, even if, as some scholars suggest, it should be understood as referring to a sprawl of settlements rather than to a single one.[60] The growth in population density and building across sites such as Gadei, Old Gai and Gao Saney may have been a result not only of new opportunities opened up by trans-Saharan trade, but also of variability of rainfall and flood patterns and in particular of the resultant shifts of sediment and fish stocks.[61]

Similar processes of rising connectivity can be found in the Americas around this time. This was a period of transition in the American south-west, as people of the Puebloan cultures moved from pit houses into larger, more elaborate and more permanent structures.[62] It was also a point where political powers began to concentrate under the leadership of single chiefdoms in the Mississippian cultures of the midwest, east and south-east of North America, which in turn led to competition that drove consolidation and expansion.[63]

In all these cases, the causes of change were complex, but the principle of a chain reaction seems to have been particularly important in the way entities galvanised each other. Certainly, demographic expansion was a factor, which was closely linked to the ability to grow and store food, and to cope with weather shocks or with long-term climatic changes. Likewise, stability was dependent on the emergence of organisational sophistication that had to adapt and expand as the powers and the claims of the centre grew – something that presented growing pains of its own.

This was always easier said than done, especially when it came to the relationship between population growth, consumption patterns and sustainability. A decline in both the quantity and size of land crabs in the Caribbean from the first to the sixth centuries resulted from human activity and over-exploitation, while precipitous falls in marine life, including reef fish, as a result of overharvesting likewise shows that food availability which supports increasing numbers of people can become quickly exhausted.[64] Coping with this equation normally required adaptation, new lifeways, migration – or starvation.[65]

Urban settlements too could be victims of their own success, as the case of Panjikent neatly shows. A magnificent jewel of a city in what is now Tajikistan, Panjikent was a booming centre along the Silk Roads, serving as a key point of exchange for Sogdian and other merchants, some of whom were engaged in long-distance trade in luxury goods. The city blossomed as trade grew, expanding rapidly in the fifth century and becoming home to magnificent palaces whose murals depicting scenes from the Indian epic *Mahābhārata*, from the Persian classic *Shāh-nāma* and from ancient Greek literature still take the breath away today.[66] Panjikent's glory came at the expense of the natural environment. Over time, the surrounding area was subject to major deforestation, while the demands made on the land both for agricultural production to feed the population and to make bricks for construction projects resulted in severe soil erosion.

Those presented challenges in any circumstances. But when there were even modest changes to precipitation levels and to water supply from springs, they not only became problematic but insurmountable. While the abandonment of what had once been a key node along the Silk Roads may have owed something to the Arab conquest of this region and to the diversion of trade routes, there were obvious consequences for cities that lived beyond their means.[67]

Perhaps not surprisingly, then, in the world of the caliphate, pressures came primarily from within. Competition between rival factions at the court could sometimes spill into dynastic upheaval and, in the worst cases, secession. A case in point was the overthrow of the Umayyad dynasty in the middle of the eighth century by the ʿAbbāsids after almost a hundred years in power – although members of the former managed to hold on to power in Spain, establishing an independent state centred on Córdoba.[68]

Revolutions like these could spark reform and change that rebooted the socio-economic and political system, primarily through a purge of the elite and their replacement with a new class and caste. As new leaders sought to win hearts and minds, they would often spend lavishly not only on their immediate client base but on public works and on patronage that could appeal more widely. Rather than an Islamic golden age, there was a series of golden ages or golden waves, overseen by rulers with different resources at their disposal and different aims.

For example, considerable effort went into gathering and translating Sanskrit texts about science into Arabic, to bringing physicians from India to instruct about medicine and to becoming better informed about other parts of the world. This was partly motivated by a genuine sense of curiosity, although, as has been recently argued, it also owed something to emulating earlier, pre-Islamic Sasanian models where rulers were champions of scholarship. There were benefits too, of providing support to and privileges for non-Muslim subjects: inclusiveness and tolerance were not just indicators of open-mindedness; they were smart politics in a world studded with minorities.[69]

Skills in subjects like astronomy and astrology were important too in providing additional tools for the legitimisation and validation of political decision-making, which had heightened significance after a change of dynastic leadership.[70] The transfer of information, knowledge and technical expertise between India, China, the Middle East, Constantinople and beyond was a hallmark of the rivalry between interconnected and interlocking empires.[71]

The explosion of literacy from the mid-eighth century, which is sometimes linked to the introduction of paper to the Middle East from China, was above all else a sign of rising prosperity. Wealth and leisure time helped generate interest in book production, as well as funding for scribes and for scholars to research, think and write. Some writers were voracious readers – like al-Jāḥiẓ, who reportedly rented bookshops so he could read volumes all night; according to one source, he was killed by a stack of volumes that collapsed on him when he was elderly and frail.[72] Others were workaholic compilers of information, like Ibn al-Nadīm, a scholar who lived and worked in Baghdad in the tenth century, who set out to make lists of the 'books of all peoples, Arab and foreign … dealing with the various sciences', recording who 'composed them and the categories of their authors, together with their relationships and records of their times of birth, length of life and times of death as well as the location of their cities', while also listing their virtues and faults.[73]

Naturally, the abundance of wealth that enabled this rich cultural world was equated with divine benediction. Both were closely linked with benign climate, and, above all, the availability of food. After all, this had been one of the messages given by God to Muḥammad in a cave near Mecca: those who were obedient would experience 'gardens of perpetual bliss', promised one verse that was later codified to create the text known as the Qur'ān.[74] God 'has promised to believers, men and women, gardens under which rivers flow, to dwell therein and beautiful mansions of everlasting happiness'.[75] Paradise would be a place where all one's needs would be catered for, from fruits to whatever else one desired.[76]

This was of course all familiar in other Abrahamic faiths – Judaism and Christianity, where God has a central role as provider of a benign environment in general and of enough food in particular. God had provided manna from heaven, a special 'fine, flake-like thing' that had to be collected before it was melted by the sun's rays, and was either eaten raw with a taste like honey, or baked into cakes that would not 'stink or get maggots in it'.[77] When Jesus had gone fishing in the Sea of Galilee, he had managed to fill the net to bursting – after the efforts of his disciples had proved fruitless.[78] Perhaps the most famous example of divine intervention to provide food, however, comes with the feeding of the 5,000, the only miracle that appears in all four gospels.[79] In Judaism, Christianity and Islam, God was not only the creator of the natural world, he was also the ultimate provider of resources, able to guarantee provisions when needed and to provide benign climatic conditions at will.

Indeed, in Islam God's control over the natural world was absolute to the extent that animals were purported to be particularly alert on Fridays, as they realised that this was the day that the end of world would take place. Muslims were warned not to slap creatures in the face or to mistreat them as 'all animals hymn the praises of God'.[80] Just as the Bible underscores the idea that God perfected all creation, the Qur'ān speaks of the order, beauty and harmony of nature as being divinely ordained. Moreover, when taken as a whole, nature has intrinsic and inherent value, not simply being useful for human beings. As some contemporary scholars contend, the earliest teachings of Islam argue that biodiversity and rich ecosystems stem from God's creation and therefore deserve respect and maintenance.[81]

Naturally, the bounty of plenty was not just the result of a benign God but also the sign of a good ruler. The Caliph al-Mutawakkil (r. 847–61) was praised by one contemporary poet who noted that it was not God alone who deserved thanks, as he wrote in rapture:

Thanks to you, vast tracts of land have become fertile.
For sure, the world cannot be barren as long as you are its
protector.[82]

Such praise went hand in hand with an expansion of irrigation and of agriculture. In Central Asia, for example, the number of oasis settlements and the area that they covered had already started to rise before the Arab conquests. They continued to do so afterwards, even though it is clear that the Arab moves into this region met with considerable resistance and deliberate destruction, at least in some locations.[83] The development of crop growing must certainly have been facilitated by the fact that, around 650, climatic conditions shifted across Central Asia, the Tibetan plateau, the steppes of Mongolia and eastern China, becoming both cooler and more humid, with additional rainfall beneficial to plant cultivation as well as to vegetation cover that enhanced livestock rearing.[84]

In this bustling, vibrant world of widening horizons, rising populations and growing wealth, 'high cuisine' was an important way of expressing cultural identities, especially for the urban bourgeoisie that in time extended beyond just the rich and powerful.[85] Although some wryly noted that Baghdad was 'a joyful land for the affluent' but 'for the destitute, an abode of anguish and sorrow', there was great demand for the best ingredients, as well as information about where to find and how to prepare them.[86]

Do not be fooled into thinking that the wealthy have different food to normal people, warned the author of one Baghdadi cookbook. The difference in flavour and experience was down to the meticulous cleanliness of the ingredients – as well as of the pots in which they were cooked. It was important, therefore, to have good hygiene practices in the kitchen, including having separate knives and chopping boards for meat and for vegetables and to use good-quality materials for handwashing.[87] Personal tastes could sometimes be quixotic, such as those of the Caliph al-Wāthiq who had a penchant for aubergines and once ate forty in a single sitting.[88] Some gourmands were dismissive about vegetarianism, claiming that dishes made only of vegetables were a fraud, often being presented to look like meat but tasting nothing like it. 'Trifling vegetable dishes are not for me,' wrote one poet in protest; 'where is my kebāb? Where are the fried dishes? The succulent roasts and the spiced meat? Bring them on!'[89]

While metropolitan concerns preoccupied most contemporary commentators in all these regions – they paid particular attention to the corridors of power – during times of demographic growth, urbanisation and rising patterns of consumption, maintaining agricultural sustainability was essential. This in turn was dependent on multiple factors that varied significantly not just from region to region but sometimes even across modest distances. Climate was of course one element; but so were distances to market, the availability of labour forces to work the land, crop specialisation, soil suitability and optimal yields.

What mattered most of all, however, was water management, and not just in terms of assessing agricultural production. Pre-industrial states were heavily dependent on their agrarian economies and above all on land tax. Trade was important, certainly, and rightly receives much attention from modern scholars. However, revenues from land were considerably higher than they were from long- or short-distance trade.[90] Not surprisingly, considerable effort went into assessing land quality, ownership and the revenues it would produce. Muslim rulers conducted regular land surveys, therefore, just as their Sasanian predecessors had done before them.[91] In addition, state officials were careful to make records of hydraulics, irrigation systems and water resources, in order to try to maximise returns that could be collected by the crown.[92]

Such evaluations naturally depended on the fact that rainfall should be consistent and – equally importantly – that demand made of the land and of the available water sources did not rise. When the balance tipped in the wrong direction, problems followed. Around the start of the ninth century, for example, a set of challenges emerged that brought with them major socio-economic and political consequences. To judge from tree-ring records from the Altai mountains in Central Asia, salinity levels in the Aral Sea and observations about the North Atlantic Oscillation shifting strongly towards positive mode, a long-term trend away from colder, more humid conditions towards warmer and drier ones for many parts of Eurasia began to emerge around c.800. The challenges this posed can be seen from the decline in the number of oasis settlements, which fell by almost 70 per cent over the decades that followed.[93]

This was not a phenomenon unique to Central Asia, as seems clear from the abandonment of towns, villages and agricultural land in western Iran as well as in the floodplain of the Euphrates – one of the most productive areas not only in the Middle East but in the world.[94] In addition to the climatic shift was ecological stress caused by rapidly increasing salinisation of soil. Wheat yields in the rich alluvial plains of Mesopotamia fell precipitously in the years c.820–50; that those of barley rose provides one indication of the imbalance in salinity levels, since the latter is much more robust than the former in soil that has become degraded.[95] The importation of coerced labourers from Africa to remove the salt layers by hand to keep fields cultivable provides another.[96]

These problems were compounded by the fact that around 800 wealthy elites had started successfully to build up landholdings, using status, connections and political pressure to influence taxation systems and water allocations.[97] This brought about short-term gains at the expense of long-term sustainability – both economic and environmental: in the early ninth century, the Abbāsid state was able to collect around 125 million dirhams per year in revenue from land tax in Iraq; a century later, the figure had fallen by almost 80 per cent.[98]

Such collapses in available funds created problems of their own, not least pressure on the leadership to explain why they could not live up to the largesse and glories of their predecessors, ranging from their magnificent building works to their territorial expansion to the lavish spending that could often seem to be a distant memory. One response was to criticise profligacy, over-the-top lifestyles and irresponsible outgoings. According to Alī ibn 'Īsā who was writing in the early tenth century, almost a third of the caliphate's annual budget was spent on the harem, on eunuchs and on senior officials at the court.[99] With expenditure like this, it was not surprising that shocks could exacerbate grievances and open the door for protest, instability and sometimes worse.

In Baghdad in 919–20, for example, there were riots as a result of food shortages that were only pacified after grain reserves were distributed at subsidised prices.[100] Two decades later, a famine struck that was so bad that 'houses, vineyards, and gardens were sold for joints of meat and cakes of bread. And men used to pick out the grains of barley from the dung of horses and asses and eat them.'[101] A few years later, lack of food in the Jazira was so terrible that 'many went mad, attacking one another mercilessly and savagely devouring each other'.[102]

Whether one can rely on such accounts is unclear, even in cases where they seem to correlate with climate data that suggest unusual weather patterns or events, such as droughts, floods or periods when it was hotter or colder than normal.[103] Of course, food shortages were not always related to climate or even to productivity as they were heavily influenced by market expectations. Some tried to mitigate these risks by buying up grain, such as the Fatimid authorities in Egypt in the eighth century – although, tellingly, this practice was abandoned because too often grain stocks had been bought above market prices and could not be sold.[104] Equally, it was inevitable that speculators would seek to capitalise on high prices and try to drive them higher – an activity that the Caliph al-Hākim dealt with by threatening punishment. 'I will cut off the head of whoever possesses any grain whatsoever,' he announced during a crop failure that followed a poor Nile flood in 1007; 'I will burn his house and confiscate his wealth.'[105]

As the Caliph's reaction makes clear, such episodes provided opportunities for the disaffected, the ambitious and the brave to chance their arm in attempts to improve their position. Economic problems that could flow from harvest failure, shock weather patterns or military instability could be exploited by rivals to the Caliph, his court and interest groups eager to capitalise on fundamental underlying structural problems flowing from the concentration of too much power in too few hands. Peripheral regions were often the breeding ground of dissent, the source of revolt and a springboard for newcomers to rise to power.

In the case of the caliphate, one of the key sources of social, economic and political problems was that reforms introduced to provide the state with a stable and secure income ultimately served to strengthen the hand of the rich and powerful further still. The creation of the *iqtā'* system during the mid-tenth century devolved tax-collection rights in exchange for services; apart from being open to abuse, it meant that the aims of the

state and of the elite were not aligned, with the latter seeking to benefit at
the expense of the former, and indeed of tenants and farmers who would
be squeezed as hard as possible for rents. This aggravated existing causes
of widespread dissatisfaction and rising inequality, further stretching a
system that was already inefficient, open to corruption and inclined to
favour large landholders at the expense of the weak.[106] Perhaps climatic
change fanned problems whose embers were already glowing, but it was
the failure to keep the rapacious magnate class under control that was
the ultimate cause of the regular crises.

It was a similar story in Tang dynasty China. Many scholars have
recently sought to associate climatic change with the fall of the ruling
family and the implosion of the empire, arguing that droughts, floods,
locust invasions and famine spread over fifty years, along with harsh
winter and weak summer monsoons inspired waves of rebellion.[107]
These cannot have helped, but the root causes of instability, revolt and
ultimately the overthrow of the last Tang Emperor in 907 lay in what
one historian called the 'violently anti-aristocratic feeling' that was
manifested by 'hatred of the old families and hatred of high officials'.[108]

These feelings owed much to the success of the wealthy in
feathering their own nests at the expense of the wider population and
in managing not only to protect these gains but to keep augmenting
them. Tang dynasty China had become a closed shop, observed Zheng
Qiao, a commentator writing in the twelfth century. Appointments
were not made on merit, but owed everything to family background,
with officials (who were themselves all drawn from the same narrow
social group) consulting genealogies and marriage ties, records which
they kept up to date and relied on as their guide to show not only
who was who, but who should be allowed to be part of the great and
the good.[109]

By the 870s, wrote one chronicler just over a hundred years later,
'waste and extravagance [at the court] became more extreme by the
day', while corruption and dishonesty were rife among bureaucrats.
Successive years of drought had caused difficulties, but the real problem
had been that the effects 'were not reported truthfully' to the authorities,
so action that would have averted suffering was not taken. The result
was that 'the common people wandered about in search of food' and,
with nobody to help them, soon 'gathered into bandit gangs, moving

about like swarms of bees'. Worse, because peace had reigned for so long, government soldiers had little experience and were often defeated by bands of marauders.[110]

Rebellions in the 870s and 880s critically weakened the state, damaged the credibility of the imperial dynasty and strengthened the hands of provincial warlords whose own machinations led to a splintering of territories controlled by the Tang after the murder of Emperor Daizong – who was given the name Ai (哀) or 'lamentable' after his death. As one historian has put it, the period that followed, known as that of the Five Dynasties and Ten Kingdoms, was the logical culmination of increasing regional development at the expense of the centre and had been decades in the making, if not more than a century, depending on one's perspective.[111]

Identifying the deep roots of problems that were affected and exacerbated rather than caused by shifting climatic conditions is also helpful in understanding the fate of the Maya culture in Central America – whose 'collapse' has become one of the most celebrated and commonly cited examples of the dangers of climate stress and environmental degradation and a clarion warning about the troubles of the present and the future. According to some, for example, climate factors brought about pressures that were so severe that catastrophe was unavoidable. 'There was nothing [the Maya] could do or could have done,' in the words of a group of leading scholars; 'in the end, the food and water ran out and they all died.'[112]

This is something of an exaggeration. The Maya did not all die – with most estimates suggesting a population today around the 9 million mark, as well as a cultural footprint that is not only recognisable but extremely important in Guatemala, parts of Mexico and elsewhere in Central America.[113] Moreover, while there was undeniably a period of profound change, some Maya polities continued to survive and flourish, with the last only falling to the Spanish in 1697 – almost 800 years after a decline that was supposedly apocalyptic.[114]

The Maya culture of Central America had blossomed for many centuries, reaching a symbolic apogee with the construction in AD 747 of Temple IV at Tikal, which had the distinction of being the tallest building in the Americas before the arrival of the Europeans at the end of the fifteenth century.[115] Tikal had long been an important urban centre, one of a series of cities, polities and settlements knitted together by extensive trade networks that facilitated the movement of luxury goods such as obsidian.[116] These networks were also closely linked to the retention of political authority by individuals and family groups that preserved some degree of autonomy from each other.[117] Long-distance reciprocal contact was maintained, including with Teotihuacan over a thousand kilometres away, which was a source of cultural reference points and even the inspiration for the reproduction of major buildings in Tikal.[118]

The distribution of power, status and wealth was not even either between cities or within them: people living in locations that were better connected and close to principal trade routes were more prosperous than those on the periphery, while those ruled over by autocratic elites saw high levels of wealth inequality.[119] A mesh of political alliances was held together by officials and diplomats who shuttled between locations and frequently appear on carved monuments, murals and polychrome vessels.

Recent excavations of a small plaza compound at El Palmar in the eastern part of the Yucatán peninsula have revealed a particularly fine burial chamber of one such individual, a diplomat named Ajpach' Waal, who held the title of *lakam* (standard-bearer) and was involved in negotiating terms between El Palmar and the ruling dynasty of Copán, located 350 kilometres to the south.[120] Ajpach' Waal had acquired jade and pyrite inlays to his teeth during puberty or as a young adult, as was common for individuals of high status, especially those in the Lowlands, as a means of displaying social distinction.[121] Pioneering research into his osteobiography – the study of his skeletal remains – reveals that the inlay had fallen out of his right canine; the fact that dental plaque had formed around it and hardened into calculus suggests that he was not able to afford a replacement, which in turn raises the question of whether his status and that of El Palmar suffered during his lifetime in the mid-eighth century.[122]

Despite regional ups and downs, long-term demographic growth over many centuries was substantial, supporting city states with populations numbering in the tens of thousands.[123] Some estimate that total population across Maya lands peaked at around 10 million, if not higher.[124] Tikal's importance had risen under the leadership of Jasaw Chan K'awiil and his son, Yik'in Chan K'awiil, who oversaw a sequence of military victories and political expansion from the very end of the seventh century.[125] This was a factor in the size of the city's population tripling or perhaps even quadrupling in the course of the next hundred years or so.[126]

Urbanisation required significant investment if settlements were to be sustainable – and able to expand. This included the creation of irrigation networks, as well as development of sophisticated engineering solutions to maximise water capture that ranged from dam building to sand-filtration technologies to cleanse water of sediments and impurities.[127] Another crucial element was tackling erosion, which was partly done through sophisticated forestry and soil management.[128] This allowed the expansion of food production based on maize, beans, squashes, sweet potato and other root crops and enabled it to meet the rising demands of densely distributed and rising populations.[129]

Speleothem data from Yok Balum Cave in Belize, along with lake-sediment cores in northern Yucatán and titanium content from the Cariaco Basin in the southern Caribbean all point to a protracted period of drought in the mid-ninth century that lasted for several decades.[130] Average rainfall levels dropped by around 50 per cent and occasionally by as much as 70 per cent, with these shifts likely the result of changes in solar activity, volcanic eruptions or both.[131] This exacerbated problems caused by rapid deforestation that has been linked to the dual need to expand agricultural land and to obtain wood to fuel fires required in order to bake calcium carbonate from shells or stone to create quicklime – a substance that can be used as a binder, for whitewashing and for construction.[132] Cutting down trees amplified drought conditions since less water evaporates from cleared land, which has a negative impact on cloud formation and on rainfall.[133]

It helped then that the Maya cultivated a wide range of plants, but what is more, that many of these were drought resistant.[134] Although it is the lack of rainfall that has attracted a great deal of attention among historians seeking to link climatic change with apparent civilisational collapse, from an ecological perspective what may have mattered more was not rainfall deficiencies but rising temperatures in the summer and their impact on maize: as modern research has shown, maize yields decline by as much as 1 per cent for each day that air temperatures are greater than 30 °C.[135] This was important in Maya culture, not only from the point of view of food availability, but also because of the symbolic relationship between political legitimacy and maize. Harvest depletion raised questions about the competence and special status of rulers, which in turn provided obvious incentives to maintain authority and acquire prestige through military conquest.[136]

Rising levels of violence in the eighth and ninth centuries therefore created instability and put pressure on trade networks. However, it also created opportunities for the accumulation and appropriation of greater levels of wealth and resources by soldiers and officials. This widened the demand for luxury goods such as ceramic vessels, and drove the evolution of new styles.[137] It also increased demands on rulers whose kingship rested on elaborate rituals such as bloodletting, sometimes involving venomous stingray spines, which 'opened a conduit between the natural and supernatural worlds'.[138] Such rituals were designed to allow elites to assert and maintain their distance from commoners – as was the case in Monte Albán culture in the Central Valleys of Oaxaca, in what is now Mexico, where rulers erected carved stones to show off their genealogy and so preserve a gap between themselves and commoners. In Monte Albán, increasingly challenging times led to rising levels of elite competition that likewise played a role in driving deurbanisation, depopulation and the decline of a functioning state apparatus.[139]

Another problem may also have come from materials used in decorative preferences and techniques employed by the Maya. Recent scholarship has drawn attention to the cinnabar that was used to produce blood-red colours in dyes and paint used for claywares and architectural ornamentation as well as in ritual activities. High in mercury, cinnabar would have been washed off buildings and artefacts during rainstorms, leaching into reservoirs on which the city depended. Over time, pollutants rose to dangerous levels, made worse during dry periods when cyanobacteria became even more concentrated and toxic than normal. The pollutants brought the sustainability of cities into question and undermined the authority of their rulers and elites; moreover, the effects of chronic mercury exposure on obesity and cognitive function may even have played a role in undermining social structures that were already under pressure.[140]

As scholars of Mesoamerica often stress, the transition from a highly connected patchwork of densely populated settlements was neither sudden nor consistent. In Oaxaca, for example, many aspects of domestic life continued uninterrupted for many centuries until the Spanish conquest.[141] In Maya lands, different urban centres faced different challenges and different experiences, in both the short and the long term: while some sites experienced severe depopulation and the breakdown of bureaucratic systems, others did not.[142]

What collapsed was not the Maya world as a whole, but rather the skeleton that held it up – the mesh of networks that linked locations together, facilitated the exchange of goods and ideas, and provided a canvas for alliances, rivalries and competitive kingship. Faced with drought, crop shortages and loss of mechanisms of control, rulers found it impossible to meet expectations and to maintain authority.[143] This was the reason why grand monuments and palaces stopped being built and why they began to be occupied not by rulers and officials but by what appear to be squatters – ad hoc groups who used the buildings for cover from the elements to cook, eat and sleep.[144]

Changes in climate, even pronounced and challenging ones, were not unusual in Mesoamerica (or indeed in other regions around the world), especially for cultures that had survived and flourished for decades, centuries or longer. Crucial, then, was the balance between environmental pressure on the one hand and social and economic fragility on the other – something worth thinking about in the present day. Hyperconnectivity such as globalisation can provide obvious benefits in terms of exchange of all kind; but these can mask the vulnerabilities and shocks that can accelerate if one or more link in the chain becomes uncoupled, intentionally or otherwise. Factories closing, ports being congested or natural resources being cut off not only create inflation, but in the worst case, can lead to socio-economic pressure, revolution and state failure.

It is also worth remembering that demographic contraction, the abandonment and decline of cities and the reduction in travel, communication and exchange might disappoint archaeologists and historians, who revel in studying grand monuments, in assessing power structures and kinship patterns. For most people, the retreat of geographic, socio-political and ecological frontiers did not necessarily equate with the catastrophe or even the decline that is often associated with the end of supposedly 'golden ages'. Likewise, transformations of human societies evidently had an impact on flora and fauna as usage of the land changed in response to demand: deurbanisation and city failure meant local ecologies were no longer used the same way or in the same scale, which meant a different set of winners and losers for animals and plants alike. And it is worth remembering that the climate pendulum can swing both ways. Long-term shifts in rainfall distribution, in aridity or in temperature do not always result in the unravelling of connections. Sometimes, they can galvanise new opportunities and spur the creation of new worlds.

12

The Medieval Warm Period
(c.900–c.1250)

They thought that the Day of Judgement had arrived.

Ibn al-Athīr on the people of Mosul (thirteenth century)

In 1965, the historian Hubert Lamb noted that evidence had been 'accumulating in many fields of investigation pointing to a notably warm climate in many parts of the world, that lasted a few centuries around AD 1000–1200'. His proposed name for this period, the Medieval Warm Epoch, has since been modified and is now usually referred to by scholars as the Medieval Climate Anomaly or the Medieval Warm Period.[1] Some too have pushed at the dating boundaries, arguing that the period of long-term generally warm climate conditions in fact dates from c.800 and lasted until 1200 or even 1250.[2]

From a European perspective, this was a time of favourable weather patterns which ensured that atmospheric circulation in the North Atlantic was a reliable source of warm, dry air which in turn resulted in a reduction in the number both of wet and cold summers and of bitterly cold winters. This created ideal conditions for agriculture, generating good harvests, inflicting few shocks and, perhaps best of all, providing a climatic context that was reliable and stable.[3] Of course, temperatures and rainfall levels do not remain constant or benign; nor does it mean that there was coherence or consistency across Europe as a whole – something that is in any event difficult to assess given that considerably less attention has been paid to the south and the east of the continent than to the north and the west.[4]

The benign climate conditions that favoured Europe had different consequences for other parts of the world, although it is important to note important regional variations. For example, while rainfall in Iran, Armenia and Palestine was significantly below average for much of this period, there is little evidence that this was true of northern Syria or of western or central Anatolia.[5] Climate impacts varied from region to region, even over relatively small areas – as was the case in what is now Bulgaria, central Greece and western Asia Minor, which do not show uniform precipitation patterns in the early Middle Ages.[6]

Tree-ring data from Central Asia, combined with reconstructions of the Aral Sea salinity, point to the climate being cold and dry, especially from around 900 onwards.[7] This chimes with evidence from the northern parts of China, though the rising cultivation of citrus trees and subtropical plants in Henan province to the south provides a reminder that experiences were not only different but could be sharply contrasting.[8] More detailed and more recent surveys drawing on peat cellulose, stalagmites, ice cores and tree rings show that many parts of what is now China were generally warmer and wetter than average during this long period.[9] Taken as a whole, however, six of the ten warmest decades globally of the last millennium were clustered in the period 950–1250.[10]

These changes have been linked by some scholars to large-scale shifts in the El Niño–Southern Oscillation (ENSO), the Atlantic Multidecadal Oscillation (AMO) and the North Atlantic Oscillation (NAO).[11] Others however have suggested that they were driven by high levels of solar irradiance and low levels of tropical volcanism.[12] The lack of the latter seems to be the more important, given that while reconstructions of radioactive beryllium (^{10}Be) and carbon (^{14}C) isotopes show that while the main phase of the Medieval Climate Anomaly corresponds with relatively high solar magnetic activity levels, these were not unusual compared to other periods. As such, reduced volcanic activity and variability of the ocean-atmosphere system appear to have been the main motor of what was a major global climate reorganisation.[13]

The warming of the tropical Indian and western Pacific oceans induced a broad range of changes to atmospheric pressure in the North

Atlantic and shifts in monsoon rainfall patterns in Africa and South Asia, and affected aridity levels in the Eurasian subtropics.[14] Much of the Pacific Rim, including San Francisco Bay and coastal Peru, was affected by drier conditions than normal, albeit at different stages between 800 and 1250.[15] There were long and unusually regular periods of hydrologic drought in California and Patagonia, as well as in the Upper Colorado Basin, although peatlands in north-eastern America do not seem to have been affected.[16]

That warming also brought change in Africa, although establishing the precise impact is more difficult because so little work has been done on data gathering and on climate reconstructions – a reflection of the way that this continent's histories have been marginalised more generally.[17] Nevertheless, information gathered from over forty sites shows uneven and highly varied patterns, with marked cooling in the Benguela Current Upwelling System that dominates the south-western coast of the continent, mirrored by warming across southern Mauritania, the Gulf of Guinea and the Congo River basin.[18]

How these shifts in long-term weather patterns affected different regions is not easy to determine: although socio-economic changes that began in the early Middle Ages may correlate with climate contexts that themselves were not uniform, constant or immediate, that is not the same as asserting that one causes the other. Even where connections seem both plausible and compelling, identifying the precise relationship between environmental and societal changes requires caution.

For example, in the southern Mediterranean, changes were modest. The eastern parts of the Roman empire that had survived the Arab attacks had regrouped. Characterised by centralised control of Constantinople and a bureaucratic, military and religious apparatus which sustained integration as well as a common Roman identity now went through a period of contraction where cities became smaller and networks less vibrant. Exchanges between the Middle East, Levant, North Africa and Spain were based on a similar model of political structure that provided protection of property rights, administered justice and collected taxes. The difference was one of scale, with cities like Damascus, Cordoba, Fustat and many others being both larger and more numerous than those in the Eastern Roman – or Byzantine world – that was centred on the Aegean, the Balkans and Greece.[19]

Both stood in sharp contrast with western and northern Europe. There, the decline and fall of Rome brought about fragmentation and atomisation. There were brief spells of consolidation, most notably during the reign of the great ruler Charlemagne who succeeded in uniting much of what is now France, the Low Countries, Germany and northern Italy into a single realm. The high water mark came with Charlemagne's coronation as Emperor of the Romans by Pope Leo II on Christmas Day in 800. This was a brief and exceptional moment in what was otherwise a period of almost no long-distance trade and a narrowing of horizons that lasted for hundreds of years.

Rather than the romantic figure of Charlemagne, who became a totemic symbol for those keen to provide a reference point for ideas about European unity, the regional emporia of Comacchio and Torcello in Italy, Verdun in France and Birka in Scandinavia were better examples of reality. Curiously, each was set in locations that were ecologically marginal and geographically peripheral; but more importantly, each was a trading zone that was an internal market, where commerce took place between local producers and local consumers rather than with those of other regions.[20]

This in turn provided a setting for a very different form of social and economic development. In the absence of a sophisticated bureaucracy, a new baronial class emerged in western Europe that was able to establish authority over both the labour force and over productive land. The magnates faced challenges from each other, of course, as well as from other competitors – namely the Church, which built up extensive landholdings and sought to protect and maximise its own socio-economic and political position. Together, these represented a superclass of dominant individuals, families and landowners who sought to concentrate power in their own hands, and retain it within kinship groups closely related by marriage or in institutional ownership that kept assets away from the king.[21]

Ideas about the 'feudal revolution' that were commonplace a few decades ago have been replaced by much more sophisticated interpretations, many of which emphasise the variety and importance of other participants in early medieval society in western Europe – such as guilds, urban groups, parishes, regional assemblies and universities.[22] Some commentators have also stressed that the initial weakness of property rights spurred innovations over time in the formalisation and consolidation of power as aristocrats built up assets and status that ultimately proved transformational.[23] The evolving role of the Church, as the recipient of endowments and distributor of alms, patronage and influence, was also a significant factor in social, institutional and ecological change.[24]

The consequent transformation of both human societies and the natural environment in the early Middle Ages was so profound that some scholars have talked of this period as being the time of 'the most significant agricultural expansion since the Neolithic'.[25] The role of new technologies in driving yields and production has long been emphasised by medieval historians. Particular attention has been paid to the importance of horse collars and to the development of heavy ploughs that were much more effective in turning the heavy clay soils of northern Europe. These improved weed control, enhanced drainage and had the twin effect of boosting yields and requiring less work by farmers, thereby freeing up time and resources that could be allocated to other activities.[26] The breaking up of larger estates into smaller units resulted in important social change, altering perceptions of the land and landscape for the peasantry as well as for the emerging baronial class.[27]

What was most important about the uplift in agricultural productivity was its relationship to urbanisation: by improving per capita income and spurring the development of transport and commercial networks, the changes in the agrarian economies of western and northern Europe set off a chain reaction that led to the growth in size and number of towns. This in turn encouraged specialisation and cultural experimentation and resulted in further migration from the country to urban settlements – and drove cycles of dynamic growth.[28]

The rise of towns and cities – and the regular arrival of newcomers and strangers – had profound effects on urban cultures as well as on those who lived in the countryside, with new customs, ideas, fashions and tastes producing an explosive transformation of Europe.[29] As long-distance trade networks developed, intellectual, cultural and geographic horizons expanded too, typified by concepts like pilgrimage to Jerusalem, a journey that was long, expensive and often risky, but that gave considerable kudos to those who were able to visit the sites where Jesus Christ had lived, died and risen from the dead.

Ideas about nature also evolved, as did concern about competition for resources that varied from region to region; these ideas were evidently influenced by changing lifestyles, as well as by engagement with flora and fauna.[30] Concepts of the natural world could be ambiguous: as one leading historian has pointed out, growing one's own food in early medieval Italy 'was both a necessity and a luxury'.[31]

For some scholars, however, climate shifts provide an invaluable key to help understand the early Middle Ages. It has been suggested, for example, that warming was at least a contributing factor in the move of the Bulgars into the Middle Volga region from around AD 800, as it was in the establishment around this time of the Volga Bulgarian state, which opened up trade routes fanning out to Scandinavia, Byzantium, the Middle East and Central Asia.[32] These networks spread goods as well as ideas and religions: when the Arab envoy Ibn Faḍlān visited the Volga Bulgars just over a century later, he reported that the ruler presided over a court complete with elaborate rituals, and with expensive materials and goods on display that had come from Constantinople and Baghdad – although he was unimpressed by the incomplete understanding of Islamic teaching.[33]

Journeys to the east were mirrored by those heading both south and west. New evidence based on mammal faeces, pollen samples and charcoal analysis suggests settlement of the Azores by Scandinavian peoples – which has been linked to anomalous winds and warmer temperatures in the northern hemisphere.[34] The expansion of Scandinavian peoples across the North Atlantic into the Faroe Islands, Iceland and Greenland in the ninth century has also been strongly linked to the retreat of the polar ice cap that allowed ice-free sailing, to the northerly migration of fish stocks and to the emergence of favourable growing conditions on land.[35] Such colonisation was not easy, for it involved not only a jump into the unknown but also leaving families and friends behind. A major eruption of the Hallmundarhraun volcano in Iceland around c.900 must have been unsettling and inspired at least some settlers to build an enormous boat-shaped structure in a 1,600-metre-long lava cave in the interior, with animals including sheep, cattle, horses and pigs apparently sacrificed as burned offerings to appease pagan gods.[36]

This was just one of dozens of eruptions in the period c.850–c.1250, with some – such as the Eldgjá volcano in 934 – proving particularly damaging to flora and fauna alike.[37]

Perhaps not surprisingly, it was mainly men who set out in the first waves of colonisation. Although Y-chromosomal and mitochondrial DNA (mtDNA) evidence suggests that Norse women were involved in expansions to the Shetlands, Orkneys and northern parts of Scotland, genomic data reveals that in Iceland most settlers were lone men who brought enslaved women from the British Isles to satisfy their sexual desires through rape and coercion.[38] Some made it as far as North America to the L'Anse aux Meadows site in Newfoundland, although the settlement proved unsuccessful.[39] Advances in dating techniques allow us to know that a Scandinavian community had become established by 1021 – when trees were cut down with metal blades used by Vikings, but not by indigenous peoples.[40]

Trade between new colonies in the North Atlantic and Scandinavia was primarily centred around low-bulk, high-value prestige goods that could be sold back home for rich rewards, most notably walrus hides and ivory tusks.[41] That produced problems of its own, with Iceland evolving into a society that was dominated by those who had arrived first and built up the best and largest landholdings; by the mid-tenth century, it was 'over-chieftained' – one reason why the national assembly, the Althing, was established, with the earliest laws concerned with protecting landholdings from new arrivals and landowners from each other. There were creative efforts to correct the manpower shortage, with texts like the *Íslendingabók* setting out how Erik the Red was able to tempt others to journey to Greenland with an astutely judged sales pitch that spoke of verdant and abundant land and of limitless opportunities that this auspiciously named island offered.[42]

The expansion from Scandinavia into the North Atlantic was part of a wider intensification not only of regional trade and knowledge networks, but of long-distance trade too – most notably to the east and to the south that in turn brought enormous volumes of silver coinage into circulation first in the Nordic and Baltic lands and then elsewhere.[43] These activities, coupled with human interventions in the landscape such as building new settlements, farming and rearing domesticated animals, changed ecosystems – as did the hunting of animals for food and trade.[44] One outcome was a world of plenty – and of equality: while evidence from Roman sites suggests men ate 50 per cent more protein than women, in Scandinavian societies in this period women and girls had access to the same food sources as men and boys and had better health outcomes as a result. Some scholars have even suggested that this may help explain why there are such high levels of female autonomy and gender equality in contemporary Scandinavia.[45]

The impact of human activities in geographically constrained locations with finite resources could be severe: within decades of the first settlers arriving in Iceland it is possible to detect soil erosion and deforestation that continued for several hundred years before long-term conservation practices were adopted.[46] Genomic analysis, combined with radiocarbon dating and use of written sources, shows that the local population of walrus was wiped out soon after the Norse settlement in Iceland, with overhunting the most obvious cause of extinction – even if warming climate and volcanism may have been additional stress factors.[47]

The pressure on managing resources led to shifts in consumption patterns, such as in Iceland with deliberate moves away from pigs and cattle to sheep, whose rising numbers may be explained also by attempts to produce wool for domestic use and for export.[48] Isotope data shows that adaptation in Greenland led to terrestrial meat-based diets being replaced over time by reliance on marine protein sources.[49]

In other words coping strategies were needed not only at times of climate shifts, but also to manage the consequences. The favourable conditions and material incentives that opened up routes between Scandinavia and the North Atlantic led to different sets of questions that were part of a constant negotiation and renegotiation between human agency and the natural environment: the arrival of any animal or plant species could have major ecological consequences. It just so happened that humans brought cascades of change in their wake as a result of interventions in the landscape: the need for settlement, food, water and other resources meant that human impact on ecosystems was profound. Plants and animals that were brought by humans, deliberately or otherwise, were part of a 'natural' set of changes that had anthropogenic causes – such as weeds, seeds and parasites that were carried in the guts of pigs, or plants carried for food, for planting or simply as insulation or packaging that then took root in a new ecological setting.[50] These outcomes, sometimes referred to as human ecodynamics, are particularly clear with the occupation of previously uninhabited locations that are then occupied and transformed by human settlement.[51]

In this sense, islands offer unique and important insights into understanding how landscapes, flora and fauna were affected – and also how quickly. Remarkably, then, the examples of Iceland, Greenland and the Faroes have obvious parallels with similar colonisation experiences of islands in the South Pacific which took place at the same time and were likewise closely related to changes in global climatic patterns.

Starting around AD 800, there were abrupt reductions in zonal sea surface temperatures in the West Pacific Warm Pool and a push of rainbands to the north. Moisture levels in the archipelagos of Vanuatu, Samoa, Tonga and Fiji began to fall, resulting in the driest period of the last two millennia. The inhabitants of these islands who had settled there almost 1,500 years earlier had not previously sought to explore islands further north – or, if they had, they had done so impermanently, leaving little or no sign of settlement. That now changed as weather patterns went through a fundamental shift, bringing winds that facilitated exploration of and journeys to Polynesia's margins.[52] Much of the long-distance travel to and from the islands was undertaken by double-hulled canoes and, as computer modelling has shown, discovery and settlement of new locations was deliberate and systematic rather than a matter of chance.[53]

Radiocarbon analyses show waves of migration first to the Cook Islands and then beyond into East Polynesia, the vast area between Hawai'i, Rapa Nui and New Zealand. Successive groups of islands were colonised not only by humans but also by livestock that they intentionally brought with them, such as pigs, and those that they presumably did not, such as rats.[54] As in the North Atlantic, settlement led to transformation of vegetation as land was cleared for crop cultivation, for fuel sources to burn or both, with appreciable soil erosion as a result. Leaf wax biomarker hydrogen isotopes confirm that these islands saw enhanced rainfall levels over a long period of time, confirming the reason for their attraction as alternatives to islands where life was becoming more difficult.[55]

That may also explain social change during this period in other Pacific island groups: increasing aridity clearly put a premium on capturing rainfall as and when it fell. As such, the investment in the building of canals, aqueducts and terraces was not only a natural response but an important one.[56] Projects like this required high-levels of co-operation, in terms of energy requirements to build and maintain such structures, and also to share equitably the benefits and proceeds. This in turn provided a context for transitions from small, dispersed communities into larger groups that over time became stratified and hierarchical.[57]

Changing lifeways were also evident in other parts of the Southern Hemisphere during the period of the Medieval Climate Anomaly, although warming started later than in the north.[58] In addition to paleotemperature reconstructions, archaeological evidence suggests that human population levels in continental Australia rose rapidly around 1000. While patterns of demographic increase may reflect migration patterns, studies of other periods suggest that major changes in population size of hunter-gatherers in Australia were triggered by high-amplitude environmental changes.[59]

Aboriginal hunter-gatherers used mobility and technologies to manage their exposure to risks in resource availability.[60] In this instance, however, it appears that higher levels of water and food availability encouraged a shift to sedentary lifeways.[61] Benign conditions meant that more people could safely live together rather than having to spread out to find resources – one reason for the striking reduction in archaeological signatures in lower-latitude settings in this period.[62] To give one example of the scale of change, a major pluvial event in southern central Australia c.1050–1100 led to Lake Callabonna being filled by around ten to twelve times more water than at its highest-known historical filling. Local populations were being presented, in other words, with new options of how to live, co-operate and flourish.[63]

Societal and environmental transitions are also evident at sites in the Caribbean starting c.900, where centuries of aridity gave way to significantly higher levels of moisture. This was a time too of rising sea levels, which forced islanders to move inland to locations such as Coralie on Grand Turk Island in the Turks and Caicos Islands.[64] The abundance of rainfall favoured agricultural surplus; but there were other outcomes too – not least rising levels of interaction between island groups and between the islands and South America. This can be attested by major transformations of pottery styles, as in the Antilles, which are often interpreted as a sign of sharply increased interactions between islands, and also as a response to the loss of confidence in traditional gods whose preservation of previously arid conditions was now seen as hostile, if not cruel.[65] On top of this was the introduction of a suite of new species of plants and animals into and across many parts of the Caribbean, which served as catalysts for change. For one thing, they reduced the previous heavy dependence of local populations on fish, crab and bird stocks, whose numbers began to recover as a result; for another, island forests were cut down to make way for flora and fauna that were introduced for the first time to the island.[66] Changes in climate, in other words, brought about changes in interaction, in belief systems and even in diets.

This happened elsewhere too around the same time. One such case was the American Bottom, the region stretching from the confluence of the Mississippi and Missouri rivers with the Kaskaskia. This region was home to dispersed, isolated single-home farmsteads and small settlements, of which Cahokia was one of the most prominent. From c.900, Cahokia exploded in size and importance, drawing in migrants from outside the wider region, in what is often called a Big Bang moment, sparking a cultural efflorescence in pottery and other arts.[67] Centred on a single, enormous 6.5-metre-high platform, Cahokia benefited from being set within a vast floodplain that offered ideal conditions for growing crops, while permanent lakes and swamps contained plentiful fish stocks that were central to Cahokian diets, and access to rivers provided water and served as trade and transport arteries.[68] Being able to expand exponentially during times of demographic growth offered possibilities, in other words, that more geographically constrained locations did not.

Temperature profiles at six sites in the North Atlantic from 200 BC–2000 AD

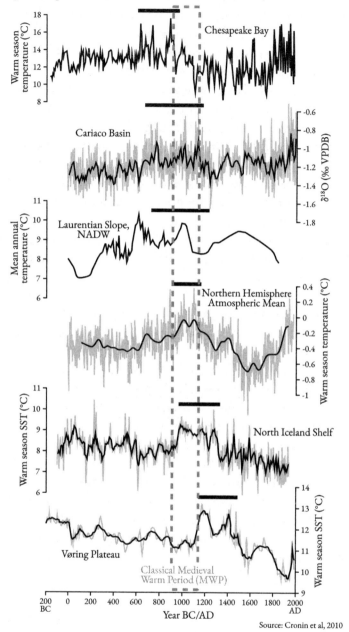

Source: Cronin et al, 2010

The Medieval Climate Anomaly was not congruous, and was pock-marked by regional as well as periodic differences. There were hiccups and one-off episodes too that caused disruption. Most obvious were significant volcanic episodes – such as the highly explosive 'Millennium' eruption of Changbaishan, situated on what is now the border between China and North Korea, which took place in c.940–50. Another is a recently identified but previously unknown tropical eruption that may have been part of a 'forgotten cluster' of explosions at the start of the twelfth century that has been linked to crop failure and poor weather across Europe; it obscured the moon, whose light was so diminished, according to one chronicler, that at nightfall 'it was completely extinguished withal, that neither light, nor orb, nor anything at all of it was seen' – a reference to a dust veil made up of ejected materials.[69]

Then there were natural disasters that were epic in proportion and consequences. On 19 July 1048, the Yellow River breached its northern bank, causing a cataclysmic flood and gouging a new channel 700 kilometres in length up to the Gulf of Bohai. Myriads drowned, 'turning into food for dish and turtles', in the words of contemporaries. Famine followed that was so bad that 'fathers and sons ate each other.' At least one million people were displaced, producing social, economic, political, environmental and humanitarian shocks that some scholars argue took eighty years to play out.[70]

The case of the catastrophe of 1048 illustrates the importance of stability for new farming techniques to take hold and for demographic growth and societal shifts that also followed. For example, levels of rainfall that were considerably higher than they had been in the past help explain transformations in Ancestral Pueblo cultures in the Four Corners region of the American south-west. Spread across where the states of Utah, Colorado, Arizona and New Mexico meet today, rain-fed farming which supported cultivation of maize began around a thousand years ago; this was especially important since maize was a food source that made up 60 per cent of the Puebloan diet, if not more.[71]

Higher food production was of course a bonus in its own right. But no less important was the fact that greater availability was connected with the familiar processes of elite control of resources and ritual, the creation and extension of regional trade networks and political, social and economic centralisation – as well as population expansion.[72] This was typified by the rise of the Great House system in Chaco Canyon in the San Juan Basin in north-western New Mexico, where these structures served as residences of the powerful, as administrative centres, as places with a ceremonial purpose – or all three.[73]

The growing complexity of these communities helped spur the extension of procurement networks from Chaco Canyon from around c.900, with marine shells from the Gulf of California, copper from west Mexico and cacao from Mesoamerica being found in increasing numbers as horizons and elite consumption demands expanded.[74] Scarlet and military macaws whose long and colourful feathers were particularly prized as indicators of prestige, wealth and spiritual status also began to be imported in large numbers from Central America. In Ancestral Pueblo communities too, they played key roles in repetitive rituals that helped enable group cohesion and solidarity, while underscoring the hierarchies that cemented and augmented power and status of those in the highest social groups.[75]

Processes of centralisation and expansion put pressure on resources, both locally and also beyond. There were ways to alleviate these by ecological interventions. In locations in the Andes, such as near Cuzco, for example, extensive planting of the fast-growing *Alnus acuminata*, which does well in poor, degraded soil, bears witness to sophisticated large-scale agro-forestry that was designed to reduce erosion or perhaps to ensure a fast-growing supply of timber. This may apply also in the Ancash highlands where a complex set of hydraulic systems was created at this time, apparently as a result of co-operation between rural communities.[76] The aim, evidently, was to re-landscape in order to mitigate against risk, and to ensure long-term sustainability of natural resources.

Key, then, was ecological awareness; but so too was the development and improvement of new technologies. Sometimes, this was spurred by the arrival of new, colonising powers. In the case of Andean societies, for example, the Wari brought about a range of new ideas as they expanded the territories and peoples under their control from around 600. The most important of these was the introduction of terraced agriculture in the high sierra, something that was supplemented by construction of advanced canal systems that were capable of discharging 400 litres per second. This was important in locations where there were significant demands on water supply: to give a sense of scale, the economic capital of the Tiwanku, allies of the Wari, was located at Chen Chen. It has been estimated that the people who lived in and around this conurbation required 250 million litres per year to sustain its population and its agricultural production. This necessitated a delicate balance not only with the requirements of fields further upstream but with other groups such as the Tumilaca.[77]

In such delicate contexts, then, population expansion, competition for water, overexploitation and of course subtle shifts in weather patterns could all present problems that could develop into existential threats. Just how serious those could be can be seen with the sack of Chen Chen and the collapse of Tiwanku in the tenth century.[78] While some scholars have linked the fall of Chen Chen and the contraction to the return of drought conditions, the sudden and dramatic dispersals of people from cultural centres point tellingly to the failure to adapt to changing circumstances by populations who were living beyond their means and capabilities.[79]

It was no coincidence, therefore, that the Chimú – effectively the heirs of Wari – invested time and energy in major infrastructure projects. These included the construction of the largest canal system in the western hemisphere along the hyperarid coast of Peru that connected the Chicama and Moche valleys. The aim was to ensure water supply to Chen Chen and the surrounding area, which both began to flourish once again. This time, in a clear sign that lessons from the past had been learned, the canal was extended further still as the city's populations or needs grew.[80] Steps like this were important at any time; during long periods of El Niño-related droughts, however, they were essential.[81]

Other locations in South America experienced different climatic changes from c.800. The steep, forested slopes of the mid-elevation Andes in northern Peru, saw unusually high levels of rainfall in this period. Conditions were so wet in this region that it seems that maize was abandoned in favour of other crops, such as potatoes, squash and beans.[82] The Chachapoya culture emerged around this time, which was also a moment of the expansion of Wari influence in this region. Key to the success of the latter was the introduction of widespread consumption of beer laced with hallucinogenic substances that expanded the numbers of those able to partake in experiences of euphoria and heightened awareness.[83]

Similar patterns could be seen in the eastern Amazon, where changes to the South American monsoon system brought a substantial shift from humid to drier conditions. Here too there were wholesale changes in diet, as well as in living patterns, marked by the rise of scattered settlements known as the Guarita phase.[84] In the southern highlands of Brazil, coastal communities not only saw an expansion of trade networks and of ceramic distribution, but underwent a demographic boom between c.800 and 1100.[85]

Such expansions excite archaeologists and historians; whether they produced such enviable outcomes for all involved is not so clear. In Japan, for example, a notably warm period starting in the late twelfth century was marked by demographic growth and higher population densities. This came at a cost, however: sharply falling life expectancies. Part of the reason for this was regular conflict and warfare that themselves reflect competition for resources, which in Japan's case was closely connected to the rise of a warrior class.[86] However, there was another, more important explanation: people living close to each other spread disease, often made worse by domesticated animals, rodents and parasites. Poor drainage and unhygienic conditions created a disease environment that could be dangerous, even deadly. New research on skeletal remains indicates that life expectancy fell as both the number and size of towns and cities rose.[87]

Curiously, there were long-term beneficiaries of epidemic disease. Some scholars argue that frequent outbreaks of smallpox – whose spread accelerated thanks to the intensification of trade as well as because of rising proximities and numbers of hosts – created 'endemic afflictions of childhood', thereby allowing immunity to build up over time.[88] Those who survived, in other words, built up resistance that proved helpful later in life. It is intriguing, then, that while phylogenetic analyses, ancient DNA (aDNA) and palaeopathological studies around smallpox are not (yet) able to shed light on smallpox in particular, there are indications that this disease spread widely across the Indian Ocean worlds during the early Middle Ages: the great polymath al-Bīrūnī writes about smallpox being blown by winds from Sri Lanka, while the emergence around the same time of the cult of the Hindu goddess Shitala as a figure of worship in Bengal – with a particular association with this disease – suggests a growing awareness of, and concern with, the transmission of infectious disease.[89]

A 'cluster of writing' about smallpox along the Silk Roads from the seventh to eleventh centuries during a time of intensified commercial, political and cultural contacts provides another illustration of how increased contact spreads disease, even if it says nothing about infection levels or mortality rates.[90] The dissemination of ideas about therapeutics, healing techniques and medical knowledge was a crucial characteristic of the regions that were connected by land and sea in Asia.[91] In the past, as well as the present, inter-connections of trade did not just help move goods, people and ideas; these networks also spread disease and death.

As it happened, there had long been extensive connections between the Indian subcontinent, South-East Asia, China and beyond: evidence from the Gupta dynasties in India attests to local, regional and long-distance contacts, diplomatic, commercial and otherwise in the fifth and sixth centuries.[92] There are clues too of maritime connections: for example, communities from southern India are recorded as living in Chinese ports in the sixth century; Tamil inscriptions of a trade guild in Takaupa in what is now Thailand point to trade relations between one side of the Bay of Bengal and the other in the ninth century; a set of copper plates from the mid-ninth century, meanwhile, inscribed in old Malayalam as well as in Arabic, Middle Persian and Judaeo-Persian show the level of cosmopolitanism in the Indian Ocean in this period. Nevertheless, while connections existed, they were relatively modest in scale.[93]

That changed dramatically from c.900, as connections, ties and exchanges rose quickly and dramatically. Climatic shifts certainly seem to have been a key part of the knitting together of ties. Cave speleothem deposits and other indicators reveal that there were regular monsoons and consistent rainfall for a three hundred years time-frame, with a short interlude in the years c.1030–70 which is usually attributed to the Oort Solar Minimum, a period when the sun's activities were significantly reduced.[94] As in other regions, what mattered as much as shifts in temperature and precipitation was the stability of climate patterns: it is certainly true that higher levels of rainfall made a major difference in particular boosting rice production across many parts of Asia – which helped improve calorie intake, freed up labour and contributed to demographic growth.[95] The low incidence of sudden or long-term shocks, however, was no less important in providing a platform for what has been described as the 'jump start' of a new era in the history of Asia: namely large, centralised states that rose in parallel.[96]

* * *

A set of empires began to grew up across South, South-East and East Asia in the early Middle Ages. One good example is provided by the Song dynasty in China which from the mid-tenth century was able to consolidate large parts of the lands that had disintegrated following the collapse of the Tang at the start of the tenth century, and establishing relations with neighbouring states like the Dali kingdom in what is now south-west China's Yunnan province in the process.[97] The success of the Song owed much to mundane, bureaucratic reforms. Instrumental in the economic boom, for example, was the widening of participation by merchants in political decision-making. Likewise, the investment in and improvements in literacy and education brought rewards, as did greater sharing of knowledge through rising book production. These all influenced imperial policy towards external trade in an age of change.[98] Benign and stable climatic conditions were important; but monetary policies, urbanisation, the rise of vibrant market towns and the networks that bound these together both domestically and internationally were what helped transform the Song into an imperial power.[99]

The success was mirrored by the rise of dynasties elsewhere which emulated, influenced and competed with each other. Strikingly, they rose as a group, fuelling each other directly and indirectly. The success of Chola dynasty in India, of Pagan in what is now Burma, of Angkor in Cambodia, of Srivijaya in the Indonesian archipelago, of Đại Việt in what is now Vietnam all took place more or less contemporaneously as part of a rapid broadening of geographic, commercial and cultural horizons across the Indian Ocean and across large parts of Asia.

Such was the intensity of these connections by the tenth century, that instead of finding whisps of evidence that show long-distance exchange, we find envoys were being received in Kaifeng in China from the Arab lands, from Chola India, from Srivijaya Sumatra and from the Champa in central-south Vietnam.[100] Dining tables in the Middle East were adorned with Chinese ceramics of such high quality, wrote one contemporary, that 'you can see water sparkle through them, even though they are ceramic'.[101]

Much of this contact was driven by trade, as well as by curiosity and information gathering, in some cases across distances of thousands of kilometres: the Mahārāja of the Srivijaya, wrote the Arab geographer al-Mas'ūdī, 'commands an empire without limits … the fastest vehicle could not in two years make the tour of the islands which are under his domination. The lands of this king produce all kinds of spices and aromatics, and no other sovereign in the world extracts as much wealth from his country.'[102]

Central to the creation of what developed into a global trading network that linked many parts of Asia, North Africa and Europe was the Chola dynasty in southern India. The origins of the Chola are not clear; either they supplanted the Pallavas who had held sway over much of this region before the ninth century or they were the beneficiaries of good timing as a stable agrarian economy emerged as a result of improvements in rainfall patterns.[103] The Cholas were formidable rulers; but they were lucky ones too.[104]

From the late tenth century, territories under Chola control underwent a series of physical transformations. The most striking of these was the transition from small shrines and places of worship into grandiose religious institutions. In addition to the resources that went into building enormous temples such as at Gangaikondacholapuram in what is now Tamil Nadu, hundreds of musicians, dancers, actors, goldsmiths, text reciters and more were employed to emphasise the power, wealth and splendour of the rulers and the divine protection they enjoyed.[105]

Chola rulers were keen to profit from maritime trade, with one ruler urging merchants to be generous to foreign visitors, to offer them hospitality and gifts as a way of ensuring preferential treatment.[106] Inscriptions dating to the second and third decades of the eleventh century suggest that Chola rulers were extending their interests more deeply into South-East Asia, presumably in order to gain control of regional and long-distance trade. In a case of expand or be damned, doing so was important to prevent access being blocked by Srivijaya through the straits of Melaka and suffer higher prices – or throttled supply as a consequence.[107]

The Chola kingdom evolved rapidly in response to the opening up to other regions and parts of the world. Monetisation was one key element in a series of steps taken that strengthened bureaucratic control over the agrarian economy. This had as its parallel the extension of cultural norms in the form of the spread of the cult of Śiva across Chola territories, as a means of promoting a common identity.[108] Like other post-Gupta dynasties in South Asia, such as the Paramāras, Cāllukyas and Rāṣṭrakūṭas, the Chola leaders also looked to connect their genealogies with the ancient past, tracing links to the sacred texts of the Purāṇas as a way of emphasising their authority – most notably in a set of famous copper plates discovered in 1905 at the shrine of the Vāṭaraṇyeśvara temple in what is now northern Tamil Nadu.[109]

Crucial too were the steps taken by successive rulers and administrators to plan for unexpected circumstances: with heavy dependence on monsoon rains, major investment went into the construction of tanks to trap and store water.[110] Adaptation and innovation were important too. The relocation of the capital first from Uraiyur to Thanjavur and then to Gangaikondacholapuram provides one example; the implementation of a fundamental reform of land tax to distinguish between the ways crops were watered, presumably to optimise central revenues for the benefit of the crown, provides another.[111]

It was a similar story in Angkor where massive storage facilities were constructed to help cater for a huge influx of inhabitants that some estimate rose to as much as 750,000 at its peak, bringing about the 'largest low density urban complex in the industrial world'.[112] The city, whose central area and periphery covered more than 1,000 square kilometres, was studded with magnificent temples, ritual dance halls and palace complexes that owed a heavy debt to southern India, to both Hindu and Buddhist influences and to a blend between the two.[113] Angkor was characterised by large-scale hydraulic systems that helped provide water to inhabitants and mitigated against sudden collapses in precipitation levels.[114] This was essential not only for social and political stability, but also for ensuring food supplies for a population whose sheer size meant there were obvious risks to even modest climatic shocks, such as droughts or floods.[115]

In other cases, such as Pagan and Đại Việt, water supplies were less of a problem thanks to the abundance of the river systems. Nevertheless, it has been suggested that higher-than-usual rainfall levels across several centuries helped reduce mortality rates from droughts in the highlands. This encouraged migration which in turn produced a boost in manpower and capacity in towns and regions that further galvanised productivity both locally and further afield.[116]

Each of these states had the good fortune to expand without obvious competition – or to absorb rivals with ease. In due course, however, they came into contact with each other and so competed for resources and for status. Market pressures could drive prices down, while rivalry over control of goods and products, as well as over transportation nodes, could lead to antagonism and in some cases military confrontation. Burmese royal interest in ports that served as transit points between the Indian Ocean and China sharpened ill-feeling locally in the eleventh century, while the struggle to control ports led to multiple conflicts between Angkor and Champa not long afterwards.[117]

The interlocking worlds of the Indian Ocean were not a new phenomenon, for even in antiquity there were close connections that linked the coasts and interior of many parts of Asia with Africa, the Mediterranean and Europe. What was different was the scale of activity: the rise of states and kingdoms that were imperial in scope and ambition created velocities of commercial and cultural exchange that were remarkable in both scale and volume. This was clear even as early as the ninth and tenth centuries, when ships carrying tens of thousands of pieces of ceramics made in China, bronzes from India, polished mirrors from Java, glassware from Egypt flitted back and forth – and occasionally ended up on the sea floor.[118]

This spurred interest in other parts of the world too. One Chinese Emperor wanted to know how elephants and rhinos were caught. 'To capture elephants,' one envoy replied, 'we use decoy elephants to get so near them that we can catch them with a big lasso. To catch a rhinoceros, a man with a bow and arrow climbs a big tree, where he watches for the animal until he can shoot and kill it. The young rhinoceros are not shot as they can be caught.'[119]

We know of rhinoceros horns, elephant tusks and rattan mats, as well as silks, textiles and umbrellas, being brought to Song China by traders from closer to home, such as from Champa, which also acted as a base for middlemen for goods from further afield, such as Javanese fabrics and aromatics from the Middle East. While it is tempting to look at exotica and the array of different kinds of things being exchanged, it is noteworthy that closer contacts also drove trends to standardisation – with a case in point being the ceramic industries of Đại Việt, Angkor and Java that over time adapted to mirror Chinese ceramic design.[120]

Then there were the cultures of the Toutswemogala and Mapungubwe kingdoms in the Limpopo–Shashi basin of what is now Botswana that grew and thrived from the eighth to the twelfth centuries.[121] Both lay to the south of Great Zimbabwe, which likewise flourished in southern Africa from the eleventh century and was centred on a settlement surrounded by massive sets of walls made up of almost 1 million pieces of stone, and with soapstone figures of birds with human lips mounted on perimeter columns.[122] These walls acted above all as statements of authority, rather than as defensive structures, built as enclosures for the most powerful members of a community numbering many thousands of people. The Hill Complex, the oldest of the enclosures, was the spiritual centre and the location of royal rituals that included appeasement of ancestors and sacrifices to the gods for clement weather. Finds of goods and luxury objects from Persia, Syria and China show that southern Africa was also involved in the rise of long-distance trade networks during this period.[123]

So were other societies, cultures, peoples and locations in Africa. The island of Kilwa played a central role in the Indian Ocean connections, linking the Swahili coast and East Africa in particular not only with maritime routes but also with southern Africa. Kilwa's prominence was partly the result of its location at the southern end of the route down which ships could sail from the north with monsoon winds, which made it an export centre for ivory, wood and above all gold from mines in what is now Mozambique; it enjoyed a rich trade in imported goods from as far away as China, attested by ceramic records dating from the eleventh century onwards.[124] Kilwa was 'one of the most beautiful towns in the world', according to Ibn Baṭṭūṭa, who nevertheless notes that its Muslim sultan and inhabitants were in a state of constant conflict with those living on the mainland.[125]

Kilwa was just one town among many dotted along the East African coast, extending from Somalia to Mozambique and northern Madagascar, which were typically home to mosques, tombs made of coral and houses of elites who were closely and directly involved with trade between the hinterland and the Indian Ocean.[126] Glass-bead assemblages provide particularly important insights into connections with the Gulf and South Asia. So too do large numbers of coins from Fatimid Egypt dating to the tenth and eleventh centuries that have been found in East Africa and Madagascar, which not only provide evidence of a north–south trade axis, but suggest Madagascar and the Comoros Islands as the likely sources of exceptionally pure rock crystal used for the magnificent ewers produced in North Africa in this period.[127]

While individual towns differed greatly in size and social structure, they were part of a wider, mutually interdependent web that fed regional trade, bound together by linguistic similarity, by Islam which had spread effectively by the twelfth century, and by rituals that helped build and deepen relationships between different rulers and peoples – of which feasting was one of the most important.[128]

The continuing development of these long-distance networks brought challenges as well as opportunities. Locations like Unguja Ukuu on Zanzibar became victims of their own success: deposits which built up from agricultural activities that supported growing populations, combined with the dumping of food remains and general waste, helped amplify sediment levels that resulted in the decline and eventual abandonment of one of the key trading hubs in East Africa.[129]

Elsewhere, the widening of connections led to states seeking to maintain monopolies over trade to protect existing interests and assert the authority of the political centre – one reason why the authorities in Song dynasty China interfered regularly in foreign trade, issuing bans, announcing reforms and following the movement of goods and traders carefully. This spilt over into other sectors as people became richer and, in some cases, more adventurous: the rise of a literati class who commented on courtly and official life, looked at history as a mirror for the present and created intellectual networks of their own was a major development, a by-product of a widening of society that was partly a result of increased international contacts.[130]

All around the world, the period from c.800 to c.1200 was one of profound change – a time when the effects of a climate reorganisation were enhanced by a lack of major volcanic activity. Migration to new regions, the development of new hydraulic technologies and the expansion of agricultural production were just some of the strategies that were adopted and modified to cope with a new set of questions that were different in different regions.

In some cases, ecological exchange had significant consequences. For example, the adoption of drought-resistant, early-maturing Champa rice by Chinese farmers following a drought in the Yangtze and Hui river valleys at the start of the eleventh century is thought to have been instrumental in providing a greater level of insurance against weather shocks in the future; the new strain not only helped guarantee calorie intakes and enabled more mouths to be fed, but in doing so also created conditions for political stability.[131] Perhaps not surprisingly, then, this was also the time when a set of other interventions in the natural landscape were carried out in East Asia, including the creation of large irrigation works, the construction of dams and deforestation to open up new areas for agricultural exploitation.[132]

Economic expansion, agrarian production and population growth were not only themes across many parts of Asia, Africa and the Americas but in Europe too where population levels also shot up, even if estimates of a tripling or even a quadrupling between c.800 and 1200 may be on the high side.[133] Some historians have noted that this set off a race between humans and their ecological and environmental settings, with the former battling to keep pace with the needs of ever-rising numbers of people that would almost inevitably end in crisis.[134]

What mattered above all, though, was not headcount in total terms, but population distribution and density. Cities like Hangzhou and Kaifeng are often thought to have been home to a million people, and while such estimates are both conveniently round and notably large, there is little escaping the fact that they were home to very substantial numbers of inhabitants.[135] As in other major cities in other regions and in other periods of history, their practical needs – for food, water and fuel, not to mention luxury goods – were substantial and not only put a strain on ecological resources but demanded supply chains that were efficient and robust. This was a problem for locations like Pagan, later known as Arimaddana-pura (or 'the City that Tramples on Enemies'), which had to contend with seawater flooding and regular river sedimentation.[136]

At Angkor, a city that was home to 3,000 temples including the magnificent Angkor Wat complex, an elaborate system of reservoirs and canals that trapped and distributed fresh water helped to supply inhabitants as well as to irrigate fields locally. Schemes such as this not only depended on a great deal of manpower for construction, but also needed constant maintenance to prevent sand and debris from blocking the canals.[137] This meant heavy labour costs and required supervision and co-ordination, as well as technical skills. The water system was designed to reduce risk of one kind, but in doing so introduced those of another kind: any lapse in or challenge to centralised authority could quickly escalate to create problems that could leave the livelihood of the inhabitants and the viability of the city in doubt.

The ease with which urban settlements could be threatened by relatively modest fluctuations in weather conditions is made clear in the middle of the twelfth century in the Levant, where any delay to the rains provoked concern and distress and where their arrival was greeted with joyful celebration. As Nūr al-Dīn, a well-known and important leader at the time, reached Baalbek, 'it happened by the predestined decree and celestial mercy that the heavens opened their fountains with rains, dews, outpourings, and heavy showers lasting from Tuesday until the following Tuesday. The water courses overflowed, the pools of Hawran were filled, the mills turned, and the crops and plants that had been withered were restored to fresh green shoots.' This fortuitous timing generated political capital for Nūr al-Dīn, with people declaring that the rains were the result of 'his blessed influence, his justice, and his upright conduct'.[138]

The people of Mosul were less fortunate at the end of the 1170s when drought and famine were so severe that citizens demanded that the sale of wine be prohibited, judging that the lack of rain was an act of divine punishment for the impiety of those who dared drink alcohol. To make matters worse, dust storms blown by strong winds had made the skies 'so dark that a man could hardly see anyone he was with', causing people to pray at all times of the day, begging God for forgiveness. 'They thought that the Day of Judgement had arrived.'[139]

The swings in fortune are captured in a treatise written by the physician 'Abd al-Laṭīf al-Baghdādī which offers a snapshot of life in Egypt at the start of the thirteenth century. While it starts with accounts of abundance – including a memorable recipe for a giant pie made with three roast lambs and some ninety chickens and other birds that would be ideal for a large picnic for family and friends – it goes on to provide harrowing details of sudden food shortages and of the spread of disease. So many died, he writes, that skulls were 'stacked up on top of each other in layers ... to an onlooker, they resembled a newly cut crop of watermelons, heaped together at the harvest'. When 'Abd al-Laṭīf saw them a few days later, 'the sun had scorched the flesh off them and they had turned white'; they now looked 'like ostrich eggs piled up'.[140] It did not take much for times of plenty to give way to horrors such as this in cities that were densely packed and where a sudden shortage of supply could not be quickly addressed.

The dry conditions were a source of bafflement for some commentators, especially those who read about the past history of the region. William of Tyre, a prominent archbishop and chronicler at the time of the Crusades, was puzzled when he read an account written by

Gaius Solinus several hundred years before about different parts of the then Roman world. 'I am surprised at Solinus' statement that Judea is famous for its waters,' wrote William in the mid-twelfth century, given that the conditions at the time of writing were arid and that households had to depend on rainfall and on their wits to survive. 'I cannot account for this,' he added, 'except to conclude that either he was not telling the truth, or that the face of the earth has changed since that time.'[141]

As it happens, evidence from lake sediment, speleothems, pollen data and tree-ring samples shows that conditions were becoming drier and colder in Anatolia, Syria and the Balkans in the second half of the twelfth century.[142] Rising aridity also seems to have been the signature in many parts of Central Asia in the same period, with evidence of progressive settlement contraction in the decades leading up to 1200 – a period that also saw long and damaging droughts on the Mongolian plains.[143] Perhaps not surprisingly, this was a time of considerable turbulence and instability among nomadic groups, whose intense competition for dwindling resources points to the gravity of the situation as it unravelled.[144]

A dramatic and seemingly sudden demographic downturn in and around Jenne-Jeno, a city on the floodplain of the Niger and Bani rivers, in c.1200 also hints at a possible role played by climatic factors. The previous decades had seen an extraordinary blossoming of the city's art and architecture which came to an abrupt end at this time, with other large urban settlements in the Niger floodplain, such as Dia and the Akumbu communities in what is now Mali, likewise undergoing major contractions.[145] In the absence of environmental data, hypotheses about climate factors is highly speculative – and perhaps even dubious, given that Jenne-Jeno's sister city of Jenne, home to the famous Great Mosque that was located just a few kilometres away, does not appear to have experienced the same negative fortunes at the same time or afterwards.[146]

In fact, population collapse could equally result from disease outbreaks or from political infighting and instability. For example, while some scholars have argued that the decline of Cahokia in North America was a form of ecocide caused by the exhaustion of natural resources (wood in particular), and other scholars have suggested that evidence of demographic decline shown by faecal stool samples is correlated to changes in summer precipitation around 1200 which affected maize yields and made life more difficult. Others still have noted that more mundane explanations may be the most plausible: leaders within Cahokia society tried to gain too much power, prompting local rebellion and infighting between settlements that spilt over into bitter conflict. The need for groups that had previously co-operated to protect themselves from each other explains why towns became fortified with defensive walls, palisades and moats – rather than changing precipitation levels.[147] Naturally, resource scarcity caused by changes to seasonal rains may have exacerbated the situation; but climatic change was likely to have been a contributing factor rather than the direct cause of decline.

Such distinctions are important, not least because of the contemporary focus on searching for lessons from societies that were apparently ecologically or environmentally unsustainable and sowed the seeds of their own demise. In the case of Angkor, for example, it has been convincingly argued that what proved difficult to overcome were not so much the decades-long droughts and intense monsoons that are indicated by archaeological evidence as well as by tree-ring and other data, but rather the variability between the two. Multi-year arid periods followed by long phases of very heavy rainfall made planning difficult and undermined the complex socio-economic systems required to manage the needs of the city and its inhabitants.[148]

As historians have also noted, a new phase in the strengthening of maritime connections, especially in the Mekong Delta, may have persuaded elites to relocate closer to the benefits and rewards of trade. This left the hydraulic networks that had made Angkor into one of the greatest cities in Asia overwhelmed by a combination of a lack of expertise, available labour, investment, leadership and oversight. Heavy expenditure on temple building, maintenance and public services was also a strain: Khmer rulers had embarked on a 'building orgy', with Jayavarman VII (r. 1181–1218) overseeing a construction programme 'never equalled by any other monarch in any other country'; this included a network of more than a hundred hospitals, each of which had a walled compound, a stone-lined pool and a 'library' building, as well as a sanctuary, ritual platform and storeroom for herbs, spices and precious items sent out three times a year from the king's warehouse. All of these were completed within four years of him taking the throne and evidently required enormous funding.[149]

Such irrational exuberance did not need much to turn the good times into bad ones. But by the early fourteenth century, a tipping point had been reached. This was a difficult period in Khmer history. There was widespread desecration of Jayavarman's temples, while artefacts were destroyed. Ritual burials of Buddha icons were carried out with idols carefully placed in beds of sand to protect them.[150] The costs of living rose too fast, and as they did so confidence in the old way of doing things faded too. The hard realities of keeping up appearances was what brought about decline, rather than catastrophic collapse brought on by climatic change.[151]

Similarly, while the decline of the Pagan kingdom in South Asia has multiple intertwining explanations, the most compelling reason for a trajectory that corresponded to that of Angkor was that it too was a victim of its own success. Successive rulers in the eleventh and twelfth centuries had proved capable of fusing ideas that bound together diverse peoples and cultures, and finding ways to express these in magnificent monumental architecture, as well as through art, literature and language and through more mundane steps such as the standardisation of weights and the monetisation of the economy.[152] Pagan's rulers invested considerable resources in religious patronage of Buddhist monasteries and institutions as a trade-off for support and confirmation of authority. Constructions such as the Ananda, Shwesandaw and Thatbyinnyu temples – to name three of the 2,000 that were built between the tenth and thirteenth centuries – were intended to serve as statements of power, not just as links to the Buddhist cycle of reincarnation: royal donations were supplemented by support from elites who hoped thereby to gain status as well as to earn merit that might ensure for them a better next life.[153]

Inevitably, over time this tipped the balance away from secular authority in favour of monastic establishments. As more land, its produce and tax revenues passed into the hands of religious devotees, the less authority the crown had over territories it nominally controlled – and the less able it was to make investments for the future, whether in trade, in military capabilities or simply to retain the loyalty of magnates.[154] Pagan had benefited from the springboard provided by benign conditions that favoured agricultural exploitation, enabling a sufficient and steady food supply that encouraged a process of urbanisation that in turn led to specialisation, to a glorious cultural flowering and to a place within vibrant local, regional and even intercontinental trade networks. In due course, that took a toll from which recovery proved impossible: it would be both an oversimplification and an exaggeration to argue that Pagan and Angkor declined because of such excesses. Nevertheless, it is hard not to acknowledge the impact of the depletion of financial resources and of what amounted to an effective transfer in royal wealth to religious foundations. But, taken together, it may well be that the most important way to understand the decline of these great cities in South and South-East Asia is as victims of their own success.[155]

Shifting consumption patterns, combined with an inability or unwillingness to adapt, also explain the failure of Norse communities in Greenland. A cooling process from the early fourteenth century saw an extension of Arctic pack ice, significantly reduced rainfall, shorter growing seasons and more demanding conditions for domestic animals. Each and all were challenging. But what may have proved more telling was that Norse Greenlanders did not adopt Inuit Arctic-adapted technologies, such as the toggle harpoon and the kayak – perhaps out of pride or because of an 'intense cultural conservatism' that impelled them to looked down on Inuit peoples and keep separate from them. Osteological and DNA evidence suggests that intermixing between settlers and Inuit was essentially non-existent.[156]

In fact, even the unwillingness to adopt tools that had proved their worth may have been less important than developments elsewhere that had nothing to do with climate or adaptation and a lot to do with market forces: Greenland's main value was a source of exports of furs and walrus hides and teeth. From the early 1300s, however, new trading networks linking Novgorod and Russian cities into the White Sea opened up new sources of animal skins and furs that provided competition for supplies from the North Atlantic, while hemp ropes offered alternatives that were cheaper and more plentiful than those made from thick and sturdy walrus hides. The market for walrus tusks, meanwhile, was depressed on the one hand by rising supplies of elephant ivory from Africa, and on the other by changing tastes and cultural shifts that included a turn away from ivory in religious art production.[157] To top it all off, as climate conditions became more challenging and economic realities more difficult, life also became more precarious for the Norse communities, who were subject to ever more attacks by Inuit (whom the the settlers called Skrælings) driven by opportunism and by competition for resources and location; these raids were devastating and demoralising.[158]

Nevertheless, just as there had been a reconfiguration of global climates starting around 800, patterns now begun to change around four centuries later, albeit neither suddenly nor consistently. The impacts started to be felt in the eastern Mediterranean and Central Asia as early as the late twelfth century, and appear to have been matched by changes that took effect in the Pacific Rim around the same time. Wetter conditions coincided with a new wave of migrations and settlements from Polynesia to Hawai'i, Aotearoa (New Zealand) and Rapa Nui (Easter Island).[159] This was also the moment of a single contact between Polynesian and South American population groups – either as a result of a group or groups of the former journeying across the entire expanse of the Pacific and returning successfully, or as a result of groups of the latter setting off and reaching Polynesian islands c.1200.[160]

The causes of population dispersals across the Pacific were complex. While a shift in climate was likely an important factor, the custom of primogeniture – which consolidated power for the benefit of a single family member – may have encouraged searches for new opportunities.[161] Whatever the case, new settlements brought about ecological change to islands that had previously not been inhabited, including deforestation and the collapse of bird and mammal species caused by human interventions, such as hunting or land clearing. On top of that was the damage done by domesticated animals that were brought intentionally by new settlers and by rodents like the Pacific rat that were transported alongside human travellers – perhaps inadvertently, but perhaps not.[162]

By the late thirteenth century, life on many Pacific islands was becoming precarious. Evidence of elevated numbers and growing strength of storms, falling sea levels and rapid reduction of food sources in coastal areas transformed many island communities. The harvesting and trading of pearl oysters across the South Pacific by inhabitants of the Cook Islands came to an end, while fishing seems to have declined sharply on Easter Island. Coastal embayments that had provided comfortable living spaces became brackish lakes or swamps in the Solomon Islands, for example. In New Zealand, the drop in temperatures meant that it was no longer possible to grow the sweet potatoes that had been brought by the first human settlers who had arrived c.1250, leading to a reliance on the roots of the bracken fern instead.[163]

When we think about the Middle Ages, we tend to focus only on western Europe and think in terms of an age of kings and barons, peasants and priests, of the rise of institutions such as the Church or guilds. Taking a more global view of this period raises important questions about the exploitation of natural resources, about the role of technological change in raising agricultural yields or about the adoption of new crops or of new strains such as Champa rice. It also raises questions about the role played by climatic shifts and about the distinction between changes in weather conditions and the challenges posed by their variations.

Taken as a whole, however, the period c.800–c.1250 was one of profound intensification of connections – within interlocking and interdependent worlds in Asia, Africa and Europe, or within communities in the Americas which emerged as central if independent hubs that had little or no interaction. It was hardly the case that this long time-frame provided conditions of peace and harmony that enabled relentless economic and demographic growth: in fact, one could argue the opposite was the case, as empires and dynasties rose and fell, states fought, were subsumed by or conquered each other or faded into obsolescence as new competitors emerged who could supply goods more quickly and more cheaply.

Nevertheless, as with other periods, it is hard to escape the fact that the fundamentals of ecological equilibrium and environmental sustainability underpinned the cultural, political, socio-economic, diplomatic and military histories of individual kingdoms, states or regions. Reliable food and water supplies were central at all times, but especially during periods of demographic expansion. Societies had to contend with finite natural resources; when those became exhausted or came under stress because of over-exploitation, because of shifts in rainfall patterns or because of conflict, disease or the failure of infrastructure such as river defences, disaster soon followed. That provides some food for thought for the present and future – as well as the past.

13

Disease and the Formation of a New World (c.1250–c.1450)

Time itself has slipped through our fingers.

Petrarch, *De rebus familiaribus* (1348)

The twelfth century saw repeated series of fractures within and beyond the Chinese world. The efflorescence that followed the collapse of the Tang 200 years earlier had seen the emergence of the Song dynasty as well as a host of other states of varying size and capabilities across East, South and South-East Asia. Kingdoms such as Đại Việt in what is now northern Vietnam, Dali in modern Yunnan province and Goryeo (Koryŏ) in the Korean peninsula had been part of a tapestry of states that rose together and benefited from increasing levels of trade as well as from cultural, political and sometimes military competition.[1]

The mesh of relationships was often uneven, complex and unstable. In 1127, the city of Kaifeng was sacked by Jürchen nomads in one of the most dramatic moments in history. At the time, Kaifeng was one of the largest cities in the world – perhaps even the largest measured by population size – and also one of the most splendid, lovingly described by Meng Yuanlao in a treatise known as *Dreams of Splendour of an Eastern Capital* which records the friendliness of the inhabitants as well as the richness of civic life before the city's fall. 'Peace stretched on day after day; people were many and all things were in abundance,' writes Meng. 'Youths with trailing locks practiced naught but drumming and dancing, the aged with white speckled [hair] recognized neither shield nor spear. Season and festival followed one upon the other, each with its own sights to enjoy.'[2]

Now devastation followed. The Emperor Huizong and his family were captured and deported to Jürchen homelands in Manchuria. 'Once I lived in heaven above, in pearl palaces and jade towers,' wrote the Empress Zhu, who was raped by her captors as she was marched northwards into the cold; 'now I live among grass and brambles, my blue robe soaked in tears. I hate the drift of snow.'[3] It was a disaster, lamented the poet Li Qingzhao:

And you should've been more cautious,
Better educated by the past.
The ancient bamboo books of history
Were there for you to study.
But you didn't see ...[4]

Disruption extended into the steppes, where peoples like the Naiman, Kereit and Qonggirad were obliged to submit to and make contributions in kind to the Jürchen overlords. The Mongols were treated so badly that, in the words of one leading scholar, they 'almost ceased to exist'.[5]

That changed in the late twelfth century, thanks to another Mongol leader who proved rather more resilient and successful. There were many reasons for the rise of Temüjin: his charisma, determination and leadership skills were crucial, as was his strategic decision-making. However, he owed his rise to his marriage to Börte, the daughter of a Qonggirad chief, which gave status to the Mongols and to Temüjin personally. To keep Temüjin in his place, Börte was kidnapped by the dominant Merkit tribe, which likely resulted in her rape; the birth of her firstborn son, Jochi, soon followed. Temüjin's response seems to have been astute – he brought up Jochi as his own, and later placed him in charge of all Merkit territories and beyond.[6]

Temüjin consolidated his power steadily in the 1180s and 1190s, perhaps helped by a period of extremely dry conditions that made life on the steppes challenging and offered opportunities for those looking to profit from the weakening of both the authority and the resources of more powerful groups.[7] By 1203, he had become master of the Orkhon Valley, home to hundreds of *balbal* stone statues and to a famous set of inscriptions proclaiming that whoever controlled this area would be the master of all the steppe nomad tribes. For nomadic peoples, this was the centre of the world; by taking control, Temüjin could benefit not only from prestige but from *sülde* – the life-affirming source of unity and power that provided a mandate for further expansion.[8]

This was important, for steppe empires required expansion to survive: growth was not only useful but essential in supplying the rewards to keep social and political structures in place. The fluidity of tribal groups and confederations meant that leaders needed to engage in the constant acquisition of material rewards – in the form either of the payment of tribute or of spoils of conquest – in order to keep interest groups, supporters, rivals and potential rivals happy.[9]

By 1206, Temüjin was master of the steppes, expanding his authority through military force, dynastic ties and relentless expansion through the elimination of rivals. That year, he gathered an assembly of the Mongol elites and representatives of all the other groups that had been defeated by or had submitted to him and was proclaimed the supreme ruler with the title Činggis Khan or universal ruler.[10] The consequences of not recognising his overlordship were then made clear: those who had defied him would be hunted down one by one and measured 'against the linchpin of a cart'. Those who were not murdered would be captured, enslaved and shared out among Mongol supporters as prizes.[11]

Achieving a dominant position on the steppe was one thing; using that platform to create the largest land empire in human history represented an achievement of a different magnitude altogether. In the decades that followed, states and dynasties in what is now China were picked off one by one, as the Western Xia, Jin, Dali and Song fell in turn leading up to the fall of the house of Ch'oe in Korea in 1258; this left Japan as the final remaining objective in East Asia. To the west, Mongols had also spread westwards like wildfire, forcing the submission of Central Asia before Činggis Khan's death in 1227, and reaching central Europe barely a decade later.

There were many explanations for these successes – including the selective use of extreme violence as a tool of control and intimidation, the organisational abilities of highly mobile scouting troops in identifying new targets, logistical brilliance in information gathering, adoption of new techniques and tactics (such as the use of artillery) and supreme innovation on the battlefield.[12]

But the fuel for success may have been provided by an extraordinary pluvial period between 1211 and 1225 in Mongolia that was the wettest in more than 1,110 years. These conditions significantly increased the carrying capacity of the landscape, producing more abundant grasses and dramatically expanding the amount of available pastureland. This provided the basis for enormous increases in the size of livestock herds, above all of horses. Činggis Khan, his followers and successors may well have been tactically brilliant, yet it was their good fortune that the Mongols not only could draw on vast resources to defeat their enemies and expand their empire, but were able to do so at exactly the right moment.[13]

The significance of this accident of timing can be underlined by noting a downturn in conditions in the later 1220s caused by another 'machine-gun effect' of multiple volcanic eruptions such as Mounts Reykanes and Reykjaneshryggur in Iceland, and Mounts Zao and Aso on the Japanese islands of Honshū and Kyūshū which erupted between 1226 and 1231 and left acid spikes on northern hemisphere ice cores. These were likely responsible for drops in temperature that are attested by tree rings in Scandinavia and the Qinghai–Tibetan plateau, perhaps exacerbated by changes to El Niño patterns in the Pacific.[14]

This period was one of severe food shortage in Korea and of catastrophic suffering in Japan, which experienced one of the worst famines in its history in the early 1230s. This was followed by an epidemic that was referred to as the 'barbarian sickness' (ibyō) and by floods that left dead bodies lining the riverbanks in Kyoto. The story was the same throughout Japan, wrote the nobleman Kageyukōji Tsunemitsu in his diary: put simply, it was a time of 'sad lamentation'. Although mortality rates across the Japanese archipelago would not have been uniform, data from censuses and from taxation and land records suggest population falls of around 20 per cent in the course of four years of woe.[15]

Around the same time in Novgorod in what is now Russia, one chronicler recorded that crops were ruined by frost, leading to so many starving to death that it was impossible to bury the bodies. 'The wrath of God was such that the people not only ate the dead but even the living would kill and eat each other; and they ate horseflesh, dogs, cats, and other animals. Whatever one could find, he would eat – moss, pine, elm, linden bark and leaves.' While the impact on the Mongols is not clear, the fact that this was the time when they expanded across swathes of territory, overwhelmed the Xia and destroyed what was left of the Jin may well indicate that these developments are best understood as knockout blows being delivered to already weakened states that were now teetering on the abyss. The prizes taken by the Mongols were in many cases low-hanging, fading fruit rather than glittering, extraordinary glories.[16]

The administrative and bureaucratic structures that the Mongols put in place as they brought more and more territory, people and cities under their sway were nevertheless impressive in their scale and their efficiency. In many cases, these were extensions or adaptations of systems that the Mongols had been exposed to and were then introduced across the empire – such as the service for bringing post and information both reliably and quickly to and from the centre. Usually referred to as the *yām*, this was a variant of the Chinese *yi* (or *li*) system of communication which had been introduced by Uighur and Kitan advisers enjoying prominent roles at the Mongol court.[17]

Another key part of the Mongols' success was the incorporation of local elites – something that runs contrary to the common assumptions today of the conquerors as brutal, bloody and ultra-violent.[18] Such is this reputation, indeed, that some scientists have claimed that the Mongol invasions killed so many people that this had an impact on the global carbon cycle and lowered atmospheric CO_2 content – a proposition that gained attention in the press around the world, generating headlines such as 'Why Genghis Khan was good for the planet'.[19]

In fact, growing evidence shows that, although the Mongols were beneficiaries of an ideal set of climatic conditions for their own needs, the world they were stepping into – at least in Central Asia – was one of urban and demographic contraction, at least partially caused by ecological and hydrological pressure as long periods of aridity forced changes of lifestyle and in some cases abandonment of settlements.[20]

While there can be little doubt about instances of extreme violence on the part of the Mongols, of rather more significance was the creation of the Pax Mongolica – a term intended to explain the essential stability of Mongol overlordship after the explosive period of expansion. Rather than devastate and destroy the world, the Mongols oversaw an intensification of trade across Eurasia, which sits at odds with the widespread depiction even today of Činggis Khan and his successors as bloodthirsty and barbaric.[21] A 'bridge of justice' should be built across the Mongol lands, one khan was told, 'for where there is justice, the world is prosperous'.[22]

The interconnected world created by the Mongol conquests facilitated commercial exchange – something the leadership was actively keen to promote.[23] The Mongols were prolific builders of cities, most notably Karakorum, which was founded in 1220 and was the recipient of heavy investment over the decades that followed, including an opulent and spectacular palace.[24] Many new towns were founded on the banks of the major rivers of Central Asia and on the shorelines of the Black Sea and the Sea of Azov.[25]

As recent experience of pandemic has reminded us, greater volumes of trade, higher levels of travel and closer links between people living in different regions accelerate the transmission of disease. It was no coincidence, for example, that the increase in population size in Song dynasty China and the expansion of territory under centralised control also saw an increase in the number and severity of outbreaks of epidemic disease.[26] While leprosy is well attested in Europe, the rash of leper houses that began to be founded in the eleventh century would most naturally seem connected with the rise of socio-economic interactions across the continent in precisely that period.[27]

The rise of the Mongol empire too seems to have been closely linked to the expansion of pathogens and disease. Multiple accounts talk of large numbers of casualties in sieges mounted by Mongol forces in the course of the thirteenth century, including the assaults on Kaifeng in 1232 and on Baghdad in 1258 which were seminal moments in the establishment of control in East and West Asia respectively. In the case of the latter, so many had died from 'pestilence' that there were not enough people to bury the dead, with the result that dead bodies were simply flung into the River Tigris. The fact that the Mongol ruler, Hülegü, moved camp at least five times in 1257 while preparing the assault on the city may reflect efforts to relocate in order to contain or stay ahead of outbreaks of disease.[28] Literary sources as well as network analysis of authors who trained in Damascus in the thirteenth century reveal how epidemics affected other parts of the Middle East at this time.[29]

The significance of this evidence has long been overlooked, as has material relating to demographic contraction and political instability in East Africa and in Ethiopia in particular.[30] In recent years, a handful of pioneering scholars have been questioning whether plague was responsible for some or all of these developments. For example, the site of Akrokrowa in Ghana was abandoned around the middle of the fourteenth century, as were multiple associated sites, with new settlement patterns being adopted that suggest a sudden shock or shocks traumatic enough to alter people's way of life. This took place precisely at the time when the Black Death was ravaging other parts of Africa as well as the Middle East and Europe.[31]

Groundbreaking research has produced startling new avenues of investigation into how the Mongols may have unwittingly created a perfect environment for plague to be spread along trade and travel routes and for it to be taken outside natural foci where it exists endemically, such as in the Tien Shan mountain range of Central Asia. One way in which this happened was the expansion of Mongol food tastes, as well as through their fur and leather requirements.

As Monica Green has suggested, marmots were prime suspects as vectors of disease transmission: textbooks written by leading dietary physicians extolled the utility of marmot meat as a source of protein, and also remarked positively on the warmth of marmot skin as well as its resistance to rain and water. It seems that the spread of the Mongols and of their dietary and fashion preferences may have played a role in helping disseminate pathogens from their natural habitat, where they could enter the human body through ingestion of meat or simply through inhalation.[32] It may be that the higher prevalence of plague was related to greater exploitation of marmots from their habitats; or it could also be that changing environmental conditions provided the impetus for the migration of marmots and other hosts to locations that brought them into closer contact with human populations.[33]

Extraordinary breakthroughs have also led to a full mapping out of the genome sequence of *Yersinia pestis* aDNA and to the phylogenetic tree of *Yersinia pestis*.[34] This shows the sudden divergence of *Y. pestis* into four branches shortly before the Black Death in a moment that geneticists have called the Big Bang. The causes, context and date of this divergence are not clear, although some have suggested a spillover event may date to the first two decades of the thirteenth century within a context of Mongol contacts with the Turfan Uighurs or the Qara Khitai.[35]

Another line of investigation has focused on the massive eruption of the Samalas volcano on Lombok in what is now Indonesia that took place in the late spring or early summer of 1257.[36] The eruption was one of the largest of the last millennium, if not the largest.[37]

Its violence led to thick tephra covering Lombok, with pyroclastic density currents up to fifty metres thick burying around half the island.[38] The eruption appears to have had an important climatic impact, including the draining of the stratospheric beryllium (^{10}Be) reservoir for over a decade, as well as resulting in an El Niño-like event in its immediate aftermath or enhancing pre-existing weather patterns.[39]

The most important of these was an exceptional period of high solar irradiance which had peaked in the late 1240s – and reached levels that have not been matched for almost eight hundred years. The effects of the Samalas eruption were global, producing intense monsoons in Asia, severe drought in the western flank of the Americas and unusual and unpredictable conditions in England where unusually strong storms in some years and 'intolerable heat' in others had an impact on harvests and on wheat prices. These uncertainties fanned baronial opposition to the crown in England, where King Henry III was faced with considerable political pressure in 1258 as a result of a severe food crisis that stemmed in part from bad weather, but also from the panicked response to rising prices. People fled from the countryside to towns and cities in search of food. As London became swamped by refugees, it was not long before bodies could be found 'in all directions, swollen and livid through hunger, lying by fives and sixes in pigsties, on dunghills, and in the muddy streets, their bodies woefully and mortally wasted'. Poor harvests put pressure on supplies, but the responses made a bad situation much worse.[40]

The middle decades of the thirteenth century were a time of intense volcanic activity. As it happens, eruptions of Zao in Japan in 1227 and of Rekjanes in Iceland in the same year and again in 1231, left a heavier signature on the dendrochronological evidence than Samalas, presumably because of the timing of the latter.[41] Two further eruptions that have recently been identified but whose locations remain unknown can be dated to 1241 and 1269. All these eruptions resulted in the mass ejection of aerosols into the atmosphere.[42] 1258 and 1259 proved to be two of the coldest summers in the northern hemisphere of the last millennium – with conditions in western Europe, Siberia and Japan proving to be particularly harsh.[43]

Volcanic eruptions were one part of the story. The behaviour of the sun was another. The period of enhanced irradiance gave way to a Grand Solar Minimum, a time of sharply reduced solar magnetic activity – first christened the Wolf Minimum in 1980.[44] A number of studies have demonstrated there were sharp changes in atmospheric radiocarbon and cooler global temperatures starting around 1260 and lasting for eighty years until the middle of the fourteenth century.[45] As astronomers note, solar minima have limited impact on temperature, with differentials typically no more than 0.3 °C.[46] What was significant, then, was that this reduced solar activity not only coincided with yet another series of major volcanic eruptions in 1269, 1276 and 1286 but also with the weakening of the El Niño–Southern Oscillation, the Asian monsoon and the North Atlantic Oscillation. The results were striking, with higher levels of moisture to the Pacific coast of South America as well to North America, ending a long period of drought in each, while also resulting in sudden reductions in monsoon rainfall in South and South-East Asia from the 1280s, which played a role in harvest failure, hunger and famine.[47]

In north-western Europe, weather became more unsettled, heightening the risk of food pressure and increasing the possibility of the spread of disease – for humans and for livestock. These pressures were compounded by the strong demographic growth that had characterised the early Middle Ages and by the resultant development and exploitation of fragile ecosystems. A case in point comes from a belt of sandy terrain stretching from Breckland in England across continental Europe through North Sea coastal regions as far as Russia.[48] Mismanagement or overuse of the top layers of loose quartz could result in heightened vulnerability to floods and to uncontrolled sand drifts that could destroy intensively cultivated arable land very quickly.[49] As one leading scholar has put it, the prospect of supply-side food shortages came at precisely the moment when societies found it hard to cope with them.[50]

Accounts from Scotland, England and Ireland paint a picture of conditions that were difficult and unpredictable, with repeated indications of crops failing and outbreaks of famine in the second part of the thirteenth century. One report of 'a great lack of productivity of the land and unfruitfulness of the sea, as well as turbulence of the air, as a result of which many people fell ill and many animals died' was typical of many that show the difficulties in trying to contend with unusual storm patterns, insect infestations, excessive rain or unusual cold.[51]

The falls in revenue at international fairs such as those held at St Giles Winchester and St Ives, which collapsed by at least 75 per cent between 1285 and the 1340s show this was a time of disruption and contraction. The dramatic decline in the value of English overseas trade handled by foreigners, and the halving of rental values of property in Cheapside in London across three decades at the start of the fourteenth century, point to the scale of the economic repercussions in this period.[52] So too do cases of the spread of sheep scab in 1279 which halved national wool output and led to supply shortages in locations that were dependent on high-quality raw materials for their own production – such as in Flanders, where riots broke out as a consequence.[53]

It has been suggested that rising numbers of cases in Scotland in the 1290s of scab – an intense reaction to the *Psoroptes ovis* mite – along with severe winters, poor summers and failed harvests played a role in fomenting dissent against King Edward I of England, especially after his treasurer, Hugh de Cressingham, sought to raise taxes in 1296–7; this provided a rallying point for anti-English sentiment, spurring revolts led by William Wallace that dominated much of the following decade.[54]

In East Asia, the century that followed 1260 saw regular drops in mean temperature, with harsh conditions in the 1270s, 1310s and 1350s attested by multiple written and climate sources from Korea, Japan and China.[55] For many parts of China in particular, the period 1300–60 was one of almost constant natural disaster, including frequent supertyphoons that devastated the coastline, regular flooding of the Yangtze and Yellow River deltas and a series of epidemics in the middle of the century that claimed hundreds of thousands of lives. In 1308 alone, according to the Yuan chronicle, bitter snowstorms on the Mongolian steppe killed huge numbers of livestock and forced almost a million people to migrate southwards – where they had to survive on handouts from the court. Famine and disease killed almost half the population in the Yue region of the Yangtze Delta in the same year, while so many perished in Jiangzhe province that 'Dead bodies lay upon each other. Fathers sold their sons, and husbands sold their wives, the sound of their crying was so loud that the Earth trembled.'[56]

This presented challenges for the imperial court and the Emperor in particular, whose authority – linked to having a mandate from heaven – was compromised by such regular and severe setbacks. Indeed, in 1297, the Yuan Emperor changed his reign title to Dade (大德, or 'Great virtue') in an attempt to end the downturn of fortunes.[57] Imperial power was not just affected in its abstract terms: failed harvests meant reduced revenues, which were then further stretched by distribution of food and disaster relief. This in turn impaired the Emperor's ability to dominate the aristocracy, which relied on regular disbursements from the centre. In 1307, Emperor Wuzong was barely able to pay half of what he had promised because 'the exchequer's coffers … [were] empty'. Four years later, the amounts paid were only a third of that figure; and those in turn had halved by 1317.[58] In other words, beneficiaries received less than a tenth of what they had been getting a decade earlier.

It was perhaps not surprising then that shortage, suffering and fear brought about social and political turmoil. Many parts of the Middle East had seen an unusually large number of freak weather events in the decades after 1260, including damaging wind storms – such as one in 1319–20 that destroyed many houses in Damascus, leaving people trapped indoors by fallen trees. The same storm struck Aleppo, accompanied by dust, hail, thunder and lightning, and uprooted oak and olive trees as well as vines. As is true of all such events, the poor were hit hardest, first through the loss of homes and livelihood, and then by the limited or non-existent resources that might enable them to start from scratch; needless to say, one additional outcome was the inflationary effect on prices that pushed commodities, goods and food to become even more unaffordable.[59]

In this context, it was no surprise that social unrest was a consistent feature of this period. Its effects were particularly clear at the start of the fourteenth century in a phase of rapid climate change that has become known as the Dantean Anomaly, after the contemporary poet, author and philosopher Dante Alighieri. Reconstructions of weather conditions in 1302–7 point to several years of dry summers, coupled with large-scale urban fires across Europe which led to steps being taken to mitigate future risks; these included the city of Siena buying the port of Talamone to help ensure food security, as well as investments by several cities in more resilient infrastructure, such as wells that were new and deeper than those that had been dug in the past.[60]

Nevertheless, the decade that followed saw problems that have led to this period being described as experiencing 'arguably the single worst agrarian and food crisis in northern and central Europe in the last two millennia'. The problem, as so often, was not a single failure of crops but back-to-back harvest shortfalls. In 1315, 1316 and 1317, torrential rains resulted in grain yields that were respectively around 40, 60 and 10 per cent of their usual levels.[61] Temperatures were also conspicuously cold, with chroniclers in northern Italy reporting that wine stored in barrels froze solid, as did wells and springs, while many trees died of cold. For this reason, and presumably as a result of high consumption, the price of wood rose sharply.[62] Scholars believe that 10–15 per cent of Europe's population died of hunger and hunger-related disease in these years in perhaps 'the single worst subsistence crisis, in terms of relative mortality, in recorded European history'.[63]

These shocks produced civil unrest across many parts of northern Europe, with a mob of men, women and children gathering and rampaging across France, attacking castles, officials of the crown, priests and lepers before targeting Jews in particular across Languedoc in 1320. Anti-semitism had a long history in Europe, most notably during the passage of elements of the First Crusade who committed atrocities in Cologne, Nuremberg and elsewhere as they made their way east towards Constantinople and Jerusalem in the mid-1090s.[64] On this occasion too, it would seem that Jews were attacked because they were perceived to be responsible for the misfortune of others, or because they were vulnerable targets that were perceived to be wealthy. As noted in the Introduction, the pogroms of the early 1320s were part of a pattern that saw the probability of persecution rise by between 1 and 1.5 per cent according to decreases in growing season temperatures in the previous five-year period. In other words, the worse the weather conditions, the greater the likelihood that minorities would be attacked.[65]

This was mirrored elsewhere: in Egypt, for example, churches and monasteries were looted and sacked in 1321, while Christians were accused of trying to set fire to mosques, with some arrested and tortured into 'confessing' their apparent crimes.[66] As in Yuan dynasty China, climate shocks presented political challenges. In the case of Muslim Egypt, Nile failures tended to result in crackdowns on minorities (including Christians), as well as enforcement of decrees against prostitution, beer drinking or the wearing of either immodest or over-luxurious clothes.[67] Such instances were also typically accompanied by the sultan ordering the construction of new mosques, the repair of existing structures, the distribution of money to urban inhabitants and the grant of enhanced powers to religious authorities in order to buy their acquiescence.[68]

Others dealt with the situation in ways that were perhaps intentionally more vague. One decree issued by Pope John XX in 1320 urged that 'sorcerers, the infectors of God's flock, flee from the midst of the House of God'. Those who 'make sacrifice to demons or adore them' or who have made 'binding pacts with them' should be identified and punished accordingly. Such pronouncements, of course, fit within a wider context of the Church hierarchy exerting control, and using accusations of heresy or 'evil deeds' to consolidate and concentrate power. Nevertheless, it is difficult not to be struck by the similarities with other times of need, of pressures on food supplies and of harsh weather – most notably, as we shall see, with systematic persecutions in the late seventeenth century, predominantly of women.[69]

Traumatic though the second and third decades of the fourteenth century were, however, one of the most striking features was the resilience of urban populations in coping and surviving. Cities like Florence, Pisa and Lucca were hit repeatedly by food shortages, by inward flows of people from the countryside and by hefty rises in wheat prices not only between 1314 and 1322 but on multiple occasions before the 1340s.[70] The inhabitants of Cairo meanwhile were understandably delighted by the visit of Mansa Musa, ruler of the Malian empire in West Africa, who spent so much gold on his way to Mecca in 1324 that its value fell, according to one contemporary.[71] Whether this was really the case, or whether deflationary pressures were a reflection of economic recovery following shock is not clear; but the fact that life returned to normal is an indication that it was possible to come out the other side of even the most difficult experiences.[72]

Ironically, then, the most significant environmental, ecological and epidemiological development in the first decades of the fourteenth century, at least in Europe, was not the impact of harvest failure but the spread of bovine pestilence that swept across the continent; this probably arrived from the Far East and was likely linked, once again, to the enhanced connectivity brought about by the creation of the Mongol empire across much of Eurasia. By 1315, the disease was ravaging central Europe; over the next five years, it devastated herds across much of what is now Germany, France, the Low Countries and Denmark before reaching the British Isles in 1319. In England and Wales, the disease killed almost two-thirds of the bovine population, with total losses in some regions balanced out by other locations which saw few or even no deaths. Nevertheless, as owners grappled with what was happening, many panicked, trying to get whatever price they could before their herds were struck – with obvious implications both for value per head of cattle and oxen and for the rural economy as a whole.[73]

Clearly the loss of assets was devastating to rural communities that were already suffering from the harvest shortfalls of previous years. But so too were consequences that played out over the longer term. One was the fact that bovines such as oxen had important roles in agricultural production, most notably in field ploughing, so their reduced numbers meant that either future crop yields would be lower or more human effort (and therefore calories) would have to be expended to produce the same return. Whether the pestilence in question was a form of anthrax, foot and mouth or rinderpest, the cold weather of the 1310s may well have had a role in reducing resistance to pathogens: colder weather, combined with smaller quantities of fodder, logically resulted in animals having to expend more energy to maintain their body temperature, making them more prone to disease – especially in the case of cows, whose immune systems tend to become weaker during the nine months of the year when they are pregnant or lactating.[74]

The consequences of this perfect storm were dramatic. Although many historians have pointed to evidence of a robust recovery in places like Dresden, Hamburg and many parts of England and a return to normal by the mid- to late 1320s, others have questioned whether the decline or loss of protein sources in diets over more than a decade may have had a role in compromising immune systems as a result of malnourishment in adolescents – exacerbating susceptibility and vulnerability to disease later in life. According to this ingenious suggestion, one of the causes of the mass suffering of the Black Death in the 1340s lay in the weather conditions and disease environment of three decades earlier.[75] Demonstrating this with certainty is not straightforward, and requires detailed data sets that allow mortality profiles to be tested empirically, as well as skeletal evidence that might support ideas about malnourishment; what is clearer is that when bad weather, crop failure and disease struck in the 1340s, it did so with a vengeance.

* * *

The Mongol expansion across Eurasia had brought about an extensive ecological reorganisation of the steppes as well as beyond. This was primarily driven by the increased demands for pasturage for livestock – enhanced by political control that gave the ability to enforce rights to pasturage. It is telling that some accounts praise individual administrators for convincing Mongol leaders not to convert newly conquered lands to pasture; others report that where once cities had flourished, mulberry trees had grown, vines had borne fruit and fields had produced good harvests, now the landscape consisted of rich pastures that were home to cattle and horses, an abundance of hay and very little grain. Optimal conditions of damp and mild weather encouraged grass growth; however, they also produced expansion in the populations of rodents such as marmots, susliks and gerbils, which thrive in grassland.[76]

An extreme drought episode between 1336 and 1339 triggered a set of chain reactions that proved devastating. The lack of rainfall, attested by the dendrochronological records, would have led to a sharp decline in vegetation levels which would in turn not only put pressure on the rodent population through rising mortality levels because of shortages of food and water supplies, but also increase susceptibility to fleas carrying pathogens. A sharp spike in burials in two East Syriac Christian cemeteries in the Chu Valley in the Issyk-Kul region of Kazakhstan, including a rash of inscriptions to 'death through pestilence' in 1338–9, provides persuasive evidence of a zoonotic crossover from rodents to humans, with fleas seeking new hosts to spread the bacterium.[77]

As one leading scholar has pointed out, it was not easy for plague to spread: not only were plague foci far removed geographically, physically and geologically from places with high population densities, but the disease had to move across multiple animal species and over long distances – including across diverse climatic zones – to spread effectively. As such, while the role of the rat has usually been the focus of scholarly attention, it is worth noting the multiplicity of vectors that likely combined to help spread plague from the late 1330s. Among these are commensals – that is to say, animals that 'share our tables', living in, around and near human settlements, eating food scraps – and wider biological systems or groups such as wild rodents, including rats, hares and rabbits, and ruminants, including cattle, camels, goats and sheep.[78]

Other spreaders of plague include predator birds that feed on rodents, including large birds of prey and migratory birds, and also carnivores and scavengers such as wolves, foxes, jackals and hyenas that were common across Eurasia and would eat infected carrion, thus spreading the disease. That *Y. pestis* has been shown to survive in flea faeces in both soil and plant likewise shows that there were multiple routes for the transmission of plague, while the disease's ability to persist within rat colonies for a hundred years without the need for importing new infection underlines how prevalent the disease can be once it is established. Some cities ravaged by the Black Death – such as Constantinople – experienced more than 230 outbreaks in the 500 years after the 1340s, averaging around one outbreak every two years.[79]

The most powerful spreaders of plague, however, were humans. The hyperconnected world created by Mongol expansions enabled high levels of economic and cultural exchange, as well as rapid communication of information along trade routes. These links were well suited to the shipping of materials such as carpets and clothes, which were ideal for the spread of fleas, ticks and lice and therefore infection, as were the traders and the animals who transported them. The long-distance movements of foodstuffs in general, and of millet in particular, likewise provided perfect conditions for 'tag-along rodents', the parasites that accompanied them and the bacterium itself.[80]

That the connections facilitating the exchange of goods, ideas and information and at the same time providing the sinews of Mongol power across much of Eurasia were the very same that spread disease and death should not surprise us: in more recent times too we have learned that thinking about globalising forces solely in socio-economic and geopolitical terms makes it all too easy to forget that air, sea, rail and road links are the ways in which pandemics spread – and do so rapidly.

In the case of the Black Death that took hold of Europe, North Africa and the Middle East in the 1340s, the shipment of grain seems to have played a key role in the catastrophes that followed. Of particular importance were worsening growing conditions in Italy since the late thirteenth century that had led to increasing demand for exports from the Mongol Golden Horde; the Horde occupied prime territory that was ideally located for shipping through ports on the Black Sea. This produced an economic boom for the Mongols, while simultaneously creating dependency of populations in southern Europe on regular shipments from afar for their calorie provision. So important was the grain that flowed towards Europe that control of the sea lanes and the goods that moved along them became a source of competition and confrontation between Italian maritime republics. The competition between Venice and Genoa was so intense that it led to a war that lasted for most of the 1290s before the latter emerged triumphant.[81]

Demographic growth in Europe in the later thirteenth and early fourteenth centuries also posed a problem. Urban populations could be struck by sudden and acute crises – as was the case in 1329–30 in Italy where major uprisings followed harvest shortfall and soaring prices. In Florence, all-out anarchy was only narrowly averted through quick action by the authorities in importing grain and selling bread to citizens at subsidised prices. Those living in the countryside were no better off; indeed, quite the opposite was the case. Repeated subdivision and subletting of land into smallholdings served as a barrier to economies of scale and provided limited incentive for innovation. In times of shortage, therefore, families had few safety nets – and often fled towards cities in search of relief from hunger and suffering. This in turn meant there were even more mouths to feed in one location, which often made a bad situation worse by driving prices even higher.[82]

From the 1330s, unsettled conditions became common – and a source of concern. In 1338, for example, one chronicler reported that locusts descended on central Europe like a snowstorm, so blinding as to block out the rays of the sun, and so cacophonous that people could not hear each other speak. The insects destroyed everything: 'everywhere they landed, no sowing, no fruits, no hay nor any other of such crops of the earth remained, but they digested all', while many 'pigs, dogs and other animals' died as a result of the infestation. 'All the men of the church and the people of Prague then made processions with holy relics and banners, and begged God's mercy to eliminate such injustice.'[83] Locusts whose eggs 'were as large as bats' descended on many parts of Italy the following year, devastating fields and causing chronic food shortage as well as disease.[84]

In this context, the collapse of relations between the Mongols and the Italian maritime republics at the start of the 1340s was particularly poorly timed, coming at a moment when 'all parts of Eurasia were experiencing exceptional levels of environmental stress'.[85] These challenges were not uniform either chronologically or geographically, with tree-ring reconstructions in northern Scandinavia and central Sweden indicative of harsher conditions than those in Novgorod and southern Finland around the same time.[86]

This took place around the same time as the accession of Janïbek Khan as the new ruler of the Golden Horde which controlled access to the Black Sea in 1342. This sparked a new round of competition between Genoa and Venice, both of which were keen to have their previous trade concessions confirmed by the new ruler. The antagonism between the two city states was such that as well as seeking to preserve their own advantages, both also sought to undermine their rival, arguing that their commercial privileges be withdrawn. As it happened, both were left unhappy. Following the murder of one of Janibek's high-ranking subjects by a western trader, the ruler of the Golden Horde decided to act against both states. He not only ordered the imprisonment of 'Latins' living in his territories, but also banned trade outright – including grain shipments.[87]

The effect was twofold: first, the blockade of shipping put further pressure on food supplies in the mid-1340s at a time of rising scarcity in Europe and in Italy in particular when harvests were badly affected by higher-than-usual levels of rainfall and also a period of cooler weather than normal.[88] Second, the embargo on grain movements inadvertently prevented the transmission of pandemic disease that would have been carried unwittingly in the cargoes of the ships and perhaps on the bodies of those who sailed them. As such, when the Golden Horde agreed peace terms with Venice and Genoa in 1347, it did not just unlock trade, it unleashed death.[89]

It has long been assumed that plague had little or no impact in China. This is now being challenged by close reading of complex sources whose significance has long been overlooked by scholars.[90] As for Europe, the Middle East, North Africa and likely parts of sub-Saharan Africa, the evidence points to wide-scale disaster: an estimated 40–60 per cent of the population perished of disease in what remains the 'highest [mortality] of any large-scale catastrophe known to humankind, save for the impact of smallpox and measles on indigenous peoples in first-contact events of the early modern period'.[91] So great was the demographic and economic collapse that metal production and atmospheric lead dropped to undetectable levels in ice-core analysis – the only time they have ever done so in at least the last 2,000 years.[92]

'The year of 1348 has left us alone and helpless,' wrote the Florentine poet Petrarch, whose son was to succumb to the disease in an outbreak a few years later. 'Where are our dear friends now? Where are the beloved faces? Where are the affectionate words, the relaxed and enjoyable conversations?' The pandemic was one 'without equal for centuries', so devastating that it had 'trampled and destroyed the entire world'. Those who have lived through pandemics more recently will recognise Petrarch's wistful observation too that 'time itself has slipped through our fingers'.[93]

The Black Death did not spread evenly across countries and states in Europe, with space–time mapping suggesting that the highest levels of virulence in France were in the warm, dry south, likely propagating from the port of Marseille, while what is now Belgium and the Netherlands were spared the worst ravages of the plague, at least in its first waves.[94] Limited coverage of plague in Polish chronicles, along with payments of tithes to the papacy that remained constant throughout the 1340s and 1350s, have led some to suggest that mortality levels were low or even negligible – and to question the impact in other regions too.[95] Some places were saved by steps taken by the authorities to force urban populations to self-isolate. In Milan, for example, immediate action to implement preventive measures led to only three households being infected – sparing the rest of the population as a result.[96] Cultural, ecological, economic and climatic factors explain why the Black Death proved devastating in many parts of Europe but left others unscathed.[97]

The first accounts of the arrival of plague in North Africa describe a disease 'worse than any seen before in the Islamic world'. It arrived in Alexandria in 1347 on a ship full of corpses drifting into the harbour, manned by a handful of surviving crew who themselves all died shortly afterwards. The pandemic spread through the city like wildfire, killing hundreds every day before reaching other towns and cities in Egypt – including Cairo, which recorded 7,000 daily deaths at its peak.[98]

Part of the problem was that cities were ideal crucibles for the spread of disease, because people lived in close proximity to each other, because of inadequate sanitation standards and because of the density of rodent populations that helped spread the plague bacterium. It is instructive, for example, that basic widening of streets, repair of buildings and the move away from wood for housebuilding in the United States in the twentieth century had an immediate effect on the size of rat colonies, producing a decline of almost 80 per cent in just two years: in other words, the layout of cities had and has a direct relationship with disease environments and as such provides an important insight into outcomes during pandemics. While the idea of filthy houses and poor hygiene standards dominate the popular imagination (and are often taken for granted by medieval historians), many cities took seriously the challenges presented by rising populations and infrastructure needs and invested heavily in creating preventative health programmes and devising ways to deal with domestic waste disposal, burials and artisanal pollution, not to mention maintaining wells, canals, bridges and roads that were of benefit to citizens individually and collectively.[99]

That the Black Death overcame many of these measures – which included procedures to contain or stop the spread of infectious disease – speaks volumes about the robustness of the pathogen and its ability to find new hosts. The decline in the number of craft workshops and textile makers in Alexandria in the 1340s and the decades that followed suggests that around half the population died as disease swept through the city.[100] In the case of Cairo, meanwhile, changes to the city were profound, reminding us that demographic disaster has an impact on the built environment and on the way that buildings are used, maintained and constructed.[101]

Socio-economic background was a factor in Cairene mortality rates during the pandemic, with those from poor households more likely to die than those with access to medical care, better levels of nutrition, more space and better domestic hygiene levels. It was the poor who suffered most during the Black Death, then, with particularly high fatalities among those who sought refuge in cities to escape trauma or simply to find food in the face of rising prices. Those drawn from the countryside to Cairo died in large numbers, as did newcomers to Dijon in France, who were more likely to die than those who already lived in the city or who had moved there before the outbreak of disease.[102]

The movement of people in the face of adversity must have played a part in the acceleration of the spread of the plague, just as in later periods pilgrims travelling to and from holy places were crucial in spreading disease.[103] Changes to land use also seem to have been an important reason why the pandemic spread in many parts of Europe: the rapid urbanisation and demographic growth of previous centuries brought ecological pressure not just in terms of exploitation of agricultural resources, but also in land-use practices and in particular the adoption of the open-field system. Even modest changes could have important outcomes. For example, in modern land-management practice, hedges are often removed to create efficiencies for crop planting. This comes at the expense of numbers and diversity of birds, and also causes an increase in vermin populations. While little is known about how hedges were maintained during the fourteenth century, if they were at all, such issues may have played a role in helping the Black Death maintain a lethal velocity, as it kept finding more animals and humans to infect and kill.[104]

On top of all this, the cocktail of catastrophe was enhanced by the fact that the 1340s was one of the most turbulent decades in global military history, not only in Europe but in the Middle East and North Africa. This was a period that saw bitter warfare between England and France, and between Scotland and England; relations between Florence and Pisa and between Genoa and Venice were not just fractious but violent, marked by repeated military confrontations; the Byzantine empire was disrupted by a brutal and long-running civil war, to say nothing of the rising threat of the Ottomans whose raids and attacks were a constant feature in this period; to the east, competition between rival descendants of Činggis Khan saw the Golden Horde to the north of the Black and Caspian Seas take on the Il-Khanate masters of Persia and the Levant, who were also involved in a protracted confrontation with Mamluk Egypt. In normal circumstances, the demands made on manpower, resources and food consumption for military forces in each of these cases would have caused strain. In a period when multiple proxies point to more unsettled, more variable and less predictable weather and therefore to harvest uncertainty, these combined to create a deadly context which ensured that a virulent pathogen circulated commercial disruption, economic compression and political turbulence. Each served to magnify the problems caused by the others, producing a downward spiral of which large-scale mortality was just one feature.[105]

Other features included major cultural changes as a result of concern about health and life expectancy, the loss of loved ones and attitudes to spending money rather than saving it, made worse by the repeated waves of plague that served as brakes on recovery of all kinds and as a near constant source of anxiety for those who had avoided death and suffering previously.[106] Waves of horror accompanied those of plague that fanned out across Germany in the late 1350s, just as life seemed to be getting back to normal.[107]

People in Scotland had heard reports of 'the foul death of England', and 'declared that it had befallen them through the revenging hand of God'. The disease struck the Scots in 1349 just as they were gathering 'with the intention of invading the whole realm of England'.[108] It was the first of four devastating waves that swept away huge numbers of people – with one-third of those who had survived the first outbreak dying in 1362–3, a third of the remainder perishing in 1380 and yet more in 1401. And of course, while naturally drawing most attention, plague was just one disease among many. In 1402, for example, dysentery spread across eastern Scotland, causing many to die 'with the overflowing of the bowels'.[109]

Cycles of plague outbreak repeatedly scarred Egypt, with deaths in 1403, 1407, 1412, 1430 and 1460 running into the thousands in each case, and sometimes the many tens of thousands. 'Most of the cities of Upper Egypt have been obliterated,' wrote al-Maqrīzī of 1412; 'Cairo and its outskirts have lost half their wealth. And two-thirds of the population of Egypt has been wiped out by famine and plague.'[110] Plague recurred repeatedly in cities in the Ottoman empire such as Salonica, Aleppo, Damascus and Trebizond for the best part of 500 years – which helped build up ideas of the Ottoman world as 'a sickened land and peoples' or 'the sick man of Europe'.[111]

The heavily Eurocentric slant of medieval history in general and of accounts of the Black Death in particular can make it all too easy to ignore the impact that plague had outside European cities and societies. As one leading historian has stressed, current knowledge about the plague in East Asia, South Asia, Central Asia, the Middle East and North Africa 'is at best fragmentary and disconnected'.[112] This is problematic, not least since genetic evidence reveals that plague found in sub-Saharan Africa today descends from the strains that caused the Black Death and suggests that the disease took hold and may be responsible for the abandonment of settlements and apparent population losses of as much as 50 per cent in West Africa. It may further explain cultural shifts, such

as the sudden prominence in Ethiopia of St Sebastian and St Roch –
saints closely associated with plague in Europe.[113]

The limited research done on its consequences beyond Europe mean
that it is not easy to assess the damage in locations that have been poorly
studied, especially in this period. And even in regions where written,
archaeological and secondary material is more abundant, there can be a
temptation to overlook how damaging the pandemic was in collapsing
connectivities established in the aftermath of the Mongol conquests.
Cities in territory controlled by the Golden Horde, for example, were
hit badly by plague – such as Caffa in the 1340s, one likely entry point
of the disease to Europe, or Saray in 1364.[114]

The decimation of the labour force through disease must have affected
agricultural production across the steppes, as well as having an impact
on harvesting and on rearing of livestock. These pressures clearly had
implications not only for trade but for supply to cities that depended
on crops, meat and dairy products as well as the textiles and fabrics
that were sourced from nomad populations. It has been convincingly
argued that the creation of a new mint and new coinage types and
the later introduction of new lightweight silver coinage were responses
to acute economic pressures that arose from the spread of pandemic
disease in the Eurasian steppes.[115] Another indication of stress was the
soaring price of peoples enslaved by the Mongols and sold on to Italian
buyers who were desperate to find labour in the face of demographic
collapse in the 1350s. The fact that many were sold by members of their
own family shows how desperate conditions were around the Black Sea
at this time.[116]

As one scholar puts it, the Golden Horde seems to have been 'an
orderly, stable, well-functioning political system' until 1359; at that
point 'the only word one can use to describe it … is "anarchy"'.[117]
Competition for power and control became intense, reflecting the
fact that there were fewer rewards and benefits available than in the
past, and that resources were dwindling at speed. If vicious infighting
provides one indication of growing crisis, the rapid expansion of other
powers into Mongol territory provides another: in the second half of
the fourteenth century, Lithuanian forces pushed south dramatically,
taking swathes of lands and cities, and by 1400 extending control right
up to the shore of the Black Sea.[118]

This was a rare case of opportunism. More common was the collapse of long-distance travel and trade, and a narrowing of horizons as societies turned inwards. Even before the pandemic, there had been signs of change across parts of Central Asia. In the 1330s, a wave of conversions to Islam marked a move away from the cosmopolitanism and laissez-faire policies of inclusivity which may not have characterised Mongol society but were certainly an important part of it.[119] This now accelerated in the period after the outbreak of the Black Death as the steppe world went through a period of socio-economic contraction. The disappearance of languages such as Syriac, Volga Bulgarian (related to modern Chuvash) and Standard Turkic (linked to modern Kazan Turkic) in the second half of the fourteenth century is most logically explained as a sign of a retreat to a single common identity at a time of pressure and duress.[120]

In Egypt, the Black Death had a devastating impact on the labour force. The problem centred on irrigation: vast amounts of manpower were required to maintain the canal system. Several accounts from the late Middle Ages put the number of those required to work on regional, large-scale irrigation in Upper and Lower Egypt well above 100,000 people, with many more involved in local community schemes – with perhaps around half the male population between the ages of fifteen and fifty participating on a seasonal basis to clear canals of silt, remove blockages and shore up dykes. Sharp population loss through disease had obvious implications for villages, let alone for more substantial networks of water distribution. In some cases, irrigation canals did not just fall into disrepair but became unusable.[121]

Not surprisingly, in all areas and regions that had been struck by the plague, landowners and the previous beneficiaries of the rich surpluses tried to retain their status and to extract the rewards of agricultural production. In England, small emerging elites in the countryside started to build larger houses, set back from the roadway to mark rising status linked to increasing stratification in village life, which was in turn accentuated by the wealthier inhabitants taking advantage of opportunities to enclose and take ownership of open land and fields.[122]

Unlike in Europe, where the aftermath of the Black Death saw the start of a social revolution that stemmed from the successes of the peasantry and the labour force in negotiating better bargaining positions that translated into better living conditions, in Egypt elites were able to protect their own interests with considerable success. This had long-term consequences that were economically regressive, throttling opportunities for social mobility, stifling innovation and creating long-term stagnation. Ironically, the principal cause of this divergence lay in the fact that the Mamluk state in North Africa was more centralised and better administered than fragmented societies in most parts of Europe. In some contexts, this was an advantage; here, it proved to be an Achilles heel that prevented reform and held back progress.[123]

The experience of plague brought about a series of important changes – including biological ones. As it happened, many of those who survived the plague may have done so because they were carrying a genetic mutation that served to offer a layer of protection to the immune system. Ironically, this mutation, known as ERAP2, is now associated with several autoimmune disorders, such as Crohn's disease, lupus and rheumatoid arthritis: in other words, alleles that protected against Black Death confer raised risk for diseases for people alive today.[124] Evidence from burial sites in London suggests that the onset of the menarche (first menstrual cycles) occurred at a younger age for adolescent women – something that can be best understood as a sign of better living conditions after the pandemic.[125]

There were cultural shifts too. For example, there was what some scholars refer to as a 'nuptial frenzy' as those who had survived the plague rushed to get married – resulting in a period of bumper fertility.[126] Great efforts were made to catalogue experiences of plague, including medical tracts explaining the symptoms and effects of the disease, as well as liturgical poetry written by Sephardic Jews recording the suffering – and also the violence – that had accompanied the Black Death.[127] Over time, writings by and for Jews came to suggest Jewish resistance to plague – usually attributed to higher levels of sanitary behaviour and prudence.[128]

The aftermath of plague also saw new fashions, diets and attitudes towards luxury goods, partly as a result of the emergence of competitive consumption, partly because smaller populations meant goods cost less, and partly because of the euphoria of having dodged death's call.[129] Protein availability not only soared in Europe because there were fewer people to feed, but as farmers and herders were forced to find new markets for their livestock – opening up what one historian has called an international meat trade.[130] It has been argued too that the deaths of so many copyists during the pandemic led to the fall in the price of paper – something that spurred literacy levels and perhaps even helped prompt the print revolution of Johannes Gutenberg and others.[131]

Systems to detect plague were also devised and developed, with varying degrees of success. While the Ottoman empire struggled to deal with regular outbreaks, public health authorities in Milan monitored plague cases with extreme vigilance following a devastating outbreak in northern Italy in the 1360s which Petrarch described as not only equal to but worse than that of the 1340s – and which killed the poet's beloved son, Giovanni. A network of early-warning stations reported new cases, with particular attention paid to main travel routes, mountain passes and the periphery of Lombardy. In the first half of the sixteenth century, surveillance systems failed, largely as a result of a long period of inter-city warfare and turbulence which put pressure on expenditure and diverted attention elsewhere. The results were dramatic. Anxiety about plague was not misplaced, as is clear from the death of half the population of Milan in 1524; it took years for the city to recover. Fear of plague bred suspicions, with some refusing to believe reports of new cases or to suspect skulduggery by nurses, gravediggers and others keen to continue collecting 'high, hazard-pay wages' and to exaggerate the situation in order to enrich themselves.[132]

Recovery from the demographic contractions of the mid-fourteenth century took a long time. By 1550, the population of north Italy stood at around five and a half million – a rise of more than 40 per cent from a century earlier. Nevertheless, this was still a long way short of where things had been on the eve of the Black Death.[133] The fact that the setback had not been reversed 200 years later speaks volumes about the scale of correction caused by the perfect storm that struck at the height of the Middle Ages.

There were counter-intuitive benefits for those who survived: the large numbers of deaths meant there were more 'cards, wagons, horses, oxen, mules, boats, ships, barns, and granaries' available per capita – in what amounted to a 'plague bonus'.[134] Ironically, climatic variability, harvest failure, dependence on long-distance trade, intense warfare and a shifting disease environment created conditions that decimated communities across three continents – but often also served as a catalyst to long-term growth. This was especially true in Europe, and above all the north of the continent. For some, the plague did not so much have a silver-lining as serve to change the world.[135]

The unusual constellation of factors that created the Black Death helps explain why seemingly similar periods did not produce similar results. In the mid-fifteenth century, for example, another phase of reduced solar activity known as the Spörer Minimum produced a period of unusual cold in north-western and central Europe, with conditions in the 1430s being particularly hostile.[136] In addition to wine freezing solid in bottles, crops failed in 1432, 1433, 1434, 1436, 1437 and 1438 in England, Germany, France, the Low Countries and elsewhere – leading to price rises not only for food but also for firewood in Paris, Cologne and Augsburg. Manorial accounts from southern England suggest sharp declines in fertility rates of ewes, and mortality rates in sheep multiple times greater in 1438 than in normal years.[137]

Large-scale eruptions in the 1450s of an as yet unidentified volcano and of the Kuwae underwater caldera in the South Pacific, which was more explosive than the massive Tambora eruption of 1815, resulted in lakes in the Alps freezing solid, so that they could be crossed on horseback. We learn of trees in Ireland not growing leaves till May and of celestial phenomena that were much commented on by chroniclers across Europe who noted that the sun had lost its power, that it shone weakly with a blue colour and that fog and haze hung in the air – like the dust veil of the sixth century.[138] The volcanic events left an indelible impression on oral traditions in Oceania, where stories were told centuries later that explained that the eruption of Kuwae was the work of a powerful sorcerer who had been tricked into committing incest with his own mother and had unleashed the cataclysm as revenge.[139]

Extreme weather events elsewhere could and did pose serious challenges. For example, a severe storm in northwestern Europe in January 1362 was so strong that a monk was blown out of a window, falling beams killed people taking shelter in churches and many famous buildings were damaged. As one scholar reminds us, while little consideration has been given to the impact of major storms in the pre-modern era, it is worth noting that an unusually strong storm in October 1987 brought down an estimated 15 million trees in Britain.[140] Storms in central Europe in December 1999 brought down 400,000 telephone and power supply lines, along with 138 million cubic metres of trees.[141] Even though much depends on tree type, wind direction and speed, tree anchorage (including root system, soil and drainage), tree density and height, as well as forestry techniques, the scale of damage that can result from such weather events is enormous and can impact all aspects of the natural environment, from animal and plant habitats to reshaping landscapes – as well as producing socio-economic shifts that result from adapting to major upheaval.[142]

Curiously, then, the centuries that followed the creation of the Mongol empire, the intensification of commercial and cultural ties across Asia, Europe and Africa and the sweeping pandemic that proved so destructive were the prelude to a long and slow period of consolidation in which states and peoples that had been on the geographic periphery of long-established political centres and of the networks that linked them together found themselves able to take advantage of new opportunities not only to expand but to explore new worlds. The results were to change the nature of the world we live in – quite literally.

14

On the Expansion of Ecological Horizons
(c.1400–c.1500)

The famine was so great that the old Mexicans sold themselves.

Annals of Chimalpahin (early seventeenth century)

The aftermath of the Black Death saw the creation of a set of new states, new worlds and new interactions. In Europe, the next century witnessed the twin trends of military and bureaucratic innovation as states fought each other almost incessantly. New technologies and tactics could not fail to emerge during the Hundred Years' War between the kings of England and France which had started shortly before the pandemic, while the need to raise taxes and armies provided a motor that drove both the centralisation of power and the professionalisation of those who ran kingdoms, controlled budgets and chose how to deploy expenditure.[1]

It was a time of change too for those able to take advantage of new opportunities. The dukes of Burgundy, for example, oversaw a rapid political and territorial expansion from the late fourteenth century, forging canny alliances with the kings of England as well as compromises with magnates and cities across the Low Countries – like Bruges and Ghent – that saw the Burgundian state become the commercial and culture powerhouse of the western half of Europe.[2] It was matched in the east by the Grand Duchy of Lithuania, whose military successes even before the great pandemic were followed by momentous victories such as Kulikovo in 1380, by the conquest of territory as far south as the Black Sea and by the invasion of Crimea in 1398.[3]

To the south-east too, things were changing rapidly, with a Serbian empire taking shape under Stjepan Dušan in the 1340s, helped first by the death by plague of his brother-in-law, the powerful Mladen Subić, which opened up a pathway to the conquest of Bosnia and Dalmatia, and then by two decades of civil war in the Byzantine empire which left the latter poorly placed to defend its northern cities and territories. New opportunities also emerged for the Ottomans, who established a foothold in mainland Europe in the early 1350s, which served as a springboard for future gains across the Balkans – which opened up following the battles of Maritsa in 1371 and Kosovo in 1389. The latter acquired totemic status in later Serbian historiography.[4]

These successes paved the way for the successful assault on Constantinople in 1453, and eventually took the sultan's armies deep into the heart of Europe. Success followed success as the Ottomans advanced deep into eastern and central Europe. By 1529, troops were poised for an assault on Vienna. The city was saved by the rain: torrential rainfall led to Ottoman heavy cannon becoming stuck in the mud. Had the sultan's forces moved two months earlier – or if the weather had stayed benign – Vienna might have fallen and the history of Europe would have been dramatically different.[5]

As it was, the Ottoman expansion into Europe paid dividends of a different sort, for the presence of an existential threat to Christian states across the continent concentrated hearts and minds: Ottoman military expeditions not only resulted in fewer violent engagements between kingdoms in Europe but also shortened conflicts by more than 50 per cent from the early sixteenth century at least until around 1600. This was remarkable given that the Ottoman surge into Europe coincided with the Reformation and the splintering of Protestant and Catholic communities. The military prowess of the Ottomans and the momentum behind the expansion of Islam and of Turks challenged ideas about the role of the Church and the moral rectitude of leaders, while the threat of further conquests provided grounds for co-operation among those most at risk. Ironically, then, the Ottomans were instrumental in driving the cohesion that enabled Protestantism to establish itself in a way that previous reformist movements had failed to do, a process that had a profound impact on the religion, politics and economy of Europe.[6]

The Ottomans expanded elsewhere too, taking on the Safavids of Persia whose ruler, Shah Ismail, was renowned for his moustache, for being 'as brave as a game cock' and for being an excellent archer. Ismail was a man who spent most of his time 'hunting, or in the company of rosy-cheeked youths, quaffing goblets of purple wine, and listening to the strains of music and song'.[7] A lightning campaign in 1514 against the Safavids resulted in a crushing defeat and led to the fall of Tabriz, a city famous for its magnificent library, its miniature painters and its expert carpet makers. This not only removed the threat to the Ottomans' eastern flank, but also freed up resources to enable an attack on Egypt, which duly fell with a whimper in 1517. The result was that the Ottomans now controlled a global empire that spanned three continents – Europe, Africa and Asia.[8]

The Ottoman encounter with Europe was part of an Age of Discovery that historians typically link with European voyages across the Atlantic and to Asia at the end of the fifteenth and start of the sixteenth centuries. This says much about how study of the past prioritises European experiences instead of providing a wider, more balanced and more meaningful context. In fact, the Ottoman field of vision expanded rapidly in this period to the east, as well as into Europe. The conquest of North Africa opened up maritime routes stretching not only into the Red Sea but into the Indian Ocean World – a web of vibrant connections that had meshed South-East and South Asia, the Gulf and East Africa, as well as reaching beyond to China, Japan and Oceania for centuries.[9]

This engagement was accompanied by rapid and almost continuous expansion along the north-western coast of the Indian Ocean, including the occupation of Aden, Mocha and Basra – which opened up new gateways to the east – as well as conquest of the coasts of Sudan and Eritrea.[10] Although control of many of these new regions was often precarious and dependent on co-operation with local rulers, these advances went hand in hand with sharply increasing interest in and the accumulation of information about peoples and places as far afield as southern India, Sri Lanka and Melaka.[11]

Horizons were being recast elsewhere, such as the Solomonic dynasty in Christian Ethiopia, whose extension and consolidation of authority and power locally continued apace. By the start of the fifteenth century, its *nägäśt* – or kings – ruled over the largest political entity in the Horn of Africa in this period, and began to dispatch diplomatic missions to Venice, Rome, Valencia, Lisbon and other cities. These were not intended to seek European technology, solicit military support or show submission, as has long been assumed by western scholars, but rather were confident displays of an ambitious and successful power that saw itself as at least the equal of contemporary societies elsewhere.[12]

Nowhere was this clearer than in the 1440s when Pope Eugene IV invited 'Prester John, illustrious emperor of the Ethiopians' to attend the Council of Florence, a landmark event that was intended to resolve schisms that had ruptured the Christian Church and that in some cases dated back not just centuries, but a full millennium. The initial response, composed in Gəʿəz, the ancient language of the Ethiopian Church, to emphasise independence and autonomy, was curt to the point of being dismissive. Although a delegation led by a certain Peṭros duly met the Pope at the Council in 1441, his message, likely delivered in Amharic, then translated into Arabic and then into Latin, left little to the imagination: the Ethiopian Church had not 'crumbled' as others had in the face of intimidation, heresy or poor leadership. That was no thanks to the papacy, he went on, pointing to 'the negligence of your predecessor Roman pontiffs' who had shown no concern for 'the sheep of Christ', let alone deigned to visit over the past 800 years, even though the first followers of Christ had done so. These were emphatic words that reflected the self-confidence of a state that could draw on the deep past to frame expressions of its power.[13]

This was a time of discovery for others too. Long before the age of European navigation across the Atlantic, sailors in Oceania were making regular return journeys that in some cases covered thousands of kilometres in double-hulled sailing canoes, leapfrogging across what one leading scholar has called a 'sea of islands' that connected tapestries of peoples, ecologies and resources. Rising levels of exchange in the Indian Ocean world, including along the coast of East Africa, also characterised a period of intensifying contacts from around the middle of the fourteenth century.[14]

In East Asia, constant environmental pressure from the 1320s onwards had produced severe famine, epidemic disease and drought so bad that land in Anhui province in China split 'with cracks like the back of a tortoise'.[15] Uprisings gathered pace against the Yuan dynasty, whose emperors, one poor peasant named Zhu Yuanzhang complained, were 'weak and failed to do their jobs'. Galvanising support among those who could barely survive because 'food was scarce, with grasses and bark serving as our nourishment', by the 1350s Zhu had become a leading force in a revolt that was gaining pace. By 1368, he had deposed the Yuan and become the master of the empire himself – and the father of a new dynasty which he named Ming, or 'Brightness', while taking for his own imperial name Hongwu, or 'Magnificent in War'.[16] This provides another example that has caught the eye of historians seeking to correlate environmental change with the fall of dynasties in China.[17]

Whereas the Yuan and the Song dynasty before them had sought to promote and prioritise long-distance maritime trade, the new Ming rulers took a very different approach. In 1371, just three years after the Hongwu Emperor seized power, a ban was imposed on seaborne commercial traffic, forbidding those living in coastal regions from setting sail in any capacity whatsoever. Foreign trade and contact with people beyond China were to be reserved for the imperial court and its officials alone.[18]

This did not mean that Ming dynasty China cut off its engagement with the world beyond. In fact, in the first half of the fifteenth century, considerable energy and expense went into equipping fleets under the command of Zheng He that were intended to be statements of Ming power. Reports written by Ma Huan, who accompanied several of these missions, provide rich detail about the rituals, wealth and interactions of interlocking political and commercial centres along the Malabar and Coromandel coasts of India and also about what is now Sri Lanka. In the latter, he wrote, people flocked to scour the sandy beaches whenever it rained to search for precious stones, which were thought to be nothing else than 'the crystallised tears of the Buddha'.[19]

Like other senior commanders on these expeditions, Zheng He was Muslim – likely a consideration for appointment for voyages that set out into regions that were experiencing a wave of Islamicisation. Muslim gravestones had become increasingly common across South-East Asia in the course of the fourteenth century, perhaps spread by refugees coming from Champa during a time of upheaval to places like Surabaya, Gresik and Cirebon in Java, each of which became what one scholar has called 'early centres of Islamic propaganda'.[20]

The Yongle Emperor, who dispatched Zheng He, issued orders in 1407 to guarantee the safety of Muslims within Ming dynasty China itself, proclaiming that 'no official, military or civilian personnel shall despise, insult or bully [Muslims] and whoever disobeys this order by doing so shall bear the consequences'. While this points to the extent and speed of the spread of Islam in the fourteenth and early fifteenth centuries, it can also be understood to demonstrate the challenges posed by the arrival of newcomers, new ideas or both.[21]

Although the fleets also reached East Africa, South-East Asia was a particular focus of the expeditions' attention. Ma Huan also wrote at length about the Majapahit kingdom, which was centred on the island of Java and knitted much of South-East Asia together. It had experienced a golden age of cultural brilliance in the fourteenth century under the Hindu King Hayam Wuruk that is richly evoked in a text known as the *Nagarakṛtāgama*; this records the building of temples and palaces and the rituals undertaken to honour ancestors and to mark phases of the moon, as well as painting a vivid picture of the arts, crafts and handiworks being carried out by skilled artisans making goods for their customers. In addition to diplomatic exchanges with Ming China, the Majapahit kingdom built up contacts with dozens of cities and states stretching from southern Thailand through the Malay peninsula, across Sumatra through the Sulu archipelago and into the Pacific Ocean. These kings may not have been quite the vassals that the author of the *Nagarakṛtāgama* seems to claim, with the payment of tribute not necessarily a reliable indicator of submission. What is less in doubt, however, is that this was a time of widening horizons and perspectives.[22]

It was a similar story in South Asia several decades later, where Babur, the founder of the Mughal dynasty, in 1505 marched south into India for the first time, seeking to expand his authority, to acquire new riches and to undergo fresh experiences. 'I had never seen a hot climate or any of Hindustan before,' he wrote, 'a new world came into view – different plants, different trees, different animals and birds, different tribes and people, different manners and customs. It was astonishing, truly astonishing.'[23]

This did not mean that he was entranced by what he saw: India, wrote Babur, 'is a place of little charm. There is no beauty in its people, no graceful social intercourse, no poetic talent or understanding, no etiquette, nobility, or manliness. The arts and crafts have no harmony or symmetry. There are no good horses, meat, grapes, melons or other fruit. There is no ice, cold water, good food or bread in the markets. There are no baths and no madrasas. There are no candles, torches or candlesticks.'[24] As others found in this period, encounters with new worlds were often uncomfortable, prompting unfavourable parallels with familiar places that were left behind.

It is perhaps not surprising, then, that the global climate records for the second half of the fourteenth century and the first decades of the fifteenth are conspicuously quiet: it seems that this was a long period of stability with few episodes of upheaval or major shocks. While demographic losses to the Black Death and the associated lowered usage of the land might explain why this was a time of continuity in Asia, Europe and Africa, the fact that similar patterns can be identified in places unaffected by the devastating plague pandemic provides an insight into the importance of multi-decade spells of stable conditions.[25]

It is striking, for example, that in Polynesia, chiefs from the Tongan island of Tongapatu began to centralise authority from the early fifteenth century, sparking social change that resulted in commoners reduced to tributary serfs and a small group of elite leaders emerging under the Tu'i Tonga, the supreme ruler. As new forms of monumental architecture developed in this period, such as mounds, altars and a massive complex of stone tombs, other islands across the region saw transformations of their material culture and rising levels of imports – most notably of stone. Oral traditions likewise commemorate the emergence of new chiefly lineages as well as the adoption of new rituals around this time.[26] Although the way to understand these developments is subject to debate, they are most logically explained as an expansion of Tongan culture, if not direct political overlordship.[27]

How these changes related to developments in Hawai'i, which had been first settled around AD 1200, is not clear: however, it seems that while voyages between these islands and central Polynesia had been relatively common, they stopped around the same time as the Tongan expansion. This may have been entirely coincidental; whatever the case, the Hawai'ian archipelago became isolated from the rest of the world and remained so until the late eighteenth century when an expedition under James Cook reintroduced the islands into global exchange networks.[28]

The case of Hawai'i was unusual, for the patterns elsewhere were ones of integration and consolidation. By the early fifteenth century, for example, a new empire was being forged by the Mexica (often referred to as Aztecs), who emerged as the dominant power in central Mexico through a combination of military success and skilful political diplomacy.[29] The world of the Aztecs rested heavily on control of water resources, evidenced by dense networks of canals not only in the principal city of Tenochtitlán which was located on an island in the great lake of Texcoco, but also right across central Mexico. These waterways greatly facilitated movement of goods and people over long distances.[30] Water was a core part of the identity of the peoples of this rising empire, recorded in pictographic records, in song and in belief systems.[31]

Management of water resources was also of crucial importance to the long-term viability of the Aztec world as a whole, as well as to Tenochtitlán itself, whose population perhaps reached 200,000 at its peak. Major investments in terracing and irrigation were vital for supporting such large numbers and densities.[32] These were also responses to threats posed by ecological conditions in the Valley of Mexico, which was subject to the twin risks of early frosts and late rains.[33]

Although Aztec rulers tried to ensure that reserves were kept in royal granaries to protect against weather shocks and food shortages, there were occasions when not even these proved enough. The so-called Famine of One Rabbit in the middle of the fifteenth century during the reign of Moctezuma I (c.1440–c.1469) was the result of almost a decade of climate turbulence, including bad frosts, droughts, locust plagues and crop failures, which overwhelmed food stocks. This led to starvation, disease and large-scale migration from cities including Tenochtitlán, Texcoco, Chalco and Xochimilco.[34]

In 1454, according to the *Annals of Chimalpahin*:

> the people died of thirst. From Chalco came foxes, ferocious beasts, lizards, etc., and they devoured the people. The famine was so great that the old Mexicans sold themselves; they took refuge in the woods where they lived unhappy and feeble. For four years there was nothing to eat in the country, so that the older Mexicans sold themselves and two divisions, it is said, delivered themselves into servitude … They put themselves into holes and died in any place they found and the lizards devoured them for there was no one to bury them.[35]

Some scholars have argued that the famine was instrumental in prompting a further wave of Aztec expansion, which might explain why priority was given to the annexation of Totonacapan, which had not been so badly affected by the disasters of the 1450s.[36] Whether or not linking the Aztec conquests to the traumatic experiences which also included children being sold into slavery is plausible, it is certainly striking that there were major upgrades to dykes, canals and aqueducts in the aftermath of the disaster. Not surprisingly, considerable effort went into increasing the amount of land that could be cultivated in order to ensure there was a bigger buffer in the future. The intensification of agricultural production was an obvious and logical response to a catastrophic sequence of events.[37]

How these difficult conditions played out in other parts of Central America are more difficult to evaluate. Drought in Yucatán appears to have played a role in prompting civil conflict and political collapse between c.1441 and 1461 at Mayapan, the largest and most important city in the peninsula following the demise of Chichen Itza four centuries earlier. While lack of rainfall posed its own problems, the compression of trade links, reductions in mobility and rising levels of violence were what drove change: even then, however, the re-emergence of a resilient network of small states shows that the failure of some created opportunities for others.[38]

In South America, the age of discovery saw the Chimú bring more territory and peoples under their control from the start of the thirteenth century. The heart of the Chimú state was the city of Chen Chen in the Moche Valley, whose population of 30,000–40,000 drew in agricultural produce from the surrounding region and beyond. Chen Chen was home to palaces, three-sided constructions called *audiencias* that provided living and working quarters for the Chimú nobility and their families, and to plazas and temples. The city was located close to the Pacific Ocean, alongside wetlands, fields, desert and mountains.[39]

By around 1310, the Chimú had moved into the Jequetepeque Valley to the north and had taken the strategically important location of Farfán by force before consolidating control over the Casma Valley to the south, where a new provincial capital was built at Manchan, at the intersection of major routes running north–south and also to the east.[40] Like many societies in the past, human and animal sacrifices were regular features in the Chimú world, given as offerings to the gods in a range of contexts. Around 1450, a mass sacrifice was made of more than

140 children and 200 camelids (llamas and alpacas) at Huanchaquito–
Las Llamas on the western coast of Peru, just north of Chen Chen.
Stratigraphic evidence from the site suggests that the sacrifice was made
following heavy rains or perhaps a flooding event which has recently
been connected to a weather event, likely associated with the El Niño–
Southern Oscillation which disrupts the marine food chain in northern
and central Peru and brings about coastal flooding. It seems plausible,
if not likely, that the offering of young boys and girls was made in an
attempt to appease the adverse weather and to bring about a return of
more clement, hospitable conditions.[41]

Sacrifices that were intended to respond to climatic and natural
disasters can also be found elsewhere in South America from around
the same period. An archaeological expedition to the summit of the
Misti volcano led to the astonishing and spectacular discovery of the
bodies of several children ritually killed and buried alongside dozens of
figurines made of gold, copper, silver and spondylus shell – as well as
ceramic and wooden vessels. The pre-Columbian Andes peoples held
belief systems that articulated ideas about the landscape and about
ancestors and ethnic identity, and involved a sacrifice ritual known
as the *capacocha* ceremony in which prestigious goods and human
sacrifices were presented as offerings to the gods. Important moments,
such as major disasters like bad weather that affected crops, were taken
as signs of angered deities that could be calmed only by a major offering.
The context for and date of this particular ritual sacrifice is not clear,
although some have linked it to a major eruption of the Misti volcano
and to the climatic dislocation that likely followed.[42]

The Inca too proved highly successful as empire builders from around
AD 1400, succeeding in creating the largest empire in the history of the
Americas before the European colonisations. They did so through a
combination of alliance-building which included copious consumption
of *chicha* (a maize-based alcoholic drink), intimidation and selective use
of force – eventually overcoming the Chimú themselves around 1470.[43]
The rise of the Inca owed much to the warm weather conditions which
opened up the potential for farming at higher altitudes, not least around
their capital city of Cuzco – as well as to the fact that climatic patterns
remained consistent for long periods. Investment in the construction
of agricultural terracing, which was so important in highland societies,
was not only a hallmark of Inca success but underpinned its resilience;

the same was true of the development of agroforestry techniques and the cultivation of a suite of crops that produced exceptionally high levels of seed protein and oil content.[44]

The Inca also developed regional exchange networks which were of central importance to ideological, cultural, economic and political control through the monopoly of acquisition and redistribution of long-distance trade goods, metals, ceramics and luxury objects. This sometimes took place through co-opting newly incorporated local elites who were able to benefit from Inca overlordship, sometimes through a light touch that left sacred sites undisturbed (such as the Yumbo site of Palmitopamba), but also sometimes through direct control.[45]

Perhaps the most important – and enduring – feature of Inca rule and empire was the enormous programme of road building to create a royal highway (*qhapaq ñan*) using labour tribute; covering an estimated 30,000 kilometres of interconnected coastal and highway routes, it was punctuated by way stations (*tampukuna*) and relay-runner posts (*wasi*).[46] The aim was to improve the speed and lower the cost of moving caravans, personnel and information between the provinces and the capital, thereby improving levels of control as well as stimulating trade.[47] The increase in the vibrancy of exchange networks and in activity more generally can be identified by the sharp rise in mite abundances from the mid-fifteenth century that are suggestive of the increased density of large herbivores, above all llamas, that were being used as part of trade caravans in the Patacancha Valley and beyond.[48]

The importance of this road network was not limited to the period of the Inca empire: its role in shaping subsequent economic development after the Spanish conquest of much of South America and later has been such that it boosted living standards, including average hourly wages, nutrition and educational achievement – with a particularly pronounced effect on women. Land near the roads rose in value as a result of the ease of accessibility and lower costs of travel and trade. This not only had long-term consequences in the Inca world and in the period of colonial rule – but beyond as well: locations close to the 'Royal road' of the Incas have today high levels of property rights and protection, more schools, greater literacy levels, and better levels of child nutrition than those further away.[49]

This has parallels with the web of the land-based Silk Roads that criss-crossed the spine of Asia. Again, locations close to primary routes developed significantly higher levels of economic activity than those situated at distance, as well as greater rates of intergroup marriage that can be identified across many centuries – right up to today.[50] The identification of such long-term impacts is revealing, instructive and, as we shall see, crucial for understanding even broader patterns of inequality which are global in their nature and which allow us to see just how far the world of the past has shaped the world of today.

Taken as a whole, the fourteenth and fifteenth centuries were a time of transition, a series of new ages of expansion and discovery – at least for those who were able to impose themselves on others. Of course, things looked rather different for cultures and societies that found their customs and lifestyles swept away – whether by conquest or by accommodation. Cahokia had been home to a thriving culture, based on agricultural exploitation of the rich, fertile soils of the American Bottom region. By around 1400, however, it had fallen into decline. Many explanations have been suggested for the dispersal of population and the abandonment of the central site located near the modern city of St Louis that was based around more than 100 burial mounds. These hypotheses include climatic change that impacted rainfall levels and flood frequency, soil erosion and deforestation due to overexploitation, and unsustainable levels of pollution caused by poor sewage clearance.[51] Each and all of these use archaeological and environmental data (including faecal matter, pollen records and tree ring evidence) to build a picture of ecocide – that is to say, a picture of resources being depleted to the point that collapse was inevitable.

In the case of Cahokia, what is perhaps most important is that use of the political centre declined over many decades, centuries even, suggesting that there was not a sudden point of no return or a conflation of factors that caused dramatic change.[52] Rather, whatever looks like a decisive moment of no return around 1400 was in fact the result of a long and drawn-out process of socio-economic and cultural changes. The most significant of these was the decentralisation of power, the emergence of local elites within Cahokia with distinct residential areas and their own mound plazas, and the resulting rise of intergroup identities, rivalries and antagonisms. While ecological exhaustion and climatic shifts cannot have helped, the key to long-term abandonment may have been tensions and conflicts between different groups that created incentives to seek new opportunities elsewhere.[53]

The same seems to have been the case in southern Brazil where previous robust trade networks sagged and subsided, just as they did in southern Africa where repeated droughts starting in the late thirteenth century seem to have been at least one of the factors in the migration of the Hima and Tutsu peoples towards Lake Victoria and of the Luo towards the Nile. There were more large-scale movements of people a century later, at a time when the Nile in Cairo was so low that it could be crossed on foot.[54]

In other cases, change came through the arrival of new overlords. An obvious case in point is Timur, the most prominent of the successors of the Turco-Mongols, masters of much of Asia, who brought swathes of territories, cities and peoples under his dominion in the late fourteenth and early fifteenth centuries. Like all empires, Timur's centralised resources drew labour, funds and expertise from all corners to support and adorn the political heart, in this case enabling the creation of architectural jewels – like the magnificent Bibi-Xonim mosque, the Ulugh Beg madrasa and the mausoleum of Timur himself, all located in Samarkand in what is now Uzbekistan – to say nothing of the art, literature and scientific scholarship that went hand in hand with imperial patronage.[55]

Conquest, expansion and change of dynasty did not always create centripetal forces, for they could also could send shock waves that resulted in fragmentation. This was the case with Timur's brutal sack of Delhi in 1398, which served as a catalyst for the splintering of a sultanate that had itself built up a position of control over much of the Indian subcontinent. Its collapse sparked a blossoming of city states and the intensification of spheres of regional interaction as tax revenues that previously flowed north were now reallocated locally. Delhi's loss was Gujarat's and Orissa's gain; the Malabar and Coromandel coasts benefited in the same way.[56]

Likewise, the recoil of the Mongols after the fall of the Yuan dynasty in China opened opportunities for others. In the 1390s in Korea, General Yi Seong-gye imposed a major land reform after seizing power that was centred on trying to distribute land more equitably than in the past. As had been the case at Pagan, one of the problems had been the concentration of land ownership in the hands of wealthy families, as well as the creation of large-scale endowments by Buddhist temples and minorities. 'In ancient times,' noted one of the new ruler's senior advisers, 'all the land belonged to the state, and the states then granted land to the people ... There was no one who did not receive land and there was no one who did not cultivate land.' Yi – who took the name of Taejo when he seized power – dramatically burned all the existing land registration records and set about a wholesale redistribution of land and favours.[57]

While some of the motivation naturally came from the desire to weaken rivals and potential rivals, another aim was to boost food production and to make more intensive use of the land. One of Taejo's grandsons, King Sejong 'the Great', took considerable personal interest in this cause, ordering the compilation of a farm manual *Straight Talk on Farming*, which stressed the importance of sowing at the right time, the correct use of effective fertiliser and the need to weed regularly, and explained how to plough during the autumn months. 'Farmers are the roots of all the nations of the world,' states the preface to the text. Moreover, it goes on, 'because all food and clothing are produced by farmers, our government must give them foremost priority'.[58]

The Lê dynasty in Đại Việt adopted a similar view after taking power in 1428 – an event celebrated with a 'Great Proclamation on the Defeat of the Ming' which declared that 'Now our Great Việt is truly a cultured country', one with its own customs, landscape and people.[59] As in Korea, a new code set out measures to protect peasant landholdings as well as public lands, with 'eighty strokes of the heavy stick' ordered as punishment for transgressors. Steps such as these were not simply acts of benign rulers – indeed it could be argued that they represented the opposite, seeking to ensure that all taxes passed directly to the crown rather than to those who might be able to conceal their assets or resist the demands of the fisc. It is noteworthy, then, that eighty strokes of the heavy stick could be administered to anyone who 'cultivates public rice land but does not make grain payment within the time limit'.[60]

As one leading scholar of the European Renaissance makes clear, by the end of the fifteenth century, perspectives had widened dramatically. Paintings were being created in Bruges that showed rugs from the Ottoman empire, metalwork from Islamic Spain and porcelains and silks from China. Pictures like the Arnolfini portrait by van Eyck showed not only the scale of trade networks that linked continents together, but also the competitive urge to acquire – itself a precondition for growth and for the presentation of status. This famous painting might be viewed as the record of a pair of individuals, but it also represents a 'celebration of ownership', not only of the picture itself but of the many lavish and expensive objects depicted.[61]

This proved to be important from an ecological and environmental perspective. The connections that had linked Asia, Africa and Europe together had not been driven by royal policy or command, except of course during phases of conquest and expansion. While it is true that such periods could lead to increases in regional and interregional trade, the principal outcomes more usually resulted in nets being cast by the political centre to drag resources towards it, rather than in the facilitation of exports. There were exceptions, such as in Song dynasty China and even during the early decades of the Mongol empire. By and large, however, the driving force behind increased levels of exchange came from merchants, from middlemen, from shipowners and from those in oasis settlements and towns whose populations were well supported by their hinterlands and well located for benefiting from the sale and resale of commodities and goods that were rare, expensive and desirable.[62]

These were the seeds of what some historians have called the capitalist world economy that gathered strength in the eighteenth century and beyond.[63] Between 1500 and 1800, global trade expanded at an unprecedented rate, growing on average by 1 per cent a year: by 1800, twenty-three times as many goods were being carried on ships as had been the case 300 years earlier – a reflection of course of increased levels of exchange, but more pertinently of the impulse to acquire, demonstrate and accentuate status, and above all of the deployment of merchant capital to respond to and feed these desires.[64]

That such demands placed strains on ecosystems had been understood even in antiquity. The point was being articulated ever more forcefully and regularly by 1500. Long before that, depletion of forests in Germany had become so acute that protection was the rule and special permission was required to clear woods. In the 1230s, Archbishop Eberhard of Salzburg expressly forbade the transformation of forests owned by the Church into arable land, so that trees could grow again.[65] A few decades later, King Henry VII of Germany declared that 'harm had come to him' and his realm as a result of 'the destruction of the forest of the kingdom' and its reuse as cultivated land – which he regarded as a calamity.[66]

By the early fifteenth century, Venice was taking steps to try to ensure control of wood supplies from the Italian mainland, recognition of the vulnerability that states could experience as a result of overconsumption of sustainable resources. With no forests of its own, the maritime city state was vulnerable to shortages – as well as price inflation. The latter was expensive; the former was hard to overcome. During an unusually cold period in the 1530s, for example, the authorities complained that the apparatus of government, as well as industry, had ground to a standstill: 'Our mint cannot function, nor can many artisans such as glassmakers, dyers and metalworkers.' This was a dire state of affairs, and a precarious one too.

Henry VIII of England had complained of precisely such a problem halfway through his reign when he passed an act that acknowledged the 'great and manifest likelihood of scarcity' as a result of 'the great decaye of Tymber and Woodes'. As one commentator put it a century later, many cut down wood but 'few or none at all doth plant or preserve'. There used to be ten times as much wood in England as there was at the time of writing, he said. This was dangerous, he added bluntly: 'so it may be conceived, no wood, no kingdome'.[67]

Such concerns were shared in many parts of the world – and not surprisingly. Wealth and power were closely linked to agricultural production, which gave rulers a strong incentive to support land clearances and the transformation of woodland into fields that could support settlements, expand cultivation and produce cash crops that were taxed as a share of each harvest.[68]

There were exceptions, such as King Krishnadevaraya Tuluva (r. 1509–29), whose poem on statecraft, *Āmuktamālyada*, advised kings to preserve and protect forests. Deforestation that cleared land to allow more agriculture should be discouraged, not least since it impinged upon the 'tribal people, who roam about in the forest and hill areas'.[69] Such concern with the rights of indigenous peoples was to prove extremely unusual in relation to other developments that were taking place at the same time in other parts of the world.

Among those expanding geographic and cultural horizons in the fifteenth century were the Portuguese. In popular history, much of the credit for voyages down the western coast of Africa and to the various islands and island groups in the Atlantic Ocean such as Madeira, the Canaries and the Azores is given to King Henry V, whose nickname 'the Navigator' provides a clue to the central role given to this ruler during a time when Portuguese engagement with new worlds rose rapidly.

Henry should better be described as a co-ordinator of the interests of financiers, merchants, navigators and cartographers who were the driving force behind the development of sugar plantations in Madeira and of the use first of Muslim and then of African forced labour. By 1444, Lançarote Passanha had founded the Lagos Company with the intention of formalising the enslavement of fellow human beings; soon ships were sailing south likewise motivated by the profits to be obtained from the import of malagueta, also known as 'grains of paradise', used as a substitute for Indian pepper, and by the discovery of gold markets at Elmina in what is now Ghana.[70]

These voyages, and perhaps most importantly the profits they generated, helped propel more journeys over longer distances. By 1475, Portuguese ships had crossed the equator going south, and two decades later had reached the southern tip of Africa. The crown benefited from expeditions that returned with lucrative cargoes – whether of human beings, foodstuffs or gold – taking a fifth of the value of goods in tax. According to some chroniclers, such as Fernão Lopes de Castanheda, who was writing several decades later, Portugal's rulers in the 1480s and 1490s were also keen champions of these maritime journeys because of their desire to wrest control of the spice, medicine and jewel trades that passed through the Red Sea from Egypt and Venice.[71]

One of those who took part in these adventures was Christopher Columbus, whose strong religious convictions and desire to use the proceeds of trade with Asia to finance a reconquest of the Holy Land from the Muslims inspired an ambitious plan to sail not south but west across the Atlantic Ocean in the hope of reaching the rich markets of China, Japan, India and South-East Asia. When he failed to win backers in Portugal for his project, he turned to Ferdinand and Isabella of the unified kingdom of Castile and Aragon, eventually setting sail in August 1492 from Palos de la Frontera in what is now southern Spain.[72]

Columbus provided an excitable account of the people and places he discovered after successfully reaching the islands of the Caribbean. Apart from the 'gold and metals' that he claimed to have found, he stressed that he had come upon a natural environment that was ideal for development. The island which he named Hispaniola was home to 'great farms, groves and fields, most fertile both for cultivation and for pasturage'. Another island, which he named Juana (Cuba), likewise was 'exceedingly fertile' and blessed with many safe harbours.[73] Particular attention was paid to the kinds of things grown by locals, including cotton and foodstuffs like kidney beans and maize; the latter 'has a very good taste when cooked, either roasted or ground and made into gruel'.[74] 'Your Highnesses must believe me', he wrote, 'that these islands are the most fertile, and temperate and flat and good in the whole world.'[75]

Reports of the ecological richness of these discoveries were matched by the accounts of those who accompanied the men who followed Columbus across the Atlantic. The Venetian Zuan Caboto (who is better known as John Cabot) set out from Bristol five years after Columbus' first voyage in search of the spice islands of South-East Asia, and instead landed on the north-eastern coast of what is now Canada. Although the rich fishing waters of the North Atlantic had been well known for centuries, the abundance of fish was almost overwhelming. The seas were 'swarming with fish', wrote the Duke of Milan's envoy in London to his patron. Cod were so numerous and easy to catch, it was said, that rather than using nets, weighted baskets simply needed to be lowered over the side of fishing boats and then hauled aboard. The fact that the first recorded cargo of cod brought back to Europe by Hugh Elyot in 1502 had a value equivalent to the annual income of a prosperous landed estate showed that there were fortunes to be made from the natural wealth of parts of the world that Europeans now found themselves able to access with ease and regularity.[76]

Alongside such excitement came considerable disappointment and confusion. Having read all the works of the great philosophers and poets, wrote the Jesuit priest and naturalist José de Acosta in the late sixteenth century, 'I was convinced that when I reached the equator I would not be able to bear the dreadful heat.' Instead, he went on, 'I felt such cold that at times I went out into the sun to keep warm.' All this made him doubt his education. 'I laughed and jeered at Aristotle's meteorological theories and his philosophy.' It was clear that the Greek scholar had no idea when he was talking about.[77] This troubled others too. It was obvious that 'the ancients, guided by inference', had got things badly wrong, noted Bernabé Cobo; those who now live in the Americas know from experience that 'it is the opposite' of what the great scholars of antiquity had assumed when it came to hypotheses about the world, its temperatures and its climate.[78]

The harshness of conditions in the Americas prompted much speculation. Some suggested that South America was full of holes and caverns of water, and that the strength of the sun caused cooling vapour to escape; others argued that heavy rains were responsible for counteracting heat and helped create a cold climate as a result. Others still threw their hands in the air. The American tropics were on the same latitudinal parallel as those of Africa, yet were much colder. 'What the causes of these differences may be, I do not know,' wrote one commentator.[79]

The realities differed sharply from expectations that the new climates would damage or destroy newcomers. Early reports of the 'New World' had emphasised that ecologies were very different, including – in the words of the English natural philosopher Richard Eden – 'Contagious ayre and extreeme heate'. So alien was the natural environment, he added, that it 'altereth the formes and qualities of [European] thynges', such as wheat and cattle.[80] Some worried that those who travelled to the Americas would be overwhelmed by the 'change of air, diet and drinking of water' that would lead to 'sore sicknesses and grievous diseases'.[81]

This in turn helped sow the seeds of an ecological hierarchy that was to find an echo in ideas that developed about race. Tobacco grown in England was 'better for the constitution of our bodies' than that grown on American soil, stated the herbalist John Gerard, author of *Great Herball, or Generall Historie of Plantes*.[82] In the minds of at least some Europeans, things grown in the Americas were smaller, more dangerous and worse than those grown back home. Animal life, wrote the Comte de Buffon in the eighteenth century, 'is less active, less varied, and even less vigorous' in the Americas; not only was the number of species smaller, animals were generally 'inferior in size to those of the old continent'.[83]

These were ideas that hardened as they became established, and influenced thinking for centuries. Writing around the same time as de Buffon, the Dutch philosopher Cornelius de Pauw claimed that 'Europeans who pass into America degenerate, as do the animals; a proof that the climate is unfavourable to the improvement of either man or animal.' The climate and natural environment of North America were such that they prevented reason itself. 'America has not yet produced one good poet, one able mathematician, one man of genius in a single art or a single science,' wrote Guillaume Raynal, one of de Pauw's contemporaries.[84] De Buffon himself was equally scathing about the peoples living in North America: the indigenous population and the waves of immigrants who had settled had certainly formed a distinct 'new people', he wrote, but it was not an impressive one, defined by 'their ignorance, and the little progress the most civilised among them had made in the arts'.[85]

Such views were not shared by all. Alexander Hamilton was dismissive of 'men admired as profound philosophers' who could be so foolish as to have 'gravely asserted that all animals, and with them the human species, degenerate in America, [claiming] that even dogs cease to bark after having breathed awhile in our atmosphere'. Such comments betrayed the 'arrogant pretensions' of their authors and of Europeans in general. Moreover, they could be easily disproved by studying scientific data that few had even bothered to gather, let alone think about.[86] Quite right, agreed Thomas Jefferson; it had taken centuries for the Greeks to produce 'a Homer, the Romans a Virgil, the French a Racine and Voltaire, the English a Shakespeare and Milton'. America was a young nation and needed more time to produce poets of similar genius.[87]

The creation in the minds of Europeans of the Americas as a 'New World' of course paid no attention to the indigenous populations who had settled and lived in these continents for tens of thousands of years before the transatlantic crossings. In the conceptualisations of early European travellers and the waves of settlers who followed them, the Americas were virgin lands, ripe for exploitation. To all intents and purposes, the ways that land had been used by local populations were irrelevant – as were the local populations themselves.

It was certainly true that the first waves of those who sailed across the Atlantic from Europe, who became known as *conquistadors* or conquerors, were motivated by the rapid rewards of movable wealth – particularly the gold, silver and jewels that were pillaged from the Mexica (or Aztec) in Central America and the Inca in South America and were piled up on the quayside in Seville in such volumes as to be compared to wheat being brought in from the harvest. But after these initial surges of pillage and looting, the Americas became primarily important as landscapes whose ecologies could be transformed and exploited.

The energy – and cruelty – with which that process took place has its own important story, as we shall see, one centred on human bondage, on slavery and on grotesque ideas about race. The terrible treatment of indigenous peoples in the Americas played a central role in these abuses, but so too did that of peoples from Africa who were torn from their families, transported across the Atlantic in horrific conditions against their will and forced to work for their 'owners' and 'masters', helping to create great fortunes for them in the process.

In some ways, then, the disappointment of many of those who visited or settled in the Americas with the environmental conditions that they found raises a question that can all too easily be overlooked – namely that of why Europeans sought to expand across the Atlantic in the first place rather than stay closer to home. After all, Portuguese and Spanish cultivators had successfully set about creating plantations in places like Madeira, the Azores and São Tomé in the second half of the fifteenth century and early sixteenth; why then did they not turn their attention to doing the same in West Africa itself? It was after all a region blessed with climate conditions that were similar to or better than those on the other side of the Atlantic, with land and soil well suited to growing crops such as sugar, rice and cotton that proved so lucrative in the Caribbean and the Americas. West Africa was also home to a labour force whose size is self-evident from the slave trade itself. Not only that, West Africa was closer to European markets and as such meant transport was quicker, less risky than crossing the Atlantic and therefore much cheaper thanks to lower transportation costs.

As one later English official put it, 'everything that thrives in ye West Indies' would thrive in West Africa. As others also noted, 'the shortness of distance, and the safe passage between England and the Africa coast, compared to the whole [transatlantic] voyage' made the idea of plantations in West Africa infinitely preferable to long-distance connections – and would likely produce three times as much sugar to boot.[88]

Although some have questioned whether soil fertility and acidity, as well as rainfall distribution patterns, were entirely appropriate for cash crops, the fact that these were successfully grown from the mid-nineteenth century suggests that there were other reasons why they were not grown at the time of European maritime expansion. São Tomé and other such locations could have been a 'stepping stone' to similar developments elsewhere along the coast of Africa; instead, the latter became a source of labour rather than a place for intensive agricultural investment.[89]

Historians who have focused on the disease environment in tropical Africa have noted that Europeans were at a major epidemiological disadvantage because of the lack of immunity to malaria and yellow fever that local populations had built up over millennia. From the outset, Europeans in West Africa were confronted by a 'striking angel with a flaming sword of deadly fevers', with the result that visitors and settlers 'tended to sizzle and die'.[90] In contrast, the biological odds swung heavily in their favour in the New World where, ironically, indigenous peoples were the ones who suffered as a result of diseases that were brought by new arrivals and the animals that were brought with them.[91]

This was all true enough, but what was more significant was the fact that the political systems in states in West Africa were highly developed to the extent that it was nigh on impossible to contemplate colonisation – at least for several centuries. In fact, until the nineteenth century, Europeans were rarely able to penetrate 'beyond a cannon shot from the coast'. The kingdoms of Kongo, Benin and Oyo and others were perfectly able to resist incursions, and were not much threatened by military pressure exerted by small numbers of people a very long way from home, whose settlements amounted to a handful of coastal fortresses and whose commercial activities depended not on coercion but on negotiation.[92]

As one scholar has put it, Europeans were convinced of the potential of Africa. The problem was that they 'failed completely' to gain access to, let alone control of, gold mines, and were unable to develop the plantations that they wanted. 'African resistance', therefore, 'resulted in Europeans taking slaves away in ships as a second-best alternative to working slaves on African plantations or mines'. Although things would change dramatically in the centuries that followed, the reality at the time of the European engagement with the Americas was as clear as it was emphatic: 'the slave trade was a symptom of African strength, not weakness'.[93]

There were many reasons why the Americas were colonised, including misinformation, poorly informed and elevated expectations, competition between settlers and of course the push towards further discoveries in what was to Europeans at least a New World that offered excitement and opportunities, albeit ones that were often disappointed. The primary reason, though, was mundane and easy to overlook. While there were many and complex motivations for the different ages of discovery that characterised all parts of the world in the fifteenth century and beyond, the least convincing was the notion of an idealistic gathering of information about new peoples and new parts of the world for the sake of learning and knowledge. What drove the next cycle in global history was the pursuit of profit. It reshaped political power, transformed ecologies and ultimately changed the climate itself.

15

The Fusion of the Old and the New Worlds
(c.1500–c.1700)

Another great pestilence struck this land, bringing death and destruction to the native population.

Diego Muñoz Camargo (late sixteenth century)

The establishment of routes across the Atlantic was one element of a much wider web of connections that tied most of the world's great landmasses together. Just five years after Columbus had set out westwards, Vasco da Gama had rounded the southern tip of Africa, headed north as far as Malindi and then made his way across the Indian Ocean, reaching the coast of what is now Kerala in southern India. Others followed swiftly in his footsteps, sailing not only along the coastline of Africa or even to the Red Sea, Gulf and South Asia but beyond, to Sri Lanka, South-East and East Asia. Within a matter of decades, ships were criss-crossing the Pacific, creating what might be reasonably described as a globalised commercial system.

This went hand in hand with a dramatic ecological transformation that was also global in its nature, scope and impact. While attention is often paid to political frontiers being reset by the forces of colonialism and by the social and economic consequences of new and even deeper contact and integrations at local, regional and intercontinental level, the reshaping of the natural environment had impacts that are difficult to exaggerate. Flora and fauna were transplanted into new settings, sometimes intentionally and sometimes not. Ecological boundaries that were demarcated by climatic conditions became boundaries for human interaction. Public imagination and conceptualisation of the natural world were reshaped in such dramatic ways as to distort how we think about history as the Old World expropriated and refashioned the New World in its image.

For example, in today's world, we think of tomatoes as being synonymous with Greek and Italian cuisine, or perhaps with that of Spain – home to tomato-throwing festivals such as 'La Tomatina' which takes place every year near Valencia. We relate paprika to goulash, the Hungarian national dish; we associate pineapples with tropical Africa or South-East Asia, chillies with India, peanuts with the satay sauces of Thailand and Malaysia, and potatoes with Sunday roasts that are the hallmarks of the British family weekend experience. Yet none of these foods is native to Europe, Africa or Asia; all are from the Americas.[1]

At stake was not the greater availability of different crops and their diffusion to different parts of the world, but a full-scale global ecological revolution. The process was that of the harnessing, exploitation and consumption of resources that changed landscapes, transformed ecosystems and shaped human settlement patterns as a result of the deployment of the labour that was needed to sow, reap, extract and ship foods, minerals, materials and goods to those able and willing to pay for them. That in turn provided motors of economic growth and social change that were disproportionately concentrated in centres of power that were able to build up and maintain control over key resources, to militarise and secure trade routes and to protect themselves from competitors and rivals both at home and abroad.

The result was the creation of global empires, above all centred in Europe, that were directly related to the relentless rolling back of commodity frontiers – the expansion of geographic boundaries to appropriate and exploit ever greater natural resources. The search for more and more materials, whether in the form of minerals or crops, brought about the wholesale transformation of landscapes, as seams of precious metals were mined and forests and flatlands turned into fields and plantations. This had ecological costs, but also had obvious economic consequences as booms in production of precious minerals or cash crops that generated the greatest profits often gave way to gluts in supply that could not be easily absorbed, which in turn led to downturns in prices.

High levels of availability accompanied by falling costs had benefits of their own, with widening access serving as a driver of social change and creating conditions well suited for an 'industrious revolution' of populations in Europe; these populations gained access to ever-increasing volumes of goods at ever-decreasing prices that initiated a cycle of rising levels of disposable wealth and greater participation in the celebration of ownership so richly shown in the Arnolfini portrait of the last chapter.[2] The consequences were significant in the Old World, but they came with a heavy price in the New, where the benefits were not shared equally or equitably either socially or ecologically.

Sugar, once a luxury product for the elite alone, serves as a perfect example of this process. Sugar plantations were created in the Atlantic on Madeira, the Canary Islands and São Tomé before being introduced by the Flemish and Dutch to Brazil and to one island of the Caribbean after another; it spread further, as production later took off in Louisiana and above all in Cuba, which by the nineteenth century was the most productive sugar island in the world. By that time Java in what is now Indonesia had become an important centre for production, as had Taiwan – with centres then being developed in Mauritius and Réunion in the Indian Ocean and Fiji in the Pacific; then vast plantations in Brazil were created to grow sugar for ethanol in industrial quantities as a form of 'sustainable' fuel.[3]

Sugar was one commodity among many – with cotton, coffee, cacao, rubber, timber, furs and many others following similar trajectories of massive expansion of exploitation that in turn depended on four interrelated factors. First, the forcible occupation of land, often through recourse to violence, with the most productive terrain seized, secured and then turned over to the production of cash crops; second, the availability of a labour force to engage in plantation, cultivation, harvesting or extraction of resources; third, a logistical infrastructure that enabled the transportation of goods and an institutional framework that protected property rights at source, during transit and on arrival; and finally, the existence of markets with growing appetites and discretionary spending power.

Some scholars have argued that the goods and products that flowed back across the Atlantic in particular fuelled the industrial revolution and the rise of Europe.[4] Indeed, Columbus' crossing and the opening up of maritime trade routes to Asia shortly afterwards have long made an impression on economists. 'The discovery of America,' wrote

Adam Smith in 1776, 'and that of a passage to the East Indies by the Cape of Good Hope' by Vasco da Gama just six years later were 'the two greatest and most important events recorded in the history of mankind'. These new routes united 'the most distant parts of the world ... enabling them to relieve one another's wants, to increase one another's enjoyments, and to encourage one another's industry'. Smith was no rosy-eyed globalist who saw the benefits of wealth being evenly distributed: it was just that 'At the particular time when these discoveries were made, the superiority of force happened to be so great on the side of the Europeans.' They took advantage of this in ways that were grotesque, committing 'with impunity every sort of injustice' in remote lands.[5]

Smith was principally concerned with the political and economic transformations which followed in the wake of the opening up of new trade routes that eventually linked all the world's continents together. By the time that he was writing in the 1770s, Europeans had spent the best part of three centuries fanning out in all directions, driven above all by the search for resources, goods and produce that could be extracted by force or acquired cheaply but that commanded higher prices elsewhere. The process of colonisation later became closely wrapped up in the promotion of values and ideas about religion, about race, about interpretation of the past and even about scientific exploration. But the motor for expansion from the 1490s was the deployment of mercantile capital and interests.

It was no surprise or coincidence, therefore, that the colonial expansions that brought misery and injustice to so many, as Smith had noted, brought different results in the countries that benefited most from the opportunities offered by a new global trading system. Those who became wealthy through commerce were determined to protect their assets, both by minimising tax demands from the crown and by limiting the powers of the sovereign to interfere in trade generally or to target its beneficiaries – entrepreneurs, risk-takers and investors. Ironically, enslavement, murder and dispossession from their land by Europeans in many corners of the world were mirrored by the entrenchment and enhancement of rights back at home: parliaments, law courts and institutions that were independent of the king were set up, often acting specifically to limit the powers of the sovereign while also defending the interests of elites who were determined to retain their independence and to use their fortunes to demand and fashion further political, social and economic reforms.[6]

Naturally, the aim of these reforms was to develop further still the sinews for economic growth and further institutional improvements. They were not uniform, with interest groups in northern Europe – in England and the Netherlands – proving far more effective than their counterparts in the south in Spain and Portugal, especially after 1650. Among other things, the relative skill of parliamentarians in preventing extraordinary taxes, curtailing warfare with neighbours and borrowing prudently led to significantly lower interest rates, which served to provide a competitive advantage in global trade, but also served to ensure lower levels of risk, thus favouring long-term investments.[7]

From a European perspective, this led to what economists refer to as the Little Divergence, a time when northern Europe pulled away from the south in terms of socio-economic and political performance, which led to waves of democratisation that although slow were regular when viewed over the long term.[8] But the path towards higher participation in the political process, and away from absolute monarchies, can be traced back to the initial bursts when the 'superiority of force' enabled Europeans to gain at the expense of those living in other parts of the world.

The first waves of those who crossed the Atlantic focused on movable wealth, and above all precious metals, jewels and fine objects. Attention turned quickly to the conquest of political systems that offered the greatest and most lucrative spoils. Chief among these were the Aztecs of Central America and the Inca kingdom in the Andes, both of which were effectively dismantled by relatively small numbers of men who had left Spain looking for fame and fortune. The invaders' success owed something to the military technologies that had been honed by centuries of warfare in Europe, particularly the use of firearms and other weapons, although identifying where and how these were decisive is not straightforward. Horses also gave the newcomers a decisive edge in communication and transportation as well as in military confrontations. The ability of individual Europeans to forge local alliances and to exploit differences with rivals among the ruling elites both within and outside their realms however also proved crucial in enabling modest numbers of outsiders to bring down what had appeared to be robust, resilient and sophisticated state structures.[9]

Precious metals flooded out of the Americas, with some vessels packed so full that they even used gold for ballast.[10] Gold and silver flooded back to Seville, where they were stacked up like wheat, often in such large volumes that the customs house (the Casa de Contratación) 'could not accommodate it all and it overflowed onto the patio'.[11] Such booty was part of a one-off, exceptional transfer of wealth that reflected large-scale appropriation from leadership structures that had themselves succeeded in centralising power and drawing in riches from all parts of their realms, and sometimes beyond it too through the collection of tribute. After this initial explosion, however, a different model was required to extract revenue, whether through crops or through mining, such as from Potosí, which accounted for more than half of global silver production for more than a century: one that was based on mass labour.[12]

Columbus himself had not only noted the possibility of relying on local populations in the Caribbean and the Americas as a workforce but had hinted at the ability to make them do so through compulsion: 'they are fit to be ordered about and made to work', he wrote, and to 'plant and do everything else that may be needed'.[13] The enslavement of the indigenous peoples of the Americas is often mentioned only in passing by historians of this period, if indeed it is mentioned at all. However, those who do discuss the way the local populations were forced to work suggest that hundreds of thousands and perhaps as many as a million people were put into bondage and made to work for Europeans who had crossed the Atlantic.[14] This was despite the fact that Queen Isabel had been horrified by the enslavement of indigenous peoples, had ordered them to be freed and returned to their homeland and had even, in 1501, declared that they were free vassals who should be treated well and should pay tribute to the crown.[15]

This view was not only shared by clerics such as Bartolomé de las Casas, who argued that God had created all humans to be equal by their nature and in their recognition of the Almighty, but also repeatedly enshrined in law, such as the Laws of Burgos in 1512, Pope Paul III's papal bull of 1537 and further legislation issued by the King of Spain in the 1540s.[16] As happened in many other cases during the creation of colonial empires, there was a profound disconnect between theory and practice, between the declarations of law on one side of the world and the hard realities on the ground in another.

The arrival of the first Europeans, along with their requirements and expectations, met with fierce resistance from indigenous peoples. The first settlement in the New World, La Navidad on the island of Hispaniola, which had been built using the remains of a Spanish ship, the *Santa María*, was destroyed by the Taíno population. In some cases, resistance took passive forms of protest against the appropriation of land, including the refusal to plant their annual crops – a ploy described by the contemporary commentator Gonzalo Fernández de Oviedo as an 'evil scheme' that cost the lives of Spanish settlers and local populations alike. The Spaniards took desperate steps to survive, eating all the domesticated animals they could find, including those they had brought with them, before turning to lizards, salamanders and snakes, 'of which there were many types, but none poisonous'. Any living creature they could find 'ended up in the fire, boiled or roasted'.[17]

Experiences such as these resulted in a range of measures designed to reduce food insecurity. One was the introduction of species that were familiar to Europeans as reliable sources of protein – pigs being the most important, above all because of their prolific reproduction rates, short gestation, large litters and ability to eat almost anything. This was one part of a major ecological upheaval that was accelerated by the introduction of sheep, goats and cattle – a process captured by one eyewitness in the early seventeenth century, who noted that there were 'immense flocks of cattle, such as horses, mules, oxen, cows, sheep and goats, which have pastures always fresh in every season', spreading out in all directions 'as far as the eye can see'.[18]

This of course had dramatic effects on native species of animals of all kinds; but it also had a major impact on topsoil and plant life. For example, in some cases, overgrazing brought about soil erosion which dramatically reduced the quality of the land; that in turn reduced the quality of forage that was available, which led to a decline in the average weight of animal stocks, affecting animal reproduction rates and thus impacting herd and flock sizes, which reduced available protein and textile sources. Deforestation likewise brought about a host of consequences, including deterioration of the water regime that in some places made land unsuitable for long-term settlement and encouraged the spread of arid-zone species. Anthropogenic change, inadvertent and otherwise, had drastic impacts in the Americas.[19]

The impact of the biological revolution was so widespread that some historians have termed it a form of 'ecological imperialism'. Native biota were usurped and transformed by the arrival of new peoples with new habits, lifestyles and demands – and by that of their domesticated animals, whose 'eating habits, trampling hooves, and droppings, and the seeds of the weedish plants they carried with them ... altered forever the soil and flora' of regions that were colonised.[20]

The Europeans brought with them a 'portmanteau biota', in part by design, in part by mistake. In addition to domesticated crops and animals, which spread to, bred with and affected domestic species of flora and fauna, there were weeds, seeds and pests that also had profound effects on all aspects of the peoples, places and living organisms they came into contact with.[21] So too did pathogens. Local populations had had no contact with or experience of a range of diseases brought by the Europeans, leaving them immunologically defenceless.

Smallpox and measles proved devastating for the inhabitants of Central America, with waves in the 1520s leading to catastrophic loss of life, with some accounts describing the number of rotting bodies left unburied as almost overwhelming.[22] The 'cocoliztli' pandemic of the 1540s was likewise disastrous, which is clear not only from written accounts but from chemical analysis of a cemetery in southern Mexico that points to ruinous population loss.[23] Subsequent study of these bodies shows that they had died after being infected with a subspecies of salmonella known as *S. paratyphi C*, a bacterial cause of enteric fever, that was perhaps brought across the Atlantic by European carriers who were either asymptomatic or survived the crossing. The fact that contemporary accounts suggest that both indigenous peoples and Europeans died during the outbreak provides an indication of its virulence.[24]

This was followed by a further outbreak of disease in 1576 that was devastating. 'Another great pestilence struck this land,' wrote Diego Muñoz Camargo, 'bringing death and destruction to the native population.' So many died, he added, that 'the native population was almost extinct'. The pandemic was accompanied by ominous celestial signs – namely 'three circles in the sun, resembling bleeding or exploding suns, in which the colours merged'.[25]

The apocalyptic scale of suffering was reported by others too, such as the Franciscan friar Juan de Torquemada, who wrote that 'a great mortality and pestilence' that spread through Spanish-controlled territory in Central America 'was so fierce that it ruined and destroyed almost the entire land. The place we know as New Spain was left more or less empty.' So many died, he added, that 'nobody had the health or stamina to help the sick or to bury the dead. Large trenches were dug in the cities and towns, and from morning till sunset, priests did nothing but carry the dead bodies and toss them into the ditches without any of the solemn rites usually reserved for the dead, because there was simply not enough time to do so. At night they covered the trenches with soil.' According to Torquemada, more than 2 million died as a result.[26] Modern research indicates that this estimate was not far off the mark. One study suggests that 80 per cent of the indigenous population died in the pandemic of the 1540s and that there was a mortality rate of 45 per cent three decades later.[27]

Some Europeans believed that indigenous peoples were being punished by God because of their belief systems which were not so much pagan as diabolical and demonic.[28] The response, therefore, was to enforce hard-line religious practices on local populations. As it happened, this also provided an opportunity for individual missionary priests to appeal for greater resources to help minister to their flocks – in a classic case of not letting a good crisis go to waste.[29]

It was not disease alone that proved devastating, however, but rather a cascading set of factors that became closely intertwined, as forced labour, slavery, resettlement and malnutrition combined to lower resistance and increase vulnerability to illness and suffering. 'I saw ... cruelty on a scale no living being has ever seen or expects to see,' wrote the Spanish friar Bartolomé de las Casas of his experiences in the earliest days of European settlement, in a horrified report designed to inform those back home of what was happening in the New World.[30] These thoughts were echoed by Jerónimo Mendieta later in the sixteenth century. The indigenous population 'was falling each and every day, consumed by inhumanity and cruelty'. The greed of the Spanish, he said, was such that not only were the settlers 'pitilessly watching them die like flies', but were 'exploiting them for the short time while they yet survive, for it will not be long before none of them remain'. Vast regions were being devastated by greed, leaving no records of the countless inhabitants who had once populated them.[31] Adverse climatic conditions made life more difficult for new arrivals and presumably for indigenous populations as well.[32]

Expeditions into what is now New Mexico in the 1540s that were inspired by excitable and exaggerated rumours of rich cities waiting to be conquered were accompanied by the use of violence against Ancestral Puebloans by the Spaniards, including rape and torture on a scale that was so horrifying that they became the subject of a royal commission set up to investigate abuses. Contemporary sources claimed that antagonisms were sharpened by competition for shelter between new arrivals and local peoples, which resulted not only in displacement of the latter, but in the burning of their homes and pillaging of sources of fuel 'to provide insurance against the cold, which was extreme'.[33]

In the eyes of some modern historians, the fact that the invading forces were woefully ill-equipped for the conditions and lacked warm clothes was decisive, with food shortages and the looting of blankets and turkeys – whose feathers were used to make cloaks – proving to be sources of friction and confrontation. The most infamous of these incidents was in 1599 when Spanish soldiers and their native auxiliaries massacred almost a thousand men, women and children at Acoma Pueblo, spurred, at least in part, by 'the struggle for warmth [which], even more than food, likely created the worst hardships'.[34]

Exceptionally cold weather in the south-east and south-west of North America played a part in this, with freezing winters and heavy snows, including in parts of California in the 1540s, while alternating patterns of droughts and storms in the last decades of the sixteenth century made life difficult for settlers in Virginia, which one eyewitness spoke of as a land of 'sterility and death'.[35] In South Carolina, outposts were abandoned under pressure from a combination of food shortages, the animosity of Guale Indians and inclement weather; as one contemporary recorded, it did 'nothing but rain all the time' when grain had to ripen. 'So here we are lost, old, weary and full of sickness.'[36]

Life became more difficult still in the late sixteenth century in the Americas – and elsewhere too, as we shall see – following a series of eruptions of Colima in Mexico in 1586 and of Nevado del Ruiz and Huaynaputina in the Andes in 1595 and 1600 respectively, as well another major volcanic event at an unknown location around 1592. While none of these was particularly large in its own right, they had a similar effect to chain-reaction explosions in the sixth century, leading to a rapid phase of cooling that brought temperatures down sharply across Eurasia and North America. In 1601, the temperatures around the northern hemisphere were some 1.8 °C below their long-term average, making the summer the coldest of the last 2,000 years – and part of the coldest decade of the same period – if tree-ring data is to be believed.[37]

The late seventeenth century was a time when there was one disaster after another in North America, with conditions so bad that many Spaniards questioned whether it was even worth holding on to the territories that had been taken. Spanish Florida was 'a wasteland', warned one commentator, that 'renders little harvest after much labour'. The entire enterprise of supporting colonies in North America was misguided, Alonso Suárez de Toledo told King Philip II of Spain; 'to maintain Florida is merely to incur expense because it is and has been entirely unprofitable nor can it sustain its own population. Everything must be brought from outside.'[38] As if to underline the scale of the challenges, the first English colony – at Roanoke in what is now North Carolina – failed, with its inhabitants reported to have been massacred, to have starved to death, dispersed or fled.[39] Perhaps not surprisingly, Suárez de Toledo reported to Philip II that whatever problems the Spanish had to face in North America, the English were not one of them.[40]

The cold did not affect all regions the same way, nor all peoples, with many different responses and coping strategies. Neutral Iroquois in eastern America shifted from cold-sensitive protein-rich beans to a diet that involved more deer hunting both for protein sources and for the animals' hides, although this in turn led to rising competition for hunting territories.[41] Other Iroquois groups migrated, relying on a decentralised clan and kinship system to ensure a balanced distribution of resources during times of scarcity. Then there were the Algonquin societies in the Chesapeake and Potomac, which responded in a different way, concentrating power and authority in the hands of a hereditary elite as part of a hierarchical social, economic and political system that marked a radical departure from previous systems of organisation.[42] Changing settlement patterns in the south-west and in eastern woodlands which included greater population densities at some sites and the construction of fortified villages reflected the emergence not only of hierarchies but of violence and of higher levels of competition for resources.[43] These were just some of the changes that are also captured in a range of oral histories of different peoples that were passed down through generations right across North America that recall a set of climatic and environmental crises and enshrine them as lessons of resilience and triumph over adversity.[44]

The histories of indigenous populations were not framed by their interactions with Europeans and new settlers, as there were complex relations not only between local groups but within them too.[45] However, the pattern was rather different in regions that were conquered or dominated by arrivals from Europe, where the scale of demographic collapse was astonishing: while precise figures are not easy to come by, some estimates suggest that the Valley of Mexico was home to 1.5 million people around the year 1500, but to just 325,000 seventy years later; by the middle of the seventeenth century, this had fallen again to as little as 70,000. In other words, the population around 1650 was just 5 per cent of what it had been before the arrival of the Europeans.[46]

The scale of loss was such that indigenous historians like Hernando de Alvarado Tezozomoc and the great Don Domingo Chimalpahin took to writing down accounts of their ancestors for fear that there would soon be no one left to recall the deeds and events of the ages before the transatlantic crossings began.[47] More recent commentators have focused on other consequences of the large fall in population size, most strikingly arguing that the loss of life on such a scale induced dramatic environmental and climatic change: one study has suggested that the demographic decline resulted in a massive reduction in land use, with tens of millions of hectares of land that had previously been cultivated reverting to prior states, impacting CO_2 levels and global surface air temperatures in the sixteenth and seventeenth centuries.[48]

The hypothesis that the 'Great Dying' of the indigenous populations of the Americas which was caused by violence, malnutrition and disease itself led to climatic change is ingenious, but it is also speculative and problematic. For one thing, it relies on assumptions about population sizes before 1492, as well as about those of a century and more later, which are very difficult to assess with a real degree of certainty – to the extent that some models concede a margin of error in calculations of almost 100 per cent.[49] For another, it is not clear that reforestation did occur in the Americas, and if it did, where it did and what its precise impact was; furthermore, even if forests did grow back up and even if plant biomass rose as a result, it is also worth noting that the sixteenth and seventeenth centuries were a time of rapid deforestation in Asia, which would (presumably) have offset some of the changes in the Americas.[50]

Perhaps the most obvious problem, however, is that the climate evidence from ice-core data points to a sharp decline in global atmospheric carbon dioxide in the 1590s, and not in the 1540s and/or 1570s, two decades that were periods of catastrophic mortality rates caused by pandemic disease, at least in many parts of Central America. The suddenness of this signature suggests that the causes of the shift had less to do with population collapse and changes to the use of land, and more to do with other, non-human factors – including volcanic eruptions that we know took place at precisely this time.

What is perhaps less contentious is the broader impact of population loss on the fate of the Americas, on Europe and on Africa. The ecological dividends of the New World had been a key factor in the early transatlantic trade, most notably sugar to start with, soon followed by tobacco which was thought to have almost miraculous medicinal qualities. Settlement and colonisation happened not by accident but by design – and both were closely linked to exploitation of new landscapes, and to the wealth that these could generate.[51]

Key, however, was availability of a workforce that could plant, grow, harvest and process the fruits of the land; this was especially important for cash crops that were labour-intensive and year-round processes. From the outset, the new arrivals from Europe saw forced labour and slavery as the obvious solution to producing sugar: this required the digging of trenches, planting of new cuttings, weeding, cutting and then crushing and processing within twenty-four hours before the juice began to ferment, through a process of boiling and refining that was often compared to the fires of hell.[52]

In Brazil, tens of thousands of people were enslaved and set to work on sugar plantations, sometimes through slaving expeditions into the interior of Bahia that also brought Europeans into conflict with each other over who could seize the lion's share of indigenous inhabitants who could be set to work to create profits for strangers from thousands of kilometres away. The large-scale population loss among those living in the Americas therefore presented a major problem. Outbreaks of dysentery in the 1550s, bubonic plague a decade later and repeated bursts of smallpox soon afterwards killed many of those working for planters in Bahia, compounded by starvation resulting from the failure to plant enough food crops under the pressure of falling population numbers.[53] 'The number of people who have died here in Bahia in the past twenty years seems unbelievable,' wrote one Jesuit missionary. 'No one ever imagined that so many people could ever be expended, far less in so short a time.'[54]

Population losses were not uniform throughout the Americas, nor even within individual regions. Those living in coastal estuaries, by rivers or near water sources that favoured waterborne disease were far more at risk than those living in the interior, where heavily forested homelands supported higher numbers of game animals as well as soils that produced surpluses. This explains why the Spanish faced regular if not constant hostility from indigenous populations on the Atlantic coast of North America for more than a century after the initial settlements, which suggests that demographic collapses were highly localised. As one leading scholar has put it, when it comes to coastal communities 'massive depopulation did not occur'.[55]

European settlers had been preoccupied with boosting the labour force even before the first waves of demographic disaster through disease and other factors. Crucial to this had been the development of the 'plantation complex' where enormous quantities of sugar as well as other cash crops could be cultivated and produced, and where Italians and Portuguese had learned from experience with agricultural production on the offshore islands in the Atlantic such as the Canaries.[56] Access to the slave markets of West Africa had played an important part in the economic and ecological exploitation of these locations; it now proved crucial in the search for profits across the ocean.[57]

By the early sixteenth century, large numbers of Africans were being transported from one side of the Atlantic to the other. So many were being made to work on the sugar plantations in Hispaniola that 'the land appears a copy or image of Ethiopia', wrote one Spanish writer.[58] However, there was some trepidation among new settlers about the shipments of large numbers of enslaved, unfree or indentured people. In theory at least, one concern was that Islam would be transported to the New World. 'In a new land like this one where faith is only recently being sowed,' stated one royal decree in 1543, 'it is necessary not to allow to spread there the sect of Mahomet or any other.'[59] These echoed long-standing fears that had led to Africans taken to Spain and Portugal before the crossings of Columbus and others being forcibly baptised and given religious instruction designed, if not to turn 'idolators' into good Christians, then at least to reduce the threats they posed.[60]

More of a concern than the possible spread of Islam was the numerical inferiority that was soon a source of deep anxiety for early European settlers in the Americas. As early as 1503, some like Nicolás de Ovando, Governor of Hispaniola, were arguing in favour of a complete ban on the trafficking of Africans across the Atlantic because they fled, joined the indigenous population and taught them 'bad customs'.[61] These worries were rooted in fear of uprisings, and were framed by claims that Muslim Africans were effective at inciting rebellions and at encouraging indigenous populations to revolt too. Such fears were not ill founded, with the first major revolts breaking out in the 1520s prompting the repeated issue of decrees by the Spanish crown that specifically forbade the sale of enslaved Muslims from Africa without a special licence.[62]

One alternative was to try to attract people to migrate voluntarily or through forms of incentivised migration. In England, these ideas had been brewing since the start of the Tudor period, primarily in relation to Ireland – which figured in the English imagination as a wilderness ripe to be civilised by settlers who would tame the 'weeds of Irish society' and turn Ireland into 'our new world'.[63]

Reports about the natural environment on the other side of the Atlantic capitalised on such rosy portrayals of virgin territories waiting to be transformed. Accounts such as that by Thomas Harriot which paid close attention to the commodities and produce that grew and could be grown in the fields and forests of North America were read carefully in Europe and in England in particular, where Queen Elizabeth I took a keen and personal interest in the opportunities these new lands offered both in their own terms and as a potential source of profits that would benefit the country and protect it against Catholic rivals and enemies closer to home.[64]

Initially, the numbers of those who crossed the Atlantic voluntarily from northern Europe were modest. In the fifty years that followed the first English attempts to settle in the Americas in the 1580s, colonists established themselves in Virginia, New England, Bermuda, Barbados and the Leeward Islands. Communities were so sparse, however, that some have suggested that there were more people from the British

Isles being enslaved in North Africa by the Moors, usually taken captive at sea, than the sum total of those who had made their way to the New World.[65]

However, the flow of settlers rose steadily throughout the seventeenth century. In many cases, the rewards of agricultural production were reaped not through coercion of a labour force controlled by fear and violence, but through co-operation and trade. However, it was not lost on some early settlers that opportunities had opened up because of the decimation of local populations through disease. In a charter of 1620 that set out the claim for what became known as New England, King James I declared that 'within these late Yeares there hath by God's visitation reigned a wonderfull plague' that resulted in 'the utter Destruction, Deuastacion, and Depopulation of that whole Territorye'.[66] The large numbers killed in this outbreak, perhaps caused by leptospirosis complicated by Weil syndrome resulting from contamination of soil and fresh water by rats brought from Europe, helped smooth the way for colonisation.[67] Ironically, however, it also paved the way for co-operation locally as competition for the best resources became less intense, and as those who survived were incentivised both to trade and to seek accommodations while being forced to regroup and rebuild strength.[68]

For Europeans, such experiences must have seemed providential, but they were also a reminder of the need to build up labour forces that could actually take advantage of opportunities opening up as if by magic. While much of the commentary about the New World, its climate and nature was whimsical, anecdotal and plain wrong, there was also a concerted effort to explain the potential rewards on offer. For example, in the 1630s, John Winthrop sent a letter back to London reporting that while Boston was characterised by 'sharp and longe' winters, 'the natives, they are near all dead of the smallpox, so the Lord hath cleared our title to what we possess'. If that was not enough of an attraction, men like the minister Francis Higginson were careful to let others know that there was 'hardly a more healthful place to be found in the world that agreeth better with our English bodies' than Massachusetts. 'Many that hath been weak and sickly in old England', he went on, 'by coming hither have been thoroughly healed and grown healthful and strong.'[69]

The climate of New England was 'most apt' for those born and bred in England, and its lands 'most fitt for the generation and habitation of our English nation', wrote Thomas Morton, whose book about his experiences in North America turned him into something of a celebrity when it was published in 1637. The 'English and Scotch' had another advantage over others, wrote Philip Vincent around the same time, namely 'a facultie that God hath given the Brittish Ilanders to beget and bring forth more children, than any other nation of the world'.[70]

The focus on being 'good breeders', as Vincent put it, was significant for it points to the problems of labour shortage and the attempts to overcome them. While having more children was an obvious solution, such population growth took time, and also required accounting for high levels of infant mortality that kept population numbers low. A quicker fix came from indenture, a contract of servitude whereby an individual agreed to work for a designated master for a set period of time, in return for passage to an agreed location on the other side of the Atlantic.[71] Efforts went into extolling the prodigious resources and rewards that were dangled to lure workers overseas. There were 'extravagant encomiums', wrote one disbelieving cynic, that promised there were islands in the Caribbean where 'Gold is more plentiful than Ice, Silver than Snow, Pearls than Hailstones.'[72]

In the case of England and to some extent France, the availability of a labour force and its migration to the other side of the Atlantic were part of a wider story of socio-economic changes in the sixteenth century that saw improvements in agriculture and gains in production which resulted in shortages of work for the peasantry. Merchant capital was quick to connect this surplus to the surging demand for workers in the New World, exploiting indenture contracts to offer opportunity, transport and work for a fixed period, normally of four to five years, followed by a cash payment at the end.[73] Some, like Francis Bacon writing in the early seventeenth century, were unimpressed by the quality of those agreeing or sometimes being forced to go to work on plantations in the New World, which were being filled with 'the scum of people, and wicked condemned men'. For others, early colonists in places such as Virginia and Barbados were 'loose vagrant people' whose interests centred on 'whoreing, thieving or other debauchery'.[74]

Perhaps not surprisingly, however, not everyone saw things the same way. In addition to developing a labour market in the colonies, the dispatch of cohorts of unskilled workers would rid England, as well as Scotland and Ireland, of potential troublemakers at home, at the same time strengthening the ties of dependence with the mother country. There were 'many thousands of idle persons' in the British Isles, wrote Richard Hakluyt in the early 1600s, who have 'no way to be sett on worke'. They are 'either mutinous and seeke alteration in the state, or at least very burdensome to the common wealthe and often fall to pilferage and thevinge and other lewdness'. If they were not sent off abroad, they were bound to end up on the gallows.[75]

Indenture contracts for the poor (whether mutinous or otherwise) offered a credit mechanism that gave those who set off overseas the ability to borrow against future returns based on their labour. Their arrival, as members of the House of Lords put it in 1640, was 'hailed with delight by planters who wanted cheap labour' on the other side of the world.[76] It was a solution that suited worker and owner alike.

Planters often saw little distinction between indentured servants who came from Europe and those shipped from Africa, with the former often being referred to as 'white slaves'.[77] In some cases, enslaved African people were heavily outnumbered by indentured Europeans: by 1645, around 24,000 people had settled on Barbados, which was fast becoming a crucial engine in the growth of the plantation economy. Some three-quarters of the population were white, with many either previously or still indentured servants.[78] Africans were much more desirable – something reflected in prices that were almost double those for white indentured workers, although this differential also reflected attitudes to investing in those whose freedom had been taken away for good rather than reverting to them after a defined period and whose labour therefore 'belonged' to their 'owner' as long as they were alive.[79]

Scholars have pointed out that many Africans in the New World were highly regarded and valued for their knowledge and expertise in particular areas. Those from the regions of Wolof, Fula and Mandinga in West Africa which had well-established equestrian and cattle-raising traditions were relied on for livestock management – skills that continued to be valued well into the seventeenth century. Experience with mining and aptitude in pearl fishing were also sought after in enslaved African workers. This finds a parallel in the way that Spanish settlers not only valued but made use of the smelting and technological skills of indigenous populations when it came to metal working in Central America; another parallel lies in the help given by Arawak peoples in South America whose agricultural knowledge and acumen were so invaluable that promises were given to them that they would be left as 'free people', commitments that were soon broken.[80]

The heavy reliance on those who were enslaved, indentured or otherwise unfree characterised Europe's engagement with the new worlds that they had stumbled into in the Americas. The extraction of resources of all kinds, from pearls to precious metals, from crops like sugar to tobacco, required manpower. Political crisis in England spurred an intensification of those demands. Protracted and bloody civil war in the 1640s resulted not only in the emergence of a new leader in Oliver Cromwell but in a major change of direction and ambition in foreign affairs. Cromwell's determination to stamp out royalists and rivals led to interventions in Ireland that resulted in more than 3 million hectares of land being confiscated from Catholic owners and handed out to his supporters, while a fleet sent to Barbados in 1651 paved the way for the conquest of Jamaica shortly afterwards as part of a wider effort to weaken Spain by taking its prized possessions in the West Indies.[81]

England's imperial ambitions transformed engagement with islands in the Caribbean as well as beyond. As early as the sixteenth century, indigenous Taíno populations across the region as well as in Central America had been decimated by overwork, malnutrition and epidemic disease.[82] Ideas for solving labour shortages were soon being sought in Africa. Supply was not only about numbers though: Spaniards in New Spain and other colonies often suggested that one African was as productive as four indigenous workers – with sums paid for enslaved people often reflecting high differentials accordingly. Perceptions about physical strength may or may not have corresponded to reality. What was more important, as one commentator noted in the 1650s, was that a coerced African labourer 'begins at three in the morning and works until eleven at night', compared to indigenous workers, who work 'from eight or nine in the morning until six in the evening'.[83]

The British decision to invest in global affairs in a direct and meaningful way through conquests of islands in the Caribbean brought about a significant acceleration in transatlantic slavery. Part of the motivation was a major yellow fever outbreak in Barbados that began in 1647 and spread not only through the Caribbean but across Central America too; this brought into sharp focus the need to find ways to exploit lucrative honeypots that could help generate valuable resources as well as revenue.

Life expectancies for Europeans who came to places like Jamaica were dismal, especially in urban areas, and, what is more, declined rather than improved in the century and a half after that island's capture by the British in 1655.[84] Yellow fever proved especially lethal to white settlers, more so than to enslaved people shipped from Africa, though the latter likely did not have immunity to this disease despite many historians' claims to the contrary.[85] Yellow fever was just one of a suite of diseases that proved devastating, alongside typhus, smallpox, influenza and malaria. Taken together, these all posed considerable threats not only to the indigenous populations, but to those from further afield – including enslaved people and the indentured and unfree from Africa, as well as European settlers of all kinds. Although the disease environment for each was different, some required particular conditions to flourish: malaria and yellow fever, two of the most dangerous and virulent diseases, were both spread by the *Aedes aegypti* mosquitoes that needed hot, wet conditions in which to breed and spread the parasite and virus to human populations.[86]

The Atlantic coastal regions of South, Central and North America – as well as the islands of the Caribbean – provided perfect breeding grounds for the mosquitoes and for these two deadly illnesses. This ecological environment, which was perfectly suited to a particular insect species and as a result ill suited to most humans, shaped political, economic and military fortunes not only across this region but in Europe too. Yellow fever and malaria, diseases transmitted in the Americas by females of the *Anopheles quadrimaculatus* mosquito, were prices to pay for the so-called Columbian Exchange – the transfer of people, foods, ideas and pathogens that followed Columbus' voyage of 1492. Millions died as a result of the epidemic diseases which were largely responsible for shaping the boundaries of what one scholar has called 'mosquito empires' formed in the centuries that followed: where mosquitoes led, only those who were rash, brave or obliged followed.[87] Europeans were not the only colonisers, in other words, who reshaped the world; so too did insects.

Until the middle of the seventeenth century, the scale of transatlantic slavery from Africa was relatively small, averaging around 2,700 souls per year – a number that can all too easily mask the horror of the loss of dignity and liberty and the traumatic experience of being settled involuntarily in poor conditions, thousands of kilometres away from

Cave paintings from Lascaux in the Dordogne, southwest France. The depiction of animals became increasingly common around 40,000 years ago.

Mohenjo-Daro, one of the main Indus Valley settlements. Planned around a grid system, the city was one of the largest in the world around 2500 BC.

Female figurine from the Indus Valley. Women were often portrayed as deities in many civilisations, including across Mesopotamia.

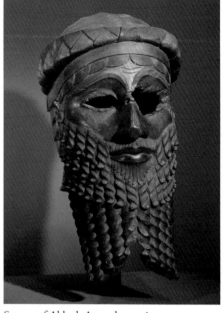

Sargon of Akkad. An early empire builder, he had 'neither rival nor equal', according to one source.

Tortoise shell that was used in Shang dynasty China to predict the future – including the weather.

Detail of a painted casket from the tomb of King Tutankhamun. Horse-drawn chariots were not just symbols of power, but methods of control.

Scene from the Ramagrama stupa at the temple complex at Sanchi, Madhya Pradesh. It depicts a visit by the great leader Ashoka to collect relics belonging to the Buddha. Buddhism was one of many religions that offered explanations about engagement with the natural world.

Gold adornment from Issyk Kul, modern Kazakhstan, of winged horses, c.4th century BC. Objects such as these showed status and wealth – and the importance of horses in the steppes of Central Asia and beyond.

Roman-era mosaic from southern France. The Romans idealised the countryside and control over nature.

Pyramid of the Sun in Teotihuacán in the heart of Mexico. The city was given its name (literally 'City of Gods') only much later.

Portrait vessel from the Moche era of South America (c.1–800 AD).

Aztec gods Cipactonal and his wife Oxomoco devising the calendar. The peoples of Central America – like others – set great store by their mathematical and astronomical calculations.

The Emperor Justinian (r. 527–65). One of the greatest of the Roman
emperors – but one whose reign coincided with a catastrophic pandemic.

Above left: Temple V at Tikal, in what is now Guatemala. The building marks an apogee of Maya culture in Central America. *Above right:* A ceramic pot of the Aztec rain god Tláloc. Offerings were given to deities who brought rains, water and fertility across Mesoamerica.

The magnificent temple complex of Angkor Wat at Angkor in modern Cambodia. The city's huge population depended on sophisticated water management systems.

Monks Mound at Cahokia, one of the largest and most important pre-Columbian settlements in North America. Cahokia's success owed much to the rich soils of the American Bottom region.

The eruption of Mount Samalas in 1257 was one of the largest in the last millennium and had global consequences. It was so violent that it created Mount Rinjani on Lombok, Indonesia, with its distinctive Segara Anak caldera.

Peter Bruegel the Elder's *Hunters in the Snow*. Painted in the mid-sixteenth century, this oil painting is often closely associated with ideas about the Little Ice Age (c.1550–1800).

Above left: Conditions on slave ships were appalling and were all about maximising profits for those with capital to invest – and no concerns about the fates of their fellow human beings. *Above right:* A sample of a potato plant from 1660. Potatoes have played an extraordinary role in global history, and not only in re-shaping diets around the world.

Opposite: A page from Thomas Jefferson's meteorological observations. The American statesman took multiple temperature readings every day for decades – including on the day of the signing of the Declaration of Independence on 4 July 1776.

Observations on the weather
Philadelphia 1776

uly.	hour.	thermom.	day	h. m.	°
	9 - 0 A.M.	81½	9	5 - 30 A.M.	75
	7 - P.M.	82.	9		77½
2.	6. A.M.	78.		6 - 30 P.M.	81½
	9 - 40' A.M.	78		9 - 45	78.
	9. P.M.	74	10.	8. A.M.	75.
3.	5 - 30 A.M.	71½		9 - 15.	76½
	1 - 30. P.M.	76		2 - 0. P.M.	80.
	8 - 10.	74.		4 - 45	82.
4.	6. A.M.	68.		6 - 30	81½
	9.	72¼		9 - 30.	78.
	1. P.M.	76	11.	5 - 30. A.M.	74.
	9.	73½		8.	76½
5.	6. A.M.	71½		9 - 40. P.M.	75.
	9.	72	12.	7. a.m.	72.
	9. P.M.	74.		9.	72.
6.	5. A.M.	74.		8 - 50. P.M.	72.
	9.	75.	13.	5 - 30. a.m.	71½
	4. P.M.	77.		11.	74
	10.	74.		2. P.M.	76
7.	6. A.M.	71.		6 - 45.	76
	10.	73.		7 - 25	76
	1. P.M.	74.		9 -	75
	3 - 20'	75		rain	
	9 - 30.	74	14.	6 - 50. a.m.	73.
8.	5 - 35' A.m	75		rain	
	9.	77½		9 - 30.	72
	2. P.M.	80.		rain.	
	5.	81.		1. P.	71½
	8 - 15'	80		rain	
	9 - 30.	79		5 - 35	70
				5.	

Cast-brass plaques currently in the British Museum. Part of what has become known as 'the Benin Bronzes', these were looted during a reprisal raid by British forces on the Oba (ruler) of Benin in 1897.

Guano was both highly prized as a fertiliser and a source of profits that some
could only dream of. This image from the mid-nineteenth century shows
bird droppings being collected along the coast of Peru.

Below left: Eunice Foote's seminal article on the effects of the Sun's rays
(1856). Foote proposed that atmospheric water vapour and carbon dioxide
could combine to create what later became known as the 'greenhouse
effect'. *Below right:* Svante Arrhenius likewise worked on the influences of
human activities on climate change, including assessing carbon dioxide
concentrations in the earth's atmosphere.

Much of the Soviet Union's new infrastructure in the twentieth century was built by coerced labour. Here prisoners are being made to work in sub-zero temperatures in the 1930s to build a canal linking the White and Baltic seas.

Below left: Rubber plantations grew at an astonishing rate in South-East Asia. Hundreds of thousands of acres of forest were cleared in the twentieth century to meet global demand. *Below right:* A poster from Mao's ill-fated 'Wipe Out the Four Pests' campaign of the late 1950s. Efforts to eliminate mosquitoes, flies, sparrows and rats had unforeseen consequences.

home.[88] The numbers being sent across the ocean against their will now rose dramatically in what has been described as a moment of profound transformation, nothing less in fact than the 'Africanisation of the Caribbean'.[89] Ecological opportunities provided by soils that lent themselves to cash crops, the efficient deployment of capital in the search for profits, the establishment of triangular trade system, the development of supply chains and the pricing of human lives all came together to create opportunities for some and misery for countless others.

16

On the Exploitation of Nature and People (c.1650–c.1750)

For God's sake [capture] it without delay.

William Beckford (1758)

The English engagement with the Caribbean established the principle of conquest and colonisation as a state enterprise. It did not take long for new institutions to be set up to formalise investment overseas. The most important of these was the Royal African Company (RAC), founded in 1660. While this had obvious parallels with the East India Company (EIC) and the Levant Company which had both been founded a few decades earlier, it was not long before the RAC branched out beyond metals and agricultural crops into slavery. Indeed, in 1663, a charter was granted to the RAC by King Charles II for 'the buying and selling, bartering and exchanging of, for, and with any negro slaves, goods, wares and merchandises whatsoever to be vended or found' in West Africa.[1]

These developments had a dramatic impact on the ecologies of the Caribbean, the Americas and Africa itself. Shipments of enslaved people rose sharply, rising almost tenfold in the course of the seventeenth century, and reaching over 80,000 per year by the middle of the eighteenth century. By 1680, enslaved people made up around half of Europe's trade with Africa; a century later, in the 1780s – the peak decade for transatlantic slavery when more than 900,000 souls were sent from the coast of Africa – it accounted for over 90 per cent.[2]

The demand for enslaved people was driven by the vast profits that could be generated from tobacco, cotton, indigo and sugar – all of which required large amounts of labour. Returns on capital were substantial and rapid, with the enslaved paying back the cost of acquisition within eighteen months, 'with god's blessing', as one visitor to the Caribbean put it.[3] The incentive to make money drove technological and political change as well. Ships were developed that were fortified and specially designed to discourage uprisings of those being transported across the Atlantic.[4]

Shipowners in England seized the opportunity to invest in building bigger, better and faster vessels – and also a lot more of them. Tonnage of English shipping grew by seven times in just over a hundred years after 1570.[5] While the Spanish and Portuguese dominated the first century of transatlantic trade, the English and later the British built up a dominant position to become by far the biggest carriers of enslaved people, transporting around 2.5 million in the eighteenth century, around 40 per cent of the total.[6] The Dutch moved quickly too, quadrupling tonnage between 1500 and 1700 as they too became so involved in the slave trade that some contemporaries contended that they 'managed the whole trade' of the colonies in the western Atlantic, furnishing islands like Barbados 'with Negroes, coppers, stills, and all other things appertaining to the engines for making sugar'.[7]

Advances like these were crucial to the development of merchant shipping fleets, and to the evolution of military forces whose mastery of the seas would later prove the bedrock of imperial power and global empires – most notably the Royal Navy. The demand for seamen far outpaced population growth in England and then Britain as a whole, and helped change perspectives. Once an isolated corner of northern Europe, the British Isles now transformed into a global hub whose population became exposed to peoples, languages, commodities and climates in other corners of the world.[8]

Long-distance trade was part of what is often referred to as a triangular system through which textiles and manufactured goods were shipped from Europe to be exchanged in Africa for enslaved people who were then transported across the Atlantic, before vessels travelled home carrying sugar, tobacco and cotton. Such trade also played an important role in the creation of insurance markets, which in turn relied on the accurate pricing of risk. This in turn was linked to mathematical models and the careful evaluation of factors ranging from the competence and experience of a ship's captain to the route being sailed to the value of the cargo being transported – whether human or otherwise. This too had long-term consequences for the emergence of financial markets and the creation of centres of commercial power that established cities like London and Amsterdam as economic powerhouses.[9]

Such efficiencies had awful consequences, most notably in driving the price of enslaved people downwards. Just over a decade after 1664, average market prices in the West Indies fell by 25–30 per cent; over the same period, supply more than doubled. In other words, coerced labourers became cheaper and cheaper, which in turn stimulated demand further still.[10] In time, that changed attitudes, hardening the hearts and minds of enslavers, who came to treat fellow humans as though they were simply disposable. It was 'cheaper to work slaves to the utmost', said one planter in the middle of the eighteenth century, 'and by the little fare and hard usage, to wear them out before they become useless and unable to do service; and then to buy new ones to fill up their places'. In one of history's strange twists and turns, John Newton – a notorious trader of West African men, women and children who never said a word in public against slavery – was the author of 'Amazing Grace', a hymn that became closely associated with the civil rights movement in the twentieth century and with those struggling for justice thanks to lyrics that include the euphoric lines 'My chains are gone, / I've been set free. / My God, my Saviour has ransomed me.'[11]

As one leading scholar has put it, enslaved people were 'systematically worked to death', with the Caribbean best described as a 'slaughterhouse'.[12] The ships that sailed across the Atlantic were designed to maximise profits by cramming as many humans as possible into the smallest amount of space, in horrific conditions with poor ventilation, shocking sanitation and perfect for the spread of disease. On one crossing, 200 captives died as smallpox took hold – with signs of the disease evidently missed before loading, when each individual would or should have been carefully inspected to ensure they were in good health.[13]

From the point of view of the merchant, death at sea was a poor use of capital. In the seventeenth century, it is estimated that 30 per cent of those who left Africa on Spanish ships and 20 per cent of those on

British ones never made it to the other side of the Atlantic. It was not long before these figures began to improve, driven by more rigorous inspections at point of sale and by better care during the crossing – though it would be hard to describe conditions as anything other than inhuman. The British again were pioneers in this regard, bringing mortality rates down to 10 per cent by the second half of the eighteenth century.[14] Captives were typically taken on deck every day to breathe fresh air and made to exercise, with the threat of a lashing from a cat-o'-nine-tails concentrating the minds of those who were reluctant.[15] This allowed the disposal of excrement and the smoking of the quarters with tar, tobacco and sulphur, before they were washed down with vinegar – steps thought to be helpful, but which offered little help against illness.[16] Nevertheless, these steps were an aspect of the efforts made to reduce loss of life, or, to put it more accurately, to improve profitability.

The relentless process of improvements had other important knock-on effects. Apart from the technological advances that boosted efficiency and provided greater returns in investment, there was a host of other advances that flowed from the maritime world. These included increasing sophistication of logistics required to provision and supply ships as well as ports and settlements that were often many thousands of kilometres apart and that required first-class administrators and bureaucrats who learned not only from their mistakes but from each other. This in turn helped professionalise the economy and for that matter government apparatus. It is hard to measure exactly what uplift these provided; but it stands to reason that they were extremely important.[17]

Those lessons were not shared well in places where personal responsibility was high, accountability low and temptation made irresistible by lack of oversight: in fact, as recent research has shown, the economics of Spanish trans-Pacific trade between Manila and Acapulco from 1570 to 1815 that transported silver as well as cochineal, sweet potato, tobacco and chocolate was compromised by overloading of vessels, endemic corruption of officials and poor decision-making related to bribery of ships' captains. These led to many late departures that took chances with the monsoon winds and ocean currents and dramatically raised the chances of shipwreck. As all the galleons were owned by the crown, losses of vessels such as the *San José* in 1694 which carried a cargo equal to 2 per cent of the Spanish empire's entire GDP had catastrophic consequences for Spain's economy.[18]

The relationship between the state and mercantile interests was different in northern Europe, though not completely clear-cut: after all, Queen Elizabeth I herself was an early investor in the slave trade, persuaded by Sir John Hawkins that 'Negroes were very good merchandise in Hispaniola and that store of Negroes might easily be had upon the coast of Guinea' to boost the royal coffers.[19] The overloading of slave ships went hand in hand not only with the search for gain but also with the dehumanisation of those being shipped. In recent years, considerable attention has been paid to questions around race, racism, slavery and the way that humans have sought to justify treatment of those of different skin colour, religious beliefs or sexualities, attention that has helped revolutionise the way we think about these issues.[20]

At the time, attitudes built on ideas and influences from the classical world, of which Europeans now claimed to be the true heirs. Herodotus, for example, opined that 'soft lands tend to breed soft men', a reference not to political leadership but to geographic bounty: 'it is impossible for one and the same country to produce wonderful crops and good fighting men'.[21] Being tough meant coming from land that required hard work; places that offered easy lives produced lazy men.

Montesquieu was heavily influenced by what he read, tweaking views that were not only widespread but repeated almost unquestioningly in texts by authors like Pliny, Strabo and Vitruvius. People 'are more vigorous in cold climates', wrote Montesquieu in *L'Esprit des lois* in 1748, exhibiting 'more confidence in oneself' as well as 'more courage' and a better sense of 'one's superiority' than those living in warmer conditions. 'The peoples in hot countries', he went on, were 'like old men': timid. Those living in Asia were 'indolent of mind and incapable of any exertion or effort'.[22]

Sweeping statements like this reveal much about finding justifications and explanations for how the cold climate of northern Europe enabled the rise of European global empires. They were also heavily imbued with ideas about race and about the right of European men to dominate other peoples and cultures in distant countries and continents. Those who lived in hot climates, said Montesquieu, were greatly in need of a wise legislator, unlike those who lived in Europe, who were, of course, ideally placed to provide such wisdom to others. Cold air restricts the body's fibres, he wrote, meaning that people lived like 'young, brave men'. In contrast to the lure of luxury experienced by those in other parts of the world, those from cold countries had 'very little sensibility for pleasure'. Indeed, Muscovites were so tough and so inured to comfort that they needed to be flayed to even feel alive.[23]

As Montesquieu realised, elaborate intellectual somersaults were needed to explain the apparently self-evident truth that those in northern climes had superior temperaments, were racially superior and deserved to rule over others. After all, if this had been the case, why was it that northern Europe had been home to barbarian tribes at the time of the Roman empire, and had produced so little by way of culture, scholarship and philosophy in comparison with the Mediterranean region? As always, Montesquieu had the answer: the Germanic tribes 'rose and quit the forests to subvert that great empire'. In the end, in other words, the cold, calm north had won out.[24]

Montesquieu and others were well aware that others had built empires in hot climates, so again manoeuvred to distinguish between the achievements of those with 'a certain vigour of body and mind' who were capable of making 'long, painful, great and intrepid actions', like Europeans, and those who lived close to or near the equator. Those who inhabited 'hot climates' suffered from cowardice which 'has almost always made them slaves'. Empires that had grown up in Mexico and Peru before the arrival of Columbus were fundamentally inferior, he argued. They were 'despotic', he said – presumably unlike their European counterparts.[25]

This was nothing compared to how those from Africa were written about, treated and reacted to – which makes for painful and difficult reading. Africans who were sold for shipment across the Atlantic were inspected by buyers as if they were animals rather than humans, even being compared to the purchase of 'black cattle'.[26] In the middle of the eighteenth century, one Lord Chancellor used a High Court judgement to confirm his opinion that 'a Negro slave ... is as much property as anything else'.[27]

Similar views were expressed in the notorious incident of the *Zong*, a ship whose captain had overloaded his vessel and made navigational errors that resulted in water supplies running low. As shortages and sickness took hold, over 130 Africans, many bound and shackled, were thrown overboard to drown. The ship's owners, a syndicate based in Liverpool, went to court to claim on their insurance for losses in a case heard by the Chief Justice, Lord Mansfield – a towering figure in maritime law. Mansfield had ruled that the fate of those who drowned 'was the same as if Horses had been thrown overboard'. This was not a case of murder, in other words, but one of dealing with excess farm animals.[28]

Those who benefited directly or indirectly from the slave trade thought little about the source of the wealth that built grand country houses, funded great art collections and improved the quality of life in comfortable surroundings at home.[29] Britain is a country, wrote one of Lord Mansfield's contemporaries, 'whose grandeur is founded on commerce' – rather than on the blood, sweat, tears and lives of enslaved black men, women and children toiling on sugar and tobacco plantations in the Caribbean and Virginia.[30]

Others did not so much turn a blind eye as convert reality into fantasy. 'Let an intelligent and educated man compare the deplorable state' of those who had been sold into slavery 'in Africa with the pleasant and easy life which they enjoy in the colonies', one delegate told the French Colonial Assembly. They should be thankful that they were 'sheltered by all the necessities of life, surrounded with an ease unknown in the greater part of the countries of Europe', with access to good healthcare, surrounded by loved ones and 'in peace with their children'. It would be hard to paint a more misleading picture. Rather more accurate were the views of the coerced labourers themselves, who cursed the way that Europeans exploited everything they came into contact with: 'The devil was in the Englishman,' said one enslaved African in Barbados; 'he makes the negro work, he makes the horse work, the ass work, the wood work, the water work and the wind work.'[31]

Some admitted to being moved by the plight, sorrow and despair of those whose lives were spent making money for others, against their will. 'My Heart hath been ready to bleed for those poor Wretches,' admitted one surgeon on a slave ship.[32] Others spoke of their sadness at seeing the separation of 'fathers from sons, husbands from wives, brothers from brothers', declaring that it was impossible not to be moved by such scenes: 'what heart, however hard it might be, would not be pierced with piteous feeling to see that company?'[33] It was dreadful to see the 'Barbarity daily exercised on the Bodies of the miserable Negros; The piercing Cryes and dolefull Lamentations that every Day enters one's Ears both in Town and Country.'[34]

Such sentiments rarely translated into more prolonged reflection, and were rather the passing thoughts of those briefly moved by a sense of compassion. It did not take long to become 'cruel and hard-hearted', and some even encouraged their children to become just that when they were young. 'The first Play-Thing put into their hands is commonly a Whip with which they exercise themselves upon a Post, in Imitation of what they daily see perform'd on the naked Bodies of those miserable Creatures, till they are come to an Age that will allow them Strength to do it themselves.'[35]

Ideas of African barbarism also took hold – dispensing with the history of West Africa and its contemporary sophistication. Dutch writers in the seventeenth century had written with admiration of Benin City, for example, describing its 'very broad streets, each about 120 feet wide', and the royal quarters that were 'easily as big as the town of Haarlem and enclosed by a remarkable wall', while the palace of the Oba (ruler) was 'so large that you can feel no End', so vast in fact that walking its length was exhausting.[36]

These accounts were replaced by representations of Africa as dangerous, barbaric and cruel. If Africans were not sold, wrote the same ship's surgeon who claimed to be upset by the 'Abuse and Death' of enslaved people, other Africans 'will surely starve them to death'.[37] Similar views were expressed to a parliamentary committee by Richard Miles, a slave trader who had 'bought some hundreds – some thousands of slaves' and claimed that if he had not done so, many would have been 'sacrificed at the burials of great men'. Another slaver confirmed that buying those who had been enslaved helped save their lives, 'preserving them from being sacrificed, or otherwise put to death'. In such warped logic, the slave trade became one of salvation rather than of suffering and sacrifice.[38]

It was not just that coerced labour from Africa was all about lining the pockets of merchants, investors and landowners – as in Barbados, which saw land prices multiply by almost twenty times in a few years and went from being a sparsely populated, nondescript island to 'one of the richest Spots on earth under the Sun' following the development of sugar plantations in the mid-seventeenth century.[39] The fortunes that were made for white plantation owners were built on the fact that Africans who were shipped across the Atlantic were far more productive, especially in tropical climates, than those who controlled and traded their lives. Nowhere was this clearer than in West Africa itself, a place described by one scholar as a place for most white men 'to get away from or to die in'.[40] In the early eighteenth century, the Royal African Company lost half those it sent from Europe to West Africa within a year. Just one out of every ten Englishmen who went to work in this region came home alive before the middle of the nineteenth century.[41] Such was the gamble of trying to strike it rich.

The main cause of such high mortality levels was the disease environment. The lack of innate immunities of European populations stood in sharp contrast to those that had been developed over thousands of years by African populations to cope with malaria, a single-cell parasite that is transmitted to humans by mosquitoes. The two most prevalent strains of the disease are *vivax* malaria, a mild form that is rarely fatal, and *falciparum* malaria, which is far more virulent and deadly, with the latter requiring higher temperatures than the former to become infectious. Classic symptoms include fever, chills and nausea and, in serious cases, impaired consciousness, coma and death. Repeated infection results in deteriorating health, including decreased ability to resist other diseases. Populations in sub-Saharan Africa have developed a vast range of immunities to malaria – including the sickle-cell trait, a blood-cell disorder that can reduce the likelihood of developing cerebral malaria after a *falciparum* infection by 90 per cent. Populations that do not present a high frequency of sickle-cell traits have other forms of innate resistance, including the HbC allele or high levels of antimalarial antibodies.[42]

Falciparum malaria had established itself in the Caribbean and South America through multiple independent introductions that were linked to the slave trade – attested by genetic and archaeological evidence, with mitochondrial DNA showing a clear link between African and South American haplotypes.[43] Settlers from Portugal and Spain may also have brought the disease with them, as malaria was endemic in both countries at the time of the conquest.[44] Strains may also have entered the New World from Asia and the western Pacific either before Columbus' crossing or as a result of the subsequent creation of trans-Pacific trade – which would help explain the high genetic diversity of *vivax* parasite in the Americas.[45]

However, malaria does not seem to have taken hold in the colonies of North America until the 1680s, when it did so suddenly and with a vengeance. A series of epidemics hit most southern US colonies, with high mortality in Virginia and South Carolina, where Charleston was particularly badly affected. *Falciparum* malaria then became established, leaving long-term impacts on the white population, such as in Christ Parish in South Carolina, where records show that 86 per cent of the population died before the age of twenty, and more than half before the age of five.[46]

The spread of malarial disease is dependent on three variables, namely the parasite itself, mosquitoes – of which several species prefer to feed on humans rather than on any other vertebrate – and climate, itself closely linked to the habitats of mosquitoes, which require enough water and hot enough temperatures to reproduce, survive and spread. The early 1680s in particular were a time of turbulent and unusual climate conditions, with major El Niño events in 1681 and 1683–4 and again in 1686–8.[47] The correlation has led some scholars to ask whether these weather anomalies played a significant role in allowing *falciparum* malaria to cross a threshold to establish itself successfully in North America.[48]

The appearance of malaria was to have profound consequences that lasted centuries – plaguing the south of what became the United States long into the twentieth century, reducing life expectancy, impacting productivity and being both an indicator and a motor of poverty in the American south.[49] As it was, the second half of the seventeenth century saw a wider shift by plantation owners in states like Virginia; they had previously had a preference for indentured English workers who spoke the same language as the owners, had similar customs and were familiar with English agricultural practices. Demand was difficult to satisfy even before the arrival of malaria – at which point those who could choose where to work actively avoided the American south if they could. Combined with this, however, was a dramatically enhanced need for a labour force that resulted from so-called landgrab in the decades after 1650 in which millions more hectares that were ideal for cultivation were seized – further stimulating appetite for the cheapest, most effective workers. Hardening racial prejudice played a role, with some like the Reverend Godwyn Morgan declaring in 1680 that the terms 'Negroe' and 'Slave' had 'by custom grown Homogenous and Convertible'. As if to underline what this meant to him and to many of his contemporaries, he added that 'Negro and Christian, Englishman and Heathen, are by the like corrupt Custom and Partiality made Opposites.'[50]

As far as colonial settlers were concerned, therefore, African manpower was the answer to multiple problems. As malaria kicked in, decimating the existing population, the desire for more coerced labourers rose sharply. Buyers were not keen to buy enslaved people from just anywhere, but had strong preferences for acquiring those from malaria-ridden regions in Africa, whose populations had high levels of resistance to the disease. This resulted in what one scholar has called a 'malaria premium': higher prices for people most likely to survive infection – and therefore prove to be better 'investments'. Captives from the Gold Coast were considered robust, strong and little affected by disease, while those from the Niger Delta were thought to be less hardy.[51]

It was not so much disingenuous as disgusting then that the depiction of blackness in general and of enslaved peoples expressly shipped because of their genetic advantages should become associated with inferiority, when the opposite was the case. Those brought across the Atlantic in subhuman conditions and subjected to lives of misery were not only the backbone of fortunes and status for their 'owners', but were doing work that the latter were poorly suited to do themselves. Far from being 'inferior', those put into chains were not only stronger but genetically better suited to the Americas than those who exploited them.

In a further surreal twist, states set about codifying the deprivation of rights of fellow human beings – both to justify the principles of enslavement and racism and to enshrine these ideas in law. Slave codes began to be passed by one state after another that formalised the status of slavery as a lifelong condition, as having a racial basis and as being an inherited condition, with coerced labourers being defined as the property of their 'owner': 'buying' another human meant controlling and benefiting from the fruits not only of their labour but that of their descendants too.[52]

This was first set in law in Virginia in 1662 whereby the legal status of 'all children born in this country shall be held in bond or free only according to the condition of the mother'. This was known as *partus sequitur ventrem* – or 'the offspring follows the womb', which among other things meant that the children of women who had been raped by owners of coerced labourers or other white men were condemned to lives of servitude, thus concealing the acts of sexual violence that had led to their conception.[53]

Controlling fertility became an important part of the lives of enslaved women, and in due course led to advances in the development of herbal remedies by black women to control the spacing of childbirth, to act as contraception and to track stages of pregnancy.[54] This was itself partly a response to the fact that an estimated 54 per cent of pregnancies among enslaved women resulted in stillbirths, infant mortality and early childhood mortality.[55] Appalling experiments on women of African descent in the first half of the nineteenth century, almost all without consent, proved foundational for modern gynaecology, obstetrics and healthcare for women – debts that are likewise little known and even less acknowledged.[56] This does not mean that the benefits have been shared equally: today in the United States the disparity between deaths of infants born to white and black mothers is actually greater than it was in the first half of the nineteenth century, while pregnancy-related mortality is three to four times higher among black women than among white women.[57]

Then there is the Mason–Dixon line which is often seen as marking the boundary between southern slave states and northern free states. This was not only a political and commercial frontier but an epidemiological one too, with *falciparum* malaria flourishing to the south – precisely where slavery was not only prevalent and defended as a principle, but eventually a fundamental cause of civil war in the United States in the 1860s.[58] The role that climatic factors had in creating the rich soils of the American south has already been noted in this book, along with the role these play in shaping US presidential elections. However, this can be developed further, with recent research suggesting that the counties with large populations of enslaved people at the time of the abolition of slavery in the 1860s are more likely today not only to vote Republican, but to oppose affirmative action and express racial resentment and sentiments towards black people.[59]

The major expansion of the exploitation of human labour deepened the ecological transformation of large swathes of land in the New World which diverted the benefits to those in the Old, much of it delivered by the manpower and lives of those who had been transported from Africa. This included the importation of coffee, tea and chocolate, of silver and raw materials that were hacked out of the ground and from the sides of mountains, and of cod from Newfoundland that found its way on to European tables by the boatload.[60] The benefits were manifold. For example, indigo production soared in the 1740s, rising from just over 2,200 kilos in 1746 to more than 62,000 just twelve months later.

Such jumps owed much to the consolidation of estates that allowed efficiencies of scale, but they owed more to the huge increases in the size of the coerced labour force working the land, such as in Jamaica where numbers almost doubled between 1740 and 1774 – a figure that excludes many tens of thousands who arrived on the island but did not survive. The sheer numbers of enslaved people being transported across the Atlantic, combined with good climatic and economic conditions, meant that prices fell – driving a permanent cycle of demand for coerced labour, and rising production.[61]

So valuable did this trade become that it was a key part in the struggle for the mastery of Europe, as well as in the creation of and competition between fledgling global empires. Naval victories by the British against the French in West Africa and the Caribbean not only sapped the finances of the latter, but made it more difficult to fund efforts against the former either locally or elsewhere. During the Seven Years' War of 1756–63, the conquest of the West Indies loomed large. One plan involved the British swapping control of Guadeloupe, which they had taken from the French, for France's territories in Canada, so great was Canada's perceived strategic value. This was preposterous, William Burke wrote in riposte to discussions in Parliament. Canada, he told MPs, 'produced no Commodity except Furs and Skins', and offered 'little Returns to make the English merchant'.[62] Guadeloupe, in contrast, produced sugar, cotton, tobacco and more besides that was worth about forty times the wealth of the trade of Canada each year.[63] Despite these entreaties, the French managed to get back Guadeloupe as well as Martinique and St Lucia – but at the price of all its possessions in North America, except for the territory of Louisiana west of the Mississippi river.

The preoccupation with controlling resources was intense. 'The negroes and stock' of Martinique, an island controlled by the French, 'are worth above four millions sterling', William Beckford had told the prime minister, William Pitt the Elder, in 1758. 'For God's sake', he said, capture it 'without delay'.[64] A prominent enslaver, Beckford had his own interests to promote – a pursuit made easier by the fact that he had the ear of the Prime Minister, who took to saying that Beckford 'had done more to support government than any minister in England', thereby surprising other parliamentarians who viewed him 'as a wild, incoherent, superficial buffoon'.[65] Beckford was motivated, above all, by concerns that were shared by many involved in the sugar industry – namely, that taxes would be levied to help support British war efforts at a time when 'the low price of sugar, high freights, high insurance, and hoops and staves' threatened to eat into their profits. Pitt obliged, overruling his own Chancellor of the Exchequer to abandon a special tax on sugar, earning the goodwill and support not only of Beckford but of many others in the colonies. It paid to have friends in high places.[66]

The volumes of sugar being imported back to Europe naturally brought prices down rapidly, enabling consumption by an increasing share of society; this in turn encouraged people to earn more money that could be spent on luxuries that were previously unavailable, unaffordable or both. This was a core part of an 'industrious revolution' that drove a rise in productivity and an increase in levels of income.[67] Some scholars have linked this to a further set of other social responses, such as growing interest and investment in new ideas, that stemmed in part from rising wages and the gains that could be obtained from innovation and technology.[68]

As such, the increase in goods, materials and foods being drawn back to Europe from the Americas in general was important from the perspective not just of ecological dividends being recirculated from one part of the world to another, but of powering a much wider division between what are often referred to today as the global north and the global south. Those in Europe did not just advance because they were able to dominate other parts of the world, or even because they could adapt ecosystems for their own benefit and reap the rewards; those rewards themselves brought further gains that themselves proved crucial. What mattered most was not so much the quantities of goods brought back to Europe as the range and novelty of what became available during the Age of Discovery. Elites secured the bulk of the profits available from transatlantic trade, although these were not always substantial. What made a difference, then, were the gains from variety, as life became sweeter and more stimulating and, furthermore, became available to rich and poor alike.[69]

The case of sugar again proves instructive. In 1700 England imported around 10,000 metric tons; a century later, this had risen to 150,000 tons. On a per capita basis, consumption of sugar in England increased twentyfold between 1663 and 1775.[70] Apart from having the obvious effect of dramatically increasing the availability of what had previously been a luxury product, this consumption of sugar also provided a calorie boost for the growing working class in Europe. It has been argued that the increase in sugar imports between 1600 and 1850 increased English welfare and living standards by an astonishing 8 per cent.[71]

Sugar availability was significant in other ways too. For example, the innovation of adding sweetener to hot drinks such as coffee and tea produced not so much a spike in demand from China as a tsunami, as consumption rose by 400 times in the course of the eighteenth century. This in turn galvanised the East India Company and others to invest in direct trade with East Asia, and in time to begin production of tea in India. The ecological transplantation of natural commodities to new locations was paralleled by that of coffee, native to Ethiopia and Yemen, which was then introduced to plantations in Java in South-East Asia and Surinam in South America by the Dutch soon after 1700, to Martinique and Saint-Domingue in the Caribbean by the French and to Jamaica by the English – by 1800 Jamaica was producing a third of the world's coffee.[72]

In some cases, there were unexpected side-effects of the transplantation of plants and the opening up of new markets. High taxes on tea and tobacco imports to Britain produced a thriving smuggling industry, with some estimates suggesting that between 50 and 90 per cent of all the latter were brought into the country surreptitiously.[73] While difficult to measure accurately, it stands to reason that there were gains arising from the improved navigational skills of sailors who had to sneak in to unwatched bays and from a new industry whose job it was to stay one step ahead of government tax authorities – perhaps coincidentally an area where Britain has long led the world: even in 2021, British tax havens in the Cayman Islands, Bermuda and the British Virgin Islands are ranked as the three top enablers of corporate tax abuse on the planet.[74] Engagement with the New World led to new possibilities and new tastes – and demanded new ways of doing things that had long-lasting consequences.

Near insatiable demand for tea which rose dramatically in the course of the nineteenth century, meanwhile, led to the production of opium in Bengal which was typically sold at auction in Calcutta in exchange for tea sold in Canton (Guangzhou) in order to avoid bans imposed by Qing dynasty emperors.[75] Trade eventually became so important to the British Exchequer that the government used military force to gain favourable trading terms, control of China's customs system, access to ports such as Shanghai and even direct sovereignty over Hong Kong – part of what has later become known in China as the 'Century of Humiliation', and a fundamental part of contemporary conceptualisations of world affairs in Beijing and beyond.[76] Again, it is hard to overstate the impact of new global connections, of new patterns in supply of and demand for commodities and of the attractions of a financial world that enabled merchant capital not only to reshape ecologies but to transform global politics.

As with sugar, increasing availability meant lower prices and greater affordability. The impact on social interaction was profound. There is 'no bourgeois household where you are not offered coffee', wrote one Parisian in the eighteenth century, 'no shopkeeper, no cook, no chambermaid who does not breakfast on coffee with milk in the morning. In public markets and in certain streets and alleys in the capital, women have set themselves up selling what they call *café au lait* to the populace.'[77]

These interactions were not just about improvements to the quality of life, but were important to the exchange of ideas, to innovation and to collaboration. It was no coincidence, for example, that tea and coffee houses played key roles in the development of the stock exchange, of the insurance industry and of political debate and in the dissemination of print media during the Age of Enlightenment – a term that suggests a time of exceptional brilliance in Europe without acknowledging the debts that were owed to the planters, pickers and diggers who were an essential part of the story.[78]

Sugar, coffee and tea were just some of the commodities that characterised a time of intensive and deepening global exchange; attention could also be paid to individual goods like tobacco, timber or furs that played a role individually and collectively in the acceleration of pre-industrial capitalism, which was centred on geographic, ecological and environmental inequality and exploitation.[79] Commodities could see explosive growth in production, as was true of cotton, with exports from the United States to Great Britain rising ninety-three times between 1791 and 1800 and then rising another seven times before 1820.[80] This owed much to the development of the Whitney gin, a device that separated cotton fibres from their seeds, and the huge

British demand in terms of domestic consumption and for export, not to mention the almost doubling in size of the United States after the Louisiana Purchase, which was followed in 1845 by the annexation of Texas. The annexation delivered land that not only could be turned over to cotton but was ideally suited to be offered as rewards to political allies and to become part of what one eminent scholar has called the 'military–cotton complex'.[81] As with the other phases of the expansion across the Atlantic, the impetus of mercantile interests and landowners, combined with a targeted and relentless search for a return on capital, proved not so much crucial as the driving force.[82]

Often, there were steep environmental prices to pay. Overwork of the land damaged soils, caused a decline in fertility and resulted in erosion. Even by the start of the eighteenth century, some were commenting that fields had turned into 'barren, rocky gullies, runaway land, waste land ... much worn out and not so fertile as it was.' According to one clergyman in Barbados in the 1730s, 'the face of the earth appeared, as it were, a dry crust, burnt up and gaping', while a contemporary noted that 'excessive drought, the number of people running off, and the miserable condition and poverty' of an island that had been the source of colossal fortunes only a century before now meant that famine and disaster seemed inevitable.[83] According to Eric Williams, one of the Caribbean's most influential historians, the ecological degradation was a blessing in disguise, helping to reduce profitability and therefore easing the way to the abolition of slavery. Commercial realities rather than compassionate sensibilities were what made the difference.[84]

Plantation agriculture in the Caribbean opened up other environmental hazards too. These included destructive landslides that were dangerous to workers and damaging to ecosystems. Rampant deforestation did not only have implications for soil run-off but magnified the threat posed by hurricanes because of the removal of trees that served as natural protection for animal and plant life alike.[85] Colonial legacies of ecological intervention remain an important factor in climate and biotic vulnerability to this day, to judge from some studies.[86]

The secret to the rise of Europe – and especially of northern Europe – was the ability to access, develop and control millions of 'ghost acres' of land that were either blessed with natural resources or that could be repurposed to produce crops and goods that were necessary and desirable thousands of kilometres away. This had the twin effect of diverting calories, energy and raw materials to Europe and so supporting economic and demographic growth that would otherwise have not been possible, and also of liberating land for other uses.[87]

Much of this was poorly understood and taken for granted, with buyers and sellers knowing and caring little about where goods, products, components or resources came from. A good example comes from hat fashion in Europe in the second half of the seventeenth century. King James I is sometimes given credit for starting the craze when he ordered twenty beaver hats when he became king of England in 1603. Sweden's successes in the Thirty Years' War influenced the popularity of tall 'cavalier's hats', with hat styles then influenced by the latest French fashions. This led to surging demands for beaver fur, which has the ability to hold its shape through felting, and for vicuña, an alternative from the Andes. In short order, this led to beaver populations in most parts of Europe being all but hunted to extinction, and to commodity frontiers being expanded elsewhere, most notably in what is now Canada and Peru. Tens of millions of beaver pelts were imported to Europe from North America, with England alone re-exporting more than twenty million between 1700–1770.[88]

Other components for these hats – such as mastic gum that was used as a stiffening agent and ostrich feathers for decoration – led to surging pressures on plant and animal life in West Africa, Sudan and the Levant where these items were in seemingly inexhaustible supply. All were parts of a process that has been termed 'Invisible Globalization' – that is to say, the centralisation of resources and the expansion of supply chains alongside patterns of overconsumption and depletion. All went unnoticed by consumers.[89]

This was true of no end of other commodities, goods and products. Animals were hunted to the edge of extinction and sometimes beyond. Demand for ivory piano keys and billiard balls in the nineteenth century in the drawing rooms of the burgeoning middle classes in Europe and North America decimated African elephants; beavers were trapped in vast numbers not only for their fur but for the castoreum that could be extracted from their anal scent glands and was used in popular treatments for fever, headaches, spasms, epilepsy and mental illness. Demand for products from whaling, including whalebone and oil made from blubber that was boiled down and used in street lighting, in miners' lamps and in lubricants for guns, watches, sewing machines and typewriters, led to the collapse of whale populations in the Atlantic and the opening up of new whaling stations as far away as the Falklands and the Pacific in the search for new supplies.[90]

Rubber booms saw another surge in the plantation agricultural economy and the intensification of monoculture; demand was spurred both by the growing use of this material and by the development of vulcanisation which stabilises rubber and allows it to be used across a much wider range of temperatures. The booms were concentrated in the Amazon forests of Brazil, where latex was collected from rubber trees, until Sir Henry Wickham smuggled tens of thousands of seeds back to Kew Gardens in London. These were then transplanted to South and South-East Asia, where they were used to establish rubber plantations that not only became central to local, regional and global economies, but led to mass migration through the familiar practice of indentured labour.[91]

Developments such as these fuelled the Great Divergence – the shift by which the western world caught up with, overtook and dominated vast parts of the world. To most Europeans, this was a story of entitlement as much as one of enlightenment, a natural outcome of inherent sophistication and progress which those living in other parts of the world could not and never would match, a result even of racial superiority. Underpinning all these ideas, however, were the cold realities of resource exploitation, of the creation and improvement of supply chains and of turning blind eyes to abuses, of not asking too many questions about who lost while others gained.

Such questions were hardly new. After all, many societies had experienced problems of over-consumption, exhaustion of natural resources or strains on ecosystems that were excessive and unsustainable. Centralised states had at their roots the principle of drawing in resources of all kinds – whether minerals or metals, animals or foodstuffs, tax revenues or human labour – from the periphery to the core. What was different in the centuries that followed Columbus, however, was the global scale on which these cycles operated. Exploitation of landscapes no longer just meant pushing geographic frontiers beyond existing territories, it meant an expansion across oceans and continents.

This in turn was enabled by advances that are easy to dismiss as dull or to overlook altogether, in matters like the logistics of shipping, including docking facilities that enabled rapid turnaround of vessels and the efficient onward distribution of goods; or like the calculation of pricing when purchasing goods at source, which in turn owed much to information gathering and analysis, taking in factors such as the size of harvest, the value of commodities or weather factors.

Calculations like these were extensive and constant, and not just for Europeans involved with trade of all kinds. For example, traders in Angola deliberately restricted the number of captives in the market place at any one time in order to drive prices up. Then there was disease, illness and malnutrition that also led to extensive loss of life: an estimated 6 million enslaved men, women and children who never even made it on to a ship, let alone across the ocean, lost their lives as a result of the transatlantic slave trade.[92]

Trading seasons for trafficking captives from Africa to the New World meanwhile were dictated by rainfall: it was difficult for merchants to move heavy cargoes during downpours that directly affected the ability to reach coastal ports from the interior. Navigational dangers increased during the tropical rainy seasons in Africa, the Guianas and north-east Brazil, while estuarial sandbars off the coast of West Africa and reefs off that of the Americas posed additional risks that rose and fell depending on season and on seasonal variations.

This was not the full extent of the relationship between slavery and climatic conditions. In fact, Atlantic rainfall in Africa not only impacted harvests, but shaped the distribution of crops, determined growing seasons and directed the farming calendar. This was important, of course, in its own right for domestic agricultural production, but it was significant too for the wider trade in terms of selling cash crops to Europe and for buying foodstuffs for enslaved Africans. As such, there were optimal times for sellers to seek to profit, with exports highest in September–October, immediately after the yam harvest, and lowest during yam planting in May–June. These rhythms suited merchants, as they also fitted around supply constraints in Atlantic Africa and allowed provisioning before the ocean crossing. As one agent of the Royal African Company put it, the 'best time for Negroes to arrive is between December & June, being a healthy time & affording plenty of provisions, and ye rest of ye Year being ye reverse'. Such realities underpinned the transatlantic slave trade.[93]

The role of climatic and weather conditions was closely linked in other ways too. For example, higher temperatures had an impact on rainfall levels and on agricultural production. Rises of just 1 °C resulted in measurable and significant reductions in exports of coerced labour – a phenomenon best explained by the rising costs of enslavement since provisions needed to be obtained for those who had been enslaved and for those who enslaved them. These trends were particularly marked in drier regions which were more sensitive to changes in temperature and rainfall and where agricultural productivity varied accordingly. Furthermore, warmer conditions resulted in higher mortality levels, both as a result of an increased disease burden and because of food scarcities, with again the results being most striking in regions that were least ecologically resilient and those where pathogens flourished most easily.[94]

As with the sources of goods that made life in Europe more interesting, more exciting and more varied, these rhythms were difficult to identify or even to see. In some ways, this is not a surprise, for invisibility characterised the way that history itself was written. The arrival of the pilgrims aboard the *Mayflower* in Plymouth Bay in 1620, for example, was seen for centuries as a seminal moment in the telling of the origins of the United States, while the landing of the *White Lion*, the first known arrival of indentured Africans at Old Point Comfort in Hampton, Virginia, a year earlier was relegated to footnotes, or not mentioned at all. The foundation of many of the most illustrious seats of learning in the United States, including Princeton, Yale, Georgetown and Harvard, owed much to the profits of slavery and in the case of University of Virginia to coerced labour itself.[95] US politics likewise owe much to the fruits of slavery, with more than 1,700 members of Congress between 1789 and the 1920s 'owning' or having once 'owned' other human beings.[96]

Not everyone was blind to the new world that was being opened up by long-distance trade. 'I never more will drink Sugar in my Tea,' wrote Aaron Thomas, ship's purser who saw for himself the backbreaking way sugar was made and the conditions it was made in; 'it is nothing but Negroe's blood'.[97] Others too were clear-sighted about just how important the exploitation of humans and nature was. 'If the negro trade was lost,' one businessman of the mid-eighteenth century observed, 'the Colonies must be lost.'[98] There was a choice to be made, in other words: wealth and glory; or compassion and fewer rewards.

Daniel Defoe, later to find fame as author of *Robinson Crusoe*, set out the equation in similar terms. 'No African trade, no negroes,' he argued; then 'no negroes, no sugars, gingers, indicoes etc; no sugar etc no islands, no islands, no continent, no continent, no trade.'[99] He could have added 'no empire, no rise of the west'. Defoe was no critic of the slave trade, in fact quite the opposite, this comment coming not from a critique but from an impassioned defence of the importance of British commerce: the slave trade was vital to trade in general; in Defoe's eyes, that justified the violence done to African men and women.[100] Some, like the Quakers, took increasingly principled stands, with Joseph Woods in 1784 questioning whether it was 'better a thousand poor unoffending people should be degraded and destroyed [than] the inhabitants of Europe should pay a higher price for their rum, rice and sugar?' Those who buy any such goods, observed a contemporary, 'become partaker in the guilt of it'.[101]

Few took such principled views, preferring to look the other way – or to benefit directly from trade. The 'discovery' of the Americas was of course nothing of the sort; indeed, despite his place in historical narratives, Columbus was not even the first European to cross the Atlantic. And yet the new arrivals reshaped and renamed the world they now stepped into and that they regarded as theirs by right. New names reflecting the triumph of Europe were layered over those of indigenous peoples. Continents, countries and states came to bear the names of their conquerors and new masters, from America to Colombia, named for Amerigo Vespucci and Columbus, from Pennsylvania, named after William Penn, to Venezuela – literally 'Little Venice', because the houses that local populations lived in on stilts surrounded by water reminded the Spanish of the Italian city.

Yet the idea that the Europeans embarked on an Age of Discovery, a golden age that is associated with a sense of curiosity and exploration, of adventure and search for knowledge obscures the fact that the driving force behind the expansion of horizons was merchant capital and the thirst for financial rewards. There were scholars, certainly, whose minds were inspired and opened by new possibilities; but, as in any day and age, scientific research has always been closely linked to the availability of resources, of funds and of time that allows the flapping of intellectual wings in place of the planting and harvesting of crops.

This model shaped the world of today in the Americas as well as in Africa. For example, regions in the Americas that were well suited to cash crops that required intensive farming and benefited from large pools of labour became places with high levels of inequality and limited distribution of rights among the population. Locations better suited to less intensive forms of agricultural production on the other hand – regions that favoured the growing of wheat, for example – proved to be more egalitarian, with better distribution of rights among the population. The short explanation for this is that crops that required lower labour input produced smaller profits and therefore meant there was less to fight over, and more reason to co-operate. This is one of the reasons why it is possible to identify a strong relationship between a country's socio-economic development and its distance from the equator.[102]

What mattered, of course, was the combination of temperature, rainfall and soil quality that in turn together determines where particular crops could – and could not – be grown. But the disease environments of tropical locations were of key importance too. In an alternative reality where African sailors had crossed the Atlantic first and taken advantage of conditions the way that the Europeans managed to do, the last 500 years of the world's history would have been very different indeed.

Whether this different scenario would have meant no transatlantic slavery, however, is another matter. For one thing, the ability of Europeans to ship millions of people across the ocean owed much to the existence of established markets for enslaved people in Africa that they could tap into easily and quickly – even if the insatiable appetites became overwhelming almost immediately. By 1516, some African leaders were already demanding a stop to the enslavement of local populations, begging for it even, for it was already clear that it brought negative and damaging results locally. African slavery was not a transatlantic issue. Around two million of the estimated seven million people enslaved or sold by the Ottomans came from sub-Saharan Africa. Some caravans are attested to have conveyed thousands of captives, while other records suggest annual sales to port cities in the Red Sea of as many as 10,000 people per year.[103]

Over the long term, the impacts of slavery on Africa were catastrophic. By 1800, the population of the continent was half of what it would have been had the slave trade not existed.[104] That of course meant that manpower that would and could have been involved either in ecological transformations of Africa or in other productive activities was deployed elsewhere and for the benefit of others.[105] Indeed, even the end of the slave trade did not immediately result in more positive outcomes; in some parts of Africa, for example, prisoners of war had previously been sold into captivity. With this option closed off, many were put to death.[106]

But there were more profound effects that changed social and political development in many parts of the continent too. Supplying captives to traders on the coast demanded constant raiding to secure near endless numbers of captives – which created a vicious and circular world of enslaving or being enslaved. That in itself had other consequences, not least demand for weapons and above all guns – areas in which Europeans had an advantage by the time of enhanced contact with Africa, an advantage maintained and furthered in part thanks to the sheer number of conflicts in Europe and between Europeans that incentivised the development of improvements in reliability of firearms.[107] The demand for guns, itself in part a function of the need both to defend against raiding and to use in raids, became a motor of intensification of the slave trade in its own right, as well as propelling the emergence of highly centralised states dominated by military elites such as Oyo, Dahomey and Asante, each of whose fortunes were closely connected to the European expansion.[108]

While some of these states consolidated, others splintered, with the Jolof confederation splitting into a series of smaller kingdoms under the pressures and demands of slave traders that were so great that some rulers in West Africa complained that it was not only prisoners of war, members of minorities and those of low status who were being sold and shipped across the seas, but high-ranking figures and even members of royal families.[109]

In this age of mounting violence and insecurity, it was perhaps not surprising that ties between villages weakened, communities became introverted and levels of trust plummeted dramatically.[110] Societies atomised and disintegrated, leading to fragmentation that encouraged differentiation along ethnic and other grounds. Research has suggested that these breakdowns developed into long-term issues which are still prevalent today in many parts of West Africa, and explain low levels of co-operation, low levels of trust and poor economic performance. Regions that provided large numbers of captives to be shipped across the Atlantic are worse off now thanks to the historical effects of slavery. In other words, it is not just that peoples and places in Africa paid a heavy price centuries ago; they continue to do so to this day.[111]

Slave raiding had a significant impact on age and gender balances, with demand being heavily skewed in favour of securing male captives of working age whose labour was most valuable across the Atlantic. The instructions given to Cesar Lawson, a slave-ship captain, by a member of the merchant consortium in Liverpool were typical. The vessel under Lawson's command was 'allowed to carry 400 Negroes, and we request that they be all males, if possible to get them, at any rate buy as few females as in your power'. It was important, Lawson was told, to 'be very particular, select those that are well formed and strong; and do not buy any above 24 years of Age'. The captain's patrons further instructed him to keep the ship 'very clean' and to maintain discipline on board. Lawson was also told to ensure that no officers or crew 'abuse or insult them in any respect'. In the world of slavery, this passed for a rare expression of kindness.[112]

Investigation of the impact of gender both in locations where enslaved people were taken from and in those they were exported to is complicated by the fact that the proportion of women and children taken across the Atlantic varied greatly by region and changed over time. Price differentials between men and women generally were much smaller in the Americas than in Africa, partly because planters soon recognised that enslaved African women had a high work rate.[113] In fact, on some estates, women made up the majority of field hands. Gender shaped work roles beyond the fields too, with men being used as mechanics, blacksmiths, carpenters, coopers, masons and so on, while women were made to cook, nurse and act as midwives – jobs that brought less prestige and fewer material rewards than the men's, which in turn affected models and expectations both within slave populations and beyond.[114]

Rape and sexual fantasies were particularly virulent among enslavers and white settlers, with some scholars arguing that ideas about abuse and the use of violence became more prominent, not less so, over time.[115] Women who chose to acquiesce, either in the hope of material rewards or to self-convince that they had choices that did not exist in reality, had little chance of seeing their offspring being freed, although again patterns were different in different locations with manumission of sexual partners and children more common in the Spanish West Indies than in most other regions.[116]

There was, of course, considerable variation in the ways that enslaved people were treated, dependent not only on the personality of the 'owner' but on the size of plantation, its location and what work a coerced labourer was made to do: those working in enslaver homes typically benefited from better food, clothing and housing than those forced to work in the fields, and endured less exposure to disease, heat exhaustion, frostbite, snakebite and more. Hierarchies were created among enslaved social groups, in other words, based on proximity to those who exploited unfree labour.[117]

The effects of the slave trade in Africa were also significant. For example, scholars have noted that the prevalence of polygyny (men having more than one wife) is strikingly high today in regions that were sources of large numbers of enslaved men, such as Guinea, Togo and Benin – where the numbers with multiple wives are three times higher than in countries in East Africa. This has been linked to skewed sex ratios caused by the strong preference for male coerced labour in the Caribbean and Brazil, the main destinations for the exports of human captives, mirrored by the demand for enslaved women from East Africa who were sold into slavery as household staff and concubines in the Middle East and India.[118]

There is evidence to suggest that these patterns were reduced in districts that received intensive Christian missions during the later colonial period.[119] This is important, as models show that the banning of polygyny reduces fertility, increases savings, produces significant uplifts in GDP per capita and reduces gender inequality – raising separate questions about the impact of slavery and the period that followed its abolition in the early nineteenth century.[120] In regions where polygyny persists, on the other hand, incidences of HIV infection rates, violence and child mortality rates are high.[121] However, there are more progressive outcomes too, including higher levels of women's participation in the labour force, an increased likelihood that women will vote and broader-minded views about women as political leaders.[122]

Such then were the profound and many impacts that resulted from the 'discovery' of the Americas that followed Columbus' crossing of the Atlantic in 1492. Global ecosystems were knitted together through transformations of landscapes, the emergence of new tastes driven by widening demand that were in turn propelled by consumption patterns and spending power, above all in coastal regions of western and northern Europe. All this came at the expense of indigenous populations in the Americas and of the millions shipped from Africa who ironically were better suited and more resilient in climate and disease environments than the Europeans who dominated, controlled and 'owned' them.

The sense of entitlement extended even further. The philosopher John Locke, for example, writing in the late seventeenth century, proposed that every person had an equal right to use natural resources, as these were provided by the 'spontaneous hand of nature'. If, however, one worked the land oneself, that land should become one's property. For Locke, human intervention changed the status of land itself from 'the common state of nature' to something that 'excludes the common right of other men'. Labour, in other words, was the foundation of private property.[123]

Ideas like this naturally had resonance as European settlers fanned out around the world, especially when they moved into lands that had not been cultivated or were lived on by nomadic and tribal peoples. As the Reverend Samuel Stoddard, a Puritan minister in Boston, put it in 1722, it was entirely reasonable to take land from the indigenous peoples as they 'made no use of it, but for hunting'. In this particular case, the local population had at least been paid a nominal sum for some of their land; they were lucky, said Stoddard, given that the land had no value in their hands. For the settlers, however, it would be rendered valuable after 'our improvements' had been made to it.[124]

It was a similar story in other parts of the world, where Dutch, British and other jurists and philosophers relied heavily on humanist ideas that private property related only to land that an owner cultivated and transformed. Anything else was *terra nullius* – virgin land that could be claimed and taken over.[125] One good example comes from Assam in India, where British authorities declared that land that was not planted with cash crops was deemed to be 'waste land'. This meant that it was deemed unowned and capable of being claimed or given out as a grant to settlers, usually for free.[126] Another example can be found in legislation in the United States, such as the Homestead Act (1862), which entitled any adult citizen or intended citizen to claim 160 acres of surveyed government land as long as they improved and 'cultivated' it, and allowed land to be taken from indigenous peoples if it was deemed suitable for agriculture or grazing – by newcomers.[127]

The story is not just one of human exploitation of nature, nor even one of humans' exploitation of each other. Insects played a role in shaping social, economic and political change, as did pathogens, precipitation patterns and soil conditions not only in the New World but beyond. One thing, however, was clear: the intensification of exchange had dramatic consequences. It seemed inevitable, therefore, that the emergence and development of new technologies was likely to produce a familiar pattern of exploitation of all kinds, of inequality and of unsustainability. The question was who would do well, and who would pay the price.

17

The Little Ice Age
(c.1550–c.1800)

There was great scarcity in the cities and villages of India … men took to eating one another.

Abū al-Faẓl, Ain-I Akbari (late sixteenth century)

In April 1939, a committee on glaciers at the American Geophysical Union delivered a report which stated that glaciers had advanced over the course of the previous century by a 'far greater extent and volume' than they had done in the past, and suggested that 'We are living in an epoch of renewed but moderate glaciation – a "little ice age".'[1] Although the committee took the long view of the duration of this epoch, suggesting a time frame of 'about 4,000 years' for global cooling, the idea of the Little Ice Age caught the imagination of historians, who typically use the label to refer to the period from the sixteenth to the nineteenth century.[2]

While the problems of trying to identify even vague start and finish points given the vast range of global, regional and local variations are obvious, many scholars have argued that it is possible to paint a broad picture of changing climatic conditions that spanned several centuries, which is attested by tree-ring data, morphostratigraphic evidence and glacier evidence.[3] Three periods of low solar activity are often noted as being key factors in climatic changes in this period – namely the Spörer Minimum (1420–1550), the Maunder Minimum (1645–1715) and the Dalton Minimum (1790–1830).[4] The Little Ice Age is said to be characterised by significantly lower average temperatures in Europe, shown for example by canals freezing in the Low Countries and by the timing of Baltic ice that blocked ports such as Tallinn and Stockholm.[5] Some reconstructions have indicated that temperatures in Sweden and Switzerland fell by as much as 2 °C and 5 °C below normal respectively.[6]

According to some assessments, the hundred years or so from the late sixteenth to the late seventeenth centuries were unique in being the only significant period of cooling in both the northern and southern hemispheres known in history.[7] Others have suggested that the Little Ice Age as a whole corresponded to a time of weaker Asian and East Asian monsoons, greater humidity in Central Asia and higher rainfall in the Indo-Pacific.[8] The concept of the Little Ice Age as a global phenomenon has taken root and become popular with historians and general readers alike.[9]

This is not entirely surprising, as the period overlaps with a time of profound social, economic, political and ecological change. The seventeenth century in particular has been described as a 'General Crisis', a time of tumult across much of Europe, Asia, Africa and the Americas, with more wars taking place around the world in the 1640s than in any other era until the 1940s.[10] As one recent magisterial book put it, climatic extremes combined with poor harvests, food shortages and famine, disease and conflict to produce a 'fatal synergy' that had dramatic impacts on human societies around the world during the period between c.1600 and c.1700.[11]

A host of transformations have been associated with the challenges posed by harsher climates. For example, it has been suggested that adaptations to the challenges presented by the Little Ice Age shaped not only the way people lived but the way they built and lived in houses and interacted with each other. In Sweden, a shift towards tiled stoves – which use less wood and retain more heat than open fireplaces – has been linked to the cooling of northern Europe and to the practicalities of needing to maximise indoor temperatures and comfort. The move away from large, multifunctional halls towards corridors and smaller rooms brought with it ideas about privacy and intimacy in personal relationships – as well as about individuality and exclusion for those who were not invited into small rooms to listen to, take part in or overhear conversations.[12]

The effects of the Little Ice Age apparently impacted European art, with paintings dating to the period 1550–1849 showing a higher proportion of clouds and darkness than earlier or later periods.[13] Paintings such as Bruegel's *Hunters in the Snow*, produced in 1565, have become iconic representations of a phase in history that is supposedly distinctive and identifiable for its coldness.[14] Social behaviour and tastes during the early modern period ranging from fashion to the growing popularity of beer – which has been associated with the cooling temperatures that affected vineyard production, forced the cultivation of wine to the south and both reduced its availability and raised its prices – have likewise been linked to the Little Ice Age.[15]

The persecution of women through accusations of and executions for witchcraft has also been linked to climatic change, adverse weather conditions generally and hailstorms, with women disproportionately being made scapegoats for poor harvests, food shortages and high prices of grain.[16] Although the estimates of excitable commentators in the eighteenth century who claimed that 9 million witches had been executed in the previous 200 years can be dismissed out of hand, there can be little doubt that both perceptions and realities of the suffering of women were extraordinarily high in the second half of the sixteenth and the first half of the seventeenth centuries.[17] The scale of persecution was astonishing. Some cases saw hundreds tried and sentenced to death.[18] Prosecutions for 'witchcraft' in Catholic and Protestant parts of Germany were similar until around 1600, when the numbers of women accused and tried rose sharply in the former – becoming twice as common than in the latter.[19] Regardless of ratio, this should all be seen within the wider context of women being blamed for societal problems, not least in the modern day for ecological stress, economic shocks and disease, including HIV/AIDS.[20]

Some historians have suggested that cooler weather may have led to high levels of clinical depression in the late sixteenth century, with the 'fashionable malady' of melancholy prevalent across royal households and intellectuals circles in England, France and Spain (in England it was known as the Elizabethan malady). Cases of the 'winter blues' were 'well suited to an age of long winters and raining summers', fuelling a rash of literary works focusing on despair – of which Montaigne's essay 'Of Sorrow' is one obvious example. Challenging climate apparently led to an escalation in cases of suicide – although this had the mirror effect, at least in popular imagination, of implying that suicide itself was the cause of bad weather.[21]

The correlation between ecological catastrophe and the expansion of glaciers in the European Alps has led some to connect concern with climatic change with the contemporary search for explanations and scapegoats.[22] Individuals like the Swiss scientist and politician Renward Cysat were blunter when it came to speculating on the causes of challenges and change. In recent years, he wrote c.1600, the weather has taken 'such a peculiar and astounding course and undergone such extraordinary alterations'. He had little doubt about what was to blame. 'The years have shown themselves to be more rigorous and severe' than in the past, he declared, 'because of our sins'. This, he said, should serve 'as a warning to future generations'.[23]

Sustained periods of cold weather have a marked effect on agricultural production: a drop of just 1 °C over a period of a few years can result in the kilocalories from solar radiation falling by around 10 per cent per square centimetre. In temperate zones, diminished sunlight as a result of lower levels of solar irradiation or cover thrown up by volcanic dust can sharply reduce growing periods of crops, pastures and forests. Moreover, cold temperatures often had associated effects – including changes to rainfall levels, and negative alterations to microbial activity in the soil that in turn affected the decomposition of organic material and thus the fertility of the land.[24]

Climate enhances vulnerability to disease – a factor that has been stressed by historians, who have pointed out that colder temperatures significantly raise the risk of the spread of disease, largely as a result of weakened immune systems that are closely connected to malnourishment. It has been pointed out that in the case of China, for example, the six centuries following 1370 saw almost 6,000 epidemics, with a cold climate raising the risk of outbreak by 35–40 per cent.[25]

Indeed, specific events that took place during the period of the Little Ice Age have been explained as being understandable primarily through the lens of unusually cold conditions and of changing climate in general. For example, heightened storm activity in the later sixteenth century, which included the incidence of severe storms rising by 400 per cent, has been cited as the decisive factor in the demise of the Spanish Armada in 1588 in conditions where wind speeds approached hurricane strength. As one author has noted, great gales destroyed more of the Spanish fleet than the combined guns of English warships.[26] It has been suggested that Sweden's status as a European great power was first compromised and then shattered by a cluster of cold winters in the 1690s and early 1700s, as Swedish armies were 'broken by cold and disease', leading to the loss of the country's Baltic possessions and the occupation of Finland by Russian forces.[27]

While the idea of the Little Ice Age may seem an attractive one, a way of explaining cultural and behavioural change, the context of disease transitions shaping the outcomes of military confrontations, it is not without its problems. For one thing, it is simply not the case that temperatures dropped simultaneously in different parts of the world for sustained periods, and certainly not over the course of many centuries. As the Intergovernmental Panel on Climate Change (IPCC) puts it, evidence does not support the hypothesis of a Little Ice Age as globally synchronous.[28]

There were long periods even in the seventeenth century when climate conditions were entirely within their normal range in the northern hemisphere, including during decades of multiple crises, such as major wars and devastating outbreaks of plague.[29] Even where temperatures dropped below average, such as in northern Europe in the 1590s, there was no such drop in other parts of the continent, such as southern Italy or the eastern Mediterranean, where tree-ring data is not in any way unusual.[30]

Marine-core data, sea-ice incidence and ice-core isotope records from this period are marked not by the presence of a persistent multi-century signal, but rather by its absence.[31] Even the advance of glaciers from c.1400 to c.1800 that are supposed to be a key marker of a new cold phase are in fact neither unusual nor markedly greater than advances made a century or two earlier.[32] As two leading scholars put it diplomatically, evidence for a Little Ice Age that is climatically distinct and clearly cooler than periods before or after 'remains elusive' even for northern Europe and the North Atlantic.[33]

Likewise, although it is tempting to suppose that solar minima and a reduction in irradiance and in the numbers of sunspots had an impact on global, regional or local climatic conditions, more careful evaluation shows that the effects were modest, if not entirely negligible. 'Grand solar minima' such as the Maunder Minimum produced a measurable difference in temperature of around 0.3 °C.[34] Indeed, studies on the likely outcome of future solar minima suggest that this is at the top end of the scale for temperature change, with a range of 0.09–0.26 °C a more appropriate outcome – which has obvious implications for any hypothesis about a Little Ice Age.[35]

Moreover, even cases where the Little Ice Age seems to have influenced change can look different when provided with wider context. It is easy to focus on Bruegel's *Hunters in the Snow*, for example, while overlooking *The Harvesters*, painted by the same artist in the same year, which evokes a warm summer, bountiful harvest and golden light. While it is true that some landscape painters in northern Europe produced a large number of winter pictures, such as Hendrick Avercamp, many others did not. Rather than acting as a guide to colder climate, it may be that paintings depicting snowy scenes represent the contemporary tastes of buyers and artists alike.[36] These tastes changed: while icy landscapes were popular in the late sixteenth century, during the chilliest decades of the Maunder Minimum a hundred years later, 'Dutch customers preferred bright, sunny scenes.'[37]

Similarly, the correlation of witchcraft trials and cold temperatures seems convincing at face value. After all, one papal bull issued in the 1480s specifically declares that evildoers 'raise and stir up hailstorms and tempests, and cause lightning to blast both men and beasts', noting that many reports had been received in Rome of occasions where 'the produce of the earth' including fruit, wheat and other crops had been destroyed by sorcerers.[38] However, some scholars have argued that rather than reflecting deteriorating climate conditions, the persecutions of the late sixteenth and early seventeenth centuries should be understood in the context of rising instances of syphilis and resultant mental illness that presented as disturbing; it may equally and also be seen as a case of men seeking to secure medicine and healthcare as a male preserve, or as a result of an economic downturn that might be related to poor yields. Likewise, other explanations might explain rising anxieties that helped spur animosities and violence, such as slowdowns in trade, increased demands by the state or breakdown between rival political factions.[39] Recent research into mass psychogenic illness also raises the question of whether the 'witch craze' of this period was a case of more and more people being caught up in accusations and counter-accusations in a self-fuelling and self-fulfilling cycle.[40]

Or there is the case of the defeat of King Charles XII at the battle of Poltava in 1709 and subsequent setbacks that proved so damaging for

Sweden. While cold weather certainly did not help, it was more telling that the Swedes had not only overextended their resources by investing in long-distance and expensive warfare, but had overreached into Russian territory, leaving their supply lines exposed and vulnerable to harassment and disruption. When combined with a set of strategically naive mistakes on the battlefield that exposed the King, his leading generals and his men to unnecessary risks, it was hardly a surprise that things turned out badly over the following years. Perhaps, in fact, the main surprise was that the fallout was not even worse.[41]

Identifying exactly what effect cooler temperatures have on trends, fashions and even individual events is not easy and requires careful judgement. So too does evaluating climatic change during a long period where there was considerable variation and fluctuation both geographically and chronologically. There were some decades – notably the 1590s, the 1680s and the 1810s – when there is evidence of substantial disruption to regular climatic patterns that saw cooler temperatures across multiple locations as a result of volcanic activity, of particularly strong El Niño events or of the two reinforcing each other. Equally, however, it is important not to treat a period of over 500 years as one that presents any consistency across either time or space.

Temperatures do seem to have dropped sharply in the early fifteenth century. Ironically, it appears that this was a result not of a weakening of climatic and solar patterns, but rather of their strengthening: the Atlantic Meridional Overturning Circulation (AMOC) usually pushes water from the tropics to higher latitudes where it then meets colder Arctic water, causing it to lose heat, become more dense, sink to the bottom of the ocean and become part of global circulation patterns. In the late fourteenth century, however, abnormally strong transfers of warm water were circulated northwards as a result of the major strengthening of AMOC, in turn causing a period of extreme sea-ice export that released enormous volumes of cold water into the North Atlantic, affecting salinity levels and leading to the decline of the AMOC.[42] The outcome was an age of intensive cooling which was reinforced by a sequence of major volcanic eruptions that served to magnify reductions of solar irradiance persisting from c.1400 until the early seventeenth century.[43]

This serves as a useful reminder of how important it is to separate out different phases, causes and outcomes in a long period that is often treated as a single phenomenon. In fact, there are important trends that do give a coherence to the centuries leading up to the start of the industrial revolution. Clearly the linking together of the world's major landmasses through the opening up of sea routes across the Atlantic and the Pacific resulted in new exchanges of goods, foodstuffs and ideas as well as in the large-scale movements of people, both through choice and through enslavement. The ecological changes that this produced were substantial, as we have already seen in the case of the Americas and the Caribbean, as were the new pathways that opened up for the spread of disease, such as the transfer of malaria and yellow fever from the Old World to the New, and of smallpox in the other direction.

The spread of these and other diseases was facilitated by intense competition for resources and power, not least in Europe itself, where states not only jostled for position in their own continent but sought to outmanoeuvre their rivals' advantages in others. One result was a dramatic rise in military confrontation, with a war between the major powers in Europe under way in 95 per cent of all years between 1500 and 1700. This itself was partly the result of the development of new technologies and their constant improvement, most obviously in the field of gunpowder. The spread of cannon brought about major changes to defensive tactics and fortifications as it became clear that town and city walls could be quickly destroyed. Among the innovations were massive earthen bulwarks, often covered with brick, which could withstand fire. The fact that they could be built in numerous locations and away from urban settlements (albeit at considerable cost) transformed warfare, changing battlefield requirements, not the least of which was the need for more men and better training. All this meant higher levels of professionali-sation, more equipment – and more money.[44] These were all fundamental parts of a military revolution which not only meant that 1600–1700 was the 'century of the soldier', as one contemporary commentator has so aptly put it, but also played a key part in the rise of west.[45]

Military innovation was in turn closely connected to wider social, economic and institutional transformations. The decades and centuries that followed Columbus' crossing of the Atlantic saw successive waves of centralisation, above all in Europe. There was a wide range of reasons for this, but constant war was perhaps the most significant. The need to put more and more men in the field required ever-greater revenues, which inspired an almost insatiable appetite for taxation. Between

1500 and 1780, therefore, the combined tax take of major European powers increased by a factor of twenty. On average, 80 per cent of government expenditure was devoted to military costs, with spending often exceeding tax revenues during times of war. In turn, this brought about a financial revolution in government debt finance.[46]

It was not just the military who became better equipped, better trained and better run as a result. One effect of the drawing of more resources into political centres was an uplift in the quantity and quality of bureaucrats whose job it was to assess, collect and allocate funds. States that invested time and energy in creating institutions, educating administrators and appointing on merit, and in applying methods that rooted out corruption, did better than those that did not. Indeed, failure to reform in some cases led not only to poor outcomes but to states being 'partitioned out of existence', as was the case with Poland. Capacity building was closely linked to the creation of institutions that were run by salaried officials appointed and judged by performance and competence – at least in theory. The development of these institutions was of crucial importance in establishing constraints on the autonomy and autocratic powers of rulers, and they thereby served as staging posts towards higher levels of accountability and increased levels of political participation.[47] Indeed, some have argued that the relative weakness of the crown may even have been 'an essential precondition for the eventual success of England's overseas enterprise' – and empire.[48]

The building of an efficient state apparatus was not a rapid process, but rather one that evolved over the course of many decades and centuries. There were nonetheless rapid accelerations that had knock-on effects not only on the role of the state, but also on urbanisation, disease and health and the natural environment. In France, for example, public revenues rose by three times in the course of just forty years between 1600 and 1640 in the face of demand from the centre. While this is striking from a purely economic point of view, no less dramatic was the effect it had on population migration. As monetary (and other) resources were sucked into the capital, so too were people, eager to take advantage of opportunities there or because those that had existed locally had vanished. Paris accounted for 60 per cent of all French population growth during the first half of the seventeenth century. The speed and scale of urbanisation meanwhile acted like a shot in the arm for the city's merchant class – who suddenly found themselves with hosts of new customers – and like a mirage for those elsewhere whose markets melted away before their eyes.[49]

The centralisation of the state and the collection of resources at its disposal were particularly pronounced in parts of northern and western Europe that were connected to Atlantic trade, demonstrating the significance of the maritime routes to Africa, the Americas and Asia which accelerated growth after 1500.[50] Urbanisation, however, produced further developments through unexpected side-effects, the most notable of which was disease. Europe's cities were 'major death traps' that were unhygienic and ideal for the spread of illnesses. London recorded twice as many burials as baptisms in many years during the seventeenth century.

Perhaps counter-intuitively, the rise of urban populations led to higher wages, with large numbers of people packed together driving demand and stimulating supply within cities and in the countryside. The rate of urbanisation shocked some, like King James I, who claimed in 1616 that the entire population was being crammed into the capital. Soon, he said, 'England will only be London, and the whole country be left waste with everyone living miserably in our houses, and dwelling all in the city.' This was hardly exceptional, he added; it simply made London like Italy – and especially Naples.[51] London, wrote John Evelyn in the 1660s, was the 'suburbs of Hell', afflicted by a 'fuliginous and filthy vapour' that hurt the lungs and ensured that 'Catharrs, Phthisicks, Coughs and Consumptions rage more in this one City than in the whole Earth besides'.[52]

Paris was no better, a city that one contemporary complained was 'alwayes dirty' and where visitors would get covered in 'black onctious oyl, that wher it sticks no art can wash it off'. Paris, he added, was so grotesque as to merit the nickname 'vagina populorum'.[53] While some complained, the reality was that large-scale urbanisation was a prerequisite for an acceleration of production and consumption patterns, a catalyst for engagement with other parts of the world and in due course a motor of the industrial revolution itself.[54]

As we shall see, demand for goods and foods stimulated global trade and came with ecological and environmental prices that were charged to the parts of the world they originated from, not only unseen but usually unpaid by those living hundreds and often thousands of kilometres away. Key to that story was the role of cities relative to their hinterlands and their ability to absorb large and growing populations. While cities drove demand, fostered innovation and drew in manpower, they were also co-dependent on their hinterlands and on agricultural production. Large urban settlements could be uniquely vulnerable to weather shocks, although risk could be mitigated in cities that had access to the sea or river systems and well-established long-distance connections.[55]

Clearly, changes to the production and availability of crops, fodder and lumber – bulky items that were heavy and expensive to transport – as a result of weather shocks or long-term climatic change had immediate and direct impacts on both urban and rural populations. Reduced availability of food brought about demographic declines through increased mortality and disease, through lower fertility levels and through people leaving cities. During the seventeenth century, for example, the Balkans and Anatolia lost half their population, with declines of 80 per cent in some regions and large numbers of rural villages simply abandoned.[56]

Food shortage had other consequences that did not just alter the relationship between town and country, but changed the character of urban life – even without catastrophic incidence of famine: reduced agricultural productivity means that workers in the rural economy have less to sell, which means that they earn less. This then affects the prices of goods and services made or sold in towns and cities, as demand falls. Employment prospects in the latter diminish as a result, making life in cities less profitable. As such, assessing temperature yield ratios and their correlation to historical wheat prices helps show that climate is a fundamental motor in powering growth, and that it is a crucial factor in elucidating economic growth and explaining why it was so uneven across Europe in the early modern period.[57]

This unevenness again shows that there was no 'one size fits all' during the Little Ice Age. For example, from the winter of 1539, a long spell of high pressure over western and central Europe was mirrored by low-pressure systems over the Atlantic and western Russia. One Russian chronicle noted that 'Springtime was cold and during all summer there were floods, and the rye did not grow and was frozen in spring, and all the meadows at the banks of the rivers and lakes were flooded,' while 'in the autumn there was a lot of rain, and the sun was not seen for 2 weeks' in November. This produced a different set of problems to continental Europe, where Lake Constance dropped so low that the lake floor could be seen, while water transport became difficult and, in some cases, impossible. Wildfires broke out in Portugal and Germany; town fires were more frequent in Germany in 1540 than any other year since 1000. As well as animals suffering from heatstroke, water shortages led to tree stress, poor vine and cereal harvests and a collapse of water power for mills – all of which led to sky-rocketing prices.[58]

High prices were closely related to a range of factors, including hoarding practices by unscrupulous traders who sought to take advantage of demand and panic; in addition, ineffective measures were adopted to alleviate suffering as meagre resources were ineptly distributed or food was not brought in from other sources elsewhere. Desperate scenes could result. In India just after the accession of Akbar to the Mughal throne in 1556, there was 'great scarcity in the cities and villages of India … men took to eating one another; some would join together and carry off a solitary man and make him their food'.[59]

Some scholars have suggested that the Atlantic Meridional Overturning Circulation (AMOC) underwent a period of significant change around the 1560s, provoking the Grindelwald Fluctuation – a reference to a marked increase in Alpine glaciers that starts at this time. This period also saw significant falls in precipitation in the Mediterranean and a rise in north-western Europe, especially during spring and summer months, which shortened growing seasons by six weeks.[60] The effects may have been felt further afield, with Shona oral traditions and other evidence from sub-Saharan Africa pointing to severe droughts, locust infestations, famine and epidemic disease in northern Zimbabwe and on the Mozambique coast in the 1560s.[61] Average temperatures in China went into a long cycle of cooling, with only three years between 1569 and 1644 warmer than normal.[62]

It was not impossible or even difficult to adapt to changed circumstances. In northern Europe, for example, many farmers switched to growing barley, oats and rye rather than wheat, which is more sensitive to cold.[63] Nevertheless, other circumstances made significant differences to experiences. For example, in 1569–73 a succession of long and severe winters brought heavy rain and disastrous flooding throughout much of Europe. Lakes, rivers and the Baltic Sea from Denmark to Finland froze as a result of temperatures that were not unusually low, but stayed low for weeks at a time. The effect on harvests was considerable, exacerbated by successive failures, leading to grain prices in central Europe reaching their highest point before 1877. Landlocked regions suffered more than those by the coast, while cities with access to the sea were less badly affected than those in the interior.[64] This was a time of considerable disruption that affected south-east Europe and the Middle East too, where one chronicler described food shortages and famine in 1574–5 as causing the worst suffering for hundreds of years.[65]

Plagues of locusts that swarmed into Italy threatened to make things worse still until Pope Pius V held a trial in St Peter's Square, attended by locusts that appeared 'in such numbers that the sun was obscured', and excommunicated them. With that, 'they soon disappeared, never to be seen again'.[66] Not surprisingly, some feared that famine and high prices would lead to unrest – as in southern Germany, where conditions were particularly bad.[67] Perhaps anxieties were so acute because climate had been so stable for many decades, and preparedness to cope with crises was declining. As such, cold and harvest failure seemed like 'a bolt of thunder after a long period of economic sunshine'.[68]

The most dramatic effects, though, were felt in the Low Countries, where tensions had been boiling because of resentment against Spanish authority, aggravated by religious animosity between Protestants and Catholics. There had been problems of food availability with low harvests even before unusually poor weather made things worse, exacerbated by war between Denmark and Sweden which made alternative supply difficult and led to a tripling of the price of wheat in some parts of Flanders over the course of six months in 1565 alone. Government ministers had already been warning of unrest when religious mobs took each other on in scenes of escalating violence that saw churches set on fire, their contents and interiors destroyed by Protestant mobs as part of the *Beeldenstorm* (literally 'image storm') that set the tone for poisonous relations in the Low Countries and that did not improve when thousands were killed by storm surges and gales in the early 1570s. The culmination of this time of upheaval was the brutal sack of Antwerp in 1576 by Spanish soldiers who had been frustrated by weather conditions during a failed siege at Leiden and had not been paid. The ferocity of the attack on Antwerp was instrumental in uniting the provinces of the northern Netherlands and led to the Union of Utrecht, which effectively created the Dutch Republic.[69]

In this instance, a wide range of factors had reinforced each other, had served to compound and deepen existing crises and had produced outcomes that were to have long-lasting significance. A similar chain reaction came with a sequence of large-scale eruptions of low-latitude volcanoes between 1580 and 1600 at Billy Mitchell in Melanesia (1580), Kelut and Ruang in Java (1586 and 1593), Ruiz in Colombia (1595) and Huaynaputina in Peru (1596), the latter being the largest eruption ever recorded in South America.[70] Indeed, its effects were so pronounced that some scholars have questioned whether there was a contemporaneous eruption elsewhere that might explain the sheer size of the signature in ice cores and tree rings in the northern hemisphere.[71] Either way, the result was the severest short-term cooling of the last 600 years – if not more.[72]

The climatic upheavals were dramatic – and global. In Scandinavia, a series of long and severe winters began in 1587 with a year without a summer – a fabled *fimbulvetr* of Norse mythology.[73] In the autumn of 1589, for example, much of Italy suffered from very heavy rainfall which caused flooding in Campania, Tuscany and Rome, and affected sowing of crops. A bad situation turned to crisis in the 1590s as harvest yields fell by two-thirds, leading to reserves becoming exhausted. Cities like Naples, Bologna and Mantua responded by expelling anyone who might be considered a burden – foreigners, students, the poor – in desperate attempts to preserve food supplies, to avoid overcrowding and to alleviate the risk of theft and potential revolts.[74] Cities saw not only sharp rises in mortality, contributing to a drop in population in and around Bologna of almost a fifth, but also a collapse in births of 44 per cent.[75]

Towns and regions such as the Po Valley saw the worst famine and the steepest demographic collapse since the Black Death. The disaster provoked long-term change. For one thing, it prompted farmers to accelerate a shift to more intensive production techniques as well as to sacrifice food variety in favour of greater calorie availability through a widespread shift to maize.[76]

For another, it helped draw parts of Europe more closely together, linking the Baltic region into southern European trade networks following the desperate search for emergency supplies by city states and local rulers during a time of crisis. Cities like Genoa, Venice and Livorno established strong links with the Baltic region, importing not only grain but also other foodstuffs, including beans, salted meat and fish, as well as metals, textiles and hides. Much of this trade was brokered and shipped by the Dutch, whose investment in the 1590s paid dividends

at the time but above all a few decades later after relations with Spain
had been stabilised. The returns on investment of 100 per cent were to
prove vital in the acceleration of northern Europe in the early modern
period in general and of Dutch capitalism in particular.[77] Such were the
curious by-products of disasters and response efforts.

Spain was already in an economic tailspin as a result of persistent
overstretch in wars in continental Europe and slowdowns in extractions
from its empire overseas. It was hit hard too by almost a decade of high
rainfall and inclement conditions, followed by a decade of drought.
As well as resulting in a death toll that some estimate was as high as
600,000 – a demographic shock from which recovery took more than a
century – the effect on livestock was particularly severe with the loss of a
third of the country's sheep, which in turn had knock-on effects for the
wool industry. All this was made worse by a major increase in taxation
intended to help the crown to make good on a debt burden that had left
it crippled and prone to taking poor political and strategic decisions. As
we have seen, this coincided with discussions about whether the imperial
project was worth pursuing or should be abandoned as too costly. Spain,
noted one author in 1621, was like a patient suffering from a critical
illness; sometimes 'you have to cut off an arm' to ensure they would live.[78]

Harvest failures in the 1590s are attested to in Scotland, Sweden and
Austria, the latter experiencing several major uprisings as the situation
turned bleak. It was said that in Ireland, starvation left the population unable
to walk and resembling ghosts. In England, things were bleak too, with
famine, great floods and in the 1590s and 1600s frosts that were so strong
that the Thames froze over and was able to host 'frost fairs'. Particularly
strong storm conditions in this period went hand in hand with sand drift
that had considerable long-term ecological impacts on the Atlantic coast
of western Europe.[79] Some scholars have pointed out the attention paid
to celestial events and climate phenomena in Shakespeare's writings in the
1590s and 1600s, and have suggested that climate was an important framing
device in tragedies and comedies written in this period.[80]

Climatic stress not only characterised South-East Africa in the late
sixteenth century but was a factor in political change. As one Portuguese
missionary put it, the region was afflicted by 'chastisements' from the
late 1580s including locust plagues that 'devoured all the crops, gardens
and palm groves' leaving them bare for the next two years, famine and a

severe outbreak of smallpox. This served to weaken the Zambezi Tonga chiefdoms, provoking social instability, sharpening local rivalries and opening the door for Portuguese intervention in this region. Initially, this took the form of military assistance provided by traders who had hitherto been confined to coastal regions; it was quickly turned into concessions over land, access to mineral resources and a role in local and dynastic politics that ultimately served as a springboard for colonial expansion – and for the economic impoverishment of Zimbabwe culture states.[81]

This was a time of environmental and ecological change in other parts of Africa, most notably the southern frontier of the Sahara which expanded by some 300 kilometres to the south. Disease environments shifted too as the habitat of the tsetse fly increased, prompting population movements and altering agricultural capacity. Dating precisely when and how this happened is important, particularly if the transitions are to be linked with the collapse of the Songhai empire and the conquest of Timbuktu in 1591 by Moroccan forces.[82] After all, Moroccan operations to the south to gain control over oases and trade networks had begun many decades earlier and were driven by the desire to access gold and salt on the one hand, and powered by rising ambitions and capabilities on the other.[83] Nevertheless, the fact that Timbuktu did not regain its prominence, its wealth or its size is to be explained, at least in part, by the onset of desertification – which also drove outflows of people from regions that were most exposed to changes in weather patterns around the end of the sixteenth century.[84]

In China, floods, unusually cold temperatures and food shortages in the 1580s produced the worst famine in a hundred years. The effects were made worse by outbreaks of epidemic disease that likely included hydrocephalic meningitis that caught hold in densely populated cities – cities, as one contemporary observer complained, that were home to houses 'so closely crowded together that there is no spare space and in the markets there is much excrement and filth'. These were perfect conditions, in other words, for 'malarious fevers, diarrhoeas and epidemics [to] follow each other without stopping'.[85] The Jesuit missionary Matteo Ricci noted that 'all the rivers in northern China' froze over in the late 1590s – a time of notably lower average yearly temperatures than normal.[86]

South-East and South Asia saw significant falls in precipitation, with rain levels well below normal. Spanish tax lists from the Philippines point to a population loss of 25 per cent between 1591 and 1608.[87] In the early 1590s, reports Abū al-Faẓl, the author of the *Akbarnāma*, 'those learned in stars announced death and scarcity', which allowed the Mughal Emperor Akbar to take emergency action to make sure that supplies were available to all.[88] This worked – to start with. Lack of rain over several years eventually took a terrible toll, with one Turkish source speaking of 'fearful famine' and 'general distress' made worse by epidemic disease. As large numbers died, leaving cities, towns and villages empty apart from 'streets [that] were blocked with dead bodies', some who were desperate resorted to cannibalism.[89]

It had been a similar story in the Ottoman empire, where famine-relief efforts at the start of the 1590s initially proved successful – notwithstanding the demands of supplying cities that were often ecologically constrained by the limitations on what their hinterlands could supply and the distribution of populations in the interiors of the Balkans, Anatolia and parts of the Middle East that were logistically difficult and expensive to support. The situation now became bleak as drought took hold and turned into the longest that the eastern Mediterranean had experienced in 600 years and by far the worst in the history of the Ottoman empire.

Rampant inflation ravaged the economy and drove prices up, leading to chaos as the government responded by increasing taxation and debasing the coinage in an attempt at fiscal stimulus. As people abandoned the countryside for cities, discontent spread – as did disease, most notably plague. Banditry was rife as strongmen took power into their own hands, leading to breakdowns of law and order, including direct challenges to central authority such as by a figure known as Karayazıcı ('Black Scribe'), who managed to bring regions and towns in what is now south-east Turkey under his control. Although this and other uprisings were eventually put down, some scholars have argued that the events of the 1590s and 1610s brought about fundamental changes in the Ottoman empire. Chief among these were a sharp reduction in sultanic authority and the transformation in the political and economic fortunes of the Janissary Corps, which henceforth became the major power broker in the internal workings of the empire.[90]

The late 1590s and the first decade of the 1600s was a traumatic period in Russian history, known as the Time of Troubles. It too was characterised by political upheaval and by chronic shortages as a result of successive years of harvest failure. One contemporary was shocked by what he saw. 'I swear to God,' wrote Conrad Bussow, 'it is the honest truth that I saw people lying dead in the street with my own eyes; in the summer people ate grass and in winter they ate hay, like cows.' The dead could be seen with straw and manure in their mouths, having evidently been trying to eat anything to stay alive, while some had even resorted to eating human waste, he wrote. 'Children were chopped up and boiled by their parents, parents by their children, guests by their hosts and hosts by their guests.' People flocked from the countryside to the city in search of food and handouts. While Bussow's assurance that 500,000 people died in Moscow alone is exaggerated, mortality rates were clearly very high indeed – with perhaps as much as a third of the population succumbing.[91]

Extensive though the global climatic rearrangement was, however, it is important to underline that in many cases the unsettled and unusual weather conditions served to accentuate existing vulnerabilities rather than act as primary causes of disaster. In many of the cases of food shortage in the late sixteenth and early seventeenth centuries, for example, problems stemmed from cities that had expanded to a size that left them exposed to risks that were themselves aggravated by the attempts of those living in the countryside to try to find safety – and things to eat. Pushing communities over the edge that were living on land that was at the limits of its carrying capacity did not require dramatic, extreme or apocalyptic weather events; rather, as many of the accounts from different parts of the world make clear, the problem was not the cold or rain or drought, but rather that it stayed cold, wet or dry for longer than people were used to – and that adaptation proved difficult, especially at speed.

Perhaps understandably, animosities rose against those who benefited from shortages and price rises – or at least those who were thought to be benefiting. In Ottoman Turkey speculators were fiercely denounced for hoarding grain and taking advantage of the suffering of others.[92] In Russia, many were stirred up by 'the devil of greed, enabled by God to punish the entire country' by holding on to grain or buying it cheaply, only to resell it at higher prices.[93] In England, some blamed foreigners, with one good example captured by a poem written on the wall of a Dutch churchyard in London in 1593, which declared that foreign merchants were responsible for high prices, before posting a dark warning to them to look after 'your goods, your children, and your dearest wives' because 'like Jews you eat us up as bread'.[94]

But hoarding and price gouging were symptoms of crisis, not its causes. In many of the cases that marked the late sixteenth and early seventeenth centuries, there were deep-rooted underlying factors that helped turn challenging situations into catastrophes. In Russia, for example, the combined impacts of inflation, increasing tax demands by the state, heavy costs of war and ineffective leadership by tsars who were divisive, indecisive or both produced intense competition within the elite – factors that were aggravated by a rising population that almost doubled during the sixteenth century.[95] The ability of monasteries to build up property and acquire tax exemptions resulted in artificial prices and a distorted market, which persisted until the start of the eighteenth century when Peter the Great sought to limit monasteries' rights to own land, assigned monks a fixed income and attempted to reduce the number of clergy as a whole.[96]

In this sense, climatic stress served to bring ongoing issues to the boil. The Ottoman experiences in the late sixteenth and early seventeenth centuries owed much to the fact that the state was engaged in military operations against the Austrians and the Persians simultaneously – at a time when the costs of warfare were increasing both in real terms and in terms of the numbers of men needed on the front lines and in support positions. This produced a draw on resources that removed margins for error – not least when it came to harvest collection.[97]

Poor leadership combined with military overstretch also brought down empires in this period – not climate. The collapse of the Tungoo empire, which was marked by the sack of many of its principal cities in 1599, is a case in point. The empire was one of the largest, if not the largest, in South-East Asian history. It had grown out of a series of spectacular military successes, shrewd diplomatic compromises and alliances to cover much of what is now Burma, Thailand, Cambodia and Vietnam. It may be that breakdowns in regional and global silver bullion markets put strain on the economy, although evidence to this effect is scant. It may be that weak monsoons prompted things to eat shortages, rising prices and perhaps a plague of rats that infested the capital in 1596. But the more prosaic answer, as one scholar has put it, is that the empire 'overheated' and that it was a victim of its own success – a polite way of saying that its structure was weak, its operation unviable and its ability to dominate the periphery from the centre poor to non-existent.[98]

The reason then that all the streets of the capital, Pegu, 'especially those which lead to the temples, are scattered with skulls and with the corpses of these wretched Peguans' was partly due to famine, as one visitor to the city observed the year after its sack by the combined armies of the Tungoo dynasty. But many lay dead because they had killed each other in street-to-street fighting, while many others had been 'killed by command of the King, who had them thrown in the river, which is hardly navigable any more even in a small boat because of the multitude of corpses'. As a result, said another European commentator, 'the former seats of great and powerful lords became the abodes of tigers and other wild beasts', with an eerie calm now hanging over a once great city that was described as 'the greatest silence on Earth that human thoughts can imagine'.[99]

The many crises of this period could and did present opportunities. In England, for example, the severe conditions of the late 1590s led to the formulation of legislation that included the Act for the Relief of the Poor of 1598, which was largely repeated in 1601. This passed on to individual parishes the responsibility for looking after the poor and the associated costs, a move that proved both revolutionary and remarkably long-lasting. Even though such ideas drew on those that dated back long before this period, the principle that households should be taxed to support their poor neighbours was one that had crucial significance for attitudes to welfare, to communities, to money and to the creation of a 'robust safety net' which was to come into play when all other options had failed.[100]

Others seized opportunities for change in different ways. Christian priests and missionaries in North America took advantage of unusual weather to proselytise the indigenous populations, exploiting precipitation shortfalls to undermine existing beliefs. Franciscans working among the Timucua of Florida in the early seventeenth century were advised to ask questions such as 'Have you made rain?'; or 'Have you conjured a rain storm or a thunderstorm with superstitions?' Local populations were told not to perform traditional rain ceremonies, as they should 'be aware that it will not rain unless God our Lord is served'.[101]

Rainmaking contests were a key part of interaction with indigenous peoples in the Americas and an important way for Europeans to try to win hearts, minds and credibility. One of the questions most often asked of Christians was about the ability to modify the weather through appealing to God. 'If we believe in your God, will it snow?' Montagnais Indians in Quebec asked French Jesuits in the early seventeenth century. 'It will snow,' came the reply, soliciting the follow-up questions of 'will the snow be deep … shall we find moose … shall we kill some?' The Jesuit replied, 'Yes; for as God knows all things, as he can do all things, and as he is very good, he will not fail to help you, if you have recourse to him, if you receive the Faith, and if you render him obedience.' This seemed to impress the listeners. 'We will think about what thou hast told us,' they said, before heading off to the woods and promptly putting what they had heard to one side.[102]

Changing religious beliefs and reconfigurations of the engagement with the natural world were not only connected to European interaction with local populations. In the late 1620s, a new wave of unusual weather brought about a combination of El Niño and a weak Azores anticyclone that had global impacts lasting several years. The Indian monsoon failed in four successive years from 1628 to 1631, followed by unusually high rainfall in 1632. The impact in India and Burma was catastrophic, with some suggesting that as many as 3 million people died in Gujarat alone. Demographic devastation was financially crippling, with the reduced revenue from some provinces meaning that administrative expenditures could not be covered for decades.[103] This came at a pivotal time in South-East Asia, just as the Dutch East India Company was establishing itself as a political as well as an economic force by taking over most of the lucrative spice trade, crippling the economies of port states like Demak, Japara and Surabaya in the process. These then fell to Sultan Agung, the ruler of Mataram, centred near modern Yojakarta on the island of Java, who oversaw the creation of a distinctive court culture that blended elements from Islam with Hinduism and Buddhism.[104]

In the 1630s, however, greater emphasis was placed on Islamic features, with Agung abandoning the Javanese calendar and its anchor around the lunisolar Śaka year for the Islamic lunar year, sponsoring patronage of Qur'ānic teaching and making great play of the importance of pilgrimages. While this may have derived from Agung's own evolving beliefs, it is striking that it followed on from a series of uprisings centred on a group of villages in central Java and above all on the holy site of Tembayat.[105] It is tempting, therefore, to associate the suffering of the early 1630s with the need to win over starving and restive populations with conciliatory measures; after all, turbulence of all kinds can be a powerful motivation for seeking explanations and finding solutions.[106]

The effects of these patterns were global, with an estimated 30 million perishing from hunger and related causes around the world before more normal conditions returned in the mid-1630s. The flooding of Potosí in South America forced the suspension of mining activities, while cataclysmic flooding in Mexico between 1629 and 1634 left fields saturated, washed away nutrients and made it almost impossible to travel, let alone transport goods and foods.[107] In Europe, 1628 was another 'year without a summer', with snow falling in Switzerland twenty-three times in the Bernese Oberland, crop failures and a notable rise in the number of witch hunts and accusations of sorcery in the Alps and Rhine basin.[108]

Far more damaging, however, were war and disease which decimated populations, transformed societies and had consequences that lasted for centuries. Wars of religion between Protestants and Catholics overwhelmed much of continental Europe in what became known as the Thirty Years' War (1618–48), a time of furious, sustained conflict and suffering. The 1630s onwards saw the start of fierce fighting between Spain and France that lasted for more than twenty years, while England was ravaged by civil war for most of the following decade. The 1640s were brutal, a time of constant unrest, suffering and turbulence within as well as between states. There were revolts and uprisings 'everywhere in the world, for example in France, England, Germany, Poland, Muscovy and the Ottoman empire', noted the Swedish diplomat Johan Adler Salvius, who was at a loss to understand the rise in violence. Perhaps 'this can be explained by some general configuration of the stars in the sky', he suggested – musings that were shared by others around the same time.[109]

To make matters worse, plague took hold, spreading from northern France in 1623 to England, the Low Countries and Germany before reaching Italy in 1629–30. Mortality rates were particularly high in major cities in northern Italy with around 30 to 35 per cent of the population of that region – some 2 million people – dying from plague.[110] The effects of war and disease were even more severe in the territories of the Holy Roman empire, with demographic declines of 35 to 40 per cent.[111] The dual effects of conflict and plague were so great that they impacted inequality into the eighteenth and perhaps even into the nineteenth century. Had Germany not had these experiences, it would probably have followed trends elsewhere and become much more unequal. While this made Germany more egalitarian, it also meant it was on the wrong side of economic divergence in Europe that left it having to play catch-up from the mid-nineteenth century onwards.[112]

The outcome was equally bad in Italy, especially when further waves of plague struck in the 1650s and led to around a million deaths in the kingdom of Naples – or somewhere between 30 and 43 per cent of the population. This was dramatically worse than north-western Europe, where plague intensity led to the deaths of around 8–10 per cent of the population in England and marginally higher in France. Plague did enormous damage in Italy because it struck so quickly and because its decimation of the urban workforce brought about shocks to production capabilities – and because deaths among elites in cities like Venice and Genoa who organised and invested in long-distance trade had material impacts on short- and long-term economic fortunes.

But perhaps most important of all was timing: plague struck at the worst possible moment, at a time when manufacturers were facing intense and rising competition from countries in northern Europe. In this sense, the disparity in mortality rates between north and south was crucial, as it allowed the former not only not to suffer but left it in a position to capitalise on its emerging advantages.[113] This was a crucial staging post in the Little Divergence – the point where northern Europe caught up with, then overtook and pulled away from the south. By 1650, English wages were 10 per cent higher than those in Italy; by 1800, they had risen to a staggering 150 per cent higher.[114]

These changes were not due only to warfare and disease. Spain's transatlantic trade had contracted sharply from the start of the seventeenth century, leading to a contagious financial crisis that brought Genoa and its banking system to its knees. Part of the reason for this was the maturing of economies in the New World that saw greater levels of internal trade combined with an increased ability of local officials, landowners and merchants to build up their own resources. Where around 30,000 tons of goods were shipped to Spain in the 1610s, less than half that quantity was being sent across the Atlantic thirty years later. Other economies were also experiencing transitions that were in some cases accelerated by wars that had substantial impacts on supply and demand. Industry in Venice contracted by half in the first decades of the seventeenth century, as did exports from Tuscany, while English sales of woollen cloth in continental Europe suffered a similar level of collapse.[115]

The great upheavals and crises struck many as extraordinarily severe and unusual. 'God Almighty has a quarrel lately with all mankind, and

given the reins to the ill spirit to compass the whole earth,' wrote James
Howell, a historian, in the middle of the seventeenth century. For more
than a decade 'there have the strangest revolutions and horridest things
happened, not only in Europe but all the world over, that have befallen
mankind, I dare boldly say, since Adam fell, in so short a revolution of
time'. It would seem, said Howell, 'the whole world is off the hinges'.[116]

Particularly harsh weather was part of the story of disruption. Rather
than taking place every five years or so, the El Niño–Southern Oscillation
(ENSO) took place twice as frequently, including in 1638, 1639, 1641, 1642
and a further eight times in the next twenty years. The western United
States and Canadian Rockies experienced prolonged periods of drought,
as did the Valley of Mexico, where processions were held invoking the
intercession of the Virgin Mary to bring rain. Challenging conditions
were the norm in many places around the world, from the coldest winter
ever recorded in Scandinavia to the failure of rice harvests in South-East
Asia, chronic food shortages in India and Central Asia and chaos in many
parts of East Asia where the monsoon was extremely weak in this period.[117]
The unusual conditions were aggravated by the eruptions of Komagatake
in 1640 and above all of Parker Peak in the Philippines a year later, which
extended drought conditions by at least three years.[118]

    This came at a particularly testing time in China, where the fall of
the Ming dynasty has often been linked to poor weather generally and
to climatic change in particular.[119] It is not hard to see why. In 1640,
poor harvests were accompanied by locust swarms, food shortages,
sky-high prices and outbreaks of disease. The next three years (1641–
4) then produced the worst drought in 500 years.[120] Zeng Yuwang, an
eyewitness who wrote about the suffering that followed, leaves little to
the imagination. First came a plague of locusts who were so many that
they piled up a foot high in people's compounds and forced Zeng to
cover his face with a fan so that he could breathe when he was out of the
house. 'I could barely stand up under the weight of the locusts clinging
to my fan and to my clothes and hat.'

    In 1642, he wrote, famine struck, causing huge loss of life. 'All along
our route home,' he wrote, 'we saw corpses scattered about in the fields,
and innumerable children abandoned by the side of the road … To
be walking properly attired down an unending road of corpses was
a nightmare the likes of which I had never known. Approaching the

village, we saw six or seven people stripping bark off elm trees' trying to feed themselves.[121]

In Suzhou, the engine room of Ming dynasty economic development where anything and anything could be bought in the early seventeenth century, where shops lined the streets and merchants houses with their delightful gardens characterised the prosperity of the city and its inhabitants, things looked bleak indeed. 'Most of the residences in the city are empty and they are falling into ruins,' recounted Ye Shaoyuan, a scholar who wrote extensively about the traumas of these times. 'Fertile farms and beautiful estates are for sale but there is no one to buy them. Formerly the city of Suzhou was prosperous and its people tended to be extravagant. It is natural that after a period of prosperity a period of depression should follow; but I never dreamed that I should have to witness these misfortunes in the days of my life.'[122]

Anxieties were heightened by reports of rebel armies taking up arms, the result of years of uprisings and unrest gathering steam under disgruntled Ming officials like Li Zicheng and Zhang Xianzhong, who captured the imagination – and gained the support – of the peasantry by promising land reform and an overhaul of the taxation system, as well as by being successful bandit leaders who were able to deliver rewards to their supporters.[123]

By the end of the 1630s, the rebel army numbered in the tens of thousands – if not more – and was not only capturing cities and taking control of provinces but was soon bearing down on Beijing itself. Worrying omens spelled trouble in a state where disorder was understood as a sign of divine disfavour. Further harbingers of doom were provided by an earthquake in early 1644, by strange-coloured pears appearing on trees, by ominous winds that rose shortly before the start of the annual veneration of Confucius and by not a single baby being born in the capital, Beijing.[124]

As rebel forces closed in on the capital in the spring of 1644 and then gained entry through the city gates, the Chongzhen Emperor apologised to his relatives that they should be part of his unlucky family, instructed his wife to commit suicide, told the younger members to disguise themselves and flee, and then hung himself from a tree. He reportedly left a letter noting that his 'inadequate virtues and weak flesh have invited punishment from Heaven'. Although his officials deserved the blame, he went on, 'I must die but am ashamed to face my ancestors.

Therefore I take off my crown and cover my face with my hair.' And with that the Ming dynasty that had ruled China for almost 300 years came to an end.[125]

While the climatic misfortunes of the 1640s cannot have helped, given the starvation and disease, and also given the loss of prestige, credibility and authority of the Emperor personally, the reality was that the fall of the Ming had been a long time coming and had deep roots. These included population growth that almost tripled from about 70 million around 1400 to more than 200 million by 1644, a rise in military spending in the late sixteenth century which meant that 76 per cent of all government expenditure went towards provisioning and equipping troops, and using them in costly engagements, particularly on the northern frontiers, and an eye-wateringly profligate waste of resources on the 'confusions of pleasure'.[126]

Lavish levels of spending on the palace and the court – which included maintaining 3,000 court ladies and an apparent 20,000 eunuchs – went hand in hand with high levels of corruption, endemic bribery being a product of low salaries and regular opportunity and temptation. Eunuchs collected imperial rents, administered tax, oversaw government storehouses and ran the secret police. This came at a high cost in regular payments, combined with inefficiencies and inflated costs as a result of regular kickbacks pocketed by eunuchs, and also at the price of the Emperor being shielded from reality as these officials grew more powerful. As one popular ditty addressed to the Emperor from the 1630s put it:

You're getting on, your ears are deaf, your eyes are gone
Can't see people, can't hear words …
How can you be so high? Come down to earth.[127]

The problems in Ming China were made worse by a cycle of desperate measures, poor decision-making and bad luck. Cuts to the postal service of some 30 per cent in 1629 were imposed in order to save money but ended up rendering efforts to deal with uprisings more difficult as information supply and orders slowed down. The ranks of the poor, hungry and disgruntled were swelled by officials who had lost their jobs in similar cost-cutting exercises. Growing banditry added to the sense of confusion and chaos, as well as to ideas about incompetence at the highest levels of government. Major changes to patterns of global commerce, over which the Ming dynasty had little control and even less understanding, were a factor too: China had been the world's great silver sink, sucking in bullion from the Americas via Manila. But from the start of the seventeenth century, trade competition from other locations in South and South-East Asia had risen sharply; Japanese decisions to cut off trade with Macao shut off an important market; while the capture of Melaka by the Dutch likewise had a major impact on Chinese silver imports.[128]

The collapse of the silver mines of Potosí in 1630, the reduced number of Chinese trading ships and the loss of galleons sailing across the Pacific because of poor seamanship and strong typhoons also proved damaging. Among those wrecked in 1638, for example, was the flagship *Nuestra Señora de la Concepción*, the largest vessel built at that time.[129] Losses such as these brought about change, since they represented major setbacks for the Spanish crown, which monopolised trans-Pacific trade. The year 1640 marked a turning point not only as the end of a period of rapid growth and high profits dating back to the 1580s, but because it saw a fundamental curtailment of shipping from Acapulco, the principal point of embarkation in the Americas to Manila, the entry point to Asia. In order to try to control the bribery that had made ships leave port overloaded, late or both, it was decided that the number of vessels travelling the route each year across the Pacific should be reduced – to one.[130] For China, it was like the oxygen supply being cut off to a patient that was already sick.

This was all made worse by dislocation in the provinces which played a major part in the collapse of central tax collection, while falling levels of agricultural production created pressures of their own: some estimates suggest the amount of land being cultivated in China fell from almost 200 million acres at the start of the seventeenth century to less than a third of that by the time of the collapse of the Ming.[131] China was trapped in a death spiral, in other words, locked in above all by the failure to adapt to or deal with mounting problems. But it means the collapse had roots that extended far deeper and lasted for far longer than climate crises in the build-up to 1644 or even in the years that preceded the fall of the Ming.

In the circumstances, then, the turbulent climate in the late 1630s and early 1640s clearly did not help; but this was one factor among a very wide range of others that dovetailed and came together to bring about the end of a dynasty. It was a similar story in many other parts of the world, as political challenges, economic contraction and demographic loss through warfare, disease and famine proved so deadly at roughly the same time. It did not take much to upset precarious balances that relied on fine margins of error.

However, it was not the same story in every part of the world. Tokugawa Japan, for example, and the Low Countries were able to navigate very similar climatic conditions that proved so devastating in China without the catastrophic problems of epidemic disease, famine and the overthrow of the ruling elite. The secret to this success lay in the mundane: the competence of officials and administrators in recognising problems, in anticipating the challenges they would bring and in planning ahead accordingly.[132] Climate was an aggravating factor, in other words, where problems already existed.

It is important to steer away from the irresistible temptation of the historian to identify watershed moments, to pinpoint events that can be described as turning points. The fall of the Ming dynasty clearly had repercussions and a high level of symbolic resonance both at the time and looking back with hindsight. However, the reality is that such transitions had much more ambiguous meanings for most contemporaries. Who sat on the throne was presumably less important than taxation demands that emanated from regional and imperial political and administrative centres. In that sense, the significance of the transition to the Qing was more obviously felt in the arrival of new hairstyles, new customs and new pastimes that were introduced at the court and then fanned outwards: frontier products like fur became the markers of elite Chinese fashion, while mushrooms from Mongolia, freshwater pearls from Manchuria and exotic foods from South-East Asia and Oceania put a raft of commodities under pressure as they were exploited for the benefit of metropolitan markets.[133]

Nevertheless, the challenges of the 'general crisis' of the seventeenth century produced important responses. The most significant of these was about putting plans in place to mitigate risk and to reduce the chances of being exposed to a range of problems being shaken into a cocktail at the same time. There were many ways to go about doing this: improving communication and efficiency; putting time, effort and resources into agricultural sciences; and opening up or taking over new lands that brought with them solutions to one of the oldest problems in human history: how to enable cities to expand and grow beyond the extent of their own hinterland. As we have seen, parts of western Europe had already done just that in the New World. Others too were about to try to do the same.

18

Concerning Great and Little Divergences (c.1600–c.1800)

I am astonished at my own moderation.

Robert Clive (1772)

The opening up of trade routes linking Europe, Africa, the Americas and Asia brought about a series of commercial, social, political, biological and ecological revolutions. The demand for resources and goods, the search for profits and the acceleration of exchange brought more and more people into ever closer contact with each other, knitting the world together in the process by linking overlapping regional networks into a globalised economy.

Taking advantage of opportunities demanded investment in skills, the development of information-gathering and the systemisation of knowledge. For example, shipping routes were standardised by the Dutch in a formal set of sailors' orders, with fleets sailing from harbour twice and, from the 1630s, three times per year for collective security – while they also sought optimal wind conditions: in a world where time was money, setting sail in adverse conditions was not just risky but costly. On average, ships sailing into easterly winds covered 218 kilometres per day; those sailing into westerlies covered just 167 kilometres – almost 25 per cent less. Winds were part of unpredictable cycles of weather patterns. For example, westerly winds were common in the 1730s and the early 1750s, but much less so in the 1740s and after 1755.[1]

Knowledge that had commercial and strategic value was kept secret. Ships' captains who were among the first waves to travel from Europe to the Americas and Asia were under orders to make maps, and to keep them secret from potential rivals. The Venetians were desperate to acquire accounts of the voyage of the Portuguese Pedro Cabral around the Cape of Good Hope to India in 1500, though this was not easy 'because the king has placed a death penalty on anyone who gives it out'. Shrewd intelligence solved the problem within three months, with one leading Venetian writing back home to say that he had been able to get hold of maps not only of the routes to India but beyond as well.[2]

Other materials were also kept secret, such as a text compiled in the seventeenth century by the botanist Georg Rumphius, who was sent out to South-East Asia by the Dutch East India Company to gather knowledge about plants. His catalogue, entitled *Het Amboinsche kruidboek*, ran to over 7,000 pages, with descriptions of more than a thousand plant species from all over the Indonesian archipelago. But this was no altruistic contribution to modern scholarship. In fact, it was considered so sensitive and commercially important that it was not allowed to be published for several decades and did not appear until 1741, some forty years after Rumphius' death.[3]

This was part of a wider set of new connections that had developed almost as soon as European sailors had reached the Americas and rounded the tip of southern Africa to gain access to the worlds of the Indian Ocean and beyond in the 1490s in a rapid, deliberate and systematic exploration of oceans, coastlines and peoples. Within the space of a few short decades, Spanish and Portuguese explorers and mariners had reached the Americas, India and the Philippines, had sailed around the Cape of Good Hope, had come into contact with Andean, Mesoamerican, Asian and Oceanic peoples and had circumnavigated the globe. Scholars and scientists chronicled and recorded the peoples, geographies and natural histories that had been encountered, compiling encyclopaedic works of extraordinary scope and scale, such as the thirty volumes produced by Francisco Hernández, who had set out for the New World accompanied by painters and engravers to help capture what he saw and discovered.[4]

Such ventures were championed and paid for by Iberian rulers who, rather than sharing with others what scholars found out, saw the chance to help understand and fashion new empires taking shape not in adjacent territories to ones that they already controlled – which was the abiding model of political expansion – but in lands far from home. The Spanish and Portuguese models differed in many ways. While the latter tended to rely on military control of specific enclaves, the former focused on establishing seats of learning in new locations. Almost all major cities in the Spanish empire were endowed with hospitals, printing presses and even universities – with the first set up in Santo Domingo in what is now the Dominican Republic in 1538, followed by Michoacán in Mexico the following year and Lima just over a decade later.[5]

There was a further purpose in supporting learning overseas, as the Dominican monk Tommaso Campanella stressed c.1600: 'This learning will make the one who possesses it master of the sea, the land and the people, and will illustrate the empire more than any other thing imaginable for making a King great,' he wrote. 'Because God Himself wants His works to be known and He gives them to he who knows them.' Empires were a manifestation of divine benediction, in other words, and therefore understanding and controlling them was a matter not just of interest but of duty.[6]

Such rosy ideas about the value of scholarship should of course be set within the context of an age of intolerance and prejudice that characterised both the Inquisition and the Reformation in Europe in the late fifteenth century and beyond. As violence erupted between Catholics and Protestants, as Jews were subjected to terrible persecution and countless innocent victims across Europe were accused of sorcery, heresy or both, science and learning became battlegrounds too. Rulers issued decrees ordering the handing over of Lutheran works on pain of fines and imprisonment; popes issued lists of forbidden books, which included texts deemed inappropriate because of where they were published or because their publishers had issued other works that were heretical.[7]

It should also be stressed that European engagement and growing familiarity with new parts of the world, new peoples and new cultures did not result in relationships based on mutual respect – indeed, far from it. As we have seen, attitudes to men, women and children from Africa developed into condescension, brutality and oppression, producing painful wounds that still scar the contemporary world; the treatment of indigenous peoples in the Americas, likewise, was above all one based on entitlement, manipulation and inequality that also has legacies today.

Such ideas took time to foment, develop and then harden – but harden they did as views about race as well as about other parts of the world became set in stone. It took several leaps of faith to underline the European sense of superiority when it came to climates that were hostile because of disease environments or uncomfortably warm. Some had their own theories about who might flourish and why. 'The Lustier and Fresher' one was, speculated Dr John Fryer, the harder it was to adapt to living in India. 'But to Old Men and Women', on the other hand, 'it seems more suitable.' Others were gloomier: one English doctor in the late seventeenth century mourned that 'we are here, as Exotick Plants ... not agreeable to the Soil'.[8]

As far as Asia was concerned, supposed 'exoticness' was no barrier to the growing conviction that Europeans were uniquely privileged among all the peoples of the world. This was self-evident, wrote Voltaire. Europeans had proved their 'great superiority of genius and courage over eastern nations'. Preconceptions and prejudices became routine, both about others and about Europeans themselves. 'Europe may be the smallest part of the world,' wrote one German scholar in the late eighteenth century, 'but it is the best.' There could be no doubt, claimed a contemporary, that Europe had attained 'the ultimate peak of perfection'.[9]

Those living elsewhere were worthy of contempt – an attitude reinforced by a flood of travel literature written by a new class of scholar gentlemen who set off around the world in pursuit of scientific knowledge and learning, snootily complaining about the 'hard and dangerous work' of investigating peoples and places that usually fell short of expectations. Timbuktu, for example, was not a glorious desert city that was home to wealth and wisdom, but a profound disappointment for one European visitor – 'nothing but a mass of ill-looking houses, built of earth. Nothing was to be seen in all directions but immense plains of quicksand of a yellowish white colour.'[10]

Racist tropes developed into sneering caricatures of other peoples' cultures. Persians were barely able to use knives, forks, plates or napkins, wrote one traveller in the early nineteenth century. Mongols and Tibetans were good natured, open and trusting, and showed none of the 'deception, cowardice and baseness of the Hindus', said the philosopher Georg Hegel in a series of lectures delivered in Berlin around the same time.[11]

In European imagination, the Ottoman empire became synonymous with plague and illness, to the point where (as we have seen) it became routinely referred to as 'the sick man of Europe', both in reference to a supposed sclerotic political system and literally as a sick land unable to deal with ill-health in a rational manner.[12] Sickness, laziness and perversion were all rolled into perceptions of the Turks. Constantinople, the Ottoman capital, 'has been not only the hot bed of every sort of Eastern vice', stated British Prime Minister David Lloyd George in 1919, but 'the source from which the poison of corruption and intrigue has spread far and wide'.[13] Such views were commonplace.

They also became central parts of reframing history in a way that celebrated 'western civilisation' at the expense of all others. 'A single shelf of a good European library', wrote the celebrated historian Thomas Macaulay in 1836, 'was worth the whole native literature of India and Arabia.' As for education in India, he opined, it was essential for the British to do their 'best to form a class who may be interpreters between us and the millions whom we govern – a class of persons Indian in blood and colour, but English in tastes, in opinions, in morals and in intellect'. India needed non-Indians to run it; this could be done only by creating and training a new 'class' who had been disconnected from their Indianness and made to think like Europeans. English was 'better worth knowing than Sanskrit or Arabic', wrote the British historian and politician Thomas Babington Macaulay; moreover, it was much easier to learn than Greek. Given that intelligent English youths could master Herodotus and Sophocles easily, how hard could it be for 'a Hindoo to read Hume and Milton'?[14]

Entitlement over other people was mirrored by entitlement over nature. As we have seen, islands in the Caribbean as well as enslaved people shipped from Africa were brutally exploited to extract crops that could be sold for high profits, most notably sugar, coffee, cotton and other cash crops. The human costs of these enterprises were catastrophic; in many cases, the ecological consequences were also dramatic – described by one scholar as 'reverse tonsures, shaved bald but for little tufts of forest left on their mountain crowns'. Exhaustion of the soil was exacerbated by deforestation which exposed the land to rain and heat that sapped the nutrients further still. This was neither sustainable nor clever business: it did not take long for it to become necessary for firewood to be imported to provide fuel for sugar furnaces, with wood eventually even being imported to the Caribbean from as far away as England.[15]

Such ecological degradation was initially limited to a relatively small number of locations – above all in north-eastern Brazil and the Caribbean. Taken as a whole, European exploitation of territories in the Americas was surprisingly constrained. For one thing, the aim of establishing colonies was above all not to increase production but to control trade. Indeed, in some cases, severe restrictions were introduced to limit exports in order to maximise the financial return to the crown. For example, concessions giving monopoly on brazilwood, a red dyewood that was much in demand for European textile makers and was so valuable that it gave its name to a vast country, were auctioned every three years; strict limits were set for volumes that could be exported, with the King of Portugal ordering the death sentence in 1605 for anyone caught smuggling. Control of the diamond trade was also enforced, with physical removal of everyone who was not involved in mining – and especially priests, who were notorious for their involvement in contraband trade.[16]

In fact, one of the most noteworthy features of the New World when looked at as a whole was how poorly it was exploited by European settlers. Spanish olive and wine producers and Portuguese salt manufacturers successfully lobbied to block production in the Americas in order to keep prices of their own domestic goods high. Before the third quarter of the eighteenth century, Spain received around 150,000 animal hides from the Americas; changes to trade policies and taxes in 1778 altered the dynamics of trade, resulting in 800,000 hides being shipped across the Atlantic the following year – and 1.4 million being sent in 1783. This was part of a tenfold increase in colonial trade between 1778 and 1796. In fact, rather than exploiting 'virgin lands', trade from the colonies in the Americas often ran at a fraction of its potential for some 300 years after the first crossing by Columbus.[17]

One result was that there were widespread environmental changes in North, Central and South America in the centuries that followed 1492 that were not caused by human activity – but quite the opposite. This was a time of major reforestation and wildlife gains in many regions. The major reductions in human populations as a result of disease, hunger, warfare and dislocation meant that land that had been cultivated became overgrown, to the benefit of wild plants and the detriment of foodstuffs like fruits and nuts. Likewise, animals that had been heavily exploited for food or status recovered – such as birds whose feathers had been valued as symbols of prestige and currency, or apex predators like jaguars who gained from expanded habitats with the thinning out of the men who had hunted them and of settlements that had displaced them. Animals whose fortunes and numbers had risen with human success, like turkeys, dogs and llamas, suffered decline as their owners, breeders and keepers died out. But one of the most curious outcomes of the European settlement of the Americas – outside the locations given over to the cultivation of a small number of valuable crops – was the significant wildlife gains across vast territories. Taken as a whole, the Americas were more heavily forested in 1800 than they had been 300 years earlier.[18]

Dramatic ecological change was not just connected to the interventions of Europeans. The peoples of the indigenous world that linked what is now California, Nevada, Utah, Arizona, New Mexico, Sonora and Baja California with the Colorado Delta and on to the east coast had long been part of regions that had been defined by geographic boundaries made up of rivers, mountains and deserts, of economies that interlocked or were distinct as a result of tools, commodities and livestock, of food systems that were based on similar plant and animal resources and water availability, and of transport and communication networks. Over time, these relationships and balances began to change, both as a by-product of what was happening far to the east and above all because of the introduction of horses, which prompted dynamic change across swathes of North America. As raiding strategies evolved, so too did new confederacies emerge under the Haudenosaunees, Cherokees, Comanches, Navajo, Apaches and others, in response to pressures posed by European settlers, to the need to defend or attack territory controlled by other indigenous peoples, and to the urge to enshrine the power of elites within what some scholars have terms 'regimes of violence'.[19]

The opening up of new lands was not limited to the Americas. In India in the late sixteenth century, for example, the expansion of the territorial boundaries of the Mughal empire brought about more liberal ideas that were connected to the incorporation of more minorities and the expedience of inclusivity. The Emperor Akbar was instrumental not only in welcoming Jains to his court, but in being influenced by their philosophies and practices. This included vegetarianism, which Akbar adopted with enthusiasm. 'It is not right that a man should make his stomach the grave of animals,' he declared, adding that he would ban the eating of meat if it were practicable. In any event, he said, 'from my earliest years, whenever I ordered animal food to be cooked for me, I found it rather tasteless and cared little for it. I took this feeling to indicate a necessity for protecting animals, and I refrained from animal food.'[20]

This should not be confused with conservationism or environmentally sustainable practices. In fact, Mughal rulers were motivated by seeking military victory, imposing public order, increasing land revenues and annexing new territories. The expansion of the empire into Bengal in the late sixteenth century was a perfect example of these aims intertwining as ambitious local rulers were forced into submission over the course of a long series of military campaigns. Local populations – many of whom were devotees of forest goddesses – were displaced as new settlers set about securing land grants before cutting down the jungle and clearing land to make way for rice cultivation. This came at a heavy price for forest dwellers, who were not inhabitants of peripheral lands that were wild and savage, but rather played hugely significant roles in the collection and cultivation of spices, resins and other non-timber products which required knowledge and skills that were difficult to acquire.[21]

Most of these 'pioneers' were Muslims, and built small rural mosques to support new settlements and communities as wild wetlands, marshlands and forests were transformed into domesticated lands. The effect was to open up new regions which eventually produced vast amounts of foods, commodities and tax revenues that helped sustain and fuel the Mughal empire in the seventeenth century.[22]

The principle was the same under the Qing dynasty which took power in the middle of the seventeenth century in much of what is now China. The new rulers were able to restore order both speedily and effectively after the chaos that had accompanied the fall of their Ming predecessors, which of course speaks volumes about the structural problems most to blame for the calamities that had proved so devastating in the 1640s. As administrative reforms kicked in, central coffers swelled as agricultural production rose sharply. Over the next two centuries, the amount of land under cultivation rose from around 100 million to 200 million acres – equivalent to a rate of 500,000 more acres per year being turned over to the growing of crops.[23]

This came with significant ecological costs. Intensive deforestation and uplift in farming resulted in high levels of erosion and soil degradation that badly affected the Yellow River and the Grand Canal. The results proved to be not just environmentally damaging but economically catastrophic: the costs of maintaining the canal systems rose fivefold in the century after the 1730s, eventually consuming as much as 20 per cent of all government spending by the 1820s.[24] This was a poor use of capital and manpower under any circumstances; but such inefficiency left Qing dynasty China badly placed to deal with the global competition that emerged in the nineteenth century.

The Qing oversaw a period of territorial expansion in all directions – to the west, to the north and to the south. By the end of the seventeenth century, the dynasty had established control over large parts of Mongolia and Xinjiang as well as Taiwan, meanwhile extending influence into Tibet.[25] By 1759, the Qianlong Emperor (r. 1735–96) was declaring that all rival states and kingdoms had been subdued and that he had brought about 'eternal peace and security on the borders'.[26]

Many of the lands that the Qing moved into did not offer manifold natural bonanzas. While expanding into the interior brought kudos, taking over steppe lands, mountains and deserts – all of which featured prominently in the newly conquered regions – did not offer obvious gains. In any event, if, when and where they did, they came at a price: goods needed to reach consumers and customers; exploiting regions with low population densities of their own that were far from towns and cities meant that transportation of high-volume, bulk items – like crops – was expensive and even financially unviable. As a result, attention was almost exclusively focused on exotic and luxury commodities, such as furs and freshwater pearls, that were light, high value and offered the best returns.[27]

In other parts of the world, cities rose up along new trade routes. For example, Lima, Panama, Havana, Buenos Aires, Rio de Janeiro, Manila and beyond all grew in response to silver mines and shipments from South and Central America.[28] The expansions of the seventeenth and eighteenth centuries meant that many parts of the world cross-fertilised, galvanised and stimulated each other. But this did not happen in China: no new cities were founded; there was limited resettlement of populations by choice or by force; and the gains of expansion were primarily existential rather than material. That was a poor equation. High costs, low production and low wages all placed drags on growth, as well as on expenditure. That all served to set Qing China on a trajectory that contrasted sharply with Europe, where acute anxieties had led to considerable efforts being made to improve yields, promote resilience and reduce the risk posed by climate shocks.

The traumas of the mid-seventeenth century had prompted considerable thought on how to get better returns from the soil. For example, Walter Blith was a passionate advocate of land management, urging farmers to study the subject more carefully, offering advice that he promised, in the manner of a modern marketing guru, would lead to a doubling or trebling of crop growths, if not a fivefold and perhaps even a tenfold return on expectations. This was just one example of burgeoning interest in agronomy and in the efforts to protect against future shortage.[29]

The devastation of the Thirty Years' War, not least in the form of heavy loss of life through war, disease and hunger, perhaps played a crucial role in focusing minds. It was probably no coincidence, for example, that in the seventeenth century, young scholars like Ludwig von Seckendorff not only spent time thinking about soil conditions, fertility of the land and jurisdiction over the land, but considered these to be essential elements for all rulers to be informed about in order to govern their states successfully. This was not just about mitigation of potential threats; it was also closely connected to questions about labour-force size and potential gains from higher levels of productivity. 'A country in which subsistence and commerce flourish can never have too many inhabitants,' wrote Johann von Justi, an influential scholar in the eighteenth century. Finding ways to support higher population densities was important, he argued, in enabling rulers to generate higher incomes.[30]

Such lessons were not lost on those who understood how science, politics and economics were all closely linked. 'Agriculture', wrote Frederick the Great, the pre-eminent figure in eastern Europe in the mid-eighteenth century, 'is the first of all the arts, without which there would be no merchants, kings, poets, philosophers.' As he observed to his correspondent, the French author and polymath Voltaire, 'making domain lands cultivable interests me more than murdering people'.[31]

Such views can easily mask widespread anxieties about production and about supply being able to keep up with demand. London alone had grown by seven times in the hundred years after the reign of Queen Elizabeth I (1558–1603), noted William Petty. What would happen if it grew by the same amount again, he wondered; would there be enough 'bread and drink-corn ... fruits, garden stuff, hay, timber, coal?'[32] One way to solve the problem, was to spawn new colonies from which resources could be extracted – which could prove something of a learning curve: England's experiences in Ireland, for example, were to provide a template in North America and in Canada in particular in relation to displacing existing populations from their lands, to the use of force within racial and religious frameworks and to ideas about supposed superiority and entitlements.[33]

Another method of boosting productivity was to work the land more intensively, through higher labour levels or through innovation. Qing China, for example, imported vast quantities of fertiliser primarily made of rapeseed, cottonseed and soybean cakes amounting to perhaps 3 billion kilos per year by 1750. This was part of a revolution in land management and also in consumption, welfare and health. Life expectancy and living standards not only matched but were superior to those almost everywhere in Europe other than south-east England, where levels were about the same. This was particularly impressive given that the population of Qing China more than doubled in the course of the eighteenth century.[34]

One explanation for how demographic growth happened was the process known as the Columbian Exchange which linked the Americas to the other continents of the world. Although this term is often used by historians to describe the new connections made in the decades and centuries after 1492, it is unsatisfactory – above all since it implies symmetry in the two-way relationship between the Americas and the rest of the world. For one thing, the movement of people was almost exclusively in one direction: as we have seen, millions were shipped against their will from Africa to the Americas, while millions more settlers in due course crossed the Atlantic from Europe; the number of those heading the other way, as visiting dignitaries or as coerced labourers, was extremely low.[35]

To be sure, silver flows from the Americas were truly transformational; but taken in broader terms, the New World was the recipient of a great deal more from the Old than the other way round. In addition to the involuntary and voluntary movements of people, countless horses, sheep, pigs, cows, chickens, geese, cats, rats and more were shipped across the Atlantic, while only squirrels, turkeys and guinea pigs came in the opposite direction. Cacao, corn, tobacco, pineapples, beans and chilli peppers were exported from the Americas, but many plants and crops were imported from Europe, Africa and Asia, including citrus fruits, rice and bananas – with all three becoming staple parts of the diet.[36]

Old World diets had more of an effect on those living in the New, at least initially: indeed, by the 1580s, indigenous populations in 190 communities which were surveyed about high mortality rates and sickness levels explained that a century earlier, before the arrival of the Spanish, people had eaten less food, consumed less salt and drunk less alcohol – while also claiming that hygiene levels had been higher. Although it was noted that the tried-and-tested remedies of local healers had been more effective than medical ideas brought by new settlers and that bans on polygamy had limited birth rates, the fact remained that the arrival of Europeans had heralded the end of an age of moderation and replaced it with one of excess.[37]

Nevertheless, while relatively few in number, there were foods that had a major impact after they were exported from the Americas. Manioc (cassava) and maize were first brought east across the Atlantic by Portuguese traders in the sixteenth century and became much prized by local farmers in West Africa above all for their robustness against drought. Manioc was drought-resistant as well as high-yielding, and, better still, not only resistant to locusts but also easy to store. It was labour-intensive, requiring soaking, grating and squeezing before being left to dry and then ground into flour; this process was vital in order to remove metabolites that have the ability to produce highly toxic hydrogen cyanide when degraded by plant enzymes. Failure to do so properly causes paralysis and poisoning.[38]

Maize too took well to African soils, providing two crops in the time it usually took for a single sorghum harvest, and moreover was both easy to store and difficult to spoil. It became such a crucial source of diets in Benin, Ghana, Nigeria, Togo, Cameroon and Angola that it is often seen today as an indigenous, traditional crop rather than a relatively recent import.[39] Both of these crops were of crucial importance in increasing the number of calories available in regions that were sources of large numbers of enslaved peoples who were sold. Ironically, therefore, they played a role in the slave trade by enabling more people to survive famine, by increasing the dependence on women in agricultural production and by enabling stores of food to be built up that reduced labour demands locally. This created pools of 'surplus' workforces that made men available for sale to traders.

Even more important, however, than maize and manioc was another crop, whose impact on global history is hard to overestimate – not least because it too mitigated risks posed by weather shocks and climatic shifts. Indeed, one could reasonably argue that it did as much to change human lives as some of the most significant medical discoveries in history or as much to change economic outcomes as events like the industrial revolution. As well as providing security against famine and disease, it changed health outcomes, drove urbanisation and reduced conflict. The humble potato changed the world.

Potatoes provide more calories, vitamins and nutrients per acre of land sown than other staple crops. The skin of a medium-sized potato contains 45 per cent of the recommended daily intake of vitamin C – unlike wheat, oats, barley, rice and maize which contain none at all; a medium potato also provides significant amounts of the recommended daily intake of vitamin B6, as well thiamin, riboflavin, niacin, magnesium, iron and zinc. In addition, potatoes need less land and yield well over ten times more calories than crops such as wheat. An acre of potatoes typically produces three times more energy than an acre of oats, wheat or barley.[40]

Potatoes can grow on land that is not suitable for the cultivation of wheat or rice – and, what is more, can be grown in between the growing seasons of other crops and on land left fallow between periods of grain cultivation. As well as being robust in poor weather conditions, potatoes provide diversification that mitigates the threat of famine. Relatively easy to store, they also allow for surpluses to be built up as contingencies during winter months for both human and animal consumption. The latter is important too: as fodder for livestock, potatoes also help feed larger numbers of pigs and cattle, which increases opportunities for meat consumption, as well as boosting quantities of manure which in turn further helps with crop production.[41]

Cultivated in the Andes for thousands of years, potatoes were not immediately appreciated in Europe after being brought back in the sixteenth century, partly because the potato belongs to the poisonous nightshade family and partly because of associations made between the lumpy, discoloured appearance of the crop and leprosy. Slowly adopted at first, potatoes started to be planted in Spain, Italy, England and Germany by around 1600, by which time they were also being introduced by sailors to ports in Africa, Asia and Oceania – although widespread cultivation in Europe, India and China did not take off until the late seventeenth and early eighteenth centuries.[42]

By this time, the potato was widely considered to have almost miraculous properties. Peter the Great had toured Europe in the late 1690s and sent a bag of potatoes back to Russia with instructions that they should be distributed to farmers in different districts. A few decades later, the Senate issued directives to grow 'earth apples which in England are called potatoes' as part of an effort not only to encourage cultivation but to counter grain failures that had led to hunger and disease in Finland and Siberia in the 1760s. It took time to catch on, partly because some were convinced that the potato was 'that forbidden fruit' which Adam and Eve had eaten in the Garden of Eden (presumably because of the name *pomme de terre*); 'whoever eats it disobeys God', said some traditionalists in Russia, 'violates the holy testament and will never inherit the Kingdom of Heaven'.[43]

Others were more pragmatic. 'The food produced by a field of potatoes', wrote Adam Smith in *The Wealth of Nations*, was 'much superior to what is produced by a field of wheat'. Smith was convinced that 'No food can afford a more decisive proof of its nourishing quality, or of its being peculiarly suitable to the health of the human constitution.' The strongest men in London and the most beautiful women in the dominions, he said, were those who were from the 'lowest rank of people in Ireland, who are generally fed with this root'.[44]

The adoption and dissemination of potatoes had remarkable effects in many different spheres. Military records of more than 13,000 French soldiers born between 1658 and 1770 suggest that adult height went up by an average of over one centimetre as a result of nutritional investments made during early life that can be directly attributed to consumption of more calories in general and of potatoes in particular.[45]

More remarkable still is the fact that the adoption of potatoes in Europe increased agricultural productivity, reducing the requirement for land in the process and thereby watering down competition for its control. Although it stands to reason that the availability of cheap food can reduce the cost of maintaining large armies and therefore make warfare more attractive, lower land values typically lessen the probability of violent conflict because incentives to arm are lower, as are the probabilities of winning a war. Statistical modelling suggests that the introduction of potatoes dramatically decreased conflict not only in Europe but in other continents and regions where it was established.[46] The introduction of sweet potatoes, first to the southern part of China and then to the north, served to reduce peasant rebellions primarily by providing insurance against rainfall shocks that led to failures of other crops.[47]

By mitigating risks of adverse weather conditions, whether temporary or part of wider, long-term shifts, potatoes opened up new opportunities for larger populations by reducing food shortages, increasing calorific intakes and improving health and life expectancies. Furthermore, they also enabled higher population densities to be supported, which in turn drove the rise and growing size of cities in the seventeenth and eighteenth centuries. It has been estimated, for example, that potatoes account for around 25 per cent of the increase in population sizes in this period – and for an even greater percentage of the increase in urbanisation.[48] This was crucial because of the primary role that cities played (and play) in fostering commercial exchange, stimulating demand and spurring innovation.

If food in general played an important role in propelling the growth of cities around the world, then so too did high wages – which are fundamental to explaining the phenomenon that has been mentioned before in this book and that historians call the Great Divergence, the phase when Europe caught up with and overtook what had long been much larger and more established economies in Asia, most notably in India and China.

There were many reasons why this happened. Some scholars who have investigated urban growth in Europe have looked at the importance of the continent having been part of the Roman empire and having access to Roman road infrastructure a thousand years or more later.[49] Others have looked at the effects of Protestantism and at the profound changes which its rise brought about for education in Europe, where countries in the north and west pulled away from those in the south and east. Martin Luther had been a passionate advocate of schooling for both boys and girls, insisting that all should be able to read the Scriptures. It was disgraceful, he argued in *A Sermon on Keeping Children in School* in 1530, that some parents were so selfish, stupid and unChristian as to leave their children ignorant or to withdraw them from school. In doing so, he said, they were serving the devil. Such admonitions had long-term impacts, with Protestant cities and lands adopting policies of education for all children and requiring the building of new schools. Strikingly, while all countries with Protestant majorities had nearly universal literacy by 1900, none with Catholic ones did, with many a long way behind.[50] This pattern was replicated between 1910 and 1938 in the United States, where educational outcomes were better in areas with high proportions of Protestants in their populations.[51]

The rise of institutions of all kinds in Europe was important, as were the introduction of the printing press and the expansion of book production which opened up ideas and knowledge to more and more people. The creation of universities was significant too, not least because they ensured increasing numbers trained in law, which had a positive effect on economic transactions by reducing the uncertainties of trade – a development that increased levels of trust as well as improving volumes and speeds of exchanges.[52]

Lowering transactional risks helped make the use of capital cheaper, which in turn helped stimulate competition. Interest rates in Europe, especially in Great Britain and the Netherlands, were much lower than they were in China: Adam Smith noted in the 1770s that while 3–4.5 per cent could be considered normal in London, current rates in China were said to be as high as 12 per cent.[53] He was not quite right. In fact, loans in China often ran at 2 per cent per month, or 24 per cent annually; in some periods, rates were more like 50 per cent per annum.[54] Although there were regional variations across South, South-East and East Asia and fluctuations too depending on the period, it is clear that the costs of taking loans and of doing business were extremely high when compared to Europe – and that these contributed to both dampening economic growth and suffocating innovation.[55]

Both economic growth and innovation were fuelled by competition, something that was readily available in Europe where political fragmentation created opportunities to test and refine ideas, to sharpen reactions and to drive change. This manifested itself in the near constant warfare which served to improve military technologies, as has been touched on already, and which proved essential when it came to the age of colonisations of Africa, Asia and Oceania in the nineteenth century. But competition fuelled scientific discovery and advance too, although these should be seen in the context of gender divergences that often are not mentioned: in northern Europe and in Britain in particular, male scholars and entrepreneurs drove innovation, creating and fuelling networks that shared and celebrated inventions, as well as providing capital for those with commercial application.[56] Women were locked out of these networks, intentionally and otherwise, and had to publish their work anonymously or not at all.[57]

The circle of men, science, money and opportunity was particularly effective in Britain, where the key elements that drove progress and ultimately resulted in the industrial revolution were high levels of pay and high productive output of the labour force. The workforce in Britain were far more productive and also better paid than anywhere else in Europe, which meant that new inventions were adopted earlier, faster and on a larger scale than anywhere else in the world. What mattered most was not schooling or literacy, but mechanical competence – something that was in uniquely high supply in Britain where skilled craftsmen introduced a constant stream of small improvements to machinery.[58] Examples included the spinning jenny, a basic and cheap hand-powered cotton-spinning machine, changes in which metals were used for gears in early textile machines and standardisation of engine size that enabled inventories of spare parts to be kept on hand that in turn saved time and money in the event of breakdown or failure.[59]

As a result, agricultural workers easily outstripped their peers in terms of time and speed. Whereas it took around seven days to reap a hectare of wheat in England at the end of the eighteenth century, the same process took more than sixteen days in France. These efficiencies enabled higher wages and a slew of further benefits for English workers, including higher calorie consumption than their French peers. It has even been suggested that because English workers were better paid, protein from meat was more readily affordable, which is particularly important for brain development in babies and infants. It seems that workers may not only have been richer and more productive than in other countries, but smarter too.[60]

'The working manufacturing people of England eat the fat, and drink the sweet, live better, and fare better, than the working poor of any other nation in Europe,' wrote Daniel Defoe in 1726; 'they make better wages of their work, and spend more of the money upon their backs and bellies, than in any other country.' Defoe could have added that, as well as providing leisure time, high wages underpinned the acquisition of skills, ranging from literacy to numeracy to craft competence, all of which were in high demand in an economy that was advancing rapidly.[61]

It was a very different story in China, where pressures to innovate and to compete were conspicuous by their absence. For one thing, only a tiny sliver of the rural population was engaged in wage labour – perhaps as little as 1–2 per cent during the late Ming dynasty.[62] Moreover, for all the territorial gains made by the Qing in the late seventeenth and eighteenth centuries, the Pax Manchurica that was so triumphantly proclaimed as a symbol of heavenly order proved to be a badly exposed Achilles heel. The push towards natural barriers such as mountains and deserts removed neighbours that were threats or competitors, and forced parallel empires out of view. The military had to contend with threats that were modest and containable from Korea, from South-East and Inner Asia and from Cossack adventurers. None prompted revolutions in military technology or tactics, and what is more, none led to administrative, social or economic reform, or to investment in innovation, productivity or industry, which were so instrumental in the rise of the west. Europe's divisions and fractured political history since the time of the Roman empire made for intense competition. Warfare and fracture had long been sources of weakness within Europe; now they became a strength. As Europe galloped forward into the future, in other words, China remained stuck in the past.[63]

Higher levels of resilience against unpredictable weather conditions helped societies deal with food shortages and upheavals in which climate had been a factor in the past. There were still one-off events that could have dramatic consequences. For example, a particularly severe storm in southern England in December 1703, described by Daniel Defoe as 'the greatest, the longest in duration, the widest in extent, of all the Tempests and storms that history gives any account of since the Beginning of time', led to thirteen Royal Navy ships being lost at sea along with 8,000 seamen. This jeopardised English naval supremacy at a testing time, coming as it did during the War of Spanish Succession, which amounted to a battle for control of the heart of the continent of Europe.[64]

Sequences of unusually frequent and severe storms in the Atlantic in the 1760s and 1770s were instrumental, meanwhile, in reshaping trade networks and shifting political alliances. A disastrous hurricane season in 1766 which saw six major storms hit the Caribbean basin brought about severe food shortages that prompted desperate appeals for help from Spanish islands being placed in newspapers in cities in the US colonies. American support brought warnings from the British government, which regarded the sale of flour and other goods as trading with the enemy and issued official demands to cease trade forthwith.[65]

Another brutal hurricane season in 1772 which resulted in terrible destruction across the Caribbean again, damaging houses, shops, hospitals and civic infrastructure in Havana followed by crop failures, presented what one scholar has called 'a onetime windfall' for merchants in Philadelphia. Five of the six richest men in the city, at that time the leading financial centre on the eastern seaboard, were already actively involved in trade with Spain, and attention now began to turn to asking what Britain's European rivalries had to do with the colonies in North America – a question that was compounded by growing concern about taxation demands and the use of unconstitutional powers.[66] This had resulted in a gathering in October 1774 that brought together representatives of twelve of the thirteen colonies to meet and issue the Declaration of Colonial Rights that proposed a boycott of British goods and sent a list of grievances to London, along with a petition to King George III.[67]

Americans began to look at the opportunities presented closer to home, both in the Caribbean and in Spanish Louisiana, where New Orleans had also experienced severe food shortages. Representatives of the newly formed Continental Congress were established in French Caribbean seaports, while channels of communication with Spanish islands were opened to discuss the possibility of trading tobacco from North America for gunpowder. In October 1775, the Continental Congress passed a resolution that authorised exports to foreign ports in exchange for weapons, ammunition, gunpowder and cash – all of which were essential given the rising tension with Britain and the adoption of a boycott of goods a few months earlier. Leading figures in North America, such as John Adams, one of the Founding Fathers and signatories of the Declaration of Independence, were convinced that there 'will be little Difficulty in Trading with France and Spain, a great deal in dealing with Portugal and some with Holland'.[68]

The realisation that the environmental and economic vulnerabilities of the American south and of the Caribbean represented commercial and political opportunities for the colonists and weak spots for the British was an important, if little commented on, part of the story of the weeks before, during and after the Declaration of Independence on 4 July 1776. Embargoes on British shipping effectively cut off Jamaica and other British colonies, creating shortages and suffering that were made worse by a violent early-season hurricane that struck in June of that year. In the French islands in the Caribbean, in contrast, there was a 'festival-like atmosphere' as traders cut deals, booked future agreements and filled warehouses to the rafters with goods.[69] There were plenty of good reasons why the French and later the Spanish entered the War of Independence on the side of the Patriots in the second half of the 1770s; but one factor was certainly that all benefited from closer integration of commercial ties in the western Atlantic and Caribbean, which owed much to the efforts to mitigate risk from adverse weather shocks.

Not all were so fortunate when it came to finding solutions to these problems. Climate conditions in India in the second half of the eighteenth century were challenging, consistently resulting in lower-than-usual agricultural productivity and higher-than-average grain prices. Regular warfare between potentates in South Asia pushed the price of agricultural input higher still as did rising rent burdens, made worse by the deterioration of central authority. This had the unfortunate effect of raising nominal wages while driving up the cost of living, serving to make India less competitive at a time when trends in Britain and elsewhere in Europe were heading in the other direction. In 1750, India had been responsible for around a quarter of the world's industrial output; by 1900, it accounted for just 2 per cent.[70]

This precipitous decline can also be explained, at least in part, by colonial policies that included a lack of investment, tariff protection that supported foreign-made goods, and the extraction of resources and labour by the East India Company that established a dominant position in much of the subcontinent by the middle of the eighteenth century.[71] This combination proved deadly in the late 1760s when a weak monsoon resulted in a poor harvest in Bengal and Bihar in 1768 which was followed a year later by even lower levels of rainfall, prompting the superintendent of Bishunpur to note that 'the fields of rice are become like fields of dried straw'.[72] The East India Company administrators in the region took little interest in the calamities that were unfolding. Their primary concern was to collect revenues in order to meet financial targets that helped enrich shareholders – so attention was focused on gathering obligations, which by the start of 1770 were reported as being on track and as expected. Although it was noted in January that a slight remission of land tax might be necessary, at the start of February officials stated that they had not 'yet found any failure in the revenue or stated payments'.[73]

By this time, the price of rice had already gone up to ten times its normal rate, and there were reports that starvation levels were so bad that people were selling their children to try to raise money. Malnutrition and disease took hold, followed by death on an almost unimaginable scale. More than 76,000 people died in Calcutta alone between July and September 1770; as many as one in five Bengalis died that year – numbering more than a million. 'The only remedy', wrote one contemporary, 'is the mercy of God.'[74]

Some East India Company officials tried to put emergency measures in place, setting up distribution centres to give out food to those who were suffering, although this proved to be a losing battle. Others, however, seized the chance to enrich themselves, buying up stocks of rice that forced prices higher still and then selling them on at huge mark-ups. A number made 'great fortunes' as a result, with one employee of previously modest means earning the modern equivalent of millions of pounds from the disaster which he promptly sent back home. Although some, like Horace Walpole, were horrified by reports coming from India, investors were delighted: the East India Company share price soared, convincing the directors to issue a dividend of 12.5 per cent – the highest that the company had ever paid out.[75]

There were to be consequences in due course, not least because the famine provoked a collapse in land values in and remittances from Bengal, which led to a sell-off that, coupled with unsold stockpiles of tea and high company debts, precipitated a downturn in fortunes that was as dramatic and rapid as the collapse of major investment banks in the financial crisis of 2008. In need of a state bail-out, senior EIC figures were hauled into Parliament to explain and justify what had happened. The fact of the matter, said Robert Clive, who had taken control of the fisc of Bengal just over a decade earlier and had enriched himself mightily, was that he could have helped himself to even more. 'I stand astonished at my own moderation,' he told nonplussed MPs.[76]

That the motivation of greed turned a difficult situation into a catastrophe was to have obvious parallels with a similar situation in Bengal in the twentieth century as millions again became exposed to the lethal combination of poor weather, bad harvest, incompetent administration and the consequences of predatory speculation. In these cases, it was human decision-making that played a significant and even a decisive role in making a difficult situation worse. The result was mass mortality on an epic scale.

Sometimes, however, it was coincidence of timing of natural phenomena that exacerbated problems. A case in point comes with the eruptions of the Laki fissure in Iceland in 1783. Between 8 June and 25 October that year, Laki produced ten stratospheric eruption episodes, with eruptions continuing until the following February. Local impacts were dire, as 80 per cent of the sheep, almost the same proportion of horses and half the cattle in Iceland died, primarily as a result of grazing lands becoming poisoned. Around one in five of the human population perished as famine and 'haze hardships' (Móðuharðindin) gripped the island for several years.[77] The effects were felt more widely too, with unusually frequent episodes of respiratory illnesses across many parts of Europe, along with multiple accounts of acute headaches and asthma attacks and high mortality rates in England in the summer of 1783.[78] The summer months saw 'a constant fog over all Europe', observed Benjamin Franklin, 'and a great part of North America'; he added that 'the rays of the sun seemed to have little effect towards dissipating it', and suggested that it was probably the result of major volcanic activity in Iceland.[79]

The cloud of haze was watched as it spread eastwards, reaching Berlin, Padua and Rome by mid-June, St Petersburg, Moscow and Tripoli in Lebanon by the end of the month, and then the Altai mountains in Central and East Asia by the start of July.[80] The summer was unusually warm across many parts of Europe: model simulations suggest that the abnormally high temperatures were the result of high pressure over northern Europe causing cold polar air to bypass western and central Europe, as well as the Middle East. The anomaly also brought about lower-than-normal rainfall in the Sahel and North Africa, and in many parts of China and South Asia. It is not impossible that, without the eruptions, conditions might have been even more challenging across the northern hemisphere.[81]

The period that followed saw significant temperature drops in the northern hemisphere, where the years 1784–6 were the coldest in the second half of the eighteenth century. Measurements from New Brunswick show that the winter of 1783–4 was the coldest in 250 years, while harbours and channels in Chesapeake Bay were closed for the longest period in recorded history as a result of build-up of ice. The Mississippi River was filled with ice fragments at New Orleans for a week in February 1784. North-west Alaska saw some of the coldest conditions of the previous millennium, while unusually low temperatures were recorded from Paris to Prague, from Lebanon to Japan; droughts and frosts in Mexico in 1784–5 were also part of the disturbed weather patterns in this period.[82]

It has been argued that these conditions were caused by a protracted El Niño event in 1782–4 that was coupled with a negative North Atlantic Oscillation phase.[83] However, recent research has shown that large high-latitude eruptions can prime the Pacific to create climatic perturbations – and that effects are particularly severe when El Niño–Southern Oscillation or La Niña episodes are already developing, magnifying the effects in the process.[84] The timing and scale of the Laki eruption was therefore not only important in its own right, but as an amplifier of other emerging climatic trends that were developing at this time.

While most parts of the world coped with the challenges posed by this period of unsettled and unusual weather well, some did not. That said much about how important underlying factors were in the context of climatic impacts, and shows that turbulence should be usually be seen as a catalyst of change rather than its primary driver. For example, the early 1780s saw famines in several locations across India, with death tolls running into the millions and leaving some regions entirely depopulated.[85] While many reports commented on the lack of rain and the effects this had on food production, non-climatic factors, most notably hostilities and warfare in southern and western India and the resulting reduction in the area of land under cultivation because of the diversion of manpower were significant. So too was the fact that crops were deliberately burned on several occasions as intentional acts of aggravation. All this heightened risk by reducing margins of error to the point that populations were left highly exposed to weather and food shocks.[86]

There were other occasions where something similar happened. For example, in Japan, a poor harvest in 1782 was followed by four years of failure that were made worse by the eruption of Mount Asama, which covered with volcanic ash a large part of the major food-producing Kanto plain surrounding the shogun's administrative capital at Edo. Some domains reported no harvest at all.[87] Ash made its way into the waterways, adding to silt build-up that was already a labour-intensive chore for villagers to deal with; now it proved deadly.[88]

As people were reduced to eating horses, cats and grass, hunger and disease took hold, resulting in a million deaths in the space of little more than four years. This led to a chronic shortage of labour, as was made clear by the fact that in the twenty years after the so-called Tenmei famine wages rose by 500 per cent while rice prices essentially remained stable.[89] The eruptions and poor weather were the straw that broke the camel's back in a finely balanced relationship that had led agricultural exploitation to develop to the edge of its ecological margin. Too much depended on harvests delivering anticipated yields and on waterways working as expected. Relatively modest alterations to both left vast populations at risk of hunger, disease – and death.

In Egypt, climate shock in the late eighteenth century triggered a set of socio-economic and political changes that had been brewing for years, decades even. Since the 1760s, local elites in the Ottoman province had grown increasingly assertive in their relationship with the central authorities, successfully building up their landholdings, not least through control over tax collection – where the incentives were to collect as much as possible from the population and pass on as little as possible to the state. Indeed, by the 1770s, they had established power bases that were not so much independent of the Ottoman empire as competing with it, sending private militias into Ottoman Syria in attempts to boost their influence and their fortunes further.[90]

The high-pressure anomaly of 1783 and the effects of the Laki eruptions deepened these existing problems. The failure of the Nile floods, which reduced irrigation by almost 20 per cent, sparked an intense period of drought, famine and poor yields. One chronicler wrote that the 'grain became scarce ... the price of wheat was on the loose ... and the poor suffered greatly from hunger'. Others commented on the lawlessness, violence and banditry which rose as shortages were accompanied by outbreaks of disease. The rich seized the opportunity to further their dominance, no doubt in part driven by their anxiety to protect their falling incomes during a time of uncertainty. This in turn reinforced determination in Constantinople to cut rapacious magnates down to size and restore control over the empire's wealthiest province.[91]

Plans were drawn up for a military occupation of Egypt that was designed to weaken the elites, depose the Mamluk emirs and impose tighter supervision over the provincial administration. A powerful force dispatched in 1786 under the command of Gazi Hasan Pasha, an experienced and trusted officer, met with immediate success. Before it could achieve its full objectives, however, it was recalled the following year when Catherine the Great ordered Russian forces to begin an offensive in the Black Sea and annexed Crimea. Ottoman efforts to push back the Russians came to nothing, as did the best-laid plans in Egypt, where as one leading scholar puts it, 'defiant rural leaders returned and quickly picked up where they had left off – embedding a system of 'crony politics that would shape Egypt for at least the next 150 years'.[92]

Some locations, in contrast, benefited from the climatic upheavals. Evidence from the region between the Niger Bend and the various parts of the Voltas in Burkina Faso and Ghana suggests a period of wet conditions, as does the fact that Lake Chad and Lake Ngami in what is now Botswana rose to very high levels in the 1780s. Of course, heavy rains present problems of their own, causing waterlogging of fields and rough seas, as seems to have happened on the Guinea coast in the early 1780s, a decade which tree-ring data from South Africa indicates was the wettest decade for 200 years.[93]

These upheavals were soon followed in 1789–93 by what has been referred to as a 'mega-Niño', an episode so strong that it has only occurred a handful of times in the last two millennia.[92] Recent scholarship that draws on climatological records from the western Pacific suggests that the event was in fact a very strong La Niña event from 1788–90 which flipped to a strong El Niño event that lasted from 1791 to 1794.[94] This was a global reorganisation of weather systems that had global consequences, some of them long-lasting, some dramatic and some both.

Cold and wet conditions made settlement of south-east Australia by the British precarious. Officials appointed to set up a new administration in Sydney commented on the inclement, tempestuous weather that made life difficult. It was almost impossible to produce bricks because of the driving rain and howling gales, while newly created roads were all but impassable. 'The rain came down in torrents, filling up every trench and cavity which had been dug about the settlement,' wrote one observer, 'causing much damage to the miserable mud tenements' that had been built by convicts shipped out to help build what looked like an unpromising new world.[95]

The loss at sea of a crucial provisioning ship not only devastated morale further still, but led to the introduction both of drastic rationing and of martial law. Finally, in September 1790, conditions seemed to be improving – only for the rains to stop and be replaced by heatwaves which were compared to the 'blast of a heated oven'. It was again all but impossible to grow food, because of the lack of precipitation. By November 1791, water restrictions were introduced, with the only source of natural water a small freshwater stream that ran into Sydney Cove. The project of colonising Australia was looking like an act of folly – until benign and stable conditions finally settled around the middle of 1794. But it had been touch and go whether it was even worth trying to make a success of it.[96]

As it happened, the rainy conditions of the late 1780s in Oceania and the Pacific helped preserve a totemic moment in history. Captain William Bligh and a handful of sailors had been cast into an open boat after mutineers took control of HMS *Bounty*, a Royal Navy vessel that had been sent into the South Pacific on a botanical mission. In the diary he kept during the long trip at sea that followed, Bligh commented not only on the cold but also on the regular rainfall that allowed stocks of water to be maintained. This was vital in helping Bligh eventually reach safety – and therefore in the story of the mutiny becoming one of the best-known episodes in history. In a normal year, notes one scholar, survival would likely have been impossible, and the story would have been one of 'the disappearance of Captain Bligh and the *Bounty*', or just another unremarkable case of a ship lost at sea, in other words.[97]

The effects of the climate upheavals in other parts of the world affected rather more people than the escapades of a handful of British sailors. In India, so many died in a famine that struck in 1791 that it became known in folklore in Bijapur as the *Doji bara* or the 'skull famine', because so many bones of unburied victims could be found lying by the side of roads; census figures from the Madras Presidency, from Andhra Pradesh, from Hyderabad, the Deccan and elsewhere give a frightening sense of the scale of mortality, once more measuring in the millions.[98]

Prolonged drought in Natal and Zululand that started in 1789 brought about the Mahlatule famine (literally 'the time we were forced to eat grass'), the most severe episode known before the mid-nineteenth century, which nonetheless served as a springboard for the reorganisation and consolidation of political control that strengthened and accelerated the rise of the Zulu kingdom.[99] In North America, a period of mild, dry winters helped spur migrations of indigenous peoples including the Cree, Blackfeet and Gros Ventre, perhaps because higher than normal temperatures expanded the pasture available for horses: this led to increases in herd size and created competition for the best grazing lands. But there were challenges too that resulted from smallpox outbreaks and from shifts in the bison population which scattered in the face of climate factors and diminished as a result of epidemic bovine disease.[100]

On the eastern seaboard, meanwhile, pronounced warming enlarged the tropical range of the *Aedes aegypti* mosquito, resulting in outbreaks of yellow fever as far north as Philadelphia. This sparked an important division between political parties in the newly independent United States, with the newly formed Federalists and Republicans blaming each other for the outbreak. The former party argued that weak immigration policy had enabled the disease to be brought from Haiti, while the latter blamed Philadelphia's poor hygiene, bad governance and worse morals. Among other things, the dispute put pressure on elected officials to act swiftly to show their competence, leading to new approaches to investment in civic infrastructure, in emergency relief and in improving the quality of medical care.[101]

In Europe, change was in the air. A cold and hard winter in France in 1787–8 had been followed by a late and wet spring that led to grain prices rising by 50 per cent – an upsurge that proved crushing for the peasantry and had knock-on effects for the wider economy: as food costs soared, sales of wine fell sharply as financial resources were used to buy bread. By the summer of 1788, unrest was building across the country, with small-scale uprisings and shows of dissent in regions that had been badly hit, such as Provence, Picardy, Brittany, Franche-Comté,

Languedoc and Poitou. Bad storms that brought hailstones large enough to kill hares and knock partridges out of trees did further damage to vines and to wheatfields. Things were so bad that it was estimated that one in five people in Paris alone were dependent on charitable relief to survive.[102]

The French King, Louis XVI, took steps to try to calm the situation, sending out calls for the people of his kingdom to draw up *cahiers* of complaints and grievances and to present them in Paris. In just three months in early 1789, over 25,000 documents were prepared – a clear indication of the scale of the problems that were brewing. Steps were taken in the winter of 1788 to address food shortages by offering trade privileges for American flour imports, including exemptions from freight duties, as well as agreed premium prices – concessions that were extended in April 1789. As one historian has put it, 'the urban merchant's windfall was the frontier settler's despair': grain being shipped across the Atlantic was a godsend for growers, traders and shippers, but bad news for local populations who were faced with shortfalls and higher prices – if not both.[103]

The fact that the late 1780s had seen a surge in migrations to frontier communities in New York, Vermont and Pennsylvania put further pressure on grain supplies, made worse by a bitterly cold winter and warnings of poor harvests. As one newspaper in Vermont put it at the start of June 1789, 'The great want of that necessary article BREAD ... will be more severely felt the next season than it is the present.'[104] By this time, acts of resistance and defiance had become commonplace in France. These ranged from petty breakdowns such as poaching to more violent protests such as the Réveillon riots in April 1789 which served as a sign of things to come. Leaflets were circulated such as 'What No One Has Yet Said' which declared that the authorities were failing in their primary duty of ensuring there was enough bread for all. Another, 'Four Cries of a Patriot of the Nation', put it more bluntly. Citizens needed to be armed, immediately; and aristocrats should be banished. What was the point of 'preaching peace and liberty to men dying of hunger? What use would a wise constitution be to a people of skeletons?'[105]

The French revolution set fire to Europe and much of the world beyond. In the years that followed the storming of the Bastille on 14 July 1789, France re-emerged not as an egalitarian kingdom but as a putative empire, with ambitions in Egypt and India, to say nothing of a series of spectacular military victories that made Napoleon Bonaparte the master of much of continental Europe. There were reverberations beyond too – including revolution in 1791 in Saint-Domingue (Haiti) which was followed by independence.

France's failure to retake the island, its most profitable colony, owed much to the organisational skills and charismatic leadership of Toussaint Louverture and to the determination of Haiti's inhabitants to pursue 'liberté, égalité and fraternité' for themselves. It owed something too, however, to the yellow fever that devastated a force sent by France to reimpose authority. The failure to retake a colony that was the most valuable real estate in the world at the time, that produced much of the world's sugar and coffee and that was responsible for 40 per cent of France's foreign trade was devastating, and led to the panic sale of Louisiana to the United States to raise much-needed funds to pay for ongoing and constant military operations in Europe.[106] This changed the political landscape of global geopolitics: it shifted the gaze of the newly independent US to the south and to the west. In doing so, it opened the doors to the conquest of a large part of the continent of North America.

Ironically, France's turmoil provided Britain with several shots in the arm. The violence of revolution as well as the upheavals that started to engulf Europe soon afterwards, even before the rise of Napoleon, served to make Britain in general and London in particular a magnet for talent from all over. Skills, capital and connections descended on London from the Low Countries, Germany and of course France itself. As one historian has elegantly put it, new arrivals were like bees bringing pollen with them to produce new blooms and, in doing so, to germinate Britain's industrial take-off.[107] Such were the unforeseen consequences of major shifts in politics, ideas and climatic change.

19

Industry, Extraction and the Natural World
(c.1800–c.1870)

Fog everywhere. Fog up the river where it flows among green airs and meadows; fog down the river, where it rolls defiled among the tiers of shipping, and the waterside pollutions of a great (and dirty) city.

Charles Dickens, *Bleak House* (1853)

Engagement with new parts of the world spurred some to take a deeper interest in what could be learned from geography, from history and from science. Writing in the middle of the eighteenth century, the philosopher David Hume considered what the authors Horace, Juvenal and Diodorus Siculus had said about the weather and climate in Rome as well as elsewhere in the empire. It would have been preferable, he notes, 'had the ancients known the use of thermometers'. Nevertheless, comparing the accounts with the present day, it is reasonable to conclude that 'the winters are now much more temperate at Rome than formerly'.[1]

In Hume's own time, he wrote, the Tiber froze about as often as the River Nile – never, in other words. Likewise, Ovid's description of the Black Sea freezing every year either spoke of a very different climate, or reveals that Ovid was lying. There was only one explanation, concluded Hume. 'Plainly', he said, human activity was responsible for causing the planet to warm. This must have been done, he went on, primarily through deforestation and the cutting down of trees 'which formerly threw a shade upon the earth, and kept the rays of the sun from penetrating it'.[2]

The question of man-made climate change was one that preoccupied many settlers in the colonies in North America, including several of the Founding Fathers. In the 1760s, Benjamin Franklin wrote to Ezra Stiles, later President of Yale, stating that temperatures were becoming milder as a result of deforestation. 'When a Country is clear'd of Woods,' he said, 'the Sun acts more strongly on the Face of the Earth.' Solar warmth 'melts great Snows sooner than they could be melted if they were shaded by the Trees'. While a 'regular and steady Course of Observations' would be needed across multiple years and taking measurements from several parts of the country to confirm it, Franklin was persuaded that real changes were happening – and that human activity was responsible.[3]

Franklin reported in the same letter that he had recently been in England where he had visited Cambridge to compare notes with John Hadley, the Professor of Chemistry. Contacts such as these were a by-product of fast-expanding global trade networks and a new age of information-gathering from around the world as Europeans began to translate voyages of discovery into extensive commercial contacts and into regional dominance and colonialism. While trade, political and military priorities had led the way, science and scientists had sometimes followed hand in hand and had sometimes done so soon afterwards, supported by rising levels of wealth that funded scholarships and academic institutions and encouraged individual curiosity.

In 1768, for example, Captain James Cook was commissioned by the Admiralty to undertake a voyage to the Pacific Ocean, with the aim of tracking the transit of Venus across the sun the following year. Missions like this were commendable, Samuel Johnson had written two decades earlier, because unlike expeditions which set off with 'intent like merchants' to trade, or had military ambitions, they were motivated solely by the joy of knowledge for knowledge's sake.[4] Such sentiments sounded reassuring, noble even. But they masked the fact that those leading the expeditions, like Cook, often had other motives too: in this case Cook was also given secret orders to search the South Pacific for a southern continent whose existence had been much speculated on and whose discovery was considered a matter of signal strategic importance to Britain and its global interests.[5]

The question of the weather, of climate and of changing conditions dominated the minds of some. Thomas Jefferson had an obsessive interest, starting a diary on 1 July 1776 just as he was drafting the Declaration of Independence, and recording two temperature readings per day for the next fifty years. Indeed, on the morning of 4 July, the day that America's independence from Britain was declared, Jefferson visited Sparhawk's stationery store in Philadelphia to buy himself a new thermometer.[6] We know from his diary that as the Declaration itself was being delivered to Congress, he was busy recording that the ambient temperature was 72.5 °F.[7] As the United States was being born, one of its principal architects was thinking about humidity and atmospheric pressure. He was presumably not entirely happy, at least about the tools at his disposal, for the day after independence he went back to Sparhawk's to buy a barometer so that his findings could be even more accurate.[8]

One of Jefferson's pet theories was about the changing climate in North America in the late eighteenth century. Summarising in a book his 'data for estimating the climate of Virginia', he set out observations about sudden temperature changes, frosts and the impact on plant and animal life. This led him to conclude that 'A change in our climate … is taking place very sensibly. Both heats and colds are become much more moderate within the memory even of the middle-aged. Snows are less frequent and less deep,' and while 'The elderly inform me the earth used to be covered with snow for about three months in every year,' it no longer was – and nor did rivers freeze often, as they used to.[9]

Jefferson's views chimed with the prevailing wisdom among scholars in North America that the climate was changing rapidly. Hugh Williamson of Harvard had written almost twenty years earlier that 'our winters are not so intensely cold, nor our summers so disagreeably warm'. This was due to land-use change from forest to open fields, which gave the earth a hard smooth surface, and rather as 'the face of a looking glass or any polished metal will reflect more light and heat' the result was a warming of the land and of the temperature. This was good news for the future, he said: 'clearing the country will mitigate the cold of our winters [and] it will also increase the heat of our summers'. As soon as trees had been felled, 'we shall seldom be visited by frosts or snows'.[10] Climate change was 'so rapid and constant', agreed Samuel Williams in 1794, that 'it is the subject of common observation and experience'. Not only that, he added, but it could be observed 'in every part of the United States'. There was no scope for this to be 'a matter of doubt'; rather, it was a matter of fact.[11]

That was all nonsense, retorted Noah Webster, who is best known for his famous dictionary. Webster took issue both with such statements and with the supporting evidence. 'Mr Jefferson seems to have no authority for his opinions' other than 'the observations of elderly and middle-aged people', he said, adding that there was plenty of evidence to suggest that climates had not changed. The claims by men like Williams that temperatures had risen by ten to twelve degrees in the last century and a half were implausible and should lead any rational commentator to conclude that such views depended on 'insurmountable difficulties' and were quite unreliable.[12]

This was less a case of climate-change denial than a demand for rigorous scholarship to back up claims properly. As it was, competing views had already developed that set out entirely the opposite hypothesis – namely that the earth was cooling. One pioneer was the Comte de Buffon, who looked into questions like the locations of oceans and continents, sea-level changes and the formation of mountains. Widely read in the second half of the eighteenth century, Buffon proposed not only that the earth had been getting colder since its creation, but that it would keep on doing so. Draining marshes, deforestation and urbanisation had certainly helped raise temperatures, but ultimately little would stop an inevitable freeze.[13]

For some, the worry was less about warming and cooling than about the problems of rising populations and the pressure of food shortages, a topic that had generated considerable discussion since the 1770s when the Bengal famine, outbreaks of wheat infestations by the Hessian fly, hurricanes in the Caribbean, the American War of Independence and a run of bad harvests in Britain and Ireland all raised fears about the impact on the poor, about the viability of the colonies and about the potential for disaster in the future.

In 1798, Thomas Malthus published a gloomy tract *On the Principle of Population*. The power of population, he wrote, 'is so superior to the power of the earth to produce subsistence for man, that premature death must in some shape or other visit the human race'. The more people were alive, the greater the difficulty in producing enough food for them all. Fortunately, he went on, such are 'the vices of mankind' that humans were often the best source of population control, most notably through fighting wars that brought death to many and served as a cap on the number of those consuming resources. Inevitably, however, this would not always work – for 'Man cannot live in the midst of plenty.' As a result, the spectre of 'gigantic inevitable famine' loomed large to resolve competition between the total available 'food of the world' and the number of people living in it.[14]

Such concerns led Sir John Banks, President of the Royal Society, to investigate ways of making warm climate plants and crops frost resistant. This was a task that gained additional urgency in the light of scientists' conviction that the world was going through a pronounced phase of climatic change, although it was a matter of disagreement whether the problem was one of cooling or warming. It was 'unquestionable', wrote the Scottish chemist John Leslie in 1804, 'that the climate, over the whole of Europe, has assumed a milder character'. It was clear, he argued, that 'our earth must grow continually warmer' thanks to the sun's rays. There could be little doubting, he added, that the climate of central and northern Europe 'has gradually become milder', for natural reasons. This had nothing to do with human activities. If it did, then the role was a marginal and peripheral one: anthropogenic activities 'have no influence whatever in altering the average of temperature'.[15]

Scholars like Harvard Professor Samuel Williams were not so sure: Williams suggested that 'the heat of the earth has been gradually increasing' as a result of colonisation and human-inspired ecological change in New England. If this was true, argued others like the influential Buffon, then it was an anomaly that would pass: the clear trend was towards cooling that would eventually cause the planet to freeze.[16]

Hypotheses and disagreements like these were in part a reflection of the awareness and realities of a rapidly changing world. The first decades of the nineteenth century saw a series of profound technological, political, socio-economic and ecological shifts that remoulded geographies, accelerated exchanges of goods and people and transformed landscapes in ways that were both dramatic and rapid. This was an age of scientific discovery and of the dissemination of information, an age of the creation, expansion and enhancement of transport, trade and communication networks, a time when improvements in communication and transportation were developed and rolled out, a time when productivity shot up as a set of industrial and scientific revolutions bore fruit.

These changes had the greatest impact in Europe, a world that in the late eighteenth century was 'shaped by bereavement, peopled with orphans and widows', where half of all children died before the age of ten and only one in ten people reached the age of sixty. Harvest failure, famine and epidemic disease were commonplace, all aggravated by squalid conditions in towns and cities where mortality rates were so high that there was constant demand for people to migrate from the countryside.[17]

Part of the stimulus for change came from the military revolutions that transformed battlefield tactics as well as from the demand for manpower by states that became increasingly centralised as a result. In the early eighteenth century, the number of casualties in even major battles in Europe amounted to a few hundred, and rarely much more than that. With soldiers carrying enough ammunition for about fifteen or twenty minutes of fire, and at a slow rate of discharge, army sizes were modest, as were levels of training. By the end of the century, however, firefights could last many hours – and the number of dead and wounded typically ran into the tens of thousands.[18] Around 1.7 million men (and a few women) who served in the French armies between 1798 and 1815 died, with a large proportion not killed in battle but dying as a result of injuries, infection or disease.[19]

Britain was able to mass-produce weapons and ammunition – helped by control of the saltpetre of Bengal and Bihar, by far the richest in the world, which produced vast quantities of nitrates, the essential ingredient in gunpowder. In the years 1808–11, during the height of the Napoleonic Wars, the British were able to supply 336,000 muskets, 100,000 pistols and 60 million cartridges to help Spanish guerrillas opposed to Napoleon, to say nothing of the production of weapons, cannon and ordnance for use by British forces in their own campaigns.[20]

The Napoleonic Wars had another curious effect too: the demand for manpower to serve in Britain's armed forces against the French produced labour shortages as men were recruited to fight, with estimated 350,000 men under arms at the peak of the conflict. Towns and regions where recruitment was heaviest prompted adoption of, investment in and improvement of labour-saving technologies – such as threshing machines. This produced long-term socio-economic benefits, even after peace returned to Europe in 1815.[21]

The enhanced role of the state created demands for higher levels of political participation, a mood that reached crisis point at St Peter's Field in Manchester in August 1819, when a crowd of perhaps 60,000 gathered to protest against the lack of parliamentary representation; this was a time when voting was a right confined to the elites, with just over 10 per cent of adult men (and no women) being allowed to vote in elections, which in some cases were not even held regularly. Magistrates called in troops, who brutally broke up the protests with a cavalry charge that resulted in deaths and many casualties. Soon known as the Peterloo Massacre, the event became notorious for the use of force against unarmed demonstrators.[22]

The demand for reform was driven by a number of factors, including economic stagnation and unemployment stemming from a conclusion to almost two decades of constant warfare after the defeat of Napoleon at the battle of Waterloo four years earlier. But depressed climatic conditions also played a role in disrupting harvests, creating price shocks that led to the cost of grain doubling and to poverty deepening across much of Europe and elsewhere around this time. In the winter of 1816–17, noted a leading newspaper in Manchester not long afterwards, workers in large manufacturing towns were without work and desperately short of food. Parishes gave what they could, but this bore no comparison to what was needed. As one influential newspaper at the time put it, Britain was 'a nation supplicating for bread – a people sinking for want of food'.[23]

This stemmed in part from measures adopted by the government following the end of the Napoleonic Wars which served to benefit landowners and the wealthy. One was the abolition of wartime income tax; another was the introduction of the Corn Laws that imposed a ban on the import of grain, which inevitably drove prices upwards and dragged people deeper into poverty.[24]

Another cause of problems, though, lay on the other side of the world. This was Mount Tambora in what is now Indonesia, whose eruption on the evening of April 1815 is the largest of the last ten thousand years. The effects locally were devastating as tens of cubic kilometres of magma were spewed out and ejected as much as forty-three kilometres into the atmosphere, while the explosions were heard 2,000 kilometres away. A tsunami fanned out, with some reports of waves as high as four metres devastating multiple islands, including Java. As many as 120,000 people lost their lives in South-East Asia as a result of the famine and disease that followed.[25]

In the three years before Tambora erupted, global temperatures had already become distinctly cooler, partly because of the eruptions of Mount Soufrière in the Caribbean and of Mount Mayon in what is now the Philippines in 1812 and 1814 respectively. If these magnified the effects of Tambora, it did not help that 1816 corresponded to an unusually weak maximum in the sunspot cycle, a phenomenon that is known to affect sea surface temperatures. The impacts around the world were so great that 1816 has become popularly known as 'the year without a summer'.[26]

The consequences were dramatic. In July 1816, *The Times* of London warned that dangers lay ahead: 'Should the present wet weather continue', the paper noted, harvests were likely to fail 'and the effects of such a calamity at such a time cannot be otherwise than ruinous to the farmers and even to the people at large.' It was a similar story in many parts of Europe, with 'melancholy accounts' being received 'from all parts of the Continent of the unusual wetness of the season; property in consequence swept away by inundation and irretrievable injuries done to the vine yards and corn crops. In several provinces of Holland, the rich grass lands are all under water, and scarcity and high prices are naturally apprehended and dreaded. In France the interior of the country has suffered greatly from the floods and heavy rains.' Mortality rates in some parts of Europe increased, most notably in Switzerland and Tuscany.[27]

It is perhaps no coincidence that a group of English writers that included Percy and Mary Shelley and Lord Byron, who were spending time in Geneva in the summer of 1816, made repeated reference to dark storms, unusual skies, violent winds and rains in their writings. Indeed, on one evening in June, the group came up with the idea of a ghost-story contest in order to entertain themselves during that long, cold summer; thus it was that Mary Shelley had the idea for *Frankenstein*, one of the most famous novels of all time, and one in which celestial anomalies, lightning strikes, thunder and storms feature prominently.[28]

A collapse in cereal crops in New England led not only to severe food shortages and price surges, but also to large-scale livestock death thanks to lack of animal feed. 'Never were such hard times,' wrote Thomas Jefferson, as people found themselves in a state of 'unparalleled distress'. It was likely, perhaps even inevitable, he wrote, that there would be local insurrections, uprisings and breakdowns of law and order as a result. Newspapers compared the situation to the biblical 'famine of Egypt', though that analogy did not allow for the scale of the financial crisis, the emotional upheaval or the abandonment of towns. One historian has even argued that Tambora was a 'primary cause of the United States' first major economic depression'.[29]

The eruption devasted other regions, such as the Indian subcontinent, where a shift in monsoon rains, a failure of trade winds and a three-year depression of the thermal cycle of South Asia not only led to major reductions in crop yields and of maritime trade, but also served to change the microbial ecology of the Bay of Bengal. In 1817, unusually early and heavy rains brought about a surge in cases of cholera that caused death on an almost unimaginable scale. The bodies of the dead and dying were gathered together, wrote one eyewitness, with funeral pyres burning non-stop to incinerate the rich and the poor, and other corpses picked over by vultures or jackals. It was 'a scene of woe which completely baffles the power of description to portray'.[30]

More than a million were estimated to have died as a result of what one report of 1820 argued was the 'distempered' state of the weather since 1815. It seems that climatic factors had indeed played a decisive role: changes in water temperature and salinity supported zooplankton that serves as cholera's main aquatic host, while unusual and unseasonal flooding served as the source of the bacterium's nutrients, at the same time delivering the pathogen into the water system of coastal regions. This was almost uniquely dangerous in Bengal because of the low-lying land in the river delta.[31]

While assessing how many people died involves wide margins of error, another indication of the devastation it caused can be seen in the widespread panic within affected communities, with large numbers of towns being depopulated as people fled. Some took to traditional methods of salvation, turning for protection to deities such as Kali and Ola Bibi, whose cult grew quickly around this time. Although climate had a role in the prevalence of cholera, diet, sanitation and hygiene were even more important factors, since cholera was above all a disease of poverty.[32] By the early 1820s, cholera had spread by land and sea through South-East Asia to China and Japan and westwards to Persia and Russia, and then on to Europe, where it took hold at the start of the 1830s.[33]

Disease, poverty and limited employment prospects all played a role in driving waves of migration from Europe. The end of the Napoleonic Wars meant that the job market was inundated with 200,000 demobilised soldiers at a time when massive government contracts to provide supplies to the military of everything from uniforms to musket balls to ropes to canvas for ships were scaled back or abandoned altogether.[34] Appetites for better futures were ravenous: a British government scheme for settlement in South Africa was set up in a bid to attract 4,000 people willing to move continent to settle in the Albany district of the eastern Cape; more than 80,000 submitted applications.[35]

This was not to say that all greeted the arrival of newcomers with glee. George Washington, the first President of the United States, was scornful of the quality of those who reached the shores of North America in search of better lives. They were nothing more than 'banditti who will bid defiance to all authority', 'worthless fellows' and a bunch of 'savages'.[36] From the point of view of those facing a protracted depression in Europe, the prospect of moving to start a new life elsewhere was an increasingly attractive one, especially in lands where new opportunities were opening up and infrastructure and facilities were constantly being improved, such as in the United States, where more and more steamboats plying the great rivers created new networks, cheaper transportation and the prospect not only of wealth but of freedom too.[37]

The numbers of those leaving the British Isles accelerated sharply. Between 1790 and 1815, around 180,000 emigrated from England, Scotland and Wales.[38] In the three decades that followed, numbers swelled dramatically, followed by a series of surges in the second half of the nineteenth century. In the seventy years after 1850, some 45 million people migrated from the Old to the New World.[39] This proved crucial for the development of the Americas as a whole, with new arrivals not only serving as fresh pools of labour, but bringing with them ideas, knowledge, cultures, genes, institutions and languages that helped promote rapid socio-economic and political development.[40] It spurred change in Europe too, with the mass exodus reducing the size of the workforce, thereby driving up wages and offering further rewards for innovation, mechanisation and industrialisation.[41]

Reports were sent back home that talked not only of opportunities in new lands, but of freedoms. As Joseph Hollingworth, a recent arrival in North America in the 1820s, put it in a letter to his relatives in Huddersfield, 'in this country there are no Lords, nor Dukes, nor Counts, nor Marquises, nor Earls, nor Royal Family to support nor no King'. Not only that, there was no sign of poverty. 'I have never seen in this Country a Beggar such as I used Daily to see in England,' and, perhaps better still, no sign of a tax collector 'taking the last penny out of the poor Mans Pocket'. It was a wonder too that the President of the United States began speeches by addressing not 'My Lords and Gentlemen' but his 'Fellow Citizens'. This was a place of dreams, remarked Hollingworth, and turning to what he called 'Old English poetry', described his new homeland as 'A land where tyranny is no more / Where we can all be free.'[42]

Underpinning such notions of freedom was a variety of expansive ideas about nature, about ecological transformation, about 'improvement' of virgin lands – and about the displacement of those who already lived there. Indigenous populations, commonly lumped together and referred to as 'Indians', were routinely dismissed as 'citizens of an inferior order' – like Jews, Gypsies, enslaved people and 'free negroes'. Native peoples were 'the very filth of civilized society', opined some, worthy to be 'left to the rapacity of noxious vermin'; it was only a matter of time before they would end in 'total extermination'. In any event, it seemed obvious to many that the lands where they hunted, farmed and subsisted should be taken over by settlers. This would involve displacing existing communities, since, as one commentator claimed, 'if any thing is certain', it is that 'savage and civilised man cannot live together'.[43]

Views like this prompted discussions about mass deportations and in due course led to government policy and legislation that expelled Chickasaw, Choctaw, Muscogee-Creek, Cherokee and other nations, pushing them west into what survivors called 'the Land of Death'. It has 'long been the policy of Government', said President Jackson in his State of the Union address in 1829, to introduce indigenous peoples to 'the arts of civilisation'. Such efforts had failed entirely, he said, as was clear from the fact that they had 'retained their savage habits'. The best solution, therefore, set out in the 1830 Indian Removal Act, was to encourage migration to the west – which in practice led to forcible deportation.[44] It was a 'great pity', wrote former US President Thomas Jefferson, 'and indeed a scandal that we let that race of men disappear without preserving scarcely any trace of their history', although he too argued that deportation would free up land for white labourers.[45]

It was a similar story elsewhere. In Canada, First Nations were pushed into reserves away from the best land, which was taken over by new settlers. In Australia, the 1830s and 1840s saw Europeans move inland into territories that some described with giddy excitement as being 'as green and fresh as Eden', forcing out the Wurundjeri, Boonwurrung and Walthaurong people who had managed and lived on grasslands for centuries, cutting off their access to water holes and in some cases even accusing them of trespass.[46] New Zealand was presented as a wilderness ready to be tamed and turned into a bucolic idyll by hard work and perseverance, with little or no reference to those who already lived there. New worlds were waiting to be transformed. All they needed were people – or, more precisely, the right kind of people. Europeans, in other words.

Mass migration not only dramatically changed demographics and population distribution but also reshaped the natural world. The number of settlers in Australia grew from 1,000 to 12,000 between 1790 and 1810, before climbing to 1.25 million fifty years later – a rise of more than a hundredfold. The population of Ontario rose by a multiple of twenty-three, from around 60,000 to 1.4 million, in roughly the same period – while those of Ohio, Indiana, Illinois, Michigan and Wisconsin did much the same, from just over 250,000 to 7 million in total. Similar shifts could be found in Alabama, Mississippi, Arkansas plus Missouri, Florida, Louisiana and Texas, which together grew from 150,000 to more than 4.6 million – and in the original thirteen colonies, plus Vermont and Maine, where numbers rose from 3.8 million to 15.9 million between 1791 and 1861.[47] In 1830, Chicago consisted of 'about half a dozen houses'; sixty years later, it had a population of 1.1 million.[48]

This pattern of expansion was not limited to the Americas and to the west. It was mirrored in the steppe region of the European part of the Russian empire, where the population increased more than eightfold between 1700 and 1800, almost trebled again before 1850 and then trebled again before 1914 – rising from around 380,000 to more than 25 million. Moreover, these numbers did not include the seasonal migrant labourers who came to work on farms each year. But it was not only population movements that explain the dramatic rise in numbers; so too did the high fertility levels among new settlers.[49] The abolition of serfdom in the 1860s did much to help loosen ties between the rural peasantry and the land, sending waves of those seeking new opportunities to lands that changed from being exploited as pastoral, partly nomadic economies to settled arable farming.[50]

Colonial expansion did not repeat the pattern in Qing China, where there was little enthusiasm for long-distance migration into Xinjiang,

Inner Mongolia and Manchuria – regions that offered few of the attractions or rewards promised by reshaping agricultural systems. It did not help that the lands conquered by the Qing in the late seventeenth and eighteenth centuries were remote and difficult to reach, or that there were no sea and river routes allowing the transport of bulk materials in both directions to be carried out easily and relatively cheaply. What mattered more, however, was that these lands afforded little by way of commodity frontiers that might render their exploitation attractive in the first place, and no obvious upside of converting challenging terrains into large arable landholdings that could enrich new owners and support large settlements locally. Regressive policies adopted by the Qing, in particular preventing recipients of land grants from buying or selling land, and the practice of tying labour to landholdings, created barriers that offered few incentives and even fewer opportunities.[51]

This acted as a brake on Chinese social, economic and even political development during the heady nineteenth century that saw vast empires take shape in other parts of the world. Past climatic and geological serendipity which created coal reserves were also to prove important at the start of an age of fossil fuels that in some ways is still responsible for the way the world is today. The exploitation of coal, combined with advances in technology that paved the way for the industrial revolution, helped to transform productivity in Europe. Britain in particular was blessed with coal-fields and a scientific community that developed, refined and improved the methods by which enhanced energy resources could be put to use. That included improving coal extraction, which lowered costs further still. The impact was astonishing. By 1850, some 18 million people in Britain used as much energy as 300 million in China.[52] This was a reflection of multiple factors. Most important of these, according to some historians, was rising demand – which in turn reflected new and evolving ways in which energy could be used.[53]

The scale of such demand was impressive. In Britain, coal production doubled between 1815 and 1830.[54] In this sense, the distribution and location of coal deposits proved extremely providential for Britain. Much turned on the location of coal-fields. While China matched Europe in its living standards, its sophisticated and commercialised agriculture, its vibrant scientific community and its advanced print culture, its coal-fields were a long way from population centres in general, and from the densely populated Yangtze Delta that was the heartland of manufacturing and production in particular.[55]

Coal-fields in Britain – above all in Northumberland and Durham – were far closer to towns and cities, where there were high energy demands. Indeed, the availability of coal spurred the growth of cities which could attract cheap labour and were either connected to new canal systems or located on the coast. Manchester and Birmingham were two obvious beneficiaries; so were Glasgow and Liverpool, whose population rose by nineteen times during the course of the eighteenth century.[56]

Part of the success of provincial cities was because transportation costs for large volumes of bulky coal were high: the cost of coal in Newcastle, for example, was one-eighth of what it was in London. Coal was important not only as a source of cheap energy, however, but also because it spurred immediate and major gains in productivity, most notably thanks to the steam engine and the railway, which combined to connect locations together and to lower the costs of transport and of exchange while increasing their speed.[57] It helped too that there was an enhanced ability and interest in supporting research and the development of new technologies which ensured ever greater efficiency thanks to profits from overseas trade that created a pool of capital looking for returns.[58]

The bondage of other human beings was crucial in this regard: what mattered above all was not the purchase and sale of enslaved peoples, but rather the fruits of their labour in the form of sugar, tobacco, coffee and cotton. As new research shows, not only would Britain have been substantially poorer and more agricultural in the absence of slave wealth, but it also benefited from the proceeds of slavery being invested in other businesses and technology. In other words, it could be argued those who toiled in servitude provided the fuel that accelerated the industrial revolution in Britain.[59]

Taken together, pools of capital, new ideas and technologies helped drive urbanisation and the growth of London in particular, which stimulated the growth of the coal trade and in doing so helped seed towns close to mines that needed manpower and capital, offered financial rewards to investors and encouraged consumption in new locations too. This powered a housebuilding boom that was accompanied by changes in living habits and architectural styles, requiring 'an entirely new style of house' as heating with coal replaced burning of wood.[60]

In China, in contrast, regions with lower resources and worse soils were the ones that saw the most rapid demographic growth – which exacerbated strains on resources rather than alleviating or solving them.[61] This too marked a different trajectory to Europe, where the creation of colonies overseas had created networks of extraction that funnelled resources from one continent to another. As we have seen, some commodities that were highly prized were cash crops, like sugar, cotton and tobacco; but there were real needs for more mundane materials too, including a number that were bulky and expensive to move. For example, by 1650, perhaps as much as 200,000 hectares of forest land had been cut down in Europe – around 40 per cent of the entire area. Almost the same again was cleared between 1750 and 1850. This was a process of land being repurposed for other uses, and also a reflection of unsustainable consumption patterns. The answer was to look to sources abroad.

One key area was the Baltic, which had long serviced the timber needs of western Europe. Mature trees needed for ships and large buildings took a hundred and twenty years to grow; moreover, substantial volumes were required: a single galleon required two thousand oaks, or around twenty hectares of forest. These needs had been instrumental in opening up trade into the Baltic and stimulating the success of the towns of the Hanseatic league that were dotted around the coast of the North and Baltic seas.[62] With industrialisation taking off, demand now rose sharply: imports of wood climbed from 2.5 million cubic metres in 1850 to 15.5 million cubic metres seventy years later, with wood-pulp imports rising even more steeply in the same period.[63]

Fundamental to the extraction of resources were radical ideas about nature, about land and about the right to remodel the environment in whatever way they wished and thought best. The natural world became something to be tamed and defeated, a notion fuelled by the conviction that human ingenuity, hard work and new tools could now shape and repurpose ecologies better and faster than ever before. Many scholars tie these attitudes directly to Europe and European religious, cultural and philosophical sensibilities. Hegel was dismissive about the way that East Asians engaged with nature and suggested that their cosmological frameworks prevented them from thinking in abstract terms or freely. His view of Africans as exemplifying 'natural man in his completely wild and untamed states' also captured the supremacist sentiment that it was for Europeans to inherit the earth, and that other races were not only inferior but unworthy and incapable of doing so. For Hegel, then, the urge to 'do violence' to nature was an aggressive statement that reflected emerging mainstream ideas, bundling whiteness, power and entitlement into a toxic framework that set Europeans at the apex of humankind and of all living animals and plants.[64]

Nature became something to be not only exploited but defeated as standing in the way of human progress. As one American engineer modestly put it when proposing the construction of a canal between the Black and Caspian seas that would supposedly double the size of the latter, change rainfall patterns and improve the soil fertility of the steppes, schemes such as this would represent 'a great triumph of a nation over Nature' which 'would be far the greatest conquest in the annals of human material progress'.[65] His scheme would restore desert lands to 'their primaeval condition, as the abode of countless millions of men and beasts'. This was important, noted one contemporary commentator, because 'the world is none too large for its present population'. Stopping the advance of nature was essential; anyone who could help do so 'will be a benefactor of his race'.[66]

Not everyone was convinced that human activity was positive and some instead worried about sustainability and about the long-term damage that was done to the environment. Alexander von Humboldt was concerned about the combination of deforestation and the increase in irrigated agriculture that turned plains into deserts. 'By the felling of trees that cover the tops and sides of mountains,' he noted, 'men in every climate prepare at once two calamities for future generations; the want of fuel and a scarcity of water.'[67]

Humboldt was hardly alone in his concern about or his awareness of the link between deforestation and aridity, which was known, as one leading historian puts it, by 'every literate person' in the nineteenth century.[68] New regions brought wealth to some and disappointment to others, observed one English visitor to Australia. Though 'Anglo-Saxon energy at last triumphs over every obstacle', this victory came at a cost: 'Nature, as if offended, withdraws her beauty from the land; the pasture gradually loses its freshness, some of the rivers and lakes run low, others become wholly dry.' Wild animals 'are no more to be found'.[69]

* * *

Anxiety about the effects of deforestation became part of mainstream scholarship – and policy. In Russia, measures to promote the conservation of forests were put in place as early as 1802, with the Ministry of State Domains establishing a forestry corps to oversee protection.[70] In due course, efforts were made to gather information about pre-existing territories and about the large swathes of land in Siberia and Central Asia which were brought under imperial control from the middle of the century. Russian scientists and landowners became increasingly concerned about rising aridity and intense and worryingly regular droughts. Many had read the works being written in the United States and in Europe and picked up on the theme of deforestation as a cause of changing climate. Cutting down trees had exposed the land in southern Russia to the easterly winds, reported a survey in the early 1840s, noting that this 'must be the main cause of the disastrous impact of droughts which have been intensifying recently'.[71]

Although the Valuev Commission, which published its findings in 1873, stated that the climate had become 'more severe and drier' thanks to land being cleared, not everyone was convinced either that this was the case or that human activity could influence climate in the first place. Senior military officers who surveyed the empire's provinces complained that ideas about changing climate were more often than not based on anecdotal evidence and on comments made by members of the local population that were of doubtful reliability.[72] Nevertheless, the common view was that the climate on the steppes was changing, and for the worse; to help understand how and why, networks of weather-measuring stations were set up across the empire, to try to build a coherent picture that relied on data rather than opinions.[73]

Similar concerns were being raised elsewhere. In Mexico, the polymath Michel Chevalier considered how to develop the economy of Mexico after it had been taken over by France in the 1860s. One of the principal problems, he argued, was that a place that had once been a veritable Eden had been turned into a 'barren and desolate wasteland' by overexploitation by the Spanish. Deforestation had been catastrophic, he wrote, not only because it led to spells of aridity and changing patterns of precipitation, but because the land had been starved of nutrients, depleting its productivity. This naturally had an impact on the diet and poverty of the local population – and led in turn to falls in productivity and competitiveness, to economic distress and to political instability. The answer, for Chevalier, was to look at 'the extent to which the country could be reforested'.[74]

Protecting forests and indeed replanting trees became a central part of British colonial policy – starting with India and the Charter of Indian Forestry, which annexed all forests that were not privately owned and declared them to be state property. Similar measures soon followed in Australia, Canada and Africa, where 'large tracts of the country' were said to be drying up as a result of too many trees being felled. Despite the claims of some scholars, the motivations of the authorities in taking control of forests had little to do with conservation: in fact, what was at stake was that colonial authorities insisted on exploiting timber resources that were vital to the extension of political and economic control. The consequences for peoples who lived in the forests – and who had done so for many generations – were disastrous.[75]

Though some raised concerns, the reality was that deforestation continued at a staggering rate in the nineteenth century and beyond. Between 1850 and 1920, around 152 million hectares of the world's tropical forests were converted to grasslands, almost two-thirds of which (some 94 million hectares) were in sub-Saharan Africa and South and South-East Asia – that is to say, in the heartlands of colonial expansion.[76] Ironically, when it came to rationalising change, the standard narrative was that local populations were poor guardians of nature and were primitive in their approach to agriculture and that the development of new landscapes was not only to their benefit but beyond their capabilities. Such claims, of course, were untrue.[77]

From 1750 to 1900, around 600,000 to 800,000 hectares of the world's most fertile arable land were opened up for exploitation. Newly settled regions in the Americas, Australia, New Zealand and southern Africa became important sources of wool, meat and grain and among the largest producing regions in the world. This was not just the result of those hunting for land and scouting for prospects, but also a function of the predatory use of claims to legal possession and land title and by insistence on the importance of 'improvement' of land and nature, which gave incomers the 'right' to take control of territory.[78] In many cases, such as in India, colonial administrations simply asserted – and enshrined that assertion in law – that all uncultivated land belonged to the state. This too was an aspect of the widely held assumptions that indigenous peoples were ignorant and careless and adopted policies that ruined forests. The British saw themselves as guardians of the environment who needed to protect the natural world from the predations and practices of peoples who had lived there for centuries and even millennia.[79]

In time, ideas like this were carried further still – namely, not only taking control of land but pushing people off it altogether. National parks established at Yellowstone in the United States, Banff in Canada and Tongariro in New Zealand in the 1870s and 1880s were based on the idea that, to protect nature, human beings needed to be excluded entirely, even if that meant forcible displacement.[80] In some cases, this led to violent protest, as in German East Africa where orders to protect forests granted the right to expel inhabitants from newly created reserves.[81]

Colonial expansion cemented the power of the global north by giving access to the best land all over the world, controlling its usage, monopolising the fruits of its production and enshrining the reality of poverty and limited freedoms for those excluded from its resources and from land 'ownership'.[82] Even today, wildlife conservation – whether to do with animals or plants – often involves benefactors with deep pockets or well-funded and well-resourced charities seeking to 'preserve' the natural world by keeping human beings out of conservation areas. In a curiously neo-colonial twist, the wealthy of the developed world protect nature from being spoiled and save it by ring-fencing it, often literally, from indigenous populations: the creation of the Messok Dja protected area in the Republic of Congo by the World Wildlife Fund, without the consent of local Baka communities, or the eviction of more than 70,000 Maasai from their lands in northern Tanzania to create a game reserve for wealthy Emiratis are just two examples among many.[83] In fact, creating national parks and protected areas does not necessarily benefit wildlife – and certainly does not do so in predictable, uniform ways.[84]

Ironically, of course, for all the concern about the effects of anthropogenic change on forests and the impact on soil erosion (and therefore on yields), the demand for goods and commodities was not merely ravenous but ecologically catastrophic. As we have seen, animals were hunted for their pelts to the brink of extinction and sometimes beyond in North America; in southern Africa, ivory was the driver of the expansion of resource frontiers. In the late 1870s, British and Boer hunters advanced north into modern Zimbabwe, northern Botswana and eastern Zambia in search of elephants. Export figures show the shocking scale of slaughter, with thousands of elephants killed each year in the second half of the nineteenth century.[85]

Ivory was highly desirable in Victorian-era Britain and the United States, as well as elsewhere, used for fashion accessories ranging from collar studs, hairbrushes and vanity sets to sewing cases, toothpicks and napkin rings.[86] Major demand came from piano manufacturers, as these instruments became popular in working-class bars and music halls and also as status symbols for the burgeoning middle classes, whether in British homes or newly settled farming communities on the Great Plains. The rise of billiards as a social pastime also increased demand; the ivory used for billiard balls had to come from soft young specimens – and from only part of the tusk at that.[87]

There were attempts to slow the trade down, if not stop it altogether, with Khama, the Tswana King, trying to introduce controls over hunting by sharply raising levies for elephants shot in his territory. This had little effect on consumers living a long way away, whose ideas about nature and the majesty of wild animals and preconceptions about the continent of Africa proved a heady cocktail that glamorised hunting and hunters; indeed big-game hunters like R. G. Cumming became household names and even outsold Charles Dickens when they wrote their memoirs filled with derring-do tales about how supposedly brave (white) men were able to push large animals to the brink of extinction thanks to their proficiency with the rifle.[88]

These were all new developments in the opening up of 'ghost acres' – that is, the colonial powers' exploitation of land, resources and commodities in other parts of the world. The British were by far the best, most organised and most determined at spawning clones in other continents, such as South Africa, North America and Australia. In each, political, legal and religious institutions were created that imitated those at home and were controlled by those who spoke the same language and had strong family ties with the mother country. The growth of the Anglosphere was explosive: the number of English-speakers rose sixteenfold between 1790 and 1930, from 12 to 200 million. It was not that the Spanish, Russians, Chinese or others who expanded into new lands or developed extractive, centralising policies in the same period did not meet with success; but as one leading historian puts it, 'it was the Anglophones who bred like rabbits'. It was the British who met with conspicuous success in creating infrastructure networks that sent resources, commodities and goods in one direction and people in the other. Despite what conventional wisdom might say, it was only in the nineteenth century that Britain became great.[89]

Of course, success came at the expense of other people, as local populations were displaced or coerced in the Americas, in Africa, in Asia and in Australia either by Europeans directly or by their descendants. Ironically, the push towards independence in the United States was not predominantly caused by the rejection of Britain, or by revulsion towards British rule and British identity; rather it was more because leading Americans felt that they were treated as not being British enough and were accorded second-class status, above all in the lack of representation in the political process in London.[90]

On the face of it, the United States was fiercely republican in character, demeanour and self-identification; in behaviour and practice, however, it proved to be an expansive, militaristic and extractive power in its own right: the Louisiana Purchase in 1803 was followed by the occupation of Florida in 1810, by the expansion of geographic horizons to the west in the decades that followed and in the 1840s by the seizure of about half of Mexico. The gains that came thereby were distributed to elites and to commercial interests, at the expense of those who were conquered, displaced or subjugated.

The processes of acquiring territory and of opening up new commodity frontiers set in motion a chain of other changes, including investment in transportation connections and a rapid period of urbanisation. In the late 1770s, the three principal settlements in Kentucky were home to a combined population of 280 people. By 1782, some 8,000 European settlers had joined them; by 1790, the number had risen to 73,000.[91] Development of bigger and faster steamships brought shipping costs down and prices with it – though not in uniform ways. For example, in the 1820s, the cost of sending freight by river from Philadelphia via New Orleans was a third of what it cost to transport it overland; a few decades later, transatlantic shipping had become so efficient and cheap that it cost less to transport flour from North America to Liverpool than from Dublin across the Irish Sea.[92]

The rise of coal-powered steamships, combined with increases in their size, speed and reliability in difficult seas, stimulated the creation of a global network of refuelling stations and in doing so galvanised the development of new ports and coastal cities where goods could be loaded and unloaded and which became important in their own right.[93] The opening up of the Suez canal in the late 1860s cut shipping times dramatically, with obvious implications for prices; the massive expansion of railways in Britain and Europe, the United States and Canada and in other continents during the nineteenth century was a similar story.

Cheaper, quicker, more reliable connections did not just boost economic exchange, but brought about dramatic social and cultural revolution too: provincial cities blossomed as they became integrated into networks giving access to ideas about art, music and literature that had previously been the preserve of the wealthy. Literacy levels in France rose by 20 per cent in the 1830s and about the same again in both the 1840s and 1850s; museums opened in the second half of the nineteenth century at great pace in the major cities in Europe, seeding discussions about the past and the present across ever wider sections of society. Not everyone approved: with operators like Thomas Cook capitalising on a booming tourism industry, some complained that visitor numbers spoiled the experience for others. English tourists, ran one complaint, were 'seemingly everywhere; there is no lemon tree without an English lady smelling its perfume, no picture gallery without at least sixty Englishmen, each with a guidebook in their hands checking everything is where it should be'. All these changes transformed connectivity, shrinking distances between regions and widening cultural horizons.[94]

So too did technological breakthroughs: the invention of a concentrated meat extract by Justus von Liebig not only proved commercially lucrative (and spawned many imitators), but also played an important role in the 'meatification' of metropolitan diets, as did mechanical refrigeration, which made the transport of meat highly profitable and much more efficient from the late 1870s.[95] Meat and protein increasingly became a part of working-class diets in London in the later nineteenth and early twentieth centuries, bringing health benefits to adult populations and aiding brain development in young people.[96] Meat consumption likewise grew in parts of Asia, such as in Japan, where the Meiji Restoration of 1868 prompted new attitudes to beef in particular, and in China. China was scouted by the beef baron William Vestey, whose family business had built up a global network that shipped millions of carcasses. He thought China offered enormous long-term potential – although one study in 1912 poured cold water on the idea of exporting to Asia because the inhabitants, 'where they are not entirely vegetarian, are too poor to buy imported meat'.[97]

There were clear winners and losers in the acceleration and deepening of globalisation that characterised the nineteenth century. The British were prime beneficiaries, above all in terms of rising living standards and availability of goods and commodities. For example, by the 1890s, Britain absorbed 60 per cent of the meat and as much as 40 per cent of the wheat that was traded globally.[98] There was good news too for low-income households, with the repeal of the Corn Laws and the rise of imports from America ensuring that the price of a loaf of bread halved between 1840 and 1880.[99]

Constant improvement of machinery expanded production, improved efficiency and applied pressure on costs. Wheat exports from the United States rose from 5 million hectolitres to 100 million in the thirty years after 1840. The introduction of mechanical reapers doubled productivity, while steam-powered grain elevators meant that 500,000 bushels of grain could be processed in ten hours at a cost of five cents per bushel.[100] Mechanisation reduced the amount of labour required to yield a hectare of wheat from 150 hours to just nine. Breeding techniques doubled milk-fat production per cow and resulted in draught horses becoming 50 per cent bigger (and therefore stronger) in the United States between 1860 and 1890.[101]

The fruits of these gains flowed to those who had capital to invest and to those who could take advantage of mass production – large-scale arable farmers in the United States and livestock owners in Australia and South America, for example, or shareholders in railway companies that paid handsome dividends. They brought despair to those who were squeezed out, however, such as cereal farmers in Britain who could not compete with the flood of imports, and to labourers who were forced to leave the countryside to look for work in towns that had low levels of hygiene and a high incidence of poverty and disease – a way of life epitomised in works such as *Bleak House* by Charles Dickens.

There were similarly few benefits in parts of the world that were either left behind or received little by way of hard infrastructure in the form of roads, schools, hospitals and railways, and little by way of soft investment in institutions, education and local capacity building. States that were notionally free from colonial rule, such as in South America, behaved as classic extractive satellite states, exporting raw materials and relying on imports for domestic consumption. The changes to the global economy brought mixed blessings for India and South Asia. Between 1810 and 1860, India lost much of its domestic textile market to Britain as prices were driven downwards, which had dramatic consequences because of the relative rise in the price of grain in the same period.

So while Europeans revelled in plentiful and cheap food, others were not so fortunate: as many as 16 million died of hunger in India in the decades between 1875 and the start of the First World War – a prolonged catastrophe that colonial administrators treated as a fact of life and one that had positive side-effects, which included forcing indebted smallholders off the land while serving as a welcome check on the growth of India's population size.[102] Huge numbers died in famines, often during times when massive consignments of wheat from India continued to be exported, especially to Britain. This mattered little, according to one blunt official writing to the Viceroy in the second half of the nineteenth century: 'still they reproduce themselves with sufficient rapidity to overcrowd every employment that is opened to them.'[103]

Problems came too from opportunistic attempts to turn profits. By the end of the 1850s, for example, the United States was the biggest producer of cotton in the world, exporting around 3.5 million bales annually – much of it grown by coerced labour on plantations in the Deep South. The Union blockade of Confederate ports during the civil war dramatically strangled trade, with just 10,000 bales exported in 1861–2, a drop of almost 99 per cent.[104] Although slavery had been banned in Britain by the Abolition Act of 1833, the British economy relied heavily on the textile industry and as such not only benefited from cotton imports but relied on them to keep its factories working. The supply failure raised concerns about shortages of materials and about threats to public order. There were riots in several cotton towns in England, as well as elsewhere in Europe. 'No crisis in modern times has been so anxiously watched,' declared *The Times* in the early 1860s in reference to the US civil war, 'nor has any European war or revolution so seriously threatened the interests of England.'[105]

Anxieties were heightened by the rise of radical ideas that were themselves closely linked to long-term socio-economic problems. Rapid and large-scale urbanisation was transforming the literal and the political landscapes of Europe, which had already been hit by a series of revolutions in 1848. These upheavals were framed by Karl

Marx and Friedrich Engels as expressions of the class struggle by the oppressed against those who controlled the means of production; in fact they owed rather more to serious food shortfalls that had triggered famine and hunger riots, most notably in Ireland, Flanders and Silesia in the mid-1840s. The violence that spread across many parts of the continent resulted in governments cancelling investment programmes and so negatively impacting mining and metal production from the spring of 1847. This contributed to the groundswell of protest and the demands for reform, freedom and greater rights that peaked the following year.[106]

Attention quickly turned to India, therefore, as an alternative source of cotton – perhaps not surprisingly given the repeated attempts to stimulate production, most of which had faltered thanks to the low quality of Indian cotton and to poor transportation networks that added to costs. The invention and widespread adoption of the Whitney gin had prompted a revolution of its own in the United States: in 1801, a cotton picker typically averaged around 28 pounds per day; by the end of the 1820s, this had risen more than fourfold, to just over 132 pounds a day, almost trebling again just over a decade or so later to 341 pounds.[107] The coerced labourers who were forced to work at these staggering rates of productivity benefited factory owners and factory workers (albeit to a much lesser extent) in cities like Manchester on the other side of the Atlantic, as efficiency in weaving mills improved by six to ten times between 1820 and 1860. Ironically, the gains made slavery even more lucrative, ensured that enslavers in the American south became richer still and reinforced their determination to hold on to the source of their wealth – forced labour.[108]

The pressure on supplies caused prices of Indian cotton to rise by almost five times in the early 1860s. A surge in land clearances followed as producers sought to capitalise on the high prices. More than a million hectares were turned over to cotton growing from other subsistence crops. Railway construction dissected Berar, a province in the heart of the Indian subcontinent, where the town of Khangaon quickly became what one contemporary called the 'largest cotton outpost of the British empire'.[109]

Others too tried to grasp the opportunity, including in Central Asia where some Russians in this period hoped the local populations would be 'our Negroes' – an aspiration that leaves little to the imagination.

During the US civil war, cotton production in Central Asia boomed, rising more than fourfold in the period 1861–4.[110] Then there was Lower Egypt where 40 per cent of all fertile land was converted to cotton cultivation, as was much of the substantial personal landholdings of the Ottoman Viceroy, Sa'id Pasha.[111]

All these opportunistic moves paid immediate dividends. However, they came at a high cost. For one thing, the settlement of the American civil war reintroduced large supplies to the market, with improved availability placing downward pressure on prices. For another, the expansion of cotton growing led to the introduction of agricultural slavery in other parts of the world, most notably in the Nile Delta, which became home to large numbers of enslaved people imported from East Africa: efforts to end slavery in one continent brought about just the opposite in another.[112]

The attraction of high returns also led to financial strains and overstretch among those who borrowed money for seeds, tools, food and labour. When prices turned, many found themselves overextended and with debts that they struggled to pay. In Egypt, this produced waves of land abandonment, bankruptcies, a growing body of landless labourers and the polarisation of social relations in the countryside as inequalities rose. Much the same happened in India, where some have argued that indebtedness, displacement and desperation – combined with the tightening suffocation of colonial demands – provide the backdrop to the Deccan riots and to the death of millions from starvation in the 1870s.

Minimal efforts went into investing in irrigation because of mistaken beliefs about the richness of the black soil of Berar and partly because of the incompetence of colonial officials who prioritised cotton over grain. The failure of wages to keep up with prices resulted in malnutrition and higher susceptibility to disease as well as starvation. Famine cycles in the 1890s struck again and again, ruining countless families and enriching those who hoarded food – and even continued to export it during years of acute crisis.[113] That starvation rates were particularly high in Berar tells its own story about attempts to cash in on short-term opportunity.[114] Such were the consequences that flowed from a conjunction of the search for profits, the unsustainable exploitation of the landscape and nature taking revenge when pushed beyond its limits.

20

The Age of Turbulence
(c.1870–c.1920)

A gallant body of Englishmen have fallen victim to their efforts to bring West Africa within the outer fringes at least of civilisation.

Daily Telegraph (18 January1897)

If the human consequences of disaster were severe and shocking, so too were the ecological implications of rapid transformations of landscapes that were motivated by the chase for a fast buck. For example, forests were hacked down to create cotton plantations. This had obvious knock-on effects for flora and fauna alike, exacerbated by the practice of paying bounties for tigers, panthers, wolves, bears and hyenas – apex predators whose disappearance produced major environmental change. Worse, land that was cleared often proved to be unsuitable or was exploited so badly that yields dried up, as (literally) did rivers, lakes and water resources as a result of soil erosion or because clearances induced changes to regional rainfall patterns.[1]

The story of cotton was one that was repeated time and again, particularly from the second half of the nineteenth century onwards when global markets became more integrated, transport networks improved and information-sharing accelerated. For example, the demand for rubber shot up as a result of Charles Goodyear's pioneering work in the 1830s on vulcanisation, the chemical process that improves elasticity, hardness and resilience, and then again by the development of the pneumatic tyre, perfected by John Dunlop in 1888.[2]

Rubber production rose in leaps and bounds from around 2,500 metric tons in 1851 to over 20,000 tons thirty years later. That was just the start of it. By 1900, some 50,000 tons was being produced; by the eve of the First World War, it was closer to 120,000 tons. During this time, rubber became 'the most important, most market-sensitive, most sought-after new commodity in the world', much in demand for bicycles and cars, as well as for a seemingly limitless new range of goods and products, from shoe soles to electrical insulation.[3]

This versatility too spurred a rush to alter the use of land and take advantage of the demands – and profits – on offer. The rate of transformation was not so much bewildering as epic. Vast amounts of rainforest in South-East Asia were cut down and replanted with *Hevea* seeds from the Amazon. In the late 1890s, around 145 hectares had been planted in Melaka and Selangor, in the Malay peninsula. By 1910, that had risen to around 220,000 hectares, with plantations being established in other states too, such as Perak. Four years later, more than 445,000 hectares had been cleared for rubber-plant cultivation. By 1914, more rubber was being exported from the Malay peninsula than all of South America combined. The Dutch East Indies followed the same pattern, with large-scale planting in the same period resulting in rubber trees covering 245,000 hectares in 1914 and almost double that amount five years later. By the 1930s, millions of hectares of the world's richest rainforests had been replaced by rubber trees by entrepreneurs who recognised that cheap land could be the basis of great fortunes, especially once cars began to be mass-produced and demand for rubber for tyres soared even more. The excitement of being a pioneer and of the rewards that came with it was palpable: as one new planter put it, he felt he had the 'morale of a conquistador', a phrase that summed up the prevailing attitudes as well as the process of extraction. The Americas had been denuded; now it was the turn of other parts of the world.[4]

Ecological reconfigurations had always followed the transplantation of crops, flora and fauna. Highly integrated global markets that were linked by increasingly efficient and cheap transport networks enabled this to happen faster and more deeply than at any point in human history. Exploration of unknown lands had the same outcome, usually motivated by the search for new resources. Central to this was a philosophical framework which asserted that uncharted parts of the world were not only wild and lived in by savages, but home to endless sources of wealth.[5] As David Livingstone put it, European expansion brought three elements that would be welcomed by all: 'Christianity, commerce and civilisation'.[6] The dovetailing of evangelical ideas about racial superiority, religious virtue and capitalism was a core element of the way that Europeans, and the British above all, saw both themselves – and the rest of the world.[7]

Rubber was just one commodity among many. Some were plant-based, like cocoa, coffee and tobacco, which were all introduced into new regions around the world. It was a process that depended in many locations on the availability of quinine, the first effective treatment of malaria, which itself came from the bark of the cinchona tree native to the Andes which spread rapidly from the 1820s.[8]

The exploitation of resources that accelerated in the nineteenth century was not limited to crops and plants. Minerals and metals too were in high demand as new technologies were developed and rapidly scaled up, while manufacturing accelerated too. A good example was tin, which played a key role in a range of industries, including textile production, mechanical engineering and military armaments. Its main use was for tin cans for preserved food – a function vital in conserving rural food surpluses and transporting them to cities, and therefore crucial to urbanisation, industrialisation and globalisation.[9] Tin production in Europe quickly became exhausted, leading to the search for supply from elsewhere, most notably South-East Asia. As with rubber, volumes grew sharply. Automation meant that daily output of cans per worker rose from 60 in 1847 to 1,000 less than thirty years later; production then went up by a factor of almost four between 1874 and 1914. In the following decades, demand was all but insatiable: in 1962, for example, the United States alone produced almost 50 billion cans, corresponding to more than 250 cans per person per year.[10]

Another highly prized commodity was whale oil, obtained from rendered blubber, which was a prime source of lamp fuel. Around 162,000 Greenland whales were killed between 1500 and 1800. Although whaling had long been part of the economy of the Arctic Sea and the North Atlantic, the industrial revolution brought about a surge in demand because the low viscosity of whale oil made it a valuable source of lubricants for use in machinery: it did not dry out, congeal or corrode metals.[11]

The United States became the epicentre of the global whaling industry, home to more than three-quarters of the worldwide fleet by the 1840s, in large part because stocks of bowhead and right whales in the Atlantic had been so overexploited by the start of the nineteenth century, forcing mariners to look elsewhere for their kills.[12] This served to open up the heart of the Pacific basin, integrating the littoral of South America in particular into global commercial networks.[13]

The global hunt for new commodities extended to other resources that were in abundant supply in the region, most notably guano, the excrement of wild birds and bats whose prodigious value as a fertiliser had been well known for many centuries before the European arrival in the Americas. Birds congregated and bred in flocks on the coast of what is now Peru, wrote one observer, flocks so enormous as to be incredible 'to anyone who has not seen them'. Inca kings had made it illegal to interfere with the birds during breeding season on pain of death, so prized was the guano – a word derived from the Quechua for 'shit' – which was spread over fields each year to help crops grow.[14]

Its value as a fertiliser rose dramatically during the age of scientific advancement, as investment in plant sciences and concern about increasing food production to feed growing populations directed attention to improving crop yields. Experiments conducted by Alexander von Humboldt in the early nineteenth century on samples that he brought back from his travels to the Pacific coast of South America revealed extraordinarily high concentrations of nitrogen-rich uric acid in guano that astonished the scientific community and sparked a global hunt to find sources before exporting them back to Europe and the United States.[15]

The British Isles, the Caribbean, Canada and South-West Africa were stripped of their supplies. But it was the coast of what became the independent state of Peru in the 1820s that proved the greatest source of guano, as well as the most lucrative. Between 1840 and 1879, almost 13 million metric tons of guano were exported from Peru's islands and coastline, with an estimated value of £100–£150 million. Most of this was shipped to Britain, though some was sold to farmers, landowners and planters in the Low Countries, Germany and the United States – as well as to islands in the Caribbean, to Mauritius and Réunion in the Indian Ocean and even to China.[16]

Guano's properties were so prodigious that it took on a role in popular culture. Joseph Conrad's *Lord Jim* includes a character excitedly talking about his plans to make a fortune by buying a cheap steamer and sailing to 'a guano island' that he had discovered, which despite lacking safe anchorage and despite lying in the path of frequent hurricanes promised to deliver untold riches.[17] One story printed in a San Francisco newspaper in the 1850s claimed that when the hatches were left open on a ship transporting guano it caused the timbers of the vessels to sprout, the masts to grow and a cherry table to grow fruit; indeed so potent was its fertilising power that cockroaches grew to enormous sizes, so large 'that they could get up the anchor and make sail on the brig'. According to the sailor who reported this story, 'there is nothing like guano to make things grow'.[18]

Other prizes lay in wait too. Huge saltpetre deposits in the Atacama desert quickly caught the eye of prospectors. Like guano, saltpetre nitrates were valuable as a fertiliser. They had another quality too: their ability to burn at an explosive rate. They were therefore of enormous interest both to miners and to armies whose artilleries became increasingly powerful in the course of the nineteenth century, especially after Alfred Nobel pioneered ways to transport and detonate nitroglycerine in the form of 'dynamite'. This set off a race to find and secure sources that were ideally both plentiful and cheap. It did not take long for attention to turn to the Atacama desert, one of the driest places on earth where rich quantities of sodium nitrate ($NaNO_3$) had built up over the course of many millions of years.[19]

As happened elsewhere, the appetite for extracting resources from South America had consequences. For one thing, it led to the flexing of muscles by those who benefited from the natural wealth to ensure that they were able to continue to do so. Blockades of Buenos Aires by British and French warships in the mid-1840s were paralleled around the same time by the advance of the United States at Mexico's expense as the former took control of more than a million square kilometres of the latter's territory: the 'storming of the Halls of Montezuma', a reference to the assault on Chapultepec castle in Mexico City, was so important that it features in the official hymn of the US Marine Corps.[20]

US ambitions soon widened further still. With the Guano Act passed by Congress in 1856, US citizens were given the right to lay claim to islands and territories on behalf of the government.[21] Several of these are still in US hands, including the Midway Atoll, famous first as a staging post for telegraph communication and flights between the United States and Asia and then as the location of the battle on which the Second World War in the Pacific turned.[22]

For another, the race to acquire natural resources led to a spending spree at both government and individual level in Peru, based on the sudden bonanza brought by guano and nitrate sales and on the belief that this would never end. New railways, roads, hospitals and city sewerage were testimony to this newfound wealth, as were the fine wines, cigars and fashions that were brought from all over the world. Reality eventually caught up with the overenthusiasm, overspending and overborrowing as Peru lurched from a costly civil war in the 1850s into hostilities with Spain in the 1860s and then, at the end of the 1870s, into the War of the Pacific (1879–84), which has been described as 'one of the largest armed conflicts ever fought in the Americas'.[23]

The adoption of new technologies and the identification of new ingredients or materials that were suddenly in high demand often brought unusual spillover consequences. The discovery by James Lind, a British naval officer, that the consumption of citrus fruits prevented scurvy led to the Royal Navy buying vast quantities of lemons – enough to supply 1.6 million gallons of lemon juice in the years 1795–1814 alone.[24] This caused production to soar, especially in Sicily, which was exporting 2.5 million cases of lemons a year to New York by the mid-1880s, with citrus cultivation on the island yielding more than sixty times the profit per hectare of any other crop. When combined with the weak rule of law, low levels of inter-personal trust, high levels of local poverty and a series of land reforms introduced in the first part of the nineteenth century, these created the perfect circumstances for the rise of groups that could exploit high margins and also benefit from conditions of uncertainty. Lind's solution to scurvy helped sow the seeds for the rise of the Sicilian Mafia.[25]

Thanks to the craze for rubber, guano and nitrates, the deepening of trade connections with South America also had far-reaching effects. In 1842, an unusual blight appeared in potato crops in Philadelphia and New York, as well as in many parts of Europe. Ireland was severely affected, in part because the population was dependent on potatoes as a source of food and calories and as a form of payment, but also because of pre-existing poverty closely correlated with pressure on the land, poor agricultural practices made worse by landlord absenteeism, and inadequate government policies. The results were dramatic, with as many as one million men, women and children dying from hunger and disease in appalling conditions. For many, the choice was simple: migrate or die, or as one leading scholar has expressed it, 'the next world or the new world'.[26]

Recent sequencing of DNA from strains of the blight suggests that it likely had an Andean origin and had been transmitted around the world among new potato varieties exported from Peru that owed much to the country's growing accessibility and its place in global commercial networks.[27] Ireland's population fell by almost 40 per cent between the mid-1840s and early 1850s: in addition to those who died, well over a million people emigrated, with most heading across the Atlantic to North America.[28] Not surprisingly, the profound suffering left scars that lasted for generations and influenced ideas about British rule, about sectarianism and about rebellion.[29] The rapid creation of large Irish communities in the US, meanwhile, became a part of mainstream political discourse in the United States in the mid-nineteenth century, as many questioned whether large influxes of migrants might not only impact prosperity but perhaps even damage the nation's institutions.[30]

That so many new arrivals in the late 1840s were less educated than those who had reached the US from Ireland beforehand was reflected in sharply lowered literacy levels and in their children's poor educational and vocational outcomes.[31] Nevertheless, as the Irish population grew, it retained pride in its roots – as is clear from the fact that today almost 40 million Americans claim Irish descent – influencing cultural events such as St Patrick's Day as well as the results of US presidential and congressional elections for more than a century and a half.[32] These dramatic demographic trends re-shaped Ireland and the United States, and can be traced back to a crop disease in South America that had piggy-backed on intensive global trade networks. Moving plants from one side of the world to another brought the risks of doing the same for pathogens.

The exodus that followed the Irish potato famine was part of a much wider set of migrations closely connected to the exploitation of foods, minerals and natural resources. As slavery in the Americas had shown, crops like sugar, tobacco, coffee, cocoa and cotton counted for little without labour to plant, cultivate, harvest and process them. The advances achieved in the nineteenth century were part of an interrelated and complex series of technological developments, deepening trade ties, rising aspirations and knowledge-sharing that above all required vast amounts of labour, almost all of which was in the wrong place. Clearing forests, reworking land and establishing new plantations therefore meant bringing in workers from locations near and far. So while the nineteenth century can be seen in terms of the reshaping of the natural environment, it should be stressed that this relied on massive changes in the human environment too. Just as crops were transplanted around the world, so too were people; strikingly, much of the movement of the latter was involuntary.

The second half of the nineteenth century and early years of the twentieth are often characterised by wistful ideas of impoverished Europeans packing up their few belongings and heading across the Atlantic where new lives awaited those willing to work hard and where new opportunities awaited, especially after the end of the civil war and the abolition of slavery. While migration to North America in the second half of the nineteenth century was substantial, the decades that followed c.1850 saw even greater mass movements of people in and around Asia. Almost 30 million Indians migrated around the Indian Ocean and South Pacific, often at the instigation of the colonial authorities, in many cases involving debt obligations whereby loans were provided in return for labour. Nearly 4 million from India moved to Malaysia; more than double that number to Ceylon (modern Sri Lanka); more than 15 million moved to Burma and around 1 million to other parts of South-East Asia, to islands in the Indian and Pacific oceans and to Africa.[33]

Movements on this scale were paralleled by the migrations of some 50 million Chinese, who relocated to South-East Asia, to the Dutch East Indies, Thailand, French Indo-China, Australia and New Zealand, as well as to Pacific and Indian Ocean islands. All this caused a major shift in patterns of global demographics. The Americas and South-East and North Asia experienced massive population growth, with numbers increasing by a factor of four or more between 1850 and 1950. While the trajectories ran in parallel, there were some fundamental differences, not the least of which was that density of settlement rose far more sharply in South-East Asia than in the United States as around the same number of migrants moved into less than half the space.[34] By 1900, there were more Indians on Mauritius than Africans, and more Indians in Natal than there were Europeans. Forty per cent of the population of Hawai'i were of Japanese origin, and almost 20 per cent were Chinese.[35]

These enormous movements of people were above all driven by the need for workers on plantations, in mines or engaged in processing materials, minerals and metals. Again, much of the movement was involuntary. Populations across Polynesia were devastated by raids that

aimed to enslave and transport adult men against their will and force
them to participate in collecting guano in Peru and preparing it for
export.[36] Indian and Chinese 'coolie' labourers were shipped across the
Atlantic under false pretences or against their will as indentured labour to
help build railways, roads and port facilities, or to work in hospitals or as
domestic staff, or to carry out backbreaking work such as picking crops.[37]

Forced sexual exploitation and rape of women were rife, underpinned
by western tropes about people living in Asia being prone to laziness,
pleasure-seeking and promiscuity. Among other things, this also
reinforced the idea that not only should women 'serve' their masters, but
that their doing so should not come at great cost. 'Some of the China
women are very good-looking,' observed Robert Hart, Inspector General
of the Imperial Maritime Customs in China. 'You can make one your
absolute possession for 50 to 100 dollars and support her at a cost of only
2 or 3 dollars per month.'[38] This was just one among countless examples
that shows how ideas about race and entitlement combined to reinforce
the belief that it was not just humans holding sway over the flora and
fauna of the world, but Europeans doing so over all other peoples too.

In this sense, the abolition of slavery in Britain, Europe and North
America was symbolically and commercially significant, but it brought
little by way of changes in attitude or behaviour. Colonial administrators
found it easy to convince themselves of their own virtues. 'There was
hard work,' wrote one official posted to India, 'but it seemed worth
doing; it was always concerned with other people's lives.' Yet physical
abuse was routine – and, when administered by Europeans, either went
unnoticed, unpunished, or all too easily excused. In India, labourers
with low work rates, who complained or did not meet their targets were
beaten and in some cases even killed.[39] So great were the losses in Congo
to maltreatment, torture, starvation and disease as the local population
were forced to gather rubber during a boom that lasted around forty
years from the 1880s until the early 1920s that every ten kilos of rubber
exported in this period came at the price of one human life. This
appalling lack of regard meant that the population in the Congo fell by
70 per cent in the course of these decades.[40]

While Europeans and their descendants who had fanned out across
the world's continents in a series of increasingly large waves were the
main beneficiaries of the fruits of the land and the fruits of human
labour, they did not benefit evenly: in fact, the proceeds went to those

with capital, rather than to those in or linked to Europe – including to those from and living in Asia, Africa, the Americas and Oceania. It was capitalism's 'ruthless terrorism', in Karl Marx's phrase, that spurred economic growth, but it also came at a heavy price.[41]

The relentless demand for commodities of course did not just put pressure on ecologies that were transformed as forests were cut down, new crops introduced and planted or hillsides split open in search of minerals, for major interventions were also needed to support, house and feed large workforces that themselves put strains on the local environment. One farm in southern Cambodia, for example, had to supply between three and five metric tons of food per day for the workforce of 3,000 who toiled on a neighbouring rubber plantation, while also maintaining 500 cows, 800 pigs and herds of sheep and goats.[42] Such projects inevitably had trickle-down effects on local economies, but the cold reality was that the lion's share of rewards, both direct and indirect, went to make the rich even richer.

It did not help that investments could be precarious because the race to create supply could sometimes overwhelm demand – pushing prices down and turning glittering El Dorados into bleak wastelands. At the height of the rubber boom Iquitos in the Peruvian Amazon rainforest fleetingly became home to some of the most expensive real estate in the world, with prices for property reputedly surpassing those in cities like New York, only to fade as new sources of rubber came on tap in other parts of the world. Or there was Irkutsk in Siberia, which by the end of the nineteenth century was home to an opera house, several cathedrals and no fewer than thirty-four schools; it was also a repository of hope and optimism about the future fuelled by rapid industrialisation, major investment, not least in railway connections, and rising living standards. 'Siberia is going to be another America,' remarked one contemporary visitor, a prediction that remains unfulfilled.[43]

Then there were the by-products of extraction that condemned local communities, as well as local wildlife and plant life, to generations of side-effects, as well as to widespread ecocide. The tailings from metal industries, for example, caused rivers to silt up from Tasmania to Perak in Malaya by increasing sediment supply to local stream systems.[44] Aquatic environments around the world were poisoned by metal pollution resulting from efforts to extract copper, zinc, lead, tin and more from the landscape.[45] Highly toxic sodium cyanide, used to concentrate gold, which was first developed in the late nineteenth century and was almost immediately employed in the Witwatersrand gold fields in South Africa, poisoned the landscape.[46] Even today, around 100 million kilos of cyanide is used annually in North America, of which more than three-quarters is assigned to gold mining, while some scientists estimate that gold mining alone generates around 1 billion metric tons of waste rock and tailings each year.[47]

The conviction that transformations of the natural environment were certain to bring about positive long-term change proved to be spectacularly ill-placed – throwing ideas about cultural and ethnic supremacy into sharp relief. The expansion of British political power in India sparked an ambitious set of new ideas to transform what looked like basic and inefficient networks of canals, small dams and terraced fields fed by water channels. These were dramatically expanded with technologies that were thought to be far superior and would prevent the devastating famines that seemed to be regular occurrences – as in 1837–8 when some 800,000 people died in the North-Western Provinces, Punjab and Rajasthan owing to the failure of monsoon rains.[48] If the problem was obvious, so too was the solution: 'all Indian famines are caused by drought', in the words of a report by the Indian Famine Commission set up in the second half of the nineteenth century after more than 5 million people had died from hunger and disease; to stop this happening, 'the first place must unquestionably be assigned to works of irrigation'.[49]

The problem, according to one British engineer, was that in 'one year a portion of the whole crop ... is destroyed by the overflowing of the rivers', while 'in another the crop is destroyed by a failure of the rains'. The answer was to open up all of India to new irrigation schemes, which would be 'a work of such magnitude ... that nothing approaching it has ever been seen in the world'.[50] The excitement of those who built and commented on the works that followed was no less breathless and self-congratulatory: a dam built in 1852 that regulated the flow of the Godavari River in Dowleswaram was described as 'the noblest feat of engineering skills which has yet been accomplished in British India'.[51]

Similar sentiments were expressed about the 700-mile-long Ganges canal which was opened two years later. One senior official who had conceived the project talked of his pride that 'a few hundred Christians in the heart of a foreign country' and surrounded by heathens had been able to create 'a work of civilisation for the benefit of these unenlightened multitudes'. The dark night of 'false religion, tyranny and war' and 'the bitter consequences of evil' had given way to the bright day 'of Christianity, good government and peace'.[52]

In the next three decades or so, more than 65,000 kilometres of new canals were built, irrigating some 5.4 million hectares – with the costs largely passed on to the Indians themselves.[53] Railways were constructed that offered returns to private investors that were guaranteed by the state, which proved a recipe for a huge programme of track-laying that turned India into the largest railway network in Asia and the fourth largest in the world. This required vast amounts of steel and iron to make the tracks, engines, wagons and carriages, as well as wood, coke and coal for sleepers and fuel. The subcontinent shrank to 'one 20th of its former dimensions', stated one British engineer, who also noted that 'the power of steam' had done much to deliver social progress by undermining 'one of the most rigid and exclusive caste systems in the world' by linking regions together, enabling the mobility of workforces and modernising the subcontinent.[54]

The scale of such changes was breathtaking. In Burma, the land devoted to rice growing rose twelvefold, turning the Irrawaddy Delta into one of the world's largest areas of rice production. The delta's population soared from 1.5 million to over 4 million in the period 1852–1900. This was mirrored by Dutch activities in the East Indies and those of the French on the Mekong; in the latter case, massive removals of mud and soil made the canalisation of the river one of the largest earth-moving exercises in human history.[55]

It would be tempting to assume that the development of infrastructure was intended first and foremost to help the local population, an objective born from a sense of magnanimity, duty and philanthropy. Of course the primary purpose was to support the concept and reality of empire. For example, investments in irrigation systems served the dual purpose of boosting agricultural yields (and therefore tax receipts) and mitigating the effects of famine, which could prove costly: in the 1870s, for example, almost £10 million was spent on famine relief – the equivalent of around £200 million today.[56]

While the expansion of the railways likewise brought opportunities for India and Indians, the increase in velocities of exchange benefited the colonial administration by boosting revenues, at the same time promoting British industries that exported raw materials in large quantities. Apart from the fact that one motive for building railways was to connect ports with the interior and thus enhance both the quantities and speed of exports and imports, there was a further important motivation. As the Governor General of India, Lord Dalhousie, told Parliament in 1853, an extensive rail network 'would enable the government to bring the main bulk of its military strength to bear upon any given point in as many days as it would now require months'.[57] The railways encouraged trade, linked regions together, spurred urbanisation, impacted land values and helped widen literacy; but above all they strengthened Britain's political, military and economic stranglehold on the subcontinent – just as they did for Russia in Siberia, for the United States in the midwest and beyond and for China in Manchuria.[58]

While colonisers helped themselves to the best of the rewards, there were local beneficiaries too, of course. Local farmers keen to improve their lot provided support, stimulus and even labour for agricultural improvement.[59] Substantial opportunities became available to those able and willing to move into regions as they were opened up through new transport links and overhauled by large-scale irrigation projects. A good example is the western Punjab, where the scale and pace of ecological transformation was dramatic. One million people moved into nine 'canal colonies' built between 1885 and 1940 for a workforce that tended to 13 million hectares of land which had previously been little more than scrub and desert but had now been turned into lush green fields by new irrigation works. This transformed Punjab into what one leading scholar has called 'the engine of agrarian growth in India'; the region was home to almost half of all canal-irrigated land in British India and the source of high levels of revenue and of manpower, both of which helped reinforce colonial rule over the subcontinent as a whole.[60] While farmers and those who worked this newly available land clearly gained from the process, control over nature provided resources for the British to strengthen their grip on India.[61]

This was not how colonial administrators themselves saw it – or at least not how they wrote about it. One major report issued in 1918 stated that the investment in India's agricultural development had been so profound and so successful that 'the terrible calamities which from time to time depopulated wide stretches of country need no longer be feared'. The interventions in the natural environment had eliminated risks of climatic stress: failure of the rains had once meant not just 'privation and hardship' but also 'wholesale starvation and loss of life'. This was not the case any longer, since the problems had all been 'scientifically studied and a system worked out'. Nature itself had been tamed.[62]

Such self-confidence went hand in hand with the certainty that knowledge and enlightenment brought from far away were greatly superior to anything that had existed or had developed locally. In a volume written by a British official in East Africa, modestly entitled *The Book of Civilisation*, the author claimed that 'Folk are poorly fed in Africa because most Africans are not good farmers, and particularly they're not good farmers because they do not know how to keep the soil fertile.' This was infuriating, he said, adding almost with a sense of despair: 'When cattle in Africa are used for their proper purposes – to provide milk for the children and meat for [them]selves, and manure for [their] fields and draw carts and ploughs – then, but not sooner will the people thrive.'[63]

Although views of the supposed inferiority of indigenous practices were typical and widespread, they were not uniform. One British agriculturist who was asked by the Secretary of State for India to assess the condition of Indian farming concluded firmly that he did 'not share the opinions which have been expressed as to Indian Agriculture being, as a whole, primitive and backward', but rather believed 'that in many parts there is little or nothing that can be improved'. In so far as it was even possible to generalise in these matters, the reality was that it was not 'inherent bad systems of cultivation' that were problematic, he wrote, but the absence of infrastructure in some districts in the subcontinent. Moreover, rather than adopt new practices from Britain, Europe or elsewhere, far better results would be achieved 'by the transference of a better indigenous method from one part [of India], where it is practised, to another where it is not'.[64]

Disdain for farming practices in Africa – and for African peoples in general – was likewise not shared by all. As one French botanist wrote, 'the indigenous cultivator is not the contemptible lay-about ... that is so often represented' by many contemporary commentators; rather, local practices not only got the best out of the land but did so in ways the European efforts had conspicuously failed to do, often at great financial as well as ecological cost.[65] British officials, wrote Archibald Church, a member of the Parliamentary Commission of Enquiry into the East African colonies, 'would do well to make a careful study of native methods of agriculture before they arrogantly assume that the methods of the European are far superior to those of the African'.[66]

Such views reflected rare cases of open-mindedness and did little to change opinions or to affect policies and practices in relation to cultivation and extraction that often made things worse, not better, replacing one set of problems with another. For example, biodiversity suffered as habitats that were home to animals and plants were cleared to make way for monoculture production.[67] In India, malaria was such a 'serious menace' as it spread along canal networks that some questioned whether the building programme would deliver any positive outcomes at all.[68] The digging of new canals often brought disputes about property rights, while poor drainage sometimes not only meant irrigation was inefficient but gave rise to unsanitary conditions that enabled disease to catch and spread.[69]

Large-scale irrigation was also problematic because, although initial results always looked promising, the threats from waterlogging and soil salinisation were no different in the modern world from what they had been in Mesopotamia and elsewhere thousands of years earlier. So it proved in Punjab, where the cold reality soon became clear, that canalisation was not the panacea that had been hoped for. By the 1940s, yields in many parts of the Punjab had fallen by 75 per cent or more; at least one million acres of former cultivated land had been made barren by unsustainable irrigation practices.[70] This was bad enough on its own terms, but even worse given the infrastructure of housing, schooling, healthcare, roads and more that had been provided for the large populations that had moved into these regions in the expectation that they would have rosy long-term futures, rather than precarious ones.[71]

Then there were the dangers of overdependence on a single or principal crop, which could produce economic downturns – and major shocks. While cocoa had been grown in South and Central America, as well as the Caribbean, from the start of the twentieth century, a massive development of plantations in West Africa eventually led to this region becoming the primary global producer of cocoa, as yields rose almost twenty times from around 40,000 tons a year to some 700,000 in the five decades after 1885. The glut led to a collapse in prices that had obvious beneficial consequences for consumers who were able to obtain this calorific bonus at increasingly low prices, but also consequences for workers and investors that were distinctly less rosy. The problem was exacerbated by the biological vulnerability that put the reliance on cocoa into sharp focus: in the 1940s, the 'swollen shoot' pathogen devastated plantations in West Africa, destroying livelihoods and stability with it, leading to riots in Accra and desperate attempts to stop the spread of the disease that eventually led to more than 100 million trees being cut down.[72]

In many other parts of Africa, human reshaping of the environment with the establishment of plantations on the one hand and of conservation zones on the other had a series of profound impacts. These ranged from forcible resettlement to competition for water, land and manpower. Settlement patterns shifted as railways were built into the interior resulting in the enlargement of local towns and markets that put ecological pressures on surrounding regions.[73] Matching impacts were effected by livestock herds that stripped vegetation from new regions where they had been forced to move, and by tribal and intertribal rivalries that were often fanned by decisions made by colonial authorities to support (and arm) one particular social group over another.[74]

Above all, however, the colonies were where resources could be claimed and used by the colonisers. Commodities like palm oil, rubber, cotton, timber, coffee, cocoa and metals were all needed for industrial production, for no end of manufactured goods, ranging from soap to clothing, from vehicle tyres to engine belts for use in factories. Soon after his appointment as Special Commissioner to Uganda, one of the first questions Harry Johnston asked was: 'what resources does the country possess for the development of a profitable trade?' He was trying to find out, of course, what had value that could be sent abroad to consumers back home.[75]

The world was a rich paradise, whose fruits were to be enjoyed by those who had inherited the keys to the garden of Eden. Nature could be tamed, just as local populations could be 'civilised'; scientific knowledge could be applied to impose and maintain control. All this powered a conviction that the world offered unlimited riches that could be developed and tapped for ever.

For example, after a tour of East Africa in 1907, Winston Churchill did not mention the people of the region, commenting instead on its fertility and natural beauty, the coolness of the air, richness of the soil and abundance of running water. Africa, he went on, 'must one day become the great centre of tropical production, play a most important part in the economic development of the whole world'. Africa, in other words, would be remodelled to suit the needs of people beyond, not those of its own people.[76] Theodore Roosevelt, who followed a very similar itinerary to that of Churchill a year and a half later just after standing down as US president, put it more bluntly. East Africa, he said, was 'a white man's country, a country that should be filled with white settlers'.[77]

This was an expression of ideas and convictions which had been developing since the first crossing of the Atlantic and which were intoxicatingly strong in northern Europe and in those who had emigrated from northern Europe to other corners of the world. Ideas about Anglo-Saxon tribes from the distant past fed into fetishised mythologises of history which held that the Germanic peoples had succeeded in overthrowing Rome thanks to their profound devotion to liberty and their determination to throw off the shackles of authoritarianism. These concepts had been forcefully articulated by Montesquieu in the eighteenth century, had proved highly attractive in Britain and Germany and were particularly seductive in the United States. The British success against Qing dynasty China in the First Opium War (1839–42) was hailed by the *New York Herald*, for example, as 'not a victory for British imperialism, but a triumph for the Anglo-Saxons'.[78] Such views were all the more striking at a time when many in the US were critical of British imperialism.

Some went further still. For example, in the 1850s, one congressman could be found musing that one day 'the two great branches of the Anglo-Saxon stock, the one pressing from the Bay of Bengal, and the other from the golden gulf of California, would meet in some beautiful group of sunny isles in the Pacific ocean, and together clasp their united hands in love and peace around the globe'.[79] If some in the United States could not hesitate to express their gratitude that the Atlantic seaboard 'was settled by colonies of the Anglo-Saxon race', others left little to the imagination about what this meant: 'history warrants us in believing in races of men, as well as of inferior animals', said Edward Everett, a man whose glittering career saw him serve as Governor of Massachusetts, US senator, representative of the United States to the United Kingdom and President of Harvard. 'The Anglo-Saxon race', he went on, 'from which we Americans trace our descent is surpassed by none other that ever existed.'[80] He meant some Americans, of course – those with pale skin.

The British were hardly immune from such high self-regard. Indeed, some even argued that Britain itself had evolved as a result. 'England has outgrown the continent of Europe,' said Benjamin Disraeli in 1866. She was 'no longer a mere European power; she is the metropolis of a great maritime empire, extending to the boundaries of the farthest ocean ... she is really a more Asiatic power than a European'. This all stemmed from the engagement with other continents, peoples and ecologies and reflected the awareness, if not the conviction, that the sources of Britain's wealth lay overseas.[81]

British rule was 'steadfastly progressive', *The Times* claimed a month after the end of the First World War, 'the most beneficent in design and execution known in the history of mankind'. These views were shared by many, such as Gertrude Bell, who wrote to her father not long afterwards, reflecting that 'truly we are a remarkable people. We save from destruction remnants of oppressed nations, laboriously and expensively giving them sanitary accommodation, teaching their children, respecting their faiths' – even if few showed much gratitude for it.[82]

Sir Michael O'Dwyer, who gained notoriety as the Lieutenant Governor of Punjab after the Jallianwala Bagh massacre of 1919 in Amritsar when British troops opened fire on peaceful protesters complaining about the arrest of pro-independence leaders, was even more emphatic. 'The British Empire in India is the greatest achievement of our race,' he wrote. 'It has been built up by the blood, the brains and the energy of our ancestors.' In any event, he insisted, 'INDIA NEVER HAD – unity, security, peace, justice, communications, public health – until the British came.'[83]

Such self-congratulation hid the mechanics of how control was ruthlessly exerted to keep local populations in place – and apart. One historian has noted that Indian regiments were 'organised to kill each other should the British desire it', a scheme attested by comments made by Sir Charles Wood, Secretary of State for India in the second half of the nineteenth century. Wood had shown his colours when he opposed support for relief in Ireland during the terrible famine of the mid-1840s, claiming that this was 'a calamity' which had been 'sent by Providence' and would help stimulate better farming practices in the long run; famine, mass starvation and death on an apocalyptic scale were a price worth paying.[84] His view of India and Indians was no more enlightened. The reason for keeping ethnic groups apart in the army, he wrote, was simple: 'If one regiment mutinies, I should like to have the next so alien that it would be ready to fire into it, so that Sikh might fire into Hindu, Gurkha into either, without any scruple in case of need.'[85]

The overwhelming dominance of colonisers offered almost unlimited and irresistible temptations.[86] The Belgian King Leopold I simply asserted that the Congo River basin was his own – sparking a set of diplomatic crises not in West Africa but in Europe, where some objected that they had been deprived by Leopold's action from undertaking their own exploitation. Eventually, Leopold's 'ownership' of territories five times the size of France was endorsed by European politicians at a conference in Berlin in 1884–5, where the primary concern was to ensure that disputes between colonial powers should be settled peacefully – in order to avoid a war close to home. This mirrored attitudes to resources, to the environment and to human life outside the settler world: all were fruits that were ripe for the taking.[87]

Africa was one of the last to be plucked, a function of long-standing ideas about the continent and its many different peoples and cultures that were deeply rooted in prejudice and racism. It was significant, though, that as had been the case with the establishment of transatlantic slavery in the sixteenth century, Europeans proved singularly poor at making inroads beyond the coasts and their immediate hinterland. This speaks of the resilience and adaptability of local political leadership, and shows that their consolidation of authority was a logical response to the threats posed by non-native traders as well as to the opportunities that they offered.

By the late nineteenth century, the accelerations brought by the industrial revolution tipped the balance decisively in favour of European outsiders, most obviously because of the improvements in weaponry which meant that more could be done more quickly by fewer men. For example, in 1897, James Phillips, the Deputy Commissioner and Consul for the Niger Coast Protectorate, set off to overthrow the Oba (king) of Benin, accompanied by half a dozen officials, two businessmen and a train of porters. Their ambush – and Phillips' death – became a cause célèbre in London. 'A deplorable catastrophe' had taken place, said the *Daily Telegraph*, which lamented that 'a gallant body of Englishmen have fallen victim to their efforts to bring West Africa within the outer fringes at least of civilisation'. The paper did not ask why this gallant body's interest and motivations might not have been welcome.[88]

Reprisals were demanded throughout the press to avenge the apparent compromising of honour, and to teach the Oba 'the wholesome lesson that not only is English faith to be trusted and English friendship to be sought after, but that English justice, when outraged, is something to be feared'.[89] The expedition to 'avenge' Phillips brought about one of the more shameful episodes of destruction, murder and theft of African cultural and political heritage, not least of the 'Benin bronzes' which today stand in some of the world's leading museums, and which have been central to calls for the return of looted artworks to the places and the peoples from whom they were taken.[90]

At the time, though, teaching the Oba and the people of Benin a lesson in how they should understand their position in the world seemed perfectly natural. After being detained, the Oba was informed that he was no longer the ruler of his own lands; 'the white man', he was told, 'is the only man who is King in this country'. The local population were to be shown 'how a country of black men ought to be governed', by a British judge sent to oversee a 'trial' of the Oba to consider his role in the death of Phillips. If any evidence was found connecting the leader to the murder, the judge told him, 'I will hang you here.'[91]

The seemingly unstoppable rise of the west caused soul-searching and even sorrow. In Vietnam, for example, some called for a 'new learning' that moved away from traditional models to linguistic, economic and political innovations. 'In ancient times', wrote one Vietnamese author in 1904, 'Asia was the source of civilisation.' Vietnam had possessed 'fertile land, a moderate climate, plenty of rice, silk worms, and forestry products and a seacoast longer than most'. But now 'we no longer have forestry products and other resources. We no longer control hundreds of goods and benefits of our country, such as cloth, crepe, velvet, silk, shoes, sandals, handkerchiefs, spectacles, umbrellas,' or dozens of other items, all painstakingly listed.[92]

Others among the colonised communities saw things in a similar way, but called for action. 'Asia has sat too long in darkness and in the shadow of death,' railed a group of radical Indian revolutionaries in exile in 1909, calling for an Asian parliament to be established made up of 'educated Indians, Osmanlis, Egyptians, Japanese, Chinese, Arabs, Armenians, Parsis, Persians, Siamese, and others' to help rise up against the domination of European imperial powers.[93] In other cases, passionate anti-colonialist calls for change brought fleeting successes – as in much of the Russian empire after the abdication of the Tsar in 1917, when extensive rights of self-determination were given to minorities in an initial blossoming of optimism and creativity, before crushing persecution set in once again. A burst of poetry, creative writing and visual arts lit up Russian Central Asia before being suffocated as the Soviet Union began to centralise and to deprive of oxygen everyone and anyone who might threaten the communist dream. In such scenarios, suspicions fell quickly and decisively on those who were ethnically distinct or lived in peripheral, frontier regions – or both.[94]

Anti-colonial attitudes hardened, often reinforced by strong ecological agendas that pointed out how lands were being stripped, overworked and degraded for the benefit of people living thousands of kilometres away. 'India's salvation', wrote Mahatma Gandhi in 1909, 'consists of unlearning what she has learnt during the past fifty years.' Modernity had brought unhappiness and oppression. 'The railways, telegraphs, hospitals, lawyers, doctors, and such like have all to go,' he went on. 'Machinery is the main symbol of modern civilisation; it represents a great sin.'[95] Urbanisation, he predicted later, was sure to lead to 'a slow but sure death for [India's] villages and villagers'.[96]

True happiness could only come from living 'the simple peasant life' and rejecting the technology, the consumption and the ravages of colonialism. 'The British Empire today', he wrote bitterly soon after the end of the First World War, 'represents Satanism … repression and terrorism.' It 'will stoop to any atrocity' to boost itself, he added; it was a source of evil and 'the height of tyranny'.[97]

Others too were struck by the pace and deleterious effects of modern life. Vsevolod Timonov was one Russian scholar who was sharply critical of the way 'Nature's harmony' was being ruined in the search for 'immediate profits'. Human activities and lifestyles meant that factories 'spew their foul-smelling gases into the atmosphere, greatly impairing the enjoyment of nature'. The result, he concluded, was that the 'climate is being ruined'.[98] Another Russian author, Leo Tolstoy, renounced alcohol, became a vegetarian and gave up handling money as part of a search for a simple, self-sufficient and notionally traditional lifestyle – which in turn inspired Gandhi to create a utopian community in South Africa based on the same principles and ideals. Tolstoy had been so influential, in fact, that Gandhi wrote to tell him of his development, to thank him for his guidance and to reveal that the ashram had been christened 'Tolstoy Farm' in his honour.[99] For Gandhi, the idea that thousands of men worked in factories and mines in conditions 'worse than [those] of beasts' and women laboured 'for the sake of a pittance' was despicable; it could hardly be described as 'civilisation', he said.[100]

The hypothesis that humanity was dangerous – to itself and the natural world – gained currency in the nineteenth century, with Ralph Waldo Emerson urging limits to how the wilderness was treated, and George Perkins Marsh warning that man wages 'an almost indiscriminate warfare upon all the forms of animal and vegetable existence around him'. Human intervention was both damaging and relentless: as 'man … advances in civilization, he gradually eradicates or transforms every spontaneous product of the soil he occupies'.[101]

The logical culmination of such thinking came in a famous essay written in the 1960s, in which Lynn White argued that Judaeo-Christian society had introduced a world view that had made people less likely to care for the environment because it promoted humans as superior to and separate from nature – with the result that they became the primary causes of ecological crisis.[102] This reveals much about Eurocentric ideas from the Enlightenment onwards which characterise 'eastern' belief systems as more environmentally friendly, and sees people living in Asia in particular as being imbued with noble, almost mystical attitudes to life, spirituality and nature; this itself is a form of orientalism. In fact, religious tradition was not the problem nor the source of the problem; greed and personal gain were.

Although it would be wrong to suggest that landscapes had been untouched, forests left intact and ecologies undisturbed until Europeans arrived to disrupt a golden age, the reality was that extraction during the colonial era, facilitated by technologies and labour forces that made land clearance quicker and more extensive than ever before, took place on scales that were unprecedented.[103] Moreover, as recent scholarship has emphasised, agricultural policies (in particular in relation to woodlands) were closely linked to population resettlement, the consolidation of authority and social engineering, and therefore to the extension of political control, especially in ecologically and geographically peripheral regions. As one scholar has put it, environmental and colonial rule went hand in hand.[104]

Nowhere was this clearer than in North America, where indigenous peoples were pushed off their lands by force and sometime by deception. Moving the 'Indians' to 'suitable lands west of the Mississippi', stated James Barbour, the Secretary of War of the United States, would 'produce the happiest benefits upon the Indian race' – without mentioning the benefits that the lands they vacated would bring to their new occupiers. Some tribes, such as the Senecas, had themselves to blame, according to officials who said that the suffering that followed forced auctions of property and migration under duress was 'their own fault' for not choosing better substitute territories to move to.[105]

Other politicians urged brutal treatment in order to claim the best lands for crops and grazing for themselves. At the start of the Black Hawk War of the 1830s, one editorial urged John Reynolds, the Governor of Illinois, to 'carry on a war of extermination until there shall be no Indian (with his scalp on) left to the north part of Illinois'.[106] The pattern of dispossession was one that extended for decades. At noon on 22 April 1889, to cite one example, a gunshot signalled the 'right' of settlers to claim land in Oklahoma that had been assigned to the Creek and Seminole peoples as part of previous settlements and pressured migrations. By the end of the day, 2 million acres had been claimed in plots of 160 acres; by sundown, new cities with populations of as many as 10,000 had been founded, with street grids planned, lots staked out and thoughts already turning to the structure of civic government.[107]

The furious pace of change offered tantalising prospects of fortunes to be made and of social mobility. It also captured the imagination of writers like Anton Chekhov, whose play *The Cherry Orchard* describes perfectly the ambiguities of the old being replaced by the new, and the challenges of adaptation, as Madame Ranevskaya, a blue-blooded landowner, struggles to come to terms with a changing world epitomised by Lopakhin, a self-made man whose father had been a peasant and grandfather a serf. The play ends with Lopakhin buying the estate where he had grown up, accompanied by the sound of the orchard being chopped down – with the repurposing of nature to suit modern needs and tastes a symbolic nod to the changing times and the 'progress' of the modern era.[108]

Such advancement came at a price. Marx expressed his concern about the relentless determination to 'exploit the earth's surface, the bowels of the earth, the air', which was driven by the desire to profit at nature's expense.[109] The rush to exploit the land brought about ravenous demand for returns on investment, and led to ecological exhaustion. The development of Alabama was paid for by capital gathered in faraway locations, from

Wall Street to cities across Europe. The black prairie lands, with their dark, fertile soils high in calcium deposits left over from previous periods of climatic change, were particularly attractive. Few cared that the switch to monoculture and heavy exploitation produced very different results to the way that the Creek people, for example, had managed their lands through sophisticated models of biodiversity that combined multicropping with careful rotation to ensure long-term sustainability.[110]

It was true that colonialism did not always lead to degradation. Imperial authorities in Japan invested considerable resources in massive tree-planting activities in Korea, planting more than a million trees in the first decades of the twentieth century and protecting forests by law – although there was also heavy investment in megaprojects such as dams, ports and other monuments that echo European policies and practices. Japanese motivations here were centred not on conservationism or attitudes to forests, but rather on the centrality of wood in the pre-industrial history of Japan, on the conceptualisation of the country as a 'luxuriantly green realm'. The reason to preserve forests was not about protecting nature, but rather the promotion of national identity, statecraft and rulership at a notional level, combined with securing access to unlimited stocks of wood for fuel and building. Taken together, this all demonstrated the prescience of the emperor and the imperial court.[111]

Taken as a whole the story of the nineteenth century – and particularly the second half – was one of the world becoming smaller and smaller, with peoples and places being brought closer together as a result of the development of railways, bigger, faster and more reliable ships and new technologies such as telegraph systems that allowed information to be shared quickly. It was not only an age of new infrastructures that accelerated globalisation but one that saw the rise of cities, which sprang up like mushrooms and became swollen by inflows of inhabitants. It was perhaps not surprising that many of the largest cities were located on the coast, with good harbour access that allowed ships to load cheaply and efficiently. Ports were funnels for commodities, natural resources and minerals extracted from colonial hinterlands, as well as valves for manufactured goods that flowed in the opposite direction, out from industrialised Europe into new markets.[112]

There was growing awareness that the intensification of exchange and of consumption came at a price – though, needless to say, that meant little to investors in railway financing across North America, Russia and Africa who barely thought about the ecological costs that came with deforestation or with the imposition of livestock, crops and mines. The construction of a railway line in Equatorial Africa proved to be one of the deadliest in history, resulting in tens of thousands of deaths from overwork, disease, malnutrition and physical abuse – but providing guaranteed profits for the French company that built it.[113]

Those with more of a conscience, open mind, or both, paid greater attention to the ways in which environmental and climatic change had significant consequences. Phenomena like the Carrington Event in 1859, a massive solar storm and coronal mass ejection that knocked out telegraph stations around the world, or the dramatic eruption of Krakatoa in 1883, which had an explosive power that was an estimated four times greater than the most powerful thermonuclear device ever detonated – or forty times the combined force of all the conventional explosives used during the Second World War – did much to focus attention on weather patterns and to spur research into how they were changing and the extent to which this was the result of human activities and interventions in the landscape.[114]

Scientists had been trying to gain a better understanding of climatic shifts for some time. In 1801, for example, the renowned astronomer Sir William Herschel wrote a paper in which he suggested that sunspots were a crucial factor in weather conditions and also in harvest yields, wheat prices and economic cycles. Others followed in the ensuing decades, including Arthur Schuster, who observed that good vintages of wine seemed to be correlated with the eleven-year solar cycle.[115] William Jevons went further in the 1870s, linking the sun's activities in the eighteenth and nineteenth centuries with prices, commercial crises and a pattern of 'unquestionable collapse' of economies.[116]

Others investigated atmospheric conditions. The French scientist and mathematician Joseph Fourier was one of the first to look at this methodically, suggesting that gases in the atmosphere served as a barrier that trapped heat and kept the earth warm – and he questioned whether 'the progress of human society' around the globe could be responsible for 'remarkable changes', including 'variations in mean temperatures'.[117] Another pioneer was Eunice Foote, who by the 1850s, realised how significant her findings were for science and for the future of the planet. Foote conducted experiments in which she heated combinations of gases in glass cylinders and observed that carbon dioxide and water vapour not only became hotter faster than other combinations, but also were 'many times as long in cooling' as cylinders containing different gases when removed from the source of the heat. 'An atmosphere of that gas would give to our earth a high temperature.'[118]

By the turn of the twentieth century, further research by John Tyndall, Samuel Pierpont Langley, T. C. Chamberlain and, most famously, Svante Arrhenius had established the principles of the greenhouse effect – although this research was driven not by any concern about rising levels of CO_2 but rather by efforts to investigate the world's geological and geophysical past. Arrhenius was not worried about global warming – indeed, quite the opposite: he wondered whether heating the earth might be beneficial and lead to a 'more equable' environment, more abundant plant life and higher food production.[119] Despite these advances, climate science was for decades pushed to one side as a fringe subject, a pursuit for amateurs, crackpots and oddball academics rather than one worthy of serious investigation.[120]

If such events brought questions about solar cycles, volcanic activity and weather patterns into public consciousness, so too did an upsurge of popular science writing and early science fiction, much of which focused on anthropogenic change, on ways in which human behaviour altered the climate for good or for ill. As early as the 1820s, authors like Faddei Bulgarin could be found pondering a world where Russian scientists had successfully warmed its Arctic coastline and turned it into a maritime idyll. A few decades later, Byron Brooks and Lysander Richards separately came up with the idea of the Sahara desert being transformed into fields through manipulation of the climate. British writers speculated about the horrors of alterations in the Gulf Stream patterns that would surely result from the construction of the Panama canal – and would bring down the empire as a result of a fundamentally changing climate.[121]

Or there was George Griffith, in whose book *The Great Weather Syndicate* the hero, Arthur Arkwright, develops a machine that changes the climate and promises to make him the 'master of the fate of the world' by enabling him and his 'syndicate' to sell bespoke weather conditions to those willing and able to pay for them.[122] Another author who wrote on a similar theme was Jules Verne, whose *Sans dessus dessous* was a biting satire of a plan by reckless investors to tilt the axis of the earth, equalising global climates in order to eliminate seasons and differences in the length of the day and night, but also so as to melt the Arctic and gain access to enormous coal reserves.[123]

What Verne and others could not have known was that sea levels were not only rising globally in the late nineteenth and early twentieth centuries but were beginning to do so at an accelerated rate.[124] Recent research pinpoints a starting date of 1863 for the sea-level rises, which do not seem to have been associated with mass loss of the Greenland Ice Sheet or with anthropogenic factors; instead, they were more likely linked to ocean circulation changes resulting from the Atlantic Meridional Overturning Circulation (AMOC), the strength of the Florida Current and the strength and position of the Gulf Stream, as well as to changing patterns in atmospheric winds, buoyancy fluxes and pressure.[125]

Works conjuring up dystopian (and utopian) futures that were framed by climatic change point to a growing interest in the ways that human activities had an impact on the natural world and the environment. This was not entirely surprising, especially in places that had industrialised early and intensively: air pollution in cities in Britain was so severe that it raised infant mortality by as much as 8 per cent, while industrial coal had a measurable and highly detrimental effect on urban life expectancy during the later nineteenth century.[126] In this period, atmospheric pollution from coal-fired industrialisation was fifty times higher than today and had a strong negative impact on health outcomes and on adult heights.[127]

City living was always noisy, bustling and chaotic. What made the nineteenth century different, however, was the scale and speed of the cities' growth. The population of Manchester quadrupled between 1801 and 1851, as people were drawn by the promise of work.[128] Such rapid expansion of urban areas, combined with poor sanitation and heavy levels of pollution that were emitted mainly from the burning of fossil fuels, shocked visitors. Friedrich Engels was struck by the 'foul air' of the city that caused 'blood-spitting, hard, noisy breathing, pains in the chest, coughs [and] sleeplessness', and where women and girls not only had to make dresses 'in almost total exclusion from fresh air' but worked in such poor light that many had trouble with their eyesight and some even went blind. This, along with the capitalist principles behind the factories that belched thick smoke and the work which was 'monotonous and demeaning', was nothing less than 'the barbarous exploitation of the workers'.[129] These conditions were mirrored all over the north-west, which in the words of a contemporary of Engels was full of 'little Manchesters'.[130]

While wealth and status have always provided one barrier to disease, they did not always offer sufficient protection. In 1841, William Harrison died just a month after being sworn in as the ninth President of the United States. Although his death has long been attributed to pneumonia, and to his decision not to wear a hat, overcoat and gloves on a bitterly cold inauguration day, it seems that what actually killed him was enteric fever, most likely caused by poor sanitation in Washington, DC, and specifically by the White House water supply being located close to marshy public ground where sewage flowed freely in the absence of a city sewer system. It seems too that two of his successors – Presidents Polk and Taylor – suffered from illness during their presidencies that may have stemmed from the same source.[131]

One reaction to the growth of cities, to pollution, to disease and to the degradation of the environment was a surge in literature, most notably in romantic poetry, which extolled the countryside and family life as an undisturbed idyll, unspoiled by human intervention. These were all a sharp contrast to the reality of industrialisation, which according to Wordsworth meant that mothers had 'no nice arts / Of needlework' to look forward to, while young boys had the 'short holiday of childhood' curtailed as they were pushed into factories as workers and 'prisoners'.[132]

It did not take much to grasp, in other words, that modernity came at a cost – and that those costs were not evenly distributed globally. Air pollution, for example, was largely restricted to places that industrialised early and quickly, above all cities in northern Europe and North America; water and riverine pollution, on the other hand, was devastating in regions where severe deforestation and land clearing had taken place. The large-scale movement of people had been instigated both by urbanisation and by the distribution of labour, whether by force, as a response to demand or as a reflection of the search for opportunity. As a result, the concentration and dispersal of people shifted more dramatically and more quickly than at any point in human history. As they did so, they brought consequences whose legacies are very much part of the challenges we face in the present day. Perhaps the most obvious and resonant was the impact of epidemic disease.

Urbanisation brought more and more people into closer contact, which not only accelerated the rhythms of commercial and cultural exchange but promoted the spread of infectious diseases. These did not only affect humans: in the autumn of 1872, for example, equine influenza took hold across North America, appearing first near Toronto and reaching the Gulf coast by the end of the year and the west coast by the spring. Although the disease rarely proved fatal (with mortality rates of around 2 per cent), it had the effect of leaving horses unable to work through exhaustion; this caused major economic disruption, in no small part because of the central role played by the animals in hauling 'coal, bales and boxes' in cities. One result was a sharp rise in the cost of goods and services, which some believed was the result of opportunistic price gouging. Another was the vulnerability of cities to fire, with one enormous blaze in Boston attributed to the lack of horses for pulling fire-tending equipment into place.[133]

Epizootic disease elsewhere had unexpected outcomes, most notably in East and southern Africa where an outbreak of rinderpest in the 1890s killed millions of cattle as well as sheep, goats and other livestock; this precipitated famine that resulted in the deaths of two-thirds of the Maasai from starvation, weakened local social and political structures, caused widespread violence and ultimately opened the door to the expansion of colonial authority at the expense of local elites.[134]

In other places, too, misfortune for some brought opportunity for others. An outbreak of measles in Fiji in 1875 led to an increase in demand for Indian labour, not least because of high immunity levels acquired during infancy in South Asian populations.[135] Pacific islander plantation workers in Queensland and elsewhere in Australia experienced unusually high mortality rates from measles, most notably during the first year, which shows how epidemiological boundaries shifted as migrant labour moved – or was moved – in order to transform and refashion landscapes for growing labour-intensive crops.[136]

As one prominent historian has put it, the intensification of intercontinental connections in the nineteenth century brought about 'the unification of the globe by disease', with trade routes, migration corridors and troop movements serving to create a 'common market of bacilli' criss-crossing the world and linking it together.[137] Epidemic and pandemic disease were part of the price to pay as human interactions and activities spread pathogens from one continent to another. Ports like

Bombay, Cape Town, Singapore, Hong Kong and Calcutta were crucial not only for the loading and unloading of goods but as transmission points in an interconnected global disease network.[138]

Other nodes were important too, of which Jeddah was perhaps the most significant. Since the time of the Prophet Muḥammad, Muslims had been expected to undertake the hajj, a pilgrimage to Mecca that involved the performance of a series of rituals. The journey became synonymous with outbreaks of cholera that intensified with the rise of steamer ships and the opening of the Suez canal. Cholera broke out in Mecca on average every three years in the nineteenth century, with eruptions in 1831, 1865 and 1893 each resulting in tens of thousands of deaths.[139]

Such events had parallels. As it was expressed at a sanitary conference in 1866, pilgrimage was 'the most powerful of all the causes which conduce to the development and to the propagation of epidemics of cholera'.[140] As well as Mecca, 'places where congregations of Hindoo pilgrims take place' were notorious for the rise in infection, which fitted into colonial tropes of the pilgrim as 'filthy, superstitious, inherently irrational and resistant to sanitation measures' introduced by the state.[141]

The Hindu festivals that are held in northern India at alternating locations on four sacred rivers – Hardwar on the Ganges, Nashik on the Godavari, Ujjain on the Shirpa and Prayag at the confluence of the Ganges, the Yamuna and the mythical Sarasvati – were a particular concern. This was especially true of the Kumbh Mela, which takes place roughly every twelve years and attracts myriads of pilgrims: the gathering in 2019 was estimated to have been attended by 50 million people.[142] These festivals became a deadly source of infection and dissemination, for example in 1867, when torrential rains saturated the ground, resulting in a major epidemic which spread despite attempts by the colonial authorities to screen pilgrims and to quarantine those showing symptoms. Disease spread despite the construction of stone kilns to burn excrement, as well as trench latrines that were then covered by dry earth – efforts that were initially so successful that one observer noted that 'not a single Anglo-Saxon, a race far more sensitive to foul smells than Natives, perceived [any smell]'. Events in 1879, 1891 and 1901 also brought serious outbreaks.[143]

Even such disasters could have silver linings. For one thing, large-scale disease encouraged scientific research and investigation by scholars and doctors such as John Snow, Filippo Pacini and Robert Koch to identify the causes of cholera, to devise treatments and eventually to identify the cholera bacillus itself.[144] For another, suffering brought about shifts in ideas about civic responsibility, with some communities like the Parsis in India taking pride in founding hospitals to tend to the sick. Ten major international conferences between 1851 and 1900 which saw researchers from all over the world share their findings and hypotheses represented high levels of collaboration.[145]

Other cases provided further evidence of the downsides of increasingly integrated transport links and high population densities. In the summer of 1889, the first cases of what appears to have been a highly virulent strain of influenza were detected in Bukhara in Central Asia. Not long afterwards, cases were being detected across the Russian empire, leading to factories and schools being closed in St Petersburg where almost 20 per cent of the population became infected. The disease spread quickly to Germany and by the end of the year was ravaging cities on the east coast of North America, before affecting populations from New Orleans to San Francisco – as well as reaching Constantinople, where half the population fell ill. Within four months, the virus had circumnavigated the globe, killing about 1 million people.[146] A new hypothesis has suggested that the pandemic might in fact have been the result of a coronavirus, rather than influenza; whichever it was, the ways in which human populations lived and travelled provided ideal routes for the pathogen to spread around the world.[147]

Concerns about the spread of disease, political fragility and economic dislocation prompted rallying calls for international co-operation. At a conference on plague prevention in 1911, for example, the Qing Viceroy of Manchuria, Xi Liang, urged delegates to work out how to develop safeguards that 'will result in the saving of human lives, not only of this country but of others also, should this terrible disease unfortunately break out elsewhere'. Efforts to implement strategies to identify infectious disease and prevent its spread became a major focus for policy planners and non-profit organisations in other parts of the world, as well as for international collaboration: the ill-fated League of Nations set up an agency in 1924 that was dedicated to health organisation, while the Rockefeller Foundation invested more money in China in pursuit of disease prevention than any country outside the United States.[148]

This attention was partly a response to the most celebrated pandemic of the last century, the Spanish flu of 1918–20, which was likewise able to piggyback on a particular set of conditions that were as advantageous for the virus as they were disastrous for the people it infected. Estimates of the numbers who died from Spanish flu are wildly divergent, with some suggesting a figure of around 17 million and others suggesting that it may have been as high as 100 million.[149] The mass demobilisation of troops following the end of the First World War, combined with low calorie consumption as a result of four years of conflict in Europe, Asia and Africa which reduced natural immunity, helped spread the disease around the world.[150]

Poor hygiene levels in hospitals treating infected patients made matters worse still, and it has been suggested that a large number of fatalities – perhaps even the majority – resulted from secondary bacterial pneumonia caused by common upper respiratory-tract bacteria.[151] Location mattered too: mortality rates in cities were high, partly because populations living in close proximity provide obvious vectors for transmissions. But death rates were also conspicuously high in cities that burned more coal; those that did experienced tens of thousands more fatalities than those that did not.[152] Urbanised, industrialised cities proved to be more fragile and vulnerable, in other words, than places that were less connected.

This did not just matter in the short term, for there were long-term consequences, as recent research on the Spanish flu has shown. The disease had profound effects on infant mortality in Brazil, for example, where it also significantly altered gender ratios.[153] Evidence from the United States surveying outcomes over many decades shows that the cohort of children *in utero* in 1918–20 had increased physical impairments, lower incomes and reduced educational attainments compared to those born before or after the pandemic.[154] No less strikingly, civic responses to the Spanish flu were closely linked to voting patterns and political extremism in Germany: areas most affected by the pandemic, and where per capita spending by local authorities was low in the following decades, saw markedly higher numbers voting for Hitler and the National Socialists in the early 1930s.[155]

Spanish flu caused the highest number of known deaths in history from a single pandemic. It has long been suspected that a key factor in its potency was the use of chlorine gas on the battlefields of Flanders and northern France, which either caused or accelerated the mutation of a virus that had originated in Asia and been brought to Europe by Allied troops.[156] It seems, however, that a series of climate anomalies in the form of torrential rains and depressed temperatures – especially during the autumns of 1917 and 1918 – also played an important role. Historians have noted that the adverse weather had a material bearing on the outcome of battles during the First World War, such as flooding of trenches, cessation of operations because of waterlogging and substantially increased casualty numbers. Heavy rains and cold were the result of an unusual spike in cold, wet marine air from the North Atlantic – the highest concentrations in a century. These also provided ideal conditions for the survival and replication of the virus in Europe, both by enhancing infectivity in pools of water and perhaps also by interrupting the migration of birds and ducks whose infected droppings contaminated water sources and helped magnify the spread of disease.[157]

The Spanish flu was a product of the suffering of the First World War that had itself left as many as 20 million dead; a result of military hostilities in Europe, Africa and Asia and also because of chronic food-supply crises – above all in the German, Ottoman and Russian empires. Russia had been the source of around a third of global wheat supply before 1914, so the closure of the Bosporus inevitably put a strain on economies around the world, exacerbated by challenging climate conditions: at the start of the war, unfavourable weather led to shortfalls from major producers such as Canada and Australia, which had both suffered from drought, the latter yielding barely a quarter of its usual output; the crop in South America was unexpectedly poor, while an early winter freeze in the United States produced transportation delays west of the Great Lakes. This prompted panic in London, where cables were sent to India urging the Viceroy to boost exports to maintain supply – and to keep prices down, as farmers and speculators in the United States in particular were already moving in to take advantage of the squeeze.[158]

The demands of the military for manpower made matters worse, with declines in grain production in Russia closely correlated with the military draft. The thinning out of the labour force brought about declines in the regions where crops were grown, and commensurate falls in yields. Peasant farms additionally reacted to conscription and to the uncertainties generated by wartime by refusing to sell grain, which deepened food crises and ultimately resulted in shortages and queues for bread. All this helped lay the ground for revolution, not least by highlighting the ineptitude of the tsarist government.[159]

In some cases, most notably Central Asia – a region that was poorly integrated into the Russian empire – ineptitude was closely linked to abuse of power by local officials responsible for overseeing conscription, which in turn led to popular dissatisfaction and then to a series of open revolts.[160] While these are often seen by modern scholars as the seeds that grew into the Russian revolution, a more useful and compelling way to understand the uprisings is as part of wider contemporaneous resistance movements in South Asia, North Africa, West Africa and Ireland and beyond that aimed to throw off colonial rule.[161]

One reason for this was the insatiable demands made on colonial societies by those who controlled them and drew on resources in ever greater volumes in increasingly interventionist ways, with mistreatment of local populations proving even more antagonistic than before the war.[162] In France, more than 350,000 hectares of forest were cut down during the First World War in order to provide wood for trench building, camps, fuel and more – which had obvious implications for ecological systems in France and for the pressures on its colonies to make up six decades' worth of tree harvests.[163]

African copper had already electrified European cities by providing millions of kilometres of cabling to help power everything from elegant soirées to factories churning out products. It now helped deliver death, destruction and ecological damage on an unprecedented scale: copper was sucked in from fields that had been opened up and exploited in Central Africa as well as elsewhere to create casings for the 1.45 billion artillery shells fired in western Europe alone, not to mention the copper and lead required for countless rounds of rifle cartridges and small-arms bullets. Their use brought about soil contamination in the killing fields of northern Europe that is still detectable today.[164]

These resources were all secured by colonial officials who thought it was their right to exploit and extract what was needed to undertake a war between European powers based on hypercompetition between small groups within the ruling elites. Millions of men were enlisted from India, from Africa and from Indo-China, not to mention those who volunteered to serve in the armed forces of Australia, New Zealand and Canada. The pressure on the colonies to serve their masters acted as a catalyst for revolutionary and anti-colonial movements which had already begun to communicate and co-operate through networks ironically flourishing in precisely the cities and ports that had fostered globalisation and cemented the economic power of the industrialised world.[165]

As the US President Woodrow Wilson put it in 1917 when trying to justify staying out of the war, the United States was 'the only one of the great White nations that is free from war today', and it would be 'a crime against civilisation' for that to change. In any event, as he told one key adviser, it was essential for the US to stay out of the conflict so that when peace eventually came it could help rebuild 'the nations ravaged by war'; this was vital, he said, so that 'white civilisation and its domination of the world' should continue unchallenged.[166]

Wilson was hardly alone. Max Weber, whose belief that agricultural productivity was low in less developed countries because peasant farmers were 'irrational' proved highly influential with economists and policy planners in the 1950s and 1960s, wrote that 'a dross of African and Asiatic savages and all the world's rabble of thieves and lumpens' stood armed to fight on the western front in 1917 – without mentioning that many of them were about to give up their lives thanks to the whims and preconceptions of a set of emperors and leaders obsessed by ideas about the balance of power in Europe.[167] Even in the 1930s, the Governor General of the Netherlands East Indies said bluntly that 'We have ruled here for 300 years with the whip and the club, and we shall still be doing it for another 300 years.'[168]

In the context of nature, the environment and climate, such views were important indications of a taxonomy and ranking that placed white Europeans at the apex of humanity; but they also represented a conceptualisation of the natural world as being at the disposal of those who saw themselves as best suited and most entitled to use and control the fruits of the land, agricultural and mineral alike, while also being their most capable guardians. The First World War is often seen as marking the end of empires and the beginning of the end of colonialism. Much depends on the eye of the beholder, for when it came to nature, the environment and anthropogenic climate change, the century that followed witnessed a profound acceleration and intensification in the way that resources were extracted, consumed and used. The consequences of the twentieth century were to shape the fate of the twenty-first – and of the future beyond.

21

Fashioning New Utopias
(c.1920–c.1950)

It is imperative to preserve the German landscape, for it is, and always was, the ultimate foundation of the power and strength of the German people.

Adolf Hitler (1936)

Judged as a whole, the century that followed the start of the First World War was a sequence of catastrophes unparalleled both in human history and in that of the natural world. Millions of people were killed as a result of wars that were conceived, or rather misconceived, in courts, chanceries, presidential offices or revolutionary camps. Millions were killed as a result of persecution and hatred founded on grotesque preconceptions about race, religion or ethnicity. Millions died as a result of famine, deliberate starvation or lack of access to basic healthcare. The suffering of the last hundred years or so has been by far the greatest in recorded history in terms of its scale and its horror.

The heavy human costs were matched by those inflicted on the natural world. The last century was one of profound ecological change that ranged from the impact of mass urbanisation to the large-scale extraction of resources required to support, service and power populations living in cities of unprecedented size. It has been a period during which the consequences of how we live have been poorly understood or little thought about – with the result that environmental and climatic changes of the present and future are being and will be shaped by what has already happened in the past, rather than simply by decisions made today.

Much of this has been driven by higher levels of exchange within and between different regions and continents and by an intensification of globalisation, whose roots long predate the modern era. New technologies provided the basis for a sharp acceleration from the eighteenth century onwards, with mechanisation, industrialisation and improvements in speed and cost of transportation by rail and by sea all providing gains that helped tie the world together. All depended on minerals like coal, iron, copper and steel, which in turn attracted attention to places holding reserves that could be exploited.

These often lay in locations that were difficult to reach or were not under the control of those most motivated to gain access to them. Oil provides one obvious example. The value of petroleum became obvious in the later part of the nineteenth century as an energy source that was easier to extract and cheaper to transport and store than coal, as well as having a higher energy density. Oil – and gas – did not replace coal, but rather served as a supplement long into the twentieth century, only displacing the latter from the 1970s as coal-fired steam engines gave way to petrol-powered combustion engines, as oil and gas heating took over from coal ovens and as hydrocarbons became a primary source of electricity production.[1]

Oil strikes in Pennsylvania and then by the Caspian Sea provided the spark for a scramble to establish further commercially viable wells in these and other locations around the world, with attention falling on Burma and the East Indies and then on Persia following a massive series of discoveries from 1907. These each provided the seeds for personal fortunes and for the rise of giant oil companies, including Standard Oil, Burmah, Shell and BP, and other operators such as the Nobel Brothers, which ultimately served as a source of wealth for Alfred Nobel and the prizes that bear his name.[2]

Production rose dramatically in response to soaring demand that was itself fuelled by innovations such as the motor car. In 1900, there were just over four thousand vehicles on the roads in the United States. Twenty years later, that had risen to almost two million.[3] Production was dominated by Model T Fords, whose success was based on streamlined, standardised design and a moving assembly line that allowed costs to be driven down and affordability up.[4]

By this time, ensuring reliable supplies had become a major area of concern for countries in Europe, whose geological and climatic history had left a continent more or less bereft of crude oil, with a few modest exceptions. Britain was particularly vulnerable, as leading politicians and officials realised. 'The only big potential supply', wrote Sir Maurice Hankey as the First World War was still raging, 'is the Persian and Mesopotamian supply.' As such, gaining 'control of these oil supplies', the Secretary to the War Cabinet went on, should be considered nothing less than 'a first-class war aim'.[5]

Oil shaped the history of the Middle East, and arguably much besides. There were other enormous resources, of course, not least in Venezuela, whose coastline is still home to the world's largest reserves.[6] But taken together it was not hard to see why the oil of Iran, Iraq, Saudi Arabia and elsewhere in the Gulf was being referred to in the 1940s by US government envoys as 'the greatest single prize in history'.[7] The lack of access to oil sources played a crucial role in the strategic unravelling of the Second World War, responsible both for the ill-fated German attempt to push south into the Caucasus to gain access to oilfields and for Japan's attack on Pearl Harbor in 1941, which was motivated at least in part by Tokyo's acute awareness of Japan's energy limitations and by its desire to have a free hand in securing oil and other minerals in resource-rich locations across South-East Asia.[8]

Oil and gas have been central to global geopolitics over the eight decades that have followed, shaping the rise of petrostates, helping pay for high-profile football teams and World Cup tournaments, Formula One races and eye-poppingly lucrative golf tournaments, while also being used as a source of oligarch wealth and latterly as a weapon of control for Russia in its relations with Europe and the west following the invasion of Ukraine in 2022.

Anxiety over energy prices has been a crucial factor in the United States' domestic politics as well as in its foreign, defence and economic affairs, whether relating to pipeline construction in North America, to permits for drilling new wells or to developing methods for unlocking shale which has helped turn the US from an importer into an exporter of all oil products, including crude and refined petroleum products.[9] The energy needs of India and China, both of which are heavily dependent on oil and gas imports, are not merely an important part of the long-term future of the world's two most populous countries, but are matters of such fundamental vulnerability as to determine their policies towards oil- and gas-producing states, as well as towards multinational companies.[10]

Oil was just one example of the competition for natural resources. Another was gold, a metal that exists on earth as a result of extraterrestrial impacts over the course of billions of years, and whose distribution in commercially viable quantities results from the haphazard points of collisions of comets, meteors and asteroids.[11] Gold has been highly prized since antiquity, a marker of wealth and status, and in the modern world is also valued for its low conductivity, which makes it useful for circuit boards and wiring in cars and household appliances, such as microwaves, refrigerators and stoves.

Gold mining is often both inefficient and highly polluting: twenty tons of soil and rock are typically required to produce enough gold to create a single ring – with much of the waste contaminated with the cyanide and mercury that are used to extract gold.[12] Mining activities in the Grasberg minerals district in Papua in Indonesia, home to the world's largest proven gold and second-largest copper reserves respectively, had already discharged more than a billion tons of metal-laden tailings into the local river systems by 2006 – with this quantity increasing significantly as production has risen sharply since.[13] The scramble for gold has been instrumental in encroachments on indigenous lands in recent years, such as in the Amazon, but previous gold rushes also brought about sizeable changes in population movements, such as in California, Colorado, Siberia and Australia. These movements in turn led to transformations of the landscape as land was cleared (usually by burning), as towns, cities and transport infrastructure were built to support miners, as ores were deposited in rivers creating long-term problems of pollution, and as livestock were introduced as sources of protein, usually after native animals had all been killed and eaten.[14]

Another example is copper, whose usage and value soared in the early twentieth century and have continued to rise ever since; it will perhaps even replace hydrocarbons as the most sought-after material as the world transitions, or seeks to transition, to more carbon-friendly technologies. Copper, according to Goldman Sachs, is the 'oil of the twenty-first century', although this label has been given to lithium, to rare earths more generally and to hydrogen, as well as to non-natural resources such as data.[15] The importance of copper can be seen in the fact that the average US-built car contains more than twenty kilos of copper, while a typical electric car requires six times the mineral inputs of a conventional vehicle.[16]

Demand for copper encouraged large-scale investment in regions and locations rich in reserves, not least the copper belts of Central Africa, where some reports in the early twentieth century suggested the presence of 'a quantity of minerals that one can practically consider inexhaustible' and of exceptionally high quality to boot. The extraction of copper and of other metals provided the impetus for railway construction in Africa, with lines connecting to port cities on the coast. It brought social change too, because manpower requirements meant that large numbers of young men were drawn into copper-producing regions with obvious consequences for gender roles in societies with high levels of male outward migration, for agricultural production which required higher levels of female participation and also for ecological systems: mining and processing resulted in enormous waste heaps, liquid-suspended tailings and the discharge of particulates into water systems, as well as substantial amounts of sulphur dioxide. All of this resulted in major damage to soil, animal and plant life and helped create virulent disease environments.[17]

The cutting down of forests for lumber for boilers, for poles to support mines and for railway sleepers did much the same, with the four largest mines in Central and southern Africa alone requiring almost 57,000 cubic metres of sawn timber per year. Furthermore, the demand for protein to feed workers helped devastate aquatic ecosystems, as fish stocks were heavily depleted by overfishing, which was facilitated by methods and techniques imported from Europe that did enormous damage.[18]

Copper demand was closely correlated with the global economy, which naturally meant that jobs and livelihoods were impacted by themes, trends and events that took place far away, out of sight. One example was the Great Depression, which had an effect on employment and settlement in Central Africa, leading to job losses as demand in other parts of the world collapsed. Another was the shock of the 1970s, when the oil crisis provoked not only sharp falls in demand for copper as economies contracted sharply and suddenly but a debt crisis in Zaire and Zambia, both of which were heavily dependent on copper revenues: the result was pressure to boost production at a time of falling prices to try to meet international obligations. Not surprisingly, this too had catastrophic environmental consequences.[19]

The list of minerals, metals and materials that were dragged towards the rich world of Europe and its settler offshoots, above all in the Americas, was – and remains – a long one. Rich, developed economies depend on vast quantities of natural resources at the lowest possible prices. Europe could not have been rebuilt as quickly nor as cheaply following the catastrophic damage of the Second World War without access to plentiful supplies of copper and other minerals from Africa. Cheap oil and gas have been the lifeblood of economic growth, rising living standards and mass consumerism, with the benefits felt most keenly by societies and states which had industrialised early and which had built institutions that protected investment.

Uranium from the Shinkolobwe mine at Katanga in southern Congo was far richer than any other source in the world – producing uranium oxide whose quality assayed as high as 75 per cent (compared to 0.02 per cent from ores in the United States and Canada). So important was Shinkolobwe to the US nuclear programme, and consequently to the Cold War, that it was deemed to be essential to US national security. Congo as a whole 'offers natural resources of extreme importance to our domestic economy', noted the officials and engineers who worked on the Manhattan Project; they went to great lengths to conceal the origin of the uranium used in the first successful atomic bomb test, claiming it derived from Canadian sources. As a report of 1951 declared, uranium from Congo was of 'capital importance to the free world'.[20]

If peace, freedom and prosperity hinged on being able to secure a wide variety of resources it was notable how few were available domestically, especially in Europe. It was apparent too that, as the benefits of extraction flowed into the developed world, states that were resource rich often had little to show for their natural wealth. This was in part the result of what has become known as the resource trap, whereby countries with oil, gas and mineral resources have either become or remained authoritarian, with limited distribution of rights and equalities through the wider population. The tendency for commodity prices to fluctuate dramatically from year to year also means that revenues can be unpredictable, dragging economies through boom-and-bust cycles, which can result in debt crises that further affect institutional development. Resource-rich governments typically underspend on health, education and social services, and typically overspend on government salaries, on fuel and food subsidies and on large monuments.[21]

One problem was that investment was concentrated around regions and facilities that were important for extraction rather than for social development. For example, Congo, home to such rich reserves of copper and uranium, and also of cobalt, tin and gold, became home by 1960 to eight international airports, thirty major airports and another hundred lesser airports, thanks to the mining industry – but there was no parallel construction of hospitals, schools and infrastructure that benefited the local population. Bribery of local officials was an intrinsic part of gaining access to reserves with the least resistance, in the fastest time and at the lowest possible price.[22]

It was significant too, of course, that many places that were rich in resources – in Africa but also elsewhere – had to deal with the consequences of colonialism, which had left patchy and sometimes poor systems of government in place. These had themselves succeeded colonial social and political structures that reduced human capital, limited capacity and made governance difficult, not least because of the way that states and provinces were set up according to the vagaries of colonial control.[23] In many locations, such as in West Africa, pre-colonial pasts also played a significant role in influencing the period after independence.[24]

But there is another important element. Although the age of colonialism drifted away in notional terms as states became independent in the course of the twentieth century, the lure of accessing the fruits of the earth proved impossible to resist. Interference in the domestic affairs of independent states was something that has defined the last hundred years or so, with obvious examples ranging from US engagement in Iran and the Middle East to intelligence operations that supported and in some cases carried out political assassinations in places as diverse as Congo, Chile, Central America and South-East Asia.

The issue was not always about natural resources, as the context was often provided by the Cold War, or by geopolitical hypothesising about the need for friendly and reliable leaders and the removal of those who were hostile. But often there was a desire to maintain control over minerals, fuel sources and even vegetation, plants and food. For example, the introduction of the banana to the US in the latter part of the nineteenth century helped spur soaring demand for a tropical fruit that was nutritious and easy to transport, with the additional advantage of continuing to ripen after being picked. The popularity and profitability of the banana trade led to US fruit companies acquiring and transforming hundreds of thousands of hectares of land in Central America and the Caribbean into plantations. In doing so, they secured economic and political powers that were so overwhelming that the term 'banana republic' was coined as a shorthand for states that were highly dependent on a single crop and whose governments and officials were in hock to the major producers.

Such was the control over the levers of power wielded by companies such as the United Fruit Company (UFC) that a familiar record emerged by the early twentieth century of corporations successfully deposing governments and installing friendly political leaders who could be trusted to protect and further the interests of investors. This was what happened in Honduras, where President Dávila in 1911 was overthrown in a coup led by the memorably named Lee Christmas, an American mercenary, who had been hired by UFC. Lavish rewards followed, including land concessions, the rights to build ports, railways and buildings, and a cash 'reward' for helping engineer the revolution.[25]

During the Cold War, interventions and coups enjoyed support from, and were sometimes co-ordinated by, the CIA, as in Guatemala. UFC owned millions of hectares there by the Second World War, was the biggest landowner and largest employer in the country and generated annual profits twice those of Guatemalan government revenue.[26] Low salary levels, often paid only on a seasonal basis, were combined with high levels of systemic racism – with all non-white workers obliged to yield right of way to white people and to remove their hats while talking to them. Indigenous workers, said Sam Zemurray, President of UFC, were 'too ignorant' to translate dissent into any meaningful form of resistance. His confidence that UFC could afford to be complacent proved to be misjudged when major land reforms were introduced to help local farmers who were unable to access or use UFC's vast land bank – of which 85 per cent lay uncultivated.[27]

Concern about what this meant for UFC's business model, its valuation and its investors led to the US government being lobbied and issued with stark warnings that the country would become a Soviet satellite unless action was taken. This prompted the CIA to carry out Operation PBSUCCESS in 1954, which deposed President Árbenz Guzmán and installed a dictator in his place. This helped trigger a civil war that lasted for almost four decades, during which a series of military leaders were kept propped up by support, weapons and money disbursed from Washington.[28]

While important individually, these examples – and the many more that could be cited alongside them – found their significance in the role they played in the rapid modernisation, industrialisation and standardisation that drove change of all kinds in the twentieth century. Without raw materials, patterns of urbanisation could not have emerged as quickly as they did, nor those of long-distance travel, nor ultimately the creation of weapons of mass destruction. They had a climate context too, though, for the growth and spread of industry brought about rises in levels of manufacturing, production, exchange and consumption over the last hundred years – and also in emissions of carbon dioxide, greenhouse gases and aerosols that have formed a central part of anthropogenic climate change.

One of the most striking periods of accelerated warming took place between the 1890s and the 1940s. Although data for many key regions around the world is either limited or non-existent, a robust pattern emerges of a phase often referred to as the Early Twentieth-Century Warming. This period saw anomalies and failures in the Indian monsoon system in the first years of the century, pronounced Arctic warming and ice retreat in the 1920s and 1930s, heatwaves in North America that were broadly contemporaneous, drought in Australia in the late 1930s and 1940s and unusually cold winters in Europe in 1940–2. Despite the obvious limitations of the data, there was evidently a rise in mean surface air temperature that was particularly prominent over high latitudes in Europe, the Atlantic, the North Pacific and Canada.[29]

The global temperature rise points to a significant change in the energy budget of the earth's atmosphere, resulting not from a single cause, but from complex interaction between a number of factors. The lack of major tropical volcanic eruptions in the first half of the twentieth century was significant, for example, with no major ejection of rock, ash and particles into the atmosphere to induce cooling. Changes to solar irradiance, which appears to have increased marginally in this period, may also have played a role, although assessing this accurately is not easy. Decadal variability in the climate system, with the Atlantic Multidecadal Oscillation (AMOC), the Pacific Decadal Oscillation (PDO) or both, might also have been a cause of warming patterns.[30]

Reconstructions of hemispheric conditions point to another factor in this period of pronounced warming: increases in greenhouse gases. Indeed, these models suggest that a significant proportion of the global climatic change up to the middle of the twentieth century resulted from anthropogenic activities, with the fingerprint of human activities most notable because warming was stronger over land than over oceans, and moreover was enhanced in the Arctic – precisely what one would expect, in other words, from industrial production and rising emissions of greenhouse gases and of fossil-fuel combustion.[31]

These in turn arose from the changes in the ways people lived, worked and communicated. Of course, these changes did not take place uniformly around the world, but in some cases, they were dramatic. In the United States, for example, the size and number of cities grew rapidly as transport networks and innovations increased speed of travel, cut shipment costs and enabled production to take place further from customers. The mileage covered by national railroad networks rose almost sixfold from around 30,000 miles in 1860 to more than 160,000 thirty years later; the size of locomotives more than doubled in the same period, allowing greater loads to be pulled, while their speed increased substantially from around 12 mph to closer to 60. This was matched by the extraordinarily rapid rise of communication networks that helped co-ordinate trade flows, allowed for price convergence and stimulated economic growth: in 1860, the United States was covered by around 50,000 miles of telegraph wires; by 1890, that had risen to nearly 20 million miles.[32]

This helped spur changes in the nature of demographic distribution, not only by linking regions more closely together, but by altering the nature of towns, turning them from distribution points for agricultural products into industrial centres in their own right. Although it is significant that the number of cities in the United States more than doubled in the years 1880–1920, more telling were the changes in the sizes of cities and in demographic distribution as rapid and large-scale urbanisation took place in the same period: cities did not just become more numerous but acquired larger and larger populations, with sixty-eight cities having more than 100,000 inhabitants by 1920, compared to twenty just four decades earlier. While around a quarter of the people in the United States lived in cities in 1880, more than half did so forty years later.[33]

These dynamic transformations ensured considerable social change as the labour force moved out of agriculture into manufacturing. Innovation, efficiency and investment in new technologies and infrastructure turned the United States into an economic powerhouse, one where by 1900 labour productivity was twice as high as in Britain.[34] One reason for this was mechanisation and the rise of factories, which replaced artisanal and craft workshops for everything from textiles to ironmongery. The reason for the growth of cities was a complex one, linked to a range of factors including the development of the steam engine, immigration and domestic migration, and moreover in the United States such growth was neither geographically nor chronologically consistent.[35]

The transformation of the US paralleled similar processes in England, continental Europe and Japan, where railways, industrialisation, urbanisation and price and wage convergence likewise formed central themes of the later nineteenth and early twentieth centuries.[36] Dramatic though they were, those processes pale by comparison with what happened in Russia and the Soviet Union following the revolutions of 1917 and the seizure of power by Lenin and the Bolsheviks. The tenets of classical Marxism not only emphasised the importance of the urban proletariat in class struggle and the creation of a new political system, but also demanded development of the means of production. As such, in addition to being an authoritarian state, the Soviet Union was centred on top-down planning and the development of massive projects that came at profound human and ecological cost.

Long before the revolution, Lenin had argued that the key to turning Russia into a Communist model state was mechanisation and the provision of mass electrification, which he had written about at length while living in exile in Siberia in the late 1890s.[37] The nascent Soviet Union, he warned, would remain a petty, agrarian state based on peasant smallholdings unless dramatic action was taken. It was vital, therefore, to modernise the country and to do so rapidly. The success of the revolution itself rested on electrification: it might take years, but electrification would guarantee against 'any return to capitalism'. Put simply, he said in a report of December 1920, Communism 'is Soviet power plus the electrification of the whole country'.

Electrification was part of a wider modernisation that would rid the Soviet Union of 'the illiterates we have', because 'we need cultured, enlightened and educated working people'. For this reason, he argued, 'our best men, our economic experts' had been brought together to make a plan that 'indicates how many million barrels of cement and how many million bricks' would be needed to carry out an ambitious plan for the State Commission for Electrification of Russia – known by the acronym GOLERO.[38]

This was a statement of intent that presaged a series of monumental construction projects conceived to fulfil ideological dreams and to satisfy political dogma. Many caused massive ecological damage. Vast tracts of forests were cleared, often wastefully and almost always unnecessarily, with supply of wood far outstripping demand; copious amounts of pesticides were used in agriculture, with rates deployed often three to five times greater per hectare compared to Europe and the United States; river after river was dammed from the 1920s onwards to enable the construction of more and larger hydroelectrical power stations to provide the power and water needed for the production of the metals and resources essential to the creation of a fully industrialised state.[39] Trofim Lysenko, an agronomist who found his way into the corridors of power in the first decades of the Soviet Union where he promoted views that were as controversial as they were influential, liked to quote as his motto words attributed to the plant breeder Ivan Michurin: 'We cannot wait for kindnesses from nature; our task is to wrest them from her.'[40]

This was a view shared by Trotsky. 'Man has already made changes in the map of nature that are not few or insignificant,' wrote the revolutionary idealist. These were nothing compared to what could, or should, be done. The time had come to cut down mountains and move them, to divert rivers and to 'earnestly and repeatedly make improvements in nature. In the end, [man] will have rebuilt the earth, if not in his own image, at least according to his own taste. We have not the slightest fear that this taste will be bad.'[41]

Electrification and resource allocation were essential too for the transformation of cities, of which Moscow was the most notable example. In June 1931, the Central Committee of the Communist Party announced a major overhaul of Moscow's urban landscape, to include the construction of a subway system, modern sewerage works, street lights, parks and new buildings that could showcase the triumphs of the working class and of the Soviet Union. The metro, noted Lazar Kaganovich approvingly, 'is a symbol of the new society that is being built', because 'into each step of the escalator penetrates the spirit of new man, our socialist labour, there lie our blood, our love, our struggle for a new man, for a socialist society'. He was not wrong, for the subway, like many of the other works undertaken in Moscow and elsewhere in the USSR, was built by political prisoners, class enemies, intellectuals, Jews and others who fell foul of this new, self-serving, self-satisfied utopia.[42]

Everything – and everyone – was deemed to be secondary to the progress of the Soviet state. Coerced labour – derived from the gulag population that was swelling to enormous size thanks to denunciations, fear and vindictiveness – was deployed to build a canal linking the White Sea with the Baltic, a project that cost tens of thousands of lives, or to find and exploit gold and other metals in the Arctic north. Over a million prisoners were sent to Magadan, on the Sea of Okhotsk in Russia's Far East where temperatures as low as –37 °C have been recorded; labour was then distributed into penal colonies in Kolyma and Chukotka to claim the fruits of the land in much the same way as Orthodox bishoprics had once sent out missionaries to claim the souls of those yet to be enlightened by the Christian faith.[43]

Enforced collectivisation of farming under Stalin was supposed to improve yields by 20 per cent as a result of increased crop planting and the use of the latest agricultural technologies. The lack of co-operation from a peasantry resistant both to new methods and to coercion, coupled with requisitioning and repression, created circumstances that resulted in famine across Ukraine and southern Russia which claimed astonishing numbers of lives – perhaps as many as 8 million in 1932–3; life expectancy for men born in Ukraine in 1932 was thirty; for those born in 1933–5, it was just five.[44] The victims were disproportionately those of Ukrainian ethnicity, a reflection of bias in policymaking in the Soviet Union – a significant feature given the invasion of Ukraine by Russia in 2022.[45]

While there were many strands to repression in the Soviet Union, one constant was the conceptualisation of the natural world as something to be tamed, whose transformation represented the ingenuity and industriousness of the proletariat. Nature offered tools that could and should serve the construction of revolutionary society. The granite, marble, iron and steel needed to improve cities for the benefit of the urban proletariat were all hacked, hewn and mined from places that were often geographically remote and always ideologically light years away from where they were used – with little thought paid to the environmental costs of extraction. 'When we have seated the USSR on an automobile and the peasant on a tractor,' Stalin proclaimed in 1929, 'let the esteemed capitalists … try to catch us up then. We will then be able to see which countries can then be "classified" among the backward and which among the advanced.'[46]

Central control and demand for implausibly high volumes of materials in impossibly short time frames led to exaggerations about production levels (which created a vicious circle by suggesting unrealistic results were possible) and to short cuts in connection with pollution, with the disposal of hazardous waste and with the health of miners and builders, whether forced to work or otherwise. For example, in 1928, Soviet authorities claimed that more than 73 million tons had been harvested – a figure likely overestimated by millions of tons. In any event, tens of millions of cubic metres of earth were moved annually by hand or by machinery, and millions of hectares repurposed every year.[47]

It would not be true to say that there were no concerns about the damage inflicted on the environment, or that no steps were taken to preserve and protect the natural world. As early as May 1918, just a few months after the Bolsheviks had seized power and as the former tsarist empire was dissolving into civil war, the new leadership passed legislation on the Basic Law of Forests. While the methods of enforcement were top-down, rather than bottom-up – put bluntly (and approvingly) by a contemporary forestry journal as aiming to 'centralise the forest economy of the country, dictate its will to the localities, and demand from them absolute economic obedience' – preservation was taken seriously in some areas by some people.[48]

There was concern among some agronomists that Soviet practices in forest preservation were resolutely antiquated. 'Remnants of tsarist practices are blocking the path to progress,' declared one article in the leading journal published in the USSR on woods and forests. While new approaches were transforming German attitudes to the landscape, the Soviet Union in the mid-1920s was characterised by 'obsolete concepts, technical backwardness, inertness, and a formulaic quality out of step with new German forestry ideas'.[49]

It did not help that there was bitter and near constant rivalry between the People's Commissariat of Agriculture and the Supreme Soviet of the National Economy about who had the right to set timber targets as well as policy in general.[50] There were disputes too about sustainability: a report in 1926 complained that 'fiscal goals overwhelmingly dominate our forest management', with too little thought being given to the effects which would leave a mark for 'fifty to eighty years'.[51] So what? retorted Fedor Syromolotov, a senior Communist figure who was a member of the Supreme Soviet of the National Economy; 'if all the forests' in regions like Smolensk, Tver, Novgorod and elsewhere 'were to be cut down, then these regions could be converted into areas suitable for the development of grain crops'. No one would suffer as a result, he went on; on the contrary, such a transition would be liberating.[52] Nevertheless, by the early 1930s nearly 3 million hectares of forests had been protected as reserves.[53]

By this time, concern about water led to the creation of an enormous forest preserve in the European part of Russia which became the largest in the world at the time. Cutting down trees within a twenty-kilometre belt along the Dniepr, Don, Volga, Ural and Dvina and multiple tributaries was made a criminal offence, with similar though smaller corridors alongside several other tributary rivers.[54]

Despite these efforts, Soviet leaders and thinkers had been clear from the outset that technology would ensure that the Soviet Union would succeed partly through the 'conquest' of nature. The White Sea canal was hailed by Maxim Gorkii, for example, as a victory of the people of the Soviet Union, not over capitalism or rivals abroad, but 'over the elements of the harsh nature of the north'. Gorkii chose not to mention that victory came at the price of tens of thousands of deaths of labourers who were made to work under the slogan 'We will instruct nature – and we will receive freedom'. Faith in technology, exaggerated support for decisions made by high-ranking party officials and the obvious consequences of dissent meant that there was little or no pushback about the pollution, increased salinity, loss of topsoil or other disastrous consequences of taking shovels and machines to change the environment to conform to the role that political tracts, textbooks and technocrats insisted it should play.[55]

Such problems were hardly confined to authoritarian states led by despots with effectively limitless powers. In Europe, the First World War had had a dramatic impact on consumption patterns. Before 1914, around 60 per cent of the energy value of the British diet came from imported foods. Although food shortages were rare and of relatively short duration during the war, there were significant shifts in what consumers ate, and were able to afford, with large increases in the consumption of sausages, bacon, margarine and condensed milk, and falls in consumption of sugar, butter, fruit and vegetables. Interventionist government policies concerning agricultural production and food requisitioning were made necessary by the war, not least by German U-boat activity leading to the loss of around 2 million metric tons of merchant ships by the autumn of 1916. These brought about significant changes in the use of the land, in food availability and in attitudes to nutrition, which continued after the war had ended.[56]

One consequence was an attempt to increase taxes from all parts of the empire after 1918 to help fill a treasury that had been heavily depleted by war. Another was the effort that went into boosting food availability by opening up more and more farmland.[57] Yet another was to try to create a circular economy by which people in Britain were encouraged to buy from producers and farmers who were local or at least based in the British empire: the Empire Marketing Board was set up in the mid-1920s to urge customers to think about where their food came from. 'Buying Empire goods means buying the produce of your own Country and of the Empire Overseas, instead of the produce of foreign countries' ran one early advertisement in a 1926 newspaper campaign headlined 'Message to the Shopping Public – British First!' Customers were told, 'Every time you buy Canadian salmon, Australian fruit, New Zealand lamb, South African wine, Indian tea, you are dealing with the very people who go out of the way to spend money on the goods made in your own country, and so to create employment, pay wages and increase prosperity here.' Before they buy, customers should always 'Ask – Is it British?' The royal family were enrolled to support these efforts, George V and Queen Mary expressing their personal sympathy and allowing it to be known that their Christmas pudding in 1927 was made solely with ingredients sourced from within the empire.[58]

Great effort therefore went into boosting agriculture in British colonies overseas – with predictable results. Colonial administrators set great store by the plough, identifying this piece of equipment as the means by which Africa and Africans could be taught how to 'improve' their lands and modernise, and what is more, in doing so to follow European norms in terms of patriarchal nuclear families.[59] Needless to say, rather than developing bountiful new fields and leading local populations into a utopian state of rapture, the massive expansion of ploughing did almost exactly the opposite: in one district in Uganda, the number of ploughs rose from just under 300 in 1923 to more than 15,000 in 1937. The results included high levels of erosion and gradual degradation of ecosystems that had previously regenerated under the light if time-consuming cultivation of the hoe. In West Africa, the experiment was so disastrous that British agronomists concluded that traditional methods of sowing and harvesting were far more effective than European methods after all.[60]

The introduction of unsustainable practices was hardly restricted to the colonies. Large swathes of the great plains of the United States had been converted to land for cash crops and for ranching in the latter part of the nineteenth century and in the early twentieth, spurred by the spread of railways, the availability of farm machinery and by high commodity prices following the outbreak of the First World War. All good things come to an end, however, and there were risks to agricultural booms – as farmers in Europe had learned the hard way in the 1870s: then, rising yields, innovation in fertiliser and soil chemistry and the availability of imports brought about a price correction that saw oversupply and a halving of prices two decades after their peak; the result was a spiral of falling land values and stagnation, most notably in Britain.[61]

Things turned out much worse in the United States as the First World War finally came to an end and, not long afterwards, so too did the American farming golden age. Encouraged by cheap credit, booming markets and expert advice, farmers had aggressively expanded wheat, corn, beef and pork production, betting on rising demand and ever higher prices. The Wall Street crash of 1929 dealt a shattering blow: prices plummeted, leaving crops worthless and making it impossible for many to meet crippling debt obligations. In 1932, half a million farmers across the midwest went on strike in protest, blocking roads with telegraph poles, deliberately letting milk and grain spoil and threatening to sell nothing to those living in cities. Franklin D. Roosevelt, the Governor of New York, had already observed what he called 'the dislocation of a proper balance between urban and rural life', which had inspired him to propose a new chapter in US politics. As he declared when opening his bid for the presidency, the time had come for 'something deeper and far more important for the future – in other words state planning'.[62]

The US farming crisis now went from bad to worse. The midwest experienced a decade of extreme heatwaves, drought and dust storms that devastated farmland, driving people into penury and hopelessness as banks foreclosed, inflicting further indignity and misery on farming communities – as described by John Steinbeck in *The Grapes of Wrath*. Dust storms lifted the topsoil that was already dry and exposed from lack of rain but also because the land had been worked almost to its limits in the preceding years. Although the 1930s were a time of warm temperature anomalies which deviated from the typical La Niña patterns that were part of the Early Twentieth-Century Warming phenomenon, reductions in vegetation and overexploitation of the land helped create a disaster.[63]

The result was a series of dust storms that one scholar has called 'the worst manmade environmental problem the United States has ever seen, whether measured in physical terms or by their human and economic impact'.[64] It was not hard to see why. Some storms were so intense that in the course of a single afternoon in April 1935 more than 300,000 metric tons of topsoil was estimated to have been whipped off the surface of the land – twice as much dirt as had been dug out to create the Panama canal over the course of seven years – leaving cities on the east coast covered in dust.[65]

Although the stark conditions which lasted for almost ten years eventually dissipated, the consequences were dramatic. By the 1940s, many areas in the Great Plains had lost more than three-quarters of their topsoil. There were significant population declines too as people moved away in search of better opportunities, or simply in order to survive. Not all areas were affected equally. However, it was not just farmland and farmers that suffered: counties which experienced high levels of erosion also saw higher levels of debt stress and bank weakness, which reduced the local supply of credit and impeded socio-economic recovery. The dust-bowl events did not just reduce land values at the time, but did so persistently and substantially, especially in the counties that were most severely affected.[66]

A report published in 1936, even before the disaster was over, had been highly critical in setting out the primary cause, which lay not in climatic anomalies and changes but in short-sighted and unsustainable human decision-making. Millions of acres of natural cover had been destroyed 'partly by over grazing, partly by excessive plowing'. Agricultural systems, techniques and expectations suited to humid conditions had been used on a semi-arid region, prompted by the high price of wheat during the First World War and the search for profits, made worse by innovations such as the tractor and the truck.[67] It did not help that the 1930s saw unusual weather patterns, including unusually dry springs and extreme heatwaves that brought record temperatures triggered by anomalous southward warm advection and continent-wide anticyclonic flows. But the dust bowl was an accident waiting to happen.[68]

The dust storms captured public imagination and that of the press. Columnists and science writers wondered whether the Plains would turn out to be the 'American Desert', echoing the conclusion of surveyors in the early nineteenth century that the High Plains were 'almost wholly unfit for cultivation' and might even serve as a barrier to the western expansion of the European population in North America.[69] One newspaper ran a column with the headline 'Erosion a World Problem', noting that 'abuse of the soil' by 'the unskilled farmer' had been devastating for many parts of the world, from Canada to Uganda, from Ceylon (Sri Lanka) to Australia. This mirrored articles that had appeared elsewhere in the world, such as in Britain, where there was considerable disquiet about the relationship between population growth, wheat and food production and degradation of the soil. Soil erosion, said Sir Daniel Hall in an issue of the *Journal of the Royal African Society* devoted to global conditions, was not a problem that was local or regional. It was a matter 'that affects the world, and in particular the British Empire'. As others writing in China, Japan and elsewhere observed, the problem truly was ubiquitous, and very serious to boot.[70]

These pessimistic and worrying accounts of the damage being done to the natural environment were part of a wider literature warning of the threat posed by humans in the hunt for resources and the pursuit of profit. The most influential and important work of this period appeared in 1939 with the title *The Rape of the Earth: A World Survey of Soil Erosion*, which not only compared land degradation with a disease, but put the blame for its spread squarely on the shoulders of Europeans and the 'European model' of trying to expand to the entire globe agricultural practices and methods that worked in one corner of it. 'Nature is in full revolt', wrote the authors, 'against the sudden incursion of an exotic civilisation into her ordered domains.' Land was being exploited 'beyond the limit of safety', they went on; the destruction of the earth's soils was 'proceeding at a rate and on a scale unprecedented in history.' Fertile regions were being turned into uninhabitable deserts.[71]

The authors, like others who produced similar tracts around this time, were hardly calling for anti-colonialism or for European settlers to withdraw from lands they had taken over, but rather the opposite: soil erosion was bound to make white territorial control more difficult given the problems it produced, so solving the challenge was essential if authority was to be maintained over potentially productive lands. It was 'increasingly clear', another author wrote around the time *Rape of the Earth* was published, that soil conditions in West Africa had become progressively worse 'as the influence of the white man has spread'. Before European colonisation, 'intertribal warfare and the ravages of disease' had taken their toll on 'man and animal alike', thus relieving pressure on the land. Now, peace brought by white settlers meant population growth, overuse of the soil, deforestation, overgrazing and other problems.[72]

By the late 1930s, some scientists were considering whether human activities might be producing other negative environmental impacts. Guy Callendar, a steam engineer, wrote a paper in which he noted that 'about 150,000 million tons of carbon dioxide' had been added 'to the air during the past half century'. The release of these emissions, he suggested, had resulted in the increase in the earth's land temperature, albeit by a small overall margin. Nevertheless, he concluded, this had obvious benefits, not least that the 'return of the deadly glaciers' that had plunged the world into Ice Ages in the past would now 'be delayed indefinitely'.[73]

The connection made by Callendar with emissions from fossil-fuel sources was not widely accepted by the scientific community, partly because of concerns about methodology and about the accuracy of the measurements he relied on.[74] There was – and indeed remains – vigorous discussion about the causes of the warming that characterised the first half of the twentieth century, and in particular about the nature, role and scale of putative anthropogenic factors.[75] Nevertheless, there were many others in the 1930s whose work pointed to warming patterns, in particular relating to the Arctic and changes that were both measurable and dramatic in Greenland and at Spitsbergen in Norway's Svalbard archipelago, where a meteorological station had been established in 1912.[76]

Amid concerns about climatic change, there were some who were thinking about conservation and preservation of the natural environment. In North America, for example, some rhapsodised about how 'tired, nerve-shaken, over-civilized people' were increasingly finding that 'going to the mountains is going home; that wildness is a necessity; and that mountain parks and reservations are useful not only as fountains of timber and irrigating rivers, but as fountains of life'.[77] National parks, wrote Stephen Mather, the first Director of the US Park Service, were 'not only show places and vacation lands but also vast schoolrooms' where people could learn 'to love more deeply this land in which they live'.[78]

Some of the most enthusiastic about linking national identity, happiness and nature were in Germany, where deeply held ideas about the protection of wildlife, of forests and of the 'right to wilderness' had taken root in the nineteenth century. These had fed into wider ideas not only about nature but about German identity itself: 'the love of nature is the root for the love of the fatherland', wrote Konrad Guenther in 1910; he later went on to argue that 'the chords of the German soul are tuned to nature'.[79] Nature, moreover, was a social equaliser: 'for only in nature is there no difference between poor and rich, high and low; only there does it cost nothing to gain a wealth of knowledge and happiness'.[80]

These idealistic views sharpened alongside poisonous ideas about racial 'purity'. 'Nature', wrote Hitler in *Mein Kampf*, 'knows no political boundaries. First, she puts living creatures on this globe and watches the free play of forces. She then confers the master's right on her favourite child, the strongest in courage and industry.'[81] Such comments delighted conservationists, who blended their views about the environment with Nazi political ideology. Conserving nature would help unite Germans, wrote Guenther, who was a vocal advocate of the notion that blond and blue-eyed people had a stronger attachment to nature than anyone else, and believed that making Germany country ecologically pure would help with its racial cleansing too.[82] It was important, wrote Wilhelm Lienenkämper, not long after Hitler's government had passed a national conservation law, to set out the methodology for 'the protection of nature from a Nazi perspective'.[83]

'We will not only create a Germany of power', said Hitler, 'but also a Germany of beauty.'[84] This was why it was important, wrote Walther Schoenichen, a prominent biologist and later Director of the Department of Conservation, to eradicate 'foreign ways of building' inspired by the 'merchant's spirit' – a poorly concealed reference to Jewish capitalism. 'In the past the German soul always drew strength from German nature and the German landscape when it became necessary to overcome foreign influences and help Germanness break through again.'[85] Again, this seemed to chime with Hitler's own views. 'It is imperative to preserve the German landscape', the Führer claimed, 'for it is, and always was, the ultimate foundation of the power and strength of the German people.'[86]

In fact, things were not quite so straightforward. For all the words of encouragement, agronomists often squabbled with each other and had less influence on what was done than they wanted.[87] Moreover, the Nazis did little to protect nature: forestry expansion was minimal and often even counterproductive. While Hitler might have liked to talk about beauty and nature, he was more interested in overseeing massive building works in cities like Berlin and in the expansion of the autobahn network. He shrugged when asked about the impact on the landscape. Although beech forests should be protected if possible during motorway construction, they would ultimately 'have to yield to the demands of such a great technological project'. In fact, the costs of landscape protection amounted to 0.1 per cent of total construction expenditure – hardly the sign of high levels of environmental concern by the Nazi leadership.[88] That Hitler recommended physical training but did little exercise himself, walking gently downhill from his Alpine idyll before being driven back up the mountain by car, also suggests that his overall attitude to nature was one of ambivalence, if not downright indifference.[89]

There was little ambiguity, however, when it came to formulating ideas about the environment in the context of foreigners, of minorities or of plants. It was necessary, urged Reinhold Tüxen, head of the Central Office for Vegetation Mapping under the Nazis, to 'cleanse the German landscape of unharmonious foreign substances' – in this case, a small forest plant against which 'a war of extermination' needed to be fought. 'As with the fight against Bolshevism', he said, 'our entire occidental culture is at stake.'[90] This extended to new territories seized by the Germans during the Second World War. In an official edict issued in 1942, the Reich Commissioner for the Consolidation of German Nationality, Heinrich Himmler, set out 'Rules for the Design of the Landscape'. For territories captured in Poland, Himmler's order ran, 'it is not sufficient to settle all people in those areas and to eliminate foreign people. Instead, the area must be given a structure which corresponds to our type of being.'[91]

That 'type of being' had been in some German minds for a while. Long before the rise of Hitler and the Nazis, there had been suggestions that the defeat of Germany's neighbours would offer great opportunities for a major ecological transformation. Victory in eastern Europe during the First World War would open up the chance to replace 'clay huts and thatched and tiled roofs' with 'charming pictures of villages and little towns'. It would be possible to 'eliminate the urban-development sins of past decades'.[92]

Similar arguments accompanied the invasion of Poland in 1939. The east offered a chance, wrote the agronomist Heinrich Wiepking-Jürgensmann, to achieve 'a golden age for the German landscape and garden designer that will surpass everything that even the most enthusiastic among us had previously dreamed'.[93] It was a theme the same author returned to the following year: 'A German farmer is more fit for life, in the sense of having a higher calling, than a Polish baron, and every German worker possesses more creativity than the Polish intellectual elite. Four millennia of Germanic evolution point to an irrevocable chain of evidence.'[94]

Another leading figure, Alwin Seifert, who became an influential figure in the German green movement of the later twentieth century, bluntly spelled out what this meant: 'If the East is to become home for Germans from all over Germany, and if it is to flourish and become as beautiful as the rest of the Reich, then it is not enough just to cleanse the towns of past Polish mismanagement and construct clean and pleasant villages. The entire landscape must be Germanized.'[95] This was to be done by Polish workers, ordered Himmler, who needed to be kept separate from Germans, presumably for fear of 'contaminating' them.

Supposed racial superiority was often couched in terms of claimed abilities when it came to environmental stewardship. 'It is only man who can leave an imprint on a landscape,' stated the anonymous author of *Der Untermensch* ('The Subhuman') in 1942.

> Therefore, we find orderly fertility, planned harmony of fields, and well-thought-out villages on the one side of Germany; beyond we see zones of impenetrable thicket, steppe, and endless primeval

forests, through which silted-up rivers are grinding their way.
This badly used yet fertile lap of black soil could be a paradise,
a California of Europe, but in reality it is run down, coarsely
untended, imprinted with the seal of a cultural disgrace without
precedent, an eternal accusation against the subhuman being and
his rule.[96]

The Slavs, in other words, knew only chaos; it was up to the Germans
to transform and break nature into service.

What made this breathtaking, racist German self-confidence worse
was that it was a poor reflection of reality. Exploitation of agricultural
production during the war proved to be highly inefficient, characterised
by poor decision-making and by a set of priorities that not only did
not make the most of the opportunities available, especially in western
Europe, but proved actively counterproductive. German incompetence,
rather than sabotage or resistance, proved telling when officials failed to
generate the resources and outcomes that they could and even should
have managed.[97]

Poor planning lay at the heart of other German failures during the
Second World War, including provisioning of the Wehrmacht during
the invasion of the Soviet Union in 1941. While the cold Russian winters
have a prominent role in public imagination as an explanation for the
German army running to a standstill at Stalingrad and elsewhere, even
before the onset of winter it was clear that the invasion was compromised
by basic logistical problems in supply lines and the failure to deliver
food, fuel and armaments to where they were most needed.[98]

It is true there was an adverse climatic context for mass starvation in
Bengal in the early 1940s. 'Famine came, ghastly, staggering, horrible
beyond words,' wrote Jawaharlal Nehru, later the first Prime Minister
of India. 'Men and women and little children died in their thousands
daily for lack for food.' In some parts of the world, 'men were dying ...
killing each other in battle.' But in Malabar, Bijapur, Orissa and above
all in 'the rich and fertile province of Bengal', it was different: 'here
death had no purpose, no logic, no necessity; it was the result of man's
incompetence and callousness'.[99]

All in all, 2 to 3 million people died from starvation and associated
disease. Nehru was right that these deaths were in vain. As Amartya Sen
argued in a seminal study of the famine that was a key reason for his

winning the Nobel prize for economics, much of the stockpiling and the resultant price spikes during the famine were due to poor decision-making by the authorities which made a bad situation worse.[100] In fact, the most severe drought conditions predated food shortages by more than a year and, what is more, the months immediately before the famine took hold coincided with above-average precipitation levels. As such, political and military factors were primarily responsible for the high levels of mortality, rather than drought per se. Grain-import restrictions imposed by colonial officials, large inbound flows of refugees to the region, above all from Burma, high levels of pre-existing malnutrition and the prevalence of malaria all combined with deadly effect. Unlike most famines in India in the later nineteenth and twentieth centuries, the catastrophe in Bengal was mainly about human error, rather than about monsoon failure and problems of soil moisture.[101]

The horrors of the Second World War finally came to an end in 1945. Six years of bloodshed had led to tens of millions of deaths – with the numbers of those killed in combat dwarfed by those who had succumbed to starvation, to disease or to the gas chamber in the Holocaust. Men, women and children perished in numbers that owed as much to human cruelty as to human ingenuity in developing tools that could kill ever more efficiently and in ever greater numbers.

The single most powerful was a new type of explosive device of such devastating power that it arguably helped steer the world into a period of relative peace and prosperity – not least since the consequences of its use were so dreadful, so terrifying and so apocalyptic that they threatened global annihilation. Weapons of mass destruction thus seemed all but unusable in war situations, with two exceptions so far: Hiroshima and Nagasaki.

The development of these weapons had aroused concerns that they would do more than destroy the targets that they were dropped on. Hitler himself 'was unable to grasp the revolutionary nature of nuclear physics' and 'the idea quite obviously strained his intellectual capacity', according to his close confidant Albert Speer. Speer questioned leading German theoretical physicists about the detonation of a nuclear bomb, and pushed for an answer about 'whether a successful nuclear fission could be kept under control with absolute certainty or might continue as a chain reaction'. The fact that he could not get a straight answer troubled him – and troubled Hitler himself, who was 'plainly not delighted with the possibility that the earth under his rule might be transformed into a glowing star'.[102]

Those working on the Manhattan Project on the other side of the Atlantic also considered whether a nuclear detonation might result in a catastrophic ignition of the atmosphere, eventually producing a report which showed that this was unlikely to happen, at least with bombs of the current size. 'Whatever the temperature to which a section of the atmosphere may be heated,' argued three leading theoretical physicists, 'no self-propagating chain of nuclear reactions is likely to be started.'[103]

While only two nuclear devices have been used in warfare, more than 400 atmospheric explosions were detonated between 1945 and 1963, when the US, UK and the Soviet Union agreed the Partial Nuclear Test Ban Treaty, which prohibited atmospheric and underwater nuclear weapons tests – with a further sixty-three atmospheric detonations taking place after this date as China began and France continued testing. The total yield of the 504 atmospheric nuclear explosions between 1945 and 1980 (the date of the last test by China at Lop Nor) was 440 megatons.[104]

Although physicists were right that detonations would not ignite the atmosphere, they misunderstood what would happen to the radioactive dust produced by the explosions. Rather than spreading out evenly before falling back to earth several years later with depleted levels of radioactivity, it turned out that there were significant variations in the geographical distribution of radionuclide deposits. What is more, there were major differences in the descent of the fallout that were closely related to latitude, with northern climes being affected much more quickly than those to the south.[105]

In this context, then, it was noteworthy that the period immediately after the Second World War corresponded with the end of the Early Twentieth-Century Warming period. In the last months of the war, cities in Japan and Germany had been devastated by Allied bombing. In the former, an area of 461 square kilometres in sixty-nine cities including Hiroshima and Nagasaki had been bombed in US B-29 Superfortress raids, producing huge columns of smoke from urban fires. This was mirrored by what happened in Germany, where more than 80 per cent of the total bombing tonnage released by Allied aircraft on cities during the war was dropped in 1944–5. Much of this was done by incendiary bombs, which US Strategic Command found were four to five times as destructive as high explosives – and they destroyed 20 per cent of all residential properties in Germany, making 7,500,000 civilians homeless in the process. This produced smoke plumes and thermal currents that pilots described as 'a black hell'.[106]

Despite the very substantial amounts of soot released by the fires, it seems that this had little effect on global surface air temperatures.[107] More important seems to have been the repositioning of the boreal Hadley cell towards the equator in the 1940s and the cooling of the northern hemisphere.[108] It seems, however, that another key factor in the changes in climatic patterns and in the stagnation of global warming in the mid-twentieth century was the high level of nuclear activity in general and the atmospheric tests in particular.

The link between climate change and weapons tests was being suggested as early as the early 1950s, when a report by the US Atomic Energy Commission and the US Air Force looking into radioactive–biological hazards discussed the possible impact of radioactive debris on upper-atmosphere ionisation, and noted that the 'loading of the atmosphere with particulate matter … may affect the weather of the earth'.[109] As it was, public fears of weather modification had already risen following a lengthy period of drought in the American midwest, while unusually cold and wet summers in Japan likewise sparked widespread debate as well as papers written by Akio Arakawa and others that linked abnormal weather with nuclear detonations both individually and collectively.[110]

The effects of weather and climate disturbance formed part of Project Sunshine, a classified American programme led by the Atomic Energy Commission, the US Air Force and the RAND Corporation which reported in 1953 on the 'hazards of radioactive debris that, by one means or another, finds its way into a human being'.[111] The threat by the Eastman Kodak Company to hold the Atomic Energy Commission liable for damages after it turned out that contamination from tests done more than 1,000 miles away had ruined X-ray film had spurred attempts to understand the effects of releases of radioactive material – especially as bombs began to grow larger and as detonations took place at higher altitudes.[112]

A Congressional committee investigating the impact of nuclear weapons in the mid-1950s noted that 'many inventions of

man – gunpowder, radio, airplanes, and television – have been blamed
for changes in weather and climate'. It was 'only natural', therefore,
'that atomic and thermo-nuclear explosions, being amongst the most
dramatic achievements of mankind, would come in for their share
of the blame'.[113] While conceding that there had been an increase
in 'unusual and undesirable weather' over the previous decade, the
committee's report claimed that apparent abnormalities did not exceed
the limits that could be explained by chance. Even so, it added, 'the
failure to detect statistically significant changes' did not act as 'proof that
physically significant changes have not been produced by explosions'.
More work was needed to prove the case either way.[114]

This was a reflection of the scientific consensus at the time: as it
had been with Guy Callendar's hypothesis about the effects of carbon
emissions, it was a question of more data, more analysis, and avoiding
rushing to conclusions.[115] Recent research, in part drawing on later
studies of the possible effects of a nuclear war, has suggested that
atmospheric explosions, especially of large hydrogen bombs and the
fine dust released as a result, were the cause of the stagnation in global
warming that took place from the middle of the twentieth century.[116]
Ironically, however, what was at the forefront of the minds of military
planners immediately after the Second World War was not whether
the climate might be changed inadvertently by new weapons of mass
destruction, but rather whether weapons could be developed that could
change and control the climate.

22

Reshaping the Global Environment
(the Mid-Twentieth Century)

We had to bang on pots until the poor sparrows were exhausted. We
did it for several days. There were many fewer sparrows after that.

Student, Chongqing Agricultural University,
on War on Pests (1958)

The idea of manipulating the weather is one that has long and deep
roots. Rituals intended to encourage rains, to protect crops, to make
harvests bounteous and to render climate conditions benign are known
from societies stretching from the ancient past to the present day, from
South Asia to the Americas. These rituals often involved a complex set
of steps designed to win the favour of animate or inanimate deities,
including the offering of foods or of sacrifices, and sometimes changes to
behaviour, such as fasting, in order to earn the goodwill of supernatural
powers.

By the nineteenth century, attempts to intervene in the weather had
become rather more determined in their methods and aims. Interest was
particularly strong in the United States, where several pioneers set about
trying to conduct experiments to see if rains could be induced. One was
James Espy, the first federally funded meteorologist, who conducted a series
of experiments in the 1840s to generate artificial precipitation by setting fire
to large tracts of forest in the hope that a giant column of heated air would
create clouds and would thus generate rain. Although these experiments
ended in failure, other scientists developed new ideas based on the supposed

correlation between battles that involved heavy use of artillery shells and the rain storms that often seemed to follow soon afterwards.[1]

Despite the lack of results, the US government took a keen interest, with Congress allocating funds to the Agriculture Department in the second half of the twentieth century for experiments to 'shock' rain from the sky through explosives – and further support when initial findings seemed promising. The follow-up proved less successful, with no rain being produced over the course of two months of incessant detonations in what observers described as full-scale imitations of a major battle. This was hardly a surprise, according to well-placed commentators: the premise was flawed, a waste of taxpayer dollars, and 'the silliest performance that human ingenuity could devise'. With that, the funding that had not yet been spent was returned to the Treasury.[2]

Rainmaking became something of an industry for confidence men in the early part of the twentieth century, who persuaded farmers to part with money in return for promising to induce rainfall that would result in bumper harvests. Men like Charles Hatfield were 'a charlatan's charlatan' – adept at staging compelling demonstrations of what seemed to be tried, tested and foolproof chemical products that made the most of the latest scientific discoveries.[3]

As is often the case, war brought about a spike in interest as well as heavy investment in new technologies that might offer strategic benefits. In Britain during the First World War, for example, the Advisory Committee for Aeronautics, overseen by the Department of Scientific and Industrial Research, ran a range of trials of innovations such as incendiary bullets for use against Zeppelin airships, model aircraft to help improve gunsights and hydraulic timing equipment for firing guns. Another project looked into producing artificial clouds.[4]

Interest in meteorology rose sharply as the value of being able to anticipate weather conditions on the battlefield became apparent. With the US entry into the war in 1917, the Signal Corps set about training a thousand men as military weather observers and forecasters – no easy job given the low regard for what one physicist called 'a guessing science'. It was not enough, noted the distinguished meteorologist Sir Napier Shaw, to rely on 'observations, map making, and forecasting'; what was needed, rather, was to develop specialist skills in mathematics and physics. The investigative field began to blossom in the 1920s, although it took time to do so: in the period 1919–23 in the US, while more than 600 PhDs were awarded in chemistry, 200 each in botany and physics and nearly a hundred in geological sciences, just two were awarded in meteorology.[5]

Advances in aeronautics and avionics led to attention being paid to dissipating fog – driven by the desire to clear landing strips for aircraft – with experiments in the 1920s using electronically charged sand, with follow-up trials on cloud formations that seemed to bear fruit. These were picked up by the national and international press, with the *New York Times* commenting that while weather modification was 'a subject in which quacks have revelled for more than a century', the lines of investigation being pursued by the military were not only promising but promised to 'change geography and history', indeed ultimately to transform 'the future of the human race'.[6]

The experiments being undertaken by the military ran out of steam in the 1920s, as did their funding; nevertheless, academic interest persisted both in seeking better understanding of weather formation and in efforts to influence it. This was helped by the establishment of the American Meteorological Society, set up to promote 'the advancement and diffusion of knowledge of meteorology, including climatology, and the development of its application to public health, agriculture, engineering, transportation by land and inland waterways, navigation of the air and oceans, and other forms of industry and commerce'.[7] Vapour transfer, ice-crystal process and the use of calcium chloride powder were just some of the ideas that were proposed and in some cases tested by scientists from Sweden to the US, from Germany to the Soviet Union. The Turkmenistan Institute of Rainfall in the USSR was reported to have been successful in 'producing rain from a cloudless sky' through the use of chemical reactions conducted on the ground or in the air.[8]

Research conducted during the Second World War into cloud-droplet size and crystal formation prompted a new wave of research into weather manipulation, with promising initial results. A team at General Electric's Research Laboratory in Schenectady, New York established that silver iodide and dry-ice particles could stimulate rainfall by providing nuclei around which moisture could cling, in a process known as cloud seeding.[9] The results were so exciting, and the implications so profound, that some leading figures in the technology community believed that 'control of the weather by man is a scientific possibility of the future', and that it might soon be feasible to 'neutralise a storm or detour it from its course' simply by 'pressing radio buttons'.[10]

For others the opportunity was not about how storms might be controlled but about how this budding new technology could be used as an offensive weapon. Vannevar Bush, who had overseen the US Office of Scientific Research Development during the war and played a key role in the Manhattan Project, wondered if it would be possible to create snow rather than rain: if so, he went on, being able to drop thousands of tons of snow on enemy troops would offer obvious strategic and military advantages.[11]

By 1947, a formal research programme had been established to look into 'the manipulation of gigantic natural forces for the benefit of mankind everywhere'. The aim of the programme – codenamed Project CIRRUS – was to boost the understanding of weather patterns in order to improve forecasting, as well as to attempt cloud modification using dry-ice granules, seeding with silver or dispensing water droplets into cumulus clouds in the hope of triggering a chain reaction to produce rain. A secret memo set out the objective of establishing the viability of weather modification from the strategical and tactical viewpoint. Not everyone was convinced, with one member of the military's Research and Development Board suggesting that money would be better spent on 'a lot of rattles and snake skins' which might be more likely to induce precipitation.[12]

Those involved with the project were more bullish, both about the experiments and about their implications. Dr Irving Langmuir, who had won the Nobel prize for chemistry in 1932 and was head of General Electric's Research Laboratory, had little doubt about the stakes involved. In August 1950, Langmuir featured on the cover of *Time* magazine above the headline: 'Can man learn to control the atmosphere he lives in?'[13] Rainmaking and weather control, he said in an interview in December that year, could be 'as powerful a war weapon as the atom bomb'. The effects of just thirty milligrams of silver iodide, Langmuir was quoted as saying, 'under optimum conditions equals that of one atomic bomb'.[14]

The potential of weather modification was immense, said Howard Orville, a former naval officer who had been appointed by President Eisenhower to serve as chair of the Advisory Committee on Weather Control. It 'may sound fantastic today', wrote Orville for *Collier's* magazine, but in the not too distant future it 'could well be a reality' that planes would be sent into the sky to break up tornados and hurricanes over Texas and elsewhere. Indeed, it might even be possible 'to influence all our weather to a degree that staggers the imagination'. What was needed was public support and funding for research. If both were given, 'we may be able eventually to make weather almost to order'.

Warming to his theme, Orville explained what this meant. For one thing, he wrote, 'Russia would be at a disadvantage,' since 'weather characteristically moves from west to east'. Being able to influence climate patterns did not just serve US citizens at home, but could be used as a weapon. Orville spelled it out: with control over the weather it would be possible to 'deluge an enemy with rain, or strike at his food supplies by withholding needed rain from his crops'.[15]

It was a topic at the forefront of much discussion in the 1950s as the Cold War took hold. The Soviet Union could be weakened by 'torrents of rain' caused by 'seeding clouds' that moved over its territory, suggested the science writer Frank Carey; alternatively, he noted, 'if an opposite effect is desired', it might be possible 'to cause destructive droughts which dry up food crops by "overseeding" those same clouds'. Fortunately, he added, echoing Orville, 'Russia could do little to retaliate because most weather moves from west to east.'[16] Just think, said the Texas senator – and future president – Lyndon Johnson, who had an even more ambitious vision: 'From space, the masters of infinity could have the power to control the earth's weather, to cause drought and flood, to change the tides and raise the level of the sea, to divert the Gulf Stream, and change temperate climates to frigid.'[17]

For all the bullish claims about the potential of climate control, the results of the experiments proved to be frustrating. While cloud seeding worked in practice as well as in principle, it was difficult, if not impossible, to produce quantities of rain that were economically viable – whether as a strategic weapon or to help farmers in the US and elsewhere.[18] Funding kept flowing, partly because of the worry that others might master weather-modification technology first. Were this to happen, the consequences would be dire, warned Orville. 'If an unfriendly nation solves the problem of weather control and gets into the position to control the large-scale weather patterns before we can,' he said, 'the results could be even more disastrous than nuclear warfare.' As the author of an article that appeared on the front page of the *New York Times* on New Year's Day 1958 put it, this could mean that 'New York City might be put under a few hundred feet of ice or a few hundred feet of water depending upon whether the temperature was raised or lowered.'[19] Professor Henry Houghton of MIT could only 'shudder to think of the consequences of a prior Russian discovery of a feasible method of weather control'; improvements to the climate of the Soviet Union 'could seriously weaken our economy and our ability to resist', regardless of whether such steps were taken with that aim in mind or were done inadvertently.[20]

These anxieties were heightened by the technological advances that the Soviet Union had made, not only in its development of nuclear weapons but also in the creation of a space programme that resulted in the launch of the Sputnik satellite in October 1957. Sputnik's launch took the United States by surprise and provoked shock verging on panic in some quarters, not just because it represented what some called a 'propaganda advantage' but because of what it revealed about Soviet ballistics and launch systems for its arsenal of warheads.[21] US scientists pored over pictures taken of the far side of the moon by Soviet spacecraft – and at the technologies used to do so.[22]

Not surprisingly, this raised concerns that the Soviets were making strides in weather modification too. Terrible drought caused by temperatures in 1946 that were much higher than usual, especially in June, resulted in harvest failure in many of the most agriculturally productive regions of the USSR.[23] This caused severe famine that lasted into 1948 and claimed more than a million lives – losses that came on top of around 24–27 million excess deaths during the Second World War.[24] One result was a top-down effort to create what one scholar has called the 'world's largest ecological engineering project': namely, a plan to change the climate of the Soviet Union.[25]

Announced on 20 October 1948, the 'Great Stalin Plan for the Transformation of Nature' was a considered attempt to counter the effects of anthropogenic climate change. That it was conceived and approved at all is remarkable, given Stalin's own certainty about human impact on the natural world. 'Geographical environment is unquestionably one of the constant and indispensable conditions of development of society,' he had written in the 1930s. But for the last

3,000 years 'geographic conditions in Europe have either not changed at all, or have changed so slightly' as to be irrelevant. Significant changes to the natural world, he went on, 'require millions of years'; this was unlike 'the system of human society' where 'a few hundred or a couple of thousand years are enough' to make a difference.[26]

The Great Plan now aimed to create 6 million hectares of new forests, a series of eight belts of woodland and the stabilisation of sands and soils, which would serve as a barrier to winds blowing from Central Asia and in so doing both cool southern Russia and induce rainfall in this region. A further set of decrees in 1950 expanded the scope of this major ecological transformation with the commissioning of projects to build dams and hydroelectric power stations, create new canal systems and plant more forests.[27]

The plan was not just ambitious but a centrepiece of propaganda within the Soviet Union: 'Which of the capitalist countries could take on a task of such a grandiose scale?' asked the head of the Ministry of Forest Management. 'None are able to cope with such a task. They are not interested in the people, but in the bags of money they protect. The robbery of their own and other people – this lies at the base of the programs of bourgeois countries.'[28]

The ambition and the triumphant overconfidence did not match outcomes. For one thing, central planning for what the transformation of nature would, could or should involve proved poor, as was so often the case with major projects in the Soviet Union, partly because of personality clashes but also because of endless bureaucratic infighting. For another, the assumptions about the science that underpinned both the aims and the methods were nowhere near as robust or advanced as had been expected.[29] As it was, days after Stalin died in March 1953, the project was shelved, the Ministry of Forest Management closed and the majority of workers employed in forest management were let go.[30] It was time for a new era, said Nikita Khrushchev in February 1956 when he came to review Stalin's rule in a famous speech at a closed session of the 20th Congress of the Communist Party in Moscow: Stalin never went anywhere, 'never met with workers and collective farmers', had little understanding of rural affairs and was completely out of his depth in rural areas. His last visit to a village was in 1928; instead, he relied on 'films that tarted up and made the real situation in the countryside look all nice and beautiful', with images of farmhouse tables groaning under the weight of turkeys and geese. No wonder his initiatives never ended in success.[31]

Stalin's other crimes, said Khrushchev, included the torture and execution of party members on false and trumped-up charges, his foreign policy mistakes and the dangers of his cult of personality – all of which were laid out to a shocked audience in a speech that lasted for hours. Stalin considered himself a genius, said Khrushchev repeatedly; and when a genius 'expresses his opinion, everyone has to repeat it and admire his wisdom' – especially if they had concentrated power in his hands as Stalin had. Stalin 'acted not through persuasion, explanation and patient cooperation with people, but by imposing his concepts and demanding absolute submission to his opinion'. The problems and failures of Soviet agriculture were laid firmly at Stalin's feet; these would now be remedied, said Khrushchev, and consigned to the past. It was time for new approaches that extended from the Soviets on the world stage to the treatment of the environment at home.[32]

Some of these initiatives were extremely ambitious. Considerable attention was paid in the US to the work being done by scholars based at multiple research institutes in the Soviet Union on cloud physics, with materials collated by US scientists and intelligence officers to show who was working on what project, where and with how much (or how little) success.[33] Soviet scientists had been looking into the melting of polar ice caps as well as contemplating 'large public works projects that would upset the entire wind circulation pattern of the Northern Hemisphere'. So advanced and ambitious was Soviet thinking that one engineer, Arkady Markin, had proposed an international project to design a dam across the Bering Straits that 'would pump the warmer waters from the Pacific into the colder Arctic Ocean' and sometimes in the opposite direction, 'cancelling out the Greenland, Labrador and other cold oceanic streams' and raising the temperature in New York, London, Berlin, Stockholm and Vladivostok by several degrees. Nevertheless, as Edward Teller, the 'father of the atomic bomb' put it, 'The Russians can conquer us without fighting through a growing scientific and technological preponderance.' The Soviet Union 'may advance so fast in science and leave us so far behind' that there would be 'nothing we can do about it … What kind of world will it be where they have this new kind of control and we do not?'[34]

Concerns like these were carefully chosen to try to persuade Congress to provide funding for current and future research into geo-engineering schemes that were outrageously ambitious. These ranged from 'the large-scale use of coloured pigments over polar ice surfaces', which would 'melt the ice, and change the local climate', to a gigantic space mirror that would focus the sun's rays as a 'giant magnifying glass' and could 'prevent frosts over orchards, or melt Atlantic icebergs, open frozen harbours' or 'light entire cities or other areas safely at night'.[35]

Then there was the raw power of nuclear energy, the 'greatest of destructive forces', said President Eisenhower in his 'Atoms for Peace' speech at the United Nations in 1953, which could nonetheless 'be developed into a great boon for the benefit of all mankind' and could be used 'to serve the needs rather than the fears of the world – to make the deserts flourish, to warm the cold, to feed the hungry, to alleviate the misery of the world'.[36] Energy would become so cheap, suggested some senior officials, that there would be little point charging for it.[37]

Such were the new powers available to physicists and engineers, suggested Edward Teller, that the time had come to put right 'a slightly flawed planet'. Apart from the opportunity 'to remedy nature's oversights', the 'new and important discipline' of 'geographical engineering' had opened up limitless possibilities. 'We will change the earth's surface to suit us,' he said. New technologies, including nuclear explosives, 'will enable men to remould many landscapes'. These changes were not limited to reshaping landscapes; nuclear energy could bring about genetic mutations in fish that would create 'new breeds of higher food value'. Not only that: high-pressure explosions would be able to turn carbon into 'the hardest, rarest, and most beautiful material on earth: diamonds. Anyone visiting the earth in a hundred or two hundred years' time,' said Ralph Sanders, a contemporary military historian, would barely be able to recognise 'geographical landmarks' – let alone the other transformations that would have taken place.[38]

Scientists in the Soviet Union were making equally grandiose promises. The 'omnipotence of human genius', claimed Arkady Markin, meant there were no limits to the 'magnificent results' that could be achieved thanks to atomic explosions, which could help remodel nature by carving 'new canyons through mountain ranges' or creating new islands, as well as 'canals, reservoirs and seas'. There was surely more to come, wrote Nikolai Rusin and Lila Flit in *Man versus Climate*: 'we are merely on the threshold of the conquest of nature'.[39] Another Soviet author suggested several other schemes might soon be viable, including melting the North Polar ice-cap, the transformation of the climate of North Africa, the creation of the Chad and Congo seas, and the irrigation of the Sahara. These would open up 'millions and millions of fertile acres' that would 'yield two and even three crops a year for the benefit of mankind'. This would help the 'struggle of African peoples for national liberation'.[40] 'In a matter of decades,' the author predicted, gigantic dams and dykes, 'pumping stations capable of handling entire seas and other facilities as yet unknown' would put humans in full control of the world's 'heating system'. The only obstacle, he went on, was 'the continued existence of capitalism' – which served as a 'ball and chain hampering man in his progress towards a happier lot.' Fortunately, he concluded, 'nothing can stop the march of history ... and victory will come as surely as day follows night.' The ability to transform and shackle the earth, he wrote, 'was limitless'.[41]

There was little to show for all the promises of this brave new world. In fact, the claims for how science might help human progress – or produce devastating new weapons that were so awesome as to create and preserve a unipolar world – had already irritated some observers, who concluded that the breakthroughs were neither as imminent nor as dramatic as promised. One senior US official poured scorn on claims that 'one ounce of a particular biological material would be sufficient to kill 200,000,000 people': they were 'fantastic and have no basis in fact'. Statements made in the Merck Report prepared for the US Secretary of War in 1946 about the possibilities arising from biological warfare were dismissed as 'extravagant, inaccurate, and unduly spectacular in the light of present scientific knowledge' – ironic given that a report written around the same time had warned of the dangers of looking too far into the future and thinking that ' "Buck Rogers" warfare has arrived or that it is likely to arrive in the next ten years'.[42]

It was certainly true, noted a high-level report for the National Research Council of the United States Academy of Sciences published in the mid-1960s, that work over the previous decade had produced results that were 'intensely interesting' and provided encouragement 'for future efforts in weather modification'. However, it went on, the overall assessment was that 'the initiation of large-scale operational weather-modification programs would be premature'. There were 'fundamental problems' that needed answering before real progress could be made. All in all, therefore, said the report's authors, 'we must emphasise that the time-scale required for success' should be measured in decades.[43]

By this time, public opinion had become not just sceptical but in some cases actively hostile to experimentation that impacted the natural environment; this was coupled with concerns about the implications of what might happen in the event of a nuclear war – or if experiments were conducted of nuclear weapons being detonated on the surface of the moon, something that was being discussed seriously and regularly in some circles in the US.[44] Prominent public intellectuals like the mathematician John von Neumann warned that deliberate anthropogenic climate manipulation could have greater effects than a nuclear war. The title of his article, 'Can We Survive Technology?', gives an insight into growing fears about how human development was creating monsters it neither fully understood nor was able to control.[45]

If this was not a cause for alarm, the plethora of press reports about high levels of strontium-90 isotopes in milk certainly were. Even *Playboy* magazine published an editorial on 'The Contaminators', warning that children might 'die before their time … or after having spawned grotesque mutations'. In a stunt designed to provide reassurance, President Kennedy allowed himself to be filmed drinking a glass of milk and announced that he was serving it at every White House meal.[46]

Such thought as had been given to the implications of the reshaping of nature had downplayed the consequences. Radioactive fallout from nuclear explosions to open up new canals in South America and Africa or to create new deep-water harbours in Alaska 'would be negligible', claimed Teller. Underground detonations would have minimal impacts, with radioactivity trapped deep below the earth's surface.[47]

These promises and commitments proved to be wide of the mark. It had been clear from the many films made for the military and the public that, while much was made of nuclear energy's positive potential, the new power could cause terrible suffering. Films such as *Operation Plumbbob: Military Effects Studies* of 1957 showed the horrendous effects on pigs who were deliberately exposed to atomic tests. Films like *Atomic Tests in Nevada* (1955) opened with shots of St George, Utah in the still of the night. 'It's pre-dawn,' said the voice-over. 'Five in the morning. Pretty deserted at this hour. Everything is closed down. Everyone's asleep.' Before the town woke and people went to work, the sky turned blinding white. All got up and went on with their daily business. 'Nothing to get excited about,' the narrator told viewers, unconvincingly; the residents had seen this many times with previous tests. It was hard, however, for those watching not to feel that this was an age of fear rather than one of hope.[48]

Protests before a high-altitude test over Johnston Island in the Pacific, controversy over Project CHARIOT – a plan involving the detonation of a series of nuclear devices to create a new harbour – and the explosion of a thermonuclear device called 'Sedan' in Nevada which exposed more than 13 million Americans (or around 7 per cent of the population) to radiation, prompted a stricter set of guidelines.[49] These were set out in April 1963 by President John F. Kennedy in National Security Memorandum 235 'governing the conduct of large-scale scientific or technological experiments that might have significant or protracted effects on the physical or biological environment'. This was followed a few months later by the Partial Nuclear Test Ban Treaty, signed amid growing anti-nuclear protests, with public anxieties heightened by the Cuban missile crisis of 1962 and the possibilities of a Third World War. There had also been an accident at the Mayak nuclear facility in Chelyabinsk in the Soviet Union, when a storage tank exploded in September 1957, resulting in the worst nuclear accident in history at the time – and still ranked behind only the disasters at Chernobyl and Fukushima in terms of the release of radioactive materials.[50] As we shall see, there were other factors too that made a rapprochement between the US and USSR propitious at this time.[51]

It was not just the United States and the Soviet Union that had been looking into transforming the natural environment or at weather modification. Within a year of announcements that the US government was examining cloud-seeding programmes, research had begun in Australia, France and South Africa; twelve months later, at least twelve countries were conducting experiments in this area – and by the end of 1950 around thirty were doing so.[52]

Although these had all tailed off by the end of the decade in the face of minimal returns on investment, ambitions to change the physical environment did not. In India, independence was the moment for a major ecological transformation that would change and modernise Indian society. That, at least, was the hope of senior officials like Sardar Bahadur Sir Datar Singh, who had been vice-chair of the Imperial Council of Agricultural Research. 'For centuries, the Indian peasant has used the old plough and sickle; for centuries, he has suffered from inhuman toil and drudgery,' he wrote. 'The time to repaint the picture has come. The primitive peasant economy dating from five thousand years old Mohenjo Daro period must be replaced by scientific development and scientific technique, so that the peasant gets leisure for educational and cultural pursuits.'[53]

One way to do this was through concerted projects such as the 'Grow More Food' programme which led to an increase in domestic grain production between 1947 and 1951; another was for the government to take control of food grains, which it did in September 1948.[54] Another way to drag the country into the modern age was by commissioning a series of mega-projects. Before independence, India had just thirty dams over thirty metres in height; now, as one senior official put it, dams served as 'the symbols of the aspirations of new India, and the blessings that stream forth are the enduring gifts from this generation to posterity'. Dams, canals, power lines, roads and more were all seen not only as motors of progress but as ways of relieving dependence on the vagaries of nature – and of climate anomalies in particular. Dams would mean that India, and Indians, would be safe even 'in the worst monsoon'. As such, they represented a new future for a people that had not been able to build, nor even desire, projects before they 'became a nation'.[55]

Little was said about the human or ecological price of embracing modernity through major construction programmes. As many as 40 million people were displaced in India by dam-building projects and as many as 10 million more through other major construction programmes. Then there was the soil salination, flooding of woodland and fields, blocking or diversion of rivers and impacts on natural drainage – all of which had effects that became clear only later in the twentieth century. This was in addition to the spread of malaria, depletion of fish stocks, rampant corruption around water procurement and disaster caused by dam failure. As one scholar has noted, the beneficiaries were the rich landed classes, while those displaced suffered 'pauperization and increased marginalisation'.[56]

Dam-building was not just about prestige and vainglory, however: in the US in particular, dams were seen as crucial for preventing hunger – and for promoting peace. President Harry S. Truman envisaged enormous dams from the Yangtze Valley to the Danube, pooh-poohing those who were sceptical. 'These things can be done,' he told one adviser, 'and don't let anybody tell you different.' When dams are built, he said, and 'when millions and millions of people are no longer hungry and pushed and harassed, then the causes of war will be less by that much'.[57]

Truman did not have India in mind when he voiced support for dam-building, not least since he thought of it as a country 'jammed with poor people and cows wandering around streets, witch doctors and poor people sitting on hot coals and bathing in the Ganges' – or so he told Chester Bowles, a leading Democrat politician who had been Governor of Connecticut, when he expressed an interest in being appointed US ambassador to the country in 1951.[58]

Nevertheless, Truman and many of his successors as president proved enthusiastic promoters of the idea that these projects would be highly beneficial, encouraging initiatives for the Nile, Tigris, Jordan, Indus, Mekong, Irrawaddy and Ganges valleys. These were led by builders who took on the status of what one scholar has called the 'technocratic warrior elite', typified by men like Harvey Slocum, the chief designer of the 226-metre-high Bhakra Nangal dam in Himachal Pradesh in India whose reservoir held more than 9 billion cubic metres of water: Slocum modestly saw himself as part of a line that linked 'Napoleon, Eisenhower, Alexander the Great, all the great generals'.[59]

Dams also offered ways for neighbouring and rival states to work together – or to challenge each other. Following Partition and the creation of the separate states of India and Pakistan in 1947, the former shut down water supply to the latter in the Bari Doab, one of the major waterways of the Indus River. This led to violent clashes that threatened to develop into full-scale war and massive migration of Muslims and Hindus from one part of South Asia to another. The dispute escalated and was quickly brought before the United Nations, where Pakistan argued that 'the withholding of water' on which 'the survival of millions' of people depended constituted 'an international wrong and ... [is] contrary to the obligations of membership in the United Nations', while India claimed rights 'over the waters of rivers flowing through her territory', and insisted in any event that international law was ill-suited in this particular case because of the unique circumstances of Partition.[60]

The issue of Kashmir, wrote David Lilienthal, a senior figure in US public administration who had served as head of the Atomic Energy Commission, 'may not be solvable, now, short of war'. India 'must have more water or starve'; Pakistan, meanwhile, is naturally 'fearful of the future'. Tensions, however, could be reduced by common sense and engineering. Matters could be greatly improved if the 'whole Indus system' was 'developed as a unit – designed, built and operated' as a single entity, like the Tennessee Valley Authority in the US.[61] Efforts to broker an agreement over water rights were paralleled by US efforts to resolve the worsening conflict in

Vietnam two decades later, which President Lyndon Johnson proposed to alleviate in exactly the same way – this time, with the construction of a massive dam and irrigation works on the Mekong River.[62]

If the narrowness of perspective around identifying and solving problems is striking, so too were the limited successes achieved – and, in some cases, the cold reality of simply making matters worse. Rivalries between the US and the Soviet Union had intensified after the Second World War as the Cold War kicked in. The theatre for competition was global. Of particular concern to the US and to Europe was the Middle East both because of its geographic position and because of its enormous oil reserves. Iran attracted considerable attention as it was considered a 'weak post in the outer wall of the Free World's defence line', and therefore in need of shoring up. One obvious problem was that three-quarters of Iran's population were tenant farmers who owned no land and few assets; another was that credit was typically available at rates that were not so much extortionate as punitive, with money loaned at rates as high as 75 per cent.[63]

Considerable efforts were made, therefore, to try to help modernise the country, led by the Ford Foundation, the largest philanthropic organisation in the United States and one with impeccable connections at the very highest levels within the US government: Paul Hoffmann, the foundation's president in the 1950s who oversaw projects in Iran, had previously overseen the implementation of the Marshall Plan – the US initiative to provide foreign aid that helped rebuild western Europe after the Second World War. The Foundation introduced microfinance programmes, connected farmers with buying agents in Europe and established projects that boosted production methods, stimulated greater community participation in local affairs and improved creditworthiness. In addition, the US government poured in aid money, rising from around $27 million per year in the period 1946–53 to an average of more than $120 million a year after a CIA-engineered coup in 1953 that removed Mohammed Mossadegh from power; of course, there was also funding for a major dam, this time at Karaj, near Tehran.[64]

These initiatives met with almost total indifference from the Iranian political establishment, whose members stood to gain little from reforms, and might even lose from them. Perhaps worse still, for all the efforts to help modernise Iran, the end results were precisely the opposite of those that had been intended: long-term dependence on the west; high spending on military equipment, primarily from US sources, that while bringing rewards for American contractors served to concentrate economic and political power in the hands of the elite in Iran; and a pool of seething resentment among the majority of the Iranian population that proved ripe for exploitation either by the hard-line Tudeh party or by religious figures such as Ayatollah Khomeini, who had little trouble pointing to the inequalities in Iran – and showing that the United States was responsible for them.[65]

It was a similar story in Afghanistan, a country that had positioned itself well during the first half of the twentieth century and ended the Second World War with $100 million in reserves. Nevertheless, Afghanistan was 'a backward country', said the prime minister, Mohammed Daoud. 'We must do something about it or die as a nation.' He was particularly keen on building a dam. The resultant scheme in the Helmand valley was a disaster. Rather than crystallising Afghan dreams, it turned into a nightmare. As well as the water table being raised too high, salination quickly became a big problem. Vast sums were spent on construction salaries as well as on the wages of technicians during construction; costs were passed on to farmers, who were also subject to inefficient tax collection designed to repay a US loan for the project. Perhaps worse, it encouraged competition from the Soviet Union, which was keen not to lose influence in the region; this led to the construction of the Jalalabad dam and major development of the Amu Darya River, funded by a loan worth three times that of the US, and on terms that had little chance of being met. This all helped undermine the credibility of the king and the government – setting the scene for turbulence later in the twentieth century which has continued to the present day.[66]

Similar interventions in the landscape were attempted in other parts of the world, by the United States as well as by the Soviet Union, as part of the battle for hearts, minds and stomachs. Outcomes often did not match expectations. For example, with Latin America considered a 'fertile field for Communist agitation', efforts were made to introduce practices and models developed in the US. In Venezuela, these included new farming methods, such as the heavy use of synthetic fertiliser to increase yields, food-procurement plans and supply-chain optimisation. These were intended to stabilise the country's economy, calm union militancy and both stimulate and reward the Venezuelan middle classes with the conveniences of modern living, such as self-service supermarkets.

In fact, it stoked suspicion and resentment that the country was being transformed, in the words of one radio commentator, into 'an immense farm of economic slaves', underpinned by a plan for American industrialists to create a monopoly in Venezuelan food supply and distribution – and to turn the country into a colony in all but name.

By the 1960s, these fears, ill-founded or otherwise, resulted in the most visible face of US interests and activity, the oil tycoon and philanthropist Nelson Rockefeller, being branded 'public enemy no. 1' not by left-wing agitators but by Venezuela's Central Bank, in US businesses being firebombed and in protesters urging an end to the 'looting of our continent' by American investors.[67]

Competition between the United States and the Soviet Union had major political, economic and military consequences across all continents; but it had profound ecological implications too. In his inaugural address following his re-election as president in 1949, Harry S. Truman had noted that 'More than half the people of the world are living in conditions approaching misery.' This meant hunger and suffering. Put simply, he went on, 'Their food is inadequate.'[68] Truman had been taken with a briefing that assured him that the US had a 'potent weapon' in its arsenal: 'immense technological resources' that could not only 'capture the imagination of the peoples of other countries', but boost production of 'food, clothing and other consumer goods'.[69]

Some had warned Truman to tread carefully, with the National Security Council advising in December 1949 that while Asia was 'the source of important raw materials, many of which were of strategic value', the President should 'scrupulously avoid responsibility for raising Asiatic living standards'.[70] Trying to do so would cause no end of trouble. Far better, as one senior diplomat put it not long afterwards, to accept that 'the hands of the clock of history are set at different hours in different parts of the world'.[71] The spectre of the Soviet Union taking advantage of global poverty to promote left-wing causes and propel states towards revolution focused minds of policymakers in the United States: rural populations in Asia in particular 'were packed into what virtually constitutes an endless village', President Truman was told by his foreign aid adviser Isidor Lubin in the early 1950s. This was nothing less than 'a breeding ground for violent revolution'.[72]

This was an important strand in the evolution of American foreign policy. Soon after the end of the Second World War, former President

Herbert Hoover visited more than forty countries and territories to report back on the challenges they faced in terms of food supply and famine. The report prepared by his Famine Emergency Committee noted that 230 million people were at risk if wheat supplies could not be found for India. Within a few years, loans, aid and expertise were being given to dozens of countries around the world, with over 2,000 technical experts working in more than thirty-five different countries. At least one reason for these varied initiatives, many of which focused on agricultural production, was that overpopulation, resource exhaustion and hunger were all thought to dovetail into political instability and communist uprisings. They were therefore framed within the context of the Cold War and thus to US national security.[73]

But there was also a genuine desire to improve the lot of others in the world by sharing the American model of development that had been so successful, at least for the principal beneficiaries – namely, the descendants of European immigrants. Improvements and innovation had led to a golden age of agricultural productivity in the 1930s and 1940s, with developments of chemical fertilisers, pesticides, hybrid seeds, breeding programmes, mechanised farm tools, antibiotics and more resulting in an annual growth rate doubling or even tripling in the middle of the twentieth century.[74] What made this even more astonishing was that US crop output – which rose from some 70 million metric tons around 1910 to 100 million in 1965 and then nearly 140 million ten years later – was produced on smaller amounts of planted land, falling from 32 million hectares in 1954 to just 22 million in 1970.[75]

This bonanza had moved into national discussion and into government policy. The American Century, wrote the publisher Henry Luce in *Life* magazine early in 1941, meant that it was the 'destiny' of the United States to share 'with all peoples' not only the American way of living, but 'our magnificent industrial products'. Above all, he went on, 'It is the manifest duty of this country to undertake to feed all the people of the world who as a result of [the] worldwide collapse of civilization are hungry and destitute.'[76] President Truman put it in similar terms in his 1949 inaugural address. 'The United States is pre-eminent among the nations in the development of industrial and scientific techniques,' he said; 'our imponderable resources in technical knowledge are constantly growing and are inexhaustible. I believe that we should make available to peace-loving peoples the benefits of our store of technical knowledge in order to help them realize their aspirations for a better life.'[77]

Although Truman claimed that 'the old imperialism ... had no place in our plans', there was a neo-colonial zeal about these efforts. It was significant therefore that what started out as an attempt to support the developing world morphed into something rather different. The post-war period had led to challenges for American farmers and producers with export markets drying up as agriculture began to recover in parts of the world that had been ravaged by conflict. Federal granaries were filled to bursting point, with storage alone costing the US government around $1 million per day, and rising to half a billion dollars a year by the early 1950s. A 'Food for Peace' programme therefore solved several problems at once: feeding the developing world especially in Asia with the fruits of American fields that would make poverty 'obsolete'; opening the door on American values while closing it on those of the Soviet Union; reducing the threat of unrest and revolution; supporting American farmers; reducing stockpiles; and lowering expenditure.[78]

It sounded too good to be true, and it was. Dumping vast amounts of American surplus food depressed prices, hurting local farmers in the process, which then affected investment in agriculture and the countryside more generally. Although the Indian prime minister Jawaharlal Nehru had said in 1948 that 'everything else can wait, but not agriculture', the failure to boost domestic production sufficiently by the following year led to discussions with the US about imports.[79] Annual imports rose sharply and steadily. Between 1954 and 1960, annual imports of American wheat to India rose from 200,000 metric tons to more than 4 million. Nehru put a brave face on things when asked about hardship in the rural communities, saying that 'lower prices are much better than higher prices'.[80]

The reality, however, was that cheap grain weakened domestic production, increased dependence on imports, depleted foreign currency reserves and, rather than aiding socio-economic development, put pressure on an economy that began to show signs of stress and crisis in the late 1950s – just as the UN Food and Agriculture Organisation and some US officials had warned.[81] That was not all: after the signing in 1956 of the PL (Public Law) 480 programme which allowed food shipments to be made from the US to countries facing a deficit, discounted grain was paid for in rupees which were then held by the American government in India. The balance rose so high that by the

1970s the US had control over as much as a third of the money supply in India, a position of extraordinary potential and actual leverage – and an economic and political problem in its own right.[82]

As had happened in Venezuela, the dominance of the US position helped fuel precisely the opposite outcome to the one intended. A bad drought and poor harvest in 1957 were accompanied by Indian farmers being forced by the government to sell grain at discounted prices; inevitably, this led to a surge of support in several states for left-wing parties promising land reform (among other things) and, in the case of Kerala, communists leading the state government.[83]

This set off alarm bells, not least when Nehru made a well-publicised visit to the Soviet Union in 1955. The Indian Prime Minister had first been to Moscow in 1927 when he had been struck by similarities between the challenges facing the USSR and those confronting India. He later admitted to being impressed by the Five-Year Plans, an industrialisation programme which while scarred by 'all its defects and mistakes and ruthlessness' nevertheless served as 'a bright and heartening phenomenon in a dark and dismal world'.[84] On this visit, Nehru was taken to see farms as well as factories, and was then promised gifts of equipment, including hundreds of tractors, harvesters and other machines as part of an effort by Moscow to promote friendships by helping cultivate lands. This was just one example among many: development projects funded by Soviet aid and loans were put in place from Cambodia to Ethiopia, from Sudan to Nepal, many of which were linked to rural modernisation that turned barren parts of the countryside into productive fields or improved yields.[85] These were on top of wide-ranging efforts by the Soviet Union to influence anti-colonial movements around the world, often with the aim of undermining western influence in regions of strategic importance or with access to valuable natural resources.[86]

Taken as a whole, such approaches seemed a challenge to the visions of freedom and democracy that were being championed by the United States. In fact, while some major programmes really were statements of intent – most notably the Aswan High Dam, which was funded by the Soviet Union to the chagrin of a shocked US State Department – Soviet economists, agronomists and development experts frequently complained that they did not have the resources to make meaningful differences in countries they were assigned to, and drew comparisons specifically with the funds available to their American peers and rivals.[87]

That Soviet achievement did not match rhetoric was true also of agricultural and ecological transformation within the USSR in the decade after the death of Stalin in 1953. Despite a testy relationship with Stalin, especially in the latter's final years, Nikita Khrushchev had emerged as a decisive power broker in Soviet politics and eventually as the supreme leader. In the months after Stalin's death, he proposed and then began to implement a massive overhaul of the countryside named the 'Virgin Lands' programme which aimed to transform Soviet agriculture. Khrushchev planned to convert millions of hectares across the Soviet Union, primarily in Siberia and Kazakhstan, into mechanised, industrial-size farming lands that dramatically altered not only the character of the natural world but also the population's diets: in 1953, consumption of meat and milk was lower than it had been in 1914.[88]

This approach owed something to the Second World War and in particular to changing demographics. In some parts of the Soviet Union, the gender balance of women to men shifted to two and even three to one – both because more men than women were killed during the war, and because of mass urbanisation as men who returned from the front moved to cities for jobs and opportunities that offered better rewards and working conditions than could be found in the countryside.[89]

But much too was owed to Khrushchev's own experiences and views about agriculture. Soviet statistics, he asserted at the start of 1954, were distorted to the point of being totally incorrect. Grain production two years earlier had not been 130 million metric tons, as the authorities had claimed, but 30 per cent lower, at 92 tons. Moreover, he said, significantly less grain was being produced than before the Second World War. What was needed was the opening up of vast tracts of land – more than 40 million hectares – and the creation of giant farms that could profit from the benefits of scale.[90] This was intended to produce more grain for human consumption, but also to generate a major increase in animal feed that would therefore lead to a boost in production of protein, milk and eggs and an improvement in living standards.[91]

A key element in this was the planting of corn: Khrushchev had seen how famine had been avoided in 1949 in Ukraine where he had been based for more than a decade by the planting of this crop, and he now became an evangelist, seeing corn as the catalyst for a new revolutionary era in the Soviet Union. Corn, he said, 'has proven itself to possess boundless potential as feed' and was 'the decisive requirement' for boosting the output of protein and dairy produce.[92] Energetic central planning yielded immediate results, with planting of corn rising fivefold between 1953 and 1955 and then doubling again in the next seven years.[93]

The programme was not just about ploughing new lands and planting new crops. It was part of a much wider programme that included novel uses of genetics, soil chemistry, machines and engineering and accountancy to upgrade an entire sector in the search for abundance. Khrushchev was an ardent believer. 'This is all nonsense,' he told one official on a visit to Egypt who tried to explain tried-and-tested local methods of cultivation. 'You're wasting your time,' he went on; 'chemical agriculture is the answer.'[94] These new techniques and technologies would improve lifestyles. 'We want Soviet people to eat to their hearts' content,' Khrushchev proclaimed, 'and not just bread, but good bread, as well as sufficient meat, milk, butter, eggs, and fruits.'[95]

The transformation of the Soviet countryside was framed as the fulfilment of political destiny. 'In the competition with America, comrades, there is no doubt victory will be ours,' said Khrushchev. 'This is because our economy, based on the teachings of Marx and Lenin, develops without the bourgeoisie, the landowners, or the exploitation of man by man.'[96] A delegation that visited North America in 1955 had confirmed as much in a report prepared after its return to the Soviet Union. 'The enormous advantages of our socialist system became clearer to us' during the visit, it explained, especially given America's 'destruction of small farmers' – something firmly in line with Khrushchev's belief that in many parts of the world agriculture was 'concentrated in the hands of a numerically small group of capitalist farmers'. It was simple, declared the report: 'We enjoy enormous advantages over the USA.'[97]

This was not true. The Soviet Union was at a chronic climatological disadvantage when compared to the United States. The thermal conditions of the USSR were poorly suited to agriculture: 80 per cent of Soviet cropland was located in what would be classified as 'the least productive thermal zone' – four times as high as was the case in the US. Moreover, while around a third of US cropland was in the most favourable zone for agricultural production, the same was true for just 4 per cent of the equivalent in the USSR. Comparative rainfall levels were also very heavily weighted in favour of North America, where moist oceanic air helps support high continental moisture levels. According to some estimates, while 56 per cent of land suitable for cereal cultivation in the United States has an optimum combination of temperature and moisture, the same was the case for just 1.4 per cent of land in the Soviet Union.[98]

This was not the only challenge the Soviet Union faced when comparing its model with that of the United States and the capitalist west where the 'American way of life' rested on ideas (which had become realities) of superabundance, choice and low prices. Efficiency in supply chains, standardisation of quality, competition between retailers and wafer-thin margins had turned western supermarkets into extraordinarily successful enterprises – and effectively into shop windows for the rest of the world. Shelves groaning under the weight of goods and products made for compelling publicity and served as important tools in Cold War rivalries: while scholarly attention usually focuses on missiles, technology and ideology, the ways that nature was exploited provided a canvas that was easy to interpret and meant more to everyday citizens than high-flown discussions of theory.

The Americans knew it too: events like the 1957 Zagreb Trade Fair were perfect for what John Logan, head of the National Association of Food Chains in the US, called 'effective propaganda for the democratic way in Eastern Europe'. Another example was an exhibition in Sokolniki Park in Moscow in 1959 allowed by the Soviet authorities to mark a thaw in relations between the USSR and the United States. It was seized on by US planners as a chance to show off 'the freedom of choice and expression, and the unimpeded flow of diverse goods and ideas' that epitomised the free world – and that stood in contrast to those in the Soviet sphere. Behold an array of devices, said Vice-President Richard Nixon during a visit, such as automatic stoves and robot floor cleaners that would 'make easier the life of our housewives'. Although Khrushchev retaliated by telling Nixon off for a typically 'capitalist attitude toward women', it was painfully obvious that American ecologies and the US business environment produced results that were far beyond those of the Soviet Union. 'We don't have stores like this in Russia,' Deputy Premier Anastas Mikoyan said during a reciprocal visit to the USA in 1959.[99]

It was vital, Khrushchev said repeatedly in meetings in Moscow, 'to overtake and surpass' the United States, both in volume of production of foods and goods and in innovation in science and technology.[100] Colonial states were 'agog' at the abundance on display in the west; it was essential then to show that the socialist model could do more than keep up, that it could do better.[101]

It was not just competition with the outside world that drove Soviet socio-economic policy. So too did fears about the dangers of failing to reform, modernise and adapt. As Khrushchev later recalled, raising living standards was important for ensuring stability and continuity at home: poor housing, bland diets and shortages were all ingredients that might individually or collectively result in mass uprisings – as indeed proved to be the case in East Germany in 1953 and in Poland and Hungary in 1956. There were concerns too that a loosening of controls that had tightened inexorably under Stalin might create unintended consequences. 'We were afraid to lose control of the country,' wrote Khrushchev; 'we didn't want some tidal wave to come along that would sweep us away.'[102]

In other words, the transformation of Soviet agriculture was part of an extensive reorientation in the USSR and its satellite states.[103] In the late 1950s, for example, ambitious new decrees ordered mass housing construction to provide apartments that not only offered improvements in ways of living but created private spaces from which the state could be excluded, at least in theory.[104] Clothing brands like Moda Polska in Poland and magazines like *Sibylle* in East Germany were launched to promote ready-to-wear fashions and the latest styles – examples of a shift towards consumerism. They were also tacit admissions that the needs of citizens, and especially those of women, had been ignored because of the overwhelming focus on production. Efforts went into the manufacture of consumer goods that would 'alleviate women's work' in the home, while one leading newspaper began a new 'home and family' page aimed at female readers that focused on fashions, domestic advice and appliances for the home. The dramatic change from the tenets set out by Lenin and his acolytes was clear from Khrushchev's statement at the 22nd Party Congress in 1961 that 'personal ownership by the toiler of a large number of things … is not at variance with the principles of communist construction.'[105]

If this sounded unconvincing, then the 'Virgin Lands' deserved an even less favourable verdict. Hundreds of thousands of new settlers were sent to Kazakhstan, putting pressure on infrastructure and creating social friction and ecological catastrophe that led to what has been called 'the worst case of ecocide' in the history of the Soviet Union – the reworking of the Aral Sea's tributaries into irrigation channels which was as ill-conceived as it has proved devastating.[106] The exposure of the dry seabed of the Aral Sea (once the world's fourth largest) had reached 87,000 square kilometres by 2010, with wind spreading 45 million metric tons of salty and contaminated dust each year and creating dust plumes that can reach 400 kilometres in length and 40 kilometres in width. This now directly affects some 5 million people, with one in two women suffering from serious gynaecological diseases as a result.[107] All in all, the transformation of the Aral Sea basin has been nothing less than a disaster.[108]

Khrushchev's master plan to reconfigure the natural environment ended in humiliation. In 1963, Moscow was forced to turn to Washington for grain imports, an admission that agricultural reforms had failed, and at the same time a damning indictment of what one US senator called 'the greatest weakness in all the Communist countries', namely 'their inability to produce food'. Other senators wanted to use the opportunity more aggressively. 'Food is a weapon in the cold war just as much as bullets or bombs,' said Strom Thurmond. Selling wheat to the Soviet Union would simply enable it to keep investing in military affairs; far better, he seemed to believe, to try to starve the USSR into democracy.[109]

The debacle cost Khrushchev his job. In October 1964, he was ousted as leader, with his colleagues and former supporters rounding on him for his 'hare-brained scheming' and in particular for his obsession with corn. As more generous recent scholarship has noted, Khrushchev was hardly to blame: the Soviet Union he had led and tried to modernise had been one ravaged by crises in agrarian production and more generally; moreover, condemning Khrushchev for driving forward a personal policy obscures the responsibility of others who had endorsed or tolerated plans to reshape the country on a monumental scale.[110]

If things did not go according to plan in the Soviet Union, at least they did not go as badly as in China. The country had been in turmoil following the Xinhai revolution of 1911–12, which deposed the last emperor, Puyi, and turned China into a republic. In the decades that followed, successive crises provoked by egregious settlements at the end of the First World War led to the rise of the Communist party; the result was civil war, which dramatically weakened resistance to Japan in the 1930s and during the Second World War – epitomised by the annexation of Manchuria in 1931 and the Nanjing massacre six years later in which somewhere between

40,000 and 300,000 people lost their lives. To make matters even worse, in February 1945, before the war in Europe had ended, Joseph Stalin made territorial demands, not least for control of the seaports Dalian and Port Arthur, as well as insisting on significant concessions over railway infrastructure – demands that were conceded by Churchill and Roosevelt without consulting the Chinese authorities.[111]

Stalin offered little by way of support or encouragement for the Chinese communists under the leadership of Mao Zedong – indeed quite the opposite. The Soviet leader contacted Mao in August 1945 to ask him to ensure that his troops avoided conflict with government forces. Mao took this to heart, issuing orders a few weeks later: 'We must stop [the] civil war and all parties must unite under the leadership of Chairman Chiang [Kai-shek] to build a modern China.' Part of Stalin's motivation was to try to ensure the withdrawal of US troops from East Asia; but there was also the lure of the industrial heartland of Manchuria, which in the autumn of that year was systematically looted by Red Army soldiers. As one eyewitness recalled, they 'stole everything in sight, broke up bathtubs and toilets with hammers, pulled electric wiring out of the plaster'; by the time they had finished, 'factories lay like raddled skeletons, picked clean of their machinery'. The value of this plunder was around $2 billion.[112]

With the fault lines of the Cold War already taking shape, a series of decisions were now made in Washington that had momentous significance. Unlike western Europe, which benefited from a massive injection of funds to help it rebuild, little or nothing was set aside to support China. Moreover, George Marshall, the architect of the regeneration of post-war Europe, was sent to China by President Truman with instructions not to back the government of Chiang Kai-shek, but to broker an agreement with Mao and the communists, persuaded by Stalin's apparent lack of interest in China, and by the soothing promises that 'Chinese democracy' under Mao would follow 'the American path'. Mao and his followers had little to lose and much to gain by making such commitments – especially when Washington imposed an arms embargo, which tied the hands of Chiang while those of his rivals were being untied and empowered with a massive injection of rifles, machine guns, aircraft and artillery from Moscow.[113]

The results were predictable and dramatic. Uncertainty and loss of confidence led to chronic price inflation, the cost of living being around 30,000 times higher in 1947 than it had been just over a decade earlier. Not surprisingly, this quickly spilled over into economic chaos and ensured the effective failure of the organs of bureaucracy as the government struggled to pay the salaries of officials, which in turn fuelled corruption and state failure. This played into the hands of the communists, who made a series of stunning gains in 1948 as one city after another fell into their hands; by the start of 1949, the Liberation Army had arrived at the west gates of Beijing.[114] A new world had been born.

What this new world would look like was far from certain. By the time the forces of Mao Zedong had established control over most of mainland China, there had already been considerable soul-searching among Chinese scholars, writers and strategists as they debated how and why China had been left behind by the countries of Europe, which had grown into global powers and suffocated China in the process during what became known as the Century of Humiliation. Many had radical ideas about what was needed to modernise the country and to turn it back into the behemoth that it had once been. One of the most vocal and authoritative was Sun Yat-sen, who was elected the first President of the Republic of China, albeit on a provisional basis, at the start of 1912. For Sun, the United States was the obvious model to replicate. 'In order to make sure of our success,' he wrote, addressing the American people, 'we intend to model our new government after yours.' There were many reasons for this; but 'above all', he wrote, it was 'because you are the champion of liberty and democracy'.[115]

He wrote a book about China's 'vital problems'. These included the British, who saw as allies and friends those who 'can render her services', though 'when her friends are too weak to be of any use to her, they must be sacrificed in her interests'. The British, he said, treat their friends no better than farmers treat silkworms – namely using them, and killing them.[116] Sun thought, wrote and spoke at length about what China needed. In 1924 he gave a speech setting out his views. Above all, China had to turn into a modern, industrial state. His vision of what this looked like was clear: a country studded with cities the size of London and New York, linked by 160,000 kilometres of railways, and connected by 1.5 million kilometres of new paved roads. This would transform a poorly connected agrarian economy into a powerhouse. About 100 million horsepower might be obtained, he suggested, from hydroelectric plants on the Yangtze and Yellow rivers. This would be enough to 'supply railways, motor cars, fertilizer factories, and all kinds of manufacturing establishments'. It was time, in other words, for China to leapfrog several stages of development, to become an advanced country and reclaim its place in the world.[117]

Although Mao had been taken with the idea of China developing along the lines of the United States, declaring that 'Chinese democracy must follow the American path,' his ideas changed radically following the seizure and consolidation of power. They sharpened again during the Korean War when he committed hundreds of thousands of troops to support the forces of Kim Il-sung. The United States was 'thoroughly dark, thoroughly corrupt, thoroughly cruel', declared one leading newspaper, closely echoing Mao's thinking; it was a country that was the garden of 'Eden of a few millionaires, [but] the hell of countless millions of poor people'. Put simply, it was the 'source of ... darkness, cruelty, decadence, corruption, debauchery [and] oppression of man by man'.[118]

Mao was after a different model. This was not to be found in the US after all, as a Central Directive issued in December 1950 made clear: 'Hate America. Despise America. And look down on America.'[119] Instead, Mao turned to Moscow for inspiration. 'Learn from the Soviet Union' was one motto adopted soon after a Treaty of Friendship had been agreed between Mao and Stalin in 1950; Russian would become compulsory in all Chinese schools; China was to follow not in American but in Soviet footsteps. As Mao confidently predicted, 'The Soviet Union's Today is our Tomorrow.'[120]

In this context, then, Khrushchev's savage denunciation of Stalin in 1956 had severe repercussions in China generally and for Mao personally. The seizure of power had come at a price of severe turbulence and violence which Mao had not only approved of but actively encouraged. He had set crude targets for identifying 'counter-revolutionaries', a deliberately broad categorisation that included the wealthy small landowners and teachers – and in some cases entire communities: for example, Shanghai, home to the largest foreign population of any metropolis in the world with the exception of New York, was 'a non-productive city, a parasitic city'. A cycle of violence had followed that was epic in scale and devastation, all encouraged by Mao. 'Killing counter-revolutionaries,' he said, 'is even more joyful than a good downpour.'[121]

It was not hard to see how the attacks on Stalin for being domineering, instigating violence and failing to introduce reforms that produced truly positive outcomes could be applied to Mao. At the 8th Party Congress in September 1956, a few months after Khrushchev's bombshell, the cult of personality was criticised while the importance of collective leadership was praised. Tellingly, 'Mao Zedong thought' was removed as a central tenet of Chinese communism in a sign of how vulnerable the leader's position had become.[122]

Highly sensitive to shifts in the direction of the wind, Mao reacted swiftly and decisively to the changes of tone and direction in Moscow. The Soviet model was not, in fact, one to follow, he said, berating those who 'copy everything and transplant it mechanically'. The USSR, moreover, had made many mistakes, especially in relation to the countryside and to rural populations – something which could not be said, Mao had the nerve to assert, about China. If that was bold, so too were his demands for what was now needed: a root-and-branch reform of the Communist party itself, which had clearly gone off the rails. Freedoms had been suppressed by those trying to take and preserve power for themselves, he said, in the process starving the people of their voice. It was important to 'let a hundred flowers bloom, let a hundred schools of thought contend'.[123] These were first-class survival instincts.

Mao needed to do more, though, than reposition his vision for China and reposition himself. Having already 'out-Khrushcheved Khrushchev' with his own brutal dismissal of Stalin, his policies and the weakness of those who had surrounded him, Mao had to come up with concrete proposals that were clear, simple and achievable. It did not take him long to find the ingredients for a perfect cocktail. These included a long-term plan, announced in 1956, for the 'chemicalisation, mechanization and electrification' of China to help boost agricultural production – just as Khrushchev was attempting in the USSR. As one formal report put it, 'the principle of ensuring food security via grain self-sufficiency needs to be the top priority of the development strategy, and this principle should never be slackened'.[124]

Mao distilled this for the masses with a single phrase: 'Man Must Conquer Nature' (*Ren ding shengrian*). There was no reason to think that humans could not affect astronomy, geology and the natural world, he wrote, criticising Stalin's famous essay which had argued the opposite.[125] Nature could – and should – be forced to obey the will of its human masters. 'When we ask the mountain to bow its head, it has to do so! When we ask the river to yield the way, it must yield!' said Mao.[126] 'Man's ability to know and change nature is unlimited,' he remarked on another occasion – with one senior acolyte commenting with approval that 'No other world leader looks down with such disdain on great mountains and powerful rivers.'[127]

These words were chosen to galvanise people into action. Dams, hydropower plants and irrigation schemes were undertaken on a colossal scale – largely driven by Mao's sense of urgency that dramatic and rapid change was needed.[128] In 1958 alone, for example, almost 600 million cubic metres of earth were moved; the following year, twelve times more earth was moved in a single week than during the construction of the Panama canal. That, at least, was what the authorities claimed. If nothing else, the claim gives an indication of the resources that were poured into modernising China – and of the ambition that lay behind it all. Agricultural yields would rise, production would gallop ahead and within fifteen years, Mao predicted, China would have caught up with the symbol of western imperialism – Great Britain. In fact it was not long before he was arguing that this could be achieved sooner, perhaps in as little as two to three years.[129]

Those who doubted the logic, methods or principles found themselves demonised and disgraced. This had been the practice even before the massive projects of the late 1950s. For example, at the start of the decade, Huang Wanli had raised concerns about plans to build the Sanmenxia – or Three Gate Gorge – dam on the Yellow River, noting that the heavy load of silt carried by a waterway colloquially known as China's Sorrow would be likely to damage the dam and cause environmental damage, to say nothing of the forced resettling of almost half a million people. For his troubles, Huang was labelled a 'rightist', the standard designation of anyone deemed suspect, and his professional career ended overnight. This happened to many others, such as Chen Xing, who argued that dam construction would lead to waterlogged land and in turn to salinity and alkalisation. Those close to Mao, like his personal secretary Li Rui, who warned that the Great Leap Forward carried risks, found that their position did not protect them from being removed, not only from their positions but from public life.[130]

Many of those identified as 'rightists' found themselves placed in camps, often in remote parts of the country where they added to the labour force of many millions sent from the cities to cut down trees, dig canals, build roads and bridges and open up new lands. Vast areas of China were transformed as a result, with workers urged on with slogans to 'destroy the forests, open the wastelands', to 'squeeze land from the rock peaks, get grain from the rocks'.[131] Villages that had achieved outstanding results were held up as paragons to be emulated, examples of what could be achieved with hard work and devotion to the cause.

One such case, Dengjiabao in Gansu province, became the subject of posters and films, not least because of the positive story it told about gender roles. Efforts had long been made to encourage women to turn away from 'unproductive' handicrafts and to play a part in collective agriculture. With yields of grain more than doubling between 1952 and 1956, the local authorities put forward ambitious plans to create 'ten thousand Dengjiabaos'.[132]

The reality at Dengjiabao was rather different: as one official put it years later, 'most of it was exaggeration. It was bragging.' Moreover, after soaring briefly, yields soon returned to their previous levels – which threatened villagers' ability to feed themselves because of state requisitioning of grain.[133] If that told one important story, then the disastrous decision to connect the Great Leap Forward with changing ecosystems and food chains told another. Densely inhabited, the large cities in China had long suffered from public health problems, of which the spread of epidemic and pandemic disease was the most obvious. In the early 1950s, the authorities had claimed that germ warfare was being conducted by the US at a time of rising tensions through insects such as infected flies, mosquitoes, spiders, ants and more being deliberately dropped on urban populations.[134]

Inevitably, the rapid modernisation of China also now had to embrace an upgrade in hygiene standards, especially in cities – to reflect the utopian socialist ideal. Thus was launched a nationwide campaign to 'Wipe Out the Four Pests', egged on by Mao who insisted at the 8th Party Congress in 1958 that 'the whole people, including five-year-old children, must be mobilised to eliminate the four pests'. The pests in question were rats, flies, mosquitoes and sparrows. The inclusion of the latter in this list was based on the assumption that sparrows ruined harvests. 'We made ladders to knock down their nests and beat gongs in the evenings, when they were coming home to roost,' remembered one school pupil.[135] Between March and November 1959, almost 2 billion sparrows were killed across China.[136]

What hadn't been considered was that while sparrows did indeed eat grain, they also consumed vast numbers of insects. The extermination of so many of these birds – they became a rare sight for years afterwards – resulted in loss of grain due to insect infestation and so had a direct impact on harvest figures. This magnified the problems caused by rapid modernisation, urbanisation and industrialisation. The result of all these efforts, in the words of one leading historian, was 'the greatest human-created famine in history'. Between 1959 and 1961, the death toll from starvation beggars belief. While it is difficult to be precise about numbers, most historians estimate that somewhere between 35 and 50 million people perished because of food shortages.[137]

The impact on the environment was devastating too: as famine kicked in, animals of all kinds were slaughtered for food, from livestock to domestic pets to rodents; plant life suffered too, with anything edible consumed by those desperately trying to stay alive. Seeds and roots were pulled from the ground and eaten, while trees were stripped of their leaves and bark. The environment took decades to recover.[138] On top of this were the ecological consequences of the huge deforestation intended to create more lands for crops. In a rare moment of candour in 1966, Premier Zhou Enlai admitted his misgivings about the damage that had been done. 'I fear that we have made a mistake in harnessing and accumulating water and cutting down so much forest cover,' he said. 'Some mistakes can be remedied in a day or a year, but mistakes in the fields of water conservancy and forestry cannot be reversed for years.'[139]

In the course of the twentieth century, innovations across multiple scientific fields, the demand for food and energy and competition between political ideologies relentlessly drove forward the exploitation of natural resources. Some steadfastly refused to learn lessons that had caused such pain elsewhere. 'A revolution is a force more powerful than nature,' said Fidel Castro in the wake of Hurricane Flora, which struck Cuba in October 1963. Winds, storms, cyclones and hurricanes 'are nothing compared to the revolution', he said. This was correct, agreed *Revolución*, the newspaper that served as Castro's mouthpiece; 'Neither a hundred "Floras" nor a hundred imperialisms can defeat us,' declared the paper the day after the hurricane had passed. Quite right, noted Raúl Roa, Cuba's Foreign Minister. Referring to the great liberator of much of South America, he declared that 'like Bolívar, if Nature opposes us, we will fight against it'.[140]

It was important to take such fighting talk with a pinch of salt, to understand declarations of defiance as expressions of political determination in the face of adversity rather than as literal statements. Nevertheless, in the middle of the twentieth century, few stopped to think about sustainability – partly out of a sense of optimism that new technologies would bring about what Henry Wallace termed in 1942 the 'century of the common man'. Wallace, at the time Vice-President of the United States, was sure that new ideas, new inventions and new technology would be crucial in spreading freedoms and in particular in boosting agricultural yields. 'Modern science', he said in a speech heralded by one commentator as 'the Gettysburg Address of World War II', had 'potentialities of which we do not yet dream'. One thing that was possible to imagine, however, was that innovation 'made it technologically possible to see that all the people of the world get enough to eat'.[141]

By the 1960s, things looked rather less rosy. There were rare beacons of light and hope – such as Martin Luther King and the civil rights movement in the United States that aimed to give equality to all, or advances in rocket science that enabled humans to walk on the moon at the end of the decade. For many, however, it felt like storm clouds were gathering. The Cuban missile crisis provided a stark reminder of how high the stakes were and how fine the line was between a world of peace and one of destruction. War in Vietnam, which spilled into South-East Asia, reinforced these concerns.

In this context, it was perhaps no coincidence that a burgeoning counterculture did not just focus on freedoms and on resistance to consumerism, but had an important ecological message. Concerns were building in the corridors of power too that consumption of resources, choices of lifestyles and the search for economic growth all put pressure on and came at the expense of the natural environment. In some quarters, deepening anxieties led some to question whether there were circumstances in which human actions and decisions might even bring about the extinction of our own species. It was time for serious change.

23

The Sharpening of Anxieties
(c.1960–c.1990)

The magnitude of the first-order effects are so large, and the implications so serious, that we hope the scientific issues raised here will be vigorously and critically examined.

TTAPS paper on 'Nuclear Winter', *Science* (1983)

The Cold War played out in many different regions of the world in many different ways. One important, but often neglected, impact that it had was on attitudes to the environment. Concerns about the existential threat to life were crucial, however. As the American anthropologist Margaret Mead noted in the late 1960s, a generation was growing up fearful of global destruction, of cataclysmic nuclear war and of an impending apocalypse that was all but inevitable. Young people, wrote Mead, 'have never known a time when war did not threaten annihilation'.[1] While the slogan 'make love not war' is often used to illustrate the anti-war movement roused by US involvement in Vietnam, the emerging ideas of the counterculture were closely linked to ecological concerns.

Beat writers like Jack Kerouac had already begun to write about nature as an escape from city life and from the mundane realities of suburban America. In *The Dharma Bums* (1958), for example, Kerouac's narrator Japhy Ryder has a vision of a 'great rucksack revolution' in which 'thousands or even millions of young Americans' abandon bourgeois existence to head to the mountains to pray, to spend their time making children laugh and old people happy, motivated by the idea of 'giving visions of eternal freedom to everybody and to all living creatures'.[2] Drugs played a role too: LSD opened doors to higher meanings than were offered by a life of work, said Timothy Leary in New York in 1966. The purpose of existence, said Leary, was 'the glorification and the worship of God', which were after all 'ancient goals' that deserved endorsement today. As such, the right thing to do was 'turn on, tune in, drop out'.[3]

Black activists in the US, such as Coretta Scott King, were prominent in the anti-nuclear movement, connecting disarmament with the fight for racial equality.[4] Women also played a crucial role in bringing concerns to the forefront of public consciousness. On 1 November 1961, around 50,000 'concerned housewives' went on strike across the US, with protests in over sixty cities including New York, Chicago, Detroit, St Louis and Los Angeles that ranged from marches to picketing of nuclear facilities to lobbying officials, with the aim of banning atmospheric atomic weapons tests.[5] This was set out in an open letter written to President Kennedy by Dagmar Wilson, a children's book illustrator who was a prominent figure in the budding movement. 'American women today,' she wrote, 'want to see an end to nuclear texting by any country.'[6]

This was part of a much longer tradition in North America and in Britain, where women had been influential in the founding of conservation programmes to protect forests, waterways and wildlife and in the creation of animal rights movements prompted by concern about treatment of laboratory animals or about conditions in zoos and wildlife reserves.[7] By the mid-twentieth century, women's roles had become more restricted than they had been a century earlier, with men dominating public space while women were typically expected to be home-makers and to accept traditional female roles, for example by being teachers or librarians or giving advice about home economics.[8]

From the early 1960s, however, that started to change. Women's magazines such as *American Home*, *Redbook* and *Good Housekeeping* began to publish regular articles about pollution, falling environmental standards and the impact of these on family life. As one recent scholar has put it, 'the environmental cause seemed a natural extension of [middle-class women's] concerns as housewives and mothers'.[9] *Silent Spring* by Rachel Carson, published in 1962, provided a rallying cry therefore for those with deep concerns about ecological damage and about the degradation not only of the idyllic dreams of the American natural world but of the American way of life.

Carson mourned the time when 'all life seemed to live in harmony with its surroundings', characterised by 'fields of grain and hillsides of orchards', where foxes barked and 'deer silently crossed the fields, half hidden in the mists of the fall mornings' – all of which had been replaced by commercial farming that relied on industrial use of pesticides. It was as though 'some evil spell had settled on the community', marked by stillness – 'a spring without voices'. Chemicals had killed all the birds; they also lay behind 'sudden and unexplained deaths, not only among adults but even among children'. Farmers themselves 'spoke of much illness among their families'. It was unbearable: 'Everywhere was a shadow of death.'[10]

Pesticides, wrote Carson, 'have been found in fish in remote mountain lakes, in earthworms burrowing in soil, in the eggs of birds – and in man himself. For these chemicals are now stored in the bodies of the vast majority of human beings, regardless of age. They occur in the mother's milk, and probably in the tissues of the unborn child.' If this was not clear enough, one only needed to turn to the dedication, in which Carson thanked the polymath Albert Schweitzer and quoted his gloomy prediction that 'Man has lost the capacity to foresee and to forestall. He will end by destroying the earth.'[11]

Silent Spring was a runaway bestseller, its sales owing much to canny marketing by publishers who sent advance copies to women in prominent positions, to groups such as the League of Women Voters and to the heads of the Children's Bureau, the National Council of Jewish Women, the National Federation of Women's Clubs and more besides. *Silent Spring* also helped influence debate in contemporary politics, even prodding President Kennedy into commissioning a report on the use of pesticides.[12]

Activism around ecological issues, including the synthetic chemicals that were the focus of Carson's criticism, took place within a broader debate about private wealth and public poverty in which the Harvard academics Arthur Schlesinger Jr and J. K. Galbraith were perhaps the most prominent voices.[13] How was it possible, Galbraith argued in *The Affluent Society*, his own bestselling book that came out a few years before *Silent Spring*, that – while many were well off – cities could be 'badly paved, made hideous by litter, blighted buildings, billboards' and cabling that 'should long since have been put underground'? How was it possible that one could enjoy abundance, but have to do so 'amid the stench of decaying refuse'? Was this, he mused, 'the American genius?'[14]

Questions like these spilled into the mainstream, featuring prominently in publications like the *New York Times*, which complained in 1960 that despite the United States enjoying levels of 'private wealth never before seen on earth', the country's 'education is underfinanced. Streams are polluted. There remains a shortage of hospital beds. Slums proliferate, and there is a gap in middle-income housing. We could use more and better parks, streets, detention facilities, water supply. The very quality of American life is suffering from these lacks.'[15]

Well-placed senior figures in US politics wrestled with this problem. 'America stands today poised on a pinnacle of wealth and power,' wrote Stewart Udall, who served in both the Kennedy and Johnson administrations as Secretary of the Interior, 'yet we live in the land of vanishing beauty, of increasing ugliness, of shrinking open space, and of an overall environment that is diminished daily by pollution and noise and blight.'[16] Lyndon Johnson put it bluntly in May 1964, just a few months after he took over the presidency following Kennedy's assassination. 'We have always prided ourselves on being not only America the strong and America the free, but America the beautiful,' he said in a speech at the University of Michigan. 'Today that beauty is in danger. The water we drink, the food we eat, the very air we breathe, are threatened with pollution ... Green fields and dense forests are disappearing.' As a result, our 'communion with nature' was being eroded. This brought ominous risks, he went on, 'For once the battle is lost, once our natural splendor is destroyed, it can never be recaptured.'[17] Urgent action was required.

Anxieties about ecological devastation were compounded by coverage of the Vietnam War. That conflict had a significant environmental slant as a result of the deliberate use by the US military of herbicides and defoliants against woodlands, crops and rice fields to degrade the landscape, to deprive the Việt Nam cộng sản (or Vietcong) forces of food and so to weaken their capabilities and demoralise them. These tactics emerged from a classified research programme intended to explore the best ways to gain military advantages via interaction and interference with nature.[18]

Between 1962 and 1971, Operation RANCHHAND sprayed around 90 million litres of herbicides over South Vietnam – including Agents

Pink, White and Blue but most famously Agent Orange, the most extensively used.[19] In 1966, scientists protested to President Johnson, 'Even if it can be shown that the chemicals are not toxic to man, such tactics are barbarous because they are indiscriminate; they represent an attack on the entire population of the region where the crops are destroyed.'[20] A second petition, signed by 5,000 scientists including seventeen Nobel prize winners, was addressed to President Johnson, demanding that he end the use of herbicides in South-East Asia.[21] What the US was doing, said Yale professor and plant biologist Arthur Galston, who had spent several years studying the ecological and health effects of herbicidal war in Vietnam on plants and humans (including US servicemen), amounted to 'ecocide'.[22]

Then there were accidents that caused considerable damage and received widespread attention in the national and international press. In January 1969, a blowout in a well being drilled by Union Oil on Platform A off the coast of Santa Barbara in California led to oil being released into the ocean at a rate of around 40,000 litres per hour for eleven days. By the time it was stopped, almost 1.4 million litres had been spilled.[23] Activists who had formed a group within days which they named 'Get Oil Out!' helped generate media coverage for an event described a year later by one journalist as an 'ecological "shot heard around the world"'.[24]

Another shot came from a blaze on the River Cuyahoga in Cleveland, where oil and other pollutants caught fire in June 1969. Although the incident was small-scale and easily dealt with, it too captured the imagination, of the press above all. 'Some river!' exclaimed the author of an essay in *Time* magazine published in the aftermath. 'Chocolate-brown, oily, bubbling with subsurface gases, it oozes rather than flows.' The river 'receives the wastes of steel mills, chemical and meat-rendering plants, and other industries', ran a story in *National Geographic* in 1970, in an issue devoted to 'Our Ecological Crisis'.[25]

These disasters, coupled with other high-profile disasters such as the *Torrey Canyon* which spilled 160 million litres of crude oil after running aground off the western coast of England in 1967 fuelled calls for action. Carl Stokes, the first black mayor of a major US city, was instrumental, giving testimony in Congress and demanding the introduction of controls to deal with the 'rape of the Cuyahoga river' and its effect on the ecology of the Great Lakes.[26] President Nixon, who had been in office for just over a week when the Santa Barbara blowout took place, was clear that change was required. America needed to use 'the resources of the sea and of the land in a more effective way and with more concern for preserving' the natural world for the 'society we want for the future'. There could be no doubt, he went on, that environmentally damaging incidents had 'frankly touched the conscience of the American people'.[27]

Nixon was reading the tea leaves of a shift in public opinion which was so profound that the *New York Times* speculated that 'rising concern about the "environmental crisis"' was 'sweeping the nation's campuses with an intensity that may be on its way to eclipsing student discontent over the war in Vietnam'. Students were organising lobby groups, organising learn-ins, protesting against unnecessary packaging and in some cases even filing complaints against university authorities for their role in ecological damage and pollution. 'Environmental issues will obviously replace other major issues of today,' said one student at the University of Washington. Thank goodness, noted a young geologist at the University of Colorado, 'people are beginning to sense [the] urgency' of the crisis. Many students were already looking forward to 'D-Day' on 22 April 1970, reported the newspaper, to mark a nationwide campaign that some believed 'could be a bigger and more meaningful event than the anti-war demonstrations'.[28]

This proved to be an accurate prediction. Urged to create 'a huge grassroots protest' by Gaylord Nelson, a senator from Wisconsin who was one of the most powerful and long-standing advocates of stricter regulations on uses of the landscape and on water and air pollutants, students, scientists and conservationists worked together to publicise what was renamed 'Earth Day'. On 22 April 1970, around 20 million Americans demonstrated and staged teach-ins about the environmental crisis and propelled these concerns to the top of political agendas around the world.[29] As the famous broadcaster Alistair Cooke put it, Earth Day was 'the first mass reminder of our decaying and polluted planet'.[30]

President Nixon moved 'to place improved quality of life at the head of the national agenda for the new decade', noted the *New York Times*.[31] He was hardly the first to do so – his predecessor, Lyndon Johnson, signed more than 300 conservation measures into law, including the Clean Air Act of 1963, the Water Quality Act 1965 and the Wilderness

Act of 1964, the latter covering more than 9 million acres of national forests.[32] Nevertheless, Nixon now swung into action, signing the National Environmental Policy Act, revising the Clean Air Act and issuing an Executive Order to create the Environmental Protection Agency – all before the end of 1970.[33]

By this time, there had already been appeals at the United Nations pointing to the 'urgent need for intensified action at the national and international level, to limit and, where possible, to eliminate the impairment of the human environment'.[34] In the build-up to the first UN Conference on the Environment, held in Stockholm in June 1972, an unofficial report commissioned by Kurt Waldheim, the UN Secretary General, stressed the fragility of 'the planet's energy system' and the dangers of 'small but fateful changes which alter the balance of the seesaw'. What was needed, the authors urged, was 'a new capacity for global decision-making and global care ... a new commitment to global responsibilities'.[35] Put simply, 'Man must accept responsibility for the stewardship of the world.'[36]

'We share your concern at the rapid deterioration of flora and fauna,' said Indira Gandhi, the Prime Minister of India, in her address to the conference. 'Some of our own wildlife has been wiped out, miles of forests with beautiful trees, mute witnesses of history, have been destroyed.' However, while it was important, even essential, to 'deal with incipient environmental imbalances', it should not be forgotten that another species 'is also imperiled': man. 'In poverty,' said Gandhi, 'he is threatened by malnutrition and disease, in weakness by war, in richness by the pollution brought by his own prosperity.' Advanced countries had become rich through dominating others and exploiting their resources. 'We do not wish to impoverish the environment any further,' she went on, 'and yet we cannot for a moment forget the grim poverty of large numbers of people. Are not poverty and need the greatest polluters?' It was important to underline that 'we inhabit a divided world'.[37]

This harked back to commitments that had been made long before about trying to bring an end to poverty and hunger in many parts of the world. Although John F. Kennedy's inaugural address as president in 1961 is best known for his challenge to 'Ask not what your country can do for you – ask what you can do for your country,' his speech made promises that were as ambitious as they were wide-ranging. 'To those new states whom we welcome to the ranks of the free,' said the new President, 'we pledge our word that one form of colonial control shall not have passed away merely to be replaced by a far more iron tyranny.' The US would help those who needed help: 'To those people in the huts and villages of half the globe struggling to break the bonds of mass misery,' Kennedy added, 'we pledge our best efforts to help them help themselves, for whatever period is required – not because the communists may be doing it, not because we seek their votes, but because it is right. If a free society cannot help the many who are poor, it cannot save the few who are rich.'[38]

This echoed the promises made by President Truman more than a decade earlier. As we have seen, Truman was almost evangelical in his view of how the US could be a force for good in the world. 'America is faced with a solemn obligation,' he had said in a speech broadcast across the nation in April 1946. It was impossible 'to ignore the cry of hungry children. Surely we will not turn our backs on the millions of human beings begging for just a crust of bread ... We would not be Americans if we did not wish to share our comparative plenty with suffering people. I am sure I speak for every American when I say the United States is determined to do everything in its power to relieve the famine of half the world.'[39]

At the heart of the problem of hunger, according to many policymakers and thinkers in the United States, was that population in the 'developing' world kept growing, 'not because birth rates are rising', as one CIA report written in the early 1970s explained, 'but because death rates, especially infant mortality, have fallen so sharply'.[40] What this meant had been a matter of considerable interest to general readers who had grappled with questions about the relationship between rising population, resource pressure and political instability that dated back to Malthus. These themes found new messengers in works such as Edward Murray East's *Mankind at the Crossroads* (1923), Warren Thompson's *Population and Peace in the Pacific* (1946) and above all William Vogt's *Road to Survival* (1948) and Fairfield Osborn's *Our Plundered Planet* (1948) – which paint ominous pictures of what the future had in store.[41]

These books proved highly influential, inducing Chester I. Barnard, the President of the Rockefeller Foundation, one of the wealthiest in the world, to ask his officers why programmes were being funded in Mexico to raise yields even though the earth's carrying capacity was already being stretched to its limits, if not beyond.[42] The logical conclusion of such perspectives was made clear in various reports, such as the 'World Food Problem' commissioned by the Rockefeller Foundation which underlined 'the conflict between population growth and unequally divided and inadequate resources', or the 'Food Crisis Report' prepared by the Ford Foundation in 1959 for the Indian government which asserted that 'the crux of the problem' facing India was the gap between the food supply and a rapidly rising population.[43]

The threat of a world facing a sky-rocketing population that would lead to mass starvation was not so much a problem to ponder in the years and decades ahead as one that was present and immediate. Americans had been told in 1946 that the situation in Europe and Asia was so dire that it was essential 'to save bread and to conserve oils and fat'. President Truman was emphatic in his message: 'Every slice of bread, every ounce of fat and oil saved by voluntary sacrifice, will keep starving people alive.' It was simple: 'Millions will surely die unless we eat less.'[44]

This was a message that was reinforced repeatedly in the 1950s and 1960s – although Paul and Anne Ehrlich's *The Population Bomb* of 1968 warned that the battle had already been lost. The chance 'to feed all of humanity is over', the authors declared in their hugely influential book. 'Hundreds of millions of people are going to starve to death.' The book's cover asserted that 'While you are reading these words, four people will have died from starvation. Most of them children.'[45]

The prospect of more and more people sharing the planet was one that added to anxieties about nuclear apocalypse and the transformation of the natural world into industrial heartlands that scarred the landscape and poisoned the soil, the water and the human population. Overpopulation now threatened to create yet another catastrophe. For some, it was obvious where blame should lie. 'The white race *is* the cancer of human history,' wrote Susan Sontag in the mid-1960s; 'it is the white race and it alone – its ideologies and inventions – which eradicates autonomous civilisations wherever it spreads, which has upset the ecological balance of the planet, which now threatens the very existence of life itself.' The Mongol hordes were far less frightening than the 'western man with his idealism, magnificent art, his sense of intellectual adventure [and] his world-devouring energies for conquest'.[46]

Others offered solutions. President Kennedy proposed 'the transfer of technology to food deficit nations' that would stimulate 'a scientific revolution which may well rival, in its social consequences, the industrial revolution'.[47] Such hopes were not entirely unfounded: research into high-yielding seeds that were responsive to high inputs of chemical fertiliser and irrigation had produced what is often referred to as the 'green revolution' – even if scholars today are often sceptical about how green this was, whether it amounted to a revolution and whether it was a legendary phenomenon rather than a real one.[48] Initial results showed that new dwarf wheat varieties, produced by cross-breeding short-strawed Japanese and Mexican strains, could produce four times as much as traditional varieties, thanks partly to improving resistance to rust and partly to resolving issues around late ripening. Similar approaches were then adopted to create new rice varieties, which were likewise early maturing, insensitive to day length and had short, stiff stems.[49] One of the most prominent pioneers, Norman Borlaug, won the Nobel peace prize in recognition of his work developing new cereal strains and then putting them 'into extensive production in order to feed the hungry people of the world'.[50]

These developments seemed to offer hope that the worst problems of rising global populations could be averted. In the late 1960s, the availability of what President Nixon called 'miracle seeds' promised a solution to the problems of global food supply.[51] The introduction of new hybrid crop varieties provided a substantial bonus, with recent studies suggesting that the calorific availability around the world was boosted by about 11–13 per cent.[52]

Ironically, in fact, the principal beneficiaries of substantially higher yields were in the countries that had already industrialised, that had developed new technologies and adopted them quickly.[53] Moreover, the surge in production generated a range of new and unexpected problems. Having been fearful of too little food being available, it was observed at a conference of leading experts, the concern was now about too much, with the Third World entering a period of surplus production: 'we worry more about idle arms than hungry mouths'.[54]

It was not wrong to be thinking of the socio-economic consequences. In South Asia, for example, improving fortunes and rising confidence precipitated a consolidation in landholdings as farmers with access to credit and know-how bought out smaller producers. In some parts of India and Pakistan, land values trebled as landlords moved in to exploit the opportunities on offer, aggravating social polarisation – especially in places where inequalities already existed.[55] As a UN study produced in 1974 expressed it, the green revolution compounded hierarchies rather than reforming them.[56]

The green revolution then was itself counterproductive, for one of the core aims had been not only to overcome nature but to soothe political instabilities. In practice, in many cases, it did precisely the opposite. In India in the early 1970s, for example, populists found support for their emphasis on the gap between the rich and the poor which was increasing as a result of improved harvests. In Sierra Leone, a country that is an integral part of the 'rice belt' of western Africa and one where rice is central to social life and economic activity, farmers who were already wealthy and integrated into rice markets could reap the rewards of new techniques, especially in lowland regions which did not favour traditional varieties of rice that were more dependent on rainfall.[57] In the Philippines, opportunities opened up for the consolidation of power by the regime and family of Ferdinand Marcos, which monopolised the supply of seeds, chemicals, loans and machinery – and controlled prices to boot.[58] The green revolution was supposed to offer 'technology as a substitute to both nature and politics, in the creation of abundance and peace'. Some scholars argue that it did neither.[59]

One reason for failure lay in the obvious fact that the green revolution was essentially seeking to overcome the ecological constraints in parts of the world that were poorly suited to large-scale agricultural production. Tropical locations that often saw intense rainfall were prone to erosion, soil run-off and the depletion of nutrients in lands whose cover had been stripped to convert to the growing of crops.[60] Overuse of synthetic pesticides and fertilisers led to the increase of heavy metals such as cadmium, lead and arsenic in the soil, whose pH levels rose as a result.[61] As one scholar has put it, 'the chief "success" of the idealised new agricultural technologies was to export the new high-yield but patently unsustainable agricultural systems of the industrial world throughout the tropics'.[62] The breathtaking scale of land degradation that results from agricultural practices associated with these initiatives is estimated to have affected nearly 2 billion hectares globally – as well as 2.6 billion people.[63]

The green revolution also had significant impacts both on ecosystems and on health. The crops introduced to India in the 1960s and later were water-intensive – with the irrigated agriculture that subsequently arose being the primary reason why the country is today experiencing water stress.[64] The planting of hybrid crops that would grow faster also led to a large decrease in the cultivation of sorghum, barley, groundnuts and more, which had repercussions for the ecological balance of plant and animal life.[65] It has been estimated that 100,000 varieties of indigenous rice were lost because of the introduction of hybrids from abroad.[66] Then there were the implications of farmers using pesticides without sufficient protection, a danger especially for women, who make up half the agricultural labour force in countries like India and who are particularly vulnerable if exposed to chemicals at a young age.[67]

Another problem came from massive population movements, both through government policies, through programmes funded by the World Bank and through the search for work and food. In Indonesia, for example, as many as 15–20 million settlers moved into the jungles of Sumatra, Kalimantan, Sulawesi and Irian Jaya, which not only changed local ecologies, but also brought widespread human rights abuses and the development of large-scale logging industries that today see around 750,000 hectares of forests cleared every year in this part of South-East Asia alone. Even by the mid-1980s, this was being called 'the World Bank's most irresponsible project'.[68]

The rise both in urbanisation across the less developed world and in the size of cities like Bombay, Manila and Mexico City brought new concerns about social and political stability and put pressure on city authorities to build infrastructure quickly enough to cope with soaring numbers of inhabitants – which in turn led to environmental degradation. There was scepticism in some places that production could keep up with demographics in the first place. When the Indian Minister of Food and Agriculture, C. Subramaniam, gave a talk at Stanford in 1968, Paul Ehrlich listened in disbelief. There was no way, wrote Ehrlich, that 'India is going to find a way to produce enough food to support some 12 million more people than they can feed today.' Millions would die, he predicted.[69]

For Ehrlich, 'Population control is the only answer.'[70] This was a policy that had been advocated since the 1950s by the World Bank, which had forecast that Indians could expect 40 per cent more income within three decades by adopting aggressive contraception programmes.[71] Borlaug was a passionate advocate too. Not enough people recognised 'the magnitude and the menace of the population monster', he insisted in December 1970. His work and that of others to develop new strains of rice simply bought time – 'breathing space' as he called it – perhaps thirty years.[72] Such dire warnings helped propel government interventions into reproductive health, which ranged from sex education and the promotion of family planning to programmes of large-scale forced sterilisation.[73]

Others did not see it that way, at least to start with. 'The more people there are, the earlier we can realize humanity's greatest ideal – communism,' ran one newspaper headline in China in the late 1950s. In the eyes of Mao Zedong, China's vast population was a positive asset, one that kept it insulated from dangers. 'We shouldn't be afraid of atomic missiles,' he told a shocked Nikita Khrushchev in Moscow in 1957. 'No matter what kind of war breaks out – conventional or thermonuclear – we'll win. As for China, if the imperialists unleash war on us, we may lose more than three hundred million people. So what? War is war. The years will pass and we'll get to work producing more babies than ever before.'[74] There was no need to put a cap on population growth or to advocate use of contraceptives, at least according to Mao. If China was home to half of the world's population in a hundred years' time, that would be fine as by then everyone would be 'college educated' and would 'naturally practice birth control'.[75]

Eventually, by the early 1970s, even China adopted measures designed to manage a population that was 50 per cent larger than it had been in 1949, introducing a family-planning campaign, raising the legal age of marriage to the mid-twenties in most regions and encouraging mothers to take more time between births.[76] By 1979, this had not produced the slowdown that was expected and a one-child policy was introduced.[77] While usually interpreted as a sign of central coercion by a Communist party determined to implement an effective modernisation programme, in fact almost all the principal ideas that underpinned the policy were borrowed from the west and from western science.[78] As is so often the case, this solution has created a new set of problems, not least that of a population that is not replacing itself and that is rapidly ageing, twin issues that are likely to have a profound impact on China's economy – and its social and political trajectories – in the future.

Many of these issues – and fears – seem remarkably familiar in today's world: the threat of nuclear cataclysm; ecological damage as a result of the pursuit of economic growth; unsustainable use of resources; demographic pressures from a rising global population on infrastructure and on food; over-reliance on new ideas and technologies that raise hopes but also open Pandora's box; regular statements by governments and intergovernmental organisations about the importance of co-operation coupled with an absence of real progress; and, most importantly of all, deep-rooted concerns about what the future holds. To these should be added concerns about climate change too.

Some scientists had become concerned that human behaviour was not just altering the natural world through pollution, pesticides and exhaustion of natural resources, but was also changing the climate itself. One paper published by Roger Revelle and Hans Suess in 1957 which looked at the increase of atmospheric carbon dioxide predicted that 'During the next few decades the rate of combustion of fossil fuels will continue to increase, if the fuel and power requirements of our worldwide industrial civilization continue to rise exponentially.' This would have ominous consequences, wrote the two scientists: 'human beings are now carrying out a large-scale geophysical experiment of a kind that could not have happened in the past nor be reproduced in the future'. The impact of the industrial revolution and the resultant addition of carbon dioxide through the burning of fossil fuels, especially since the middle of the nineteenth century, meant that 'Within a few centuries we are returning to the atmosphere and oceans the concentrated organic carbon stored in sedimentary rocks over hundreds of millions of years.' Revell and Suess did not venture to guess what the consequences would be, but they were certain they would be far-reaching.[79]

Other research around the same time began to produce alarming results. As we have already seen, interest in weather patterns, in climatic conditions and in short- and long-term changes had been a key part of military planning since the early twentieth century, if not before. At the height of the Cold War, as the Pentagon had put it, 'The Department of Defense has a vital interest in the environmental sciences since the military services must have an understanding of, and an ability to predict and even to control, the environment in which it is required to operate' – not least since guided-missile systems required as much information as possible about the lower and upper atmospheres, ionospheric conditions, geodesy and geomagnetism and more besides.[80]

Considerable energy and resources went into polar research, with major expeditions and bases set up in the Antarctic in the late 1940s with Operation HIGHJUMP and a decade later at Camp Century in Greenland under the authority of the US Army Corps of Engineers' Snow, Ice, and Permafrost Research Establishment (SIPRE), which included investigations into carbon dioxide monitoring not only in the present day but also in the past – as did monitoring stations elsewhere, such as at Mauna Loa in Hawai'i.[81]

Camp Century in particular proved a revelation: chosen as a site for Project ICEWORM, a proposed nuclear arsenal of 600 ballistic missiles, the scientists who were based there made a series of discoveries drilling into ice cores under the direction of Henri Bader, who had previously worked on carbon dioxide bubbles trapped in the ice sheets of Alaska. Using a drill rig brought in from Oklahoma, the team at Camp Century helped provide empirical evidence of previous climatic conditions dating back thousands and even tens of thousands of years – and in so doing helped provide perspective for long-run climate conditions that showed both the scale and the rate of change in the contemporary world compared to the past.[82]

Much work was also being done in the Soviet Union in this period on climatic change in general and on human impact in particular by scholars like Evgenii Fedorov.[83] One leading light was Mikhail Budyko, whose groundbreaking work on the relationship between the lower atmosphere and the earth's surface was picked up on with great interest outside the USSR by climatologists in the US and elsewhere.[84] One of Budyko's areas of investigation was the anthropogenic generation of heat in large quantities – and the question whether, where and how this might affect local, regional and potentially even global climates. Research revealed the polar ice–albedo feedback, whereby decreases in snow and ice in the polar region are intensified by solar heating that further decreases the snow and ice area and amplifies global warming.[85] This all suggested that human behaviour and activities were in the process of effecting 'major climatic change in the near future. As a result,' Budyko wrote in 1969, 'changes in climate that are natural are to be replaced in time by changes that are created and shaped by mankind.'[86]

Human impacts on climate became a subject of considerable discussion within the scientific community. One paper commissioned by the American Petroleum Institute, a trade association representing the oil and gas industry, reported that prospects 'for the future must be of serious concern' given the amounts of carbon being released by the burning of fossil fuels.[87] Another paper, this one published in the journal *Science* in 1970, looked not only at fossil fuels but at the dust particles, particulates and air pollution they generated and above all at the cities which were home to 'by far the most pronounced and locally far-reaching effects of man's activities'. The 'noise' of natural climatic fluctuations could easily mask anthropogenic influences; what was urgently needed, therefore, was 'an adequate worldwide monitoring system to permit early assessment of these changes'.[88]

There were papers that considered when the present interglacial period would end, or examined historical global climate conditions, asserting that the world was currently in a cool cycle that would last for another 8,300 years.[89] Other studies written around the same time underlined the way ozone was being destroyed by nitrous oxide and could be further degraded by the advent of supersonic transport because of the high altitudes at which emissions would be released, or evaluated the effects of chlorofluorocarbons (CFCs) on the ozone layer. All served to concentrate minds on what the future might hold.[90]

Fears spilled over into the public domain. Even in the 1950s, the popular press carried articles that painted a bleak picture of a world about to enter a new ice age that might lead to a 'real estate boom in the Sahara'.[91] In the 1970s, such ideas were now taken up with gusto. Colder winters herald the dawn of a new ice age, promised the *Washington Post* in January 1970; 'Is mankind manufacturing a new ice age for itself?' wondered the *LA Times* four days later; a new ice age was predicted by the start of the twenty-first century, reported the *Boston Globe*, a few months afterwards – just a few examples among a vast array of similar coverage across print media.[92]

The gloomy, cold world that lay around the corner proved both persistent and irresistible. 'Tell-tale signs are everywhere,' said *Time* magazine in 1974; indications of global cooling were everywhere, and were already responsible for drought in sub-Saharan Africa, Central America, the Middle East and India. The changes were partly due to changes in the sun's behaviour – although 'Man, too, may be somewhat responsible for the cooling trend' thanks to 'dust and other particles being released into the atmosphere as a result of farming and fuel burning' that was 'blocking more and more sunlight from reaching and heating the surface of the earth'.[93] *Newsweek* followed a year later with the claim that while 'meteorologists disagree about the cause and extent of the cooling trend ... they are almost unanimous in the view that the trend will reduce agricultural productivity for the rest of the century'.[94]

This was not in fact the case at all: most scientists working on environmental and climatic change were wary of making sweeping statements about the present, let alone issuing catastrophising predictions about the future. Reports for the National Science Board in the US in 1974 noted apparent trends in cooling, but pointed out that 'major advances' were needed in order to establish whether, how and where emissions, pollutants or particulates were affecting current climates.[95] A report by the US National Academy of Sciences a year later suggested that 'a major climatic change would force economic and social adjustments on the worldwide scale' and therefore reiterated the need for more research; the NAS acknowledged that 'The climates of the earth have always been changing,' and it was not known 'How large these future changes will be'.[96] This was the line that Secretary of State Henry Kissinger took when addressing the General Assembly of the United Nations in April 1974: scientists needed urgently to investigate 'the possibility of climatic changes in the monsoon belt and perhaps throughout the world'.[97]

Nevertheless, some scholars expressed their opinion forcefully – and at the highest levels. The authors of one paper on global cooling wrote to President Nixon in 1972 to warn that the prospect of 'a global deterioration of climate, by order of magnitude larger than any hitherto experienced by civilized mankind, is a very real possibility and indeed may be due very soon'. This was circulated by the White House to several bodies 'for review and appropriate action'.[98]

What climatological changes meant for 'intelligence problems', national security and global affairs was set out in a CIA report prepared later that year. 'Climate has not been a prime consideration of intelligence analysis because, until recently, it has not caused any significant perturbations to the status of major nations.' This was because conditions in the twentieth century were the most benign for agriculture they had been for the best part of a millennium – right back to the eleventh century, according to the report's authors.[99]

Recent events had served to spook the spooks: drought in Burma, Costa Rica, Honduras and Pakistan, poor harvests in North Korea, the Philippines and the USSR, cold-damaged crops in Japan, the worst floods in a century in the Great Lakes of North America, unusually heavy rainfall in North Vietnam and poor weather, droughts and floods in the Soviet Union and China in the early 1970s had served to show that 'Climate is now a critical factor.' In particular, 'The politics of food will become the central issue of every government.'[100] The CIA noted a large and growing body of scientific work that indicated that 'A global climatic change was underway' and that this 'would create worldwide agricultural failures in the 1970s'.[101]

A separate, parallel CIA report looked at the implications in more detail. 'If climatologists who believe a cooling trend is underway prove to be right', its authors declared, there would 'almost certainly be an absolute shortage of food' around the world, led by drops in output in the Soviet Union and China because of shorter growing seasons, as well as more frequent monsoon failures in South and South-East Asia and in southern China.[102] 'Moreover, in periods when climate change is underway,' they continued, 'violent weather – unseasonal frosts, warm spells, large storms, floods, etc. – is thought to be more common.' All this would have 'an enormous impact' not only on the balance between food and population but on 'the world balance of power', largely because the US's geography made its ecologies less vulnerable to climatic change: this was likely to lead to anti-American sentiment on the part of countries which either were already dependent on the US or would become so.[103]

There was a strong chance of social and political upheaval, said the report's authors, as 'rural masses' became 'less docile' under pressure of famine and as the living standards of urban middle classes in sub-Saharan Africa, East Africa and India fell in response to food shortages and sharp price rises.[104] In the worst-case scenario, they warned, 'Massive migration backed by force would become a very live issue. Nuclear blackmail is not inconceivable.' As far as poor countries were concerned, it was likely that the population 'problem' would be solved 'in the most unpleasant fashion'. This meant mass starvation.[105] When George Will of the *Washington Post* got hold of a copy of this report, he summarised its findings bluntly: if the climate change occurs, he wrote, 'there will be megadeaths'.[106]

Some senior figures in the US administration believed that it was possible to leverage agricultural, climatological and economic power into gains. 'Food is a weapon,' said Nixon's secretary of agriculture, Earl Butz, and was 'now one of the principal tools in our negotiating kit'.[107]

The problem was that, despite having strong cards to play, the US had a weak hand when it came to energy. And this helped determine policy in ways that were far more influential than warnings about climate change, and furthermore went a lot further in encouraging lower consumption of fossil fuels, in promoting investment in renewable and clean sources of power and in provoking discussions about sustainability.

Ironically, then, the impulse towards lower consumption of fossil fuels came not as a result of warnings from scientists or from intelligence briefings, but as a result of events in October 1973 that took place thousands of kilometres away in the Middle East after a coalition of Arab states launched a surprise attack on Israel on the Jewish holy day of Yom Kippur – which gave its name to the ensuing war. To apply pressure on the US, the Arab nations that were part of OPEC (the Organisation of Petroleum Exporting Countries) cut oil production and then placed an embargo on oil shipments to the United States, as well as on those to other countries that were either supportive of and sympathetic to Israel or were thought to be. The result was a major energy crisis.

Within weeks, the US was facing shortages and what President Nixon in a televised address to the nation on 7 November called 'a serious national problem'. The United States had 'grown and prospered in recent years' by being able to rely on oil imports. The war in the Middle East had changed this, leaving the country facing 'the most acute shortages since World War II'. As a result, dramatic action was now needed by the American people: in the short run, that meant 'we must use less energy – that means less heat, less electricity, less gasoline'. In the long run, he went on, 'it means that we must develop new sources of energy' to provide for energy independence in the future.[108]

He spelt out a radical set of measures that would now come into effect. These included nationwide changes for every household. 'To be sure that there is enough oil to go around for the entire winter, all over the country,' said Nixon, 'it will be essential for all of us to live and work in lower temperatures.' That meant lowering 'the thermostat in your home by at least 6 degrees'; this had been endorsed by his personal doctor, who had told him that 'you really are more healthy' in a cool environment than in a warm one. Offices, factories and 'commercial establishments' were required to reduce temperatures by ten degrees – 'either by lowering the thermostat or curtailing working hours' if that was the only alternative.[109]

Sweeping changes were announced across the federal government. Energy consumption was being and would be further cut across 'every agency and every department in government'; state governors were encouraged to look at plans 'slightly altering the school year' (presumably to take advantage of longer hours of daylight during the summer) and at curbing 'unnecessary lighting' in communities; initiatives would be introduced to encourage greater use of public transport and car sharing; every government vehicle would have its speed capped at 50 miles per hour (except in emergencies) to conserve fuel; and a national highway speed limit would be set, based on combustion engines' optimal efficiency, to help save hundreds of thousands of barrels of oil a day. 'We must all co-operate to change,' said Nixon.[110]

The US should be inspired by the recent moon landing, as well as by the technological achievements of the Manhattan Project, the President went on, to develop 'the potential to meet our own energy needs without depending on any foreign energy supplies'. Announcing a new plan, which he christened Project Independence, Nixon pledged that by 1980 it would be possible for America to meet its energy needs from its own resources.[111]

Concerns about energy availability, rising prices, the environment and dependency on foreign exports with its implications for the economy and for national security all have resonance in today's world. So too do the promises and commitments by governments to solve problems with deep roots through a series of ambitious announcements that deliver little by way of action. It is true that the energy crisis of the early 1970s left a deep imprint on the United States, the most obvious of which is that the speed limit of 55mph which was signed into law a few weeks after the presidential address remains in place half a century later. Early studies showed that these restrictions cost Americans almost 2 billion hours a year in lost time, but that lower speeds saved lives as well as fuel.[112] But few who take to the roads today, in electric vehicles or otherwise, link the speed they are allowed to travel with emergency measures intended to limit energy consumption.

One of the challenges, of course, was the power of the fossil-fuel lobby in the US which made moves towards cleaner energy difficult to achieve, as well as the resistance of voters to any increase in taxation to fund long-term programmes. The problems were epitomised during the presidency of Jimmy Carter (1976–80). 'The choices facing the members of Congress are not easy,' he said, when announcing his National Energy Plan in November 1977 in a nationwide address. 'With every passing month,' he said, 'our energy problems have grown worse. This summer we used more oil and gasoline than ever before in history,' with reliance on imports increasing rather than decreasing. This created inflationary pressures that were out of the hands of the US government, said Carter, who quoted his Secretary of Defense, Harold Brown, as saying that 'The present deficiency of assured energy sources is the single surest threat ... to our security and to that of our allies.' This was one reason why it was essential to create the new Department of Energy to oversee and co-ordinate responses to an extremely serious challenge.[113]

We need to 'cut back on consumption', said Carter, 'shift away from oil and gas to other sources of energy' and 'encourage production of energy here in the United States'. While supporting domestic fossil-fuel producers, he went on, the government would use tax incentives and penalties 'to hasten the shift from oil and gas to coal, to wind and solar power, to geothermal, methane, and other energy sources'. This was difficult, the President acknowledged, because America was facing 'long-range, future challenges', and politicians were elected for only short periods in office. Nevertheless, he concluded, 'I hope that, perhaps a hundred years from now, the change to inexhaustible energy sources will have been made.'[114]

Carter was not the first to suggest investment in research and development in clean energy. At the start of the 1970s, Nixon had introduced measures in Congress that included plans to improve energy efficiency as well as investment in technologies that enabled moves to cleaner fuels, including solar power, geothermal sources and hydrogen-based fusion reactors.[115] The money made available, however, was derisory and never likely to open up resources that were commercially viable. Carter, on the other hand, spoke with the zeal of an evangelist. 'The world has not prepared for the future,' he had said in a televised address to the nation soon after taking office. While advocating a boost in coal usage, he also set out ambitious goals to insulate homes and new buildings, and to develop and expand solar energy. These were all necessary, he said, 'to protect our jobs, our environment, our standard of living, and our future'. It was simple: 'We must not be selfish or timid if we hope to have a decent world for our children and grandchildren.'[116]

Not enough people agreed with him. Part of the problem lay in geopolitical turbulence in the late 1970s which saw OPEC hiking oil prices once again by 50 per cent in 1979, threatening to tip global economies – including in the US – into recession. Matters were made worse by Carter's tin-eared response. 'In a nation that was proud of hard work, strong families, close-knit communities and our faith in God, too many of us now tend to worship self-indulgence and consumption,' he said in July 1979, chastising voters who were due to vote in presidential elections just a few months later. There was 'a growing disrespect for government and for churches and for schools', he added. 'It is the truth and it is a warning.' Personal greed was the problem. 'Human identity is no longer defined by what one does, but by what one owns.'[117] These admonitions went down badly, with Carter's popularity plunging to unprecedented levels. This was capitalised on by Ronald Reagan, whose defence of the 'common sense and common decency of ordinary men and women, working out their lives in their own way', fell on fertile ground and swept him into the White House.[118]

Looking back now, it is hard to see how the opportunities to engage with energy shifts were missed. In the summer of 1979, for example, Carter had announced a billion-dollar funding package for solar and other renewables while showing off new solar panels that had been fitted to the White House roof. 'In the year 2000, this solar water heater behind me, which is being dedicated today, will still be here supplying cheap, efficient energy,' he said. 'A generation from now, this solar heater can either be a curiosity, a museum piece, an example of a road not taken, or it can be just a small part of one of the greatest and most exciting adventures ever undertaken by the American people.'[119]

Rather than a world of clean, renewable energy, the pathway of the following decades was one that led to an extraordinary rise in energy consumption, fossil-fuel burning, carbon emissions and pollutants – propelled above all by rising and intensive international trade and globalisation. Ironically, one of the catalysts for this lay in the compromising of the US presidential system; and another in weather-modification programmes that had been developed during the Vietnam War.

A treasure trove of thousands of documents relating to US military activities in South-East Asia had been handed over to the press by Daniel Ellsberg, a disillusioned researcher who had been involved in compiling a history of the US role in Indo-China from the end of the Second World War to the late 1960s. Known as the Pentagon Papers, these began to appear in print in a series of scoops and revelations in the *New York Times* and *Washington Post* that had readers riveted – and outraged by the number and range of covert operations that had been authorised, and by the disclosure that the administration of Lyndon Johnson had systematically lied 'not only to the public but also to Congress'.[120]

Stories began to appear in the summer of 1971 and continued unabated after the Supreme Court ruled that efforts by the US government to block publication violated the First Amendment of the Constitution and could not be justified in law.[121] One of the most striking revelations was about long-term efforts to manipulate the weather in South-East Asia during the Vietnam War. A report that had appeared even before the Pentagon Papers were released had alleged that 'Air Force rainmakers' had 'succeeded in turning the weather against the North Vietnamese' in a hush-hush project codenamed Intermediary Compatriot that had begun in 1967 and had increased rainfall over jungle road networks during the wet seasons.[122]

This report had caused alarm in some quarters in Washington, not least within the Senate Subcommittee on Oceans and International Environment, which demanded a response from the Secretary of Defense, who first declined to reply on the grounds that it would threaten national security and then testified in the Senate that no weather modification had been attempted, stating that 'we have never engaged in that type of activity over North Vietnam'.[123]

It was highly embarrassing, therefore, when a detailed account of precisely that activity appeared in the summer of 1972 in a lengthy exposé in which the journalist Seymour Hersh set out how, where and why a concerted programme had been developed. As one official with detailed knowledge of the operation explained, 'We were trying to arrange the weather pattern to suit our convenience.'[124] This was a reference to the Project POPEYE, the new codename chosen for INTERMEDIARY COMPATRIOT after the latter's moniker had been revealed despite being classified.[125]

As it later emerged, the objective of POPEYE was 'to produce sufficient rainfall' along communication lines in North Vietnam and southern Laos by seeding clouds with iodine to 'interdict or at least interfere with truck traffic' and, in so doing, to interrupt supplies. Initial experiments were conducted in Laos without the knowledge of Lao authorities and in conditions of utmost secrecy, 'unknown to other than a severely limited number of U.S. officials'. During this test phase, 'more than 50 cloud seeding experiments were conducted'. The results were described by the Department of Defense as 'outstandingly successful', with more than 80 per cent of the clouds that were seeded producing rain soon afterwards, with sufficient downpours 'to have contributed substantially to rendering vehicular routes ... inoperable'. One US Special Forces camp in Vietnam was 'inundated with nine inches of rain in four hours', seemingly taking servicemen by surprise.[126]

The results were very promising, early reports claimed, and provided strong evidence that the techniques could have a significant impact on enemy movements, supplies and communications; this could be enhanced by bombing bridges and river crossings to create bottlenecks. There were potential side-effects, however. For one thing, 'the proposed program would drastically change the weather patterns over the next few months', according to the request presented to the Secretary of State, Dean Rusk, 'to inaugurate operations at once'. For another, as the memorandum conceded, 'There would be some hypothetical effect of an adverse nature in Thailand where ... normal rainfall might be somewhat diminished,' although this was not worth worrying about; changes to precipitation levels and timings were nonetheless likely to have 'appreciable consequences outside the target areas'. There were risks to confidentiality, such as 'planned weather experiments in India', the possibility of a US seeding aircraft being downed or of leaks in the press. This was why the proposal to move forward was dependent on the authorisation of the President.[127]

As it later emerged in Senate hearings, POPEYE was intended 'to deny the enemy the use of roads by: softening road services, causing landslides along roadways, washing out river crossings [and] maintaining saturated soil conditions beyond the normal time span'.[128] Over the five years between its inception and its termination two days after Hersh's revelations, more than 2,500 sorties were flown by US aircraft with target priorities set by intelligence-gathering officers based at Tan Son Nhut in South Vietnam, at a cost of around $3.6 million per year.[129] Aircraft whose roles 'were not dedicated exclusively to the cloudseeding missions' over Laos and northern Cambodia were operated out of Thailand, whose government was neither asked for approval nor informed of the purpose and nature of these sorties.[130]

These disclosures were the tip of the iceberg. In Senate hearings in April 1972, it emerged that the US had been involved in weather interventions in the Philippines three years earlier and had been in discussion with that country's government about 'potential hurricane modification'. US Navy personnel had selected, seeded and 'kept alive' rainclouds off Okinawa in 1971 to help with drought alleviation. Discussions had been held 'informally' with Canada about cloud-seeding over the Great Lakes and with the British about 'hurricane work' in the Bahamas.[131]

In addition to this there was Project GROMET, a top-secret plan to try to mitigate drought in India in 1966–7 in which President Johnson had taken a personal, even obsessive interest, examining weekly rainfall maps so closely that he knew 'exactly where the rain fell and where it failed to fall'. On this occasion, the US consulted with the Indian Prime Minister, Indira Gandhi, whose government gave approval, even though it took steps to ensure that American involvement and the initiatives were not made public. As it turned out, the interventions were not successful and, with the arrival of abundant monsoon rains in the summer of 1967, not needed.[132]

The nature and extent of these weather modifications came as a surprise. 'The seeding techniques' that had been developed by the US military 'are now in use in almost every country in the world', one senior official told shocked senators in a prepared statement. Collaborations had been undertaken with dozens of institutions in the US as well as with 'numerous private corporations', while there had also been 'contact with individuals interested in' climate changes in 'India, Philippines, Taiwan, Chile, Israel, Rhodesia, Mexico, Portugal, France, Italy, Argentina and Australia'.[133]

This was 'extremely distressing', protested Claiborne Pell, chair of the hearings in the Senate in April 1972, some of which were conducted behind closed doors. 'If we do not restrict military use of current environmental modification techniques,' he said, 'we risk the danger of the development of vastly more dangerous techniques whose consequences may be unknown and may cause irreparable damage to our global environment.'[134] The committee recommended that the

US government 'seek the agreement of other governments' in pursuit of an international treaty banning the 'use of any environmental or geophysical modification as a weapon of war'.[135]

That overture was of particular significance for the Soviet Union and for Washington's relations with Moscow. In the late 1960s the USSR had undertaken a huge programme to build up its nuclear arsenal, while investing in an anti-ballistic missile (ABM) defence system that threatened to offer a decisive advantage in models of how a military confrontation might play out. This eventually led to the Strategic Arms Limitation Talks (SALT) which began in 1969 and concluded in the signing of an initial agreement in Moscow three years later.[136]

Co-operation such as this was part of an encouraging thaw in relations that opened the door for other agreements. Leading policymakers and scientists had built up a rapport at events like the regular Dartmouth conferences held in New Hampshire which provided the opportunity for US–Soviet discussions.[137] These contacts were now parlayed into bilateral talks about anthropogenic climate interventions that started in the summer of 1974 and led to the outlines of an agreement a year later which was then submitted to the United Nations as the Environmental Modification Convention and adopted on 10 December 1976.[138]

The convention banned 'environmental modification techniques', namely 'techniques for changing ... the dynamics, composition or structure of the Earth, including its biota, lithosphere, hydrosphere and atmosphere, or of outer space' for military purposes. Examples were offered of phenomena that could be caused by such techniques: 'earthquakes, tsunamis; an upset in the ecological balance of a region; changes in weather patterns (clouds, precipitation, cyclones of various types and tornadic storms); changes in climate patterns; changes in ocean currents; changes in the state of the ozone layer; and changes in the state of the ionosphere'.[139]

In a further demonstration of co-operation and openness, a delegation of scientists had spent three weeks in the Soviet Union in May–June 1976 to discuss weather-modification research and cloud physics and to learn how cloud seeding was being used over 5 million hectares in the Caucasus, Moldavia, Central Asia and Soviet bloc countries such as Bulgaria and Hungary; Soviet administrators and scientists claimed that these were already 'very successful ... and that the operations will continue to enlarge in the years to come'. The talks were constructive and amicable with comparisons of hailstorms in the Caucasus and Colorado and discussions of the merits of using rockets to inject ice nuclei into supercooled clouds, and of the optimal techniques for fog dissipation. Access was granted to multiple research institutes, including in Moscow, Leningrad, Tbilisi, Kiev and Nalchik. What struck the visitors most, however, was the age of those leading the research programmes: they were all noticeably younger than their predecessors, which could be taken as a sign of the growing interest in and commitment to the field by the Soviet authorities.[140]

Personal relationships and scholarly interactions such as these between scientists were to prove important during the years that followed. Of central importance was not the deliberate use of weather-modification programmes, alterations in global temperatures or even the effect of emissions on the atmosphere, but rather modelling the possible impact of war between the US and the Soviet Union. As one study published in 1975 put it, even during a period of détente – a warming of ties between the two superpowers – it was important to underline what the consequences of nuclear warfare might be, so that such knowledge might act as a deterrent to the use of these powerful weapons.[141] The impact of a nuclear exchange would include extended periods, perhaps lasting months, when fires would 'strongly restrict the penetration of sunlight to the earth's surface'. In such a scenario, 'it is likely that agricultural production in the Northern Hemisphere would be almost totally eliminated, so that no food would be available for the survivors of the initial effects of the war'.[142] The effect of such studies was profound. As one scholar has written, 'In the United States, the sharpest dispute about climate change in the 1980s was not about carbon dioxide but rather about the possibility of "Nuclear Winter".'[143]

Anxieties were soon intensified by a series of publications that also modelled the impact of large-scale nuclear confrontation between the US and the Soviet Union. Scholars working in both countries presented hypotheses a few months apart in 1983 that grabbed public attention, and stoked fears of what was at stake in the rivalry between two starkly different socio-economic and political systems. A paper published by a group of scholars headed by Richard Turco in the journal *Science*, using 'new data and improved models' which also drew on studies of dust storms on Mars, looked at the effect of 'sooty smoke' that would follow from wildfires and extensive urban fires. While 'most of the world's population could probably survive the initial nuclear exchange', wrote the authors, a major military engagement would result in 'significant surface darkening over many weeks, subfreezing land temperatures persisting for up to several months ... and dramatic changes in local weather and precipitation rates'. The result, they went on, would be a harsh 'nuclear winter'. Even more worrying was the observation that 'relatively large climatic effects could result even from relatively small nuclear exchanges ... if urban areas were heavily targeted' because of 'massive smoke emissions'.[144]

A paper published in the Soviet Union not long afterwards reached similar conclusions about the consequences of nuclear war: black smoke would envelop the whole earth, blocking out the sun's light and leading to dramatic drops in temperature so that all fresh water would freeze, all harvests would fail and ecologies would be destabilised. There would be mass extinctions of animals, plants and microorganisms; all terrestrial biota would be affected.[145] Intelligence analysts in the US were dubious about this. Soviet research on 'nuclear winter' was 'derived almost entirely from US ideas, data, and models'. Moreover, scientists in the USSR 'consistently reported more severe climatic changes than are usually found in similar research in the West'.[146]

US intelligence and scientific assessments were that the Soviets' calculations were not just derivative but crude, as well as being based on results that took forty hours on their clunky BESM-6 computer but only eight minutes on the latest Cray-1 machine used in the United States. As such, it was hard to avoid the conclusion that Moscow was developing a well-directed propaganda campaign to encourage disarmament movements, push for reductions in military spending and sow discord abroad – all in the USSR's interests.[147]

Nonetheless, it was worth considering how to address a scenario that Turco and his colleagues suggested could lead to reductions in surface temperatures to -17 °C within thirty days of a nuclear attack – with a base-case scenario of subfreezing conditions lasting for about three months and only returning to normal levels after about a year.[148] Although more accurate modelling in the US downgraded some of these assumptions and suggested a 'nuclear autumn' rather than a nuclear winter, the doomsday scenario caught the public imagination as 'an end-of-the-world story that fit the times' – sitting alongside disasters in the 1980s such as drought and famine in Ethiopia, the global AIDS epidemic, the catastrophe at the Chernobyl nuclear facility and more which framed humans as their own worst enemy.[149]

Certainly, there were well-placed figures within the Soviet Union who took the threat of nuclear disaster seriously. The physicist Sergei Kapitsa, whose father Pyotr won the Nobel prize for physics, took part in a round-table discussion in the Senate during a visit in December 1983 at the invitation of Senators Edward Kennedy and Mark Hatfield to consider the effects of nuclear war. A well-known TV broadcaster who hosted a weekly science programme in the USSR, Kapitsa reminded attendees of the explosion of Mount Tambora in 1815 – and of the poem 'Darkness' by Lord Byron that was written the following year, which he said was well known in the Soviet Union because it had been translated into Russian by the writer Ivan Turgenev. As the poem puts it:

I had a dream, which was not all a dream.
The bright sun was extinguish'd, and the stars
Did wander darkling in the eternal space,
Rayless, and pathless, and the ice earth
Swung blind and blackening in the moonless air.[150]

'Nuclear weapons have ceased to be an instrument of war,' Kapitsa said in a speech at the United Nations a month later, in which he again referenced the Tambora eruption and Byron's poem which he called 'by far the best description of a nuclear winter to be found in literature'. He also cited Mary Shelley's *Frankenstein*, which showed, he said, the dangers of the interface between humans and technologies that were not fully understood.[151]

There were many factors that moved US–Soviet relations towards discussions and actions around disarmament. The characters of both Ronald Reagan and Mikhail Gorbachev – the latter blowing fresh air into the sclerotic Soviet system after he became leader – were important, as was the personal relationship between the two men. Advances in the development of other military offensive and defensive tools such as the Strategic Defense Initiative which were very prominent in the media and beyond were significant, even if some scholars argue that the role these played was both more complicated and more limited than is often thought.[152] The Soviet invasion of Afghanistan, the travails of the US in the Middle East, Iran and elsewhere and the domestic pressures they produced were also ingredients that went into the pot of geopolitical change, disarmament talks and superpower co-operation in the 1980s.

Concerns about pollution, stronger environmental laws, better waste disposal and natural resource depletion were not only prominent issues across the United States and many parts of the west, but consistently ranked as the most important ones locally – which fed into political agendas, campaigning and the strengthening of green movements.[153]

This was mirrored in the Soviet Union, where there had been growing calls to focus on ecological protection rather than economic growth, to improve air quality, to stop harmful mining, to clear up industrial waste, to stop and reverse desertification and to protect the Aral Sea and Lake Baikal (the two most high-profile cases of anthropogenic devastation).[154] These calls became easier – and louder – following Gorbachev's reforms based on the principles of *glasnost* ('openness') and *perestroika* ('rebuilding'), which made it easier for citizens in the Soviet Union to demand action from the government. Local, regional, national and global environmental issues ranked highly as concerns of the Soviet population and were evidenced by mass demonstrations.[155]

There were parallels in other parts of the world, with the Chipko movement in the Himalayan foothills, which drew international attention to the relentless loss of forest cover, serving as an inspiration to others and as a warning that degradation of the environment was happening everywhere on the planet – and needed to be slowed down if not stopped.[156] The 1980s marked the peak of global deforestation, with tens of millions of hectares of rainforest cut down during that decade, largely in the form of clearances in the Amazon.[157] Protests groups and movements, from Brazil to Mexico, from West Africa to the Middle East, from Canada to Central America, mushroomed at this time demanding changes to the way consumption in rich countries was driving exploitation of nature and natural resources and causing substantial damage too.[158]

Environmental protection provided an obvious, mutual and indeed easy overlap in US–Soviet relations, and offered benefits in the presentation of both superpowers as sympathetic and benign global leaders. At their first meeting, in Geneva in November 1985, Reagan and Gorbachev discussed and agreed a raft of issues, from reaffirming the complete prohibition of chemical weapons to undertaking to meet regularly in the future. They also gave commitments 'to contribute to the preservation of the environment – a global task – through joint research and practical measures'.[159]

The opportunity to do so in practice came quickly. On top of fears of the potential impact of nuclear war, of rising pollution and of ecological degradation came yet another worrying concern about climatic change that might have devastating consequences. Scientists working on the ozone layer, which sits in the earth's stratosphere and absorbs almost all of the ultraviolet light emitted by the sun, had been concerned about its depletion since the 1970s, although suggestions that the damage was being done by the release of CFCs, often used in aerosols and as solvents, refrigerants and fire-fighting agents, were savaged by those working in the commercial sector.[160] By the mid-1980s, further work had emphatically established the link, and the worry about the rate of change and its effects had made it into mainstream media.[161]

International efforts to reduce and phase out chlorofluorocarbons led to the Vienna and then the Montreal Protocols being signed in March 1985 and September 1987 respectively, with Kofi Annan, later UN Secretary General, referring to the latter as 'perhaps the single most successful international agreement' overseen by the United Nations. These efforts have resulted in the likely recovery of the ozone layer to 1980 levels in the second half of the twenty-first century.[162] The subject was important in all US–Soviet discussions during this period, such as when Reagan and Gorbachev met in Washington just a few months after Montreal, when both leaders agreed to sponsor 'joint studies in global climate and environmental change through cooperation in areas of mutual concern, such as protection and conservation of stratospheric ozone'.[163]

While such expressions of co-operation are often more meaningful as positive gestures and statements of intentions not backed up by results, looking back now the 1980s in many ways were a golden age, a time of genuine resolve to try to counter major problems through working together and even a time of optimism that it might be possible to find global solutions to global problems. The agreement about ozone in 1987 was one example; but other major initiatives were also adopted, such as the Convention on Biological Diversity after the United Nations agreed in 1988 to hold a major conference on environment and development. The UN General Assembly declared that it was 'deeply concerned by the continuing deterioration of the state of the environment and the serious degradation of the global life-support systems, as well as by trends that, if allowed to continue, could disrupt the global ecological balance, jeopardize the life-sustaining qualities of the Earth and lead to an ecological catastrophe'. It recognised that 'decisive, urgent and global action is vital to protecting the ecological balance of the Earth'. The only question was what steps should be taken, where and by whom.[164]

As some realised, the problem was not just ozone. In June 1988, James Hansen, chief scientist of NASA's Goddard Institute for Space Studies, gave testimony to the US Senate, stating that 'The greenhouse effect has been detected and it is changing our climate now.' Addressing the media straight afterwards, he put it bluntly: 'It's time to stop waffling.' Action was needed, not words.[165]

Words, though, were what followed. Climate change had been important enough an issue for Vice-President George H. W. Bush to talk about it on the campaign trail during his successful run for the presidency in 1988. 'I'm an environmentalist – always have been,' he said. 'Those who think we are powerless to do anything about the "greenhouse effect" are forgetting about the "White House effect",' he said, promising to bring the Soviet Union, China and others to the table to discuss global warming.[166]

It sounded encouraging: the United Nations Conference on Environment and Development – known as the Earth Summit – held in Rio de Janeiro in June 1992, set out to agree ways of dealing with 'dangerous human interference with the climate system', including through regulating greenhouse-gas emissions, while making allowances for 'those countries, especially developing countries, whose economies are particularly dependent on fossil fuel production, use and exportation'. Although the nations gathered in Rio noted that 'there are many uncertainties in predictions of climate change', they acknowledged that 'the global nature of climate change calls for the widest possible cooperation by all countries and their participation in an effective and appropriate international response'.[167] This was a real breakthrough, said Bush. It was time, he said, to take 'concrete action to protect the planet'. After all, 'our children' would 'judge us by the actions we take from this day forward. Let us not disappoint them.'[168]

Like the conference on 'Changing the Atmosphere: Implications for Global Security' in 1988 that led to non-binding commitments by the participating governments to seek a 20 per cent reduction in CO_2 emissions by 2005, the UN Framework Convention on Climate Change promised much but delivered little. Although seen as a landmark agreement at the time, the reality was that the commitments eventually signed by 192 countries to stabilise 'greenhouse gas concentrations in the atmosphere at a level that would prevent dangerous anthropogenic interference with the climate system' produced few tangible results.[169]

This was a missed trick, not least because of the extraordinary opportunity provided by the end of the Cold War. The early 1990s, said President George H. W. Bush at Rio, was an 'unprecedented era of peace, freedom, and stability [which] makes concerted action on the environment possible as never before'. There was no progress and there were few breakthroughs. Further rounds of negotiation, such as a new protocol agreed in 1992 and signed at Kyoto in 1997 which set out the principle that countries had 'differentiated responsibilities' – namely, that richer countries which had industrialised first should bear a heavier burden – had flawed outcomes too.[170] Not only that, but after the conference the United States, the world's biggest consumer of fossil fuels, refused to ratify the Kyoto agreement without amendments, with the Senate rejecting it by a vote of 95–0.[171]

Part of the reason was that, while Bush had seemed keen on climate in public, he was fundamentally 'uninterested' in it personally, as a journalist reported in 1992. 'He never sat for a full-dress scientific briefing on it or exercised control over administration policy, even after infighting among administration officials became public, or leaders of other industrialised nations pledged action,' delegating all decisions to an official whose 'personal belief' was that 'global warming projections were alarmist'.[172]

It was not just President Bush who realised that saying the right things about climate helped win votes while doing something about it lost them. Bill Clinton faced the same equation when he became president. Climate change was 'a real problem', he admitted in calls to British Prime Minister Tony Blair in recently declassified telephone records. There was no question, he said, that 'something has to be done', from using cleaner energy supplies to working with the car industry to improve efficiency and thereby reduce emissions. But political divisions in Congress meant that although there was 'broad acknowledgement' that climate change was a problem, the chances of taking meaningful steps to address it were slim indeed.[173]

It might be naive to think that any initiatives might ever have reached a successful conclusion, although recent research suggests that the Montreal agreement on ozone will be responsible for global temperatures being at least 1 °C cooler – and 3–4 °C lower in the Arctic – by the middle of the twenty-first century than they would otherwise have been.[174] As it happened, however, the prospect of their doing so melted away. In the summer of 1989, a chain reaction began that eventually led to the fall of the Berlin Wall, to the reunification of Germany, to the replacement of communist regimes across Europe by democratically elected governments, to the splintering of the Soviet Union as its former constituent republics declared independence one by one and ultimately to the USSR ceasing to exist in December 1991.

In retrospect, this was a golden opportunity for bridge-building, rapprochement and mutual agreements; in the event, history took a different course. For Russian nationalists, the fall of the Soviet Union became a subject of shame and distress – the 'greatest catastrophe' of the twentieth century, according to President Vladimir Putin speaking in 2005.[175] It had major significance for the rest of the world, albeit for different reasons, because the collapse of the USSR gave rise to two seismic shifts. The first was that the vast natural resources that had been under the economic and political control of Moscow for decades suddenly became available for intensive exploitation on global markets. The second was that, in the months and years that followed, the shock of what had happened in 1989 in eastern Europe and the USSR had a profound effect on thinking in Beijing, which had almost succumbed to similar demands for reforms and freedoms when mass protests led by students reached Tiananmen Square in the heart of the Chinese capital that summer. The outcome was a fundamental reorientation in Chinese domestic, foreign and economic policies.

It is hard to overstate the importance of these two developments; taken together, they helped mould a new world that arguably rivalled the European arrival in the Americas in the 1490s. The decades that followed 1989 have proved to be by far the most intensive period of commercial exchange and integration – or globalisation – in history, in terms of scale and intensity as well as of speed. Needless to say, the impacts on local, regional and global climate have been epic – and unprecedented in human and natural history. The consequences will shape the world for generations to come.

24

On the Edge of Ecological Limits
(c.1990–today)

Широкий простор для мечты и для жизни
Грядущие нам открывают года.
(Wide spaces for dreams and for life
Are being opened up by the coming years.)

Russian National Anthem

The last decades of the twentieth century saw massive and relentless growth in demand for natural resources and raw materials. The search for supplies that were plentiful, cheap and easy to exploit was a global one. Bauxite mines were developed as reserves ran out in the US and France, with Jamaica and Guinea both becoming leading suppliers for industrial production in the developed world. To this could be added iron from West Africa, phosphates from Morocco and Senegal, copper and gold from Papua New Guinea and nickel from New Caledonia in the South Pacific, where exports rose at least a hundredfold between 1950 and 1976.[1]

The intensification of global trade has not only continued, it has accelerated rapidly, spurred on by the development of transportation networks that have enabled goods to be moved around the world more quickly and more cheaply than at any time in the past. New technologies have brought people closer together through the sharing of knowledge, harmonisation of information (and prices) and enhanced ability to do business. These trends were evident well before the digital revolution which enabled orders to be placed in real time: the opening up of Soviet airspace for civil aviation in 1985, which was partly the result of a softening of enmities between the USSR and the west and partly a reflection of Moscow's need to find sources of foreign currency during a period of deteriorating economic fortunes, did not just dramatically reduce typical journey times between Europe and Asia, but helped pave the way for rapid economic co-operation and investment by bringing businesses and business leaders into more regular contact.[2]

The end of the Cold War was the catalyst for further deepening of commercial ties and economic growth. The collapse of the Soviet Union provided opportunities for its rich resources to be sold on global markets, free of political doctrine and with no strings attached, while investment in the USSR by western businesses improved efficiency, boosted production, funded new operations, fields, mines and pipelines and pushed down prices. The collapse also brought about a large fall in industrial emissions as production fell and in some cases ground to a halt; moreover, higher prices and lower purchasing power severely reduced consumption of livestock products, resulting in a halving of cattle and pig numbers in the former Soviet Union between 1992 and 2011. The reconfiguration of food systems, including the abandonment of cropland, was dropped and the restructuring of agricultural trade resulted in a massive reduction in global greenhouse emissions.[3] Uncertainties that impacted fossil-fuel production in the twenty years after the 1991 dissolution of the USSR may also have been responsible for a very significant fall in methane emissions that correlates closely with the economic and political turmoil in the years that followed.[4] The fall of the Soviet Union was bad for political idealists, but it seems to have been good for global climate – at least in the short term.

Seismic shifts were taking place in other parts of the world too. Although the impetus for China's integration into global markets can be traced back to President Nixon's visit to Beijing in the early 1970s and then the award of Most Favoured Nation status under the Carter administration, it was the decision of the leadership in Beijing in the early 1990s to open up to foreign investment that proved transformational: suddenly, a massive pool of cheap labour that could make goods at a low price became available, alongside the tantalising prospects offered by a market of more than a billion people that appeared certain to grow quickly in the years that followed.

The pace of that growth has proved mind-boggling. The global economy quadrupled in size in the three decades after 1990, an astonishing rate spread over such a short period and despite regular punctures caused by the Iraq War of 1990, the 'Asian crisis' of 1998, the attacks of 9/11 and their aftermath, the financial crisis of 2008 and the coronavirus pandemic (some estimates suggest that the latter cost the US economy alone some $16 trillion).[5] The expansion of international and global trade agreements, along with investment in logistical capabilities – such as enormous cargo ships, the largest of which now carry over 20,000 containers, and port facilities able to handle traffic – spurred the closer integration of markets, stimulated the creation of intercontinental supply chains and boosted global economic growth.

Membership of the World Trade Organisation (WTO) brought down tax barriers, putting downward pressure on prices that triggered a series of booms – at least for those well placed to benefit from them. For example, average taxes on imports in Colombia fell by more than three-quarters after it was admitted to the WTO in 1995, and those in India fell from over 80 per cent to an average of 30 per cent. While the US economy has more than tripled in size in the three decades after 1990, that of China grew by forty-five times in the same period, with nominal GDP rising from around $310 billion in 1990 to over $14 trillion in 2020. To give just one indication of the scale of change, there were an estimated 20,000 private vehicles on the road in China in 1985; today, there are more than 240 million.[6]

A series of political, economic, social, technological and digital revolutions since the early 1990s have transformed the world we live in. But perhaps the most important of all the changes has been the transformation of the natural world, the remodelling of ecological systems and the impacts on current and future local, regional and global climates. For example, intensive farming in the midwest of the United States has lost almost 60 billion metric tons of topsoil since 1860 – a process that degrades soils by removing organic matter and nutrients, reduces crop yields and increases agricultural costs.[7] An estimated 36 billion metric tons of soil are eroded globally every year, with losses predicted to rise quickly in sub-Saharan Africa, South America and South-East Asia.[8] Heavy use of pesticides in soils, along

THE EARTH TRANSFORMED

with contamination by heavy metals and plastics, has not only affected land quality and yields, but when ingested also damages the human cardiovascular system.[9]

Unsustainable exploitation of resources has obvious consequences once those resources become exhausted. For example, the High Plains Aquifer in the western portion of the Great Plains region of North America was formed around 65 million years ago from sediment eroded from the Rocky Mountains and carried by streams flowing towards the Mississippi River. The Aquifer contains enough water to cover the state of Colorado to a depth of almost fourteen metres. Today, it is recharged only by rainfall that seeps into the soil. Its deposits are being used faster than they are being replaced, largely to provide irrigation for what is often referred to as the 'breadbasket of the world'. This is not news: even in 1978, the Lieutenant Governor of Kansas, Shelby Smith, warned that Kansas had 'major water problems, and a crisis is on the horizon'. Although the rate of water decline slowed down, some sections of the Aquifer are now completely exhausted. As one recent report observed, the High Plains Aquifer was formed over millions of years; it is 'being depleted in the span of one human lifetime'.[10]

If this is damaging, so too is deforestation. Tens of millions of hectares of forest have been lost, with tropical forests the primary source of new agricultural land in the last years of the twentieth century.[11] Indeed, as much as 99 per cent of deforestation in the tropics is driven by agricultural expansion.[12] In South-East Asia, much land has been cleared for the cultivation of palm oil, the most common vegetable oil in the world and an ingredient found in more than half of all packaged products sold in the United States, including lipstick, soap and ice cream.[13] Ironically, in a classic case of one step forward and two steps back, forest clearance for plantations was also encouraged by the identification of palm oil by the European Union as a suitable biofuel to help reduce reliance on fossil fuels.[14]

It is a similar story in the Amazon, where massive land clearances have taken place in response to global demand for consumables. Some 63 per cent of the tree-cover loss across all forest types in the Amazon was the result of opening up land for beef and dairy production, with land conversion for cattle pasture in Brazil particularly acute.[15] Although deforestation slowed in the early years of the twenty-first century, rates hit a fifteen-year high in 2021, driven by fires lit to clear land illegally even before enforcement of environmental laws was scaled back under President Jair Bolsonaro.[16] In the counties of the Congo basin – Cameroon, Central African Republic, Democratic Republic of the Congo, Equatorial Guinea, Gabon and Republic of Congo – home to the second-largest area of humid tropical forest in the world, an estimated 16 million acres were lost in the years 2000–14 as a result of clearances for agriculture and logging; these losses would seem likely to accelerate given that the region is forecast to see a fivefold population increase by 2100.[17]

Major land clearances that are connected to beef, meat and dairy have also driven forest loss. Since 2000, for example, the amount of soy plantation in Brazil has doubled to 34 million hectares, resulting not only in loss of tropical rainforest but also in the negative impact of the Cerrado, a global biodiversity hotspot which distributes fresh water to the largest basins in South America.[18] Around three-quarters of global soy production is used for animal feed, particularly for chicken and pig consumption, helping meet demand in a world that has become richer, more interconnected and more populous in recent decades, with the number of people sharing the planet and its resources rising from 3 billion in 1960 to almost 8 billion in 2019.[19] It is not hard to understand the link between environmental degradation and the collapse of ecosystems, the loss of biodiversity and the obvious long-term consequences of decisions made when we choose what to eat. These pressures are likely to become more intense, with demand for meat, milk and eggs projected to grow strongly in coming decades.[20]

The impact of forest loss goes far beyond the dinner table in parts of the world that import palm oil, soy or beef planted, grown or reared in newly cleared lands. For one thing, around 1.6 billion people depend on forests for their livelihoods, above all in developing countries.[21] For another, the loss of forest cover has dramatic impacts on plant and animal habitats and on biodiversity: according to the United Nations Environment Programme, forests are home to around 80 per cent of all amphibian, 75 per cent of bird and 68 per cent of mammal species.[22] As such, dramatic remodelling of landscapes has deep and serious consequences for all forms of life.

Deforestation has a significant influence on climate patterns. For example, in the decade after 2000, palm cultivation was thought to be responsible for between 2 and 9 per cent of total worldwide emissions from tropical land use.[23] Average losses of more than 3 million hectares of forest per year in South-East Asia alone in the period 2001–19 have meant that more than 420 million metric tons of carbon are released into the atmosphere every year – a state of affairs made worse by the fact that forests are being cut down at increasingly high altitudes and on steeper slopes, where carbon densities are higher than in the lowlands.[24]

The ecosystem productivity of the Amazon rainforest has been declining since the 1980s, with increased tree mortality, fire feedbacks that amplify drought and reduced evapotranspiration resulting in shifts in moisture patterns, precipitation levels and forest viability.[25] These changes have been so pronounced that the Amazon has gone from being an absorber into a source of carbon emissions – with release much greater in the eastern regions where anthropogenic activities are concentrated.[26] Understanding the impact of other significant factors, such as methane, nitrous oxide, biogenic volatile organic compounds and aerosols is also important, as these have often been overlooked in assessments of current and projected changes across the diverse Amazon region.[27]

Although there are wide discrepancies between models of future changes, a series of recent studies have suggested that the major role that the Amazon system plays in global climate is at increasing risk of sudden collapse, with serious consequences for us all.[28] In addition to deliberate forest clearances, forest fires have already become increasingly frequent, fierce and extensive. In 2021, for example, the equivalent of around ten football pitches was lost to forest fires every minute – with over 5 million hectares burned in Russia alone (in addition to a million hectares that were cleared deliberately).[29] One recent report suggests that extreme fires will increase sharply in coming decades, with higher burning incidence in the Arctic accelerating the thawing of permafrost peatlands that are then susceptible to fire and to the release of irrecoverable terrestrial carbon, which is then released into the atmosphere, exacerbating global warming.[30]

At the COP26/UN Climate Change Conference in Glasgow in November 2021, a total of 141 countries vowed to 'halt and reverse forest loss and land degradation by 2030'.[31] On the evidence of recent years, decades and centuries, that would seem like an ambitious target. Just as repurposing of land and forests has dramatically changed the world we live in, so too has globalised trade altered ecosystems and plant and animal habitats – including our own. To be sure, and as we have seen, the opening up of trade and transport networks in the past has introduced new species and led to major ecological transformations.

However, the hyperconnected globalised trade and transport networks of the modern world that have brought producers and consumers closer together and made it easier for humans to move around the world have also led to the expansion, relocation and invasion of alien species into new locations that have resulted in the extinction of native species, disrupted food chains and produced significant changes in the natural environment on an unprecedented scale and at an astonishing speed.[32]

These networks also carry significant implications for human health, welfare and finances, given many have a major impact on activities related to economic productivity, or have financial consequences: for example, an infestation of brown tree snakes in Guam has caused thousands of hours of power outages as the creatures disturb or become trapped in electrical power lines and service stations, causing as many as 200 outages in a single year – at a cost of millions of dollars in damage, repair costs and lost productivity.[33] The spread of the common coqui frog in Hawai'i, meanwhile, has been linked to a decline in real estate values in places where infestation levels are high because its loud mating song is such a disturbance to local (human) residents.[34]

The emerald ash borer, native to East Asia, was first identified killing trees in Michigan and Ontario in 2002; two years later, 15 million trees were dead or dying. The entire stock of 8 billion ash trees in the US are vulnerable to this pest – which if lost would cost forestry more than $280 billion, not to mention the costs of removal of dead urban trees for an additional $20–$60 billion.[35] Then there are the Asian and citrus long-horned beetles, originally from South-East Asia, which some estimate might together kill 30 per cent of trees in US cities (more than a billion, in other words), valued at $669 billion, and which are already killing ash

trees in Russia and spreading westwards towards Europe.[36] An outbreak
in Kent in the UK, most likely from infested imported wood packaging,
required a six-year programme of trapping and surveillance by the
Animal and Plant Health Agency and the Forestry Commission, which
eventually led to a triumphant and relieved statement by the Minister
for Biosecurity.[37] Or there is the fall armyworm moth which is highly
damaging to many crops and to maize, sorghum and rice in particular,
and which despite being native to the Americas was first reported in
West Africa in 2016 and a year later was the fastest-spreading major pest
in the world.[38]

Taken as a whole, the consequences for world agriculture if the
spread of invasive pests and pathogens is not stopped runs to hundreds
of billions of dollars per year – with China, the United States, India
and Brazil facing the highest potential costs from around 1,300 species
that are particularly dangerous. Relative to GDP, however, the majority
of the twenty countries most at risk are located in sub-Saharan Africa.[39]
Pests do not just destroy ecosystems: animals such as termites can also
destroy built infrastructure, and are likely to do so more often as colony
sizes and geographic distribution rise sharply in the coming decades;
this has climate implications too since these animals are a substantial
source of methane emissions.[40]

On top of this comes crop disease from parasitic plants, viruses, fungi
and bacteria, which are thought to be the cause of the loss of around 10
per cent of global food production each year. These are typically dealt
with through the application of chemicals or antibiotics, though these
are losing their efficiency thanks to the natural development of bacterial
resistance.[41] This is in addition to measurable declines in nutritional
values in multiple crops in recent decades, presumably as a result of use
of fertilisers, pesticides and the more aggressive farming methods that
place a premium on crop size and yield.[42]

However, the most important environmental transformations have
resulted from the ways in which human populations have become
concentrated in recent decades. Cities and urban areas are the
source of most major climate-change impacts: although living close
together encourages high velocities of exchange, cities are centres of
consumption rather than production. Urban populations require food,
water and energy which need to be brought over distance – sometimes
considerable ones – and rarely only from the hinterland or immediate

vicinity. Factories and manufacturing are located in or near cities in order to access labour forces or transportation, power and digital networks, but the materials that supply them are usually brought from other locations – again often ones that are distant.

Transportation is responsible for around a quarter of global energy-related CO_2 emissions, and even more in many developed countries, accounting for about 29 per cent of emissions in the US as a whole and around 41 per cent of those in California. In some cases, more emissions are produced by inefficient production than by the transportation of goods over long distances; indeed, as well as the socio-economic benefits of trade, there are sometimes cases where transportation actually decreases emissions even when goods are not produced in a 'cleaner' way in different locations.[43]

Nevertheless, urbanisation is a driver of multiple environmental problems and not only because of the needs of high-density populations. Despite cities being synonymous with 'civilisation' in the literal meaning of the world (Latin *civitas* – city), the reality is that cities occupy only a tiny fraction of the world's land surface – perhaps as little as 3 per cent.[44] Despite this, rising urbanisation has meant that more than half the global population now live in urban areas, with this number projected to rise to 70 per cent by 2050. Given current demographic trends, this means that an additional 2.5 billion people will be living in cities within the next thirty years – which has obvious implications for demands on resources of all kinds, for infrastructure natural and otherwise and for emissions of carbon, greenhouse gases and heat.[45]

This comes on top of the rate of urbanisation over the last thirty years which has been jaw-dropping in scale. Construction in urban areas in China quadrupled between 1990 and 2010, with time-series satellite imagery showing that built-up land areas in parts of Chengdu grew by 300 per cent in the six years after 1996.[46] China's urban population rose from around 18 per cent to almost 60 per cent in forty years, with hundreds of millions of people moving to cities in what is the largest and fastest rate of urbanisation in history.[47] China is estimated to have used more concrete in 2011–13 than the United States did in the whole of the twentieth century.[48]

Urbanisation in other parts of the world – including Nigeria, India, Brazil and Indonesia – has been epic too, with cities such as Mexico

City, Lagos, Manila, Mumbai, Jakarta, Dhaka and Cairo now each having populations of at least 20 million and in some cases considerably more. Before the coronavirus took hold, all ten of the fastest-growing cities in the world by GDP in the next fifteen years were forecast to be in India; it is still too early to say whether these projections will hold.[49] What is clearer is that the distribution of urbanisation levels and growth rates across continents and regions is uneven, with more than 80 per cent of people living in urban areas in North America, Latin America and the Caribbean, compared to just 40 per cent in sub-Saharan Africa.[50]

Cities give rise to profound socio-economic inequalities, with more than two-thirds of the world's urban population experiencing widening income inequality since 1980 – which means that almost 3 billion people live in cities where realities and prospects are worse than they were a generation ago.[51] Although slum conditions have improved over the last fifteen years, an estimated 1 billion people – or one in four of all the world's urban population – live in housing that is non-durable or overcrowded, or lack access to safe water and sanitation or security against eviction.[52]

As well as being centres of consumption, cities and their populations generate vast amounts of waste, putting pressure on infrastructure as well as on the natural environment as a result of heat stress, water scarcity, energy demands and difficulties of sanitation treatment.[53] Sometimes, the challenges are not only overwhelming, but a source of health hazards. In Lagos, for example, less than half the population in high-density areas of the city have access to flush toilets, resorting to open pit latrines – with limited handwashing facilities available.[54] Cities in high-income countries are able to pay to remove waste out of sight and out of mind, as is the case with New York City, where more than 3 million metric tons of rubbish every year are moved out of the city to incineration and recycling plants and to landfill at a cost of more than $450 million.[55] These options are not available, however, in most of the world's largest cities, where disposal is often either rudimentary, hazardous or non-existent.

While the impacts of oil and gas on climate receive a great deal of attention, those of the waste sector are often ignored – despite the fact that the latter account for almost 20 per cent of total anthropogenic emissions, primarily as a result of anaerobic decay of organic materials in landfill.[56] Landfill waste is expected to grow at more than double the rate of population growth in the years leading up to 2050 – which is likely to lead to a significant rise in methane concentrations that in turn have a major impact on global warming. Recent research using satellite data on landfill sites in Delhi, Mumbai, Lahore and Buenos Aires reveals that city-level emissions are considerably higher than usually reported, which underlines the importance of the development and implementation of policies to mitigate the effect that they have on atmospheric conditions.[57]

This research also confirmed the importance of identifying 'superemitter' sites that produce a disproportionately large volume of emissions, where the rewards for reduction can be high. There are obvious lessons, therefore, for by-products created by cities around the world, not least since cities generate more than 70 per cent of greenhouse-gas emissions, which are closely linked to global warming. More than half of these are produced by just twenty-five 'megacities', all of which are located in China, apart from Moscow and Tokyo.[58]

Urbanisation, combined with rapid industrialisation in low-income countries and the intensification of international trade, has led to falls in air quality, which, as we have already seen, leads to a range of detrimental health outcomes. Particulate pollution in India, Pakistan, Bangladesh and Nepal has risen by 47 per cent since the start of the century, with some parts of India recording $PM_{2.5}$ concentration levels of 107 µg/m^3 – more than twenty-one times World Health Organisation guidelines. Poor air quality means that life expectancy in several provinces east of Kinshasa in the Democratic Republic of Congo or in Mixco in Guatemala is more than three and a half years less than it should be, while across South-East Asia, where 99.9 per cent of the population live in areas that exceed the WHO guidelines, average life expectancy is reduced by one and a half years for every man, woman and child – a total loss of almost 960 million person-years. Taking a global average, the impact of particulate pollution on life expectancy is three times greater than that of alcohol, six times that of HIV/AIDS and eighty-nine times that of conflict and terrorism.[59]

Potential gain in life expectancy from permanently reducing PM$_{2.5}$ from 2020 concentrations to the WHO Guideline in the 10 most populated countries

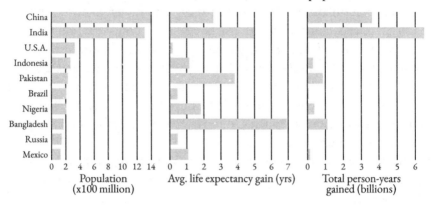

Life expectancy impact of PM$_{2.5}$ and unassociated causes/risks of death, Global

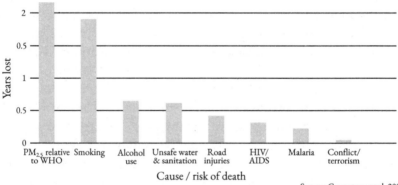

Source: Greenstone et al, 2022

That air quality is significantly better in high-income countries is partly a testimony to legislation, but it owes much to the fact that manufacturing – and its dirty by-products – have been outsourced to other parts of the world that as a result bear the environmental, health and human consequences. Despite this, the per capita greenhouse-gas emissions of cities in Europe, the United States and Australia are significantly higher, because of higher consumption patterns, lifestyle choices and energy availability.[60] Those who are wealthy, in other words, do more direct and indirect damage to the environment and to climate than those who are not.

Underpinning this has been the development and adoption of one technology in particular: air conditioning. According to one prominent economist, air conditioning ranks alongside the civil rights movement in the reshaping of US demographics and politics in the latter part of the twentieth century.[61] The ability to control temperature and to maintain it at a constant level transformed not only how people lived but where, with offices, factories, homes and leisure facilities springing up in locations that had previously been too hot to be practical as major urban settlements. Such has been the impact of air conditioning that studies suggest it has been responsible for up to 80 per cent of the decline in heat-related mortality in the United States alone.[62] The ability to cool classrooms and workplaces in warm regions is vital for productivity and cognition, with studies showing that student performances in standardised maths tests fall as temperatures rise from the low 20s °C, while thermal stress also affects simple cognitive and manual tasks such as handling a steering wheel.[63]

Air conditioning, and the associated energy requirements, has allowed humans to create artificial climate environments that are independent of their natural surroundings. Put differently, this has meant that urban metropolises could be built in locations that would not otherwise be sustainable – and whose futures are dependent on air-conditioning units and on power being supplied to them. As one leading commentator has pointed out, there are already more than 350 major cities today where the average maximum summer temperature is over 35 °C; given current warming patterns, more than 600 more cities might well fall into the same category by 2050 – resulting in 1.6 billion people living in challenging conditions that far exceed the optimal temperature for the human body that medical literature consistently places in the range of 15–20 °C.[64]

Air conditioning requires vast amounts of energy: in Saudi Arabia, for example, 700,000 barrels of oil per day are burned, primarily to keep premises cooler than they would otherwise be. Around 70 per cent of all energy consumption in Saudi Arabia is spent on air conditioning. Although there has been some progress in clean energy production as recently as 2017, all of this came from fossil fuel energy sources.[65] As things stand today, air conditioners and fans account for 10 per cent of global electricity consumption – with demand likely to triple or even quadruple by the end of this decade; some estimate that there will be more than 9 billion cooling appliances being used by 2050.[66] In this context, rapid population growth in drought-prone places – such as the south and mountainous west of the United States – that adds to existing pressures on water, as well as on infrastructure, transportation and energy, is not just hard to understand but difficult to believe.[67]

This falls into a wider pattern of behaviour relating to the choices that are made on the basis of apparent certainties and assumptions that tomorrow's world will be as benign as today's. For example, across the United States, almost 4 million houses have been built in flood zones which are exposed to tropical cyclones, floods and other hazards; in Florida alone, one in six single-family houses have been built in floodplains. Taken as a whole, this means that US housing stock located on floodplains is overvalued by almost $44 billion, even before implications of rising sea levels, more frequent and more extreme storms and other hazards are considered.[68]

If decisions to move towards rather than away from risk seem perplexing, so too do countless other choices we make. Nearly three-quarters of all the energy produced by humans is squandered as waste heat; although this does not directly warm the atmosphere and has a negligible impact on climate change, the wastage is testimony to the profligate way we treat the world around us.[69] In the UK, for example, almost 10 million metric tons of food, worth almost £20 billion, are thrown away each year. Getting this food from the field, pasture or coop to the rubbish bin required energy to sow, tend, reap, harvest, feed, pasture, slaughter and transport not only to the point of sale and then to the larder or fridge, but also to compost heap or rubbish bin. As such, it represents 36 million metric tons of greenhouse-gas emissions that were generated because of inefficiency.[70]

When widened out with data from elsewhere, the UN Environment Programme and the climate action group WRAP suggest that 931 million metric tons of food were wasted globally in 2019 – the equivalent of 23 million fully loaded forty-ton trucks, which if lined up bumper to bumper would circle the earth seven times. Almost two-thirds of this food is wasted at household level, with a global average of 74 kilos per capita of food thrown away or not eaten each year – with little difference between lower-middle and high-income countries.[71] An estimated 8–10 per cent of global greenhouse-gas emissions are associated with food that is not consumed.[72] Our inability to budget and plan meals efficiently comes at a cost to plants and animals, to soil, to the atmosphere – and to each other.

So, for example, the fashion industry as a whole is estimated to contribute around 10 per cent of global greenhouse-gas emissions – more than the aviation and shipping industries combined.[73] Some believe that clothes production may account for a quarter of the world's carbon budget by 2050.[74] A significant part of the energy and resources that go into clothes production is squandered: in the UK alone, it is estimated that consumers have unworn clothes in their cupboards that are worth almost $50 billion.[75] This is the tip of the iceberg: around the world, the equivalent of a rubbish truck of textiles is burned or deposited in landfill every second of every minute of every hour of every day of the year because of clothes and fabrics that are no longer wanted or cannot find a buyer.[76] At least 39,000 metric tons of this end up being dumped in the Atacama desert, one of the world's driest regions, where it can take hundreds of years to biodegrade, if it biodegrades at all.[77]

Moreover, clothes production is extremely water intensive: making a single cotton shirt requires 2,700 litres of fresh water – the equivalent of a person's drinking needs for two and a half years – and 7,500 litres to make a single pair of jeans, drinking water for someone for seven years.[78] This clearly has implications in the context of a world where by 2010 a quarter of the world's population was already affected by water scarcity, with 17 per cent of the European Union's territory and more than 10 per cent of its population already also exposed.[79] These pressures are rising quickly, with demand for water projected to exceed supply by 40 per cent by the end of this decade – before factoring in what climate change will do to availability.[80] It does not help that poor infrastructure means that in some places water is wasted – with more than 3 billion litres estimated lost to leaks every day in England and Wales in the twelve months to March 2021, and an estimated 20–40 per cent of Europe's available water likewise lost unnecessarily.[81]

A long list of other examples could be given to illustrate the consequences of lifestyle choices. A study of drinking-water habits in Barcelona showed that the environmental impact of bottled water was up to 3,500 times greater than tap water, and that switching either to tap or filtered water had major benefits because of reduced use of resources and raw materials.[82] Around 500 billion plastic bottles are produced every year – the equivalent of more than sixty for every man, woman and child in the world. According to one study a few years ago, fewer than half of the 20,000 bottles or so that are sold every second around the world were collected for recycling, with just 7 per cent of those turned into new bottles.[83] One senior executive at Coca-Cola, whose factories are thought to produce more than 100 billion throwaway bottles a year, commented that the company would not abandon single-use plastic bottles because they were popular with customers, noting that 'Business won't be in business if we don't accommodate consumers.'[84]

Consumer demands may sate short-term desires – at costs that can be overlooked or obscured. The popularity of ship cruises, for example, has helped drive the construction of more and larger vessels that take customers on voyages of a lifetime. According to recent analysis, in 2017 emissions of noxious oxides around the coasts of Europe by the world's largest cruise operator, Carnival Corporation, were nearly ten times greater than those of all 260 million cars in Europe put together – with obvious consequences for marine and coastal life of all kinds, as well as enhanced risks to human health, especially in the main cruise ports such as Venice, Palma and Barcelona.[85] Then there is the boom in space tourism which threatens to deplete the ozone layer and to produce soot emissions that are 500 times greater than those of the aviation industry.[86]

The digital age that has powered a revolution in communication, information and connectivity has also served to boost consumption by putting pressure on prices: internet retailers do not need to have expensive shops in town centres, to employ staff to restock shelves that look attractive to customers or to be based physically or even legally in countries where orders are placed. Given also the ease with which one can order from mobile devices, it is perhaps not surprising that some of the largest companies in the world – from Apple to Alphabet, from Alibaba to Amazon, from Meta to Verizon – are directly and indirectly linked to boosting patterns of exchange. To give one example, in 2019, Alibaba's annual Singles' Day sale on 11 November saw sales of around $13 billion in a little over ninety seconds; the day as a whole resulted in the dispatch of 1.29 billion parcels.[87] In 2020, nearly 4 billion packages were shipped as a result of Singles' Day sales.[88] In the course of the previous year, China had consumed more than 9 million tons of plastic packaging – equivalent to the weight of 130 million adults, and carbon emissions that would take 700 million trees to neutralise.[89]

Inefficiency and wastage plague other sectors too. Many medicines that are produced become useless or have to be destroyed because they are susceptible to physical or chemical deterioration – a feature that makes them difficult to formulate, store and transport; as a result, almost half of all biologics, including vaccines, are ruined before they can be used.[90] As well as the cost of ingredients, manufacture and transportation, the difficulties of cold-chain and logistics systems means that countries that have poor transport and energy infrastructure, have challenging climates or geographies or both, or have large rural or semi-urban populations experience considerably more problems in delivering medicines such as vaccines. This leads to a range of outcomes that impact incomes, social development and political liberalisation.[91]

Or there is the military, whose energy expenditure is vast – even in times of peace. A new F-35A fighter plane consumes almost six litres per kilometre on a typical training sortie, and generates almost twenty-eight metric tons of carbon dioxide emissions if it uses its full capacity without refuelling. Financial and environmental costs rise sharply during periods of conflict: since 2001, when the United States has been heavily committed to operations in Syria, Iraq and Afghanistan, as well as in other arenas such as the South China Sea, the Department of Defense has been responsible for around 80 per cent of the entire energy consumption of the US government. Indeed, the Department is the world's largest institutional user of petroleum and the single largest institutional producer of greenhouse gases in the world, with energy primarily expended on fuel for aircraft, but also for other vehicles and vessels, as well as on heating, lighting and powering military facilities – which include 560,000 facilities with over 275,000 buildings at 800 bases, located on 11 million hectares of land in the US and elsewhere around the world.[92]

While the scale of the US military dwarfs those of other countries, many of whose energy expenditures are difficult to calculate accurately, it is nevertheless clear that defence comes with a very high price tag. Ironically, the link between climate change and war was at the forefront of the minds of participants at the Toronto Conference on Changing Atmosphere in 1988, where the delegates declared in an agreed statement that human activities amounted to an 'unintended, uncontrolled, globally pervasive experiment whose ultimate consequences could be second only to a global nuclear war'.[93]

It has taken a long time for this message to sink in. A 2019 study by the British Academy of Film and Television Arts (BAFTA) and the environmental organisation Albert, supported by Deloitte, looked at almost 130,000 TV programmes shown by four major broadcasters in the UK between September 2017 and September 2018. 'Climate change' and 'global warming' were mentioned 3,125 times and 799 times respectively. To put that in perspective, 'gravy' was mentioned 3,942 times, 'cheese' almost 33,000 times and 'dog' 105,245 times.[94] In a follow-up report published in the autumn of 2021, climate change was mentioned marginally more often than 'goldfish', slightly less often than 'Shakespeare' and just over twice as often as the word 'motherfucker'.[95] This would suggest that awareness of and concern about the world of tomorrow – and today – are not as high as they could and perhaps should be.

According to the World Meteorological Association, the decade 2010–20 was the warmest since modern record-keeping began in the 1880s.[96] This included a drought event in Europe that was the most intense in centuries and reduced crop yields in countries and regions most affected by as much as 40 per cent.[97] In the south-western United States, meanwhile, the years since 2000 have been the driest since at least AD 800 thanks to what some scientists refer to as a megadrought, with temperatures above average and precipitation well below, leading to the decline of two of North America's largest reservoirs, Lake Mead and Lake Powell, both of which reached their lowest levels on record.[98] The year 2019 was the warmest on record in the Arctic, resulting in the loss of almost 660 billion metric tons of ice, more than double the average of the previous two decades.[99] Glacial retreat in the Peruvian Andes that is almost certainly linked to human activities has raised the threat to towns and communities as a result of the increased probabilities of major flooding.[100] Severe storms and extreme rainfall that occurred when three tropical cyclones and two tropical storms hit Madagascar, Malawi and Mozambique in the space of just six weeks in early 2022 are also part of shifting weather conditions that can be associated with anthropogenic climate change.[101]

What makes these so significant is that they are part of a globally coherent pattern of warming. As we have seen, while there have been many epochs in the past that have experienced particularly cold or warm periods – such as the Little Ice Age, the Medieval Climate Anomaly or the Roman Warm Period – these were not universal, but rather were particularly pronounced in one or more regions, and even on one or more continents. In contrast, the last 150 years show near coherence all around the world. For 98 per cent of the planet, the twentieth century was the warmest period of the last two millennia. This is not only unprecedented; it is also not a coincidence.[102]

At the heart of the acceleration of warming have been resource depletion, manufacturing, urbanisation and population growth, all of which have relied heavily on vast consumptions of energy and of power produced by carbon in particular. Even though recent years have seen large investments in renewable energy sources (such as hydro, geothermal and above all wind and solar power), around 80 per cent of the energy used around the world comes from the burning of fossil fuels.[103] The burning of fossil fuels releases carbon dioxide into the air which intensifies the greenhouse effect by trapping heat in the atmosphere, causing the earth's average air temperatures to increase.

Rising population levels, greater urbanisation and new production and transport technologies as well as more frequent commercial interaction have all played a part in driving demand for more energy in recent decades: as the influential writer David Wallace-Wells put it, around 85 per cent of the burning of carbon-based fuel has been carried out since the end of the Second World War – while more than half has been since the first episode of *Seinfeld* was broadcast. The result is that there is more carbon in the atmosphere than there has been for millions of years.[104]

How human activities interact with, affect or mitigate natural changes in the climate is a matter of considerable discussion – primarily because of the technical difficulties of weighing up complex evidence and data. For example, the rapid warming of global surface temperatures was reported to have slowed down in the early part of the twenty-first century, with unusually low growth trends in surface and tropospheric temperatures, as well as those of upper ocean heat content and sea level – in what has become known as the 'global warming slowdown' (or 'hiatus'). It is not only the reasons for this that are contested; so too is the premise, with disagreement about whether selection or measurement bias (or both) influenced conclusions, or even if changes in instrumentation might have distorted data.[105]

Despite the spillover from such discussions, which can convince those who want to be convinced that there is no anthropogenic impact on climate, a survey of almost 90,000 peer-reviewed climate-related papers published since 2012 suggests that the consensus about human-caused climate change among scientists working in this field exceeds 99 per cent. This stands in sharp contrast to members of the 117th Congress of the United States, of whom more than a quarter both in the House of Representatives and in the Senate – including more than half the

Republican members of the former and 60 per cent of the latter – have made statements either doubting or refusing to accept the scientific evidence for anthropogenic climate change.[106]

In fact, the chances that some of the most significant changes – such as the earth's growing energy imbalance – are occurring naturally rather than as a result of human activities is extremely slim, to be measured as below 1 per cent probability.[107] Study after study reveals rapid transformations that when taken together paint not just a compelling but an ominous picture. For example, two major glaciers in the Antarctic are losing ice at the fastest rate for 5,500 years.[108] Climate modelling drawing on a period from around 15 million years ago when atmospheric carbon dioxide levels and global temperatures were similar to those expected at the end of this century suggests that a chain reaction may result in Antarctica being unable to maintain a large ice sheet.[109] This means that there is an elevated risk of the collapse of the West Antarctic Ice Sheet, which would bring with it projected global sea-level rises of three to four metres – if not more – as a result of the mass melting of ice.[110]

Although high geothermal heat flow beneath the Thwaites glacier is a contributor to ice loss, unusual mean temperature anomalies, such as in the spring of 2020 when the highest temperature over the Antarctic was recorded – some +4.5 °C above average – clearly add to the risks of sudden collapse.[111] So great have been the impacts of glacial ice melt since the 1990s that the earth's axis has shifted as a result of the redistribution of the planet's water; moreover, as well as showing that this is the result of human factors that cause global warming and the heating of polar regions, new research suggests that the movement of the pole has also been affected by groundwater depletion of terrestrial water storage, for example in northern India – where 351 billion cubic metres of water was drawn in 2010.[112]

Not all the problems are caused by humans. Tundra fires in Arctic Alaska are accelerating permafrost degradation – which in turn unlocks a vast store of frozen plant and animal matter that magnifies other warming factors through the release of carbon stocks into the atmosphere.[113] Massive fires in Siberia in the summer of 2021 dwarfed all the others on the planet combined and formed what NASA called a 'vast, thick, and acrid blanket' that covered most of Russia, releasing the estimated equivalent of 505 million metric tons of carbon.[114] This was broadly equal to fires that took hold in the Amazon five years earlier, when the 2015–16 El Niño resulted in extreme drought that paved the way for megafires.[115]

Such events intertwine with the wide range of other drivers of warming processes, which in turn create feedback loops that make bad situations even worse: as the atmosphere warms up, more water evaporates from oceans, rivers and lakes, rising up into the atmosphere where water vapour traps more heat, amplifying the initial warming. In this way, it is possible to reach spirals from which there is little or no chance of escape. If carbon dioxide concentrations reach high enough levels, stratocumulus clouds that are prevalent in the subtropics and also cover 20 per cent of the low-latitude oceans may become unstable and vanish, triggering further global warming.[116] There is much discussion about and research into similar 'tipping points' by which precarious situations are made worse and worse in a series of climate domino effects.[117]

Many examples could be given – including collapse of ice caps, the loss of almost all mountain glaciers, permafrost melt and carbon release, disruption to ocean circulation and massive northern hemisphere tree loss due to fire.[118] Warming conditions in Greenland have already resulted in 3.5 trillion tons of ice melt from the surface of the island into the ocean in the last decade alone.[119] The point of no return has already been passed for future ice loss – meaning that change is 'baked in', regardless of any steps taken to address emissions. The prognosis is ominous, according to one recent study, which projects a best-case scenario of global sea-level rises of almost eleven inches (twenty-eight centimetres) by the end of the century, and almost treble that in the worst-case. This has dire consequences for the hundreds of millions who currently live in coastal communities less than one metre above sea level.[120]

The oceans and other bodies of water offer another example. Heatwaves affecting the oceans have become more frequent, last longer and are more intense, resulting in damage to and loss of coral reefs, kelp forests and seagrass meadows.[121] Ocean warming has had a significant and detrimental effect on fish and invertebrate populations.[122] These losses come on top of those caused by industrialised fishing, which has reduced the biomass of large predatory fish to about 10 per cent of pre-industrial levels – with serious consequences for ecosystems.[123] Warming oceans seem likely to change these further, both because warming water temperatures increases metabolic rates which leads to predators eating more, and because of the likelihood of large species moving away from their historical ranges and latitudes.[124]

Oxygen levels in the world's oceans and freshwater lakes are declining rapidly, falling by 5.5 per cent at the surface and almost 20 per cent in deep waters of the latter since 1980. This is important since the concentration of dissolved oxygen in aquatic systems plays an important role in supporting biodiversity as well as in regulating greenhouse-gas emissions and the quality of drinking water.[125] Similarly, since oceans trap and absorb 90 per cent of greenhouse gases, the deoxygenation that has followed as a result of global warming not only has obvious implications for ecosystems, but will continue for centuries even if all carbon dioxide emissions were to stop immediately.[126] Indeed, some studies suggest that changes to the oceans are such that they have already passed the point of no return.[127] Climate change is not something to worry about in the future, in other words, nor even in the present: rather, it has already created problems that cannot be avoided.

Some of these challenges are now obvious. For example, field experiments suggest that warmer night-time temperatures reduce rice grain yield and quality.[128] Even very modest changes to two major field crops in North America, corn and soy, show that yields fall by half a per cent for each day when the temperature is a single degree warmer than the optimal 29 °C. This means that as the world gets hotter, growing food becomes more difficult, and much more expensive. Some studies suggest that there will be huge financial and production losses by 2050 based on most current climate models.[129]

Photosynthetic algae, which flourish in oceans, lakes and rivers when exposed to more light and to hotter weather conditions, can form blooms that are not only toxic but affect other organisms in the food web.[130] These blooms, which can cover thousands of square kilometres, can also be triggered and fuelled by the iron aerosols carried in smoke and ash – as demonstrated by the widespread bloom formation in the Southern Ocean following the Australian wildfires of 2019–20.[131]

The warming world is forcing the redistribution of life on earth in other ways too, and at unprecedented speed. For example, migratory birds play a fundamental role in long-distance seed dispersal, with seeds carried towards either warmer or cooler latitudes depending on plant fruiting periods and on northward or southward avian migration. One recent study showed that 86 per cent of plant species in a sample set were dispersed by birds migrating south, and only 35 per cent carried north. Another found that earlier onset of spring increases the risk of massive bumblebee declines because of shrinking food availability – which has obvious implications for the 'vital pollination services' bees (and other species) provide, not least for vegetables, fruits and many kinds of crops.[132] With climatic boundaries already shifting towards cooler latitudes, plant as well as animal habitats and ecosystems and food-chain networks are already being reconfigured.[133]

Of course, these include the spread of infectious diseases. Mosquitoes are active in tropical regions all year round, but in other locations go into diapause or seasonal dormancy in response to cold exposure. As autumns and winters become warmer, mosquitoes may increase their annual activity time as well as their distribution northwards, an important development given that many species carry viruses that induce human and/or wildlife diseases, including St Louis and Eastern equine encephalitis, dengue and West Nile virus.[134] Some estimate that in the worst case scenario about 8.5 billion people – or about 90 per cent of the world's projected population – will be at risk of malaria and dengue fever by 2078 as a result of global warming and the expansion of disease belts northwards.[135]

As the coronavirus pandemic that took hold in 2020 reminds us, diseases that jump species can be devastating. Specialists in this field already knew long before the pandemic that about 60 per cent of human infections are estimated to have an animal origin, while around 75 per cent of all new and emerging infectious diseases are ones that jump from animals to humans. The trade and transport networks that form the backbone of modern globalisation serve not only to move goods and people around the world faster than ever before, but also allow diseases to spread more quickly than ever before – as the recent coronavirus pandemic showed all too clearly.[136]

While important lessons will have been learned about future prevention, in a warming world it is also crucial to understand that not only do disease environments alter as temperatures and climates change; so too do diseases themselves. Almost 60 per cent of known infectious diseases have at some point been aggravated by climate hazards, such as drought, wildfire, extreme rainfall, floods and rising sea levels, which enhance specific aspects of pathogens, such as improving climate suitability for reproduction, accelerating the life cycle, increasing seasons or length of potential exposure, improving the chances of pathogen vector interactions and increasing virulence. In addition, climatic hazards can be responsible for diminishing human capacity to cope with pathogens, for example by compromising immunity to disease through heat stress, reducing access to medical care as a result of extreme weather events or through malnutrition, whether through lack of access to food or because of reduced concentration of nutrients in crops as a result of exposure to elevated carbon dioxide levels.[137]

Taking all these factors together, then, the world of today and tomorrow looks terrifying. Multiple models predict rises in sea levels as a result of extreme ice-melting events in Greenland as well as from melting Antarctic ice sheets.[138] Others predict that the threat of intense tropical cyclones will have doubled by 2050, extending into areas where exposure is currently low and where populations densities are high, putting millions of people at risk – not least in low-income countries such as Cambodia, Laos, Mozambique and many Pacific island nations.[139] The climate in Alaska may be so profoundly affected later this century that not only will the number of thunderstorms treble, but extreme conditions will lead to flash flooding, landslides and wildfires caused by lightning.[140] Slow-moving, intense storms that produce high levels of rainfall may be fourteen times more frequent across Europe by the end of the century.[141]

Then there are assessments which suggest that by 2053 a quarter of the land area of the United States, stretching from the northern border of Texas and Louisiana through Iowa, Indiana and Illinois – currently home to more than 100 million Americans – will be exposed to summer temperatures above 125 °F (just over 50 °C) if current demographic distribution patterns are maintained.[142] Increasing evidence suggests that summers in northern hemisphere mid-latitudes have already lengthened, whereas spring, autumn and winter have shortened – a pattern that will continue without climate-change mitigation to the point where six-month-long summers may become commonplace.[143]

The likelihood of multiple heatwaves covering regions the size of Iran or Mongolia (the eighteenth- and nineteenth-largest countries in the world respectively) occurring simultaneously across the northern hemisphere have become six times greater since the 1980s, with concurrent events growing larger and more intense during the warm season of May–September.[144] If the current trajectory of emissions and warming is maintained, the average temperature in Milan may reach 50 °C by 2100, according to Luca Mercalli, President of the Italian Meteorological Society – and 8 °C higher across Italy compared to today, as the Mediterranean as a whole bears the brunt of extreme weather.[145]

Such conditions present extraordinary challenges for human life in the absence of artificial cooling that is not affordable or available to all. Hot weather is closely correlated with rises in suicide rates, deterioration in mental health and sharp declines in cognitive abilities, with verbal reasoning, spatial awareness and attention span in particular affected by the heat.[146] When combined with humidity, things become precarious. Even modest global warming will put hundreds of millions of people at risk in densely populated regions of South-West Asia, in South Asia in the Indus and Ganges river valleys and in eastern China as a result of the 'wet bulb' effect which makes the fittest humans unable to tolerate more than a few hours of exposure even under shaded and ventilated conditions.[147]

The composition and nature of oceans and seas that are already being transformed are likely to be further affected in the future, according to scientists. Freshwater is accumulating in the Arctic Ocean, for example, with the Beaufort Sea, the largest oceanic freshwater reservoir in the northern hemisphere, increasing its freshwater content by over 40 per cent since the start of this century. The timing and scale of release of this water into the North Atlantic, and the magnitude of salinity anomalies, have major consequences for the strength of the Atlantic Meridional Overturning Circulation (AMOC) which itself has a significant influence on the climates of the northern hemisphere.[148] This is particularly important given the slowdown of the AMOC – also known as the Gulf Stream System – in recent decades to the point where it is now weaker than at any time in the last millennium, a downturn that has itself been linked with anthropogenic global warming.[149]

Or there is the Caspian Sea, the world's biggest inland body of water, which some projections suggest will experience a decline in water level of at least nine metres by the end of the twenty-first century – resulting in 'a loss of 25 per cent of the Caspian's total area and the uncovering of some 93,000 km² of dry land, an area roughly the size of Portugal'. Ironically, the melting of glaciers across Central Asia, a region with severe water stress, has provided a short-term boost to water availability that is expected to peak during this decade. There are already signs of things to come, with a drought in Kazakhstan in 2012 resulting in the loss of 1 million hectares of crops and hot conditions across a broad swathe of this region in 2021 leading to mass livestock deaths.[150]

Then there are the ice fields in the Himalaya mountain range which are projected to decline by one-third if carbon emissions fall rapidly and by as much as two-thirds if they don't. The glaciers store water for some 240 million hill and mountain people who live across the eight countries of the Hindu Kush Himalayan region, and for 1.65 billion who live in the ten river basins downstream and benefit directly and indirectly from the glaciers' resources and whose livelihoods, rich and diverse cultures, languages, religions, traditional knowledge systems – and lives – are at risk.[151]

Some models provide disturbing forecasts of what is in store for humanity in the decades ahead. Even if strong climate-mitigation measures are put in place, according to one recent study, around 1.5 billion people will be living in a climate that has historically been considered beyond the temperature niche sustainable for human life – a figure which in worst-case scenarios for population growth and climate change rises to 3.5 billion people, or around 30 per cent of the projected global population.[152] Perhaps not surprisingly, thoughts have turned to what the responses might be, in particular to the prospect of massive migrations – and of violent conflict.[153]

Guessing which regions and areas might be worst – or first – affected is difficult, as is assessing the ways that problems might brew, escalate or proliferate. Twelve of the seventeen countries most at risk from water stress are located in the Middle East and North Africa, where mortality risk because of excessive heat stress is forecast to intensify by a factor of 2–7 by the last decades of this century if global warming is limited, and by significantly more if it is not.[154] Then there is South-East Asia, where by 2050 daily high tides will flood areas that are currently home to almost 50 million people – to say nothing of the 77 per cent of the population of the region as a whole who live along the coast or in low-lying river deltas.[155] Or perhaps one should focus on the countries of the western Sahel, ranked among the most vulnerable in the world, where a rise in temperatures over the last five decades, combined with less frequent rainfall and an increase in the frequency and severity of extreme weather events, exacerbates high levels of extreme poverty, rapid population growth and fragile governance – a blend that helps explain a power vacuum that is being filled by organised-crime networks, terrorist organisations and a range of violent non-state actors, including affiliates of both ISIS and Al-Qaida.[156]

The concerns are such that many governments have started to engage with planning how to deal with the effects of climate change. For example, in a major review published in 2010, the US Department of Defense noted that climate change would 'shape the operating environment, roles, and missions that we undertake', and warned that 'assessments conducted by the intelligence community indicate that climate change could have significant geopolitical impact around the world, contributing to poverty, environmental degradation, and the further weakening of fragile governments. Climate change will contribute to food and water scarcity, will increase the spread of disease, and may spur or exacerbate mass migration.'[157] Significant resources have gone into forming committees, writing reports and preparing plans to deal with the fact that, as President Obama put it in 2016, 'Climate change poses a significant and growing threat to national security, both at home and abroad.'[158]

Not least among the problems is the cost of maintaining US military facilities in the face of climate change. As early as 1990, some were asking what the implications were for the armed forces, for their operations, facilities and systems. By 2018, the Pentagon was reporting that around half its installations had experienced climate-change-related effects, while a year later it was admitting to recurrent flooding, drought, wildfires and desertification across dozens of its facilities.[159]

Other countries face major challenges too. More than 80 per cent of Russia's gas and 15 per cent of its oil production, as well as non-ferrous and rare earth metals, are located in the Arctic regions, as are almost $250 billion of fixed assets. Changes in climate are projected to affect 20 per cent of buildings and other infrastructure, requiring a total spend of almost $85 billion to mitigate them as the permafrost that covers much of the region melts.[160] This is partly because of the reduced load-bearing capacity of the standard reinforced concrete piles used in the second half of the twentieth century, which are being undermined by permafrost degradation and changes to the strength properties of the soil.[161] One survey suggested that an increase in temperature of 1.5 °C above present-day averages could potentially result in the deformation of almost the whole of the city of Yakutsk, as well as affecting roads and railways in the surrounding area.[162] Studies on other parts of the world have likewise flagged the risks posed to the structural integrity of buildings by changing temperatures.[163]

As a recent major report by the Ministry of Natural Resources and the Environment in Russia observed, in addition to Moscow and other major cities being at serious risk because of rising temperatures, water contamination and pollution, melting permafrost in the country's northern regions threatens to release 'dangerous chemical, biological and radioactive substances into the human habitat'.[164] The growing number of cases of anthrax and of tick-borne encephalitis and borreliosis (Lyme disease) in Siberia provides yet another reason to be fearful about what the future has in store.[165]

Those fears play a real and increasing role in our daily lives – and particularly those of the next generation. A major survey of 10,000 children and young people (aged 16–25) across ten countries found that more than half felt sad, anxious, angry, powerless, helpless and guilty about climate change, although relative levels of emotion about each varies between individuals. Almost 50 per cent said that their feelings about climate change negatively affected their day-to-day lives and functioning, while 75 per cent admitted that they found thinking about the future frightening. Investigators found that while anxiety among young people is a complex topic, the climate crisis produced psychological stress that resulted in responses that included confusion and a sense of betrayal and abandonment because of adult inaction in relation to climate change.[166]

These concerns do not always extend to taking positive steps: music festivals in the UK, whose audiences are generally young people, generate 23,500 tonnes of waste a year, including plastic bottles, abandoned tents and food waste. Despite all ticket holders at Glastonbury in 2022 signing a 'Green Pledge' and many cheering Greta Thunberg as she warned that the world was 'approaching the precipice' and 'total natural catastrophe', festivalgoers left around 2,000 tonnes of waste behind – or 10 kilos per person.[167]

Nevertheless, some polls and surveys have even suggested that young adults are having fewer children because of concerns about climate change.[168] These seem to include the Duke and Duchess of Sussex, whose comments in an interview in *Vogue* that 'this place is borrowed', that 'we should be able to leave something better behind for the next generation' and that 'we've got to try to pay a little of it back. And get together to try and heal some of the harm, and at least slow down climate change' were widely interpreted as a conscious decision not to have more than two children for the earth's long-term benefit – not least by a British charity that focuses on population control, which hailed them as 'a role model for other families' and announced that they would be given a special award.[169]

With 40 per cent of the world's land degraded and half its population suffering from the impacts, it is hard not to be gloomy about the future.[170] The chances of limiting global warming to 1.5 °C – the goal set in the Paris climate agreements of 2015 – are slim, if they have not been missed already.[171] One recent study put the chances of limiting global average temperature change to the Paris targets at 0.1 per cent based on current projections.[172] In the words of António Guterres, Secretary General of the United Nations, in the summer of 2022, the Paris target is 'on life support' and in recent months 'its pulse has weakened further'.[173] Around 30 per cent of the world's population is already currently exposed to climatic conditions that put lives at risk for more than twenty days a year. By 2100, this will rise to almost half if drastic reductions in greenhouse-gas emissions take place, and to almost three-quarters if emissions continue to rise.[174]

With scientists testing hypotheses about the temperature-change thresholds for mass extinctions, declaring that even modest climate modifications to habitats have dramatic effects on plant and animal species, assessing whether the sixth mass extinction is not just possible but already under way or warning that more thought should be given to humanity's 'endgame', it is not entirely surprising that many feel the time has come for more dramatic action to force politicians and decision-makers to address these problems head-on, rather than just paying lip service.[175]

Nor is it difficult to be sympathetic. During the summer of 2022, when drought conditions, water shortages and heat stress developed into what the European Commission Joint Research Centre called the worst for at least 500 years, temperatures across Europe reached record levels, hitting 40 °C in the UK, France and the Iberian peninsula, and the month of July was the driest on record.[176] With the source of the River Thames drying up, the depth of the Rhine falling below thirty centimetres and forcing barge traffic to be hauled by road, and nuclear reactors in France shutting down or running on limited capacity because of the lack of water required to cool them, the responses from European leaders included the Prime Minister of Spain advising business people not to wear ties to meetings; the Swiss Prime Minister suggesting couples take showers together to conserve water; lights being turned off at major tourist attractions in Greece at 3 a.m.; and no hot water being allowed in showers in public buildings, swimming pools, sports halls and gyms in some cities in Germany. Although in some countries more stringent measures were later proposed (in any event largely in response to surging energy prices), initial reactions hardly provided assurance that effective measures were being put in place or that political leaders understood the scale of the current challenges – to say nothing of those of the future.[177]

The anticipated economic shocks of the future connected to crop failures, food and water shortages, rising prices, mass migration, rising levels of violence and increased prospects of warfare, and the apocalyptic ways in which they are described, are enough to turn blood to ice. Without further action to reduce greenhouse gases, said the IMF in October 2020, the planet would reach temperatures 'not seen in millions of years, potentially with catastrophic consequences'. These include disruption to economic activity and lower productivity, as well as more severe natural disasters, increased prevalence of infectious disease, deterioration in human health outcomes and possible loss of life.[178] 'Who cares if Miami is six metres underwater in 100 years?' said one senior investment banker in the summer of 2022. The 'average loan length' at his bank was seven years, he said, adding that 'What happens to the planet in year seven is actually irrelevant to our loan book.'[179] Some deliver the news with more sangfroid. 'Climate change is likely to affect monetary policy one way or the other,' said one senior member of the European Central Bank.[180] Putting it simply, said Larry Fink of BlackRock, 'climate risk is investment risk'.[181]

Just how great the financial risks are, on top of threats to the existence of humans, other animals and plants, is hard to estimate given the variables and uncertainties. However, some scholars have suggested that the average income in many countries will decline by 75 per cent by 2100 if climate change continues on current trajectories. The countries that will be worst hit are those that are already poorest, with more basic medical care, less well-developed infrastructure and institutions that are not as robust as in wealthier parts of the world.[182]

Ironically, many of the regions most exposed are ones that have suffered from high levels of pollution thanks to manufacturing that has moved away from high-income states, attracted by cheap labour forces and low environmental controls, in a form of neo-colonialism that has seen the needs of the wealthy provided for at the expense of the poor. It has been estimated, for example, that nearly 2.5 trillion metric tons of materials were extracted and used globally between 1970 and 2017; while high-income countries (as classified by World Bank criteria) consumed 75 per cent of this, lower-middle-income and low-income countries collectively consumed less than 1 per cent.[183]

Such are consumption inequalities that it has been estimated that New York City uses more energy than all of sub-Saharan Africa put together.[184] Despite being home to one-fifth of the world's population, Africa accounts for less than 3 per cent of energy-related carbon dioxide emissions – with the lowest per capita emissions of any region. In a telling sign of how resources continue to be exploited in the modern world, Africa contains 60 per cent of the best solar resources globally, but only 1 per cent of installed solar power, despite this already being the cheapest source of energy across the continent.[185]

This forms part of a wider story of climate, resource, geographic and socio-economic inequality: for example, while many in high-income countries worry about the future financial consequences of climate change, the reality is that lower-income countries are already suffering the pain of reduced circumstances both because of shifting patterns and because of the lack of climate finance. According to African Development Bank assessments, Africa as a whole has been losing 5–15 per cent of its GDP per capita growth because of climate change and related impacts. Despite being home to almost a fifth of the world's population (as well as the location of substantial natural resources), Africa has accounted for just 3 per cent of historic worldwide emissions of carbon dioxide.[186] Globally, the bottom half of the world's population by income produces the same amount of emissions as the richest 1 per cent.[187] Wealthy Americans have substantially bigger carbon footprints than those with fewer means, primarily because they own larger homes which require more heat, light and energy; in very affluent suburbs, emissions can be fifteen times higher than those in nearby neighbourhoods.[188] There are also significant implications about race and ethnicity, with research showing that people of colour are disproportionately exposed to lower air quality and higher health hazards, at least in the United States, because they typically live closer to emission sources.[189]

It seems particularly unfair, therefore, that damage from natural disasters, extreme weather and rising temperatures is greater in developing countries than in those that are wealthy and therefore more able to deal with individual and multiple setbacks.[190] That they can do so owes much to their own ecological and climatological good fortune in being located at latitudes that are particularly well suited for productivity: it has been shown that 13 °C is the optimal temperature for human productivity – which declines at higher temperatures. It is even more galling, then, that while incomes in poor countries are likely to fall sharply as a result of climate change, those in rich ones may actually rise. Apart from everything else, global warming increases inequality.[191] Indeed, it even increases inequality within low-income states, where the poor are most badly affected by climate change.[192]

Even if the Paris Agreement goals that were adopted in 2015 are met, especially the aim to limit global warming to 2 °C, exposure to dangerous heat levels will increase by 50–100 per cent across much of the tropics, and by a factor of 3–10 in many regions in mid-latitudes, which will experience deadly heatwaves that have thus far been rare on an annual basis.[193] As it happens, global warming of 1 °C, a threshold we have already passed, puts us at risk of triggering a series of catastrophic chain reactions in the natural world.[194] As if that was not enough, climate change seems likely to reorder global geopolitics. While many will suffer in the coming decades, new opportunities will also open up as habitats are transformed. Of twenty-two countries that stand to benefit, more than half are located in the former USSR and in central and eastern Europe including the Baltic States, Ukraine, Armenia, Belarus and Russia.[195]

These benefits will not flow quickly or easily, as a draft report by the Russian Ministry of Natural Resources and the Environment made clear: Russians should prepare for epidemics, crop failures, famine, pest infestations, forest fires and exposure to chemical, biological and radioactive substances – as well as heavy costs for fixing and repairing damage done to cities and to infrastructure in the largest country on earth.[196]

Some, however, have focused on the upside rather than the downside. Vladimir Putin, for example, once quipped that climate change would be a good thing, enabling Russians to spend less on fur coats, while being able to benefit from bigger and better harvests.[197] As it happens, investment in technologies, efficiencies and soil science meant that Russia's agricultural exports rose sixteenfold in the period 2000–18. Wheat exports doubled in the five years after 2015, making Russia the largest wheat exporter in the world and responsible for a quarter of the global market.[198]

While it is important not to oversimplify, it would not be unreasonable to argue that Russia's past, present and future ecological bonanzas played a role in strategic calculations when the decision was taken to invade Ukraine in February 2022 and to weaponise the dividends of its natural environment in order to put pressure on Ukraine, on Europe and beyond. These bonanzas were the oil, gas and natural resources formed by ancient climatic change, as well as the crops and other foods that are vitally important for calorie intake around the world today, all enhanced by the confidence that Russia's environmental hand of cards will improve while those of others become more difficult. As one former senior intelligence official put it, a year before the assault on Ukraine, 'Global ecological disruption is arguably the 21st Century's most underappreciated security threat.'[199] If, how, when and where resources are withheld, fought over or interrupted by states or for that matter by non-state actors will serve to exacerbate other stresses and challenges – not least those presented by climatic change. They deserve considerable attention.

Conclusion

The summer of 2022 might have been enough to convince even the most sceptical of people that something strange is afoot within global weather systems. Record heatwaves in Europe, the worst drought in many decades in Africa, nearly eight times the average rainfall in Pakistan that displaced tens of millions of people, flash floods in Death Valley in the USA that saw three-quarters of a year's average rainfall in three hours, the highest-ever recorded rate of rainfall in South Korea with almost 15 centimetres falling per hour, the wettest year in Australia's modern history, winter temperatures in the southern hemisphere in Paraguay that soared above 40 °C and almost as high in South Africa, and a long and severe drought in China that followed the hottest summer on record, which was called the most severe heatwave ever recorded anywhere and was unparalleled in world climatic history, brought the issue of climate change on to the front pages of newspapers around the world.[1]

Some, however, are unwilling to be swayed. 'Current evidence', stated the UK's Brexit negotiator Lord Frost, 'does not support the assertion that we are in a climate "emergency".' It was preposterous, he went on, that 'medieval technology like wind power' was being recommended for use in the modern world. 'We have all got used to being hectored by the government and by a huge body of intellectual and NGO [non-governmental organisation] opinion to make sacrifices to save the planet. We are told to stop travelling, live local, eat less, stop eating meat, turn our lights out, and generally to stop being a burden.' This was all nonsense, in other words.[2]

Similar views are not hard to find in the corridors of power, especially in democratic countries where freedoms of opinion, of expression and of the press are not only highly prized but of signal importance. 'For the past eighteen years', Senator Ted Cruz stated while chairing his first hearing on climate change, 'there has been no significant warming whatsoever.' Current models used to understand global climate trends 'are profoundly wrong' and, he went on, 'inconsistent with the evidence and the data'.[3] Climate change is 'a hoax', said former US President Donald Trump, who had previously said it was not a hoax. People now 'just talk about climate change. The climate's always been changing.' He insisted that there was nothing to worry about, and added, echoing Cruz, that scientists who said otherwise were not to be trusted.[4]

Two British prime ministers who took office in 2022 agreed that clean energy was not a priority. We should make 'sure our fields are used for food production and not solar panels', intoned Rishi Sunak. 'I'm somebody who wants to see farmers producing food, not filling in forms,' said Liz Truss, 'not filling fields with paraphernalia like solar farms. What we want is crops.'[5] It was not clear why it had to be one or the other or why it could not be both; and in any event, even if the UK government were to quintuple all the solar capacity it has committed to establishing by 2035, the amount of land covered by solar farms would be around 0.5 per cent of the land currently used for farming – or just over half the amount of land currently covered by golf courses.[6] Still, the message was clear: renewable energy, climate change and concerns about the future need not be taken seriously.

Some of these beliefs are fuelled by an energetic industry that has grown up to misinform, to magnify and distort reports about climate and climate science for a range of reasons that includes mischief, domestic political agendas, foreign interventions and genuine misgivings. Analysis of millions of social media accounts shows that in the course of a normal day around a quarter of original postings about climate change on Twitter are made by automated bots operated by a range of 'bad actors' seeking to sow discord through social media. Bots are disproportionately likely to promote 'denial research', with as many as 38 per cent of tweets about 'fake science' being generated automatically – and then often retweeted by human users, as well as by other bots to reach bigger and bigger audiences.[7]

Some climate sceptics point out – rightly – that forecasts that look into the future can be highly speculative, and they also seek to dampen alarm by noting, again quite correctly, that economic growth, new technologies and adaptation may alleviate the problems that lie ahead and, in some cases, may even solve them.[8] That too, however, requires faith and confidence; moreover, what history in general and this book in particular show is that there have been a great many times in the past when societies, peoples and cultures have proved unable to adapt. Indeed, in some respects, the human story of progress is about batons being repeatedly dropped and picked up by others.

The question, then, is not so much whether to adapt, but how, where and when to do so. And in that sense it is certainly true that there is plenty of good news, much to celebrate and reasons to be optimistic. For example, it would not take much for progressive decision-making, supported, if necessary, by appropriate investment and regulation, to reduce some of the astonishing wastage of resources that occurs every year – of food, of water, of energy and more. This does not need to come at a cost. For example, total water consumption in Australia declined by 40 per cent between 2001 and 2009 while GDP grew by almost a third during the same period.[9] A National Air Quality Plan introduced in China in 2013, and the announcement of a 'war against pollution' the following summer helped spark a decline in particulate pollution in China of almost 40 per cent in the years up to 2020. Beijing's air pollution alone fell by 55 per cent, adding around four and a half years to the average inhabitant's life expectancy as a result.[10]

A switch to low-energy LEDs (light-emitting diodes) has already generated major savings in the European Union, where policy measures have been introduced to ban inefficient lighting systems; some estimates suggest that similar steps in low-income countries could save $40 billion of electricity and prevent 320 million metric tons of carbon pollution annually.[11] In fact, and despite often acute pessimism, many countries have made considerable progress. Members of the European Union, for example, collectively reduced greenhouse-gas emissions by almost 25 per cent between 1990 and 2019, and seem likely to reduce these by another 15 per cent in the next decade.[12]

Or there is the United States, where progress over the last twenty years combined with current federal and state policies means that the world's largest economy is on track to reduce emissions so substantially that, despite population growth, industrial productivity and higher levels of international and global trade, greenhouse-gas emissions in 2030 are likely to be at least 24 per cent and perhaps as much as 35 per cent below what they were in 2005. Although this falls short of the pledges and ambitions set out in the Paris Agreement of 2015, it is nevertheless a sign of considerable progress.[13] The Inflation Reduction Act of 2022 which included by far the biggest climate and energy investments in American history was hailed by some commentators as likely to play a crucial role in speeding up a 'green transition' on which much depends in the future.[14]

Steps like these can be built on quickly, with solar and wind capable of meeting as much as 90 per cent of energy demands in many industrialised countries, even without new storage capacity being built.[15] Indeed, in the spring of 2021, California was producing enough clean power from renewable energy sources to supply nearly 95 per cent of its in-state needs and, if the Diablo Canyon nuclear plant is included, produced more than 100 per cent of its electricity needs for the first time.[16] In 2019 the UK energy grid went for more than two weeks without burning coal to make power for the first time in almost 150 years – a sequence apparently broken by millions tuning in on their televisions and turning on their kettles to watch the finale of the TV show *Love Island*.[17]

A survey of 29,000 fossil-fuel power stations in more than 200 countries showed that a small group of 'superemitter' plants – just 5 per cent of the total – produced almost 75 per cent of global emissions produced by electricity generation, a figure that would fall dramatically if they were made more efficient and/or switched from coal or oil to natural gas, while carbon-capture technologies that are already available could cut emissions fully in half.[18]

There are other good reasons to remain upbeat. Some scientists argue that many climate models are overly pessimistic and over-rely on worst-case scenarios, especially when it comes to key green technology costs. In fact, one recent study that draws on empirically grounded research shows that a rapid green energy transition would not only produce a 'greener, healthier and safer global energy system with reduced air pollution, more stable pricing and reduced climate damage', but that it would 'likely result in overall net savings of many trillions of dollars'. A very good outcome, in other words.[19]

Then there are the new ideas that are emerging about how to reduce damage to the environment. For example, recent research shows that raising or lowering the altitudes of less than 2 per cent of aircraft flights could reduce the climate impact inflicted by vapour trails made up of hot exhaust gases as they meet cold, low-pressure air – since this tiny minority are responsible for 80 per cent of the radiative forcing in the atmosphere by altering the balance between radiation emitted by the sun and heat emitted by the earth, resulting in changes in the climate. The costs of doing so are minimal, with researchers calculating that the diversion would add less than 0.1 per cent to fuel consumption.[20]

Similarly, studies on mitigating the climate impacts and carbon emissions of ships – which carry more than nine-tenths of global trade – suggest that reducing speeds by 10 per cent would result in a 13 per cent reduction in emissions as a result of reduced demands on engine power, which in turn would mean that voyages might require as much as 40 per cent less energy. Reductions in speed would reduce underwater noise for the benefit of aquatic life and greatly lessen the chances of whale strikes, thereby improving marine biodiversity.[21]

These are just a handful of examples where good research and clear thinking can help find low-hanging fruit that can make significant and immediate differences. Many, many others can also be cited: for instance, indiscriminate voiding of excreta by cattle contributes to greenhouse-gas emission as well as resulting in soil and water contamination, with emissions higher when animals are given more space to graze in. It has been shown, however, that cattle can be trained to control their micturition reflex and use a latrine for urination, with significant environmental and climatic benefits.[22]

Scientists have developed a plant-based emulsifier rich in protein and antioxidants that could replace eggs and dairy in foods such as mayonnaise, soups and sauces and would help reduce the impact of poultry.[23] Substituting 20 per cent of meat from cattle with imitation meats made from plants or with cultured meats made from animal cells or from fermentation-derived microbial protein could cut both annual global deforestation and related carbon dioxide emissions by half.[24]

New methods have been proposed and successfully tested which break down substances known as 'forever chemicals' that are used as water-, oil- and stain-resistant barriers for fabrics, make-up and food containers such as frying pans and which both avoid the very harsh techniques currently used to break them down and do so without creating damaging by-products – thereby helping the natural environment.[25] Enriching waters of lakes with particular bacteria can break down plastic pollution, helping to remove it from ecosystems.[26] Bioengineered acceleration of the photosynthesis process of soybean plants increases the efficiency of the chemical reaction, resulting in higher yields with no fall in quality, with obvious implications not only for soybean but for other crops too.[27]

Such then are the wonders of science and of scientific research. Sometimes, it is true, the process is one of two steps forward and one step back. Switching away from fossil fuels, for example, can increase pressures on different resources and materials that can be easily obscured by the elation of switching to notionally carbon-neutral technologies. Thus, while the declared intention to move to renewable energy such as wind power is laudable, it is easy to forget – or never to realise – that to produce a quarter of global energy in this way would require at least 450 million metric tons of steel, which in turn need the fossil-fuel equivalent of more than 600 million metric tons of coal.[28] Perhaps one answer lies in new materials: researchers at Michigan State University have made composite resin for turbine blades that can be broken down and recycled into gummy bears.[29]

Likewise, the switch to electric vehicles (EVs) in many countries, states and cities can make it easy to forget both that these need to charge and recharge, bringing about a higher demand for electricity, and that EVs produce high levels of pollution. As it is, synthetic tyres are a leading source of microplastics which are found in high concentrations not only next to roads but in rivers, in seas and even in the Arctic, with almost 7 million tons of particles from tyres and non-exhaust sources such as vehicle brakes emitted each year.[30] In fact, car tyres produce far more particle pollution than exhausts of modern cars – perhaps as much as 1,800 times more.[31] This is significant, since models with large batteries, capable of travelling up to 500 kilometres between charges, are much heavier than petrol and diesel models, and emit up to 8 per cent more fine particles as a result.[32]

Certainly, thinking about climate change, about the overexploitation of natural resources and about a world transforming in front of our eyes can even extend into mundane and seemingly petty issues. Will we still be playing or watching sports that take place outdoors and depend on good weather, such as cricket – the second most followed sport in the world, but which will be the hardest hit of all the major pitch sports by changing climates?[33] Will winter sports in Europe all but disappear, given the projected collapse of Alpine snow?[34] Should anyone buy a seaside property given that sea-level rises of between twenty-seven and seventy-eight centimetres are apparently all but guaranteed because of the impact of 110 trillion metric tons of melt from Greenland's ice sheet?[35]

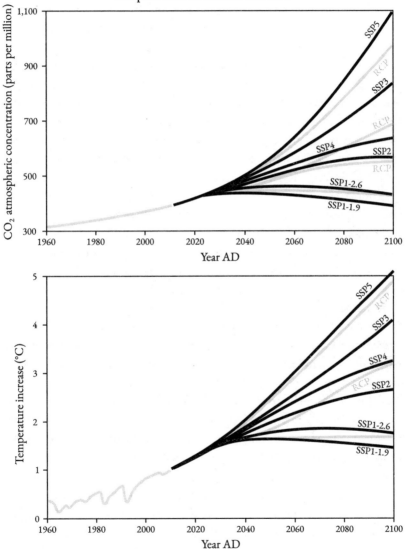

Predicted CO_2 atmospheric concentration and temperature increase to 2100 AD

Source: O'Neill et al, 2016

Will the famous nightclubs of Ibiza be a thing of the past, as temperatures in Spain soar to levels that make other destinations not only more sensible and enjoyable for dancing and partying, but also survivable?[36] Will the blue seas of the Caribbean still be picture-postcard beautiful if toxic algal blooms that have already spread in a chain from Africa right across the Atlantic Ocean continue to expand?[37] Will what we know of as the 'Mediterranean diet' disappear thanks to the soaring cost of olive oil as crops fail in the absence of rain and in scorching heat – and if so, will this affect life expectancy of populations whose longevity has long been attributed to how they live and what they eat?[38]

Will tourists still visit the Taj Mahal, the Great Wall of China or Petra if doing so comes at a risk to life? What will happen to the meaning of Islam if the hajj – the pilgrimage to Mecca, which involves walking around the sacred Ka'ba and is one of the pillars of the Muslim faith – becomes not only impractical but dangerous because of excessively high temperatures? What will become of the Kumbh Mela in India, where the sacred Ganges itself may reduce to a trickle, or indeed dry up altogether?[39]

How should one factor rapidly falling birth rates in most of the developed world into decisions that may substantially change as global populations levels fall – or at least do so in the more temperate regions of the earth? Will collapsing demographics lead to much lower demand on resources, less pressure on the environment and lower energy requirements, and if so, how and when will they do so?

It may well be that such questions become irrelevant, for it may be that what causes the greatest threat to our existence is not climate change and the horrors that lie ahead later in this century. Climate projections rely on assumptions that progress up to 2100 and beyond will be linear – that is to say, they look ahead at where current factors and trends are likely to lead us. However, there are plenty of things that could happen that render all projections about climate change redundant at a stroke. One is the prospect of major warfare.

There has been much discussion in recent years about the link between a warming world and violence, and in particular about 'water wars' in the future, as states fight over resources that become limited by global warming, overconsumption or both. What few had thought hard about was the prospect of the use of nuclear weapons, at least until President Putin put Russia's nuclear arsenal on alert early on during the invasion of

Ukraine. In the last thirty years, the use of nuclear weapons has seemed inconceivable, largely because of the dreadful consequences it would bring, but also because many had assumed that the end of the Cold War marked a decisive termination to the threat of 'mutually assured destruction' that had characterised strategic thinking in both Washington and Moscow for much of the period after the Second World War.

And yet, as António Guterres, Secretary General of the United Nations, said in a speech in August 2022, the threat of nuclear confrontation has become as high as it was during the Cold War. Indeed, as he underlined, 'humanity is just one misunderstanding, one miscalculation away from nuclear annihilation'.[40] New analysis using the latest climate modelling shows that the smoke from the use of significant numbers of warheads would destroy much of the ozone layer over the course of fifteen years.[41] Even a relatively small-scale nuclear scenario, such as a localised war between India and Pakistan, would have an effect on crops – reducing global calorie consumption by 7 per cent, and particularly affecting agriculture in mid- and high-latitude countries such as the United States and Russia.[42]

Then there are other events that could have severe effects on human life on earth. These include solar winds that have major impact on earth's magnetosphere, solar storms that could destroy power-grid transformers, costing the US economy more than $1 trillion and taking years to recover from. So high are risk levels that the US has formally passed laws to 'predict and detect' space weather events in the form of 'solar flares, solar energetic particles and geomagnetic disturbances'. President Obama's Executive Order of 2016 on 'Coordinating Efforts to Prepare the Nation for Space Weather Events' requires collaboration between the secretaries of Defense, Homeland Security, Interior, Commerce and Energy, along with the Administrator of NASA, to 'minimize the extent of economic loss and human hardship'.[43]

Solar storms represent major challenges. In July 2012, a coronal mass ejection measured at an initial speed of around 2,500 kilometres per second. Had this taken place a week earlier, it would have passed much closer to earth, with grave consequences for satellites, aircraft, power systems and possibly human society as a whole – because of our reliance on modern technologies, which are extremely vulnerable to any form of electromagnetic disruption.[44]

Then there are risks of lunar flooding which NASA expects to occur in the mid-2030s when the lunar cycle amplifies rising sea levels to create increasing high-tide floods that surge in low-lying regions, and earthquakes which can cause major disruption; or there are tsunami events in the world's great oceans or even in the Mediterranean where UNESCO has said the chance of a tsunami striking at-risk coastal areas by 2030 is nothing less than 100 per cent.[45]

The threat of impactors is also a very real one. For example, the asteroid first named 1989FC and then rechristened 4581 Asclepius passed 680,000 kilometres from the earth in March 1989; had it approached six hours earlier, it would have struck the planet, with devastating consequences (the angle and the location of impact would both have helped determine how bad things would have been).[46] Another asteroid, 99942 Apophis, has been identified as one of the most hazardous threats to the earth after its discovery in 2004. Recently, NASA concluded that it certainly would not strike our planet – at least not for another hundred years.[47] Nevertheless, the development and deployment by NASA of the Double Asteroid Redirection Test (DART), a planetary defence system, at the end of 2021 provides an insight into the level of threats posed by extra-terrestrial objects.[48]

But by far the biggest risk to global climate comes from volcanoes. Although considerable thought and attention have gone and are going into planning for a warming world, almost no investment of time, planning or funding has been spent on the potential implications of major volcanic eruptions. This is despite the fact that new evidence shows that eruptions with a volcanic explosivity index (VEI) of magnitude 7 occur around once every 625 years – and those with VEI of magnitude 8 around every 14,300 years – much more frequently than previously thought.[49]

With the last VEI 7 taking place in 1815 at Mount Tambora, the clock is ticking, and indeed may be ticking faster than in the past: again, recent investigations have shown that volcanism and volcanic activity are closely connected to the melting of ice sheets and to sea-level rise, suggesting a causal link between pressure on the earth's crust and mantle.[50] If this is indeed correct, we may be facing an accelerated timetable for the next mega-eruption that would inject vast amounts of ash and gases into the atmosphere and make discussions about climate change redundant, possibly at the cost of millions or even hundreds of millions of lives as temperatures suddenly cool, harvests fail and plants and animals die. Some estimate the chance of a major eruption before

2100 as one in six – in other words hundreds of times more likely than asteroid and comet impact combined.[51]

In fact, so poor is general knowledge about the impact of volcanoes that while the news of a big underwater eruption of Hunga Tonga-Hunga Ha'apai in Tonga on 15 January 2022 was reported around the world, less well covered was the scientific analysis of what had happened. The eruption had more explosive force than a hundred simultaneous detonations of the atomic bomb dropped on Hiroshima in 1945.[52] A plume of ash and dust was forced into the atmosphere, reaching higher than any other on record, with volcanic heat and superheated moisture from the ocean acting like 'hyper-fuel for a mega-thunderstorm', according to NASA scientists – which generated almost 600,000 lightning strikes in three days.[53] Not only was it the most powerful eruption ever observed in the modern era; unlike most terrestrial volcanoes that create cooling events, in the case of Hunga Tonga-Hunga Ha'apai so much water was vaporised and sent into the atmosphere that it might lead to surface warming and intensify existing climate trends.[54]

The question is not if a major volcanic eruption will take place, but when. In March 2021, the US Geological Survey warned that Mauna Loa, the world's largest active volcano, 'continues to awaken from its slumber'. While noting that an eruption 'is not imminent, now is the time to revisit personal eruption plans'. Ominously, its update quoted Benjamin Franklin and was headed 'Volcano Watch – "By failing to prepare, you are preparing to fail."'[55] Moreover, although massive eruptions by single volcanoes feature vividly in public imagination, it may be that clusters of even relatively minor explosions from smaller active volcanoes are of greater concern and potentially pose a more serious threat to global temperatures, supply chains and travel and communication networks.[56]

Other phenomena may also affect the current projections, directions and realities of climatic change. More than fifty countries have ongoing climate-modification programmes, for example to disperse fog, enhance rain and snowfall and suppress hail.[57] 'Cloud seeding is one of the most promising solutions in Saudi Arabia,' commented Ayman Ghulam, Chief Executive Officer of the National Centre of Meteorology in Riyadh, speaking of a country which has an average of ten centimetres of rain per year and is likely to be one of the worst affected by climate change.[58] Russia used cloud-seeding technology to ensure that skies were clear above Moscow for May Day celebrations in May 2016, as did China before the Beijing Olympics to make conditions ideal for athletes and viewers and to show the country in the best possible light.[59]

China has been particularly active in climate and weather modification, developing schemes that energise rain particles by firing 'low-frequency, high-intensity acoustic waves [to] excite the cloud body, vibrating it', a process that can be controlled remotely and at low cost.[60] With artificial rainfall responsible for an increase in precipitation of more than 230 billion cubic metres between 2012 and 2017, Chinese state authorities have announced major subsequent upgrades to and expansions of such activities, including a bold announcement in 2020 of a series of 'breakthroughs in fundamental research and R&D in key technologies that would create rain and snow across five and a half million square kilometres – while also suppressing hail across 580,000 square kilometres.' Taken together, these would help with 'ecological protection and restoration', as well as being fundamental to major emergency responses to forest fires and mitigating the effects of high temperatures and droughts.[61]

An important element in this is the framing of nature as something to be 'tamed' – in other words, as something that can be controlled at will, rather than setting environmental boundaries or requiring adaptation. Describing clouds as 'airborne water reservoirs', for example, sets up the idea that the weather, climate and nature as a whole can and should be used to meet human requirements; this sits within wider suggestions that ecologies are being 'modernised', and that ingenuity, technology and sheer determination can mitigate and even remove large-scale environmental challenges.[62]

Choice of language has proved important with scientists elsewhere, with a major study produced by the US National Academy of Sciences in 2015 choosing to use the term 'climate intervention' rather than 'geoengineering' or 'climate engineering' or modification, not to assert the ability to control the weather but rather because the term better captures the imprecision and uncertainties of the outcomes when changes are made to atmospheric conditions.[63]

There is considerable activity in the field of weather modification in the United States, with over 850 non-federal programmes initiated (and in many cases completed) since 2000, as recorded by the office of the US Secretary of Commerce via the National Oceanic Atmospheric Administration, as required by law.[64] Although some scholars note that reports often seem to overstate the amount of precipitation that has been generated, and that such activities create little environmental downside (including contamination by the silver iodide used in cloud seeding), studies suggest that costs are relatively low compared to the value of water. In other words, overall benefits seem to outweigh the negatives.[65]

Many cloud-seeding operations are classified, and it is unclear what their aims, scope and methods are, or what their implications will be for other countries and regions whose weather systems – and precipitation levels in particular – may be affected by non-natural changes.[66] It goes without saying that programmes to 'modify weather patterns to divert massive amounts of water through the sky from a place where it's abundant to another that's dry' can have major implications for ecosystems in both locations, and indeed in others as well.[67]

One recent report noted that, leaving aside the fact that 'current observing systems are insufficient to quantify the effects' of modification programmes, there were also considerable 'political, social, legal, economic, and ethical dimensions' that were unclear. Above all, concluded a high-level group of researchers, 'there is significant potential for unanticipated, unmanageable, and regrettable consequences' that might result from human interference with natural weather systems.[68] In other words, attempts to influence, modify or control the climate might end up making things worse.

It is not clear quite what the status is of the latest and edgiest research conducted behind closed doors. Even thirty years ago there were proposals to look at ways of countering the effects of global warming. In a wide-ranging policy document produced in 1992 by scientists in the US collaborating across multiple disciplines, many different mitigation proposals were set out – from the introduction of energy-efficient lighting to fuel-efficiency programmes for cars and heavy trucks, from the use of clean and renewable energy to eliminating paddy-rice production, reducing the use of nitrogenous fertiliser, bringing down the numbers of ruminant animals and fixing leaks in natural-gas pipelines.

A host of other more creative suggestions were also put forward. These include the creation of 'space mirrors' in earth's orbit to reflect sunlight; using guns to fire particles to form and maintain a dust cloud in the stratosphere in order to increase sunlight reflection and therefore keep the earth cool; the placing of 'billions of aluminized, hydrogen-filled balloons in the stratosphere' to do something similar by providing a reflective screen that stops sunlight from reaching earth; burning sulphur 'in ships or power plants' to stimulate low marine clouds in order to reflect sunlight; and dumping iron in the oceans to stimulate the generation and growth of CO_2-absorbing phytoplankton. 'We need to know more about them because measures of this kind may be crucial if greenhouse warming occurs,' said the US report. Moreover, it went on, while 'all have large unknowns concerning possible environmental side-effects', it was worth noting that 'some of these options are relatively inexpensive to implement'.[69]

By 2003, few of the new ideas seemed to show promise, with the National Research Council guardedly declaring that 'there still is no convincing scientific proof of the efficacy of intentional weather modification efforts', and that while there were some hopeful signs, the evidence had yet to be robustly tested. Nevertheless, recent years had yielded 'many promising developments and advances'.[70] The Council therefore recommended that a co-ordinated national programme be developed to look into weather modification, and also at the inadvertent consequences that might flow from the use of new techniques and tools.[71]

Just over a decade later, sufficient progress had been made to allow a technical evaluation of the impacts of climate modification with a major survey offering glimpses into ideas about the removal of carbon dioxide from the atmosphere (known as carbon capture), and also into the latest thinking about ways to cool the planet by increasing the reflection of solar radiation. Attempts to achieve the latter 'should not be deployed at this time', according to this report, published in 2015. Other steps to address global warming should be looked at urgently, advised the researchers, who recommended that further work be undertaken on how to slow down or reverse global warming. It was clear, however, that dramatic reductions in carbon dioxide emissions remained the best route.[72]

As a follow-up study published in 2021 put it, even if solar geoengineering were possible it neither addresses the cause of climate change and global warming – namely, the increasing concentrations of greenhouse gases in the atmosphere – nor solves related problems, such as ocean acidification.[73] Although this is true, more research into large-scale modification is ongoing, including into its possible effects for all life on earth.[74] It would be reasonable to suppose that the volume of work will rise sharply in coming years, leading to more and perhaps better suggestions for what might be done to prevent worst-case scenarios emerging. It would be reasonable too to conclude that in the years and decades ahead some states, and even non-state actors, may choose to test and even implement strategies that offer (or seem to offer) solutions that have detrimental consequences for others on the planet.

The problems and challenges that we face today are of course in many ways completely different to those faced by our earliest human ancestors. One thing, however, remains the same: the fact that the natural environment around us, and the climate that supports it, frames our existence. Nonetheless, we have come to believe that technology can overcome our limitations, that our reshaping and remodelling of nature can alleviate, circumvent or overcome all obstacles and barriers that determine not only where we live but how we live.

That feeling of confidence is not without cost. According to the UN, as much as 40 per cent of the world's land is now degraded. At current rates, an area the size of South America will be degraded by 2050.[75] 'Overshoot Day' – a notional benchmark that flags the date each year on which consumption of resources surpasses the earth's capacity to regenerate, as a way to focus minds on sustainability – keeps falling earlier and earlier in the year, moving from around October in the 1990s to late July in 2022.[76]

It is not impossible, of course, that humanity proves able to adapt, perhaps by changing the way we live and the choices we make; perhaps thanks to new technologies and ideas; perhaps through higher levels of collaboration, brought on either by enlightened governance or by crisis and necessity. It is worth bearing in mind, however, that much of human history has been about the failure to understand or adapt to changing circumstances in the physical and natural world around us, and about the consequences that ensue.

In that sense, then, environmental factors – including the climate – are not actors in the story of our species, which sometimes make interventions that bring down empires, lead to societal collapse or catch people by surprise. Rather, they provide the very stage on which our existence plays out, shaping everything we do, who we are, where and how we live. And like most stages, it can be all too easy to think only about what happens on them – what the protagonists do and say – without thinking about the fabric of the set itself. Actors come and go; but if the theatre closes or collapses, that marks the end for us all.

Like all animals and plants, humans flourish in habitats that suit them; as for all animals and plants, life is difficult, if not impossible, in those habitats that do not. We have been uniquely resourceful in finding ways to modulate those habitats and to refashion nature to suit our own needs – whether through building cities, through creating artificial water systems that enable the growing of crops where they otherwise could not grow, or through creating artificial ecosystems by means of innovation, trial and error and by developing technologies that allow us to manipulate hostile conditions. Our is a story of resourcefulness, resilience and adaptation.

Those qualities, however, can lead to a false sense of security, to the illusion that challenging times will one day revert to normal – which a historian can help remind us is nothing more than a mirage of wishful thinking. At the heart of the problems of today and tomorrow lies the fact that we are living on the edge of our means and indeed beyond them, reliant on everything to go right and with little margin of error for things to go wrong. This has created vulnerabilities, fragility and risk in the past, as this book has tried to show, and does so in the present as well.

Our species has been a part of this planet's history for a tiny sliver of its existence. While we conceptualise the natural past in terms of mass extinctions and think of these as almighty horrors, the reality is that nature does not care who wins or loses and does not choose one form of biota over another: the issue is always about adaptation and survival. It is worth remembering that we owe our presence on earth to previous, dramatic climate change and to the fluke circumstances that have made this planet well suited to our own existence.

Climate has shaped the earth since the beginning of time, with shifts in long-term patterns dictating the location of resources and materials that humans have found useful – such as coal, oil and gas – but which have no relevance to other plants and animals, except as a result of the ways in which we use them. It goes without saying, or at least it should do, that the world will keep spinning on its axis and rotating around the sun, however many of us – or however few of us – are around to witness and enjoy it. One thing is certainly clear: if we and future generations cannot prevent or adapt to global warming, then we go the way of a vast number of other species from the past. Our loss will be the gain of other animals and plants.

In *Paradise Lost*, John Milton wrote that expulsion from the Garden of Eden brought consequences. The short-sightedness, greed and disobedience of Adam and Eve, humanity's common ancestors, so angered God that he 'called forth by name His mightie Angels' and ordered them to shift the earth's axis, to change climate so that the earth was affected 'with cold and heat Scarce tollerable', and to make thunder 'rowle with terror'. Paradise had been climatically perfect, never affected by 'pinching cold and scorching heate'. Humans have long been the architects of their own climatic downfall, in other words.[77]

Returning to paradise is something that Milton thought about too, as is clear from his *Paradise Regained*. He was following a long tradition. Writing in the second century, St Irenaeus imagined the time of Christ's second coming and the joys which that would bring and the abundance that would greet the faithful. The Lord would surely declare, he wrote, that 'a grain of wheat would produce ten thousand ears, and that every ear should have ten thousand grains, and every grain would yield ten pounds of clear, pure, fine flour. Vines would have ten thousand branches, each with ten thousand twigs, each with ten thousand shoots, each of which would have ten thousand clusters, each with ten thousand grapes' – each of which would be magnificently juicy. 'All other fruit-bearing trees and seeds and grass would produce in similar proportions.' No one, that is to say, would go hungry.[78]

Similar promises of plenty can be found in almost every major world literature, not least in the Upaniṣads, which declare that 'the earth is like honey for all the creatures and all the creatures are like honey for this earth', or the Qur'ān, which notes that in paradise there would be 'soft couches' set in 'shady groves', filled with couples in a state of bliss enjoying fruits and everything else they might care for.[79] In Thomas More's fictional *Utopia*, food 'groweth everywhere without labour', while for some indigenous populations in North America idealised locations of paradise were not in new or post-life locations, but rather situated in the same place but in earlier times – when food and resources were more abundant.[80]

* * *

In the real world, however, we are taking extraordinary risks with our futures. Humans take advantage of nature's resources for food, water and shelter, says a major report on the economics of biodiversity that was published in the spring of 2021. And yet we also use nature as a sink for our waste products, such as carbon dioxide, plastics and pollution. This is the result not just of short-sightedness, says Sir Partha Dasgupta, the author of the report, but of stupidity: 'Governments almost everywhere exacerbate the problem by paying people more to exploit Nature than to protect it, and to prioritise unsustainable economic activities.'[81]

In fact, as the report goes on to say, we are living well beyond our means. At present, 'we would require 1.6 Earths to maintain the world's current living standards', an assessment that reveals critical shortcomings in how little thought and how little action has gone into tackling problems that reveal 'deep-rooted, widespread institutional failure'.[82] In the final analysis, however, as the UK government's Office for Budget Responsibility recently put it, it is easy to answer the question of how the problem of climate change is solved: it will be nature, rather than human action, that ultimately brings net emissions towards zero.[83] It will do so through catastrophic depopulation, whether through hunger, disease or conflict. With fewer of us around to burn fuel, cut down forests and tear minerals from the earth's crust, the human footprint may become drastically reduced – and we will move closer to the sustainable, lush paradise of our fantasised past. Perhaps we will find our way back there through peaceful means; a historian would not bet on it.

Acknowledgements

This has been a wonderful project to work on. Like many people, I have been thinking about climate change for a long time and trying to understand how global warming will affect the coming years as well as future generations. Being able to think about, read about and study the history of climate change, the role that extreme weather and long stable periods have played in the past, has been not only a great pleasure but a very challenging and rewarding journey too.

The process of writing this book has forced me to engage with new types of source material, above all from the sciences, and to learn how to interpret them; it has pushed me to look at the histories of peoples and places in regions that I have not worked on in great detail before, broadening my horizons considerably and making me a better historian in the process. I am acutely aware of the privilege that I have as a historian based at one of the world's great universities to enjoy the freedom to develop my ideas, to interact with colleagues and to be ambitious about which subjects I engage with.

This book has been brewing for several decades. In the first instance, however, I owe a debt of thanks to Jim Cuno, President of the Getty Center in Los Angeles, who invited me to the United States in 2017 as President's Council Fellow to benefit from the Center's extraordinary resources, to work on climate history and to give a preliminary lecture that offered me a chance to order my thought and crystallise my ideas. All ideas need a catalyst and a context, and I am hugely grateful to the Getty Center and its trustees for providing a glorious and generous setting which proved fundamental in helping take a project from the drawing board into something more ambitious than I had ever imagined.

I am grateful to my colleagues and students at Oxford for providing a relentlessly stimulating environment and to the staff at the Bodleian Library for their world-class collection and near endless patience in helping me track down material that was often obscure and difficult to find. I must thank the Provost and Fellows of Worcester College, Oxford, my friends and colleagues who work on Late Antique and Byzantine Studies, on Global and Imperial History and related fields for their help and support over many years. A similar level of support from the A. G. Leventis Foundation and the Stavros Niarchos Foundation has been crucial. I am very grateful to the trustees for their continued encouragement and backing.

I am also extremely grateful to the Provost and Fellows of King's College, Cambridge and in particular to Professor Robin Osborne, Lorraine Headon, Professor David Good and Dr Katie Campbell, as well as Alison Traub and Professor Stephen Toope, who have been instrumental in supporting the studies of the peoples, cultures and countries of the Silk Roads and opening new doors that have helped with my research in general as well as with this book in particular.

As ever, my agents Catherine Clarke and Zoe Pagnamenta have been my guardian angels, as has the team at Knight Ayton, always encouraging me and making me think I am more interesting and able than I really am. My editors, Alexis Kirschbaum and Michael Fishwick, provided a perfect balance of warm cheer and cold steel that has worked wonders in the past. I am grateful to both and to my copyeditor, Peter James, whose keen eye for detail I learned to admire long ago.

Lauren Whybrow, Genista Tate-Alexander, Hayley Camis and Jonny Coward have been a pleasure to work with in making sure this book reads and looks as good as it does. I'm very grateful to Mike Athanson for his wonderful maps. Jo Carlill was fantastic at tracking down images for the plates. And a special thanks, as with my last books, to Emma Ewbank for a magnificent cover. They say one should not judge a book by its cover; with *The Earth Transformed*, I am happy if readers do.

I've had a happy time over the years at Bloomsbury, as well as at Knopf, Spectrum, Rowohlt Berlin and my other publishers around the world, and thank them all for their continued confidence and backing. I am grateful too to Professor Chris Stringer for his generosity in providing invaluable advice and comments about human evolution and to Dr Vicki Smith for her guidance on the date of the Ilopango eruption of AD 431. Thanks too to Michael Drolet, my colleague at Worcester College, for pointing me towards Michel Chevalier.

I could not have managed to write this book without our children's support, encouragement and occasional teasing about how long it was taking to write and about why the same topics seemed to come up again and again at meal times. Thank you Katarina, Flora, Francis and Luke: you are all a lot older than when I started this book. I will miss you asking how much more I still have left to write; and what date I've got up to in my most recent chapter. I suspect I'll break my promise that I won't ever write another book; but you have all supported me more than you can imagine.

I lost my father in 2018. Not a day has gone by when I have not missed him. I used to speak to him every day about history, politics and his real passion, geology. I'm so sorry that I have not been able to do so while writing this book. I also missed my mother and my siblings terribly during the lockdowns of the global pandemic of 2020–2 when I could not see them in person for many months at a time.

But this book is dedicated to Jessica, the love of my life. For more than thirty years she has seen me turn half-baked ideas into something more promising, always telling me I could do it, suggesting ways I could do it better and, above all, being a pillar of support, happiness and laughter day in and day out, come rain or shine. She has inspired me every day for many, many years, always saying the right thing at the right time; she is the rock on which this book and my life are built. I could never have done this without her support and encouragement. She has always looked to the future with optimism and courage and reminded me to do the same. I will clasp her hand, and those of our children, ever more tightly – inspired by her urging that we must always be hopeful, even as we all head into an uncertain future. For that, and for so much more, this book is dedicated to her.

Notes

The endnotes for this book are extremely extensive and run to more than 200 pages. To spare the readers the extra weight of carrying these pages around, I decided to post all the notes on www.bloomsbury.com/theearthtransformed where they can be downloaded, consulted and searched at leisure.

Image Credits

1. Lascaux. Photo: © 2023 RMN-Grand Palais/Dist. Photo SCALA, Florence
2. Mohenjo-daro, Indus valley. Photo: Saqib Qayyum, March 2014. CC BY-SA 3.0. https://commons.wikimedia.org/wiki/File:Mohenjodaro_-_view_of_the_stupa_mound.JPG
3. Female figurine from the Indus Valley Civilisation. Harappa. Photo: Ismoon, 2021. CC0 1.0.
   https://commons.wikimedia.org/wiki/File:Female_figurine_3._Mature_Harappan_period._Indus_civilization_(detail).jpg
4. Sargon of Akkad; materials: bone, gold and lapislazuli; Iraqi National Museum, Baghdad.
   Photo: INTERFOTO/Alamy
5. Chinese cracked turtle shell. 18.4cm (L)×11.1cm (W). Photo: Courtesy of the Institute of History and Philology, Academia Sinica
6. Detail of Painted Casket of Tutankhamun. Photo: Roger Wood/Corbis/VCG via Getty Images
7. Ramagrama stupa. Photo: Dharma from Sadao, Thailand, 2017. CC BY 2.0. https://commons.wikimedia.org/wiki/

File:Ashoka%27s_visit_to_the_Ramagrama_stupa_Sanchi_
Stupa_1_Southern_gateway.jpg

8. Gold adornment from Issyk Kul, modern Kazakhstan. Photo: Peter Frankopan

9. Mosaic from Saint-Romain-en-Gal.Photo: DEA/J. E. BULLOZ/ De Agostini via Getty Images

10. Teotihuacan. Photo: Peter Frankopan

11. Vessel from the Moche Apogee Epoch, Larco Museum, Lima, Peru. Photo: Peter Frankopan

12. Detail from Codex Borbonicus Aztec manuscript, 1562-63. Palais Bourbon, Bibliothèque.
    Photo: De Agostini via Getty Images

13. Emperor Justinian, Byzantine mosaic in the presbytery of the Basilica of San Vitale. Photo: DEA/A. DAGLI ORTI/Getty Images

14. Temple V – Tikal. Photo: Peter Frankopan

15. Tlaloc from Templo Mayor. Photo: Peter Frankopan

16. Angkor Wat. Photo: Peter Frankopan

17. Monks Mound at Cahokia. Photo: Matthew Gush/Alamy

18. Segara Anak caldera. Photo: Robby Oktawianto/EyeEm/Getty Images

19. Pieter Bruegel The Elder, *Hunters in the Snow (Winter)*, 1565 (oil on wood). Kunsthistorisches Museum, Vienna, Austria. Photo: Fine Art Images/Heritage Images/Getty Images

20. Diagram of the 'Brookes' slave ship, 1801. British Library shelfmark 1881.d.8 (46) 522.f.23
    Photo: © British Library Board/Bridgeman Images

21. Sample of potato plant 1660, Sloan Herbarium. Photo: © The Trustees of the Natural History Museum, London.

22. Thomas Jefferson temperatures July 1776 from Massachusetts Historical Society: Coolidge Collection of Thomas Jefferson Manuscripts, 1705-1827, Reel 15, Memorandum book, 1776-1778, Image 128, Special Colls. Jefferson. Photo: Collection of the Massachusetts Historical Society

23. Cast brass plaques from Benin City. British Museum, London. Photo: Andreas Praefcke /Wikimedia.org. PD-self

24. Sailors visiting a guano bed off the coast of Peru 1880. Hand-coloured woodcut. Photo: North Wind Picture Archives/Alamy

25. Eunice Newton Foote, *Circumstances Affecting the Heat of the Sun's Rays* (1856), The American Journal of Science and Arts. Second

Series, Vol XXII (1856). Photo: Archive.org/Missouri Botanical Garden/The Biodiversity Heritage Library.

26. Photogravure after a photograph of Svante August Arrhenius. Photo: SSPL/Getty Images

27. Construction of the White Sea-Baltic Canal (Belomorkanal). Photo: Laski Diffusion/Getty Images

28. Rubber-tapping. Photo: The Granger Collection/Alamy

29. Ding Hao, *Exterminate the four pests! Chu siha!* Feb 1958. Photo: Private Collection, International Institute of Social History, Amsterdam. pc-1958-025 (chineseposters.net, Private collection)

30. A mushroom cloud after the explosion of a French atomic bomb above the atoll of Mururoa, also known as Aopuni. 1971. Photo: Galerie Bilderwelt/Getty Images

31. Peace march on the United Nations Plaza. Photo: Bettmann/Getty Images

32. Collier's magazine cover, May 28, 1954. Weather made to order by HT Orville, Illustration by Frederick (Fritz) Siebel. Photo: Courtesy of Novak Archive/Paleofuture

33. Film poster for the 1986 film *When the Wind Blows*. Photo: Courtesy of www.themoviedb.org

34. Propaganda poster from the Virgin Lands Campaign. Text reads, 'Let us gather vast crops from the virgin lands'. Photo: Universal History Archive/Universal Images Group via Getty Images

35. Earth Summit on 12 June 1992 at Rio de Janeiro. Photo: DANIEL GARCIA/AFP via Getty Images

36. Photo taken during an aerial survey mission by Greenpeace at East Kotawaringin district in Central Kalimantan province on Indonesia's Borneo Island on 24 February 2014 shows cleared trees in a forest located in the concession of Karya Makmur Abadi which is being developed for a palm oil plantation. Photo: BAY ISMOYO/ AFP via Getty Images

37. A view of Kartavya Path engulfed in dense smog on 7 November 2022 in New Delhi, India.
Photo: Arvind Yadav/Hindustan Times via Getty Images

38. Aerial view of plumes of smoke rising out of the oil refinery towers in Houston, Texas, USA.
Photo: simonkr/Getty Images

Chart Credits

1. 'Synoptic frequency of extreme marine heat across ocean basins from 1900–2019', adapted from K. R. Tanaka and K. S. Van Houtan, 'The recent normalization of historical marine heat extremes', PLOS Clim 1(2) (2022)

2. 'Deep ocean temperature from the Palaeocene to the present', adapted from a graph by Hunter Allen and Michon Scott, using data from the NOAA National Climatic Data Center © NOAA Climate.gov

3. 'Global mean surface temperature change over the past 24 kyr' from M. B. Osman, J. E. Tierney, J. Zhu et al, 'Globally resolved surface temperatures since the Last Glacial Maximum', *Nature* 599, 239–244 (2021) © Springer Nature

4. 'Isotopic ratio profiles at three sites in Italy from 1000 BC–1000 AD', M. Bini, G. Zanchetta, E. Regattieri, I. Isola, R. N. Drysdale, F. Fabiani, S. Genovesi, J. C. Hellstrom, 'Hydrological changes during the Roman Climatic Optimum in northern Tuscany (Central Italy) as evidenced by speleothem records and archaeological data', *Journal of Quaternary Science* 35 (2020) © 2020 John Wiley & Sons, Ltd

5. 'Temperature profiles at six sites in the North Atlantic from 200 BC–2000 AD', used with permission from T. Cronin, K. Hayo, R. Thunell, G. S. Dwyer, C. Saenger, D. Willard, 'The Medieval Climate Anomaly and Little Ice Age in Chesapeake Bay and the North Atlantic Ocean', *Palaeogeography, Palaeoclimatology, Palaeoecology* 297 (2010)

6. 'Potential gain in life...' and 'Life expectancy impact...' adapted from B.C. O'Neill, C. Tebaldi, D. P. van Vuuren, V. Eyring, P. Friedlingstein, G. Hurtt, R. Knutti, E. Kriegler, J.-F. Lamarque, J. Lowe, G. A. Meehl, R. Moss, K. Riahi and B. M. Sanderson, 'The Scenario Model Intercomparison Project (ScenarioMIP) for CMIP6', *Geosci. Model Dev* 9 (2016)

7. 'Predicted CO_2 atmospheric concentration and temperature increase from 2100 AD', adapted from 'Air Quality Life Index Annual Update', June 2022, awli.epic.uchicago.edu

Index

A Note on the Author

Peter Frankopan is Professor of Global History at the University of Oxford and Senior Research Fellow at Worcester College, Oxford. *The Silk Roads: A New History of the World*, published by Bloomsbury in 2015, was a No. 1 *Sunday Times* bestseller and remained in the top 10 for nine months after publication. It was named one of the 'Books of the Decade' 2010–2020 by the *Sunday Times*. *The New Silk Roads: The Present and Future of the World* was published by Bloomsbury in 2018 and won the Human Sciences prize of the Carical Foundation in 2019.

A Note on the Type

The text of this book is set Adobe Garamond. It is one of several versions of Garamond based on the designs of Claude Garamond. It is thought that Garamond based his font on Bembo, cut in 1495 by Francesco Griffo in collaboration with the Italian printer Aldus Manutius. Garamond types were first used in books printed in Paris around 1532. Many of the present-day versions of this type are based on the *Typi Academiae* of Jean Jannon cut in Sedan in 1615.

Claude Garamond was born in Paris in 1480. He learned how to cut type from his father and by the age of fifteen he was able to fashion steel punches the size of a pica with great precision. At the age of sixty he was commissioned by King Francis I to design a Greek alphabet, and for this he was given the honourable title of royal type founder. He died in 1561.

SEDIMENT TRANSPORT
IN ALLUVIAL STREAMS

SEDIMENT TRANSPORT IN ALLUVIAL STREAMS

JÁNOS BOGÁRDI

Member of the Hungarian Academy of Sciences
University Professor

AKADÉMIAI KIADÓ · BUDAPEST 1974

TRANSLATED BY

ZOLTÁN SZILVÁSSY

ISBN 963 05 0278 X

© AKADÉMIAI KIADÓ, BUDAPEST 1974

PRINTED IN HUNGARY

To my wife

PREFACE

Professor János Bogárdi has been my friend for many years, but our strongest connection is through our common field of interest: sediment transport and the laws of the alluvial river. His contributions in this field are well known the world over and prove his desire not only to describe, but to understand the behavior of the flows in these channels. He thoroughly appreciates the fact that reliable predictions of flow behavior for design purposes can be made only on the basis of the full understanding of the basic relationships.

In this book he attempts to transmit to the reader such an understanding as he has acquired himself during the many years of research and of practical work in this field. He has guided the development of measuring devices for field use and their mode of application in rivers. Many measurements of sediment transport and of the corresponding flow parameters have been made in Hungarian rivers and are used as examples in his book. They represent a welcome addition to the relatively few well documented prototype measurements available in the literature. These measurements were all made in the alluvial streams of the Hungarian plain, under exclusion of mountain torrents. Bed material finer than 1 mm is hardly represented, reducing considerably the influence of fluid viscosity on the flow characteristics.

The Hungarian Academy of Sciences may be highly commended for making this most valuable work available to the world in the English language.

Hans Albert Einstein

AUTHOR'S PREFACE

Increasing difficulties have been encountered when attempting to describe sediment transport in alluvial streams and the results obtained in a comprehensive manner. The broadening scope of water resources management has multiplied the number of problems associated with sediment transport. Tremendous efforts are being made all over the world to provide theoretically well founded answers to the problems arising in engineering practice. The volume of knowledge that was confined initially to a narrow domain has expanded considerably.

The general development of technology has provided additional stimulus to this expansion. The theory of sediment transport has also entered its "atomic age". Instruments and equipment have not only become more sophisticated, but permit physical variables of unknown magnitude a decade ago to be measured.

The theory of sediment transport has been dealt with extensively and amply in the literature. The inclusion of all efforts and advances would be practically impossible and no attempt is made at completeness in this respect. The achievements of numerous recognized investigators have had to be omitted. This however, must by no means be mistaken for an underestimation of their significance and importance and does not imply disagreement with these results.

The objective in writing this book was to present a reasonably comprehensive review of research into sediment transportation and of the results achieved thus far, including the original contributions of the author.

The theory of sediment transport has commanded my attention since 1935. The first observations and studies were conducted in Hungary, on the Danube. During a study trip to the United States I was given opportunity to carry on sediment studies at the Hydraulic Laboratory of the State University of Iowa. Since 1938 studies and observations have been carried out on practically all major streams in Hungary. Field observations and studies for a long time were performed under my personal guidance at the Hungarian Hydrographic Institute and later at its successor, the Research Institute for Water Resources Development, Budapest. More recent observations have already been performed by the staff members of the Research Institute for Water Resources Development.

Since most of my measurements and observations have been performed in Hungary, the number of references to sediment transport in Hungarian rivers and to relevant studies is obviously large but the results of Hungarian observations are believed to provide useful data also for foreign investigators. It should be noted here that the sediment conditions in Hungarian rivers are dealt with in much greater detail in the Hungarian version of this book.

9

Sincere appreciation and thanks are due to the Research Institute for Water Resources Development for the valuable assistance received. First of all, the generosity of the Institute made the publication of this book possible. But thanks are due to the management and staff of the Institute for having made available the results and data of their measurements and observations, as well as for the valuable assistance afforded in the work of data processing.

A stimulus for an English edition of this book was received some ten years ago from the world-famed hydraulician Prof. Hunter Rouse who suggested the translation of my book published in 1955. The English version of this completely revised book is a somewhat delayed response to this encouragement.

It may be of interest to add that the translation of my book into one of the major languages was also urged by Prof. I. V. Egiazaroff, the outstanding authority on sediment transport. The desirability of a more widely accessible version has since been stated repeatedly by several fellow investigators dealing with sediment transport problems abroad. I trust I have succeeded in meeting their expectations.

Sincere appreciation is due also to Prof. H. A. Einstein who, following the invitation of the publisher – the Publishing House of the Hungarian Academy of Sciences – introduced by his preface this book to the wide English reading public.

During the past five years I have carried on investigations within the research group of the Academy at the Department for Hydraulic Engineering, Budapest Technical University. For their assistance in my research work I am indebted to my collaborators at the Department for Hydraulic Engineering and Water Management, Budapest Technical University.

For the effective support in getting this book published acknowledgments are due to the Hungarian Academy of Sciences, especially to the Department of Technical Sciences of the Academy. The valuable aid afforded by the Publishing House and Press of the Hungarian Academy in writing, editing and printing this book is gratefully acknowledged.

For their valuable suggestions and ideas in the final compilation of the material I am deeply indebted to the two most competent reviewers of the book, Dr. Z. Hankó and Dr. K. Stelczer. Their helpful advices have resulted in numerous improvements in the composition and presentation of the material.

For the translation of the Hungarian text into English my thanks are due to Mr. Z. Szilvássy, and for the linguistical revision, to Dr. G. Dienes who handled also the editorial work.

Mr. András Csákvári, staff editor of the publisher was of great help to me in preparing the final text for printing.

It is my pleasant task to express my thanks to each of my collaborators, Mr. Z. Ambrus, Dr. L. Dávid, Mr. K. Hampel, Mr. Gy. Hrehuss and Dr. E. Szücs, who performed computation work, prepared the illustrations and derived relations in compiling the material for this book.

The pleasing appearance of the drawings testifies to the skill of Mrs. Á. Buday.

I am obliged finally to record my sincere appreciation to my devoted secretary, Mrs. K. Hampel who, besides typing the manuscript, handled most efficiently the ramified tasks of administration related to the publication of this book.

The efforts and skill of my collaborators in their respective fields of activity have greatly contributed to the appearance of this volume.

J. L. Bogárdi

CONTENTS

  15

In spite of all efforts no uniform set of notations could be adopted. Beside new uniform symbols introduced on several occasions, it was often found necessary to retain the original notations of some of the authors.

The dimensions generally involved in considerations on sediment transport are those of length (L), time (T), mass (M) or force (F) and temperature (Θ). The metric system has been adopted throughout, except for a few empirical formulae specified originally in the foot-pound system. Following the method which has recently found widespread use, a distinction has been made between the units of mass and force, using the notation kg (kilogramme) for the former and kp (kilopond) for the latter. Of course, in accordance with the requirements of engineering practice, the technical system of units has been adopted, viz. the basic unit is the kilopond (kp). It should be noted that the use of the international system (SI = Système international) has not been considered desirable since it is compulsory only in a few European countries (e.g. the Federal Republic of Germany). The description of the system of units used in this book, together with the conversion factors of some, is given in the List of Symbols.

The Progress Reports of the Task Committee on Preparation of Sedimentation Manual, Committee on Sedimentation, published in successive volumes of the Journal of the Hydraulics Division, ASCE, have been studied carefully and drawn upon freely. However, the division into chapters of the progress reports, as well as the manner of treatment adopted in them differs radically from the grouping and treatment adopted in this book, yet for this very reason no superfluous overlapping or unwanted parallelism will be observed between the present book and the progress reports.

A number of familiar general principles and descriptions are discussed, but always with the objective of providing the necessary information for those engaged in research on the theory of sediment transport and only to the extent considered necessary for this purpose.

In compiling most of the material for this book an endeavour was made to treat of sediment transport as of a physical phenomenon in order to eliminate in this way the inconsistencies unquestionably existing in some of the widely known sediment transport relations. The inclusion of such details must not be taken for an underestimation of the reader, their only objective being to afford an exact formulation of the problem.

Theories and relations of sediment transport are used in practice by engineers. With this in mind various relations and theories have been made directly suitable for practical use wherever this proved possible. In doing so empirical relationships were also included but not without examining their physical foundations. It is therefore fully consistent to regard also sediment transport, as a physical phenomenon while introducing observation data and making use of the empirical relationships.

Some of the empirical relationships are generally believed to yield the desired value with a very wide range of scatter. Nevertheless, these have also been included, especially in cases where it was considered essential to provide some information.

It should be noted further that reference is made to a number of results obtained in Hungary which may appear disproportionately high compared to the results of observations abroad. The purpose of including such data was to offer opportunities for comparing these with observation data obtained by investigators on other water courses and to draw further conclusions therefrom. Of course, these data may also be of interest to the practicing engineer.

The book is divided into three parts. The first part is devoted to the theory of sediment transport, the second, to sediment transport in alluvial streams, whereas the third part presents a description on the processing of sediment observation data, on the methodological problems involved and on the practical value of the results obtained.

The theory of sediment transport is dealt with in three chapters.

The first chapter is concerned with studies on the sediment and its movement. It deals with the general principles of theoretical studies as well as with the personal views of the author in certain respects.

The second chapter is devoted to the movement of bed load. The laws governing variable critical tractive forces and critical velocities are described in detail together with illustrative examples. The latest results on bed load wear are also summarized here.

The third chapter in the first part deals with the movement of suspended sediment by observing the general transport theory as applied in thermodynamics and by introducing new balance equations. Starting from the general balance equations, the theory of turbulent sediment transport and especially the interesting theories of Soviet investigators have been collated.

In the second part sediment transportation in streams has been described in five chapters.

In the first chapter the relationships on the basis of field observation data are introduced and physically interpreted.

The second chapter deals with the properties of alluvial streams in the context of sediment movement and sums up the relevant relations without any claim at completeness.

The third chapter is devoted to the regime theory. In the light of latest research this theory is unquestionably related to the general theory of sediment transport.

In the fourth chapter the general principles underlying the influence of sediment transport on river regulation are dealt with.

The fifth chapter of part two is devoted to the problems of hydraulic similarity in sediment transport. The volume of information presented here may appear disproportionately large at a first glance. Considering, however, that the advanced theory of hydraulic similarity includes, besides problems of model testing, also that of hydraulic analogy of streams, it will be appreciated that similarity theory is highly relevant to the theory of sediment transport. For this reason it appeared necessary to summarize here the basic concepts of hydraulic similarity.

In the third part the conclusions arrived at, and information obtained from sediment observations and studies are discussed.

The third part is divided into two chapters.

In the first chapter the processing of observation data and the methodological problems related thereto are outlined. The examples quoted for the processing of observation data relate, in general, to streams in Hungary. This is due to the high number of available data and also to the advanced state of sediment observations in Hungary which, although started at a relatively late date, have attained a high international standard and even display certain novel features.

The second chapter gives a brief summary of sediment transportation in Hungarian streams together with the regularities and characteristics thereof. As mentioned already the wealth of data presented here may prove of interest to investigators abroad in their research work.

The copious bibliography includes the publications discussed or mentioned in the text. As shown by the long list of references, the theory of sediment transport has been studied extensively and from different angles by a very great number of investigators. A number of papers of considerable interest have nevertheless been omitted from the list. This, however, is not a sign of disagreement on the part of the author with the conclusions arrived at in them but is due exclusively to the abundance of publications on sediment movement, the complete listing of which would call practically for a separate volume.

PART ONE
THEORY OF SEDIMENT MOVEMENT

1.1. INVESTIGATIONS ON SEDIMENT AND ITS MOVEMENT

1.1.1. SEDIMENT IN ALLUVIAL STREAMS

1.1.1.1. Sources of sediment. In addition to water, solids are also conveyed in channels. Regardless of their origin and provenance, these solids are referred to collectively as sediment.

The sediment in alluvial channels consists of mineral and organic matter. The organic sediment originates from a wide variety of wastes discharged mostly through the sewers of major settlements into the streams. Since the appearance of wastes, that is, of organic sediment, is irregular, being limited to certain occasions, and their movement is of a random character, studies concerned with sediment transportation in streams focus their attention exclusively on the mineral matter.

Most sediments transported in alluvial channels are of natural-mineral origin. The laws governing their movement apply, however, to the movement of other solid granular material as well. This circumstance is exploited in laboratory experiments where granulated coal, glass or even synthetic material is used to study the movement of natural sediment. In engineering practice this process is reversed: the transportation and movement of a wide variety of granular materials is designed with due consideration to the laws governing the movement of natural sediments.

In early hydraulic engineering, sediment transported in streams gave rise to numerous difficulties, but the full significance of sediment transportation in alluvial channels was not realized.

The interest devoted to sediment transportation in streams increased with the projects in hydraulic engineering becoming more ambitious and with the methods and procedures of water management becoming increasingly sophisticated.

The problems of sediment transportation are of a highly complex haracter. The origin of sediment is difficult to trace, since large areas and many aspects of human activity are involved. The phenomenon responsible for the appearance of sediment is erosion, so that the relevant problems are of consequence for agricultural and forest areas alike as well as for the safety and continuous existence of human settlements and a wide variety of structures.

It will be readily appreciated that the sediment originated from scouring the bottom and the banks of rivers may present a hazard to the existence of natural and artificial channels alike.

The sediment, once born, may be set into motion by a suitable transporting medium, and this movement, just like the origin, may give rise to a variety of problems. Numerous transporting media are conceivable, but the present considerations will be restricted to water. Over the headwater reaches of rivers large boulders may also be transported, especially at times of floods, and the hydraulic engineering structures there may be severely damaged or even destroyed thereby.

On the other hand, the problems caused by the fine suspended sediment may prove equally serious. Reference is only made here to industrial and communal water supply, were one of the gravest problems is the removal of suspended particles.

Problems are encountered finally when the sediment is deposited either temporarily or permanently. The deposited sediment may cause unwanted silting in streams, while at times of flood it may cause serious damages within the flood bed and in human settlements alike. In many instances the operation of reservoirs may be jeopardized by settling sediment and, where rivers discharge into major streams, even the recipient may be gradually filled.

In other instances the sediment may prove beneficial. This is exemplified by the rich silt deposits in flood plains whereby agricultural production may be greatly increased in some alluvial valleys.

The significance of problems associated with sediment will be appreciated by considering the volumes of sediment originating by erosion and transported in streams.

Depending on geographical location, on geologic, climatic and physical conditions, on the plant cover in the catchment areas and on numerous other factors, the sediment volumes transported in water courses on our Globe range between extremely wide limits. The amount of fine sediment material transported in some streams during floods is large enough to approach the phenomenon of mud flow — about 56 to 58% by weight — in which the loess and clay particles become practically plastic. Sediment concentration is expressed in percentages by weight, in which the weight ratio of the sediment and the transporting water is expressed as percentages. According to data published by E. W. Lane, the sediment transported in the Young Ting river in China may attain as much as 55.7% by weight. The sediment transported in some of the major and well known rivers of the Earth may also become extremely great under certain conditions. Figures as high as 39 and 14.4% by weight have been recorded for the Yellow river and the Colorado respectively. The sediment transported by the rivers in Europe is insignificant in comparison. The highest sediment concentration over the Hungarian reach of the Danube is 0.1% by weight. The highest sediment concentration in the Volga is of the same order of magnitude. Of the major rivers in Hungary sediment concentration is highest in the Tisza river, but even the highest figure remains below 0.35 to 0.4% by weight. The greatest sediment load of the Hungarian rivers is carried by the Hernád, in which the highest concentration observed was 2.93% by weight at Hidasnémeti.

Sediment transportation in the rivers of our Globe can be illustrated even more strikingly by considering the annual mean sediment volumes. The volume of sediment transported annually depends, obviously, also on the magnitude of the catchment area. It is for this reason that, concerning the annual volume of sediment, the large streams are at the head of the lists. Drawing on data published by J. N. Holeman, *Table 1.1.1 −1* shows rivers with an annual mean sediment load higher

Table 1.1.1—1

Rivers transporting more than 100 million Mp sediment annually

River	Country	Catchment area [10³ km²]	Annual mean sediment transport [10⁶ Mp]	[Mp/km²]	Average discharge at the mouth [m³/sec]	Annual average runoff volume [10⁹ m³]	Mean sediment concentration [kp/m³]
1. Yellow	China	673	1,889,000	2,805	1,500	473	39.9
2. Ganges	India	955	1,451,000	1,520	11,750	3,705	3.92
3. Brahmaputra	Bangla Desh	665	726,000	1,092	12,180	3,839	1.89
4. Yangtze	China	1,941	499,000	257	21,800	6,870	0.727
5. Indus	Pakistan	969	436,000	450	5,550	1,750	2.50
6. Ching	China	57	408,000	7,155	57	18	227.0
7. Amazonas	Brasil	5,780	363,000	63	181,100	57,090	0.0636
8. Mississippi	USA	3,221	312,000	97	17,830	5,620	0.565
9. Irrawaddy	Burma	430	300,000	697	13,560	4,273	0.702
10. Missouri	USA	1,370	218,000	159	1,950	615	3.54
11. Lo	China	26	191,000	7,350	–	–	–
12. Kosi	India	62	172,000	2,772	1,810	570	3.02
13. Mekong	Thailand	795	170,000	214	11,040	3,480	0.488
14. Colorado	USA	637	135,000	212	156	49	27.6
15. Red	North Vietnam	119	130,000	1,092	3,900	1,230	1.05
16. Nile	Egypt	2,980	111,000	37	2,830	892	1.25

Table 1.1.1—2

Annual mean sediment transport observed by continents

Continent	Catchment area considered [km²]	Annual mean sediment transport	
		[10² Mp]	[Mp/km²]
North America	6,388,500	547,400	85.95
South America	9,892,000	552,000	56.07
Africa	8,154,000	136,200	24.57
Australia	1,072,000	42,900	40.33
Europe	3,513,500	110,400	31.56
Asia	10,910,000	5,818,000	536.20
Total	39,930,000	7,266,900	average 182.30

than 100 million Megaponds. Heading the list is the Yellow river the catchment area of which is hardly larger than one-tenth of the catchment drained by the largest stream of the Earth, the Amazonas river, yet which carries annually over five times more sediment into the sea than the Amazonas.

The mean water discharges for the estuary sections of individual rivers have also been entered in the table and the mean sediment concentrations, as well as the annual sediment yield per unit area of the catchment have been computed from the annual averages. Eleven of the 16 rivers included in the tables are in the southern part of Asia, three in North America, one in South America and one in Africa, which alone testifies that the largest sediment volumes are transported by rivers in Asia.

Sediment transportation in the water courses of the Globe have received attention from a large number of investigators. Compiling data on sediment transportation in rivers, it will be perceived that observation data are available for about one-third of the area which may be regarded as a potential source of sediment. Of course, the measurement and observation data are not uniform as far as reliability is concerned, so that their comparison and any conclusion drawn from them on the remaining two-thirds of the area involve necessarily crude approximations. In recent times sediment transportation by the rivers of the Globe has been studied in detailed by J. N. Holeman. A brief description of sediment conditions in the major streams of the Earth will be presented on the basis of the data compiled by him.

Bearing in mind that 71% of the Earth's surface is covered by the oceans and that 13 million sq.km. of the remaining 149 million sq.km. of continental and island area are occupied by the Antarctic and 34.5 million sq.km., by closed basins and deserts which do not contribute sediment to the oceans, the water and sediment runoff to the oceans originates from a catchment of altogether 101. million sq.km.

Total annual mean sediment transport by continents

Continent	Total catchment area [km²]	Annual mean sediment transport	
		[Mp/km²]	[10³ Mp]
North America	20,730,000	85.95	1,780,000
South America	19,410,000	56.07	1,090,000
Africa	19,930,000	24.57	490,000
Australia	5,180,000	40.33	210,000
Europe	9,320,000	31.56	290,000
Asia	26,920,000	536.20	14,430,000
Total	101,490,000		18,290,000

Taking into account all measurement and observation data published in the literature, Holeman has established for each continent the extension of catchment areas on which such data are available and the annual mean volume of sediment originating from this area, estimating thus the annual mean specific sediment rate per unit catchment area. The data thus obtained are shown in *Table 1.1.1−2*. The sediment load per unit area of catchment is the figure of greatest interest. It will be perceived that the specific sediment yield in Asia is more than 6 times as high as in North America, further that these figures are relatively low for Africa and Europe.

The total annual mean sediment yield from each continent is estimated by extrapolation by taking into consideration the total catchment area producing sediment and the specific sediment yield figures. Proceeding in this manner, the annual mean sediment yield for each continent has been entered into the 1st column of *Table 1.1.1−3* and these have been combined to find the total figure for the Globe.

It will be seen therefrom that, according to the investigations of Holeman, the total volume of sediment transported by the rivers of the Globe in an average year amounts to 18.29 thousand million (18.29×10^9) Mp. In view of the questionable reliability of some of the observation data and of the uncertainty introduced by extending specific figures to the entire area of continents, this figure cannot be accepted unless its approximate character is recognized. In this context it should be noted that the annual mean volume of sediment transported in the rivers of the Globe was estimated in 1926 by H. Twenhofel at 16.2, in 1960 by Fournier at 58, while in 1952 by Lopatin at 12.6 thousand million Mp. The figure given by Holeman is seen thus to occupy an intermediate position between the above extreme values and considering that his estimates are based on the most recent data, his figure may be regarded as the most reliable of all.

When considering the mean sediment volume transported annually into the oceans by the water courses of the Globe, allowance should be made for the fact that this forms no more than a certain part of the gross erosion. The sediment volume which can be carried potentially by the streams is always smaller than, or at the most equal to, the sediment volume originating by erosion. The ratio of the two expressed as percentages, is termed *the sediment yield ratio*.

The sediment yield ratio is a complex function of the characteristics of the catchment and of the climatic conditions prevailing there. The magnitude of this figure is affected, obviously by the sizes, slope, petrographic and topographic conditions of the catchment area, as well as by the amount and distribution of precipitation and the runoff resulting therefrom. Although extensive investigations have already been made into the influence of these factors, no relations of general validity could so far be established.

Investigations thus far have shown the sediment yield ratio to range between very wide limits. Detailed studies performed in the catchment of the Potomac river in North America have shown, for instance, that of the total eroded sediment volume no more than 5% are transported by water into the sea. According to other detailed studies practically the entire sediment volume produced by erosion finds access to the sea.

The formation of sediment can be traced back to the weathering and decaying of rocks. Coarse sediment is, in general, composed of fragments of various rocks. In the fine sediment fractions, especially in suspended sediment, crystals of minerals are also encountered.

Concerning mineralogical composition, sediments usually contain fragments and crystals of a very great number of rocks and minerals.

The magnitude of sediment particles ranges from boulders weighing several hundred kiloponds down to very finely grained suspended matter. Consequently, the sediment in rivers consists mostly of a mixture of different particle sizes.

In engineering practice fractions larger than 0.002 mm are regarded as sediment. In this respect the particles performing Brownian movement and smaller than 0.002 mm, together with the substances dissolved in water are not regarded sediments.

Sediment particles may range in shape from the approximately spherical gravels to flat sheet-like scales and may assume all conceivable intermediate forms. The edges may be sharp or rounded off by wearing, depending on the distance travelled in the river. The mineralogical composition of sediments, the magnitude, shape and specific gravity of sediment particles will be discussed in detail in *Section 1.1.2*.

The main agent responsible for sediment in the catchment area is *erosion by water*. Erosion, like the transportation of sediment formed in the course of erosion, as well as the periodic or permanent deposition of this sediment are continuous geological processes constantly changing the surface configuration of the Earth. Even the present surface topography is the result of erosion processes which took place in geological times. Erosion is controlled by natural conditions and thus the formation of sediment is variable in both time and location, it is controlled by geologic and climatic conditions and even by the quality of the plant cover over a particular area.

The above considerations apply to *natural erosion* which is a continuous process. The conditions governing erosion may be changed as a result of human interference, mostly by deforestation and agricultural activities, accelerating thereby the rate of erosion. In distinction to natural erosion this artificial type of erosion is usually referred to as *accelerated erosion*. As a consequence of accelereted erosion due to human interference the rate of sediment formation is increased and the phenomenon of natural erosion is fundamentally modified.

The rate of erosion is controlled by the balance prevailing between the erosive force and the erosive resistance of the soil. The erosive force is understood as the effect tending to scour the soil particles, whereas erosive resistance is the property of the soil resisting erosion. The magnitude of the erosive force depends primarily on the magnitude and intensity of precipitation, whereas the erosive resistance depends mainly on the quality and type of the soil, as well as on the vegetation offering protection to the soil.

Under climates rich in precipitation, the erosive force is naturally greater, but is offset by dense vegetation, so that eventually the destruction caused by erosion is relatively small and less sediment is carried into the water courses. Under dry climates, on the other hand, the erosive force is relatively small, but it is less effectively resisted by sparse vegetation so that the destructive force of erosion is considerable. As a consequence, relatively more sediment is carried into the water courses.

Denudation is increased under both humid and arid climates by the artificial acceleration of erosion. Its influence, however, is to a certain extent greater under humid climates where a much greater resisting force is diminished by human interference. A characteristic property of natural and accelerated erosion alike is that it tends to extend gradually upwards attacking eventually the entire watershed. The rate of sediment formation is thus gradually accelerated, and increasing volumes of sediment are washed into the water courses.

Concerning the location of occurrence, both natural and accelerated erosion may be *areal* or *local* erosion.

Areal erosion extends over large areas and, especially in agricultural areas, takes the form of accelerated erosion. Local erosion is a consequence of particular conditions and occurs also at structures such as bridge piers, bottom outlets, etc.

Areal erosion takes most frequently the form of *layer erosion* by which the soil over sloping surfaces is eroded practically by layers. Gully erosion is also classified as areal erosion, in which case erosion is concentrated in the path of minor or greater rivulets. This type of erosion results eventually in deep gullys which alone or in combination with denudation prevent any kind of regular human activity.

Extensive studies have been performed with the objective of determining the soil loss caused by erosion, i.e. the rate of sediment formation. A relationship of general validity is, obviously, very difficult to establish since, besides the slope of the soil and the type of precipitation, the phenomenon of erosion is influenced by a great number of other factors.

29

Let us consider first the expressions commonly used for estimating the *soil loss caused by areal erosion.*

In 1947, based on the analysis of about 40,000 storm data relating the soil loss E (acre-in), G. W. Musgrave published a coefficient representing the erodability of the soil I (in), a coefficient R representing the plant cover, the percentage slope S of the soil, the length L (ft) of the slope and the 30 minute storm depth P_{30} (in) of two-year recurrence in the form

$$E = \dot{I}RS^{1.25}L^{0.35}P_{30}^{1.75} \qquad (1.1.1-1)$$

The expression has proved successfully for estimating the average erosion over extended periods of time from large areas.

As a result of continued research work American investigators have succeeded in deriving a relationship of general validity suitable for estimating short-term erosion from smaller areas. This relationship is claimed to be universal and takes the form

$$A = RKLSCP \qquad (1.1.1-2)$$

where A (Mp/ha.year) = the annual average soil loss,
  R = the storm factor,
  K = the coefficient of soil erodability,
  L = the length of the slope,
  S = a factor indicating the inclination of the slope,
  C = representative of the crop structure,
  P = the method of cultivation.

The practical application of the relationship is facilitated by the detailed instruction accompanied by diagrams compiled by the authors for determining the magnitude of the terms involved therein in particular cases.

The phenomenon of sediment formation caused by *local erosion* is mentioned in engineering practice usually as *scouring* or *degradation.* Whereas sediment formation due to areal erosion has been determined with the help of observations and measurements in the field, the attempts made at the determination of scouring were based mostly on experiments and theoretical considerations. Theoretical investigations of this kind have been conducted by E. N. Laursen who has summarized the general properties of scours in the following four principles:

a) The extent of scouring equals the difference of the sediment-transporting capacity in the region under considerations and of the sediment supply arriving to the same location.

b) The extent of scouring tends to decrease at the same rate as the flow cross-section increases.

c) Depending on local and initial conditions scours will always tend to a definite limit value.

d) Scours approach this limit value asymptotically in time.

30

The prerequisite for the validity of the above general property is that fluid movement ceases to exist as the field of flow approaches infinity. Another condition is that the decrease of sediment-transporting capacity is a continuous, monotonous function of the enlargement of cross-section and, before fluid movement ceases, this value attains zero.

The first general principle related to scouring is expressed symbolically by the expression

$$\frac{d}{dt} F(B) = g(B) - g(S) \qquad (1.1.1-3)$$

where B denotes a mathematical description of the boundary surface so that the term

$$\frac{d}{dt} F(B)$$

is the extent of scouring with respect to time t. The rate at which sediment is removed from the scouring area as a function of the boundary surface and location is expressed by $g(B)$, while the rate at which sediment is supplied to the same area is represented by $g(S)$.

The remaining three general principles serve as boundary conditions for the solution of the equation. In any particular case the rate of sediment supply and the sediment-transporting capacity must be known before Eq. $(1.1.1-3)$ can be used. In the majority of cases these relations are unknown, and it is difficult to meet the boundary conditions. For this reason a solution is impossible unless simplifying assumptions are introduced and experimental methods are resorted to.

Whenever the local sediment-transporting capacity is higher than the rate of supply, the equation assumes positive values and scouring occurs. If, on the other hand, the local sediment-transporting capacity is smaller than the rate of supply, the term

$$\left(\frac{d}{dt}\right) F(B)$$

becomes negative and sediment is deposited.

And finally if the sediment-transporting capacity and the rate of supply are balanced – including the case when both are zero – the term

$$\left(\frac{d}{dt}\right) F(B)$$

becomes also zero, and the channel remains unchanged.

In an integrated form Eq. $(1.1.1-3)$ is expressed by the following symbolic function

$$F(B) = F_1[g(B), g(S), t] \qquad (1.1.1-4)$$

implying that *channel development is a function of the sediment-transporting capacity, the rate of sediment supply and time.*

31

The understanding of the phenomenon of scouring was greatly promoted by the study of scouring caused by water jets. Since the first fundamental studies by H. Rouse, many such experimental studies have been reported on. These experiments have contributed to the theoretical understanding of the phenomenon of scouring.

Channel degradation due to river regulation works—including the construction of dams—may also be regarded as local erosion. Besides the above engineering measures, the rate of sediment supply related to the sediment-transporting capacity may be increased or decreased by a variety of natural phenomena. If the rate of sediment supply decreases, the channel will be degraded, if on the other hand the rate of the supply is greater than the transporting capacity, deposits will occur. Scours occur primarily downstream of dams, whereas silting is observable over the backwater reach created by the dams. These problems will be dealt with later in greater detail. In this context it should only be noted that Eq. (1.1.1−3) applies also to channel development of this nature. In this case sediment originating from the reach of scouring appears as sediment supply. In this manner the change in channel configuration will be proportionate to the rate of change of sediment transport G_S with the distance x along the water course, i.e.

$$\frac{\partial}{\partial t} F(B) = \frac{\partial}{\partial x} G_s \qquad (1.1.1-5)$$

Eq. (1.1.1−5) provides the theoretical description of the rate at which the channel is degraded or silted. However, owing to the complexity of boundary conditions, no solution is possible unless simplifying assumptions are introduced.

According to origin, sediment can be classified into two groups: sediment originating from the catchment area, and that scoured from the bottom and banks of the channel itself.

In order to indicate the place of origin the terms wash load and bed material load have been introduced in the literature.

Wash load is understood as that part of the sediment material transported, which is composed of particles finer than the bed material.

Unlike the former, the term *bed material load* indicates sediment consisting of fractions of the same size as the bed material.

Under this terminology the wash load originates exclusively in the catchment area or from the banks. It should be obvious, however, that the bed material load may originate not only from the channel bottom, but also from the catchment. For this reason, concerning the origin of sediment it is deemed advisable to classify sediment into that originating from the catchment and that from the channel.

Attempts should always be made to prevent the formation of sediment. Aside from benefits in soil conservation and melioration, the reduction of sediment volume is desirable also in hydraulic engineering practice. In fact, reduced sediment volumes in water courses would greatly simplify the engineering measures associated with water management.

Nevertheless any attempt at excluding sediment competely from water courses would be unsuccessful. Once the sediment is carried into the stream, it must be regarded as a fundamental property of the latter and, consequently, the entire sediment volume be taken into consideration when attempting to achieve balanced conditions. Consequently any effort to reduce the sediment volume must be confined to the place of its origin, namely to the catchment area.

Numerous methods are conceivable for retarding sediment formation. A familiar method yielding most direct results consists of afforestation and protection of vegetation in the catchment area. In agricultural areas appropriate cultivation methods, such as contour line ploughing or occasionally terracing may be applied to prevent or retard sediment formation. . Since the sediment is carried to the water courses mainly over gullies, the control thereof and the construction of checking dams across minor water courses in the catchment may also prove successful in reducing the sediment volume entering the recipient. In certain cases favourable topographical condition may also be utilized for creating sediment retention basins which are effective in reducing the sediment volume carried into the stream. Any detailed study of these methods would, however, exceed the scope of the present book.

1.1.1.2. The movement of sediment. Sediment entering the stream from the catchment area is carried downstream by the transporting medium, namely water. During the movement of water the potential energy is transformed into kinetic energy and part of the latter is consumed for transporting the sediment.

Moving sediment, consuming energy, invariably reduces the velocity of flow which, in turn, reduces the sediment-transporting capacity. The upper limit of transporting capacity is governed by this circumstance.

The condition under which sediment is transported is, in general, simple to describe. Already in the early stages of research into sediment movement two conditions were distinguished: *sediment moving along the bottom was termed bed load, whereas that transported in suspension in water was referred to as suspended sediment.*

Extensive investigations of the conditions of sediment transportation shortly revealed, however, that the classification into bed load and suspended sediment was unsatisfactory for describing certain boundary conditions of sediment movement.

As to the manner in which sediment is transported in the channel, a wide variety of definitions have been published in the literature on sediment transportation. Besides bed load and suspended sediment, a third type of sediment movement, namely *saltation* is often distinguished. Numerous other terms have been used beyond the foregoing ones concerning the manner of sediment movement. In view of the wide variety of terms used, some 25 to 30 years ago it was found necessary to introduce a more or less standard terminology. The terms contact load, bottom wash load, bed load identical with the channel material, suspended load, saltation load, etc. were then introduced in this way. Unfortunately, the standard terminology has not found general acceptance, but this was to be expected owing to the diversity of aspects emphasized as research advanced and to the consequent necessity of introducing new terms.

As long as the scope is a general treatment of sediment transportation unrelated to particular studies, the classification into two types is believed to be satisfactory. The saltation type of movement is considered together with the movement of bed load, and thus *sediment is preferably classified as* a) *bed load* and b) *suspended sediment*.

a) *Bed load* is transported along the bottom by sliding and rolling. It is thus essentially in contact with the bottom except for very short distances. In fact, it is conceivable that a bed load particle sliding or rolling along the bottom is forced to clear a larger particle or other obstacle and on such occasions its contact with the bottom is interrupted for a short distance.

When considering the movement of bed load, *one of the most important problems consists in determining the boundary conditions at which the sediment particle resting at the bottom is just set into motion. The other important problem* – encountered also in connection with suspended sediment movement – *is concerned with the determination of the rate of bed load transport.*

The volume of bed load transported in water courses is highly variable in natural streams.

The rate of bed load transport depends, besides the cross-sectional dimensions of the water course, also on the regime of flow therein. In some channels, or over some channel reaches, bed load is transported beyond certain stages only. This applies especially to minor rivers in mountain regions, where the energy at low stages is insufficient for conveying sediment. At falling stages the sediment particles, starting with the coarse fractions, are gradually deposited and general sediment transportation is not started again until a new flood wave passes down the river. In major plain-land streams the phenomenon of sediment transportation is a continuous one, at least if a longer reach of the river is considered. However, concerning the volume of sediment transported, considerable differences may be encountered even in plain-land rivers. It should be noted already in this context that the determination of the rate of bed load transport presents one of the most difficult problems. The problem is a highly complex and involved one so that, in spite of the great number of investigations and observations conducted for obtaining a clear picture, no satisfactory solution has been found as yet.

b) In contrast to bed load, the most important property of the *suspended sediment* is that the suspended particles move at a velocity which is closely the same as that of the water. The movement of the suspended sediment is in general more balanced than that of bed load. Changes are less pronounced and occur invariably with a certain transition. The forces maintaining sediment in suspension are, of course, subject to continuous variations entailing corresponding variations in the quality and quantity of the suspended sediment. If the force keeping sediment in suspension is reduced, the coarse particles gradually settle to the bottom, whereas if the suspending force is increased, further larger fractions may be

34

picked up. Such changes are always gradual, starting with the finer particle sizes. Suspended sediment is characteristic mostly of flat river reaches. Over steep sections the reason for the usually smaller proportion of suspended sediment is the absence of fine sediment material, rather than the insufficient magnitude of the suspending force.

The active forces, as well as the relations thereof to the hydraulic parameters of the channel, further their effect on the quality and quantity of sediment will be considered in detail in connection with the transportation of both bed load and suspended sediment.

The wash load is composed usually of fine-grained material and the bulk thereof is transported as suspended sediment. As long as the rate of sediment supply does not surpass the sediment-transporting capacity, the suspended sediment is transported practically without any consequence, without changing the configuration of the channel which, in contrast, is modified by the bed material load or bed load.

Bed load may be transported over a *smooth bottom*, but its movement is most frequently accompanied by the development of *ripples, dunes or antidunes*. The different bed forms will be discussed in detail in *Section 1.2.2*, in connection with the different boundary conditions of bed load movement.

A special type of bed load movement is referred to as sand bar travel, a phenomenon often encountered in alluvial channels. Any changes in the shape or dimension of sand bars is due, obviously, to the movement of bed load. Extensive investigations have shown that the rate of sand bar travel can be related to the Froude number, as well as to some parameter of bed load mobility, for instance the ratio of flow velocity and the settling velocity of the size fraction under consideration. Sand bar travel is closely related to river regulation, and the relevant investigations will not be discussed in detail here.

It will be clear by now that the sediment may be extremely variable as far as its material, particle size, shape, specific gravity and grain size distribution are concerned. The differences due to the origin and provenance of the sediment are obvious. However, the origin of the sediment alone leaves a number of problems unexplained. For instance, the circumstance that the diameter of a granite particle may attain or exceed 70 mm over the section of the Danube in Germany, and that 10 − 15 mm are the maximum particle diameter over the section upstream of Budapest is clearly related to bed load transportation in the river. *The properties of the water course appear to influence and modify the sediment material, establishing a balance between these properties and those of the sediment.*

The hydraulic parameters characteristic of the water course are indicative of the type of the sediment transported therein. The sediment in rapid, steep rivers or river sections is overwhelmingly coarse, consisting of large fractions. In slow streams flowing at mild slopes the sediment, on the other hand, is finely grained.

The hydraulic properties of water courses are accordingly characteristic of the sediment transported. Naturally, this conclusion can be reversed, in that *the sediment transported by a water course is characteristic of the water course itself.*

It will be appreciated from the foregoing that a complete description of a particular water course is impossible, unless the sediment conditions are taken into consideration along with the hydraulic properties. The relationships expected to exist between the hydraulic properties and the sediment conditions of a water course may be applied in particular cases also for the quantitative description of sediment transportation. The fundamental objective of theoretical and experimental research alike is invariably to relate the hydraulic parameters to the quality and quantity of sediment. The relationships determined either theoretically or experimentally provide the means for a more detailed understanding of the complex phenomenon of sediment transportation in alluvial channels.

For the sake of completeness it should be noted at the outset that studies and investigation conducted so far have demonstrated the impossibility of determining positively sediment transportation in natural channels by relying exclusively on relationships determined theoretically or in laboratory experiments. The basic importance of sediment observations in the field is emphasized by this circumstance.

1.1.2. CHARACTERISTICS OF SEDIMENT AND BED MATERIAL

1.1.2.1. Size, shape, specific gravity and granulometry of sediment. Sediment and bed material alike, as solid inorganic matter due to the weathering, decay and fragmentation of rocks, can be described in a variety of manners. For describing sediment and bed material their most essential properties involved in sediment transportation are to be selected. It should be obvious, moreover, that the properties adopted should be applicable as far as possible to bed load and suspended sediment alike and even to the material covering the bed.

For describing the sediment material it is essential to obtain information on the individual properties of sediment particles of which the sediment material is composed.

Beyond the description of individual sediment particles, for practical purposes it may be even more important to establish the characteristics of the entire sediment material. Whereas the individual properties of single particles assume importance during the theoretical treatment of sediment transportation only, the properties of the combination of particles forming the sediment material must be taken into consideration when dealing with sediment transportation as a physical phenomenon.

The most important property of individual sediment particles is their dimensions, i.e. the particle size. This would be simple to describe if the particles were spherical or other regular solid bodies. Natural sediments, however, are far from being regular in shape and, in most instances, not even the approximation by spheres is permissible. In view of the foregoing it should be obvious that one single dimension, namely the diameter, if spheres are assumed, is insufficient for characterizing the

36

Table 1.1.2 — 1

Classification of sediment according to size

Nomenclature	Millimetres	Microns
Very large boulders	4,000 — 2,000	
Large boulders	2,000 — 1,000	
Medium boulders	1,000 — 500	
Small boulders	500 — 250	
Large debris	250 — 130	
Small debris	130 — 64	
Very coarse gravel	64 — 32	
Coarse gravel	32 — 16	
Medium gravel	16 — 8	
Fine gravel	8 — 4	
Very fine gravel	4 — 2	
Very coarse sand	2.00 — 1.00	2,000 — 1,000
Coarse sand	1.00 — 0.50	1,000 — 500
Medium sand	0.50 — 0.25	500 — 250
Fine sand	0.25 — 0.125	250 — 125
Very fine sand	0.125 — 0.062	125 — 62
Coarse silt	0.062 — 0.031	62 — 31
Medium silt	0.031 — 0.016	31 — 16
Fine silt	0.016 — 0.008	16 — 8
Very fine silt	0.008 — 0.004	8 — 4
Coarse clay	0.004 — 0.0020	4 — 2
Medium clay	0.0020 — 0.0010	2 — 1
Fine clay	0.0010 — 0.0005	1 — 0.5
Very fine clay	0.0005 — 0.00024	0.5 — 0.24

sediment. Additional difficulties are due to the fact that the particle size or diameter depends in general also on the method by which it is determined.

Starting from the torrent headwater reaches down to the flat estuary sections, sediment sizes vary within an extremely wide range and include boulders of several hundred kiloponds weight down to the finest clay particles in major rivers. The sediment classification recommended by the American Geophysical Union is shown in *Table 1.1.2 — 1*.

The particle commonly involved in sediment transportation studies is seldom greater than 100 to 250 mm, but is invariably larger than 0.002 mm.

As far as possible, a single dimension is desirable for describing the sediment size. The difficulties mentioned before make it clear that, although a variety of such sizes have already been suggested in the literature, none of them has proved entirely suitable.

According to the generally accepted classification, the size of the sediment particles is commonly expressed by one of the following three linear dimensions.

a) *The settling diameter* is the diameter of a sphere having a specific gravity identical with that of the particle, the fall velocity of which is the same as that of the particle under consideration, assuming the fluids to be identical.

b) *The sieving diameter* is the smallest sieve opening through which the particle under consideration just passes.

c) *The nominal diameter* is the diameter of a sphere having a volume identical with that of the particle under consideration.

The settling and sieving diameters are most readily determined. This is why these are used almost exclusively in practice.

The settling diameter is used mostly for characterizing particles smaller than 0.1 mm, the sieves required for similarly small fractions being extremely difficult to produce. Therefore the particle size is determined with the help of a wet analysis relying on the settling (fall) velocity.

The settling diameter of natural sediments is unfortunately an inexactly defined dimension, for it depends also on the properties of the fluid in which the sedimentation test is performed. In the case of regular spheres the settling diameter is not affected by the quality of the fluid. Natural sediment particles are, however, never regular spheres and thus any change in the fluid properties which affect settling involves a change in the effect of shape. In order to eliminate the discrepancies resulting therefrom, a standard sedimentation diameter has been introduced recently, where the sedimentation test is performed in clear distilled water of 24 deg. C temperature.

In the determination of the settling diameter the settling or fall velocity assumes paramount importance, and will, therefore, be considered in detail subsequently.

The sieving diameter is used almost exclusively for size fractions greater than 0.1 mm. The mesh openings used for the sieve analysis form a geometrical sequence. The sizing analysis by sieving seems to be extremely simple to perform. In exact tests, however, minor deviations in sieve mesh widths, the thickness of the sediment layer on the sieve and the duration of sieving should also be taken into consideration.

The nominal diameter is seldom used in sediment transportation studies, and its significance is rather theoretical than practical.

Besides the three particle diameters mentioned above, increasing use has been made recently of the *triaxial dimensions* (*a, b, c*) for describing particle sizes. Here *a* is used in general for denoting the greatest, *b* the intermediate and *c* the smallest of the perpendicular dimensions.

The triaxial dimensions are believed to be less suited for describing the particle size, being representative rather of particle shape.

The particle shape is important not only when determining the fall velocity or the settling diameter, but plays an essential role in the movement of the particle itself. A variety of methods is used for describing the shape of sediment particles.

The volume constant k has been introduced by Heywood for describing the shape of sediment particles. The volume constant is defined as the ratio of the particle volume and diameter d, raised to the third power, of the sphere enveloping the horizontal projection of the particle in the most stable position. Accordingly

$$k = \frac{\text{particle volume}}{d^3} \qquad (1.1.2-1)$$

In the case of spheres

$$k = \frac{\frac{\pi d^3}{6}}{d^3} = \frac{\pi}{6} = 0.524$$

The volume constant of sediments in alluvial channels is usually smaller than 0.5 ranging commonly around 0.4. The shape factor of Heywood can be determined rather accurately especially for particles greater than 0.1 mm and describes fairly well the particle shape.

The surface constant (f) suggested by Heywood is less frequently applied for describing the shape of particles. It is defined as the ratio of the surface area of the sediment particle and the diameter raised to the second power of the circle enveloping the horizontal projection of the particle. Accordingly

$$f = \frac{\text{surface area of the particle}}{d^2} \qquad (1.1.2-2)$$

in the case of spheres

$$f = \frac{\pi d^2}{d^2} = \pi$$

The surface constant of natural sediment materials may be greater or smaller than π, but it is usually smaller.

J. S. McNown and J. Malaika assumed the sediment particles to be mostly of an ellipsoidal shape, and used the ratios of dimensions a_1, b_1 and c_1 measured along three perpendicular axes to describe the particle shape. With a_1 denoting the half-axis of the ellipsoid coinciding with the direction of movement and the two other half-axes perpendicular thereto being denoted by b_1 and c_1, the shape is characterized by the ratios $a_1/\sqrt{b_1 c_1}$, further b_1/c_1.

Depending on the relative magnitude of the half-axes, altogether eight different cases can be distinguished, the corresponding shape effects having been determining experimentally by McNown and Malaika.

The shape factor

$$\phi = \frac{V_t}{V_e} \qquad (1.1.2-3)$$

has been introduced by L. Ivicsics for describing the particle shape. In the formula V_t is the actual volume of the particle while V_e is the volume of the ellipsoid of revolution, the axes of which are defined as follows: the principal axis is the greatest linear dimension $(2a_1)$ of the horizontal projection of the particle in stable position, while the minor axis is the second largest dimension $(d = 2b_1)$ measured also in the horizontal projection in a direction perpendicular to the first. The axis of revolution coincides with the direction of $2a_1$. Accordingly

$$V_e = \frac{4}{3} \pi a_1 b_1^2$$

If the actual volume of the particle equals the volume of the ellipsoid of revolution, the shape factor Φ becomes unity. In alluvial streams the shape factor Φ of the sediment ranges mostly from 0.2 to 0.9. Low values of Φ indicate usually flat, scaly particles.

The triaxial dimensions a, b, c have been introduced recently for describing the particle shape. With a denoting the longest, b the intermediate and c the shortest dimension of the particle along three perpendicular axes, the triaxial shape factor becomes

$$SF = \frac{c}{\sqrt{ab}} \tag{1.1.2-4}$$

Using the triaxial dimensions, the *flatness index i* has been introduced by Cailleaux, and defined as

$$i = \frac{a + b}{2c}$$

The flatness index has been adopted in the Hungarian standard specifications as well.

According to investigations by E. Török on the Danube, the magnitude of the flatness index i is practically the same for the same types of rock.

None of the shape factors has proved to be perfect, each showing certain drawbacks. In the case of the triaxial shape factor, for instance, the value thereof is affected by the axis selected first, since the magnitude of the remaining two is already determined by the selection of the former.

The extent of wearing has also been used for describing particle shapes. According to Tester the extent of wearing is the length ratio of worn edges to the original ones, i.e. the extent K of wearing is, with the notation of *Fig. 1.1.2–1*,

$$K = \frac{(AB + BC + CD + DA) - (aa' + bb' + cc' + dd')}{AB + BC + CD + DA} \tag{1.1.2-5}$$

or

$$K = \frac{\Sigma l - \Sigma l'}{\Sigma l} \tag{1.1.2-6}$$

The extent K of wearing expressed as a percentage value is characteristic of the roundness of the sediment particle.

40

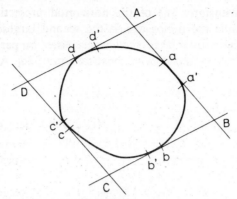

Fig. 1.1.2—1. Definition sketch for measuring bed load wear

An arbitrary classification has also been suggested by Tester. Accordingly
for $K = 81 - 100\%$ the particle is rounded
for $K = 61 - 80\%$ the particle is slightly rounded
for $K = 41 - 60\%$ the particle is slightly angular
for $K = 21 - 40\%$ the particle is angular
for $K = 0 - 20\%$ the particle is strongly angular
Another measure used for describing the shape of sediment particles is *angularity*
which is understood as the ratio of actual edge length to the original one. With
reference to the notation of *Fig. 1.1.2—1*

$$\text{angularity} = \frac{aa' + bb' + cc' + dd'}{AB + BC + CD + DA} = \frac{\Sigma l'}{\Sigma l} \qquad (1.1.2-7)$$

For describing the shape of sediment particles the *"degree of rolling"* has been
used by Mrs. Pécsi (E. Donáth) and E. Szádeczki-Kardos. The degree of rolling
is expressed in terms of the distance travelled by the sediment particles, and of the
length of the convex parts, as well as of straight parts on the horizontal projection of the gravel particles. The rolling degree is used commonly in geological
studies.

Another parameter indicating the properties, especially wearing, of sediment
particles, is the *frictional or sliding angle* of the sediment.

According to studies by K. Stelczer:

in a wet condition the sliding angle of surfaces with natural roughness is
$\alpha = 21 - 35°$;

in a dry condition the sliding angle ranges from 19 to 39°.

A property particular to each sediment is *specific gravity* which can be computed by any suitable method from the weight and actual volume of the sediment.
The specific gravity of sediments transported in alluvial streams varies within a
rather narrow range. The specific gravity of the lightest mineral components is
2.1, whereas that of the heaviest ones may be up to 2.8 [p/cm^3].

41

For *mineralogical analyses* the sediment is usually divided into the heavy fractions with a specific gravity greater than 2.75 and the light-weight fractions having specific gravities lower than the above value. The heavy fraction is in general no more than $1-5\%$ of the sediment material, but often it is only 1% or even less.

The differences observable in the specific gravity of individual sediment particles are even smaller if the entire sediment material is considered. The specific gravity of sediment material in alluvial streams is mostly around 2.65. It is for this reason that in studies concerning sediment transportation a specific gravity $\gamma_1 = 2.65$ $[p/cm^3]$ is commonly assumed.

*

For a general description of the sediment material its *pore volume* should also be specified. This is obtained by relating the difference of the apparent and actual volumes to the apparent volume.

In discussing the theory of sediment transportation the concept of *sediment density* has been introduced by Soviet investigators as the ratio of sediment volume to the entire volume.

Under natural conditions the bulk density of deposited sediment material may also be of interest. This is logically always lower than the specific gravity of the sediment particles of which the deposit consists. The bulk density of deposited sediment may be used in estimating the percentage loss of reservoir volume on account of silting.

Extensive investigations have been carried out by E. W. Lane and W. A. Koelzer with the objective of determining the bulk density of a wide variety of deposited sediments. The bulk density of such sediments is affected by the mechanical grain size distribution of the material deposited, by the surroundings of the deposit and by the time elapsed since deposition. Gravels and coarse sands attain the final bulk density practically upon deposition. On the other hand, the initial bulk density of silt and clay deposits is usually very low and increases gradually with time. Studies into the bulk density of sediment deposits assume importance in the dimensioning of reservoirs.

The sediment transported in alluvial water courses always consists of a mixture of sediment particles of different size, specific gravity and shapes. In practical problems the entire sediment mass is of primary interest, and therefore information on the size, specific gravity, shape yet even mineralogical composition is of paramount importance.

Differences in shape, specific gravity and mineralogy are essential in many respects but, since for a particular sediment material the variations in these properties are limited to a rather narrow range and since these changes have fairly small impact on the movement of the entire sediment, these variations are neglected in most instances.

In studies on sediment material, *the distribution and relative proportions of particle sizes* or of the sieving and sedimentation size fractions introduced in lieu of these are essential. This is why the first step in obtaining information on a particular sediment material consists of separation into different size fractions and the determination of the percentages by weight of the individual size fractions. Once these percentages are available, the most important property of sediment materials, namely the granulometric curve, can be traced. The determination of the granulometric curve is commonly referred to in the literature as the *mechanical analysis*.

A variety of methods have been suggested for tracing the *granulometric curve*. In the case of coarse sediments an arithmetic scale can be used, whereas a semi-logarithmic plot may be advisable if the sediment contains appreciable pro-portions of fine grains. In recent times arithmetic and logarithmic probability plots have found widespread application for representing the granulometric curve.

The grain size distribution of the sediment material is shown without distortion in an *arithmetic plot*. The composition of bed load material of the Danube in the Dunaremete gaging section is shown in *Fig. 1.1.2−2*.

An arithmetic plot of the granulometric curve is a visual indication of the size fractions comprised in the particular sediment material. Since, however, well defined index numbers characterizing sediment composition are necessary, for computations associated with sediment transportation such numbers representing the size and granulometry of the sediment have been introduced by definition. To a certain extent these index numbers deviate from those used in soil mechanics and material testing. It should be realized that the introduction of similar index numbers is unavoidable even if semilogarithmic and probability plots are used.

The mean diameter may be regarded as the most important index number. It is denoted by d_g [mm] which is obtained, according to *Fig. 1.1.2− 2*, by equating the areas under and above the granulometric curve, i.e. by making the horizontally and vertically shaded areas equal. In the relevant literature on the mean particle diameter the subscript is often omitted, denoting the mean particle diameter briefly by d only.

If the percentages by weight pertaining to the individual size fractions d are denoted by p, the mean diameter is obtained numerically as

$$d_g = \frac{\sum\limits_{p=0}^{p=100} d\, \Delta p}{\sum\limits_{p=0}^{p=100} \Delta p} = \frac{F_a + F_b}{100} \qquad (1.1.2-8)$$

The median particle diameter, denoted d_m [mm] is the particle diameter pertaining to 50% (see *Fig. 1.1.2−2*).

As a numerical value for the *fineness of the sediment* an index number has been introduced by Schoklitsch. This has been defined as the ratio of the areas above and below the granulometric curve, so that with reference to *Fig. 1.1.2−2*

$$s = \frac{a}{b} \qquad (1.1.2-9)$$

Fig. 1.1.2—2. Granulometric curve of bed load sample from Dunaremete, arithmetic plot

Sediment factor *s* is a dimensionless number. When comparing the *s* factors of several sediments, it should be remembered to plot the granulometric curves of all sediment materials in diagrams where the largest particle size is the same. The largest particle diameter of the diagram should be selected to accommodate even the largest-size fraction encountered. Under conditions prevailing in Hungary this value is usually 100 mm (see *Fig. 1.1.2—2*).

Factor *s* may assume any arbitrary positive value. The higher its value, the coarser the sediment material.

In earlier investigations the fineness of the sediment was commonly described by the linear fineness which was defined as the number of sediment particles that could be placed end to end along unit length.

For denoting the uniformity of grain size distribution, the *uniformity coefficient* *M* has been suggested by Kramer. The uniformity coefficient *M* has been defined as the ratio of the area F_a and the area F_b under, respectively, above the median particle diameter d_m. Accordingly, with the notations of *Fig. 1.12—2*.

$$M = \frac{F_a}{F_b} \qquad (1.1.2-10)$$

The uniformity coefficient is also a dimensionless number. In the case of sediments composed of identical particles the granulometric curve will be a vertical straight line at a given particle diameter. Consequently $F_a = F_b$ and thus $M = 1$. If the sediment consists of a mixture of different size fractions, the value of *M* will invariably be lower than unity.

The granulometric curve is essentially an integral curve, indicating the percentages of particles smaller or larger than a particular diameter present in the sediment material under consideration. Valuable information is often obtained by plotting the *frequency distribution curve* of the particles. The frequency distribution curve

44

Fig. 1.1.2—3. Frequency distribution curve of bed load material from Dunaremete

is the differential curve of the granulometric curve. The frequency distribution of the bed load material at Dunaremete indicated in *Fig. 1.1.2—2* is shown in *Fig. 1.1.2—3*. Here the ordinate pertaining to the individual particle sizes d indicates the frequency expressed as percentages by weight of the particles comprised in a 1 mm wide interval in the vicinity of d. If the width of the interval were n mm instead 1 mm, then the frequency of the particles comprised in the n mm wide interval in the vicinity of the particle diameter, d would be np, instead of the weight percentage p indicated in *Fig. 1.1.2—3*.

In the differential curve the maximum percentage by weight p_{max} is observable at the same particle size where the granulometric curve displays a point of counterflexure. The vertical line passing through the center of gravity of the area enclosed by the differential curve and the horizontal axis is defined by the mean particle diameter d_g.

Fig. 1.1.2—4. Granulometric curve of suspended sediment in the Danube, semilogarithmic plot

Fig. 1.1.2−5. Granulometric curve of suspended sediment in the Danube, arithmetic plot

The mean diameter, the uniformity coefficient of granulometry, as well as the index number of sediment fineness can be determined graphically from the arithmetic plot of the granulometric curve.

The granulometric curve is most commonly represented in a semilogarithmic plot, which is the only possible method of representation if the greatest and smallest particles present in the sediment material differ from one another by several orders of magnitude. The granulometry of suspended sediment in the Medve gaging section of the Danube is represented by a semilogarithmic plot in *Fig. 1.1.2−4.* The grain size distribution of the same suspended sediment is shown in an arithmetic plot in *Fig. 1.1.2−5,* whereas the corresponding frequency distribution curve is illustrated in *Fig. 1.1.2−6.*

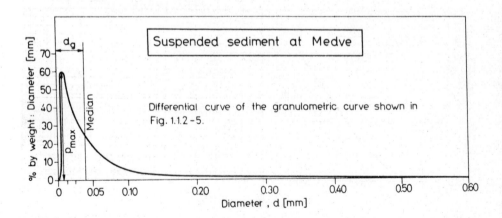

Fig. 1.1.2−6. Frequency distribution curve of suspended sediment in the Danube

46

Fig. 1.1.2–7. Arithmetic probability plot of the granulometric
curve of suspended sediment in the Danube

The median particle diameter is obtained visually from the semilogarithmic plot
of the granulometric curve, in the same manner as in the case of arithmetic plotting.
On the other hand, the mean diameter, the uniformity coefficient of granulometry
and the index number of sediment fineness must be determined by computation if
a semilogarithmic plot is used.

In certain cases it is common practice to use the ratio of the largest and mean
particle diameters for describing the quality of sediment material consisting of
different size fractions. The ratio d_{max}/d_g is preferred especially by Soviet investigators.

It should be noted in this context, that in theoretical studies on sediment transportation a wide variety of particle diameters have been used in the literature. For
instance the diameters d_{35} and d_{90} have been used by Einstein, respectively by
Meyer-Peter, denoting the diameters at 35 and 90 per cents by weight passing.

The *arithmetic probability plot* can be used to advantage if the granulometry of
the sediment shows a normal distribution. In this kind of plotting, sediments with
a normal size distribution are represented by a straight line. From the arithmetic
probability plot the mean particle diameter is obtained directly at 50% probability
and the standard deviation σ is obtained similarly from the expression

$$\sigma = d_{84.1} - d_{50} = d_{50} - d_{15.9} \qquad (1.1.2-11)$$

where $d_{84.1}$, d_{50} and $d_{15.9}$ denote diameters at 84.1%, 50% and 15.9% of the sediment
material passing. It should be noted, however, that the arithmetic probability

47

Fig. 1.1.2—8. Logarithmic probability plot of the granulometric curve
of suspended sediment in the Danube

plot is rarely suited for representing natural sediment materials, these being of
normal distribution in exceptional cases only.

The suspended sediment at Medve considered before has been represented as an
example in the arithmetic probability plot in *Fig. 1.1.2 — 7*. The granulometric curve
will be seen to plot to a line which is by no means a straight one.

The *logarithmic probability* plot has become popular recently for representing
the granulometric curve. This is entirely similar to the arithmetic probability plot,
the only difference being that the particle sizes are plotted to a logarithmic scale.
In this method of representation the granulometric curve of natural sediment
materials is more often approximated by a straight line. Where it is truly possible
to replace the granulometric curve by a straight line, d_{50} will become equal to the
geometrical median diameter which — displaying the same properties as the mean
diameter — is also denoted by d_g.

The geometrical standard deviation σ_g is obtained from the expression

$$\sigma_g = \sqrt{\frac{d_{84.1}}{d_{15.9}}} \qquad (1.1.2-12)$$

It is interesting to note that low values of σ_g are usually associated with small
d_g values, frequently in large streams. In the case of coarse sediment materials, i.e.
where d_g is relatively great, the geometrical standard deviation σ_g is also relatively
higher.

48

The granulometry of suspended sediment taken from the Medve gaging section on the Danube river is represented in a logarithmic probability plot in *Fig. 1.1.2−8*. The grain size distribution curve in the figure is not represented by a straight line, not even the section between 84.1 and 15.9% is striaght. It has been demonstrated by G. H. Otto, who has conducted detailed studies on the representation of granulometric curves in the logarithmic probability plot, that in this case the geometrical median diameter d_g is given as the intersection of the line connecting the 84.1 and 15.9% values with the line indicating 50%.

The geometrical standard deviation σ_g is, according to Eq. (1.1.2−12),

$$\sigma_g = \sqrt{\frac{0{,}068}{0.0077}} = 2.95$$

`and is thus seen to be rather high.

A drawback of the probability method of representation is that its use is restricted to the types of sediment granulometry in which the curvature of the grain size distribution curve is of a constant sign, with points of counterflexure occurring at the most at low and at very high percentages only. The application of the method is found impossible in the case of curves with a pronounced "S" curvature.

1.1.2.2. The mineralogical composition of sediment. The sediments in alluvial streams comprise fragments of several kinds of rock and crystals of a wide variety of minerals. The mineralogical composition of the sediment may vary from river to river, yet even from section to section on the same river. Moreover, variations in sediment mineralogy may be observable even on the same river, or river section, in different seasons and as a function of river regime. This is the reason why repeated samples must be taken from several sections if detailed information is desired on the mineralogy of sediment carried by a particular water course. No general rule can be given for the spacing of sampling sections and the frequency of sampling should also be selected by careful judgement. On smaller rivers 2−3 sampling points and samples taken from these at low and high stages are believed to be sufficient. On major streams the spacing of sampling sections may vary between very wide limits, such as 15 to 100 km, depending on the number of tributaries. On major streams it is advisable to take samples at low and high stages occurring in different seasons.

Information on the mineralogical composition is a valuable contribution to the characteristics of sediment material, since fragments of rocks and crystals of minerals are typical of both the specific giavity and the shape and, in many instances, even of particle size.

From the mineralogy of sediment conclusions may be drawn, in certain instances, concerning the place of sediment origin. It should be obvious, however, that the accurate determination of the place of origin is impossible without extensive and lengthy explorations.

As an illustrative example, data are given subsequently on the mineralogical composition of sediment transported by the Danube and the Tisza rivers, and an attempt will be made to summarize the information obtainable therefrom.

It is of interest to note that petrographic studieson the comm on Hungarian–Czechoslovak section of the Danube have recently been performed by E. Hornis and E. Török.

To our knowledge extremely thorough and detailed studies have been performed in Austria and Czechoslovakia on the mineralogical composition of sediment transported by the Danube. Any detailed account of the results obtained would exceed by far the scope of this book, so that the present considerations will be confined to the mineralogy of individual sediment samples.

The bulk of sediment in, Danube originates in the Alps. Concerning its mineralogical composition, the fragmented, worn particles of about 20 to 25 different rocks are contained therein. The majority of sediment consists of quarz, limestone and crystalline shale. Beyond these considerable amounts of amphibole, piroxene and granite are contained.

The conventional sediment-petrographical methods have been used for the analyses* including the application of the binocular and polarized-light microscope.

In order to prepare the sediment particles for analysis the carbonate and limonite layer has been removed first using a 30% solution of HCl, whereafter they were thoroughly rinsed with distilled water. Bromoform adjusted to 2.75 specific gravity was then used for separating the sediment material into heavy and light-weight fractions. The mineralogical composition of the material prepared in this way was determined under a polarized-light microscope. A drawback of this method is that the minerals approximating in specific gravity that of the discriminating limit are difficult to separate. For this reason some minerals are encountered among the heavy and light-weight fractions alike in the tables showing the mineralogical composition. It should be noted here that the inclusion of quartz among the heavy fractions can be traced back to ore impurities.

The tables showing the analytical results indicate the mean, maximum and minimum particle sizes present in the sediment sample, while as an indication of particle shape the percentage of minerals of spherical, rounded, prismatic, flat or fragmented-irregular form is also given. The ratio r of the longest and shortest dimension of mineral components is also an indication of particle shape in the case of bed load and bottom material. For spherical particles $r = 1$. Higher values of r indicate elongated minerals.

*It should be noted here that all sediment samples have been analysed for mineralogical composition at the Chair for Mineralogy and Geology, Budapest Technical University. The analytical work was performed by P. Kertész and I. Meizl under the guidance of the late professor F. Papp.

Analytical results* for a suspended sediment and a bed load sample taken from the Nagymaros section of the Danube (see *Fig. 3.1.2—3)* have been compiled in *Tables 1.1.2—2* and *1.1.2—3*.

From the table containing the analytical results obtained on the suspended sediment the mean particle size and the *r* value of the minerals have been omitted, their determination being uncertain owing to the cohesion of small particles.

These tables show the percentage occurrence of heavy and light-weight fractions, together with the mineralogical composition of material for the corresponding fractions and, on the basis of these figures, for the total sample.

No data are given on the mineralogy of the material at Nagymaros, as it is found more expedient to describe the material composed of coarse fractions by the analysis of individual gravels.

Most gravels are well-rounded, though their shape is greatly influenced by the quality of rock at the place of origin. In general, most gravels are approximately ellipsoidal, their petrography being rather variable. Crystalline shale (with quartz and muscovite as the main minerals) of 7 by 4 cm size, quartzite of 1 cm size, gneiss (including quartz, feldspar, biotite and muscovite minerals) of 1 cm size, brown muscovitic sandstone (with limonite, quartz and muscovite minerals) of 1 cm size, weathered biotite-granite (with biotite, quartz, orthoclase and oligoclase minerals) of 2 cm size, further several smaller quartz and limestone gravels were found among them. A thin section prepared from a gravel of sericite shale taken from the bottom material at Nagymaros has shown the dominant minerals to be quartz, sericite, biotite, chlorite, appreciable amount of limonite and little feldspar.

The mineralogical composition of sediment at Nagymaros is rather consistent, although certain differences are observable in the amount of ores.

From among the heavy minerals amphiboles, limonite and biotite are predominant in the suspended sediment, whereas granate and amphiboles in the bed load and limonite, biotite and amphiboles in the bed material.

From among the light-weight minerals the suspended sediment contains considerable amounts of quartz, muscovite and calcite, the bed load quartz, plagioclase and quartzite, the bed material, on the other hand, quartz and plagioclase.

Concerning the origin of the sediment material, most reliable information is obtained from the gravels of the bed material and the minerals of the bed load.

The gravels of the bed material stem from metamorphic rocks, mainly from the Alps, although the possibility that the material from the Csallóköz talus of the Danube has been washed into the Nagymaros basin cannot be excluded. The granite gravels found in the bottom material is likewise of Alpine origin.

*In the discussion of both theoretical and empirical relationships reference will be made to several rivers in Europe, as well as numerous rivers in Hungary and gaging stations along them. The geographical location of these is shown in three figures. *Fig. 3.1.2—1*, indicates the major rivers in Europe together with the corresponding catchment areas *Fig. 3.1.2—2* shows the catchment of the Danube (including all Hungarian rivers), while in *Fig. 3.1.2—3* the rivers of Hungary and the network of sediment observation stations in Hungary have been entered.

Table 1.1.2—2

Mineralogical composition of suspended sediment in the Danube at Nagymaros

Mineral component	Spherical particles	Rounded particles	Prismatic particles	Laminar particles	Fragment-ed irregular particles	%-age present
			percentage			

Heavy fraction (specific gravity greater than 2.75), 5% of the material

Mineral component	Spherical	Rounded	Prismatic	Laminar	Fragmented irregular	%-age present
Magnetite	—	100	—	—	—	6
Hematite	—	100	—	—	—	6
Limonite	100	—	—	—	—	18
Amphibole	—	—	100	—	—	25
Turmaline	—	—	100	—	—	2
Biotite	—	—	—	100	—	15
Muskovite	—	—	—	100	—	5
Chlorite	—	—	—	100	—	15
Quartz	—	—	—	—	100	2
Granate	—	—	—	—	100	4
Hyperstene	—	—	100	—	—	2
						100

Light-weight fraction (specific gravity smaller than 2.75), 95% of the material

Mineral component	Spherical	Rounded	Prismatic	Laminar	Fragmented irregular	%-age present
Quartz	—	—	—	—	100	55
Calcite	—	—	—	—	100	15
Muskovite	—	—	—	100	—	18
Chlorite	—	—	—	100	—	2
Plagioclase	—	—	—	—	100	4
Limonite	100	—				6
			as coating			100

Heavy and light-weight fractions combined

Mineral component	Spherical	Rounded	Prismatic	Laminar	Fragmented irregular	%-age present
Quartz	—	—	—	—	100	52.35
Muskovite	—	—	—	100	—	17.35
Calcite	—	—	—	—	100	14.25
Limonite	100	—	—	—	—	6.60
Plagioclase	—	—	—	—	100	3.80
Chlorite	—	—	—	100	—	2.65
Amphibole	—	—	100	—	—	1.25
Biotite	—	—	—	100	—	0.75
Magnetite	—	100	—	—	—	0.30
Hematite	—	100	—	—	—	0.30
Granate	—	—	—	—	100	0.20
Turmaline	—	—	100	—	—	0.10
Hyperstene	—	—	100	—	—	0.10
						100.00

Table 1.1.2—3

Mineralogical composition of bed load in the Danube at Nagymaros

Mineral component	Particle size mm	Spherical	Rounded	Prismatic	Laminar	Fragmented, irregular	Average value of r	%-age present
		particles						
		percentage						
Heavy fraction (specific gravity greater than 2.75), 10% of the material								
Magnetite	0.2	—	100	—	—	—	1.3	7
Limonite	0.3	—	100	—	—	—	1.1	3
Pirite	0.15	—	—	—	—	100	1.4	2
Ilmenite	0.1	—	—	—	—	100	1.0	1
Green amphibole	0.5	—	—	75	—	25	1.5	15
Antofillite	0.4	—	—	100	—	—	1.4	0.5
Hyperstene	0.45	—	—	100	—	—	2.0	3
Augite	0.5	—	—	100	—	—	1.4	2
Turmaline	0.3	—	—	100	—	—	17.0	0.2
Biotite	0.3	—	—	—	100	—	33.0	4
Chlorite	0.3	—	—	—	100	—	33.0	5
Muskovite	0.3	—	—	—	100	—	33.0	2
Sillimanite	0.4	—	—	100	—	—	9.8	0.1
Granate	0.2	—	—	—	—	100	1.3	55
Quartz	0.5	—	100	—	—	—	1.3	0.2
								100.0
Light-weight fraction (specific gravity smaller than 2.75), 90% of the material								
Quartz	0.5	13	21	—	—	66	1.3	75
Plagioclase	0.4	—	—	—	—	100	1.3	10
Calcite	0.3	—	20	—	—	80	1.4	10
Muskovite	0.6	—	—	—	100	—	33.0	5
Limonite								—
Chlorite			as coating rare particles				33.0	—
								100
Heavy and light-weight fractions combined								
Quartz	0.5	12	29	—	—	59	1.3	67.52
Plagioclase	0.4	—	—	—	—	100	1.3	9.00
Calcite	0.3	—	20	—	—	80	1.4	9.00
Granate	0.2	—	—	—	—	100	1.3	5.50
Muskovite	0.6	—	—	—	100	—	33.0	4.70
Amphiboles	0.5	—	—	75	—	25	1.5	1.55
Magnetite	0.2	—	100	—	—	—	1.3	0.70
Chlorite	0.3	—	—	—	100	—	33.0	0.50
Biotite	0.3	—	—	—	100	—	33.0	0.40
Hyperstene	0.45	—	—	100	—	—	2.0	0.30
Limonite	0.30	—	100	—	—	—	1.1	0.30
Pirite	0.15	—	—	—	—	100	1.4	0.20
Augite	0.5	—	—	100	—	—	1.4	0.20
Ilmenite	0.1	—	—	—	—	100	1.0	0.10
Turmaline	0.3	—	—	100	—	—	17.0	0.02
Sillimanite	0.4	—	—	100	—	—	9.8	0.01
								100.00

The most frequent mineral present in the bed load is quartz, some of which originates from metamorphic rocks. These may result from the total fragmentation of metamorphic rock debris still encountered at the surface, and from sedimentary rocks during the formation of which debris material has found access to the deposit from metamorphic areas as well. Another portion of quartz originates primarily from some acidic volcanic rock and secondarily from sedimentary rocks such as sands and sand stones. The second possibility is a more likely one. Consequently the majority of quartz, together with part of the quartz from metamorphic rocks originate from the Upper Oligocene sand stones encountered along the Danube. These are the likely sources of granates as well, although some of the granates originate from the granate-bearing andezites commonly encountered in the Dunazug and Börzsöny ranges. Plagioclases, amphiboles, piroxenes and biotites have found access to the Danube by the comminution of andezites encountered in the immediate vicinity. Most of the calcite can be traced back to the calcite veins developed in the fissures of the andezite in the hydrothermal phase. Owing to its chemical composition, but mainly to its softness, this mineral is uncapable of resisting transportation over longer distances. Most of the chlorite is washed from the Upper Oligocene sands and sandstones into the Danube. Among the minerals included in the tables the occurrence of sillimanite is worthy of special interests; this has been transported into the Danube from the metamorphic inclusions encountered in the andezite rocks in the Börzsöny range at Szob and Zebegény.

The high proportion of calcite, limonite and moscovite is conspicuous among the minerals of the suspended sediment. The higher proportion of calcite, carbonates and limonite can be explained by the fact that most of the calcium carbonate ($CaCO_3$) continuously formed in the rivers is transported in the form of suspended sediment.

The character of rocks is truly reflected by the sediment in the Tisza river. The mineralogical composition of samples taken from the sediment and bedmaterial at Tiszabő (see *Fig. 3.1.2−3)* has been determined in detail.

According to the analysis of the sediment samples from Tiszabő, the mineralogical composition of suspended sediment, bed load and bed material is rather consistent, although the relative proportion of ores is variable. The results of analyses performed on samples from Tiszabő have been compiled in *Tables 1.1.2−4, 1.1.2−5* and *1.1.2−6.*

Among the heavy minerals present in the suspended sediment, bed load and bed material, limonite, ilmenite, muscovite, amphibole, piroxene and chlorite, among the light-weight minerals, quartz and plagioclase are found to predominate. The heavy mineral components represent $0.0-1.4\%$ of the total material.

Piroxene, amphibole and chlorite originate from the andezite area between Tokaj and Sátoraljaújhely. Plagioclase, quartz, granate and some of the ilmenite stems from the same area. The carbonate rock fragments determined in the bed material originate from the catchment of the Hernád river and from the limestone dolomite area around Košice.

1.1.2.3. The fall velocity of sediment particles. Any particle of a specific gravity greater than that of water will, when placed into water, sink to the bottom under the influence of gravity, i.e. will tend to perform downward motion, which is counteracted by the resistance of water. The drag resistance will depend on the size and shape, the surface quality of the particle, on the density and viscosity of the fluid, as well as on the fall velocity of the particle. The drag resistance is composed of the shape resistance and the frictional force developed on the surface of the particle. Obviously, the effects of gravity force, as well as of the shape and frictional resistance arise simultaneously. Concerning the magnitude of shape resistance and the resistance due to surface friction experiments have indicated the shape resistance to predominate in the case of larger particles, whereas in the case of the smaller ones, friction plays the decisive role.

Depending on their size, specific gravity, shape and on the temperature of water, the distance travelled downward by the settling particles will be different, i.e. the fall velocity of particles will be different in accordance with the factors mentioned above.

1. The fall velocity of spherical particles. Sediment particles are most conveniently replaced by spheres. It is for this reason that the majority of experimental and theoretical data apply to the fall velocity of spherical particles. Although natural sediments are never regular spheres, it appears expedient to discuss first the fall velocity of regular spheres.

The first exact formula for the fall velocity of spherical particles was published in 1851 by Stokes. According to the Stokes law a solid particle having a specific gravity greater than that of the fluid will settle under the action of gravity, after certain initial acceleration with constant velocity in the fluid at rest, assuming the particle to be large enough to overcome the forces giving rise to Brownian movement. According to the assumption introduced by Stokes this constant velocity depends, besides the submerged weight of the particle, exclusively on the viscosity of the fluid. The downward force acting on the particle equals, accordingly, the effect of gravity minus the bouyant force exerted by the fluid on the particle, so that the downward force is

$$G' = \frac{\pi d^3}{6} g(\rho_1 - \rho) \qquad (1.1.2.-13)$$

where d [cm] = the diameter of the particle,

ρ_1 and ρ [psec^2 cm^{-4}] = densities of the particle and fluid, resp.

g [cm sec^{-2}] = acceleration due to gravity.

The drag force acting against gravity is

$$E = 3 \pi d \mu \omega \qquad (1.1.2-14)$$

where μ [p sec cm^{-2}] = the coefficient of absolute viscosity

ω [cm sec^{-1}] = the fall velocity.

Table 1.1.2—4

Mineralogical composition of suspended sediment in the Tisza River at Tiszabő

Mineral component	Particle size, mm	Spheri-cal	Round-ed	Prisma-tic	Lami-nar	Average value of r	%-age present
				particles			
				percentage			

Heavy fraction (specific gravity greater than 2.75), 0.9% of the material

Granate	0.02—0.1	100	—	—	—	—	10
Amphibole	0.03—0.08	80	20	—	—	—	10
Phyroxene	0.04—0.07	70	30	—	—	—	7
Turmaline	0.01—0.03	—	—	100	—	—	3
Chlorite	0.04—0.18	—	—	—	100	—	10
Muskovite	0.02—0.25	—	—	—	100	—	27
Ilmenite	0.02—0.07	—	100	—	—	—	3
Limonite	0.03—0.17			Irregular			30
							100

Light-weight fraction (specific gravity smaller than 2.75), 99.1% of the material

Quartz	0.01—0.22	85	15	—	—	—	65
Feldspar	0.07—0.13	60	40	—	—	—	1
Plagioclase	0.04—0.10	50	50	—	—	—	1
Muskovite	0.02—0.24	—	—	—	100	—	8
Clayey particles	0.01—0.20	—	—	—	—	—	25
							100

Heavy and light-weight fractions combined

Quartz	0.01—0.22	85	15	—	—	—	65
Feldspar	0.07—0.13	60	40	—	—	—	1
Plagioclase	0.04—0.1	50	50	—	—	—	1
Muskovite	0.02—0.25	—	—	—	100	—	8
Chlorite	0.04—0.18	—	—	—	100	—	0.0x
Granate	0.02—0.1	100	—	—	—	—	0.0x
Amphibole	0.03—0.08	80	20	—	—	—	0.0x
Pyroxene	0.04—0.07	70	30	—	—	—	0.0x
Turmaline	0.01—0.03	—	—	100	—	—	0.0x
Ilmenite	0.02—0.07	—	100	—	—	—	0.0x
Limonite	0.03—0.17			Irregular			0.x
Clayey particles	0.01—0.20						25
							100

Note: "0.0x" and "0.x" denote quantities of one-hundredth and one-tenth order of magnitude, respectively, but defying any accurate determination

56

Table 1.1.2—5

Mineralogical composition of bed load in the Tisza River at Tiszabő

Mineral component	Particle size, mm	Spherical	Rounded	Prismatic	Laminar	Average value of *r*	%-age present
		particles percentage					
Heavy fraction (specific greater than 2.75), 1.2% of the material							
Granate	0.2—0.7	100	—	—	—	1 —1.1	10
Muskovite	0.1—0.9	—	—	—	100	1.2—1.6	19
Biotite	0.3—0.5	—	—	—	100	1.3—1.5	1
Chlorite	0.4—0.7	—	—	—	100	1.2—1.8	10
Amphibole	0.3—0.6	—	20	80	—	1.7—2.6	16
Pyroxene	0.2—0.4	—	—	100	—	1.6—2.7	17
Turmaline	0.1—0.2	—	—	100	—	2 —3	4
Epidotite	0.1—0.2	—	—	100	—	1.5—2.5	2
Magnetite	∼0.1	100	—	—	—	∼1	1
Ilmenite	∼0.1	—	100	—	—	1.2—1.5	8
Limonite	0.1—0.8	Irregular					12
							100
Light-weight fraction (specific gravity smaller than 2.75), 98.8% of the material							
Quartz with inclusions	0.2—0.8	—	100	—	—	1.1—1.9	69
Encrusted quartz	0.2—0.7	—	100	—	—	1.2—1.9	11
Plagioclase	0.3—0.6	—	35	65	—	1.7—2.3	7
Microline	0.4—0.5	—	30	70	—	1.6—2.3	1
Muskovite	0.3—0.8	—	—	—	100	1.4—1.3	12
							100
Heavy fraction (specific greater than 2.75), 1.4% of the material							
Quartz with inclusions	0.2—0.8	—	100	—	—	1.1—1.9	68
Encrusted quartz	0.2—0.7	—	100	—	—	1.2—1.9	11
Microline	0.4—0.5	—	30	70	—	1.6—2.3	1
Plagioclase	0.3—0.6	—	35	65	—	1.7—2.3	7
Muskovite	0.1—0.9	—	—	—	100	1.2—1.6	12
Biotite	0.3—0.5	—	—	—	100	1.3—1.5	0.0x
Chlorite	0.4—0.7	—	—	—	100	1.2—1.8	0.x
Granate	0.2—0.7	100	—	—	—	1 —1.1	0.x
Amphibole	0.3—0.6	—	20	80	—	1.7—2.6	0.x
Pyroxene	0.2—0.4	—	20	80	—	1.6—2.7	0.x
Turmaline	0.1—0.2	—	—	100	—	2 —3	0.0x
Epidotite	0.1—0.2	—	—	100	—	1.5—2.5	0.0x
Magnetite	∼0.1	100	—	—	—	∼1	0.0x
Ilmenite	∼0.1	—	100	—	—	1.2—1.5	0.0x
Limonite	0.1—0.8	Irregular					0.x
							99

Note: "0.0x" and "0.x" denote quantities of one-hundredth and one-tenth order of magnitude, respectively, but defying any accurate determination

Table 1.1.2—6

Mineralogical composition of bed material of the Tisza River at Tiszabő

Mineral component	Particle size, mm	Spheri-cal	Round-ed	Prisma-tic	Lami-nar	Average value of r	%-age present
		particles					
		percentage					
Granate	0.2—0.7	100	—	—	—	~1	11
Pyroxene	0.3—0.4	70	30	—	—	1.8—3.2	16
Ilmenite	0.2—0.3	—	100	—	—	1.2—1.7	6
Epidotite	0.2—0.3	—	—	100	—	1.9—2.7	2
Amphibole	0.3—0.7	20	80	—	—	1.8—3.1	14
Chlorite	0.2—0.5	—	—	—	100	1.3—1.5	13
Limonite	0.2—0.4	Irregular					5
Calcite, or dolomite	0.4—0.6	—	100	—	—	1.4—1.6	6
Muskovite	0.6—1.2	—	—	—	100	1.3—1.7	27
							100

Light-weight fraction (specific gravity smaller than 2.75), 98.6% of the material

Mineral component	Particle size, mm	Spheri-cal	Round-ed	Prisma-tic	Lami-nar	Average value of r	%-age present
Plagioclase	0.4—0.8	20	45	35	—	1.4—1.6	7
Calcite, or dolomite	0.5—0.7	—	100	—	—	1.5—1.7	2
Quartzite particle	0.8—1.2	—	100	—	—	1.2—1.4	12
Quartz with inclusions	0.4—1.1	15	85	—	—	1.1—1.6	68
Encrusted quartz	0.5—0.7	—	100	—	—	1.2—1.8	11
							100

Heavy and light-weight fractions combined

Mineral component	Particle size, mm	Spheri-cal	Round-ed	Prisma-tic	Lami-nar	Average value of r	%-age present
Quartzite particle	0.8—1.2	—	100	—	—	1.2—1.4	12
Quartz with inclusions	0.4—1.1	15	85	—	—	1.1—1.6	68
Encrusted quartz	0.5—0.7	—	100	—	—	1.2—1.8	11
Plagioclase	0.4—0.8	20	45	35	—	1.4—1.6	7
Muskovite	0.6—1.2	—	—	—	100	1.3—1.7	0.x
Chlorite	0.2—0.5	—	—	—	100	1.3—1.5	0.x
Granate	0.2—0.7	100	—	—	—	~1	0.x
Pyroxene	0.3—0.4	70	30	—	—	1.8—3.2	0.x
Amphibole	0.3—0.7	20	80	—	—	1.8—3.1	0.x
Epidotite	0.2—0.3	—	—	100	—	1.9—2.7	0.0x
Calcite, or dolomite	0.4—0.7	—	100	—	—	1.4—1.7	2
Ilmenite	0.2—0.3	—	100	—	—	1.2—1.7	0.0x
Limonite	0.2—0.4	Irregular					0.0x
							100

Note: "0.0x" and "0.x" denote quantities of one-hundredth and one-tenth order of magnitude, respectively, but defying any accurate determination

The latter will be constant if the downward force acting on the particle is just balanced by the drag force. Equating accordingly Eqs (1.1.2−13) and (1.1.2−14) the familiar Stokes law is obtained

$$\omega = \frac{1}{18}\,g\,\frac{(\rho_1 - \rho)\,d^2}{\mu} = \frac{2}{9}\,\frac{\rho_1 - \rho}{\mu}\,gr^2 \qquad (1.1.2-15)$$

where r [cm] = the radius of the particle.

There are certain limitations to determining the fall velocity on the basis of the Stokes law. The limiting conditions are as follows:

a) The settling solid particles should be regular spheres;

b) The particles should be solids having a smooth surface. No slip takes place between the fluid and the particle, but friction develops between the water layer adhering to the moving particle and the water at rest;

c) The particle settles in a fluid space of infinite extension;

d) The particles are large enough to permit the fluid to be assumed homogeneous relative to their size;

e) The resistance to the settling of the particles depends exclusively on the viscosity of the fluid.

Let us consider hereafter the case most frequently encountered in practice and deviating from the above assumptions.

Condition *a)* is usually not satisfied in practice. The effect of particle shapes other than spherical will be considered subsequently.

Condition *b)* is readily satisfied since in practice the particles usually meet this condition. Experiments carried out thus far have shown no slip to take place between the water and the sediment particle.

Condition *c)* is very simple to meet partially in practice. In fact, for the gravity force and the drag resistance to become of equal magnitude, i.e. for the development of the fall velocity, it is necessary that the particle cover a certain distance of acceleration. Experiments have shown this distance or the acceleration period to be very small, e.g. in the case of particles of 0.05 mm diameter the fall velocity may be regarded as constant after a time of 0.0003 sec has elapsed.

It will be seen from the foregoing that condition *c)* concerning infinite settling depth is satisfied even at the smallest settling depth.

However, according to the pertinent condition underlying the Stokes law, the boundary of the fluid space must be at a theoretically infinite distance not only in the direction of settling, but also perpendicular thereto. If this condition is not satisfied, the drag resistance to the movement of the particles is no longer described by the relation $E = 3\pi d\mu\omega$ expressed by Eq. (1.1.2−14). According to practical experience, if the distance between the side walls of the basin or vessel is greater than 2 to 3 cm, the lateral boundary of the fluid may be regarded as infinite as far as settling is concerned. Of course, this applies only to particle sizes within the validity limits of the Stokes law. Experiments by J. S. McNown have revealed that the drag resistance to the movement of a particle of diameter d settling in a cylinder of D_0 diameter increases owing to the presence of a lateral boundary and can be obtained if the drag resistance computed according to Stokes from the expression $3\pi d\mu\omega$ is multiplied by a factor K. It should be noted that this consideration applies, obviously, only to particles within the validity limits of the Stokes law. The magnitude of K depends on the ratio of d and D_0 as

$$K = 1 + \frac{9d}{4D_0} + \left(\frac{9d}{4D_0}\right)^2 \qquad (1.1.2-16)$$

Considering Eqs $(1.1.2-14)$ to $(1.1.2-16)$ it will be perceived that the fall velocities ω and ω_D of a particle settling in a fluid space of infinite extension in a direction perpendicular to that of settling and in a cylinder of diameter D_0 are related to each other by the factor K, so that

$$\frac{\omega}{\omega_D} = 1 + \frac{9d}{4D_0} + \left(\frac{9d}{4D_0}\right)^2 \qquad (1.1.2-17)$$

In the case of particles of 0.05 mm diameter mentioned before, assuming for instance a cylinder of 20 mm diameter, $K = 1.0056$, indicating that the effect on fall velocity is an extremely small one.

Sediment materials occurring in practice invariably meet condition $d)$, for even the smallest settleable particle size may be regarded as extremely large relative to the irregularities in fluid structure.

Studies into the validity of condition $e)$ have revealed the existence of a limit particle size, the magnitude of which depends on the properties of the fluid and the solid particles, beyond which the fall velocities obtained by the Stokes law are greater than actual ones, owing to the neglected inertia effects. From the results of pertinent investigations it has become apparent that if the fluid is water and the specific gravity of the solid particles is $\gamma_1 = 2.65$ [p/cm^3], the fall velocity is obtained exactly by the Stokes law up to the $d = 0.05$ mm size fraction. By introducing an error of practically no consequence, the fall velocity can be computed up to $d = 0.08$ mm from the Stokes law, assuming the fluid to be water and the specific gravity of the sediment material to be $\gamma_1 = 2.65$ [p/cm^3].

Assuming the specific gravity of sediment to have the constant value of 2.65 p/cm^3, in the case of water whose variation in density with temperature is negligible, the Stokes law is expressed as

$$\omega = 9.19 \cdot 10^{-4} \frac{d^2}{\mu} \text{ [cm/sec]} \qquad (1.1.2-18)$$

where d should be substituted in mm, while μ in p sec/cm^2 units.

The variation of the coefficient μ of absolute viscosity, of specific gravity γ and of density ρ with temperature is shown for water in *Fig. 1.1.2-9*. Since in the case of water of 20 deg. C temperature $\mu = 1.024 \cdot 10^{-5}$ [psec/cm^2] and substituting d in mm units, the Stokes law assumes the form

$$\omega = 89.83 d^2 \text{ [cm/sec]} \qquad (1.1.2-19)$$

60

Fig. 1.1.2—9. Specific gravity, density and viscosity of water as functions of temperature

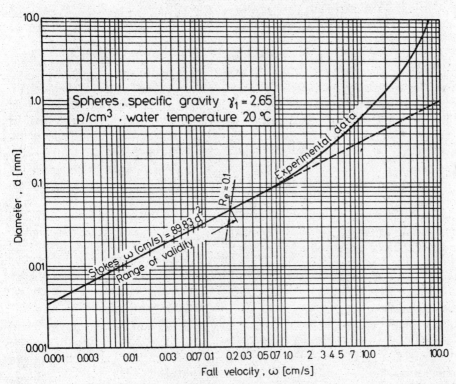

Fig. 1.1.2—10. Fall velocity of spherical sediment particles of $\gamma_1 = 2.65$ [p/cm³] specific gravity in water of 20°C temperature

61

Table 1.1.2—7

Absolute viscosity (μ_t) of water of temperature t, related to the viscosity (μ_{20}) of water of 20°C temperature

Water temper- ature, °C	$\dfrac{\mu_t}{\mu_{20}}$	Water temper- ature, °C	$\dfrac{\mu_t}{\mu_{20}}$	Water temper- ature, °C	$\dfrac{\mu_t}{\mu_{20}}$	Water temper- ature, °C	$\dfrac{\mu_t}{\mu_{20}}$
0	1.79	11	1.28	22	0.960	33	0.752
1	1.74	12	1.24	23	0.940	34	0.737
2	1.68	13	1.21	24	0.917	35	0.723
3	1.62	14	1.17	25	0.894	36	0.708
4	1.56	15	1.14	26	0.875	37	0.694
5	1.52	16	1.11	27	0.856	38	0.681
6	1.48	17	1.08	28	0.838	39	0.669
7	1.43	18	1.06	29	0.820	40	0.656
8	1.39	19	1.03	30	0.801	41	0.643
9	1.35	20	1.00	31	0.785	42	0.631
10	1.31	21	0.982	32	0.769	43	0.601

Since $\mu_{20} = 1.024 \times 10^{-5}$ [p · sec · cm^{-2}], to obtain the coefficient of absolute viscosity at any temperature multiply the ratio μ_t/μ_{20} by 1.024×10^{-5}

The Stokes law applying to water of 20 deg. C temperature is represented graphically in *Fig. 1.1.2—10* (see the full and dashed straight lines).

The viscosity (μ_t) of water at different temperatures has been related to viscosity at 20 deg. C temperature (μ_{20}) in *Table 1.1.2—7*. In water of a temperature other than 20 deg. C the fall velocity of particles within the validity ranges of the Stokes law is obtained by reading from *Fig. 1.1.2—10* the fall velocity corresponding to d and dividing this by the ratio of viscosities. Mathematically

$$\omega_t = \frac{\omega_{20}}{\dfrac{\mu_t}{\mu_{20}}} \text{ [cm/sec]}$$

From the ratios indicated in *Table 1.1.2—7* it will be perceived that within the validity ranges of the Stokes law the influence of temperature on fall velocity is appreciable. For instance at 0 deg. C, the fall velocity is 1.79 times less, i.e. only about one-half of the fall velocity in water of 20 deg. C. In view of the climates prevailing in countries in the northern hemisphere, it is always advisable to estimate fall velocities with a margin of safety in water of 0 deg. C temperature, for instance, when dimensioning settling basins.

Returning to the assumptions introduced in the derivation of the Stokes law, it has been stated already that conditions under *b)*, *c)* and *d)* are readily satisfied in practice. Condition *a)*, i.e. the departure of the solid particles from the spherical shape will be considered together with condition *e)*.

Consider hereafter condition *e)* which appears to be the most essential one because it limits the applicability of the Stokes law to size fractions finer than 0.05−0.08 mm. The resulting differences are of special significance in practice, where the task is often to estimate the fall velocity of fractions coarser than 0.1 or even 0.3 mm, and sometimes even the fall velocity of fine gravels may be of interest. For this reason the drag resistance is expediently determined in a manner to be applicable to fractions of arbitrary size.

The drag resistance acting on spherical particles moving in a fluid is determined in general by using the fundamental relationship of Newton.

In the case of a sphere of d [cm] diametre settling at the constant fall velocity ω [cm/sec] in a fluid of density ρ [psec²/cm⁴] and viscosity μ [psec/cm²] and denoting the drag resistance by E [p], the physical phenomenon of settling will be described by the five independent physical quantities listed above, so that the relationship

$$F(E, \omega, d, \rho, \mu) = 0 \qquad (1.1.2-20)$$

applies, or regarding ω, d and ρ as the basic quantities, and introducing the resulting two independent dimensionless groups, the relationship

$$F_1\left(\frac{E}{\omega^2 d^2 \rho}, \ \frac{\omega d \rho}{\mu} \right) = 0 \qquad (1.1.2-21)$$

is obtained.

The above expression solved for drag resistance yields

$$E = \omega^2 d^2 \rho \, F_2\left(\frac{\omega d \rho}{\mu} \right) = \omega^2 d^2 \rho \, F_2(Re) \qquad (1.1.2-22)$$

since $\omega d \rho / \mu$ denotes essentially the fall velocity Reynolds numbers of the sediment.

In Eq. (1.1.2−22) area A can replace d^2, and writing $\rho \omega^2/2$ for $\rho \omega^2$, the hydrodynamic pressure can be introduced and, finally, replacing $F_2(Re)$, namely the function depending on the Reynolds number, by the dimensionless resistance coefficient C_D, the general form of drag resistance is obtained as

$$E = \frac{1}{2} C_D \rho A \omega^2 \qquad (1.1.2-23)$$

or, since the particle moving in the fluid has been assumed to be a sphere of diameter d, i.e. $A = \pi d^2/4$, we have

$$E = \frac{1}{8} C_D \rho \pi d^2 \omega^2 \qquad (1.1.2-24)$$

In the above expression C_D is a dimensionless resistance coefficient, the magnitude of which depends on the Reynolds number. According to *Fig. 1.1.2−11* the relationship between the Reynolds number *Re* and the friction coefficient C_D is a

Fig. 1.1.2—11. Drag coefficients C_D vs. Reynolds number

hyperbolical one as long as the Reynolds number remains below a certain limit value. The hyperbolical relationship is valid with full mathematical exactness only for Reynolds numbers lower than $Re = 0.1$, where, in computing the Reynolds number, d should be substituted in cm, ω in cm/sec, ρ in psec^2/cm^4 and μ in psec/cm^2 units. Nevertheless, for practical purposes it is permissible to use the expression

$$C_D = \frac{24}{Re} \qquad (1.1.2-25)$$

also at Reynolds numbers up to $Re = 0.4$.

Substituting Eq. (1.1.2−25) into the expression developed by Newton for the drag resistance and given under Eq. (1.1.2−24), the condition

$$G' = \frac{\pi d^3}{6}(\rho_1 - \rho)g = E$$

yields the Stokes law expressed by Eq. (1.1.2−15).

In the general case, by equating gravity force to the Newtonian expression of drag resistance and assuming spherical particles, the relationship

$$\frac{\pi d^3}{6}(\rho_1 - \rho)g = \frac{1}{8}C_D \rho \pi d^2 \omega^2$$

is obtained, whence the fall velocity is

$$\omega = \sqrt{\frac{4}{3}\frac{g}{C_D}\frac{\rho_1 - \rho}{\rho}d} \qquad (1.1.2-26)$$

Eq. (1.1.2−26) is, obviously, impossible to use unless the function $C_D = C_D(Re)$ is known.

The resistance coefficient has been suggested by C. W. Oseen in the form

$$C_D = \frac{24}{Re}\left(1 + \frac{3}{16}Re\right) \qquad (1.1.2-27)$$

The curve representing the above expression gives a fair approximation of the experimental curve $C_D = C_D(Re)$ up to $Re = 1$, as indicated in *Fig. 1.1.2−11*.

Introducing the value of the resistance coefficient suggested by C. W. Oseen into Eq. (1.1.2−26), the resulting expression can be used for determining the fall velocity with the desired accuracy up to $Re = 1.0$ values.

It should be noted that in the case of water of 20 deg. C temperature and sediment of $\gamma_1 = 2.65$ [p/cm³] specific gravity, the mathematically exact validity limit of the Stokes law is the value $Re = 0.1$ − as mentioned before − and this corresponds to a particle diameter of $d = 0.05$ mm. It has also been pointed out that for practical purposes the validity of the Stokes law can be extended up to the value $Re = 0.4$, corresponding to $d = 0.08$ mm, implying that it is practically permissible to apply the Stokes law to the settling of sediment smaller than 0.08 mm diameter. For the sake of completeness it should be added, that the $Re = 1.0$ value in the Oseen formula is associated with a maximum particle size of $d = 0.114$ mm.

The relationship $C_D = F(Re)$ has been represented in a graphical form in *Fig. 1.1.2−11* on the basis of a number of experiments. Any attempt to use the diagram for determining the fall velocity of a sediment particle of diameter d and specific gravity γ_1 in a fluid of γ specific gravity and v viscosity would involve a lengthy procedure of trial and error. Several methods have been suggested in the literature for eliminating time-consuming trials. The chart constructed by H. Rouse is shown in *Fig. 1.1.2−12* and can be used for determining the fall velocity not only of particles greater than 0.05 mm, but also of spheres having a specific gravity other than 2.65 p/cm³.

When using the chart the distance AC is first plotted on the straight edge of a sheet of paper. When determining the fall velocity or the particle diameter, point C should always be plotted on the base line.

For determining the fall velocity:

a) the product of $\rho' = \dfrac{\rho_1 - \rho}{\rho}$ and the particle diameter d, as well as of ρ' and the kinematic viscosity v is formed;

b) the values of $d\rho'$ and $v\rho'$ are noted on the two corresponding scales;

c) locating point C on the value indicated on the base line the paper is oriented in a manner that it should pass through the value $d\rho'$ and at point A the fall velocity ω and the Reynolds number Re are obtained.

Fig. 1.1.2–12. Chart for determining the fall velocity. After Rouse

For determining the particle diameter:

a) the product $\rho'v$ is formed and marked on the base line;

b) point C is made to coincide with this value and the distance CA is rotated as long as point A coincides with the fall velocity ω specified in advance;

c) with the straight line CA in this position the value $\rho'd$ is obtained, which yields the desired particle diameter d after division by ρ'.

Fig. 1.1.2—13. Fall velocity of quartz spheres in clear water, as function of diameter and temperature

Returning to *Fig. 1.1.2—10*, the Stokes law is represented therein — as mentioned before — by a straight line whose validity range has been indicated by a full line, whereas the inapplicable section, by a dashed one. Using data obtained at the California Institute of Technology, the fall velocity : particle diameter relationship has been completed in the figure for values higher than $Re = 0.1$, assuming water of 20 deg. C temperature and spherical sediment particles of $\gamma_1 = 2.65$ p/cm^3 specific gravity.

It should be noted here that the data of *Fig. 1.1.2—10* must not be used in combination with the data in *Table 1.1.2—7* for determining the fall velocity at values greater than $Re = 0.1$ and in water of a temperature other than 20 deg. C in the manner mentioned in connection with the Stokes law. For instance if $d = 0.3$ mm, then, since from *Fig. 1.1.2—10* $\omega_{20} = 4.2$ cm/sec, for water of 0 deg. C we would have $\omega_0 = 4.2/1.79 = 2.35$ cm/sec, which is in conflict with practical experience according to which in water of 0. deg. C the fall velocity is $\omega_0 = 3$ cm/sec. The discrepancy is logical, since beyond the validity limit of the Stokes law the relation between ω and $1/\mu$ is not a linear one.

For quartz spheres of $\gamma_1 = 2.65$ p/cm^3 specific gravity, the ω versus d relation for different water temperatures is given in handbooks either in a tabulated or in graphical form. For instance, in the case of quartz spheres of 2.65 p/cm^3 specific gravity and clear water of 0, 10, 20, 30 and 40 deg. C temperature the diameter : fall velocity relation is illustrated in *Fig. 1.1.2—13*.

5*

67

Numerous experimental relations have been described in the relevant literature, in which the fall velocity of spherical sediment particles of different diameters d and specific gravities is specified in terms of the density and viscosity of the fluid. The values obtained from these relationships show drastic differences, which is probably due to the circumstance that particles differing in shape from spheres have been used in many of the settling tests.

Some of these relations will be described briefly for the sake of completeness. For the validity range $Re = 1$ to 30 the expression

$$\omega^{3/2} = \frac{(gd)^{3/2} \dfrac{\rho_1 - \rho}{\rho}}{11.2 \sqrt{v}} \qquad (1.1.2-28)$$

has been suggested by Prandtl for determining the fall velocity.

The results of experiments performed by Richards have been processed by A. P. Zegzhda and therefrom I. I. Levi has derived the following fall velocity formulae: for $Re = 30$ to 400

$$\omega^{1.8} = \frac{gd^{1.2} \left(\dfrac{\rho_1 - \rho}{\rho} \right)}{4.4 \, v^{0.2}} \qquad (1.1.2-29)$$

for Re values greater than 400

$$\omega = 1.2 \sqrt{gd \frac{\rho_1 - \rho}{\rho}} \qquad (1.1.2-30)$$

In the above expressions $v = \mu/\rho$ indicates the coefficient of kinematic viscosity.

For sediment of 2.65 p/cm^3 specific gravity and water of 10 deg. C temperature, D. Ya. Sokolov has derived from experiments the empirical relation

$$\omega = 36 \sqrt{d} \qquad (1.1.2-31)$$

the validity of which is restricted to the range $Re = 30$ to 800.

The expressions mentioned thus far have a rather narrow range of validity. Attempts have been made therefore to develop a relationship for the fall velocity which can be applied to all Reynolds numbers (i.e. particle sizes) of practical interest. A similar expression has been developed experimentally in recent times by W. W. Rubey. Accordingly if $\rho' = \dfrac{\rho_1 - \rho}{\rho}$ and μ is viscosity, then the fall velocity is

$$\omega = \sqrt{\frac{2}{3} \rho' gd + \frac{36\mu^2}{\rho^2 d^2}} - \frac{6\mu}{\rho d} \qquad (1.1.2-32)$$

68

For small μ and great d values the approximate expression

$$\omega = \sqrt{\frac{2}{3}\rho' gd}$$

(1.1.2−33)

has been suggested.

On the other hand, for high μ or very small d values

$$\omega = \frac{6\mu}{\rho d}\left(\sqrt{1 + \frac{\rho' g\rho^2 d^3}{54\mu^2}} - 1\right)$$

Remembering that for arbitrarily low z values

$$\sqrt{(1 + z)} \approx \left(1 + \frac{z}{2}\right)$$

it is permissible to write

$$\omega = \frac{6\mu}{\rho d}\left(1 + \frac{\rho' g\rho^2 d^3}{108\mu^2} - 1\right) = \frac{\rho' g\rho d^2}{18\mu}$$

and thus the Stokes law is obtained

$$\omega = \frac{1}{18} g \frac{(\rho_1 - \rho)d^2}{\mu}$$

The Rubey formula involves, implicitly though, the relationship of two dimensionless numbers, namely the Reynolds number and the Froude number. In fact with the substitutions

$$Re = \frac{\omega d}{v}$$

and

$$Fr = \frac{\omega^2}{gd}$$

Eq. (1.1.2−32) of Rubey is rewritten into the form

$$Fr\,Re + 12Fr = \frac{2}{3}\rho' Re$$

(1.1.2−34)

The validity of Eq. (1.1.2−34) is apparent, since Eq. (1.1.2−26) developed by Newton on the basis of the drag resistance can also be transformed into a *Re* versus *Fr* relation.

The fall velocities computed from the expressions given in the foregoing for $\gamma_1 = 2.65 \ p/cm^3$ specific gravity and 20 deg. C water temperature, when plotted

Fig. 1.1.2−14. Fall velocity vs. particle diameter according to various autnors

against the particle diameter d in a log-log plot, yield drastically different relations in the case of $d > 0.1$ mm values as indicated in *Fig. 1.1.2−14*. For this reason *the fall velocity of regular spherical particles is most expediently determined with the help of Fig. 1.1.2−11 and Eq. (1.1.2−26)*. As mentioned before, the computation work is greatly facilitated by using the chart illustrated in *Fig. 1.1.2−12*.

2. The fall velocity of particles other than spherical. When determining the fall velocity of irregular particles accuracy can be increased by taking into consideration the effect of irregular shape on the fall velocity.

Being influenced by a wide variety of factors the shape of sediment particles displays a great variability. The effect of particle shape on fall velocity is variable, being smaller at low fall velocities and more appreciable at higher velocity. For instance, experiments conducted by McNown and J. Malaika at *Re* values lower than unity with particles of different shapes show that the influence of particle shape is considerable in this range.

Several methods have been suggested for taking the effect of particle shape on fall velocity into consideration. A number of theoretical considerations and the results of experiments based on them have been published in the relevant literature. Any detailed discussion of these methods would lead too far and therefore attention will be confined here to some of the approaches of interest in the study of sediment transportation.

A simple graphical method has been suggested by Heywood for considering *the influence of particle shape on fall velocity*. Heywood has introduced the volume constant k [see Eq. (1.1.2−1)] of the particle into the dimensionless expression of the resistance coefficient C_D.

With the introduction of the volume constant k Heywood has developed the expression

$$C_D = \frac{8k}{\pi} \frac{(\rho_1 - \rho)gd}{\rho\omega^2} \qquad (1.1.2-35)$$

for the resistance coefficient.

Heywood's graphical method is based on the actual Reynolds number Re, which is related to a fictitious Reynolds number Rs computed from the velocity and diameter determined by the Stokes law. The actual Reynolds number is

$$Re = \frac{\omega d \rho}{\mu} \qquad (1.1.2-36)$$

the fictitious Reynolds number is

$$Rs = \frac{\omega_s d_s \rho}{\mu} \qquad (1.1.2-37)$$

In the graphical method of Heywood differences arise according to whether it is desired to determine the fall velocity pertaining to a particular particle diameter d, or the particle diameter d pertaining to a particular ω value.

a) *Finding ω for known d values:* In this case the fictitious fall velocity ω_s is computed from the actual particle diameter d according to the Stokes law. Thus

$$\omega_s = \frac{1}{18} \frac{(\rho_1 - \rho)gd^2}{\mu} \qquad (1.1.2-38)$$

The particle diameter d_s, on the other hand, is obtained from the expression

$$C_D = \frac{8k}{\pi} \frac{(\rho_1 - \rho)gd_s}{\rho\omega^2} \qquad (1.1.2-39)$$

In this manner the fictitious particle diameter d_s corresponding to the actual fall velocity ω is obtained.

The value of d_s is accordingly

$$d_s = \frac{C_D \rho\omega^2 \pi}{8k(\rho_1 - \rho)g} \qquad (1.1.2-40)$$

Thus

$$\frac{Re}{Rs} = \frac{\omega d}{\omega_s d_s} \qquad (1.1.2-41)$$

Combining the above values of ω_s and d_s with Eq. (1.1.2−41):

$$\frac{Re}{Rs} = \frac{6k}{\pi} \frac{24}{C_D Re} \qquad (1.1.2-42)$$

71

b) *Finding d for known ω values:* If ω is known and the task is to determine the corresponding particle diameter d, then, in contrast to the foregoing procedure, the fictitious particle diameter d_s is computed with the actual ω value according to the Stokes law

$$\omega = \frac{1}{18} g \frac{(\rho_1 - \rho) d_s^2}{\mu} \tag{1.1.2-43}$$

On the other hand, the fictitious fall velocity ω_s is computed with the actual particle diameter d using Eq. (1.1.2−35).

The ratio of the two Reynolds number becomes thus

$$\frac{Re}{Rs} = \frac{\omega d}{\omega_s d_s} = \left(\frac{C_D Re}{24} \frac{\pi}{6k} \right)^{1/2} \tag{1.1.2-44}$$

For spherical particles $k = \pi/6$ and thus logically

$$\frac{Re}{Rs} = \left(\frac{C_D Re}{24} \right)^{1/2} \tag{1.1.2-45}$$

Since in the case of $Re < 0.4$, Eq. (1.1.2−25) is valid, so that $C_D = 24/Re$, it will be realized that, in the relationships derived for both ω and d, the ratio $Re/Rs = 1$ demonstrating truly the validity of the Stokes law.

For irregular particle shapes and for seven different mixtures of water and glycerine the values of $24/C_D Re$ have been determined from experimental data. The Rs values related to Re have been determined by Heywood using the expressions

$$\frac{Re}{Rs} = \frac{6k}{\pi} \frac{24}{C_D Re}$$

and

$$\frac{Re}{Rs} = \left(\frac{C_D Re}{24} \frac{\pi}{6k} \right)^{1/2}$$

and the corresponding values have been represented graphically.

In *Fig. 1.1.2 − 15* the left-hand side curve Ⓐ, in combination with the family of curves Ⓐ on the right-hand side is used for determining the fall velocity pertaining to a particular particle diameter d. If it is desired to find the diameter d pertaining to a particular fall velocity ω, then the curve Ⓑ on the left-hand side, in combination with the family of curves denoted by Ⓑ on the right-hand side, should be used.

Attention should be called to the fact that when using *Fig. 1.1.2 − 15* the fall velocity or the diameter pertaining to a particular ω value is determined for water of 20 deg. C temperature and sediment material of $\gamma_1 = 2.65$ [p/cm³] specific gravity if the shape factor is 0.1, 0.2, 0.3, 0.4 or $\pi/6 = 0.524$.

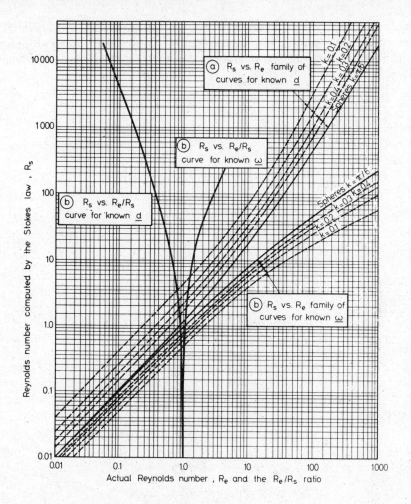

Fig. 1.1.2—15. $Re/Rs = F(Rs)$ and $Re = F(k, Rs)$ relations. After Heywood

Fig. 1.1.2 — 15 in combination with *Fig. 1.1.2 — 10* and *Table 1.1.2 — 7* can thus be used for determining ω in waters of different temperature. Thus the method of Heywood is suitable for determining the fall velocity of sediment materials with a different volume constant and in waters of different temperature. The only assumption involved *in this method* is that *the specific gravity of the sediment material* under consideration *is constant at* $\gamma_1 = 2.65$ p/cm³. Since, however, the specific gravity of most sediments likely to settle under actual conditions ranges around the above value with only slight differences, the graphical method of Heywood can be used successfully in almost every problem encountered in practice.

The graphical method of Heywood will be illustrated by the following example.

Let us find the fall velocity of a sediment particle of $\gamma_1 = 2.65$ p/cm^2 specific gravity in water of 20 deg. C temperature, for which the envelope sphere has a diameter $d = 1$ mm and the volume constant is $k = 0.2$. Since, according to *Fig. 1.1.2−10*, the fall velocity of a 1 mm diameter particle is from the Stokes law round $\omega_s = 90$ cm/sec,

$$Rs = \frac{d_s\,\omega_s\,\rho}{\mu} = \frac{0.1 \cdot 90 \cdot 1.0175 \cdot 10^{-3}}{1.024 \cdot 10^{-5}} = 894$$

On the curve $k = 0.2$ in the family of curves ⓐ on the right-hand side of *Fig. 1.1.2−15*, $Re = 70$ corresponds to $Rs = 894$. The desired fall velocity is thus

$$\omega = \frac{Re\mu}{d\rho} = \frac{70 \cdot 1.024 \cdot 10^{-5}}{0.1 \cdot 1.0175 \cdot 10^{-3}} = 7 \quad [\text{cm/sec}]$$

On the left-hand curve ⓐ in *Fig. 1.1.2−15* the ratio $Re/Rs = 0.175$ corresponds to $Rs = 894$. The fall velocity of a spherical sediment particle of 1 mm diameter is thus

$$\omega = \omega_s \frac{Re}{Rs} = 90 \cdot 0.175 = 15.7 [\text{cm/sec}]$$

(The result obtained can be checked with the help of *Fig. 1.1.2 − 10* where from the ω versus d curve the fall velocity $\omega = 15.7$ [cm/sec] is actually obtained at $d = 1$ mm.)

Comparing the fall velocities of the spherical sediment particle with that of one having a volume constant $k = 0.2$, it will be seen that the fall velocity of the latter is less than one half of that of the spherical particle.

Experiments have been conducted by L. Ivicsics in the laboratory for determining the fall velocity of sediment particles having different shapes and diameters ranging from 0.16 to 1.5, as well as from 10 to 50 mm. He assumed the phenomenon of settling to be influenced by acceleration g due to gravity, by the particle diameter d, the kinematic viscosity v, the relative density $\rho' = \dfrac{\rho_1 - \rho}{\rho}$ and by the shape factor ϕ defined by him with Eq. (1.1.2−3), and succeeded in demonstrating that the resultant fall velocity is actually governed by two dimensionless groups formed of the five fundamental quantities listed above. Introducing the fall velocity Reynolds and Froude numbers of the sediment, the numerical form of the theoretical relation was found by correlation to be

$$\frac{Fr}{\phi\rho'} = 0.117 \left[Re\,(1 + \phi) \right]^{0.5} \tag{1.1.2−46}$$

Introducing into the above expression the fall velocity Reynolds and Froude numbers of the sediment, the actual fall velocity is eventually obtained as

$$\omega = 0.238\,d \sqrt[3]{\frac{g^2\,\phi^2\,(1 + \phi)\,\rho'^2}{v}} \tag{1.1.2−47}$$

74

As the fall velocity increases, the significance of the Reynolds number tends to decrease gradually, since the effect of the force due to the internal friction of the fluid becomes very slight compared to the effect of the gravity force. For this reason the expression

$$\frac{Fr}{\phi(1 + \phi)\rho'} = \text{Constant} \qquad (1.1.2-48)$$

has been introduced by Ivicsics for describing the process of settling of particles ranging from 10 to 50 mm in size. The above expression, solved for ω yields the equation

$$\omega = 0.914 \sqrt{g\phi(1 + \phi)\rho' d} \qquad (1.1.2-49)$$

In the experiments the value of ϕ varied from 0.2 to 0.9. It follows from the definition of the shape factor ϕ that the relations cannot be suggested for use around $\phi = 1$ values.

Allowance for the effect of particle shape on fall velocity has been made recently with the help of the shape factor $SF = c/a\sqrt{ab}$ defined by Eq. (1.1.2−4).

The departure from spherical shape, i.e. the shape effect can be observed within the validity range of the Stokes law, i.e. for $Re < 0.1$, in that the expression given by Eq. (1.1.2−13) for the submerged weight G' of the particle is no longer equal to the drag resistance given by Eq. (1.1.2−14), but equals the K-fold value thereof, where K denotes a factor greater than unity, depending on SF.

Values of the factor K involved in the expression

$$G' = K(3\pi\mu\omega d) \qquad (1.1.2-50)$$

have been given for sediment particles of different shapes in a graphical form by McNown, classified according to the ratio b_1/c_1 and in terms of $a_1/\sqrt{b_1 c_1}$.

Beyond the validity limit of the Stokes law a modified dimensionless resistance coefficient C_D has been introduced by McNown in order to allow for the shape effect. The dimensionless resistance coefficient is found accordingly from the expression

$$C_D = K\frac{24}{Re} \qquad (1.1.2-51)$$

where the magnitude of K is given in the form of a graph, in terms of the Reynolds number, classified according to the ratio of the dimensions measured along the axes a_1, b_1 and c_1, the shape factor $a_1/\sqrt{b_1 c_1}$ being determined by these dimensions.

In the foregoing considerations on the fall velocity of particles other than spherical the term particle diameter has been used implicitly without qualification. However, it has already been mentioned (when the concept of the settling diameter was introduced) that this diameter is not constant, but subject to variations with the specific gravity, density and viscosity of the fluid used in the settling test. This

Fig. 1.1.2—16. Fall velocity vs. sieve diameter, with water temperature and the shape factor
SF as parameters. After *Sedimentation Manual (ASCE, HY4,* July, 1962)

implies, for instance, that the settling diameter determined in water of "*t*" temperature is valid exclusively at the particular temperature "*t*". Since the settling
diameter depends on the fluid used and on the properties thereof, it cannot be regarded as a sediment parameter of the same significance as, for instance, the
nominal diameter or the shape factor.

Motivated by such considerations, the standard fall velocity and the standard
settling diameter have been introduced for more exact investigations.

The standard fall velocity is understood as the average fall velocity of a sediment
particle in distilled water of 24 deg. C temperature and of infinite extension. *The
standard settling diameter* has been defined as the diameter of a sphere of the same
specific gravity, the standard fall velocity of which equals that of the particle under
consideration.

Although the settling diameter of particles other than spherical depends on the
temperature of water used for its determination, the influence of slight variations
in temperature is small enough to be neglected in most practical problems.

The particle size of coarse sediments is determined usually by sieving, and it is
therefore expedient to understand the relation between the sieving diameter and
the fall velocity for different shape factors *SF*. The fall velocity versus sieving
diameter relation is illustrated in *Fig. 1.1.2 — 16* after the Inter-Agency Committee
on Water Resources for shape factors *SF* = 0.5, 0.7 and 0.9, determined in clear
distilled water of 0, 10, 20, 24, 30 and 40 deg. C temperature. On the other hand,
the relation between the sieving and the standard settling diameters is shown, again

76

Fig. 1.1.2—17. Sieve diameter vs. standard settling diameter for different shape factors. After *Sedimentation Manual (ASCE, HY4, July, 1962)*

after the same reference, in *Fig. 1.1.2 − 17* for different shape factors. Both diagrams apply to natural sediment material of 2.65 p/cm^3 specific gravity and yield directly the fall velocity if the shape factor, the temperature of water and the sieving diameter are known.

In the majority of cases the fall velocity is required in flowing, sediment-carrying water. This fall velocity is no longer characteristic of the sediment material since it depends, obviously, on hydraulic factors, chiefly the flow velocity and turbulence of water, secondarily on the degree of pollution of the water course. Nevertheless, for practical reasons it is deemed advisable to discuss briefly the problem of fall velocity in flowing, sediment-carrying water.

In sediment-carrying water the fall velocity may be affected primarily by the proximity of individual sediment particles.

In early investigations the fall velocity was found to be influenced to any appreciable extent at extremely high sediment concentrations only. Recent research, however, has revealed that the reduction in fall velocity may be substantial even at low sediment concentrations.

Fig. 1.1.2—18. Fall velocity of quartz particles in sediment carrying water. After Schoklitsch

The reduction in fall velocity with sediment concentration is shown in *Fig. 1.1.2—18*, on the basis of data obtained by Schoklitsch for quartz particles. In this figure the fall velocity versus particle diameter relation is shown for clear water and for four different sediment concentrations C [kp/m³], all for water of about 10 deg. C temperature. The bulk densities γ_z computed according to sediment concentration have also been entered for the individual curves.*

From *Fig. 1.1.2—18* it will be seen that the influence on fall velocity becomes appreciable at very high sediment concentrations only. In fact, according to the experiments of Schoklitsch, in sediment concentrations of round 55 kp/m³ the fall velocity of 0.5 mm quartz particles was found to be reduced by about 7%, whereas that of one mm large particles, by no more than about 3.4%. It may be concluded therefrom that, in view of sediment concentrations occurring in natural alluvial streams, the reduction in fall velocity due to the presence of sediment can safely be neglected in practice.

The ratio of the fall velocity ω in clear water and the fall velocity ω_c at a sediment concentration c per cent by dry weight has recently been studied by McNown and Pin-Nam Lin who relate the variations in this ratio to the sediment concentration c in terms of the sediment fall velocity Reynolds number $Re = \omega d / \nu$. The results of their theoretical and experimental investigations are shown in

*For the definition of γ_z, see *Section 1.3.2*.

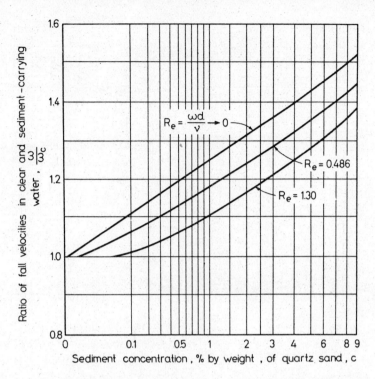

Fig. 1.1.2—19. Ratio of fall velocities in clear and sediment carrying water vs. sediment concentration, with the fall velocity Reynolds number as parameter. After McNown and Lin

Fig. 1.1.2—19. The authors note that the validity of their relation is confined to Reynolds numbers smaller than 2. In contrast to earlier assumptions the figure reveals that the fall velocity is noticeably reduced at rather low sediment concentrations already.

It should be realized finally that the fall velocity is modified in flowing water as well.

The reduction in fall velocity in flowing water is closely related to the circumstance that the movement of sediment-carrying water is turbulent practically without exception. Consequently the reduction of fall velocity in flowing water can be attributed to turbulence. Although several experiments have been conducted concerning the reducing effect of turbulence on fall velocity, the problem is not fully understood as yet. In earlier practice, for instance, the fall velocity in water at rest was used in considerations on settling, and the retarding effects of turbulence were allowed for by a variety of approaches.

Relying on the experimental results of Bestelli, Velikanov and others, Levin relates the reduction in the magnitude of fall velocity under the influence of turbulence to the main velocity v of flow and to the depth D of water. The reduction in fall velocity is accordingly

$$\omega_1[\text{m/sec}] = v\eta$$

where

$$\eta = \frac{0.132}{\sqrt{D}}$$

In the above expression D and v should ·be substituted in m and m/sec units.
The actual fall velocity in water of velocity v is, according to Levin, eventually

$$\omega_t = \omega - \omega_1 \qquad (1.1.2-52)$$

The reduction in fall velocity has been related by S. F. Saveliev also to v and D by the expression

$$\omega_1 = 0.0282 \frac{v}{D^{0.2}} \qquad (1.1.2-53)$$

The majority of such formulae derived by other investigators are formally similar.

Rather detailed attention has been devoted in the foregoing to the fall velocity of sediment, this playing an important role especially in the movement of suspended sediment. Moreover the detailed discussion of this problem is justified also by the circumstance that hydraulic engineers are often confronted with the necessity of determining the settling conditions of certain sediment materials themselves.

1.1.3. EARLIER THEORIES ON SEDIMENT TRANSPORT IN STREAMS

1.1.3.1. The tractive-force formula of Du Boys. The term "tractive force", or "force d'entrainement" was introduced in 1879 by the French engineer P. Du Boys. At that time the energy equation of D. Bernoulli and L. Euler's fundamental equation of hydrodynamics had been known for more than 120 years. The fundamentals of river hydraulics had already been established by the French hydraulicians, headed by A. De Chézy. In 1786, almost 100 years before Du Boys, a theoretical expression was derived by P. Du Buat for the frictional force developed between the channel bottom and the column of water moving above it. Following the assumption of Du Buat, the friction developed on the channel bottom was offered by Du Boys as an explanation for the movement of the sediment. The concept of the tractive force is thus closely associated with the movement of bed load.

In his approach Du Boys assumed the flow to be steady and uniform, in which the kinetic energy of water remains constant. The potential energy of water is continually reduced as a consequence of the vertical distance travelled (i.e. movement) and is converted into kinetic energy. In principle it would follow that the kinetic energy should increase without attaining an upper limit. If the original velocity of flow is v, after a certain time dt it should increase to $v + dv$. The increment dE of kinetic energy would be

$$dE = \frac{\gamma D}{2g}\left[(v + dv)^2 - v^2\right]$$

if the mass of the water column of height D and unit area, specific gravity γ is, in the case of g acceleration due to gravity, $\gamma D/g$. Expanding the expression and neglecting terms of higher order, we obtain

$$dE = \frac{\gamma D}{g}v\,dv$$

If the surface slope is S (and since steady, uniform flow is assumed, this is at the same time the slope of the bottom), the acceleration parallel to the slope is $dv/dt = gS$, thus

$$dE = \gamma\,DSv\,dt \qquad\qquad (1.1.3-1)$$

Actually the kinetic energy remains constant since, according to the assumption of Du Boys. the increment is consumed by the work performed by the friction force τ_0 over the distance $v\,dt$. Accordingly

$$\tau_0 v\,dt = dE = \gamma\,DSv\,dt$$

whence

$$\tau_0 = \gamma DS \qquad\qquad (1.1.3-2)$$

The Du Boys formula can be written in a general form as well. This is the expression of the general tractive force, which is essentially identical with the expression of Du Buat. Accordingly, the sum of tractive forces acting along the full wetted perimeter P of any given channel cross-section is given as

$$\tau_{\ddot{o}} = F\gamma S$$

In this expression F denotes the cross-sectional area pertaining to the wetted perimeter P. The average tractive force along unit width of the wetted perimeter P is

$$\tau_{av} = \frac{\tau_{\ddot{o}}}{P} = \frac{F}{P}\gamma S$$

Since F/P is the hydraulic radius R, the average tractive force becomes

$$\tau_{av} = \gamma RS \qquad\qquad (1.1.3-3)$$

The average tractive force is related invariably to a complete cross-section of a channel. In natural water courses, especially rivers, the hydraulic radius plays a more important role, since the depth varies between wide limits. For this very

Fig. 1.1.3—1. Ratio of tractive force
and friction. After Mavis

reason, the expression of the average tractive force, in contrast to the Du Boys formula, is applied to advantage especially in problems related to river regulation.

The relation between tractive force and friction is illustrated, in general, by the following example. Let I and II denote (see *Fig. 1.1.3—1)* two tanks connected by a pipe through which the same discharge passes continuously. The flow into tank I occurs at the same rate as water is withdrawn from tank II, so that the differential level between the two tanks h_v assumes a constant value corresponding to the frictional resistance developed in the pipe through which they communicate. Let the cross-sectional area of the connecting pipe be F, the wetted perimeter (the internal perimeter of the pipe) be P. Under head h_v the water in the pipe assumes a certain velocity which, in accordance to the assumption introduced, does not increase as a consequence of frictional resistance developed along the wall of the connecting pipe. With γ denoting the specific gravity of water, the accelerating force will become $\gamma h_v F$. The frictional force acting over unit area of the pipe wall, should be τ_0. Since the velocity of flow remains constant, the frictional forces in the pipe of length L just balance the accelerating forces. Thus

$$\gamma\, h_v F = \tau_0 PL$$

whence

$$\tau_0 = \gamma\, \frac{F}{P}\, \frac{h_o}{L}$$

However, h_v/L equals the surface slope S and F/P equals the hydraulic radius R, which denotes a quantity comparable to water depth. The formula becomes thus

$$\tau_0 = \gamma\, RS$$

It will be appreciated that in the interpretation of Du Boys the magnitude of the tractive force equals the friction developed on the channel bottom. Du Boys

82

assumed an increase in the kinetic energy of flow to be offset exclusively by the work performed by friction on the channel bottom, i.e. by the tractive forces. However, other resistances also arise, namely

a) internal friction,

b) vortices (turbulence),

c) air resistance,

d) friction developed along the banks, etc.

The energy required for overcoming the resistances listed above are derived necessarily from the conversion of potential energy into its kinetic counterpart, i.e. from the increment energy $\gamma\,DSv\,dt$. The assumption of Du Boys is thus seen to be invalid.

Thus the most serious objection to the Du Boys formula is that only part of the increment kinetic energy is consumed by the friction forces developed on the bottom. H. Engels and 1. Schober have succeeded in demonstrating experimentally that the actual friction force developed on the bottom covers only part of the expression $\gamma\,DS$. For the actual friction force they have found the value

$$\tau'_0 = \alpha(\gamma\,DS)$$

where α increases as the depth of flow decreases but remains invariably smaller than unity.

A further drawback of the Du Boys tractive force formula is its failure of demonstrating that the internal forces of flow are also tractive forces. This is due to the circumstance that only the friction forces developed along the channel bottom are taken into consideration. During the discussion of suspended sediment transportation a detailed demonstration will be presented of the fact that, as a consequence of velocity fluctuation in turbulent flow, internal energies actually contribute to sediment transportation.

All considered, it is. misleading to call tractive force the quantity expressed by the Du Boys formula since this may suggest incorrect conclusions concerning the role of the formula. Nevertheless, the term tractive force being generally accepted by now, any modification thereof would appear inadvisable.

The original assumption according to which the tractive force is exclusively the force by which sediment is set into motion is obviously obsolete by now, although its role in theoretical investigations has not diminished, but rather increased. *In fact the tractive force as the product of slope and depth is a parameter eminently suited for characterizing the type of flow.* This possibility is actually exploited in studies concerned with sediment transportation. The tractive force as a parameter is frequently introduced in the determination of the different boundary conditions and of the rate of transport alike. Indeed, it has played an almost exclusive role until recently because, on the basis of earlier assumptions, the magnitude of the tractive force alone was believed to characterize the movement of sediment. Although this assumption has been disproved for a long time by experimental evidence, expressions still arise is which the tractive force assumes predominance in determining the boundary conditions and rates of transport. Studies in which depth and slope were considered separately and the recognition of the importance of relative roughness have demonstrated the inadequacy of characterizing the movement of sediment exclusively by the tractive force, i.e. by the product of slope and water depth. Pertinent recent advances will be expounded in Chapter 1.2.

1.1.3.2. Earlier theories of major significance. As in all domains of science also in sediment transportation, the present state of knowledge has been attained gradually. In the majority of cases earlier results are completed and somewhat modified or, in fortunate cases, made more exact by later research. In other instances old theories are invalidated and replaced by new, modified concepts. This process is a logical one in the development of science since the complex laws governing material and substances are approached and discovered by a gradual process only.

A number of earlier results have become obsolete by now and are of historical interest only while others with certain modifications and additions remain still applicable.

1. *The critical tractive force.* Advances in the theory of sediment transportation may be assumed to have started with the publication of the tractive force formula by Du Boys.

In the earliest stages the critical value of the tractive force, τ_c, was widely used for describing the boundary condition between movement and no-movement. The method proved highly successful since — especially in laboratory experiments — both depth and slope could be measured with a rather high degree of accuracy.

The classical theory, in which the critical condition is characterized in terms of the tractive force, is referred to as *the frictional drag theory.* The force displacing the sediment acts accordingly on an area proportionate to the projection of a particle of diameter d and, in the incipient stages of movement, this equals exactly the submerged weight of the sediment particle. The resulting expression is

$$\tau_c = \text{constant} \cdot d\,(\gamma_1 - \gamma) \qquad (1.1.3-4)$$

implying that the tractive force pertaining to the incipient movement of a sediment particle of given diameter d and submerged weight $(\gamma_1 - \gamma)$ is constant. For this very reason this relation may be called *the law of constant tractive forces.*

A number of critical tractive force expressions, derived on the basis of laboratory experiments, have been published in the literature. Such expressions have been suggested among others by H. Krey, A. Schoklitsch, Y. L. Chang, and E. Eisner.

The formula of H. Kramer

$$\tau_c = \frac{100}{6} d_g \frac{(\gamma_1 - \gamma)}{M} \qquad (1.1.3-5)$$

is deemed worthy of being mentioned separately, since the term of "constant tractive forces" has been introduced on its basis.

Using an approach similar to that of *Kramer* for deriving the critical tractive force E. Indri has introduced the particle diameter and the uniformity coefficient *M*.

For sediments belonging to fractions smaller than 1 mm:

$$\tau_c = 13.3 \, d_g \frac{(\gamma_1 - \gamma)}{M} + 12.16 \qquad (1.1.3-6)$$

whereas for fractions greater than 1 mm:

$$\tau_c = 54.85 \, d_g \frac{(\gamma_1 - \gamma)}{M} - 78.48 \qquad (1.1.3-7)$$

has been derived on the basis of experiments carried out by him and other in-vestigators.

From experiments carried out at the U.S. Waterways Experiment Station, Vicksburg, the expression

$$\tau_c = 29 \sqrt{\frac{d_g}{M}(\gamma_1 - \gamma)} \qquad (1.1.3-8)$$

has been developed and named the modified Kramer formula.

As a result of sediment measurement experiments at Iowa with six different sediment materials, Te-Yun Liu has derived the expression

$$\tau_c = 45.7 \, d_g \qquad (1.1.3-9)$$

where the mean particle diameter d_g is introduced in mm units to obtain the tractive force in p/m² units. It is emphasized, however, that the expression applies exclusively to the sediment materials used in the experiments (mean diameter = = 1.4 to 4.4 mm, specific gravity = 2.66 p/cm³).

Combining all measurement data available the critical tractive force for dif-ferently graded sediments (mean diameter 0.2 to 6.5 mm, specific gravity 2.57 to 2.70 p/cm³) has been expressed by Te-Yun Liu in terms of the mean diameter and the uniformity coefficient as

$$\tau_c = 6.1 \left[\frac{d_g}{M}(\gamma_1 - \gamma) \right]^{1.5} + 21.34 \, [\text{p/m}^2] \qquad (1.1.3-10)$$

The value obtained by this expression is, however, an approximate one only. Discrepancies as high as $\pm 27\%$ between the values computed by the formula and the actually observed ones have been encountered.

In 1936 experiments were performed by A. Shields with a sediment of specific gravity γ_1 and diameter d, in water of specific gravity γ and viscosity ν for determin-ing the critical tractive force. The results of these experiments are shown in

85

Fig. 1.1.3−2. With D denoting depth, S the slope and $U_* = \sqrt{gDS}$ the shear velocity, the figure yields

$$f_c = \frac{\tau_c}{(\gamma_1 - \gamma)d} = F\left(\frac{U_* d}{\nu}\right) = F(Re_{*s}) \qquad (1.1.3-11)$$

saying that for given γ_1, γ and d values the critical tractive force is a function of the sediment shear velocity Reynolds number.

In 1960, J. Valembois introduced the grain parameter

$$G = \left(\frac{\rho_1 - \rho}{\rho}\right) \frac{gd^3}{\nu}$$

and, using the results of J. Goddet from 1959, he suggested, like Shields's approach, the relation

$$G = F(R_{*s}^2)$$

for estimating the critical tractive force. It is of interest to know that in 1963 the dimensionless number

$$D_* = \left(\frac{\rho' g}{\nu^2}\right)^{1/3} d = \frac{d}{\nu^{2/3} g^{-1/3}} \left(\frac{\rho_1 - \rho}{\rho}\right)^{1/3}$$

was introduced by Bonnefille and retaining the parameters f_c and Re_* he succeeded in transforming the relation of Shields into a three-variable one.

The relationship or similarity of the grain parameter G, of D_* and subsequently of the dimensionless numbers d/A obtained from the ratios of potential dynamic velocities will be recurred to in *Section 1.2.3*.

Considering Eq. (1.1.3−4) it will be appreciated that, *in contrast to the early frictional theory, the dimensionless resistance coefficient f_c is not constant, consequently, the magnitude of the critical tractive force τ_c cannot be constant either.*

The relation of Shields has found general acceptance and the resistance coefficient f_c is still involved in various investigations. Originally not even a graphical relation between f_c and Re_{*s} was determined by Shields who confined to determining the range in which the experimental data scattered. The curve shown in *Fig. 1.1.3−2* was traced by H. Rouse. The experiments of Shields have demonstrated eventually that for a given sediment material and under given conditions of observation the magnitude of the critical tractive force is influenced also by the temperature of water.

Let us emphasize that these are the first investigations demonstrating the variability of the critical tractive force τ_c.

Experiments conducted by the author and Yen in 1937−38 at Iowa have shown the magnitude of τ_c to depend also on roughness conditions n.

These rather early observations concerning the variability of the critical tractive force will be discussed in greater detail in *Section 1.2.4*, in connection with the critical considerations on the constant critical tractive forces.

Fig. 1.1.3−2. Resistance coefficient f_c vs. sediment shear velocity Reynolds number. After Shields

The critical tractive forces indicated by the curves shown in *Fig. 1.1.3−3* have been recommended by E. W. Lane for use in connection with irrigation canals. For coarse bed materials, larger than about 5 mm in size, this relation reduces to

$$\tau_c = 0.0801 \ d_{75} \ [\text{kp/m}^2] \qquad (1.1.3-12)$$

where d_{75} [mm] denotes the particle size at 75% of the bed material passing. The data of Shields have also been entered into the figure. For coarse materials the data of Lane and Shields are in fair agreement, whereas in the case of fine sediment particles differences as high as ten-fold are observable.

Starting from·the relation of Shields the expression

$$f_c = \frac{4}{3 C_D (a_r + 5.75 \ \lg 0.63 \ d)^2} \qquad (1.1.3-13)$$

has been derived by I. V. Egiazaroff. Here C_D is a dimensionless resistance coefficient which depends on the fall velocity Reynolds number $Re_s = \omega d/v$, the quantity a_r depends on the Reynolds number at the channel bottom and has generally a value of 8.5. In deriving Eq. (1.1.3−13) Egiazaroff assumed at a particular velocity distribution that in the critical condition the velocity to which the particle is subjected may be taken identical with the fall velocity of sediment particles of comparable size and specific gravity in clear water at rest.

For spherical quartz particles $C_D = 0.4$ and recalling the value $a_r = 0.8$, we obtain $f_c = 0.06$, which is in fair agreement with the data observed by Shields at high Re_{*s} numbers (see *Fig. 1.1.3−2*).

In deriving general criteria for the different boundary conditions of sediment movement, the boundary condition of incipient movement, i.e., the critical condi-

87

Fig. 1.1.3—3. Critical tractive force vs. particle diameter, according to the investigations of Lane and Shields. After *Sedimentation Manual, ASCE, HY2,* March, 1966

tion was also characterized by the author in 1958. From these investigations (for details, see *Section 1.2.3)* it was concluded that for $d \geqq 0.0145$ cm,

$$\tau_c = 0.0774 \, d \, [\text{p/cm}^2] \tag{1.1.3—14}$$

while for $d \leqq 0.0145$ cm,

$$\tau_c = 0.00182 \, d^{0.118} \, [\text{p/cm}^2] \tag{1.1.3—15}$$

A graphical representation of the relation is shown in *Fig. 1.1.3—4.* The discriminating value of 0.0145 cm is an indication of the fact that for particles

88

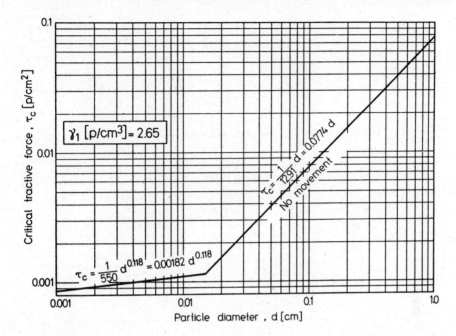

Fig. 1.1.3—4. Critical tractive force vs. particle diameter for bed load of $\gamma_1 = 2.65$ p/cm³ specific gravity

smaller in size the magnitude of the critical tractive force depends but slightly on the particle diameter d. In other words the movement of these fine particles is governed by the internal forces of flow, rather than by the tractive force.

The afore-mentioned expressions reflect invariably the law of constant critical tractive forces. The relations of Shields constitutes the only exception in which the variation of f_c entails a variation in τ_c as well.

2. Critical velocities. The idea of using, besides the tractive forces, also the velocity and especially the mean velocity for describing the incipient condition of movement was a logical one, since the mean velocity was found easy to measure at a given cross-section and discharge. The bottom velocity was also used for determining the critical condition although the determination thereof is rather uncertain.

The classical theory in which the critical condition is described in terms of the critical velocity (either mean or bottom velocity) *is referred to as the impact theory.* An impact force of a magnitude depending on flow velocity, is exerted by water on an area proportional to the projection of the sediment particle of diameter d and, in the critical stage of incipient movement, this impact force equals the submerged weight of the sediment particle. The resulting expression is

$$v_c = \text{constant} \cdot \sqrt{gd \frac{(\gamma_1 - \gamma)}{\gamma}} \qquad (1.1.3-16)$$

89

Fig. 1.1.3−5. Definition sketch of bottom velocity

according to which a constant critical velocity pertains to sediment of a given *d* and submerged specific gravity $(\gamma_1 - \gamma)$. On the model of the tractive forces, this theorem may be called *the law of constant critical velocities.*

For a theoretical determination of the mean and bottom velocities it would be necessary to introduce assumptions concerning the distribution of velocities over depths but, since the critical mean and bottom velocities at which the sediment is picked up from the bottom is usually determined by actual measurements, no detailed attention will be devoted here to the vertical velocity profile.

There being no direct means available for measuring bottom velocities, the values derived from the velocity profile are by no means unambiguous. More or less arbitrary assumptions have therefore been introduced for defining the bottom velocity. One of the methods commonly adopted for this purpose will be described subsequently.

In the critical condition (at general sediment transport) the moving layer of sediment or the sediment grains in the top layer under the moving sediment particles are just in the incipient stage of movement. Consequently at the top plane of the particles the velocity of flow differs from zero. Below the top plane of the uppermost sediment layer at rest there is rapid decrease in flow velocity and between the particles of the underlying layer no appreciable flow is assumed to exist, i.e., the velocity will be zero. As indicated in *Fig. 1.1.3−5*, the bottom velocity v_{cf} is determined by the intersection of the extended continuous line connecting the observed velocity data at the top plane of the uppermost sediment layer at rest. Beyond this point the flow velocity decreases continuously to become zero at the bottom plane of the layer.

90

Fig. 1.1.3—6. Critical bottom velocity vs. average particle diameter

The above assumption concerning the definition of bottom velocity is in fair agreement with the investigations of H. A. Einstein who in alluvial streams assumes the thickness of the "bottom layer" — in which the movement of the bottom layer takes place — to equal twice the particle diameter.

A large number of formulae have been published in the literature on the critical mean and bottom velocity.

The oldest of these was perhaps the sixth-power law of velocity. Since according to Eq. (1.1.3—16) v_c^2 is proportional to d and, by raising both sides to the third power, the quantity d^3 characteristic of the particle weight is seen to be proportional to the sixth power of velocity.

Hereafter numerous formulae have been developed by H. Sternberg, V. Airy, A. Schoklitsch, H. Kramer, E. Indri, M. A. Velikanov, A. P. Bochkov and many others for estimating the critical velocities.

Several formulae on the critical velocities have been developed from experimental results and been found to reflect the theoretical relation expressed by Eq. (1.1.3—16). Some of these are concerned with the critical mean velocity v_c, while others, with the critical bottom velocity v_{cf}.

From the results of a series of measurements carried out at Iowa City the critical bottom velocity in terms of the particle diameter has been derived by F. T. Mavis in the form

$$v_{cf} = 15.2 d_g^{4/9} \sqrt{\gamma_1 - 1} \ [\text{cm/sec}] \qquad (1.1.3-17)$$

where d_g [mm] = the mean particle diameter
γ_1 [p/cm³] = the specific gravity of sediment.

91

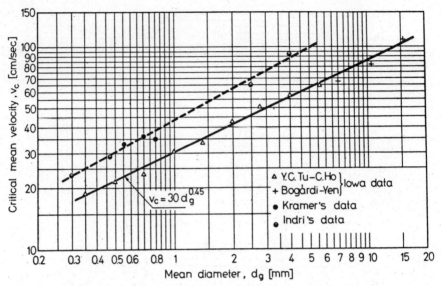

Fig. 1.1.3—7. Critical mean velocity vs. average particle diameter

From experimental results obtained also at Iowa City the expression

$$v_c = 22.9 d_g^{4/9} \sqrt{\gamma_1 - 1} \ [\text{cm/sec}] \qquad (1.1.3-18)$$

has been suggested by the author and C. H. Yen for the relationship existing between the critical mean velocity and the particle size.

In experiments on critical bottom velocities the specific gravity of sediment varied from 2.61 to 2.64 p/cm^3 whereas in those on the critical mean velocity, from 2.61 to 2.70, i.e., between rather narrow limits.

For this reason the author and Yen assumed γ_1 to be constant and suggested, on the basis of *Fig. 1.1.3—6*, the expression

$$v_{cf} = 21.5 d_g^{0.38} \ [\text{cm/sec}] \qquad (1.1.3-19)$$

and from *Fig. 1.1.3—7*, the expression

$$v_c = 30 d_g^{0.45} \ [\text{cm/sec}] \qquad (1.1.3-20)$$

for the approximate estimation of the critical bottom and mean velocities, respectively. In *Fig. 1.1.3—7* the relation derived from the experiments of Kramer and Indri is entered. The considerable difference between the two relations reflects the approximate character of such expressions.

Eqs (1.1.3—17) to (1.1.3—20) have been developed only for particle sizes greater than 1.0 and 0.3 mm, respectively.

The results of experiments conducted at the Chair for Hydraulic Engineering, Budapest Technical University, using coarse sand graded from 0.1 to 10 mm and of $\gamma_1 = 2.7$ $[p/cm^3]$ specific gravity, as well as with ground coal of $\gamma_1 = 1.54$ $[p/cm^3]$ specific gravity are shown in *Figs 1.1.3—8* and *1.1.3—9*. From these figures different relations will be seen to apply to particles smaller and greater

Fig. 1.1.3—8. Critical bottom velocities based on experiments at the Chair for Hydraulic Structures, Budapest Technical University, Budapest, Hungary

Fig. 1.1.3—9. Critical mean velocities based on experiments at the Chair for Hydraulic Structures, Budapest Technical University, Budapest, Hungary

Fig. 1.1.3—10. Characteristics of flow and sediment related in the critical condition. After Ippen and Verma

than 1 mm in size, indicative of the same circumstance as the discrepancy observed at the size limit 0.145 mm for the critical tractive forces (see *Fig. 1.1.3—4.*). In the case of *sand:*

$$\text{if} \quad 0.1 < d_g < 1.0 \,[\text{mm}]$$

$$v_{cf} = 20d_g^{0.10} \,[\text{cm/sec}] \tag{1.1.3—21}$$

$$v_c = 33d_g^{0.14} \,[\text{cm/sec}] \tag{1.1.3—22}$$

$$\text{if} \quad 1.0 < d_g < 10 \,[\text{mm}]$$

$$v_{cf} = 20d_g^{0.43} \,[\text{cm/sec}] \tag{1.1.3—23}$$

$$v_c = 33d_g^{0.47} \,[\text{cm/sec}] \tag{1.1.3—24}$$

In the case of granulated *coal:*

$$\text{if} \quad 0.1 < d_g < 1.3 \,[\text{mm}]$$

$$v_{cf} = 11.3d_g^{0.27} \,[\text{cm/sec}] \tag{1.1.3—25}$$

$$\text{if} \quad 1.3 < d_g < 4 \,[\text{mm}]$$

$$v_{cf} = 10d_g^{0.85} \,[\text{cm/sec}] \tag{1.1.3—26}$$

94

The ratio of the critical edge velocities v_{cf} (see *Fig. 1.1.3–5)* and the fall velocity ω pertaining to particle size d under consideration has been determined by A. T. Ippen and P. R. Verma in terms of the slope S of the energy gradient, of specific gravity γ_1 and of the quantity k_e characteristic of hydraulic roughness. As will be seen from *Fig. 1.1.3–10* the mathematical expression of the relationship is

$$\frac{v_{ce}}{\omega} = 0.12 \left[S^{\frac{1}{4}} \frac{d}{k_e} (\gamma_1 - 1) \right]^{-0.3} \qquad (1.1.3-27)$$

All expressions mentioned in the foregoing comply with the law of constant critical velocities.

Departing from the afore-mentioned investigations, I. I. Levi has included in his considerations the relative roughness as the ratio of flow depth D to particle size d, i.e. D/d.*

The expressions derived by Levi are for uniform particle sizes:

a)   for $10 < \dfrac{D}{d} < 60$

$$v_c = 1.4 \sqrt{gd} \left(1 + \ln \sqrt{\frac{D}{7d}} \right) \qquad (1.1.3-28)$$

b)   for $\dfrac{D}{d} > 60$

$$v_c = 1.4 \sqrt{gd} \ln \frac{D}{7d} \qquad (1.1.3-29)$$

In the case of *graded sediment material* the mean particle diameter d_g is replaced by the ratio of the maximum diameter d_{max} to the mean particle diameter d_g. The eventual form thus obtained is

a)   for $10 < \dfrac{D}{d_g} < 60$

$$v_c = 1.4 \sqrt{gd_g} \left(1 + \ln \sqrt{\frac{D}{7d_g}} \right) \left(\frac{d_{max}}{d_g} \right)^{1/7} \qquad (1.1.3-30)$$

b)   for $\dfrac{D}{d_g} > 60$

$$v_c = 1.4 \sqrt{gd_g} \ln \frac{D}{7d_g} \left(\frac{d_{max}}{d_g} \right)^{1/7} \qquad (1.1.3-31)$$

* The relative roughness is expressed by the ratio d/D. The inverse thereof, the ratio D/d is called the relative smoothness, but it is often used as a measure of relative roughness. Following this practice the "relative roughness D/d" term in the present book will be understood as the measure of relative roughness d/D.

By including the relative roughness, Levi succeeded in allowing, to a certain extent, for the variation of critical velocities, but the influence of slope is still neglected in his expressions. In more recent investigations, besides relative roughness, the influence of slope is also taken into account, as will be demonstrated subsequently.

3. Bed load transport. Attempts have been made to determine the rate of bed load transportation by a theoretical approach, comparing the sediment-transporting capacity of the stream with the properties of the sediment material. It has been assumed, among other things, that the work expended for transporting the sediment is proportionate to the work performed by the moving water, or that the weight of sediment transported is proportionate to the transporting force, or to the output thereof. Whichever of the two assumptions is adopted, or even if another similar theory is introduced, the conclusion eventually arrived at is invariably that for a particular sediment material the rate of transport depends on the hydraulic factors of the stream. The early relations of bed load transport can be thus classified according to the hydraulic factor of the stream taken into consideration.

In one group of the relations the bed load transport by weight G_B is related to the tractive force, in a second group, to the water discharge and the slope, whereas in a third group, to the velocity of flow.

The rate of bed load transport has been expressed in terms of the tractive force, e.g., in the expressions of the US Waterways Experiment Station, Vicksburg, by Te-Yun Liu and Chang.

The formula of the US Waterways Experiment Station is

$$G_B = \frac{k}{n}(\tau_0 - \tau_c)^m \tag{1.1.3-32}$$

where $m = 1.5$ to 1.8, while n is Manning's roughness coefficient. The difference $(\tau_0 - \tau_c)$ may be regarded as the effective tractive force controlling movement. The same concept will be encountered in connection with water discharge and velocity (effective discharge and effective velocity).

According to Chang

$$G_B = \frac{kn}{\tau_c^2}\tau_0(\tau_0 - \tau_c) \tag{1.1.3-33}$$

Te-Yun Liu, too, has adopted the effective tractive force for expressing the weight of sediment transported:

$$G_B = c_2(DS - D_cS_c)^n \tag{1.1.3-34}$$

where D and S denote the depth and slope, respectively, of the stream, while D_c and S_c, the corresponding critical depth and critical slope.

96

Experiments conducted by Liu himself have failed to verify the validity of this formula, since extremely wide differences were obtained for the values of c_2 and n. Thus Te-Yun Liu gives no numerical values for c_2 and n.

Numerous authors, including MacDougall, G. K. Gilbert, E. Meyer-Peter, A. Schoklitsch and L. G. Straub have attempted to relate bed load transport to discharge and slope.

According to MacDougall, if the water discharge per unit width is q, the critical value thereof is q_c and S denotes the slope, then the bed load transport per unit width of a channel is

$$q_B = a\, S^n(q - q_c) \qquad\qquad (1.1.3 - 35)$$

where n ranges from 1.25 to 2.0.

According to *Gilbert*

$$q_B = \frac{a S^{1.59}}{d^{0.58}}\, q^{1.02} - b \qquad\qquad (1.1.3 - 36)$$

In his original expression, Gilbert related the bed load transport to slope, to the water discharge and to sediment properties. The above formula has been derived from the results of experiments made in order to test the original relation. In the formula a and b are constants.

Straub started from the assumption that the weight of the bed load quantity transported is a function of the transporting force, the latter being related to hydraulic factors. The resulting expression will differ depending on the hydraulic factor introduced into the calculations. Adopting the slope and water discharge, the formula becomes

$$G_B = \psi \left(\frac{S^{1/4}}{c^{1/2}}\right) Q^{3/5} (Q^{3/5} - Q_c^{3/5}) \qquad\qquad (1.1.3 - 37)$$

where ψ = characteristic of the bed load
c = velocity coefficient.

The rate of bed load transport has been expressed in terms of velocities, or of effective velocities by J. Donat, L. Mühlhofer, F. Schaffernak, B. V. Polyakov, G. B. Lopatin, V. N. Goncharov, I. I. Levi, N. A. Velikanov and others. The expressions of Donat and Mühlhofer will be mentioned here.

According to Donat

$$q_B = \frac{\psi}{D}\, v^2 (v^2 - v_c^2) \qquad\qquad (1.1.3 - 38)$$

By this expression—the second power of velocity being involved—the tractive force is essentially introduced into the calculations, although in an implicit form.

From his investigations made on the Inn river, the bed load transport per unit width has been expressed with the help of the square of velocities by Mühlhofer:

$$q_B = kv^2(v^2 - v_c^2) \qquad (1.1.3-39)$$

The expressions mentioned above are the results of the first attempts to determine the bed load transport and should by no means be used for numerical computations. These relations are rather of a historical interest.

The expressions of Du Boys, Schoklitsch, Meyer-Peter and Levi will be discussed in detail in *Sections 1.2.6* and *1.2.7*, as it is deemed advisable to include these into the theoretical considerations on the bed load transport relationships.

On the other hand, the expressions given by Lopatin, Goncharov and other Soviet investigators, will be discussed in *Section 2.1.3*, these being based, at least in part, on the results of field observations.

The first theory resting on a firm physical foundation has been introduced by Einstein. The method consists essentially of introducing a function, describing the transportation of bed load, defining in this manner the rates at which the different size fractions of the bed load are transported by the different discharges in a particular channel.

With the help of this function the bed load transport equation is derived, by which a general relationship is established between the bed load transported, the parameters of the stream and the composition of the bed load. The theory makes thus possible the estimation of the quantity of different size fractions transported under steady conditions.

The theory and method of Einstein will be discussed in detail subsequently.

4. Abrasion of bed load. Proceeding downstream along water courses the sediment will, in general, be found to decrease in size. This decrease in sediment size along the river has been attributed initially to abrasion exclusively. Although the reduction in the weight or diameter of sediment particles is attributable to wearing, it should be equally realized that the size of sediment particles is reduced, especially over steep sections, on account of fragmentation and weathering as well. The reduction of particle sizes as a result of wearing, fragmentation and weathering was named mechanical wear in the early stages of investigations.

More recent research into sediment transportation mechanics has revealed, besides mechanical wearing, a *sorting process* as a second potential cause of sediment size reduction. In fact, proceeding downstream, both slope and velocities tend to diminish, accompanied by a corresponding decrease of the force available for sediment transportation, as a consequence of which the coarse particles are gradually sorted out from the mixture transported.

Abrasion was initially offered as the only explanation for the reduction of sediment sizes downstream along the river.

Numerous theories have since been published in the literature for determining the rate of abrasion. The fundamental assumption common to all is that the reduction in sediment weight, i.e. abrasion, is a function of the distance s travelled by the particle and the original weight G_0', or other property of the particle.

A great number of laboratory experiments have been made with the objective of determining the rate of sediment abrasion. The device used in the majority of these experiments consisted of a steel cylinder, into which the sediment was introduced together with water and which was rotated about its axis. The theoretical length of the path travelled in the drum was computed from the speed of revolution and the time elapsed.

Adopting the approach of H. Sternberg, A. Schoklitsch assumed the abrasion of sediment dG' to be proportionate to the original weight G' and the distance s travelled, so that

$$dG' = cG' \, ds \qquad (1.1.3-40)$$

where c is a factor of proportionality. Separation of the variables and integration yields

$$\ln G' = -cs + C_1$$

Since the original weight is $G' = G_0'$, for $s = 0$, we have

$$C_1 = \ln G_0'$$

Consequently

$$\ln G' = -cs + \ln G_0'$$

or

$$G' = G_0' \, e^{-cs} \qquad (1.1.3-41)$$

where G_0' = the original weight
   G' = the weight at the end of distance s,
   c = the specific abrasion.

Extensive experiments have been performed also by E. Düll for determining sediment abrasion. According to his fundamental assumption, abrasion is proportionate to the surface, rather than to the weight, of the sediment particles, so that if F denotes the surface area of a sediment particle,

$$dG' = - cF \, ds \qquad (1.1.3-42)$$

or

$$\frac{dG'}{ds} = - cF$$

However, area F is proportionate to the weight of the particle. For instance, in the case of a spherical sediment particle of specific weight γ_1, diameter d and weight G'

$$F = d^2\pi \quad \text{and} \quad \frac{G'}{\gamma_1} = \frac{\pi d^3}{6}$$

whence

$$F = 4.83 \left(\frac{G'}{\gamma_1}\right)^{2/3}$$

so that the area is seen to increase as the 2/3-rd power of volume. With another coefficient the same expression applies to cubic and prismatic shapes.

The general form of the above expression is

$$F = mG'^n$$

Introducing this value of F into the afore-mentioned differential equation

$$\frac{dG'}{ds} = -cmG'^n$$

or in general form

$$\frac{dG'}{ds} = z = -kG'^n$$

where k is an abrasion coefficient, the magnitude of which depends on the sediment material, while the exponent n is given with a general validity by the abrasion curve.

Düll has found the value 0.55 for n. Since, in keeping with the foregoing considerations, $n = 2/3$ should have been obtained, the experiments showed abrasion to be related but partly to surface area. Using the value $n = 0.55$,

$$\frac{dG'}{ds} = -kG'^{0.55}$$

which upon integration becomes

$$s = -\frac{1}{k} \int G'^{-0.55} \, dG'$$

$$s = -\frac{1}{0.45k} G'^{0.45} + C$$

In the initial stage of abrasion $s = 0$ and $G' = G'_0$ so that

$$C = \frac{1}{0.45k} G'^{0.45}_0$$

which term is introduced into the equation of s to obtain the abrasion theorem of *Düll* as

$$G' = (G_0'^{0.45} - 0.45ks)^{\frac{1}{0.45}} \qquad (1.1.3-43)$$

The particle is worn completely if $G' = 0$. In this case $G_0^{0.45} = 0.45\ ks$, or complete abrasion occurs at the end of the distance

$$s = \frac{1}{0.45k} G_0'^{0.45}$$

Measurements of Düll have shown $k = 0.031$ for limestone of $G' = 541$ p weight (in the case of 2.61 p/cm³ specific gravity, the corresponding particle diameter is 73.6 mm) which, in turn, gives the distance

$$s = \frac{1}{0.45 \cdot 0.031} 541^{0.45} = 1216 \text{ km}$$

Consequently, a sediment particle of about 70 to 75 mm diameter would theoretically be worn completely in the Danube between Vienna and Lom in Bulgaria.

The most important result of experiments made in connection with sediment abrasion is that they yielded data on the potential rates of abrasion. The loss in sediment weight on account to abrasion has been demonstrated to be substantial.

Information on sediment abrasion has failed, however, to throw light on the actual cause of reduction in sediment size. More recent investigations have shown the loss in weight to be too great to be attributable to mechanical wearing alone. According to the results of measurements performed over the Hungarian Upper Reach of the Danube at R.St. 1855 km (Oroszvár) the mean diameter of sediment was 32 mm, whereas at R.St. 1806 km (Medve) this was no more than 9 mm. It would be illogical to assume that the appreciable reduction in particle size over a distance of 49 km occurred as a result of abrasion only.

Let us estimate the reduction in particle size over the 49 km long distance by taking an average value of the abrasion coefficient into consideration, as well as the actual abrasion coefficient which would correspond to the actual reduction in particle size.

Assuming a sediment specific gravity of 2.60 p/cm³, the weight of a 32 mm diameter sediment particle, i.e., the original weight is

$$G_0' = \frac{\pi 3.2^3}{6} 2.6 = 44.6 \text{ p}$$

The weight reduced by abrasion over the 49 km long distance is

$$G' = \frac{\pi 0.9^3}{6} 2.6 = 0.99 \text{ p}$$

According to Düll's abrasion theorem

$$G' = (G_0'^{0.45} - 0.45ks)^{\frac{1}{0.45}}$$

Taking the average value $k = 0.031$ for the "abrasion coefficient"

$$G' = (44.6^{0.45} - 0.45 \cdot 0.031 \cdot 49)^{\frac{1}{0.45}} = 33.21 \text{ p}$$

indicating that the particles of 44.6 p weight should retain a weight of 33.21 p after having travelled the 49 km long distance. This contrasts with the 0.99 p weight actually observed. Assuming the particles to be spherical, the diameter of a particle of 33.21 p weight (and 2.6 p/cm³ specific gravity) would be 29 mm, thus 20 mm larger than 9.0 mm.

The abrasion coefficient corresponding to the actual loss in weight would be

$$k = \frac{1}{0.45 \cdot 49} (44.6^{0.45} - 0.99^{0.45}) = 0.2378$$

which, in view of the highest value $k = 0.044$ found in the experiment of Düll, appears to be extremely high.

The formula of Schoklitsch leads to the same conclusion. Accordingly

$$G' = G_0' e^{-cs}$$

where c is the specific abrasion, s the distance in m units, travelled by the particle and e is the base of the natural logarithm.

Adopting for specific abrasion the average value $c = 0.00001$, the weight

$$G' = 44.6 \, e^{-0.00001 \cdot 49000} = 27.32 \text{ p}$$

is obtained, comparing fairly well with that found by Düll's theorem.

It appears thus safe to conclude from both relations that the reduction of a 32 mm diameter particle of medium hardness over a distance of 49 km to 9 mm is not attributable exclusively to abrasion.

It will be perceived from the above numerical example that in particular cases the sorting process may result in a substantially greater reduction of particle sizes than mechanical wearing.

In the early stages of research the phenomenon of abrasion was given a wide variety of interpretations. In laboratory experiments abrasion was regarded as one of the factors responsible for the diminution of particles along the stream. In observations performed in the field, on the other hand, it was regarded to include the processes of fragmentation, weathering, attrition yet even sorting.

In contemporary investigations the sorting process is excluded primarily from the concept of abrasion, and even diminution by increments (fragmentation, weathering) is distinguished from gradual size reduction, that is, from abrasion and attrition proper.

5. *Suspension of sediment.* A number of explanations have been offered in the literature for the causes maintaining the sediment in suspension.

According to one of the simple assumptions the sediment is set in suspension whenever the buoyant force corresponding to the velocity head becomes equal to the submerged weight of the sediment. The assumption, however, leads obviously to the velocity corresponding to the initial stage of movement. Thus it may be accepted as an explanation for starting movement but not for continued suspension. The suspending force has been suggested to be proportionate to the velocity gradient. The idea is obviously misleading as it would imply that no suspended sediment would be present in the water layers where flow velocity is highest, the velocity gradient being zero there. This, however, is in conflict with practical experience.

The suspension of sediment has been attributed in recent theories to the internal forces acting in turbulent flow. Since the sediment, owing to its specific gravity greater than that of water, tends to settle continually with respect to the surrounding fluid at a rate corresponding to its fall velocity, no continuous suspension of sediment particles is conceivable unless this settling is continually counteracted by a lifting force in the fluid.

The upward movement of particles is due to turbulent mixing. This is the process responsible for the continued exchange of fluid between adjacent horizontal layers as a consequence of velocity pulsations in turbulent flow.

Although starting from different assumptions, all recent theories explaining the suspension of sediment are founded on *the theory of turbulent velocity pulsations.*

Of the relevant theories the *diffusion* or *turbulent sediment transport theory* is in rather fair agreement with the regularities of suspended sediment movement. The statements on turbulent sediment transport are believed to be the most classic ones. However, this theory has its considerable drawbacks as well. Several approaches of a novel character have been introduced with the aim of eliminating them.

One of these familiar theories is referred to as the gravitational theory, or a modified alternative thereof, in which the analysis is carried out by resolving the sediment-carrying water into two components, namely the fluid and solid phases.

The energy balance equations of pulsation have been recently applied to sediment-carrying flow.

6. *Suspended-sediment transport.* The bulk of sediment transported in suspension consists of wash load or very fine grained material which the water courses are always capable of carrying. Suspended sediment transportation is thus mostly unrelated to the hydraulic parameters of the water course. Opinions generally agree on the fact that suspended - sediment transport is controlled almost exclusively by the quantity of sediment entering the water course, i.e., by the sediment supply. There being no causal relation between the suspended sediment

103

load and the hydraulic factors, it would be essentially impossible to establish a relationship between them.

The rate of the sediment supply is governed by the properties of the catchment area and of the climatic conditions, named collectively the hydrological factors. In principle, suspended sediment transport should be related to these. Remembering, however, that the regime of rivers, i.e., the variations in discharges and flow velocities are controlled by the very same hydrological factors (the size and shape of the catchment area as well as by the volume and distribution of precipitation), it seems logical to assume that symptomatic relations can be introduced for relating suspended sediment transportation, too, to discharge and flow velocity. These symptomatic relations will be associated, logically, with probability theory, since great numbers of factors affecting sediment transportation can still not be allowed for.

Symptomatic relations of this nature offer in principle the only means for describing suspended sediment transportation. These apply always to a particular river or river section.

In many cases it will nevertheless be found impossible to determine the total suspended sediment load on the basis of relationships involving water discharge or flow velocity. The problem is related to the particle size of suspended sediment. No explanation is deemed necessary for the fact that in the case of sediments finer than a certain size, the role of discharges and flow velocities, that is, of the hydraulic factors, is considerably less important than where the sediment is more coarsely grained. Where the supply of very fine sediments from the catchment area, or the channel to the water course is abundant, the river is capable of transporting it without particular conditions. This is why in cases where fine suspended sediment has a very large share in the total sediment load, the symptomatic relations with water discharge and flow velocity become invalid.

For instance, sediment observations performed on the Colorado River have shown the weight of suspended sediment particles greater than 0.01 mm to be proportionate to discharge raised to a certain power, and the weight of fractions finer than that, not to be related thereto. The total suspended sediment discharge was demonstrated moreover to be unrelated to discharge. These investigations were made by E. W. Lane and S. Shulits according to whom 0.01 mm is thus the potential size limit.

Similar conclusions have been arrived at also by J. W. Johnson, according to whom the suspended load consisting of particles greater than 0.05 mm is related to water discharge.

The sediment transported in rivers in Hungary is generally fine-grained, but the percentage of fractions finer than 0.01 is rather low. This is why it was found possible almost invariably to establish for these rivers relationships between the suspended sediment load and the water discharge or flow velocity. These will be recurred to in detail later.

Another method for determining the suspended sediment load involves observations in the field. Sediment concentration is determined from water samples

104

retrieved in several verticals, and even from several points in the same verticals. The great volume of sampling can sometimes be avoided if we succeed in estimating the mean sediment concentration from a few representative concentration values on the basis of regularities determined by preliminary studies.

Once the mean sediment concentration and discharge in a section are known, the weight of sediment transported in unit time is found as the product of the two values.

A number of relationships have been published in the literature, from which the suspended sediment load is computed with the help of the mean concentration. Neither of the formulas involving the mean sediment concentration can be used unless at least one concentration value is known.

The determination of the mean sediment concentration or of the suspended sediment load will be discussed in detail subsequently.

1.1.3.3. Research into sediment transport. Although the problems associated with the movement of sediment in alluvial streams have received attention for a relatively long time, no appreciable advances have been achieved in this field until recent times.

Extensive investigations and research have succeeded in throwing light on many physical, morphological and hydrological aspects of the phenomenon of sediment transportation. In spite of the considerable advances and the results attained thereby, it would be misleading to assume that all problems related to sediment transportation have been clearly formulated and solved.

A complete *historical review* of the development in the theory of sediment transportation would be very difficult to present. Nevertheless for the sake of completeness it is deemed necessary to mention, however briefly, the main stages in this process of development.*

According to early records sediment transportation in streams was first studied in China. Problems related to the regulation of the Yellow River were studied from 1565 to 1591, i.e. for 27 years by C. H. Pan who published the results of his studies in 1590, in 14 volumes. The early endeavours of the Chinese in the research on sediment transportation in alluvial streams were not unmotivated. As pointed out in *Section 1.1.1*, incredibly large volumes of sediment are transported by the Yellow River and the other large rivers in China at times of floods.

The vast volumes of sediment present serious obstacles to navigation and increase continually the grave hazard of flood disasters. Sediment transportation has received continuous attention in China and many scientific results of great importance have been attained in this work.

The early research in China was followed by the studies of D. Guglielmini in Italy, who examined besides the regulation of water courses, also the phenomenon

---

* A detailed description of the history of fluvial hydraulics and in this connection of the hydraulics of sediment movement is to be found in the book "Hydraulics of sediment transport" by W. H. Graf, published in 1971.

of sediment transportation in his work *Opera omnia*. Mention should be made further of P. Frizi who in 1762 published a paper on problems related to the regulation of river beds and gullies.

The first investigators are known to have been followed by the French hydraulicians who adopted a theoretical approach, based on practical experience, to phenomena taking place in alluvial channels. The famous velocity formula of A. Chézy became familiar in 1768 and was followed by studies of L. G. Du Buat concerning the frictional force arising on the channel bottom.

Relying on the scientific results of the French hydraulicians, field observations on sediment transportation in alluvial streams were started at the end of the 18th and early in the 19th centuries. These observations were meant to determine the suspended load transported in streams. The first of such observations on record were made in 1808 to 1809 by Grosse and Subours on the Rhône river. These were followed by the observations of Blohm from 1837 to 1854 on the Elbe and by those of Baumgarten on the Garonne river. On the Mississippi the first observations were performed in 1838 by Captain Talcott, while in connection with the studies of A. A. Humphreys and H. L. Abbot sediment transportation in the Mississippi was investigated by Forshey from 1851 to 1852.

Following the first sediment observations, an increasing number of reports can be found in the literature on alluvial rivers. In Hungary, the first observations were performed on the Danube at Budapest by M. Balló in 1871 and 1872. These were followed by the measurements of D. Pasteiner in 1901 – 1902 on the Tisza river and by those of H. Horusitzky on the Vág river in 1903. The first observations in Russia were performed between 1875 and 1900 by V. M. Lokhtin. The suspended sediment in the Danube was studied by Wolfsbauer at Vienna, in 1878, while in 1890 the problems of sediment discharge in the Danube were studied in considerable detail by A. Penck. In 1905 a sampling device constructed especially for this purpose was used by S. P. Maksimov to observe the suspended-sediment discharge in the Volga.

The advances in the field observation of sediment transportation were, naturally, accompanied by continued research on the theory of sediment transport. Considering theoretical development in this field, greatest significance may be attributed to the theory of P. Du Boys who introduced in his studies on alluvial rivers the tractive force, a concept still in use. In the endeavours of Du Boys an attempt was already made to apply the contemporary knowledge on hydraulics in determining theoretically the mechanics of sediment discharge in alluvial rivers.

Following Du Boys, publications on research into the theory of sediment transportation appeared at an increasing rate. Motivated by the significant role played by sediment transportation in the planning, designing and implementation of hydraulic engineering projects, research was extended to an increasing number of problems related to sediment movement. As an outstanding example of these efforts the studies performed by R. G. Kennedy in 1894 to 1895 on non-silting and non-scouring channels are worthy of being mentioned separately. In 1897 the Russian engineer V. M. Lokhtin discussed the stability of alluvial channels.

In Hungary conclusions of considerable theoretical interest were published in 1906 by Ö. Bogdánfy in his book The Hydraulics of Alluvial Rivers.

Early measurements and observations in the field were made in order to facilitate the realization of river regulation projects. These efforts were mainly concerned with the aversion of damages caused by natural water courses.

Development in the field of theoretical research proceeded logically at an increasing rate. Progress in the theory of sediment transportation was greatly accelerated by the introduction of laboratory experiments in hydraulics. Prior to the beginning of laboratory work, the criteria for the initial movement of sediment particles were expressed in terms of velocities by W. Airy. A similar approach was later adopted by W. W. Rubey and others.

Among the laboratory experiments on sediment transportation those made in 1914 by G. K. Gilbert in California are of outstanding significance. The studies on sediment movement by A. Schoklitsch were published simultaneously.

Significant contributions to the theory of sediment transportation mechanics were made by N. E. Zhukovsky who devoted detailed attention to sediment transportation in alluvial rivers in several publications.

In 1919 the concept and theory of non-scouring and non-silting channels, introduced earlier by Kennedy, were improved by R. K. Linsley. The movement of bed load was studied under laboratory conditions in 1922 by F. Shaffernak, who developed a method for estimating the rate of bed load in alluvial rivers. Extensive measurements were made between 1927 and 1938 by B. V. Polyakov with the objective of determining the movement of suspended sediment in the Volga. In 1929 G. Lacey published his paper on non-scouring and non-silting channels, reflecting the importance of sediment transportation in artificial canals as well, especially those conveying irrigation water. The laws governing turbulent flow were introduced by V. M. Makkaveev to the study of suspended sediment transportation. He was followed by M. P. O'Brien who introduced the theory of turbulent sediment transportation. A bed load trap was used in 1931 by R. Ehrenberger for studying the bed load discharge in the Danube at Vienna. Bed load transportation was studied as a physical phenomenon by E. Indri and F. T. Mavis. Considerable advances in the development of the theory of sediment transportation may be attributed to E. Meyer-Peter, P. Polya and R. Müller followed by A. A. Kalinske and L. G. Straub. The studies on stable channels have been improved and advanced by E. W. Lane, T. Blench and C. C. Inglis.

An experimental approach was adopted by H. Kramer, later by A. Shields for the study of bed load transportation. Almost every detail of the phenomenon of sediment discharge received attention by V. Vanoni whose results greatly contributed to the better understanding of this problem. By his studies founded on the mechanics of fluids, H. Rouse succeeded in clearing a number of theoretical problems in sediment movement. The bed load function and equation of H. A. Einstein may be regarded to have opened a new chapter in the field of theoretical research.

Results of considerable interest were attained by A. I. Losievsky and V. N. Goncharov in improving bed load measurements. In Hungary regular field observations on bed load discharge were started in 1933 by K. Töry on the Upper Danube in which the author had the opportunity of participating after 1935. A bed load trap involving no screen was designed in 1942 to 1944 by Z. Károlyi, and is still in use, which certain modifications, in a number of countries.*

Sediment problems related to canalized river sections were considered by F. Orth and G. I. Shamov.

Sediment transportation in alluvial channels was studied in great detail by V. I. Egiazaroff. A special theory was derived by M. A. Velikanov for describing the regularities observed in the movement of suspended sediment. Results of great interest were attained also by I. I. Levi, G. B. Lopatin, M. A. Dementiev, A. K. Ananyan, A. V. Karaushev, Y. Ibad-Zade, G. Labaye, and J. Chabert.

Of the more recent investigations, special mention must be made of the results attained by M. Albertson, D. B. Simons, E. V. Richardson, A. M. Laursen, H. K. Liu and R. J. Garde, who have examined the criteria governing various boundary conditions and the regime of sediment transportation. The similarity criteria of sediment movement have been improved by Ning Chien and S. Yalin. The physical foundations of sediment transportation have been studied by R. R. Bagnold, the silting of reservoirs, by L. C. Gottschalk, channel development, by H. W. Anderson, while suspended sediment discharge, by N. H. Brooks.

The complex phenomenon of sediment transportation is being studied presently by a great number of scientists. Of these, mention should be made of J. F. Kennedy who deals with bed forms, of R. Pedroli and C. Erkek who are concerned with bed load discharge, of G. I. Barenblatt, F. Frankl, V. G. Sanoyan and N. A. Mikhailova whose interest is focused on suspended sediment, of J. Zeller, D. I. H. Barr, and J. G. Herbertson who, besides general aspects, deal with numerous detail problems in sediment transportation, further of T. Ackers who studies alluvial streams, as well as of L. B. Leopold and I. Maddock who have conducted investigations on the interrelations existing between the geometry and sediment transport of alluvial streams.

Of the Hungarian investigators Z. Károlyi, in more recent times J. Csoma, Z. Hankó, L. Rákóczi, K. Stelczer and I. V. Nagy, have made noteworthy contributions to our understanding of sediment transportation phenomena.

Although it is fully appreciated that the above list of references is necessarily an incomplete one, it is believed to reflect the main features of development in the theory of sediment transportation. In the course of gradual advancement started with the publication of the theory of Du Boys, the first studies were concerned with the forms of sediment transportation. The distinction between bed load and suspended load was made in the early stage of investigations. Significant progress in the theory of sediment transportation mechanics may be asso-

*In the present book the Hungarian Upper Danube will be understood to be the river section between Dévény and Gönyü, disregarding any other division into sections.

ciated with the introduction of the concepts of channel stability and of the non-scouring and non-silting channel. A better understanding of the fundamentals of fluid mechanics and hydrodynamics are believed to have contributed greatly to the understanding of sediment transportation phenomena. Progress in research on turbulent flow has offered explanation to a great number of problems encountered in connection with sediment transportation.

Parallel to theoretical research a number of sediment traps and samplers have been devised for sediment observations in the field.

Besides the problems caused by sediment in general river regulation practice, the sediment problems encountered in connection with a wide variety of hydraulic structures have been tackled in the course of development. For solving sediment problems arising at river barrages extensive investigations have become necessary.

The problems encountered in the design of non-scouring and non-silting canals have demonstrated the great significance of sediment movement in irrigation projects. Sediment problems have proved to be no longer negligible in a wide variety of water uses. The removal of sediment from water has become an important stage of treatment.

Gradual development has led eventually to the recognition of the necessity of taking sediment transportation into consideration in practically every hydraulic project to ensure a technically and economically sound design and construction, as well as undisturbed operation of all hydraulic structures.

1.1.4. ADVANCES IN THE THEORY OF SEDIMENT TRANSPORT

1.1.4.1. Theoretical relationships in sediment transport. In studies on the mechanics of sediment transportation the principle of cause and effect has been applied from the very beginning. In examining various sediment transportation phenomena attempts have been made to determine the magnitude of relevant quantities as the resultant effect in terms of the quantities dominating the phenomenon.

The publication of the tractive force formula by Du Boys has initiated laboratory investigations for determining the incipient stages of movement with the help of the critical tractive force τ_c. From these investigations relationships between the critical tractive force τ_c, the diameter d and the specific gravity γ_1 of the sediment material have been derived. Since τ_c is logically related to velocity, the critical magnitude thereof, namely v_c, has been related to particle size and specific gravity. The rate of bed load transport has also been related to the tractive force τ and to the critical magnitude τ_c thereof, or to velocity v and to the critical value v_c thereof. The wearing of sediment has been related, again on the basis of laboratory experiments, to the distance travelled and to the weight of sediment particles.

Along with the causal relationships, symptomatic relations were developed in the early stages of research into sediment transportation. Initially such relations were not applied deliberately; only the obvious closeness of correlation prompted investigators in their quest for such symptomatic relationships.

In sediment transportation as in any other stochastic process it is the statistical parameters, rather than the instantaneous values of individual variables, that can be related to one another. This is why probability methods, namely correlation computations, are to be applied for determining causal and symptomatic relationships alike. Nevertheless, in analogy to the approach followed in other fields of engineering practice, approximate functional relationships are applied also in sediment transportation, though at the cost of certain simplifying assumptions.

The numbers named after Froude, Cauchy, Reynolds and Weber were the first dimensionless parameters in hydraulics and fluid mechanics. Their main field of application was initially the domain of similarity mechanics. However, owing to the possibility of their physical interpretation, their potential fields of application expanded considerably with time. Although their physical significance and meaning was not always recognized immediately, they were nevertheless introduced at a fairly early stage for describing various properties of flow.

Certain dimensionless numbers can be given a physical interpretation from a number of aspects. The most general formulation appears to have been given by Rouse who expressed one aspect of physical interpretation as follows: "Any numerical coefficient characterizing flow is essentially a simple mathematical symbol of the dimensionless combination of variables characteristic of flow." For instance the Froude and Reynolds numbers mentioned before may be regarded physically as the ratio of inertia to gravity forces, respectively of the inertia to viscous forces, their numerical value being characteristic of subcritical and supercritical, respectively of laminar and turbulent flow. Another possible aspect of physical interpretation may be that the Froude and Reynolds numbers, being characteristic of the type of flow, or of the dynamic conditions of movement, can be used as substantial parameters in all relationships in which the type and dynamic conditions of movement are involved.

Shields, Kalinske and Lane were the first to use dimensionless numbers in the theoretical relationships describing sediment transportation. Their introduction was a fortunate consequence of their potential physical interpretation.

In view of the considerable advantages resulting from their use, dimensionless numbers have found widespread application in subsequent research. Many of the dimensionless parameters, of which a great number have been introduced differ from one another often in name or form only, without being essentially independent. Considering the methods of expression, application, mathematical form and the name of dimensionless numbers involved in sediment transportation studies, the absence of a uniform system will become unquestionably conspicuous. For this reason a discussion on some of the properties of dimensionless numbers appears to be fully justified.

The ratio of two physical quantities or the power products thereof may be dimensionless. In fluid mechanics — and thus obviously in sediment studies as well — dimensionless numbers are grouped on the basis of certain arbitrary approaches.

110

The ratio of two quantities defined in identical terms will be necessarily dimensionless, since quantities defined in identical terms will have obviously identical dimensions. If two quantities defined in identical terms are involved in one and the same system, their ratio may be termed a *simple quotient*. However, if the two quantities defined in identical terms are involved in two different systems, their ratio may be referred to as a *conversion factor or scale ratio*. Scale factors or scale ratios are associated specifically with the domain of model testing.

Two- or more-dimensional quantities involved in the same system may also be combined to form a dimensionless number. The method of their determination is dealt with in similarity theory, that is, in one of its chapters, dimensional analysis. In principle, the number of dimensionless numbers is infinite. The "infinite number" of dimensionless groups exists only in theory, because some of them are not independent and can thus be defined as a function of independent parameters. Actually, of the multitude of dimensionless numbers, only those independent of one another and capable of being given a physical interpretation are essential. In view of the aspects of physical interpretation outlined above, it should be clear that the dimensionless numbers that can be given a physical interpretation play the predominant role in sediment research, too.

Several advantages accrue from the introduction of dimensionless parameters: the number of variables involved in a particular relationship is thereby reduced and since they are unrelated to the system of units used, computation work is facilitated. However, as will be appreciated from the foregoing, their greatest advantages lies in the fact that by their physical interpretation a phenomenon, or a particular property thereof, is especially emphasized.

Dimensionless numbers and their applications may be accompanied by certain drawbacks as well. The most important of these is that in the dimensionless form the relative magnitude of physical quantities is mostly obscured. Even gross errors may become imperceptible in this way. In many instances errors may remain hidden even if the relationship itself is invalid. A further drawback is that the relationships expressed in dimensionless form are much less visual than dimensional equations. Thus in sediment transportation the dimensional relation between the critical velocity or critical tractive force and the particle diameter and sediment specific gravity indicates clearly, at the first glance, that a higher critical value belongs to greater diameters and specific gravities. In engineering practice this apparently insignificant advantage of visualization must not be underrated, since engineering work in the preliminary and designing stages is invariably directed at the determination of the appropriate dimensions, i.e., the magnitude of dimensional quantities.

It would, however, be misleading to gain the impression from the foregoing considerations that the application of dimensionless numbers is generally objectionable. On the contrary, dimensionless numbers are in many cases practically unavoidable.

Dimensional analysis has been recognized as the general method by which dimensional and dimensionless physical quantities characterizing a particular phenomenon are combined into dimensionless numbers or parameters, describing the phenomenon by relating these to one another.

Where the relationship existing between the variables of the particular phenomenon under consideration can be expressed in an analytical form (by a mathematical model), the application of dimensional analysis is out of place and similarity theory is to be used. In fact, dimensional analysis alone conveys no information whatsoever on the interrelation of the variables dominating the phenomenon. The variables involved in the phenomena are themselves insufficient for deciding which of the variables is essential, in what phase of a process and at what stage it becomes negligible. It is for this reason that the dimensionless groups obtained by dimensional analysis are applicable only for the more visual representation of experimental data.

Nevertheless, dimensional analysis and the dimensionless numbers developed by this method have proved extremely important in sediment investigations. In fact, the relationships are in most cases too complex, so that their mathematical model is not known in advance. In such cases dimensional analysis frequently offers the only possibility for determining dimensionless parameters. It should be realized, however, that the actual relationship cannot be determined unless experimental results are taken into consideration.

In sediment research dimensional analysis has been applied in a variety of ways, differing from one another in one or more respects.

The general method in dimensional analysis is to derive dimensionless groups from the dimensional and dimensionless physical quantities governing the phenomenon. Thus, for instance, if a phenomenon belonging to the domain of sediment transportation is known from the initial conditions to be described by the viscosity v and density ρ of the fluid, further by the particle size d and density ρ_1 of the sediment, as well as by the depth D, slope S of flow and by gravitational accelerational g, then dimensionless groups can be formed of the $n = 7$ physical quantities

$$v, \ \rho, \ d, \ \rho_1, \ D, \ S, \ g \tag{1.1.4--1}$$

The number of basic dimensions is $m = 3$. Consequently, the number of independent dimensionless parameters is $7 - 3 = 4$. As regards their formal composition, the dimensionless groups depend on the quantities adopted as basic physical quantities. Basic physical quantities may be selected arbitrarily with the only restriction that their number should equal the number m of the basic dimensions and each of the m basic dimensions should be involved at least once in them. Adopting thus the basic quantities D, ρ and g or else D, ρ_1 and v, different dimensionless groups, and, accordingly, two formally different relationships will be obtained. It should be obvious, that each of these two relationships may describe the phenomenon positively, indicating that these can be derived from one another and consequently that they are interdependent. As far as the determination of the relationship is concerned it would be thus immaterial which of the two relationships is adopted, and, in principle, even dimensionless numbers of a form other than those of the foregoing should yield the same result.

The effect of individual physical quantities and thus of the dimensionless groups derived therefrom on the phenomenon under consideration may be different. The influence of some parameters on the unknown quantity may be decisive, whereas others may be neglected without introducing an error of major consequence. This is the circumstance permitting the relationships to be simplified and, since eventually these are determined on the basis of experimental results, the number of quantities to be measured, to be reduced. In the course of experiments, measurements on one or several physical quantities are almost unavoidably omitted, allowing for their influence by approximation only. The form adopted for the relationship assumes significance in such cases. The form to be given preference is logically that in which the non-measured physical quantities are involved in the parameters of negligible influence.

A case frequently encountered in laboratory practice is where the properties v and ρ of the fluid, as well as the density ρ_1 of the sediment are kept constant, and only particle diameter d, the depth D and slope S of flow are varied. In this case it is unadvisable to adopt either d, D or S as the basic quantities, these being involved in each of the dimensionless numbers so that the magnitude of each dimensionless parameter is affected by their variation. In such cases a form obtained by adopting other basic quantities should be applied, since the variables d, D and S can be confined in this manner to individual dimensionless numbers.

It will be appreciated from the foregoing that for deriving an unknown relationship, dimensionless numbers must be produced in a wide variety of forms. The work required is usually lengthy and tedious, which is a drawback of dimensional analysis.

Another method of applying dimensional analysis in sediment research consists of replacing one or several of the physical quantities describing the phenomenon by a derived quantity related to these. Thus, for instance, quantities g and S were replaced by Yalin with the derived quantities

$$\Delta\gamma = g(\rho_1 - \rho) \tag{1.1.4-2}$$

and

$$U_* = \sqrt{gDS} \tag{1.1.4-3}$$

The seven physical quantities in Eq. (1.1.4−1) are thus replaced by the quantities

$$v, \ \rho, \ d, \ \rho_1, \ D, \ \Delta\gamma, \ U_* \tag{1.1.4-4}$$

and consequently the relationship is obtained in a new form. Being derived according to Eqs (1.1.4−2) and (1.1.4−3) from the foregoing, the description given of the relationship by the new form is a positive one just as that given by the foregoing expressions.

Derived physical quantities are in general introduced on the basis of preliminary research into the phenomenon under consideration. Studies on sediment transportation have revealed the importance of the shear velocity $U_* = \sqrt{\tau_0/\rho}$

113

and the suitability of $\Delta\gamma$ for representing the densities of the fluid and the sediment. In this way the replacement of the physical quantities in Eq. (1.1.4−1) by those involved in Eqs (1.1.4−2) and (1.1.4−3) may be regarded as advantageous.

The replacement of the physical quantities characterizing the phenomenon by derived quantities may, however, involve several drawbacks. On the one hand, inconsistencies may be introduced into the logical system of notations adopted for the physical quantities, on the other hand, derived quantities are involved in some dimensionless groups. The selection of the most suitable form of expression may be *a priori* restricted by this circumstance.

Relationships are frequently determined on the basis of *hydraulic similarity*. No relationship whatsoever can be established by the principle of similarity alone. Although we are justified in postulating that if the relationship retains its validity for physical phenomena of different dimensions and properties (in the present case, for different kinds of flow transporting sediment), it may then be regarded as a criterion of similarity. It should be remembered, nevertheless, that rather than ensuring similarity, the problem here is the determination of expressions and relationships by permitting the determination of the desired quantity.

Obviously, in particular cases experiments performed by using similarity criteria may also prove successful.

For determining relationships the concept of *potential dynamic velocities* has most recently been introduced by D. I. H. Barr. The approach appears to be a very promising one. With due allowance for the physical character of the phenomenon, the physical quantities characterizing the phenomenon have been combined by Barr into quantities having the dimension of velocity, referred to as potential dynamic velocities, which, being independent, are suitable for determining any particular quantity involved in the phenomenon. The method of Barr will naturally yield good results, provided the most suitable potential dynamic velocities are selected in advance. It is, however, extremely difficult to select in advance the most suitable and independent potential dynamic velocities. To overcome this difficulty a mathematical method has been developed by the author permitting the relation to be formulated in a variety of ways without being obliged to adopt in advance the potential dynamic velocities. Aside from velocities, the method can be applied also if other potential dynamic quantities of any arbitrary dimension are introduced. A corresponding method has been developed by the author for potential dynamic accelerations and potential dynamic lengths as well. These will be described in detail in *Subsection 1.1.4.2*.

The procedure by which a dimensionless equation of n terms is derived from a dimensionally homogeneous equation of $(n + 1)$ terms is applied as a separate method in several papers published by Barr. The terms of the dimensionally homogeneous equation may have, clearly, any dimension. (The dimension may be thus the force acting on unit mass, velocity or even length.)

It should be noted finally that in later papers Barr introduced the linear proportionalities which are essentially identical with the method developed by the

114

author using potential dynamic lengths. The description of the method of linear proportionalities will be given in *Section 1.2.8* discussing the investigations of Barr and Herbertson.

1.1.4.2. The introduction of theoretical relations. In any relation describing or defining a physical phenomenon, the correct selection of the quantities characterizing the phenomenon, namely of the variables, is of fundamental importance. Whichever method is adopted for determining a relation, an error is introduced if one or several of the variables affecting the phenomenon are neglected, and the magnitude of the error will depend on the weight of the neglected variable. *The correct selection of physical quantities is thus seen to be an essential prerequisite in any method.* This alone is, however, an unsatisfactory and insufficient condition since of the quantities selected only those independent of one another are to be taken into consideration. The physical quantities are in general combined into dimensionless groups, and the relation itself is formulated in a dimensionless form. However, the application of dimensional relations is also readily possible. With dimensionless numbers there is again the possibility of using interdependent groups as independent ones.

As mentioned before, it is generally recognized that in the conventional application of dimensional analysis, the dimensionless groups depend formally on the quantities selected as basic physical quantities. The use of derived quantities instead of the variables may also impose restrictions. In order to permit the relations to be analysed in different forms without a priori restrictions a new mathematical method has been developed by the author. The method will be introduced first in connection with the potential dynamic velocities.

It seems pertinent to discuss first the concept of *potential dynamic velocities* and the generalization thereof introduced by the author.

The term potential dynamic velocity will be remembered to have been introduced by I. D. Barr who used these velocities for determining relations on the basis of similarity, relying on independent dimensionless groups selected in advance with the help of theoretical considerations. In the method developed by the author, the independent dimensionless groups are determined on an analytical basis without being selected in advance.

Any quantity can be described in terms of dimensional and dimensionless physical quantities. By subjecting these to different mathematical operations, quantities having the dimension of velocity can be formed. It should be clear, that these are not actual velocities and are not even identical with the resultant velocities associated with movement but constitute only possible, i.e. *potential velocities.*

The term is believed to be relevant because these velocities depend on the physical quantities controlling the movement of the liquid and imply thus a certain possibility, ability, i.e. potentiality. It should be noted in this context that the shear velocity $U_* = \sqrt{gRS}$ introduced long ago in fluid mechanics is also one of these potential dynamic velocities.

Depending on the type and number of dimensional and dimensionless physical quantities found necessary or desirable for describing a particular phenomenon, the potential dynamic velocities will be of a different number. It should be appreciated further that, if all potential dynamic velocities are formed, some of these will be obtainable from one or several velocities, indicating that not all of the conceivable potential dynamic velocities will be independent. The phenomenon will be described positively by the truly independent ones. If it is desired to specify the relation characterizing a particular phenomenon in a form reduced to some resultant velocity, the independent potential dynamic velocities can be applied directly. Obviously, dimensionless relations can also be formulated. The ratios of independent potential dynamic velocities lead in fact to independent dimensionless groups, so that these define on a mathematical basis the independent dimensionless numbers by which the phenomenon is uniquely described. Thus the independent complete system of simple physical variables can be replaced essentially by the independent complete system of parameters having the dimension of velocity, derived from these quantities.

It is considered pertinent to illustrate the formulation of potential dynamic velocities in connection with the phenomenon of sediment transportation.

Let g [m/sec^2] denote acceleration by gravity, D [m] the mean depth of flow, B [m] the width of the channel, d [m] the diameter of the sediment particle, v [m^2/sec] the coefficient of kinematic viscosity, ρ [kp sec^2/m^4] and ρ_1 [kp sec^2/m^4] the densities of the fluid and sediment, respectively and S [$-$] the slope of the energy line.

Introducing the dimensionless ratio

$$\frac{\rho_1 - \rho}{\rho} = \rho' \qquad (1.1.4-5)$$

the phenomenon of sediment transportation will be described by five dimensional and two dimensionless — altogether by seven — physical quantities:

$$g, \ D, \ B, \ d, \ v, \ \rho', \ S \qquad (1.1.4-6)$$

In selecting the physical quantities, the sediment (its size, granulometry, shape) has been assumed to be completely described by the particle diameter d and in the case of a given fluid by the quantity ρ'.

The seven physical quantities involved in Eq. (1.1.4−6) are clearly independent.

The five independent dimensional physical quantities g, D, B, d and v, the dimensions of which comprise only length and time, can be combined into $5 - 2 + 1 = 4$ independent potential dynamic velocities. All other derived quantities having the dimension of velocity are obtainable from the four independent velocities and are thus no longer independent.

From the four independent potential dynamic velocities and from the two dimensionless physical quantities (ρ', S) no more that two additional independent potential dynamic velocities can be formed by any arbitrary operation or grouping. Consequently, for describing the phenomenon of sediment transportation under the afore-mentioned conditions, the number of independent potential dynamic velocities, that can be combined into a variety of groups, will invariably be six. Considering an independent velocity group comprising six terms, it should be clear that additional velocities can also be formed, but these will depend on the six-term group mentioned above.

In principle, it would be thus sufficient to write a single independent velocity group of six terms for describing the physical phenomenon. However, if a six-term independent velocity group of this kind were to be selected without guidance from previous experience and considerations, this would very likely prove useless owing to the limited range of available experimental data, or because of the absence of observation data on one of the variables. It is therefore expedient to form more than six independent potential dynamic velocities, of which six-term velocity groups of several different compositions can be selected. This would moreover enable us to analyse parameters (or dimensionless numbers) mentioned earlier in the literature, or to be introduced in the future in any conceivable form.

Using the five dimensional physical quantities adopted at the start, a method resembling dimensional analysis may be applied for determining the independent parameters of velocity dimension which will, naturally, be the potential dynamic velocities v_i. The dimension matrix should be written in the "System of units" $z_1 = \text{m/sec}$ and $z_2 = \text{m}$, and the logarithm of the dimension x_i of the individual variables should be y_i, i.e. $y_i = \ln (x_i)$:

	z_1	z_2
y_v	1	0
y_g	2	-1
y_D	0	1
y_B	0	1
y_d	0	1
y_v	1	1

Expressing from the first two rows z_1 and z_2 as functions of y_v and y_g:

$$z_1 = y_v$$

$$z_2 = 2y_v - y_g$$

the expressions

$$y_D = 2y_v - y_s$$

$$y_B = 2y_v - y_g$$

$$y_d = 2y_v - y_g$$

$$y_v = 3y_v - y_g$$

117

are obtained. Rearranging terms, y_v is obtained as

$$y_v = \frac{1}{2}(y_D + y_g) = \frac{1}{2}(y_B + y_g) = \frac{1}{2}(y_d + y_g) = \frac{1}{3}(y_v + y_g)$$

Taking the exponential form of the relations and introducing the physical variables, the following four independent potential dynamic velocities result:

$$v_1 = \sqrt{Dg}, \quad v_2 = \sqrt{Bg}, \quad v_3 = \sqrt{dg}, \quad v_4 = \sqrt[3]{vg} \qquad (1.1.4-7a)$$

Another independent system is obtained if g in the second row of the dimensional matrix is replaced by some other variable. For instance, with the basic dimension v the dimension matrix becomes

	z_1	z_2
y_v	1	0
y_v	1	1
y_g	2	-1
y_D	0	1
y_B	0	1
y_d	0	1

and since

$$z_1 = y_v, \quad z_2 = -y_v + y_v$$

thus

$$y_g = 2y_v + y_v + y_v = 3y_v - y_v$$
$$y_D = y_B = y_d = -y_v + y_v$$

whence

$$v_1' = \sqrt[3]{vg}, \quad v_2' = v/B, \quad v_3' = v/D, \quad v_4' = v/d \qquad (1.1.4-7b)$$

become the four independent potential dynamic velocities.

Any system can be adopted as basis and, from the potential dynamic velocities involved in any system, additional potential velocities can be derived as indicated by the relation

$$\frac{v_i^3}{v_j^2} = v_K$$

For instance

$$\frac{v_2^3}{v_1^2} = \frac{B^{3/2}\, g^{3/2}}{Dg} = \frac{B^{3/2}\, g^{1/2}}{D}$$

118

As mentioned before, the five independent dimensional basic quantities are combined into more than four potential velocities. Let us write, for instance, from Eqs (1.1.4−7a) and (1.1.4−7b) the seven velocities

$$\sqrt{gD}, \quad \sqrt{gB}, \quad \sqrt{gd}, \quad v/D, \quad v/B, \quad v/d, \quad \sqrt[3]{gv} \qquad (1.1.4-7)$$

of which no more than four are independent.

Including the two dimensionless numbers, any operation or grouping will result in only two additional independent dynamic velocities. Consequently, the number of independent potential dynamic velocities will be six.

If each of the velocities involved in Eq. (1.1.4−7) is multiplied or divided (whereby the operation is immaterial) by the two dimensionless independent physical quantities (ρ', S) or by any of these raised to an arbitrary power, additional fourteen velocities are obtained. Of the altogether twenty-one potential dynamic velocities produced in this manner, no more than six will be independent.

The twenty-one velocities derived under the above restrictions may be entered into the following seven columns and three rows:

$$\sqrt{gD}, \quad \sqrt{gB}, \quad \sqrt{gd}, \quad v/D, \quad v/B, \quad v/d, \quad \sqrt[3]{gv} \qquad (1.1.4-8)$$

$$\sqrt{gDS}, \quad \sqrt{gBS}, \quad \sqrt{gdS}, \quad (v/D)S, \quad (v/B)S, \quad (v/d)S, \quad \sqrt[3]{gvS} \qquad (1.1.4-9)$$

$$\sqrt{gD\rho'}, \quad \sqrt{gB\rho'}, \quad \sqrt{gd\rho'}, \quad (v/D)\rho', \quad (v/B)\rho', \quad (v/d)\rho', \quad \sqrt[3]{gv\rho'} \qquad (1.1.4-10)$$

The above twenty-one terms may be combined in a large number of ways into six independent velocities.

The number of possible sixth-order combinations for the twenty-one quantities is

$$\binom{21}{6} = 54\ 264.$$

However, some of these combinations do not comprise six independent velocities. Some combinations are encountered in which only four independent velocities occur, but the 54,264 combinations include some which do not comprise all of the five dimensional and both dimensionless quantities and consequently, concerning all quantities describing the phenomenon, they cannot be regarded to form six independent velocities.

In selecting the truly independent six-term velocity combinations the following rules should be observed:

a) The velocities selected should comprise each of the seven physical quantities (g, D, B, d, v, ρ', S) at least once.

b) From each row no more than four velocities may be selected, but these should be independent.

c) The velocities selected must satisfy the condition that none of their possible ratios should have the same value. In other words the quantities S, ρ', S/ρ', or their inverse values should occur only once among the ratios.

119

The rules depend on the number of physical quantities included, as well as on the number of velocities formed, and are thus subject to variations for each particular case. With n denoting the number of all dimensional and dimensionless physical quantities and m the number of basic units, the number of independent potential dynamic velocities is $s = (n - m + 1)$. Since, however, the s potential dynamic velocities can be combined into $(s - 1)$ independent dimensionless groups, the number of independent dimensionless groups will be $(n - m)$, which is obviously in full agreement with Buckingham's dimensional analysis.

In terms of any velocity group comprising six independent members selected in this manner, a unique description can be given of the physical phenomenon. Since any six-term velocity group can be combined to form five independent velocity ratios, this statement applies to the velocity ratios as well. It will be appreciated from the foregoing that the particular independent velocity group used for characterizing the phenomenon is irrelevant, any difference being a formal one only. As far as the relation is concerned, it is moreover immaterial whether the relation is characterized by the velocities themselves or by dimensionless parameters formed from the ratios of these velocities.

From the above example it may be inferred that in principle it is possible to describe the phenomenon with the help of any one of the independent velocity groups. Since however, the method derived in this manner reflects the velocities or velocity ratios on which the phenomenon may mathematically depend, some of the velocities or velocity ratios may be omitted from the actual relations on the basis of experimental results. (This means, naturally, at the same time that dimensionless quantities may also drop out, these being also obtainable as velocity ratios.)

The circumstance that a particular phenomenon may depend mathematically on an independent variable, yet considering the physics of the phenomenon the effect thereof is found negligibly small, will be illustrated by the following example.

Locus and time may be regarded obviously as independent quantities. Consequently the variations in acceleration due to gravity may be studied in terms of these quantities. There is ample experimental evidence to indicate that gravitational acceleration depends, with a fair degree of approximation, on geographical location only and that time is not involved at all in this relation.

Experimental results will indicate, moreover, which of the potential dynamic velocities or velocity ratios is predominant for the phenomenon under consideration. A more or less clear picture of the role of the individual parameters is obtained as the experimental results are processed. The potential dynamic velocities and dimensionless parameters that can be neglected without introducing an appreciable error will emerge, and so will the manner in which each of the parameters is to be taken into consideration. It should be remembered that in the course of the experiments one or several physical quantities may not be observed or may be measured approximately only.

Considering the importance of individual potential dynamic velocities or dimensionless groups, as well as the unavoidable errors introduced during experi-

120

mentation, the practical importance of the velocity or dimensionless group considered negligible will be readily appreciated.

From the 21 potential dynamic velocities involved in Eqs (1.1.4−8) to (1.1.4−10), the following group involving six independent velocities should be selected

$$\sqrt{gD}, \quad \sqrt{gd}, \quad v/B, \quad v/d, \quad \sqrt{gdS}, \quad \sqrt{gd\rho'} \qquad (1.1.4-11)$$

If it is desired to determine the critical velocity v_c pertaining to the incipient motion of sediment of size d and density ρ', it is possible to express mathematically this velocity in terms of the six independent velocities in Eq. (1.1.4−11). Consequently, under these particular initial conditions the critical velocity is given by the relation

$$v_c = F(\sqrt{gD}, \quad \sqrt{gd}, \quad v/B, \quad v/d, \quad \sqrt{gdS}, \quad \sqrt{gd\rho'}) \qquad (1.1.4-12)$$

The formal structure and numerical figures of the relation of critical velocity must be determined, naturally, by experiments.

Critical velocities have already been mentioned in *Section 1.1.3*. It should only be noted here that, according to the classic impact theory, the critical velocity only depends on the potential dynamic velocity $\sqrt{gd\rho'}$ in the theoretical relation expressed by Eq. (1.1.4−12), so that according to Eq. (1.1.3−16)

$$v_c = F(\sqrt{gd\rho'})$$

A more detailed discussion of the critical velocity will be presented in *Section 1.2.5*.

The quantities comprised in Eq. (1.1.4−6) can also be combined into a dimensionless relation for describing the phenomenon. For this purpose the six independent potential dynamic velocities in Eq. (1.1.4−11) must be combined into corresponding five independent dimensionless groups.

Dimensionless groups are formed by dividing the velocities in Eq. (1.1.4−11) for instance by $\sqrt{gd}$:

$$\frac{\sqrt{gD}}{\sqrt{gd}} = \sqrt{\frac{D}{d}} \qquad (1.1.4-13a_1)$$

$$\frac{v/B}{\sqrt{gd}} = \frac{v}{B\sqrt{gd}} \qquad (1.1.4-13b_1)$$

$$\frac{v/d}{\sqrt{gd}} = \frac{v}{d\sqrt{gd}} = \frac{v}{g^{1/2}d^{3/2}} \qquad (1.1.4-13c_1)$$

$$\frac{\sqrt{gDS}}{\sqrt{gd}} = \sqrt{\frac{DS}{d}} \qquad (1.1.4-13d_1)$$

$$\frac{\sqrt{gd\rho'}}{\sqrt{gd}} = \sqrt{\rho'} \qquad (1.1.4-13e_1)$$

121

In the initial stage of investigation it may often be found practicable to intro-duce certain dimensionless parameters. For instance it may be advantageous to include slope S. Since dimensionless numbers raised to any power or multiplied by each other remain dimensionless, the ratio of two parameters may be used as a new one, in place of one of the parameters.

Since

$$\frac{\sqrt{\frac{DS}{d}}}{\sqrt{\frac{D}{d}}} = \sqrt{S}$$

of the parameters given by Eqs $(1.1.4-13a_1)$ to $(1.1.4-13e_1)$ $\sqrt{DS/d}$ is omitted and replaced by $\sqrt{S}$ as the new dimensionless parameter.

Dimensionless groups may also be introduced by combining the six velocities into five arbitrary ratios instead of dividing the remaining ones with a selected velocity. The advantage is that the five independent ratios may be selected in a manner to include, from the very beginning, certain parameters considered essential among the dimensionless numbers. For instance, from the six velocities given by Eq. $(1.1.4-11)$ the independent ratios 1/2, 2/4, 5/2, 6/2 and 1/3 can be formed. In this case the following dimensionless groups result:

$$\frac{\sqrt{gD}}{\sqrt{gd}} = \sqrt{\frac{D}{d}} \qquad (1.1.4-13a)$$

$$\frac{\sqrt{gd}}{v/d} = \frac{g^{1/2}d^{3/2}}{v} = \left(\frac{d}{v^{2/3}g^{-1/3}}\right)^{3/2} \qquad (1.1.4-13b)$$

$$\frac{\sqrt{gdS}}{\sqrt{gd}} = \sqrt{S} \qquad (1.1.4-13c)$$

$$\frac{\sqrt{gd\rho'}}{\sqrt{gd}} = \sqrt{\rho'} \qquad (1.1.4-13d)$$

$$\frac{\sqrt{gD}}{v/B} = \frac{g^{1/2}D^{1/2}}{v}B \qquad (1.1.4-13e)$$

In accordance with the initial conditions, the relationship is uniquely described in terms of the five dimensionless groups given by Eqs $(1.1.4-13a_1)$ to $(1.1.4-13e_1)$ or by Eqs $(1.1.4-13a)$ to $(1.1.4-13e)$.

Sediment will be transported by the flowing water as soon as the quantities involved in Eq. $(1.1.4-6)$ assume a certain value. Where the weight q_B [kp/m sec] of sediment transported during unit time in unit width of the channel is to be determined, the first step should consist of introducing a resultant velocity measuring q_B. Since the submerged weight of the sediment under consideration is $g(\rho_1 - \rho)$ and D is the depth of flow, the expression

$$\frac{q_B}{g(\rho_1 - \rho)D} \qquad (1.1.4-14)$$

will give the quantity of sediment expressed in volumetric units transported during unit time over unit area of the cross-section. The expression given by Eq. (1.1.4−14) has the dimension of velocity and may thus actually be regarded as a resultant velocity by which sediment load is measured. If this resultant velocity (which is a measure of sediment transport) is divided, for instance, by the potential dynamic velocity v/D, i.e., if the dimensionless parameter

$$\Phi_{B_1} = \frac{q_B}{g(\rho_1 - \rho)D} : \frac{v}{D} = \frac{q_B}{g(\rho_1 - \rho)v} \qquad (1.1.4-15)$$

is formed as a measure of sediment transport, Φ_{B_1} will be obviously a function of the five dimensionless groups involved in Eqs (1.1.4−13a) to (1.1.4−13e).

Thus, in accordance with the initial conditions, the sediment transport is given by the symbolic relation

$$\Phi_{B_1} = F\left(\frac{D}{d}, \ \frac{d}{v^{2/3} g^{-1/3}}, \ S, \ \rho', \ \frac{g^{1/2} D^{1/2}}{v} B \right) \qquad (1.1.4-16)$$

The relation itself can be determined on the basis of experimental results only. Studies of this nature will be described in *Section 1.2.9.*

Comparing the potential dynamic velocities with the dimensionless numbers commonly used, it will be realized that certain relations exist between them. The relations between the potential dynamic velocities and the dimensionless numbers will be expressed eventually with the help of some actual or resultant velocity.

It should be clear that by introducing the resultant mean velocity v and the resultant fall velocity ω, the potential dynamic velocities given by Eqs (1.1.4−8), (1.1.4−9) and (1.1.4−10) can be expressed in terms of the Reynolds and Froude numbers:

$$Re = \frac{vD}{v} \qquad (1.1.4-17)$$

$$Fr = \frac{v^2}{gD} \qquad (1.1.4-18)$$

as well as in terms of the familiar settling velocity Reynolds number and settling velocity Froude number:

$$Re_s = \frac{\omega d}{v} \qquad (1.1.4-19)$$

$$Fr_s = \frac{\omega^2}{gd} \qquad (1.1.4-20)$$

123

For instance the shear velocity $U_* = \sqrt{gDS}$ is related to the Fr number and the resultant velocity v as

$$\sqrt{gDS} = v \sqrt{\frac{S}{Fr}} \qquad (1.1.4-21)$$

or the potential velocity v/d

$$\frac{v}{d} = \frac{\omega}{Re_s} \qquad (1.1.4-22)$$

Differences will result depending on whether the potential dynamic velocities can be introduced into the Froude number or the Reynolds number. Reviewing the potential dynamic velocities it will become clear that each of them involving the acceleration due to gravity g is a Froude type potential dynamic velocity, whereas those involving the kinematic or dynamic viscosity coefficient v or μ, respectively, may be regarded as Reynolds type potential dynamic velocities.

It should be obvious, moreover, that the potential dynamic velocities involving both g and v may be referred to as Froude−Reynolds type potential dynamic velocities.

By this classification a perfect system is created for the known dimensionless numbers and the different forms of potential dynamic velocities.

For the sake of completeness it should be noted that, when considering hydraulic phenomena in which the influence of surface tension and elastic forces is not negligible, the dimensional physical quantities will comprise the surface tension H [kp/m] and Young's modulus of elasticity E [kp/m²]. Potential dynamic velocities will consequently result in which H or E is involved. On analogy to the foregoing, these will be related to the Wr or to the Ca numbers and may be regarded as Weber type or Cauchy type potential dynamic velocities.

In studies on the phenomenon of sediment transportation Froude type and Reynolds type potential dynamic velocities are involved almost exclusively. Therefore we shall only deal with these.

The use of potential dynamic velocities will be seen to entail a number of advantages. In fact, velocity may be regarded as the kinematic quantity most characteristic of phenomena related to movement. In sediment transportation, just as in any other problem in hydraulics, the task mostly consists of determining the ensuing velocities. The selection of velocities is thus amply justified. It should be realized at the same time that the exclusive use of velocities is not made compulsory by any restriction or imperative theorem. In principle any dimension could be adopted.

In some cases the introduction of *potential dynamic accelerations* may be preferable. The application of acceleration as a kinematic quantity may be motivated by its being related to the acting forces. Indeed, any acceleration may be regarded as a force acting on unit mass and, considering the predominant forces in the phenomenon, this circumstance may be extremely advantageous.

124

Considering the phenomenon of sediment transportation used also in the generalization of potential velocities, four of the five dimensional physical quantities g, D, B, d, v can be written whilst, including the two dimensionless quantities S and ρ', another two, that is, altogether six independent potential dynamic accelerations can be written.

Logically, on the analogy of the potential velocities, accelerations may also be formed. In this manner the five dimensional quantities can be combined into the "accelerations"

$$g, \quad g\frac{d}{B}, \quad g\frac{B}{d}, \quad g\frac{D}{d}, \quad \frac{v^2}{D^3}, \quad \frac{v^2}{B^3}, \quad \frac{v^2}{d^3} \qquad (1.1.4-23)$$

so that, in combination with S and ρ' — observing the restrictions mentioned before — eventually twenty-one potential dynamic accelerations are obtained:

$$g, \quad g\frac{D}{B}, \quad g\frac{D}{d}, \quad g\frac{B}{d}, \quad \frac{v^2}{D^3}, \quad \frac{v^2}{B^3}, \quad \frac{v^2}{d^3} \qquad (1.1.4-24)$$

$$gS, \quad g\frac{D}{B}S, \quad g\frac{D}{d}S, \quad g\frac{B}{d}S, \quad \frac{v^2}{D^3}S, \quad \frac{v^2}{B^3}S, \quad \frac{v^2}{d^3}S \qquad (1.1.4-25)$$

$$g\rho', \quad g\frac{D}{B}\rho', \quad g\frac{D}{d}\rho', \quad g\frac{B}{d}\rho', \quad \frac{v^2}{D^3}\rho', \quad \frac{v^2}{B^3}\rho', \quad \frac{v^2}{d^3}\rho' \qquad (1.1.4-26)$$

In selecting the truly independent six-term combinations of accelerations, the same three rules should be complied with as in the case of velocity. Any six-term group of accelerations selected in this manner will give a unique description of the physical phenomenon, in the present case, of sediment transportation subject to the initial restrictions.

Concerning the result it is thus immaterial which of the independent acceleration groups is used for describing the phenomenon. Any difference observable may be a formal one only.

It should be clear moreover that the theoretical relations derived with the help of accelerations will be identical with those determined with the help of velocities. Since regardless of whether velocities or accelerations are involved and since it includes all possible alternatives, the method outlined above must necessarily comprise a group consisting of six independent velocities and one of six independent accelerations which yield exactly the same result.

No further explanation is considered necessary to appreciate that the potential dynamic accelerations, too, can be expressed with the help of the dimensionless numbers generally used.

Potential dynamic accelerations, as pointed out already, may be regarded as a force acting on unit mass. The accelerations involving g may be termed potential gravity force acting on unit mass, whereas those including v may be treated as potential viscous forces. In hydraulic phenomena affected by surface tension or by the modulus of elasticity, accelerations that may be regarded as potential surface and potential elastic forces will clearly exist. In phenomena related to sediment transportation the effect of the two latter forces are, as mentioned already, usually small enough to be neglected.

It should be noted finally that, for ease of treatment, in certain cases the introduction of *potential dynamic lengths*, besides velocities and accelerations, may also be justified.

Adopting again the example of sediment transportation referred to in the generalization of potential velocities, the five dimensional basic quantities may be combined into the potential lengths

$$D, \ B, \ d, \ \frac{v}{\sqrt{gD}}, \ \frac{v}{\sqrt{gB}}, \ \frac{v}{\sqrt{gd}}, \ \frac{v^{2/3}}{\sqrt[3]{g}} \qquad (1.1.4-27)$$

of which, however, not more than four are independent. Introducing also the dimensionless numbers S and ρ' altogether six independent potential lengths can be written.

With the restrictions mentioned in the foregoing, twenty-one potential dynamic lengths can be written also in this case:

$$D, \quad B, \quad d, \quad \frac{v}{\sqrt{gD}}, \quad \frac{v}{\sqrt{gB}}, \quad \frac{v}{\sqrt{gd}}, \quad \frac{v^{2/3}}{\sqrt[3]{g}} \qquad (1.1.4-28)$$

$$DS, \quad BS, \quad dS, \quad \frac{v}{\sqrt{gDS}}, \quad \frac{v}{\sqrt{gBS}}, \quad \frac{v}{\sqrt{gdS}}, \quad \frac{v^{2/3}}{\sqrt[3]{gS}} \qquad (1.1.4-29)$$

$$D\rho', \quad B\rho', \quad d\rho', \quad \frac{v}{\sqrt{gD\rho'}}, \quad \frac{v}{\sqrt{gB\rho'}}, \quad \frac{v}{\sqrt{gd\rho'}}, \quad \frac{v^{2/3}}{\sqrt[3]{g\rho'}} \qquad (1.1.4-30)$$

In selecting the independent six-term length groups the rules given in connection with velocities is to be observed.

With the help of potential dynamic lengths, relations are determined in the same manner as in the case of the velocities and accelerations. It should be obvious, moreover, that the theoretical relations derived with the help of lengths will be identical with those obtained by using velocities or accelerations. In the same way as each independent six-term velocity group had a counterpart independent six-term acceleration group that yielded a result identical with that obtained with the help of velocities, corresponding length terms are also bound to exist.

It should be added that also the potential dynamic lengths can be expressed with the help of the dimensionless numbers generally used.

Let us remember that these potential dynamic lengths and the ratios thereof are referred to as linear proportionalities by Barr and Herbertson.

1.1.5. TRENDS, METHODS AND MEANS OF CONTEMPORARY RESEARCH

1.1.5.1. Recent trends in sediment research. A serious drawback of research into the movement of sediment and, in this way, also of the knowledge gained thereby is that most results are of but theoretical character, and their practical application is still unsolved except for some particular phenomena. The development of closer relationships between theory and practice is made difficult by the circumstance that the theoretical results that could be generalized in principle are not directly applicable owing to differences in the properties of streams, whereas the experiences gained on particular rivers, although valid for the river under consideration, are frequently unfounded theoretically and thus unsuited for being generalized.

Some advance in this respect may be anticipated from the circumstance that the theoretical problems in sediment transportation and the practical consequences thereof in water management problems command increasing attention, and the opportunities offered by modern technology are made use of by a great number of scientists all over the world in conducting important research with the help of sophisticated experimental, measuring, observing and data-processing equipment.

Sediment transportation phenomena associated with water management problems are being studied at present under an extremely wide variety of aspects. In these studies three principal trends may be distinguished.

Significant endeavours are made to take hydrological properties and factors into consideration in determining the sediment transport in water courses.

The second trend of research is concerned with the morphology of channels, including the macro-, mezo- and micro-configurations and the influence thereof on the movement of sediment.

A third group of research activities is concerned with the comparison and checking of theoretical results against data obtained by measurements and observations in the field.

In connection with the first trend of research it should be noted that the influence of hydrological factors and properties is most conspicuous in the origin of the sediment in the catchment and its access to the channel, yet is still discernible in sediment phenomena in the bed through the regime of flow in the channel. The influence of hydrological factors on sediment transport is manifold. In many cases these effects are amenable to qualitative observation only, but the impact of some factors on sediment transport can be determined quantitatively as well.

The second trend is concerned with the shape, magnitude and movement of irregularities occurring in the channel of alluvial streams.

The paramount importance of bed forms for sediment movement is generally recognized by now. Although in alluvial streams the mezoforms extending to an entire cross-section and the macroforms characteristic of longer sections are of primary interest yet, considering the physical aspects of the phenomenon, the study of microforms is also essential.

The third trend is not of recent origin. In fluvial hydraulics and in all investigations related thereto, attempts have been made at the very beginning to check the results obtained theoretically against measurements in the field. A novel feature in the comparison of theoretical and experimental results with actually observed ones is that in recent times this has been extended to every detail of sediment transportation and that such comparisons are made systematically. In checking theoretical results against field observation data new problems awaiting solution arise inevitably. This circumstance presents, however, no obstacle to these efforts as it has been demonstrated by recent results that various sediment transportation phenomena are much more closely interrelated than assumed ever before. The theoretical results are thus seen to form a closed system and, while detail problems are solved individually and by successive approximation, the continuous comparison and co-ordination of the results obtained is nevertheless believed to be necessary.

The three trends of research on sediment transportation comprise substantially all investigations in this domain. It would thus be superfluous to list various research subjects separately. Yet in order to make future research as efficient as possible, it is deemed advisable to focus interest on the solution of certain tasks.

One of these important tasks would be the introduction of regular sediment observations on a routine basis, even by making them obligatory. The results of theoretical research are in fact of little value unless supported by data of observations performed in the field. The objective in sediment observations should be the attainment of the same highly organized and regular observation, data collection and processing work which has already been achieved in hydrometry and hydrography on practically all water courses.

The determination of rates of sediment transportation should be made accessible to practice by further investigations. The critical evaluation and checking of a great number of sediment transport relations appears to be inevitable. Research should be conducted for developing methods that are well founded physically and guarantee that, with due allowance for the properties of a particular water course, the actual rates of sediment transport are obtained.

Increasing use should be made of the opportunities offered by the applications of a variety of tracer materials. A number of interesting results have already been achieved by the experimental application of such substances. In the solution of particular problems additional information on this extremely complex physical phenomenon may well be expected in this way.

Modelling techniques of alluvial streams are believed to be in need of being perfected. The methods commonly used are extremely ramified and concerned in general with discrete properties of sediment transportation only, so that they should be co-ordinated to develop eventually a method of testing that is general enough for the conditions of a particular problem and suited also for application to problems of detail.

The rapid advances in nuclear techniques, automation and electronics should be exploited for the construction of new measuring, observing and data-processing

128

devices. Increasing use is being made of sophisticated measuring and observing devices in both field observations and laboratory studies. Their widespread application would enable scientists and engineers to measure numerous factors in the movement of water and sediment alike which have so far been unaccessible to observation. The significance of considerably improving the accuracy and reliability of observations is almost beyond estimation.

Electronic computers are being extensively used for processing measurement and observation data. Regular mechanical data-processing may permit alternatives that would be time-consuming and expensive enough to be prohibitive.

1.1.5.2. Methods and means of research. Concerning the methods used for describing the phenomenon of sediment transportation and for determining theoretical relations between the physical quantities governing movement, a detailed treatment has been presented in *Section 1.1.4.*

For the verification and quantitative determination of every theoretical, symbolical relation, experimental methods should be adopted. The term "experiment" should be understood here in its broadest sense, i.e., any measurement, observation and data collection on a variable relevant to a particular phenomenon should be regarded an experiment. Observations, measurements and the collection of data are carried out in part in the field, on the water course itself, but the same kind of work may be performed also on flow phenomena reproduced under laboratory conditions.

Both methods are inevitable when studying sediment transportation. The methods applied to the processing of data are largely the same, regardless whether the measurements have been performed in the prototype or in a laboratory model. The differences in their respective validities should, of course, be appreciated. The results of observations performed in the field apply to the particular river or river section only. The results obtained in the laborarory are of more general validity, since the hydrological properties of particular water courses do not enter the investigations. The results of field measurements are directly applicable to the river on which they have been made. The results of laboratory tests should be evaluated separately and converted to the prototype to make them suitable for practical use.

The methods and devices used in sediment research will be discussed chiefly in accordance with the classification into bed load and suspended load. The methods and means of research into bed material and sedimentation will be dealt with separately. A detailed description of measuring devices would exceed the scope of the present volume. For these the reader is referred to the Bibliography.

Nor shall we embark upon the details of the many observation procedures. However, in connection with the development and operation of measuring devices particular methods of measurement will also be outlined.

1. Methods and devices of bed load measurements

a) *Bed load traps.* The most important measuring device used for the determination of bed load transport is the bed load trap or sampler which is lowered to the bottom to collect the bed load transported along the bottom measuring directly the amount of bed load transported during the period of measurement.

The bed load traps now in use have been evolved as a result of lengthy and tiresome work.

It should be noted at the outset that critical remarks concerning the validity of sampler measurements are still being voiced by several investigators. This aversion in the early stages of measurements using bed load traps was even greater. A number of objections to their use should be recognized as unquestionably justified, these being still the least reliable devices of sediment measurements. Their introduction has, however, proved necessary since every effort involved in a great volume of research and experiment has remained unsuccessful in the general determination of bed load transport. The attempts to determine the bed load transport directly from the particular conditions of the channel have failed similarly. Determined in these cumulative measurements is the total volume of bed load transported in a certain period. Suitable conditions are provided at the estuary of the stream where the total transported sediment volume is in general deposited. In a delta estuary, the sediment volumes deposited in the recipient sea, lake or river observed around the estuary may be used for estimating the sediment volume transported during a given period of time. It should be realized that in such cases part of the suspended sediment is also measured along with the bed load, as in the absence of flow a considerable portion of the suspended load tends to settle out.

Cumulative measurements offer no information whatsoever on variations in bed load transport with time. The results obtained in this manner contribute little to our understanding of the relationships unquestionably existing between the bed load volume and several of the hydraulic properties of the water course.

It is these reasons that may have prompted investigators to start the highly uncertain measurements by using the bed load traps.

The bed load traps are commonly classified into three groups. The first samplers were *box type traps* where the sampler frame was covered by a closely spaced mesh screen. Samplers of this type were used in 1908 by Schaffernak for his measurements on the Mura river. Samplers of this type were later constructed by Mühlhofer, Ehrenberger, Nesper and also by the Hungarian Water Service for measurements on the Upper Danube.

The second group of bed load samplers comprises the *pan type* and *pit type samplers* in which the moving bed load is accumulated in successive depressions or collecting bars. Examples for these groups are the bed load traps of Losievsky and of Polyakov.

Both box type and pit type samplers offer considerable resistance to flow as a consequence of which the entering velocity and, in turn, the transported sediment volume are greatly reduced.

The third and most up-to-date group of bed load traps may be referred to as *pressure difference samplers* where a suitable design is used to restore the original flow velocity to obtain thus a representative bed load sample. The first of the

130

pressure difference samplers was used in 1925 by Goncharov in his measurements on the Kuban river. The bed load sampler developed at the Leningrad Hydrotechnical Scientific Research Institute also belongs to this group.

After a long period of development a sampler without a mesh screen was constructed also for bed load measurements in Hungary. The principles underlying the design were elaborated by Z. Károlyi. On the basis of laboratory experiments a perforated dividing wall was mounted in the interior of the sampler to retain the entering bed load, permitting thus the clear water to emerge through the port at the rear of the sampler without unwanted turbulence.

The results of bed load measurements made with different bed load traps have shown the weight of bed load trapped in the sampler to differ from the weight of bed load actually transported. Especially great differences were observable with the first mesh-screen type samplers calling attention in the early stage of bed load measurements to the necessity of calibrating such equipment.

In connection with the calibration of bed load samplers the investigations by Shamov at Leningrad are of fundamental importance on account of establishing the efficiency of the samplers by Losievsky — Polyakov and the Leningrad Hydrotechnical Scientific Research Institute. In these measurements the efficiency of the Losievsky sampler was 0.38, that of the Polyakov sampler 0.46, while that of the Leningrad Research Institute 0.75 on the average. These efficiency figures imply that not more than 38, 46 and 75% of the actual bed load are measured by the afore-mentioned samplers. The investigations of Shamov have shown further the differential pressure samplers to be superior to the box type and pan type samplers alike.

At the Hydraulic Experimental Institute, Zürich, models to scales of 1 : 5, 1 : 10 and 1 : 25 have been used by Einstein to determine the efficiency of the sediment sampler devised by Nesper. The results have shown the average efficiency of the box type bed load sampler of Nesper to be about 0.45.

In the experiments of Einstein a certain periodicity was observed in bed load transport. The pulsations observed in the quantity of bed load transported have shown a period of about 15 minutes and one about 10 to 16 hours.

In Vienna, laboratory tests were made by Ehrenberger to determine the efficiency of a bed load sampler developed by himself. The sampler of Ehrenberger is of the box type in which, as in the case of other samplers, the efficiency is affected by the extent to which the sample box is filled. The variation in efficiency with bottom velocity was studied by Ehrenberger with the sampler box empty and filled to 10 — 30%. The efficiency of sampling was found to diminish as both the fullness of the box and the bottom velocity increased. The very high efficiency of the Ehrenberger type bed load sampler is believed to be attributable to the fact that, in contrast to other calibration experiments, the tests were performed in a flume with a metal bottom rather than one with a movable bed. The sediment material used in the tests belonged to the 50, 30, and 10 mm fractions, and the variation in efficiency with the sampler box filled to 10% was studied at different bottom velocities. The efficiency of sampling was found to be higher in the case of greater fractions.

Extensive tests have been performed also at the Swiss Federal Water Management Bureau for the calibration of its bed load sampler. The laboratory tests were mainly concerned with the relationship between the time and efficiency of sampling. The rate of bed load transport has also been taken into consideration. At higher rates of this transport the Swiss experiments have shown the efficiency of the sampler increased together with the sampling period. The improvement of efficiency is probably due to stabilization following the disturbance caused during the first minutes after lowering the sampler until it is settled firmly on the bottom.

The efficiency of a variety of samplers has been studied thoroughly by G. Labaye. The conclusion arrived at from these studies was that the efficiency of box type samplers is generally around 0.5, whereas that of differential pressure type samplers, or such designed without mesh screen may, under favourable conditions, attain values as high as 0.9. In view of the great variety of factors affecting bed load transportation, the determination of sampler efficiency will be recognized to present a serious problem. Investigations made so far have demonstrated the fact that, as far as the quantity of bed load is concerned, the rate of transport is a periodical phenomenon. Besides the natural periodicity observable in bed load transport, the properties of different samplers, the method of measuring applied and the duration of sampling complicate the problem. The discrepancies and variations may be especially large in sediment observations on water courses transporting large volumes of coarse bed load on the bottom.

Parallel to Hungarian measurements, separate studies are conducted at the Water Management Research Institute in Prague for determining the efficiency of the bed load sampler developed by Károlyi.

Laboratory experiments of P. Novak have shown the efficiency of the Hungarian bed load sampler to be 45%. More recent Hungarian investigations have revealed this value to be rather low, the efficiency being more likely to exceed 55 to 60%.

Details of the Károlyi type sampler and its version modified by the Water Management Institute in Prague are also presented in W. H. Graf's book (1971).

Sediment measurements made in Czechoslovakia have yielded a number of interesting experiences. The primary objective of these studies is to throw light on the reliability of the sampler by repeated measurements in the same vertical, as well as by using sampling periods of different duration.

It should be noted here that in the absence of accurate data on the efficiency of Hungarian samplers, investigations have been based invariably on actual measurement data.

Comparing the relative merits of different bed load samplers it appears safe to conclude that those operating on the principle of differential pressure show the highest degree of reliability. Several designs of this type have been published in the literature, most of them being a modified version of the Hungarian sampler of Károlyi.

The questionable reliability of sampler data has discouraged research to a certain extent. Investigations concerning bed load samplers have been discontinued.

However, in view of continuing need for some kind of a more reliable measuring device, several endeavours have been made in recent times. A critical review of all known sampler types and research into the development of a new sampler were started by the U.S. Geological Survey in 1966. Renewed interest in bed load samplers has been displayed also in the Soviet Union. Attempts at the improvement of bed load samplers are being made in the Netherlands, in Japan, in the German Democratic Republic as well as in the German Federal Republic.

b) *Bed load noise detectors*. Prompted by the need for information on bed load transport, a number of devices have been used experimentally besides direct measurements with samplers. The experiments concerned with the measurement sof bed load noise are deemed worthy of being mentioned separately.

Experiments for measuring the noise of bed load generated during its transportation in the Inn river were conducted by Mühlhofer around 1930. Similar experiments were made by French investigators in 1942. In both instances the bed load noise detectors proved difficult to handle and the device lowered to the bottom greatly modified flow conditions.

In 1951 experiments aimed at the development of a suitable type of bed load noise detector were started at the Budapest Technical University. The experiments were led by L. Ivicsics. The design consists of a stream-lined metal casing with stabilizing fins in which a crystal microphone is housed for detecting the noise generated by the moving bed load. The noise detector is submerged about 80 cm below the surface.

The bed load noise detector has been tested on the Danube. The measurements were found to be of a qualitative rather than of a quantitative character and showed the instrument to be suitable for measuring the noise of bed load larger than about 1 mm in diameter.

The intensity of bed load noise permits conclusions concerning the bands of bed load movement, the location of the highest transport rate and changes in bed load transport. The instrument is expected to yield information on bed load quantities as well, since noise intensity is recorded with a high degree of accuracy. For the time being the bed load noise detector has been used for experimental measurements only.

In recent times extensive laboratory studies have been made by P. Johnson and T. C. Muir for determining bed load transport with the help of a noise detector. According to them the rate of transport depends, besides noise intensity, also of the depth of flow D, on the particle diameter d and on flow velocity v.

c) *Tracers*. It has been realized that information on the characteristics of bed load movement would be much easier to gain if it were possible to trace the movement of either the entire bed load mass or individual particles. It has been repeatedly suggested to observe and record the movement of bed load by underwater photography or occasionally with the help of divers. Experiments have been undertaken with both methods but none of these has found wider application, since they alter flow conditions in the vicinity of the bottom, and this disturbs the actual movement of bed load. Both methods would require sophisticated technical equipment and considerable expenses. The observation data would remain nevertheless imperfect, as it appears hardly possible to detect and record the periods spent by individual bed load particles in movement and at rest. It was thus suggested to use tracer materials moving together with the natural bed load but having properties clearly discernible therefrom. Tracers may be of different kinds, but must be, as far as possible, of the same specific gravity, shape, mechanical composition, etc. as the natural bed load.

The objective of using tracers is to obtain information on the rate and direction of bed load transportation, on the periods of movement and rest of bed load particles, that is to offer general information on the phenomenon by moving together with the natural bed load material. Beyond qualitative information on sediment transportation, tracers may be helpful in some instances to estimate the quantity of transport, so that data may be obtained on the boundary condition of initial movement and even on the volumes of bed load transported.

(i) *Heavy mineral tracers.* In early tracer applications material having a specific gravity greater than that of the natural bed load, namely crushed or ground rocks containing heavy minerals, were used. The heavy mineral tracer was launched in pre-determined quantities into the channel and bed load samples were taken at certain intervals of time and distance. Owing to their higher specific gravity, the heavy minerals were readily settled out. It will be understood that the use of heavy minerals does not yield acceptable results, since their movement differs considerably from that of natural bed load material.

(ii) *Luminescent tracers.* Radiation emitted by excited atoms returning to their original state is referred to as luminescence. If bed load particles are coated with a luminescent dye and subject to ultraviolet radiation, the particle will radiate a bright colour corresponding to the dye applied and is thus readily detactable even among a large number of uncoated particles. Glue used for applying the selected dye to the particles is to form a thin layer on the particle surface otherwise it would materially change the size and specific gravity thereof. A drawback of luminescent coats is that they wear off in a rather short time and tend to adhere to unlabelled particles as well. Luminescent tracers should be applied preferably on particles of the natural bed load material. Reliable coating is possible, however, only of grains larger than 0.2 mm, for which reason finer fractions are made of an artificial tracer material, usually finely ground glass of luminescent properties. Luminescent ground glass has radiating properties not only at the surface but inherent to the material retaining this properties for a practically unlimited period. This property is of advantage in field observations where bed load transportation phenomena are studied over several years. For similar long-term studies radioactive tracers of a long half-life would be required, but these present serious radiation hazard to the environment.

134

The natural bed load material is always composed of different size fractions· In such cases luminescent tracers are especially advantageous, since different colours can be used for the different fractions. Critical values of the tractive force and flow velocity can be determined in this manner for each size fraction separately in laboratory experiments, since the initial movement of luminescent particles is readily observable under a torch emitting ultraviolet light. Obviously, the rate at which individual bed load particles travel can also be determined.

In the laboratory, luminescent tracers can be used also for determining the rate of bed load transport. In principle this method resembles bed load measurements made with the help of radioactive isotopes. The tracer is introduced at a specified rate continuously for a predetermined period, and, at different distances downstream of the point of introduction, different concentrations will be observed as a consequence of mixing. At different distances from the point of introduction the number or weight of labelled particles is determined at different points of the cross-section and is related to the unlabelled particles, and the curves describing variations in concentration are plotted on the individual sections; thus the rate of bed load transport will be proportionate to the area under the concentration curve.

The concentration of labelled particles is found by sampling. A less tiresome method which can be applied occasionally consists of expressing concentration in terms of the number of particles observed over the unit area of the bottom surface.

The same principle can be applied in natural alluvial streams for determining the rate of bed load transport with the help of luminescent tracers. Measurements of this type are, however, adversely affected by the difficulties of retrieving samples from alluvial channels. In fact, the sampler would be required to obtain samples from the same area of constant magnitude of the channel, which is obviously a difficult task in natural streams.

Luminescent tracers can be applied successfully also in natural streams for observing the bands and velocity of bed load travel. In such cases labelled particles are detected by repeated sampling.

(iii) *Radioactive tracers.* In most recent studies on bed load transport radioactive tracers are mentioned to have been widely used and with the greatest hope of success. Owing to the radiation emitted by the tracer material, the labelled particles can be spotted even in a large volume of inactive bed load material.

Several methods are known for producing radioactive tracers. One of the obvious modes consists of activating the natural bed load material in a nuclear reactor. The advantage of this solution is that the tracer material will be identical with the natural bed load. The application of this method is restricted by the limited capacity of reactors, as well as by the circumstance that impurities present in the natural sediment particles respond to activation to a different extent than the bed load material, and the uniform activity desired is not obtained.

A number of experiments have used activated natural bed load material, for studying especially littoral drift and sedimentation in estuaries, with isotopes such as ^{32}P, ^{110}Ag and ^{51}Cr.

Another method widely used for labelling bed load particles with a radiating substance consists of applying the isotope to the surface of natural bed load particles; the isotope is incorporated in the glue forming a thin film on the particle surface. This method is preferred especially in the Soviet Union.

According to another method of isotope labelling, ^{51}Cr is applied with the help of sodium silicate on sand grains in a solution of hydrochloric acid. An alternative method consists of using a chlorine solution of ^{51}Cr in which the sand is boiled. The potential isotopes for such surface treatment are, besides ^{51}Cr mentioned before, ^{59}Fe, ^{192}Ir, ^{140}La, ^{198}Au and ^{110}Ag.

For studying coarse fractions of bed load, the isotope is often introduced into the particles themselves. The practice commonly applied is to drill a small hole into the particle in which the isotope of the required quantity is introduced and the hole covered with a swelling type of cement. This method is laborious and time-consuming but has proved very successful. For labelling bed load particles in this manner ^{140}Ba, ^{132}Ta, ^{124}Sb, ^{65}Zn, ^{95}Zr and ^{181}Hf have been used.

A widely used nuclear method of bed load investigation consists of using, instead of natural bed load, an artificial tracer resembling bed load as far as shape, specific gravity, particle size and mechanical composition are concerned. Radioactive ground glass is used most frequently. In this method the radioactive substance is either added to the aggregates before smelting, or a glass containing a substance that can be activated is manufactured. In this method the isotopes ^{46}Sc, ^{24}Na and ^{64}Zm have been used to advantage.

In selecting the nuclear substance it is important to eliminate radiation hazards to the environment. In this respect the initial radiation of the isotope is also of great importance. It is equally desirable that the tracer should cease radiating one to two weeks after the termination of measurements, i.e. the tracer should lose its activity for fear of preventing a repeated investigation over the same section. Of interest, in this respect, is the length of time $t_{1/2}$ during which the radiation intensity of a particular radioactive substance is halved. This is termed half-life which, depending on the nature of study, should be longer than a few hours but preferably shorter than one or two months. If the radiation intensity at $t = 0$ is N_0, the intensity of radiation at time $t = t$ is

$$N_t = N_0\, e^{\frac{0.693t}{t_{1/2}}} \qquad (1.1.5-1)$$

indicating that the intensity of radiation after a certain time depends on the half-life. For instance, after a period five times as long as half-life, the intensity of radiation is not more than 3%, whereas after 10 times the half-life it is not more than about 0.1 % of the original value.

For further details on the application of radioactive isotopes the reader is referred to the Proceedings of the XXth International Congress on Navigation (Baltimore, 1961, Section II, Subject V) and to the bibliography enclosed.

For detecting nuclear radiation either the familiar GM tubes or scintillation counters are used.

GM tubes consist essentially of gas-filled tubes in which an ionization process is triggered by nuclear radiation, resulting in an electric pulse. This is then amplified and counted mechanically.

In scintillation detectors a scintillating substance is used to emit a light pulse when exposed to nuclear radiation. The light pulse is converted and amplified in a photo cathode tube into an electric pulse which is further amplified and recorded by electronic equipment. Scintillation probes are used for detecting various types of radiation. Their significance is especially great for detecting gamma radiation. The scintillating element is mostly a sodium iodide crystal.

The sand and gravel particles forming the sediment material emit some radiation even in their natural state. This is termed natural radioactivity. This radiation is weak enough to remain undetected by detectors in moving water. It is, however, a component of "background" radiation, which is due to the bed material, to water, as well as to cosmic rays. The intensity of background radiation should be determined carefully before any experiment in the field is started and should be subtracted from the measurement data.

Radioactive tracers lend themselves for determining critical values of the tractive force and flow velocity, as well as of the rate at which the bed load particles travel. They are used to advantage in similar studies, especially in natural water courses, since no sampling is necessary for tracing and finding the labelled particles, for which purpose scintillation probes towed along the bottom can be used.

Several methods are known for determining bed load transport with the help of radioactive isotopes.

If the rate of bed load travel v_s, the thickness m of the bed load layer in movement and the bulk density γ_t of bed load are known, the bed load discharge in unit width and unit time is obtained as

$$q_B = v_s m \gamma_t [\text{kp/sec m}] \qquad (1.1.5-2)$$

The magnitude of γ_t is usually known and approximately constant, while that of v_s is rather easy to mesure with the help of radioactive tracers. There is, however, a great deal of uncertainty in the determination of the thickness m of the layer in motion. For this purpose core samples are taken most frequently and m is assumed identical with the average penetration depth of the tracer substance. In several experiments m has been identified with the average height of the moving dunes and measured by ultrasonic sounding. The values obtained for m are nevertheless very uncertain in both methods.

For estimating the total amount of bed load passing a particular cross-section it is further necessary to know the full width of the band in which bed load is transported. Noise detectors or even tracers are suitable for obtaining fairly reliable values on this quantity.

The extent to which the tracer material undergoes mixing (dilution) may also be used for estimating the bed load discharge. If a tracer of weight K [kp] is introduced into a band of width B and the ratio by numbers of labelled particles to unlabelled ones, i.e. concentration, is established for downstream sections, then the area T [sec] under the curve connecting concentration values plotted against time, will be proportionate to bed load transport. The weight in unit time and unit width is thus obtained from the expression

$$q_B = \frac{K}{BT} \text{ [kp/sec m]} \qquad (1.1.5-3)$$

For using this expression it is essential to determine concentration. This can be found by sampling. Samples should be taken from the moving layer only, otherwise the concentration data obtained will be misleading. The difficulties arise in connection with sampling itself.

In one version of the method mentioned above the tracer material is introduced continuously, and variations in concentration are recorded continuously in the measuring cross-section. Once steady conditions are attained, and with the dimensionless ratio C_k denoting the mean-concentration, the bed load discharge is

$$q_B = \frac{q_j}{BC_k} \text{ [kp/sec m]} \qquad (1.1.5-4)$$

where q_j [kp/sec] is the rate at which the tracer is introduced over width B.

The use of Eqs (1.1.5−3) and (1.1.5−5) is restricted to steady flow conditions.

A number of difficulties are still encountered when attempting to estimate bed load discharge from nuclear tracer data. Eq. (1.1.5−2) appears to be most suitable although here the determination of the moving layer thickness is of questionable accuracy.

In an effort to eliminate the uncertainty of determining the layer thickness m, the pulse density balance of radioactive tracers has been adopted by G. Courtois and G. Sauzay for estimating the bed load transport. The principle underlying their method is that the deeper the tracer penetrates, the lower the count recorded by the detector. Consequently the curve connecting identical activity values will enclose a larger area if the depth of penetration is smaller. In this case some relation is bound to exist between the thickness m of the moving layer and the total count detected in a particular case. When using a single probe it is claimed that q_B can be determined with an error of 25%. Accuracy can be improved by using several probes.

(iv) *Magnetic tracers.* Ferromagnetic substances may also be used as tracers. Natural sand is obtained from the point under study and is mixed with fine-grained ferromagnetic material. By spreading the mixture on the bottom, information on the movement of bed load is obtained from differences in the magnetic properties of the original and labelled bed load. The principal properties of the magnetic tracer produced of the natural bed load are identical with those of the original sand.

138

In the German Democratic Republic an instrument has been developed recently which, in combination with ferromagnetic tracers, is suitable for determining the rate of bed load transport. The device consists essentially of a cylinder filled with magnetic material in which a secondary magnetic field is induced by an external magnetic field. The intensity of the secondary field depends on the volume or height of the cylinder and thus on the quantity of the magnetic tracer material contained therein. The cylinder is installed suitably on the bottom, and the height of the magnetic tracer in the cylinder is reduced as a consequence of bed load movement. The decrease in height is measured accurately by changes in magnetic field intensity.

Magnetic tracers can further be used for determining the rate and direction of movement alike. The use of magnetic tracers involves no hazards at all.

(v) *Measuring structures*. A variety of measuring structures have been repeatedly constructed on minor water courses for determining the bed load transport. At such structures the entire bed load volume arriving is retained and recorded continuously by a variety of devices. At these structures recording instruments are mounted for continuously measuring stages, discharges or even velocities.

Measuring structures are used mainly for research purposes, although the data obtained are of immediate use on the particular water course.

Measuring structures for determining bed load discharge have been constructed especially in the United States, in Switzerland and in the Soviet Union.

2. *Methods and equipment for measuring suspended load*

a) *Suspended-sediment samplers*. For obtaining information on the magnitude of the suspended load transported, water samples retrieved with the help of samplers are analysed most frequently. Using the sampler a certain volume of sediment: water mixture is scooped from the river. The sediment is allowed to settle and the weights and particle sizes characteristic of the suspended load are determined by separate measurements. The suspended load is substantially simpler to measure in the field than the bed load. It should be added that in contrast to bed load traps, the suspended-sediment samplers are very reliable measuring devices.

A wide variety of samplers are currently in use. In the early measurements the water sample was taken from the surface using a simple vessel. With advances in the theory on sediment transportation the necessity arose of taking samples from different depths. The main consideration was to ensure, logically, that the sample taken should be truly representative of the sediment at the particular depths.

Concerning the correct design of samplers as well as the determination of errors introduced by their use and the percentage differences of results obtained by different procedures, a large number of laboratory experiments have been made. The experiments performed by the Collaborating Agencies are worthy of being mentioned because of their thoroughness. In these the influence of the location and magnitude of the intake port, of the entering velocity and of sediments of different concentration and size have been studied. The velocity of entrance into the sampler is commonly called the sampling velocity. As indicated by experimental studies the reliability of samplers is largely influenced by the relative velocities of sampling and flow. Highest reliability of operation may be expected from instruments for which the sampling velocity is always identical with the velocity of flow, i.e. where the ratio of the two velocities equals unity. The difference and thus the error committed is greatest if the sampling velocity is substantially lower than the velocity of flow. In such cases a sediment volume greater than the actual is collected by the sampler. In cases where the sampling velocity is higher than flow velocity the difference is considerably smaller and the concentration of the sample is but slightly lower than the actual value.

The accuracy attainable by samplers is greatly influenced also by the particle size of the sediment. Experimental results have shown the influence of size to be negligible up to about 0.06 mm diameter. Beyond this size, however, the differences observable with various samplers tend to become appreciable.

There is finally ample experimental evidence to demonstrate the importance of keeping the intake port of the sampler perpendicular to the direction of flow in order to permit the streamlines to enter directly, without deflection into the vessel. The reliability of samplers is affected also by the shape and size of the entrance port.

The studies on the efficiency of samplers have resulted in the evolution of highly accurate designs. Of these the American samplers US D-43 and US P-46 should be mentioned. In these devices the hydrostatic pressure and air pressure are automatically balanced at each depth, preventing thus the initial rapid inflow of the sample. The sampler itself consists of a streamlined bronze casing, which accommodates the exchangeable glass vessel for collecting the sample and an air tank of a volume five times as large as that of the glass vessel. The air tank and the collecting vessel are interconnected. During lowering, both the entrance port and the air vent are closed, whereas the pressure balance vent is opened. Water is permitted thus to enter the air tank, creating therein a pressure always corresponding to the particular depth.

The samplers US DH-48 and US D-49 have been recently introduced by the Oxford Sediment Laboratory of the US Department of Agriculture (USDA). Detailed data of the sampler US DH-48 are presented also by W. H. Graf.

A device of high accuracy is the "turbidisonde" of Neyrpic, designed at the Grenoble Hydraulic Laboratory. The sampler is operated with the help of compressed air. Upon lowering to the desired depth the supply of compressed air is discontinued, relieving suddenly the overpressure in the flask so that water is free to enter. The entrance velocity is controlled automatically to the velocity of flow by the depression of a Venturi tube incorporated especially for this purpose. The sampling period is considered to have started at the moment at which the air supply is shut off. After the predetermined sampling period the air valve is opened the compressed air preventing additional water from entering so that sampling is terminated.

140

The simplest stopper bottle is commonly used for sampling in Hungary. The use of this sampler would be impermissible in the case of coarser suspended sediment since the entrance velocity differs from the velocity of flow, neither is the entrance port perpendicular to flow direction. Nevertheless, in view of the fact that the suspended sediment in Hungarian rivers is generally very fine, the simple stopper bottle has proved successful in use.

For measurements in Hungary a Tait–Binckley tape sampler has also been constructed. It is interesting to note that the greatest difference of results obtained with the stopper bottle and the Tait–Binckley sampler has been found to be not more than ±5%.

Measurements have recently been made in Hungary also with the Polyakov sampler. Here the sampling velocity is identical with the flow velocity. Samplers of the Polyakov type are very simple, reliable, and the results obtained with them were found to be accurate.

The common feature of the afore-mentioned samplers is that they permit samples to be retrieved from any vertical of the stream and from any depth thereof.

The mean concentration in a vertical is determined by means of depth-integrating samplers. In the depth integration method the sample is taken continuously during the time of lowering the sampler from the surface to the bottom (and occasionally when raising it from the bottom to the surface).

The mean concentration with respect to time in a particular point is determined by point integration measurement. In this method the sampler is kept at the same depth during the sampling period.

b) *Nuclear concentration meters*. The advances in nuclear techniques have been used also for measuring sediment concentration. Several methods are known, most of which are based on the attenuation of radiation, the extent of which depends on whether the water carries sediment or not.

One of the first devices was the "Parametrics" concentration meter named after the firm producing it. The attenuation of X-rays in sediment-carrying and in clear water is measured by the device. The ratio of the two is a function of the suspended-sediment concentration. The device must be calibrated. From the calibration curve the concentration of the suspended load is read off directly in terms of the ratio of values measured in sediment-carrying and clear water.

An isotope ^{109}Cd is used as the radiating source. The Parametrics device has proved highly suitable for measurements in remote sites since it is capable of recording continuously the concentration at a particular point of the cross-section. The attenuation of X-rays in sediment-carrying and clear water is measured automatically, this feature making it highly suitable for routine measurements.

In connection with the uses of isotopes in hydrology detailed attention to nuclear concentration meters has been devoted by the UN International Atomic Energy Agency (IAEA), Vienna. A device called the IAEA meter has been constructed by the International Atomic Energy Agency, by which the concentration of the

141

suspended sediment is measured again in terms of the relative attenuation of X-rays in sediment-carrying and clear water. The IAEA concentration meter is manually operated and the clear water measurements must be repeated periodically. In this meter ^{109}Cd and ^{241}Am isotopes are used as X-ray sources. The meter is unsuited for routine measurements.

A concentration meter operating on the same principle has been developed by the Oxford, Mississippi Sediment Laboratory, USDA. This meter is also manually operated, less suited for routine work but eminently suited for laboratory studies. ^{109}Cd isotop is used as the radiating source. It is interesting to note that initially the meter was used also for measuring soil moisture and silting in reservoirs.

c) *Automatic samplers.* From the very beginning of sediment observations pumping has been used for taking samples. This method may be classified essentially as an alternative of the samplers listed under a). In recent times, however, the procedure of sampling by pumps has been automated. From a particular point of the selected vertical the samples are withdrawn automatically at predetermined intervals of time, the samples being discharged into a calibrated settling bottle. After settling, photographs of the sample are taken automatically by a special device and the sediment-free water is returned to the river. At each sampling some of the material is stored for granulometric analysis at the laboratory.

Several automatic samplers are presently in operation. In the sampling gage several samplers are mounted above one another, taking samples successively at rising stages. Automatic sampling gages of this type are usually mounted on the wall or on a pier of a hydraulic structure, so that the samples are taken from the edge of flow. Concentration representative of the full cross-section cannot be obtained unless a correction factor depending on particular conditions is introduced.

Automatic samplers are often incorporated into the structure itself. With these samplers the samples are analysed automatically and the results are recorded on punched cards in a form suitable for processing by mechanical computation.

3. *Bed material samplers.* In studies concerning the sediment transport in alluvial channels, bed material samplers play an important role. The relationship existing between the sediment transported and the material covering the channel bottom make the analysis of the bed material with the help of samples essential. The bed material samplers are very simple devices and operate perfectly in contrast to bed load samplers, as far as their reliability is concerned. A wide variety of bed material samplers is used in practice. In view of the fact that bed material studies related to sediment transportation are necessarily concentrated on the composition of the top layers lining the bed, the samples retrieved by the bed material samplers come usually from the top layers of the channel material. The majority of such samplers are designed to scrape the desired bed material sample from the bottom.

Some bed material samplers operate on the clamshell principle. Typical for these is the US DM-54 bed material sampler. Lowered to the bottom, the bucket automatically collects the sample, immediately closes to provide water-tight closure. In this way the sample remains unaffected during the period of hoisting.

The Hungarian sampler consists of a steel pipe closed at one end and flared conically at the other. The sampler is lowered to the bottom and towed at the end of a cable downstream from a boat. The dimensions, and thus the weight of the bed material sampler, depend on the quality and type of the bed material.

4. *Methods and means of measuring deposited sediment.* In observations on sedimentations in reservoirs, one of the most important problems consists in the determination of the sediment volume accumulated, deposited in the storage spaces. Obviously, the original storage volume is also of interest.

For determining the volume of sediment deposited in the reservoir two methods may in general be recommended.

In the first method the volume of silting is estimated as the difference between the original storage space and that determined by a survey at the time of study. For this method to be applicable the original storage volume must be available. Any error in the determination of the original storage space may drastically distort the result, especially if silting is small in comparison with the original reservoir volume. This method yields, in general, questionable results when applied to existing reservoirs, because accurate contour line maps of these are rarely available.

In the second method the volume of sediment deposited is measured directly. For using this method a greater volume of measuring work and special measuring devices are necessary. This is offset by the advantage of obtaining detailed information on reservoir silting, regardless whether accurate survey data on the original storage space are available or not.

The thickness of the deposited sediment layers is determined by means of special sounding rods. Attached to a line, the rod is plunged with great force from a boat, into the water, causing it to penetrate the soft silt layer deposited, coming to rest in the original bottom material. Upon careful retrieval the quality of material retained in the annular spaces of the probe yields information on the thickness of the deposited sediment layer. In shallow reservoirs up to about 10 m depth, the thickness of the silted layer can be determined by means of a normal sounding rod as well.

Regardless of the method applied for determining the volume of sediment deposited, the actual reservoir volume at the time of measurement must be determined somehow. In shallow reservoirs soundings rods, in deeper ones, a sounding weight fastened to a line is used for measuring depth. Echo type sounders have been introduced recently.

In field measurements a predetermined pattern should be followed in determining depths and sediment layer thicknesses. Measurements are usually performed along profiles selected in advance. Water depths and the thickness of the sediment layer are measured in verticals spaced uniformly along the profile. In smaller reservoirs the spacing will range from 5 to 20, in larges ones, from 20 to 50 m. Once the profiles are plotted, areas and from these the volumes may be estimated by any suitable method.

Sometimes full details on the bottom contour are of interest. From such measurements a contour line map is plotted. From the measurement data the lines are obtained by interpolation. The density of the sounding points is governed by the configuration of sediment deposits. A dense network is necessary where the contour of the sediment surface is rugged. The position of sounding points is recorded by one of the familiar methods. Surveys for contour line mapping are appreciably more laborious than surveys by long profiles. For this reason they are justified only in cases where accurate contour line maps of the original reservoir are available.

Undisturbed core samples are taken from the silt layer for determining the specific gravity, granulometry and bulk density of the sediment deposited. A wide variety of samplers can be used for this purpose.

Data on sediment bulk density are essential for conversion from volume to weight. The density of silt deposits is variable with time. For the pertinent extensive investigations reference is made to the attached bibliography.

In recent times nuclear methods have been adopted for sediment density measurements.

Such measurements rely on the principle of attenuation, according to which the intensity I_0 of the incident monochromatic radiation is attenuated in a uniform material of a constant mass absorption coefficient μ across a layer of thickness x according to expression

$$I = I_0 e^{-\mu x} \qquad (1.1.5-5)$$

The single-probe and two-probe methods developed at the Oxford Sediment Laboratory are founded on the reflexion principle. In these the attenuation of rays is measured. The radiation emitted from the source is scattered back by the surrounding medium to the detector. ^{226}Ra and ^{137}Cs isotopes are used as radiation sources. The probes are calibrated, and density is thus determined in terms of the activity observed. Several measurements have been made by J. R. McHenry at the Oxford Sediment Laboratory and applied by him to a smaller reservoir.

The two-probe method has been found suitable for determining the density of silt layers not thicker than 2.5 cm, regardless of the quality of the material above and under this layer. The density of a round 1 m thick silt layer was determined successfully in water 3 to 5 m deep.

1.2. BED LOAD

1.2.1. THE MOVEMENT OF BED LOAD

As pointed out in the foregoing, bed load is transported along the bottom by rolling, sliding or occasionally in jumps, by saltation. The bed load particle starts moving whenever subjected continuously, or at least with short interruptions,

144

to forces having a resultant sufficiently great to overcome the resultant of forces tending to impede motion. The main direction of movement is parallel to the bottom, i.e. practically horizontal.

In the mechanical sense, the movement of bed load appears to be simple when compared with the other properties of sediment transportation. The rate of sediment movement and the volumes of bed load transported are governed by the quality of the bed load and the magnitude of forces acting thereon.

The movement of bed load is readily observable in a laboratory glass flume or in shallow and clear water even in alluvial channels. According to variations with time, the movement may be classified as steady or unsteady depending on whether the rate of bed load travel at a particular point is constant or variable with time. Movement may further be classified as continuous or intermittent depending on whether the bed load quantities entering and leaving a particular volume are identical or different. When the quantity of bed load leaving a given volume is smaller, deposition will occur, and when larger, the channel is scoured.

Bed load transportation will thus be seen to be subject to variations, but the movement itself is a physical phenomenon readily recognizable. The beginning of movement may be regarded as the boundary case of incipient sediment motion. In principle the statements made in connection with movement may thus be extended to this boundary condition. Conversely, the boundary condition of incipient sediment motion is significant for bed load transportation since the acting forces are greater than in the boundary condition. Actually the movement of bed load is defined by the acting forces being greater than those in the boundary condition.

In the case of a cohesionless bed load material a particle on the bottom is exposed to a drag force acting parallel to the bottom, and to a hydrodynamic uplift force perpendicular thereto. Both forces are exerted by the flowing water. The particle is further subjected to gravity force (the weight of the particle) and to a buoyant force.

In the majority of investigations the drag force is alone taken into consideration, and the uplift force, depending in principle on the same hydraulic factors of flow as the drag force, is neglected.

Neglecting the uplift force, C. M. White has expressed the submerged weight of a bed load particle of d diameter and γ_1 specific gravity as

$$W_1 = c_3 d^3 (\gamma_1 - \gamma) \qquad (1.2.1-1)$$

where γ is the specific gravity of water, and has assumed that in the boundary condition of incipient movement a drag force $F = \tau_c c_1 d^2$ is exerted by the critical tractive force τ_c. The arm of force F about the point of support is $c_2 d$ (see *Fig. 1.2.1−1*) so that the moment tending to displace the particle is

$$M_0 = \tau_c c_1 c_2 d^3 \qquad (1.2.1-2)$$

Fig. 1.2.1—1. Interpretation of the
frictional theory. After White

The resisting moment of the same magnitude is due to the submerged weight W_1 acting on the arm c_4d and has the magnitude

$$M_r = d_3 c_4 d^4 (\gamma_1 - \gamma) \qquad (1.2.1-3)$$

Since in the boundary condition of incipient sediment motion $M_0 = M_r$, the critical tractive force becomes

$$\tau_c = c_5 (\gamma_1 - \gamma) d \qquad (1.2.1-4)$$

Assuming coefficient c_5 to be constant, the above expression becomes identical with Eq. (1.1.3—4) of the classic frictional-drag theory.

If the bottom is inclined at angle α to the horizontal, further if the angle of internal friction of the bed load material under water is Θ, the critical tractive force is

$$\tau_c = c_6 (\gamma_1 - \gamma) \, d \cos \alpha \, (\text{tg } \Theta - \text{tg } \alpha) \qquad (1.2.1-5)$$

In the case of a horizontal bottom $\alpha = 0$. In laminar flow White's experiments have yielded the value $c_6 = 0.18$ so that

$$\tau_c = 0.18 (\gamma_1 - \gamma) d \, \text{tg } \Theta \qquad (1.2.1-6)$$

In turbulent flow White has found the magnitude of τ_c to be reduced to about half of the original value, attributing this effect to turbulent velocity fluctuations. White may thus be regarded as one of the first investigators to recognize the influence of turbulent velocity fluctuations on the tractive force.

Rather little attention has been devoted to the analysis of forces affecting the bed load transport. A. J. Sutherland has remarked pertinently that most investigators appear to rest content with the opinion according to which the only force to be taken into consideration is the frictional drag. There is, however, ample evidence for the influence of some kind of uplift force. The main evidence of this kind is the pulsation of vertical velocity in turbulent flow, the existence of a velocity gradient other than zero, as well as the possibility of pressures acting from below on the bed load particle.

Investigations reported in the literature support the existence of uplift forces.

The first investigation of this nature was made by H. J. Jeffreys in 1929. Starting from the assumption of irrotational flow in an ideal fluid, he described the flow pattern around a cylinder of infinite length and diameter d, situated perpendicular to parallel flow of velocity v_p by the complex potential

$$w = \frac{\pi d}{2} v_p \operatorname{cth} \frac{\pi d}{2z} \qquad (1.2.1-7)$$

According to Jeffreys the cylinder will thus start to rise if

$$v_p > 0.59 \sqrt{\frac{\gamma_1 - \gamma}{\gamma} gd} \qquad (1.2.1-8)$$

Considering sand of 2.65 [p/cm³] specific gravity and water

$$v_p^2 > 0.575 \, gd \qquad (1.2.1-9)$$

Experimental results have shown the bed load particles to be lifted at velocities appreciably higher than given by Eq. (1.2.1−9). The difference is explained by the fact that the uplift force exerted by the same flow velocity v_p on approximately spherical particles is substantially smaller than in the case of a cylinder at rest on the bottom.

The role of turbulence in bed load transport as well as the fact that the acting forces tend to pulsate rather than remain constant, have been recognized also by Kalinske and Einstein.

An understanding of the conditions prevailing in the layer of mixing between the fluid and the bottom would appear essential. However, the number of studies on this problem is small.

Interesting results have been obtained by Einstein and El-Samni concerning the forces acting on 68.6 mm half-spheres located in a hexagonal pattern on a smooth bottom. The magnitude of the uplift force was estimated from the differential pressure between the highest point and the base of the half-sphere. The differential pressure is given as

$$\Delta p = C_L \frac{\rho v^2}{2} \qquad (1.2.1-10)$$

The magnitude of C_L was found to be 0.178 and constant. The velocity v was measured at distance $0.35\,d$ from the theoretical boundary.

Simple harmonic oscillation of a grid mounted in a frame was adopted by H. Rouse to induce turbulent flow, and the fine bed load on the bottom was set into motion by changing the frequency. The movement of bed load was found to be initiated by the periodic eruption and spreading of turbulent vortices.

Fig. 1.2.1—2. Variations in velocity fluctuations with time.
After Sárosi and Kaposi

In turbulent flow Southerland assumes periodic vortices to impinge on the bed load particles at the bottom and to be thus immediately responsible for their movement. The velocity of water particles in the vortex is expected to increase until striking the bottom and, depending on the direction of their revolution, the frictional force is also likely to increase. Consequently, according to Southerland, in the boundary condition of incipient movement

— the viscous layer is disrupted by the vortices which impinge on the bed load particle at the bottom,

— the local frictional force is increased by rotation within the vortices. Once the critical magnitude of the frictional force is exceeded, the bed load particle is set into motion,

— over a bed covered by dunes, movement is started in the zone where turbulence is most intensive.

In these experiments turbulent flow was generated by means of a pulsating jet. For observing the movement of fluid particles hydrogen bubbles served as tracers. Flow velocities were measured with the help of hot-plate flow meters. The intensity of the jet was controlled according to the amplitude and frequency of pulsation. The experiments have shown a well-defined critical value of jet intensity to pertain to the boundary condition of incipient movement. The interesting observations and conclusions have greatly contributed to the knowledge of bed load transport.

The influence of velocity fluctuations on the critical velocity has been studied under the guidance of the author at the Chair for Hydraulic Engineering, Budapest Technical University by the Research Group of the Academy of Sciences. The experiments in the laboratory glass fume were conducted by L. Sárosi and L. Kaposi. Velocity fluctuations were measured with an Ott type revolving-vane current meter combined with a compensograph. In this way the pulses emitted by the current meter were converted with the help of an integrator into a signal

148

Fig. 1.2.1—3. Fluctuation in momentary velocity at Section I, size fraction 1.47—2.27 mm, in damped and undamped flow. After Sárosi and Kaposi

Fig. 1.2.1—4. Fluctuation in momentary velocity at Section II, size fraction 1.47—2.27 mm, in damped and undamped flow. After Sárosi and Kaposi

proportionate to the instantaneous velocity, the signal being recorded by the compensograph on paper tape. Although the accuracy of recording velocity fluctuations with the revolving-vane current meter was limited, this type of instrument was adopted because of the possibility of utilizing the results of laboratory measurements also in alluvial streams.

Velocity fluctuations were measured and recorded at a single representative point in each of two cross-sections in the glass flume. The variation of instantaneous velocity v with time t is shown in *Fig. 1.2.1 — 2*. The mean velocity with respect to time at the point of observation is denoted $\bar{v}$. The magnitude of velocity fluctuations may be taken into consideration in several different ways. As a first approximation the value T^x [(cm/sec) sec] was introduced and determined from the hydrograph of instantaneous velocities by connecting the prominent peaks

149

Fig. 1.2.1—5. Fluctuation in momentary velocity at Section I, size fraction 2.27—4.47 mm, in damped and undamped flow. After Sárosi and Kaposi

Fig. 1.2.1—6. Fluctuation in momentary velocity at Section II, size fraction 2.27—4.47 mm, in damped and undamped flow. After Sárosi and Kaposi

with a continuous line and by measuring the area enclosed by the two lines with a planimeter.

Since experiments were started just a short time ago, only the 1.47 to 2.27 mm and the 2.27 to 4.47 mm fractions could be studied so far.

By increasing velocities, i.e. discharges the intention was to approach, as far as possible, the steady condition at which the size fraction under consideration just starts moving. Experiments were run for each size fraction with highly turbulent and well damped flow. The hydrograph of instantaneous velocities and the mean value with respect to time of the critical velocity determined therefrom are

Fig. 1.2.1—7. Critical velocity vs. index of velocity fluctuation for the 1.47—2.27 mm and 2.27—4.47 mm size fractions. After Sárosi and Kaposi

shown in *Figs 1.2.1—3* and *1.2.1—4* for the smaller size fraction for damped and undamped flow in sections I and II.

The same quantities are shown in *Figs 1.2.1—5* and *1.2.1—6* for the larger size fraction.

It will be seen from the four figures that in the case of damped flow, i.e. where turbulence is smaller and thus also T^x is smaller, the critical condition occurs at a higher mean velocity with respect to time than in the case of undamped highly turbulent flow.

It appears thus safe to conclude from the rather small number of measurements and from the rather arbitrary parameter T^x that in highly turbulent flow lower velocities are capable of picking up particles at rest on the bottom.

For the two size fractions under consideration the turbulence parameter T^x has been illustrated separately in *Fig. 1.2.1—7* together with the corresponding mean value $\bar{v}_c$ with respect to time of the critical velocities measured at the representative points. As will be seen from this graph, the critical velocity tends to increase as the turbulence of flow decreases.

In subsequent experiments the variations in the critical mean velocity of the flume will be determined and the influence of depth, flume width, slope and relative roughness will be studied simultaneously.

From the investigations described in the foregoing it will be appreciated that in particular cases the properties of turbulent flow are of paramount importance for sediment transportation. Nevertheless, for lack of reliable observation data, the influence of turbulence cannot be taken into account and consequently no general relationship is known for describing bed load transportation and for revealing directly the effect of turbulence. This drawback is partly offset by the

151

circumstance that the properties of turbulence are to a certain extent expressed by the type of flow, as well as by the properties of water and the bed load material.

Further experiments are believed to be of utmost importance for clarifying the effect and role of turbulence in bed load transportation.

1.2.2. THE BOUNDARY CONDITIONS OF MOVEMENT

1.2.2.1. *Initial movement and variations of the stream bed.* Under certain conditions the particles of loose, cohesionless bed load covering the bottom are set into motion. At the moment movement starts, the forces acting on the bed load particles at rest on the bottom are exactly equal to the resistance of the bed load particles to movement. It has been pointed out that these forces are still impossible to estimate accurately. It may be stated, however, that the velocity of flow or the tractive force has attained the limit value, at which the forces acting on the bed load particles are just balanced by the resistance of the particles to movement.

Consequently the particles of bed load covering the bottom will start moving as soon as the velocity of flow has attained a certain value. The boundary condition between movement and no movement is referred to as the critical condition.

The general movement of bed load particles starts as the velocity is further increased. The originally smooth, uniform bed remains initially smooth, minor disturbances occurring only at still higher flow velocities. The uniformity of the bed is disrupted and replaced by variable bed forms and configurations. These are the consequences of local scours and deposits, caused by disturbances in bed load movement. The interrelations between the bottom and the flow, as well as the resulting bed form depend on the depth, velocity and turbulence of flow, moreover on the properties of water and the bed load material.

In the first stage and especially in the case of fine-grained bed load material small waves, called sand ripples are observable. The unevenness becomes more pronounced as the tractive force or velocity is increased, the ripples being replaced by dunes on the bottom. These are triangular in section with a mild upstream slope followed by a steep downstream one. The dunes travel downstream at a velocity that is small relative to the velocity of flow. A few projecting bed load particles on the originally smooth bottom or any other disturbing factors are sufficient to initiate the formation of dunes.

Sand ripples and dunes are essentially identical bed forms except for size; the dunes are in fact sand ripples but more pronounced and of greater dimensions. It is for this reason that *in recent publications sand ripples and dunes are treated collectively as dunes.*

The dunes are smoothed and the bed becomes stable as the forces acting on the bed load particles are further increased. This condition in bed load transportation is known under the term of boundary condition of transition. This boundary condition remains often unobservable and the dunes are followed immediately by the development of antidunes. In this condition bed load transportation is influenced

152

also by the waves at the water surface and the resulting scours and deposits take the form of extended sinusoidal waves in section. Antidunes tend to travel slowly upstream against the direction of flow.

In spite of the considerable attention that has been devoted to this problem, no generally acceptable explanation has been offered for the development of the different bed forms. The development of dunes has been attributed by Karman to turbulence, whereas by Liu, to instability at the interface of the fluid and the bed load layer at the bottom. Bed forms have been studied by Exner, followed recently by Kennedy in their development with time. Starting from the height of bed forms H. Ertel, D. B. Simons and A. Führböter have studied these in terms of the bed load transport. The theoretical and experimental investigations of Kennedy are of great significance for they have yielded several results of practical interest. Thus, for instance, Kennedy has found the development of dunes to depend on the magnitude of the Froude number, on flow depth D and on the extent to which local velocities are reduced by bed load transportation.

For a detailed description of investigations concerning the development of bed forms, the reader is referred to the papers listed in the bibliography enclosed.

The bed forms are of great interest to the practising engineer in view of their considerable influence on roughness conditions and of their modifying affect on the rate of bed load transport, on which several experiments have provided evidence.

The bearing of bed forms on sediment transportation is difficult to determine not only because of the complexity of the problem, but also because of the small number of observation data available. The pertinent statement made by Kennedy is that the reports on experiments describing in detail the bed forms observed are rather small in number. The objective of most experiments was to determine the critical conditions, the roughness or the sediment transport with but little attention to bed forms. It should be obvious, however, that the movement and bed load transportation are necessarily related to the geometry of the bottom.

In the present book an endeavour has been made to take the influence of bed forms into consideration wherever possible—for instance in connection with the critical condition—but, owing to the lack of a sufficient number of observation data, in most cases it was found impossible to undertake investigations of this nature.

The importance of bed forms has been appreciated in all recent experiments and observations so that the studies initiated in this domain may well be expected to attain the desired results in the near future.

In sediment transportation the initial condition of movement, the development of sand ripples, dunes, transition and antidunes, the boundary conditions of their formation, further the variations in bed load transport may be referred to collectively as *the regime of bed load transportation* or, more generally, as *the regime of sediment movement*.

The term is a highly appropriate one since it includes all relevant boundary conditions of bed load movement. The term has been introduced by M. L. Albertson and his co-workers.

Starting with the incipient condition of movement, several relevant boundary conditions may be distinguished in bed load transportation.

The incipient condition of movement is a phenomenon that is clearly observable and highly conspicuous since it is characterized by the starting movement of bed load particle. As will be seen subsequently, this condition is difficult to define uniquely although ample experimental and theoretical evidence is available for its determination.

The boundary conditions following that of incipient movement, although readily observable, are difficult to determine positively in the absence of observation data. In a few publications, relations have been advanced for these boundary conditions but they have been developed from a small number of observations only and cannot thus be excepted to be of general validity. Further extensive investigations are therefore necessary to develop reliable relations on the boundary conditions of different bed forms.

In sediment transportation the incipient condition of movement may be regarded as the most important and will thus be discussed in greater detail subsequently.

1.2.2.2. The boundary conditions of movement and no movement. In studies on bed load transport in alluvial streams the boundary condition at which the movement of bed load is just about to start is referred to as critical. In the critical condition the tractive force is called the critical tractive force while the velocity, the critical velocity. The concepts of critical slope, critical depth, etc. may be introduced similarily. The results of a great number of investigations will be found impossible to utilize and to compare unless a unique definition of the critical condition can be given. However, beyond the unique definition, the ready recognition by simple visual inspection of the critical condition is equally essential.

Considered as a phenomenon, the incipient movement of bed load particles is of a statistical character, so that *it is impossible to determine a definite critical condition. It is only the occurrence of the most probable, expected condition that can be determined.*

Introducing certain simplifying assumptions practically all studies made so far describe the critical condition essentially in terms of the expected values of the critical parameters.

A wide variety of definitions of the critical condition have been offered in the literature but, unfortunately, not all of them are unambiguous. And this, in turn, is partly responsible for the fact that the results of observations, however thoroughly performed, display certain discrepancies.

With a view to determining the critical condition extensive experiments have been undertaken by H. Kramer at Dresden.

In his experiments Kramer distinguished the following stages in bed load transportation:

a) *Stationary condition* in which no bed load is transported.

b) *The condition of slight movement* in which a certain, at any rate countable number of the finest bed load fractions are set into motion. In this condition movement is still of a local character only. The term "countable" should be understood to mean that focusing attention to a certain area, say 1 cm², it is possible to count the particles moving there.

c) *The conditions of medium movement* in which particles of average size move in quantities no longer countable by inspection. Transportation is no longer of a local character although the quantity of the bed load transported is insignificant. The bed form is still unaffected in this condition.

d) *The condition of general movement* in which even the largest particles start moving.

In view of the above classification the tractive force at which all particles are set into movement is termed critical by Kramer. This value is at the same time regarded as the lower limit of the critical tractive force. The upper limit of the critical tractive force is, on the other hand, the value at which the disturbing effect of sand ripples is still moderate. The critical value defined by Kramer is slightly higher than the actual.

The critical condition was studied before Kramer by Gilbert and Schaffernak and by many others following him.

A more detailed description of the investigations concerned with the determination of the critical condition will be omitted here. The methods suggested for this purpose will be mentioned in connection with the individual relations, in so far as this is considered necessary. In fact the results obtained by the different investigators cannot be compared successfully unless the methods applied for these investigations are also taken into consideration.

In view of the fact that several relations developed by the author will also be described subsequently, it is deemed pertinent to present a separate description of the method used for determining the critical condition.

For this purpose, use has been made of the observations by Schaffernak who gradually increased the transporting capacity of flow in his experiments. The bed load particles at rest on the bottom were found to start oscillating first, to be shifted intermittently without, however, being set into motion. By increasing the transporting capacity of flow, the sediment particles dropped into the water were observed to perform continuous movement, without being accompanied by the movement of bed load at the bottom. In the series of experiments at Iowa, the first typical condition was named the condition of *static equilibrium*, the second, that of *kinetic equilibrium*. The actual critical condition becomes visually observable as soon as some of the bed load particles at rest on the bottom are set into movement.

In this manner, starting from the stationary condition, after attaining and exceeding two clearly discernible preceding states the critical condition becomes observable. This contributes to the reliability of observation and makes determination unequivocal.

It should be noted here that in most experiments a state of movement beyond the critical condition suggested by the author has been described, i.e. one in which — using the terminology of Kramer — movement has become general. A limit value greater than the critical is used also by Velikanov and Levi.

155

It should be appreciated that in any description of the critical condition it is essential to specify the condition regarded as relevant.

Considering the hydraulic factors of flowing water, a wide variety of methods may be adopted for describing the critical condition. Accordingly, the factors introduced for describing the critical condition are also of a wide variety. Attempts have been made to relate the critical condition to depths, to velocities and slopes of flow and even to water discharges. Several investigators have introduced, logically, the product of slope and depth, i.e. the tractive force as a measure of the critical condition.

In determining the critical condition the relationship between the hydraulic factors of flow and the characteristics of the bed load material is invariably established. In studies related to the critical condition the main factors used for describing bed load are particle size and specific gravity. Besides these quantities the granulometry of bed load material and sometimes even the particle shape have been included.

Aside from the statistical fluctuation of critical values, most recent investigations have shown the magnitude of these to depend also on the characteristics of flow. In other words, the incipient movement of a particular bed load particle is controlled for instance by a variable critical tractive force, depending on the conditions of observations. These investigations will be considered more extensively in *Sections 1.2.4* and *1.2.5*.

Although closely related to the theory of sediment transportation, the description of the critical condition is of considerable importance in other problems of hydraulic engineering practice as well. The stability of canals in different soils has been a concern to hydraulic engineers for long. The stability of canals — and especially the control of bottom scouring — is obviously related to the critical condition corresponding to the bed material of such canals.

Once the relationship between the hydraulic factors of flow and the characteristics of the bed load material in the critical condition is known, it is possible to specify different limit values for this condition. However, owing to variations in the critical value pertaining to the same bed load material, these limit values will obviously approximate ones only.

In general practice the limit values of velocity, namely critical bottom velocity or mean velocity, are usually specified, but often critical values are established for the depth and slope or for the product of the two, i.e. for the tractive force. According to these simplifying assumptions, the bed load will remain stationary as long as the velocity, depth or slope of the flow remain below the critical values pertaining to a particular bed load material.

A criterion adopted exceptionally for describing the critical condition is that the quantity of bed load transported in this condition is zero. Consequently by introducing the weight of bed load with zero value into the bed load transport relations, the boundary condition of incipient bed load movement is logically established. In practice, however, these relations are of no general validity for they include not only the desired limit value, but also the values below the critical condition.

156

It should be emphasized here that in practical problems the critical condition is controlled not only by the properties of the bed load material and by the hydraulic factors of flow in the strict sense of the word, but also by the characteristics of the channel, such as the configuration of the bed, the ratio of width and depth, as well as by roughness.

From among the great number of investigations into the critical condition it is proposed to mention only the results obtained for the critical tractive force, for the critical bottom and mean velocities. This is justified by the circumstance that in practical problems the critical condition is described almost exclusively in terms of velocities or of the tractive force.

1.2.3. CRITERIA FOR THE BOUNDARY CONDITIONS OF BED LOAD MOVEMENT

The exact formulation and distinction of boundary conditions in bed load transportation constitutes a problem of considerable importance. The approach commonly adopted for the recognition and determination of these boundary conditions has usually been a graphical one. In the studies made by considering a bed load material of particle size d, specific gravity γ_1 and a fluid of viscosity v and specific gravity γ the critical values are assumed to remain invariable. In this respect the graphical relations would obviously need revision. Since, however, these variations have been determined approximately for the critical condition only, and since these graphical relations concerning the other boundary conditions are still in use, their description here appears to be justified.

The investigations by H. K. Liu on the development of sand ripples have greatly contributed to our understanding of the different boundary conditions in bed load transportation.

The development of sand ripples is governed, just as bed load transportation in general, by the complex interaction of several factors. Without embarking upon details it should be noted that a number of theories have been forwarded on the development of sand ripples.

Instability of the interface was suggested by Liu as an explanation for the development of sand ripples, relying on studies into the flow of several fluid layers of different densities and moving at different velocities, with special regard to the stability of the interface. In his studies he included also the results of G. H. Keulegan, who considered the interface of two fluid layers, the lower of which was at rest initially. The conclusions arrived at by Liu are in fair agreement with the findings of H. L. Drydon who studied the flow of air above a solid plate, regarding the latter as a fluid of infinite viscosity. The transition from laminar into turbulent flow in the boundary layer is related to the instability of interfaces. Liu found sufficient experimental evidence to regard the bed load at the bottom as a fluid, appearing to support the conclusion of Keulegan, according to whom the soil boundary of the channel may be regarded as a fluid of infinite viscosity.

Liu identifies the interface between the fluid and the bed sediment with the laminar boundary layers. Consequently, the development of sand ripples is related to interface instability. The interrelations and mutual influences between the two are obvious but, in view of the present state of knowledge, this relations would be very difficult to formulate definitely. Liu assumes the instability of the laminar boundary layer to be described by the dimensionless number U_*d/v where $U_* = \sqrt{gDS}$ is the shear velocity, d the particle diameter of bed load at rest on the bottom, while v is the kinematic viscosity of the fluid. According to his assumption, sand ripples may develop on the bed if the flow is capable of transporting the bed load, and when the stability of the interface between the bed-load-covered bottom and the water is disrupted.

In a number of laboratory experiments Liu has observed sand ripples to appear shortly after the occurrence of the critical condition. By writing, in the familiar manner, the frictional drag force acting on the bed load particle at rest on the bottom and equating it with the resistance offered by the particle to movement and by describing this resisting force with the help of the most characteristic property of the bed load particle, namely in terms of the fall velocity, Liu has found eventually that in the boundary condition of sand ripple development the dimensionless number U_*/ω characteristic of the mobility of the bed load particle is definitely related to the parameter U_*d/v representing the instability of the boundary layer.

Relying on the results of experiments made in order to study the development of sand ripples Liu has determined graphically the relation between the parameters U_*/ω and U_*d/v. The curve representing the relation

$$\frac{U_*}{\omega} = F\left(\frac{U_*d}{v}\right) \tag{1.2.3-1}$$

is shown in *Fig. 1.2.3−1*. Although the experimental results obtained by several investigators, using different bed load materials, have been entered into the graph, the relationship between the two parameters will be seen to be a positive, definite one.

Following the first attempts of Liu, investigations were started by M. L. Albertson, D. B. Simons and E. V. Richardson who were among the first to review the results of Liu and to establish thereby the first criterion of general validity for the boundary conditions of bed load transportation.

The parameter U_*d/v, which these authors termed the sediment shear velocity Rheynolds number, can be related to the thickness

$$\delta' = 11.6 \frac{v}{U_*} \tag{1.2.3-2}$$

of the laminar boundary layer, and written preferably in the form

$$11.6 \frac{d}{\delta'} = \frac{U_*d}{v} \tag{1.2.3-3}$$

158

Fig. 1.2.3—1. The U_*/ω ratio vs. sediment shear velocity Reynolds number at the boundary condition of sand ripple formation. After Liu

Eq. (1.2.3 − 3) implies essentially that the shear velocity Reynolds number of bed load is about twelve times the ratio d/δ'. The ratio d/δ' being representative of hydraulic roughness, the relation suggested by Liu can be given a hydromechanical interpretation.

Albertson and his collaborators came to the conclusion that sand ripples could not develop unless the flow was turbulent and a laminar sublayer existed within the boundary layer. This conclusion implies at the same time that, besides the instability of the interface, the development of sand ripples is related to a certain extent also to turbulence above the boundary layer.

Albertson and his collaborators assumed that relations similar to that applying to the boundary conditions of sand ripple formation were bound to exist at the other boundary conditions of bed load transportation, namely at the boundary conditions of incipient bed load movement, of dunes, transition and the development of antidunes. Completing the data of Liu for smaller and larger particle sizes they succeeded in plotting *Fig. 1.2.3 − 2* from which the quantitative separation of the different conditions of movement will be clearly appreciated.

The relation showing the boundary condition of bed load transportation has been represented by Albertson and his collaborators after Shields and, with due regard to the relations plotted for the other conditions of movement, they succeeded in slightly modifying the original relation of Liu. The modified curve of Liu is shown with a dashed line in *Fig. 1.2.3 − 2.*

In addition to the relations of U_*/ω and $U_* d/v$, the ratio d/δ' has also been included in *Fig. 1.2.3 − 2* and indicated on a second horizontal scale.

In the experiments on which *Fig. 1.2.3 − 2* is based the specific gravity of the bed load materials was $\gamma_1 = 2.65$ p/cm^3 and the temperature of water varied between

159

Fig. 1.2.3−2. The U_*/ω ratio vs. sediment shear velocity Reynolds number at different boundary conditions of bed load movement. After Albertson et al.

rather narrow limits and may thus be taken as 20 deg. C with fair approximation.

From this graph Albertson and his co-workers have drawn an important conclusion: they have established, for instance, extreme values for the development of individual conditions of movement in terms of the d/δ' values.

It should be noted here that in the course of their studies on alluvial channels at the Laboratoire National d'Hydraulique at Chatou, France, J. Chabert and J. L. Chauvin succeeded in deriving detailed graphic relationships between the parameters U_*d/ν and U_*/ω at the boundary conditions of smooth bed, of sand ripples and of dune development for different bed load materials.

Considering the criteria defining the boundary conditions of sediment transportations R. J. Garde and K. G. Ranga Raju have made interesting comments on the graphical relations of Liu, of Albertson and his co-workers.

In *Figs 1.2.3−1* and *1.2.3−2* a well defined condition of bed load movement may be associated with each value of the tractive force, provided the bed load material and fluid viscosity are maintained constant. It will be appreciated therefrom that, as long as the tractive force remains constant, the condition of bed load transportation remains unchanged regardless whether flow occurs at small depth and steep slope, or at great depth and mild slope. *Fig. 1.2.3−2* has been plotted by Albertson and his co-workers on the basis of laboratory experiments in which the depth of flow was usually small, and the slope very steep. For this reason Garde and Ranga Raju considered the relationship of Albertson and his col-

160

laborators inapplicable to alluvial streams in which flow occurs usually at great depth and mild slope.

The above remark by Garde is essentially a positive indication of the fact that the critical tractive force pertaining to a particular bed load material is a variable quantity.

In 1957—58, relying on the studies made by Liu and Albertson and co-workers, the author made an attempt at a quantitative separation of the different boundary conditions with the objective of describing the condition of movement for a particular combination of particle size d, slope S and flow depth D with the help of a single parameter.

In the log-log plot of *Fig. 1.2.3—2* the corresponding pairs of values pertaining to identical temperatures and particle sizes are situated along a straight line rising at 45° from left to right. It should be obvious that, by keeping the particle size unchanged and varying the temperature, the 45° straight line of this particular particle size will be shifted parallel to itself. If the temperature is kept constant and the particle size is increased, then the corresponding points will be arranged along a 45° straight line displaced downward to the right for larger particles. The 45° inclination of the straight lines and the parallel displacement thereof with changes in temperature and particle size do not imply a new relationship within the problem. The magnitude of displacement with a change in particle size appears, however, to permit certain new conclusions to be drawn. In subsequent investigations allowance is made for this circumstance.

With the help of the 45° (or approximately 45°) straight lines pertaining in the figure to the individual particle sizes the influence of a change in particle size on the parameters $U_* d/\nu$ and U_*/ω is readily determined. The relation will depend on whether the bed load is at rest or its movement is accompanied by the development of sand ripples, dunes, transition or antidunes.

As will be perceived from the figure, at a given temperature and size d the condition of movement is controlled by the magnitude of U_*. If, however, the individual conditions of movement are separated by certain numerical values of U_*, the desired new variable may be expected to depend exclusively on the depth of flow D, on slope S and on the particle size d, or on a parameter involving these three quantities. The ratios d/D or d/S are potential parameters of this type and so is the dimensionless *bed stability factor* $b=d/DS$ introduced by the author in 1942 in Hungarian bed load research.

Since

$$DS = \frac{U_*^2}{g}$$

thus

$$b = \frac{d}{DS} = \frac{gd}{U_*^2}$$

(1.2.3—4)

Fig. 1.2.3–3. Particle size vs. channel stability factor at different boundary conditions of bed load movement

From Eq. (1.2.3−4) the bed stability factor will be seen to equal the inverse of a Froude number in which the characteristic length is the particle size d, whereas the velocity involved is the shear velocity. The Froude number thus formulated has been termed the sediment shear velocity Froude number on the analogy of the shear velocity Reynolds number of sediment.

The two dimensionless numbers are preferably denoted as follows:

$$Fr_* = \frac{U_*^2}{gd} \qquad (1.2.3-5)$$

$$Re_* = \frac{U_* d}{\nu} \qquad (1.2.3-6)$$

With the above considerations the variable numerically defining the different conditions of movement should depend on Fr_* or on the parameter b.

For all particle sizes (represented by the 45° straight line) in *Fig. 1.2.3−2* the quantity

$$b = \frac{gd}{U_*^2} = \frac{1}{Fr_*} \qquad (1.2.3-7)$$

162

has been computed with the help of the sediment shear velocity Reynolds number for incipient bed load movement, for the boundary condition of smooth bed (the boundary condition of sand ripple formation), as well as for the boundary conditions of dunes, transition and antidunes. The corresponding pairs of values computed in this way are plotted in *Fig. 1.2.3−3*. In the log-log plot the points pertaining to the condition of movement, the formation of sand ripples, dunes, transition and antidunes are seen to be situated along parallel straight lines indicating that the quantities $b = 1/Fr_*$ and d are related by an expression of the form

$$b = \frac{1}{Fr_*} = \frac{gd}{U_*^2} = \beta d^N \qquad (1.2.3-8)$$

From the figure $N = 0.882$, while the magnitude of β depends on the conditions of movement. The straight lines being parallel to one another, the value of N is constant, consequently the condition of movement is defined exclusively by the magnitude of

$$\beta = \frac{1}{Fr_* \, d^{0.882}} \qquad (1.2.3-9)$$

According to *Fig. 1.2.3−3* the boundaries of the individual conditions of movement are characterized by the following β values:

boundary condition of incipient movement	$\beta = 550$
boundary of sand ripple formation	$\beta = 322$
boundary of dunes	$\beta = 66$
boundary of transition	$\beta = 23.8$
boundary of antidunes	$\beta = 9.65$

The bed load remains thus stationary at the bottom if β is greater than 550, the bed remains smooth if β is greater than 322, sand ripples may be formed if $66 < \beta < 322$, dunes may occur if $23.8 < \beta < 66$, whereas if $9.65 < \beta < 23.8$ the bed is in the state of transition, and antidunes are possible if $\beta < 9.65$.

The boundary condition of incipient movement is defined for particle sizes smaller than $d < 0.0145$ cm by the straight line inclined at $N = 0.882$ corresponding to the value $\beta = 550$, whereas for particle sizes greater than $d > 0.0145$ cm, by the horizontal straight line at

$$\frac{gd}{U_*^2} = 12.91 \qquad (1.2.3-10)$$

The straight lines sloping at 0.882 and characterizing the bed forms following the boundary condition of incipient movement join the horizontal straight line pertaining to the condition of no movement and, from the point of intersection in the direction of increasing particle sizes, the boundary proceeds along the horizontal line at $gd/U_*^2 = 12.91$.

Concerning bed load transportation in alluvial channels and even the condition of movement certain approximate conclusions may be drawn from *Fig. 1.2.3 – 3.*

For a bed load material of $\gamma_1 = 2.65$ specific gravity and consisting of well rounded particles in water of 20 deg. C temperature:

a) bed load of any size will remain stationary as long as

$$b = \frac{gd}{U_*^2} \geq 12.91$$

b) bed load particles of about 0.01 to 0.15 mm in size may remain stationary even if

$$b = \frac{gd}{U_*^2} < 12.91$$

c) in the case of particles larger than about 0.25 to 0.30 mm no bed load can be transported over a smooth bed,

d) at size fractions greater than about 2.0 mm no sand ripples are possible and logically no bed load is transported over a smooth bed,

e) no dunes and sand ripples are formed of fractions greater than about 5 to 6 mm and logically no bed load is transported over a smooth bed,

f) at particle sizes greater than about 15 mm transition, dunes and sand ripples are excluded and thus bed load movement over a smooth bed is likewise impossible.

From Eq. (1.2.3 – 8) it will be realized that the relation between U_* and particle size d can also be determined with the different conditions of movement. Denoting the parameter $(g/\beta)^{1/2}$ by ε, the relation becomes

$$U_* = \left(\frac{g}{\beta}\right)^{1/2} d^{0.059} = \varepsilon d^{0.059} \tag{1.2.3 – 11}$$

Considering the different values of β, the boundary conditions of bed load transportation are represented according the relation

$$U_* = F(d) \tag{1.2.3 – 12}$$

in *Fig. 1.2.3 – 4;* consequently, since the magnitude of ε depends exclusively on β, the boundary of the different conditions is also uniquely determined by ε.

According to Eq. (1.2.3 – 8) the quantity β is a dimensional one. Since in *Fig. 1.2.3 – 3* lengths are expressed in cm units, the dimension of β is cm$^{-0.882}$.

The quantity ε is similarly a dimensional one and has the dimension cm$^{0.941}$ sec^{-1}, according to Eq. (1.2.3 – 11).

Specific gravity is not involved in the parameter $b = gd/U_*^2$ since, in the experiments on the basis of which the parameter has been introduced, the bed load material was invariably river gravel or sand of a specific gravity $\gamma_1 = 2.65$ p/cm^3 with fair approximation. A form of the parameter in which materials of different

164

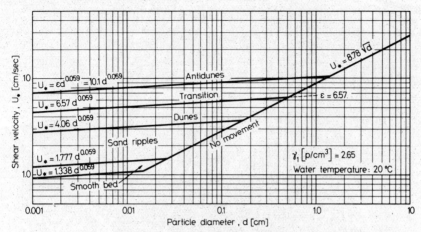

Fig. 1.2.3—4. Particle size vs. shear velocity at different boundary conditions of bed load movement

specific gravities or densities can be taken into consideration is

$$b = \frac{1}{Fr_*} \frac{(\rho_1 - \rho)}{\rho} \qquad (1.2.3-13)$$

The numerical values given in the foregoing for the parameter β apply to a bed load material having a submerged specific gravity $2.65 - 1 = 1.65$. If it is desired to include in the numerical value of the parameter β the specific gravity of bed load, then from Eq. $(1.2.3-13)$ the new form of Eq. $(1.2.3-8)$ will become

$$\beta_{\gamma_1} d^N = \frac{1}{Fr_*} \frac{1}{1.65} \frac{(\rho_1 - \rho)}{\rho} \qquad (1.2.3-14)$$

The foregoing parameter values may be denoted as $\beta_{2.65}$ since they apply to bed load of $\gamma_1 = 2.65$ specific gravity.

For a bed load material of arbitrary specific gravity γ_1 the magnitude of β_{γ_1} is obtained from the expression

$$\beta_{\gamma_1} = \beta_{2.65} \frac{(\gamma_1 - \gamma)}{1.65\gamma} = \beta_{2.65} \frac{(\rho_1 - \rho)}{1.65\rho} \qquad (1.2.3-15)$$

Eq. $(1.2.3-8)$ defining the boundary conditions of bed load transportation has been rewritten by Z. Hankó who expressed the quantity $\tau_0/(\gamma_1 - \gamma)$ having the dimension of length in terms of the particle diameter d [cm]. Since

$$U_*^2 = gDS = \frac{gd}{\beta d^N} \qquad (1.2.3-16)$$

165

Fig. 1.2.3—5. Particle size vs. ratio of tractive force to differential specific gravity at different boundary conditions of bed load movement. After Hankó

in the case of depth D and slope S the tractive force τ_0 is

$$\tau_0 = \gamma DS = \frac{1}{\beta}\, d^{0.118}\, \gamma \qquad (1.2.3-17)$$

while the relation introduced by Hankó is

$$\frac{\tau_0}{(\gamma_1 - \gamma)} = \frac{1}{\beta}\, d^{0.118}\, \frac{\gamma}{(\gamma_1 - \gamma)} \qquad (1.2.3-18)$$

When using Eq. (1.2.3—18) the straight lines defining the different boundary conditions are obtained by substituting successively the corresponding values of β. As mentioned before, a bed load of 2.65 p/cm³ specific gravity was used in the experiments from which *Fig. 1.2.3—3* was constructed. Consequently any relation derived therefrom is limited in its validity to bed load of 2.65 specific gravity. For this reason the value $\gamma/(\gamma_1 - \gamma) = 1/1.65$ must be used.

For example the numerical form of the relation describing the boundary condition of incipient movement is accordingly

166

$$\frac{\tau_0}{(\gamma_1 - \gamma)} = 0.00182 \, d^{0.118} \frac{1}{1.65} = 0.001103 \, d^{0.118} \qquad (1.2.3-19)$$

With the help of Eq. (1.2.3−18), *Fig. 1.2.3−5* is constructed.

In connection with Eq. (1.2.3−8) and *Fig. 1.2.3−3* representing the latter it is necessary to point out an important fact. Since the dimensionless quantity gd/U_*^2 cannot be a unique function of the dimensional particle diameter d, it should be obvious that the horizontal axis of the figure must be scaled theoretically to a quantity d/A, where A is an actual length or the combination of quantities resulting eventually in a length dimension. It should be clear, moreover, that A must be composed of physical quantities which preserve a constant magnitude within the validity limits of *Fig. 1.2.3−3*. In fact, if the magnitude of A were permitted to vary, the validity of the relations represented in the figure would be destroyed. This, however, is impossible in view of the experimental results used in plotting them.

This inconsistence may be eliminated by considering the occurrence of the different boundary conditions of sediment movement as a physical phenomenon and by taking into account all the physical quantities that are of potential influence during the experiments.

The approach described in *Section 1.1.4.* yields combination A of length dimension and thus the dimensionless parameter d/A.

The channel will be assumed to be very wide compared to the depth of flow and it will be assumed further that the sediment is described adequately by its size, d and by the dimensionless ratio $\rho' = \rho_1 - \rho/\rho$ representing the densities.

With the above simplifying assumption the different boundary conditions of sediment transportation as physical phenomena are defined by gravitational acceleration g [cm/sec²], by the mean depth of flow D [cm], by the particle diameter of the bed load d [cm], by the kinematic viscosity of the fluid v [cm²/sec], by the slope of the hydraulic grade line S [−] and the density ρ' [−].

Of the four independent dimensional physical quantities g, D, d and v, the dimensions of which involve length and time alone, $4 - 2 + 1 = 3$ independent potential dynamic velocities can be formed. Including the dimensionless physical quantities S and ρ' no more than two additional independent potential dynamic velocities can be written, irrespective of what mathematical operation or combination is adopted. Remembering the initial conditions, the phenomenon is thus described by altogether $3 + 2 = 5$ independent potential dynamic velocities. It is found, however, expedient to write more than five independent potential dynamic velocities. Remembering *Section 1.1.4.* altogether 15 velocities are formed which are tabulated in five columns and three rows as follows:

$$\sqrt{gD}, \quad \sqrt{gd}, \quad v/D, \quad v/d, \quad \sqrt[3]{gv} \qquad (1.2.3-20)$$

$$\sqrt{gDS}, \quad \sqrt{gdS}, \quad (v/D)S, \quad (v/d)S, \quad \sqrt[3]{gvS} \qquad (1.2.3-21)$$

$$\sqrt{gD\rho'}, \quad \sqrt{gd\rho'}, \quad (v/D)\rho', \quad (v/d)\rho', \quad \sqrt[3]{gv\rho'} \qquad (1.2.3-22)$$

167

Fig. 1.2.3−6. Parameter $\dfrac{d}{\nu^{2/3}g^{-1/3}}$ vs. channel stability factor at different boundary conditions of bed load movement

water on the boundary conditions of sediment transportation will not be reflected by these figures if these are derived from *Fig. 1.2.3−3* or *1.2.3−6*. If it is intended to determine the effect of viscosity, the results of actual experiments performed with water of different temperatures should be compared. If experiments were performed with bed load of 2.65 specific gravity, for instance, in water of 10 deg. C temperature, and if the relations indicating the different boundary conditions in the chart constructed therefrom did not change in the ratio of $A_{20}°$C and $A_{10}°$C, then the change differring from the ratio $A_{20}°$C$/A_{10}°$C would express the influence of the temperature drop from 20 to 10 deg. C on bed load transportation.

Starting from this consideration the author has performed several experiments for determining the effect of viscosity. Unfortunately, the number of experiments made at water temperatures other than 20 deg. C is too small to permit any reliable determination of the relations describing the different boundary conditions.

According to Eq. (1.2.3−9), as well as to

$$\beta_1 = \frac{gd}{U_*^2}\left(\frac{d}{\nu^{2/3}\,g^{-1/3}}\right)^{-N} \tag{1.2.3−29}$$

170

the magnitude of β and β_1 depends on the quantities d, D and S. In other words, the regime of movement of bed load of a particular size is uniquely defined by depth and by the slope of flow. This is obviously in agreement with the law of constant critical values and, as pointed out previously, is in fact incorrect. *Figs 1.2.3−3, 1.2.3−4* and *1.2.3−6* may thus be used for approximate computations only. Obviously, the other conclusions arrived at from the figures will also be of an approximate character only.

Fig. 1.2.3−3 was subject to critical discussion by Garde and Ranga Raju in their studies mentioned before. Since this figure is also founded on laboratory experiments, the remarks made in connection with the relation of Albertson and co-workers obviously apply to it. Same as the expressions of Albertson and partners, the relations indicated in this figure are not generally applicable to natural water courses either.

In 1959 Garde and Albertson described the different boundary conditions of bed load transportation by relating the dimensionless resistance factor f_0 to the Froude number. The parameter

$$f_0 = \frac{\tau_0}{(\gamma_1 - \gamma)d} \qquad (1.2.3-30)$$

plays an important role in estimating the rate of bed load transport, as will be seen in *Section 1.2.6* in Eq. (1.2.6−5). The Froude number

$$Fr = \frac{v}{\sqrt{gR}} \qquad (1.2.3-31)$$

where R is the hydraulic radius, is known to represent the relation between bed forms and waves appearing at the surface. From the appearance of sand ripples to the development of dunes, bed forms exert a slight influence on the water surface as well. The role of the Froude number remains insignificant as long as the height of sand ripples or dunes is negligible in comparison with the depth of flow. But as soon as the relative height of dunes to the depths of flow becomes appreciable, the Froude number, too, assumes added significance.

On the strength of the foregoing considerations Garde and Albertson introduced the criterion $f_0 - Fr$ for describing the boundary conditions of bed load transportation.

Using the measurement data listed in *Table 1.2.3−1* they succeeded in estimating the $f_0 - Fr$ criteria shown in *Fig. 1.2.3−7*. Sand ripples and dunes are seen to be separated from the transition range by a well defined line. The boundary between transition and the antidunes is less pronounced. The rule of general validity derived from the figure seems to be that antidunes may develop around $Fr \simeq 1$ values.

Beside the wide scatter in the values of antidunes, a drawback of the $f_0 - Fr$ criterion is that in addition to the hydraulic radius R, to the particle diameter d, to the slope S and to the difference in specific gravities $(\gamma_1 - \gamma)$, the magnitude of the resultant velocity v is also necessary. Now it will be appreciated that, owing to

171

Table 1.2.3—1

Data of laboratory experiments and field observations in natural channels for determining the boundary conditions of sediment transport. After Garde and Ranga Raju

No.	Name of watercourse, or author	Particle diameter, d [mm]	Flow velocity, v [cm/sec]	Symbol
1.	Gilbert — A Sand	0.305	64.01 — 97.53	◇
2.	Gilbert — C Sand	0.506	48.76 —100.58	◇
3.	Gilbert — F Sand	3.170	60.96 — 99.06	◇
4.	Shen	1.12	4.938— 24.54	◁
5.	Shen	3.17	12.44 — 26.06	▷
6.	Shen	0.80	18.53 — 1.524	◇
7.	Simons & Richardson	0.28	16.15 —149.35	◇
8.	Simons & Richardson	0.45	21.31 —188.36	◇
9.	Kennedy	0.088—0.233	62.48 — 65.53	◇-
10.	Barton and Lin	0.18	21.64 —109.72	□
11.	Laursen	0.10	32.61 —102.41	◻
12.	Kalinske and Hsia	0.011	25.63 — 83.21	◻
13.	Sind canals (India)	0.021—0.196	46.94 —113.08	○
14.	Punjab canals	0.17 —0.43	33.22 — 99.06	▽
15.	Canals in the US	0.096—0.805	41.45 — 78.33	⩢
16.	U. P. canals (India)	0.047—0.365	58.83 —124.36	◇
17.	Middle Loup River	0.305	56.99 —112.47	◇
18.	Pigeon Roost Creek	0.40	22.86 —228.6	○
19.	Rio Grande River	0.30	67.05 —234.69	◻
20.	Colorado River	0.33	64.31 —104.54	◻
21.	Mississippi River	0.31	101.80 —223.72	◻
22.	Tiberis River	0.30	73.76 — 94.49	○
23.	Waikato River (New-Zeeland)	0.51	17.68 — 57.91	○
24.	Niobrara River	0.28	74.06 —108.2	◇
25.	Mountain Creek	0.90	39.01 — 73.46	○
26.	West Goose Creek	0.33	41.45 —135.03	○
27.	San Louis Valley canals	20—78	88.39 —199.03	+

the variable effect of bed forms on bed resistance, the estimation of velocity is highly unreliable.

In order to eliminate this difficulty a new criterion was introduced in 1963 by Garde and Ranga Raju, in which velocity v is absent. The parameters of the new criterion are determined by a resistance law applying to alluvial channels. With the help of dimensional analysis it is demonstrated that the resistance law of alluvial channels can be expressed by a general relation of the form

$$\frac{v}{\sqrt{\dfrac{(\gamma_1 - \gamma)d}{\rho}}} = F\left(\frac{R}{d},\ \frac{S\gamma}{(\gamma_1 - \gamma)},\ \frac{g^{1/2}\,d^{3/2}}{v}\right) \qquad (1.2.3-32)$$

In alluvial streams, resistance and the regime of bed load transport are closely interrelated. It appears thus safe to assume that the different boundary conditions

172

Fig. 1.2.3—7. Resistance factor f_0 vs. Froude number at different boundary conditions of bed load movement. After Garde and Albertson

of bed load transportation are controlled by the three parameters on the right-hand side of Eq. (1.2.3 – 32) or, neglecting the effect of viscosity, as a first approximation, by the relative roughness R/d and by the parameter $S\gamma/(\gamma_1 - \gamma)$.

Using the data shown in *Table 1.2.3 – 1* the relation between R/d and the parameter $S\gamma/(\gamma_1 - \gamma)$ is indicated in *Fig. 1.2.3 – 8* by the two dashed straight lines, one of which applies to the boundary condition between the range of sand ripples and dunes and the range of transition, while the second separates the transition range from that of the antidunes.

173

Fig. 1.2.3−8. Relative roughness R/d vs. parameter $\dfrac{S\gamma}{(\gamma_1 - \gamma)}$ at different boundary conditions of bed load movement. After Garde and Ranga Raju

The parameter of Shields

$$f_c = \frac{\tau_c}{(\gamma_1 - \gamma)d}$$

indicating the boundary condition of incipient movement − see Eq. (1.2.3−3) − can also be written as the product of the two dimensionless parameters involved in *Fig. 1.2.3−8:*

$$f_c = \frac{\tau_c}{(\gamma_1 - \gamma)d} = \frac{\gamma RS}{(\gamma_1 - \gamma)d} = \frac{S\gamma}{(\gamma_1 - \gamma)} \frac{R}{d} \qquad (1.2.3-33)$$

implying that, in the log-log plot, each $f_c =$ constant value is represented by a straight line inclined at 45° from left to right.

From the relation of Shields (see *Fig. 1.1.3−2)* Garde and Ranga Raju adopted the value $f_c = 0.05$ for coarse bed load material with fair approximation and indicated the boundary condition of incipient movement in the figure with the full straight line inclined at 45°.

From *Fig. 1.2.3−8* Garde and Ranga Raju arrived at the following conclusions:

174

a) The condition of bed load movement referred to as transition occurs only in a narrow range of depth or slope, especially at high R/d values.

b) The straight lines separating the boundary conditions of bed load movement are inclined at less than 45° to the horizontal axis R/d. On the other hand, for a given combination of d and $(\gamma_1 - \gamma)$, the constant magnitude of the tractive force is indicated by a straight line of 45° slope. This circumstance supports the conclusion that the regime of bed load transport may be variable even if the tractive force is constant. This is in conflict with the law of constant tractive forces pertaining to a given set of d and $(\gamma_1 - \gamma)$ values and thus with the laws represented in the six *Figs 1.2.3−1* to *1.2.3−6*. It will be perceived therefrom that the regime of bed load movement is not described by the tractive force alone, since it is affected also by the parameters R/d and $S\gamma/(\gamma_1 - \gamma)$. According to Garde, this inconsistency is probably due to the great differences observable in the R/d and $S\gamma/(\gamma_1 - \gamma)$ values.

The advantage of the new criterion over the one suggested by Garde and Albertson is that velocity is eliminated therefrom since it is a quantity difficult to determine.

The final conclusion of Garde and Ranga Raju is that the tractive force is not always a suitable parameter for describing the regime of bed load transportation and that the criterion involving the quantities R/d and $S\gamma/(\gamma_1 - \gamma)$ may be used as a fair approximation.

In *Section 1.2.4*, in connection with the law of variable tractive forces, the correctness of the conclusions by Garde and Ranga Raju will be demonstrated numerically.

Considering the individual criteria describing the boundary conditions of bed load movement it will be seen that the parameters involved in them are interrelated, and thus not each of them may be accepted as an independent variable.

In the criteria mentioned in the foregoing the following parameters are involved:

$$\frac{U_*}{\omega}, \quad \frac{U_* d}{\nu}, \quad \frac{d}{\delta'}, \quad \frac{gd}{U_*^2} = \frac{1}{Fr_*}, \quad \frac{d}{\nu^{2/3} g^{-1/3}}, \quad f_c = \frac{\tau_c}{(\gamma_1 - \gamma)d},$$

$$Fr = \frac{v}{\sqrt{gR}}, \quad \frac{R}{d}, \quad \frac{S\gamma}{(\gamma_1 - \gamma)}$$

Studying the relations existing between these parameters, $U_* d/\nu$ will be seen to depend on d/δ' according to Eq. (1.2.3−3).

The dimensionless parameter

$$\frac{d}{\nu^{2/3} g^{-1/3}} = \frac{d}{A}$$

has been introduced in the foregoing as the ratio of potential dynamic velocities formed of physical quantities describing the boundary conditions of bed load movement. According to Eq. (1.2.3−24a), the parameter has been obtained

175

Finally

$$\frac{R}{d} = \frac{\tau_c}{(\gamma_1 - \gamma)d} \frac{(\gamma_1 - \gamma)}{S\gamma} = \frac{f_c}{\dfrac{S\gamma}{(\gamma_1 - \gamma)}}$$ (1.2.3−41)

and

$$\frac{S\gamma}{(\gamma_1 - \gamma)} = \frac{\tau_c}{(\gamma_1 - \gamma)} \frac{d}{R} = \frac{f_c}{R/d}$$ (1.2.3−42)

or combining Eqs (1.2.3 − 38) and (1.2.3 − 39)

$$\left(\frac{R}{d}\right)\left(\frac{S\gamma}{(\gamma_1 - \gamma)}\right) = f_c = \frac{U_*^2}{gd} \frac{\gamma}{(\gamma_1 - \gamma)}$$ (1.2.3−43)

which is a further demonstration of the relationships existing between the in-dividual parameters.

When combining several criteria it may occur occasionally that, concerning the physical quantities describing the phenomenon, not each of the parameters defining the boundary conditions of bed load movement will be independent.

Interrelated parameters which may be derived from each other are most readily eliminated from consideration by adopting the approach described in *Section 1.1.4* and used in the foregoing for deriving the theoretical relation given by Eq. (1.2.3−26).

1.2.4. INTRODUCTION OF THE VARIABLE CRITICAL TRACTIVE FORCES

1.2.4.1. Variation of the critical tractive forces. As pointed out previously in *Section 1.1.3*, the experiments performed by Shields in 1936 have demonstrated the critical tractive force τ_c to be a variable quantity. If the value of τ_c pertaining to a given particle diameter d and submerged specific gravity $(\gamma_1 - \gamma)$ were constant, then $f_c = \tau_c/(\gamma_1 - \gamma)d$ would also be constant and would thus be unaffected by $Re_* = U_*d/v$. On the other hand, from *Fig. 1.1.3−2* illustrating the experiments of Shields, the variation of f_c with Re_* will be appreciated. In the sediment shear velocity Reynolds number the kinematic viscosity v of water is the only variable not involved in f_c. It follows from this circumstance that τ_c varies with water temperature. From the figure f_c will be seen to vary at values $Re_* \leqq 600$ and to assume the constant value 0.06 beyond $Re_* = 600$.

In the experiments of Shields the lowest value was approximately $Re_* = 1.8$ or, by introducing − according to Eq. (1.2.3−3) − the ratio of the particle diameter d to the thickness δ' of the laminar sublayer, the lowest value is expressed as $d/\delta' = = 0.155$. The highest value in Shields's experiments was $Re_* = 200$ and $d/\delta' = 17.3$.

Fig. 1.2.4—1. Resistance coefficient f_c vs. ratio of particle diameter
to thickness of boundary layer. After V. Nagy et al.

Experiments similar to those of Shields were made by I. V. Nagy, G. Karádi
and Gy. Kalmár, but the range studied was appreciably wider. In the experiments
of Kalmár the lowest values were $Re_* = 0.41$, or $d/\delta' = 0.035$, whereas the
highest values were $Re_* = 1,100$ or $d/\delta' = 95$. The results of these investigations
are shown in *Fig. 1.2.4—1*. From the figure it will be perceived that, concerning
the relation

$$f_c = F\left(\frac{d}{\delta'}\right) \tag{1.2.4—1}$$

three different ranges can be distinguished.

a) For values of d/δ' smaller than unity (corresponding to $Re_* < 12$) the experimental points satisfy the equation

$$f_c = \frac{1}{67}\,(d/\delta')^{-0.5} \tag{1.2.4—2}$$

The range $1 > d/\delta' > 0.035$ is that of a hydraulically smooth bed. In the case of
bed load specific gravities and water temperatures most commonly encountered,
this corresponds to the 0.05 mm $< d <$ 0.5 mm size fraction so that the critical
condition or movement of this fraction is characterized by the magnitude of U_*.

b) In the range $1 < d/\delta' < 100$ (corresponding roughly to $12 < Re_* < 1,200$)
the transitions between the hydraulically smooth and rough bed becomes prevalent. At common water temperatures and bed load specific gravities the particles
greater than 0.2 and smaller than 15 mm may be set into motion.

c) At $d/\delta' > 100$ (corresponding to $Re_* > 1,200$) the bed is hydraulically
rough. Considering, as before, water temperatures and bed load specific gravities
commonly encountered, this range applies to particles larger than 15 mm.

12*

Fig. 1.2.4–2. Variation in the critical tractive forces with Manning's roughness at 7.1 mm particle size. After Bogárdi and Yen

Fig. 1.2.4–3. Variation in the critical tractive forces with Manning's roughness at 10.6 mm particle size. After Bogárdi and Yen

According to the experiments made by V. Nagy and his co-workers for $d/\delta' > > 100$, the highest value of f_c is 0.055. Consequently in this range

$$\tau_c = 0.055\,(\gamma_1 - \gamma)d \qquad (1.2.4-3)$$

Converted to the familiar units of measurement, this expression yields, with fair approximation, Eq. (1.1.3−14) which is valid for coarse bed load material.

The experiments by V. Nagy and co-workers, just as those of Shields, have demonstrated the critical tractive force to vary with the temperature of water since

180

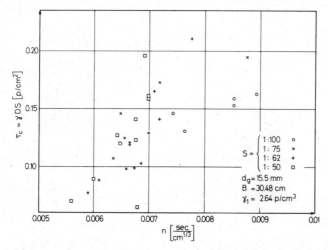

Fig. 1.2.4—4. Variation in the critical tractive forces with Manning's roughness at 15.5 mm particle size. After Bogárdi and Yen

among the physical quantities defining d/δ', the only variable not involved in f_c is viscosity v depending on temperature.

The experiments made in 1937—38 by the author and C. H. Yen at Iowa shortly after the studies of Shields, have also demonstrated the variability of the critical tractive force. As mentioned earlier in paragraph 1 of *Subsection 1.1.3.2*, in the Iowa experiments the critical tractive force was found to vary with the roughness of the laboratory flume.

For different slopes and depths of flow, and for well sorted bed load material of 7.1, 10.6 and 15.5 mm diameter, the relationship between the critical tractive force and Manning's roughness n is illustrated in *Figs 1.2.4—2, 1.2.4—3* and *1.2.4—4*. It is clearly demonstrated that for given bed load material the magnitude of the critical tractive force increases with the roughness coefficient n. Since the particle size d, the specific gravity γ_1 and the flume width B was constant in the individual figures, the roughness coefficient varied logically as a function of the depth and slope of flow. Moreover, since the critical tractive force τ_c is positively shown to vary with the coefficient n of bed roughness, it should be obvious that also the critical tractive force varies with different combinations of flow depth and slope.

The experiments at Iowa thus also support the conclusion that the critical value of the tractive force pertaining to a particular bed load material is variable.

In connection with the critical tractive force it should be noted that, for a bed load of given particle size and at certain slopes, its magnitude may also be influenced by the bottom slope. The influence of bottom slope was neglected for a long time and several investigators, including Kreuter, Schaffernak, Schoklitsch,

Sediment				Critical tractive force, in p/m²,						
Type	Av. adm., mm	Spec. grav. [p/m³]	1 : 50	1 : 62	1 : 75	1 : 80	1 : 100	1 : 111	1 : 125	
Kramer	I.	0.71	2.70							
Kramer	II.	0.56	3.70							
Kramer	III.	0.80	2.70							
Te-Yun Liu	I.	4.4	2.66					231.8		
Te-Yun Liu	II.	3.4	2.66					198.2		
Te-Yun Liu	III.	2.3	2.66					131.2		
Te-Yun Liu	IV.	1.4	2.66					70.2		
Te-Yun Liu	V.	3.6	2.66					225.7		
Te-Yun Liu	VI.	1.8	2.66					85.4		
Bogárdi—Yen	I.	10.6	2.63	965.0	1,155.7	1,280.2		1,548.4		
Bogárdi—Yen	II.	7.1	2.61	624.8	566.9	563.9		618.5		
Indri	1.	0.3	2.63							
Indri	2.	0.47	2.70							
Indri	3.	2.5	2.70						238.5	238.0
Indri	4.	4.0	2.70				407	405.0		

Gilbert and Krey have even concluded that the magnitude of the critical tractive force applying to a certain size fraction is unaffected by the bottom slope.

In the Iowa experiments the author and Yen observed that within certain limits of particle size and slope the magnitude of the critical tractive force applying to the same bed load material was influenced by changes in the bottom slope.

For a more detailed analysis of the problem experiments were performed to study the influence of changes in the bottom slope on the magnitude of the critical tractive force, using the same bed load material.

In *Table 1.2.4 — 3* the critical tractive forces observed at different bottom slopes and different bed load fractions are compiled from available data.*

The critical tractive force has been plotted against bottom slope in *Fig. 1.2.4 — 5*, where it is seen to be unaffected by the bottom slope for particles of 7.1 mm diameter and smaller. However, the critical tractive forces determined for the 10.6 mm size fraction display a definite decreasing trend as the bottom slope is increased. It may be concluded therefrom that up to a certain particle diameter the magnitude of the critical tractive force is not influenced by the bottom slope.

* Few such data have been published in the literature. Even where observations were made at variable bottom slopes, no detailed data are given.

condition at different bottom slopes

observed at bottom slopes								Mean tract. force, τ_e [p/m²]	Note
1 : 200	1:333	1 : 400	1:500	1:600	1 : 800	1:1000	1:∞		
		52.7		50.7	50.7	52.0		52.0	Mixed fractions
		41.3		41.3	35.2	36.5		39.0	Type I: $d = 0.15$ to 5.0 mm
		49.0		49.6	46.7	49.8		49.0	Type II: $d = 0.15$ to 1.8 mm
									Type III: $d = 0.25$ to 5.0 mm
183.0		201.3			186.0			201.3	Mixture composed of 0.3 to
155.5		152.5			103.7			152.5	7.0 mm size fractions
109.8		109.8			94.6			109.8	
61.0		54.9			54.9			61.0	
216.6		152.5			149.4			186.0	
76.2		82.4			79.3			80.7	
									Sieved, particles of uniform
								593.5	size
	19.4		18.0				19.0	18.8	Mixed fractions
30.5	29.6		29.9				30.2	30.2	Type 1: $d = 0.01$ to 1.0 mm
245.0								240.5	Type 2: $d = 0.01$ to 1.0 mm
407.5								406.5	Type 3: $d = 2.0$ to 3.0 mm
									Type 4: $d = 3.0$ to 5.0 mm

There seems to be a particle size limit — apparently between 7 and 10 mm — beyond which the critical tractive force is influenced by the bottom slope. It seems permissible to conclude that the influence of the bottom slope at particle sizes greater than the limit mentioned before, becomes apparent between inclinations 1 : 50 and 1 : 100. The slope limits are probably considerably wider, but the particle size limit appears to be of an importance superior thereto.

Experiments involving greater particle sizes and flatter bottom slopes would be necessary before any conclusion of general validity could be drawn from the above observations. In the Iowa experiments this proved unfortunately impossible. It is regrettable, moreover, that the experiments made by the author with 15.5 mm material have only yielded approximate results in this respect. The flume available was in fact too narrow for the 15.5 mm bed load material and, owing to strong undulation in the critical condition, the depth of flow was found difficult to measure accurately. Nevertheless, it was established that the magnitude of the critical tractive force varied with the bottom slope.

For the 10.6 mm size fraction the author and C. H. Yen succeeded in observing, at the critical condition, both the oscillation of particles and the tractive forces occurring during the uninterrupted movement of originally moving (launched)

Fig. 1.2.4—5. Critical tractive force vs. bottom slope

Table 1.2.4—2

Variation in tractive force with bottom slope

	Tractive force, in p/m², observed at bottom slopes					Note
	1 : 38	1 : 50	1 : 62	1 : 75	1 : 100	
At the critical condition (τ_c)	—	954.0	1,115.6	1,280.2	1,548.4	Sieved river gravel, particles of uniform size
Continuous transport of moving particles (τ_m)	649.2	774.2	826.0	1,018.0	1,255.8	
Particle vibrations (τ_r)	594.4	643.1	752.9	853.4	1,011.9	The average diameter $d_g = 10.6$ mm, the spec. gravity $\gamma_1 = 2.63$ p/cm³

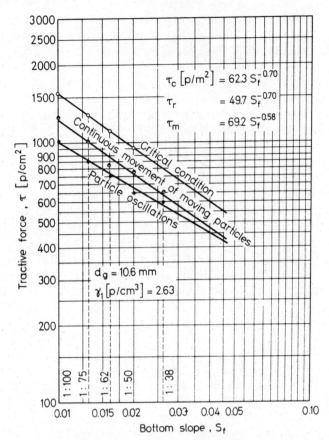

Fig. 1.2.4—6. Tractive force vs. bottom slope for 10.6 mm
diameter bed load material

bed load particles at variable bottom slopes. The experimental data are compiled
in *Table 1.2.4—2*. In *Fig. 1.2.4—6* the tractive force is plotted against bottom
slope. From the graph the following three relations can be established:

$$\tau_c \ [p/m^2] = 62.3 \ S_f^{-0.70} \qquad\qquad (1.2.4-4)$$

$$\tau_r \ [p/m^2] = 49.7 \ S_f^{-0.70} \qquad\qquad (1.2.4-5)$$

$$\tau_m [p/m^2] = 69.2 \ S_f^{-0.58} \qquad\qquad (1.2.4-6)$$

The three equations apply exlusively to the 10.6 mm size fraction and to bottom
slopes varying from 1 : 38 to 1 : 100.

When extending in *Fig. 1.2.4—5* the line applying to the 10.6 mm size bed load
it will be seen that at a bottom slope of about 1 : 20 ($S_f = 0.05$) the critical
tractive force becomes zero, that is, the tractive force of the flowing water is not
required for shifting the bed load, in other words, movement may start owing to

185

the steep slope alone even in stationary water. The slope 1 : 20 is roughly equivalent to an inclination of about 3 degrees which, if the extension is justified, would be at the same time the natural angle of internal friction under water of bed load material of 10.6 mm size.

For fine sand, gravel and boulders the angles 10, 25 and 40 degrees, respectively, are mentioned by Schoklitsch as the underwater angle of friction of bed load material. The difference is thus seen to be very wide so that any extension of the measurement data is impermissible, these being only valid in the range of slopes from 1 : 100 to 1 : 50 (1 : 38).

The dependence of the critical tractive force on bottom slope is in support of the statement that it is unadvisable to use the critical tractive force for describing the critical condition.

Section 1.2.3 has been devoted to the remarks of Garde and Ranga Raju, of Albertson and co-workers and of the author made in connection with *Figs 1.2.3 – 2* and *1.2.3 – 3*. Accordingly it is highly relevant whether the tractive force is obtained as the product of a small depth and steep slope or as that of great depth and flat slope.

The above remarks of Garde and Ranga Raju apply to various boundary conditions of sediment transportation. Consequently, this general conclusion applies to the critical condition as well.

In connection with *Fig. 1.2.3 – 8* it has been stated by Garde and Ranga Raju that the regime of bed load movement may be variable even in the case of a constant tractive force. They conclude therefrom that the tractive force alone is unsuited for describing the critical condition.

An effort will be made subsequently to take into consideration the factors which cause the critical tractive forces to vary.

1.2.4.2. The law of variable critical tractive forces. Considering the variation of the critical tractive force it is obvious that, in contrast to the early frictional drag theory, the factor f_c in the expression $\tau_c = f_c(\gamma_1 - \gamma)/d$ is not a constant value. Shields and more recently V. Nagy and co-workers have demonstrated experimentally f_c to vary with water temperature. In the experiments made by the author and Yen f_c was found to vary with bed roughness.

The concept of a constant critical tractive force pertaining to a given bed load material of particle size d and of submerged specific gravity $(\gamma_1 - \gamma)$ has to be discarded on the strength of the foregoing considerations. Moreover, since most earlier results are founded on the assumption of a constant critical tractive force τ_c, all conclusions are in need of being revised.

Investigations into the variability of the critical tractive force τ_c have demonstrated that, instead of the product of depth and slope, the influence of depth D, of slope S and of other hydraulic quantities affecting the critical condition must be considered separately.

For these investigations the available results of earlier laboratory experiments have been adopted. The highest and lowest values of the hydraulic quantities involved in the experiments have been compiled in *Table 1.2.4.–3*.

186

Table 1.2.4—3

Hydraulic parameters of observations used in determining the critical tractive force

Condition of movement	Depth of flow, D [cm]		Water temperature, t [°C]		Particle diameter, d [mm]		Slope, S		Spec. gravity of sediment γ_1 [p/cm³]	
	Max.	Min.	Max.	Min.	Max.	Min.	Max.	Min.	Max.	Min.
Critical	46.1	1.52	27	7.6	15.49	0.021	0.066	0.000055	2.65	2.59
At the boundary of dune development	59.44	12.50	33.8	10.0	15.49	0.18	0.0209	0.00037	2.65	2.65

The data used were published by J. Bogárdi, L. Ivicsics, L. Rákóczi, Guy—Simons—Richardson, Barton—Liu et al.

187

Fig. 1.2.4—7. Resistance coefficient f_c vs. sediment shear velocity Reynolds number, with relative roughness $D/10d$ as parameter

Let us examine first the validity of the relation $f_c = F(Re_*)$ put forward by Shields, relying on the results of laboratory experiments mentioned above. From *Fig. 1.2.4 — 7* the measurement points will be seen to scatter irregularly about the curve of Shields. This implies that, under observation conditions other than those in the measurements of Shields, a different critical tractive force will be obtained, since the magnitude of τ_c is influenced besides Re_* by other physical quantities as well. Remembering the variation of the critical tractive force with bed roughness it will be logical to attempt a grouping of the scattered points according to the relative roughness D/d. The relative roughness values entered at the individual experimental points give no positive indication that D/d is necessarily the third parameter that affects the variation of τ_c, but a simple inspection will suffice to indicate the essential role of relative roughness in the magnitude of τ_c. The D/d = constant curves traced with dashed lines in *Fig. 1.2.4 — 7* demonstrate the effect of relative roughness.

Extensive investigations have recently been performed at the Institute of Hydraulics, Bologna University, with the objective of studying wave phenomena, hydraulic similarity and the critical conditions in alluvial channels. The results of these experiments have been reported in several papers by G. B. Supino and co-workers, A. Rubatta, F. Lazzarri, G. L. Bragadin, G. Scarpi and L. Montefusco.

In his experiments G. Scarpi used plastic parallelepipeds of $\gamma_1 = 1.2 - 1.3$ p/cm³ specific gravity and 2.4 to 8.7 mm side length, to study the critical condition. The

Table 1.2.4—4

Characteristics of sediment material used by Scarpi and Montefusco

No.	Sediment material Symbol		Spec. gravity, γ_1 [kp/m³]	Fall velocity, ω [cm/sec]	Average size, in mm units		
					d_1	d_2	d_3
1.	GF		1,209.5	7.98	2.38	2.93	3.99
2.	OF		1,284.1	10.23	2.54	2.99	3.12
3.	SC		1,333.4	11.43	2.64	3.56	3.99
4.	E_1		1,190.0	13.82	7.77	8.16	8.70
5.	E_2		1,190.0	0.0987	3.86	4.03	4.16
6.	GF mixed	30%					
	E_1	70%					
7.	OF mixed	27%					
	E_1	73%					
8.	SC mixed	30%					
	E_1	70%					
9.	E_2 mixed	26%					
	E_1	74%					
10.	GF mixed	50%					
	SC	50%					

depth of flow varied from about 3 to 14 cm, while slopes ranged from 0.00185 to 0.0004. The difference with respect to the experiments of Shields is that, instead of the resistance coefficient f_c, the critical value of the parameter U_*/ω is plotted against $Re_* = U_* d/\nu$. The data on the material used in the experiments, together with the values of the parameters observed, are indicated in the first four rows (materials denoted *GF*, *OF*, *SC* and E_1) in *Table 1.2.4—4*. The full line in *Fig. 1.2.4—8* indicates the relevant section of Shields's curve whereas the dashed line is used to connect the results of his experiments.

The relation of Shields is not corroborated by the experiments of Scarpi. The difference is attributable primarily to the effect of shape.

Using the data of Scarpi the critical condition was determined for additional six bed load materials by L. Montefusco in 1968/69 (see *Table 1.2.4—4*, rows 5—10). Of these new materials five were produced by mixing the former materials in certain percentage proportions. The bed load particles were again parallelepipeds in form.

For the case of incipient movement Montefusco plotted the relation of U_*/ω and $Re_* = U_* d/\nu$ (see *Fig. 1.2.4—9*) while in *Fig. 1.2.4—10* U_*/ω was plotted against the fall velocity Reynolds number $\omega d/\nu$, entering in both graphs the data of Scarpi and the relation of Shields.

The numerical values of the parameters are also given in *Table 1.2.4—5*. The value of Shields's coefficient

$$f_c = \frac{\tau_c}{(\gamma_1 - \gamma)d}$$

189

Fig. 1.2.4—8. U_*/ω vs. sediment shear velocity Reynolds number at the critical condition. After Scarpi

having also been indicated, the relation $f_c = F(Re_*)$ has been plotted by the author in *Fig. 1.2.4—11*. Supporting the results of Scarpi it is inferred from the three figures that Shields's relation cannot be accepted as of general validity. It is pointed out in a paper by Suppino that one of the basic objectives in the rapid publication of their results was to caution investigators using Shields's relation.

Considerations concerning the variations of the critical tractive force will be started preferably by clearing the theoretical foundations of the relations de-

Fig. 1.2.4—9. U_*/ω vs. sediment shear velocity Reynolds number at the critical condition. After Montefusco

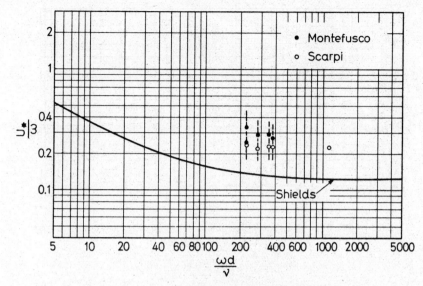

Fig. 1.2.4—10. U_*/ω vs. sediment fall velocity Reynolds number.
After Montefusco

Table 1.2.4—5

Parameter values in the experiments by Scarpi and Montefusco

No.	Sediment material Symbol		$f_c = \dfrac{\tau_c}{(\gamma_1 - \gamma)d}$	$\dfrac{U_* d}{\nu}$	$\dfrac{U_*}{\omega}$	$\dfrac{\omega d}{\nu}$
1.	GF		0.064	56	0.246	228
2.	OF		0.059	65	0.218	298
3.	SC		0.055	87	0.222	394
4.	E_1		0.061	240	0.222	1,076
5.	E_2		0.066	84	0.224	376
6.	GF	30%	0.110	71	0.324	228
	E_1	70%				
7.	OF	27%	0.101	83	0.281	298
	E_1	73%				
8.	SC	30%	0.079	104	0.266	394
	E_1	70%				
9.	E_2	26%	0.104	107	0.284	376
	E_1	74%				
10.	GF	50%	0.072	58	0.261	228
	SC	50%				

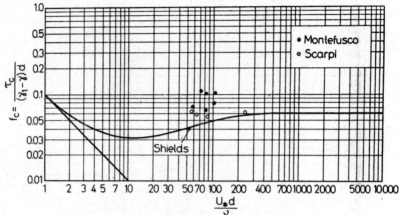

Fig. 1.2.4—11. Resistance coefficient f_c vs. sediment shear velocity Reynolds number. After Montefusco

scribing the critical condition and by examining the former structure of these relations.

The approach adopted in *Section 1.2.3* for determining the parameter

$$\frac{d}{A} = \frac{d}{v^{2/3} g^{-1/3}}$$

with the channel stability factor

$$b = \frac{gd}{U_*^2} \frac{(\rho_1 - \rho)}{\rho}$$

will again be adopted (see Eq. (1.2.3−27)).

Assume accordingly the critical condition to be controlled by the following physical quantities

$$g,\ D,\ d,\ v,\ S,\ \rho' \tag{1.2.4−7}$$

Of the dimensional and dimensionless physical quantities the 15 potential dynamic velocities given under Eqs (1.2.3−20), (1.2.3−21) and (1.2.3−22) are written. Any independent five-term velocity combination of these will be suitable for describing the critical condition.

Observing the rules described in *Section 1.2.3* the following group of five independent velocities is selected:

$$v/d,\ \sqrt[3]{gv},\ \sqrt{gDS},\ \sqrt{gdS},\ (v/d)\rho' \tag{1.2.4−8}$$

192

The five velocities under Eq. (1.2.4−8) are now combined into the ratios 2/1, 3/4, 3/1 and 5/1:

$$\frac{\sqrt[3]{gv}}{v/d} = \frac{d}{v^{2/3}\,g^{-1/3}} \qquad (1.2.4-9a)$$

$$\frac{\sqrt{gDS}}{\sqrt{gdS}} = \sqrt{\frac{D}{d}} \qquad (1.2.4-9b)$$

$$\frac{\sqrt{gDS}}{v/d} = \frac{U_* d}{v} \qquad (1.2.4-9c)$$

$$\frac{(v/d)\rho'}{v/d} = \rho' \qquad (1.2.4-9d)$$

The critical condition is thus uniquely defined by the four dimensionless parameters given by Eqs (1.2.4−9a) to (1.2.4−9d). If the resultant tractive force at the critical condition is τ_c and, in the manner described already in *Section 1.2.3*, the ratio τ_c/ρ, as the square of a resultant velocity, is divided by the square of the potential dynamic velocity $\sqrt{gd\rho'}$, then in accordance with Eq. (1.2.3−25) the dimensionless parameter

$$\frac{U_*^2}{gd}\frac{\rho}{(\rho_1 - \rho)} = f_c$$

is already obtained, which is a measure of the resultant tractive force τ_c. This parameter is a function of the dimensionless quantities involved in Eqs (1.2.4−9a) to (1.2.4−9d) i.e.,

$$f_c = F\left(\frac{d}{v^{2/3}\,g^{-1/3}},\ \frac{D}{d},\ \frac{U_* d}{v},\ \rho'\right) \qquad (1.2.4-10)$$

As indicated by Eq. (1.2.4−10), the dimensionless resistance coefficient f_c may depend, under the initial conditions assumed, on the sediment shear velocity Reynolds number $Re_* = U_* d/v$ and also on the relative roughness D/d, on ρ' and on the dimensionless number $d/(v^{2/3}g^{-1/3})$. The actual relation can be found from experimental results.

In checking the theoretical relation in Eq. (1.2.4−10) against experimental results it was found that the influence of the dimensionless parameters $U_* d/v$ and ρ' is usually small enough to be neglected in comparison to the other two parameters.

Using the experimental results mentioned in the foregoing the three-variable relation

$$f_c = F\left(\frac{d}{v^{2/3}\,g^{-1/3}},\ \frac{D}{d}\right) \qquad (1.2.4-11)$$

13

Fig. 1.2.4—12. Resistance coefficient f_c vs. relative roughness with

$$\frac{d}{v^{2/3}g^{-1/3}}$$ as parameter, at the critical condition

has been plotted in *Fig. 1.2.4—12*. For each

$$\frac{d}{v^{2/3}g^{-1/3}} = \text{constant}$$

value f_c is, according to *Fig. 1.2.4—12*, related to the relative roughness D/d by a hyperbolic relationship. In the figure the relations have been plotted for three values (1, 10 and 100) of $d/(v^{2/3}g^{-1/3})$. Of course, further experiments are necessary to check the validity limits of the relations, since the data available apply to a rather narrow range.

For instance according to *Fig. 1.2.4—12* in the case of a bed load material with $d = 0.047$ cm and $\gamma_1 = 2.65$ p/cm^3 and at the depth $D = 4.7$ cm, the critical tractive force or f_c is found in the following manner:

If the temperature of water is 20 deg. C, then $v^{2/3}g^{-1/3} = 0.0047$ cm and thus

$$\frac{d}{v^{2/3}g^{-1/3}} = 10$$

194

and $D/d = 100$. These two parameters in the figure define the value $f_c = 0.062$. The critical tractive force is then

$$\tau_c = 0.062 \cdot (2.65-1) \cdot 0.047 = 0.0047 \ [\text{p/cm}^2]$$

The critical value of slope is computed from the expression $\tau_c = 0.0047 = \gamma\, 4.7S$ as $S = 0.001$.

Considering all values to remain constant, if with steeper slopes f_c increases beyond 0.062, the particular bed load particles will be set into motion. If, on the other hand, the value of f_c remains smaller than this limit value, that is, the slope is flatter than required for attaining the critical condition, the sediment will remain stationary. The individual relations

$$\frac{d}{v^{2/3} g^{-2/3}} = \text{constant}$$

pertaining to

$$f_c = \frac{a}{(D/d)^2} \tag{1.2.4-12}$$

values reflect essentially the extremely great influence of relative roughness. The quantity a involved in Eq. (1.2.4$-$12) is not constant, but varies with the parameter $d/(v^{2/3}g^{-1/3})$. This variation is described by the equation

$$a = 620\,000 \left(\frac{d}{A}\right)^{-2.75} \tag{1.2.4-13}$$

considering which f_c is defined by the three-variable expression

$$f_c = 620\,000 \left(\frac{d}{A}\right)^{-2.75} \left(\frac{D}{d}\right)^{-2} \tag{1.2.4-14}$$

Taking the particle size, the specific gravity of the bed load particle as well as the temperature of the water as constant, the magnitude of f_c will obviously depend, to a high extent, on relative roughness D/d. The value of f_c increases rapidly as the relative roughness diminishes, which clearly implies that for the same bed load material low D/d values are accompanied by rather steep slopes at the critical condition.

Since the magnitude of $f_c = \tau_c/(\gamma_1 - \gamma)d$ is influenced in an entirely analogous manner by D/d and S, it is obvious that besides Eq. (1.2.4$-$11) a relation exists by which f_c is expressed in terms of $d/(v^{2/3}g^{-1/3})$ and of S. In other words, the existence of Eq. (1.2.4$-$11) involves the existence of the relation

$$f_c = F\left(\frac{d}{v^{2/3} g^{-1/3}}, \ S\right) \tag{1.2.4-15}$$

When introducing the potential dynamic velocities we said that these relations could be expressed in any arbitrary form with their help. Accordingly, a five-term group of independent potential dynamic velocities which leads eventually to Eq. (1.2.4−15) is bound to exist.

In fact selecting from the velocities Eq. (1.2.3−20) and (1.2.3−21), as well as Eq. (1.2.3−22) the independent five-term velocity group

$$\sqrt{gD}, \quad v/d, \quad \sqrt[3]{gv}, \quad \sqrt{gDS}, \quad \sqrt{gD\rho'} \qquad (1.2.4-16)$$

and forming the velocity ratios 3/2, 4/1, 5/1 and 4/2, the dimensionless parameter

$$\frac{\sqrt[3]{gv}}{v/d} = \frac{dg^{1/3}}{v^{2/3}} = \frac{d}{v^{2/3}\,g^{-1/3}} \qquad (1.2.4-17a)$$

$$\frac{\sqrt{gDS}}{\sqrt{gD}} = \sqrt{S} \qquad (1.2.4-17b)$$

$$\frac{\sqrt{gD\rho'}}{\sqrt{gD}} = \sqrt{\rho'} \qquad (1.2.4-17c)$$

$$\frac{\sqrt{gDS}}{v/d} = \frac{U_* d}{v} \qquad (1.2.4-17d)$$

define positively the resultant dimensionless number characterizing the critical condition, i.e.

$$f_c = F\left(\frac{d}{v^{2/3}\,g^{-1/3}}, \quad S, \quad \rho', \quad \frac{U_* d}{v}\right) \qquad (1.2.4-18)$$

The theoretical relation under Eq. (1.2.4−18) is in complete analogy with Eq. (1.2.4−10), since f_c depends clearly also on S besides D/d, because

$$f_c = \frac{\gamma}{(\gamma_1 - \gamma)} \frac{D}{d} S$$

The three-variable relation under Eq. (1.2.4−15) is plotted in *Fig. 1.2.4−13*. According to the figure, in the case of

$$\frac{d}{v^{2/3}g^{-1/3}} = \text{constant}$$

values, the relation between f_c and the slope S is a parabolical one. In *Fig. 1.2.4−13*, similarly to *Fig. 1.2.4−12*, the relations are traced for three values (1, 10, 100) of $d/(v^{2/3}g^{-1/3})$. In connection with these relations it should again be pointed out that their validity limits must be established by the results of additional experiments since the experimental data used for their construction remain within a rather narrow range.

196

Fig. 1.2.4—13. Resistance coefficient f_c vs. slope with $\dfrac{d}{v^{2/3}g^{-1/3}}$ as parameter, at the critical condition

On the basis of *Fig. 1.2.4—13*, for $d = 0.047$ cm, $\gamma_1 = 2.67$ p/cm³ and a water temperature of 20 deg. C

$$\frac{d}{v^{2/3}\,g^{-1/3}} = \frac{0.047}{0.0047} = 10$$

and for $S = 0.001$ we have $f_c = 0.062$.

Once the value of f_c is known, the critical tractive force τ_c is obtained, as in the foregoing example, as

$$\tau_c = 0.062 \cdot (2.65 - 1) \cdot 0.047 = 0.0047 \;[\text{p/cm}^2]$$

The critical depth pertaining to the critical condition is found again from the value of τ_c, taking $S = 0.001$ into consideration. Accordingly

$$D = \frac{0.0047}{0.001} = 4.7 \text{ cm}$$

If all values are taken as constant and f_c exceeds 0.062 with increasing depth, the bed load particles under consideration will start moving. If, however, f_c remains lower than this limit, that is, the depth is smaller than that necessary for attaining the critical condition, the sediment will remain stationary. The relations

$$f_c = c\,S^{0.66} \tag{1.2.4-19}$$

pertaining to individual

$$\frac{d}{v^{2/2}g^{-1/3}} = \text{constant}$$

values reflect the influence of slope. Naturally, the value c involved in the expression is not constant but varies with the parameter $d/(v^{2/3}g^{-1/3})$. This variation is expressed by the equation

$$c = 57.8 \left(\frac{d}{A}\right)^{-0.89} \tag{1.2.4-20}$$

so that f_c is described by the three-variable equation

$$f_c = 57.8 \left(\frac{d}{A}\right)^{-0.89} S^{0.66} \tag{1.2.4-21}$$

Assuming the size and specific gravity of bed load particles as well as the temperature of water to remain constant, it will be seen that f_c is less affected by the slope S than by the relative roughness D/d. The influence of slope is even an opposite one, since f_c decreases with flatter slopes. In the case of the same bed load material at flat slopes the critical condition occurs at relatively greater depths.

Summarizing the foregoing considerations the computation procedure is as follows:

a) For a bed load material of given particle diameter d and specific gravity γ_1, and in the knowledge of water temperature the magnitude of f_c is found from *Fig. 1.2.4–12* for each depth of flow D and therefrom the critical tractive force τ_c is obtained. Once the critical tractive force is known, the slope S necessary for attaining the critical condition is found in combination with the other data.

b) Again for a given bed load material and water temperature the magnitude of f_c is found from *Fig. 1.2.4–13* for each value of slope, wherefrom τ_c and the depth D necessary for attaining the critical condition can be computed.

Since the dimensionless resistance coefficient is

$$f_c = \frac{\gamma DS}{(\gamma_1 - \gamma)d} = \frac{\gamma}{(\gamma_1 - \gamma)}\frac{D}{d}S \tag{1.2.4-22}$$

it is deemed advisable to indicate separately the theoretical relation of f_c, D/d and S. This theoretical relation is illustrated in *Fig. 1.2.4–14* which, in combination with *Fig. 1.2.4–12*, yields directly the slope S necessary for attaining critical conditions, while in combination with *Fig. 1.2.4–13* the corresponding depth D is obtained.

It has been mentioned already that various boundary conditions of sediment movement are likely to display a certain similarity to the critical condition of

198

Fig. 1.2.4—14. Theoretical relation between the resistance coefficient f_c, the relative roughness and the slope

incipient movement. We are justified in anticipating that the boundary condition of sand ripples, dunes, transition and antidunes can be expressed in a form similar to the theoretical relations given under Eq. $(1.2.4-10)$ or $(1.2.4-18)$.

Making use of the experimental data available, the boundary condition of dune development has also been considered. For the boundary condition the relation

$$f_c = F\left(\frac{d}{v^{2/3}\,g^{-1/3}},\; \frac{D}{d}\right) \qquad (1.2.4-23)$$

has been constructed in *Fig. 1.2.4—15*, while the relation

$$f_c = F\left(\frac{d}{v^{2/3}\,g^{-1/3}},\; S\right) \qquad (1.2.4-24)^{\bullet}$$

is shown in *Fig. 1.2.4—16*. For

$$\frac{d}{v^{2/3}\,g^{-1/3}} = \text{constant}$$

values the relation of Eq. $(1.2.4-23)$ is again represented by hyperbolae, whereas the relation of Eq. $(1.2.4-24)$, by parabolae. According to *Fig. 1.2.4—15*, the incipient development of dunes is influenced by the relative roughness D/d to an even higher extent than observed at the incipient stage of movement. Accordingly, as will be perceived from *Fig. 1.2.4—16*, the influence of slope S will be even more pronounced. The relations are plotted in both *Figs (1.2.4—15)* and *(1.2.4—16)* for three values (1, 10, 100) of $d/(v^{2/3}g^{-1/3})$.

199

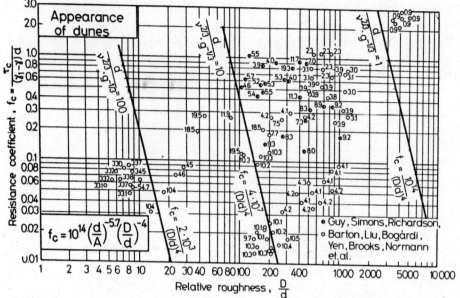

Fig. 1.2.4—15. Resistance coefficient f_c vs. relative roughness with $\dfrac{d}{v^{2/3}g^{-1/3}}$ as parameter at the boundary of dune formation

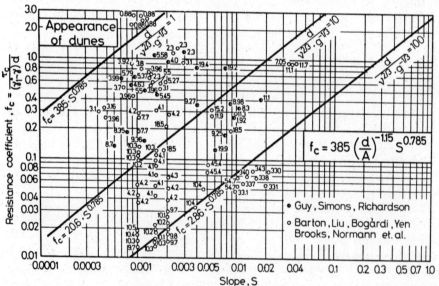

Fig. 1.2.4—16. Resistance coefficient f_c vs. slope with $\dfrac{d}{v^{2/3}g^{-1/3}}$ as parameter at the boundary of dune formation

200

In view of the rather small number of observation data these relations should be regarded as approximate ones only.

For tentative estimations the two graphs have been relied upon in determining the numerical relation of f_c with the variables d/A and D/d, as well as with d/A and S under conditions of incipient dune development:

$$f_c = 10^{14} \left(\frac{d}{A}\right)^{-5.7} \left(\frac{D}{d}\right)^{-4} \qquad (1.2.4-25)$$

$$f_c = 385 \left(\frac{d}{A}\right)^{-1.15} S^{0.785} \qquad (1.2.4-26)$$

It should be emphasized that further experiments are necessary for determining the validity limits of the relations introduced above. From the experiments covering a wide range it may perhaps be concluded that the relations under Eqs (1.2.4−12) and (1.2.4−19) are not hyperbolae, respectively parabolae, i.e. in a log-log plot the relations will not be represented by straight lines even if the values $d/(v^{2/3}g^{-1/3})$ are constant.

It may be expected that the relations improve by taking into consideration the effect of $U_* d/v$ and ρ'. In this respect further experiments are necessary.

In connection with Eqs (1.2.4−11), (1.2.4−15), (1.2.4−23) and (1.2.4−24), as well as *Figs 1.2.4−12, 1.2.4−13, 1.2.4−15* and *1.2.4−16* representing these relations, the following considerations should be remembered.

Since, according to *Table 1.2.4−3*, the specific gravity γ_1 of the bed load hardly differs from 2.65 p/cm³, the relations plotted in *Figs 1.2.4−12* and *1.2.4−13* (and even that in *Figs 1.2.4−15* and *1.2.4−16* relating to the development of dunes) is valid only for a specific gravity $\gamma_1 = 2.65$ p/cm³. This implies that *the combined use of the pairs of corresponding figures is impermissible unless the specific gravity is $\gamma_1 = 2.65$.*

In principle it seems conceivable that observation data for γ_1 values varying between wide limits would have yielded relations other than those plotted in the afore-mentioned figures. Neither would it be surprising that the combined use of the resulting new graphical relations would be permissible even at specific gravities other than 2.65 if the relations determined in this way were connected on the basis of the actual γ_1 value (rather than 2.65).

In fact the graphical relation shown in the four figures under consideration are to be used − theoretically − only in cases where the specific gravity of the bed load is 2.65 p/cm³. At the present state of our knowledge, however, there is no reason why pairs of corresponding figures should not be used separately for approximate estimations even if the specific gravity is other than 2.65. It should be realized that in such cases not all effects due to specific gravity are taken into account, yet the error resulting from their being neglected is not likely to be of a considerable magnitude.

The fact that the corresponding figures are not to be used in combination for a bed load material having a specific gravity other than 2.65, will be illustrated by the following example:

Let the particle size of bed load be $d = 0.046$ cm, its specific gravity $\gamma_1 = 3.65$ p/cm^3 and the depth of flow be $D = 4.7$ cm. From *Fig. 1.2.4 – 12* the magnitude of the critical tractive force is determined approximately in the following manner:

Since, in water of 20 deg. C temperature, $v^{2/3}g^{-1/3} = 0.0047$ cm, so that

$$\frac{d}{v^{2/3}g^{-1/3}} = 10 \quad \text{and} \quad D/d = 100$$

he resistance coefficient pertaining to these values according to *Fig. 1.2.4 – 12* is $t_c = 0.062$, and thus

$$\tau_c = 0.062 \cdot (3.65 - 1) \cdot 0.047 = 0.00777 \ [\text{p/cm}^2]$$

With the above values the critical slope S at the condition of incipient movement is found from

$$\tau_c = \gamma \, DS = 0.00777 = 1 \cdot 4.7 \cdot S$$

whence the critical slope $S = 0.001645$.

A simple check will reveal that this value of S, when used in combination with *Fig. 1.2.4 – 13*, will yield an entirely different critical tractive force, indicating clearly that in the case of bed load having a specific gravity other than 2.65 the two figures must not be used simultaneously.

Eqs (1.2.4 – 11) and (1.2.4 – 21) expressing the law of variable critical tractive forces describe essentially empirical relations, on the one hand, between the critical resistance coefficient f_c as well as the parameter d/A and the critical value (D_c/d) of the relative roughness, on the other hand, between f_c as well as d/A and the critical value (S_c) of slope. The relation between the parameter d/A, the critical values of relative roughness and slope is described by the three-variabe expression obtained by combining the foregoing two empirical relationships; thus

$$(D_c/d)^2 S_c^{0.66} \left(\frac{d}{v^{2/3}g^{-1/3}} \right)^{1.86} = 10\ 730 = \text{constant} \qquad (1.2.4 - 27)$$

Consequently, according to these investigations, for given d and v values at the critical condition the power product according to Eq. (1.2.4 – 27) of relative roughness, slope and the parameter d/A is a constant value.

According to the law of constant critical tractive forces, in the case of a specific gravity of 2.65 p/cm^3 the particle size d would be proportionate to the product (DS) of depth and slope, i.e.

$$d = \text{constant} \ (DS) \qquad (1.2.4 - 28)$$

The above expression will prove to be misleading by estimating the magnitude of d from Eq. (1.2.4$-$27). Accordingly,

$$d = 1.619775 \cdot 10^{-30} \left(\frac{1}{v^{2/3} g^{-1/3}} \right)^{13.286} D_c^{14.286} S_c^{4.714} \qquad (1.2.4-29)$$

saying that the particle diameter does not depend on the product $(DS)_c$ but on the product of the D_c and S_c values raised to different powers.

If, besides the magnitude of the parameter d/A, the actual value of the slope S is also known, the relation under Eq. (1.2.4$-$27) can be applied to determine the critical magnitude of relative roughness:

$$\frac{D_c}{d} = 103.7 \left(\frac{d}{v^{2/3} g^{-1/3}} \right)^{-0.93} S^{-0.33} \qquad (1.2.4-30)$$

On the other hand, if besides the parameter d/A the actual magnitude of the relative roughness D/d is known, again Eq. (1.2.4$-$27) can be applied for estimating the critical slope:

$$S_c = 1.283 \cdot 10^6 \left(\frac{d}{v^{2/3} g^{-1/3}} \right)^{-2.815} \left(\frac{D}{d} \right)^{-3.032} \qquad (1.2.4-31)$$

Experimental results have shown the above relations to be valid if

$$1 < \left(\frac{d}{v^{2/3} g^{-1/3}} \right) < 2 \cdot 10^2; \quad 5 < \left(\frac{D}{d} \right) < 2 \cdot 10^3 \text{ and } 5 \cdot 10^{-5} < S < 2 \cdot 10^{-2}$$

Eqs (1.2.4$-$30) and (1.2.4$-$31) can be used to advantage especially for solving problems encountered in practice.

Adopting a similar approach, Eqs (1.2.4$-$25) and (1.2.4$-$26) relating to the boundary condition of incipient dune development can also be rearranged to yield the expression

$$\left(\frac{D_c}{d} \right)^4 \left(\frac{d}{v^{2/3} g^{-1/3}} \right)^{4.55} S_c^{0.785} = 2.6 \cdot 10^{11} = \text{constant} \qquad (1.2.4-32)$$

or for known d and S the critical value of relative roughness becomes

$$\frac{D_c}{d} = 714 \left(\frac{d}{v^{2/3} g^{-1/3}} \right)^{-1.14} S^{-0.196} \qquad (1.2.4-33)$$

Conversely, if besides d, the relative roughness D/d is known, the critical value of slope is obtained as

$$S_c = 354 \cdot 10^{12} \left(\frac{d}{v^{2/3} g^{-1/3}} \right)^{-5.8} \left(\frac{D}{d} \right)^{-5.1} \qquad (1.2.4-34)$$

In the boundary condition of dune development the ranges of validity are as follows:

$$1 < \left(\frac{d}{v^{2/3}g^{-1/3}} \right) < 3.3 \cdot 10^2; \ 5 < \frac{D}{d} < 5 \cdot 10^3 \text{ and } 4 \cdot 10^{-4} < S < 4 \cdot 10^{-2}$$

The law of variable critical tractive forces has been evolved from the results of laboratory experiments. The particle diameter of bed load material used in these experiments ranged, according to *Table 1.2.4 – 3*, from 0.02 to 15.5 mm, that is, between rather wide limits, very much like that of natural bed load materials. Some of the experiments were performed at flat slopes (5 to 15 cm/km) comparable to those common in alluvial streams. In other laboratory experiments, however, slopes as steep as 200 to 600 cm/km were used, such as occur in mountain streams or torrents only. The departure of depths at the laboratory and in actual streams is even greater. As indicated by the table, the greatest depths of flow in the experiments hardly attained 60 cm and this is practically the lowest value occurring in natural streams.

The law of variable critical tractive forces was verified in every respect by laboratory experiments. It would be of extremely great interest, however, to check the validity of these variable laws also for flat slopes and relatively great depths commonly occurring in natural streams. Unfortunately, very few similar observations have been performed so far.

In the course of bed load research started at the Research Institute of Water Resources Development in 1964, the wearing of gravel particles belonging to the 20 to 40 mm size fraction and labelled by ^{124}Sb, ^{65}Zn $-$ ^{95}Zr and ^{181}Hf isotopes was studied by K. Stelczer. In these experiments a scintillation probe devised especially for this purpose was used for tracing the movement of these labelled gravel particles. During the measurements in 1967 he succeeded in tracing the movement of some of the gravel particles along the bottom. The data relating to flow depths, slopes, the size and other properties of bed load particles have been compiled in *Table 1.2.4 – 6*. As concluded by Stelczer, the movement of the particles was slow enough to be regarded with fair approximation as the critical condition. Estimating the tractive forces from observed depth and slope values and plotting the corresponding pairs of τ and d values in the manner described before (see *Fig. 1.1.3 – 4*), the points should be expected to lie in the range indicating, movement. However, as will be seen from *Fig. 1.2.4. – 17* based on the law of constant tractive forces, the experimental points are in the range of no movement. This circumstance has been noted by Stelczer in connection with several of his observations, from which he drew eventually the conclusion that the law of constant tractive forces was misleading.

The observation data shown in *Table 1.2.4 – 6* have been used for studying the condition of movement of these bed load particles, adopting the law of variable critical tractive forces.

Table 1.2.4—6

Data on bed load observations in the Dunaremete gaging section

No.	Depth of flow, D [cm]	Slope, S	Particle size, d [cm]	Spec. gravity, γ_1 [p/cm³]	Water temperature*, t [°C]	Kinematic viscosity, ν [cm²/sec]	$A = \nu^{2/3} g^{-1/3}$ [cm]
1.	320	0.00022	1.985	2.65	20	$1.008 \cdot 10^{-2}$	0.0047
2.	290	0.00019	3.145	2.65	20	$1.008 \cdot 10^{-2}$	0.0047
3.	270	0.00019	3.025	2.65	20	$1.008 \cdot 10^{-2}$	0.0047
4.	260	0.00016	1.400	2.65	20	$1.008 \cdot 10^{-2}$	0.0047
5.	300	0.00016	2.400	2.65	20	$1.008 \cdot 10^{-2}$	0.0047
6.	280	0.00012	1.845	2.65	20	$1.008 \cdot 10^{-2}$	0.0047
7.	260	0.00012	3.400	2.65	20	$1.008 \cdot 10^{-2}$	0.0047
8.	340	0.00023	1.550	2.65	20	$1.008 \cdot 10^{-2}$	0.0047
9.	290	0.00018	1.940	2.65	20	$1.008 \cdot 10^{-2}$	0.0047
10.	300	0.00016	2.695	2.65	20	$1.008 \cdot 10^{-2}$	0.0047
11.	300	0.00018	3.480	2.65	20	$1.008 \cdot 10^{-2}$	0.0047
12.	300	0.00018	1.975	2.65	20	$1.008 \cdot 10^{-2}$	0.0047
13.	300	0.00018	2.030	2.65	20	$1.008 \cdot 10^{-2}$	0.0047
14.	300	0.00018	3.545	2.65	20	$1.008 \cdot 10^{-2}$	0.0047
15.	290	0.00012	3.590	2.65	20	$1.008 \cdot 10^{-2}$	0.0047
16.	260	0.00018	1.535	2.65	20	$1.008 \cdot 10^{-2}$	0.0047
17.	270	0.00018	2.960	2.65	20	$1.008 \cdot 10^{-2}$	0.0047
18.	300	0.00020	3.940	2.65	20	$1.008 \cdot 10^{-2}$	0.0047
19.	290	0.00020	2.290	2.65	20	$1.008 \cdot 10^{-2}$	0.0047
20.	260	0.00020	2.300	2.65	20	$1.008 \cdot 10^{-2}$	0.0047
21.	260	0.00019	1.330	2.65	20	$1.008 \cdot 10^{-2}$	0.0047
22.	270	0.00010	2.495	2.65	20	$1.008 \cdot 10^{-2}$	0.0047
23.	270	0.00010	1.970	2.65	20	$1.008 \cdot 10^{-2}$	0.0047
24.	270	0.00010	1.660	2.65	20	$1.008 \cdot 10^{-2}$	0.0047
25.	290	0.00010	3.420	2.65	20	$1.008 \cdot 10^{-2}$	0.0047
26.	310	0.00018	3.695	2.65	20	$1.008 \cdot 10^{-2}$	0.0047
27.	260	0.00010	4.180	2.65	20	$1.008 \cdot 10^{-2}$	0.0047
28.	250	0.00010	2.558	2.65	20	$1.088 \cdot 10^{-2}$	0.0047
29.	260	0.00010	2.295	2.65	20	$1.008 \cdot 10^{-2}$	0.0047
30.	260	0.00010	2.385	2.65	20	$1.008 \cdot 10^{-2}$	0.0047

* Water temperatures were not measured. For simplicity of computations $t = 20°C$ has been assumed

For the purposes of this study either the expression

$$f_c = F\left(\frac{d}{\nu^{2/3} g^{-1/3}}, \frac{D}{d}\right)$$

and the relevant *Fig. 1.2.4—12*, or the expression

$$f_c = F\left(\frac{d}{\nu^{2/3} g^{-1/3}}, S\right)$$

Fig. 1.2.4—17. Evaluation of observations on the Danube, on the basis of constant critical tractive forces

and the relevant *Fig. 1.2.4—13* can be adopted. Obviously, the two expressions and the two figures are interrelated and the alternatives of approach differ only inasmuch as in one of them the actual depth of flow is adopted for estimating the slope necessary for attaining the critical condition, while in the other the actual slope is adopted for estimating the critical depth corresponding thereto. Since in the afore-mentioned two figures the highest value of

$$\frac{d}{v^{2/3}\, g^{-1/3}} = \frac{d}{A}$$

was 100, in view of the values around 300 to 900 occurring here, the d/A lines have been extended to 1000 using the three-variable relations

$$f_c = 620\,000 \left(\frac{d}{A}\right)^{-2.75} \left(\frac{D}{d}\right)^{-2}$$

according to Eq. (1.2.4—14) in *Fig. 1.2.4—18*, and

$$f_c = 57.8 \left(\frac{d}{A}\right)^{-0.89} S^{0.66}$$

according to Eq. (1.2.4—21) in *Fig. 1.2.4—19*.

The computed values necessary for representing the experimental pairs of points are compiled in *Table 1.2.4—7*.

Considering *Fig. 1.2.4—18*, if the f_0 values pertaining to the individual size fractions are computed from the actual depth and slope of flow, it will be seen that—since the ratio d/A is unaffected by slope and depth—the corresponding

206

Fig. 1.2.4—18. Evaluation of observations on the Danube, on the basis of variable critical tractive forces, according to the relation between f_c, D/d and d/A

pairs of f_0 and D/d values (indicated by a + symbol in the figure) are grouped around the $d/A = 10$ to 100 lines regardless of the actual value of d/A being around 300 to 900. This, obviously, implies that the f_c values characteristic of the critical condition are obtained if the experimental results are plotted by circles according to the actual values of D/d and d/A, while maintaining the depth of flow constant. From these f_c values, in turn, the slope at which the critical condition just occurs is computed for each experimental point. These critical S_c values are substantially lower than the original S slopes indicated in column 8 of *Table 1.3.4—7*. From this circumstance it is inferred, however, that the bed load fraction under consideration was already in motion at the time of experiment.

Values computed from the bed load observations

No.	$\tau_0 = \gamma\, DS$ [p/cm²]	$f_0 = \dfrac{\tau_0}{(\gamma_1 - \gamma)d}$	$\dfrac{d}{A}$	$\dfrac{D}{d}$	$f_c = F\left(\dfrac{d}{A},\ \dfrac{D}{d}\right)$	$\tau = f_c\,(\gamma_1 - \gamma)d$ [p/cm²]
	1.	2.	3.	4.	5.	6.
1.	0.0704	0.02152	422	161.3	$1.44 \cdot 10^{-6}$	$4.72 \cdot 10^{-6}$
2.	0.0551	0.01062	669	92.2	$1.22 \cdot 10^{-6}$	$6.34 \cdot 10^{-6}$
3.	0.0513	0.01028	643	89.3	$1.46 \cdot 10^{-6}$	$7.3\ \cdot 10^{-6}$
4.	0.0416	0.01800	298	185.7	$2.82 \cdot 10^{-6}$	$6.52 \cdot 10^{-6}$
5.	0.0480	0.01213	511	125.0	$1.42 \cdot 10^{-6}$	$5.63 \cdot 10^{-6}$
6.	0.0336	0.01105	393	151.8	$1.95 \cdot 10^{-6}$	$5.94 \cdot 10^{-6}$
7.	0.0312	0.00557	723	76.5	$1.44 \cdot 10^{-6}$	$8.08 \cdot 10^{-6}$
8.	0.0782	0.03060	330	219.2	$1.53 \cdot 10^{-6}$	$3.91 \cdot 10^{-6}$
9.	0.0522	0.01630	413	149.5	$1.79 \cdot 10^{-6}$	$5.74 \cdot 10^{-6}$
10.	0.0480	0.01179	573	111.2	$1.28 \cdot 10^{-6}$	$5.70 \cdot 10^{-6}$
11.	0.0540	0.00940	740	86.2	$1.07 \cdot 10^{-6}$	$6.15 \cdot 10^{-6}$
12.	0.0540	0.01660	420	152.0	$1.63 \cdot 10^{-6}$	$5.30 \cdot 10^{-6}$
13.	0.0540	0.01610	432	147.7	$1.58 \cdot 10^{-6}$	$5.30 \cdot 10^{-6}$
14.	0.0540	0.00923	753	84.6	$1.05 \cdot 10^{-6}$	$6.16 \cdot 10^{-6}$
15.	0.0348	0.00808	764	80.8	$1.11 \cdot 10^{-6}$	$6.58 \cdot 10^{-6}$
16.	0.0468	0.01850	327	169.4	$2.62 \cdot 10^{-6}$	$6.64 \cdot 10^{-6}$
17.	0.0486	0.00995	630	91.2	$1.53 \cdot 10^{-6}$	$7.47 \cdot 10^{-6}$
18.	0.0600	0.00925	837	76.2	$0.98 \cdot 10^{-6}$	$6.38 \cdot 10^{-6}$
19.	0.0580	0.01536	487	126.6	$1.55 \cdot 10^{-6}$	$5.85 \cdot 10^{-6}$
20.	0.0520	0.01371	489	113.0	$1.94 \cdot 10^{-6}$	$7.36 \cdot 10^{-6}$
21.	0.0494	0.02252	283	195.5	$2.92 \cdot 10^{-6}$	$6.40 \cdot 10^{-6}$
22.	0.0270	0.00655	531	108.1	$1.69 \cdot 10^{-6}$	$6.95 \cdot 10^{-6}$
23.	0.0270	0.00831	419	137.0	$1.98 \cdot 10^{-6}$	$6.45 \cdot 10^{-6}$
24.	0.0270	0.00985	353	162.6	$2.34 \cdot 10^{-6}$	$6.42 \cdot 10^{-6}$
25.	0.0290	0.00514	727	84.8	$1.15 \cdot 10^{-6}$	$6.50 \cdot 10^{-6}$
26.	0.0558	0.00915	785	83.9	$0.96 \cdot 10^{-6}$	$5.85 \cdot 10^{-6}$
27.	0.0260	0.00377	890	62.2	$1.12 \cdot 10^{-6}$	$7.74 \cdot 10^{-6}$
28.	0.0250	0.00598	544	98.7	$2.38 \cdot 10^{-6}$	$10.0\ \cdot 10^{-6}$
29.	0.0260	0.00685	489	113.2	$1.94 \cdot 10^{-6}$	$7.35 \cdot 10^{-6}$
30.	0.0260	0.00661	506	109.0	$1.92 \cdot 10^{-6}$	$7.57 \cdot 10^{-6}$

A similar result is obtained if the f_0 and S slopes computed again from the actual depth of flow and slope are plotted as in *Fig. 1.2.4−19*. The points indicated by the $+$ symbol are, in the figure, between the $d/A = 10$ to 100 lines, although the actual d/A values are, as in the foregoing case, in the range of 300 to 900. The f_c values pertaining in this figure to the corresponding values of actual slope S and actual d/A values are now used to compute the depth of flow at which the critical condition actually occurs at the original slopes. These critical depths are shown in column 11 of *Table 1.2.4−7* from which, compared with the original depths D in column 12, it will be seen that the critical condition would have occurred at a depth appreciably smaller than the actual.

in the Dunare mete gaging section

Critical slope, S_c	Actual slope, S	$f_c = F\left(\dfrac{d}{A}, S\right)$	$\tau_c = f_c (\gamma_1 - \gamma)d$ [p/cm^2]	Critical depth, D_c [cm]	Actual depth, D [cm]
7.	8.	9.	10.	11.	12.
$1.47 \cdot 10^{-8}$	$2.2 \cdot 10^{-4}$	$10.2 \cdot 10^{-4}$	$3.34 \cdot 10^{-3}$	15.2	320
$2.18 \cdot 10^{-8}$	$1.9 \cdot 10^{-4}$	$6.3 \cdot 10^{-4}$	$3.28 \cdot 10^{-3}$	17.3	290
$2.7 \cdot 10^{-8}$	$1.9 \cdot 10^{-4}$	$6.48 \cdot 10^{-4}$	$3.24 \cdot 10^{-3}$	17.2	270
$2.5 \cdot 10^{-8}$	$1.6 \cdot 10^{-4}$	$11.5 \cdot 10^{-4}$	$2.66 \cdot 10^{-3}$	16.6	260
$1.87 \cdot 10^{-8}$	$1.6 \cdot 10^{-4}$	$7.1 \cdot 10^{-4}$	$2.82 \cdot 10^{-3}$	17.6	300
$2.12 \cdot 10^{-8}$	$1.2 \cdot 10^{-4}$	$7.65 \cdot 10^{-4}$	$2.33 \cdot 10^{-3}$	19.4	280
$3.10 \cdot 10^{-8}$	$1.2 \cdot 10^{-4}$	$4.35 \cdot 10^{-4}$	$2.44 \cdot 10^{-3}$	20.3	260
$1.15 \cdot 10^{-8}$	$2.3 \cdot 10^{-4}$	$12.9 \cdot 10^{-4}$	$3.3 \cdot 10^{-3}$	14.3	340
$1.98 \cdot 10^{-8}$	$1.8 \cdot 10^{-4}$	$9.18 \cdot 10^{-4}$	$2.94 \cdot 10^{-3}$	16.4	290
$1.90 \cdot 10^{-8}$	$1.6 \cdot 10^{-4}$	$6.45 \cdot 10^{-4}$	$2.86 \cdot 10^{-3}$	17.9	300
$2.05 \cdot 10^{-8}$	$1.8 \cdot 10^{-4}$	$5.5 \cdot 10^{-4}$	$3.16 \cdot 10^{-3}$	17.5	300
$1.77 \cdot 10^{-8}$	$1.8 \cdot 10^{-4}$	$9.05 \cdot 10^{-4}$	$2.94 \cdot 10^{-3}$	16.3	300
$1.77 \cdot 10^{-8}$	$1.8 \cdot 10^{-4}$	$8.85 \cdot 10^{-4}$	$2.94 \cdot 10^{-3}$	16.3	300
$2.05 \cdot 10^{-8}$	$1.8 \cdot 10^{-4}$	$5.36 \cdot 10^{-4}$	$3.14 \cdot 10^{-3}$	17.4	300
$2.28 \cdot 10^{-8}$	$1.2 \cdot 10^{-4}$	$4.15 \cdot 10^{-4}$	$2.96 \cdot 10^{-3}$	24.6	290
$2.55 \cdot 10^{-8}$	$1.8 \cdot 10^{-4}$	$11.3 \cdot 10^{-4}$	$2.86 \cdot 10^{-3}$	15.9	260
$2.77 \cdot 10^{-8}$	$1.8 \cdot 10^{-4}$	$6.34 \cdot 10^{-4}$	$3.08 \cdot 10^{-3}$	17.1	270
$2.13 \cdot 10^{-8}$	$2.0 \cdot 10^{-4}$	$5.34 \cdot 10^{-4}$	$3.47 \cdot 10^{-3}$	17.3	300
$2.02 \cdot 10^{-8}$	$2.0 \cdot 10^{-4}$	$8.65 \cdot 10^{-4}$	$3.26 \cdot 10^{-3}$	16.3	290
$2.38 \cdot 10^{-8}$	$2.0 \cdot 10^{-4}$	$8.65 \cdot 10^{-4}$	$3.24 \cdot 10^{-3}$	16.2	260
$2.46 \cdot 10^{-8}$	$1.9 \cdot 10^{-4}$	$13.5 \cdot 10^{-4}$	$2.97 \cdot 10^{-3}$	15.6	260
$2.57 \cdot 10^{-8}$	$1.0 \cdot 10^{-4}$	$4.88 \cdot 10^{-4}$	$2.01 \cdot 10^{-3}$	20.1	270
$2.39 \cdot 10^{-8}$	$1.0 \cdot 10^{-4}$	$6.0 \cdot 10^{-4}$	$1.95 \cdot 10^{-3}$	19.5	270
$2.38 \cdot 10^{-8}$	$1.0 \cdot 10^{-4}$	$7.03 \cdot 10^{-4}$	$1.93 \cdot 10^{-3}$	19.3	270
$2.24 \cdot 10^{-8}$	$1.0 \cdot 10^{-4}$	$3.68 \cdot 10^{-4}$	$2.08 \cdot 10^{-3}$	20.8	290
$1.89 \cdot 10^{-8}$	$1.8 \cdot 10^{-4}$	$5.2 \cdot 10^{-4}$	$3.16 \cdot 10^{-3}$	17.5	310
$2.97 \cdot 10^{-8}$	$1.0 \cdot 10^{-4}$	$3.1 \cdot 10^{-4}$	$2.14 \cdot 10^{-3}$	21.4	260
$4.0 \cdot 10^{-8}$	$1.0 \cdot 10^{-4}$	$4.8 \cdot 10^{-4}$	$2.02 \cdot 10^{-3}$	20.2	250
$2.83 \cdot 10^{-8}$	$1.0 \cdot 10^{-4}$	$5.3 \cdot 10^{-4}$	$2.01 \cdot 10^{-3}$	20.1	260
$2.91 \cdot 10^{-8}$	$1.0 \cdot 10^{-4}$	$5.1 \cdot 10^{-4}$	$2.01 \cdot 10^{-3}$	20.1	260

It is thus concluded eventually from both investigations that, according to the law of variable critical tractive forces, the bed load considered in the Dunaremete section of the Danube was actually not at rest but in a condition of movement.

As demonstrated by the above investigations, the law of variable critical tractive forces also applies to natural conditions, i.e. to alluvial streams. It should be noted, however, that as indicated by the foregoing computations the extension on *Figs 1.2.4—12* and *1.2.4—13* to values as high as these is impermissible. It is suggested therefore that, relations other than the three-variable relations determined on the basis of laboratory experiments apply to great depths of flow and small slopes. The invalidity of the relation will be appreciated by considering

Fig. 1.2.4—19. Evaluation of observations on the Danube, on the basis of variable critical tractive forces, according to the relation between f_c, S and the parameter $\dfrac{d}{v^{2/3}g^{-1/3}}$

the fact that at similarly great depths of flow of around 300 cm, the critical condition occurs practically in the absence of slope, in spite of the relatively coarse-grained bed load material. Conversely, at the original and rather moderate slopes the critical condition would have occurred already at 15 to 20 cm depths.

The investigation has thus succeeded in verifying the law of variable critical tractive forces, but has also revealed the necessity of revising the relations beyond the range of experimental values.

In the investigations described so far the size of bed load particles has been characterized in general by a single dimension, the particle diameter d, only. This circumstance is essentially equivalent to the assumption of a bed load material consisting of identical particles, or that the limits of the size fraction are close enough to permit the use of the mean diameter.

Although the bed load in alluvial streams is invariably composed of a wide range of particle sizes, it is usually considered permissible to describe the graded bed load material by the mean diameter in particular sections of the stream. A number of investigations and observations have been reported, according to which the discrepancy introduced by using the mean particle diameter is negligibly small in comparison to the errors due to other assumptions and simplifications necessarily introduced.

In our considerations the mean particle diameter characterizing the bed load material is used throughout, unless a definitely well sorted bed load material is specified. The use of the mean particle diameter is justified all the more so since the fractions applied vary, as a rule, within a very narrow range.

In *Section 1.2.5*, where the variable critical velocity is introduced, the particle size *d* defined above will be used for characterizing the bed load material.

For the sake of completeness it should be noted that the literature has reported on attempts to make allowance for the granulometry of the bed load. Investigations of this nature have been made by Egiazaroff according to whom, if the weighted mean particle diameter of the bed load mixture is *d*, then

$$f_c = \frac{0.06 \, \Phi/C_x}{(\lg 19 \, d_i/d)^2} \qquad (1.2.4-35)$$

in the critical condition applying to the fraction of size d_i. Here Φ is the shape factor of the particles and C_x is a drag coefficient representing friction.

From his experiments Egiazaroff has found $\Phi = 2/3$ for spherical particles and $C_x = 0.4$ for particles smaller than 5 mm and thus $0.06\Phi/C_x = 0.1$.

1.2.5. THE LAW OF VARIABLE CRITICAL VELOCITIES

1.2.5.1. The variation of critical velocities. Paragraph 2 of *Section 1.1.3*, discussing the commonly accepted relations for computing the critical velocities, points out (see *Fig. 1.1.3—7*) that the critical mean velocity pertaining to a particular bed load material of given size *d* and specific gravity γ_1 may vary with the circumstances of observation. Reference has also been made to the investigations of Levi, that is, to Eqs (1.1.3—28) to (1.1.3—31), according to which the magnitude of the critical mean velocity is computed with allowance to relative roughness.

These statements based on discrete series of measurements are supplemented expediently by investigations on which the variation of critical velocities is taken into account from a different angle.

In the experiments at Iowa made with bed load materials larger than about 7 to 10 mm, and with bottom slopes ranging from 1 : 50 to 1 : 100, the critical tractive force was found to decrease as the bottom slope was increased, so that it is believed to be justified to examine the variation of critical velocities with bottom slope.

Using the experimental data available, the critical mean velocities observed for bed load materials of given particles size and of specific gravity at different bottom slopes have been compiled in *Table 1.2.5—1*. From this table the critical mean velocities will be seen to be independent of the bottom slope. The same

Critical mean velocities observed

Observer	Type	Av. diam., d [mm]	Spec. grav., γ_1 [p/cm³]	1:50	1:62	1:75	1:80	1:100	1:111	1:125
		Sediment					Critical mean velocity, v_c cm/sec			
Kramer	I.	0.71	2.70							
	II.	0.56	2.70							
	III.	0.80	2.70							
		5.70	2.66							
		4.0	2.66							
		2.8	2.66							
		2.0	2.62							
Tu Y. C.—Ho C.		1.4	2.63							
		1.0	2.63							
		0.7	2.68							
		0.5	2.62							
		0.35	2.62							
	I.	10.6	2.63	79.6	85.0	83.2		78.6		
Bogárdi—Yen	II.	7.1	2.61	68,0	64.3	67.0		72.5		
	III.	15.5	2.64	109,1	110.0	109.7		106.7		
	1.	0.3	2.63							
	2.	0.47	2.70							
Indri	3.	2.5	2.70						59.4	56.3
	4.	4.0	2.70				94.4	84.8		

conclusion can be drawn from *Table 1.2.5 – 2* in which the critical bottom velocities observed for bed load materials of given particle size d and of specific gravity γ_1 at different bottom slopes have been compiled. From the experimental data tabulated it is thus inferred that for any given combination of d and γ_1 values neither the critical mean velocity nor the critical bottom velocity is related to the bottom slope – of course, within the range of experimental values.

The incipient motion of bed load has been demonstrated in the foregoing to depend greatly on turbulent velocity fluctuations. Disregarding the influence of these, or assuming the extent thereof to be identical in different cases, it should be obvious that the incipient motion of bed load is controlled by the velocities acting in the vicinity of the bottom, i.e. by the bottom velocities. It should be remembered, moreover, that at identical bottom velocities the mean velocity of flow in a cross-section depends, in general, on the depth of flow. Consequently, for given d and

212

t different bottom slopes

								Av. mean velocity, $\bar{v}_c$ [cm/sec]	Note
1:200	1:333	1:400	1:500	1:600	1:800	1:1000	1:∞		
		35.4		31.9	36.4	40.2		36.0	Mixed fractions
		35.3		31.0	31.6	33.6		32.9	Type I: $d = 0.15$ to 5.0 mm
		32.5		34.2	36.7	36.5		34.9	Type II: $d = 0.15$ to 1.8 mm
									Type III: $d = 0.25$ to 5.0 mm
								64.8	Sieved particles of uniform size.
								57.3	The critical mean velocities were
								50.1	observed at different bottom
								42.6	slopes but since these proved
								33.5	identical for the same bed load
								30.3	material, only the average values
								23.4	of individual experimental runs
								21.5	are given
								18.8	
								81.6	Sieved, particles of uniform size
								69.0	
								108.9	
	25.5		25.0				18.9	23.1	Mixed fractions
29.0	30.6		24.8				29.3	28.4	Type 1: $d = 0.01$ to 1.0 mm
76.4								64.0	Type 2: $d = 0.01$ to 1.0 mm
99.4								92.9	Type 3: $d = 2.0$ to 3.0 mm
									Type 4: $d = 3.0$ to 5.0 mm
									The mean velocities are interpolated values

v_1 values the critical mean velocity should be expected to vary with dpeth. This variation of the critical mean velocity is often neglected. Yet, as mentioned by Lane, it was stated as early as in 1915 by E. A. Moritz in connection with the stability of irrigation canals that "the degradation of small canals is known to occur at lower mean velocities than that of large ones".

Several of the critical mean velocity relations described in the foregoing are compared in *Fig. 1.2.5—1*. Different relationships can be read from the figure to yield different critical mean velocities for the same particle diameter d. The differences are, however, rather small implying that, in the laboratory experiments made by various investigators, neither the depth of flow D nor any other factor of major influence on mean velocity was varied to any appreciable extent.

Extensive investigations have been made by Z. Hankó into the causes responsible for the differences in critical mean velocities computed from different re-

Table 1.2.5—2

Critical bottom velocities observed at different bottom slopes

Observer	Sediment			Bottom velocity, v_{cf} [cm/sec.], observed at the bottom slopes							Av. mean velocity, v_c [cm/sec]	Note
	Type	Av. diam., d [mm]	Spec. gravity, γ_1 [p/cm³]	1 : 50	1 : 62	1 : 75	1 : 100	1 : 200	1 : 400	1 : 800		
Te-Yun Liu	I.	4.4	2.66				38.4	36.3	36.3	40.3	37.8	Mixed fractions graded from 0.3 to 7.0 mm
	II.	3.4	2.66				33.6	34.2	33.5	31.7	33.2	
	III.	2.3	2.66				26.8	29.9	31.4	30.8	30.8	
	IV.	1.4	2.66				21.4	24.7	28.6	26.8	25.3	
	V.	3.6	2.66				35.7	40.0	41.4	38.1	38.4	
	VI.	1.8	2.66				28.1	27.8	28.9	28.7	28.4	
Bogárdi—Yen	I.	10.6	2.63	54.2	53.9	53.0	52.7				53.4	Sieved, particles of uniform size
	II.	7.1	2.61	43.3	43.6	43.6	46.6				44.3	
	III.*	15.5	2.64	63.4	63.4	55.8	62.8				61.2	
Tu, Y. C.	**	5.7	2.64								40.0	Sieved, particles of uniform size. Values were observed at different bottom slopes, but since these proved identical for the same bed load material, no details according to bottom slope are given
	**	4.0	2.64								30.0	
	**	2.8	2.64								27.0	
	**	2.0	2.64								26.0	
	**	1.4	2.64								24.0	
	**	1.0	2.64								18.0	

* The experiments with material III were performed in a narrow, 30.48 cm wide flume, while in the experiments with materials I and II the flume width was 83.82 cm.

** Extrapolated values.

lations. Slight changes in the conditions of observations were found to result possibly in considerable differences.

The influence of flow depth on critical mean velocity is illustrated strikingly by comparing the critical mean velocity determined for the same bed load material in a laboratory flume with the critical mean velocity observed in alluvial channels. In the experiments at Iowa several tests were run by the author and Yen for determining the critical mean velocity using a bed load material of $d = 15.5$ mm particle size and of $\gamma_1 = 2.64$ p/cm^3 specific gravity in a $B = 30.48$ cm wide flume. The velocity profile observed at the critical condition is shown in *Fig. 1.2.5−2*. According to the figure the critical mean velocity was $v_c = 101$ cm/sec, while the critical bottom velocity was $v_{cf} = 70$ cm/sec.

The velocity profile shown in *Fig. 1.2.5−3* has been observed by the author in the Hungarian Upper Danube (at Dunaremete, R. St. 1821.4 km) with a bottom material or moving bed load of comparable size. According to the figure, the critical mean velocity was $v_c = 173$ cm/sec, while the critical bottom velocity was $v_{cf} = 75$ cm/sec. The critical mean velocities observed in the laboratory and in the field will be seen thus to differ greatly owing to the great differences in depth. When plotting the velocity profile observed in the laboratory into the velocity profile observed in the field, the bottom velocities will be seen to show a fairly good agreement in spite of the wide difference in mean velocities.

In 1967 extensive investigations were made by C. R. Neill with natural bed load material graded from 6.2 to 29.1 mm and of $\gamma_1 = 2.54$ to 2.49 p/cm^3 specific gravity, as well as with acetate cellulose of $\gamma_1 = 1.31$ p/cm^3 specific gravity, to determine the critical mean velocity v_c. The critical mean velocities observed for the same bed load material were grouped according to the depth of flow D into three ranges (the depth intervals being 3 to 6 cm, 9 to 12 cm and 15 to 18 cm). The effect of depth is shown in *Fig. 1.2.5−4*. In each of the three depth ranges the critical mean velocity was found to vary with the 0.47th power of the mean particle size d_g (termed the effective diameter by Neill) which is almost identical with the exponent 0.45 obtained by the author and Yen in the Iowa experiments.

Plotting in the graph the relation

$$v_c = 30 \, d_g^{0.45} \qquad (1.2.5-1)$$

illustrated in *Fig. 1.1.3−7*, and remembering that in these experiments depth D varied from 2.7 to 14.4 cm, it will become clear that this relation does not agree with the three depth ranges introduced by Neill. As an explanation for this difference it is presumed that the magnitude of the critical mean velocity depends, aside from particle size and depth of flow, also on other hydraulic factors.

Neill has also adopted a dimensionless approach for processing his experimental results. By introducing the relative roughness d_g/D and the dimensionless parameter

$$\frac{\rho v_c^2}{(\gamma_1 - \gamma)d_g}$$

215

Fig. 1.2.5—1. The critical mean velocity vs. mean particle diameter relation, after several authors

Fig. 1.2.5—2. Velocity profile measured at the laboratory, for 15.5 mm particle size, in the critical condition

Fig. 1.2.5—3. Velocity profile measured in the Danube, for the 13.6 to 15.2 mm size fraction, in the critical condition

Fig. 1.2.5—4. The critical mean velocity vs. particle diameter relation, at different depths. After Neill

the relation

$$\frac{\rho v_c^2}{(\gamma_1 - \gamma)d_g} = F\left(\frac{d_g}{D}\right) \qquad (1.2.5-2)$$

is plotted in *Fig. 1.2.5—5*.

The parameter on the left-hand side of Eq. (1.2.5—2) was termed the "mobility number" by Neill. The mobility number is obviously proportionate to the expression

$$f_c = \frac{\tau_c}{(\gamma_1 - \gamma)d_g}$$

since $\tau_c = \gamma DS = \rho U_*^2$ and since, according to the Chézy formula,

$$\frac{v_c}{U_*} = \frac{c}{\sqrt{g}}$$

further

$$\rho U_*^2 = \frac{g}{c^2}\rho v_c^2 \qquad (1.2.5-3)$$

Fig. 1.2.5−5. The mobility number vs. relative roughness relation. After Neill

it is clear that

$$f_c = \frac{\tau_c}{(\gamma_1 - \gamma)d_g} = \frac{g}{c^2}\frac{\rho v_c^2}{(\gamma_1 - \gamma)d_g} \qquad (1.2.5-4)$$

whence

$$\frac{\rho v_c^2}{(\gamma_1 - \gamma)d_g} = \frac{c^2}{g}f_c \qquad (1.2.5-5)$$

From *Fig. 1.2.5−5* Neill arrived at several interesting conclusions.

The first of these is that since the submerged specific gravity of the acetate-cellulose globules is not more than 1/5th of the submerged specific gravity of the other substances used in the experiments and since experimental points relating to this material plot in the same range as the other points, it is logical to assume that the differences in the specific gravity of the bed load material are allowed for adequately in the mobility number.

The second conclusion of interest is that since the position of the experimental points relating to the glass and acetate-cellulose globule is the same as that of those relating to the irregular natural bed load material, the influence of the shape factor of particles is practically negligible.

In *Fig. 1.2.5−6* the experimental results of Mavis, Ho, Tu, the Linton Hydraulic Laboratory, Schaffernak and Mayer-Peter − Müller are shown together with those of Neill. In the interest of safety against scouring, the straight line fitting to the scattered points is traced at the lower boundary of the experimental data. The equation describing this straight line is

$$\frac{\rho v_c^2}{(\gamma_1 - \gamma)d_g} = 2.5 \left(\frac{d_g}{D}\right)^{-0.2} \qquad (1.2.5-6)$$

Fig. 1.2.5–6. The mobility number vs. relative roughness relation, based on experiments by Mavis, Ho, Tu, the Linnton Hydraulic Laboratory, Schaffernak, Meyer-Peter—Müller and Neill. After Neill

As noted by Neill, Eq. (1.2.5–6) applies to parallel, uniform, two-dimensional flow and smooth bed conditions, to particles larger than 3 mm, if the size fraction is not wider than twice the mean particle diameter d_g (the effective diameter), further if the particles are rounded and the relative roughness d_g/D is from 0.01 to 0.5.

With water used as fluid and introducing the expression D/d_g of relative roughness defined before, the relation becomes

$$\frac{v_c^2}{g\left(\dfrac{\rho_1}{\rho}-1\right)d_g} = 2.5\left(\frac{D}{d_g}\right)^{0.2} \qquad (1.2.5-7)$$

For 2.65 p/cm³ specific gravity

$$v_c = 6.37 \cdot d_g^{0.4}\,D^{0.1} \;[\text{m/sec}] \qquad (1.2.5-8)$$

where both the particle diameter d_g and the depth D should be introduced in m units.

For the depths $D = 30$ m, $D = 10$ m, $D = 3$ m, $D = 1$ m and $D = 0.3$ m the relation under Eq. (1.2.5–8) is plotted in *Fig. 1.2.5–7*.

The considerable influence on the critical mean velocity of relative roughness, respectively, of the particle size and the depth of flow separately are clearly indicated in *Figs 1.2.5–6* and *1.2.5–7* alike.

It is of interest to know that Neill has attempted to compare his experimental results with the relation of Shields illustrated in *Fig. 1.1.3–2*. (Similar investi-

Fig. 1.2.5—7. The critical mean velocity vs. particle diameter relation for bed load material of $\gamma_1 = 2.65$ p/cm^6 specific gravity, for different depths. After Neill

gations concerning the critical tractive force τ_c and f_c have been described in *Subsection 1.2.4—2*). Since in the experiments of Shields no data were available on slope, the relationship between the tractive force τ_c and the critical mean velocity v_c was estimated on the basis of the velocity distribution

$$\frac{v}{U_*} = 6.5 + 5.75 \lg \frac{D}{d_g}$$

derived for hydraulically rough channels from Keulegan's logarithmic expression. As revealed by the formula, the sand roughness was identified with the particle diameter d_g in his computations. The results of these computations are shown for the constant values $f_c = 0.06$, 0.04 and 0.02 in *Fig. 1.2.5—8*. The experimental points in the figures are, of course, the same as those in *Fig. 1.2.5—6*. In *Fig. 1.2.5—8* the experimental data are seen to be scattered at random about the $f_c = $ constant lines. These experiments of Neill are thus in support of the earlier conclusion that the magnitude of the critical tractive force and, in turn, of the critical mean velocity also depends on physical quantities other than the sediment shear velocity Reynolds number.

Neill concluded his investigations concerning the relation of Shields by stating that in hydraulically rough channels the resistance coefficient f_c is likely to be unaffected by Re_{*s}, and its magnitude may be expected to increase together with

220

Fig. 1.2.5—8. Mobility number vs. relative roughness, classified according to f_c = constant values. After Neill

relative roughness d_g/D. Neill represented his theory concerning the variations of f_c schematically in *Fig. 1.2.5—9*. In discussing the law of variable critical velocities it will be demonstrated that the variation of critical mean velocities is indeed influenced by several hydraulic properties of flow.

Fig. 1.2.5—9. Assumed resistance coefficient f_c vs. sediment shear velocity Reynolds number relation. After Neill

Fig. 1.2.5 — 10. Critical bottom velocity vs. average particle diameter according to several authors. After Stelczer

As to the variation of critical mean velocity with depth it appears that the bottom velocity, although difficult to determine or measure, is suitable for describing the condition of incipient movement, as it seems to characterize positively the critical condition.

A number of relations have been derived for determining the critical bottom velocity. Some of these are analysed in detail in *Subsection 1.1.2.3.*

For the sake of completeness a few such relations are shown in *Fig. 1.2.5 — 10.* Even if the two extreme relations of Levi ① and Velikanov—Bochkov ⑦ are disregarded, the differences will be seen to remain considerable. It is concluded therefrom that the critical bottom velocity controlling the condition of incipient movement depends greatly on the general distribution of velocities, as well as on the velocity fluctuations typical of turbulent flow.

For obtaining a better understanding of the problem extensive laboratory investigations have been performed by K. Stelczer. He assumed the velocity distribution and velocity fluctuations to be influenced in laboratory experiments primarily by the width of the experimental flume. In order to clear the role of flume width, experiments were run in flumes of four different widths ($B_1 = 15$ cm, $B_2 = 35$ cm, $B_3 = 50$ cm and $B_4 = 100$ cm) using a bed load material graded from about 1 to 24 mm. The results of these experiments are shown in *Fig. 1.2.5 — 11.* The critical bottom velocity pertaining to the boundary condition of incipient motion of the same particle size will be seen to be usually higher in narrower flumes.

The experimental results of Stelczer are displayed even more visually in *Fig. 1.2.5 — 12* where essentially the three-variable relation

$$v_{cf} = F(B, d) \qquad (1.2.5-9)$$

222

Fig. 1.2.5—11. Critical bottom velocity vs. average particle diameter for different flume widths. After Stelczer

is represented. As will be perceived from the figure, the critical bottom velocity was hardly influenced by the flume width B at small particle sizes of about 1 to 2 mm diameter, whereas at the greater size fractions the influence was considerable. In the experiments of Stelczer the greatest flume width was 1 m, and from the figure it may be anticipated that in even wider flumes the magnitude of the critical bottom velocity will remain essentially the same, since the d = constant lines approach asymptotically the velocity values pertaining to the B = 100 cm flume width.

The results of Stelczer seem to suggest that the critical bottom velocity is not a constant value either and is, for this reason, unsuited for describing uniquely the boundary condition of incipient motion.

Remembering the inevitable inaccuracies and uncertainties affecting the determination or measurement of the bottom velocity, the use of the critical value of the mean velocities is still believed advisable. The essential prerequisite thereof is, naturally, to determine in advance the manner in which, and the extent to which the mean velocities vary.

Considering the laws of physics governing the phenomenon an attempt will be made subsequently at determining the critical mean velocities, with due allowance to all physical quantities affecting the boundary condition of incipient motion.

1.2.5.2. The law of variable critical velocities. The theoretical study into the variation of critical velocities is expediently founded on the impact force theory. According to this theory, the impact force by which the bed load particle is displaced is exerted by the flowing water and, in the boundary condition of incipient motion, this force is balanced by the submerged weight of the particle.

223

Fig. 1.2.5−12. Critical bottom velocity vs. flume width for different bed load sizes. After Stelczer

If the velocity of flow related to the bed load particle is v, the impact force is

$$H = \Phi\left(\frac{\pi d^2}{4}\right) v^2 \frac{\gamma}{g} \qquad (1.2.5-10)$$

where Φ depends on the area exposed to the impact force of water and on the inclination of the slope. The submerged weight of the particle is

$$G' = \frac{\pi}{6} d^3 (\gamma_1 - \gamma) \qquad (1.2.5-11)$$

At the instant in which the particle starts moving $H = \phi G'$, where ϕ is a function of slope inclination and friction, so that denoting the critical velocity at the boundary condition of incipient motion by v_c, we have

$$\Phi\left(\frac{\pi d^2}{4}\right) v_c^2 \frac{\gamma}{g} = \phi\left[\frac{\pi d^3}{6} (\gamma_1 - \gamma)\right] \qquad (1.2.5-12)$$

Solving Eq. (1.2.5−12) for v_c and assuming the proportionality factors to be constant, further combining them into a single constant with the numerical values it is found that

$$v_c = \text{constant} \cdot \sqrt{g d \rho'} \qquad (1.2.5-13)$$

224

where

$$\rho' = \frac{\gamma_1 - \gamma}{\gamma} == \frac{\rho_1 - \rho}{\rho}$$

In analogy to the law of constant tractive forces, on the basis of Eq. (1.2.5−13) it was supposed that for a given bed load material of size d and specific gravity γ_1

$$\frac{v_c}{\sqrt{gd\rho'}} = t_{c_1} = \text{constant} \qquad (1.2.5-14)$$

Since it has been demonstrated that the law of constant tractive forces is misleading, it appears logical to conclude that t_{c_1} will also be subject to variations comparable to the variations of the resistance coefficient f_c assumed there.

On the basis of measurement data ranging between the limits indicated in *Table 1.2.5−3* it will be endeavoured now to determine the resistance coefficient t_{c_1} and the variations thereof.

Table 1.2.5−3 will be noted to differ from *Table 1.2.4−3* for the data of Neill have also been included. (As will be shown later, the resistance coefficient is expediently considered in other forms, as t_{c_2} and t_c, as well.)

Adopting an approach similar to that followed in the case of critical tractive forces, the study into the variations of critical velocities will also be started by clarifying the theoretical groundwork and formal structure of the relations describing the critical condition.

Since the critical condition has been assumed to be described positively by the physical quantities

$$g, \ D, \ d \ v, \ S, \ \rho'$$

it is irrelevant, whether the critical tractive force τ_c or the critical mean velocity v_c is considered. In this way the method described in *Section 1.2.3* can again be adopted and the most appropriate five-term velocity groups can be selected from the fifteen potential dynamic velocities under Eqs (1.2.3−20), (1.2.3−21) and (1.2.3−22).

The group comprising the following five independent velocities should be selected:

$$v/d, \ \sqrt[3]{gv}, \ \sqrt{gDS}, \ v/D, \ \sqrt{gd\rho'} \qquad (1.2.5-15)$$

The above velocities can be combined into the four independent velocity ratios

$$\frac{\sqrt[3]{gv}}{v/d} = \frac{d}{v^{2/3}g^{-1/3}} \qquad (1.2.5-16a)$$

$$\frac{v/d}{v/D} = \frac{D}{d} \qquad (1.2.5-16b)$$

Table 1.2.5 — 3

Hydraulic parameters of observations used in determining the critical mean velocities

Condition of movement	Depth of flow, D [cm]		Water temper- ature, t [°C]		Particle diameter, d [mm]		Slope, S		Spec. gravity of sediment, γ_1 [p/cm³]		Mean velocity, v_c [cm/sec]	
	Max.	Min.	Max.	Min.	Max.	Min.	Max.	Min.	Max.	Min.	Max.	Min.
Critical	46.1	1.52	27	7.6	20.0	0.021	0.066	0.000055	2.65	2.49	113.0	14.5

The data used were published by J. Bogárdi, L. Ivicsics, L. Rákóczi, Guy—Simons—Richardson, Neill, Barton—Liu et al.

$$\frac{\sqrt{gDS}}{v/d} = \frac{U_* d}{v} \qquad (1.2.5-16c)$$

$$\frac{\sqrt{gd\rho'}}{v/d} = \frac{g^{1/2} \rho'^{1/2} d^{3/2}}{v} \qquad (1.2.5-16d)$$

The velocities under Eq. (1.2.5−15) can be combined also into velocity ratios involving the term $U_* D/v$:

$$\frac{\sqrt[3]{gv}}{v/d} = \frac{d}{v^{2/3} g^{-1/3}} \qquad (1.2.5-16a_1)$$

$$\frac{v/d}{v/D} = \frac{D}{d} \qquad (1.2.5-16b_1)$$

$$\frac{\sqrt{gDS}}{\sqrt{gd\rho'}} = \left(\frac{DS}{d\rho'}\right)^{1/2} \qquad (1.2.5-16c_1)$$

$$\frac{\sqrt{gDS}}{v/D} = \frac{U_* D}{v} \qquad (1.2.5-16d_1)$$

If the resultant mean velocity of flow at incipient motion is v_c, then the ratio t_{c_1} −see Eq. (1.2.5−14)−characterizing this resultant velocity is described theoretically by the following two relations:

$$\frac{v_c}{\sqrt{gd\rho'}} = t_{c_1} = F\left(\frac{d}{v^{2/3} g^{-1/3}}, \frac{D}{d}, \frac{U_* d}{v}, \frac{g^{1/2} \rho'^{1/2} d^{3/2}}{v}\right) \qquad (1.2.5-17a)$$

$$\frac{v_c}{\sqrt{gd\rho'}} = t_{c_1} = F\left(\frac{d}{v^{2/3} g^{-1/3}}, \frac{D}{d}, \frac{DS}{d\rho'}, \frac{U_* D}{v}\right) \qquad (1.2.5-17b)$$

In contrast to Eq. (1.2.5−14), the relations under (1.2.5−17) indicate that the resistance coefficient t_{c_1} is not constant, but is likely to be a function of the four dimensionless parameters given under Eqs (1.2.5−16a) to (1.2.5−16d) or Eqs (1.2.5−16a$_1$) to (1.2.5−16d$_1$).

From the experimental results available it has been concluded that the influence of the dimensionless parameters $Re_{*s} = U_* d/v$, and $Re_* = U_* D/v$ is negligibly small in comparison with the other parameters. (The effect of $U_* d/v$ and $U_* D/v$ will be considered subsequently.)

Neglecting with this simplification the effect of the sediment shear velocity Reynolds number Re_{*s}, and the shear velocity Reynolds number Re_*, further the influence of the parameters

$$\frac{g^{1/2} \rho'^{1/2} d^{3/2}}{v},$$

Fig. 1.2.5—13. t_{c_1} vs. D/d at the critical condition with
$$\frac{d}{v^{2/3}g^{-1/3}} \text{ as parameter}$$

and $DS/d\rho'$, in *Fig. 1.2.5—13* the relation

$$t_{c_1} = F\left(\frac{d}{v^{2/3}\,g^{-1/3}}\,,\ \frac{D}{d}\right) \tag{1.2.5—18}$$

has been plotted. However, owing to the rather narrow range in which the values of t_{c_1} vary, it was found impossible to determine positively the lines corresponding to

$$\frac{d}{v^{2/3}g^{-1/3}} = \text{constant}$$

values, although the magnitude of this parameter shows a definite decreasing trend with increasing values of D/d. The experimental data available are thus insufficient to permit the relation under Eq. (1.2.5—18) to be used successfully.

In a second attempt the five-term group of independent velocities

$$v/d, \quad \sqrt[3]{gv}, \quad \sqrt{dDS}, \quad v/D, \quad \sqrt{gD\rho'} \tag{1.2.5—19}$$

should be selected from the potential dynamic velocities under Eqs (1.2.3—20), (1.2.3—21) and (1.2.3—22). The velocities under Eq. (1.2.5—19) are combined into the four independent velocity ratios:

$$\frac{\sqrt[3]{gv}}{v/d} = \frac{d}{v^{2/3}\,g^{-1/3}} \tag{1.2.5—20a}$$

$$\frac{v/d}{v/D} = \frac{D}{d} \tag{1.2.5—20b}$$

228

Fig. 1.2.5−14. t_{c_2} vs. D/d at the critical condition with $\dfrac{d}{v^{2/3}g^{-1/3}}$ as parameter

$$\frac{\sqrt{gDS}}{\sqrt{gD\rho'}} = \sqrt{\frac{S}{\rho'}} \qquad\qquad (1.2.5-20c)$$

$$\frac{\sqrt{gDS}}{v/D} = \frac{U_* D}{v} \qquad\qquad (1.2.5-20d)$$

At the boundary condition of incipient motion the resultant mean velocity of flow v_c should be characterized by the ratio $t_{c_2} = v_c/\sqrt{gD\rho'}$. In this case the parameter t_{c_2} is described theoretically by the relation

$$\frac{v_c}{\sqrt{gD\rho'}} = t_{c_2} = F\left(\frac{d}{v^{2/3}\,g^{-1/3}}, \; \frac{D}{d}, \; \frac{S}{\rho'}, \; \frac{U_* D}{v}\right) \qquad (1.2.5-21)$$

Neglecting the parameters S/ρ' and $U_* D/v$ in the definition of t_{c_2}, the relation

$$\frac{v_c}{\sqrt{gD\rho'}} = t_{c_2} = F\left(\frac{d}{v^{2/3}\,g^{-1/3}}, \; \frac{D}{d}\right) \qquad (1.2.5-22)$$

is plotted in *Fig. 1.2.5−14*. Although there is a certain scatter of data, it will be perceived from the figure that the parameter t_{c_2} can be expressed directly in terms of the ratio D/d. According to the figure this relation is expressed numerically by the equation

$$\frac{v_c}{\sqrt{gD\rho'}} = t_{c_2} = 1.7\left(\frac{D}{d}\right)^{-0.405} \qquad\qquad (1.2.5-23)$$

229

In *Fig. 1.2.5 – 14* the values

$$\frac{d}{v^{2/3}\,g^{-1/3}}$$

are seen to decrease regularly as the ratio D/d increases but, owing to the narrow range of data, it was found impossible to determine the lines indicating discrete constant values. On the other hand, the value of $d/(v^{2/8}g^{-1/3})$ is seen to be positively related to D/d. On the strength of this circumstance it was found possible to determine graphically in *Fig. 1.2.5 – 15* the numerical relation of these two parameters by selecting in *Fig. 1.2.5 – 14* the values

$$\frac{d}{v^{2/3}g^{-1/3}} = 1,\ 10 \text{ and } 100$$

(indicated by dashed circles in the figure). According to *Fig. 1.2.5 – 15*, this relation is represented by the expression

$$\frac{d}{v^{2/3}\,g^{-1/3}} = 6\,920 \left(\frac{D}{d}\right)^{-1.18} \tag{1.2.5-24}$$

As demonstrated by the numerical forms given by Eqs (1.2.5 – 23) and (1.2.5 – 24) of the relations determined, it is possible to express t_{c_2} in terms of $d/(v^{2/3}g^{-1/2})$. In fact, the two relations are combined into the relation

$$\frac{v_c}{\sqrt{gD\rho'}} = t_{c_2} = 0.085 \left(\frac{d}{v^{2/3}\,g^{-1/3}}\right)^{-0.34} \tag{1.2.5-25}$$

indicated in *Fig. 1.2.5 – 16*.

From *Figs 1.2.5 – 14, 1.2.5 – 15* and *1.2.5 – 16* the following conclusions may be drawn.

Within the range of experimental data *Fig. 1.2.5 – 14* is suitable for estimating the critical mean velocity v_c. It should be recalled, of course, that since a bed load of $\gamma_1 = 2.65$ p/cm^3 or similar specific gravity has been used in all experiments, this relation is valid only as long as the specific gravity is actually 2.65.

A further objection to *Fig. 1.2.5 – 14* is the complete lack of information on the slope pertaining to the critical condition. This implies that for a given set of bed load material and fluid as well as depth of flow, repeated attempts must be made to determine the critical slope at which the mean flow velocity assumes exactly the critical value v_c determined with the help of *Fig. 1.2.5 – 14*. In this respect *Fig. 1.2.5 – 14* and even *Fig. 1.2.5 – 16* display a close resemblance to *Figs 1.2.5 – 6* and *1.2.5 – 7* of Neill, also failing to yield information on slope S. The neglect by Neill of slope as one of the independent variables governing the phenomenon (the boundary condition of incipient motion) is theoretically questionable. For this very reason these relations are of little value to the designing engineer. Nevertheless in some cases of practical interest they may be used to advantage since they

Fig. 1.2.5—15. $\dfrac{d}{v^{2/3}g^{-1/3}}$ vs. D/d on the basis of Fig. 1.2.5.—14

yield the critical mean velocity, that is, for example the highest non-scouring velocity of flow.

From the foregoing it follows that the *theoretically correct approach consists of including the slope S in determining the critical velocity* v_c. This is done expediently by introducing the parameter

$$t_c = \frac{v_c}{\sqrt{gDS}} = \frac{v_c}{U_*} \qquad (1.2.5-26)$$

When using the parameter t_c the critical velocity is found in terms of the five-term independent group of velocities mentioned in *Section 1.2.4* and given under Eq. (1.2.4—8), and the velocity ratios under Eqs (1.2.4—9a) to (1.2.4—9d) to which these velocities are combined.

Experience gained in the processing of experimental data has shown the desirability of studying first the relation

$$\frac{v_c}{U_*} = F\left(\frac{U_* d}{v}, \frac{D}{d}\right) \qquad (1.2.5-27)$$

The desirability of this study is underlined by the fact that in the considerations related to the critical tractive force the predominant influence of the relative

Fig. 1.2.5—16. t_{c_2} vs. $\dfrac{d}{\nu^{2/3}g^{-1/3}}$ on the basis of

Figs 1.2.5—14 and 15

roughness D/d has been demonstrated first in connection with the relations resembling the presentation adopted by Shields. The relation under Eq.(1.2.5—27) has been plotted in *Fig. 1.2.5—17* where concerning the critical mean velocity the role of the parameter t_c is comparable to that of the parameter f_c introduced by Shields. However, in *Fig. 1.2.5—17* the scatter of data is too great to permit the $D/d =$ constant lines to be traced. This fact may be interpreted as an indication of the circumstance that the influence of the sediment shear velocity Reynolds number Re_{*s} on the critical mean velocity is insignificant.

Reviewing Eqs (1.2.5—18), (1.2.5—22), (1.2.5—23), (1.2.5—25) and (1.2.5—27) considered in the foregoing with the aim of determining the critical mean velocity, it appears logical to conclude that consideration should be given also to the forms of theoretical relations in which the dimensionless resistance coefficient $f_c = \tau_c/(\gamma_1 - \gamma)d$ of Shields is involved as an independent variable.

For this purpose the five-term independent group of velocities

$$\sqrt{gDS}, \quad \sqrt{gd\rho'}, \quad \nu/d, \quad \nu/D, \quad \sqrt{gd} \qquad (1.2.5-28)$$

should be selected from the velocities given under Eqs (1.2.3—20), (1.2.3—21) and (1.2.3—22). These are combined into the independent velocity ratios

$$\frac{\sqrt{gDS}}{\sqrt{gd\rho'}} = \sqrt{f_c} = \sqrt{\frac{\tau_c}{(\gamma_1 - \gamma)d}} \qquad (1.2.5-29a)$$

$$\frac{\sqrt{gDS}}{\nu/d} = \frac{U_* d}{\nu} \qquad (1.2.5-29b)$$

232

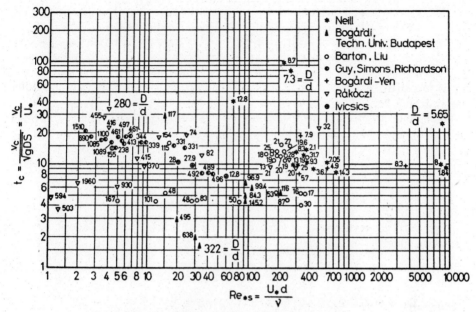

Fig. 1.2.5—17. v_c/U_* vs. Re_{*s} at the critical condition with
D/d as parameter

$$\frac{v/d}{v/D} = \frac{D}{d} \qquad\qquad (1.2.5-29c)$$

$$\frac{\sqrt{gd\rho'}}{\sqrt{gd}} = \sqrt{\rho'} \qquad\qquad (1.2.5-29d)$$

Using the parameters in Eqs (1.2.5—29a) to (1.2.5—29d), the ratio of the critical mean velocity and of the shear velocity is given theoretically by the relation

$$\frac{v_c}{U_*} = F\left(\frac{\tau_c}{(\gamma_1 - \gamma)d}, \ \frac{U_* d}{v}, \ \frac{D}{d}, \ \rho'\right) \qquad (1.2.5-30)$$

The theoretical relation under Eq. (1.2.5—30) has opened the way for studying several three-variable relations. Of these the relations

$$\frac{v_c}{U_*} = F\left(\frac{D}{d}, \ \rho'\right) \qquad\qquad (1.2.5-31)$$

and

$$\frac{v_c}{U_*} = F\left(\frac{\tau_c}{(\gamma_1 - \gamma)d}, \ \frac{U_* d}{v}\right) \qquad (1.2.5-32)$$

have proved of no avail, although the variation with D/d and f_c followed the expected trend.

233

The three-variable relation

$$\frac{v_c}{U_*} = F\left(\frac{D}{d}, \frac{\tau_c}{(\gamma_1 - \gamma)d}\right) \qquad (1.2.5-33)$$

was found to be slightly more positive but the f_c = constant lines could not be traced definitely in this case either.

In further studies an attempt was made to introduce, instead of the sediment shear velocity Reynolds number, the shear velocity Reynolds number

$$Re_* = \frac{U_* D}{\nu}$$

and the slope S.

For deriving relations of a similar theoretical form the independent five-term velocity group

$$\sqrt{gD}, \quad \sqrt{gDS}, \quad \sqrt{gdS}, \quad \sqrt{gd\rho'}, \quad \nu/D \qquad (1.2.5-34)$$

should be selected from the 15 velocities given in Eqs (1.2.3−20), (1.2.3−21) and (1.2.3−22). These are combined into the four dimensionless parameters

$$\frac{\sqrt{gDS}}{\sqrt{gD}} = \sqrt{S} \qquad (1.2.5-35a)$$

$$\frac{\sqrt{gDS}}{\sqrt{gdS}} = \sqrt{\frac{D}{d}} \qquad (1.2.5-35b)$$

$$\frac{\sqrt{gDS}}{\sqrt{gd\rho'}} = \sqrt{f_c} = \sqrt{\frac{\tau_c}{(\gamma_1 - \gamma)d}} \qquad (1.2.5-35c)$$

$$\frac{\sqrt{gDS}}{\nu/D} = \frac{U_* D}{\nu} \qquad (1.2.5-35d)$$

whence the parameter $v_c/U_* = t_c$ is defined theoretically by the relation

$$\frac{v_c}{U_*} = F\left(S, \frac{D}{d}, \frac{\tau_c}{(\gamma_1 - \gamma)d}, \frac{U_* D}{\nu}\right) \qquad (1.2.5-36)$$

Eventually the theoretical relation under Eq. (1.2.5−36) has been used for examining the relations

$$\frac{v_c}{U_*} = F\left(\frac{\tau_c}{(\gamma_1 - \gamma)d}, S\right) \qquad (1.2.5-37)$$

234

Fig. 1.2.5—18. v_c/U_* vs. D/d at the critical condition with $\dfrac{d}{v^{2/3}g^{-1/3}}$ as parameter

and

$$\frac{v_c}{U_*} = F\left(\frac{\tau_c}{(\gamma_1 - \gamma)d}, \ \frac{U_* D}{v}\right) \qquad (1.2.5-38)$$

which, however, proved to be of as little use as the foregoing relations under Eqs (1.2.5—18), (1.2.5—27), (1.2.5—31), (1.2.5—32) and (1.2.5—33).

Within the range defined by the available observation data the optimum result was obtained with the help of the theoretical relation

$$\frac{v_c}{U_*} = t_c = F\left(\frac{d}{v^{2/3}\, g^{-1/3}}, \ \frac{D}{d}, \ \frac{U_* d}{v}, \ \frac{g^{1/2}\, \rho'^{1/2}\, d^{3/2}}{v}\right) \qquad (1.2.5-39)$$

determined with the help of the five-term independent groups of velocities given by Eq. (1.2.5—15) and the velocity ratios under Eqs (1.2.5—16a) to (1.2.5—16b) to which these were combined. Assuming the influence of Re_{*s} and $(g^{1/2}\, \rho,^{1/2}d^{3/2})/v$ to be negligible, the relation

$$\frac{v_c}{U_*} = F\left(\frac{D}{d}, \ \frac{d}{v^{2/3}\, g^{-1/3}}\right) \qquad (1.2.5-40)$$

has been constructed. The plot of this relation in *Fig. 1.2.5—18* reveals clearly that the lines of the values

$$\frac{d}{v^{2/3}\, g^{-1/3}} = \text{constant}$$

(1, 10 and 100 in the figure) could be determined with a greater reliability than before.

Fig. 1.2.5—19. Coefficient a vs. $\dfrac{d}{v^{2/3}g^{-1/3}}$
on the basis of *Fig. 1.2.5—18*

Since at the values

$$\frac{d}{v^{2/3}\,g^{-1/3}} = 1,\ 10\ \text{és}\ 100$$

each of the functions

$$\frac{v_c}{U_*} = a\left(\frac{D}{d}\right)^n$$

is known, by expressing the relation between the coefficient a and the ratio

$$\frac{d}{v^{2/3}\,g^{-1/3}}$$

according to *Fig. 1.2.5 — 19* and taking into consideration the numerical expression

$$a = 0.000\,044\left(\frac{d}{v^{2/3}\,g^{-1/3}}\right)^{1.8} \tag{1.2.5—41}$$

236

the three-variable numerical relation

$$\frac{v_c}{U_*} = 0.000\,044 \left(\frac{d}{v^{2/3}\,g^{-/13}}\right)^{1.8} \left(\frac{D}{d}\right)^{1.6} \qquad (1.2.5-42)$$

could also be determined.

Before illustrating by numerical examples the practical application of the empirical relation under Eq. (1.2.5−42) it is found expedient to attach a few supplementary remarks to Eqs (1.2.5−23) and (1.2.5−25).

According to these two relations the expression

$$\frac{v_c}{\sqrt{gD\rho'}} = t_{c_2}$$

is proportionate to the −0.405th power of the relative roughness D/d and to the −0.34th power of the parameter d/A. The two relations have been obtained by the adjustment of observation data and appear to imply in this form that t_{c_2} and the critical mean velocity v_c depend practically in the same way on D/d and d/A. This distortion resulting from adjustments can be eliminated by determining the three-variable relation of $v_c/\sqrt{gD\rho'}$ or, since in the present case ρ' is constant, of $v_c/\sqrt{gD}$ to the two afore-mentioned parameters.

By introducing for S the value of the critical slope discussed in the foregoing section and expressed by Eq. (1.2.4−31), in terms of the ratios d/A and D/d, into the term

$$\frac{v_c}{U_*} = \frac{v_c}{\sqrt{gDS}}$$

on the left-hand-side of Eq. (1.2.5−42), it becomes actually possible to write $v_c/\sqrt{gD}$ in terms of the above two parameters. In this way the relation

$$\frac{v_c}{\left[1.283\cdot 10^6\, gD \left(\dfrac{d}{v^{2/3}\,g^{-1/3}}\right)^{-2.815} \left(\dfrac{D}{d}\right)^{-3.032}\right]^{1/2}} =$$

$$= 4.4\cdot 10^{-5} \left(\frac{d}{v^{2/3}\,g^{-1/3}}\right)^{1.8} \left(\frac{D}{d}\right)^{1.6} \qquad (1.2.5-43)$$

is obtained which is rearranged to the form

$$\frac{v_c}{\sqrt{gD}} \cong 0.05 \left(\frac{d}{v^{2/3}\,g^{-1/3}}\right)^{0.39} \left(\frac{D}{d}\right)^{0.08} \qquad (1.2.5-44)$$

The relation under Eq. (1.2.5−44) is applied in a manner similar to Eqs (1.2.5−23) and (1.2.5−25), indicating plainly that the magnitude of v_c is much more affected by d/A, i.e. by the particle size of bed load than by the relative roughness.

237

On the basis of *Fig. 1.2.5−18*, for any given combination the particle size d, depth of flow D and for water temperature, nothing more than the ratio v_c/U_* can be determined. It should therefore be realized that another approach must be adopted for finding the critical slope S_c needed for computing the magnitude of U_*. Otherwise the critical mean velocity v_c will be found impossible to be computed from the ratio v_c/U_*. For this purpose *Fig. 1.2.4−12* of the foregoing section may be used to advantage from which the parameter f_c is obtained for a given ratio D/d and for known values of $d/(v^{2/3}\,g^{-1/3})$, and the critical slope S_c is computed from the expression

$$f_c = \frac{\tau_c}{(\gamma_1 - \gamma)d} = \frac{\gamma D S_c}{(\gamma_1 - \gamma)d}$$

For example, compute the critical velocity v_c pertaining to a depth of flow $D = 9.4$ cm, to particle size $d = 0.047$ cm, to water temperature 20 deg.C., i.e. $v^{2/3}\,g^{-1/3} = 0.0047$ cm, together with the slope at which this velocity v_c occurs at given depth D.

In *Fig. 1.2.5−18* for $D/d = 9.4/0.047 = 200$, and for

$$\frac{d}{v^{2/3}\,g^{-1/3}} = \frac{0.047}{0.0047} = 10$$

we find the value

$$\frac{v_c}{U_*} = \frac{v_c}{\sqrt{gDS}} = 11.6$$

From *Fig. 1.2.4−12* the magnitude of the parameter f_c pertaining to $D/d = 200$ and

$$\frac{d}{v^{2/3}\,g^{-1/3}} = 10$$

is

$$f_c = \frac{\gamma D S_c}{(\gamma_1 - \gamma)d} = 0.0155$$

Thus the slope at which the critical condition occurs is

$$S_c = \frac{0.0155 \cdot (\gamma_1 - \gamma)d}{\gamma D} = \frac{0.0155 \cdot (2.65 - 1) \cdot 0.047}{1 \cdot 9.4} = 0.000\,127$$

at which

$$U_* = \sqrt{gDS} = \sqrt{981 \cdot 9.4 \cdot 0.000\,127} = \sqrt{1.17} = 1.08 \text{ cm/sec},$$

so that the critical mean velocity becomes:

$$v_c = 11.6 \cdot 1.08 = 12.5 \text{ cm/sec}$$

238

The critical tractive force is computed eventually as

$$\tau_c = f_c(\gamma_1 - \gamma)\,d = 0.0155 \cdot 1.65 \cdot 0.047 = 0.0012 \text{ p/cm}^2$$

In engineering practice it is often necessary to predict the particle size pertaining to a given combination of flow depth, slope, water temperature, or the mean velocity corresponding thereto, beyond which the larger bed load particles will remain immobile. A procedure of trial and error must be recurred to for solving problems of this nature, by reversing the example given above.

Let the depth of flow $D = 9.4$ cm, the slope $S = 0.000,127$, the water temperature be 20 deg.C and the mean velocity computed therefrom or actually observed $v_c = 12.5$ cm/sec. It is desired to find the particle size that will be exactly in the boundary condition of incipient movement.

With $U_* = \sqrt{981 \cdot 9.4 \cdot 0.000,127} = 1.08$ cm/sec,

$$\frac{v_c}{U_*} = \frac{12.5}{1.08} = 11.6$$

As a first approach assume $D/d = 100$, so that the desired particle size $d = 9.4/100 = 0.0094$ cm. Since at 20 deg.C, $v^{2/3}\,g^{-1/3} = 0.0047$,

$$\frac{d}{v^{2/3}\,g^{-1/3}} = 20$$

and from *Fig. 1.2.5 – 18* the value of D/d corresponding thereto and to the parameter $v_c/U_* = 11.6$ is around 20 to 30. Therefore a second attempt is necessary, using a smaller particle size or a higher value of D/d which is essentially the same for a given D value.

The second trial will be made with such values as $D/d = 250$, or $d = 9.4/250 = 0.0376$ cm. Thus

$$\frac{d}{v^{2/3}\,g^{-1/3}} = \frac{0.0376}{0.0047} = 8.02$$

which, in combination with $v_c/U_* = 11.6$, corresponds in *Fig. 1.2.5 – 18* to D/d around 300 to 320. The desired particle size is necessarily larger than this, and so a smaller ratio D/d is to be assumed for the particular depth D.

Repeated trials will yield $D/d = 200$ as the correct value indicating, according to the example detailed above, that the bed load particles of $d = 0.47$ cm diameter will be exactly in the boundary condition of incipient movement.

In the knowledge of depth D, of slope S, of particle size d, of water temperature (i.e. $A = v^{2/3}\,g^{-1/3}$) and of the observed or computed mean velocity v, a problem frequently encountered in practice is to decide whether critical conditions prevail for particles of the size d or bed load is transported by the stream. The solution of such problems will be illustrated by the following example.

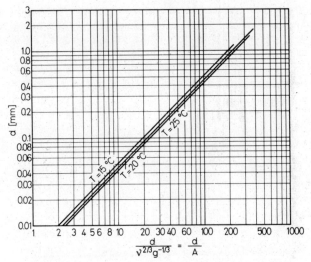

Fig. 1.2.5−20. $\dfrac{d}{v^{2/3}g^{-1/3}}$ vs. particle diameter d
for different water temperatures

Let $D = 5.62$ cm, $d = 0.0509$ cm, $S = 0.06$, $v = 94.7$ cm/sec and $A = 4.69 \cdot 10^{-3}$ cm.

With these values $D/d = 110.5$, $d/A = 10.85$.

From *Fig. 1.2.5−18* the value $v_c/U_* = 5.21$ corresponds to the above pair of $D/d = 110.5$ and $d/A = 10.85$ values.

If the prevailing conditions are actually critical for the particular particle size, the critical slope computed from the parameter

$$f_c = \frac{\gamma D S_c}{(\gamma_1 - \gamma)d} = 0.047$$

corresponding in *Fig. 1.2.4−12* to $D/d = 110.5$ and $D/A = 10.85$ must be identical with the given $S = 0.06$ value.

From $f_c = 0.047$

$$S_c = \frac{0.047 \cdot (2.65 - 1) \cdot 0.0509}{1 \cdot 5.62} = 0.0007$$

with unchanged depth of flow the slope pertaining to the critical condition is thus substantially flatter than the actual slope. It follows that the particular bed load fraction will be transported by the stream.

Of course, if $S = 0.0007$, the critical velocity will also be much lower than the prevailing $v = 94.7$ cm/sec velocity. In fact, with the critical slope S_c we obtain $U_* = \sqrt{981 \cdot 5.62 \cdot 0.0007} = 1.97$ and thus, from the ratio $v_c/1.97 = 5.21$, the critical velocity is obtained as $v_c = 10.26$ cm/sec.

As revealed by the foregoing computation, for any particular particle size the depth of flow and slope should be regarded as corresponding values governing the critical condition.

The close correlation of the slope S_c and the velocity v_c pertaining to the critical condition at a given combination of particle size and depth of flow will now be illustrated by a brief analysis attached to the foregoing numerical example.

With the original $S = 0.06$ and $v = 94.7$ cm/sec figures $U_* = \sqrt{981 \cdot 5.62 \cdot 0.06}$ $= 18.17$ and thus $v/U_* = 94.7/18.17 = 5.21$. With this value as well as with the unchanged parameters $D/d = 110.5$ and $d/A = 10.85$ a point is obtained in *Fig. 1.2.5 – 18* which, considering the hydraulic factors of slope and the particle size, seems to correspond completely to the critical condition. However, as demonstrated in the first part of the example, this is at variance with actual conditions. This approach will thus be seen to lead to an obviously incorrect result although each of the parameter values meets the criteria of critical conditions represented in *Fig. 1.2.5 – 18*. Nevertheless the computation will be misleading since the slope corresponding to the given combination of depths and particle size has been neglected.

Since the temperature of water is generally different in each particular problem and in view of the inconvenience of estimating the particle size from the parameter $d/v^{2/3} g^{-1/3}$, at variable v values, the relations

$$\frac{d}{v^{2/3} g^{-1/3}}$$

have been plotted in *Fig. 1.2.5 – 20* for $T = 15$, 20 and 25 deg.C.

From the considerations expounded in the foregoing on the application of *Fig. 1.2.5 – 18* and on the three-variable relation Eq. (1.2.5 – 42) plotted in this figure, it has been inferred that as far as the critical condition is concerned the depth of flow and the slope should be regarded as corresponding pairs of values for any given particle size. This implies briefly that this figure and this relation can be used exclusively in combination with *Fig. 1.2.4.– 12* or another similar relation. In other words no correct result will be obtained, unless the critical velocity pertaining to the given d/A value is identical with the resultant velocity pertaining to the corresponding values of depth and slope prevailing at the critical condition.

It should be noted further that in *Fig. 1.2.5 – 18* the individual $d/A =$ constant lines could only be traced approximately owing to the limited number and rather narrow range of experimental data. For this reason the approximate character of the relation represented in the figure and expressed by Eq. (1.2.5 – 42) should be realized. As additional observation data become available and further investigations are made, the relation is expected to be subjected to modifications. It should be remembered, moreover, that the laws governing the variations of critical velocities have been derived exclusively from results of laboratory experiments. Consequently, these must not be applied directly to alluvial streams and rivers. In problems associated with the latter, extensive investigations are invariably necessary and a number of approaches must be adopted for estimating the critical mean velocities.

Concerning the use of *Fig. 1.2.5 – 18* it should be pointed out in conclusion that this *applies only to a bed load material of* $\gamma_1 = 2.65 \ p/cm^3$ *specific gravity.* This statement, in contrast to those made in the foregoing in connection with the critical tractive force, should be completed by the restriction that for bed load of a specific gravity other than 2.65 there is no way in which the relations discussed above could be used for determining the critical mean velocity v_c.

1.2.6. RATE OF BED LOAD TRANSPORT

1.2.6.1. Classification of bed load transport formulas. The most difficult problem related to sediment transport in alluvial streams probably consists of detemining the rate of transport. Research into the determination of transport rates started with the theoretical consideration of Du Boys who himself has suggested a formula for predicting the rate of bed load transport.

The formulae advanced for estimating the transport rate are aimed almost without exception at determining the bed-load-transporting capacity, that is, the maximum weight of bed load the stream is capable of transporting. It should be obvious that the actual rate of transport will differ from this limit value. The prerequisite for the two values to become equal is a sediment supply equalling exactly the transporting capacity.

Several different approaches have been adopted to answer the problems of determining the transport rate.

a) *Theoretical relations* have been derived on the basis of certain assumptions.

b) *Laboratory experiments* have been performed, in the course of which observations were made on the rate of transport, on the hydraulic characteristics of flow, and the observed values were related to each other.

In a number of investigations theoretical and experimental methods have been applied in combination; moreover, the results derived from experimental data have invariably been processed under a certain theoretical aspect.

c) The rate of bed load transport has also been determined with the help of *measurements made in the field,* and the values thus obtained have been used for deriving empirical relations between the transport rate and the hydraulic characteristics of the stream. Provided the actual rate of transport can be measured with the desired degree of accuracy, this approach appears to offer the most successful and most reliable method of determining the bed load transport. Unfortunately, the measured rates of transport, especially those obtained by means of samplers, are of questionable reliability. For this reason the results obtained in this way are almost completely neglected by many investigators although, in many instances, measurements of this kind offer the only possibility of obtaining an at least approximate information on bed load transport.

Using the afore-mentioned three approaches several bed load transport formulae have been derived which, however, yield drastically different results.

The bed load transport formulae can be classified according to a number of aspects.

In some of the formulae the rate of bed load is expressed in terms of the tractive force or in terms of discharge and slope whereas in several others the velocity of flow is introduced.

A number of transport formulae have been suggested in which the rate of bed load is related to the part greater than the critical value of the actual tractive force, flow velocity or discharge, this part being usually referred to in the relevant literature as the effective tractive force, flow velocity or discharge.

Several criteria have also been introduced which are claimed to offer suitable checks for the theoretical correctness of the bed load transport formulae. An attempt will be made subsequently to examine these problems, the objective here being the determination of the conditions under which the relations can be accepted as theoretically sound.

As an example it should be noted that in 1946 M. A. Velikanov associated the theoretical correctness of transport formulae with the manner in which these depend on the velocity of flow. According to him, a relation is theoretically well founded if the bed load transport is proportionate to the fourth power of flow velocity. This criterion is apparently unsupported by any physical explanation and is rather of an empirical than of a theoretical character.

Obviously no formula may be regarded as correct, unless it is well-founded theoretically and can be given a sound physical explanation. In this interpretation all criteria needed for describing a physical phenomenon in terms of mathematics have a bearing on the correctness of bed load transport formulae.

It is equally important to assign such numerical values to the coefficients and constants of relations which yield results comparable to the actual rate of bed load transport.

A wide variety of interpretations have been given in the literature to the rate of bed load transport or to the weight of bed load transported. Any attempt at introducing a uniform nomenclature, however advisable this may seem, is bound to come up against extremely great difficulties. In certain respects this would be even disadvantageous, for it would make research achievements difficult to identify. Consequently, although a certain general notation will be adopted, various relations will be defined individually in the subsequent part.

Of the relations determined by any of the three methods mentioned in the foregoing, those resting on a theoretical and experimental foundation will be discussed preferably under the same heading, in distinction to those derived from the results of field measurements. The reason for doing so is that the latter apply invariably to a particular water course and no generalization is possible unless a similar relation is established by measurements performed on another water course. The relations originating from field measurements will be excluded from the present considerations and will be recurred to in the second part of this book.

When considering the relations derived by theory or from experimental results, it should be remembered that their application to natural streams is impossible until a number of additional problems are cleared, since they reflect usually the results of experiments performed under more or less ideal conditions of observations.

1.2.6.2 Theoretical relations. Without any attempt at completeness some of the relations of hystorical or theoretical interest will be considered subsequently.

In the first endeavour at a theoretical understanding of bed load movement it was assumed by Du Boys (1879) that the bed load moves in layers so that the top layer of a thickness identical with the particle diameter d is transported at the highest velocity, with the velocity decreasing to 0 at the bottom layer according to a linear relationship.

The relation derived eventually is

$$q_B = C_B \tau_0 (\tau_0 - \tau_c) \qquad (1.2.6-1)$$

where q_B (kp/sec m) is the rate of transport, τ_0 (kp/m^2) and τ_c (kp/m^2), the actual and the critical tractive force, respectively, while C_B (m^3/kp sec) is a dimensional coefficient. The relation is theoretically unfounded since no layers can be distinguished in the movement of bed load. Any movement of the bed load in layers or in sheets must be due necessarily to some local and temporary combination of several factors.

The tractive force being by definition proportionate to the square of flow velocity, Eq. (1.2.6−1) is in keeping with the conditions suggested by Velikanov, because q_B is proportionate to the fourth power of flow velocity, v^4.

According to Eq. (1.2.6−1) the rate of transport is proportionate to $(\tau_0 - \tau_c)$, the effective tractive force. Theoretically this conclusion is objectionable because the critical tractive force τ_c has been shown in connection with the law of variable critical tractive forces to be essentially a fictitious value that does not exist in bed load transportation.

In analogy it should be noted here that in considerations on bed load movement the critical velocity v_c, as well as the critical discharge q_c are nonexistent fictitious velocities or discharges just like the critical tractive force.

The circumstance that in a particular case it is possible to use the effective values $(\tau_0 - \tau_c)$, or $(v - v_c)$ and $(q - q_c)$ for computing the rate of transport implies obviously that in particular series of experiments the hydraulic characteristics of flow are such that the variability of τ_c, v_c and q_c is negligible.

The role of the effective tractive forces in the determination of q_B can be illustrated in the following way.

According to the law of variable critical tractive forces, in the relation

$$\tau_c = f_c(\gamma_1 - \gamma)d \qquad (1.2.6-2)$$

244

the dimensionless resistance coefficient of Shields

$$f_c = \frac{\tau_c}{(\gamma_1 - \gamma)d} \qquad (1.2.6-3)$$

for a bed load of particle size d and specific gravity γ_1 and for a fluid of given specific gravity γ, is not a constant value but one which depends on several other hydraulic properties of flow. If v (m²/sec) is the kinematic viscosity of water, g (m/sec²) is acceleration due to gravity, D(m) the hydraulic radius or the mean depth of flow and S is the slope of the energy grade line, then in accordance with the law of variable critical tractive forces the dimensionless resistance coefficient f_c depends, besides the specific gravities γ_1 and γ, further the particle diameter d, also on the dimensionless ratio

$$\frac{d}{v^{2/3} g^{-1/3}} = \frac{d}{A} \qquad (1.2.6-4)$$

and either on the relative roughness D/d or on the slope S.

In analogy to f_c prevailing at the critical condition the coefficient

$$f_0 = \frac{\tau_0}{(\gamma_1 - \gamma)d} = \frac{\gamma DS}{(\gamma_1 - \gamma)d} \qquad (1.2.6-5)$$

is computed with the actual values of flow depth and slope and thus since

$$\tau_0 - \tau_c = (f_0 - f_c)[(\gamma_1 - \gamma)d] \qquad (1.2.6-6)$$

for a given combination of γ_1, γ and d, although f_0 is constant, the magnitude of f_c will be variable depending on the reduction of either depth or slope or of both so that it is obviously unsuited for describing the rate of transport unequivocally.

The variation of f_c and, in turn, of $(f_0 - f_c)$ is strikingly illustrated by the following numerical example.

Let the diameter of the bed load particle be $d = 0.047$ cm, the depth of flow $D = 9.4$ cm, the slope $S = 0.000254$, and the water temperature 20 deg. C. According to the three-variable graphical relation

$$f_c = F\left(\frac{d}{v^{2/3} g^{-1/3}}, \frac{D}{d}\right) \qquad (1.2.6-7)$$

(see *Fig. 1.2.4−12*), since $D/d = 200$ and $d/(v^{2/3}g^{-1/3}) = 10$, the coefficient $f_c = 0.0155$.

From Eq. (1.2.6−5)

$$f_0 = \frac{\gamma DS}{(\gamma_1 - \gamma)d} = \frac{1 \cdot 9.4 \cdot 0.000\,254}{(2.65 - 1) \cdot 0.047} = 0.031$$

will be constant and thus

$$(f_0 - f_c) = 0.031 - 0.0155 = 0.0155$$

However, if the dimensionless resistance coefficient f_c is determined from the three-variable graphical relation

$$f_c = F\left(\frac{d}{v^{2/3} g^{-1/3}}, \ S\right) \tag{1.2.6-8}$$

(see *Fig. 1.2.4–13*), the value corresponding to $S = 0.000254$ and $d/A = 10$ will become $f_c = 0.0255$.

Since f_0 is unchanged, $f_0 = 0.031$, from Eq. (1.2.6–8) the effective value becomes $(f_0 - f_c) = 0.031 - 0.0255 = 0.0055$, i.e. appreciably smaller than the value computed with the value of f_c found on the basis of the relation expressed by Eq. (1.2.6–7).

This difference is explained by the law of variable critical tractive forces. In fact, the $f_c = 0.0155$ value determined on the basis of Eq. (1.2.6–7) would only reflect the critical condition if the slope corresponding to this value in Eq. (1.2.6–8) were $S = 0.000127$. The actual slope is, however, $S = 0.000254$, or twice as steep, and so the bed load is transported.

On the other hand, if the actual slope were considered on the basis of the relation under Eq. (1.2.6–8), the relative roughness $D/d = 77$ would correspond at the critical condition to the resulting $f_c = 0.0255$ as indicated by Eq. (1.2.6–7), so that the depth of flow would be not more than $D = 77 \cdot 0.047 = 3.62$ cm. The actual depth is $D = 9.4$ cm, i.e. greater and, therefore, bed load is transported.

It will be clearly perceived from the foregoing that for a given combination of d, γ_1, γ, D and S values the quantities f_c or τ_c pertaining to incipient motion, i.e. to the critical condition cannot be determined uniquely. In such cases fictitious critical values can only be considered and, depending on whether S, D or both are decreased simultaneously, different values will be obtained for f_c. Since, however, in bed load transportation under particular conditions both D and S are fixed, the f_c or τ_c quantities describing the critical condition are necessarily nonexistent, fictitious values.

Consequently, for reasons explained above, the relation of Du Boys cannot be accepted as physically or theoretically well founded and, owing to the inclusion of effective tractive forces, the relation can be determined only on the basis of a series of experiments for a rather limited range of validity.

The assumption on which the transport relation of A. A. Kalinske is founded implies that the movement of the bed load is not a steady one but fluctuates and varies in time in accordance with the turbulent velocity pulsations.

On the basis of theoretical considerations A. A. Kalinske has derived the relation

$$\frac{q_B}{U_* d \gamma_1} = 2.5 \theta \left(\frac{\tau_c}{\tau_0}\right) = F\left(\frac{\tau_c}{\tau_0}\right) \tag{1.2.6-9}$$

Fig. 1.2.6—1. Kalinske's bed load transport relation for uniform bed load material. Experimental data of several authors. After Zeller

where $U_* = \sqrt{gDS}$, the shear velocity while Θ denotes a function that cannot be determined analytically. The relation under Eq. (1.2.6—9) has been plotted in *Fig. 1.2.6—1*. Although the experimental results of several authors have been entered, the correlation in the graph will be seen to be a fairly close one. This circumstance may be regarded to support the conclusion that the theoretical foundations of the relation are sound and physically justified. The relation is presented in a dimensionless form and is one of the first theoretically correct relations.

A drawback of Kalinske's relation is that the function $F(\tau_c/\tau_0)$, as mentioned before, can be determined by experiment only. This implies clearly the same as has been noted in connection with the relation of Du Boys, namely that τ_c is not a unique value but is, in fact, a non-existent fictitious value. Since, however, in any experimental determination an actual dimensionless measure of the transport rate is established, the error introduced thereby is negligible, especially under more or less comparable conditions of observations. It should also be obvious from the foregoing that this relation cannot be applied to natural water courses.

Since several dimensionless parameters representing the weight of bed load q_B [kp/sec m] transported in unit time and unit width will be introduced in the following, it is advisable to adopt a uniform system of notation.

H. A. Einstein used the notation Φ for his parameter measuring the rate of transport. Accepting and adopting this notation for the different transport parameters, we shall use a subscript consisting of the first letter of the author by whom it was introduced. Accordingly, the parameter of Kalinske will be denoted subsequently as Φ_K in other words the notation

$$\Phi_K = \frac{q_B}{U_* d\gamma_1} \tag{1.2.6-10}$$

will be introduced.

Relying upon theoretical considerations and taking into account the experimental results obtained by himself and by several other investigators, I. I. Levi related the rate of bed load transport — exceptionally in (m³/sec m) units — in terms of the mean and critical velocities v and v_c, respectively, of the relative roughness d/D and of the sediment Froude number $v/\sqrt{gd}$ by the expression

$$q_B = 0.002 \left(\frac{v}{\sqrt{gd}}\right)^3 d(v - v_c) \left(\frac{d}{D}\right)^{0.25} \tag{1.2.6-11}$$

and expressed the ratio thereof to discharge as

$$\Phi_{Le} = 0.002 \left(\frac{v}{\sqrt{gd}}\right)^3 \left(\frac{d}{D}\right)^{1.25} \left(1 - \frac{v_c}{v}\right) \tag{1.2.6-12}$$

The relation of Levi may be regarded as a certain transition between the theoretical and empirical relations. Theoretically the rate of transport is indeed a function of the Froude number and of relative roughness. On the other hand, the relation may be rejected, since the specific gravities of both bed load and water are omitted, further a fictitious critical velocity, nonexistent in bed load movement is also involved. As to the velocities it has generally been recognized by now that the incipient movement of bed load is controlled by the law of variable critical velocities. The theoretical considerations concerning the critical tractive force made in connection with Du Boys' relation and the conclusions drawn from the numerical example introduced there apply to the variable critical velocity.

It should be noted further, that Levi's relation satisfies the criterion of Velikanov, since the rate of transport is proportionate to v^4.

A relation founded on probability theory was introduced by H. A. Einstein (1942) and C. B. Brown (1943). They assumed that the probability of a particular bed load grain to start moving within a certain period of time could be related to the rate of transport, to the diameter of the particle, to its specific gravity and to a certain time factor which depends on the ratio of the fall velocity and the diameter of the bed load particle. The same probability can be expressed as a function of the ratio of the forces exerted by flow and of the resistances to

248

movement. The rate of transport formula of Einstein—Brown is obtained by equating the two probabilities.

With μ (kp sec/m^2) denoting the coefficient of dynamic viscosity of the fluid, v (m^2/sec) the coefficient of kinematic viscosity, ρ_1 (kp sec^2/m^4) and ρ (kp sec^2/m^4) the densities of the bed load and the fluid, respectively, $\rho'_{.} = (\rho_1 - \rho)/\rho$ then, according to W. W. Rubey, the fall velocity of a bed load particle of d diameter is from Eq. (1.1.2−32)

$$\omega = \sqrt{\frac{2}{3}\,\rho'\,gd + \frac{36\mu^2}{\rho^2 d^2}} - \frac{6\mu}{\rho d} \qquad (1.2.6-13)$$

The time factor is

$$F = \frac{\omega}{\rho'^{1/2}\,g^{1/2}\,d^{1/2}} = \sqrt{\frac{2}{3} + \frac{36v^2}{gd^3\left(\dfrac{\gamma_1}{\gamma}-1\right)}} - \sqrt{\frac{36v^2}{gd^3\left(\dfrac{\gamma_1}{\gamma}-1\right)}} \qquad (1.2.6-14)$$

The transport parameter which, in distinction to Einstein's parameter, will be denoted by Φ' is

$$\Phi' = \frac{q_{\mathrm{B}}}{\gamma\,\sqrt{g\left(\dfrac{\gamma_1}{\gamma}-1\right)}\,F d^{3/2}} \qquad (1.2.6-15)$$

This latter has been termed the intensity of transport by the authors. The intensity of bed load transport Φ' is a function of the parameter Ψ which is called the intensity of flow. The parameter is essentially the inverse of the dimensionless resistance coefficient f_0 expressed by Eq. (1.2.6−5) in the foregoing, so that

$$\Psi = \frac{d}{DS}\,\frac{(\rho_1 - \rho)}{\rho} = \frac{(\gamma_1 - \gamma)d}{\tau_0} \qquad (1.2.6-16)$$

On the basis of a variety of experimental results the relation of Φ' and Ψ has been represented for bed load of uniform particle size in the semilogarithmic plot of *Fig. 1.2.6−2*.

For bed load of uniform particle size the numerical form of the relation is

$$\Phi' = \frac{e^{-0.391\Psi}}{0.465} \qquad (1.2.6-17)$$

For a bed load material comprising fractions of different size the relation is shown in *Fig. 1.2.6−3*, where the diameter d_{40} (i.e. the diameter at 40% by weight of the material passing) is regarded as effective. The scatter of experimental results is considerable.

Fig. 1.2.6—2. The Einstein—Brown rate of transport relation for uniform bed load material, indicating the results of several authors

Fig. 1.2.6—3. The Einstein—Brown rate of transport relation for bed load of mixed particle sizes, indicating the results of several authors

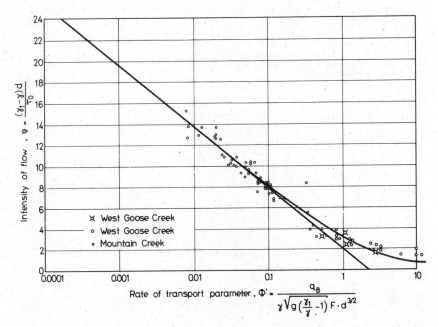

Fig. 1.2.6—4. Evaluation of the Einstein—Brown rate of transport relation on the basis of observations on three creeks. After Einstein

The Einstein—Brown relation is a rather complex one and since the dimensionless parameter F can only be computed from the fall velocity which, in turn, is difficult to determine, the use of this relation is cumbersome for practical purposes.

Although the determination of the rate of transport by this formula involves lengthy computation work, the relation is physically well founded and theoretically sound beyond doubt. Moreover, as will be perceived from *Fig. 1.2.6—4*, the results of field measurements on three minor water courses fit very well to the curve. On the other hand, observation data obtained on major streams have failed to support this relation; thus considerable differences have been experienced when processing measurement data obtained for instance on the Danube, the Tisza, Sajo and Hernad rivers.

The greatest advantage of the Einstein—Brown relations is that essentially it is the first theoretical relation emphasizing that the rate of transport q_B is primarily a function of the parameter Ψ.

The parameter Ψ has already been shown to be substantially proportionate to the inverse of the parameter f_0 but it is also obvious that

$$\Psi = \frac{gd}{U_*^2} \frac{\rho_1 - \rho}{\rho} = \frac{1}{Fr_{*s}} \frac{\rho_1 - \rho}{\rho} \qquad (1.2.6-18)$$

Consequently it is also proportionate to the inverse of the sediment shear velocity Froude number.

Fig. 1.2.6—5. Evaluation of the Einstein—Brown rate of transport relation on the basis of several experimental results. After Rouse

Practically all of the theoretically well founded rate-of-transport formulae will be demonstrated subsequently to depend on the parameters Ψ or f_0.

H. Rouse has shown the Φ' vs. Ψ relation to be represented even more strikingly in a log-log plot. According to *Fig. 1.2.6—5*

$$\Phi' = 40 \left(\frac{1}{\Psi}\right)^3 \qquad (1.2.6-19)$$

For a bed load of $\gamma_1 = 2.65$ (p/cm³) specific gravity and a fluid of $v = 0.01$ (cm²/sec) kinematic viscosity Rouse has succeeded in demonstrating that the dimensionless number F involved in Eq. (1.2.6–14) is 0.81 with a fair degree of approximation up to 1–10 mm particle diameters. Thus the relation under Eq. (1.2.6–19) assumes the form

$$\frac{q_B}{\gamma \sqrt{g\left(\frac{\gamma_1}{\gamma} - 1\right)} F d^{3/2}} = 40 \left(\frac{\tau_0}{(\gamma_1 - \gamma)d}\right)^3 \qquad (1.2.6{-}20)$$

whence the rate of transport is

$$q_B = 40 \frac{0.81 \sqrt{g\gamma}}{(\gamma_1 - \gamma)^{5/2}} \frac{\tau_0^3}{d^{3/2}} = C_s \frac{\tau_0^3}{d^{3/2}} \qquad (1.2.6{-}21)$$

With the values $\gamma = 1$ (p/cm³), $\gamma_1 = 2.65$ (p/cm³) and $g = 981$ (cm/sec²) we have $C_s = 290$ (cm$^{13/2}$/sec p²) or introducing the depth of flow D and the particle diameter d in cm units, in the range $0.1 < d(\text{cm}) < 1.0$

$$q_B = 290 \frac{\tau_0^3}{d^{1.5}} = 290 \frac{D^3 S^3}{d^{1.5}} \; [\text{p/sec cm}] \qquad (1.2.6{-}22)$$

On the basis of additional investigations a new relation, differing to a certain extent from the foregoing one was derived by H. A. Einstein in 1950. Therein the intensity of transport was expressed by the parameter

$$\Phi = \frac{q_B}{\gamma_1} \left(\frac{\rho}{\rho_1 - \rho}\right)^{1/2} \left(\frac{1}{gd^3}\right)^{1/2} \qquad (1.2.6{-}23)$$

while for the intensity of flow he retained the parameter Ψ.

In the case of a bed load material composed of uniform particles the rate of transport is given by

$$\Phi = F(\Psi) \qquad (1.2.6{-}24)$$

where the probability p of a particle being set into motion is expressed as

$$p = 1 - \frac{1}{\sqrt{\pi}} \int_{-B_*\Psi - 1/\eta_0}^{+B_*\Psi - 1/\eta_0} e^{-t^2} dt = \frac{A_* \Phi}{1 + A_* \Phi} \qquad (1.2.6{-}25)$$

and $A_* = 43.5$, $B_* = 0.143$, $\eta_0 = 0.5$, while t is a variable for integration.

For bed load of uniform particle size, Eq. (1.2.6–24) is shown in *Fig. 1.2.6–6*.

For bed load material comprising several fractions the rate of transport is determined by the relation of

$$\Phi_* = \frac{i_G}{i_g} \Phi \qquad (1.2.6{-}26)$$

253

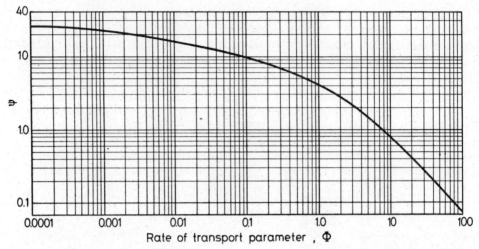

Fig. 1.2.6—6. Einstein's rate of transport relation for uniform bed load material. After Zeller

and of

$$\Psi_* = \xi Y \frac{(\beta/\beta_x)^2}{\theta} \Psi \qquad (1.2.6-27)$$

that is by

$$\Phi_* = F(\Psi_*) \qquad (1.2.6-28)$$

In the above expression i_G per i_g denotes the relative area of the bottom covered by a bed load particle of a particular diameter. ξ, Y, $(\beta/\beta_x)^2$ and Θ are correction factors allowing for the effect of the non-uniform particle sizes.

The rate-of-transport relation suggested by Einstein is theoretically perfect and physically well founded. From the relation the rate-of-transport parameter will be seen to depend again on Ψ, the intensity of flow. If the bed load is composed of fractions of different size, the rate of transport is to be computed for each separately, — an extremely lengthy and cumbersome task. In this respect a certain simplification is possible, and for particle sizes within not too wide limits Einstein has suggested the use of the diameter pertaining to 35% by weight passing in the computations.

Einstein's method was somewhat modified in 1955 by B. R. Colby and C. H. Hembree. The modification first of all affected his method of determining the full rate of transport since this applies essentially to the transport of predominantly suspended load. The principle underlying the methods has remained unaffected by these modifications. In the modified method the velocities and depth of flow are measured, the correction factors are slightly altered and the depth is used instead of the hydraulic radius R'_b.

254

Owing to its complexity Einstein's relation is only valid for a limited range exactly on account of the universal constants. Several investigators believe that the use of this relation is restricted to plain-land streams. Certain objections can be raised to the distinction of the hydraulic radius according to particle and shape resistance. This distinction is not always simple to perform.

Nevertheless, on the basis of experimental results and observations in the field, it is believed safe to state that *among the rate-of-transport relations presently known that of Einstein has proved most reliable.*

Adopting an approach similar to that of Einstein a transport relation was derived in 1958 by S. Sato, H. Kikkawa and K. Ashida. C_L is a coefficient representing the lift exerted by turbulence, r is the portion of the unit surface area exposed to the lifting force, U_* is the shear velocity, whence at any arbitrary distance y above the bottom the velocity is $u = aU_*$, the velocity of the bottom layer is $u_0 = bU_*$, further τ_0 and $\tau_c = f_c(\gamma_1 - \gamma)d$ are the actual and the critical tractive forces. With the above notations for determining the rate of bed load transport q_B, the expression

$$q_B = r\frac{bC_L a^2}{2\sqrt{2\pi}}F_1\left(\frac{\tau_c}{\tau_0}\right)\tau_0 U_* \qquad (1.2.6-29)$$

was derived on the basis of theoretical considerations.

After certain simplifications found permissible by experiments, the function $F_0(\tau_c/\tau_0)$ could be expressed as 2.517 times the function $F(\tau_c/\tau_0)$ pertaining to τ_c/τ_0 shown in *Fig. 1.2.6 – 7.* Thus

$$F_1(\tau_c/\tau_0) = 2.517 F(\tau_c/\tau_0) \qquad (1.2.6-30)$$

and Eq. (1.2.6 – 29) assumes the new form

$$q_B = 2.517 r\frac{bC_L a^2}{2\sqrt{2\pi}}F(\tau_c/\tau_0)\tau_0 U_* \qquad (1.2.6-31)$$

In dimensionless form the latter becomes

$$\Phi_{\text{S-K-A}} = \frac{q_B}{\tau_0 U_* F(\tau_c/\tau_0)} = 2.517 r\frac{bC_L a^2}{2\sqrt{2\pi}} = A' \qquad (1.2.6-32)$$

Eq. (1.2.6 – 32) is theoretically sound but, owing to the complexity of the terms on the right-hand side and to the difficulty of assigning a physical interpretation to the coefficients r, b, C_L and a, in the present form it is impracticable.

For this reason Sato and his co-workers assume A' to depend primarily on the distribution of the bottom velocity, or even more so on the ratio of the mean velocity in the bottom layer and the shear velocity. Moreover, since the ratio of mean velocity and shear velocity can in general be expressed in terms of a factor representing roughness, it is justified to assumed that A' is related to Manning's

Fig. 1.2.6−7. The rate of transport
relation suggested by Sato et al.

roughness coefficient n, which implies naturally that

$$\Phi_{S-K-A} = F(n) \tag{1.2.6−33}$$

saying that the rate of transport is a function of the roughness coefficient n.

Using the results of Gilbert and those of experiments performed at the Public Works Research Institute of the Ministry of Housing, Japan, the relation expressed by Eq. (1.2.6−33) has been determined graphically as shown in *Fig. 1.2.6−8*. According to the figure for $n \geqq 0.025$

$$\Phi_{S-K-A} = \frac{q_B}{\tau_0\, U_*\, F(\tau_c/\tau_0)} = 1 \tag{1.2.6−34}$$

for $n \leqq 0.025$

$$\Phi_{S-K-A} = \left(\frac{1}{40\,n}\right)^{3.5} \tag{1.2.6−35}$$

Sato and his co-workers have found the relations under Eqs (1.2.6−34) and (1.2.6−35) to be suited for practical use. As will be perceived from *Fig. 1.2.6−7*, for low values of τ_c/τ_0 and relatively large n values the use of the relation

$$q_B = \tau_0\, U_* \tag{1.2.6−36}$$

is considered permissible to alluvial streams.

256

Fig. 1.2.6—8. Bed load transport parameter of Sato et al. vs. Manning's roughness coefficient, according to different experimental results

As admitted by Sato and his co-workers, their relations are to be checked against further experimental and empirical evidence.

The transport relation suggested by Sato and his co-workers, although founded on theoretical considerations, is to be regarded rather as an empirical formula.

1.2.6.3. Experimental relations. Relying first of all on the experimental results of Gilbert, the relation

$$q_B = \frac{7000}{d^{1/2}} S_0^{3/2} (q - q_c) \qquad (1.2.6-37)$$

was derived in 1934 by A. Shoklitsch for estimating the weight of bed load transported in unit width and unit time. In the expression q_B is the rate of bed load transport (kp/m sec), d the particle diameter in mm, S_0 is the bottom slope in ‰, q is the water-discharge/unit width (m³/sec m), while q_c is the critical discharge at incipient motion. The latter is computed by Schoklitsch from the expression

$$q_c = 1.944 \cdot 10^{-5} \frac{d}{S_0^{4/3}} \qquad (1.2.6-38)$$

For a bed load material composed of fractions of different size, rates of transport determined for each fraction are to be summarized.

The relation of Schoklitsch has found widespread use in practice but in many cases, especially in that of plain-land streams, the computed results disagreed drastically with those actually observed.

No physical interpretation whatsoever can be given to the formula of Schoklitsch and, owing to the fictitious critical discharge q_c involved therein, its theoretical soundness is also questionable.

Besides the familiar dimensionless parameter f_c for characterizing critical conditions a relation based on experimental results was developed in 1936 by Shields for estimating the rate of transport q_B. In this relation the rate of transport is expressed in a dimensionless form and therefore his endeavours should be regarded as entirely original.

In his considerations Shields proceeds from the assumption that the rate of transport is necessarily a function of the dimensionless resistance coefficient

$$f_0 = \frac{\tau_0}{(\gamma_1 - \gamma)d}$$

the critical value thereof controlling the incipient motion of bed load. Also, since in the critical condition, if $\tau_0 = \tau_c$, there is no bed load transport, the parameter characteristic of the rate of transport is logically

$$(f_0 - f_c) = \frac{\tau_0 - \tau_c}{(\gamma_1 - \gamma)d} \qquad (1.2.6-39)$$

The approach adopted by Shields is a highly logical one and made him draw the conclusion that the parameter given by Eq. (1.2.6–39) must not be regarded as the only possible parameter for characterizing the transport rate, but other dimensionless numbers more or less closely related thereto are also conceivable for this purpose. Nevertheless he eventually found that the application of the parameter under Eq. (1.2.6–39) was advisable.

By dimensional analysis, neglecting the effect of viscosity, he found the ratio of the transport rate q_B and discharge q (both related to weight transported in unit time) to depend on some function in which the Froude number, the relative roughness, the submerged specific gravity of bed load in water, the slope and some shape factor are involved. These, in turn, can be expressed by some function F_2 of the parameter under Eq. (1.2.6–39). According to his basic assumption

$$\frac{q_B}{q} F_1\left(\frac{v^2}{gD}, \ \frac{d}{D}, \ \frac{(\gamma_1 - \gamma)}{\gamma}, \ S, \ \text{shape factors}\right) =$$

$$= F_2\left[\frac{(\tau_0 - \tau_c)}{(\gamma_1 - \gamma)d}\right] \qquad (1.2.6-40)$$

Fig. 1.2.6—9. Shields's transport equation

which — by introducing the function F_1 in the form $F_1 = (\gamma_1 - \gamma)/\gamma S$ and with due consideration to experimental results — eventually yields — the empirical relation

$$\frac{q_B(\gamma_1 - \gamma)}{q\gamma S} = 10\,\frac{(\tau_0 - \tau_c)}{(\gamma_1 - \gamma)d} \qquad (1.2.6-41)$$

With notations introduced earlier the parameter on the left-hand side of Eq. (1.2.6—41) will hereafter be denoted by Φ_s and thus Shields's rate of transport parameter becomes

$$\Phi_S = 10\,\frac{(\tau_0 - \tau_c)}{(\gamma_1 - \gamma)d} \qquad (1.2.6-42)$$

The relation under Eq. (1.2.6—41) has been determined on the basis of experimental results as indicated in *Fig. 1.2.6—9.*

Considering its essential features the relation of Shields may be regarded as physically sound. The introduction of $(\tau_0 - \tau_c)$ is, however, questionable as mentioned in connection with the relation of Du Boys. Owing to its fictitious value τ_c cannot be determined in a unique manner.

In connection with the parameter Φ_S it is of interest to note the ratio of two resultant quantities (q_B and q) are involved therein, each of which depends on the same independent physical quantities. No objection can be raised to the introduction of such a ratio, but q_B cannot be computed unless q is known. This problem will be recurred to in the examination of the rate of transport parameters.

Shields himself has claimed no general validity for his formula the purpose thereof having been only to offer guidance to designing engineers.

From the results of extensive experimental investigations in 1948 Meyer-Peter and Meyer-Peter — Müller derived a rate of transport formula of general validity. The publication of the relation was precedeed by almost 20 years of experimental work and, aside from the Einstein relation, this is probably the most widely used in engineering practice. The general use of this relation is not restricted to Europe. The transport relation itself has undergone several modifications during the long experimental period. In its first form it was published in 1934 as

$$q^{2/3} S = ad + bq_B^{2/3} \qquad (1.2.6-43)$$

which is solved for the rate of transport q_B (kp/sec m). In the expression S is the slope, d (m) the particle diameter, q (m³/sec m) the discharge while y and b are dimensional constants having the values $a = 0.17$ and $b = 0.004$ as long as the foregoing dimensions are used. Eq (1.2.6−43) applies to coarse-grained (5 to 30 mm) natural bed load material.

In the course of further experiments granulated coal and barite were used besides the natural bed load material and eventually the following relation of general validity, known as the Meyer-Peter — Müller relation was arrived at

$$\gamma R_s S_R = \frac{Q_0}{Q} \left(\frac{k_s}{k_r} \right)^{3/2} \gamma D S_e =$$

$$= A'' (\gamma_1 - \gamma) d + B'' \left(\frac{\gamma}{g} \right)^{1/3} q_B^{2/3} \left(\frac{\gamma_1 - \gamma}{\gamma_1} \right)^{2/3} \qquad (1.2.6-44)$$

Besides the notations introduced before

R_s = hydraulic radius related to bottom resistance,
S_R = slope of the energy gradient related to bottom resistance,
Q_0 = discharge causing the bed load to be transported, m³/sec,
Q = total discharge, m³/sec,
k_s = Strickler's coefficient of bottom roughness,
k_r = the share of k_s due to the bed load particles, and
$\quad$ $0.5 < k_s/k_r < 1.0$
S_e = slope of the energy gradient,
A'' = 0.047 and
B'' = 0.25 dimensionless parameters.

The Meyer-Peter relation is used extensively for mountain streams, for instance, in Switzerland.

The relation is physically well founded and theoretically correct. In its practical application, however, several difficulties are encountered including the determination of the effective particle size, which is replaced by the diameter at 90% by weight passing. This simplifications is not fully convincing. Several investigators have declared the formula to be useless if large volumes or very slight quantities of bed load are transported. On the other hand, the formula has been used successfully on a number of streams, especially were the bed load material was of a uniform granulometry.

In view of its physical and theoretical soundness, the relation, together with that of Einstein, should be regarded as the most suitable rate-of-transport expression.

In 1958, based on his experiments made at Iowa, as well as on other experimental data available M. A. Laursen constructed a graphical relation for determining the rate of total sediment transport q_t (m³/sec m) in unit width and unit time. In this relation the sediment transported was expressed in volumetric units. In principle this relation lends itself also for the determination of the rate of bed load and suspended load transportation, q_B and q_s, respectively. However, the sediment materials used and the hydraulic characteristics of flow realized in these experiments only cover a range within which the total sediment transport may be taken identical with the suspended load, without introducing an error surpassing that of measurement. In fact, the rate of bed load transportation q_B hardly attained one per cent of the total sediment transport q_t. Owing to this circumstance it would appear more correct to discuss the relation of Laursen together with the methods suggested for determining the movement of suspended sediment. However, in view of the fact that several attempts have recently been made to consider the transport of bed load and suspended sediment together, it is believed justified to mention this formula in the present chapter.

Starting from theoretical considerations, Laursen arrived at the conclusion that the parameter mentioned before

$$\frac{\sqrt{\tau_0/\rho}}{\omega} = \frac{U_*}{\omega} = t \qquad (1.2.6-45)$$

is one of the most important indicators of bed load transport. He claims the other important parameter to be the tractive force of which only a part, remaining after deductions for frictions and other resistances, is an effective conribution to bed load transport. Accordingly, rather than the full value (γDS), only the part thereof computed from roughness and mean velocity and denoted by τ_0' is taken into consideration by Laursen. Adopting Manning's formula, and Strickler's expression for finding the roughness coefficient n the effective tractive force is given as

$$\tau_0' = \frac{v^2 d^{1/3}}{30 D^{1/3}} \qquad (1.2.6-46)$$

261

It is pointed out by Laursen that, barring the case of dune-covered beds, the substitution $\tau_0' = \tau_0$ is permissible in the majority of cases.

Further considerations led him to the conclusion that if the critical tractive force pertaining to a particular size fraction is τ_c, the rate of transport is characterized essentially by the value $(\tau_0/\tau_c - 1)$.

Relying finally rather on practical experience than on theoretical considerations, allowance is made in the transport rate parameter for the 7/6th power of relative roughness, i.e. $(d/D)^{7/6}$ as well.

The rate of transport is expressed in terms of the ratio of the discharge q and the sediment q_t transported in unit width and unit time, both expressed as percentages by weight. In other words the parameter

$$\bar{c} = \frac{q_t}{q} \frac{\gamma_1}{\gamma} 100 \quad (\%) \tag{1.2.6-47}$$

or, since the specific gravity of sediment material is in general 2.65, the expression

$$\bar{c} = 265 \frac{q_t}{q} \quad (\%) \tag{1.2.6-48}$$

is introduced.

With the foregoing, the transport parameter Φ_L is written in the form

$$\Phi_L = \frac{\bar{c}}{\left(\dfrac{d}{D}\right)^{7/6} \left(\dfrac{\tau_0'}{\tau_c} - 1\right)} \tag{1.2.6-49}$$

and the relation

$$\Phi_L = F\left(\frac{U_*}{\omega}\right) \tag{1.2.6-50}$$

is determined on the basis of experimental results. The graphical plot of the relation is shown in *Fig. 1.2.6−10*.

Since the graphical relation yields not more than the transport rate for a single-size fraction, the total rate of transport of sediment including different p fractions is computed as

$$\bar{c} = \Sigma p \left(\frac{d}{D}\right)^{7/6} \left(\frac{\tau_0'}{\tau_c} - 1\right) F\left(\frac{U_*}{\omega}\right) \quad (\%) \tag{1.2.6-51}$$

The use of the relation

$$\frac{d}{v^{2/3} g^{-1/3}} = F\left(\frac{gd}{U_*^2} \frac{\gamma_1 - \gamma}{\gamma}\right) \tag{1.2.6-52}$$

according to Eq. (1.2.3−27) or *Fig. 1.2.3−6* has permitted the author to determine the values U_*/ω at the different boundary conditions of bed load movement,

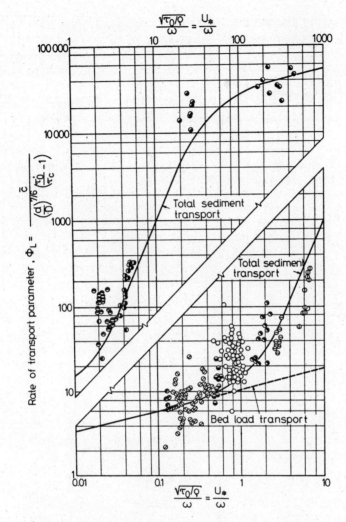

Fig. 1.2.6—10. Laursen's total sediment transport relation

for individual size fractions and to construct the three-variable relation

$$\Phi_L = F\left(\frac{gd}{U_*^2} \frac{(\gamma_1 - \gamma)}{\gamma}, \quad \frac{d}{\nu^{2/3} g^{-1/3}} \right) \qquad (1.2.6-53)$$

illustrated in *Fig. 1.2.6—11.*

The graphical relation introduced by Laursen and by the author should be regarded as one representing experimental results. Although no direct physical interpretation is possible, the relation is mathematically unobjectionable. An obvious drawback is that no allowance is made for the law of variable tractive forces.

263

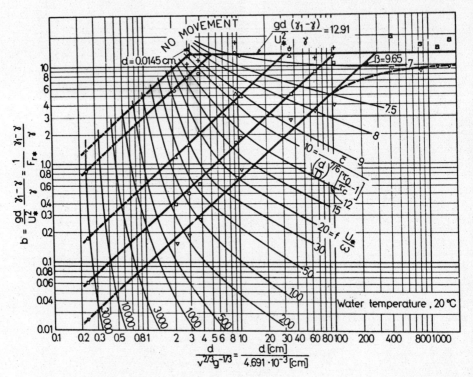

Fig. 1.2.6−11. Channel stability factor vs. $\dfrac{d}{v^{2/3}g^{-1/3}}$ related to Laursen's transport parameter

For determining the rate of bed load transport I. V. Egiazaroff (1949−1965) introduced the parameter

$$p'' = \frac{q_B}{\gamma q} \qquad (1.2.6-54)$$

i.e. the ratio of discharge q and the weight of bed load transported in unit width and unit time converted to volumetric units using the specific gravity of water. Having introduced subsequently the effect of slope, the transport parameter derived eventually on the basis of different considerations related p'' to the square root of slope as

$$\Phi_E = \frac{p''}{S^{1/2}} = \frac{q_B}{\gamma q S^{1/2}} \qquad (1.2.6-55)$$

From experimental evidence obtained by himself and others Egiazaroff has found, for the case of completely developed turbulence, a close correlation to exist between Φ_E and the ratio of the effective tractive force $(\tau_0 - \tau_c)$ and the crit-

264

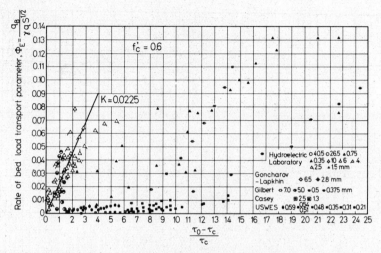

Fig. 1.2.6—12. Egiazaroff's transport relation for fully developed turbulence (cf. the large symbols in the plot)

ical value τ_c thereof. The relation thus obtained is

$$\Phi_{\mathrm{E}} = K \frac{(\tau_0 - \tau_c)}{\tau_c} = K \left(\frac{RS}{f_c \rho' d} - 1 \right) \qquad (1.2.6-56)$$

since

$$\tau_0 = \gamma RS, \quad \tau_c = f_c(\gamma_1 - \gamma)d \quad \text{and} \quad \frac{(\gamma_1 - \gamma)}{\gamma} = \frac{(\rho_1 - \rho)}{\rho} = \rho'$$

The relation under Eq.(1.2.6−56) is shown in *Fig. 1.2.6−12* and the measurement data relating to completely developed turbulence (indicated by large symbols in the figure) will be seen to display a close relationship, whereas in the range of incomplete turbulence the data (indicated by small symbols in the figure) will be seen to scatter considerably.

Further investigations indicate the possibility of determining a relation similar to Eq. (1.2.6−56) for the ranges of completely developed turbulence, transition and laminar flow, even for both hydraulically smooth and rough beds by introducing the factor $\xi = v_y/v_0$, where v_y is the velocity in the main direction of flow at the center of gravity of the particle, while v_0 is some representative constant velocity. The relation itself is of the form

$$\Phi_{\mathrm{E}} = K\xi \frac{(\tau_0 - \tau_c)}{\tau_c} \qquad (1.2.6-57)$$

which, for complete and incomplete turbulence, has been plotted in *Fig. 1.2.6−13*. For both plots Egiazaroff assumes the value $f_c' = 0.6 = $ constant. This coefficient

Fig. 1.2.6—13. Egiazaroff's modified transport relation for the ranges of fully developed turbulence, transition and laminar flow

is found from Shields coefficient $f_c = \tau_c/(\gamma_1 - \gamma)d$, from the resistance coefficient $\lambda = 2\tau_c/v^2$, $\xi_c = v_{yc}/v_0$ and the coefficient of friction C_x, from the relation

$$f_c = \frac{2}{3} f'_c \frac{\lambda}{C_x \xi_c^2} \qquad (1.2.6-58)$$

Considering the values of τ_0 and τ_c and introducing the notation

$$\rho' = \frac{\rho_1 - \rho}{\rho} = \frac{\gamma_1 - \gamma}{\gamma}$$

the rate of bed load transport is found from the expression

$$q_B = K \frac{\xi}{f_c \rho'} \gamma q S^{3/2} \frac{R}{d} \left(1 - f_c \rho' \frac{d}{RS}\right) \qquad (1.2.6-59)$$

266

The scatter observable in *Fig. 1.2.6−13* has been attributed by Egiazaroff to particle shape and to occasional variations in the coefficient f'_c.

It is of interest to note that Eq. (1.2.6−59) contains the relative roughness and the Shields parameter which − as will be recalled − is essentially identical with the sediment shear velocity Froude number.

As mentioned in *Chapter 1.2.3*, Egiazaroff has attempted to express the Shields resistance coefficient for any particular fraction d_i in a bed load material of mixed size composition. Accordingly

$$f_{ci} = \frac{\tau_c}{(\gamma_1 - \gamma)d} = \frac{0.06\phi/C_x}{(\lg 19d_i)^2} \qquad (1.2.6-60)$$

where d is the weighted diameter of the mixed bed load particles, d_i is the diameter of the fraction under consideration, ϕ is the shape factor, and C_x the coefficient of frictional resistance.

For computing f_{ci} in the case of complete developed turbulence, on the basis of more recent investigations, Egiazaroff suggested the formula

$$f_{ci} = \frac{0.1}{\left(\lg 19 \dfrac{d_i}{d}\right)^2} \qquad (1.2.6-61)$$

With due consideration to Eq. (1.2.6−61) the transport parameter of the fraction d_i in a mixture of different fractions becomes

$$\Phi_E = K \left(\frac{RS}{f_{ci}\,\rho'\,d_i} - 1\right) \qquad (1.2.6-62)$$

Egiazaroff's transport relation as stated by himself in the course of his studies is based essentially on the concept of effective energies $(N_0 - N_c)$*. $N_0 = \tau_0 v$ and $N_c = \tau_c v_c$. The basic idea underlying the approach of Egiazaroff is that the relative effective tractive forces $(\tau_0 - \tau_c)/\tau_c$ can be replaced by the relative effective energy. Thus theoretically in the case of incomplete turbulence

$$\Phi_E = K \frac{(N_0 - N_c)}{N_c} \qquad (1.2.6-63)$$

Owing to drag resistances, an energy N_0' smaller than the complete energy N_0 is available for transporting the bed load. With R' as the hydraulic radius remaining after substractions for drag resistances,

$$\frac{N_0'}{N_0} = \frac{\omega_{(C)}\,\tau_0'}{\omega\tau_c} = \frac{\omega_{(C)}\,R'\,S}{\omega f_c\,\rho'\,d} \qquad (1.2.6-64)$$

---

* N_0 and N_c are essentially the actual, respectively, critical output per unit surface area.

where $\omega_{(C)}$ is the fall velocity reduced by the sediment concentration C, while ω is the fall velocity in clear water.

By the introduction of the concept of relative effective energy the formula may be classified among the physically well-founded ones, but further investigations are believed to be necessary until it can be put to practical use.

Bed load transportation has been investigated in smooth and solid channels by R. Pedroli (1963). Owing to the very assumption of solid channel, these investigations are by no means suited for determining the rate of bed load transport in alluvial streams. The objective of these experiments was essentially to acquire information on the rate of transport in alluvial channels, from the transport relation applying to solid channel sections constructed on natural streams.

By dimensional analysis Pedroli has succeeded in deriving, for the rate of transport q_B, a relation

$$q_B = F(\tau_0, \ d, \ \gamma_1, \ \nu, \ g) \tag{1.2.6-65}$$

In dimensionless form Pedroli's relation is

$$\frac{\tau_0^{8/5} \, g^{3/5} \, d^{1/5}}{\gamma_1^{8/5} \, \nu^{6/5}} = 1.6 + 0.065 \, \frac{q_B}{\gamma_1 \nu} \tag{1.2.6-66}$$

where, following the convention introduced earlier, the dimensionless transport parameter of Pedroli will be denoted by Φ_P:

$$\Phi_P = \frac{q_B}{\gamma_1 \nu} \tag{1.2.6-67}$$

For particles of $d = 2.65$ and 5.2 mm, Eq. (1.2.6$-$66) is shown in *Fig. 1.2.6$-$14*.

Solving Eq. (1.2.6$-$66) for q_B and assuming that $\nu = 1.2 \cdot 10^{-6}$ (m²/sec) — corresponding to water of 13 deg. C temperature — $g = 9.81$ (m/sec²) and $\gamma_1 = 2,700$ (kp/m³), the simple form eventually obtained becomes

$$q_B = 7.63 \, \tau_0^{8/5} \, d^{1/5} - 0.075 \tag{1.2.6-68}$$

Pedroli's approach is basically correct, the only objection being that the rate of transport depends eventually on τ_0, irrespective of the values which slope S and depth D of flow assume separately. There is, indeed, ample experimental evidence to show that the critical condition as well as the rate of bed load transport itself are characterized by the different values of S and D separately (considering also the relative roughness D/d) rather than by the product SD.

Extensive studies have been conducted into the rate of bed load transport by J. Garde and M. L. Albertson (1961) who compared the formulae of Einstein, Meyer-Peter and Kalinske and, relying on experimental data reported in the literature, introduced the parameters

$$q_B^* = \frac{q_B}{U_* \gamma_1 d} \tag{1.2.6-69}$$

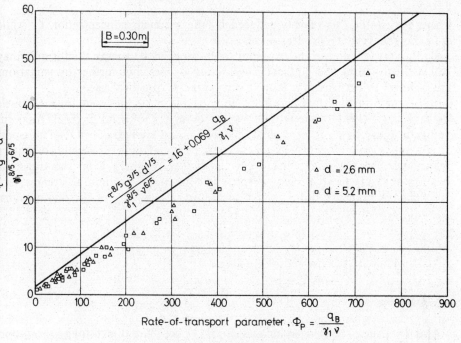

Fig. 1.2.6—14. Pedroli's transport relation

and

$$\tau^* = \frac{\tau_0}{(\gamma_1 - \gamma)d} \tag{1.2.6—70}$$

in the attempt to determine the relation

$$q_B^* = F(\tau^*) \tag{1.2.6—71}$$

As will be perceived from Eq. (1.2.6—69), the rate of transport parameter of Garde and Albertson, denoted in keeping with our convention as Φ_{G-A}, is essentially identical with Kalinske's parameter given by Eq. (1.2.6—10), i.e. $\Phi_{G-A} = = \Phi_K$. It should be evident further that the parameter of Eq. (1.2.6—70) is, according to Eqs (1.2.6—5) and (1.2.6—16), identical with the parameters f_0 and $1/\Psi$, respectively.

The relation given by Eq. (1.2.6—71) is thus well founded both physically and theoretically and is apparently more exact than Kalinske's formula Eq. (1.2.6—9), since here the non-existent fictitious quantity τ_c is not involved.

In spite of the considerable scatter of the observation data in *Fig. 1.2.6—15* constructed on the basis of a wide variety of experimental results, the theoretical groundwork of the relation will be realized as sound. Moreover the range of scatter is still much narrower than in the case of similar relations where the width

269

B of the experimental flume, the depth D of flow, the slope S, the particle diameter d, the specific gravities γ and γ_1 as well as the kinematic viscosity v range between wider limits.

For bed load transported over a smooth bottom Garde and Albertson have derived a relation according to *Fig. 1.2.6 – 16*. The plot is to be regarded as almost perfect and accordingly it is in fair agreement with the relations of Einstein and Kalinske converted appropriately and entered also into the graph.

In the course of further investigations they succeeded in determining similar relations for bed load transport with ripples and dunes on the bottom. As mentioned in their paper, after several preliminary investigations they found a family of curves to be most suited for representing the relation in the case of dunes on the bottom. In this type of presentation the ratio of the resultant mean velocity v and the shear velocity U_*, namely v/U_* has been introduced as the third parameter. This relation is illustrated in *Fig. 1.2.6 – 17*. An almost perfect correlation will be seen to exist between the three parameters of the relation

$$q_B^* = F\left(\tau^*,\ \frac{v}{U_*}\right) \tag{1.2.6–72}$$

In the original relation of Eq. (1.2.6 – 71) the resultant rate of bed load transport q_B has been assumed to depend on the acceleration by gravity g, on the depth of flow D, on slope S, on specific gravities γ and γ_1 of water and bed load, respectively, as well as on the particle diameter d.

Mathematically this assumption implies that the resultant rate of transport is uniquely determined by the six independent physical basic quantities

$$q_B = F(g,\ D,\ S,\ \gamma,\ \gamma_1,\ d) \tag{1.2.6–73}$$

It should be realized that Eq. (1.2.6 – 71) is a dimensionless expression of the relation under Eq. (1.2.6 – 73), obtained by neglecting certain dimensionless groups.

It happens that under the assumption expressed by Eq. (1.2.6 – 73) the six independent physical basic quantities involved determine, in analogy to the rate of bed load transport, also the resultant mean velocity v of the stream, so that the relation

$$v = F(g,\ D,\ S,\ \gamma,\ \gamma_1,\ d) \tag{1.2.6–74}$$

also holds.

If, in keeping with this assumption, the phenomenon were governed exclusively by the six independent physical quantities, then both q_B and v would be resultant quantities and could thus be derived on the basis of Eqs (1.2.6 – 73) and (1.2.6 – 74) from each other and would consequently be no longer independent. In this case Eq. (1.2.6 – 72) would be theoretically incorrect since the resultant rate of transport q_B would be determined, besides the independent variables, by an additional mean velocity v, which depends on the same variables.

270

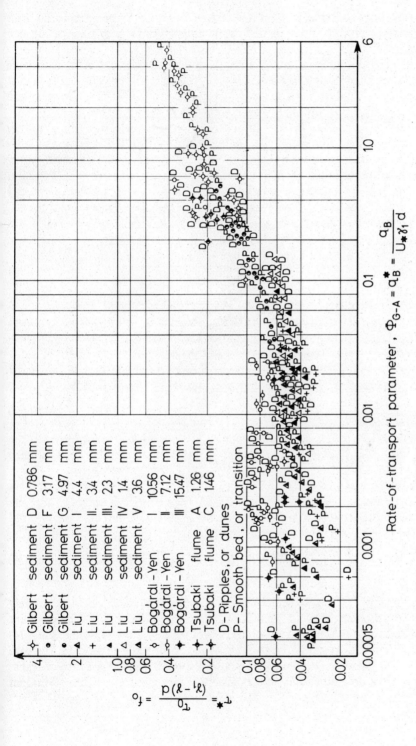

Fig. 1.2.6—15. Resistance coefficient f_0 vs. the transport parameter of Garde and Albertson showing experimental results of several authors

Rate-of-transport parameter, $\Phi_{G-A} = q_B^* = \dfrac{q_B}{U_* \gamma_1 d}$

$\tau_* = \dfrac{\tau_0}{(\gamma - \gamma_1)d} = f_0$

Gilbert	sediment	D	0.786	mm
Gilbert	sediment	F	3.17	mm
Gilbert	sediment	G	4.97	mm
Liu	sediment	I	4.4	mm
Liu	sediment	II.	3.4	mm
Liu	sediment	III.	2.3	mm
Liu	sediment	IV	1.4	mm
Liu	sediment	V	3.6	mm
Bogárdi – Yen		I	10.56	mm
Bogárdi – Yen		II	7.12	mm
Bogárdi – Yen		III	15.47	mm
Tsubaki	flume	A	1.26	mm
Tsubaki	flume	C	1.46	mm

D – Ripples, or dunes
P – Smooth bed, or transition

Fig. 1.2.6—16. Transport relation of Garde and Albertson for smooth bed

Fig. 1.2.6–17. Resistance coefficient f_6 vs. transport parameter of Garde and Albertson for different v/U_* parameter values

18

Actually both the rate of transport q_B and the mean velocity v are affected, besides the six independent physical quantities mentioned in the foregoing, by other independent variables that have been neglected in these considerations. The influence of the neglected variables (for instance, of the turbulent velocity fluctuations, of factors, other than particle size, controlling roughness, etc.) on the resultant value of q_B and v is in general manifest in different ways. Thus for instance if v is observed and is consequently regarded as an independent variable in the determination of q_B, it becomes possible to express the effect of the physical quantities neglected in the original assumption. In this case the introduction of the resultant quantities observed as "fictitious independent variables" should invariably entail an improvement of the relation, by making it closer. For this very reason, the use of such "fictitious independent variables" is theoretically beneficial and not objectionable.

The exceptionally close correlation observable in *Fig. 1.2.6—17* can be attributed to the afore-mentioned causes. In fact, by including the resultant mean velocity v, partial allowance is made for the effect of the neglected independent variables.

The only remark to be added to the foregoing considerations is that the statements relating to the expression under Eqs (1.2.6—72), (1.2.6—73) and (1.2.6—74) apply, of course, to other physical phenomena as well.

When describing phenomena in the mechanics of fluids some physical quantities are often neglected partly for the sake of simplicity, partly for lack of information on factors involved. This is why the resultant values observed directly are often adopted as independent variables. A typical example will be encountered in Section *2.1.4*, in determining empirical relations on suspended sediment transport.

The role of the "fictitious independent variables" is important also in problems of hydraulic similarity. As an example it should be noted that besides specifying the law of velocity distribution it is found necessary to include the relation expressed by the Froude number which is otherwise regarded as a "consequence".

1.2.7. EXAMINATION OF TRANSPORT RELATIONSHIPS

1.2.7.1. Comparison of different transport relationships. It will be found expedient to compare first of all the transport relations derived by theoretical and experimental methods. The point is that for the relations founded on field observations it is difficult to find a common theory or regularity which would permit such a comparison to be made.

A number of transport relations founded on actual observations, several highly reliable ones, have been reported in the literature. Such relations of practical interest have been developed first of all by Soviet investigators (e. g. Polyakov, Shamov, Lopatin, Karaushev, Goncharov). They will be dealt with in *Section 2.1.3*.

The relations of Einstein and Meyer-Peter have already been mentioned as the most reliable ones as to their theoretical and physical foundation. It is therefore obvious that most endeavours have been made to collate these two relations.

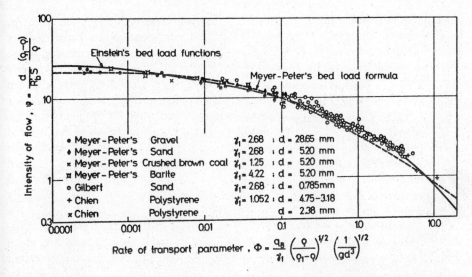

Fig. 1.2.7–1. Comparison of the transport relations by Einstein and Meyer-Peter—Müller for uniform bed load material 0.8 to 30 mm in diameter. After Ning Chien

In his investigations made in 1956 Ning Chien demonstrated that, like the relation of the parameters Ψ involved in Eq. (1.2.6–16) and Φ in Eq. (1.2.6–23) shown for identical particle sizes by Eq. (1.2.6–24), the transport relation of Meyer-Peter and Müller can also be written in terms of Einstein's parameters Ψ and Φ. According to him the new form of the Meyer-Peter—Müller relation is

$$\Phi = \left(\frac{4}{\Psi} - 0.188\right)^{3/2} \qquad (1.2.7-1)$$

From a plot showing the relations under Eqs (1.2.6–24) and (1.2.7–1) simultaneously, the perfect agreement of the two will be clearly perceived. As indicated by *Fig. 1.2.7–1* the agreement is especially good within the range

$$10^{-4} \leqq \Phi \leqq 10$$

In 1949 N. G. Mostafa showed Kalinske's transport relation to be structurally similar to Einstein's relation.

Considering Laursen's Eq. (1.2.6–50) and the relation derived therefrom by the author—Eq. (1.2.6–55),—these will be seen to resemble in structure the relation of Einstein, since according to Eq. (1.2.6–18)

$$\frac{gd}{U_*^2} \frac{\gamma_1 - \gamma}{\gamma} = \Psi$$

in fact, from Eq. (1.2.6 – 18)

$$\Phi_L = F\left(\Psi, \; \frac{d}{v^{2/3} \, g^{-1/3}}\right) \tag{1.2.7-2}$$

By following the theoretical approach used by Sato, Kikkawa and Ashida in deriving their transport relation, the formal composition thereof will be found similar to Einstein's relation.

Examining the parameters Φ_{A-G} in Eq. (1.2.6 – 69) and τ^* in Eq. (1.2.6 – 70), H. J. Garde and M. L. Albertson in 1961 succeeded in demonstrating that most of the theoretically and physically correct transport relations can be expressed in the form of the relation $q_B^* = F(\tau^*)$ introduced by them. The relations of Meyer-Peter, Einstein and Kalinske have been examined in detail from this aspect.

In examining Meyer-Peter's transport relation they adopted the form introduced by Ning-Chien under Eq. (1.2.7 – 1) and demonstrated that it is possible to write both parameters Ψ and Φ as functions of q_B^* and τ^*, respectively.

Regarding the parameter Ψ this sould be readily apparent, since

$$\Psi = \frac{d}{RS} \frac{g(\rho_1 - \rho)}{g\rho} = \frac{(\gamma_1 - \gamma)d}{\tau_0} = \frac{1}{\tau^*} \tag{1.2.7-3}$$

On the other hand, the parameter Φ can be written in the form

$$\Phi = \frac{q_B}{U_* \, \gamma_1 \, d} \frac{U_* \, d\rho^{1/2}}{(\rho_1 - \rho)^{1/2}} \left(\frac{1}{gd^3}\right)^{1/2} \tag{1.2.7-4}$$

or

$$\Phi = q_B^* \frac{(gRS)^{1/2} \, \rho^{1/2}}{g^{1/2} (\rho_1 - \rho)^{1/2}} \, d^{-1/2} = q_B^* \left[\frac{gRS}{d} \frac{\rho}{g(\rho_1 - \rho)}\right]^{1/2} \tag{1.2.7-5}$$

whence it becomes obvious that

$$\Phi = q_B^* \, \tau^{*1/2} \tag{1.2.7-6}$$

Combining Eqs (1.2.7 – 6) and (1.2.7 – 1)

$$q_B^* \, \tau^{*1/2} = (4\tau^* - 0.188)^{3/2} \tag{1.2.7-7}$$

Eq. (1.2.7 – 7) is indeed an evidence for the possibility of expressing Meyer-Peter's transport relation in terms of q_B and τ^*.

Einstein's relation is $\Phi = F(\Psi)$. Remembering that, according to Eqs (1.2.7 – 3) and (1.2.7 – 6), both, Φ and Ψ can be expressed in terms of the parameters q_B^* and τ^*, it is apparent that Einstein's relation can also be written in the form $q_B = F(\tau^*)$.

Examining the parameters Eq. (1.2.6 – 50) of Laursen, and of the author under Eq. (1.2.6 – 53), it should be considered that the quantity Ψ involved in Eq. (1.2.7 – 2) is essentially identical with the inverse of τ^*, that is, $\Psi = 1/\tau^*$, and thus it will become clear that this transport parameter can also be written in the form introduced by Garde and Albertson under Eq. (1.2.6−71).

In its original form the relation of Kalinske under Eq. (1.2.6−9) shows a strong resemblance to that of Garde and Albertson. In Kalinske's relation the parameter on the left-hand side is, as pointed our already, identical with q_B^*. Supposing, in keeping with the law of constant tractive forces, that it is possible to express τ_c in terms of the particle diameter d, the function on the right-hand side can also be written in terms of τ^*. This, however, implies that Kalinske's relation is comparable with that introduced by Garde and Albertson.

J. Zeller in a paper published in 1963 applied certain transformations to the general relation of Meyer-Peter − Müller given under Eq. (1.2.6−44) and succeeded in demonstrating that this can be expressed in a form similar to the relation of Du Boys under Eq. (1.2.6−1). In fact, with the substitutions $\gamma R_c S_R = \tau_0$ and $A''(\gamma_1 - \gamma)d = \tau_c$ in Eq. (1.2.6−44) and introducing the dimensional constant

$$8 \left(\frac{g}{\gamma}\right)^{1/2} \left(\frac{\gamma_1}{\gamma_1 - \gamma}\right) = K$$

depending on the specific gravities of the bed load and water, Eq. (1.2.6−44) can be rewritten in the form

$$q_B = K(\tau_0 - \tau_c)^{3/2} \qquad (1.2.7-8)$$

No objections can be raised to the foregoing substitutions, since the first is the actual tractive force, whereas the second may be regarded, as far as dimensions are concerned, as the critical tractive force. A constant value of A'' would imply, however, that to a bed load of a particular specific gravity and particle size a critical tractive force of constant magnitude would pertain, regardless of the conditions of observations. The law of constant critical tractive forces has already been demonstrated to be misleading, and this implies − as taken into consideration also by Meyer-Peter − that the magnitude of A'' depends on the rate of transport, i.e. eventually on the hydraulic properties of the stream.

From the above considerations of Zeller it is inferred that Eq. (1.2.6−44) may be found difficult to use, since no details are given on the manner in which the variability of A'' is to be taken into consideration.

When discussing the comparison of the different rate-of-transport relations it is of interest to remember the studies of V. A. Vanoni, M. H. Brooks and J. F. Kennedy in 1961. In these studies the transport curves representing the formulae of Du Boys, Schoklitsch, Shields, Einstein − Brown, Meyer-Peter, Meyer-Peter − Müller and Einstein were checked against the results of field observations on four rivers, namely the Colorado, Niobrara, West Goose Creek and Mountain Creek. The results of these investigations are shown in *Figs. 1.2.7−2, 1.2.7−3*, and *1.2.7−4* for the Colorado and Niobrara rivers respectively for the West Goose Creek. From these figures the considerable difference between the rates of bed load transport G_B [kp/sec] obtained by the different transport relations is

Fig. 1.2.7—2. Total sediment load observed on the Colorado river compared with diverse transport relations. After Vanoni

to be clearly seen. It is of interest to note, morevover, in connection with these investigations, that the observation points plot within the range determined by the different transport relations. Nevertheless, differences as wide as 50 and even 100 per cent are often encountered. From these figures it will be perceived further that some of the formulae consistently yield steeper transport curves than others. Thus, for instance, the relation of Einstein and of Meyer-Peter—Müller are, in general, steeper than the others. A fact demonstrated by the figure is that the curves computed according to the formulae of Einstein and Meyer-Peter—

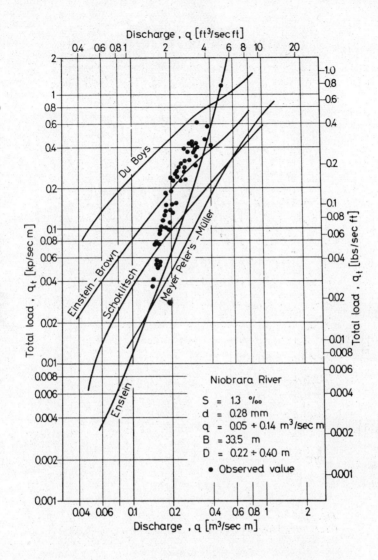

Fig. 1.2.7—3. Total sediment load observed on the Niobrara River compared with diverse transport relations. After Vanoni

Müller are in a better agreement with the trend of curves representing observation data.

The rate of bed load transport in the Rhine at Brugg is shown in *Fig. 1.2.7—5* based on the observations by Nesper and compared with some of the transport relations. The bed load transported by the Rhine over this section is rather coarse. The Einstein—Brown relation has been computed and entered into the figure

Fig. 1.2.7—4. Total sediment load observed on the West Goose Creek compared with diverse transport relations. After Vanoni

for three different particle diameters, namely those pertaining to 35, 40 and 57 per cent by weight passing. The differences will be seen to be very wide also in *Fig. 1.2.7 — 5.*

A perhaps even more visual comparison of various transport formulae is to be found in the studies of L. Pernecker and H. Volmers dating from 1965.

Denoting the submerged weight of bed load transported in unit width and unit time as q'_B (kp/sec m) the transport rate parameter

$$G_* = \frac{q'_B}{\rho U_*^3} \qquad (1.2.7-9)$$

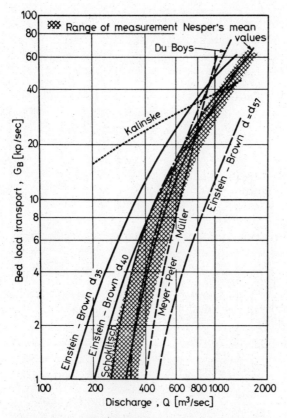

Fig. 1.2.7−5. Total sediment load observed on the Rhine compared with diverse transport relations. After Nesper and Zeller

is introduced and plotted on the basis of a number of experimental data against

$$F_* = \frac{\rho U_*^2}{g(\rho_1 - \rho)d} \qquad (1.2.7-10)$$

In this manner the relations of Meyer-Peter, Einstein−Brown, Einstein and Kalinske have been compared (see *Fig. 1.2.7.−6*).

Relating Kalinske's parameter Φ_K in Eq. (1.2.6−9) to the weight of bed load in submerged condition, the parameter G_* can be expressed in terms of the parameter

$$\Phi'_K = \frac{q'_B}{(\gamma_1 - \gamma)U_* d} \qquad (1.2.7-11)$$

281

From Eqs (1.2.7−9) and (1.2.7−11)

$$G_* = \Phi'_K \frac{(\gamma_1 - \gamma)d}{\tau_0} \qquad (1.2.7-12)$$

Since according to Eq. (1.2.6−70)

$$\frac{(\gamma_1 - \gamma)d}{\tau_0} = \frac{1}{f_0} = \frac{1}{\tau^*}$$

this becomes

$$G_* = \frac{\Phi'_K}{f_0} = \frac{\Phi'_K}{\tau^*} \qquad (1.2.7-13)$$

From the foregoing it follows also that

$$F_* = \frac{\rho U_*^2}{g(\rho_1 - \rho)d} = \frac{\tau_0}{(\gamma_1 - \gamma)d} = f_0 = \tau^* \qquad (1.2.7-14)$$

or that it is essentially identical with the well-known parameter introduced earlier by several authors.

Since most transport relations were demonstrated by Garde and Albertson as early as in 1961 to reduce to the form

$$q_B^* = \Phi_K = F(\tau^*) = F\left(\frac{\tau_0}{(\gamma_1 - \gamma)d}\right) = F(f_0) \qquad (1.2.7-15)$$

Pernecker and Vollmers' statement that the transport relations can in general be expressed as some form of the relationship between G_* and F_* is obviously correct.

Fig. 1.2.7−6 is truly representative and presents a clearer picture than *Figs 1.2.7−2* to *1.2.7−5* by Vanoni and Nesper. The obvious reason for this is that Pernecker and Vollmers −instead of the discharge (Q) and the total sediment transport (G_B)−have related the parameter measuring the rate of transport to the parameter f_0 by which the movement of bed load is primarily influenced.

In *Fig. 1.2.7−6* the authors suggested the use of the approximate relation

$$G_* = 25F_* - 1 \qquad (1.2.7-16)$$

In the present system of notations this relation is rewritten into the form

$$\frac{q'_B}{U_* \tau_0} = 25 \frac{\tau_0}{(\gamma_1 - \gamma)d} - 1 \qquad (1.2.7-17)$$

In order to facilitate the practical application of *Fig. 1.2.7−6* Pernecker and Vollmers have constructed the nomogram indicated in *Fig. 1.2.7−7*.

282

$$G_* = \frac{q'_B}{\rho U_*^3} = \Phi_K \cdot \frac{(\gamma_1 - \gamma)d}{\tau_0} = \frac{\Phi'_K}{f_0} = \frac{\Phi'_K}{\tau^*}$$

Rate of transport parameter, G_*

EINSTEIN–BROWN $G_* = 40\,F_*^{2/3}$
$F_* > 0.06$

$G_* = 25\,F_* - 1$

MEYER–PETER $G_* = 8\left(1 - \frac{0.047}{F_*}\right)^{3/2}$

EINSTEIN $G_* = \dfrac{F_*^{3/2}}{\Phi_*}$

$\left[\Phi_* = F\left(\psi = \dfrac{1}{F_*}\right)\right]$

KALINSKE $G_* = \dfrac{2.5\,F\left(\dfrac{\tau_c}{\tau_0}\right)}{F_*}$

$\left[\dfrac{\tau_c}{\tau_0} = \dfrac{0.12}{F_*}\right]$

- Einstein, uniform size
- Einstein, mixed sand grains
+ Unknown
○ Simons, Richardson, Haushild
  (no suspended matter added)
× Brooks
⋄ Shinohara, Tsubaki
✦ After Garde
  (Bogárdi-Yen, USWES, Gilbert: F,G,H)

$$F_* = \frac{\rho U_*^2}{g(\rho_1 - \rho)d} = \frac{\tau_0}{(\gamma_1 - \gamma)d} = f_0$$

Fig. 1.2.7—6. Comparison of diverse transport relations. After Pernecker and Vollmers

Fig. 1.2.7—7. Diagram for using the diverse transport relations. After Pernecker and Vollmers. The values q'_B obtained in dyn/cm.sec units are multiplied by $1.0197 \cdot 10^{-4}$ to obtain the sediment transport in kp/m.sec units)

The bed load transport relations were examined in 1968 by S. Shulits and R. D. Hill primarily for their potential practical application. Adopting the determination of the rate at which bed load is transported in alluvial streams, altogether 14 transport relations were examined and compared by them.

The relations were classified according to whether they are based on the discharge, the tractive force or on the relative roughness.

Of the formulae relating the rate of transport to the discharge, those of Schoklitsch (1934 and 1943), Meyer-Peter (1934), Casey (1935) and Haywood (1940), of the expressions including the tractive force those of Straub (1935), of the Water Ways Experiment Station (1935), Shields (1936), Kalinske (1947), Meyer-Peter— Müller (1948) and Elzermann—Frijling (1951) whereas of those based on relative roughness the transport formulae of Laursen (1957) and Rottner (1959) were examined.

The relation suggested by Einstein (1950) for estimating the rate of bed load transport was considered separately.

The comparative studies of Shulits are of great interest and direct attention to numerous difficulties associated with the transport relations. Omitting details it is only noted briefly that Shulits regards none of the transport relations as of general validity. As far as practical applications are concerned he considers the formulae of Schoklitsch (1934) based on discharge and those of Straub as well as of Meyer-Peter—Müller based on the tractive force as most suitable ones. This conclusion was drawn by checking the above 14 transport relations against the available data of laboratory experiments allowing, in general, for a discrepancy of ±30%.

The reason why Shulits selected these three relations was not because these were found to be the most accurate ones, but because they satisfy most closely the arbitrary tolerance limit of ±30%.

The author fully endorses Shulits's conclusion that in general no transport relation must be accepted as correct unless verified somehow by actual observation data gained on alluvial streams and that appropriate corrections will be necessarily introduced on the basis of such observations.

A very valuable contribution by Shulits is that he has compiled computer programes for all of the afore-mentioned 14 transport relations.

The conclusions drawn from the comparison of the different transport relations are not too encouraging and, as revealed by *Figs 1.2.7—2, 1.2.7—3, 1.2.7—4* and *1.2.7—5*, some of the factors affecting the rate of transport are still far from being understood. It was Zeller who pointed out the necessity of taking into consideration, in contemporary research, all phenomena that may be of potential influence on the rate of transport. The most important ones of these are believed to be

a) the influence of fluctuations in the concentration of suspended sediment and water temperature on the distribution of velocities in the vicinity of the bottom and on the movement of the bed load,

b) the influence of bed forms on energy losses, on velocity distribution and on bed load movement,

c) the influence of river regime on bed load movement and channel development (especially in the case of mixed bed load fractions).

1.2.7.2. Bed load transport parameters. The rate of bed load transport is measured by the weight of bed load transported in unit width and unit time, i.e. by the quantity q_B (kp/sec m). Exceptionally the rate of transport is defined on a volume basis and, in distinction, the notation Q_B (m³/sec) is introduced.

In the physical interpretation the rate of transport q_B is a resultant value which depends on the independent variables representing the stream and water, as well as the bed load material [see Eq. (1.2.6−73)].

Instead of q_B it is found advisable to introduce some dimensionless parameter as a measure of q_B, which may be referred to briefly as the transport parameter. Considering the phenomenon of bed load transportation, the transport parameter may be regarded as mathematically and physically exact if it involves q_B as the only unknown resultant value, whereas all the remaining physical quantities originate from known independent variables. In this formulation the transport parameter can also be given a physical interpretation.

In support of the above statement consider, for example, Kalinske's transport parameter

$$\Phi_K = \frac{q_B}{U_* \gamma_1 d}$$

given by Eq. (1.2.6−69). Dividing the weight of bed load q_B (kp/sec m) by the specific gravity γ_1 of the bed load, the transport rate is obtained in terms of volume. Dividing further this volume by the particle size d, the term $q_B/\gamma_1 d$ will yield the weight of bed load transported in unit width and unit time expressed by volume and related to unit particle size. This term has the dimension of velocity, so that it is a resultant velocity that is a measure of the rate of bed load transport. If this velocity measuring the rate of transport is divided by any of the potential dynamic velocities (see *Section 1.2.5*) combined of the independent physical quantities dominating the phenomenon, the desired dimensionless, mathematically and physically exact transport parameter is obtained. In the case of Φ_K this potential dynamic velocity will be seen to be the shear velocity U_*.

Under this formulation a great number of different transport parameters are conceivable. Before entering upon a discussion of the potential applications of this possibility it is deemed advisable to examine the mathematical and physical foundations of the transport parameters discussed so far.

No dimensionless transport parameter is involved in the relations of Du Boys, Schoklitsch or Meyer-Peter−Müller. Kalinske's parameter has been dealt with above and found mathematically exact and physically well founded.

The parameter of Garde and Albertson is identical with that of Kalinske, so that it need not be discussed separately.

Shields's transport parameter introduced under Eq. (1.2.6−41) is essentially a measure of the ratio of the resultant rate of transport q_B and the resultant discharge q (inasmuch as q may be regarded essentially as a resultant value comparable to the function in Eq. (1.2.6 – 74)).

No mathematical objection can be raised to the introduction of the ratio of two resultant quantities, namely q_B and q. This involves, however, the disadvantages that the computation of q_B is impossible unless q is measured. This is why a rather close correlation is found when using Shields's expression under Eq. (1.2.6 – 41). In fact, by including the resultant discharge q Shields succeeded in taking into consideration, under identical conditions of observation, all effects of the independent variables since the magnitude of this discharge is found by direct measurement, rather than by some unknown relation of questionable reliability.

Levi, too, has adopted the ratio of q_B and q as the transport parameter, and all statements made in the foregoing in connection with Shields's parameter apply also to this case.

The transport parameter of Einstein – Brown given by Eq. (1.2.6 – 15) can be rewritten, with due allowance for the relation of the time factor F given by Eq. (1.2.6 – 14), into the form

$$\Phi' = \frac{q_B}{\gamma \omega d} \qquad\qquad (1.2.7 - 18)$$

The physical interpretation that can be given to Eq. (1.2.7 – 18) is that the transport rate q_B (kp/sec m) is related to unit water volume, unit particle size and unit fall velocity.

If it is desired to produce the parameter with the help of the potential dynamic velocities introduced in *Section 1.1.5*, the resultant velocity measuring the rate of transport will become $q_B/\gamma d$ denoting the rate of transport related to unit water volume and particle size. If the fall velocity ω is regarded, besides the physical quantities dominating the phenomenon, as an independent potential dynamic velocity, the ratio of the two will yield logically Φ'. In this case, however, allowance must be made for the circumstance that ω cannot be regarded as an independent potential dynamic velocity unless not more than two of the physical quantities γ_1, v and d are involved among the independent physical basic quantities taken originally into consideration. Since, however, in the dimensionless parameter Ψ in Eq. (1.2.6 – 16) determining Φ' the independent physical quantities γ_1 and d are already involved, it should be evident that in determining the parameter Φ' the kinematic viscosity v must not be introduced as an independent physical quantity.

Of course, in the interpretation of the parameter Φ' it is permissible to regard ω as a resultant fall velocity, related positively to a bed load material of given size and specific gravity and to a fluid of known viscosity. In this case the ratio of the resultant transport rate q_B and the resultant fall velocity ω is defined by the parameter Φ'. Consequently, what is to be measured in this case for computing q_B, is the fall velocity ω which, as pointed out in connection with Shields parameter, is beneficial for the closeness of correlation.

A fair number of formulae are available for computing the fall velocity ω. Such computation, however, involves the risk of leaving some of the properties of the bed load under consideration unaccounted for.

Einstein's parameter Φ under Eq. (1.2.6 − 23) can be given the following interpretation. The term q_B/γ_1 denotes the volume of bed load transported in unit width and unit time. On dividing this by d, the term $q_B/\gamma_1 d$ denotes the resultant velocity measuring the volume of bed load transported in unit width and unit time, related to unit particle diameter. Combining this with the potential dynamic velocity $\sqrt{gd\rho'}$ mentioned in *Section 1.1.5*, the parameter Φ is already obtained. Einstein's parameter Φ is thus mathematically correct and can be given a physical interpretation.

Laursen's transport parameter in Eq. (1.2.6 − 49) is the ratio of the two resultant quantities q_t and q, just like the parameter of Shields. The relation is mathematically correct, but q_t cannot be computed unless q is known.

The questionable term in the parameter is the critical tractive force τ_c which, as has already been pointed out during the examination of the relations of Du Boys and Kalinske, is a fictitious value to which no unambiguous interpretation can be given. Nevertheless the rather close correlation observable between the graphical relation of Laursen and that of the author is evidently due to the fact that the observations were made under almost identical conditions.

Nor can a mathematical objection be raised to the parameter Φ_{S-K-A} introduced by Sato and his co-workers. The variations of the critical tractive force τ_c are apparently taken care of by the function $F(\tau_c/\tau_0)$. A physical interpretation is possible by regarding q_B/τ_0, namely the rate of transport per unit tractive force as the resultant potential dynamic velocity.

The transport parameter of Egiazaroff in Eq. (1.2.6 − 55) is mathematically correct but, since both q_B and q are resultant quantities, its applications is restricted to cases where the discharge q is known in advance.

As mentioned repeatedly in the foregoing the introduction of the critical tractive force τ_c is theoretically questionable, this being a fictitious value, impossible to determine positively.

This inconsistency may be expected to be eliminated by introducing the concept of effective energies. It is believed for this reason that by introducing the effective energies the relation of Egiazaroff can considerably be improved, and further research into the relevant details appears to be warranted.

In analogy to Einstein's parameter Φ the transport parameter of Pedroli in Eq. (1.2.6 − 66) can be assigned a physical interpretation by regarding it as the resultant velocity measuring the bed load volume transported in unit width and unit time and related to unit particle diameter, $q_B/\gamma_1 d$. Relating this to the potential dynamic velocity v/d discussed in *Section 1.1.5*, the transport parameter of Pedroli is obtained directly. Consequently Pedroli's transport parameters appears to be correct in all respects.

In the course of his investigations the author has introduced several parameters which differed more or less from the foregoing but resembled them in their mathematical and physical foundations. The transport parameters introduced in different forms served the objective of applying a wide variety of relations for determining the rate of bed load transport.

In the foregoing the parameter of Pernecker and Vollmers has been shown to be essentially identical with Kalinske's parameter and thus to be mathematically and physically correct as established already for Kalinske's parameter Φ_K.

The author was the first to introduce the parameter

$$\Phi_B = \frac{q_B}{(\gamma_1 - \gamma)} \frac{1}{D} \left(\frac{1}{gd}\right)^{1/2} \left(\frac{\gamma}{\gamma_1 - \gamma}\right)^{1/2} \qquad (1.2.7-19)$$

Physically $q_B/(\gamma_1 - \gamma)$ yields the rate of transport in unit width and unit time, expressed as volume related to the submerged specific gravity. By relating it, instead of unit width, to unit cross-sectional area, i.e. dividing by the depth of flow D, the term $q_B/(\gamma_1 - \gamma)D$ will become a resultant velocity that is a measure of the rate of transport. Combining the latter with the potential dynamic velocity $\sqrt{gd\rho'}$ in *Section 1.1.5* the expression under Eq. (1.2.7–19) is obtained.

The dimensionless number Φ_B in Eq. (1.2.7–19) is proportionate to the rate of bed load transport and the formal resemblance to Einstein's bed load transport parameter is apparent.

Mathematically the difference between the two is that instead of the term $1/d^{3/2}$ involved in Φ, the term $(1/D)(1/d^{1/2})$ appears in Φ_B.

The parameter Φ was derived by Einstein on the basis of considerations concerning the scouring probability of bed load particles. The author has introduced Φ_B as the ratio of the resultant velocity measuring bed load transport and of the potential velocity $\sqrt{gd\rho'}$. The physical considerations underlying the two parameters are thus seen to be radically different. However, since both are proportionate to the rate of bed load transport, they are equally suitable for determining the latter. Being both dimensionless numbers, they are equally applicable as a similarity criterion of bed load transportation.

If the rate of the transport related, with the help of the submerged specific gravity, to volume and to unit cross-sectional area, that is, the term $q_B/(\gamma_1 - \gamma)D$, as a resultant velocity is divided by the potential dynamic velocity v/D, the author's parameter Φ_{B_1} is obtained

$$\Phi_{B_1} = \frac{q_B}{(\gamma_1 - \gamma)v} \qquad (1.2.7-20)$$

It is also possible to introduce slope S into the transport parameter expression if the resultant velocity $q_B/(\gamma_1 - \gamma)D$ is related to the potential dynamic velocity v/DS in *Section 1.2.5:*

$$\Phi_{B_2} = \frac{q_B}{(\gamma_1 - \gamma)vS} \qquad (1.2.7-21)$$

19

289

An additional parameter is obtained if the resultant velocity $q_B/(\gamma_1 - \gamma)D$ is divided by the potential dynamic velocity v/d mentioned in *Section 1.1.5:*

$$\Phi_{B_3} = \frac{q_B}{(\gamma_1 - \gamma)v} \frac{d}{D} \qquad (1.2.7-22)$$

The parameter Φ_{B_3} is thus seen to contain the relative roughness as well. Inasmuch as relative roughness is described usually by the ratio D/d, as a last parameter the product of Φ_{B_1} and D/d is also introduced. Thus

$$\Phi_{B_4} = \frac{q_B}{(\gamma_1 - \gamma)v} \frac{D}{d} \qquad (1.2.7-23)$$

It should be noted in conclusion that in the most recent investigations a method frequently applied is to relate the total load transported in unit time and denoted as G_t (p/sec) or the suspended sediment load G_s (p/sec) to the discharge Q expressed in terms of weight G (p/sec) and to regard this ratio as the rate of transport parameter. A parameter of this type has been expressed also by J. G. Herbertson in the form G_t/G, but Q is always maintained as an independent variable since for a particular channel width either depth or slope is regarded as an independent physical quantity.

The investigations of Herbertson will be discussed in greater detail subsequently.

1.2.7.3. Physical quantities controlling the rate of bed load transport. The transport relationships considered so far and even those to be discussed subsequently have in general been derived from the results of laboratory experiments and thus rather represent, as already mentioned, the bed-load-transporting capacity which is, in fact, an upper limit of bed load transport.

In the transport relations considered so far several physical quantities describing the properties of fluid and of bed load as well as the type of flow have been encountered. These include no quantities characterizing the turbulence of flow although this may be expected considerably to affect the movement of bed load. The reason for this obviously impermissible neglect of turbulence parameters is the complete absence of relevant observation data. Thus in the course of subsequent research, just as during the past investigations, we are compelled to rest satisfied with the assumption that the characteristics of stream flow, of sediment and of water are, to the certain extent, indicative of the characteristic of turbulence as well.

When bed load of particle size d and of density ρ_1 is examined and only water of density ρ is assumed to act as the transporting medium, then — upon introducing the dimensionless ratio

$$\frac{\rho_1 - \rho}{\rho} = \rho'$$

the rate of transport is controlled by the following physical quantities:

g (m/sec^2), acceleration due to gravity, R (m) the hydraulic radius, D (m) the depth of flow, B (m) the width of the channel or bed, S the slope of the energy gradient, d (m) the diameter of the bed load particle, ρ' a dimensionless number characteristic of the specific gravity of the sediment material and finally v (m^2/sec) the kinematic viscosity of water.

The physical quantities controlling the rate of transport can be grouped also in a manner that slope S or the depth of flow D is neglected and discharge Q is adopted instead as the independent physical quantity. The three kinds of grouping applied most commonly in research are obtained in this way for the independent physical quantities:

$$g, R, D, B, S, d, \rho', v \qquad (1.2.7-24)$$

$$g, R, D, B, Q, d, \rho', v \qquad (1.2.7-25)$$

$$g, R, Q, B, S, d, \rho', v \qquad (1.2.7-26)$$

A grouping other than that indicated by Eqs $(1.2.7-24)$ to $(1.2.7-26)$ is, of course, also conceivable, provided that, under the afore-mentioned assumptions, the rate of transport is controlled by eight independent physical quantities.

In the groupings under Eqs $(1.2.7-25)$ and $(1.2.7.-26)$ certain restrictions are observable since for any particular width B the discharge depends on both depth D and slope S of flow. These cases will be recurred to later.

The magnitude of the dependent, or with the terminology used in this book, of the resultant quantities depends on the physical quantities that are adopted as the independent ones. In the grouping under Eq. $(1.2.7-24)$ the discharge Q, the characteristic velocity v and the rate of bed load transport q_B are the dependent variables or the resultant values. In the grouping according to Eq. $(1.2.7-25)$ the resultant values are v, slope S and q_B. Finally if the independent physical quantities are adopted according to Eq. $(1.2.7-26)$, the resultant values become v, the depth of flow D and q_B.

Several simplifying assumptions and omissions have been encountered in the foregoing investigations where, for practicability or for compelling reasons, the effect of one or several independent physical quantities have been neglected. One of the simplifying assumptions most frequently adopted is that of $R = D$, which is considered generally permissible once the ratio B/D is higher than 10 to 20. Otherwise beyond $B/D = 5$ the channel is usually regarded as "wide".

Further common simplifications involve the neglect of variations in ρ' or of the variations of B; occasionally the dependence of v on temperature is disregarded

1.2.8. RATE OF TRANSPORT AT GIVEN PARTICLE SIZES, AT CONSTANT DEPTH, SLOPE OR DISCHARGE

Although the most limited for practical application, the relations in which several of the quantities d, ρ', v, D, S and B, in certain combinations are of constant magnitude, are still of some interest.

Barr and Herbertson assumed ρ_1 and ρ and consequently ρ' to remain unchanged and the channel to be wide, where any variation in B is negligible. With these assumptions the resultant total sediment transport G_t (p/sec) has been described with the help of the following physical quantities

$$g, R, D, d, Q, v \qquad (1.2.8-1)$$

It should be noted in this context that the sum of bed load and suspended load transports, i.e. the total rate of sediment transport is denoted by G_t, whereas G_B and G_s denote the rates of bed load and suspended load transport, respectively. Each of the three transport rates is expressed in p/sec units. The corresponding rates of transport related to unit width are q_t for total load, q_B for bed load and q_s for suspended load, always in p/sec m units.

Several five-term independent groups of dynamic lengths can be derived from the six-dimensional physical basic quantities in Eq. (1.2.8–1) (see *Section 1.1.5*) using either the method of potential dynamic lengths introduced by the author or the method referred to as linear proportionalities by Barr and Herbertson. The latter adopted the group

$$\frac{Q^{2/5}}{g^{1/5}}, \quad R, \quad D, \quad d, \quad \frac{v^{2/3}}{g^{1/3}} \qquad (1.2.8-2)$$

and combined these into the following four independent dimensionless numbers:

$$\frac{Q^{2/5}/g^{1/5}}{v^{2/3}/g^{1/3}} = \frac{Q^{2/5} g^{2/15}}{v^{2/3}} \qquad (1.2.8-3a)$$

$$\frac{D}{R} \qquad (1.2.8-3b)$$

$$\frac{d}{R} \qquad (1.2.8-3c)$$

$$\frac{d}{v^{2/3} g^{-1/3}} \qquad (1.2.8-3d)$$

Now the 2/5th root is taken of Eq. (1.2.8–3a), that is, $Qg^{1/3}/v^{5/3}$, and Eq. (1.2.8–3d) is raised to the 1.5th (i.e. 3/2) power, that is $d^{3/2} g^{1/2}/v$; if then the resultant rate of transport is G_t while G is the discharge Q expressed in terms of weight: G [p/sec] $= Q\gamma$, the dimensionless number G_t/G measuring the rate of transport is given by the following formal function

$$\frac{G_t}{G} = F\left(\frac{Qg^{1/3}}{v^{5/3}}, \quad \frac{d^{3/2} g^{1/2}}{v}, \quad \frac{d}{R}, \quad \frac{D}{R}\right) \qquad (1.2.8-4)$$

Assuming in this theoretical relation $d = $ constant and $D = R$, so that d/R varies exclusively with depth, assuming moreover the variation of $(d^{3/2} g^{1/2})/v$ is

292

Fig. 1.2.8 – 1. Total sediment load vs. discharge at 4.2 mm
particle size. After Barr and Herbertson

small enough to be neglected, for a bed load of size d and density ρ_1 it is found
that

$$\frac{G_t}{G} = F\left(\frac{Qg^{1/3}}{v^{5/3}}, \frac{d}{R}\right) \qquad (1.2.8-5)$$

which implies essentially that for any particular $R = D$ depth of flow the rate
of sediment transport G_t depends exclusively on discharge Q.

The relation under Eq. $(1.2.8-5)$ has been plotted in *Fig. 1.2.8 – 1* for a sediment of $d = 0.42$ mm particle sizes and for four different depths of flow D, in
other words, for four different relative roughnesses, since d is constant. The
influence of relative roughness on the ratio G_t/G at any given particle size will
clearly be perceived from the figure. It should be remembered, of course, that
at a particular Q the ratio G_t/G increases with increasing values of $d/R = d/D$ as
a consequence of the fact that at lower depths the channel is capable of conveying
the same discharge Q evidently at a considerably steeper slope, i.e. at a higher
velocity only.

293

Fig. 1.2.8−2. Bed load vs. relative roughness at B=59.74 em
flume width and at different discharges and particle sizes.
After Barr and Herbertson

The transport parameter G_t/G in *Fig. 1.2.8−1* multiplied by 10^6 yields the sediment concentration C (p/m³). The weight of 1 m³ water is, in fact, almost exactly 10^6 p. Thus actually

$$\frac{G_t}{G/10^6\,[\text{p/m}^3]} = \frac{G_t}{G}\,10^6\,[\text{p/m}^3] = C\,[\text{p/m}^3]$$

and the rate of sediment transport is expressed in terms of the sediment concentration or in p.p.m (parts/million) units. For instance, the transport parameter

294

Fig. 1.2.8 – 3. Bed load transport vs. discharge at 0.305 mm particle size and different depths. After Herbertson

$G_t/G = 3 \cdot 10^{-3}$ in *Fig. 1.2.8 – 1* indicates a sediment concentration $C = 3,000$ [p/m³]. The same applies to the bed load transport parameters in *Figs 1.2.8 – 2* to *1.2.8 – 7* to be discussed subsequently. Since *Fig. 1.2.8 – 1* is constructed on the basis of Stein's data which relate to the total rate of sediment transport including bed load and suspended load alike, the relation of Barr and Herbertson implies evidently that the rate of suspended sediment transport is essentially a function of discharge Q. It should be remember that the quantity of sediment transported in suspension is in general appreciably greater than that of bed load.

Fig. 1.2.8−4. Bed load transport vs. slope at 0.377 mm particle size, B = 0.4 m flume width and at different discharges. After Herbertson

Fig. 1.2.8−5. Bed load transport vs. slope at 5.15 lit/sec discharge and 0.377 mm particle size in flumes of different width. After Herbertson

As will be demonstrated later in Part II, "Sediment and Water Courses", in *Chapter 2.1*, "Empirical relations", it is possible to determine similar relations for alluvial streams even in cases where the particle size d and the depth of flow D vary between certain limits.

Neglecting the variations of v entirely it is possible to use Eq. (1.2.8−5) for determining the variation of G_B/G with the relative roughness d/D at a particular discharge Q. In *Fig. 1.2.8−2* the variation of the bed load transport parameter G_B/G with d/D is shown for some combinations of Q = constant and d = constant values. The figure is highly instructive since with B = constant it clearly reflects that for increasing d/D, i.e. lower depths values−Q being constant−slope S increases and the increase thereof induces rapidly increasing transport rates of the small (about 0.5 mm) size fractions.

The difference between *Figs 1.2.8−2* and *1.2.8−1* is only a formal one and, unlike the first, the second has been constructed by Barr and Herbertson using the observation data on bed load of Gilbert. In these experiments the specific gravity of bed load was approximately $\gamma_1 = 2.65$ p/cm³.

Fig. 1.2.8−6. Bed load transport vs. slope in a flume of 0.4 m width, at 10.27 lit/sec discharge and sediment material of different sizes. After Herbertson

Fig. 1.2.8−7. Bed load transport vs. slope in a flume of 0.4 m width, at 20.78 lit/sec discharge and sediment material of different sizes. After Herbertson

Eq. (1.2.8−4) offers the possibility of transforming *Fig. 1.2.8−2*, the new form applying to particular values of d and ρ_1 to a wide channel (neglecting variations of B) and to a constant temperature. These assumptions imply that the three-variable family of curves

$$\frac{G_B}{G} = F(Q, \ D) \qquad\qquad (1.2.8-6)$$

has been constructed *(Fig. 1.2.8−3)*. This figure is based on data measured by Gilbert.

As will clearly be perceived from *Fig. 1.2.8−3*, for a particular combination of d and Q values the transport parameter increases with decreasing depth D, indicating that the slope S is bound to become steeper involving disproportionately higher rates of transport.

It should be evident from the foregoing that in *Figs 1.2.8−1, 1.2.8−2* and *1.2.8−3* the transport parameters G_t/G and G_B/G have been determined by Barr and Herbertson as functions of discharge Q and depth D for particular values of d and ρ_1. With $d = $ constant, the independent variables are Q and d/D.

Instead of depth D and of the hydraulic radius R, slope S and the channel width B, respectively, have been adopted by Herbertson. In this way he used the six independent variables

$$g, \ B, \ Q, \ d, \ S, \ v \qquad (1.2.8-7)$$

for describing the rate of transport.

Using the method described earlier he combined these into the independent five-term group of potential dynamic length

$$\frac{Q^{2/5}}{g^{1/5}}, \ B, \ d, \ \frac{v^{2/3}}{g^{1/3}}, \ \frac{v^{2/3}}{Sg^{1/3}} \qquad (1.2.8-8)$$

which yielded the independent ratios

$$\frac{Q^{2/5}/g^{1/5}}{v^{2/3}/g^{1/3}} = \frac{Q^{2/5} g^{2/15}}{v^{2/3}} \qquad (1.2.8-9a)$$

$$\frac{d}{B} \qquad (1.2.8-9b)$$

$$\frac{v^{2/3}/g^{1/3}}{v^{2/3}/g^{1/3}S} = S \qquad (1.2.8-9c)$$

$$\frac{d}{v^{2/3}/g^{1/3}} = \frac{dg^{1/3}}{v^{2/3}} \qquad (1.2.8-9d)$$

from which the desired transport parameter is given evidently by the relation

$$\frac{G_B}{G} = F\left(\frac{d}{B}, \ \frac{Qg^{1/3}}{v^{5/3}}, \ \frac{d^{3/2} g^{1/2}}{v}, \ S \right) \qquad (1.2.8-10)$$

Instead of Eq. (1.2.8−9d) it is obviously permissible to introduce the dimensionless parameter

$$\frac{B}{v^{2,3}/g^{1/3}} = \frac{Bg^{1/3}}{v^{2/3}}$$

so that the relation

$$\frac{G_B}{G} = F\left(\frac{d}{B}, \ \frac{Qg^{1/3}}{v^{5/2}}, \ \frac{B^{3/2} g^{1/2}}{v}, \ S \right) \qquad (1.2.8-11)$$

is also valid.

Neglecting minor variations of v, both theoretical relations under Eqs (1.2. 8−10) and (1.2.8−11) are suitable for determining the transport parameter vs. slope S function for a particular combination of channel with B and particle

298

diameter d and for different Q = constant discharges. The decisive influence of slope on bed load transport at flume width B = 0.4028 m and particle size d = 0.377 mm is shown in *Fig. 1.2.8−4* since with the same discharge higher rates of transport are induced at steeper slopes (although, the discharge being constant, this implies a reduction of depths).

Neglecting as before minor variations of v, from Eq. (1.2.8−11) it is possible to determine the transport parameter vs. slope relation for a given combination of discharge and particle size and for different flume widths B. As will be seen from *Fig. 1.2.8−5*, at the particular values of d = 0.377 mm particle size and Q = 5.15 lit/sec discharge the change in the transport parameter vs. slope relation becomes appreciable only at flume width smaller than about 20 cm. *Fig. 1.2.8−5* is of great interest in that it demonstrates that the influence of flume width is not predominant, at least within the range of values of practical interest.

Using Eq. (1.2.8−10) or Eq. (1.2.8−11) it is possible to investigate the transport parameter vs. slope relation at a given combination of discharge and flume width values and for different particle sizes d. In *Fig. 1.2.8−6* which applies to B = 40.28 cm flume width and Q = 10.27 lit/sec discharge Herbertson traced the transport parameter vs. slope relation for seven different size fractions ranging from about 0.3 to 5 mm. In *Fig. 1.2.8−7* the G_B/G vs. slope relation is illustrated for the afore-mentioned seven size fractions at the same B = 40.28 cm flume width but at a discharge of Q = 20.78 lit/sec.

From *Figs 1.2.8−6* and *1.2.8−7* alike it is concluded that for particle sizes smaller than about 0.8−1 mm the relation remains essentially unchanged. The relation applying to the size fractions greater than about 1 mm is, however, seen to be radically different.

The relations indicated in *Figs 1.2.8−1* to *1.2.8−7* are severely restricted by applying only to particular combinations of particle size and depth or discharge and particle size or to a given flume width. The effect of flume width could be determined for constant values of discharge and particle size, whereas that of particle size, for given values of constant width and discharge only. In this respect the relations considered in this Chapter are of very limited practical value. Nevertheless these investigations are of interest not only because of the theoretical conclusion but also because of the possibility of using them for the approximate estimation of actual transport rates.

1.2.9. RECENT EFFORTS TO DETERMINE
UNIVERSAL BED LOAD TRANSPORT FORMULAS

1.2.9.1. Relationships concerning the total rate of sediment transport. No transport relation is of general validity unless the particle size, the slope, the depth of flow, the specific gravity of bed load, the temperature of water and even the width of the channel may assume any arbitrary value. The results of investigations conducted thus far have demonstrated the extreme difficulties encountered when attempting to derive an exact relation satisfying these requirements. Remembering that practically no combination of variables has been left unexplored, the difficulty of the task undertaken will be even more appreciated. Nevertheless, further investigations will not be useless for, even though failing to reveal an exact transport relation, they may be expected to contribute to our understanding of several detail problems.

The examination will be started by determining the transport parameter Q_t/Q which is a measure of the rate of total sediment transport, where

$$Q_t[\text{m}^3/\text{sec}] = \frac{q_t[\text{p/sec m}]B[\text{m}]}{(\gamma_1 - \gamma)[\text{p/m}^3]} = \frac{G_t[\text{p/sec}]}{(\gamma_1 - \gamma)[\text{p/m}^3]}$$

or the volume of sediment transported in unit time and expressed in terms of the submerged specific gravity of the sediment, and Q [m³/sec] is the discharge. It should be noted in this context that the transport parameter Q_t/Q is the least useful for practical purposes. This is impracticable to apply, since discharge Q cannot be regarded as a pure independent variable. In fact, besides slope, Q is also a function of depth implying that a definite value of the slope S pertains to any arbitrary value of D and Q. With this restriction Q may be used to replace S as the independent variable.

Assume the rate of sediment transport to be dominated by the physical quantities

$$g, D, B, d, Q, v, \rho' \qquad (1.2.9-1)$$

Of the physical quantities in Eq. (1.2.9−1) potential dynamic velocities should be combined and the following six-term group of independent velocities selected:

$$\sqrt{gD}, \ \sqrt{gd}, \ \sqrt{gB}, \ \sqrt[3]{gv}, \ \frac{v^2}{Q}, \ \frac{v^2}{Q}\rho' \qquad (1.2.9-2)$$

which combine into the five dimensionless groups given below

$$\frac{\sqrt{gD}}{\sqrt{gd}} = \sqrt{\frac{D}{d}} \qquad (1.2.9-3a)$$

$$\frac{\sqrt{gd}}{\sqrt[3]{gv}} = \sqrt{\frac{d}{v^{2/3}g^{-1/3}}} \qquad (1.2.9-3b)$$

$$\frac{\sqrt{gd}}{\sqrt{gB}} = \sqrt{\frac{d}{B}} \qquad (1.2.9-3c)$$

$$\frac{\sqrt[3]{gv}}{v^2/Q} = \frac{Qg^{1/3}}{v^{5/3}} \qquad (1.2.9-3d)$$

$$\frac{\frac{v^2}{Q}\rho'}{v^2/Q} = \rho' \qquad (1.2.9-3e)$$

300

Provided the original assumption is valid, the phenomenon of sediment transportation is uniquely described by the five independent dimensionless groups under Eqs (1.2.9−3a) to (1.2.9−3e), so that the transport parameter is determined as

$$\frac{Q_t}{Q} = F\left(\frac{D}{d}, \; \frac{d}{v^{2/3}g^{-1/3}}, \; \frac{d}{B}, \; \frac{Qg^{1/3}}{v^{5/3}}, \; \rho' \right) \qquad (1.2.9-4)$$

In order to facilitate the graphical processing of experimental data, three-variable relations have in general been composed. The six-variable relation under Eq. (1.2.9−4) has been examined as a wide variety of three-variable combinations. Owing to the inevitable neglect of three-variables, none of these relations has proved useful, although it was possible to arrive at some qualitative conclusion from each of them.

As an example the three-variable relation

$$\frac{Q_t}{Q} = F\left(\frac{d}{B}, \; \frac{D}{d} \right) \qquad (1.2.9-5)$$

is shown in *Fig. 1.2.9−1*, including the results of experiments related to the total rate of transport. As will be perceived from the figure there is no possibility for tracing the $D/1000 \, d$ = constant lines but, if these are still entered with gross approximation as dashed lines, it will become apparent that at the same d/B value the parameter Q_t/Q increases together with $D/1000 \, d$ or, since d and B are maintained constant, with the depth of flow. The rate of sediment discharge itself depends on the magnitude of Q. Consequently Q acts as an independent variable. With increasing D the discharge increases even if the slope S remains constant. For these reason Q_t increases logically at a higher rate than the discharge Q. This, of course, is essentially not more than one of the potential explanations for the increase of Q_t/Q with increasing values of $D/1000 \, d$. The general conclusion arrived at from *Fig. 1.2.9−1* is that the rate of sediment transport depends in an extremely complex manner on the independent variables and, consequently, it is found impossible to determine positively their influence with the help of the three-variable relation under consideration.

One of the drawbacks associated with the grouping according to Eq. (1.2.9−1) of the independent variables is that slope S is omitted although it is logical to expect that its role in sediment movement is considerable. Maintaining the total discharge Q and the depth of flow in the channel constant, the only way for regarding the slope as an independent variable is to eliminate the width B of the channel. Accordingly, the rate of sediment transport is assumed to be dominated by the independent physical quantities

$$g, \, D, \, d, \, Q, \, v, \, S, \, \rho' \qquad (1.2.9-6)$$

301

Fig. 1.2.9—1. Total sediment transport vs. the ratio of particle size to flume width with the relative roughness as parameter

The basic quantities in Eq. (1.2.9−6) are combined into independent potential dynamic velocities of which the following six-term group is adopted

$$\sqrt{gD}, \quad \sqrt{gd}, \quad \sqrt[3]{gv}, \quad \frac{v^2}{Q}, \quad \sqrt{gDS}, \quad \frac{v^2}{Q}\rho' \qquad (1.2.9-7)$$

These are combined into the following five dimensionless groups:

$$\frac{\sqrt{gD}}{\sqrt{gd}} = \sqrt{\frac{D}{d}} \tag{1.2.9-8a}$$

$$\frac{\sqrt{gd}}{\sqrt[3]{gv}} = \sqrt{\frac{d}{v^{2/3} g^{-1/3}}} \tag{1.2.9-8b}$$

$$\frac{\sqrt[3]{gv}}{v^2/Q} = \frac{Qg^{1/3}}{v^{5/3}} \tag{1.2.9-8c}$$

$$\frac{\sqrt{gDS}}{\sqrt{gD}} = \sqrt{S} \tag{1.2.9-8d}$$

$$\frac{\dfrac{v^2}{Q}\rho'}{v^2/Q} = \rho' \tag{1.2.9-8e}$$

The rate of transport is thus described by the formal function

$$\frac{Q_t}{Q} = F\left(\frac{D}{d}, \frac{d}{v^{2/3} g^{-1/3}}, \frac{Qg^{1/3}}{v^{5/3}}, S, \rho'\right) \tag{1.2.9-9}$$

The theoretical relation under Eq. (1.2.9−9) has also been examined with the help of several relations involving different combinations of three variables. Of these the relation

$$\frac{Q_t}{Q} = F\left(\frac{D}{d}, S\right) \tag{1.2.9-10}$$

has proved to be of greatest interest. It is shown in *Fig. 1.2.9−2* without regard for the quality of the bottom, whereas for smooth bed and dunes it is shown in *Figs. 1.2.9−3* and *1.2.9−4*, respectively. In all three figures the transport parameter will be seen to increase at constant relative roughness D/d as the slope becomes steeper and, at the same slope, to increase also as the relative roughness D/d is increased. Although the relation is rather poorly defined, the S = constant (in the figure 10,000 S = constant) lines can still be traced approximately. It is of interest to know that the S = constant lines are arranged in identical patterns in each of the three figures indicating that, when the rate of transport is determined in terms of the relative roughness and slope, the quality of the bed does not play an important role, at least not within the range of values used during the experiments.

Since in each of the three figures the S = constant lines are parallel in the relation

$$\frac{Q_t}{Q} = a_1 \left(\frac{D}{d}\right)^{1.95} \tag{1.2.9-11}$$

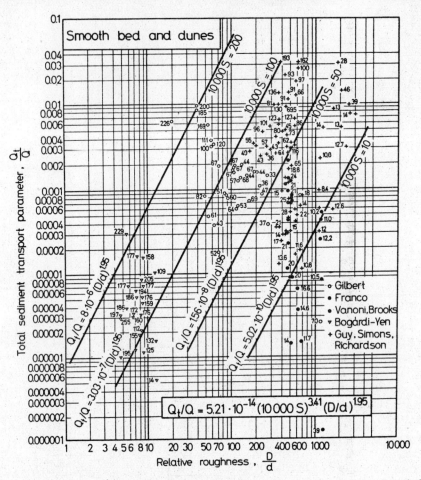

Fig. 1.2.9−2. Total sediment transport vs. relative roughness at smooth bed and dunes, with slope as parameter

it was possible to determine the magnitude of a_1 pertaining to individual 10,000 $S =$ = constant values or the variation thereof with 10,000 S which, in turn, was used in determining the three-variable relation

$$\frac{Q_t}{Q} = 5.21 \cdot 10^{-14} (10\,000\ S)^{3.41} \left(\frac{D}{d}\right)^{1.95} \qquad (1.2.9-12)$$

This relation is consequently valid for *Figs 1.2.9−2, 1.2.9−3* and *1.2.9−4* alike, at least approximately.

The rather loose relation shown in *Figs 1.2.9−2* to *1.2.9−4* is probably due to the circumstance that the rate of total sediment transport has been taken into consideration from a number of widely different experiments. As a further ex-

Fig. 1.2.9—3. Total sediment transport vs. relative roughness at smooth bed only, with slope as parameter

planation let us mention the discharge Q which, though representing the width of the channel at a given combination of slope and depth, does not reflect all properties of the experimental flumes. Particle sizes ranging between wide limits (from 15.49 to 0.137 mm) logically contribute to the scatter of data, since the particle diameter is not fully characterized by the parameter D/d. As a further explanation of the apparent differences it should be noted that the differences in temperature have not been taken into account either.

The extreme values of the physical quantities involved in the experiments used for plotting *Figs 1.2.9—1* to *1.2.9—4* have been compiled in *Table 1.2.9—1*. It should be noted that the ground coal of $\gamma_1 = 1.3$ [p/cm³] specific gravity used by Franco is involved in *Fig. 1.2.9—1* only. The experiment made with a material of $\gamma_1 = 2.67$ [p/cm³] in *Figs 1.2.9—2* and *1.2.9—4* indicates that slightly steeper slopes are necessary for moving these than in the case of a sediment of 2.65 [p/cm³] specific gravity.

20   305

Bed form	Discharge, Q [m³/sec]		Flume width, B [m]		Depth of flow, D [m]		Particle diameter, d [m]	
	Max.	Min.	Max.	Min.	Max.	Min.	Max.	Min.
Smooth and dunes	0.636	0.00482	2.4384	0.2011	0.589	0.0177	$15.49 \cdot 10^{-3}$	$0.137 \cdot 10^{-3}$
Smooth	0.347	0.00516	2.4384	0.2011	0.589	0.0272	$10.56 \cdot 10^{-3}$	$0.137 \cdot 10^{-3}$
Dunes	0.636	0.00482	2.4384	0.2011	0.5761	0.0177	$15.49 \cdot 10^{-3}$	$0.137 \cdot 10^{-3}$

The data originate from experiments by Guy, Simons,

Fig. 1.2.9—4. Total sediment transport vs. relative roughness at dune-covered bed only, with slope as parameter

in the experiments used for plotting

to 1.2.9—4

Slope, S		Water temperature, t [°C]		Spec. gravity of bed load, γ_1 [kp/m³]		$\dfrac{D}{1000\,d}$		Rate of transport, Q_t [m³/sec]	
Max.	Min.	Max.	Min.	Max.	Min.	Max.	Min.	Max.	Min.
0.0232	0.00018	34.3	4.45	2670	1300	3.09	0.00467	0.0155	$3.29 \cdot 10^{-9}$
0.0232	0.00018	26.7	10.5	2650	2650	3.09	0.00495	0.0000974	$3.29 \cdot 10^{-9}$
0.0229	0.00039	34.3	4.45	2670	2650	2.69	0.00467	0.0155	$4.27 \cdot 10^{-8}$

Richardson, Gilbert, Vanoni, Brooks, Bogárdi—Yen and Franco

Fig. 1.2.9—5. Total sediment transport vs. slope at smooth bed and dunes, with relative roughness as parameter

Bed form and particle size	Discharge, Q [m³/sec]		Flume width, B [m]		Depth of flow, D [m]		Particle diameter, d [m]	
	Max.	Min.	Max.	Min.	Max.	Min.	Max.	Min.
Smooth and dune bottom	0.636	0.00482	2.4384	0.2011	0.589	0.047	$15.49 \cdot 10^{-3}$	$0.137 \cdot 10^{-3}$
$0.1 < d < < 0.2$ mm	0.631	0.00482	2.4384	0.2668	0.589	0.0711	$0.19 \cdot 10^{-3}$	$0.137 \cdot 10^{-3}$
$0.3 < d < < 0.6$ mm	0.636	0.00516	2.4384	0.2011	0.338	0.0763	$0.54 \cdot 10^{-3}$	$0.305 \cdot 10^{-3}$
Smooth	0.347	0.00516	2.4384	0.2011	0.589	0.0272	$10.56 \cdot 10^{-3}$	$0.137 \cdot 10^{-3}$
Dunes	0.636	0.00482	2.4384	0.2011	0.5761	0.0177	$15.49 \cdot 10^{-3}$	$0.137 \cdot 10^{-3}$

The data originate from experiments by Guy, Simons, Richardson,

In the course of further investigations an attempt was made to determine the rate of total transport with the help of the parameters Φ_B, Φ_{B_1}, Φ_{B_2}, Φ_{B_3} and Φ_{B_4} introduced by the author, as well as by using Einstein's parameter Φ. In these relations the total sediment, including bed load and suspended load, will still be considered implying that in the parameters mentioned above q_B is replaced essentially by q_t.

Assume the rate of sediment transport to be dominated by the basic physical quantities

$$g, D, B, d, v, S, \rho' \qquad (1.2.9-13)$$

Of the potential dynamic velocities into which these can be combined, let us select the following six-term group of independent velocities:

$$\sqrt{gD}, \quad \sqrt{gd}, \quad v/B, \quad \sqrt{gDS}, \quad \sqrt[3]{gv}, \quad \sqrt{gd\rho'} \qquad (1.2.9-14)$$

These, in turn, determine the following five dimensionless groups:

$$\frac{\sqrt{gDS}}{\sqrt{gD}} = \sqrt{S} \qquad (1.2.9-15a)$$

$$\frac{\sqrt{gD}}{\sqrt{gd}} = \sqrt{\frac{D}{d}} \qquad (1.2.9-15b)$$

$$\frac{\sqrt{gDS}}{\sqrt{gd\rho'}} = \sqrt{\frac{\tau_0}{(\gamma_1 - \gamma)d}} = \sqrt{f_0} \qquad (1.2.9-15c)$$

the experiments used for plotting

to 1.2.9—9

Slope, S		Water temperature, t [°C]		Spec. gravity of bed load, γ_1 [kp/m³]		$\dfrac{D}{1000\ d}$		Rate of transport, Q_t [m³/sec]	
Max.	Min.	Max.	Min.	Max.	Min.	Max.	Min.	Max.	Min.
0.0232	0.00024	34.3	4.45	2670	2650	3.09	0.00467	18.46	0
0.0046	0.0007	26.0	12.3	2650	2650	3.0	0.48	6.14	0
0.017	0.00029	34.3	7.0	2650	2650	0.72	0.054	6.83	$0.1637 \cdot 10^{-4}$
0.0232	0.00024	26.7	10.5	2650	2650	3.09	0.00495	0.526	0
0.0229	0.00068	34.3	4.45	2670	2650	3.03	0.00467	18.64	$0.856\ \cdot 10^{-4}$

Gilbert, Vanoni, Brooks, Bogárdi—Yen and Franco

$$\frac{\sqrt[3]{gv}}{v/B} = \frac{B}{v^{2/3}\,g^{-1/3}} \qquad (1.2.9-15d)$$

$$\frac{\sqrt{gd}}{\sqrt[3]{gv}} = \sqrt{\frac{d}{v^{2/3}\,g^{-1/3}}} \qquad (1.2.9-15e)$$

Any of the afore-mentioned transport parameters will be a unique function of the five independent dimensionless parameters under Eqs (1.2.9— 15).

Considering for example the parameter

$$\Phi_{B_1} = \frac{q_t}{g(\rho_1 - \rho)v}$$

then

$$\Phi_{B_1} = F\left(S,\ \frac{D}{d},\ f_0,\ \frac{B}{v^{2/3}\,g^{-1/3}},\ \frac{d}{v^{2/3}\,g^{-1/3}}\right) \qquad (1.2.9-16)$$

will become the six-variable relation that describes the total rate of sediment transport.

The relation under Eq. (1.2.9— 16) has been examined in a variety of forms. Different combinations of three-variable relations have been formed, moreover, these have been varied with the different parameters.

Disregarding the parameter representing channel width and particle size, further the parameter f_0, the three-variable relation

$$\Phi_{B_1} = F\left(S,\ \frac{D}{d}\right) \qquad (1.2.9-17)$$

309

Fig. 1.2.9−6. Total sediment transport vs. slope at smooth bed and dunes, 0.1 to 0.2 mm particle size, with relative roughness as parameter

is obtained, a graphical representation of which is to be seen in *Fig. 1.2.9−5* based on the experimental results comprising the range of values indicated in the first row of *Table 1.2.9−2*. Regardless of the considerable scatter observable in the figure, it is possible to establish approximately the $D/1000\,d$ = constant lines. These lines having been found parallel in the relation

$$\Phi_{B_1} = aS^{2.62} \qquad (1.2.9-18)$$

the value of a pertaining to individual $D/1000\,d$ = constant values, or the variation of a with $D/1000\,d$ could be determined. The numerical form of the three-variable relation is finally

$$\Phi_{B_1} = 1.99 \cdot 10^9 \left(\frac{D}{1000\,d}\right)^{1.97} S^{2.62} \qquad (1.2.9-19)$$

In view of the fact that a wide variety of sediment particle sizes were used in the experiment on which this relation is based, it was logical to assume that a higher

310

Fig. 1.2.9—7. Total sediment transport vs. slope at smooth bed and dunes, 0.3 to 0.6 mm particle size, with relative roughness as parameter

degree of accuracy could be obtained by determining similar relations for individual size fractions. The relation under Eq. (1.2.9—17) has accordingly been plotted separately for the size fractions $d = 0.1$ to 0.2 mm in *Fig. 1.2.9—6* and for $d = 0.3$ to 0.6 mm in *Fig. 1.2.9—7*. The ranges of the variables in the experiments used for plotting *Figs 1.2.9—6* and *1.2.9—7* have been entered into the second, respectively third rows of *Table 1.2.9—2*. It is of interest to note that neither of the figures displays an appreciable difference over *Fig. 1.2.9—5* from which it is inferred that the numerical relation under Eq. (1.2.9—19) retains its validity for any arbitrary size fraction separately. In certain respects this circumstance may be regarded to support the general validity of the relation given by Eq. (1.2.9—19) and represented in *Fig. 1.2.9—5*.

It has been suggested further that the relation under Eq. (1.2.9—17) or Eq. (1.2.9—19) may be influenced by the configuration of the bed, i.e. by whether it is smooth or covered with dunes.

311

	Discharge, Q [m³/sec]		Flume width, B [m]		Depth of flow, D [m]		Particle diameter, d [m]	
	Max.	Min.	Max.	Min.	Max.	Min.	Max.	Min.
Bed load only	0.0660	0.00516	0.915	0.2011	0.2083	0.0177	$15.49 \cdot 10^{-3}$	$0.23 \cdot 10^{-3}$

The data originate from experiments by Gilbert,

Fig. 1.2.9—8. Total sediment transport vs. slope at smooth bed only, with relative roughness as parameter

312

the experiments used for plotting

to 1.2.9—12

Slope, S		Water temperature, t [°C]		Spec. gravity of bed load, γ_1 [kp/m³]		$\dfrac{D}{1000\ d}$		Rate of transport, Q_t [m³/sec]	
Max.	Min.	Max.	Min.	Max.	Min.	Max.	Min.	Max.	Min.
0.0232	0.000207	31.0	4.45	2670	1300	0.698	0.00462	0.526	$0.323 \cdot 10^{-4}$

Bogárdi—Yen, Garde and Franco

Fig. 1.2.9—9. Total sediment transport vs. slope at dunes only, with relative roughness as parameter

In order to examine this possibility the available data have been used for plotting the relations applying to smooth bed and to dunes in *Figs 1.2.9−8* and *1.2.9−9*, respectively. The ranges of values which the variables may assume in these two figures are indicated in the forth and fifths rows of *Table 1.2.9−2*. Although the number of observation data available is rather limited it could definitely be established that the original relation determined for various particle sizes and from data disregarding the configuration of the bed retained its validity for both cases. This circumstance may be accepted as a further evidence of the possibility of using the relation under Eq. (1.2.9−19) in general for estimating approximately the rate of sediment transport, in spite of the inevitable scatter caused by the disregarded variables.

All transport relations in the previous subsection apply to the total sediment transport. Concerning the experiments on which they are based the relations describing the total rate of transport are classified into two groups. In some of the experiments, and this applies primarily to the coarse fractions, the sediment moved almost exclusively by rolling along the bottom. In these cases $q_t \cong q_B$. On the other hand, in some experiments, where the particle sizes were very small, the suspended load predominated over the share transported as bed load, so that q_B became small enough to be neglected in comparison. In these cases $q_t \cong q_s$.

In connection with the total transport relations it should be emphasized that these are rather of an informative character since, owing to the neglect of considerable differences, they could be determined in an approximate manner only.

1.2.9.2. Relationships concerning the rate of bed load transport. In the second group of investigations only bed load will be considered, and the transport q_s of suspended load, even if it should occur, will be disregarded in determining the transport parameter. The extreme values of data in the experiments considered are shown in *Table 1.2.9−3*.

The relations discussed in the foregoing and used for determining the transport parameters apply logically also to the case where it is desired to determine the rate of bed load transport only. Of course, in such cases q_B, rather than q_t should be entered into the transport parameter.

In determining the rate of bed load transport it appears first expedient to write the dimensionless parameters under Eq. (1.2.9−15) and thus the theoretical relation under Eq. (1.2.9−16) in a form including the specific gravity of bed load directly in the relation. The basic physical quantities in Eq. (1.2.9−13), as well as the six-term group of independent velocities under Eq. (1.2.9−14) will be retained accordingly and, instead of the parameter under Eq. (1.2.9−15e), the expression

$$\frac{\sqrt{gd\rho'}}{\sqrt{gd}} = \sqrt{\rho'}$$

314

will be introduced. For example the transport parameter

$$\Phi_B = \frac{q_B}{(\gamma_1 - \gamma)} \frac{1}{D} \left(\frac{1}{gd}\right)^{1/2} \left(\frac{\gamma}{\gamma_1 - \gamma}\right)^{1/2}$$

will thus be determined by the theoretical relation

$$\Phi_B = F\left(S, \frac{D}{d}, f_0, \frac{B}{v^{2/3} g^{-1/3}}, \rho'\right) \qquad (1.2.9-20)$$

On the basis of the theoretical relation of Eq. (1.2.9−20) a number of three-variable relations have been studied in different combinations. However, each of these has failed to yield acceptable results. The most probable explanation for the considerable differences appears to be the circumstance that the rate of transport is dominated by f_0 to such a high extent that the effect on the transport rate of the dimensionless numbers representing the influence of the remaining independent variables is, in view of the rather narrow range of variations, almost of a random character in comparison to f_0.

Although the experimental data available related almost exclusively to a bed load material of $\gamma_1 = 2.65$ p/cm³ specific gravity, − considering the limited number of observation data on bed load of 1.3 and 2.67 p/cm³ specific gravity − an attempt was made to determine the rate of transport in terms of ρ' besides f_0.

The three-variable relation

$$\Phi_B = F(f_0, \rho') = F\left(f_0, \frac{\gamma_1 - \gamma}{\gamma}\right) \qquad (1.2.9-21)$$

has been plotted in *Fig. 1.2.9−10*. According to previous graphical investigations it is permissible to write this relation in the exponential form

$$\Phi_B = a \left(\frac{\gamma_1 - \gamma}{\gamma}\right)^{n_1} f_0^{n_2} \qquad (1.2.9-22)$$

The relation has been converted into the linear form

$$\lg \Phi_B = \lg a + n_1 \lg \left(\frac{\gamma_1 - \gamma}{\gamma}\right) + n_2 \lg f_0 \qquad (1.2.9-23)$$

and the resulting three-variable relation has been determined using an electronic computer Type Minsk 22.*

Correlation computations resulted in the following three-variable relation

$$\Phi_B = 0.0412 \left(\frac{\gamma_1 - \gamma}{\gamma}\right)^{-1.0486} f_0^{2.455} \qquad (1.2.9-24)$$

* The computer programme of the relation has been written and computations have been performed at the Automation Research Institute of the Hungarian Academy of Sciences by K. Bozóky Szeszich, Associate Professor, Budapest Technical University.

Fig. 1.2.9−10. The bed load transport parameter Φ_B vs. the resistance coefficient f_0 with relative specific gravity as parameter

The difference found at $(\gamma_1 - \gamma)/\gamma = 1.65$ and 1.67 values was small enough to be neglected. The relation applying to these bed load materials of almost the same specific gravity is thus

$$\Phi_B = 0.024 f_0^{2.455} \qquad (1.2.9-25)$$

in *Fig. 1.2.9−10*.

For $(\gamma_1 - \gamma)/\gamma = 0.3$

$$\Phi_B = 0.146 f_0^{2.455} \qquad (1.2.9-26)$$

A simple visual inspection of the three-variable relation under Eq. (1.2.9−24) will prove it to be unacceptable. This will become even more apparent when considering the ratio β of the observed rate q_{Bm} of transport in unit width and unit time to the corresponding value q_{Bsz} computed using the three-variable relation.

316

In fact the arithmetic mean of the ratio

$$\beta = \frac{q_{Bm}}{q_{Bsz}}$$

is

$$\bar{\beta} = \frac{\sum\limits_{n=1}^{n=N} \beta_n}{N} = 5.35$$

or the squared arithmetic mean of β is

$$\bar{\beta}_g = \sqrt{\frac{\sum\limits_{n=1}^{n=N} \beta_n{}^2}{N}} = 10.91$$

yielding for the standard deviation of β values

$$\sigma_\beta = \sqrt{\frac{\sum (\beta_n - \bar{\beta})^2}{N}} = 9.51$$

The arithmetic and squared arithmetic mean values, as well as the standard deviation of β will be seen to be excessive so that this three-variable relation is unsuited even for approximate estimates. As will be perceived from Eq. (1.2.9−24), the exponent of the parameter

$$\rho' = \frac{\gamma_1 - \gamma}{\gamma}$$

is extremely close to unity, implying essentially − and this is probably the only benefit of this three-variable relation − that the magnitude of the transport parameter Φ_B is inversely proportionate to the value of ρ'.

Einstein's transport parameter

$$\Phi = \frac{q_B}{\gamma_1} \left(\frac{\rho}{\rho_1 - \rho} \right)^{1/2} \left(\frac{1}{gd^3} \right)^{1/2}$$

has been examined in a similar manner. Regarding the three-variable relation

$$\Phi = F(f_0, \rho') \tag{1.2.9−27}$$

as a three-variable correlation, on the basis of available observation data in the manner described before, the expression eventually obtained is

$$\Phi = 14.91 \left(\frac{\gamma_1 - \gamma}{\gamma} \right)^{-1.165} f_0^{3.714} \tag{1.2.9−28}$$

Bed form	Discharge, Q [m³/sec]		Flume width, B [m]		Depth of flow, D [m]		Particle diameter,	
	Max.	Min.	Max.	Min.	Max.	Min.	Max.	Min.
Smooth and d in s	0.0660	0.00516	0.823	0.2011	0.2083	0.0177	0.01549	0.000305

The data originate from experiments by Gilbert, Bogárdi—Yen and Garde

At $(\gamma_1 \quad \gamma)/\gamma = 1.65$ and 1.67 hardly any difference was apparent, so that at this relative specific gravity this relation is described in *Fig. 1.2.9—11* by the expression

$$\Phi = 8.21 f_0^{3.714} \qquad (1.2.9-29)$$

In the same figure the relation pertaining to the relative specific gravity $\rho' = 0.3$ is

$$\Phi = 60.8 f_0^{3.714} \qquad (1.2.9-30)$$

Although this three-variable relation will be perceived to be superior to the foregoing one, it is not considered suitable for practical use because of the very wide scatter of data relating to bed load of 2.65 specific gravity used in the overwhelming majority of experiments. For the sake of completeness the values of $\beta = q_{Bm}/q_{Bsz}$ are again given. The arithmetic mean is $\bar{\beta} = 1.99$, the squared arithmetic mean is $\bar{\beta}_g = 3.43$, whereas the standard deviation of the ratio of specific transport rates actually observed and computed is $\sigma_\beta = 2.794$. Here again it will be observed that the magnitude of the transport parameter Φ is in an approximately inverse proportion with ρ' since the exponent of ρ' is -1.165 and thus almost equal to -1.

Finally, for the sake of completeness also the three-variable relation

$$\Phi_{G-A} = q_B^* = \frac{q_B}{\gamma_1 \, dU_*} = F(f_0, \rho') \qquad (1.2.9-31)$$

has been determined in the manner described before as a correlative relation.

Before a more detailed description of these examinations it is deemed expedient to repeat that, according to Eq. (1.2.7—6),

$$\Phi_{G-A} = q_B^* = \Phi(\tau^*)^{-1/2} = \Phi f_0^{-1/2}$$

saying that it is possible to obtain the transport parameter q_B^*, directly from Eqs (1.2.9—28) to (1.2.9—30).

the experiments used for plotting

15 and 17

Slope, S		Water temperature, t [°C]		Spec. gravity of bed load, γ_1 [kp/m³]		$\dfrac{D}{1000\,d}$		Rate of transport, Q_t [m³/sec]	
Max.	Min.	Max.	Min.	Max.	Min.	Max.	Min.	Max.	Min.
0.0232	0.00035	31.0	11.0	2650	2650	0.589	0.00462	0.526	$0.323 \cdot 10^{-4}$

$$\Phi = 14.91 \cdot \left(\frac{\gamma_1 - \gamma}{\gamma}\right)^{-1.165} \cdot f_0^{3.714}$$

Bed load transport parameter, $\Phi = \dfrac{q_B}{\gamma_1}\left(\dfrac{\rho}{\rho_1 - \rho}\right)^{1/2}\left(\dfrac{1}{gd^3}\right)^{1/2}$

$f_0 = \dfrac{\tau_0}{(\gamma_1 - \gamma)d}$

○ Gilbert
● Franco
▽ Bogárdi-Yen
△ Garde

Fig. 1.2.9—11. The bed load transport parameter Φ vs. the resistance coefficient f_0 with relative specific gravity as parameter

319

Bed form	Discharge, Q [m³/sec]		Flume width, B [m]		Depth of flow, D [m]		Particle diameter,	
	Max.	Min.	Max.	Min.	Max.	Min.	Max.	Min.
Smooth and dunes	0.0660	0.00516	0.823	0.2011	0.197	0.0177	0.01549	0.000305

The data originate from experiments by Gilbert and Bogárdi—Yen

The theoretical results were nevertheless checked against correlation computation and for the magnitude of the transport parameter $\Phi_{G-A} = q_B^*$ a result actually comparable to Eq. (1.2.7—6) has been obtained:

$$\Phi_{G-A} = q_B^* = 14.91 \left(\frac{\gamma_1 - \gamma}{\gamma} \right)^{-1.165} f_0^{3.214} \qquad (1.2.9-32)$$

For $\rho' = 1.65$ and 1.67 values this relation in *Fig. 1.2.9—12* is represented by the expression

$$q_B^* = 8.21 f_0^{3.214} \qquad (1.2.9-33)$$

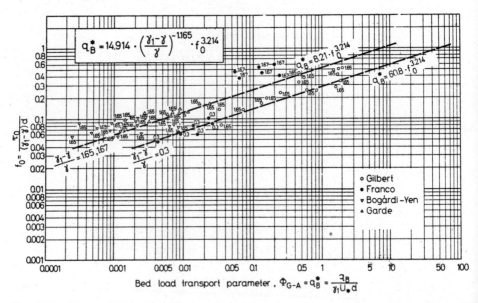

Fig. 1.2.9—12. The bed load transport parameter Φ_{G-A} vs. the resistacne coefficient f_0 with relative specific gravity as parameter

the experiments used for plotting

16 and 18

Slope, S		Water temperature, t [°C]		Spec. gravity of bed load, γ_1 [kp/m³]		$\dfrac{D}{1000\,d}$		Rate of transport, Q_t [m³'sec]	
Max.	Min.	Max.	Min.	Max.	Min.	Min.	Max.	Max.	Min.
0.0232	0.0017	22.0	11.0	2650	2650	0.279	0.00462	0.526	$7.44 \cdot 10^{-4}$

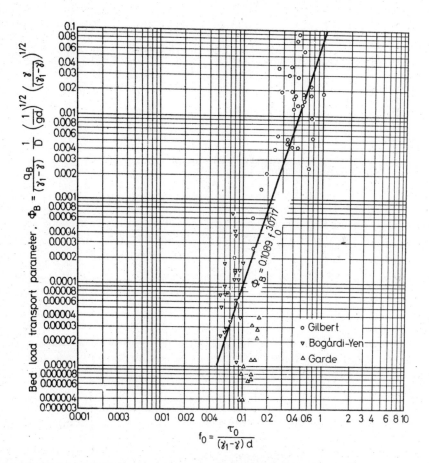

Fig. 1.2.9—13. The bed load transport parameter Φ_B vs. the resistance coefficient f_0 according to experiments by Gilbert, Bogárdi—Yen and Garde

Fig. 1.2.9—14. The bed load transport parameter Φ_B vs. the resistance coefficient f_0 according to experiments by Gilbert and Bogárdi—Yen

whereas for $\rho' = 0.3$ the corresponding expression is

$$q_B^* = 60.8\,f_0^{3.214} \tag{1.2.9-34}$$

The remarks applying to *Fig. 1.2.9—12* or to the three- and two-variable relations represented thereon are, in keeping with the foregoing, the same as made in connection with *Fig. 1.2.9—11*. Of course, the arithmetic and geometric mean value, as well as the standard deviation of β is identical with the values computed for the relation derived for Φ.

From the three-variable relations of Φ_B, Φ and q_B^* considered in the foregoing it will be inferred that the transport parameter depends primarily on the parameter f_0. Remembering that only a few data of the experiments included in *Table 1.2.9—3* apply to bed load materials having a specific gravity substantially differing from 2.65 p/cm³, it appears logical to examine the possibilities of determining two-variable relations from which ρ' is omitted.

322

Fig. 1.2.9—15. The bed load transport parameter Φ vs. the resistance coefficient f_0 according to experiments by Gilbert, Bogárdi—Yen and Garde

For each of the transport parameters the two-variable relations have been computed first by omitting the data of Franco. The extreme values of the physical quantities are indicated in *Table 1.2.9—4*. For these computations a computer has again been used. The omission of Franco's data entails, of course, that the relations obtained will apply exclusively to a bed load material of $\gamma_1 = 2.65$ p/cm^3.

According to *Fig. 1.2.9—13*

$$\Phi_B = 0.1089 f_0^{3.0717} \tag{1.2.9—35}$$

and the corresponding values of β are $\bar{\beta} = 4.25$, $\bar{\beta}_g = 8.36$ and $\sigma_\beta = 7.97$.

Although this relation represents a slight improvement over Eq. (1.2.9—24) the scatter of data is too wide to make it suitable for practical application.

Fig. 1.2.9—16. The bed load transport parameter Φ vs. the resistance coefficient f_0 according to experiments by Gilbert and Bogárdi—Yen

In Franco's data the temperature differences are rather large. Prompted by this observation it has been attempted to establish the relation of Φ_B and f_0 by observing the ranges indicated in *Table 1.2.9—5* and omitting the data of Garde which display similarly large temperature differences.

The equation describing this relation represented graphically in *Fig. 1.2.9—14* is

$$\Phi_B = 0.1136 f_0^{2.6867} \qquad (1.2.9-36)$$

with $\bar{\beta} = 1.81$, $\bar{\beta}_g = 3.2$ and $\sigma_\beta = 2.64$.

Simple visual inspection of the graph will reveal this relation to be the closest one for Φ_B, so that regardless of the still observable differences this is considered suitable for approximate practical computations.

The relation

$$\Phi = 21.99 f_0^{4.121} \qquad (1.2.9-37)$$

324

Fig. 1.2.9—17. The bed load transport parameter Φ_{G-A} vs. the resistance coefficient f_0 according to experiments by Gilbert, Bogárdi—Yen and Garde

obtained by mechanical computation has been plotted in *Fig. 1.2.9—15*, where $\bar{\beta} = 1.61$, $\bar{\beta}_g = 2.476$ and $\sigma_\beta = 1.873$. Here the data of Garde have been entered into the computation.

Of all the relations considered so far the last one may be regarded as the closest, demonstrating essentially the fact that, even if the data related to temperature, to bed forms, to flume width, etc. are neglected, the rate of bed load transport *is found most reliably from the relation existing between Einstein's transport meter Φ and the parameter f_0.*

It is interesting to note that if the Φ vs. f_0 relation is determined by omitting the data of Garde, the differences and, in turn, the values of β will become relatively higher. In fact in the relation

$$\Phi = 22.20 f_0^{4.056} \qquad (1.2.9-38)$$

according to *Fig. 1.2.9—16*, $\bar{\beta} = 1.759$, $\bar{\beta}_g = 2.86$ and $\sigma_\beta = 2.255$.

325

Fig. 1.2.9—18. The bed load transport parameter Φ_{G-A} vs. the resistance coefficient f_0 according to experiments by Gilbert and Bogárdi—Yen

In connection with the three-variable relations discussed before it has been demonstrated that the relation of q_B^* and f_0 is determined unequivocally by the relation of Φ and f_0. Nevertheless, as a check on computations and for the sake of completeness the function

$$q_B^* = 21.99 f_0^{3.621} \qquad (1.2.9-39)$$

obtained by mechanical computation has been plotted in *Fig. 1.2.9—17*. The values of β are, of course, exactly the same as those mentioned in connection with Eq. (1.2.9—37).

The relation computed by omitting the data of Garde

$$q_B^* = 22.20 f_0^{3.556} \qquad (1.2.9-40)$$

has finally been plotted in *Fig. 1.2.9—18* for purposes of verification.

326

Fig. 1.2.9−19. The bed load transport parameter Φ_{G-A} vs. the resistance coefficient f_0 at sediment materials of different specific gravity with v/U_* as parameter

Since the relations discussed in the foregoing have been derived on the basis of experimental results other than those used by Garde and Albertson, it was found expedient to determine and demonstrate the graphical relation existing between the transport parameter Φ_{G-A}, as well as the parameters f_0 and v/U_*. (The original relation of Garde and Albertson is represented by Eq. (1.2.6−72) and *Fig. 1.2.6−17.)*

As will be perceived from *Fig. 1.2.9−19*, we have succeeded in establishing a rather close correlation on the basis of available experimental data. It should be realized, moreover, that the remarks made in connection with *Fig. 1.2.6−17* apply also to the family of curves plotted in this figure. Regardless of this fact the graph is also considered suitable for practical use provided that, besides the independent physical basic quantities dominating the phenomenon, observation data are available on the resultant mean velocity v as well.

It is to be concluded that, as expected, attempts have failed to determine a relation suitable in all respects for estimating the rate of bed load transport. Differences as great as 80 to 160% will be apparent even in the case of the relations given by Eqs (1.2.9−36) to (1.2.9−40) recommended for approximate estimation. These drastic differences are believed to remain impossible to eliminate as long as we-succeed in developing a method for taking into consideration the effects of water temperature, of flume width and of other circumstances controlling the conditions of observations.

In conclusion it should be emphasized that each of the foregoing relations applies to bed load materials of uniform particle size.

1.2.10. THE WEARING OF BED LOAD

1.2.10.1. The wearing of bed load particles in movement and at rest. In the broadest interpretation the particle sizes of bed load carried along alluvial streams diminish under the combined effect of the following physical phenomena.

Wearing the diminution of particle sizes caused by friction of moving bed load particles on one another and on particles at rest at the bottom.

Attrition: the diminution of stationary bed load particles caused by the bed load moving above them.

Fragmentation: diminution of particle sizes by desintegration under the impact of a larger particle or caused by collision at high velocity.

Weathering: diminution by cracking or spalling due to repeated cycles of heating and cooling, freezing and thawing, drying and wetting of particles exposed on bars to rapid water level fluctuation.

Dissolution: diminution of particle sizes due to the chemical effect of water.

Sorting: diminution reflected in the granulometry of bed load due to the temporary or permanent elimination of larger bed load particles from transport.

The familiar theories on bed load wear are mentioned in *Subsection 1.1.3.2*

Widely divergent opinions prevail as regards sorting, fragmentation, weathering and dissolution. Neither have comprehensive studies been undertaken into these phenomena. On the other hand, the reduction in particle size or the loss of weight of particles due to wearing proper has been studied extensively in recent years. In these recent studies allowance has been made for the fact that the movement of bed load is an intermittent one and accordingly wearing is composed of two portions namely of the weight loss of moving particles due to wearing and of the attrition of stationary particles caused by the particles moving in their vicinity.

This distinction of the wearing process into parts occurring in movement and at rest appears to be logical and is substantiated also by the observation data published.

It should be realized, however, that the bed load particles at rest have acquired the stationary condition essentially as a consequence of a sorting process. Thus sorting is still involved in the reduction of particle size representing the overall effect of wearing and attrition of the particles in movement and at rest. It is possible to eliminate this conflict by defining sorting as the permanent deposition of bed load particles or at least their becoming stationary for extended periods of times, e.g. months or years.

From among the wide variety of interpretations given to the phenomenon of size reduction or wearing the classification of K. Stelczer is worthy of being mentioned. He regards the size reduction of bed load either as a result of hydrodynamic changes or as the consequence of mechanical wearing.

According to him hydrodynamic changes are reflected in the process of sorting. Mechanical wear, on the other hand, may be gradual comminution, such as fragmentation and weathering, and continuous comminution which is composed essentially of wearing and attrition.

The analytical development of relations expressing the wearing of bed load particles in movement and at rest, as well as the experiments made for checking these relationships will be discussed subsequently in detail on the basis of investigations by K. Stelczer.

K. Stelczer has performed his investigations at the Research Institute for Water Resources Development, Budapest, while the field measurements, on the Danube, in the section at Dunaremete. The basic approach in deriving his relations is based on the recognition of the fact that the process of wearing cannot be studied separately, only in combination with the phenomenon of bed load movement. This approach implies that different laws apply to the wearing of sediment in motion and to that at rest, further that the intermittent movement of bed load in the stream must also be taken into consideration. Once this is recognized, it follows that wearing cannot be regarded simply proportionate to the distance travelled. This recognition has provided at the same time an immediate explanation of the fact that relatively very low rates of wearing per unit distance have been observed in laboratory experiments.

Considering thus the process of wearing in combination with the phenomenon of bed load transport, the gradual diminution of particle sizes will be seen to be composed of the wear suffered by moving particles and of the size reduction of stationary particles by attrition. Under this approach the wearing of bed load particles should be considered as a function of time.

In earlier investigations the rate of wearing was related to the volume or weight of sediment. Since the effect of particle shape is not reflected properly either in the weight or in the volume of bed load, in recent studies wearing has been related to the particle diameter. In this way the effect of particle shape is included along with weight in the relations, which is all the more important as the magnitude of friction force responsible for wearing is influenced decisively by the shape effect.

Starting from the above considerations analytical expressions have been derived for expressing the wear of moving and stationary bed load considering in each case both prismatic and spherical particles.

Fig. 1.2.10−1. Wearing of prismatic and spherical moving sediment particles with distance travelled as a function of time. After Stelczer

1. Wearing of moving particles

a) *Wearing of prismatic particles.* Bed load particles of weight G_0, submerged specific gravity $(\gamma_1 - \gamma)$, base area A, of height y_0 and prismatic in shape are assumed to slide along the bottom. With reference to *Fig. 1.2.10−1* at time t having travelled the distance s the weight of the prism is G and its height y.

Wearing of the prism is assumed with a fair degree of approximation to be uniform over every part of the base area and over the finite distance Δs, the weight G is assumed to be constant as far as the frictional force is concerned.

Adopting the assumption introduced by Sternberg and Schoklitsch that the weight loss ΔG over the distance Δs, i.e. wearing, is proportionate to the work derformed, i.e. to the product of the friction force fG and the distance Δs, it is permissible to write

$$- \Delta G = k'(fG)\Delta s \qquad (1.2.10-)$$

330

The weight G and the weight loss ΔG of the prism is expressed in terms of volume and of the submerged specific gravity.

$$G = (\gamma_1 - \gamma)V = (\gamma_1 - \gamma)Ay, \quad \Delta G = (\gamma_1 - \gamma)\Delta V = (\gamma_1 - \gamma)A\Delta y$$

Introducing the notation $K_1 \, [\text{km}^{-1}] = fk'$ and rearranging terms the expression

$$-\Delta y = K_1 y \Delta s \qquad (1.2.10-2)$$

is obtained.

Changing to infinitesimal values the expression is solved for y, and the rate of bed load travel $v_h = ds/dt$ is introduced as a constant value over the distance under consideration. Hereafter wearing is described by the differential equation

$$-\frac{dy}{y} = K_1 v_h \, dt \qquad (1.2.10-3)$$

Integrating between the corresponding limits $y - y_0$ and $0 - t$ and with the notation $K_1 v_h = k_1 \, [\text{hours}^{-1}]$ the height y after time t of the prismatic bed load particle of y_0 original height is expressed as

$$\ln y - \ln y_0 = -k_1 t \qquad (1.2.10-4)$$

or

$$y = y_0 \, e^{-k_1 t} \qquad (1.2.10-5)$$

b) *Wearing of spherical particles.* Let the diameter of a spherical bed load particle of weight G_0 and submerged specific gravity $(\gamma_1 - \gamma)$ be y_0. According to *Fig. 1.2.10—1* at time t, after travelling the distance s the diameter is reduced to y. The loss in weight ΔG is again expressed with the help of the work performed by the frictional force over the distance Δs or, according to Eq. (1.2.10—1),

$$-\Delta G = k'(fG)\Delta s$$

The original and reduced weight of the spherical bed load particle are expressed by the relations

$$G = \frac{4\pi}{3} \left(\frac{y}{2}\right)^3 (\gamma_1 - \gamma)$$

and

$$\Delta G = \frac{4\pi}{3} \left[\left(\frac{y}{2}\right)^3 - \frac{y}{2} - \left(\frac{\Delta y}{2}\right)^3 \right] (\gamma_1 - \gamma)$$

Introducing the notation $K_1 \, [\text{km}^{-1}] = fk'$ after the necessary substitutions and reductions the wearing of spherical particles is expressed by the differential equation

$$-\frac{3}{y} \, dy + \frac{3}{y^2} \, dy^2 - \left(\frac{dy}{y}\right)^3 = K_1 \, ds \qquad (1.2.10-6)$$

Neglecting small terms of second and third order and introducing the notation $ds = v_h\,dt$, further after integration between the corresponding limits $y_0 - y$ and $0 - t$, the wearing of spherical particles is described as

$$\ln y - \ln y_0 = \frac{K_1 v_h}{3} t \qquad\qquad (1.2.10-7)$$

or introducing the wearing coefficient $K_1 v_h = k_1$ as

$$y = y_0\, e^{-\frac{k_1}{3} t} \qquad\qquad (1.2.10-8)$$

The relations under Eqs (1.2.10−5) and (1.2.10−8) are formally and substantially identical and indicate the possibility of characterizing the wear of moving bed load by the reduction of a longitudinal dimension.

The two equations are essentially identical with the expressions derived by Sternberg and Schoklitsch for bed load wear. Nevertheless they differ from these in several important respects, in that wearing is described with the help of a longitudinal dimension which is in general more representative of the frictional force, rather than by relating it to volume or weight. Moreover by introducing the rate of bed load travel $v_h = ds/dt$ the phenomenon is related to time rather than to the distance travelled.

2. Wearing of stationary particles. The wearing of stationary bed load particles is assumed to be due to the bed load moving over it. In order to simplify the problem the quantity of bed load moving in a particular location is assumed to be constant, so that the surface subject to friction is exposed continuously to the constant weight G_B of moving bed load.

a) *Wearing of prismatic particles.* The weight of a prismatic bed load particle is G_0, its submerged specific gravity $(\gamma_1 - \gamma)$, its base area A and its height y_0. The loss in weight ΔG will be proportionate to the work of bed load of constant weight G_B moving over the prism, performed over the distance Δs (see *Fig. 1.2.10−2)*

$$-\Delta G = k''(f G_B)\Delta s = K_2 G_B \Delta s \qquad\qquad (1.2.10-9)$$

where $K_2\ [\mathrm{km}^{-1}] = k''f$.

The loss in weight is

$$\Delta G = \Delta V(\gamma_1 - \gamma) = (\gamma_1 - \gamma)A\Delta y,$$

and thus

$$-(\gamma_1 - \gamma)A\Delta y = K_2 G_B \Delta s \qquad\qquad (1.2.10-10)$$

332

Fig. 1.2.10−2. Wearing of prismatic and spherical stationary sediment particles with distance travelled as a function of time. After Stelczer

Changing to infinitesimal values and substituting $ds = v_h \, dt'$

$$- (\gamma_1 - \gamma)A \, dy = K_2 G_B v_h \, dt'$$

which, upon integration between the corresponding limits $y_0 - y$ and $0 - t'$, yields

$$- (\gamma_1 - \gamma) A (y - y_0) = K_2 G_B v_h t' \qquad (1.2.10-11)$$

Dividing by $(\gamma_1 - \gamma)A$ and introducing the wearing coefficient as

$$k_2' \, [\text{mm/óra}] = \frac{K_2 G_B}{(\gamma_1 - \gamma)A} v_h$$

333

the wearing of a prismatic bed load particle will be described by the expression

$$y = y_0 - k_2' t' \qquad (1.2.10-12)$$

The rate of moving bed load transport G_B being a function of location, the magnitude of k_2' is logically also subject to variations with location.

b) *Wearing of spherical particles.* According to *Fig. 1.2.10−2* the stationary bed load particle of y_0 initial diameter is worn by the time t to the section of height z under the influence of bed load G_B travelling over it at velocity v_h. The loss in weight is again proportionate to the work performed by the bed load G_B over the distance Δs, so that

$$- \Delta G = K_2 G_B \Delta s$$

From the figure

$$\Delta G = (\gamma_1 - \gamma)\,\Delta V = (\gamma_1 - \gamma)\,\rho^2\,\pi \Delta z$$

and

$$\rho^2 = y_0 z - z^2$$

With these values

$$- (\gamma_1 - \gamma)\,\pi\,(y_0 z - z^2)\,\Delta z = K_2 G_B \Delta s \qquad (1.2.10-13)$$

Changing to elementary quantities and with the substitution $ds = v_h \, dt'$

$$- (\gamma_1 - \gamma)\,\pi\,(y_0 z - z^2)\,dz = K_2 G_B v_h \, dt' \qquad (1.2.10-14)$$

After integration between the corresponding limits $y_0 - z$ and $0 - t'$, the rearrangement of terms yields

$$- (\gamma_1 - \gamma)\,\pi \left[y_0 \left(\frac{z^2}{2} \right) - \frac{z^3}{3} \right] = (\gamma_1 - \gamma)\,\frac{y_0^3 \pi}{6} - K_2 G_B v_h \, t' \qquad (1.2.10-15)$$

The height z of the worn sphere section is very difficult to compute from Eq. (1.2.10−15). A simplified relation is obtained by determining the diameter y of a sphere having a volume identical to the section remaining. The projection of this imaginary sphere of diameter y and of a volume identical to the worn sphere is traced with a continuous line in *Fig. 1.2.10−2*. For the case of a sphere of y_0 initial diameter reduced to a section of height z, the diameter y of the sphere having a volume identical to the section can be shown to be

$$y = \sqrt[3]{z^2 (3y_0 - 2z)} \qquad (1.2.10-16)$$

whence

$$z^2 = \frac{y^3}{3y_0 - 2z}$$

334

Fig. 1.2.10—3. Reduction in particle diameter with distance travelled as a function of time in intermittent movement. After Stelczer

combining the above expression for z^2 with Eq. (1.2.10—15) and dividing the resulting equation by $(\gamma_1 - \gamma)\pi/6$ and introducing the wearing coefficient of stationary bed load as

$$k_2 \,[\text{mm}^3/\text{óra}] = \frac{6K_2 G_B v_h}{(\gamma_1 - \gamma)\pi}$$

the wearing of stationary spherical bed load particles is described by Stelczer as

$$y = \sqrt[3]{y_0^3 - k_2 t'} \qquad (1.2.10-17)$$

Since the shape of natural bed load particles is much more truly represented by a spherical shape, Eq. (1.2.10—17) will be used subsequently for estimating the wear of stationary bed load.

Assuming the shape to be spherical and with due regard to the foregoing considerations the wearing of bed load is stated by K. Stelczer in the following general form.

Inasmuch as a bed load particle of diameter d_0 is transported for time t_1 (see *Fig. 1.2.10—3*), during which its diameter is reduced by Δd_{m_1} to d_1', whereafter it is deposited at point (1) and remains stationary for the time t_1', during which its diameter is reduced by Δd_{a_1} to d_1, the relation of wear can be written in the following form:

$$\Delta d_1 = \Delta d_{m_1} + \Delta d_{a_1} = (d_0 - d_1') + (d_1' - d_1) = d_0 - d_1 \qquad (1.2.10-18)$$

335

In keeping with Eqs (1.2.10−17) and (1.2.10−8)

$$d_1 = \sqrt[3]{d_1'^3 - k_2 t_1'} = \sqrt[3]{d_0^3 e^{-k_1 t_1} - k_2 t_1'} \qquad (1.2.10\text{−}19)$$

so that the resultant size reduction Δd_1 becomes

$$\Delta d_1 = d_0 - \sqrt[3]{d_0^3 e^{-k_1 t_1} - k_2 t_1'} \qquad (1.2.10\text{−}20)$$

or written in a general form the reduction in the diameter of bed load particles moving intermittantly is given by the expression

$$\Delta d = d_0 - \sqrt[3]{d_0^3 e^{-k_1 t} - k_2 t'} \qquad (1.2.10\text{−}21)$$

where d_0 is the original diameter of the bed load particle, t and t' are the times spent in movement and at rest, expressed in hours, k_1 [hours^{-1}] and k_2 [mm^3/hour] are the wearing coefficient of moving and stationary bed load, respectively.

1.2.10.2. Laboratory experiments on the wearing of bed load particles in movement and at rest. At the Research Institute for Water Resources Development aboratory experiments have been made with four different types of rock for determining the wearing coefficients k_1 and k_2 of moving and stationary bed load. The average values obtained for the wearing coefficients are shown in *Table 1.2.10−1*.

Table 1.2.10−1

Wearing coefficients of moving and stationary bed load according to rock types, based on laboratory experiments

Type of rock	k_1 [l/hour]	k_2 [mm^3/hour]
Volcanic weathered	$11.10 \cdot 10^{-3}$	$0.718 \, q_B$
Sedimentary	$6.75 \cdot 10^{-3}$	$0.436 \, q_B$
Metamorphic	$1.53 \cdot 10^{-3}$	$0.099 \, q_B$
Quartz-quartzite	$0.58 \cdot 10^{-3}$	$0.037 \, q_B$

The values in the Table are related to the specific rate of transport q_B [p/cm sec] and thus the cœfficients tabulated have essentially the dimension mm^4/p.

The intermittent transport of bed load may be visualized as one in which a period of movement is invariably followed by one of variable duration spent at rest and thus intervals of movement and rest alternate periodically (see *Fig. 1.2.10−3*). The cycles of movement and rest are repeated as long as the particle is buried or becomes suspended. In each period the time spent in movement and at rest is very short, and consequently wearing is slight. For this reason several cycles are combined for easing computation. Such combination is possible if the following conditions are satisfied:

a) during the period of extended length resulting from the combination of several cycles the particle must not be deposited permanently or entering into suspension,

b) the rate of bed load travel v_h should be fairly constant,

c) over the section under consideration the rate of transport should remain fairly constant, otherwise the wearing coefficient k_2 cannot be regarded as constant.

The studies into bed load wear offer also the possibility of determining the rate of bed load transportation. Several investigators including D. D. Hubbel, W. W. Sayre and Rossinsky have, for estimating the rate of transport, introduced the virtual velocity v_{hv} of bed load and developed relations by taking the magnitude of the mobile area into consideration.

The virtual velocity v_{hv} is a fictitious velocity computed from the distance travelled by the particle and from the total time spent in movement and at rest.

The virtual velocity of bed load is affected by an extremely large number of factors. The magnitude of this velocity is influenced, besides the characteristics of the bed load material, by the physical properties of the water itself, by the hydraulics of flow and by the characteristics of the channel.

At the laboratory of the Research Institute for Water Resources Development the bottom velocity v_f, the bottom slope S_f and the particle diameter d have been considered primarily among the various factors affecting the virtual velocity.

Laboratory experiments were performed in a 1 m wide glass flume, the bottom of which was covered by bed load material obtained from the experimental Danube reach. In these experiments nine types of bed load particle were studied of which three belonged to the fraction of large particles, three to the medium fraction and three to the small fraction, these fractions having been determined in the course of field experiments. The physical properties of the bed load particles are tabulated in *Table 1.2.10 − 2*. The particles studied were distinguished from

Table 1.2.10 − 2

Diameter, weight and specific gravity
of Danube gravels used in the laboratory experiments

No.	Diameter [mm]	Weight [p]	Spec. gravity [p/cm³]
	of gravel particles		
1	32.60	45.60	2.51
2	37.1	54.80	2.56
3	32.1	57.20	2.61
4	19.2	13.20	2.69
5	20.3	11.70	2.60
6	21.6	14.25	2.46
7	12.6	2.50	2.50
8	11.3	2.58	2.58
9	11.2	1.60	2.66

the bed material in the flume and from other fractions by the application of different colours.

The laboratory experiments were closely related to the results of field observations. In the first series of experiments the bottom slope of the glass flume and the virtual velocity of the labelled bed load particles were adjusted so as to correspond to the average bottom slope and to the average virtual velocity of labelled particles over the first 500 m long distance travelled by the labelled particles ·during the field observations in 1965. (The bottom velocity v_f in the glass flume differed, of course, in the present case from that observed in the field, in order to make allowance for scale effects in the glass flume.) In this series of experiments the slope of the glass flume was 10%.

In the subsequent series of experiments the bottom of the glass flume was horizontal, but the bottom velocity obtained in the previous series was maintained. The virtual velocity of particles obviously assumed then another value than that found in the first series.

In the third series of experimental runs the bottom velocity was kept unchanged but the bottom of the glass flume was adjusted to a 10% negative slope.

In the laboratory experiments the effective length of the glass flume, i.e. the distance over which the virtual velocity of bed load was observed, attained 7.90 m.

In each series of experiments, comprising 20 to 30 runs, measurements on each bed load particle included

— the distance travelled in a single displacement and the time required for travelling this distance,

— the length of time spent at rest between successive displacements.

The results obtained offered opportunity for studying several characteristics of bed load movement.

Of probably the greatest interest is the fact that these laboratory experiments have furnished data on the basis of which it has become possible to compare the virtual velocity v_{hv} of bed load particles and the actual velocity v_h of bed load travel. Moreover data have become available on the bottom velocity v_f observed simultaneously. These velocities are compiled in *Table 1.2.10−3*.

Table 1.2.10−3

Velocities observed at the laboratory

Bottom velocity, v_f [cm/sec]	Bottom slope, ⁰/₀₀	Virtual bed load velocity, v_{hv} [cm/sec]	Bed load velocity, v_h [cm/sec]
83.5	0	0.014	16.4
92.3	0	0.026	22.6
80.0	+10	0.024	20.2
84.6	−10	0.005	12.3

The velocity of bed load travel will be observed in the Table to have been 1/4 to 1/7 of the bottom velocity of flow, that is approximately

$$0.25\, v_f \geqq v_h \geqq 0.15\, v_f \qquad (1.2.10-22)$$

It will also be seen from the Table that the virtual velocity of bed load was about 1/1000 to 1/2000 of the actual velocity of travel, thus

$$0.001\, v_h \geqq v_{hv} \geqq 0.0005\, v_h \qquad (1.2.10-23)$$

The analysis of experimental results obtained in the laboratory has shown the magnitude of virtual bed load velocity to be controlled primarily by the bottom velocity and the bottom slope. The influence of particle size, on the other hand, has been found to be negligibly small.

Relying on the foregoing conclusions K. Stelczer has used the results of laboratory observations for determining the relation of the virtual velocity v_{hv} to the bottom velocity v_f and the bottom slope S_f.

The resulting three-variable relation, reflecting the average of over hundred observations,

$$v_{hv} = F(v_f,\, S_f) \qquad (1.2.10-24)$$

is shown in *Fig. 1.2.10−4*.

The close relation observable in the figure is obviously due to the narrow range of bottom velocities, and to the equalizing effect of forming averages.

From the data obtained on the movement of bed load it has become possible to determine first of all the time intervals t' spent at rest and t spent in movement. In fact, by determining the virtual velocity of bed load with the help of the approximate relation under Eq. (1.2.10−24), the time required $T = (t + t')$ for travelling unit distance is readily found. If the actual velocity v_h of bed load travel is known, it is possible to compute the time t necessary for travelling unit distance.

Fig. 1.2.10−4. Virtual velocity vs. bottom velocity at different bottom slopes. After Stelczer

Table 1.2.10—4
Data on gravel particles launched and retrieved

Year	No.	Rock type	Distance travelled [km]	Total time, $T = (t + t')$ [hours]	Original weight, G_o [p]	Loss in weight, ΔG [p]	Original diameter, d_o [mm]	Loss in diameter, Δd [mm]
1965	1	Quartz	0.384	648	2.6080	0.0016	13.80	—
1965	2	Quartz	0.136	888	67.5000	0.0180	39.05	—
1965	3	Quartz	0.358	936	2.7255	0.0005	14.85	—
1965	4	Quartz	0.376	1,056	2.3150	0.0001	13.90	—
1965	5	Quartz	0.346	864	2.4890	0.0014	13.75	—
1965	6	Volcanic weathered	0.392	936	9.3500	0.1322	20.85	—
1966	1	Volcanic weathered	1.105	1,135	6.4781	0.0330	21.46	—
1966	2	Volcanic weathered	1.610	1,805	8.4664	0.3731	24.23	0.73
1966	3	Volcanic weathered	1.560	1,925	12.8711	0.2156	26.24	0.69
1966	4	Quartz	0.080	7,416	2,132.0000	14.0000	141.70	0.12
1967	1	Quartz	1.390	1,513	13.9672	0.0021	23.44	0.52
1967	2	Volcanic weathered	1.380	1,678	20.0404	0.3007	32.37	0.43
1967	3	Volcanic weathered	1.475	1,679	44.1811	—	42.05	0.36
1967	4	Metamorphic	1.690	1,701	6.9167	0.0986	19.43	0.54
1967	5	Volcanic weathered	1.420	1,703	15.0865	0.5451	27.74	0.12
1967	6	Sedimentary	1.736	1,749	10.3194	0.0796	23.35	0.18
1967	7	Metamorphic	1.570	1,752	36.0646	0.1885	37.35	0.05
1967	8	Quartz	1.854	1,894	8.1542	0.0061	19.37	0.07
1967	9	Quartz	1.458	1,994	15.0983	0.0096	24.67	0.48
1967	10	Metamorphic	1.428	2,018	19.5813	0.0328	29.95	0.02
1967	11	Metamorphic	1.401	2,037	50.0705	0.0799	41.77	0.54
1967	12	Volcanic weathered	1.450	2,040	9.9100	0.6352	23.51	0.66
1967	13	Volcanic weathered	1.410	2,060	12.9044	2.3453	22.96	0.25
1967	14	Metamorphic	1.416	2,062	61.1204	0.1728	40.47	0.07
1967	15	Metamorphic	1.320	2,085	74.8218	0.1551	43.62	0.05
1967	16	Quartz	1.588	2,181	4.0122	—	17.75	0.05

Year	No.	Rock type	Distance travelled [km]	Total time, $T = (t + t')$ [hours]	Original weight, G_0 [p]	Loss in weight ΔG [p]	Original diameter, d_0 [mm]	Loss in diameter, Δd [mm]
1967	17	Metamorphic	1.320	2,184	32.4474	0.0523	35.30	0.13
1967	18	Metamorphic	1.436	2,231	75.4187	0.2367	40.37	0.15
1967	19	Volcanic weathered	1.480	2,232	19.5007	0.5337	30.60	0.45
1967	20	Volcanic weathered	1.568	2,234	10.3610	0.1917	24.50	0.18
1967	21	Quartz	1.626	2,252	2.7730	0.0040	14.49	0.04
1967	22	Sedimentary	1.422	2,374	22.7747	0.0950	29.65	0.03
1967	23	Sedimentary	1.452	2,375	12.8594	0.0826	25.64	0.17
1967	24	Sedimentary	1.512	2,378	9.4362	0.0158	20.94	0.47
1967	25	Quartz	1.328	2,422	46.1924	—	37.15	0.05
1967	26	Volcanic weathered	1.324	2,590	71.1823	0.0763	45.85	0.40
1967	27	Volcanic weathered	1.490	2,737	55.1860	1.4435	45.76	0.29
1967	28	Quartz	1.516	2,852	23.8194	0.0080	30.94	0.13
1967	29	Volcanic weathered	1.462	2,855	18.0469	0.6974	28.32	0.67
1967	30	Metamorphic	1.484	2,856	11.9044	0.0174	25.99	0.07
1968	1	Quartz	1.606	2,902	7.7438	0.0071	21.27	0.12
1968	2	Quartz	1.870	3,020	42.9905	0.0221	39.22	0.07
1968	3	Volcanic weathered	2.024	3,021	46.4950	2.9350	38.40	0.40
1968	4	Volcanic weathered	1.988	3,071	12.0194	0.4935	26.65	0.53
1968	7	Quartz	1.625	3,239	6.0525	0.0355	18.02	0.05
1968	9	Quartz	1.185	3,383	60.1675	0.0240	38.27	0.35
1968	10	Volcanic weathered	1.242	3,405	40.4149	1.5232	38.12	2.40
1968	11	Volcanic weathered	1.100	3,430	28.5502	1.1615	33.55	1.13
1968	14	Quartz	1.260	3,572	8.0078	0.0110	21.07	0.12
1968	15	Quartz	2.146	3,719	41.7744	0.0487	38.07	0.07

Table 1.2.10—5

Actual and theoretical specific losses in diameter and weight

Rock type	Specific loss in diameter, $\Delta d/d_0 T$ 10^{-6} [hours^{-1}]		Specific loss in weight, $G/G_0 T$ 10^{-6} [hours^{-1}]		
	Actual	Computed by Stelczer's formula	Actual	According to Düll's formula	According to Schoklitsch's formula
Volcanic weathered	16.65	17.82	24.43	9.50	16.35
	13.65	14.35	8.67	7.05	16.15
	9.55	7.15	8.93	4.29	2.38
	6.10	4.25	—	—	—
	11.40	10.35	21.20	14.70	4.89
	11.21	13.75	31.40	15.15	3.12
	13.90	14.15	88.10	12.95	3.94
	6.58	6.58	12.20	1.79	4.00
	3.29	11.50	8.28	14.65	4.06
	3.37	2.44	0.41	4.50	3.12
	2.32	3.43	9.55	0.55	1.67
	8.30	6.43	13.50	8.36	3.01
	3.44	6.40	20.80	6.76	6.03
	6.51	16.40	13.34	11.90	4.47
	18.50	5.11	11.10	3.86	3.28
	9.88	7.46	11.85	4.00	2.64
	Σ 144.65 $M_1 = 9.04$	Σ 147.57 $M_1 = 9.22$	Σ 283.76 $M_1 = 18.92$	Σ 119.97 $M_1 = 7.998$	Σ 79.11 $M_1 = 5.27$
Sedimentary	2.94	13.20	4.40	13.90	3.82
	0.43	3.40	1.76	5.85	2.25
	2.79	4.76	2.71	7.75	2.26
	9.45	8.02	0.70	0.92	2.28
	Σ 15.61 $M_1 = 3.40$	Σ 29.38 $M_1 = 7.34$	Σ 9.57 $M_1 = 2.39$	Σ 28.42 $M_1 = 7.10$	Σ 10.61 $M_1 = 2.65$
Metamorphic	10.90	6.35	8.37	8.33	0.68
	2.75	3.20	2.98	3.59	1.43
	7.95	2.98	0.83	3.72	1.04
	0.24	2.46	0.78	2.36	1.04
	2.98	2.38	1.37	2.42	1.03
	0.77	0.55	0.99	1.82	0.97
	1.65	0.65	0.73	2.51	0.46
	1.66	2.32	1.40	1.84	0.94
	0.94	2.56	0.51	3.39	0.74
	Σ 29.84 $M_1 = 3.204$	Σ 23.45 $M_1 = 2.6054$	Σ 17.96 $M_1 = 1.993$	Σ 29.98 $M_1 = 3.33$	Σ 8.33 $M_1 = 0.9144$
	Σ 19.24 $M_1 = 1.48$	Σ 18.25 $M_1 = 1.40$	Σ 9.25 $M_1 = 0.84$	Σ 22.62 $M_1 = 2.065$	Σ 14.22 $M_1 = 1.29$

Rock type	Specific loss in diameter, $\Delta d/d_0 T$ 10^{-6} [hours^{-1}]		Specific loss in weight, $G/G_0 T$ 10^{-6} [hours^{-1}]		
	Actual	Computed by Stelczer's formula	Actual	According to Düll's formula	According to Schoklitsch's formula
Quartz-quartzite	3.38	1.97	0.99	2.25	0.52
	1.36	2.18	0.39	3.06	4.94
	1.42	0.81	0.32	1.70	0.40
	1.29	2.06	—	—	—
	1.23	3.37	0.65	3.68	3.36
	0.56	0.78	—	—	—
	1.47	0.79	0.12	1.02	2.81
	2.30	1.63	0.32	1.77	0.27
	0.59	0.34	0.17	2.57	0.50
	0.85	2.40	1.82	1.80	0.25
	2.70	0.31	0.12	1.22	0.28
	1.60	1.33	3.89	1.12	0.42
	0.49	0.28	0.46	2.43	0.47
	Σ 19.24	Σ 18.25	Σ 9.25	Σ 22.62	Σ 14.22
	$M_1 = 1.48$	$M_1 = 1.40$	$M_1 = 0.84$	$M_1 = 2.065$	$M_1 = 1.29$

1.2.10.3. Field observations on the wearing of bed load particles in movement and at rest. The movement of natural bed load labelled with radioactive isotopes has been studied by K. Stelczer in the Dunaremete section of the Danube. The primary objective of these observations was to check the wearing relation described in the foregoing and to compute numerical values for the wearing coefficient but as a corollary result the rates of wearing actually observed have been compared with the values obtained using the familiar relations of Schoklitsch and Düll.

The observation results have offered the possibility of determining the limits within which the periods of movement and rest can be summed. The observations permitted finally the actual determination of the periods t and t' spent in movement and at rest, respectively.

The labelled particles were launched first in 1965 in the Dunaremete section and their travel was traced with the help of a scintillation probe. The type of rock to which the labelled particles belonged, the distances travelled, the total time psent in the bed, the original weight and diameter of the particles, as well as the loss in weight and diameter determined by actual measurements after retrieval have been compiled in *Table 1.2.10−4*.

The actual specific reduction in diameter for various types of rock has been compared with the value computed by Stelczer's Eq. (1.2.10−21), as well as the actual specific loss in weight has been compared with the values found from Düll's simplified expression

$$G = G_0 - ksG_0^{0.55} \qquad (1.2.10-25)$$

and from Eq. (1.1.3−4!) suggested by Schoklitsch in *Table 1.2.10−5*.

Table 1.2.10—6

Actual and theoretical average specific losses in diameter and weight

Rock type	Average specific loss in diameter		Average specific loss in weight		
	Actual	Computed by Stelczer's formula	Actual	According to Düll's formula	According to Schoklitsch's formula
Volcanic weathered	9.04	9.22	18.92	8.00	4.36
Sedimentary	3.41	7.35	2.39	7.10	2.65
Metamorphic	3.21	2.61	1.99	3.33	0.91
Quartz-quartzite	1.48	1.40	0.84	2.06	1.29

Table 1.2.10—7

Percentage ratio of average specific losses in diameter and weight, computed by the different formulae, to the actual values

Rock type	The ratio of the average, specific loss in diameter according to Stelczer, to the actual value, in %	The ratio of the average, specific loss in weight according to Düll, to the actual value, in %	The ratio of the average specific loss in weight according to Schoklitsch, to the actual value, in %
Volcanic weathered	102	42	23
Metamorphic	81	167	45
Quartz-quartzite	94	245	153

It will be perceived from the Table that the specific reduction in diameter computed by Stelczer's formula is in very good agreement with the actual loss in diameter of the particles retrieved. It is concluded therefrom that the separation of the wearing process into phases of movement and rest has proved entirely successful. It will be seen also that the formulae of Düll and Schoklitsch on the specific loss in weight yield misleading results. It has been pointed out already that this stems from the fact that these formulae are based on laboratory experiments and reflect exclusively the loss in weight suffered during the period of movement.

In *Table 1.2.10—6* the average specific losses in diameter and weight computed for four different types of rock have been compared with the mean values obtained from Stelczer's formula, as well as with the arithmetic mean of values computed according to Düll and Schoklitsch.

Omitting the data on sedimentary rocks, in *Table 1.2.10—7* the average specific losses in diameter and weight computed by the different formulae have been

Table 1.2.10—8

Average values of the virtual bed load velocity,
data from 1964 to 68

Year	Virtual velocity, v_{hv}
1964	$\dfrac{500 \text{ m}}{25 \text{ days}} = 20 \text{ m/day} = 0.023 \text{ cm/sec}$
1965	$\dfrac{500 \text{ m}}{21 \text{ days}} = 24 \text{ m/day} = 0.028 \text{ cm/sec}$
1966	$\dfrac{1000 \text{ m}}{39 \text{ days}} = 26 \text{ m/day} = 0.030 \text{ cm/sec}$
1967	$\dfrac{1000 \text{ m}}{45.5 \text{ days}} = 22 \text{ m/day} = 0.025 \text{ cm/sec}$
1968	$\dfrac{2000 \text{ m}}{41 \text{ days}} = 49 \text{ m/day} = 0.056 \text{ cm/sec}$

expressed as percentages of the actual values. It will be noted that the values computed with Stelczer's formula agree with the actual values for metamorphic rocks up to 81 %, for quartz-quartzite to 94 %, whereas for vulcanic weathered rocks to 102 %. This close agreement may be accepted as a verification for the correctness of Eq. (1.2.10 − 21). On the other hand, as clearly reflected by the last two columns of the table, the loss in weight computed by the formulae of Düll and Schoklitsch differs drastically from the actual values.

The nuclear-tracer experiments performed in the Dunaremete section have permitted the determination of the virtual velocity of bed load under natural conditions. The average values of the actual virtual bed load velocities obtained in the course of observations between 1964 and 1968 are shown in *Table 1.2.10 − 8*.

Although the figures in this last table will be seen to differ from those observed under laboratory conditions and compiled in *Table 1.2.10 − 3*, the agreement as far as orders of magnitude are concerned may still be regarded satisfactory.

The most important result of the experiments performed by K. Stelczer at the Research Institute for Water Resources Development, Budapest, is that they have contributed to a better understanding of the phenomenon of bed load wearing and that they have resulted in the development of a reliable relation on the diminution of particle sizes.

Moreover, the determination of virtual velocities, as well as of the periods of movement and rest has established a starting basis for further investigations by which it will become eventually possible to estimate the rate of bed load transport.

1.3. SUSPENDED SEDIMENT

1.3.1. THE MOVEMENT OF SUSPENDED SEDIMENT

Under certain conditions some of the bed load particles picked up from the bottom, as well as the fine-grained material entering the stream are maintained and transported in suspension. No further explanation is deemed necessary for the fact that, in order to keep the sediment particles in suspension, some lifting force is bound to act, permitting the solid particles of a specific gravity appreciably greater than that of water to perform continuous movement at greater distances above the bottom in spite of their tendency to settling.

Viewed physically the movement of suspended sediment is a much more complex phenomenon than that of bed load. The entrance of sediment particles into suspension may be regarded as a phenomenon subsequent to the initial movement of bed load, i.e. the critical condition of incipient motion.

The movement of suspended sediment is readily observable in alluvial streams and in laboratory flumes alike.

A rather simple explanation can be offered for the incipient condition of sediment suspension. In this initial condition the sediment particle at rest on the bottom is subjected to the frictional force and to the hydrodynamic lift perpendicular to the former. Additional forces acting on the particle are gravity and the buoyant force. The extended suspension of the particles is, however, rather difficult to explain. It should be clear, that under the influence of the continually acting gravity force the suspended sediment particles tend to settle continuously and thus no extended suspension would be possible unless the settling particles were replaced by new ones entering into suspension and if the effect of gravity force were offset by forces tending to prevent settling.

In *Section 1.2.1*, in the discussion of bed load movement, the lifting forces are identified as the internal forces of turbulent flow. In analogy to the incipient condition of bed load movement, the following explanation has been offered by Sutherland for the movement of suspended sediment:

— first the force acting on the particles is increased by circulatory movement within the vortices, and the particles are accelerated. In this manner the particles are lifted from the bottom and, under the effect of vertical velocity fluctuations, continue to move upwards, in sofar as the magnitude of this velocity component is greater than the fall velocity;

— besides the velocity fluctuations there are other influences to promote the upward movement of sediment particle. Pressure differences within a vortex and momentum exchange at the collision of adjacent sediment particles may be quoted as examples.

Extended investigations have been performed by Ya. A. Ibad-Zade on the initial suspension of sediment. Supporting his theoretical conclusions by experimental results he succeeded in demonstrating that suspension is started once the ratio of the actual and the critical velocity, v and v_c, respectively, attains 1.3.

346

As long as this ratio remains between 1 and 1.3, the sediment is transported as bed load only.

Although it seems fully justified to state that the movement of suspended sediment is positively related to the properties of turbulent flow, all efforts have so far failed to derive exact relations that are satisfactory in all respects.

Attempts to relate the quantity of suspended sediment to the energy consumed by turbulent fluctuations have proved successful in some applications to alluvial streams. However, even these have failed to offer an exact and unique solution.

In subsequent chapters attemps will be made to explain the phenomenon of suspended-sediment movement, starting from the general transport equations and introducing the balance equations of suspended sediment movement.

In the most general case of suspended sediment movement the concentration of sediment is subject to variations with respect to both time and space.

In alluvial streams the movement of suspended sediment is regarded to be steady and uniform, meeting the condition

$$\frac{\partial C}{\partial t} = \frac{\partial C}{\partial x} = 0$$

where C = the sediment concentration
x = the main direction of flow.

In artificial settling installations, where the objective is exactly to retain the suspended sediment, the invariability with time, i.e. $\partial C/\partial t = 0$ is retained and uniform settling, i.e. $\partial C/\partial x = $ constant is assumed or, taking into account that

$$\frac{\partial}{\partial y} \left(\frac{\partial C}{\partial x} \right) = 0 \,,$$

the condition will become

$$\frac{\partial}{\partial x} \left(\frac{\partial C}{\partial x} \right) = 0$$

The balance equations of suspended sediment movement will be introduced in a general form, permitting their application to the afore-mentioned uniform steady type, to variable steady and even to unsteady types of movement. It should be noted in this context that all theories on the movement of suspended sediment in alluvial streams take uniform steady conditions into consideration.

A special case of suspended-sediment movement consists of the transport of water: solid mixtures in pipelines, i.e. the transportation of slurries. The requirement here is, obviously, to transport the largest possible volume of solids at the minimum possible work. In this type of movement the granular material is transported in suspension and as bed load alike.

No satisfactory theory has been developed so far for the transportation of slurry. As will be demonstrated, the problem of slurry convayence is solved on the basis of some theoretical considerations, invariably by empirical relationships.

347

Before any detailed discussion on the balance equations of suspended sediment movement, it is necessary to clarify several concepts associated with the concentration of suspended sediment.

1.3.2. SEDIMENT CONCENTRATION AND ITS DESCRIPTION

In *Sections 1.2.6* to *1.2.9* dealing with the movement of bed load some quantities have already been introduced for measuring the weight and volume of moving bed load material.

Thus q_B [kp/sec m] is the weight of bed load transported in unit time and unit width, q'_B [kp/sec m] is the submerged weight of bed load transported in unit time and unit width, G_B [kp/sec] is the total weight of bed load transported in the cross-section, while Q_B [m³/sec] is the total bed load transport in the cross-section, expressed in volumetric units.

In the same sections notations have been introduced for the total load transported as bed load and in suspension, as well as for the rates of transport. Thus q_t [kp/sec m] is the total weight of sediment per unit width and unit time, the volumetric counterpart thereof is q_{th} [m³/sec m] while the symbols G_t [kp/sec] and Q_t [m³/sec] are the total sediment counterparts of the above quantities.

Similar notations can be introduced, of course, for suspended sediment as well. Thus q_s [kp/sec m] is the weight of suspended sediment transported in unit time through the entire area above unit width, G_s [kp/sec] is the weight of suspended sediment transported in unit time in the entire cross-section, finally Q_s [m³/sec] is the volume of suspended sediment transported in unit time in the entire cross-section.

Besides the quantities mentioned above and provided with the subscript "*s*" it was found necessary to introduce other quantities for describing the movement of suspended sediment.

The first of these may be regarded as most essential in suspended sediment transport and is referred to as sediment concentration. This is understood as the weight of sediment transported in suspension in 1 m³ volume of the sediment-water mixture. The sediment concentration is denoted C and expressed usually in p/m³ or kp/m³ units. The term sediment concentration without any qualifying remark is understood invariably as the sediment concentration C [kp/m³].

Besides the sediment concentration C the quantity of sediment carried by water in suspension is commonly expressed in terms of other quantities as well. One of these is the percentage concentration by weight.

The sediment concentration expressed as percentage by weight should be denoted by C_s. With the specific gravity of water being γ [kp/m³], that of the sediment γ_1 [kp/m³] and the concentration thereof C [kp/m³], the total weight of 1 m³ sediment water mixture becomes

$$\left[\left(\gamma - \frac{\gamma C}{\gamma_1}\right) + C\right]$$

(1.3.2—1)

348

and thus the sediment concentration expressed as percentages by weight is

$$C_s = \frac{\gamma_1 C}{\gamma(\gamma_1 - C)} \cdot 100 \ (\%) \qquad (1.3.2-2)$$

From the known percentage by weight C_s concentration is found as

$$C = \frac{\gamma_1 \gamma C_s}{100 \gamma_1 + C_s \gamma} \ [\text{kp/m}^3] \qquad (1.3.2-3)$$

It should be noted that, e.g. in the mining industry, the rate of slurry transport is often expressed by the ratio of the weight of solids contained in the slurry and the weight of the slurry (i.e. the mixture of solids and water). Since the weight of solids in 1 m³ slurry is C and the total weight of 1 m³ solids water mixture is given by Eq. (1.3.2−1), the slurry concentration used in mining, expressed as percentage by weight, is

$$C_{s_1} = \frac{C}{\left(\gamma - \dfrac{\gamma C}{\gamma_1}\right) + C} \qquad (1.3.2-4)$$

Another potential method for expressing the quantity of sediment consists of relating the volumes of sediment and water. The concentration expressed in this way may be termed volumetric concentration and denoted by C_{T_1}. If the sediment concentration is C [kp/m³], the volume of sediment is (C/γ_1) times the total volume and the volume of water is $(1 - C/\gamma_1)$ times the total volume, the relative volumetric concentration of sediment is found from the expression

$$C_{T_1} = \frac{C/\gamma_1}{1 - C/\gamma_1} = \frac{C}{\gamma_1 - C} \qquad (1.3.2-5)$$

In terms of C_{T_1} the sediment concentration C is expressed as

$$C = \frac{C_{T_1}}{1/\gamma_1 + C_{T_1}/\gamma_1} = \frac{C_{T_1} \gamma_1}{1 + C_{T_1}} \qquad (1.3.2-6)$$

Sediment concentration can be expressed also by relating the volumes of the sediment and the sediment water mixture. In the case of concentration C the volume of sediment is C/γ_1 whereas the combined volume of water and sediment equals unity, the volumetric concentration is

$$C_T = \frac{C}{\gamma_1} \qquad (1.3.2-7)$$

The volumetric concentration C_T and the sediment concentration C are related by the simple expression

$$C = \gamma_1 C_T \qquad (1.3.2-8)$$

In his investigations into the movement of suspended sediment the volumetric concentration has been adopted also by Velikanov. However, in contrast to Eqs (1.3.2−5) and (1.3.2−7) he expresses the concentration of sediment as the ratio of the volume of settled sediment and the volume of the sediment water mixture. By expressing the concentration of sediment in this manner he claims to have made it possible to determine sediment concentration by direct measurements, because what remains to be determined is only the volume of the settled sediment. In distinction, the volumetric sediment concentration used by Velikanov is denoted by C_v. If the weight of suspended sediment contained in unit volume of sediment water mixture is C and the bulk density of settled sediment is γ_t, the total volume of settled loose sediment is C/γ_t and therefore, the total volume being unity, the volumetric concentration introduced by Velikanov becomes

$$C_v = \frac{C}{\gamma_t} \qquad (1.3.2-9)$$

It should be noted that appreciable differences between the volumetric concentrations C_{T_1} and C_T become observable at very high sediment concentrations only. At the sediment concentrations C commonly encountered in alluvial streams the quantities C_{T_1} and C_T can be exchanged mutually without introducing an appreciable error. For instance if $C = 100$ kp/m^3, then C_{T_1} exceeds C_T by not more than 4%, assuming the sediment to have a specific gravity $\gamma_1 = 2.65$ Mp/m^3.

Velikanov's volumetric concentration differs, however, appreciably from the foregoing two values. From Eqs (1.3.2−7) and (1.3.2−9) $C_v = C_T(\gamma_1/\gamma_t)$. Assuming the values of practical interest $\gamma_1 = 2.65$ and $\gamma_t = 1.8$ Mp/m^3, we obtain $C_v = 1.471 \, C_T$, implying that Velikanov's volumetric concentration exceeds the volumetric concentration C_T according to Eq. (1.3.2−7) by 47.1%. Consequently the volumetric concentrations C_T and C_{T_1} must not be used instead of Velikanov's volumetric concentration regardless whether the concentration is high or low.

In the relevant literature sediment concentration is often specified as parts per million, and even this is often expressed as percentages. This method of specifying sediment concentration is preferred in the Anglo-Saxon literature. It is abbreviated as p.p.m. For instance, if the sediment concentration is 50 p.p.m, then $C = 50$ p/m^3, and if the sediment concentration is 50 p.p.m.-percentage, then $C = 0.5$ p/m^3.

A special concept in the determination of sediment transport has been introduced by Laursen as $\bar{c}$ [%], which is the ratio of the total sediment transport q_{th} [m^3/sec m] in unit time and unit width, and of the discharge q [m^3/sec m] expressed as percentage by weight.

350

Since the specific gravity of water is $\gamma = \sim 1{,}000 \text{ kp/m}^3$, while that of sediment normally carried by streams is usually $\gamma_1 = 2{,}650 \text{ kp/m}^3$,

$$\bar{c} = \frac{q_{th}\,\gamma_1}{q\gamma} \cdot 100 = 265 \frac{q_{th}}{q} \ (\%) \tag{1.3.2-10}$$

Remembering that the sediment concentration C is the weight of sediment in pond-force units present in 1 m³ water,

$$C = \frac{q_{th}}{q}\,2\,650\,000 \text{ p/m}^3, \qquad \bar{c} = \frac{C}{10\,000} \tag{1.3.2-11}$$

or

$$C \ [\text{p/m}^3] = 10\,000 \ \bar{c} \tag{1.3.2-12}$$

Besides sediment concentration it is of interest also to determine the bulk density of the sediment water mixture.

If the weight of sediment present in 1 m³ sediment water mixture is C [kp/m³], the bulk density of the mixture is

$$\gamma_z = \gamma - \frac{\gamma C}{\gamma_1} + C \tag{1.3.2-13}$$

The bulk density γ_z of the sediment water mixture is used primarily in connection with problems of slurry transport.

1.3.3. BALANCE EQUATIONS OF SUSPENDED-SEDIMENT TRANSPORT

1.3.3.1. The general transport theory. Many theories involving a wide variety of assumptions have been introduced for describing the movement of suspended sediment. These assumptions are manifold and highly different in character, making any direct comparison between the different theories very difficult. It appeared thus logical to apply the transport theory introduced in thermodynamics and to adapt it to the movement of suspended sediment in order to examine the results of earlier investigations on a uniform basis. In the light of this theory various approaches to the transport of suspended sediment can be reviewed and arranged systematically with relative ease. The application of the transport theory to the movement of suspended sediment implies, moreover, that it is possible to use the transport theory successfully in many other domains of engineering practice.

When considering technical processes, two basic principles are preferably adopted as starting fundamentals, the validity of which has already been verified beyond doubt.

According to the first principle *the state of any system can be described uniquely with the help of a finite number of "state parameters".*

351

The second principle involves *adherence to the laws of conservation which are valid in every field of technical science*. All considerations and consequences rely on these laws.

In mechanics the state of any object is uniquely defined by its energy, mass and volume. If this object (system) is divided into several parts, then its energy, mass and volume are divided accordingly. If the distribution is uniform and considering $1/c$th part of volume V, then this part will carry $1/c$th parts of energy E and mass m

$$\frac{E}{\Delta E} = \frac{m}{\Delta m} = \frac{V}{\Delta V} = c \qquad (1.3.3-1)$$

In other words, there exists a homogeneous, primary relationship between E, m and V (increasing any of the three quantities c-fold, the remaining two will also increase to c-fold of the original value). As will be recalled, these physical quantities are referred to as *extensive quantities*.

The first principle may be formulated also in the following manner: the state of any particular system is uniquely determined by a finite number (in the present case 3) of relevant extensive quantities. It is important to emphasize the term "relevant", since theoretically the number of extensive quantities may be infinitely large. Here, however, only those defining the state are to be considered.

Concerning the above three relevant extensive quantities the second principle implies that in closed systems the energy, mass and volume remain unchanged. Naturally, this principle retains its validity also when two systems interact, yet are closed, i.e. isolated from their environment. Two such systems may be, e.g. two gases separated from each other by a moving system permitting only mechanical interaction to take place. The piston will be displaced towards the space where a lower pressure prevails as long as the pressures on the two sides become balanced.

Interaction may also take place if one of the systems is a fluid, separated by its own surface from the vapours above. In similar cases (considering closed vessels) the total mass remains constant, but molecules may pass from the fluid into the vapour and vice-versa.

To each interaction an extensive quantity may be assigned, the change of which is proportionate to the change in energy accompanying the particular interaction. The corresponding "proportionality factors" may be given a two-fold physical interpretation. On the one hand, these indicate the energy, represented by a unit change of the corresponding extensive quantity, on the other hand, they are quantities tending towards equalization. In other words, during interaction energy is transferred from one system into the other, as long as the characteristic quantities become equal. These quantities may be termed stresses or potentials (examples for which are the mechanical stress p, the chemical potential μ, or the electrostatic potential U).

In contrast to the extensive quantities, the common feature of all relevant quantities tending towards equalization and of a potential character is that they are unaffected by size. If a balanced system is subdivided then e.g. temperature T, stress p and the chemical potential μ of the individual parts will have the same value as in the original system. Expressed in another form this means that these quantities tending towards equalization are 0-order, homogeneous functions of the extensive quantities. Physical quantities of this nature are termed *intensive quantities*.

Intensive quantities may have an infinite number of types. Intensive quantities are, e.g., the energy per unit volume $e = E/V$ or, in other words, the energy density, further the mass density $\rho = m/V$ or the relative concentration $c_i = m_i/\Sigma_i m_i$ of the ith component. Moreover, any quantity that can be formed as the ratio of two extensive quantities may be intensive.*

No detailed explanation is believed to be necessary for their homogeneous, 0-order relationship. E. g. in the case of mass density, the relation

$$\rho = \frac{m}{V} = \frac{cm}{cV} \qquad (1.3.3-2)$$

is trivial.

It should be noted, however, that in the case of T, p and μ the quantities are not generally intensive ones but are *relevant intensive quantities*. The term relevant indicates here the role these quantities play in individual interactions. In each interaction energy is transferred, the direction of which is controlled by the gradient of the relevant intensive quantities. These are always the partial derivatives of energy with respect to the relevant extensive quantity.

A relevant extensive quantity and a relevant intensive quantity may thus be assigned to each interaction. The change in energy resulting from interaction is proportionate to the change in the relevant extensive quantity, the factor of proportionality being the relevant intensive quantity.

The trend to equalization of the relevant intensive quantities plays a decisive role during interactions. If the barrier between the two systems is removed, the extensive quantities will flow from one system into the other as long as the relevant intensive quantities become equal. Thereafter the two systems will be balanced. Two related systems are not balanced, unless the relevant intensive quantities are uniformly distributed. Therefore *the necessary and adequate condition of equilibrium is the homogeneous distribution of the relevant intensive quantities.*

The significance of the distinguishing extensive and intensive quantities is not merely a formal one. The possibility of describing, with their help, the interactions between two (or more) systems ("objects") is far more substantial.

Consider a volume element interacting with its environment (see *Fig. 1.3.3–1*).

The state of the elementary volume is described by a finite number of extensive quantities x_i. Within the elementary volume a change in the magnitude of any extensive quantity x_i may be due to two causes:

---

* The various characteristics of sediment concentration and specific weight have been defined in *Section 1.3.2* as the ratio of two extensive quantities.

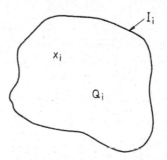

Fig. 1.3.3−1. Volume element interacting with its environment.
A change in the extensive quantity owing to source Q_i and current I_i

a) there is a source Q_i within the volume,
b) there is outflow I_i across the surface enclosing the volume.*
For the extensive quantity x_i the following balance equation is written:

$$\frac{dx_i}{dt} = Q_i - I_i \qquad (1.3.3-3)$$

where Q_i is the source and I_i the surface current.

The quantities involved in the equation apply to the entire volume element. When considering technical processes it is, however, required to know also local values at particular points within the volume. The change-over to local values is possible by considering the values related to unit volume, i.e. the densities of extensive quantities involved in the balance equation. The extensive quantity x_i within volume V equals the volume integral of its density v_i:

$$x_i = \int_V v_i \, dV \qquad (1.3.3-4)$$

All sources within the volume are

$$Q_i = \int_V q_i \, dV \qquad (1.3.3-5)$$

where q_i = source density.

The surface current density related to a particular extensive quantity should be denoted as $\mathbf{J}_i$. The total quantity flowing across the surface equals the surface integral of surface current density over the closed surface F enclosing the volume V

$$I_i = \oint_F \mathbf{J}_i \cdot d\mathbf{F} \qquad (1.3.3-6)$$

Introducing the density values into the balance equation

$$\frac{d}{dt} \int_V v_i \, dV = \int_V q_i \, dV - \oint_F \mathbf{J}_i \cdot d\mathbf{F} \qquad (1.3.3-7)$$

* By agreement, outflow is considered a current of positive, while inflow as one of negative sign.

354

The balance for the ith extensive quantity is expressed by the above equation (still applying to the entire volume!). The second term on the right-hand side is a surface integral which is transformed into a volume integral by applying the Gauss – Ostrogradsky theorem:

$$\oint_F (\mathbf{J}_i \cdot d\mathbf{F}) = \int_V \text{div } \mathbf{J}_i \, dV \qquad (1.3.3-8)$$

Combining terms and transferring the differentiation with respect to time under the integral sign

$$\int_V \left(\frac{\partial v_i}{\partial t} + \text{div } \mathbf{J}_i - q_i \right) dV = 0 \qquad (1.3.3-9)$$

Regardless of the limits of integration the integral cannot assume 0 value, unless the integrand itself is zero.*

The general balance equation is thus obtained as

$$\frac{\partial v_i}{\partial t} + \text{div } \mathbf{J}_i = q_i \qquad (1.3.3-10)$$

where the only restriction concerning v_i was that it denoted the density of some extensive quantity. It may thus denote, e.g. the energy density e, the mass density ρ, etc., alike.

The current density of extensive quantities (within a system having a stationary mass center) is defined by the inhomogeneity of the intensive quantities.

It has been recognized for long that various physical processes that are variable in time are described by laws of the form

$$\frac{dx}{dt} = L(y - y_0) \qquad (1.3.3-11)$$

where the left-hand side represents the variation of an extensive quantity with time, and the right-hand side is the difference between the corresponding intensive quantity multiplied by a suitable coefficient, the so-called conductivity or transfer coefficient.

Examples for these are Newton's cooling law, Ohm's law, the Fick law, which relate to internal energy, electric charge and mass current, respectively. The seepage law of Darcy is also familiar, expressing the volume flow of fluid in terms of the differential head. In each of these cases the equalization of an intensive quantity (temperature, electric tension, chemical potential, pressure head) is considered, which involves invariably the flow of an extensive quantity (internal energy, electric charge, mass, volume).

By the middle of the 19th century physical phenomena in which the flow of an extensive quantity is not exclusively caused by the inhomogeneity of the cor-

---

* Disregarding the so-called 0-dimension multitudes.

responding relevant intensive quantity had been recognized. (An example for this is thermal diffusion where differential temperature results in a mass current.)

With due allowance for the so-called cross-effects (thermo-mechanical, thermo-electric, electro-kinetic, etc. phenomena), the fully generalized definition of current density was formulated by L. Onsager, Nobel price winner, in his papers published in 1930 and 1931. In these current density was stated to be controlled by the inhomogeneity not only of the "pertinent", but of all intensive quantities simultaneously.

The degree of inhomogeneity is indicated by the nabla operator. Inasmuch as the relevant intensive quantity is a scalar physical quantity, the nabla operator denotes the gradient thereof

$$\nabla y_l \equiv \text{grad } y_l \tag{1.3.3-12}$$

The statement conveyed by the Onsager relation is that the current density of the ith extensive quantity is expressed as the summarized product of the gradient of the individual intensive quantities y_l and the corresponding conductivities L_{il}:

$$\mathbf{J}_i = \sum_{l=1}^{m} L_{il} \text{ grad } y_l \tag{1.3.3-13}$$

The conductivities L_{il} depend on the material properties of the medium. Materials which are poor conductors for the current of certain extensive quantities, i.e. for which the corresponding conductivities are low, act as insulators for the particular extensive quantity.

The density of the so-called conductive current of individual extensive quantities is defined by the Onsager relationship. In cases where the mass center of the system is also displaced (macroscopic movement also occurs), the extensive quantities (that are the material properties) also follow this movement, and this is termed a convective current. Convective current densities are expressed in a very simple form. If at any arbitrary point the density of the ith extensive quantity is v_i and the velocity of this point is $\mathbf{v}$, then the density of the convective current is $v_i\mathbf{v}$. The total current density (the sum of convective and conductive current densities) is thus

$$\mathbf{J}_i = v_i \mathbf{v} + \sum_{l=1}^{m} L_{il} \text{ grad } y_l \tag{1.3.3-14}$$

Introducing the total current density into the general balance equation expressed by Eq. (1.3.3−10),

$$\frac{\partial v_i}{\partial t} + \text{div} \left[v_i \mathbf{v} + \sum_{l=1}^{m} L_{il} \text{grad } y_l \right] = q_i \tag{1.3.3-15}$$

No expression of general validity, comparable to that of current density, exists for describing the source density q_i involved in the above expression. All that

356

can be said of source density is that it is the rate per unit time and unit volume at which a particular extensive quantity is generated (or reduced). The problem in various domains of technical science is to clarify for any particular process

    a) the extensive and intensive quantities that are relevant to the process,

    b) the numerical values of conductivities, and

    c) the actual form of source densities.

With the available information on the formal questions the basic equations governing individual processes can be formulated.

For describing particular processes, besides the balance equations, the so-called *unambiguity conditions* must also be specified. These may be listed as follows:

    a) *The domain of interpretation*—the range within which the variables (including the geometric ones) involved in the equations may assume values. Concerning the geometric variables this is equivalent to the definition of the perimeter of the system under consideration, i.e. to the description (frequently in the form of a drawing) of the geometrical shape delimiting the system from its environment.

    b) *Boundary conditions*—specification of the interaction between the system and its environment. The function of the boundary conditions is to express the potential interactions across the boundary of the system between the system proper and its environment within the period under consideration.

    c) *Initial conditions*—definition of the state in which the system is at the instant selected for starting considerations. When considering steady processes (constant with respect to time), obviously no initial conditions exist.

    d) *Condition equations*—specifications of the physical properties of the "operating medium" of the system.

All these conditions can be formulated accurately for particular problems only. That is why they are called unambiguity criteria. Mathematically, these are the prerequisites for the unique solution of the set of differential equations describing the phenomenon, while in the physical sense, the criteria for the unambiguous description of the particular system.

The skeleton of the transport theory has been outlined above. For a detailed treatment thereof reference is made to the work of I. Fényes (see Bibliography) who has made valuable contributions to the development of the theory itself.

1.3.3.2. Balance equations of suspended-sediment transport. * It is deemed necessary to derive the general balance equation of suspended-sediment transport first. Remembering the foregoing considerations this should present no undue difficulties, once the relevant extensive and intensive quantities are determined and the actual form of the source densities is found.

Considerations being concerned here with water, it is logical that the mass, momentum, kinetic and internal energy of water are the most important param-

---

* Similar equations for suspended sediment transport were developed first by the author and E. Szücs in a paper published in *Acta Technica* No. 1—2, 1970. In subsequent chapters parts of this paper, some condensed and some enlarged, will be found.

eters to be introduced. The same extensive quantities apply to sediment although the composition of the latter is not uniform, the individual particles being different in size. (Any allowance for differences in material properties would make even the general treatment too complicated. For this reason the multitude of particles having the same material properties but being of different sizes will be understood under the term sediment.) Individual fractions will be denoted by the subscript k.

The extensive quantities to be taken into consideration are as follows:

m	= the mass of the fluid,
$m\mathbf{v}$	= the momentum of the fluid,
$(1/2)mv^2$	= the kinetic energy of the fluid,
$c_v mT$	= the internal energy of the fluid (c_v is specific heat, T the temperature),
m_k	= the mass of sediment particle "k",
$m_k \mathbf{v}_k$	= the momentum carried by the sediment particle "k",
$(1/2)m_k \mathbf{v}_k 2$	= the kinetic energy of the sediment particle "k",
$c_k m_k T_k$	= the internal energy of the sediment particle "k".

The corresponding relevant intensive quantities are the velocity of flow $\mathbf{v}$, the hydrostatic pressure p and the temperature T. These will permit the current densities to be written according to Eq. (1.3.3−14) in the form

$$\mathbf{J}_i = v_i \mathbf{v} + \sum_{l=1}^{m} L_{il} \text{ grad } y_l \qquad (1.3.3-16)$$

In the mass balance the conductive current (diffusion) will be neglected in comparison to its convective counterpart.* Introducing the values ρ and ρ_k for the mass density of fluid and sediment, respectively, the corresponding current densities become

$$\mathbf{J} = \rho \mathbf{v}, \text{ and } \mathbf{J}_k = \rho_k \mathbf{v}_k \qquad (1.3.3-17)$$

In the momentum balance, the convective current is the dyadic product of the vectors of momentum density and flow velocity:

$$\mathbf{J}_{conv} = \rho \mathbf{v} \circ \mathbf{v} \qquad (1.3.3-18)$$

The conductive current is a stress tensor which−in turbulent flow−is the mean value with respect to time of the dyadic product of pulsation velocity:

$$\mathbf{J}_{cond} = \overline{\rho' \mathbf{v}' \circ \mathbf{v}'} \qquad (1.3.3-19)$$

The components thereof are known as the Reynolds stresses.

---

* The chemical potential has been omitted from among the relevant intensive quantities, since molecular diffusion has been neglected.

The current density of kinetic energy is obtained directly from the current density of momentum, by applying the scalar multiplicator $(1/2)\mathbf{v}$ to the vector of momentum density.

It is further required to define the source density. The mass of fluid has no source and the sediment, considered as a whole, is likewise source-free. However, the mass of individual (kth) fractions suffers a change q_k by impact, the number of larger particles decreasing, that of smaller once increasing as a result of comminution. The impact forces (momentum exchange) occurring at collisions are responsible for the desintegration of particles. This implies at the same time that in connection with the source density of momentum it is insufficient to consider the gravitational field $\rho\mathbf{g}$ alone. The collision of individual particles (the ith with the kth) is always accompanied by a momentum exchange $\mathbf{E}_{ik}$ which must be taken into consideration as a momentum source (or sink), even if it does not result in comminution.

Neither must the effect of fluid on the sediment be forgotten, this being responsible for the conveyance of particles. The momentum exchange between water and the kth sediment particles is $\mathbf{E}_k$, during which the momentum imparted to the sediment particle is equal to the momentum lost by the fluid. Consequently, the momentum exchange between water and sediment should be entered into the equation relating to water as a negative source, while as a positive source in the equation relating to sediment.

The source terms relating to the interaction between water and sediment, as well as between sediment and sediment should be entered into the balance equations of kinetic energy in a similar manner. Some kinetic energy is, logically, converted into internal energy as a consequence of friction (i.e. dissipation occurs). Concerning kinetic energy this represents a negative source, while a positive one for internal energy.

Subsequent considerations will be confined to *isothermal conditions*, in that the dissipation of kinetic energy will be regarded negligibly small. It will be readily perceived that under such conditions the balance equations of both internal and kinetic energy become superfluous. In fact, in the absence of dissipation the full kinetic energy of the entire system is conserved and any exchange of kinetic energy between the individual components occurs always in combination with an exchange of momentum. Consequently, the balance equations of kinetic energy and momentum are interrelated.

Let us now introduce the corresponding terms into the balance equations, assuming the number of particles in the kth fraction to be N_k, the total number of particles being

$$\sum_{i=1}^{n} N_i = N$$

Considering *the mass balance:*

for water

$$\frac{\partial \rho}{\partial t} + \text{div } \rho \, \mathbf{v} = 0 \tag{1.3.3-20}$$

for the kth sediment fraction

$$\frac{\partial \rho_k}{\partial t} + \text{div } \rho_k \, \mathbf{v}_k = q_k \tag{1.3.3-21}$$

The balance equations of momentum (including various sources and assuming turbulent flow) are
for water

$$\frac{\partial \rho \, \mathbf{v}}{\partial t} + \text{Div } \left(\rho \mathbf{v} \circ \mathbf{v} + \overline{\rho' \mathbf{v}' \circ \mathbf{v}'} \right) = \rho \mathbf{g} - \sum_{k=1}^{n} \mathbf{E}_k \frac{N_k}{N} \tag{1.3.3-22}$$

for the kth sediment fraction

$$\frac{\partial \rho_k \mathbf{v}_k}{\partial t} + \text{Div } \left(\rho_k \mathbf{v}_k \circ \mathbf{v}_k + \overline{\rho_k \mathbf{v}'_k \circ \mathbf{v}'_k} \right) = \rho_k \mathbf{g} + \mathbf{E}_k +$$

$$+ \sum_{\substack{i=1 \\ (i \neq k)}}^{n} \mathbf{E}_{ik} \frac{N_i}{N} \tag{1.3.3-23}$$

The term $\mathbf{E}_k$ on the right-hand side of the equations is the source density of momentum due to momentum exchange between the component of mass m_k and water, while $\mathbf{E}_{ik}$ denotes the source density of momentum due to momentum exchange between particles of mass m_k and all other particles.

The relevant intensive quantity of momentum exchange is velocity. The change in momentum is proportionate to the difference in velocities. For the interaction between water and sediment

$$\mathbf{E}_k = L_k \left(\mathbf{v}_k - \mathbf{v} \right) \tag{1.3.3-24}$$

while for the interaction between two sediment particles of different mass

$$\mathbf{E}_{ik} = L_{ik} \left(\mathbf{v}_k - \mathbf{v}_i \right) \tag{1.3.3-25}$$

where L_k and L_{ik} are the corresponding proportionality factors (the determination of which will be dealt with in detail subsequently), while $\mathbf{v}_k$, $\mathbf{v}_i$ and $\mathbf{v}$ are the velocities of the sediment fractions k and i, as well as of water, respectively.

Let us consider the condition of equilibrium. Obviously no particle is in equilibrium unless the resultant of forces to which it is subjected is zero. The forces acting on the particle are gravity and the change in momentum per unit time, resulting from collisions with other particles. These are the terms involved on the right-hand side of the momentum balance equation – Eq. (1.3.3–23) – written

360

for the sediment. In the case of equilibrium this becomes zero, so that

$$\rho_k \mathbf{g} = -\mathbf{E}_k - \sum_{\substack{i=1 \\ (i \neq k)}}^{n} \mathbf{E}_{ik} \frac{N_i}{N} = -L_k (\mathbf{v}_k - \mathbf{v}) - \sum_{\substack{i=1 \\ (i \neq k)}}^{n} L_{ik} (\mathbf{v}_k - \mathbf{v}_i) \frac{N_i}{N} \qquad (1.3.3-26)$$

The term $\mathbf{E}_{ik}$ is omitted if only particles of the same kind (of mass m_k) are present in the water. What we are concerned with in such cases is the manner in which the combined momentum of all particles undergoes a change. Collisions between particles of the same mass but of different velocity result, naturally, in an exchange of momentum, but leave the total momentum of the particles unaffected.

Consequently for water in which only particles of mass m_k are present and which is stationary, i.e. $\mathbf{v} = 0$, under equilibrium conditions it follows from Eq. $(1.3.3-26)$ that

$$|\rho_k \mathbf{g}| = \gamma_k = -|L_k \mathbf{v}_k| = -L_k \omega_k \qquad (1.3.3-27)$$

Here $\mathbf{v}_k$ is the velocity of a particle (of mass m_k and specific gravity γ_k) which is in equilibrium in a stationary fluid. This has been defined as the settling velocity ω_k. The conductivity of the momentum source is thus

$$L_k = -\frac{\gamma_k}{\omega_k} \qquad (1.3.3-28)$$

i.e. the negative value of the ratio of specific gravity and settling velocity. In the physical sense L_k denotes the proportionality factor indicating the momentum imparted to the particles moving at velocity $\mathbf{v}_k$ by the fluid flowing at velocity $\mathbf{v}$ during unit time and per unit volume.

The equations relating to the entire sediment are obtained by summing the equations written for the kth fraction. For simplicity of treatment the sediment will be considered in the manner outlined above, as a multitude consisting of discrete fraction. (In the case of a uniform distribution the summation would be replaced by integration.) The different fractions are denoted by a numerical subscript $(1, 2, \ldots, k, \ldots, n)$. The fractions of mass $m_1, m_2, \ldots, m_k, \ldots, m_n$ consist of particles the number of which is $N_1, N_2, \ldots, N_k, \ldots, N_n$. The total number of particles is $N = N_1 + N_2 + \ldots + N_k + \ldots + N_n$. With this in mind the equation for the entire sediment is obtained from the momentum balance equation of an individual fraction. The combined momentum density is expressed as the weighted sum of the momentum densities of individual fractions. Thus, with ρ_1 denoting the weighted density of the sediment fractions and $\mathbf{v}_h$ the velocity thereof

$$\rho_1 \mathbf{v}_h = \frac{1}{N} \sum_{i=1}^{n} N_i \rho_i \mathbf{v}_i \qquad (1.3.3-29)$$

The right-hand side of the momentum balance is summed up accordingly and, in analogy to the foregoing, it is assumed that the force exerted by the fluid on all particles is proportionate to the difference of the average velocity v_h of the particles and the velocity $\mathbf{v}$ of the fluid

$$\sum_{i=1}^{n} \frac{N_i}{N} \rho_i \mathbf{g} + \sum_{i=1}^{n} \frac{N_i}{N} \mathbf{E}_i = \rho_1 \mathbf{g} + L(\mathbf{v}_h - \mathbf{v}) \qquad (1.3.3-30)$$

where ρ_1 is the mean density of the particles and L is a factor of proportionality.

The term $\sum_{i=1}^{n} \mathbf{E}_{ik}$ is eliminated from the summation, since the momentum of the entire sediment remains unaltered by the momentum exchange occurring during collisions between individual particles. The momentum of the entire sediment is assumed an internal force.

Considering again the condition of equilibrium (where the gravitational force just equals the momentum exchange of fluid-particle interaction) and the fluid is stationary, i.e. $\mathbf{v} = 0$, then Eqs (1.3.3−26) and (1.3.3−27) for the entire sediment become

$$|\rho_1 \mathbf{g}| = \gamma_1 = -|L\mathbf{v}_h| = -L\bar{\omega} \qquad (1.3.3-31)$$

where γ_1 is the weighted specific gravity of the entire sediment in equilibrium and v_h is the velocity of the latter in a stationary fluid. This has been defined as the resultant settling velocity ω of the sediment. The factor of proportionality is thus

$$-L = \frac{\gamma_1}{\bar{\omega}} \qquad (1.3.3-32)$$

From the foregoing it will be recalled further that $\mathbf{E}_i = L_i(\mathbf{v}_i - \mathbf{v})$, and for $\mathbf{v} = 0$, $\mathbf{E}_i = -L_i\omega_i$, so that

$$\left| \sum_{i=1}^{n} \frac{N_i}{N} \mathbf{E}_i \right| = L\bar{\omega} = \sum_{i=1}^{n} \frac{N_i}{N} L_i \omega_i \qquad (1.3.3-33)$$

Since $\bar{\omega}$ is the mean of velocities ω_k, i.e. the settling velocity of the mass center of the entire sediment

$$L = \sum_{i=1}^{n} \frac{N_i}{N} L_i \qquad (1.3.3-34)$$

whence

$$-L = \sum_{i=1}^{n} \frac{N_i}{N} \frac{\gamma_i}{\omega_i} = \frac{\gamma_1}{\bar{\omega}} \qquad (1.3.3-35)$$

This expression is an especially striking illustration of the relationship between the settling velocities inasmuch as we are justified in assuming that all particles

362

have the same specific gravity, so that $\gamma_i = \gamma_1 = $ constant. In this case

$$\frac{1}{\overline{\omega}} = \sum_{i=1}^{n} \frac{N_i}{N} \frac{1}{\omega_i}, \quad \text{or} \quad \frac{N}{\overline{\omega}} = \sum_{i=1}^{n} \frac{N_i}{\omega_i} \qquad (1.3.3\text{--}36)$$

The source density of interaction between the fluid and sediment, on the right-hand side of the momentum balance, can be specified in two different ways: either the resultant settling velocity and the resultant specific gravity of the entire sediment mass must be known, or the values relating to the component particles of the mass and the relative number of particles must be available.

The comminution process resulting from collisions between the particles has been neglected in the foregoing treatment. If the process of comminution is also taken into consideration, the source densities q_k related to the individual fractions assume values other than zero. An attempt at the exact description of this process is known to have been made by Gy. Fáy and B. Zselev who followed and improved the approach of Kolmogorov. The theory appears still to be far from complete, so that the process of comminution will remain disregarded subsequently.

Neither has the transfer of internal energy been taken into consideration or, in other words, sediment transportation has been regarded an isothermal process, in which the dissipation of kinetic energy is negligible.

Before summarizing the general set of equations describing the regularities controlling the movement of suspended sediment the following remarks on the mass-balance equations relating to water and to the entire sediment seem to be welcome.

In turbulent flow the instantaneous values of individual physical quantities vary in a random manner and, consequently, instead of using instantaneous values, the mean values thereof with respect to time and the mean values of the product of pulsation terms (correlations) with respect to time are to be entered into the computations. In general, the mean value with respect to time of the mass current density ρv is formed

$$\overline{\rho \, \mathbf{v}} = \overline{\rho} \, \overline{\mathbf{v}} + \overline{\rho' \, \mathbf{v}'}$$

The first term on the right-hand side of this expression represents the convective mass current density, the second term being the so-called turbulent diffusion. In analogy to molecular diffusion, turbulent diffusion may be expressed as the product of conductivity ε and gradient of mass density

$$\overline{\rho' \, \mathbf{v}'} = -\varepsilon \operatorname{grad} \overline{\rho}$$

As far as the mass balance is concerned, this applies to both water and the sediment. For this reason, in the general set of equations this will be indicated in the mass balance equations, related to the entire sediment. However, in the mass balance equation of water this will be disregarded, the gradient of water density being regarded zero as far as sediment transportation is concerned.

The general set of equations describing the regularities of suspended sediment transport is in a summarized form:

For water

$$\frac{\partial \bar{\rho}}{\partial t} + \operatorname{div} \bar{\rho}\, \bar{\mathbf{v}} = 0 \tag{1.3.3-37}$$

$$\frac{\partial \bar{\rho}\, \bar{\mathbf{v}}}{\partial t} + \operatorname{Div}\left(\bar{\rho}\, \bar{\mathbf{v}} \circ \bar{\mathbf{v}} + \overline{\rho' \mathbf{v}' \circ \mathbf{v}'}\right) = \bar{\rho}\, \mathbf{g} + \frac{\gamma_1}{\omega}(\bar{\mathbf{v}}_h - \bar{\mathbf{v}}) \tag{1.3.3-38}$$

For the kth sediment fraction, assuming collision without comminution, i.e. $q_k = 0$:

$$\frac{\partial \rho_k}{\partial t} + \operatorname{div} \rho_k \bar{\mathbf{v}}_k = 0 \tag{1.3.3-39}$$

$$\frac{\partial \rho_k \bar{\mathbf{v}}_k}{\partial t} + \operatorname{Div}\left(\rho_k \bar{\mathbf{v}}_k \circ \bar{\mathbf{v}}_k + \overline{\rho_k \mathbf{v}'_k \circ \mathbf{v}'_k}\right) =$$

$$= \rho_k \mathbf{g} - \frac{\gamma_k}{\omega_k}(\bar{\mathbf{v}}_k - \bar{\mathbf{v}}) + \sum_{\substack{i=1 \\ (i \neq k)}}^{n} \mathbf{E}_{ik} \frac{N_i}{N} \tag{1.3.3-40}$$

For the entire sediment

$$\frac{\partial \rho_1}{\partial t} + \operatorname{div}(\rho_1 \bar{\mathbf{v}}_h - \varepsilon \operatorname{grad} \rho_1) = 0 \tag{1.3.3-41}$$

$$\frac{\partial \rho_1 \bar{\mathbf{v}}_h}{\partial t} + \operatorname{Div}\left(\rho_1 \bar{\mathbf{v}}_h \circ \bar{\mathbf{v}}_h + \overline{\rho_1 \mathbf{v}'_h \circ \mathbf{v}'_h}\right) = \rho_1 \mathbf{g} - \frac{\gamma_1}{\omega}(\bar{\mathbf{v}}_h - \bar{\mathbf{v}}) \tag{1.3.3-42}$$

The above set of equations expresses the conservation of the fluid mass — Eq. (1.3.3 — 37), — of the individual sediment fractions — Eq. (1.3.3 — 39) — and of the entire sediment — Eq. (1.3.3 — 41) as well as of the total momentum of the fluid-sediment system — Eqs (1.3.3 — 38), (1.3.3 — 40) and (1.3.3 — 42).

The source of momentum is represented, besides the gravity field, by the momentum exchange of magnitude

$$\frac{\gamma_1}{\omega}(\bar{\mathbf{v}}_h - \bar{\mathbf{v}}) \tag{1.3.3-43}$$

between the fluid and the entire sediment, and by the momentum exchange taking place for individual sediment fractions as a result of collision with sediment particles of "other size". The sum of these will be realized to equal zero when related to the entire water sediment system, for these are "internal forces".

The set of equations written above is an expression of one of the firmest theorems in physics, namely the law of conservation of mass and of momentum. For this reason we are justified to regard it as the most general relationship of sediment

364

movement. In this form, however, it is, of course, not suited for practical computations.

Various fundamental equations commonly applied in hydraulics are derived, in general, by introducing certain assumptions. The above equations permit clear formulation of these assumptions and a methodical review of the different theories together with the (explicit or implicit) assumptions underlying them.

In every attempt at describing sediment movement the process has been assumed to be a steady one. It follows therefrom that the first term in Eqs (1.3.3−37) to (1.3.3−42), namely the derivative with respect to time of the density of extensive quantities, equals zero. Consequently, the concentration distribution of sediment is constant in time.

When considering the movement of suspended sediment in alluvial streams it is commonly assumed further that concentration C undergoes no changes in the main direction x of flow ($\partial C/\partial x = 0$, or with the notations used in the balance equations, $\partial \rho_1/\partial x = 0$).

The primary objective of various theories concerning the movement of suspended sediment is to estimate the manner in which the concentration is distributed. For simplifying the solution in all known theories the stream is assumed infinitely wide. Variations across width (in the plane perpendicular to the direction of flow) are neglected and the problem is thus reduced to a single dimension. Still the number of variables involved in the resulting equations is greater than the number of equations available.

A closed set of equations can be arrived at by two different approaches:

a) The relationships existing between the individual parameters are determined experimentally.

b) Assumptions concerning the relationship between the unknown and known quantities are introduced.

The assumptions introduced offer a convenient means for differentiating between the different theories.

A fundamental drawback of all "sediment transport equations" is, in contrast to the set of equations derived in the foregoing, that the differences in particle sizes are neglected therein. Whichever simplifying assumption is introduced, it would be essential to specify the particle size distribution of the sediment, namely the granulometric curve before the above balance equations are put to use. This would be unavoidable even if the average or mean particle size were considered. In fact different grain size distributions may belong to the same characteristic size (even if the diversity of the methods of computing mean "sizes" from numbers, surfaces or volumes is disregarded) and therefore the results of different experiments may reveal appreciable differences.

It should be noted further that, in contrast to investigation into the transport of suspended sediment in alluvial streams, only variations with time can be regarded as zero when considering the process of settling of suspended sediment, whereas the changes in the main direction or flow differ from zero. The only simplification that is possible to introduce is to assume a constant rate of change.

The fundamental equations of some of the more familiar theories will now be derived, relying in general on the original publications by the authors. It is proposed to demonstrate at the same time that each of the various theories represents a particular case of the general balance equations. In fact, depending on the terms of the equation, neglected as small in comparison with the others, the fundamental equations of various theories are obtained.

1.3.4. THE THEORY OF TURBULENT SEDIMENT TRANSPORT

In the theory of turbulent suspended sediment transport the internal forces in turbulent flow are offered as an explanation for the suspension of sediment.*

It will be recalled that the rate of momentum exchange between two adjacent layers of the fluid depends on the shear stress developed at the interface between them. In laminar flow the magnitude of the shear stress is

$$\tau = \mu \frac{dv}{dy} = v\rho \frac{dv}{dy} \tag{1.3.4-1}$$

as will be readily seen from the definition given to the absolute coefficient of viscosity μ.

Essentially μ $(\mu = v\rho)$ is a conductivity, in that it denotes the momentum current induced by unit differential velocity. In laminar flow the magnitude of μ is assumed to remain unaffected by velocity. In turbulent flow this assumption would yield misleading results.

In turbulent flow the $\mu(v)$ relation is a highly complex one. For this very reason in the case of turbulent flow the coefficients ε' and ε are introduced instead of μ and v respectively, permitting the momentum current to be expressed in a form comparable to that of laminar flow:

$$\tau = \varepsilon' \frac{dv}{dy} = \varepsilon\rho \frac{dv}{dy} \tag{1.3.4-2}$$

The coefficient ε of turbulent mixing is mentioned also under the name "coefficient of eddy viscosity" or mechanical viscosity.

In turbulent flow there is also a process of molecular mixing so that the shear stress is expressed substantially in the form

$$\tau = v\rho \frac{dv}{dy} + \varepsilon\rho \frac{dv}{dy} \tag{1.3.4-3}$$

According to experimental evidence there is a difference of orders of magnitude between μ and ε', in that turbulent mixing exceeds many times its molecular counterpart. For this very reason the first term on the right-hand side in Eq.

---

* Often referred to as diffusion theory in the literature.

(1.3.4−3) is negligibly small in comparison with the second, so that the shear stress in turbulent flow is commonly computed from Eq. (1.3.4−2).

The tractive force introduced by Du Boys will be recalled to equal essentially the shear arising between the bottom and the water column above it. Consequently, denoting the shear stress arising at the bottom by τ_0 and the slope of the energy grade line by S in a flow of depth D while γ is the specific gravity of water, we have,

$$\tau_0 = \gamma DS = \rho g DS \qquad (1.3.4-4)$$

At any arbitrary distance y above the bottom the shear stress is $\tau = \gamma(D - y)S$ or

$$\tau = \tau_0 \left(1 - \frac{y}{D}\right) \qquad (1.3.4-5)$$

This implies that the shear stress varies according to a linear relation with the distance above the bottom.

For the sake of completeness it should be noted that in both laminar and turbulent flow the magnitude of the shear stress can be expressed also in terms of the dimensionless friction coefficient λ. It will be recalled from hydraulics that, in flow of velocity v and depth D, the head loss over distance L is

$$h_v = \lambda \frac{L}{D} \cdot \frac{v^2}{2g}$$

whence

$$\lambda = \frac{2g DS}{v^2}$$

since

$$\frac{h_v}{L} = S,$$

and thus

$$g DS = \frac{\lambda v^2}{2}$$

so that the shear stress expressed in terms of the friction coefficient λ becomes

$$\tau_0 = \lambda \frac{\rho v^2}{2} \qquad (1.3.4-6)$$

The coefficient of eddy viscosity ε' or ε, which is a conductivity comparable to μ, can be expressed by introducing the characteristics of turbulent flow.

Assume the flow to be two-dimensional, in which the main velocity (along x) is v, its pulsation (the fluctuation of the main velocity) is v', the vertical velocity

Fig. 1.3.4−1. Mixing length defined
on the basis of the velocity profile

component (along y) is u and the pulsation thereof is u'. In turbulent flow the magnitude of various physical quantities is subject to continuous variations with respect to time. Therefore, instead of the physical quantities, their statistical characteristics (expected value, standard deviation, etc.) are used in computations. The departure from the expected value (approximately the mean value*) is called pulsation. Evidently, the mean value of pulsations with respect to time equals zero, so that

$$\bar{v}' = 0, \quad \bar{u}' = 0 \tag{1.3.4−7}$$

The intensity of turbulence is described by the correlation of pulsation velocities, namely by the turbulent stress tensor

$$\begin{bmatrix} \overline{u'^2} & \overline{u'v'} \\ \overline{u'v'} & \overline{v'^2} \end{bmatrix} \tag{1.3.4−8}$$

For the approximate description thereof the concept of the mixing length has been introduced by Prandtl as follows:

Assuming the flow to be two-dimensional, let $\bar{v} = \bar{v}(y)$, with $\bar{u} = 0$. Consider a fluid particle at height $(y_1 - l)$ having the velocity $\bar{v}(y_1 - l)$, that has been raised to height y_1 as a result of transversal momentum change (see *Fig. 1.3.4−1*). The velocity of the fluid particle is smaller than the velocity of its environment by the velocity difference

$$\Delta v_1 = \bar{v}(y_1) - \bar{v}(y_1 - l) \cong l \left(\frac{d\bar{v}}{dy} \right)_1 \tag{1.3.4−9}$$

* The statistical mean value is indicated by a horizontal bar above the symbol.

368

Another fluid particle is transferred from the position $(y_1 + l)$ to height y_1 (in this case $v' > 0$), and thus the velocity difference relative to the velocity of its environment is

$$\Delta v_2 = \bar{v}(y_1 + l) - \bar{v}(y_1) \cong l\left(\frac{d\bar{v}}{dy}\right)_1 \qquad (1.3.4-10)$$

The quantities Δv_1 and Δv_2 may be regarded as turbulent velocity fluctuations. Considering absolute values the mean value of velocity fluctuations is

$$|v'| = \frac{1}{2}\left(|\Delta v_1| + |\Delta v_2|\right) = l\left|\left(\frac{d\bar{v}}{dy}\right)_1\right| \qquad (1.3.4-11)$$

From the foregoing it follows that the mixing length equals the distance a fluid particle is required to travel in a direction perpendicular to the flow in order that the differential velocity between the original and the terminal positions be equal to the mean value of velocity fluctuation in the direction of flow. The mixing length l is consequently the statistical mean value of the extent of turbulent eddy penetration related to a given horizontal datum.

Eventually the instantaneous value of longitudinal velocity fluctuation at instant t_1 is

$$v' = l\frac{d\bar{v}}{dy} \qquad (1.3.4-12)$$

where both v' and l are variable with respect to time. The actual value at the instant t_1 of the mixing length is denoted by l. In other words l is the factor of proportionality (conductivity) representing the magnitude of velocity pulsation due to unit gradient of the average velocity.

The xy component of the turbulent stress tensor is

$$\tau_{xy} = \rho\,\overline{u'\,v'} \qquad (1.3.4-13)$$

It is possible, however, to express the value of v' also according to Eq. (1.3.4–12) as the product of the mixing length and of the velocity gradient. Thus eventually

$$\tau = \rho\,\overline{u'\,l}\,\frac{d\bar{v}}{dy} \qquad (1.3.4-14)$$

Comparing Eqs (1.3.4–14) and (1.3.4–2) it will be perceived that the mixing coefficient is

$$\varepsilon = \overline{u'\,l}$$

This formulation of the mixing coefficient applies to the case of momentum exchange and in distinction the notation ε_m will also be introduced, i.e.,

$$\varepsilon_m = \overline{u'\,l} \qquad (1.3.4-15)$$

An expression describing the distribution of sediment carried in suspension in a fluid is derived according to the turbulent theory of sediment transport as follows:

Consider a plane parallel to the water surface in the interior of flow. As mentioned before, when examining the movement of suspended sediment, we invariably assume steady conditions in which the distribution of sediment concentration remains constant in time. Since the forces acting on the sediment particles are of a magnitude other than zero, the equilibrium is a dynamic one, in that the amount of sediment passing the imaginary plane downward under the action of gravity equals the amount carried upward by the forces acting within the fluid.

If the fall velocity of the sediment particles is ω cm/sec and $\bar{C}$ is the mean value of concentration with respect to time, then the convective current induced by gravity is $\bar{C}\omega$, indicating the amount of sediment that will settle in unit time over unit area of the plane.

In turbulent flow, where the vertical component of velocity fluctuation is u' and the instantaneous concentration is C, the mean value of the product $u'C$ with respect to time, i.e., $u'C$ will denote the amount of sediment actually rising across unit area of the assumed datum plane. The instantaneous concentration becomes $C = \bar{C} + C'$, where $\bar{C}$ is the mean value of concentration, while C' is the pulsating part of concentration. Thus

$$u'C = u'\bar{C} + u'C' \qquad (1.3.4-16)$$

Remembering that the mean value of vertical velocity fluctuations with respect to time is $\bar{u}' = 0$, it will be seen that

$$\overline{u'C} = \overline{u'C'} \qquad (1.3.4-17)$$

It follows from the assumption of dynamic equilibrium that the turbulent diffusion current and the gravitational convective current are of equal magnitude, but of different sign, so that

$$\overline{u'C} + \omega\bar{C} = 0 \qquad (1.3.4-18)$$

or, remembering Eq. (1.3.4−17),

$$\overline{u'C'} + \omega\bar{C} = 0 \qquad (1.3.4-19)$$

The value $\overline{u'C'}$ representing the current density of turbulent diffusion of sediment is found in analogy to momentum exchange described in the foregoing.

Introducing the mixing length l, of Prandtl, the pulsation of sediment concentration is, according to *Fig. 1.3.4−2*,

$$\Delta C_1 = \bar{C}(y_1 - l) - \bar{C}(y_1) = l\left(\frac{d\bar{C}}{dy}\right)_1$$

Fig. 1.3.4—2. Pulsation of sediment concentration
defined in terms of the mixing length

or

$$\Delta C_2 = \bar{C}(y_1) - \bar{C}(y_1 + l) = l \left(\frac{\mathrm{d}\bar{C}}{\mathrm{d}y}\right)_1$$

Since in turbulent flow ΔC_1 and ΔC_2 may be regarded as the fluctuation of
sediment concentration, the mean value of concentration fluctuations becomes

$$|\bar{C}'| = \frac{1}{2}\left(|\Delta C_1| + |\Delta C_2|\right) = l\left|\left(\frac{\mathrm{d}\bar{C}}{\mathrm{d}y}\right)_1\right| \qquad (1.3.4-20)$$

Eventually the instantaneous value of pulsation of sediment concentration is

$$C' = l\frac{\mathrm{d}\bar{C}}{\mathrm{d}y} \qquad (1.3.4-21)$$

where both C' and l are subject to variations in time.

Introducing the expression for concentration fluctuation C' into Eq. (1.3.4—19)

$$\overline{u'l}\frac{\mathrm{d}\bar{C}}{\mathrm{d}y} + \omega\bar{C} = 0 \qquad (1.3.4-22)$$

Comparing the above expression with Eq. (1.3.4—14) it will become apparent
that $\overline{u'l}$ denotes a kind of turbulent mixing coefficient. Since the present considerations apply to sediment transfer, this mixing coefficient will be denoted by
ε_h, so that in the case of sediment transfer

$$\overline{u'l} = \varepsilon_h \qquad (1.3.4-23)$$

24*

371

In early theoretical studies $\varepsilon_h = \varepsilon_m$ was assumed, that is, the coefficient applying to the mass current of sediment was assumed to equal that introduced for momentum current. Several experiments have since been performed to find out whether or not these two coefficients are identical.

I. M. Hassan has found the two coefficients to be in direct proportion, so that $\varepsilon_h = \beta \varepsilon_m$. According to his experiments $\beta = 1.5$ for sediment of 0.10 mm diameter, and $\beta = 1.3$ for sediment of 0.16 mm size. These results imply that for the mass of sediment the mixing coefficient is of a higher value than for momentum. The correctness of these conclusions has been questioned by several investigators. M. E. Laursen has claimed the reverse to be true, i.e., $\varepsilon_h < \varepsilon_m$, and thus $\beta < 1$.

Considering that the density of suspended sediment is greater than that of water M. R. Carstens infers that sediment transfer is only possible over distances shorter than that of water particles. Since actually ε_m is the mixing coefficient of the fluid, it is necessarily equal to, or greater than, the coefficient ε_h of the sediment.

The number of investigations made so far is too small and the results are too conflicting to permit any conclusion concerning the relative magnitude of ε_m and ε_h. Considering further that the validity of the turbulent sediment transport theory is unaffected by the answer given to this problem, the corresponding details will be omitted here. It should be noted also that in determining the magnitude of the sediment-mixing coefficient ε_h it is in general unavoidable to introduce simplifying assumptions by which an error appreciably greater than that resulting from inaccuracies in ε_m and ε_h may be incorporated.

Writing the sediment-mixing coefficient in the form

$$\varepsilon_h = \frac{\varepsilon_h'}{\rho}$$

and substituting the value C for the mean value of sediment concentration $\bar{C}$ with respect to time, Eq. (1.3.4−22) assumes the form

$$\frac{\varepsilon_h'}{\rho} \frac{dC}{dy} + \omega C = 0 \qquad (1.3.4-24)$$

Separating the variables in Eq. (1.3.4−24) and assuming two-dimensional turbulent flow under equilibrium conditions, the variation in sediment concentration is described by the differential equation

$$\frac{dC}{C} = -\frac{\omega \rho \, dy}{\varepsilon_h'} \qquad (1.3.4-25)$$

which, upon integration, becomes

$$\ln C = -\omega \rho \int_0^y \frac{dy}{\varepsilon_h'} + K \qquad (1.3.4-26)$$

In a point at distance a above the bottom, let the concentration be C_a, then

$$\ln C_a = -\omega\rho \int_0^a \frac{dy}{\varepsilon_h'} + K \qquad (1.3.4-27)$$

Subtracting the two expressions

$$\ln C - \ln C_a = -\omega\rho \int_a^y \frac{dy}{\varepsilon_h'} \qquad (1.3.4-28)$$

or

$$C = C_a \, e^{-\omega\rho \int_a^y \frac{dy}{\varepsilon_h'}} \qquad (1.3.4-29)$$

whence

$$C = C_0 \, e^{-\omega\rho \int_0^y \frac{dy}{\varepsilon_h'}} \qquad (1.3.4-30)$$

Eq. (1.3.4−29) is the familiar O'Brien−Christiansen concentration distribution expression. *The theory itself is referred to as the diffusion or turbulent sediment transport theory.*

It has been mentioned already that various theories advanced so far for describing the transport of suspended sediment are particular cases of the general balance equations introduced in *Subsection 1.3.3.2.* This, of course, applies also to the O'Brien−Christiansen theory of turbulent sediment transport.

What is considered in deriving the theory of turbulent sediment transport is nothing more than the mass balance equation of sediment, i.e., the expression Eq. (1.3.3−41)

$$\frac{\partial \overline{\rho}_1}{\partial t} + \operatorname{div} (\overline{\rho}_1 \overline{\mathbf{v}}_h - \varepsilon_h \operatorname{grad} \overline{\rho}_1) = 0$$

and thus source-free conditions ($q = 0$) are a priori assumed. For describing sediment concentration the value C is introduced rather than $\overline{\rho}_1$ and steady ($\partial C/\partial t = 0$) two-dimensional flow is considered. The average velocity $\mathbf{v}_h$ of the sediment equals its fall velocity $-\omega$. Thus

$$\operatorname{div} (-C\omega - \varepsilon_h \operatorname{grad} C) = 0 \qquad (1.3.4-31)$$

or after expansion

$$C \operatorname{div} \omega + \omega \operatorname{grad} C + \varepsilon_h (\operatorname{div} \, \operatorname{grad} C) + (\operatorname{grad} \varepsilon_h \operatorname{grad} C) = 0 \qquad (1.3.4-32)$$

373

In the above expression $\operatorname{div} \omega = 0$ and, since the fall velocity ω is parallel to the y direction,

$$\omega \operatorname{grad} C = \omega \frac{\partial C}{\partial y} \qquad (1.3.4-33)$$

Consequently

$$\varepsilon_h (\operatorname{div} \operatorname{grad} C) + (\operatorname{grad} \varepsilon_h \operatorname{grad} C) + \omega \frac{\partial C}{\partial y} = 0 \qquad (1.3.4-34)$$

Thus, in the case of two-dimensional flow,

$$\varepsilon_h \left(\frac{\partial^2 C}{\partial x^2} + \frac{\partial^2 C}{\partial y^2} \right) + \left(\frac{\partial \varepsilon_h}{\partial x} \frac{\partial C}{\partial x} + \frac{\partial \varepsilon_h}{\partial y} \frac{\partial C}{\partial y} \right) + \omega \frac{\partial C}{\partial y} = 0 \qquad (1.3.4-35)$$

In the theory of turbulent sediment transport the concentration C is assumed to vary exclusively with y, so that

$$\frac{\partial C}{\partial x} = 0 \qquad (1.3.4-36)$$

Accordingly

$$\varepsilon_h \frac{\partial^2 C}{\partial y^2} + \frac{\partial \varepsilon_h}{\partial y} \frac{\partial C}{\partial y} + \omega \frac{\partial C}{\partial y} = 0 \qquad (1.3.4-37)$$

or

$$\frac{\partial}{\partial y} \left(\varepsilon_h \frac{\partial C}{\partial y} \right) + \omega \frac{\partial C}{\partial y} = 0 \qquad (1.3.4-38)$$

In view of the fact that (for identical particles) the fall velocity ω does not vary with location,

$$\frac{\partial \omega}{\partial y} = 0 \qquad (1.3.4-39)$$

thus

$$\frac{\partial}{\partial y} (\omega C) = \omega \frac{\partial C}{\partial y} + C \frac{\partial \omega}{\partial y} = \omega \frac{\partial C}{\partial y} \qquad (1.3.4-40)$$

Eq. (1.3.4−38) assumes therewith the new form

$$\frac{\partial}{\partial y} \left(\varepsilon_h \frac{\partial C}{\partial y} + \omega C \right) = 0 \qquad (1.3.4-41)$$

Integrating

$$\varepsilon_h \frac{\partial C}{\partial y} + \omega C = \text{constant} \qquad (1.3.4-42)$$

374

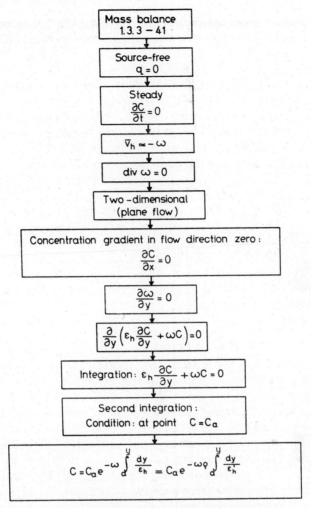

Fig. 1.3.4—3. Derivation of the fundamental equation
of turbulent sediment transport theory

For determining the constant it should be remembered that concentration distribution has been assumed originally to remain unchanged in time, implying that, in any arbitrary section y, the convective current moving downward at fall velocity equals the conductive current carried upward by turbulent diffusion. Thus

$$\varepsilon_h \frac{\partial C}{\partial y} + \omega C = 0 \qquad (1.3.4-43)$$

which is actually identical with the fundamental expression under Eq. (1.3.4—24) of O'Brien—Christiansen.

The derivation of the fundamental equation of the theory of turbulent sediment transport according to the general balance equation is shown in the block diagram of *Fig. 1.3.4–3*.

Eq. (1.3.4–30) implies that the highest concentration occurs at the bottom where its value is C_0. With increasing y values the concentration C decreases gradually to attain a minimum value at the surface, i.e. at $y = D$.

In order to estimate the concentration at different depths with the help of Eq. (1.3.4–30), it is necessary to determine the sediment concentration C_0 at the bottom. This quantity is, however, very difficult, almost impossible to observe, for the suspended sediment in the boundary layers near the bottom is mixed with the bed load. For this reason most investigators accept the validity of the resulting expressions for the flow space above the boundary layer only.

On the strength of the above considerations the variation in sediment concentration with depth is usually estimated with the help of Eq. (1.3.4–29) in terms of the concentration C_a measured at distance a above the bottom.

Obviously, neither Eq. (1.3.4–30) nor Eq. (1.3.4–29) can be applied unless the variation of $\varepsilon_h = \varepsilon_h'/\rho$ is known. Assuming ε_h' to be constant over the entire depth of flow, Eq. (1.3.4–29) will yield to direct integration, and the variation of concentration with depth is then expressed as

$$C = C_a \, e^{-\frac{\omega\rho(y-a)}{\varepsilon_h'}} \qquad (1.3.4\text{–}44)$$

It should be noted in this context that starting also from the assumption of a constant sediment-mixing coefficient a relation similar to Eq. (1.3.4–44) was developed experimentally by H. E. Hurst and Chang.

Actually, in alluvial streams the assumption of ε_h' being constant over depth appears to be questionable. The determination of the manner in which ε_h' is related to depth is one of the most difficult problems in the theory of sediment transport. Added difficulties are due to the fact noted before, namely that not even the ratio of ε_h' and ε_m' is fully understood. The approach generally adopted consists of assuming — in the absence of more accurate information — ε_h' to equal the mixing coefficient ε_m'. Under this assumption the sediment-mixing coefficient is found from the expressions of the shear force given by Eq. (1.3.4–9) or (1.3.4–2) as

$$\varepsilon_h' = \varepsilon_m' = \frac{\gamma DS(1 - y/D)}{dv/dy} \qquad (1.3.4\text{–}45)$$

Inasmuch as the variation of the main velocity with depth is known, the dv/dy component of the velocity gradient can be computed at any depth y and so can the magnitude of ε_h' from Eq. (1.3.4–45). It should be noted here that in practical computations the slope S of the energy grade line is invariably taken equal to the slope of the surface. Unfortunately the measurement of slope is for the time being one of the least accurate and least reliable operations in hydrographic practice. For this very reason any determination of the surface slope is necessarily of an approximate character.

The integral involved in the concentration distribution equation is preferably evaluated graphically. The variation of ε_h' and subsequently of $1/\varepsilon_h'$ with depth is plotted according to Eq. (1.3.4−45). The area of the $1/\varepsilon_h'$ diagram between a and depth y under consideration yields already the value of the integral. Computations concerning the variation of sediment concentration with depth will be illustrated in *Subsection 3.1.1.2.* on the methodological problems associated with the processing of measurement data, in connection with sediment observations on the Tisza River at Szeged.

Instead of the velocity profile traced from direct current measurements, the variation of velocity with depth is often expressed in an analytical form.

The velocity distribution according to Prandtl−Kármán

$$\frac{v}{v_k} = 1 + \frac{\sqrt{\frac{\tau_0}{\rho}}}{\kappa v_k}\left(1 + \ln\frac{y}{D}\right) \qquad (1.3.4-46)$$

was introduced by H. Rouse. Here v is the velocity at depth y above the bottom, v_k is the mean velocity in the vertical, while κ denotes Kármán's universal constant.

From Eq. (1.3.4−46) the velocity gradient is

$$\frac{dv}{dy} = \frac{\sqrt{\frac{\tau_0}{\rho}}}{\kappa y} = \frac{U_*}{\kappa y} = \frac{\sqrt{gDS}}{\kappa y} \qquad (1.3.4-47)$$

and therewith the expression given for the sediment-mixing coefficient in Eq. (1.3.4−45) assumes the form:

$$\varepsilon_h' = \varepsilon_h \rho = \frac{\gamma DS(1 - y/D)}{\sqrt{gDS}/\kappa y} = \rho \kappa y \sqrt{gDS}\left(1 - \frac{y}{D}\right) \qquad (1.3.4-48)$$

or

$$\varepsilon_h = \kappa y \sqrt{gDS}\left(1 - \frac{y}{D}\right) \qquad (1.3.4-49)$$

According to Eq. (1.3.4−48) or (1.3.4−49) the sediment-mixing coefficient approaches zero value at the bottom and at the surface, while it attains maximum at mid-depth.

Combining the above expression of the sediment-mixing coefficient with Eq. (1.3.4−29) and performing the integration, the distribution of sediment concentration over depth is described, according to Rouse, by the relation

$$C = C_a\left[\frac{a(D - y)}{y(D - a)}\right]^{\frac{\omega}{\kappa\sqrt{gDS}}} \qquad (1.3.4-50)$$

377

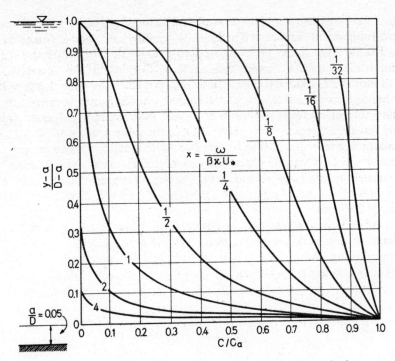

Fig. 1.3.4—4. Relative concentration vs. relative depth, with the dimensionless x quantity as parameter. After Vanoni

Adopting an approach similar to that of O'Brien but using the velocity distribution law of Keulegan, an expression identical with that of Eq. (1.3.4—50) has been derived by Einstein.

With data on the fall velocity, on the surface slope and on the sediment concentration C at any particular depth a, it is possible to compute the concentration figure at any depth y. It should be remembered that the validity of the expression does not extend to the boundary layer at the bottom.

The exponent $x = \omega/\kappa\sqrt{gDS}$ is frequently expressed in terms of the mean velocity and of the friction coefficient f involved in the Weissbach — Darcy formula. This was the approach adopted by Rouse as well. Accordingly

$$x = \frac{\omega}{\kappa v_k \sqrt{f/8}}$$

(1.3.4—51)

as will be readily perceived, remembering that $\sqrt{g} = c\sqrt{f/8}$ and $c\sqrt{DS} = v_k$, where c is the velocity coefficient of Chézy.

A family of curves representing the solution of Eq. (1.3.4—50) was constructed by Vanoni. In constructing the chart Vanoni adopted the value $a = 0.05\,D$ as the lower boundary depth beyond which the suspended and bed load are mixed.

In *Fig. 1.3.4—4* each curve represents the variation of the ratio C/C_a with relative depth for different values of x. The lower the x value, i.e., in the case of constant depth D and slope S the finer the sediment material, the greater the sediment concentration C will be at the same depth y. Conversely, the higher the value of x, the lower the sediment concentration C will be at the same depth y. On the other hand, for constant x values C decreases with increasing y values, considering the value of a. This is in agreement with the regularity generally observed, in that sediment concentration is found to decrease gradually from the bottom towards the surface. According to Eq. (1.3.4—50), at the surface, where $y = D$, concentration C is zero, whereas at the bottom, where $y = 0$, concentration C becomes infinitely large. Actually none of these extreme values is possible, and this is one of the main objections to the concentration distribution described by Eq. (1.3.4—50).

The use of Vanoni's chart will be described in the discussion of methodological problems, in connection with sediment conditions at Szeged.

Remembering that $\kappa = 0.4$ and introducing the parameter $\eta = y/D$, from Eqs (1.3.4—29) and (1.3.4—49)

$$C = C_a \exp\left(-\frac{\omega}{0.4\sqrt{\tau_0/\rho}} \int_a^\eta \frac{d\eta}{\eta(1-\eta)}\right) \qquad (1.3.4-52)$$

The plot of the term $\displaystyle\int_a^\eta \frac{d\eta}{\eta(1-\eta)}$ against depth will result in a curve that can be replaced for all practical purposes by a straight line. This implies that the sediment-mixing coefficient ε_h may be assumed constant and replaced by its mean value ε_{hk}. It should be noted that taking the sediment-mixing coefficient as constant is equivalent to assuming the variation of velocity with depth to be described by a parabola of second order.

From. Eq. (1.3.4—49) the mean sediment-mixing coefficient which is regarded constant is

$$\varepsilon_{hk} = \frac{D\sqrt{\tau_0/\rho}}{15} \qquad (1.3.4-53)$$

Introducing the mean sediment-mixing coefficient into Eq. (1.3.4—29), the expression

$$C = C_a \exp\left(-\frac{15\omega}{D\sqrt{\tau_0/\rho}} \int_a^y dy\right) \qquad (1.3.4-54)$$

is obtained. Upon integration and introduction of the dimensionless parameter

$$t = \frac{\omega}{\sqrt{\tau_0/\rho}} = \frac{\omega}{\sqrt{gDS}} = \frac{\omega}{U_*} \qquad (1.3.4-55)$$

379

for the variation of sediment concentration with depth the simple relation

$$C = C_a \, e^{-15t \left[\frac{(y-a)}{D}\right]} \qquad (1.3.4-56)$$

is written.

If the sediment concentration C_0 at the bottom is adopted for expressing concentration C at depth y, then $a = 0$ and thus

$$C = C_0 \, e^{-15t\eta} \qquad (1.3.4-57)$$

In a Napierian semilogarithmic plot Eqs (1.3.4−56) and (1.3.4−57) of sediment concentration distribution over the depth of flow will be represented by a straight line passing through the point determined by concentration C_a and by depth a, and inclined at $-15t$. Of course, if the semilogarithmic plot is constructed on the basis of Brigg's logarithm, the inclination of the straight line will become $-6.5t$.

The dimensionless parameter $t = \omega/\sqrt{\tau_0/\rho}$ plays an important role in the movement of suspended sediment. Owing to fall velocity ω the magnitude of the parameter depends on the particle size of the sediment material and the physical properties of the fluid, while by involving the shear velocity $U_* = \sqrt{\tau_0/\rho}$, it is affected also by the properties of flow, namely the water depth and the surface slope. The significance of the parameter t in sediment transport is thus readily understandable.

It is possible to express the parameter t also with the help of the mean velocity and the roughness coefficient n [sec/m$^{1/3}$], characteristic of bed roughness. For this end the hydraulic radius should be substituted in Manning's formula by the depth of flow, $\sqrt{DS} = v_k(n/D^{1/6})$. Thus

$$t = \frac{\omega}{\sqrt{g} \cdot v_k \dfrac{n}{D^{1/6}}}$$

or eventually

$$t = \frac{0.319\omega}{v_k \dfrac{n}{D^{1/6}}} \qquad (1.3.4-58)$$

Expressing velocity with the help of the Chézy formula,

$$t = \frac{\omega}{\sqrt{g}\,\dfrac{v_k}{c}} = \frac{0.319\,\omega c}{v_k} \qquad (1.3.4-59)$$

since Chézy's velocity coefficient $c = D^{1/6}/n$ [m$^{1/2}$/sec].

380

Fig. 1.3.4—5. Relative concentration vs. relative depth, with the dimensionless quantity t as parameter

It should be noted that for computing t from Eqs (1.3.4—58) and (1.3.4—59) alike the fall velocity ω should be substituted in cm/sec, while c and v_k, in metre and second units.

The distribution of concentration over depth at different values of t is shown in *Fig. 1.3.4—5* constructed by the Collaborating Agencies. As will be perceived from the figure, at parameter values lower than $t = 0.001$ concentration is practically constant over the entire depth D. Assuming the velocity of flow to be $v = 3$ m/sec, the depth $D = 3$ m, the roughness coefficient $n = 0.025$, at the parameter value $t = 0.001$, the fall velocity is $\omega = 0.0002$ cm/sec, corresponding to a particle size $d = 0.0016$ mm, i.e., a material belonging to the colloidal fraction, if $\gamma_1 = 2.65$ p/cm^3. The clay and finest silt fractions will thus be seen to be distributed uniformly over the entire flow depth.

For the rapid determination of the parameter value according to Eqs (1.3.4—58) or (1.3.4—59) it is possible to construct a chart, from which the magnitude of t is found in terms of v, $n/D^{1/6}$, or c and ω.

In the theory of turbulent sediment transport a definition other than that given in the foregoing can also be given to the turbulent mixing coefficient. It is deemed of interest to note that almost simultaneously with O'Brien a similar theory was developed by V. M. Makkaveev for describing the movement of suspended sediment.

Considering Bazin's parabolical velocity distribution Makkaveev obtained ε_h = constant, and thus the distribution of concentration is described by the expression

$$C = C_a e^{-\frac{\omega D}{\varepsilon_h}\left(\frac{y}{D} - \frac{a}{D}\right)} \qquad (1.3.4-60)$$

which is rewritten into the form more suitable for practical computations

$$\lg C = \left[\lg C_a + 0.434 \frac{\omega a}{\varepsilon_h}\right] - 0.434 \frac{\omega D}{\varepsilon_h}\left(\frac{y}{D}\right) \qquad (1.3.4-61)$$

For the coefficient of turbulent diffusion A. V. Karausev has developed the expression

$$\varepsilon = \frac{gD}{Mc} v \qquad (1.3.4-62)$$

where c = Chézy's coefficient
$\qquad M$ = a function of the latter.

Starting from this relation, Karaushev obtained for the vertical velocity distribution the expression

$$v = v_0 \sqrt{1 - P\left(1 - \frac{y}{D}\right)^2} \qquad (1.3.4-63)$$

where v = the flow velocity at distance y above the bottom
$\qquad v_0$ = the velocity at the surface
$\qquad v_k$ = the mean velocity
$\qquad D$ = the depth of flow
$\qquad P$ = dimensionless parameter found from one of the following expressions:

$$P = \frac{Mv_k^2}{cv_0^2} \qquad (1.3.4-64a)$$

$$P = 0.57 + \frac{3.3}{c} \qquad (1.3.4-64b)$$

Here

$$M = 0.7\,c + 6 \qquad (1.3.4-65)$$

and

$$\frac{v_k}{v_0} = 0.9 \frac{c-1}{c} \qquad (1.3.4-66)$$

382

The relations applying to the parameters retain their validity in the range $10 < c \leqq 65$. Beyond $c > 65$

$$M = 48 = \text{constant}$$

According to Karaushev a separate concentration distribution diagram is computed for each size fraction of the sediment. The resultant vertical concentration profile is obtained as the weighted average of these partial distributions.

For simplicity the subsequent discussion on the work of Karaushev will be confined to mono-disperse particles, the mean fall velocity of which is found from the expression

$$\omega = \frac{1}{C} \sum_{i=1}^{i=m} C_i \omega_i \qquad (1.3.4-67)$$

On substitution of the coefficient of turbulent diffusion and velocity with the corresponding values into Eq. (1.3.4−61) of Makkaveev and after integration

$$\ln C - \frac{N\omega}{v_0 \sqrt{P}} \text{arc sin} \left(\frac{D-y}{D} \sqrt{P} \right) + C_2 = 0 \qquad (1.3.4-68)$$

where

$$N = \frac{MC}{g} \qquad (1.3.4-69)$$

With the constant C_2 determined, the equation is rewritten into the form

$$\ln \frac{C}{C_0} = \frac{N\omega}{v_0 \sqrt{P}} \left[\text{arc sin} \left(\sqrt{P} \frac{D-y}{D} \right) - \text{arc sin} \left(\sqrt{P} \right) \right] \qquad (1.3.4-70)$$

where C_0 is the concentration at the bottom.

Introducing for the surface velocity the mean velocity

$$C = C_0 \exp\left[-N \sqrt{\frac{C}{M}} \frac{\omega}{v_k} \left(\text{arc sin} \sqrt{P} - \text{arc sin} \sqrt{P} \frac{D-y}{D} \right) \right] \qquad (1.3.4-71)$$

or

$$C = C_0 \exp\left[-N \sqrt{\frac{C}{M}} \frac{\omega}{v_k} \beta(y) \right] \qquad (1.3.4-72)$$

where

$$\beta(y) = \text{arc sin} \sqrt{P} - \text{arc sin} \sqrt{P} \frac{D-y}{D} \qquad (1.3.4-73)$$

Retaining the parameter $\eta = y/D$, the relation

$$v = \sqrt{\frac{gDS}{\kappa}} \ln\left(1 + \frac{\eta}{\alpha} \right) \qquad (1.3.4-74)$$

383

of Jasmund–Nikuradze was used by Velikanov for describing the velocity distribution, wherein $\kappa \cong 0.4$ (Kármán's universal constant) while α is the relative roughness according to Nikuradze

$$\alpha = \frac{d}{30D} \qquad (1.3.4-75)$$

with d denoting the particle diameter.

Computing the value of ε from Eq. (1.3.4–45) and introducing it into Eq. (1.3.4–30) we have

$$\frac{C}{C_a} = \left[\frac{(1-\eta)}{\alpha+\eta} \cdot \frac{\alpha + \dfrac{a}{D}}{1 - \dfrac{a}{D}} \right]^{\frac{\omega}{\kappa\sqrt{gDS}(1+\alpha)}} \qquad (1.3.4-76)$$

With $\eta = 1$, this expression yields $C = 0$. In the extreme case of $\omega = 0$. i.e., zero fall velocity, $C = C_a$, indicating a uniform concentration distribution over depth.

In evaluating the integral Velikanov assumed $a = 0$ and $\alpha \ll 1$, resulting in the expression

$$\frac{C}{C_a} = \left[\frac{\alpha(1-\eta)}{\alpha+\eta} \right]^{\frac{\omega}{\kappa\sqrt{gDS}}} \qquad (1.3.4-77)$$

A shortcoming of Velikanov's diffusion theory is that the maximum concentration of the sediment is disregarded in Eq. (1.3.4–76) and that concentration at the surface tends to zero.

Assuming that

$$\alpha \ll 1$$

$$\alpha \ll \eta$$

$$\alpha \ll a$$

he obtained that

$$\frac{C}{C_a} = \left[\frac{1-\eta}{\eta} \cdot \frac{a/D}{1 - \dfrac{a}{D}} \right]^{\frac{\omega}{\kappa\sqrt{gDS}}} \qquad (1.3.4-78)$$

Taking the logarithm of both sides a form more suited for computation was developed:

$$\ln C = \left[\ln C_a + \frac{\omega}{\kappa\sqrt{gDS}} \ln \frac{a/D}{1 - \dfrac{a}{D}} \right] + \frac{\omega}{\kappa\sqrt{gDS}} \ln \frac{1-\eta}{\eta} \qquad (1.3.4-79)$$

Knowing thus the fall velocity, the surface slope and the concentration of sediment at distance a above the bottom, the sediment concentration C at any

384

arbitrary depth y is found by simple computation. The relation does not apply to the boundary layer along the bottom.

In conclusion it may be stated that the basic equation of the theory of turbulent sediment transport was derived from the general mass balance equation by introducing certain assumptions. Integration of the basic equation yields an expression for the distribution of concentration. The validity of the results is governed by the assumptions introduced (see *Fig. 1.3.4—3)*. These are as follows:

a) The process is a steady one.

b) Collisions between particles do not result in comminution and the particles are of identical size.

c) The flow may be regarded two-dimensional.

d) Variations in concentration occur in the vertical direction only.

e) The mean value of the vertical component of the flow velocity of water is much smaller than the fall velocity and can thus be neglected.

The applicability of the relations derived depends on these assumptions being satisfied.

1.3.5. THE GRAVITATIONAL THEORY
OF SUSPENDED-SEDIMENT TRANSPORT

The theoretical relations governing the movement of suspended sediment have been studied in considerable detail by M. A. Velikanov. The foundations of this theory emerged from his work in 1944, with minor refinements resulting from his investigations between 1946 and 1956. In the gravitational theory attention is focused on the energy balance of sediment transport, considering the fluid and solid components separately.

Before embarking upon a more detailed discussion of the gravitational theory, it is deemed advisable to outline the interpretation given by Velikanov to the kinematics of sediment-laden water (or dispersion, in his terminology).

The fluid phase is regarded as the active component of dispersion, which performs work by lifting and transporting the solid particles. The solid phase is the passive component which is carried into suspension while decreasing the energy of the fluid. The entire volume of the disperse medium is assumed to be filled completely by each of the two phases separately.

As a starting point Velikanov assumes the steady, open-channel flow of a homogeneous fluid to be governed by two conflicting forces, namely gravity, responsible for moving the fluid along the slope, and the resistant force tending to retard movement. Under balanced conditions in the flow of clear water the work performed by gravity may be assumed, as a first approximation, to equal the work performed by the resisting forces. In sediment-laden streams, on the other hand, the work of suspension must be added to that of the resisting forces. In this way allowance must be made for the work of suspension in the energy equation.

Velikanov describes sediment concentration in terms of the volumetric concentration C_v introduced by him [Cf. Eq. (1.3.2—9)]. With ρ_1 denoting the density of sediment* and ρ the density of water, the overall density of the dispersion becomes

$$\bar{\rho} = \rho_1 C_v + \rho(1 - C_v) = \rho(1 + aC_v) \qquad (1.3.5-1)$$

where

$$a = \frac{\rho_1 - \rho}{\rho} = \rho' = \frac{\rho_1}{\rho} - 1$$

is the relative difference in densities.

Steady two-dimensional flow is also considered in the investigations of Velikanov. The main velocity of the fluid part is v, the vertical component of velocity is u, while the corresponding velocity components for the solid part are v_h and u_h respectively.

With these notations the source-free balance equation of the mass of fluid and solid becomes

$$\text{div}\left[\mathbf{v}\,\rho(1 - C_v)\right] = 0 \qquad (1.3.5-2)$$

$$\text{div}\left[\mathbf{v}_h\,\rho_1\,C_v\right] = 0 \qquad (1.3.5-3)$$

The assumption of constant concentration distribution leads to the conclusion that the mean value of the vertical mass current with respect to time is zero:

$$\rho\,\overline{u(1 - C_v)} = 0 \qquad (1.3.5-4)$$

$$\rho_1\,\overline{u_h\,C_v} = 0 \qquad (1.3.5-5)$$

Remembering that $u = \bar{u} + u'$, $C_v = \bar{C}_v + C'_v$ and $u_h = u - \omega$, Eqs (1.3.5-4) and (1.3.5-5) are rewritten into the form

$$\bar{u} - \overline{uC_v} - \overline{u'\,C'_v} = 0 \qquad (1.3.5-6)$$

$$\bar{u}\bar{C}_v + \overline{u'\,C'_v} - \omega\bar{C}_v = 0 \qquad (1.3.5-7)$$

The above equations result in three kinematic relations

$$\bar{u} = \omega\bar{C}_v \qquad (1.3.5-8)$$

$$\bar{u}_h = -\omega(1 - \bar{C}_v) \qquad (1.3.5-9)$$

$$\overline{u'\,C'_v} = \omega\bar{C}_v(1 - \bar{C}_v) \qquad (1.3.5-10)$$

From these Velikanov arrived at the following conclusions:

* Essentially the density of settled sediment; or if the bulk density of the settled sediment is γ_t, then $\rho_1 = \gamma_t/g$.

386

Eq. (1.3.5−8) implies that the mean value of the vertical velocity component with respect to time is, in contrast to homogeneous fluids, greater than zero. The magnitude of the vertical velocity component decreases also towards the surface, together with the reduction in volumetric density.

The rising velocity of sediment is, according to Eq. (1.3.5−9), invariably lower than the fall velocity ω. The term $\overline{u'C_v'}$ is a statistical characteristic of the average rate of sediment transport from one water layer into the other. As will be perceived from Eq. (1.3.5−10) the product $\overline{u'C_v'}$ becomes zero if $\bar{C}_v = 0$ or $C_v = 1$. In these two cases, however, there is obviously no sediment transportation. With increasing $\bar{C}_v$, the product $\overline{u'C_v'}$ also increases initially but starts to drop after having reached a certain peak value. This is attained where

$$\frac{d[\bar{C}_v(1 - \bar{C}_v)]}{d\bar{C}_v} = 0 \tag{1.3.5−11}$$

i.e., at $\bar{C}_v = 0.5$. According to Velikanov the sediment transfer capacity of turbulent flow is greatest in this case, implying at the same time that the theoretical maximum of volumetric concentration is also $\bar{C}_v = 0.5$. Actually, however, the maximum value which volumetric concentration is capable of attaining ranges − as stated by Velikanov − between 0.40−0.42. The volumetric concentration $\bar{C}_v = 0.40$ corresponds to a sediment concentration of $C = 720$ kp/m^3, if the specific gravity of the sediment is $\gamma_1 = 2650$ kp/m^3 and the bulk density of the settled sediment is $\gamma_t = 1800$ kp/m^3. This sediment concentration is still substantially higher than that observed in the streams carrying the greatest sediment load on Earth.

The kinematic relations expressed by Eqs (1.3.5−8), (1.3.5−9) and (1.3.5−10) are valid for any arbitrary concentration value. At very low concentrations, approximately

$$\bar{u} = 0 \tag{1.3.5−12}$$

$$\bar{u}_h = -\omega \tag{1.3.5−13}$$

$$\overline{u'C_v'} = \omega\bar{C}_v \tag{1.3.5−14}$$

The gravitational theory has been developed by Velikanov using the following approach:

In an elementary volume $(\delta_x \cdot \delta_y \cdot 1)$ the weight of the fluid part contained is

$$(1 - C_v)\rho g \, \delta x \, \delta y \tag{1.3.5−15}$$

while the submerged weight of the solid part in the same elementary volume is

$$C_v(\rho_1 - \rho)g \, \delta x \, \delta y \tag{1.3.5−16}$$

the actual weight being

$$C_v \rho_1 \, g \, \delta x \, \delta y \tag{1.3.5−17}$$

The work performed in unit time by the fluid part equals the product of the weight of the fluid part and of the absolute slope during unit time:

$$(1 - C_v)\rho g v S \; \delta x \; \delta y \qquad\qquad (1.3.5-18)$$

where v is the main velocity, S the relative slope and $h = vS$ the absolute slope.

Both the relative volumetric concentration C_v of the sediment and the main velocity are subjected to pulsations, so that the work performed by the fluid part in unit time must be determined as the mean value over time of the expression under Eq. (1.3.5–18). In steady uniform flow Velikanov assumes no correlation likely to exist between the pulsations of the main velocity and concentration, so that the term $\overline{C_v' v'}$ is negligible. Thus the mean value over time of the work performed by the fluid part due to the slope S becomes

$$\rho g S (1 - \bar{C}_v) \bar{v} \; \delta x \; \delta y \qquad\qquad (1.3.5-19)$$

The work performed in unit time by the solid part is found as the product of the total weight of the soil part and of the absolute slope $h = vS$. Thus

$$\rho_1 g S \, C_v v \; \delta x \; \delta y \qquad\qquad (1.3.5-20)$$

is the work due to the slope of the solid part. In the mean value over time of Eq. (1.3.5–20) the term $\overline{C_v' v'}$ is again neglected:

$$\rho_1 g S \bar{C}_v \bar{v} \; \delta x \; \delta y \qquad\qquad (1.3.5-21)$$

The work due to the settling of the solid part is also taken into consideration by Velikanov. Considering that the sediment of density ρ_1 settles in a medium of density ρ, the difference in specific gravity $(\rho_1 - \rho)g$ must be entered into the computation. The fall velocity of the sediment is according to Eq. (1.3.5–9) found as $\omega(1 - \bar{C}_v)$. The work performed by the solid part during settling is consequently

$$(\rho_1 - \rho)g\omega \, C_v (1 - \bar{C}_v) \; \delta x \; \delta y \qquad\qquad (1.3.5-22)$$

Taking the pulsation of sediment concentration C_v into consideration, the work performed in unit time by the settling solids becomes equal to the mean value over time. Thus

$$(\rho_1 - \rho)g\omega \, \bar{C}_v (1 - \bar{C}_v) \; \delta x \; \delta y \qquad\qquad (1.3.5-23)$$

The work performed by the resisting, i.e., friction forces has been expressed with the help of the momentum current, in keeping with the theory relating to turbulent flow. This work, too, is of course computed separately for the fluid and the solid parts.

Concerning the fluid part, since the fluid is assumed to fill the entire volume, the momentum transferred across the horizontal elementary area $\delta x \cdot 1$ is computed with the density $\rho(1 - C_v)$, with the main velocity v and with the vertical velocity

388

component u. The momentum current is accordingly

$$\rho(1 - C_v)vu \, \delta x \qquad (1.3.5-24)$$

Since both the sediment quantity and the velocities v and u are subject to pulsation, Velikanov determines the mean value of Eq. (1.3.5-24). In doing so he neglects the correlation existing between the pulsation of the main velocity and concentration, as well as the average of the product sum $\overline{v'u'C_v'}$ referred to as the "third moment".* Introducing in this manner the fundamental relations under Eqs (1.3.5-8) and (1.3.5-10) and taking into consideration the variation of momentum over the elementary vertical distance δy, the work performed in unit time by the frictional forces on the fluid part is expressed as the product of velocity v and of the differential quotient of momentum current density:

$$\rho \, \frac{d}{dy} [(1 - \bar{C}_v) \overline{v'u'}] \bar{v} \, \delta x \, \delta y \qquad (1.3.5-25)$$

Concerning the solid part, the work performed by the frictional forces is again computed on the basis of the mean value over time of the momentum current. In analogy to Eq. (1.3.5-24), with u_h denoting the vertical velocity of the sediment, the momentum current becomes

$$(\rho_1 C_v v) u_h \, \delta x \qquad (1.3.5-26)$$

Writing $u_h = \bar{u} - \omega$ on the strength of Eqs (1.3.5-8) and (1.3.5-9), and neglecting the correlation between the main velocity and the pulsation of concentration, further the "third moment", the mean value over time of the momentum current becomes

$$\rho_1 \overline{C_v v'u'} \, \delta x \qquad (1.3.5-27)$$

On the other hand, the work of the frictional forces is, with due allowance to the variation over δy,

$$\rho_1 \frac{d}{dy} (\overline{\bar{C}_v v'u'}) \bar{v} \, \delta x \, \delta y \qquad (1.3.5-28)$$

The work necessary for keeping the solid part, i.e., the sediment in suspension must also be taken into account. There is no need to determine this work separately, since its magnitude is logically identical with that performed during the settling of the solid part. Consequently, the work necessary for keeping the solid part in suspension is equal to the work expressed by Eq. (1.3.5-23):

$$(\rho_1 - \rho)g\omega\bar{C}_v(1 - \bar{C}_v)\delta x \delta y \qquad (1.3.5-29)$$

---

* The "third moment" is here the first central moment of the three variables, i.e., the expected value of the product of deviations from the expected value of the three variables.

Velikanov's assumption imply that the work performed by the fluid part is required to cover the friction work of the fluid part and the settling work of the solid part alike, the sediment being maintained in suspension by the fluid part. It follows therefrom that the work under Eq. (1.3.5−19) must equal the sum of work expressed by Eqs (1.3.5−29) and (1.3.5−25). In the case of unit volume, rather than of the elementary volume $\delta x \cdot \delta y \cdot 1$,

$$\rho g S \left(1 - \bar{C}_v\right) \bar{v} = \left(\rho_1 - \rho\right) g\omega \, \bar{C}_v \left(1 - \bar{C}_v\right) + \rho \frac{\mathrm{d}}{\mathrm{d}y} \left[\left(1 - \bar{C}_v\right) \overline{v'u'}\right] \bar{v} \qquad (1.3.5-30)$$

Eq. (1.3.5−30) is the first basic equation of the gravitational theory. The physical interpretation given by Velikanov to the terms involved in the first equation is as follows: the left-hand side indicates the loss in potential energy over unit length of flow, the second term on the right-hand side is the work performed by the resistance, that is identical with turbulent friction, the first term representing the work of suspension.

Concerning the work performed by the solid part it is assumed by Velikanov that the work due to the slope vS of the solid phase and the work by settling at velocity $\omega(1 - \bar{C}_v)$ added to each other are necessarily equal to the frictional work of the solid phase. In other words, the sum of Eqs (1.3.5−21) and (1.3.5−22) equals the work expressed by Eq. (1.3.5−28).

Changing here again to unit volume

$$\rho_1 g S \, \bar{C}_v \, \bar{v} + \left(\rho_1 - \rho\right) g\omega \, \bar{C}_v \left(1 - \bar{C}_v\right) = \rho_1 \frac{\mathrm{d}}{\mathrm{d}y} \left(\bar{C}_v \, \overline{v'u'}\right) \bar{v} \qquad (1.3.5-31)$$

which is the second basic equation in Velikanov's gravitational theory.

Velikanov derives the third basic equation by combining Eqs (1.3.5−30) and (1.3.5−31):

$$g S \left[\rho(1 - \bar{C}_v) + \rho_1 \, \bar{C}_v\right] = \frac{\mathrm{d}}{\mathrm{d}y} \left\{\rho\left[(1 - \bar{C}_v) + \rho_1 \, \bar{C}_v\right] \overline{v'u'}\right\} \qquad (1.3.5-32)$$

or introducing the notation $(\rho_1/\rho) - 1 = \rho' = a$, the final form of the third basic equation of the gravitational theory is obtained as

$$g S \left(1 + a\bar{C}_v\right) = \frac{\mathrm{d}}{\mathrm{d}y} \left[(1 + a\bar{C}_v) \overline{v'u'}\right] \qquad (1.3.5-33)$$

Velikanov claims these equations to provide answers to the following two questions:

a) What is the quantity of a particular sediment material which a fluid stream of known hydraulic properties is capable of carrying?

b) What is the law controlling the variation of sediment concentration over the depth of flow?

Velikanov's equations can be derived directly from the general balance equations written in *Subsection 1.3.3.2*. The criteria permitting this to be done define, at the same time, the validity limits of Velikanov's theory:

a) The process is a steady one, consequently the first term in all equations is zero.

b) The polydisperse character of the fluid is neglected and the sediment is taken into consideration with the average concentration $\bar{C}_v$ only. Eq. (1.3.3−37) becomes thus

$$\text{div}\left[\rho \mathbf{v}\left(1 - \bar{C}_v\right)\right] = 0 \qquad (1.3.5-34)$$

while Eq. (1.3.3−41) is written into the form

$$\text{div}\left[\rho_1 \mathbf{v}_h \bar{C}_v\right] = 0 \qquad (1.3.5-35)$$

A further restriction is that even the expected values of the current densities are zero. This yields Eqs (1.3.5−4) and (1.3.5−5) from which the kinematic relations under Eqs (1.3.5−8), (1.3.5−9) and (1.3.5−10) are derived in the manner described before.

c) Eq. (1.3.5−33) is simply the two-dimensional momentum transport equation of the combination of water and sediment, i.e., the combined form of Eqs (1.3.5-38) and (1.3.5−42) under the assumption that the convective momentum current is negligible (in other words the process is considered in a system of co-ordinates moving with the main velocity of flow). The transverse gradient of the conductive momentum current is only taken into consideration, i.e., the terms $\overline{v'^2}$ and $\overline{u'^2}$ are disregarded. Mass density is replaced by the resultant density

$$\bar{\rho} = \rho(1 - \bar{C}_v) + \rho_1 \bar{C}_v \qquad (1.3.5-36)$$

The left-hand side of Eq. (1.3.5−33) is thus the momentum source density, whereas the right-hand side is the divergence of the momentum current density.

d) Eqs (1.3.5−30) and (1.3.5−31) are the balance equations of kinetic energy, again for the two-dimensional case. The left-hand side of both equations contains the source density of kinetic energy, i.e., the work performed by external forces.

It has already been pointed out that the balance equation of kinetic energy can be derived from the momentum balance equation as the scalar product of the latter by the flow velocity v. This is the reason why not more than two of the three Eqs (1.3.5−30), (1.3.5−31) and (1.3.5−33) are independent (as mentioned also by Velikanov).

The block diagram of the manner in which the gravitational theory of suspended sediment transport is derived is shown in *Fig. 1.3.5−1*.

Even in cases where the depth of flow D, the surface slope S, the density ρ_1 and the fall velocity ω of the sediment as well as the relative roughness $\alpha = \delta/D$ are available from suitable measurements, further simplifying assumptions must be introduced for determining the three unknown quantities $\bar{C}_v$, $\bar{v}$ and $\overline{v'u'}$.

391

Fig. 1.3.5—1. Derivation of the fundamental equations of gravitational theory

By integrating the expression under Eq. (1.3.5–33) Velikanov obtains the relation

$$-\overline{u'v'} = gS \frac{\int_y^D (1 + a\bar{C}_v)\,dy}{1 + a\bar{C}_v} \qquad (1.3.5-37)$$

In this manner he determines the variation of the correlation moment $\overline{v'u'}$ over depth in terms of the volumetric concentration of the sediment. The term $\overline{v'u'}$ is always of a negative sign, since the simultaneous pulsations of the main velocity and the vertical velocity component are opposite in sense.

392

Of the three unknown functions one, e.g. $\overline{v'u'}$ is expressed with the help of another, e.g. $\bar{C}_v$ and combining $\overline{v'u'}$ with Eq. (1.3.5−30) or (1.3.5−31), the resulting differential equation involves the functions $\bar{v}(y)$ and $\bar{C}_v(y)$ expressing the variation of the main velocity and the mean concentration, respectively, with depth. Inasmuch as one of the functions is specified, it is possible to determine the other. Of course, the variation of concentration over depth is unknown, the objective being exactly the determination thereof. On the other hand, a number of measurements have been made already for determining the velocity profile, which resulted in the development of several empirical relations.

Here again Velikanov adopts the logarithmic velocity distribution of Jasmund − Nikuradze determined for rough bottoms:

$$v = \frac{\sqrt{gDS}}{\kappa} \ln \left(1 + \frac{\eta}{\alpha} \right) \qquad (1.3.5-38)$$

where $\eta = y/D =$ the relative depth

$\alpha = \delta/D =$ the relative roughness.

The velocity distribution expressed by Eq. (1.3.5−38) applies exclusively to homogeneous fluids, i.e., to clear water. In sediment-carrying flow the distribution of velocities will be different, namely the velocities will be lower according to the interpretation given to Eq. (1.3.5−37) by Velikanov.

The velocity profile in sediment-carrying flow being unknown, Velikanov adopts the one described by Eq. (1.3.5−38) as a starting approximation.

From Eq. (1.3.5−37) it follows that

$$\frac{d}{dy}(\overline{v'u'}) = gS \left[1 + a \frac{d\bar{C}_v}{dy} \frac{\int_y^D (1 + a\bar{C}_v)\, dy}{(1 + a\bar{C}_v)^2} \right] \qquad (1.3.5-39)$$

which is combined with Eq. (1.3.5−31). Introducing the main velocity according to Eq. (1.3.5−38) and replacing y by the relative depth, the following equation is arrived at

$$\frac{dC_v}{d\eta} \frac{1}{C_v(1 + aC_v)^2(1 - C_v)} \int_\eta^1 (1 + aC_v)\, d\eta +$$

$$+ \frac{1}{\ln\left(1 + \dfrac{\eta}{\alpha}\right)} \cdot \frac{\kappa a \omega}{(1 + a)\, S\sqrt{gDS}} = 0 \qquad (1.3.5-40)$$

Velikanov uses the notation

$$\beta = \frac{\kappa a \omega}{(1 + a)\, S\sqrt{gDS}} \qquad (1.3.5-41)$$

393

where the bars above the symbols indicating a mean value has already been omitted for simplicity.

Eq. $(1.3.5-40)$ cannot be integrated directly, unless certain simplifying assumptions are introduced. The most important of these is to replace the main velocity in each vertical by the mean velocity. Accordingly, the multiplicator is replaced by its mean value, i.e., the approximate value

$$\int_0^1 \ln\left(1 + \frac{\eta}{\alpha}\right) d\eta \approx \ln\frac{1}{\alpha} - 1 \qquad (1.3.5-42)$$

is introduced. For simplicity of expression Velikanov applied the notation

$$m = \frac{1}{\ln\dfrac{1}{\alpha} - 1} \qquad (1.3.5-43)$$

For cases of low sediment concentration additional simplifying assumptions are introduced. Since according to his experience the volumetric concentration of sediment in most alluvial streams is seldom higher than $1-2^0/_{00}$, the terms $(1 - C_v)$ and $(1 + C_v)$ may be set equal to unity. The error introduced thereby is claimed by Velikanov to cause a difference in the third decimal only, provided, of course, that the concentration is low.

With the foregoing simplifications Eq. $(1.3.5-40)$ may be rewritten into the following simple form

$$\frac{dC_v}{d\eta}\frac{1 - \eta}{C_v} + m\beta = 0 \qquad (1.3.5-44)$$

whence upon integration

$$\ln C_v = m\beta \ln (1 - \eta) \qquad (1.3.5-45)$$

For $y = 0$ also $\eta = 0$ and $C_v = C_{v0}$ so that

$$\ln C_{v0} = 0 \qquad (1.3.5-46)$$

Eqs $(1.3.5-45)$ and $(1.3.5-46)$ combine eventually into the expression

$$C_v = C_{v0} (1 - \eta)^{m\beta} \qquad (1.3.5-47)$$

Velikanov admits Eq. $(1.3.5-47)$ to be an approximate one describing the variation of concentration with depth with an accuracy meeting most practical requirements, in the case of low sediment concentrations.

Velikanov suggests an approximate relation for higher sediment concentrations as well. According to him high sediment concentrations are to be expected where the main velocity of flow is very high and the particle size of the suspended sediment is very small. These imply, on the other hand, that the ratio ω/v^3 and accordingly

394

Fig. 1.3.5.−2. Volumetric concentration
vs. function ψ. After Velikanov

the parameter β is relatively very low, as indicated by Eq. (1.3.5−41). In such cases however the sediment concentration may be regarded practically uniform, and thus we are justified in assuming that

$$\frac{\int\limits_{\eta}^{1}(1 + aC_v)\,d\eta}{1 + aC_v} \approx (1 - \eta) \qquad (1.3.5-48)$$

With the approximate value of Eq. (1.3.5−48) the differential equation under Eq. (1.3.5−40) assumes the simple form

$$\frac{dC_v}{C_v(1 - C_v)(1 + aC_v)} = \frac{m\beta}{1 - \eta}\,d\eta \qquad (1.3.5-49)$$

which upon integration becomes

$$\psi = \psi_0(1 - \eta)^{m\beta} \qquad (1.3.5-50)$$

Here ψ is a function of C_v and ψ_0 corresponds to the function value $\psi(C_{v0})$.

Thus for the case of high sediment concentrations Velikanov has developed a relation similar to Eq. (1.3.5−47) with the difference, however, that rather than sediment concentrations, certain functions thereof are related to one another.

The ψ versus C_v relation has been plotted by Velikanov in *Fig. 1.3.5 − 2*. It will be perceived therefrom that up to a volumetric concentration of $C_v = 0.30$ the curve $\psi(C_v)$ is identical with the $\psi = C_v$ straight line. Consequently, as long as the volumetric concentration of sediment C_v is higher than 0.30, the value

Fig. 1.3.5—3. Changes in relative concentration with parameters η and β, at relative roughnesses $\alpha = 1/500$ and $1/1000$. After Velikanov

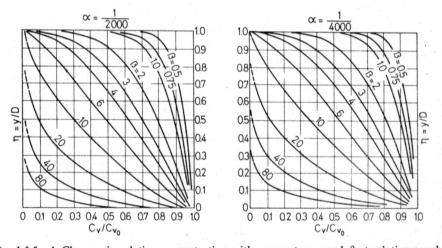

Fig. 1.3.5—4. Changes in relative concentration with parameters η and β at relative roughnesses $\alpha = 1/2000$ and $1/4000$. After Velikanov

$\psi(C_v)$ should be determined from this curve with known C_v values. For sediment concentrations higher than $C_v = 0.5$ the curve is shown by a dashed line in *Fig. 1.3.5—2* since these are beyond the theoretical limit.

For cases of low and high sediment concentrations Velikanov suggests thus the use of Eqs (1.3.5—47) and (1.3.5—50), respectively, to describe the variation of concentration over depth.

396

Velikanov applies also a mechanical integrator for solving the differential equation given by Eq. (1.3.5−40). Solutions are produced for four different values of relative roughness $\alpha = \delta/D$. For each of the relative roughness values $\alpha = 1/500$, $1/1000$, $1/2000$ and $1/4000$ the C_v/C_{v0} versus η relation has been determined for 11 different values of the parameter β. In this way within the range $\beta = 0.5$ to $\beta = 80$ the relation between relative sediment concentration and relative depth of flow is described by 11 curves for each relative roughness value. Remembering that, in the vicinity of the bottom, the suspended sediment tends to become mixed with the bed load and thus its concentration does not follow the general relation, Velikanov has dotted the family of curves under the assumption that the parameter η_0 corresponding to C_{v0} is 0.002, rather than 0. The families of curves corresponding to the four different relative roughness values are shown in *Figs 1.3.5−3* and *1.3.5−4*.

As will be seen from these figures, at low values of parameter β the sediment is approximately uniformly distributed over the depth of flow, whereas at high values of β the distribution of sediment concentration displays considerable differences.

*

The theories of sediment transport, especially the diffusion and gravitational theories, have met with much criticism. One of the lively discussions on this subject ensued at the All-Union Conference on fluvial phenomena (Dementyev 1952; Karaushev 1953; Proskuryakov 1953: Saraskina 1952). Another debate was conducted in the academy publication Izvestiya AN SSSR (Arkhangelsky, Velikanov, Greshaev, Karaushev, Levi, Makkaveev, Teverovsky, Fidman in 1952). The lively interest is displayed especially by the debate published in volume 1952 of Izvestiya Akademii Nauk SSSR. In the course of this debate much sharp criticism was voiced.

We do not intend to embark here upon the details of this debate but, since besides the shortcomings of the gravitational theory several contributors including Velikanov himself made critical comments on the turbulent sediment transport theory (known as the diffusion theory), it is believed advisable to present a brief description and summary of the discussion.

Several contributors have mentioned as a general advantage of the gravitational theory the fact that the transport of suspended sediment is described by Velikanov with the help of the dynamic relations of flow. An objection to the diffusion theory was that the interaction of the solid and fluid phases was neglected in the transport of the suspended sediment. Starting from the general dynamic relations, G. Karádi succeeded in developing the basic equation of the diffusion and gravitational theories alike and found no substantial differences to exist between the two theories as long as the flow is a steady one. Of course, the simplifying assumptions introduced in the two theories are different, and therefore the conclusions arrived at are not identical.

One of the objections to the gravitational theory made by V. M. Makkaveev and A. D. Greshaev is that the concentration resulting at the surface is zero even in the cases of rather high sediment concentrations and small particle sizes. This radically contradicts the results of field observations. It should be noted here that the Rouse—Vanoni relation of the diffusion theory—Eq. (1.3.4— 50)—is also objectionable in this respect. On the other hand, Eqs (1.3.4—29), (1.3.4—44), (1.3.4—56) and (1.3.4—57) of the diffusion theory determine a concentration other than zero at the surface.

Makkaveev questions Velikanov's assumption according to which the role played by the solid phase is a passive one only. He believes the work necessary for suspension to be composed of the work performed by the fluid and the solid phases alike. In his reply Velikanov emphasizes that he regards the solid phase to be passive only insofar as any movement thereof—excepting settlement—is due to the influence of the flowing water alone.

In the case of higher concentrations Greshaev believes the gravitational theory to be preferable to the diffusion theory. In his contribution Greshaev questioned the validity of the basic kinematic relations advanced by Velikanov under Eqs (1.3.5—4) and (1.3.5—5). According to him once the volume occupied by the solid phase is taken into consideration, the reduction in cross-section caused by the solid phase must also be allowed for. In this context Velikanov refused the remarks of Greshaev by noting that the velocity u indicates the velocity computed by considering the flow cross-section between the particles.

As another shortcoming of the gravitational theory Greshaev mentions that Velikanov neglects the increment resistance caused by the presence of sediment. The remarks by I. I. Levi and A. V. Karaushev are concerned with the same problem. Both question the validity of the logarithmic velocity distribution for sediment-carrying flow. Of course, the relation developed for clear water was used by Velikanov for lack of observation data on sediment-carrying flow.

Greshaev also questions the use of the value $\bar{u}_h = -\omega(1 - \bar{C}_v)$ in Eq. (1.3.5—9). In fact $\bar{u}_h$ is obtained as an average value over an extended period of time, whereas Velikanov applied Eq. (1.3.5—9) to express the work performed during unit time (which may be very short).

Greshaev believes also Eqs (1.3.5—24) and (1.3.5—26) to be unfounded since the solid and fluid phases pass simultaneously through the area of $(\delta x \cdot 1)$ magnitude.

It will be recalled that Velikanov in solving the differential equation under Eq. (1.3.5—40) assumed the terms $(1 + a\bar{C})$ and $(1 - \bar{C}_v)$ to equal unity. This simplification is, according to Greshaev, unjustified since it is exactly the unknown $\bar{C}_v$ value that is involved in the equation. Greshaev criticized especially the simplification in Eq. (1.3.5—48), where the value of $\bar{C}_v$ is very high.

A. E. Ivanov has called attention to the fact that in developing the gravitational theory Velikanov neglected the rotation and the effect of collisions between particles, which may assume significant proportions in suspended-sediment transport.

Theoretical objections were raised by B. A. Fidman to the separation of the solid and fluid phases in these investigations. The theory suggested by Makkaveev is considered more reliable than the gravitational theory by I. I. Levi. Makkaveev as will be remembered, performed extensive studies into the diffusion theory.

According to E. N. Teverovsky the phenomenon of suspended sediment transport is not described correctly by the diffusion theory. On the other hand, the neglect of the energy due to turbulence of stream flow by Velikanov is mentioned as an objection to the gravitational theory: this energy should also be included among those necessary for suspension. It should be noted here that Teverovsky regards the transport of suspended sediment and that of slurry in pipelines as identical phenomena.

The gravitational theory is considered superior to the others by M. N. Arkhangelsky who has qualified the experiments supporting the correctness of the diffusion theory as misleading. Among the objections raised to the diffusion theory he considers the neglect of variations in the mixing coefficient as the most important one.

Concluding the debate Velikanov stated that the diffusion theory was in need of being revised in the light of recent research achievements on turbulent flow and that modifications and justified objections suggested during the discussion should be allowed for in the gravitational theory as well.

A number of critical comments on the gravitational theory have been published also by G. I. Barenblatt (1953), A. N. Kolmogorov (1954) and A. K. Dyunin (1960). The most important remark is that of Kolmogorov, refined and made more specific by Barenblatt, according to whom the energy spent by the moving fluid for transporting the sediment is covered by the energy of pulsation rather than directly by the mean energy of flow as assumed by Velikanov. This approach is in full agreement with the now widely accepted view according to which the pulsation velocity components prevailing in the fluid current are made responsible for suspending the solid particles.

The debate concerning the correctness of the gravitational and diffusion theories has proved very beneficial. A number of new circumstances, earlier unaccounted for, were raised in the course of the discussion. It is not yet possible to settle the controversy, for both theories are pregnant with simplifying assumptions involving necessarily biased results.

1.3.6. THE THEORY OF TURBULENT SEDIMENT TRANSPORT WITH ALLOWANCE FOR THE ENERGY OF PULSATION

Both the diffusion and the gravitational theory of sediment transport were strongly criticized around 1950 by Kolmogorov and his followers.

As to the former, they admitted that some results were useful but declared that the theory itself was unacceptable, since the basic assumption, namely that the dynamics of fluid flow are unaffected by the sediment, is unfounded and, at the same time, unnecessary.

In connection with the gravitational theory they emphasized that Velikanov was the first to appreciate the necessity of introducing the mutual interference between sediment and the fluid and to take into account the work necessary for suspending the sediment. At the same time, they raised the objection that the reduction in pulsation energy resulting from this work was neglected.

In his papers published in 1953 one of Kolmogorov's co-workers, I. G. Barenblatt undertook the effort to eliminate these drawbacks.

For this purpose he considered a type of flow where both the relative volume and the particle size of sediment are small, moreover in which the instantaneous accelerations of flow are small enough to be neglected in comparison with the acceleration due to the gravitational field. Molecular diffusion of sediment is likewise assumed to be negligibly small. With these assumptions the equation of fluid movement is*

$$\frac{\partial}{\partial t} \rho (1 - C) u_i + \sum_{j=1}^{3} \frac{\partial}{\partial x_j} \rho (1 - C) u_i u_j = - \frac{\partial sp}{\partial x_i} +$$

$$+ \sum_{j=1}^{3} \frac{\partial \tau_{ji}^{(1)}}{\partial x_j} - \rho (1 - C) g_i - f_i \qquad (1.3.6-1)$$

where ρ = the density of the fluid,
$\quad\quad C$ = the concentration of the sediment,
$\quad u_i, u_j$ = the components along x_i, x_j of flow velocity of the fluid, $i = 1, 2, 3$ and $i = 3$ is the subscript of axis x pointing upward,
$\quad\quad p$ = the full hydrodynamic pressure of the disperse system,
$\quad\quad s$ = the share of pressure acting on the fluid phase,
$\quad\quad \tau_{ji}^{(1)}$ = the component j, i of the viscous stress tensor of the fluid,
$\quad\quad g_i$ = the component along x_i of the gravity force,
$\quad\quad f_i$ = the component along x_i of the interaction force between the sediment and the fluid.

The equation of motion of the sediment is similarly

$$\frac{\partial}{\partial t} \rho_s C u_{si} + \sum_{j=1}^{3} \frac{\partial}{\partial x_j} \rho_s C u_{si} u_{sj} = - \frac{\partial (1 - s)p}{\partial x_i} +$$

$$+ \sum_{j=1}^{3} \frac{\partial \tau_{ji}^{(2)}}{\partial x_j} - \rho_s C g_i + f_i \qquad (1.3.6-2)$$

where subscript s denotes values applying to the sediment, and $\tau_{ji}^{(2)}$ is the component j, i of the stress tensor due to interaction between the particles.

---

* In order to facilitate comparison with the papers published in the literature the original notations used by Barenblatt have in general been retained and modified but exceptionally. Thus for instance the simple C is used to denote concentration.

400

The equation of movement of the disperse medium is obtained by adding the two equations:

$$\frac{\partial \rho V_i}{\partial t} + \sum_{j=1}^{3} \frac{\partial \Pi_{ij}}{\partial x_j} = -\frac{\partial p}{\partial x_i} + \sum_{j=1}^{3} \frac{\partial T_{ji}}{\partial x_j} - \bar{\rho} g_i \qquad (1.3.6-3)$$

where the resultant density is

$$\bar{\rho} = \rho(1 - C) + \rho_s C \qquad (1.3.6-4)$$

the flow velocity along i of the mass center of the medium of unit volume is

$$V_i = \frac{\rho(1 - C) u_i + \rho_s C u_{si}}{\bar{\rho}} \qquad (1.3.6-5)$$

the density of convective momentum flow is

$$\Pi_{ij} = \rho(1 - C) u_i u_j + \rho_s C u_{si} u_{sj} \qquad (1.3.6-6)$$

while the conductive counterpart thereof is

$$T_{ij} = \tau_{ij}^{(1)} + \tau_{ij}^{(2)} \qquad (1.3.6-7)$$

According to Barenblatt, inasmuch as the concentration is low, tensor $\tau_{ji}^{(2)}$ is small in comparison with tensor $\tau_{ji}^{(1)}$ which, in this case, is of the same structure as in the case of a homogeneous viscous fluid.

The equation of mass conservation for the fluid and the solid particles:

$$\frac{\partial}{\partial t} \rho(1 - C) + \sum_{j=1}^{3} \frac{\partial}{\partial x_j} \rho(1 - C) u_j = 0 \qquad (1.3.6-8)$$

$$\frac{\partial}{\partial t} \rho_s C + \sum_{j=1}^{3} \frac{\partial}{\partial x_j} \rho_s C u_{sj} = 0 \qquad (1.3.6-9)$$

The mass balance equation of the two-phase medium is obtained by combining Eqs (1.3.6−8) and (1.3.6−9):

$$\frac{\partial \bar{\rho}}{\partial t} + \sum_{j=1}^{3} \frac{\partial \bar{\rho} V_j}{\partial x_j} = 0 \qquad (1.3.6-10)$$

Multiplying Eq. (1.3.6−8) by ρ and dividing Eq. (1.3.6−9) by ρ_s and adding the resulting two equations, the continuity equation of the medium is obtained

$$\sum_{j=1}^{3} \frac{\partial}{\partial x_j} [(1 - C) u_j + C u_{sj}] = 0 \qquad (1.3.6-11)$$

Eqs (1.3.6−3), (1.3.6−10) and (1.3.6−11) are the basic equations of Barenblatt's theory.

Since the particles are assumed to be small and the acceleration of the fluid is assumed to be low relative to the acceleration by gravity, it follows that the horizontal components of the instantaneous velocities of the particles and the fluid coincide, whereas the vertical components differ by a given quantity, the difference in velocities being equal to the fall velocity. In other words the inertia of the particles is neglected by Barenblatt. In a general form this condition is written as

$$u_{si} = u_i - \delta_{ij}\omega \qquad (1.3.6-12)$$

where

$$\delta_{ij} = \begin{cases} 0, & \text{if } i \neq j \\ 1, & \text{if } i = j \end{cases}$$

The fall velocity ω is introduced by Barenblatt as a familiar function of concentration C.

With allowance to Eq. (1.3.6–12), Eqs (1.3.6–3), (1.3.6–10) and (1.3.6–11) can be rewritten into the forms

$$\frac{\partial \bar{\rho} V_i}{\partial t} + \sum_{j=1}^{3} \frac{\partial \bar{\rho} V_i V_j}{\partial x_j} = -\bar{\rho} g_i + \sum_{j=1}^{3} \frac{\partial T_{ji}}{\partial x_j} - \frac{\partial p}{\partial x_i} -$$

$$- \rho \rho_s \frac{\partial}{\partial x_3}\left[\frac{\omega^2 C(1-C)}{\rho} \right]\delta_{i3} \qquad (1.3.6-13)$$

$$\frac{\partial \bar{\rho}}{\partial t} + \sum_{j=1}^{3} V_j \frac{\partial \bar{\rho}}{\partial x_j} = (\rho_s - \rho)\bar{\rho}\frac{\partial}{\partial x_3}\left[\frac{\omega C(1-C)}{\bar{\rho}} \right] \qquad (1.3.6-14)$$

$$\sum_{j=1}^{3} \frac{\partial V_j}{\partial x_j} = -(\rho_s - \rho)\frac{\partial}{\partial x_3}\left[\frac{\omega C(1-C)}{\bar{\rho}} \right] \qquad (1.3.6-15)$$

Concerning V_i, p and $\bar{\rho}$ the set of equations Eq. (1.3.6–13) to (1.3.6–15) forms a closed system.

Hereafter the equations are averaged, i.e. the expected mathematical values of the terms involved in the equations are formed.

Both the relative volume and mass of the particles are assumed to be small, so that

$$C \ll 1; \quad aC \ll 1, \qquad (1.3.6-16)$$

where

$$a = \frac{\rho_s - \rho}{\rho}$$

With these assumptions the fundamental set of equations becomes:
The momentum equation of the inhomogeneous fluid

$$\frac{\partial V_i}{\partial t} + \sum_{j=1}^{3} \frac{\partial V_i}{\partial x_j} = -(1 - aC)g_i + \sum_{j=1}^{3} \frac{\partial T_{ij}}{\partial x_j} - \frac{1}{\rho}\frac{\partial p}{\partial x_i} \qquad (1.3.6-17$$

402

The continuity equation:

$$\sum_{j=1}^{3} \frac{\partial V_j}{\partial x_j} = -\omega a \frac{\partial C}{\partial x_3} \qquad (1.3.6-18)$$

The mass balance equation:

$$\frac{\partial C}{\partial t} + \sum_{j=1}^{3} V_j \frac{\partial C}{\partial x_j} = \omega \frac{\partial C}{\partial x_3} \qquad (1.3.6-19)$$

In view of the small sediment volume Eq. (1.3.6−18) is rewritten:

$$\sum_{j=1}^{3} \frac{\partial V_i}{\partial x_j} = 0 \qquad (1.3.6-20)$$

Averaging the momentum, the mass balance and the continuity equations and neglecting the terms

$$\overline{V_i' \frac{\partial V_j'}{\partial x_j}} \quad \text{and} \quad \omega \overline{C'^2}$$

the resulting expressions are

$$\frac{\partial \overline{V}_i}{\partial t} + \sum_{j=1}^{3} \overline{V}_j \frac{\partial \overline{V}_i}{\partial x_j} = -\sum_{j=1}^{3} \frac{\partial \overline{V_i' V_j'}}{\partial x_j} - (1 + a\bar{C}) g_i +$$

$$+ \sum_{j=1}^{3} \frac{\partial \overline{T}_{ji}'}{\partial x_j} - \frac{1}{\rho} \frac{\partial \bar{p}}{\partial x_i} \qquad (1.3.6-21)$$

$$\frac{\partial \bar{C}}{\partial t} + \sum_{j=1}^{3} \left(\overline{V}_j \frac{\partial \bar{C}}{\partial x_j} + \frac{\partial \overline{C' V_j'}}{\partial x_j} \right) = \omega \frac{\partial \bar{C}}{\partial x_3} \qquad (1.3.6-22)$$

$$\sum_{j=1}^{3} \frac{\partial \overline{V}_j}{\partial x_j} = -\omega a \frac{\partial \bar{C}}{\partial x_3} \qquad (1.3.6-23)$$

In connection with the right-hand side of Eq. (1.3.6−23) it is pointed out by Barenblatt that the two-phase character of the fluid need only be taken into account in the mass balance equation and in the pulsation energy equation. In other cases the right-hand side may be taken to equal 0.

The balance equation of pulsation energy in two-phase fluid flow is introduced hereafter by Barenblatt, following the approach of Kolmogorov. In doing so the flow considered is one in which the fall velocity of sediment is of an order of magnitude comparable to the pulsation velocity, this being small in comparison with the mean velocity of flow.

The kinetic energy of unit volume of two-phase fluid is

$$E = \frac{1}{2} \rho \sum_{i=1}^{3} V_i^2 \approx \frac{1}{2} \rho \sum_{i=1}^{3} V_i^2 \qquad (1.3.6-24)$$

After averaging this becomes

$$\bar{E} = \frac{1}{2}\rho \sum_{i=1}^{3} \overline{V_i^2} + \overline{\rho' V_j'}\,\bar{V}_j + \frac{1}{2}\rho \sum_{i=1}^{3} \overline{V_i'^2} = E^0 + B \qquad (1.3.6-25)$$

where E^0 is the kinetic energy of unit volume of two-phase fluid, expressed with the mean velocity

$$E^0 = \frac{1}{2}\rho \sum_{i=1}^{3} \overline{V_i^2} \qquad (1.3.6-26)$$

and B is the average pulsation energy

$$B = \overline{\rho' V_j'}\,\bar{V}_j + \frac{1}{2}\rho \sum_{i=1}^{3} \overline{V_i'^2} \qquad (1.3.6-27)$$

From the balance equation of pulsation energy the change in pulsation energy is obtained as

$$\frac{dB}{dt} = \frac{d\bar{E}}{dt} - \frac{dE^\circ}{dt} \qquad (1.3.6-28)$$

Allowing for the fact that

$$\frac{d}{dt} = \frac{\partial}{\partial t} + \sum_{j=1}^{3} V_j \frac{\partial}{\partial x_j}$$

and neglecting the terms $\overline{E'(\partial V_j'/\partial x_j)}$ of small order of magnitude Barenblatt obtained the following expression for the energy balance of two-phase fluid flow

$$\frac{\partial B}{\partial t} + \sum_{j=1}^{3} \bar{V}_j \frac{\partial B}{\partial x_j} = -\overline{\rho' V_3'}g - \sum_{j=1}^{3} \overline{\frac{\partial p'}{\partial x_j} \cdot V_j'} + \sum_{j=1}^{3} \frac{\partial q_j}{\partial x_j} -$$

$$- Q - \sum_{j=1}^{3} \frac{\partial}{\partial x_j}\left[\frac{1}{2}\rho \sum_{i=1}^{3} \overline{V_i'^2 V_j'}\right] - \sum_{i=1}^{3}\sum_{j=1}^{3} \frac{1}{2}\rho \overline{V_j' V_i'}(\bar{\varepsilon}_{ij}) \qquad (1.3.6-29)$$

where

$$\varepsilon_{ij} = \frac{\partial V_i}{\partial x_j} + \frac{\partial V_j}{\partial x_i}$$

$q_j = \overline{V_i' T_{ji}'}$ is the component along x_j of the current density vector of the pulsation energy resulting from molecular mixing; $Q = 1/2 \cdot \overline{(T_{ij}' \varepsilon_{ij}')}$ is the pulsational energy dissipation occurring in unit volume of the two-phase fluid.

The physical interpretation given by Barenblatt to the terms on the right-hand side of the equation is as follows: the first term represents the loss in pulsation energy consumed by lifting the particles, a loss which may be of considerable magnitude owing to the high value of the multiplicator g even at low concen-

404

trations; the second term represents the gain in pulsation energy resulting from the work of pressure pulsation in pulsating flow (this term is small enough to be neglected); the third term represents the pulsation energy gain resulting from molecular mixing; the fourth term represents the dissipation of pulsation energy; the fifth term is the gain in pulsation energy due to turbulent mixing while the sixth term is the gain in pulsation energy resulting from the energy of averaged flow.

By introducing certain simplifications to the momentum equation Barenblatt obtained the momentum equation of sediment in turbulent flow. The average values in two-dimensional homogeneous steady flow are

$$\bar{V}_3 \frac{d\bar{V}_1}{dx_3} + \frac{d\overline{V_1' V_3'}}{dx_3} = \text{constant} \qquad (1.3.6-30)$$

$$- \bar{V}_3 \frac{d\bar{C}}{dx_3} - \frac{d\overline{C' V_3'}}{dx_3} + \omega \frac{\partial \bar{C}}{\partial x_3} = 0 \qquad (1.3.6-31)$$

$$\frac{d\bar{V}_3}{dx_3} = - \omega a \frac{d\bar{C}}{dx_3} \qquad (1.3\ 6-32)$$

$$- \bar{V}_3 \frac{dB}{dx_3} - a\rho \overline{C' V_3'} g - Q - \frac{d}{dx_3}\left(\frac{1}{2} \rho \sum_{i=1}^{3} \overline{V_i'^2 V_3'} \right) -$$

$$- \rho \overline{V_1' V_3'} \frac{d\bar{V}_1}{dx_3} - \frac{1}{2} \rho \overline{V_3'^2} \frac{d\bar{V}_3}{dx_3} = 0 \qquad (1.3.6-33)$$

Integration of Eq. (1.3.6−32) yields

$$\bar{V}_3 = - a\omega \bar{C} + \text{constant} \qquad (1.3.6-34)$$

The mean value of the vertical mass current being 0, the constant of integration is also assumed to be 0. Combining Eqs (1.3.6−34) and (1.3.6−31) and integrating the expression obtained, we have

$$\overline{C' V_3'} = \omega \bar{C} ,$$

where the term of ωC^2 order of magnitude is neglected. This implies essentially that the turbulent conductive current density $\overline{C' V_3'}$ is taken equal to the convective current density $\omega \bar{C}$.

Hereafter Barenblatt derived the work of suspension for unit volume of the two-phase fluid as

$$- \overline{\rho' V_3'} g = - ag \rho \omega \bar{C}(1 - \bar{C}) \qquad (1.3.6-35a)$$

For small values of C

$$- \overline{\rho' V_3'} g = - ag\rho \bar{C}\omega \qquad (1.3.6-35b)$$

405

Integration of Eq. (1.3.6–30) yields the expression

$$\overline{V_1' V_3'} = -V_*^2 + Cx_3 \qquad (1.3.6-36)$$

where V_* is a constant having the dimension of velocity.

The set of fundamental equations describing the two-dimensional flow of the two-phase fluid is thus obtained by Barenblatt as

(I) $\qquad \overline{V_1' V_3'} = -V_*^2 + \bar{C}x_3$

(II) $\qquad \overline{C' V_3'} = \omega \bar{C}$

(III) $\qquad ag\rho\omega\bar{C} + Q + \dfrac{1}{2}\rho\dfrac{d}{dx_3}\left(\sum_{i=1,3}\overline{V_i'^2 V_3'}\right) + \rho\overline{V_1' V_3'}\dfrac{d\bar{V}_1}{dx_3} = 0$

In the case of $d\bar{V}_1/dx_3 \cong 0$ the third term in Eq. (III) is negligible.

The set of equations (1.3.6–30) to (1.3.6–33) is not a closed one. In order to make it a closed one certain assumptions on the relations existing between the unknown quantities are to be introduced. The assumptions introduced by Barenblatt are as follows:

$$\overline{V_i' V_j'} = \frac{2}{3} b\,\delta_{ij} - v_1\,\varepsilon_{ij} \qquad (1.3:6-37)$$

$$\frac{1}{2}\sum_{j=1}^{3}\sum_{i=1}^{3}\overline{V_i'^2 V_j'} = -\sum_{j=1}^{3} v_2\frac{\partial b}{\partial x_j} \qquad (1.3.6-38)$$

$$\sum_{j=1}^{3}\overline{C' V_j} = -\lambda\sum_{j=1}^{3}\frac{\partial \bar{C}}{\partial x_j} \qquad (1.3.6-39)$$

Eqs (1.3.6–38) and (1.3.6–39) are essentially in agreement with the conduction law described in *Subsection 1.3.3.1*. The conductivities v_1, v_2 and λ are assumed by Barenblatt to be scalar quantities. The intensive quantity b is, on the other hand, the pulsation energy imparted to unit mass of the two-phase fluid. The set of fundamental equations assumes therewith the form

$$v_1\frac{d\bar{V}_1}{dx_3} = V_*^2 - \bar{C}x_3 \qquad (1.3.6-40)$$

$$\omega\bar{C} + \lambda\frac{d\bar{C}}{dx_3} = 0 \qquad (1.3.6-41)$$

$$ag\omega\rho\bar{C} + Q - \frac{d}{dx_3}\left(v_2\frac{db}{dx_3}\right) - \rho v_1\left(\frac{d\bar{V}_1}{dx_3}\right)^2 = 0 \qquad (1.3.6-42)$$

Inasmuch as the work performed by the flow for keeping the particles in suspension is small, i.e. the term $a\omega g\rho\bar{C}$ is small in comparison with the other terms involved in Eq. (1.3.6–42), the set of equations can be separated into the independent equations of fluid current and mass balance:

$$v_1 \frac{d\bar{V}_1}{dx_3} = V_*^2 - \bar{C}x_3 \qquad (1.3.6-43)$$

$$Q - \frac{\rho}{2} \frac{d}{dx_3}\left(v_2 \frac{db}{dx_3}\right) - \rho v_1 \left(\frac{d\bar{V}_1}{dx_3}\right)^2 = 0 \qquad (1.3.6-44)$$

$$\omega\bar{C} + \lambda \frac{\partial\bar{C}}{\partial x_3} = 0 \qquad (1.3.6-45)$$

In order to make the general set of equations closed Barenblatt introduced the fundamental assumptions of Kolmogorov, which is formulated as follows:
The characteristics v_1, v_2 and λ of flow and the dissipation of pulsation energy

$$Q/\bar{\rho} \approx Q/\rho$$

related to unit mass of the mixture can be determined with the help of b and a number l having the dimension of length. From dimensional homogeneity it follows that

$$v_1 = ql\sqrt{b}$$

$$v_2 = q_1 l\sqrt{b}$$

$$\lambda = q_2 l\sqrt{b}$$

$$Q = K\rho \frac{b^{3/2}}{l}$$

where q, q_1, q_2 and K are universal constants. These may be assumed arbitrarily to a certain extent, and so $q = 1$ imposes no restrictions. Hereafter, relying on experimental data, Barenblatt established that $q_1 = q_2 = 1$.
The set of fundamental equations describing steady, two-dimensional flow which is homogeneous on the average in the horizontal direction becomes thus

$$l\sqrt{b} \frac{d\bar{V}_1}{dx_3} = V_*^2 - Kx_3 \qquad (1.3.6-46)$$

$$\omega\bar{C} + l\sqrt{b} \frac{d\bar{C}}{dx_3} = 0 \qquad (1.3.6-47)$$

$$a\omega g\bar{C} + K\frac{b^{2/3}}{l} - \frac{d}{dx_3}\left(l\sqrt{b} \frac{db}{dx_3}\right) - l\sqrt{b}\left(\frac{d\bar{V}_1}{dx_3}\right)^2 = 0 \qquad (1.3.6-48)$$

The set of equations obtained is closed concerning the variables involved therein provided l is known as a function of co-ordinates, or the relation of l to the unknown variables can be established.

Neglecting the turbulent diffusion and applying Eqs (1.3.6−46) and (1.3.6−47) the pulsation energy of flow is described by the expression

$$b = \frac{V_*^2 - Kx_3}{\kappa^2}\left[1 + agq_2\frac{d\bar{C}}{dx_3}\left(\frac{d\bar{V}_1}{dx_3}\right)^2\right]^{1/2} \qquad (1.3.6-49)$$

where κ is a universal constant having, according to Minsky, a value around 0.5.

It will be appreciated from the last expression that for unit mass of a two-phase fluid the pulsation energy is smaller than in a homogeneous fluid, since $d\bar{C}/dx_3$ is smaller than 0.

Barenblatt claimed the dimensionless expression

$$K = -agq_2\frac{d\bar{C}}{dx_3}\left(\frac{d\bar{V}_1}{dx_3}\right)^2 \qquad (1.3.6-50)$$

to be analogous with the Richardson number which is one of the characteristics of thermally inhomogeneous turbulent flow.

In the set of equations obtained by Barenblatt allowance is made for the effect of the suspended particles on the dynamics of flow. Inasmuch as the term representing the work of suspension is small in comparison with the other terms involved in the balance equation of pulsation energy, the fundamentals of the diffusion theory are obtained.

In conclusion Barenblatt points out that, besides the assumptions introduced, others may also prove suitable for making the foregoing set of equations closed.

It is, of course, possible to derive also Barenblatt's equations from the general balance equations. For this purpose the following assumptions are to be introduced:

a) The process is a steady one.

b) Collisions between particles do not result in comminution and the sediment particles are uniform in size.

c) The flow may be regarded two-dimensional.

d) Concentration varies in the vertical direction only.

e) Instantaneous accelerations are negligibly small in comparison with acceleration due to gravity.

f) The velocity component along x of the sediment is identical with the velocity component of water in the same direction, whereas the component along y is smaller by the fall velocity than the velocity component of water in the y direction.

With these assumptions Eq. (1.3.6−1) is obtained directly from Eq. (1.3.3−38). The differences in notation are as follows:

	In the general balance equations	In Barenblatt's equation
The density of fluid	$\bar{\rho}$	$\rho(1 - C)$
The convective momentum current density	$\bar{\rho}\mathbf{v}\circ\mathbf{v}$	$\rho(1 - C)\mathbf{v}\circ\mathbf{v}$
The conductive momentum current density*	$\overline{\rho\mathbf{v}'\circ\mathbf{v}'}$	$\mathsf{U}sp - \boldsymbol{\tau}^{(1)}$
Interaction force between sediment and fluid	$\dfrac{\gamma_1}{\omega}(\mathbf{v}_h - \mathbf{v})$	$-f_i$

* U is the unit tensor.

In a similar manner Eq. (1.3.6−2) corresponds to Eq. (1.3.3−42) with the following differences in notation

	In the general balance equations	In Barenblatt's equation
The density of sediment	ρ_1	$\rho_s C$
The convective momentum current density	$\rho_1\mathbf{v}_h\circ\mathbf{v}_h$	$\rho_s C\mathbf{u}_s\circ\mathbf{u}_s$
The conductive momentum current density	$\overline{\rho_1\mathbf{v}_h'\circ\mathbf{v}_h'}$	$\mathsf{U}(1-s)p-\boldsymbol{\tau}^{(2)}$

It should be clear moreover that with due allowance to differences in notation the corresponding counterparts are Eqs (1.3.6−8) and (1.3.3−37), further (1.3.6−9) and (1.3.3−41).

The contribution made by Barenblatt to the theory of suspended sediment transport is a very valuable one. His main merit is that he succeeded in giving an entirely general formulation to the mathematical foundations of this complex phenomenon.

1.3.7. RECENT SEDIMENT TRANSPORT THEORIES

A number of theories have been developed on the transport of suspended sediment in alluvial streams. The scope of this book does not permit a detailed description of each of them. Even the foregoing sections contain only a brief outline of the most widely known three theories.

We shall now quote or just mention some more recently published theories.

The list is headed by the theory developed by F. I. Frankl which will be considered in somewhat greater detail since the equations involved are highly relevant to the movement of suspended sediment.

1.3.7.1. The theory of F. I. Frankl. Frankl has established a set of equations allowing for the continuity, momentum and energy equations of both the mean and the pulsation current (1953–1960).

In deriving his equations Frankl considered the process to take place within volume V enclosed by surface F. The function C representing the presence of the solid phase is introduced; it assumes value 1 where a solid particle is present, and value 0 where there is no solid particle. The mean value of the function C over a volume $\Omega < V$ is the mean concentration $\bar{C}_A$ related to this volume

$$\bar{C}_A = \frac{1}{\Omega_A} \int\limits_{\Omega_A} C \, dV \qquad (1.3.7-1)$$

Frankl's set of equations for the fluid and the sediment are written in the following form:

a) The *mass balance equations* for the fluid and the sediment:

$$\frac{\partial(1-\bar{C})}{\partial t} + \sum_{k=1}^{3} \frac{\partial}{\partial x_k} (1-\bar{C})\hat{u}_k = 0 \qquad (1.3.7-2)$$

$$\frac{\partial \bar{C}}{\partial t} + \sum_{k=1}^{3} \frac{\partial}{\partial x_k} \bar{C}\hat{u}_{sk} = 0 \qquad (1.3.7-3)$$

b) The *equations of the momentum balance* (three scalar equations for the fluid and three scalar equations for the solid particles, in the case of $i = 1, 2$ and 3):

$$\frac{d}{dt}\left[\rho(1-\bar{C})\hat{u}_i\right] = \left|\frac{\partial}{\partial t} + \sum_{k=1}^{3} \frac{\partial}{\partial x_k}\hat{u}_k\right|[\rho(1-\bar{C})\hat{u}_j] =$$

$$= -\sum_{k=1}^{3}\left[(1-\bar{C})\frac{\partial p_{ik}}{\partial x_k} + \frac{\partial \Pi_{ik}}{\partial x_k}\right] - R_i + \rho(1-\bar{C})X_i \qquad (1.3.7-4)$$

$$\left(\frac{\partial}{\partial t} + \sum_{k=1}^{3}\frac{\partial}{\partial x_k}\hat{u}_{ks}\right)(\rho_s\,\bar{C}\hat{u}_{is}) = -\left[\bar{C}\,\frac{\partial p_{ik}}{\partial x_k} + \frac{\partial \Pi_{iks}}{\partial x_k}\right] +$$

$$+ R_i + \rho_s\,\bar{C}X_{is} \qquad (1.3.7-5)$$

c) The *equations of the energy balance:*

$$\left(\frac{\partial}{\partial t} + \sum_{k=1}^{3}\frac{\partial}{\partial x_k}\hat{u}_k\right)\left[\rho(1-\bar{C})\frac{(\hat{w})^2}{2}\right] =$$

$$= \hat{u}_i\left\{-\sum_{k=1}^{3}\left[(1-\bar{C})\frac{\partial p_{ik}}{\partial x_k} + \frac{\partial \Pi_{ik}}{\partial x_k}\right] - R_i + \rho(1-\bar{C})X_i\right\} \qquad (1.3.7-6)$$

$$\left(\frac{\partial}{\partial t} + \sum_{k=1}^{3}\frac{\partial}{\partial x_k}\hat{u}_{ks}\right)\left[\rho_s\bar{C}\frac{(\hat{w}_s)^2}{2}\right] =$$

$$= \hat{u}_{is}\left[-\sum_{k=1}^{3}\left(\bar{C}\,\frac{\partial p_{ik}}{\partial x_k} + \frac{\partial \Pi_{iks}}{\partial x_k}\right) + R_i + \rho_s\,\bar{C}X_{is}\right] \qquad (1.3.7-7)$$

d) The *equations of the pulsation energy*:

$$\left(\frac{\partial}{\partial t} + \sum_{k=1}^{3} \frac{\partial}{\partial x_k} \hat{u}_k\right)\left[\rho(1 - \bar{C})\frac{(\hat{w}')^2}{2}\right] =$$

$$= -\frac{1}{2}\sum_{k=1}^{3}\left(\frac{\partial \hat{u}_i}{\partial x_k} + \frac{\partial \hat{u}_k}{\partial x_k}\right)\Pi_{ik} + A - \frac{\partial k_i}{\partial x_i} \qquad (1.3.7-8)$$

$$\left(\frac{\partial}{\partial t} + \sum_{k=1}^{3} \frac{\partial}{\partial x_k} \hat{u}_{ks}\right)\left[\rho_s \bar{C}\frac{(\hat{w}'_s)^2}{2}\right] =$$

$$= -\frac{1}{2}\sum_{k=1}^{3}\left(\frac{\partial \hat{u}_{is}}{\partial x_k} + \frac{\partial \hat{u}_{ks}}{\partial x_k}\right)\Pi_{iks} + A_s - \frac{\partial k_{is}}{\partial x_i} \qquad (1.3.7-9)$$

In the foregoing equations the bar above the symbols indicates averaging in the general sense over time and volume, whereas the prime denotes the departure (pulsation) from the mean value. The symbol ^ denotes averaging over the elementary volume part (occupied by the fluid or by the solid particles) and over time.

In the equations:

ρ, ρ_s = the densities of the fluid and the solid particle, respectively;

p_{ik} = the component of the molecular stress tensor of the disperse medium;

$$A = -(1 - \bar{C})\overline{u'_i \frac{\partial p_{ik}}{\partial x_k}}$$

$$\qquad (1.3.7-10)$$

$$A_s = -\bar{C}\overline{u'_{is}\frac{\partial p_{ik}}{\partial x_k}}$$

is the work performed in the turbulent flow space by the pulsation of molecular stress;

$$k_i = \rho(1 - \bar{C})\overline{u'_i \frac{(w')^2}{2}} \qquad (1.3.7-11)$$

$$k_{is} = \rho_s \bar{C}\overline{u'_{is}\frac{(w'_s)^2}{2}} \qquad (1.3.7-12)$$

the current density of turbulent energy;

$$\Pi_{ik} = \rho(1 - \bar{C})\widehat{(u'_i u'_k)} \qquad (1.3.7-13)$$

$$\Pi_{iks} = \rho_s \bar{C}\widehat{(u'_{is} u'_{ks})} \qquad (1.3.7-14)$$

the components of the turbulent stress tensor generated by the pulsation current of the fluid and the solid particles;

$$R_i = C'\overline{\frac{\partial p_{ik}}{\partial x_k}} \qquad (1.3.7-15)$$

the components of the interaction force between the particles and the fluid;

X_i and X_{is} are the components of the external force;

$$\frac{1}{2}(\hat{w})^2 = \frac{1}{2}\hat{u}_i\,\hat{u}_i \qquad (1.3.7-16)$$

$$\frac{1}{2}(\hat{w}_s)^2 = \frac{1}{2}\hat{u}_{is}\,\hat{u}_{is} \qquad (1.3.7-17)$$

for the fluid and the solid particles the energy of mean flow;

$$\frac{1}{2}(\hat{w}'^2) = \frac{1}{2}\widehat{(u_i'\,u_i')} \qquad (1.3.7-18)$$

$$\frac{1}{2}(\hat{w}_s'^2) = \frac{1}{2}\widehat{(u_{is}'\,u_{is}')} \qquad (1.3.7-19)$$

is the pulsation energy.

The set of equations is not closed either for the fluid or for the solid particles. The number of unknowns is considerably greater than that of the equations. In order to make the set a closed one Frankl suggested in 1955 the following simplifying assumptions:

a) The flow space of the fluid is assumed to be known and unaffected by the presence of the solid particles.

b) The equations concerning the solid particles will only be taken into consideration, neglecting thereby all components of turbulent stress.

c) In determining fluid resistance the concept of conditional diffusion velocity is introduced for the movement of particles. The diffusion velocity v_d is the velocity at which the suspended particles are required to move in the current assuming a given constant concentration gradient, supposing that the density of particles does not differ from the density of the fluid.

With these assumptions the following closed set of equations was obtained for the averaged values (neglecting the symbol of averaging):

$$\frac{\partial C}{\partial t}\sum_{k=1}^{3}\frac{\partial}{\partial x_k}(Cu_{ks}) = 0 \qquad (1.3.7-20)$$

$$\rho_s\left(\frac{\partial u_{is}}{\partial t}+\sum_{k=1}^{3}u_{ks}\frac{\partial u_{is}}{\partial x_k}\right) = -\frac{\partial p}{\partial x_i}+\frac{1}{C}R_i+\rho_s\,X_{is} \qquad (1.3.7-21)$$

$$R_i = -\frac{g}{2}\,C\,\frac{\mu^2}{r^2}(u_i\,C-u_i-v_{id}) \qquad (1.3.7-22)$$

finally from the relation $Cv_d = -b\ \mathrm{grad}\ C$:

$$v_{di} = -b\,\frac{\partial\ln C}{\partial x_i} \qquad (1.3.7-23)$$

412

where u_i and u_s = the velocity components of the fluid and sediment, respectively
μ = viscosity,
r = the radius of spherical solid particles of uniform size.

There is an obvious relationship between Frankl's equations and the general balance equations. Frankl's Eqs (1.3.7—2) and (1.3.7—3) are obtained directly from Eqs (1.3.3—37) and (1.3.3—41) provided that the concentration C is used instead of the densities ρ and ρ_1 of the fluid and sediment, respectively:

$$\bar{C} = \frac{\rho_1}{\rho_1 + \rho}$$

In fact, with this substitution, after dividing the mass balance equations by $-(\rho_1 + \rho)$, Eq. (1.3.3—37) yields

$$\frac{\partial}{\partial t}\left(\frac{\rho}{\rho_1 + \rho}\right) + \mathrm{div}\left(\frac{\rho}{\rho_1 + \rho}\,\mathbf{v}\right) = 0$$

or

$$\frac{\partial}{\partial t}(1 - C) + \mathrm{div}\left[(1 - C)\mathbf{v}\right] = 0 \qquad\qquad (1.3.7—24)$$

In a similar manner from Eq. (1.3.3—41)

$$\frac{\partial \bar{C}}{\partial t} + \mathrm{div}\,(\bar{C}\,\bar{\mathbf{v}}_h - \varepsilon\,\mathrm{grad}\,\bar{C}) = 0 \qquad\qquad (1.3.7—25)$$

The conductive current density $\varepsilon\,\mathrm{grad}\,\bar{C}$ is neglected by Frankl. Eqs (1.3.7—24) and (1.3.7—25) are identical with Frankl's relations in Eqs (1.3.7—2) and (1.3.7—3) and, as mentioned before, correspond to Eqs (1.3.3—37) and (1.3.3—41).

Eqs (1.3.3—38) and (1.3.3—42) are the counterparts of Frankl's Eqs (4.3.7—4) and (1.3.7—5) with the notation
a) the fluid density is $\rho(1 - \bar{C})$,
b) the sediment density is $\rho_s\bar{C}$,
c) the conductive momentum current $\rho\mathbf{v}' \circ \mathbf{v}'$ is represented by the stress tensor Π,
d) the density of the external force field is $\mathbf{X}$,
e) the interaction between the fluid and sediment is denoted by $\mathbf{R}$.

Eqs (1.3.7—6) and (1.3.7—7) of the energy balance differ, as mentioned before, from the momentum balance (in the absence of dissipation) only in that each term is multiplied externally by the flow velocity v.

The balance equations of the pulsation energy, Eqs (1.3.7—8) and (1.3.7—9), are obtained from the energy balance equations written for the instantaneous values if, after averaging over time, the correlation terms formed of the products of terms containing average values and pulsations are separated.

It will be perceived thus that the equations adopted by Frankl as the starting point in his considerations differ from the general balance equations in their notation only. The set of equations derived by him and expressed by Eqs (1.3.7−20) to (1.3.7−23) include eventually not more than the mass-and-momentum balance of the sediment. The remaining equations were necessary for determining the interaction force **R** involved in the latter. According to Frankl

$$\mathbf{R} = B\left[\bar{\mathbf{v}}(1 - \bar{C}) - \text{grad}\,(\ln \bar{C})\right] \tag{1.3.7−26}$$

where $B = g\mu^2/2r^2$,

g = acceleration due to gravity,

μ = viscosity,

r = a "shape factor" including the characteristic dimension.

The first term within the straight bracket is the convective mass current of water, the second being the conductive mass current of sediment. The interaction force is thus, according to Frankl, proportionate to the difference of these two currents.

Frankl's two equations resulting from the derivations, Eqs (1.3.7−20) and (1.3.7−21) are in vectorial form

$$\frac{\partial C}{\partial t} + \text{div}\,(C\,\mathbf{v}_h) = 0 \tag{1.3.7−27}$$

$$\frac{\partial \rho_1 \mathbf{v}_h}{\partial t} + \text{Div}\,(\rho_1\,\mathbf{v}_h \circ \mathbf{v}_h) = -\,\text{grad}\,p + \mathbf{R} + \rho_1\,\mathbf{X} \tag{1.3.7−28}$$

which, as explained before, are the counterparts of Eqs (1.3.3−41) and (1.3.3−42), respectively.

Regardless of the foregoing unavoidable simplifications, Frankl has greatly contributed to the improvement of the theory of suspended sediment transport by developing a set of equations involving the continuity, momentum and energy equations of both the mean and the pulsation current.

1.3.7.2. The theory of A. K. Ananyan. The hydraulic conditions of river bends were considered by A. K. Ananyan with the objective of solving the following problem of practical interest:

a) to determine mass distribution in cases where transverse currents are also present;

b) to establish the influence of sediment (related to clear water) on flow conditions in bends;

c) to determine friction losses in river bends.

It is established at the outset that the equations include a number of particular conditions for which no allowance could be made in the general mathematical treatment and thus it is of special importance to check the relations developed against experimental results.

As a starting basis he adopted the set of equations derived by Barenblatt (and described in *Section 1.3.6*) using the same assumptions. In keeping with the problem considered the mass-and-energy balance equations are rewritten into cylindrical co-ordinates with r denoting radial and y vertical co-ordinates. Flow conditions

414

are assumed to by symmetrical about the axis so that

$$\frac{\partial}{\partial \phi} = 0$$

which is naturally identical with assuming two-dimensional flow conditions.

The conductive mass density is specified in accordance with the conductivity law as the product of the mass gradient and of the turbulent conductivity coefficient. The dissipation of energy is then neglected, implying in the present case that the energy balance of turbulent flow is not affected appreciably by the presence of sediment. It is assumed further that in determining the velocity distribution it is sufficient to take only the momentum balance equation of clear water into consideration. For determining the concentration distribution, on the other hand, not more than the mass balance equation of sediment is necessary.

The process considered is a steady one in which the sediment particles suffer no change in size by collision. The sediment is assumed to be a monodisperse substance, i.e. one consisting of uniform particles, or the influence of different particle sizes is assumed to be negligible. The assumptions include also the approximation that the vertical velocity of sediment differs from the velocity of water by the fall velocity only. With these assumptions the fundamental equation of Ananyan, written in vectorial form in accordance with Eq. (1.3.3–41), becomes

$$\bar{v} \operatorname{grad} \bar{C} = \operatorname{div} (\varepsilon \operatorname{grad} \bar{C}) + \omega \frac{\partial \bar{C}}{\partial y} \qquad (1.3.7-29)$$

Since the problem considered forms a particular case of the subject discussed here, a more detailed treatment of this theory will be omitted. It should be noted nevertheless that in a paper containing detailed experimental data the theory of suspended sediment transport is presented in a highly visual manner.

1.3.7.3. The theory of I. V. Nagy. In an attempt to eliminate the shortcomings of various theories on the movement of suspended sediment V. Nagy has set out to describe the pulsation velocity components as a function of concentration, with due regard to their fundamental importance for the entire process of suspension. This makes it necessary to include also the dissipation of energy. Besides the dissipation of the kinetic energy of the fluid an essential role is attributed to fluid friction at the interfaces, to the friction and collision of the sediment particles with water particles and among one another, since all these entail energy losses. Owing to differences in the specific gravities of particles, further to the relative velocity of sediment particles and of fluid particles small eddy trails are generated which also consume energy. The movement of suspended sediment forms thus a highly involved particular case of energy dissipation.

Starting from Frankl's equations V. Nagy relied on theoretical considerations for introducing different concentration functions which are then used for writing transcendent equations. Solutions for these are then found with the help of experimental data. The experiments performed thus far by V. Nagy are reported to be in support of these assumptions. Further observations are expected to permit the development of a method suitable for practical purposes.

For details reference is made to the papers listed in the attached bibliography.

1.3.7.4. The theory of V. G. Sanoyan. Sanoyan has adopted Frankl's equations as a starting basis. Momentum balances are determined for the fluid and solid phases. The work expended for keeping the sediment in suspension is written in the energy balance, whereafter the instantaneous resisting force is introduced as the difference of the interaction forces and the buoyant forces. The general expression of suspension work is obtained in this manner. Sanoyan states that in accordance with the conductivity law it is possible to introduce two kinds of assumptions; consequently two relations are derived for the work of suspension.

Sanoyan confines his considerations to the case of two-dimensional flow and introduces several simplifying assumptions which he justifies by the order of magnitude of the factors involve. Adopting Velikanov's theorem concerning the constancy of the efficiency of sediment transport, he determines the concentration of sediment by the graphical relation of the parameters

$$\frac{\omega a C_T (1 - 2C_T)}{R^{1/2} S^{3/2} (1 + a C_T)} \tag{1.3.7-30}$$

and

$$\frac{\omega C_T}{R^{1/2} S^{3/2}} \tag{1.3.7-31}$$

formed from the hydraulic characteristics of the sediment and of the transporting stream. In these parameters ω is the fall velocity, C is the sediment concentration, R is the hydraulic radius, S is the slope of the energy grade line and $a = (\rho_s - \rho)/\rho$ is the ratio of sediment and water densities.

Measurement data have shown a close relationship to exist between the parameters expressed by Eqs (1.3.7−30) and (1.3.7−31).

Sanoyan presented his approach in detail at the Budapest Symposium on River Regulation and Sediment Transport in 1968.

1.3.8. DETERMINATION OF THE MEAN SEDIMENT CONCENTRATION

The variation of sediment concentration with depth is represented with the help of the concentration curve. It has been mentioned that for estimating the distribution of concentration over the depth of flow at least one concentration value must be determined by measurements even if theoretical relations are applied. However, once concentration measurements are preformed, there is no objection

416

whatsoever to performing simultaneous measurements at several depths. For this reason the variation of concentration with depth is usually determined in practice by direct measurements.

Knowledge of the variation of concentration with depth is of interest primarily in theoretical studies on sediment conditions in alluvial streams. However, in some practical problems the distribution of concentration may also assume importance. In theoretical research and in the practical problems mentioned before the variation of concentration with depth is determined preferably by analytical methods and by observations alike. In this way an opportunity is afforded for checking the validity of the theoretical relations.

Nevertheless in the majority of practical problems the primary objective is to determine the mean concentration in individual verticals and, from these values, the mean concentration in individual cross-sections.

For the sake of clarity the mean concentration in verticals is usually distinguished from the mean concentration in entire cross-sections by using different notations. In this book, however, no separate symbol will be introduced for the mean concentration in verticals in order to make the treatment as simple as possible.

Inasmuch as the suspended sediment material consists of coarser grains of considerable weight, very great differences are observed in concentrations at different depths. In such cases the concentration of sediment in the vicinity of the bottom is substantially greater than in the water layers close to the surface. Exceptionally sediment concentration values may be observed near the surface. Conversely, the variation of sediment concentration with depth is much less pronounced if the suspended sediment consists of fine grains. In the extreme case of very fine silt fractions the sediment concentration is practically unrelated to depth, the sediment being distributed almost uniformly over the entire depth.

It follows that in an exact method the concentration distribution curves must be determine separately for each size fraction, i.e. for the size fractions defined practically by two limit particle sizes. Nevertheless, what engineering practice is primarily concerned with is the aggregate concentration and so the aggregate concentration curve is usually determined first. It should be clear that the concentration curve constructed on the basis of aggregate sediment concentration does not coincide with the theoretical relations describing the variability of sediment concentration over depth.

Concentration curves may also be constructed, moreover, on the basis of the average particle diameter of the suspended sediment. Inasmuch as the suspended sediment material is graded between not too wide limits the concentration curve constructed on the basis of the average particle diameter does not differ appreciably from the curve determined on the basis of theoretical relations. In connection with the description of sediment conditions in the water courses in Hungary the concentration curves constructed for the individual size fractions will be introduced and compared with the curves representing the theoretical relations. Hereafter the aggregate concentration curve obtained with the average particle size will be demonstrated and compared again with the theoretical concentration curve determined for the average particle diameter (see the gaging station Szeged on the Tisza river, in *Subsection 3.1.1.2*).

As mentioned before, the overwhelming majority of practical problems are concerned with the determination of the mean concentration value rather than of the variation of concentration over depth. Once the concentration curve is traced, the mean concentration is found by simple graphical methods based on the balancing of areas. In many instances, however, the variation of concentration over depth cannot be made available. In such cases the mean concentration is found either by an observation method or by some analytical approach. Such a procedure for determining the mean concentration is usually much less expensive, since the additional measurements necessary for determining the variation with depth becomes superfluous.

For determining the mean concentration analytically, with the help of Eqs (1.3.4−56) and (1.3.4−46) representing the distribution of concentration over depth and the velocity of flow, respectively, the following method has been suggested by the Collaborating Agencies:

The full amount of sediment transport of fall velocity ω, moving in unit width of the stream, is obtained by integrating for the full depth the product of concentration and fall velocity. Considering Eqs (1.3.4−56) and (1.3.4−46)

$$G_s = P v_k \, DC_a \, e^{15t \frac{a}{D}} \qquad (1.3.8-1)$$

where $P = C_k/C_0$, the ratio of actual mean concentration in the vertical and of sediment concentration at the bottom. The parameter P is a function of

$$t = \frac{\omega}{\sqrt{\tau_0/\rho}} = \frac{\omega}{U_*}$$

of the roughness coefficient n and of the depth of flow D. Thus

$$P = F\left(t, \; \frac{n}{D^{1/6}}\right)$$

Function P is a highly complex one but, by computing its values for different relative roughnesses $(n/D^{1/6})$, its variation with t can be represented. From the family of curves thus obtained the ratio P is found directly at any arbitrary t value from the corresponding curve $(n/D^{1/6})$. The family of curves constructed by the Collaborating Agencies is shown in *Fig. 1.3.8−1*.

It should be realized that even these relations will yield exact values of the mean concentration in individual verticals for individual size fractions only. In cases where both particle size, specific gravity and particle shape of the suspended sediment material are rather uniform, the mean concentration related to the aggregate concentration may be determined in many instances with the help of the mean diameter by applying the above method to individual verticals.

418

g. 1.3.8—1. Relative concentration vs. parameter t at different relative roughnesses. According to Collaborating Agencies

Eq. (1.3.8—1) divided by the water discharge in unit width, i.e. by $v_k D$, the ʒan concentration is found from the expression

$$C_k = PC_a e^{15t \frac{a}{D}} \qquad (1.3.8-2)$$

the expression

$$t = \frac{\omega}{\sqrt{\tau_0/\rho}}$$

the dimensionless parameter mentioned before, while C_a is the sediment con-ʒtration at the relative depth a/D above the bottom.

For mean concentration two different concepts have been introduced by Velikanov. Computing the sediment volume contained in the volume of water-sediment mixture enclosed by two cross-sections, the mean sediment concentration related to volumes is obtained. It should be remembered that sediment concentration is anyway expressed by Velikanov normally with the volumetric ratio of the sediment.

For practical computations Velikanov introduces the mean concentration transport, expressing sediment concentration again with the help of volumetric concentration. The mean value of concentration transport is determined by relating the total sediment transport in unit width expressed as volume to the entire discharge of sediment carrying water in the same width.

Accordingly, with v denoting the main velocity, D the depth of flow, and C_v the volumetric concentration of sediment at any arbitrary depth y above the bottom, the total sediment transport in unit time is

$$p = C_{v0} \int_0^D \frac{C_v}{C_{v0}} v \, dy \qquad (1.3.8-3)$$

whence, considering the velocity distribution and changing to the relative depth $\eta = y/D$,

$$p = \frac{C_{v0} D \sqrt{gDS}}{\kappa} \int_0^1 \frac{C_v}{C_{v0}} \ln\left(1 + \frac{\eta}{\alpha}\right) d\eta \qquad (1.3.8-4$$

The discharge of sediment-carrying water is

$$q = \frac{D \sqrt{gDS}}{\kappa} \int_0^1 \ln\left(1 + \frac{\eta}{\alpha}\right) d\eta \qquad (1.3.8-5$$

so that the mean concentration transport becomes

$$C_{vk} = \frac{p}{q} = C_{v0} \frac{\int_0^1 \frac{C_v}{C_{v0}} \ln\left(1 + \frac{\eta}{\alpha}\right) d\eta}{\int_0^1 \ln\left(1 + \frac{\eta}{\alpha}\right) d\eta} \qquad (1.3.8-6)$$

Velikanov introduces the notations $C_v/C_{v0} = \phi^\beta$ and

$$N = \int_0^1 \phi^\beta \ln\left(1 + \frac{\eta}{\alpha}\right) d\eta$$

420

Table 1.3.8—1

Ratio of the mean concentration discharge to that along the bottom at different relative roughnesses and values of the parameter β, according to Velikanov

$\frac{1}{\alpha}$ \\ β	Values of N/N_0 for										
	0.50	0.75	1.0	2.0	3.0	4.0	5.0	10.0	20.0	40.0	80.0
500	4.728	4.428	4.171	3.491	2.985	2.586	2.279	1.339	0.702	0.283	0.107
1000	5.396	5.129	4.902	4.118	3.629	3.189	2.825	1.741	0.925	0.414	0.181
2000	6.042	5.810	5.547	4.823	4.269	3.803	3.417	2.205	1.205	0.583	0.264
4000	6.710	6.491	6.269	5.515	4.916	4.400	4.097	2.658	1.521	0.765	0.359

as well as for the case $\beta = 0$

$$N_0 = \int_0^1 \ln\left(1 + \frac{\eta}{\alpha}\right) d\eta$$

yielding for the mean concentration transport the expression

$$C_{vk} = C_{v0} \frac{N}{N_0} \qquad (1.3.8-7)$$

For determining the ratio N/N_0 at different values of $1/\alpha$ and β Velikanov has compiled *Table 1.3.8—1*.

Considering a number of concentration distributions actually observed, Velikanov has found an approximate relation to exist between the ratio C_{vk}/C_{v0} and the values α and β. Accordingly

$$\frac{C_{vk}}{C_{v0}} = \frac{1}{1 + B_a \beta} \qquad (1.3.8-8)$$

where B_a assumes the following values for different values of α:

α	B_a
1/ 500	0.240
1/1000	0.200
1/2000	0.178
1/4000	0.158

Velikanov has also studied the possibility of expressing approximately the mean concentration in terms of a single parameter, namely the parameter β.

Remembering the expression of parameter β under Eq. (1.3.5−1) it should be clear that a close relationship is likely to exist between β and the values of $1/C_v$. In his computations concerning the relation of β and $1/C_v$ the correlation factor $r_{11} = 0.93$.

In the boundary layer at the bottom the suspended sediment is in contact with bed load, and thus Velikanov assumes the sediment concentration at the bottom C_{v0} to be related somehow to the value $1/\beta$ i.e.

$$C_{v0} = \frac{c}{\beta} \qquad (1.3.8-9)$$

The magnitude of the coefficient c is determined by Velikanov under the assumption that the minimum value of the parameter β is about 0.40, whereas the maximum value of C_{v0} may be about 0.41 as mentioned earlier. In this way

$$c = \beta_{\min} C_{v \max} \approx 0.16 \qquad (1.3.8-10)$$

From Eqs (1.3.8−8), (1.3.8−9) and (1.3.8−10)

$$C_{vk} = \frac{0.16}{\beta(1 + B_a\beta)} \qquad (1.3.8-11)$$

As a further simplification Velikanov introduces the value $B_a = 0.20$ and thus

$$C_{vk} = \frac{0.16}{\beta(1 + 0.20\beta)} \qquad (1.3.8-12)$$

Velikanov has found the results of a number of observations to agree very well with those obtained by the approximate relation under Eq. (1.3.8−12).

Besides the analytical determination of mean concentration, repeated attempts have been made at the development of a sampling procedure permitting the mean concentration to be determined directly or with the help of some coefficient.

Of course, a method yielding the mean concentration in a vertical on the basis of a single sample taken from a certain depth would present the optimum solution. A family of curves have been constructed by the Collaborating Agencies for three particular relative roughnesses i.e. three different $(n/D^{1/6})$ values. From these the factor pertaining to concentration at any depth is found in terms of the parameter t. Correspondingly in *Figs 1.3.8−2, 1.3.8−3* and *1.3.8−4* the variation of the factor pertaining to different depths with t is represented by a separate curve. From the figures it will be perceived that the mean concentration in the vertical is approximated most closely by the concentration of the water sample taken from a depth of $0.6-0.8D$. At these depths the factor will be seen almost to equal unity over a rather wide range of t values.

From the figures it will be perceived further that, inasmuch as t is smaller than the parameter value $t = 0.01$, the concentration observed at practically any depth

422

Fig. 1.3.8—2. The ratio of concentrations at different depths to mean concentration vs. parameter *t* at 0.0121 relative roughness. According to Collaborating Agencies

may be regarded, with fair approximation, as the mean concentration. This circumstance is again believed to support the conclusion that a suspended sediment material consisting of very fine grains is distributed practically uniformly over the entire depth of flow.

It is suggested, however, that when determining the mean concentration on the basis of a water sample taken from a single depth, drastic errors may be introduced by the pulsation of concentration, as well as by the design of the particular sampler used. This is why attempts are believed to be justified at determining the mean concentration by samples taken from several depths.

Considerable efforts have already been made to evolve a reliable method of water sampling. Unfortunately, all these have failed to produce a-theoretically exact solution.

423

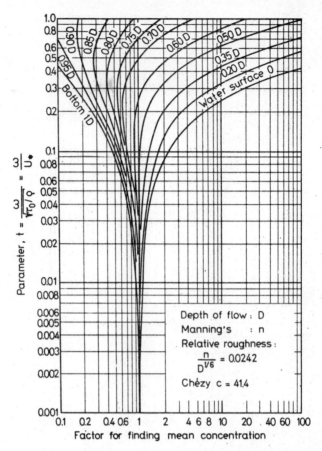

Fig. 1.3.8—3. The ratio of concentrations at different depths to mean concentration vs. parameter *t* at 0.242 relative roughness. According to Collaborating Agencies

Of the sampling methods described in the literature three have found wider application:

a) In the method of Straub, samples are taken from two-tenths and eight-tenths of the depth of flow. For computing the mean concentration five-eighths of the concentration observed at 0.2D are added to three-eighths of the concentration measured at 0.8D depth. In mathematical form

$$C_k = \left(\frac{5}{8} C_{0.2D} + \frac{3}{8} C_{0.8D} \right) \qquad (1.3.8-13)$$

Accurate results are obtained by this sampling method especially in cases where the distribution of concentration follows a linear relation or is approximately such.

424

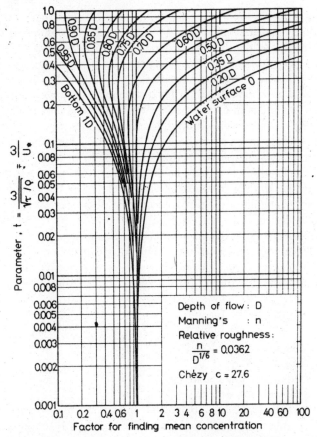

Fig. 1.3.8—4. The ratio of concentrations at different depths to mean concentration vs. parameter t at 0.0362 relative roughness. According to Collaborating Agencies

b) In the method of Luby samples are taken from the centres of bands carrying identical discharge. From the vertical selected at mid-width of the band it is suggested to take a number of samples corresponding to the desired accuracy. Five samples from each vertical are claimed to afford in general the necessary accuracy.

c) In the case of integrating sampling the sampler is lowered continuously from the surface to the bottom and raised again to the surface and the sample is collected continuously during its travel. The samplers filling at each depth at a rate corresponding to the velocity of flow afford the most accurate results.

According to other practical experience, the mean concentration in a vertical is obtained approximately by observing the concentration at six-tenths of depth. In Hungarian practice this method has been rejected owing to the drastic errors which examinations have shown to be potentially introduced thereby.

In Hngarian practice the mean concentration in individual verticals is determined with the help of integrated samples. In each vertical, water samples are taken at tenth-points of depth and the mean concentration in the vertical is determined from the combined sample. Since the sediment material transported in the streams of Hungary is usually very fine, this solution has proved adequate. Several field checks have revealed that the mean concentration computed from the integrated water sample is in close agreement, within the errors inherent to measurement, with the mean concentration determined on the basis of point samples. It is of interest to note that this technique of sampling is especially suited where less skilled personal is available for performing the field work.

Similarly to the method adopted for determining the mean concentration in individual verticals, ample practical evidence indicates that the mean concentration in any particular stream cross-section is obtained by taking samples at three points, namely at one-sixth, one-half and five-sixths of width from six-tenths of depth and by taking the mean value of the concentration of these samples.

Starting from the consideration that in alluvial streams the mean concentration C_k [p/m³], is a function of the tractive force and of the particle size of sediment, G. V. Lopatin suggests, for the mean concentration, the formula

$$C_k = \frac{4D^{0.5} S}{n^2 \omega} \qquad\qquad (1.3.8-14)$$

where D = the mean depth of flow [m]
  S = the slope,
  n = the roughness coefficient
  ω = the fall velocity. [m/sec]
Measurements performed on the Volga, Don and several other rivers have shown the concentrations obtained with the help of Eq. (1.3.8−14) to be in rather close agreement with the observed values.

In tests performed in Hungary these methods have proved unsuccessful. For this reason the mean concentration C_k in a cross-section is obtained as the ratio of the total sediment weight G_s, carried in suspension and computed from the mean concentrations in individual verticals, to the discharge Q, i.e.

$$C_k = \frac{G_s}{Q} \qquad\qquad (1.3.8-15)$$

The suspended sediment transport is found by halving the bands between verticals, in a manner comparable to that adopted for computing the water discharge. The position of verticals is selected in general by observing the rules specified for flow velocity measurements and, since the velocity of flow is measured along with each sediment measurement, the verticals of sediment observations are in Hungarian practice identical with the verticals of flow velocity measurement. It should be noted further that occasionally, after some checking, the number of sediment observation verticals is usually reduced, that is, water samples are not retrieved from all velocity measurement verticals.

1.3.9. SUSPENDED-SEDIMENT TRANSPORT
UNDER UNBALANCED CONDITIONS

Under balanced conditions the concentration of sediment at the same depth is constant with respect to time — disregarding pulsations — moreover, if also the channel dimensions remain constant, it does not change in successive cross-sections along the main direction of flow, provided, of course, that the same depth is always considered.

In alluvial streams, however, completely balanced conditions occur but rarely. Differences occur primarily in the main direction from one cross-section to the other. Under unbalanced conditions concentration may suffer changes in time as well, either decreasing or increasing depending on whether some of the sediment transported is gradually deposited or additional particles are carried into suspension from the bed material.

In deriving the balance equations — Eqs (1.3.3 − 37) to (1.3.3 − 42) — it will be remembered that only the comminution process due to collision has been neglected, while sediment transport has been regarded an isothermic process. Consequently these balance equations apply to sediment transport under both balanced and unbalanced conditions.

In the theories discussed in the preceding sections the equations describing sediment transport have been determined by introducing a wide variety of assumptions. An assumption common to almost each theory is that the process is a steady one (i.e. constant in time), that the sediment concentration suffers no change in the main direction x of flow and that the flow is two-dimensional.

In suspended-sediment transport under unbalanced conditions either the first or the second of the above assumptions is to be omitted, the change in concentration with respect to either time or flow being indicative of the fact that the movement of the suspended sediment is unbalanced. However, in view of the complexity of the phenomenon certain simplifying assumptions are unavoidable also when considering the transport of suspended sediment under such unbalanced conditions.

With due regard to the foregoing it is deemed advisable to examine the potential simplifying assumptions separately and to formulate exactly their physical implications.

Recalling, for the sake of completeness, also the criteria introduced a priori in deriving the general balance equations the potential simplifying assumptions are in general as follows:

a) The process is a steady one

$$\frac{\partial}{\partial t} = 0 \qquad (1.3.9-1)$$

i.e. the variation with time in the density of extensive quantities is negligibly small.

b) The process is a two-dimensional one, consequently it is sufficient to consider the $x − y$ plane only. In this case (i) the component along z of all physical quantities (vectors, tensors) equals zero, (ii) in the horizontal plane variations along z perpendicular to the main direction x are negligible

$$\frac{\partial}{\partial z} = 0 \qquad (1.3.9-2)$$

c) The concentration of sediment (or the mass density of sediment,
(i) varies at a constant rate along the main direction x of flow

$$\frac{\partial C}{\partial x} = \text{constant}, \quad \text{or} \quad \frac{\partial}{\partial x}\left(\frac{\partial C}{\partial x}\right) = 0 \qquad (1.3.9-3)$$

(ii) or it remains constant along the main direction x

$$\frac{\partial C}{\partial x} = \frac{\partial \rho_1}{\partial x} = 0 \qquad (1.3.9-4)$$

d) The sediment particles suffer no change in size as a result of collisions. In other words, the mass balance of individual sediment fractions is source-free (i.e. the mass of each fraction is conserved separately)

$$q_k = 0 \qquad (1.3.9-5)$$

e) The sediment is monodisperse, i.e. it consists of uniform particle sizes, or the influence of different particle sizes is small enough to be neglected. Consequently Eqs (1.3.3−39) and (1.3.3−40) applying to individual fractions need not be taken into consideration.

f) The equation of the energy balance is source-free, the dissipation of energy being negligible. As a consequence thereof the process may be considered isothermic, the balance equation of internal energy becoming superfluous and therefore the balance equation of kinetic energy is not needed either (since in this case it is not independent of the momentum balance). Although in some cases the process is considered isothermic, the balance equation of kinetic energy is still included with the momentum balance. Naturally, in the course of subsequent derivation, the former is eliminated.

g) The pattern of flow is unaffected by the presence of sediment, thus the energy and momentum exchange between water and sediment is negligible as far as the energy and momentum of water are concerned. In other words, this implies that the term

$$\frac{\gamma_1}{\omega}(\mathbf{v}_h - \mathbf{v})$$

involved in Eq. (1.3.3−38) is very small in comparison with the other terms of the equation. It follows moreover that, since $\gamma_1 > \bar{\varrho}g = \gamma$ (the specific gravity of sediment is greater than that of water), it is the ratio $(\mathbf{v}_h - \mathbf{v})/\omega$ that is to be assumed to be smaller by orders of magnitude than the product $\bar{\varrho}g$. This assumption is satisfied if $\bar{\mathbf{v}}_h \simeq \bar{\mathbf{v}}$, i.e. the travelling velocity of sediment is comparable to the flow velocity of water (the inertia of the sediment is negligible small). This assumption is often formulated by equating the velocity components along the main direction x of flow

$$\bar{v}_{hx} = \bar{v}_x \qquad (1.3.9-6)$$

whereas the vertical components along y differ from one another exactly by the fall velocity:

$$\bar{v}_{hy} = \bar{v}_y - \omega \qquad (1.3.9-7)$$

h) The current densities due to turbulent movements may be expressed (in accordance with the law of conductivity) instead of the correlation of pulsation terms, as the product of a turbulent conductivity and the gradient of the corresponding intensive quantity. Thus, for instance, the mass current density becomes

$$\overline{\rho' \mathbf{v}'} = - \varepsilon_h \operatorname{grad} \bar{\rho} \qquad (1.3.9-8)$$

while the momentum current density is

$$\overline{\rho' \mathbf{v}' \circ \mathbf{v}'} = - \varepsilon_m \operatorname{Grad} \bar{\mathbf{v}} \qquad (1.3.9-9)$$

i) The conductive momentum current density occurring as a result of turbulent pulsation (i.e. the turbulent stress) is much smaller than the convective momentum current density, so that the former is negligible:

$$\overline{\mathbf{v}' \circ \mathbf{v}'} \ll \bar{\mathbf{v}} \circ \bar{\mathbf{v}} \qquad (1.3.9-10)$$

j) The vertical component of the flow velocity of water (considering its mean value with respect to time) is much smaller than the fall velocity and is negligible in comparison with the latter

$$\bar{\mathbf{v}}_y \ll \omega \qquad (1.3.9-11)$$

k) The turbulent conductivity of sediment is ϵ_h or, omitting the subscript h, the conductivity tensor ε is

$$\begin{bmatrix} \varepsilon_{xx} & \varepsilon_{xy} & \varepsilon_{xz} \\ \varepsilon_{yx} & \varepsilon_{yy} & \varepsilon_{yz} \\ \varepsilon_{zx} & \varepsilon_{zy} & \varepsilon_{zz} \end{bmatrix} \qquad (1.3.9-12)$$

where ε_{ij} $(i, j = x, y, z)$ denotes the conductivity of current in the direction j due to the gradient in the direction i.

The magnitude of this tensor is in general taken into consideration under three assumptions, describing essentially the potential deformations of the tensor.

(i)

$$\varepsilon \Rightarrow |\varepsilon| = \varepsilon \qquad (1.3.9-13)$$

429

i. e., the tensor is regarded a scalar quantity.

(ii)
$$\varepsilon_{ij} = \varepsilon_{ji}$$
(1.3.9−14)

i. e., the tensor is regarded a symmetrical one.

(iii)
$$\varepsilon_{ij} \neq 0, \quad \text{if} \quad i = j,$$

but
$$\varepsilon_{ij} = 0, \quad \text{if} \quad i \neq j$$
(1.3.9−15)

i. e., the tensor is assumed a diagonal one.

If the process is two-dimensional, then

$$\varepsilon_{ij} = 0, \quad \text{for every} \quad i = z, \quad \text{or} \quad j = z \quad \text{case.}$$
(1.3.9−16)

Under unbalanced conditions the equations describing the variation in sediment concentration may be written into several forms, depending on the manner in which the potential simplifying assumptions are grouped.

The general differential equation frequently quoted in the relevant literature is:*

$$v\frac{\partial C}{\partial x} = \omega\frac{\partial C}{\partial y} + \frac{\partial \varepsilon_x}{\partial x}\frac{\partial C}{\partial x} + \frac{\partial \varepsilon_y}{\partial y}\frac{\partial C}{\partial y} + \varepsilon_x\frac{\partial^2 C}{\partial x^2} + \varepsilon_y\frac{\partial^2 C}{\partial y^2} \quad (1.3.9-17)$$

expressing the mass balance of sediment in a steady two-dimensional process (cf. *a* and *b*), introducing also the assumptions *d, e, g, h, j* and *k* (iii). According to assumption *b*, the turbulent conductivity has only the components ε_y and ε_x in the vertical and the main flow directions, respectively, and ε_y varies with depth (direction *y*), while ε_x along the main direction *x*. No functions being available to describe these variations, or those of the main velocity *v* along *y* or *x*, every attempt at finding a general solution for the differential equation under Eq. (1.3.9−17) has remained unsuccessful so far.

For this reason it was found inevitable to introduce certain assumptions in order to simplify the general differential equation describing suspended sediment transport under unbalanced conditions. The assumption most commonly introduced (No. *k* (iii)) is that ε_x and ε_y are equal or, at least, in a certain proportion to each other.

In connection with the theory of turbulent sediment transport it has been mentioned that by assuming a parabolic velocity distribution the determination of the sediment-mixing coefficient becomes greatly simplified. Denoting the surface velocity by v_{fs}, the expression describing the parabolic velocity distribution is obtained in the form

$$v = v_{fsz} - b(D - y)^2$$
(1.3.9−18)

---

* *v* is the component along *x* of the flow velocity of water.

430

In Eq. (1.3.9−18) a constant b is involved, while D denotes the full depth of flow. In this case the velocity gradient becomes

$$\frac{dv}{dy} = 2bD \left(1 - \frac{y}{D}\right) \qquad (1.3.9-19)$$

According to Eqs (1.3.4−4), (1.3.4−5) and (1.3.4−45)

$$\varepsilon_y = \frac{\tau_0 \left(1 - \dfrac{y}{D}\right)}{\rho \dfrac{dv}{dy}} \qquad (1.3.9-20)$$

Combining Eqs (1.3.9−19) and (1.3.9−20), we eventually have

$$\varepsilon_y = \frac{\tau_0}{2bD\rho} \qquad (1.3.9-21)$$

implying that, in the case of a parabolic velocity distribution, ε_y is unaffected by depth y.

Assuming further $\partial\varepsilon_x/\partial x$ and $\partial^2 C/\partial x^2$ to be negligible (No. $c(i)$) and remembering that, according to Eq. (1.3.9−21), $\partial\varepsilon_y/\partial y = 0$, then

$$v \frac{\partial C}{\partial x} = \omega \frac{\partial C}{\partial y} + \varepsilon_y \frac{\partial^2 C}{\partial y^2} \qquad (1.3.9-22)$$

is obtained as a differential equation describing the variation of sediment concentration.

Assuming moreover in the above differential equation the concentration to remain unchanged along x(No.$c(ii)$) or $\partial C/\partial x = 0$, then

$$0 = \omega \frac{\partial C}{\partial y} + \varepsilon_y \frac{\partial^2 C}{\partial y^2} \qquad (1.3.9-23)$$

becomes the differential equation from which, assuming sediment transport under equilibrium conditions, intergations yields the differential equation under Eq. (1.3.4−24).

It will be readily perceived that the differential equation under Eq. (1.3.9−17) is essentially a counterpart of Eq. (1.3.3−41) by substituting concentration C for the density ρ_1 and by assuming, according to a) and d), the process to be steady and source-free. Eq. (1.3.3−41) is then rewritten into the form

$$\text{div}\,(C\,\mathbf{v}_h - \varepsilon\,\text{grad}\,C) = 0 \qquad (1.3.9-24)$$

431

which, in the form corresponding to the two-dimensional case according to assumption b) (and noting that div $\mathbf{v} = 0$),

$$v_{hx}\frac{\partial C}{\partial x} + v_{hy}\frac{\partial C}{\partial y} = \frac{\partial}{\partial x}\left(\varepsilon\frac{\partial C}{\partial x}\right) + \frac{\partial}{\partial y}\left(\varepsilon\frac{\partial C}{\partial y}\right) \qquad (1.3.9-25)$$

According to assumption k (iii), each element (except for the components xx and yy) of tensor ε equals zero. Omitting the double subscript the two tensor components other than zero are denoted by ε_x and ε_y. According further to assumption g), $\mathbf{v}_h = \mathbf{v} - \omega$ and, by assumptions j), $v_y \ll \omega$. Thus from Eq. (1.3.9−25)

$$v_x\frac{\partial C}{\partial x} - \omega\frac{\partial C}{\partial y} = \frac{\partial \varepsilon_x}{\partial x}\frac{\partial C}{\partial x} + \frac{\partial \varepsilon_y}{\partial y}\frac{\partial C}{\partial y} + \varepsilon_x\frac{\partial^2 C}{\partial x^2} + \varepsilon_y\frac{\partial^2 C}{\partial y^2}$$

which is formally identical with Eq. (1.3.9−17).

It should be noted that the differential equation of A. A. Kalinske differs from Eq. (1.3.9−17) only in that he neglects the variation of conductivity with location. Thus Kalinske describes the variation in sediment concentration by the equation

$$v\frac{\partial C}{\partial x} = \omega\frac{\partial C}{\partial y} + \varepsilon_x\frac{\partial^2 C}{\partial x^2} + \varepsilon_y\frac{\partial^2 C}{\partial y^2} \qquad (1.3.9-26)$$

With the assumptions detailed in connection with Eq. (1.3.9−17) the general mass balance equation under Eq. (1.3.3−41) can be adopted as a starting point in deriving Eq. (1.3.9−26), considering also as a special condition that

$$\frac{\partial \varepsilon_{xx}}{\partial x} = 0 \quad \text{és} \quad \frac{\partial \varepsilon_{yy}}{\partial y} = 0 \qquad (1.3.9-27)$$

The differential equation (1.3.9−17) was adopted also by S. Bruk in dimensioning settling basins.

Under steady conditions, i.e. where the distribution of sediment concentration is constant in time (a), E. Dobbins adopted the differential equation

$$v_x\frac{\partial C}{\partial x} = \varepsilon_y\frac{\partial^2 C}{\partial y^2} + \frac{\partial C}{\partial y}\left(\omega + \frac{\partial \varepsilon_y}{\partial y}\right) + \varepsilon_x\frac{\partial^2 C}{\partial x^2} \qquad (1.3.9-28)$$

for expressing the mass balance of sediment in settling.

It is obvious that this equation is obtained directly from Eq. (1.3.9−17) with the assumption $\partial \varepsilon_x/\partial x = 0$. Physically this assumption implies that conductivity varies with depth only.

With these considerations no further demonstration is deemed necessary for the fact that the equation of Dobbins can also be derived from the mass balance expressed by Eq. (1.3.3−41).

432

In the Progress Report* of the Task Committee on Preparation of Sedimentation Manual, Committee on Sedimentation, the variation of sediment concentration for two-dimensional unsteady flow is described as

$$- v_x \frac{\partial C}{\partial x} - v_y \frac{\partial C}{\partial y} + \varepsilon_x \frac{\partial^2 C}{\partial x^2} + \frac{\partial \varepsilon_x}{\partial x} \frac{\partial C}{\partial x} + \varepsilon_y \frac{\partial^2 C}{\partial y^2} +$$

$$+ \frac{\partial \varepsilon_y}{\partial y} \frac{\partial C}{\partial y} + \omega \frac{\partial C}{\partial y} = \frac{\partial C}{\partial t} \qquad (1.3.9-29)$$

assuming continuity, div $v = 0$. This equation differs from Eq. (1.3.9−25) only in that $\partial C/\partial t \neq 0$, i.e. the variation of concentration in time has already been allowed for, further in that assumption $g)$ has been applied directly in determining the velocity of sediment. It will thus become clear that Eq. (1.3.9−29) can also be derived from the fundamental equation (1.3.3−41).

In the report of the Task Committee, Eq. (1.3.3−24) describing balanced conditions has been obtained from Eq. (1.3.9−29) by introducing the assumptions listed before.

Considering steady turbulent flow and assuming that transverse variations in velocity, in the turbulent characteristics and in concentration are negligibly small, W. W. Sayre has recently derived the differential equation

$$\frac{\partial C}{\partial t} + v_x \frac{\partial C}{\partial x} = \frac{\partial}{\partial y} \left(\varepsilon_y \frac{\partial C}{\partial y} \right) + \omega \frac{\partial C}{\partial y} + \varepsilon_x \frac{\partial^2 C}{\partial x^2} \qquad (1.3.9-30)$$

for the case of low sediment concentrations. The two components ε_x and ε_y of conductivity are taken into consideration as the product of their mean value ε_{av} and of a quantity $\Psi(y)$ depending on the depth of flow. The theoretical approach adopted by Sayre is of considerable interest. Considering his basic assumptions, however, this method would be applicable only to special cases of sediment transport in alluvial channels.

Omitting further details it should only be noted that with assumption $g)$ and neglecting $\partial \varepsilon_x/\partial x$ Eq. (1.3.9− 30) is identical with Eq. (1.3.9−29).

Laboratory experiments were performed by Apmann and Rumer in 1970 in order to study the variation of the diffusion coefficient. As a starting basis they adopted the equation of convective diffusion

$$\frac{\partial \bar{C}}{\partial t} = v_{hx} \frac{\partial \bar{C}}{\partial x} + v_{hy} \frac{\partial \bar{C}}{\partial y} + v_{hz} \frac{\partial \bar{C}}{\partial z} =$$

$$\qquad (1.3.9-31)$$

$$\frac{\partial}{\partial x} \left(\varepsilon_x \frac{\partial \bar{C}}{\partial x} \right) + \frac{\partial}{\partial y} \left(\varepsilon_y \frac{\partial \bar{C}}{\partial y} \right) + \frac{\partial}{\partial z} \left(\varepsilon_z \frac{\partial \bar{C}}{\partial z} \right)$$

---

* Progress Report, Task Committee on Preparation of Sedimentation Manual Committee on Sedimentation, Hydraulic Division. *Proc. of ASCE*, HY 5, September 1963.

Eq. (1.3.9−31) written in adherence to the notations introduced earlier is identical with the mass balance equation (1.3.3−41) determined for the sediment under the following assumptions:

Supposing that div $\bar{v}_h = 0$ and that, under assumptions d), e) and h), assumption k(iii) applies to conductivity, ε i.e. the tensor is diagonal, further that the simplifying assumptions b), c(i) and j) are valid, Eq. (1.3.9−31) assumes the form

$$v\frac{\partial\bar{C}}{\partial x} - \omega\frac{\partial\bar{C}}{\partial y} = \varepsilon_y\frac{\partial^2\bar{C}}{\partial y^2} + \frac{\partial\varepsilon_y}{\partial y}\frac{\partial\bar{C}}{\partial y} \qquad (1.3.9-32)$$

The equation becomes even more simple if both velocity and diffusivity are considered constant in the flow space. Normalizing Eq. (1.3.9−32), i.e. introducing the notations

$$\bar{s} = \bar{C}/C_0, \quad \bar{x} = x/D, \quad \bar{y} = y/D, \quad \bar{z} = \omega D/\bar{\varepsilon} \quad \text{and} \quad R = \bar{v}D/\bar{\varepsilon}$$

where C_0 = a characteristic concentration,
$\quad D$ = depth of flow,
$\quad \bar{\varepsilon}$ = mean value of diffusivity,
$\quad \bar{v}$ = mean velocity,
the dimensionless form:

$$\frac{\partial^2\bar{s}}{\partial\bar{y}^2} + \bar{z}\frac{\partial\bar{s}}{\partial\bar{y}} = R\frac{\partial\bar{s}}{\partial\bar{x}} \qquad (1.3.9-33)$$

is obtained.

The main merit of these studies is that they have resulted in determining the variation and numerical value of the diffusion coefficient.

* * *

A few examples have been introduced in the foregoing for mass balance equations applying to unbalanced conditions pointing out that these are particular cases of the general balance equations.

In order to facilitate comparisons to be made the assumptions introduced in connection with the theories mentioned have been grouped according to a)−k) in *Table 1.3.9−1*.

Sediment transport under unbalanced conditions has been studied extensively by Kalinske. From his investigations he concludes that Eqs (1.3.9−22) and (1.3.9−23) can be applied successfully to a number of practical problem. He agrees with the conclusion that the assumption of a parabolic velocity profile results in but slight differences from the actual distribution. On the other hand, he regards the neglect in the variation of the sediment-mixing coefficient with depth y as a source of appreciable errors.

In engineering practice it would be of great interest to devise a method for determining directly whether balanced conditions prevail in a stream for the

434

Table 1.3.9—1

Possible simplifications by different authors in the treatment of suspended-sediment movement (+ indicates simplification, − no simplification)

Author and No. of formula	Possible simplifications														Special	
	a)	b)	c(i)	c(ii)	d)	e)	f)	g)	h)	i)	j)	k(i)	k(ii)	k(iii)	$\frac{\partial \varepsilon_{zz}}{\partial x}=0$	$\frac{\partial \varepsilon_{yy}}{\partial y}=0$
General (1.3.9 − 17)	+	+	−	−	+	+	The energy balance not included	+	+	The momentum balance not included	+	−	−	−	−	−
Kalinske, A. A. (1.3.9 − 26)	+	+	−	−	+	+		+	+		+	−	−	+	+	+
Dobbins, E. (1.3.9 − 28)	+	+	−	−	+	+		+	+		+	−	−	+	+	−
Sed. Manual (1.3.9 − 29)	−	+	−	−	+	+		+	+		+	−	−	+	+	−
Sayre, W. W. (1.3.9 − 30)	−	+	−	−	+	+		+	+		+	−	−	+	+	−
Apmann, R. P.— Rumer, R. R. (1.3.9 − 32)	−	+	+	−	+	+		+	+		+	−	−	+	+	−

movement of suspended sediment. In developing such a method, the hydraulic properties of the channel and the material lining the bed arise as dominant factors. The influence of the hydraulic properties of the stream in the strict sense of the word and of the channel material on sediment transport should be obvious. Thus for instance, over steep sections where the velocity of flow is high, the material of the channel and similarly that of the sediment consist mostly of coarse gravel. The majority of the latter is transported along the bottom. At mild slopes and low velocities the bed material consists of fine-grained soils and, accordingly, fine-grained sediment is carried both in suspension and as bed load. Several attempts have been made to apply these observations, and varying degrees of success have been attained. Such investigations have resulted in establishing relations between the bed material and the hydraulic properties of the stream which apply to balanced conditions.

Starting from the logical assumption that the composition and concentration of suspended sediment depend also on the composition of the bed material, Lane and Kalinske have developed a relationship between the concentration along the bottom C_0 of suspended sediment composed of particle sizes pertaining to a particular fall velocity ω and the part of bed material described also by the concentration C_f pertaining also to ω. Under balanced conditions, i.e., in the case of a non-scouring and non-silting channel, the volume of sediment deposited under the action of gravity will be recalled to equal the volume of material raised from the bottom and maintained in suspension by turbulent flow. Considering therefore that, if the instantaneous vertical velocity at the bottom is greater than the fall velocity of the particular size fraction, the rising and suspension of the bed material start. Lane and Kalinske have found the volume of sediment characterized by the fall velocity ω and carried into suspension from the bottom to be proportionate, on the one hand, to the relative quantity of this fraction present in the bed material and, on the other, to the magnitude of the vertical velocity and to the duration of time during which the velocity becomes high enough to lift the sediment from the bottom.

As a conclusion drawn from these considerations they suggest that the ratio of the concentration of suspended sediment along the bottom and of the concentration of bed material pertaining to the same size fraction, i.e. the ratio C_0/C_f is a function of the parameter t explained in the foregoing:

$$\frac{C_0}{C_f} = \phi(t) \qquad (1.3.9-34)$$

The physical interpretation offered for this function appears to be correct In fact, under balanced conditions, according to Eqs (1.3.4−56) and (1.3.4−57) any value of

$$t = \frac{\omega}{\sqrt{\dfrac{\tau_0}{\rho}}} = \frac{\omega}{U_*}$$

436

Fig. 1.3.9—1. Concentration ratio of suspended sediment and bed material vs. parameter *t*.
After Lane and Kalinske

defines already the ratio C/C_0 indicating in turn that sediment concentration is
essentially a function of the parameter *t*.

The parameter *t* seems to be highly suited for describing the movement of suspended sediment, the fall velocity ω being characteristic of sediment quality and
primarily of its particle size, whereas $U_* = \sqrt{gDS}$ depends on the hydraulic
properties of the water course.

For determining the relation under Eq. (1.3.9 − 34) the results of field observations were adopted first by Lane and Kalinske. This resulted in the relation
illustrated in *Fig. 1.3.9—1*, showing a definite relation between C_0/C_f and *t* regardless of the considerable scattering of measurement data. Lane and Kalinske
suggested Eq. (1.3.9 − 34) for sediment transport under balanced conditions, i.e.
for non-scouring, non-silting channels. Since the shear velocity U_* is governed
by the hydraulic characteristics of the stream, whereas the concentration C_f of
a material having a certain fall velocity ω depends on the composition of bed
material, it should be obvious that the sediment concentration C_0 at balanced conditions can be found from *Fig. 1.3.9—1*. If the actual concentration is higher than
C_0, the excess part of suspended sediment will settle, and if it is lower, the channel
will start scouring. Consequently if the point representing the pair of values
ω/U_* and C_0/C_f lies above the curve silting may be expected, if it is below
the curve, scouring occurs. Since the relation shown in *Fig. 1.3.9—1* applies to

balanced conditions, it is possible to make certain predictions concerning suspended-sediment transport in particular water courses. This circumstance should be attributed a very great significance in engineering practice.

According to the figure, for values of t close to unity the rate of sediment transport in the stream is practically zero, whereas at low values of t the concentration of suspended sediment may be very high. The value of t is controlled, as mentioned, by the ratio of the fall velocity and the shear velocity. It assumes thus small values if at the same shear velocity ω is low, i.e. the sediment is very fine. Conversely, if an unchanged particle size (i.e. ω) is assumed, the shear velocity and, in turn, the sediment-transporting capacity are high.

One of the objections that can be raised in connection with *Fig. 1.3.9—1* is that the small number of observation data may include some that do not apply to actual balanced conditions. In this respect no further details are given by the authors. For the purpose of checking, the results of some observations made on rivers in Hungary have also been entered into the figure. On the basis of these data the curve appears to be acceptable in general. Nevertheless some improvement of the relation is believed possible by including the criteria concerning channel stability or stable beds.

For the sake of completeness it should be noted that from laboratory experiments Kalinske and Hsia have concluded that the relation

$$\frac{C_0}{C_f} = \phi\left(\frac{\omega}{U_*}\right)$$

is not of general validity. The examination of the data has shown the influence of the shear velocity U_* on the ratio C_0/C_f to be greater than allowed for and, it is even conceivable — since recent experiments relate to very small fractions — that fine-grained materials differ in their behaviour from coarse sediment.

In deriving their first relation Lane and Kalinske assumed the flow to be completely turbulent, that is, that turbulence extends down to the bottom material. This assumption is likely to hold true in the case of high shear stresses and coarse bed material, but does not apply to low shear stresses and fine-grained material.

For this reason Kalinske has adopted a different approach in recent investigations to take the effect of viscosity into consideration. As a consequence of diffusion he claims $T(C_f - C_0)$ to be a measure of the quantity of sediment carried into suspension. Here T is the diffusion coefficient related to unit path length, C_f and C_0 are, in accordance with the foregoing interpretation, the concentrations of the bottom material and the suspended sediment, respectively.

Under balanced conditions sediment is carried into suspension and settled at identical rates, i.e. $T(C_f - C_0) = \omega C_0$, implying that the ratio C_0/C_f is a function of ω/T.

Lane and Kalinske have succeeded in demonstrating, that the magnitude of T depends on the shear velocity U_*, on the thickness δ of the boundary layer, and on the particle diameter d of the sediment.

Fig. 1.3.9—2. Concentration ratio of suspended sediment and bed material vs. *t*, with Re_* as parameter. After Kalinske

439

It is thus possible to express T as a function of U_* and the ratio d/δ. It will be recalled that the thickness of the boundary layer is usually taken proportionate to the ratio v/U_*, where v is the coefficient of kinematic viscosity.

We are thus justified in assuming that

$$T \propto U_* \, \phi' \left(\frac{U_* d}{v} \right) \tag{1.3.9-35}$$

or that T varies in proportion to the product of the shear velocity and some function ϕ'.

It should be obvious hereafter that the ratio C_0/C_f is expressed as the function of two dimensionless quantities

$$\frac{C_0}{C_f} = \phi \left(\frac{\omega}{U_*}, \ \frac{U_* d}{v} \right) \tag{1.3.9-36}$$

or introducing the notation $\omega/U_* = t$ and $U_* d/v = Re_*$

$$\frac{C_0}{C_f} = \phi(t, \ Re_*) \tag{1.3.9-37}$$

The relation between the three parameters has been represented by Kalinske with a family of curves in *Fig. 1.3.9−2* where continuous lines connect the points representing pairs of C_0/C_f and t values pertaining to the same Re_* value.

The family of curves traced with a full line in *Fig. 1.3.9−2* represents the results of laboratory experiments so that these apply truly to balanced conditions. Nevertheless Kalinske himself notes, that further investigations are necessary before Eq. (1.3.9−37) can be applied to practical problems.

1.3.10. APPLICATION OF THE RELATIONS ON SUSPENDED-SEDIMENT TRANSPORT IN HYDRAULIC ENGINEERING

In hydraulic engineering and at hydraulic structures a number of problems arise as a consequence of the movement and settling of suspended sediment. Of these the hydraulic transport of granular materials and the removal of sediment from the water of alluvial streams by settling assume special significance since the theory of sediment transport is directly applicable to these. For this reason it is believed advisable to deal more in detail with these two classic applications of the theory of suspended-sediment transport to hydraulic engineering problems.

1.3.10.1. Slurry transport. The first attempt at the excavation and transportation of granular materials by hydraulic methods dates back to the end of the 19th century. Rapid advances in technology have made since the transport of granular materials in water an important method of present technology. Although the sphere of application is limited by several factors, low costs and continuous operation have rendered it attractive in earth moving, mining and in other branches of industry alike.

The theoretical and practical problems associated with slurry transport are related, on the one hand, to the laws of hydromechanics and, on the other, to the designing and production of mechanical equipment suitable for transporting slurry in high concentrations. What we shall examine are only the hydromechanical aspects of slurry transport since the movement of slurry in pipe-lines combines particular cases of suspended sediment and bed load movement.

Considerations are started again from the mass balance, momentum balance and energy balance of the two different media so that the general balance equations (1.3.3 − 37) and (1.3.3 − 42) given in *Section 1.3.3* also apply to the case of slurry transport. The unambiguity criteria associated with the set of equations (e.g. the condition equations describing the physical properties of the flowing medium) are extremely complex, making any theoretical treatment extremely difficult. This may be offered as an explanation for the fact that, although a number of investigators have concentrated (especially during the last fifty years) on the theory of slurry transport, no method of direct use for practice is as yet available.

Owing to the complexity of the problem, the theoretical treatment is replaced partly or entirely by empirical relations. Unfortunately, the results obtained in this manner can only be used under operating conditions resembling those of the original experiment. No suitable techniques have been designed as yet for obtaining general conclusions from these empirical relations.

For practical purposes research is called upon to develop a simple method for determining two fundamental quantities, namely the friction loss and the most efficient transport velocity. The first of these is necessary for determining the power demand and for designing the slurry pump, whereas the second is of interest to the dimensioning of the pipeline as well as for determining the rate of transport or output.

Each of the two quantities is affected by a number of parameters. Thus the friction loss and the transport velocity are functions of the physical properties of the material transported and of the transporting fluid, of the composition of the mixture, of the slurry, of the hydraulic properties of the pipeline etc. However, these two quantities are also interrelated. At constant granulometry, slurry concentration, temperature and equipment, the friction loss will become minimum at a certain velocity (here and subsequently the mean velocity will be understood). The velocity pertaining to the minimum loss is commonly referred to as a critical velocity, this indicating a limit condition, below which some solid particles tend to settle to the bottom of the pipe, whereas higher velocities involve greater losses.

The flow velocity necessary for transporting slurry must be logically higher than the velocity needed for initial sediment movement.

The equation describing the process is expected to provide information on the type of relation existing between the transport velocity, the turbulent characteristics of flow and the friction loss, and to yield an expression for estimating optimum equipment dimensions and operating instructions. It is obvious that a theory meeting these requirements is extremely difficult to develop and that no satisfactory solution has so far been offered.

One of the methods commonly adopted consists of determining the characteristics of slurry transport in terms of dimensionless numbers. The similarity transformation of Eqs (1.3.3−37) to (1.3.3−42) yields, besides $Fr = v^2/gD$, the dimensionless parameter $B = v/\omega$ which may be regarded as the settling number. The latter is of considerable significance in slurry transport.

Studies have been reported in the literature where endeavours were made to determine the volumetric concentration C_T in terms of a Froude number formed of the transport velocity and the pipe diameter, using the particle size as a parameter.

Nevertheless these experimental results could not be generalized either. Owing to the considerable scattering of the results the most efficient velocity or, with the term introduced before, the critical velocity is still determined for each particular case with the help of empirical relations. The details concerning the determination of critical velocities will be discussed in connection with the various methods.

The energy required for slurry transport is estimated by introducing simplifying assumptions.

A brief review of the theories involved is deemed advisable.

The right-hand side of the energy balance in slurry transport contains the source of kinetic energy which −neglecting dissipation−is composed of the work required for overcoming pipe friction and for transporting the slurry. The pressure loss Δp due to the work of friction is, in accordance with Bernoulli's theorem, proportionate to the density $\rho v^2/2$ of kinetic energy, so that

$$\Delta p = \zeta \frac{\rho}{2} v^2$$

where ζ is a function of the coefficient λ of pipe friction, of pipe length L and of pipe diameter D. Hence (for clear water) the Darcy−Weissbach relation

$$\left(\frac{\Delta p}{\gamma}\right)_v = \lambda \frac{v^2}{2g} \frac{L}{D} \tag{1.3.10−1}$$

is obtained.

As an approximation it is assumed that when transporting slurry of bulk density (or specific gravity) γ_z the coefficient of pipe friction is modified as compared with that applying to clear water, thus the resistance coefficient λ_z is used instead of λ applying to clear water. Consequently the pressure loss $(\Delta p)_z$ expressed with the help of the specific gravity γ_z of slurry becomes

$$\frac{(\Delta p)_z}{\gamma_z} = \lambda_z \frac{v^2}{2g} \frac{L}{D} \tag{1.3.10−2}$$

Comparing Eqs (1.3.10−1) and (1.3.10−2) it will be perceived that in the case of identical velocities v, pipe length L and pipe diameter D

$$\frac{(\Delta p)_z}{\gamma_z \lambda_z} = \frac{(\Delta p)_v}{\gamma \lambda}$$

or

$$(\Delta p)_z = \frac{\gamma_z}{\gamma} \frac{\lambda_z}{\lambda} (\Delta p)_v$$

and thus

$$\frac{\Delta p}{\gamma} = \lambda_z \frac{\gamma_z}{\gamma} \frac{L}{D} \frac{v^2}{2g} \qquad (1.3.10-3)$$

indicating that the ratio of head losses applying to slurry and to clear water is given as

$$\frac{\gamma_z}{\gamma} \frac{\lambda_z}{\lambda}$$

The second term of head loss is due to the work performed in transporting the slurry. The solid substance of volumetric concentratin C_T and specific gravity γ_1 is transported over a distance L through a pipe of cross-sectional area F at a slurry velocity v_h. The work of transport performed during time Δt is

$$C_T(\gamma_1 - \gamma)LFv_h \, \Delta t \qquad (1.3.10-4)$$

Owing to the frictional and transport work performed, the pressure of the fluid is reduced by Δp, while its energy during time Δt by

$$\Delta p F v \, \Delta t \qquad (1.3.10-5)$$

From Eqs (1.3.10−4) and (1.3.10−5) it follows that the head loss attributed to slurry transport is

$$C_T \frac{(\gamma_1 - \gamma)}{\gamma} \frac{v_h}{v} L \qquad (1.3.10-6)$$

The total head loss is consequently

$$\frac{\Delta p}{\gamma} = \lambda_z \frac{\gamma_z}{\gamma} \frac{v^2}{2g} \frac{L}{D} + C_T \frac{(\gamma_1 - \gamma)}{\gamma} \frac{v_h}{v} L \qquad (1.3.10-7)$$

Information on the dimensionless resistance coefficient λ_z applying to the slurry and the velocity v_h of the slurry would, of course, be necessary to make any practical application of Eq. (1.3.10−7) possible. λ_z differs from the resistance coefficient λ in clear water and is a function of the grain size distribution too. Although v_h is closely related to fall velocity ω, the two are not identical since,

443

beside particular fall velocity ω, it is affected by C_T and even by the velocity v of water.

The attempts at determining λ_z and v_h by a theoretical approach have failed to yield results of practical significance. Therefore, by introducing apparently logical assumptions the characteristics of the phenomenon have been determined empirically.

One of the approaches involved is the determination of the slurry-transporting capacity of water flowing in the pipe. If this is known, the loss is found directly at any particular slurry concentration. Relating the second term on the right-hand side of Eq. (1.3.10−7), i.e. the head needed for transporting the slurry, to the full head loss on the left-hand side, i.e. by forming the ratio

$$\eta = \frac{C_T \left(\dfrac{\gamma_1 - \gamma}{\gamma} \right) \dfrac{v_h}{v} L}{\Delta p / \gamma} \qquad (1.3.10-8)$$

we obtain the part of the total head loss required for transporting slurry of concentration C_T.

Since $(\Delta p / \gamma)/L$ is the slope S of the energy grade line,

$$\eta = C_T \frac{(\gamma_1 - \gamma)}{\gamma S} \frac{v_h}{v} \qquad (1.3.10-9)$$

In alluvial streams S. Bruk (1966) assumed $v_h \cong \omega$ and found for η values as low as 0.5 to 1.5%. This implies that at low sediment concentrations (the general case in alluvial streams) only a small fraction of the total energy of flow is expended for transporting sediment.

Starting therefrom Bruk assumed that in the case of slurry transport η is still small enough, so that the term representing frictional resistances on the right-hand side of Eq. (1.3.10−7) is responsible for the dominant part of head loss. For this reason he feels justified to express η as the ratio of the two terms involved on the right-hand side of this relation

$$\eta = \frac{C_T \left(\dfrac{\gamma_1 - \gamma}{\gamma} \right) \dfrac{\omega}{v} L}{\lambda_z \dfrac{\gamma_z}{\gamma} \dfrac{v^2}{2g} \dfrac{L}{D}} \qquad (1.3.10-10)$$

or introducing the notation

$$\frac{2(\gamma_1 - \gamma)}{\lambda_z \gamma_z} = A \qquad (1.3.10-11)$$

to write

$$\eta = A \frac{C_T \omega}{v} \frac{gD}{v^2} \qquad (1.3.10-12)$$

444

whence the "efficiency" K becomes

$$\frac{\eta}{A} = \frac{\eta \lambda_z \gamma_z}{2(\gamma_1 - \gamma)} = K \qquad (1.3.10-13)$$

This was used for estimating the slurry concentration

$$C_T = K \frac{v}{\omega} \frac{v^2}{gD} \qquad (1.3.10-14)$$

In other words, it is possible to express the slurry concentration as the product of the Froude number, the efficiency K and of the settling number B

$$C_T = KB \ Fr$$

Bruk claims that the above relation yields useful results also in open channel flow if the hydraulic radius or flow depth is introduced and a factor K' is used instead of K.

Both K and K' will, of course, be variable since neither η nor A is constant.

Using the approach of A. Führböter, Bruk has represented the variation of η in terms of U_*/v, where $U_* = \sqrt{gRS}$ in *Fig. 1.3.10−1*. Regardless of the fact that the mean particle diameter d_g and, accordingly, the fall velocity ω and even the concentration C_T varied between rather wide limits, the relation will be seen to be a close one.

These investigations of Bruk have shown research in this direction to yield promising results.

It should be noted here that Bruk has adopted a similar approach also for computing the sediment-transporting capacity of alluvial streams. For details, reference is made to *Section 2.1.4*.

Eq. (1.3.10−7) is applied to problems associated with slurry transport by introducing a variety of simplifying assumptions.

The commonest of these assumptions is $v_h \cong \omega$. Instead of λ_z the coefficient for clear water λ is used, and the error introduced is taken into account by applying an empirical coefficient β to the second term on the right-hand side of the equation.

$$\frac{\Delta p}{\gamma} = \lambda \frac{\gamma_z}{\gamma} \frac{v^2}{2g} \frac{L}{D} + \beta C_T \frac{(\gamma_1 - \gamma)}{\gamma} \frac{\omega}{v} L \qquad (1.3.10-15)$$

According to another practical solution, the slope S_z of slurry transport is computed from the relation

$$S_z = S \frac{\gamma_z}{\gamma} + \delta S_z \qquad (1.3.10-16)$$

using the slope S for clear water and a correction factor δ.

445

Fig. 1.3.10—1. Ratio η vs. parameter U_*/v for slurries of different particle size and concentration. After Führböter and Bruk

A method has also been suggested where S_z is computed by using the ratio γ_z/γ to multiply slope S for clear water:

$$S_z = S \frac{\gamma_z}{\gamma} \qquad (1.3.10-17)$$

Further details concerning the computation of S_z will be given in connection with different methods developed for computing slurry transport.

In the case of slurry transport in vertical pipes the most essential difference over horizontal pipes is that the mean velocity of slurry, besides transporting solid particles, contributes immediately to the process of suspension. The minimum velocity must be selected to be capable of transporting even the coarsest fraction, otherwise these may accumulate and cause clogging at the bottom of the pipe. The velocity of water transporting the solids in vertical pipes is determined usually by empirical methods.

The necessary pressure head in vertical pipes is estimated approximately under the assumption that this differs but slightly from the head needed for transporting clear water. Accordingly if the vertical difference between sections 1—1 and 2—2 of a vertical pipe is H, the cross-sectional area of the pipe is F, then, assuming

446

steady flow between the two cross-sections in the equilibrium of forces, it is sufficient to multiply the volume HF instead of the specific gravity of clear water by the specific gravity γ_z of the slurry adding to the force thus obtained the force T due to wall friction.

Denoting the pressure differences between the two cross-sections by $(p_1 - p_2)$, and assuming velocity to remain unchanged between the two sections, the equilibrium of forces is expressed as

$$F(p_1 - p_2) = \gamma_z \, HF + T \qquad (1.3.10-18)$$

The shear stress arising at the wall is

$$\tau = \gamma \, RS_t \qquad (1.3.10-19)$$

where $R = F/P$, the hydraulic radius,
$\quad\; S_t$ = the slope of the energy grade line in a smooth pipe,
$\quad\; P$ = the wetted perimeter of the vertical pipe,
while the force due to wall friction is

$$T = \tau PH = \gamma \, HFS_t \qquad (1.3.10-20)$$

which is then substituted into Eq. (1.3.10−18). Rearranging terms the necessary pressure head is obtained from an expression similar to Eq. (1.3.10−7):

$$\frac{p_1 - p_2}{\gamma} = H\frac{\gamma_z}{\gamma} + HS_t \qquad (1.3.10-21)$$

Regardless of the simplifying assumptions introduced during the derivation, the expression has proved to yield good results in practice.

A number of investigators have adopted an approach similar to the foregoing in determining experimentally the pressure head needed in vertical pipes.

The number of data available on slurry transport in inclined pipes is relatively small. The transport velocity and the necessary pressure head in inclined pipes are also determined usually by an experimental method.

Before embarking upon a detailed description of the most commonly used methods for estimating slurry transport it is deemed necessary to make the following comments on the relation existing between transport velocities and head losses.

In velocity ranges below and above the critical velocity the losses, as has been mentioned, tend to become higher. In the range to the right of v_{cr} in *Fig. 1.3.10−2* the comparison of losses in slurry transport and in clear water flow yields three possible cases. At increasing velocities the curve applying to the slurry most commonly merges with the curve applying to water (diagram *b*). In the presence of coarse particles, the curve applying to the slurry remains throughout the range above the curve applying to water (diagram *c*), whereas in the case of slurries comprising colloidal fractions a range is encountered where the curve applying to the slurry is situated below that applying to water (diagram *a*).

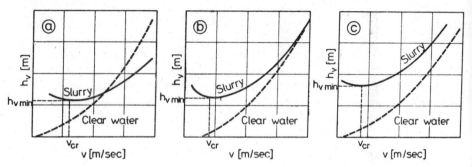

Fig. 1.3.10—2. Flow velocity vs. head loss for clear water and slurries of very fine, medium and coarse gradation. After Pásztor and Szivák

When selecting the normal transport velocity it is clearly of advantage to adhere to the critical velocity, the energy required being lowest in its vicinity. However, since variations are likely to occur in the granulometric composition of the material to be transported, a margin of safety over the critical velocity should be observed in selecting the normal operating velocity. Conflicting aspects may also become predominant especially when transporting coarse-grained material. In such cases the settling of the coarsest fractions may be tolerated increasing thereby essentially the service life of the pipe-line also at the cost of some losses in energy.

* * *

Some of the most commonly used slurry transport relations will be described subsequently.

The relation of the critical velocity v_{cr} and friction losses to the properties of slurry have been determined in each of these methods experimentally.

In describing the individual methods attempts have been made at using a consistent system of notation. Thus in all expressions mentioned v_{cr} (m/sec) is the critical velocity, D (m) is the pipe diameter, γ_z, γ and γ_1 (Mp/m^3) are the specific gravities of the slurry, of water and of the solids transported, respectively, ω (m/sec) is the fall velocity, g (m/sec^2) is the acceleration due to gravity and R (m) is the hydraulic radius of the pipe.

The resulting formulae being, however, usually of an empirical character, very often widely divergent interpretations are given even to generally accepted concepts. For this reason, in order to avoid misunderstanding, the definition of individual factors will be given separately.

1. *The method of G. N. Roer.* Relying on a great number of laboratory and field observations, Roer has suggested the following formula for estimating the critical

448

velocity

$$v_{cr} = 8.72D^{0.473}[(\gamma_z - \gamma)\omega]^{0.326}\,\frac{\gamma_1^{0.0814}}{\gamma^{0.488}}\,\frac{1}{\varDelta^{0.17}} \qquad (1.3.10-22)$$

where $\varDelta$ = the roughness coefficient.

With $\gamma_1 = 2.65$ and $\gamma = 1$ the expression reduces to

$$v_{cr} = 9.4D^{0.473}[(\gamma_z - \gamma)\omega]^{0.326}\,\frac{1}{\varDelta^{0.17}} \qquad (1.3.10-23)$$

In determining the roughness coefficient Roer has made allowance also for the material deposited in the pipe. Accordingly $\varDelta$ is found from the formula

$$\varDelta = (d_{95\%}^{0.6} + 0.5)\left(\frac{\gamma_z}{1.075}\right)^{5.88} \qquad (1.3.10-24)$$

Eqs (1.3.10−22) and (1.3.10−23) on the critical velocity apply to the transport of a solid material consisting of uniform particles. This is usually not the case in practice. After determining the grain size distribution curve of the material to be transported, Roer suggests the formula

$$v'_{cr} = v_{cr}\left(\frac{d_{av}}{d_{95\%}}\right)^{0.2} \qquad (1.3.10-25)$$

for modifying the critical velocity computed for uniform material. In the formula

v'_{cr} = the critical velocity applying to the material of mixed particles (m/sec),

d_{av} = the mean particle diameter of the material (mm),

$d_{95\%}$ = the diameter at 95% by weight passing (mm).

No instructions are given by Roer as to what particle size to adopt in estimating the fall velocity to be used for computing v_{cr} pertaining to uniform particles. In view of the fact that the exponent of ω is 0.326, no great error is likely to be introduced when using ω pertaining to d_{av}.

The magnitude of head loss is found by applying a correction factor to the specific head loss of water:

$$S_z = S\gamma_{zm} \qquad (1.3.10-26)$$

where S_z = the specific head loss in transporting slurry,

S = the specific head loss when conveying the same water discharge,

γ_{zm} = the (dynamic) specific gravity of slurry in movement, given as

$$\gamma_{zm} = 3.7D^{0.119}\,\frac{\omega^{0.2}}{v_{cr}^{0.071}}\,\varDelta^{0.0095}\gamma_1^{0.05}(\gamma_z - \gamma) + \gamma \qquad (1.3.10-27)$$

or in the case of $\gamma_1 = 2.65$, $\gamma = 1$ and $\Delta = 0.006$

$$\gamma_{zm} = 3.7 D^{0.119} \frac{\omega^{0.2}}{v_{cr}^{0.071}} (\gamma_z - \gamma) + 1 \qquad (1.3.10-28)$$

The friction loss applying to clear water is determined by Roer according to Pavlovsky, using a roughness coefficient $n = 0.0012 - 0.010$.

2. *The method of A. P. Yufin.* In this method several considerations of a theoretical nature are involved, as shown primarily by the fact that a greater number of variables are introduced. For a solid material consisting of uniform particles the formula suggested for estimating the critical velocity is

$$v_{cr} = 9.5 \sqrt[3]{gR} \sqrt[4]{\omega} \sqrt[12]{\frac{v}{k}} (\gamma_z - 0.4) \qquad (1.3.10-29)$$

where v_{cr} = the critical velocity for slurry of uniform grains [m/sec],
$\quad v$ = the kinematic viscosity of the fluid [m²/sec].
The absolute roughness is taken into account according to Nikuradze, assuming fully developed turbulence:

$$\frac{1}{\sqrt{\lambda}} = 1.74 + 2 \lg \left(\frac{r}{k} \right) \qquad (1.3.10-30)$$

and

$$\varepsilon = \frac{k}{r}$$

where λ = the resistance coefficient of Darcy−Weissbach,
$\quad r$ = the pipe radius [m],
$\quad \varepsilon$ = the relative roughness.
In his experiment he found roughness to become constant at velocities higher than critical. This constant roughness was characterized approximately by the value $k = 0.00015$ m. Thus in the case of a uniform material with d up to 10 mm of a slurry temperature of 20 centigrade, i.e. $v = 0.01$ (m²/sec) viscosity and a pipe diamter greater than $D = 200$ mm, Eq. (1.3.10−29) reduces to

$$v_{cr} = 9.8 \sqrt[3]{D} \sqrt[4]{\omega} \left[\frac{\gamma_z}{\gamma} - 0.4 \right] \qquad (1.3.10-31)$$

The use of the above formula is facilitated by the graph shown in *Fig. 1.3.10−3*
For pipe diameters smaller than 200 mm the formula assumes a different form

$$v_{cr} = 0.2 d_{av}^{0.65} e^a \sqrt{\frac{\gamma_z}{\gamma}} D^{0.54} \qquad (1.3.10-32)$$

450

Fig. 1.3.10—3. Nomograph for finding the critical velocity by the formula of Yufin

where d_{av} = the mean particle diameter of the material [mm], and

$$\alpha = 2.86/d_{av}^{0.13}$$

If the slurry to be transported consists of a mixture of different particle sizes, Yufin suggests the application of a uniformity coefficient:

$$\Delta_0 = \frac{3 d_{10\%}}{d_{90\%}} \qquad (1.3.10-33)$$

where $d_{10\%}$ and $d_{90\%}$ are the particle diameters pertaining to 10 and 90% by weight passing, respectively. Using this value the critical velocity becomes

$$v'_{cr} = v_{cr} \sqrt[8]{\Delta_0} \qquad (1.3.10-34)$$

The following formulae are used for computing the friction loss or the hydraulic gradient.

For materials consisting of uniform particles, transported at the critical velocity

$$S_{cr} = 0.8 \frac{\gamma_z}{\gamma} \sqrt{\frac{\gamma_z}{\gamma} - 1} \frac{\sqrt{\omega}}{\sqrt[3]{gR}} \sqrt[6]{\frac{v}{k}} \qquad (1.3.10-35)$$

At constant roughness and 20 centigrades slurry temperature

$$S_{cr} = 0.73 \frac{\gamma_z}{\gamma} \sqrt{\frac{\gamma_z}{\gamma} - 1} \frac{\sqrt{\omega}}{\sqrt{gD}} \qquad (1.3.10-36)$$

The use of the above expression is facilitated by the chart given in *Fig. 1.3.10 – 4*.

For materials consisting of different particle sizes the uniformity coefficient should be used in the form $\sqrt[9]{\Delta_0}$

If the transport velocity is higher than critical, a different formula is to be used for computing the friction loss or the gradient S_z:

$$S_z = S + \left[S_{cr} - S \left(\frac{v_{cr}}{v} \right)^2 \right] \sqrt[4]{\frac{v_{cr}}{v}} \qquad (1.3.10-37)$$

where S = the gradient in clear water,
     S_{cr} = the gradient resulting at critical slurry velocity,
     v = the actual velocity (m/sec).

Yufin's experiments show that the efficiency of transport improves as the clay content of the slurry to be transported increases. Thereupon he established a relationship between the shear stress of slurry and its clay content, which he used for developing the relationships needed for determining various parameters. He succeeded similarly in developing a method to be applied in the case of partial settling out.

452

Fig. 1.3.10—4. Nomograph for finding the critical slope by the formula of Yufin

For determining the entrance and exit hydraulic gradient S_{en} and S_{ex}, respectively or slurry transport in vertical pipes Yufin suggests the following empirical formulae

$$S_{en} = S \left(1 + 145 C_T \frac{gD}{v^2} \frac{\omega}{\sqrt{gD}} \right) \qquad (1.3.10-38)$$

$$S_{ex} = S \left(1 - 250 C_T \frac{gD}{v^2} \frac{\omega}{\sqrt{gD}} \right) \qquad (1.3.10-39)$$

For further details concerning the investigations made by Yufin the reader is eferred to the papers listed in the literature.

453

3. *The method of R. Durand.* The method has been evolved from an extensive experimental programme. The grain size distribution of the material transported in the experimental runs invariably consisted of several fractions. In his experiments Durand used mainly river sands and gravels. Initially the material was graded between narrow limits whereas in later experiments wider size ranges were used.

The pipe diameters and slurry properties varied in the experiments between the following limits:

pipe diameter	40−700 mm
max. particle size	0.03−100 mm
concentration	50−600 p/lit
specific gravity of solids	1.5−3.95 kp/lit.

On the basis of theoretical considerations he assumed the hydraulic characteristic of slurry transport to depend on the ratio of fall and transport velocities, as well as on the ratio of Reynolds numbers formed with the help of the fall and transport velocities. From this he concluded that different relations would apply to the laminar, transition and turbulent zones of settling.

With the objective of creating closely controlled experimental conditions he classified the solid materials into three ranges of gradation:

A) uniform mixtures (with particle diameters smaller than 0.03 mm)
B) transition range (with particle diameters from 0.03 to 0.05 mm)
C) heterogeneous mixtures.

The last range (C) was divided into three subranges:
a) suspensions (with sizes from 0.05 to 0.20 mm),
b) intermediate group (diameters from 0.20 to 2.00 mm),
c) slurries transported by rolling (diameters above 2.00 mm).

In turbulent flow no settling was found to take place and thus the mixture could be regarded uniform. The critical velocity assumed a value around the boundary separating the laminar and turbulent ranges. Head losses in turbulent flow resembled those in clear water whereas in laminar flow values higher than for clear water were obtained.

No results were given for the transition range.

In connection with slurries comprising different sizes he has concluded that the particles are sorted along the cross-section of the pipe.

For determining the critical velocity a formula was given for heterogeneous slurries only:

$$v_{cr} = F_1 \sqrt{2gD \frac{\rho_z - \rho}{\rho}} \qquad (1.3.10-40)$$

where F_1 = a factor depending on d_{av} and on concentration,
  ρ_z = the density of the mixture (kpsec²/m⁴),
  ρ = the density of the fluid (kpsec²/m⁴).
According to Eq. (1.3.10−40)

$$F_1 = \frac{v_{cr}}{\sqrt{2gD\,\dfrac{(\rho_z - \rho)}{\rho}}} \qquad (1.3.10-41)$$

is essentially the square root of the Froude number formed of the critical velocity and the pipe diameter.

The relationship between the particle diameter d, concentration C_T and F_1 is illustrated in *Fig. 1.3.10−5*. For particular values of the particle size and concentration, v_{cr} is found once the pipe diameter D is known.

It will be perceived from the figure that if d_{av} is greater than 1 mm, the magnitude of F_1 is not affected at all by concentration C_T.

For the head loss Durand gives the following formula:

$$S_z = S(1 + \phi C_T) \qquad (1.3.10-42)$$

where S_z = the head loss of slurry,
  S = the head loss of clear water,
  ϕ = a coefficient depending on the mean size, the fall velocity thereof and on the pipe diameter,
  C_T = the concentration of slurry in % by volume.

He succeeded in eliminating ϕ from the expression by stating that it is constant if the term $v/\sqrt{gD}$ is constant.

The formula eventually obtained is

$$S_z = S\left[1 + K\,\frac{gD^{3/2}}{v^3}\,\frac{\omega^3}{\left(gD\,\dfrac{\rho_z - \rho}{\rho}\right)^{3/2}}\right] \qquad (1.3.10-43)$$

Fig. 1.3.10−5. Parameter F_1 vs. average particle size, for different concentrations. After Durand

455

Fig. 1.3.10—6. Graphic plot of Durand's friction loss formula. After Lackey

In this expression K is an experimental constant the magnitude of which ranges in general from 160 to 240 but for which no exact values are given.

No numerical data are given by Durand on his experiments with slurries graded between wider limits. He points out nevertheless that in low concentrations these display properties resembling those of mixed materials, whereas in higher concentrations, those of uniform materials. He observed further that in the presence of fine fractions slurries having a coarse composition are conveyed at a reduced friction loss.

Durand's equation on friction loss is reproduced in a dimensionless form after J. B. Lackey in *Fig. 1.3.10—6*, for solids having a specific gravity of 2.65 and for velocities higher than critical. The equation plotted is

$$\frac{S_z - S}{S_z} = \text{constant} \left(\frac{\sqrt{gD}}{v} \right)^3 \left(\frac{1}{\sqrt{C_d}} \right)^{3/2} = k \left(\frac{v^2}{gD} \sqrt{C_d} \right)^{-3/2} \quad (1.3.10-44)$$

where S_z = the friction loss of slurry over unit length of pipe, expressed as height of column of clear water,

S = the friction loss of clear water at the same v and D values,

C_d = the resistance coefficient of particles,

v = the transport velocity.

456

Table 1.3.10—1

Values of the correction factor K according to Tsarevsky

Slurry to be transported		Correction factor K												
Ratio by weight $S:F$	Spec. gravity	Clay and sandy clay without crumbs $d = 0.005-0.05$ mm $\omega = 0.003-0.15$ cm/sec			Average clayey sand and sand $d = 0.05-1.0$ mm $\omega = 0.15-13.0$ cm/sec			Sand containing little gravel $d = 1.0-5.0$ mm $\omega = 13.0-30.0$ cm/sec			Coarse sand containing much gravel $d = 5.0-20.0$ mm $\omega = 30.0-60.0$ cm/sec		
		transport velocity [m/sec]											
		1.0	2.0	3.0	1.5	2.0	3.0	2.0	3.0	4.0	2.5	3.0	4.0
1 : 20	1.05	1.25	1.15	1.10	1.30	1.20	1.10	1.40	1.35	1.20	1.60	1.50	1.30
1 : 12	1.08	1.40	1.30	1.25	1.40	1.40	1.20	1.70	1.40	1.35	1.80	1.60	1.50
1 : 10	1.10	1.45	1.40	1.30	1.60	1.45	1.40	1.90	1.70	1.50	2.00	1.80	1.60
1 : 8	1.12	1.45	1.40	—	1.60	1.45	—	1.90	1.65	—	—	—	—
1 : 5	1.19	1.60	1.45	—	1.60	—	—	—	—	—	—	—	—

4. *The method of A. M. Tsarevsky.* Essentially, Tsarevsky has developed a simple form of Roer's formula by using integers for the coefficient and exponent involved therein.

He has also developed simplified expressions for the roughness and uniformity coefficients. For the critical velocity he suggests the expression

$$v_{cr} = \frac{3.20\sqrt{D}\sqrt[3]{\gamma_z - 1/\omega}}{(0.5d_{95\%} + 1)^{0.2}} \left(\frac{d_{0-80\%}}{d_{av}}\right)^{0.2}$$ (1.3.10—45)

where, in addition to the notations introduced before,
$d_{0-80\%}$ = the mean particle diameter of the fractions from $0-$ to 80% by weight passing.

For the friction loss Tsarevsky gives the extremely simple formula

$$S_z = S K$$ (1.3.10—46)

where the values of K are compiled in *Table 1.3.10—1.*

For computing the friction loss of water either Manning's or Pavlovsky's method can be used.

5. *The graphical method of Gy. Maurer.* The methods described thus far in general result in rather complex expressions. Therefore several attempts have been made to eliminate lengthy computation work by simple graphical or tabular procedures. (Advances in computer techniques have since made direct computation more attractive than tabular or graphical methods). Of these the following charts are given after Gy. Maurer: the chart of G. N. Roer's method in *Fig. 1.3.10—7;* the chart of Y. B. Slates, converted to the metric system in *Fig. 1.3.10—8;* and the chart of P. P. Dyakov in *Fig. 1.3.10—9.*

The three charts permit the determination of the critical velocity v_{cr} and the head loss (m) per 100 m of slurry pipeline h_v expressed as height of water column, provided that the amount of slurry transported Q and the pipe diameter D are given.

The result obtained from these charts is necessarily an approximate one since neither the characteristics of the solid particles to be transported, nor the concentration of slurry is taken into consideration.

6. *The method of I. G. Haskelberg.* In the experiments underlying the method the pipe diameter ranged from 100 to 600 mm, whereas the particle size of the solids, from 0.24 to 32.5 mm.

The critical velocity is found from the expression

$$v_{cr} = 6.5 K_0^{'0.36} \frac{\sqrt{gD}}{C_D^{0.25}}$$ (1.3.10—47)

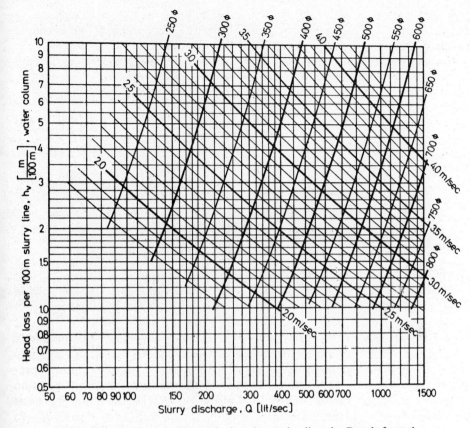

Fig. 1.3.10—7. Chart for dimensioning slurry pipe lines by Roer's formula

while the friction loss, or the slope of the hydraulic grade line is found from

$$S_z = S(1 + K_0' A_v A_c) \qquad (1.3.10{-}48)$$

where

$$A_v = 165 \left[\frac{v^2}{gD} \right]^{-1.4}$$

$$A_c = 0.84(\sqrt{C_D})^{-1.4}$$

K_0' = a factor depending on the volumetric concentration of the slurry,
C_D = the average resistance coefficient of spherical particles.
Values of K_0' are tabulated in terms of the volumetric mixing ratio of slurry, and C_D is given also in tabulated form in terms of a variable A_c, this depending on the relative magnitude of individual fractions in the material. These values are also tabulated. For details reference is made to the papers listed in the literature.

459

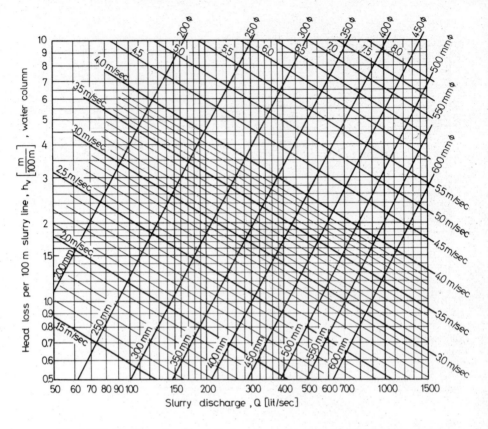

Fig. 1.3.10—8. Chart for dimensioning slurry pipe lines by the formula of Slates

7. *The method of A. Z. Yevilevich.* The author has collected a great number of data of both European and American origin, and these are checked against the results of experiments conducted for several years. The resulting charts apply to sludge to be removed from sewage treatment plants.

In these charts the friction loss is plotted against slurry discharge for 150, 200 and 250 mm pipe diameters, adopting the sludge quantity expressed as percentage of water content as parameter.

The method is suggested for the case of sludge having a specific gravity from 1.09 to 2.15 and an organic content of 70 to 90% in the dry residue.

In *Fig. 1.3.10—10* the loss h_v is plotted for 250 mm diameter pipes against the slurry discharge Q and the percentage sludge content.

8. *The method of S. A. Korzhaev.* In view of the uncertainties involved in the experimental results and computations, as well as for practical considerations Korzhaev has compiled *Table 1.3.10—2*, showing the preferable transport velocities for different pipe diameters and types of soil.

460

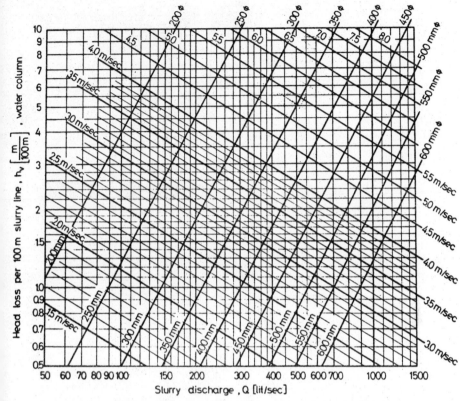

Fig. 1.3.10—9. Chart for dimensioning slurry pipe lines by the formula of Dyakov

9. *The method of Goryunov.* The results of extensive experiments and ample operating experience underlie the method developed by Goryunov for estimating the friction loss. No attention is paid to the determination of the critical velocity.

According to him when transporting slurry, the Darcy—Weissbach formula of friction loss assumes the form

$$h_v = (\lambda + \lambda_z) \frac{Lv^2}{D2g} \qquad (1.3.10-49)$$

where λ = the resistance coefficient of clear water,
λ_z = the resistance coefficient of slurry (complementary resistance coefficient).

The magnitude of λ is found, according to Nikuradze, as described in connection with Yufin's method. After 100 to 200 hours of operation absolute roughness was found to become constant around $k = 0.15$ mm in agreement with the experiences of Yufin.

Fig. 1.3.10—10. Head loss in $D = 250$ mm diameter pipe. After Yevilevich

Table 1.3.10—2

Velocities suggested by Korzhaev for a given combination of pipe diameter and slurry material

Type of soil	Velocities [m/sec] recommended for given pipe diameters [mm]					
	150	200	250	300	400	500
Fine sand	2.2	2.3	2.5	2.6	2.9	3.2
Coarse sand	2.5	2.7	2.8	3.0	3.3	3.6
Sandy gravel d max = 50 mm	3.1	3.3	3.5	3.7	4.1	4.5

462

Table 1.3.10—3

Goryunov's "conventional concentration" in terms of concentration C and bulk density of slurry

Conventional concentration, C_G [%]	0	5	10	15	20	25	30	35	40
Soil in 1 m³ of slurry [kp]	0—25	26—75	76—125	126—170	171—210	211—250	251—290	291—330	331—370
Bulk density of slurry [Mp/m³]	1.0—1.015	1.016—1.05	1.051—1.081	1.081—1.105	1.106—1.130	1.131—1.155	1.156—1.180	1.181—1.205	1.206—1.23
Solid : fluid ratio by weight ($S : F$)			1 : 10 1 : 9	1 : 6	1 : 5	1 : 4	1 : 3.5	1 : 3	1 : 2.5

Fig. 1.3.10—11. Grain-size distribution curves for materials *A* and *B* with the boundaries of the particle ranges 1 to 8 of Goryunov

Dimensional analyses have yielded the relation

$$\lambda_z = f\left(Fr \frac{d}{D} C_G\right) \tag{1.3.10—50}$$

where Fr = the Froude number,

d/D = the ratio of particle size to pipe diameter,

C_G = the "conventional" concentration of slurry according to Goryunov.

From his experiments Blatch has demonstrated that λ_z is unaffected by the relative roughness of the pipe. Ample experimental evidence supports also the fact that, disregarding small pipe diameters ($D > 100$ to 200 mm), λ_z is unrelated to D and, since a constant value may be assumed for the acceleration due to gravity g, λ_z will be perceived to be unrelated, for a particular type of soil, to the denominator $\sqrt{gd}$ of the Froude number, so that eventually

$$\lambda_z = f(v, C_G) \tag{1.3.10—51}$$

Goryunov has tabulated values of the "conventional concentration" C_G in *Table 1.3.10—3*.

Soils are classified according to granulometry into eight groups following the method illustrated in *Fig. 1.3.10—11* where the inclined straight lines indicating the boundaries of groups extend between the horizontals corresponding to 90 and 30% by weight passing since, according to experimental results, particles outside of this range do not affect appreciably the magnitude of λ_z.

For the soil types thus defined the relation $\lambda_z = f(v, C_G)$ is given by Goryunov in a tabulated form. The validity limits of the tabulated values are

$$v(\text{m/sec}) : 1.0 - 5.5$$

$$C_G(\%): 5 - 40$$

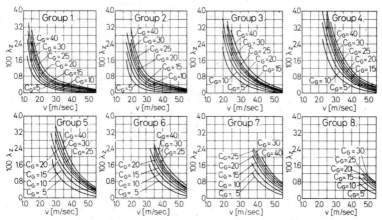

Fig. 1.3.10—12. λ_z vs. velocity v for different standard concentrations C_G for the eight soil groups of Goryunov

Instead of the lengthy tables, values of λ_z relating to the eight soil types have been plotted against concentration C_G and velocity v in *Fig. 1.3.10—12.*

For rapid computations a simplified alternative of Goryunov's method is suggested according to which, in the case of slurries comprising silt and sandy gravel and of pipe diameters from 300 to 350 mm, a combined resistance coefficient comprising two different kinds of resistance coefficient is used as follows:

for v smaller than 3.0 m/sec $\qquad \lambda_t = 0.025 - 0.032$

for $v = 3.0$ to 4.0 m/sec $\qquad \lambda_t = 0.024 - 0.030$

for v higher than 4.0 m/sec $\qquad \lambda_t = 0.023 - 0.27$

10. *Method suggested in a contemplated Soviet Standard Specification.* A standard specification comprising the entire field of advanced slurry transport in pipe lines is being compiled in the Soviet Union. The first part thereof has been published as a contemplated specification. The formulae included in these tentative specifications are described below after a report by VITUKI.

The formula suggested for the critical velocity is

$$v_{cr} = 8.3 \sqrt[3]{D} \sqrt[6]{C\psi} \ \text{[m/sec]} \qquad (1.3.10-52)$$

where

$$C = \frac{\gamma_z - \gamma}{\gamma_1 - \gamma}$$

and γ_z is the bulk density of slurry.

The head loss is found from

$$S_z = \frac{S_{min}}{3}\left[\left|\frac{v}{v_{min}}\right|^2 + \frac{2v_{min}}{v}\right] \text{[m/rm]} \qquad (1.3.10-53)$$

Here

$$S_{min} = 4.6 S \sqrt[6]{C\psi} \qquad (1.3.10-54)$$

$$S = \lambda_0 \frac{v_{min}^2}{2gD} \qquad (1.3.10-55)$$

$$\lambda_0 = \left(\frac{0.55}{\lg\dfrac{Re}{8}}\right)^2 \qquad \cdot \qquad (1.3.10-56)$$

$$v_{min} = 5.3\sqrt[6]{C\psi D} \qquad (1.3.10-57)$$

where v = the mean velocity of slurry (m/sec),
ψ = a coefficient depending on granulometry according to the table below:

d_{av}(mm)	ψ
0.05 — 0.1	0.0204
0.1 — 0.25	0.0930
0.24 — 0.5	0.404
0.5 — 1.0	0.755
1.0 — 2.0	1.155
2.0 — 3.0	1.5
3.0 — 5.0	1.77
5.0 — 10.0	1.94
10.0 — 20.0	1.97
20.0 — 60.0	1.68

$Re = vD/v$ is the Reynolds number in the expression of which the mean velocity v should be substituted in cm/sec, the pipe diameter D in cm, the kinematic viscosity v in cm²/sec units.

For $v = v_{min}$ Eq. (1.3.19 − 53) yields $S_z = S_{min}$, consequently the lower limit of the head loss formula is $v = v_{cr}$ implying that the formulae must not be used until flow in the full cross-section is started, i.e. where no settling occurs.

In the afore-mentioned report by VITUKI the head loss vs. velocity, as well as the critical velocity vs. concentration and particle diameter relations are hereafter given for concentrations ranging from 5 to 25%, for eight different average particle diameters and two different pipe diameters (314 and 400 mm) on the

466

Fig. 1.3.10—13. Critical velocity vs. volumetric concentration for different particle sizes according to the new Soviet draft standard specifications as plotted at VITUKI

asis of relevant experiments. The specific gravity of solids was assumed at 2.60 p/m³.

In examining the experimental results, the head loss is found to be greatly ffected by the mean particle diameter, in that the head loss in transporting the nest fraction ($d_{av} = 0.05 - 0.1$ mm) is 5 to 6 times smaller than in the case f the coarsest fraction ($d_{av} = 5 - 20$ mm). Minimum head loss occurs at $v = v_{cr}$ nd losses tend to increase rapidly as the mean particle size increases.

The influence of concentration is low for slurries with $d_{av} = 0.25$ mm but creases beyond this value.

With increasing concentration the critical velocity is the higher, the coarser e grain size composition is. The effect of the mean particle diameter is reflected / the fact that up to about a mean diameter of 1.0 mm the value of v_{cr} increases

Fig. 1.3.10—14. Critical velocity vs. particle sizes for different volumetric concentration according to the new Soviet draft standard specifications as plotted at VITUKI

rapidly but beyond this limit the particle size is no longer of appreciable influence. To illustrate this statement *Figs 1.3.10 — 13* and *1.3.10 — 14* are given for $D = 31$ mm pipe diameter. In Fig. 1.3.10 — 14 dashed lines indicate measurement data.

11. *Comments on the methods listed above.* The comparative study of the methods suggested by Roer, Yufin, Durand, Tsarevsky and Goryunov has been performed by D. Pásztor and A. Szivák, for the materials "A" and "B" shown in *Fig. 1.3.10 — 11* and for a solid : fluid = 1 : 4 ratio. As will be perceived, for *Fig. 1.3.1 — 11* material "A" is more finely graded, comprising fractions from fine sand to coarse silt, whereas material "B" is graded from 40 mm gravel to fine sand.

Within the ranges considered, critical velocities are compared in *Fig. 1.3.10 — 1* and head losses, in *Fig. 1.3.10 — 16* after Pásztor and Szivák. In these figures the ratio by weight of the solid (S) and fluid (F) phases is again 1 : 4.

Fig. 1.3.10—15. Critical velocity vs. pipe diameter relations suggested by different authors
After Pásztor and Szivák

Fig. 1.3.10—16. Head loss vs. transport velocity relations suggested by different authors. After Pásztor and Szivák

A further comparison is made possible by the study of J. Marton and I. V. Nagy, although this considers one material only. Each of the computation methods considered was used for determining the critical velocity pertaining to the discharge $Q = 0.2$ m³/sec, except Goryunov's method which is, of course, unsuited for this purpose and for determining the head loss. The material in this example had a specific gravity of 2.65, and that of slurry was 1.09, the material was graded from 0.01 to 16.0 mm and d_{av} was 1.68 mm. The results are tabulated in *Table 1.3.10—4.*

Considering the empirical relations introduced for determining the critical velocity it will be perceived that these can be written in the general form

$$v_{cr} = A x_1^{\alpha_1} x_2^{\alpha_2} \ldots x_n^{\alpha_n} = A \prod_{i=1}^{n} x_i^{\alpha_i} \qquad (1.3.10-58)$$

where A = constant,

$x_1, x_2, \ldots x_n$ = physical characteristics of slurry transport.

$\alpha_1, \alpha_2, \ldots \alpha_n$ = exponents of these characteristics.

Table 1.3.10—4

Critical velocities and head losses computed using different formulae

$Q_z = 0.2$ [m³/sec]; $\gamma_1 = 2.65$ [p/cm³]; $\gamma_z = 1.09$ [p/cm³]; $D = 300$ [mm]; $d_{mean} = 1.68$ [mm]

Characteristics	Roer	Yufin	Durand	Kor-zhaev	Goryunov	Haskelberg	Dyakov	Slates
v_{cr} [m/sec]	2.35	1.95	0.99	3.16	—	2.72	2.84	2.84
S_z [m/rm]	0.030	0.0448	0.0478	0.0373	0.051	0.046	0.038	0.0185

469

Concerning the critical-velocity formulae suggested by Roer, Yufin, Durand, Tsarevsky, Haskelberg and in the contemplated Soviet Standard Scpecifications, the values of the constant A, and the exponents of the pipe diameter D, of the difference in specific gravities $(\gamma_z - \gamma)$, of the fall velocity ω, of the specific gravities γ_1 and γ of the solids and the water, respectively, of the roughness coefficient Δ, of the acceleration by gravity g, of the hydraulic radius R and of the mean diameter d_{av} have been compiled in *Table 1.3.10−5. As clearly reflected by the table, no direct comparison is possible of the principles underlying the individual methods.*

However, on the basis of comparative studies, it is believed of interest to make the following comments on the individual methods.

Roer (1). − In spite of the complexity of the relations, not all parameters controlling the hydraulic characteristics are involved in them. Therefore these yield acceptable results only within a narrow range.

− The head loss relation displays no minimum, which is in contrast with theoretical and practical considerations alike.

− No instructions are given for the determination of ω in the case of mixed slurry.

− According to the head loss relation, the difference between the head losses of slurry and water increases continuously with increasing velocity, which is in contrast with practical experience.

− The formula is well suited to coarse slurries; the values for head loss are excessive and thus overconservative.

Yufin (2). − The relations are simpler than those of Roer and include a greater number of parameters. For these reasons they are applicable in a wider range considering granulometry and the specific gravity of solids alike.

− The head loss displays a minimum and with increasing velocity the difference between head losses of water and slurry shows a decreasing trend.

− By the uniformity coefficient actual mixed granulometries are fairly well represented.

− The method is primarily suited to slurries including finer fractions and yields results in good agreement with those actually observed.

Durand (3). − The critical velocity relation is simple to use.

− The number of parameters involved is apparently low, but actually several are included implicitly in the variable F_1, the magnitude of which has been established experimentally.

− This implies, at the same time, that the chart for F_1 applies to a rather narrow range only, consequently the method is limited in application to finer slurries.

− In estimating the head loss uncertainty is introduced by the experimental factor K, for which no exact value is given.

Tsarevsky (4). − The value for v_{cr} is excessive.

− The tabulated values for determining friction losses are ready to use.

− The results are economical in the case of fine-grained materials, no values

470

Table 1.3.10—5

Exponents pertaining to diverse variables, for use in formulae of the critical velocity, as given by different authors

Author	No. of equation (1.3.10—)	Value of constant, A	Exponent of								
			Pipe diameter, D	Difference in spec. gravity $(\gamma_z - \gamma)$	Fall velocity	Spec. gravity of sediment, γ_z	Spec. gravity of water, γ	Roughness coefficient, Δ	Acceleration by gravity, g	Hydraulic radius, R	Particle diameter, d
Roer $\begin{cases} \\ \end{cases}$	—22)	8.72	0.473	0.326	0.326	0.0814	0.488	—0.17	0	0	0
	—23)	9.4	0.473	0.326	0.326	0	0	—0.17	0	0	0
Yufin	—29)	9.5	0	0	0.25	0	1	0	0.333	0.333	0
Durand	—40)	$f(d_1, C)$	0	1/2	0	0	—1/2	0	1/2	1/2	0
Tsarevsky	—45)	32	1/2	1/3	—1/3	0	0	0	0	0	0.2
Haskelberg	—47)	6.5	0	0.36	0	0	0	0	1/2	1/2	0
U.S.S.R.	—52)	8.3	1/3	1/6	0	—1/6	—1/6	0	0	0	$\psi^{1/6}$

are tabulated for higher concentrations, and thus applications are limited mainly to coarse materials.

Maurer (Roer, Slates, Dyakov) (5).

Slates

— An empirical method ready to use,

— applications limited to approximate and checking computations,

— the values obtained are rather low since, for including the wearing effect of slurry, low friction losses are assumed.

Dyakov

— An empirical method ready to use,

— applications limited to approximate and checking computations,

— practice has shown the values obtained to be fair averages, which makes the method preferable for approximate computations.

Haskelberg (6). — The method is rather complex. In spite of the variety of tables used, considerable computation work is required.

— For comparison with other methods one single datum is available, and this does not permit evaluation.

Yevilevich (7). — No relation is given for v_{cr}.

— In keeping with its objective, application is limited to fine-grained silt slurries of high organic content.

— This is the method used for dimensioning the 70 km long, 400 mm diameter sludge-transporting line at Moscow.

Korzhaev (8). — An extremely simple, readily applied method.

— Head losses are not determined.

— Recommended for approximate or checking computations only.

Goryunov (9). — The critical velocity is not determined directly. When applying the method, v_{cr} must be found or checked by some other approach.

— Actual conditions are well allowed for in determining friction losses, in that the difference related to losses in water tends to decrease with increasing velocity.

— A wide velocity range is covered, since the minimum of friction loss is also given.

— Owing to the steep boundary lines, the "soil groups" are not readily related to actual soils and yield values higher than necessary.

* * *

As indicated by the comperative studies dealt with in the foregoing, present information on slurry transport is founded, in general, on the evaluation of experimental results. Although no direct physical support can be given to the individual methods, their practical significance is considerable since they summarize experiences gained during various experiments.

In designing slurry transport equipment it is found invariably of advantage to perform preliminary experiments allowing for particular conditions. A comparison of the results of preliminary experiments with experience gained in the derivation of the different methods is likely to make the operation of the contemplated slurry transport system more reliable.

A problem awaiting solution is the development of a uniform, consistent method of evaluating experiments carried out under different conditions. Similarity methods are expected to assume special significance in this respect.

For checking actual operating conditions of slurry transport and for collating theoretical results and those actually observed, *measurements of slurry concentration and discharge* are of great interest. A brief review of various methods of observation will subsequently be represented after M. Kozák.

With some exceptions, the methods to be described are unsuited for directly measuring concentration by volume or by weight. On the other hand, they afford data – mostly on bulk density – directly and positively related to the former.

The most direct method of measuring concentration consists of the retrieval of samples. According to the technique adopted, samples can be taken by interrupting the pipeline or from the closed pipeline itself.

In the first method the *pipeline is tapped* at any arbitrary point, the sample is taken simply at the discharge and is subject to detailed analysis. The method yields accurate results on instantaneous concentration and can be applied to slurries of any arbitrary composition. A drawback is the considerable requirement in labour and space.

Sampling from the continuous pipeline is feasible especially under laboratory conditions. In this method a probe suitably designed and mounted is used for retrieving samples from any point of the pipe cross-section.

The principle underlying concentration *measurement by weight* is that the density of slurry is proportionate to concentration. Measurement is carried out by supporting a given length of the pipeline on scales, the section being connected flexibly to the adjacent pipes. An accuracy of 5 to 10% is claimed for this method. Its advantages consist in yielding data continuously without interference in operation.

The methods founded on *the measurement of differential pressure* are based on the assumption that the differential pressure between the end points of an arbitrary pipe section is proportionate to the density of the fluid transported. This is the principle underlying the method of Dyakov applied to a horizontal and an inclined section, the method of Sejhet applied to two vertical sections, the method of Ivanova in which pressures are measured at the crown and invert of a pipe, as well as the method of Kozák where these measurements are made at two inclined pipe sections.

Another method of obtaining data on slurry concentration consists of measuring a physical property, such as the transparency or electric conductivity of the slurry.

The *photo-electric method* is based on light transmissibility, but the results obtained are not unambiguous. This is because the transparency of the slurry is influenced also by the character of the solid phase. Thus for instance a slurry of lower concentration but including some clay will be less transparent than one of higher concentration but containing no clay.

Because of its inaccuracy the method based on *measuring resistivity* has failed to find wider acceptance.

A number of errors are involved in the method based on *conductivity measurement*, this physical parameter not being positively related to concentration. The concentration meter Altocon developed in the Netherlands operates on this principle; the disturbing effect of salts and temperature on conductivity is balanced with the help of a separate measuring cell on an electric bridge. It is possible to combine the equipment with the water discharge meter Altoflux, from which the meter Altocol has been developed for measuring the quantity of solids. Of course, this family of instruments is completed by integrators, yielding cumulative data. Special control rooms are necessary for their operation so that their application is of potential interest only for permanent slurry transport installations.

The discharge meter *Altoflux* operates on the principle of magnetic induction. Slurry is conveyed in a rubber pipe, through a constant magnetic field and the electric force induced by the intersection of lines of force is measured.

One of the factors governing the penetration of *radiation* emitted by a radioactive source is concentration of the material irradiated. This is the principle underlying nuclear density measurement, in which a radioactive source is mounted in a pipe cross-section, and concentration is measured in terms of the attenuation of radiation intensity passing the cross-section.

Nuclear density meters are highly sophisticated instruments, and especially trained personel is needed for their operation.

An instrument of this type has been developed at the University of Heavy Industry, Veszprém, for 150 mm diameter pipes having a measuring range of 1.2 to 2.4 Mp/m^3 in specific gravity of slurry, and one of 0 to 1.5 parts by weight in concentration.

The simplest method of measuring the slurry discharge consists of *dyeing*, the application of which is limited however to long pipelines and its accuracy decreases with velocity.

Another simple method involves the *measurement of volumes* either at the end of the slurry line or with the help of a branch line mounted at an intermediate point and controlled by a double butterfly valve. The accuracy attainable can be improved by increasing the dimensions of the collecting tank.

An accuracy of 5 to 8 % can be attained by the method utilizing the *shape of the slurry jet*. By measuring the jet co-ordinates at a suitable point of the trajectory the relevant formulae of mechanics are applied to compute the discharging velocity and hence the mean velocity in the pipe. Multiplied by the cross-sectional area of the pipe this yields the discharge.

The measurement of slurry discharge *by means of a contraction in pipe* is identical in principle with that applied in the case of clear water. Two factors should, however, be remembered. The contraction must be calibrated for the slurry, since the discharge coefficient depends in general also on concentration. On the other

474

hand, owing to violent pulsations, pressures must not be transmitted directly to the differential pressure gage, but should first be balanced and damped out in a cell.

A device of this type has been constructed by Yufin: its accuracy is 5% when transporting slurry of 10 mm greatest particle size.

Further details on the transport and measurement of slurry are found in the papers listed in the attached literature. An exhaustive treatment of the relevant problems is presented in the book of W. H. Graf published in 1971.

1.3.10.2. The settling of sediment in flowing water. The movement of suspended sediment has been considered in the foregoing. Although it is recognized that in alluvial streams variations in sediment concentration are partly due to random pulsations, it has been found necessary to assume balanced conditions in most cases. In spite of this a separate section has been devoted to unbalanced conditions, describing the relevant differential equations.

It has been demonstrated that no unequivocal solution of general validity is available at present, and so we do not wish to complicate the problem of suspended-sediment transport in alluvial streams by including unbalanced conditions. What can be predicted with any degree of reliability is not more than the scouring or silting character of the channel section under consideration.

The problem of sediment settling in a moving fluid is, however, closely related to that of suspended sediment movement under unbalanced condition. This is the reason why the hydraulic aspects entering the settling of suspended sediment transported by a moving fluid will be reviewed in brief, without any attempt at completeness, and rather with the objective of outlining the potential approaches.

In the case of settling, the problem consists of ensuring the reduction of sediment concentration with respect either to time or to location, occasionally by the combination of both changes. Thus in principle any of the differential equations described in *Section 1.3.9* could be applied by introducing additional simplifying assumptions.

A number of such approaches have been reported in the literature. A detailed discussion thereof would, however, exceed the scope of the present book so that only the solution suggested by E. Dobbins will be discussed briefly and the assumptions of Lamble examined.

For describing the variation in concentration along length (x) and depth (y) Dobbins has adopted the differential equation (1.3.9−28):

$$v\frac{\partial C}{\partial x} = \varepsilon_y \frac{\partial^2 C}{\partial^2 y^2} + \frac{\partial C}{\partial y}\left(\omega + \frac{\partial \varepsilon_y}{\partial y}\right) + \varepsilon_x \frac{\partial^2 C}{\partial x^2} \qquad (1.3.10-59)$$

This is impossible to solve unless the magnitude of ε_x ,as well as the variation of v and ε_y along y are known. Attempts at determining this have remained, however, unsuccessful thus far. In the solution of the differential equation the separation of the variables appears also to present an unsurmountable problem.

For this reason, in accordance with Eqs $(1.3.9-18)$ to $(1.3.9-21)$ Dobbins assumed ε_y to remain constant, i.e. $\partial\varepsilon_y/\partial y = 0$, and introduced assumption c(i) listed in *Section 1.3.9*, i.e. the assumption of $\partial C/\partial x = $ constant, or

$$\frac{\partial}{\partial x}\left(\frac{\partial C}{\partial x}\right) = \frac{\partial^2 C}{\partial x^2} = 0$$

The physical interpretation given to the latter is that concentration along the main direction x varies at a constant rate, i.e. settling has a constant rate.

With these assumptions and omitting the subscript in the conductivity ε_y Eq. $(1.3.10-59)$ reduces to

$$v\frac{\partial C}{\partial x} = \varepsilon\frac{\partial^2 C}{\partial y^2} + \omega\frac{\partial C}{\partial y} \qquad (1.3.10-60)$$

which is, of course, identical with the differential equation $(1.3.9-22)$ developed under comparable simplifying assumptions.

Now if any point under consideration at a constant distance above the bottom moves with the velocity $v = \mathrm{d}x/\mathrm{d}t$, then (in the moving system of co-ordinates) the variation in concentration with time is expressed as

$$\frac{\partial C}{\partial t} = \varepsilon\frac{\partial^2 C}{\partial y^2} + \omega\frac{\partial C}{\partial y} \qquad (1.3.10-61)$$

Dobbins has solved Eq. $(1.3.10-61)$ verifying the solution by experimental results. The solution is valid, provided the following additional assumptions hold true: sediment concentration is uniform in the entire inflow cross-section, the values of ε and the flow velocity are constant in the entire settling basin. Of course, the solution affords only an approximate expression of the delaying effect of turbulence on settling, since a more accurate result could be obtained with the help of Eq. $(1.3.10-59)$ only.

The solution of Dobbins was modified by T. R. Camp in a manner to yield the settling percentage directly. Excluding the case of once settled sediment becoming again suspended, the settling percentage is, according to Camp, the function of three dimensionless parameters, namely $\omega D/2\varepsilon$, α_n and ω/ω_0.

The structural composition and physical interpretation of the settling percentage as well as of the three dimensionless parameters is described preferably after the results of Camp published in 1937.

According to him the rate of settling is controlled by the characteristics of sediment settling, as well as by the hydraulic properties of the settling basin. *In an ideal basin* the sediment will move with a resultant velocity composed of the velocity of flow and its own proper fall velocity, implying that the paths travelled by individual sediment particles will form parallel straight lines. From *Fig. 1.3.10—17* it will be perceived that all particle sizes having a fall velocity greater than a certain value ω_0 will settle; this being governed by the length L and depth D of the basin and by the velocity v of passing water. Of the fractions,

476

Fig. 1.3.10—17. Settling of sediment in rectangular flow-through basins

however, for which ω is smaller than ω_0, only a certain part will settle out, namely the percentage indicated by the ratio $\overline{bc}/\overline{ac}$ shown in the figure. From the similarity of triangles $D/L = \omega_0/v$, so that

$$\omega_0 = \frac{Dv}{L} = \frac{Dbv}{Lb} = \frac{Q}{Lb} ; r_r = \frac{\omega}{\omega_0} = \frac{bL\omega}{Q} \qquad (1.3.10-62)$$

In the above expressions L is the length, b is the width of the basin, while Q is the discharge passing.

The ratio $\omega_0 = Q/Lb$ is referred to by Camp as the overflow rate or as the discharge per unit surface area of the settling basin.

The settling percentage r_r is the rate at which sediment of a fall velocity $\omega < \omega_0$ is settled out. Eq. (1.3.10−62) is substantially identical with Hazen's formula and is an expression of the fact that, at a particular discharge, the quantity of sediment settling at a fall velocity $\omega < \omega_0$ is in linear proportion with the surface area and is unrelated to depth. The overflow rate ω_0 is in fact the desired fall velocity at which the full sediment quantity could be settled out in a particular settling basin. All the particles settling at a fall velocity higher than ω_0 will settle to the bottom.

The quantities $\alpha_1, \ldots, \alpha_n$ are the successive real positive roots of the transcendent equation

$$2 \operatorname{ctg} \alpha = \frac{\alpha}{\dfrac{\omega D}{2\varepsilon}} - \frac{\dfrac{\omega D}{2\varepsilon}}{\alpha} \qquad (1.3.10-63)$$

The relation between the settling percentage and the three dimensionless parameters has been plotted graphically by Camp after computing the values of α_n which, according to Eq. (1.3.10−63), also depend on the parameter $\omega D/2\varepsilon$, for each point to an accuracy of six decimals by trial and error and thus eliminating

477

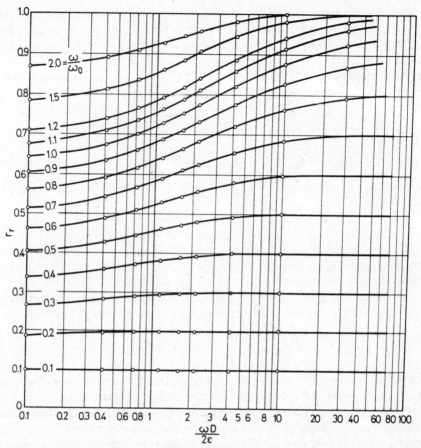

Fig. 1.3.10—18. Settling percentage r_r vs. $\omega D/2\varepsilon$ with ω/ω_0 as parameter. After Camp

them in advance. The result is shown by the family of curves in *Fig. 1.3.10—18* from which the settling percentage is obtained in terms of the parameters $\omega D/2\varepsilon$ and ω/ω_0.

The family of curves can, of course, not be used unless the value of ε applying to a particular settling basin is known. In the derivation ε has been assumed to be constant, implying a parabolic velocity profile. Determining the magnitude of ε in this manner and assuming arbitrarily the value 0.024 for the friction coefficient f — provided average roughness conditions prevail — the desired parameter becomes, according to Camp,

$$\frac{\omega D}{2\varepsilon} = 122 \frac{\omega}{v} = 122 \frac{\omega_0}{v} \frac{\omega}{\omega_0} = 122 \frac{D}{L} \frac{\omega}{\omega_0} \qquad (1.3.10-64)$$

478

The approximate dimensioning of settling basins is thus made possible by the solution of Dobbins, in combination with Camp's parameters, on the basis of the differential equation describing suspended-sediment transport under unbalanced conditions.

If for instance it is desired to settle out 85% of the 0.005 mm fraction at $v = 1$ cm/sec flow velocity, the family of curves at $r_r = 0.85$ and

$$\frac{\omega D}{L\varepsilon} = 122 \quad \frac{\omega}{v} = 122 \quad \frac{0.0013}{1} = 0.16$$

yields the value $\omega/\omega_0 = 1.8$, whence $\omega_0 = 0.0013/1.8 = 0.000722$ and the length of the settling basin becomes

$$L = \frac{300}{0.000722} \cdot 1 = 414000 \text{ cm},$$

i. e. 4140 m.

If the conductivity of sediment were zero, i.e., if in a basin of $D = 300$ cm depth the $d = 0.005$ mm fraction were to settle from water flowing at $v = 1$ cm/sec velocity exclusively under the action of gravity, the necessary length L of the basin would be appreciably shorter. It should be evident that the settling period

$$\frac{D}{\omega} = \frac{300 \text{ cm}}{0.0013 \text{ cm/sec}} = 231{,}000 \text{ sec}$$

involves a length $L = 2310$ m for 100% settling at a flow velocity $v = 1$ cm/sec whereas only $L_1 = 0.85 \, L = 1963.5$ m at the desired settling of 85%.

Lamble has introduced certain simplifying assumptions in solving the differential equation (1.3.9−17) following the approach to be outlined below.

Considering the process of settling in suspended sediment transport under unbalanced conditions at the entrance to the settling basin, at $x = 0$ the concentration $C(0,y)$ variable with depth y is evidently greater than the concentration that would pertain under balanced conditions to the particular hydraulic and sediment characteristics and which can be found e.g. from Eq. (1.3.4−57). This latter concentration is constant along the main direction x, but is variable with y so that $Ce(y)$. In mathematical form

$$C(0, y) > Ce(y) \tag{1.3.10−65}$$

At the entrance, $x = 0$, the concentration $C(0,y)$ is greater than $Ce(y)$ at the same point by some "excess' concentration $C'(0,y)$:

$$C(0, y) = Ce(y) + C'(0, y) \tag{1.3.10−66}$$

With increasing values of x the concentration $C(0,y)$ changes and, since settling is considered, it assumes a value $C(x,y) < C(0,y)$ at any arbitrary point x. However, as long as the process of settling lasts, its value will remain greater by some

479

"excess" concentration $C'(x,y)$ than $Ce(y)$ which is unrelated to x:

$$C(x, y) = Ce(y) + C'(x, y) \qquad (1.3.10-67)$$

Consequently at the point (x,y) the actual concentration is regarded by Lamble as the sum of the balanced concentration and an excess concentration. In analogy to concentration, a similar equation is written for the sediment transport $q_s(x)$, $q_s(e)$ and $q_s'(x)$ transported in unit width and unit time:

$$q_s(x) = q_s(e) + q_s'(x) \qquad (1.3.10-68)$$

Since $q_s(e)$ is unrelated to x, we have $dq_s(e)/dx = 0$.
Consequently

$$\frac{dq_s(x)}{dx} = \frac{dq_s'(x)}{dx} \qquad (1.3.10-69)$$

Excluding the possibility of bottom material or sediment once settled being carried again into suspension, Lamble assumes that the variation of specific sediment transport $dq_s(x)/dx$ can be expressed approximately by the negative value of the product $\omega C(x,0)$ so that

$$\frac{dq_s(x)}{dx} = -\omega C(x, 0) \qquad (1.3.10-70)$$

where $C(x,0)$ denotes concentration at the bottom at point x. It is assumed moreover that concentration at the bottom is proportionate to the mean concentration $C_K(x)$ at point x:

$$C(x, 0) = \lambda C_K(x) \qquad (1.3.10-71)$$

or

$$\frac{dq_s(x)}{dx} = -\omega \lambda C_K(x) \qquad (1.3.10-72)$$

where λ is some unknown function of x.
In the cross-section under consideration, where D is the depth of flow, v is the mean velocity and $C_K(x)$ is the mean concentration, the specific sediment transport $q_s(x)$ is

$$q_s(x) = C_K(x)vD \qquad (1.3.10-73)$$

or

$$\frac{d}{dx}(C_K(x)vD) = -\omega \lambda C_K(x) \qquad (1.3.10-74)$$

whence

$$\frac{d[C_K(x)]}{C_K(x)} = -\lambda \frac{\omega}{v} \frac{dx}{D} \qquad (1.3.10-75)$$

480

Introducing the parameter

$$\zeta = \frac{\omega}{v}\frac{x}{D} \qquad (1.3.10-76)$$

Eq. (1.3.10−75) assumes the form

$$\frac{d[C_K(x)]}{C_K(x)} = -\lambda d\zeta \qquad (1.3.10-77)$$

In general $\lambda = \lambda(x)$ is always greater than unity, since the concentration at the bottom is greater than the mean value for the cross-section. According to Lamble, if $\lambda = 1$, a concentration higher than actual is obtained. If, on the other hand, the value $\lambda(\infty)$ at point $x = \infty$ is introduced for $\lambda(x)$, the theoretical concentration will be smaller then the actual. A general solution is possible by determining approximately the function

$$\lambda = \lambda(\lambda_\infty, \zeta) \qquad (1.3.10-78)$$

using the known extreme values $\lambda_0 = \lambda$ at the entrance ($x = 0$) and $\lambda_\infty = \lambda$ at $x = \infty$.

For determining Eq. (1.3.10−78) Lamble has adopted a graphical approach relying on experimental data. Concentration is likewise determined from a family of curves in terms of ζ and λ_∞.

As will be realized from Eq. (1.3.10−76), ζ is evidently a term comparable to the settling percentages r_r of Camp in Eq. (1.3.10−62), provided length x (or L) influencing the rate of settling and the characteristics of the sediment to be settled and of the basin are known. The determination of the turbulent conductivity of sediment, or some function thereof, is thus seen to be inevitable also in Lamble's method. The practical application of the charts suggested by him is cumbersome, since it calls for the assumption or approximate determination of certain values in advance.

The merit of his method consists in the introduction of the concept of "excess concentration" which is expected in further research to contribute to obtaining better insight into the complex problem of settling.

PART TWO
SEDIMENT AND WATER COURSES

2.1. EMPIRICAL RELATIONS

2.1.1. RELATIONS DETERMINED ON THE BASIS
OF FIELD MEASUREMENTS

The wide variety of difficulties encountered in the theoretical study of sediment transport has prompted investigators to determine sediment transport in alluvial streams by direct measurements and observations in the field.

The methods and equipment used in field measurements have been discussed in *Section 1.1.5*. The measuring devices have been shown to afford reliabilities and accuracies ranging within wide limits. The samplers used for the determination of suspended sediment yield reliable information on the suspended-sediment transport. On the other hand, the term accuracy cannot even be mentioned in connection with the devices used for observing bed load movement, moreover the results obtained in many cases cannot be accepted even as coarse approximation. The fact that bed load traps nevertheless play a role in the determination of bed load transport, may be attributed to the circumstance that no bed load transport formula of general validity could be developed so far.

A large number of papers describe empirical relations suggested on the basis of a wide variety of considerations. In this connection attention is called to the book "Sediment Transport in Open Channels" edited by K. I. Rossinsky and published by the Water Management Institute of the Academy of Sciences of the Soviet Union in 1970.

The relations determined from measurements and observations in the field apply, in general, to a particular stream and frequently to a particular cross-section of a stream only. This is because the particular properties of the stream are represented in full in these empirical relations. In fact sediment transport in alluvial streams is not controlled exclusively by hydraulic factors.

A considerable part of data on sediment transport originates from laboratory observations in which the hydraulic factors assume predominance. Consequently these are highly suited for obtaining better insight into the fundamental properties of sediment transport. On the other hand, their direct application to practical problems is usually inadmissible owing exactly to the different properties of alluvial streams.

Bearing the above considerations in mind, before embarking upon the description of empirical relations concerning bed load and suspended sediment transport, it is deemed advisable, to examine the influences resulting form the properties particular to individual water courses.

2.1.2. THE INFLUENCE OF HYDROLOGICAL FACTORS
ON SEDIMENT TRANSPORT

Sediment transport in alluvial streams has been recognized to be affected by a number of factors including some of non-hydraulic character. The character, the regime of flow, including sediment transport, in natural streams are influenced besides hydraulic factors by several circumstances, referred to collectively as hydrological factors. These affect primarily the development and formation of sediment in the catchment area, as well as its entrance into the stream yet also influence the processes taking place in the stream channel itself.

In view of the complex interrelations existing between them, a complete list of hydrological factors is almost impossible to compile. The most important of these is probably the quantity and distribution of precipitation, the geologic structure of the catchment area, its relief and plant cover. The geological structure of formations in which the channel is embedded may also be classified among the hydrological factors. Since the formation of sediment by winter precipitation is different from that occurring under the action of rainfalls in spring, summer or autumn, the sequence of seasons may also be regarded as a hydrological factor.

The manner in which sediment transport in alluvial streams is affected by hydrological factors may assume an extremely wide variety of forms. In many instances a close correlation can be established between sediment transport and one or several hydrological factors. Many of these relations are of a symptomatic character in which no determinative relation is known to exist between the variables involved but each of them is in a causal relation with some other factor or combination of factors. Of course, the applicability of such relations to water courses is not affected at all by this circumstance.

The great importance of hydrological factors will be appreciated by comparing the sediment-transporting capacity of streams with actual sediment transport figures. The sediment-transporting capacity has been demonstrated in the foregoing to be controlled by hydraulic factors. Consequently the sediment-transporting capacity is essentially an upper limit of the quantity of sediment a stream is capable of carrying. The actual sediment transport is almost invariably less, implying that the sediment transported in the streams is in general smaller in quantity than the theoretical limit. Since the sediment-transporting capacity is determined uniquely by the hydraulic factors according to the laws of physics, the only possible explanation for the fact that it differs from the actual sediment transport is that, owing to the influence of hydrological factors, the sediment supply to the stream is insufficient.

Besides the foregoing theoretical considerations on the influence of hydrological factors several numerical examples could be quoted to demonstrate the predominant significance of the properties of alluvial streams. Examples of this type belong to the domain of empirical relations on bed load and suspended sediment which will be discussed in greater detail in *Sections 2.1.3.* and *2.1.4.*

486

Fig. 2.1.2—1. Mean velocity vs. average bed load particle diameter relation for the Danube

Nevertheless it is deemed advisable to mention here some of the relations illustrating, with special clarity, the influence of hydrological factors on sediment transport in alluvial streams.

It is readily observable that, proceeding downstream along water courses, the particle size of the sediment transported tends to decrease. The reduction in particle size is especially conspicuous in the bed load transported along the bottom. The reduction of bed load sizes along a river is clearly illustrated by observations made along the Hungarian section of the Danube. Between Dunaremete and Baja (see *Fig. 3.1.2—3)* the mean particle diameter of bed load samples collected with the help of sediment traps decreased from round 25 mm to 0.15 mm. The relation of the mean particle diameter d_g of bed load versus the mean velocity v in the cross-section has been plotted in *Fig. 2.1.2—1* for seven gaging sections on the Danube. Proceeding downstream a definite relation will be found to exist between the reduction in particle size and the mean velocity of flow (which also decreases downstream). Mathematically the relation is expressed as

$$d_g = 0.15 + 0.47v^{8.13} \qquad (2.1.2-1)$$

where the particle diameter d_g is obtained in mm units if velocity v is substituted in m/sec units.

The example presented in the figure for the Danube is quoted in support of the fact that along a particular stream the mean particle size of bed load and the mean velocity of flow vary according to the same regularity in accordance with the properties particular to the stream.

Of course, no hydraulic explanation can be quoted in support of Eq. (2.1.2—1). No parallel can be drawn even to the general quadratic relation between particle size and critical velocity. Essentially none of the known theoretical relations between particle size and the hydraulic factors of a channel can be offered as an explanation for Eq. (2.1.2—1). It should be obvious, therefore, that a wide variety

487

of hydrological and morphological factors affecting the particle size of bed load is incorporated in this relation.

An additional remark should be attached to the foregoing considerations. It has been pointed out that in general no law of hydraulics can be quoted to explain the relation between sediment transport in alluvial streams and hydrological factors. Considering, however, that any such relation, regardless whether determinative or symptomatic, reflects conditions actually existing in nature, these must never be in conflict with the laws of hydromechanics. In other words, in *Fig. 2.1.2–1* to each particle diameter a velocity higher than the critical mean velocity corresponding to this particular grain size is bound to pertain. In fact, this is the guarantee for the movement of the particle size considered. When running checks on the basis of these principles it should be remembered, however, that these relations apply invariably to average values. The particle diameter is the mean diameter of all sediment moving in the entire cross-section, and mean velocity is related to the entire cross-section.

In connection with the foregoing considerations it should be noted that in alluvial streams any sediment transport relation must necessarily be determined on the basis of average values. This circumstance is obviously an additional obstacle to the generalization of theoretical relations.

The influence of hydrological factors will often be recognize also in the movement of suspended sediment.

Observation results on most streams have shown the same sediment concentration C to occur at gradually decreasing mean velocities proceeding downstream along the water course. In *Fig. 2.1.4–14* to be discussed more in detail in *Section 2.1.4*, the relation between sediment concentration C_k and mean velocity v_k in the cross-section is shown for seven gaging stations on the Danube river. It has been pointed out that, in general, the sediment actually transported is less than the transporting capacity of a particular stream. This circumstance may explain the fact that in upstream cross-sections an essentially higher mean velocity pertains to the same sediment concentration than in cross-sections farther downstream. Of course, it is possible to examine the mean velocity pertaining to instantaneous discharge, to wetted perimeter, to roughness conditions, etc. in relation to sediment transport. However, no explanation can be given for the circumstance that in any particular cross-section higher sediment concentrations are accompanied by higher velocities. The problem whether sediment concentration increases in the entire length of the river, in any cross-section, as an exponential function of mean velocity (see *Fig. 2.1.4–14)*, is thus left unanswered. Some explanation is deemed necessary for this circumstance since from the foregoing it would follow that up to a certain limit an increase in sediment concentration does not necessarily entail an increase in velocity on the basis of hydraulics.

An answer to this problem can be given by considering the hydrological factors of the stream. At times of intensive rainfalls higher sediment volumes are formed and the discharge increases accordingly yet cannot be conveyed unless the mean velocity also increases.

Considering the example of the Danube, it will be clear that the increase in sediment concentration with mean velocity follows a symptomatic relation on other rivers as well since both the formation and transport of sediment and the velocity of flow are related to a third phenomenon, namely the magnitude, distribution and duration of precipitation on the catchment area.

In analogy to the foregoing it is possible to express sediment concentration also in terms of discharge. The exponential relation

$$C_k = dQ^l \qquad\qquad (2.1.2-2)$$

could be determined for a number of water courses with a fair degree of accuracy.

Once the above relation can be made applicable to several cross-sections on a particular stream, it becomes possible to examine the variation of these relations along the stream. In *Section 2.1.4*, the relationship between C_k and Q will be shown to remain essentially unchanged along the Danube, Tisza and Hernád rivers (see *Figs 2.1.4−12, 2.1.4−16 and 2.1.4−20)*. More precisely, variations are found to occur only in the coefficient d involved in the exponential function. The exponent l was found to remain essentially constant over the entire length of each of the rivers under considerations.

It should be noted in this context that a constant l value has been determined for all rivers on the Kamchatka peninsula by A. I. Stepanova.

The exponent l is a measure of the variation in sediment concentration C with variations in discharge Q. Considering again that apart from hydraulic factors the prevailing sediment concentration is controlled primarily by the amount of sediment available which in turn depends on the characteristics of the stream, it should be obvious that the magnitude of l is controlled by the properties of the catchment, the precipitation conditions, etc. i.e. collectively by the hydrological factors of a particular stream.

The properties of the catchment, as well as precipitation conditions can be described by a wide variety of parameters. In the present investigations the long-term mean discharge (Q_k), the significant greatest and lowest discharges (Q_{hw} and Q_{lw}), the area of the catchment F, as well as the distance of the gaging section from the headwaters (L) have been taken into consideration.

The magnitude of the catchment area and the distance of the gaging section of the headwaters is expressed most relevantly by the average width $B = F/L$ of the catchment area, including also the influence of catchment shape as well which, in turn, is a factor controlling the quantity of sediment entering the stream.

The mean discharge Q_k is alone characteristics of suspended sediment transport as it represents the depth and, to a certain extent, also the distribution of precipitation.

The ratio Q_{hw}/Q_{lw} characteristic of the flashiness of river regime is also expected to affect the magnitude of l.

The ratio $q_k = Q_k/F$, termed the specific runoff and formed as the ratio of mean discharge Q_k and the magnitude of catchment area, is also characteristic of sediment transport on the basis of hydrological consideration.

Data on hydrology and suspended sediment transport for 12

River Gaging section	Greatest discharge, Q_{hw} [cm³/sec]	Smallest discharge, Q_{lw} [cm³/sec]	Catchment area, F [km²]	Distance from origin L [km]	Coefficient, d	Exponent, $l = Y$
					for use in $C = dQ^l$	
	1.	2.	3.	4.	4.	6.
Danube						
Dunaremete	*9,000*	*575*	131,901	1,008.8	10^{-10} 1.23	2.57
Nagybajcs	*9,000*	*580*	*132,000*	1,033.3	10^{-10} 1.23	2.57
Dunaalmás	*9,000*	*585*	171,380	1,082.5	10^{-10} 1.23	2.57
Nagymaros	9,260	590	183,262	1,139.7	10^{-10} 1.23	2.57
Dunaújváros	8,700	615	189,026	1,253.7	10^{-10} 1.23	2.57
Fajsz	*8,500*	*620*	191,758	1,327.6	10^{-10} 1.23	2.57
Baja	*8,000*	*625*	207,947	1,354.9	10^{-10} 1.50	2.57
Tisza						
Záhony	4,090	48.0	32,459	326.6	10^{-5} 4.86	1.44
Rázompuszta	4,070	53.0	49,350	439.1	10^{-5} 3.10	1.44
Polgár	4,500	62.0	62,710	472.1	10^{-5} 3.04	1.44
Tiszabő	3,850	64.0	67,358	594.2	10^{-5} 2.64	1.44
Tápé	*4,000*	*70.0*	*108,800*	787.8	10^{-5} 2.60	1.44
Szeged	4,700	90.0	138,579	790.7	10^{-5} 2.24	1.44
Hernád						
Hidasnémeti	500	3.20	4,515	188.9	10^{-4} 4.2	1.63
Pere	350	*3.00*	*4,800*	223.2	10^{-4} 4.6	1.63
Gesztely	337	2.40	5,105	259.8	10^{-4} 5.0	1.63
Maros						
Deszk	1,600	21.0	*29,800*	*740*	10^{-4} 3.0	1.44
Sebes-Körös						
Körösszakál	580	0.24 R *2.00*	2,476	154.6	10^{-3} 1.5	1.16
Fekete-Körös						
Remete	540	0.40 R *1.40*	3,844	163.1	10^{-3} 2.5	1.00
Sajó						
Kazincbarcika	*400*	*1.00*	4,003	136.2	10^{-4} 1.5	2.33
Miskolc	450	1.82	6,188	173.5	10^{-3} 1.6	1.02
Berettyó						
Berettyóújfalu	260	0.13 R *0.20*	4,001	157.3	10^{-3} 6.0	1.53

rivers in Hungary, based on data of observations before 1954

Average width of catchment, $B = X_1$ [km]	Mean discharge, $Q_k = X_2$ [m³/sec]	Ratio of greatest to smallest discharge, Q_{hw}/Q_{lw}	Specific runoff, $q_k = X_4$ [l/sec km²]	Expected value of the dependent variable, Y'_ζ	Deviation from expected value, $\Lambda = Y - Y'_\zeta$	Squared deviation, Λ^2	Deviations of the dependent variable from the mean value, $y = Y - \bar{Y}$	Squared mean deviation, y^2
7.	8.	9.	10.	11.	12.	13.	14.	15.
130.8	*1,900*	15.6	14.4	2.57	0.00	0.0000	0.86	0.7396
126.5	*2,000*	15.5	15.2	2.57	0.00	0.0000	0.86	0.7396
158.3	*2,250*	15.4	13.1	2.56	0.01	0.0001	0.86	0.7396
161.0	2,340	15.7	12:8	2.53	0.04	0.0016	0.86	0.7396
150.8	2,340	14.1	12.4	2.57	0.00	0.0000	0.86	0.7396
144.5	*2,350*	13.7	12.2	2.57	0.00	0.0000	0.86	0.7396
153.3	*2,360*	12.8	11.3	2.56	0.01	0.0001	0.86	0.7396
99.4	340	85.2	10.5	1.47	−0.03	0.0009	−0.27	0.0729
112.2	464	76.8	9.4	1.43	0.01	0.0001	−0.27	0.0729
132.6	530	72.6	8.4	1.44	0.00	0.0000	−0.27	0.0729
113.3	550	60.1	8.2	1.53	−0.09	0.0081	−0.27	0.0729
138.1	*700*	57.1	6.4	1.54	−0.10	0.0100	−0.27	0.0729
175.4	810	52.2	5.9	1.59	−0.15	0.0225	−0.27	0.0729
23.9	29.0	156	6.4	1.53	0.10	0.0100	−0.08	0.0064
21.5	*29.0*	117	6.0	1.60	0.03	0.0009	−0.08	0.0064
19.7	29.6	140	5.8	1.44	0.19	0.0361	−0.08	0.0064
40	161	76.2	5.4	1.34	0.10	0.0100	−0.27	0.0729
16.0	24.0	290	9.7	1.37	−0.21	0.0441	−0.55	0.3025
23.6	21.5	R *386*	5.6	1.08	−0.08	0.0064	−0.71	0.5041
29.4	*23.0*	400	5.7	1.32	1.01	1.0201	0.62	0.3844
35.7	34.0	247	5.5	1.35	−0.33	0.1089	−0.69	0.4761
25.4	8.2	*1,300*	2.05	1.41	0.12	0.0144	−0.18	0.0323

Table 2.1.2—1

River Gaging station	Greatest discharge, Q_{hw} [cm³/sec]	Smallest discharge, Q_{lw} [cm³/sec]	Catchment area, F [km²]	Distance from origin, L [km]	Coefficint, d	Exponent, $l = Y$
					for use in $C = dQ^l$	
	1.	2.	3.	4.	5.	6.
Zala						
Zalaapáti	140	0.20	1,528	114.3	10^{-2} 1.6	0.48
Balatonhidvég	140	0.20	1,900	127.1	10^{-3} 4.7	0.88
Fenékpuszta	140	0.20	2,621	138.0	10^{-3} 3.2	0.86
Szamos						
Csenger	1,080	14.5	15,003	387.5	10^{-4} 2.0	1.74
Rába						
Szentgotthárd	380	6.0	3,080	105.6	10^{-4} 1.8	1.78
Körmend	430	7.0	4,702	142.6	10^{-5} 3.1	2.08
Sárvár	480	7.0	5,560	213.0	10^{-4} 2.9	1.50
Lapincs						
Szentgotthárd	160	3.0	1,993	87.0	10^{-4} 3.0	1.87
$N = 30$	Σ					51.19
Mean value:						$\bar{Y} = 1.71$

For the water courses and gaging sections, see *Fig. 3.1.2—3*.
Italicized figures denote estimated values.
Italicized figures accompanied by an *R* indicate observation data from Rumania.

The parameters listed in the foregoing were selected after lengthy investigations (in 1956) once the quantities B, Q_k, q_k and the ratio Q_{hw}/Q_{lw} had been found eminently suited for determinating the exponent l involved in Eq. (2.1.2—2).

The values of d and l determined on the basis of sediment measurements up to the end of 1953 on twelve rivers in Hungary at altogether 30 gaging stations are compiled in *Table 2.1.2 — 1*. The first four columns of the Table represent the characteristics of the catchment, while the values of d and l are entered in columns 5 and 6. Since the variation of exponent l is what we are studying for purposes of correlation computation, the dependent variable will be $l = Y$ in column 6. The four independent variables are $B = X_1$, $Q_k = X_2$, $Q_{hw}/Q_{lw} = X_3$ and $q_k = X_4$ tabulated in columns 7 to 10.

The location of the gaging stations indicated in the Table is shown in *Fig. 3.1.2—3*.

Continued)

Average width of catchment $B = X_1$ [km]	Mean discharge, $Q_k = X_2$ [m³/sec]	Ratio of greatest to smallest discharge, Q_{hw}/Q_{lw}	Specific runoff $q_k = X_4$ [l/sec km²]	Expected value of the dependent variable, $Y_5^{\hat{Y}}$	Deviation from expected value, $\Delta = Y - Y_5^{\hat{Y}}$	Squared deviation, Δ^2	Deviations of the dependent variable from the mean value, $y = Y - \bar{Y}$	Squared mean deviation, y^2
7.	8.	9.	10.	11.	12.	13.	14.	15.
13.4	6.0	700	3.9	0.64	−0.16	0.0256	−1.23	1.5129
14.9	6.0	700	3.2	0.76	0.12	0.0144	−0.83	0.6889
19.0	6.0	700	2.3	0.98	−0.12	0.0144	−0.85	0.7225
38.7	119	74.5	7.9	1.69	0.05	0.0025	0.03	0.0009
29.2	20.0	63.3	6.5	1.89	−0.11	0.0121	0.07	0.0049
33.0	30.2	61.5	6.4	1.84	0.24	0.0576	0.37	0.1369
26.1	34.0	68.5	6.1	1.31	0.19	0.0361	−0.21	0.0441
22.9	10.0	53.3	5.0	1.93	−0.06	0.0036	0.16	0.0256
				50.41	0.78	1.4606	−0.11	10.5428

$$\overline{Y}_5^0 = 1.68$$

Viewed from the deterministic angle, the following general remarks are believed to be appropriate concerning the relation of the dependent to the independent variables.

The average width B of the catchment is positively related to the exponent l since at greater B values the rate of suspended-sediment transport increases rapidly with the discharge Q.

A similarly positive relation is seen to exist between l and Q_k, since sediment formation is increased obviously by an increase in long-term average runoff.

On the strength of simliar considerations the relationship between l and q_k is also expected to be positive.

The relation of Q_{hw}/Q_{lw} with the exponent l will be a negative one since on rivers having a flashy regime the increase in the rate of suspended sediment transport with discharge is likely to be less rapid than in rivers having a more balanced regime. On rivers with a flashy regime rainfalls of high intensity may result in high rates of sediment transport but, considering the relatively low frequency of such extreme events, this eventually entails smaller amounts of sediment transported than under a more balanced river regime.

As to width B of the catchment, it should be noted that under certain circumstances it may be related to exponent l in a negative way as well. In fact, at identical average runoff values which imply essentially identical depth and distribution of rainfall, the amount of sediment entering the river from a narrow catchment may be greater than that washed in from a wide one.

From measurement data obtained in Hungary and abroad, the magnitude of exponent l may be different for different rivers and sometimes even for different cross-sections on the same river.

Concerning the magnitude of l five different cases may be distinguished:

a) For $l > 1$, according to Eq. (2.1.2−2), the sediment concentration C increases or decreases at a higher rate then that at which the discharge Q increases or decreases.

From *Table 2.1.2−1* it will be perceived that on rivers in Hungary, except the Fekete-Körös and Zala rivers, l assumes values higher than unity. From this circumstance it is inferred that in catchments having a climate and geological structure similar to that of Hungary the value of l will generally be greater than unity. This is believed to apply to large parts of Europe.

b) For $l = 1$, the sediment concentration obviously varies in the same proportion as the discharge Q. This case is an exceptional one. Of all the rivers in Hungary the Fekete-Körös alone displays the value $l = 1$.

c) For $0 < l < 1$, the rate of variation in C is smaller than that in Q. This case is typical of regions with little precipitation. A value in this range has been observed in Hungary on the Zala river only, but is commonly observed in the arid parts of the United States. For all water courses in Kamchatka $l = 0.23$.

d) For $l = 0$, suspended sediment transport is unaffected by variations in discharge. This represents evidently an extreme case rarely encountered. Under such circumstances sediment transport is not related to the depth and distribution of precipitation.

e) For $l < 0$, the sediment concentration C varies inversely as the discharge. No such value of l is likely to occur on rivers in Hungary and generally in Europe. Negative values of l have, in fact, been observed on several rivers in the United States.

The relationship between the dependent variable $l = Y$ and the independent variables $B = X_1$, $Q_k = X_2$, $Q_{hw}/Q_{lw} = X_3$ and $q_k = X_4$ was determined first numerically by correlation. The programme was run on a Minsk 22 type electronic computer at the Automation Research Institute of the Hungarian Academy of Sciences.

Computations performed with the data in *Table 2.1.2−1* have shown the partial correlation coefficients between the dependent variable and the four independent

494

variables to be

$$r_1 = 0.581$$
$$r_2 = 0.779$$
$$r_3 = -0.516$$
$$r_4 = 0.749$$

implying that l is most closely related to the long-term average discharge and to the average specific runoff. A rather close relation is still found to exist with the width B of the catchment and even with the ratio Q_{hw}/Q_{lw} characteristic of the regime.

As a result of these computations the five-variable relation

$$Y_5^0 = a + b_1 X_1 + b_2 X_2 + b_3 X_3 + b_4 X_4 \qquad (2.1.2-3)$$

was obtained in the numerical form

$$Y_5^0 = 1.594 - 0.004246\ X_1 + 0.000614\ X_2 -$$
$$- 0.000534\ X_3 + 0.0174\ X_4 \qquad (2.1.2-4)$$

The criterion for the linear computation of multiple correlation — as will be recalled — is that the corresponding partial correlation coefficients and the factors b should have identical signs. According to Eq. (2.1.2 −4), r_1 and b_1 are of opposite signs indicating that the desired relation is not even approximately linear.

For the sake of completeness it should be added nevertheless that the total correlation coefficient $R^2 = 0.694$, so that $R = 0.832$, indicating a rather close relationship.

It is of interest to examine the influence of individual independent variables on the magnitude of the dependent variable. The parameters

$$C_1 = r_1 \gamma_1; \quad C_2 = r_2 \gamma_2; \quad C_3 = r_3 \gamma_3; \quad C_4 = r_4 \gamma_4 \qquad (2.1.2-5)$$

are formed in the familar way, where r_1, r_2, r_3 and r_4 are the partial correlation coefficients, while

$$\gamma_1 = b_1 \frac{\sigma_1}{\sigma_0}; \quad \gamma_2 = b_2 \frac{\sigma_2}{\sigma_0}; \quad \gamma_3 = b_3 \frac{\sigma_3}{\sigma_0}; \quad \gamma_4 = b_4 \frac{\sigma_4}{\sigma_0} \qquad (2.1.2-6)$$

are the products of factors b and the ratios of the individual standard deviations (σ_1, σ_2, σ_3, σ_4) of the corresponding independent variables and the standard deviation (σ_0) of the dependent variable.

Computations have yielded the following values for the parameters:

$$C_1 = -0.241$$
$$C_2 = 0.723$$
$$C_3 = 0.134$$
$$C_4 = 0.0772$$

indicating that the value of l is influenced mostly by $X_2 = Q_k$.

495

According to Eq. (2.1.2−6) the sign of the γ values is controlled by the sign of the factors b. Since, however, the sign of the factors b is necessarily identical with the sign of the partial correlation coefficients r, it should be obvious that all index numbers C are bound to be positive. The sign of C_1 will be seen to be a negative one because, as indicated before, r_1 and b_1 are of opposite signs. As demonstrated by the foregoing computations it is entirely misleading to assume the relation to be linear; some graphical method is expediently resorted to for determining the relation.

Adopting the coaxial method the relation between the five variables is indicated in *Fig. 2.1.2−2* showing the final family of curves only. In this figure the method of determining the expected value of the exponent l is shown for the Körmend gaging section on the Rába river. The value found for Körmend is $l^0 = Y_5^0 = 1.84$ and thus the difference over the actual value $l = 2.08$ is*

$$\varLambda = Y - Y_5^0 = 2.08 - 1.84 = 0.24$$

In *Fig. 2.1.2−2* the Kazincbarcika gage displays the only appreciable difference. It is concluded therefrom that the hydrological conditions of the Sajó river differ appreciably from those of other rivers in Hungary.

Although graphical correlation analysis offers no means for determining the total correlation coefficient or the total conditional standard deviation by obtaining the expected Y values from the figure for each of the 30 gaging stations (column 11) and by forming the difference of actual and expected values in columns 12 and 13 as well as the squares $(\varLambda^2)$ thereof, approximate values can still be computed for the total correlation coefficients and the total conditional standard deviation.

If $\overline{Y}$ denotes the arithmetic mean of the dependent variable, then the deviation from the mean value at the νth value is

$$y_\nu = Y_\nu - \overline{Y} \tag{2.1.2−7}$$

According the numerical computation the expected value $y^{()}$ of the deviations from the mean value y is for the νth group of values

$$\lambda_\nu = y_\nu - y^0 \tag{2.1.2−8}$$

At the νth group of variables, similarly to the differences over the mean value, at the actual values the deviation of $Y^{()}$ from the actual Y is

$$\varLambda_\nu = Y_\nu - Y_\nu^0 \tag{2.1.2−9}$$

As an approximation it is permissible to assume that

$$\overline{Y} = \overline{Y^0} \tag{2.1.2−10}$$

the numerical demonstration of which will, however, be neglected.

---

* Including all measurements, $l = 2.18$ as shown in *Fig. 2.1.4−24*. Since our correlation computations are based on measurements prior to 1954, the value $l = 2.08$ has been retained.

Fig. 2.1.2—2. Exponent *l* involved in the expression $C = dQ^l$ related to the hydrological characteristics of the watercourse

Besides Eqs (2.1.2−7) to (2.1.2−10) the relation

$$\overline{Y}_v = \overline{Y_v^0} + y_v^0 \qquad (2.1.2-11)$$

also applies.

With the foregoing in mind, Eq. (2.1.2−9) can also be written in the form

$$\Lambda_v = (\overline{Y} + y_v) - (\overline{Y}_v + y_v^0) = y_v - y_v^0 = \lambda_v \qquad .(2.1.2-12)$$

Taking thus $\Sigma \Lambda^2$ instead of $\Sigma \lambda^2$, the square of the correlation coefficient becomes, according to columns 13 and 15 of *Table 2.1.2−1*,

$$R^2 = 1 - \frac{[\lambda\lambda]}{[yy]} = 1 - \frac{1.4606}{10.5428} = 0.862 \qquad (2.1.2-13)$$

and the total correlation coefficient itself is then

$$R = 0.928$$

Fig. 2.1.2−3. Coefficient d involved in the expression $C = dQ^l$ vs. the exponent l

The standard deviation of the dependent variable is

$$\sigma_0 = \sqrt{\frac{[yy]}{N}} = \sqrt{\frac{10.5428}{30}} = 0.593 \qquad (2.1.2-14)$$

whereas the total conditional standard deviation of the dependent variable is

$$\sigma_y^0 = \sqrt{\frac{[\lambda\lambda]}{N}} = \sqrt{\frac{1.4606}{30}} = 0.221 \qquad (2.1.2-15)$$

or substantially smaller than the above.

Using the coaxial method we have succeeded therefore in determining, with a fair degree of accuracy, the relation of the exponent l to the four independent variables selected.

The factor d involved in Eq. (2.1.2−2) is impossible to determine on the basis of hydraulics, whereas considering the hydrological factors a much more complex approach would be required for doing so. Nevertheless it is believed expedient to examine the values of the factor d in the light of available observation data. The relation of d and the exponent l, further that existing between d and the long term mean discharge Q_k have been plotted in *Figs 2.1.2−3* and *2.1.2−4*, respectively. Except for the gaging stations on the Danube and the Szentgotthárd gage on the Lapincs creek, both figures indicate a positive relation. Evidently none of

498

Fig. 2.1.2—4. Coefficient d involved in the expression $C = dQ^l$ vs. the mean discharge Q_k

these relations can be generalized, although they reflect, beyond doubt, the similarity of properties of water courses in Hungary. From the figures it will be perceived that the relation does not apply to major streams where the catchment is composed of areas differing in climate, topography and soil conditions. This is clearly exemplified by the gaging stations on the Danube.

The influence of hydrological factors on suspended-sediment transport has been demonstrated by a number of investigators.

E. Rémy-Berzenkovich (1966) has studied the influence of hydrological factors in several water courses in Germany and the properties of the catchment on the exponent m in the relation

$$Q_s = bQ^m \qquad (2.1.2{-}16)$$

This relation is identical with the relation $G_s = pQ^j$ to be described later and since $C = G_s/Q$, the sediment concentration C is related by definition to the sediment transport G_s. Of course, equations $j = l + 1$ and $d = p$ are also valid.

For the mean sediment concentration and the annual mean sediment discharge in the rivers on the Kamchatka peninsula A. I. Stepanova has suggested the empirical relations

$$C_k = dQ^{0.23} \ [\text{p/m}^3]$$ (2.1.2−17)

and

$$G_s = pQ^{1.23} \ [\text{kp/sec}]$$ (2.1.2−18)

respectively. In both equations Q (m³/sec) is the annual mean discharge, while the coefficients d and p depend on the particular properties of individual water courses. Stepanova has determined the magnitude of the latter by dividing the peninsula into four zones.

In the German Democratic Republic similar investigations have been carried out by L. Bauer and W. Tille (1966) concerning the influence of hydrological factors on suspended-sediment transport.

For details the reader is referred to the papers listed in the attached bibliography.

2.1.3. EMPIRICAL RELATIONS OF BED LOAD TRANSPORT

The theoretical aspects and experimental methods of determining the rates of bed load transport have been discussed in detail in *Sections 1.1.3, 1.2.6* and *1.2.7.*

In connection with the description of theoretical and experimental relations of bed load transport, the essential aspects concerning the basic features, fields of application and practical applicability of empirical relations have also been outlined.

For estimating the bed load transport in alluvial streams several modified forms of the theoretical and experimental relations have been suggested. Such modifications have been introduced especially in connection with the formulae of Schoklitsch and Meyer-Peter and even with the bed load transport equation of Einstein. The objective of such modifications is always to make the relations suited for general practical use.

The empirical relations include first of all the hydraulic factors of the water course which are amenable to accurate observation and which can be derived from general hydrographic measurements. It is essential to check such empirical relations against the data of field observations, and in many cases these relations themselves, are derived from the results of field measurements.

The devices and methods used for measuring bed load transport in the field have been described in *Section 1.1.5.* Of these the results obtained with the help of sediment traps and by cumulative measurements are used primarily for deriving empirical relations. Of the more recent methods the results of measurements made by luminescent and radioactive tracers are of considerable interest but, for the time being, are unsuited for use in such relations.

500

Disregarding the order of publication and of importance, and without wishing to present a complete list, we shall mention some of the more widely used empirical relations.

Starting from the theoretical conclusion of Velikanov, Polyakov suggests the relation

$$q_B = Av^4 \qquad (2.1.3-1)$$

relating thus the weight of bed load transported in unit time and unit width to the fourth power of velocity.

Bed load transport has been expressed by Lopatin and Goncharov in terms of the difference between the actual (v) and the critical velocity (v_c).

According to Lopatin

$$q_B = \frac{aS^{4/3}}{d_g^{1/3}} (v - v_c) \ [\text{kp/secm}] \qquad (2.1.3-2)$$

where a is a constant assuming different values for different water courses.

The relation of Goncharov is

$$q_B = Ad_m \frac{v^3}{v_c^3} \left(\frac{d}{D}\right)^{0.1} (v - v_c) \ [\text{kp/secm}] \qquad (2.1.3-3)$$

where A = a constant,
$\quad d_m$ = the mean particle diameter.

In a recent formula Goncharov has introduced the ratio η of the fall velocities v_t and ω observed in turbulent flow and in still water, respectively, further the limit velocity v_H characteristic of the no-movement condition of the bed material:

$$q_B = 1.2 [1 + \eta] d_m v_H \left(\frac{v}{v_H}\right)^{4.3} \ [\text{kp/secm}] \qquad (2.1.3-4)$$

For $d_m \geq 1.5$ mm, $\eta = 1$.

The limit velocity is determined from the characteristics of the water course and the bed load.

Both the ratios and the differences of velocities are involved in Shamov's relation:

$$q_B = K \left(\frac{v}{v_c}\right)^3 (v - v_c) \left(\frac{d_m}{D}\right)^{1/4} \ [\text{kp/secm}] \qquad (2.1.3-5)$$

where K is a factor representing the grain size distribution of the bed load. For computing the magnitude of v_c Shamov has suggested the expression

$$v_c = 3.7 d_m^{1/3} D^{1/3} \qquad (2.1.3-6)$$

For the bed load discharge in the entire cross-section A. V. Karaushev suggests the relation

$$G_B = K_* D^\phi S^\beta (d_g \omega)^{-\psi} Q \qquad (2,1.3-7)$$

where Q = the water discharge,

D = the mean depth,

S = the slope,

d_g = the mean particle diameter having a fall velocity ω

K_* = an empirical coefficient.

ϕ, β and ψ = exponents to be determined experimentally.

On the basis of extensive measurements on the Enns river Rémy-Berzenkovich suggests a relation of the form

$$G_B = C(Q - Q_c)^n \qquad (2.1.3-8)$$

for computing the total bed load transport. With the substitutions $C = (7,000/i\sqrt{d})S^{3/2}$ and $n = 1$ and considering the specific water discharges q and q_c, the formula assumes a structure similar to Eq. (1.2.6−27) suggested by Schocklitsch.

Starting from the assumption that the conditions underlying the formula of Meyer-Peter − Müller expressed by Eq. (1.2.6−44) apply also to the Danube and assuming the specific gravities of bed load and water to be constant, J. Csoma has introduced the expression

$$q_B^{2/3} = 856.016 DS - 57.909 d_g \qquad (2.1.3-9)$$

for estimating the rate of bed load transport on the Hungarian Upper Danube. In this expression q_B is obtained in kp/sec m units if D and d_g are introduced in m units. For particle sizes from 1 to 50 mm in diameter the use of the expression is greatly facilitated by the chart shown in *Fig. 2.1.3−1.*

An accuracy of several decimals is believed to be unjustified by O. Haszpra for numerical constants. For this reason he suggests the expression

$$q_B = (856 DS - 58 d_g)^{3/2} \, [\text{kp/msec}] \qquad (2.1.3-10)$$

the practical use of which is facilitated by the nomographs shown in *Figs 2.1.3−2* and *2.1.3−3.* For use in the expression shown in these nomographs d_g should be introduced in mm units.

An expert group of the Netherlands Engineering Consultants (NEDECO) has worked for several years on the regulation of the Niger and its tributaries. Introducing the ratio $(\gamma_1 - \gamma)/\gamma = \rho'$ they have expressed the rate of bed load transport in unit width and unit time by the formula

$$Q_B = 6.5 d^{3/2} \rho'^{1/2} g^{1/2} \left(\frac{\mu DS}{\rho' d} - 0.047 \right)^{3/2} \, [\text{m}^3/\text{secm}] \qquad (2.1.3-11)$$

which can also be derived from the Meyer-Peter − Müller formula. In this expression μ is the ripple coefficient the magnitude of which is determined by the ratio of the hydraulic radii applying to the channel and to the full cross-section.

502

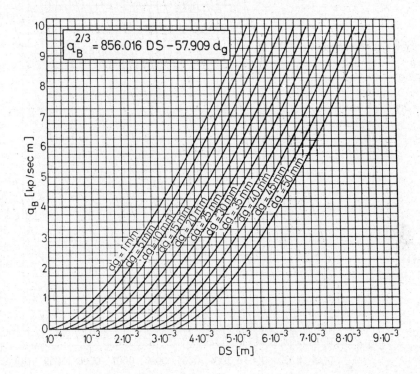

Fig. 2.1.3—1. Nomograph for estimating bed load transport. After J. Csoma

Having determined the values of Einstein's bed load and intensity parameters Φ and Ψ, respectively, from the literature, C. Erkek has examined the relation $\Phi/\Psi = F(\Psi)$ in *Fig. 2.1.3—4.* Although, as he admits, the values obtained from different figures are inaccurate, the relation between the two parameters has proved to be a very close one. According to the figure the numerical relation

$$\frac{\Phi}{\Psi} = 10\Psi^{-4.333} \qquad (2.1.3-12)$$

or $\Phi = 10\,\Psi^{-3.333}$ affords a surprisingly good description of bed load transport in the seven water courses considered.

Considering Eqs (1.2.6—23) and (1.2.6—16) of Φ and Ψ, respectively, further assuming the acceleration due to gravity and the specific gravity of water to be constant, Erkek introduces the relation

$$q_B = 0.994\gamma_1[(\gamma_1 - \gamma)d^3]^{1/2}\left[\frac{\tau_0}{(\gamma_1 - \gamma)d}\right]^{10/3} \qquad (2.1.3-13)$$

503

$$q_B = (856\ DS - 0.058\ d_g)^{3/2}$$

where

q_B [kp/sec m] = Bed load transport in unit width

D [m] = Depth of flow

S [-] = Surface slope

d_g [mm] = Mean particle diameter

Fig 2.1.3—2. Solution of the simplified Meyer-Peter—Müller transport equation derived by J. Csoma. After O. Haszpra

Eq. (2.1.3—12) was found to yield misleading results for rivers in Hungary. As will be s en in *Fig. 2.1.3—5*, bed load transport observed at the gaging stations on the Danube, Tisza and Sajó rivers is much more accurately described by the relation

$$\Phi = 0.014 \Psi^{-3.33} \tag{2.1.3—14}$$

W. H. Graf has introduced the shear intensity

$$\Psi_A = \frac{(\rho_1 - \rho)}{\rho}\ \frac{d}{SR} \tag{2.1.3—15}$$

504

$$q_B = (856\,DS - 0.058\,d_g)^{3/2}$$

where

q_B [kp/sec m] = Sediment transport in unit width

D [m] = Depth of flow

S [−] = Surface slope

d_g [mm] = Mean particle diameter

Conditions:

1) Bed load transport in the stream
   is near saturation

2) The specific gravity of the
   sediment is 2600 kp/m³

Key:

Example:

$DS = 0.002$

$d_g = 15$ mm

From the nomograph

$q_B = 0.77$

By computation

$q_B = 0.7725$

Difference 3.25 ‰

Fig. 2.1.3−3. Nomograph for solving the simplified Meyer-Peter−Müller transport equation derived by J. Csoma. After O. Haszpra

Fig. 2.1.3−4. The bed load parameter Φ vs. the intensity Ψ of the water course for alluvial channels. After Erkek

and the transport parameter

$$\Phi_A = \frac{C_T v R}{\left(\dfrac{\gamma_1 - \gamma}{\rho}\right)^{1/2} d^{3/2}} \tag{2.1.3−16}$$

measuring the total sediment transport. Relying on the results of measurements performed by Gilbert, Ansley, further by Guy and co-workers at the laboratory

505

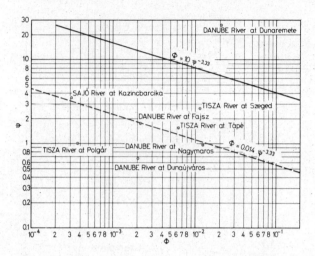

Fig. 2.1.3−5. The bed load parameter Φ vs. the intensity Ψ of the water course for gaging station on the Danube, Tisza and Sajó rivers

as well as by Einstein on alluvial streams, he has developed the graphical relation

$$\Phi_A = 10.34 \, \Psi_A^{-2 \cdot 52} \qquad (2.1.3-17)$$

which may be regarded extremely close.

Here the use of the notations Φ_A and Ψ_A is greatly confusing, these being substantially identical with the parameters Ψ and Φ introduced by Einstein under Eqs (1.2.6−16) and (1.2.6−23). In fact

$$\Psi_A = \frac{(\rho_1 - \rho)}{\rho} \, \frac{d}{SR} = \frac{(\gamma_1 - \gamma)d}{\gamma RS} = \frac{1}{f_0} = \Psi \qquad (2.1.3-18)$$

and

$$\Phi_A = \frac{C_T vR}{(\gamma_1 - \gamma/\rho)^{1/2} d^{3/2}} = C_T vR \left(\frac{\rho}{\rho_1 - \rho}\right)^{1/2} \left(\frac{1}{gd^3}\right)^{1/2}$$

or since

$$C_T = \frac{C}{\gamma_1} = \left(\frac{q_B/vR}{\gamma_1}\right)$$

actually

$$\Phi_A = \Phi = \frac{q_B}{\gamma_1} \left(\frac{\rho}{\rho_1 - \rho}\right)^{1/2} \left(\frac{1}{gd^3}\right)^{1/2} \qquad (2.1.3-19)$$

In view of the fact that Ψ_A and Φ_A are essentially identical with the parameters Ψ and Φ, Eq. (2.1.3−17) can be compared directly with Erkek's Eq. (2.1.3−12)

506

and with the relation used in Hungary and given by Eq. (2.1.3 – 14). The constant factors used by Erkek and Graf are almost identical and about seven-hundred times as great as that involved in the Hungarian relation. Graf has taken pains to emphasize that his relation applies to the total sediment transport, i.e. to the sum of suspended sediment and bed load, whereas in the Hungarian relation bed load transport is only considered. The ratio of about seven-hundred, as will be detailed in *Section 2.1 – 5*, appears to represent a rather fair mean value for the ratio of suspended sediment and bed load. From this it appears permissible to infer that, although in his paper specific reference is made to bed load transport only, Erkek's relation applies to total sediment transport. On the other hand, the exponents are ~~almost~~ identical in the relation used in Hungary and in that suggested by Erkek, whereas a major difference is observed in the formula of Graf. The relation expressed by Eq. (2.1.3 – 14) and limited to bed load transport must not be regarded even as a tentative one, since even the limited number of available data are scattered over a very wide range.

Using a different approach D. B. Simons and his co-workers have derived a transport formula on the basis of bed forms, i.e. essentially by taking the type of bed load movement into consideration. With v_h denoting the travelling velocity of ripples and dunes and h their average height their formula is

$$q_B = (1 - \lambda) v_h \frac{h}{2} + C_1 \qquad (2.1.3 - 20)$$

where the porosity of bed load

$$\lambda = \frac{\text{total volume} - \text{solid volume}}{\text{solid volume}},$$

while C_1 is the part of bed load transport which is not related to the movement of sand ripples and dunes and which becomes 0 as the bed becomes completely covered by dunes. Eq. (2.1.3 – 20) is applied successfully to narrow and straight channels in which the flow is uniform so that the mean values of v_h and h are accessible to reliable determination. In a water course were v_h and h are subject to variations with respect to time and location, the bed forms can be determined within a certain time interval using an echograph.

A common drawback of all empirical relations is that they involve unknown coefficients the magnitude or variation of which cannot be determined reliably except by direct measurements. It has been repeatedly emphasized that no relation of general validity is believed to be available as yet. Although measuring devices and methods in current use are of questionable reliability, yielding inaccurate results, direct measurements still appear to offer the most practicable method.

When the weight of bed load transported in a particular water course is related to the hydraulic chacteristics of the water course, the properties thereof will be included with the full weight in the relations thus determined. Therefore by examining the relationships between bed load weight and hydraulic factors for indiридual rivers or individual cross-sections, it becomes possible to derive certain relations.

If the relationships between the hydraulic factors of a stream and the bed load transported therein are established from data of direct bed load measurements, theoretical relations afford a certain means for checking the reliability of direct bed load measurements.

The weight of bed load transported has been related to stages, to discharges and to flow velocities at most bed-load-measuring stations in Hungary.

Subsequent considerations will be based on the relations established by these direct measurements.

In studying bed load transport along a water course no direct relations to stages can be determined on account of the different character of stages in individual cross-sections. Similar studies can be performed only on the basis of stages corresponding to one another.

Considering the flow regime and hydraulic factors of streams, the mean velocity v_k and the discharge Q are the factors of primary potential interest. In bed load transport studies the introduction of mean velocities is expected to offer advantages.

Studies concerning relationships with mean velocities and discharges alike have been performed for the Danube, Tisza, Hernád and Rába rivers, since observation results on two or more sediment-measuring stations are available on these four water courses. The rivers in question and the measuring stations thereon are shown in *Fig. 3.1.2−3*.

On the Danube at Dunaremete, Nagybajcs and Baja measurements have also been made after 1953. Since these recent measurements display no changes compared to earlier ones, the examinations will be based on the relations determined from data obtained before 1954.

The $G_B = F(v_k)$ relations for the Danube are plotted in *Fig. 2.1.3−6*. It will be perceived therefrom that the relation of G_B and v_k is an exponential one ($G_B = \alpha_1 v_k^{\beta_1}$) and that the weight of bed load transported varies at all measuring stations as the 6.67th power of mean velocity. The station at Nagybajcs is the only exception where, owing to the reduced number of observations, the relation is less reliable than at the other stations. Apart from Nagybajcs, proceeding downstream along the river gradually decreasing mean velocities are shown in *Fig. 2.1.3−6* to be sufficient for transporting the same weight of bed load. This is due evidently to the reduction in particle size clearly observable on the Danube. Thus for instance, the bed load at Fajsz and Baja consists of nothing more than sand which is transported at lower velocities than the gravel at Dunaalmás − Nagymaros or even the very coarse gravel material at Dunaremete. Comparing the individual stations the reduction in mean velocities downstream along the river necessary for transporting the same weight of bed load implies that, assuming for instance at Baja the same mean velocity as at Dunaremete, the weight of bed load at Baja would be $6.0/0.0174 = 344.3$ times as great as at Dunaremete, since G_B Dunaremete/G_B Baja $= 0.0174/6.0 = 0.0029$. In *Fig. 2.1.3−6* the ratio

508

Fig. 2.1.3—6. Bed load transport vs. mean velocity relation for different gages on the Danube

related to bed load transport at Baja has been determined for all bed-load-measuring stations except for Nagybajcs.

Consider hereafter the relationship between bed load transport and mean velocity *on the Tisza* river.

After 1953 a greater number of measurements on the Tisza river have been made at Szeged only, but these reflect no changes as against earlier conditions. For this reason the conditions before 1954, i.e. before the operation of the Tiszalök dam will be examined.*

Measurement data are available at four gaging stations on the Tisza river, namely Polgár, Tiszabő, Tápé and Szeged. The relations obtained by averaging the scattered points are shown in *Fig. 2.1.3—7.* In each of the four relations the weight of bed load will be seen to vary as the 4.59th power of flow velocity.

The flow velocities pertaining to the same weight of bed load display a more irregular variation here than on the Danube. On the other hand, the differences in mean velocities are appreciably smaller than on the Danube, as illustrated by the close spacing of lines in *Fig. 2.1.3—7.* The particle size of bed load material in the Tisza river decreases downstream of Polgár. From the identical rate of change it is concluded that an uniform relationship exists along the river between the bed load weight transported and the mean flow velocity. Bed load transport at various stations on the Tisza river has also been related to the relation for Szeged, i.e. the one farthest downstream, assuming the mean velocity to remain constant. Whereas on the Danube the ratios related to the downstream station showed a consistently increasing trend, on the Tisza river a reduction, however slight, is observable when proceeding downstream. This circumstance may be

---

* Under the influence of the barrage constructed at Tiszalök (Rázompuszta) bed load transport in the river has undergone minor changes.

Fig. 2.1.3—7. Bed load transport vs. mean velocity relation for different gaging stations on the Tisza river

attributed primarily to the relatively large volume of bed load discharged by the Maros river as a consequence of which the bed load transport at Szeged is appreciably greater than over other sections of the Tisza river upstream thereof. The ratio of bed load weights pertaining to the same mean velocity related to Szeged are indicated for various stations in *Fig. 2.1.3—7*.

The measurements *on the Hernád* river after 1953 indicate no changes to have occurred over earlier condition. Thus the relations established before 1954 will be examined also in the case of the Hernád river.

The relation between bed load weight and mean velocity is indicated in *Fig. 2.1.3—8* for the three measuring stations on the Hernád river, namely Hidasnémeti, Pere and Gesztely. On the Hernád the weight of bed load will be seen to vary at different rates with mean velocity at the three stations, as indicated by the different slopes of the straight lines representing the relations.

Fig. 2.1.3—8. Bed load transport vs. mean velocity relation for gaging stations on the Hernád river

Fig. 2.1.3−9. Bed load transport vs. mean velocity relation for gaging stations on the Rába
river

In contrast to the conclusions arrived at in connection with the Danube and
Tisza rivers, the inconsistency in the bed load weight versus mean velocity relations on the Hernád river may be surprising. Considering, however, that the
Hernád is canalized by several dams, an explanation may be offered for this
circumstance. On canalized water courses the greatest change is introduced in
the mean velocity. Consequently in such cases no consistent variation should
be expected.

On the Rába river measurements have been made after 1953 at two stations,
namely at Szentgotthárd and Körmend. According to *Fig. 2.1.3−9*, the relations
applying to the two stations are almost identical.

Examining the changes in bed load weight and mean velocities along the rivers,
neglecting the Hernád the regime of which is strongly influenced by the dams
constructed on it, we can conclude that the weight of bed load transported varies
as the same power of mean velocity along the three rivers considered. Differences
are found, however, in the bed load weights transported at the same flow velocities
on the individual rivers from station to station. If there are considerable changes
in the particle size of bed load along the river, as is the case for instance in the
Danube, then the magnitude of mean velocity pertaining to the same bed load
weight will be variable just like the particle sizes. Since the changes in particle size
are known to be controlled primarily by the properties of the water course, it
should be evident that the variation along the river of the relations $G_B = F(v_k)$
is also due mostly to the hydrological properties and, in a reduced degree, to the
hydraulic relations.

The relation between bed load weight and discharge ($G_B = p_1 Q^{j_1}$) along the
rivers has been compared for the Danube, the Tisza, the Hernád and the Rába
rivers.

As will be seen from *Fig. 2.1.3−10*, the relations determined on the Danube
for individual stations display a greater variability when related to velocities.
Although at Dunaremete, Dunaújváros, Fajsz and Baja the weight of bed load

Fig. 2.1.3—10. Bed load transport vs. discharge relation for gaging stations on the Danube

transported increases as the same power of discharge, the relations applying to Dunaalmás and Nagymaros, further to Nagybajcs differ substantially from the former. For this very reason it is impossible to establish general relations according to which the discharge required for transporting the same weight of bed load would vary consistently proceeding downstream from station to station.

For the sake of completeness *Fig. 2.1.3—10* shows how the bed load weight transported at the same discharge varies at Dunaremete, Dunaújváros and at Fajsz, adopting the relation at Baja as a basis of comparison. According to the figure at Dunaremete, at the same discharge the bed load transport is

$$\frac{10^{-8} \cdot 34}{10^{-8} \cdot 2.35} = 14.5 \text{ times}$$

as large as at Baja. This is as expected since at Dunaremete the discharge of, for instance, 1500 m³/sec is obviously of a lower duration percentage than at Baja. The ratio of the relations at Dunaalmás and Nagymaros equals unity, the relations for the two stations being identical.

In connection with the relations involving discharge it is very likely necessary to consider that, depending on the hydrological properties of the river, discharges are bound to vary along its length. Consequently the discharge versus bed load transport relations can be compared — as will be demonstrated subsequently — on the basis of discharges of identical percentage duration.

As indicated in *Fig. 2.1.3—11* the weight of bed load transported varies as the same power of discharge at all stations considered on the Tisza river. Apart from the identical exponent of discharge, however, no other regularity could be established in the relation of discharge to bed load transport on the Tisza river. In connection with the relations based on discharge it is nevertheless observable that the differences between the individual stations are confined to a much narrower range than on the Danube. Bed load transport pertaining to the same dis-

Fig. 2.1.3.—11. Bed load transport vs. discharge relation for gaging stations on the Tisza river

charge has been related to that at Szeged, and the relevant ratios have been entered into *Fig. 2.1.3—11.* The circumstance, for instance, that at the same discharge the bed load transport at Polgár is 2.53 times as great as that at Szeged, clearly shows the possibility of comparing relations based on discharges also on the Tisza river only when adopting discharges of the same percentage duration as the basis of comparison.

The relations applying to three stations on the Hernád river have been compared in *Fig. 2.1.3—12.* At each of the three stations the weight of bed load transported will be seen to vary as the same power of discharge. It is interesting to note that the exponent of discharge is almost identical for the Hernád and Tisza rivers, namely 2.66 and 2.74. It should be pointed out further that, whereas the relations based on velocities display a very high degree of variability, the relations based on discharges, at least as far as the exponent of discharge is concerned, are consistent on the Hernád river. However, not even *Fig. 2.1.3—12* is suited for establishing a relationship of general validity applying to the changes in bed load transport along the river. The discharge relations will therefore be compared also on the Hernád river on the basis of discharges of the same percentage duration.

The G_B versus Q relations applying to two stations on the Rába river are shown in *Fig. 2.1.3—13.*

Summarizing the results of investigations concerning the variation of the bed load transport versus discharge relations along a river we can conclude that, for a particular water course, G_B varies in general as the same power of discharge, but *no regularity whatsoever can be established on the variation along the river in the relations based on discharges.*

Fig. 2.1.3—12. Bed load transport vs. discharge relation for gaging stations on the Hernád river

Fig. 2.1.3—13. Bed load transport vs. discharge relations for gaging stations on the Rába river

As mentioned previously, discharges vary necessarily along a river under the influence of hydrological factors. For this reason a comparison of bed load transport rates observed at discharges of the same percentage duration should be resorted to when desiring to compare the relations based on discharges,

The rates of bed load transport corresponding to stages and discharges of 25, 50 and 75% duration have been compiled for all stations on the Danube, Tisza, Hernád and Rába rivers in *Tables 2.1.3—1, 2.1.3—2, 2.1.3—3, and 2.1.3—4*

Table 2.1.3—1

Bed load transport rates at stages and discharges of 25, 50 and 75% duration
at several gaging stations on the Danube

Gaging station	Distance from mouth [km]	Dura-tion [%]	Stage, h [cm]	Discharge, Q [m³/sec]	Bed load transport, G_B [kp/sec] from		Mean bed load transport [kp/sec]
					$G_B = F(h)$	$G_B = F(Q)$	$\frac{6. + 7.}{2}$
1.	2.	3.	4.	5.	6.	7.	8.
Dunaremete	1,825.5	25	389	1,900	8.100	6.400	7.250
		50	348	1,530	4.800	3.900	4.350
		75	306	1,280	2.600	2.650	2.625
Nagybajcs	1,801.0	25	366	2,650	0.500	0.680	0.590
		50	286	1,920	0.075	0.080	0.0775
		75	223	1,420	0.013	0.011	0.012
Dunaalmás	1,751.8	25	335	2,900	1.600	1.600	1.600
		50	273	2,200	0.570	0.500	0.535
		75	217	1,620	0.165	0.135	0.150
Nagymaros	1,694.6	25	294	2,940	1.000	1.250	1.125
		50	228	2,200	0.440	0.380	0.410
		75	172	1,620	0.175	0.110	0.1425
Dunaújváros	1,580.6	25	365	3,200	1.170	1.000	1.085
		50	295	2,450	0.620	0.560	0.590
		75	227	1,800	0.270	0.270	0.270
Fajsz	1,506.7	25	453	3,360	1.950	2.100	2.025
		50	349	2,705	1.350	1.320	1.335
		75	251	2,085	0.850	0.700	0.775
Baja	1,479.4	25	538	3,446	1.800	1.950	1.875
		50	435	2,720	1.080	1.120	1.100
		75	341	2,100	0.590	0.620	0.605

respectively. It is obvious that, on the basis of stages and discharges, different bed load transport rates are obtained even at identical percentage duration values since the relationship between bed load transport and stages or discharges can be regarded but approximately as a functional relation. In the Tables both values of bed load transport are indicated, in the present investigations, however, the use of the arithmetic mean of the two values is deemed preferable.

The variation along the river in the mean value of bed load transport determined on the basis of stages and discharges of 25, 50 and 75% duration is illus-

Table 2.1.3—2

Bed load transport rates at stages and discharges of 25, 50 and 75% duration
at several gaging stations on the Tisza river

Gaging station	Distance from mouth [km]	Dura-tion [%]	Stage, h [cm]	Discharge, Q [m³/sec]	Bed load transport, G_B [kp/sec] from		Mean bed load transport [kp/sec]
					$G_B = F(h)$	$G_B = F(Q)$	$\frac{6. + 7.}{2}$
1.	2.	3.	4.	5.	6.	7.	8.
Polgár	491.250	25	168	615	0.170	0.250	0.210
		50	22	323	0.035	0.045	0.040
		75	−49	193	0.0115	0.0115	0.0115
Tiszabő	369.200	25	320	745	0.520	0.570	0.545
		50	105	420	0.125	0.120	0.1225
		75	−17	272	0.033	0.037	0.0350
Tápé	176.300	25	316	795	0.225	0.108	0.1665
		50	116	440	0.039	0.022	0.0305
		75	0	280	0.0086	0.0067	0.0076
Szeged	170.405	25	316	1,118	0.650	0.640	0.645
		50	116	657	0.175	0.148	0.1615
		75	0	417	0.057	0.046	0.0515

trated for the Danube, Tisza and Hernád rivers in *Figs 2.1.3 — 14, 2.1.3 — 15 and 2.1.3 — 16*, respectively.

From *Fig. 2.1.3 — 14* constructed with the data compiled in *Table 2.1.3 — 1* it will be perceived that, except for Dunaremete, the rate of bed load transport pertaining to stages and to discharges of identical duration shows a remarkable consistency on the Danube. Of course, the rate of bed load transport at Duna-remete is substantially higher than at the other stations. The conspicuously low value at Nagybajcs is probably due to the poorer reliability of the relation established on the basis of a small number of measurements. It is of interest to note that bed load transport on the Danube increases almost proportionately with increasing duration percentages, suggesting that here bed load is transported continuously at low and high stages and discharges alike. Of course at the discharges of lower percentage duration bed load transport is materially greater than at discharges of higher percentage duration. The difference is especially great at Dunaremete' and Dunaalmás where, for instance, bed load transport at a discharge of 25% duration is several times greater than that at a discharge of 75% duration.

Table 2.1.3—3

Bed load transport rates at stages and discharges of 25, 50 and 75% duration
at several gaging stations on the Hernád river

Gaging station	Distance from mouth [km]	Dura-tion [%]	Stage, h [cm]	Discharge, Q [m³/sec]	Bed load transport, G_B [kp/sec] from		Mean bed load transport [kp/sec]
					$G_B = F(h)$	$G_B = F(Q)$	$\frac{6. + 7.}{2}$
1.	2.	3.	4.	5.	6.	7.	8.
Hidasnémeti	83.6	25	37	20.0	0.0035	0.0050	0.00425
		50	6	9.5	0.00052	0.00070	0.00061
		75	−8	6.5	0.00017	0.00024	0.00020
Pere	61	25	60	26	0.0052	0.0050	0.0051
		50	34	14	0.0010	0.0010	0.0010
		75	16	8.5	0.00017	0.00027	0.00022
Gesztely	22.4	25	80	31	0.030	0.048	0.039
		50	50	16	0.0079	0.0090	0.0085
		75	31	9.2	0.0029	0.0020	0.00245

Table 2.1.3—4

Bed load transport rates at stages and discharges of 25, 50 and 75% duration
at two gaging stations on the Rába river

Gaging station	Distance from mouth [km]	Dura-tion [%]	Stage, h [cm]	Discharge, Q [m³/sec]	Bed load transport, G_B [kp/sec] from		Mean bed load transport [kp/sec]
					$G_B = F(h)$	$G_B = F(Q)$	$\frac{6. + 7.}{2}$
1.	2.	3.	4.	5.	6.	7.	8.
Szentgotthárd	181.7	25	10	34	0.0059	0.0067	0.0063
		50	−12	27	0.0028	0.0037	0.0032
		75	−29	22	0.0011	0.0022	0.0016
Körmend	147.9	25	60	39	0.0029	0.0067	0.0048
		50	32	28	0.0013	0.0013	0.0013
		75	12	20	0.0004	0.0011	0.0007

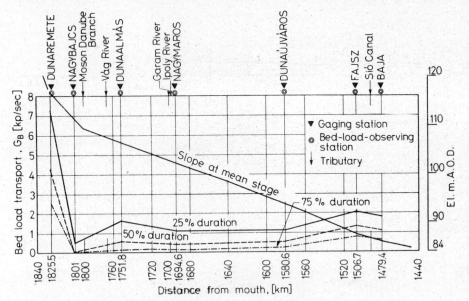

Fig. 2.1.3—14. Changes in mean bed load transport estimated for stages and discharges of 25, 50 and 75% duration along the Danube

Fig. 2.1.3—15. Changes in mean bed load transport estimated for stages and discharges of 25, 50 and 75% duration along the Tisza river

The surface profile at mean stages has also been entered into *Fig. 2.1.3—14.* The inclusion of the surface slope will clearly indicate that, besides other properties of the river, bed load transport depends to a great extent on hydraulic factors.

The rates of bed load transport pertaining to discharges and stages of identical percentage duration have been illustrated in *Fig. 2.1.3—15* for the Tisza river. The transport rate at Tiszabő is remarkably high, but this is only partly due to

518

Fig. 2.1.3.—16. Changes in mean bed load transport estimated for stages and discharges of 25, 50 and 75% duration along the Hernád river

the steeper slope upstream of Tiszabő. It will be noted that the rates of bed load transport at discharges of 50 to 75% duration are not excessive even at Tiszabő. The rate of bed load transport at Szeged is influenced evidently by the bed load discharged by the Maros river.

Bed load transport at discharges of identical percentage duration is shown in *Fig. 2.1.3 — 16* along the Hernád river. Whereas the rates of transport at the two upstream stations are almost identical, at Gesztely the measurements have shown bed load to be transported at a substantially higher rate in the Hernád. The variations observable in this river would be very difficult to explain. Since bed load transport in the Hernád is influenced by dams, any variation therein could reliably be determined only from data of a considerably higher number of stations.

Since data on bed load transport in the Rába river have been observed at two stations only, no attempt has been made at a graphical comparison based on stages and discharges of identical duration.

From the foregoing investigations we may conclude that variations in bed load transport along a river are examined preferably with the help of relations based on mean velocities. The results obtained thus far demonstrate that the role of particle sizes is also important in the variation of bed load transport rates. Future research should thus be concentrated on further elucidating the influence of particle sizes.

The rather questionable reliability of methods and devices used for measuring bed load transport rates obviously affects the results of investigations completed so far. It would therefore be misleading to assume that a complete understanding of the problem has been achieved, although research has succeeded in establishing

519

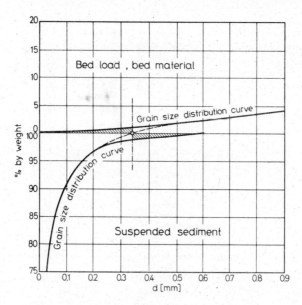

Fig. 2.1.3—17. The limit particle size between suspended sediment and bed load in the Rattendorf gaging section on the Gail river. After Kresser

several relations concerning bed load transport. Extensive measurements in the field and theoretical studies on bed load transport in alluvial streams are still needed before the hydraulic factors of a river can be separated from the influence of other properties and determined individually.

It would be of great practical advantage if the limit particle size separating bed load from the suspended sediment were known for particular rivers or, at least, for several cross-sections on the same river.

Based on investigations in the United States and in Italy the limit particle size has been estimated at 0.35 mm by Gallo and Rotundi.

Kresser is of the opinion that the limit particle size is controlled by the combination of hydrological and hydraulic properties of streams. Theoretically the limit particle size would be defined by the diameter of the largest sediment particles maintained in suspension or, conversely, by the diameter of the smallest particles contained in the bed load. In other words the percentage by weight of the limit particle size approaches theoretically zero in both the suspended sediment and the bed load. Considering the granulometry of bed load and suspended sediment it should be obvious that actually no such limit size exists since, regardless of the particle size adopted at the limit value, certain amounts thereof would occur in the bed load and the suspended sediment alike.

Considering the lower part of the granulometric curve of bed load or bed material, and the upper part of the curve representing the suspended sediment in the case shown in *Fig. 2.1.3—17*, the fractions smaller than 0.2 mm are negligible in the bed load, while the fractions larger than 0.5 mm are similarly small

Fig. 2.1.3.—18. Determination of the limit particle size between suspended sediment and bed load, based on the $Fr = v^2/gd = 360$ value for several rivers in Europe. After Kresser

in the suspended sediment. Kresser assumes the limit particle size to be somewhere between these to values. Connecting the two grain size distribution curves by a smooth curve (indicated by the dashed line in the figure) the intercept at 0.34 mm is regarded the limit particle size. A further assumption introduced by Kresser is that the criterion for deciding whether a particle of diameter d is transported in suspension or as bed load is the magnitude of the sediment Froude number $Fr = v^2/gd$.

In a log-log plot of diameter d versus mean velocity v, each $Fr = $ constant value is represented by a straight line inclined at 2 : 1 as shown in *Fig. 2.1.3—18*.

Kresser has used the limit particle sizes determined from the grain size distribution curve as described above in plotting the corresponding pairs of v and d values for four rivers. It is remarkable to note that the points plotted coincide with the $Fr = 360$ line with great accuracy. Consequently inasmuch as the mean velocity in a particular cross-section is known, the limit particle size between bed load and suspended sediment is obtainable from the relation

$$\frac{v^2}{gd} = 360 \qquad (2.1.3-21)$$

or with the help of the straight line $Fr = 360$ indicated in *Fig. 2.1.3—18* by a dash-dotted line. Observations made on a number of streams in Europe have demonstrated Eq. (2.1.3—21) to be valid.

2.1.4. EMPIRICAL RELATIONS FOR TRANSPORT OF SUSPENDED SEDIMENT

Suspended-sediment transport is controlled primarily by turbulent conductivity, as well as by particle diameter and specific gravity, or in general by the fall velocity of sediment material. The theoretical process is modified by hydrological factors in keeping with the properties of a particular stream without, however, contradicting the fundamental laws governing the mechanics of fluids.

In empirical relations it is customary to express sediment concentration or the weight of sediment transported in suspension with the help of the hydraulic factors prevailing in a water course, primarily in terms of flow velocity v, discharge Q and slope S. In alluvial streams v, Q and S being closely related to stages h, it is readily understandable that stages are often involved in empirical relations on suspended sediment transport.

The principle common to all such empirical relations is that higher velocities, greater discharges, steeper slopes or higher stages are invariably accompanied by higher rates of sediment transport. This experience gained from measurements and observations in the field has led to the conclusion that the sediment-transporting capacity of the stream increases simultaneously with increasing v, Q, S and h values. Consequently for practical purposes suspended-sediment transport in streams is described preferably with the help of the sediment-transporting capacity.

It should be noted that even if we could reliably compute the sediment-transporting capacity, this would only yield the amount of sediment transported under conditions of saturation. Alluvial streams are known, however, to transport in general less sediment than the saturation value. In this way the relations derived in terms of the sediment-transporting capacity from actually measured data on suspended sediment are indeed applicable exclusively to the particular water course. This is because the sediment transport rates actually observed include various hydrological properties of the stream.

Regardless of this consideration it is deemed advisable to include the sediment-transporting capacity as well in examining empirical relations.

Denoting the bulk density of the water sediment mixture by γ_z, its discharge by Q_z, its velocity by v and if the fall of the energy grade line is h_v over a distance L, i.e. $S = h_v/L$, then the total work performed in unit time by the stream over a distance L is

$$\gamma_z Q_z h_v = \gamma_z Q_z SL \qquad (2.1.4-1)$$

If the suspended sediment of γ_1 specific gravity and ω fall velocity is transported at the rate Q_s, then the work needed in unit time for maintaining it in suspension over a distance L is

$$(\gamma_1 - \gamma)Q_s \omega \frac{L}{v} \qquad (2.1.4-2)$$

The work in unit time expressed by Eq. (2.1.4−2) can be interpreted in two different ways. On the one hand, it can be assumed to represent the share of the total energy expended for maintaining the particles in suspension yet, on the other hand, it can be regarded to equal the part of the total energy consumed by turbulent pulsation, since the particles are maintained in suspension by turbulent mixing. In deriving empirical relations, this theoretical distinction is, of course, of no significance.

By relating the work performed in unit time for keeping the sediment in suspension to the total energy consumed in unit time by the sediment water mixture, i.e. by forming the ratio

$$\eta = \frac{(\gamma_1 - \gamma)Q_s \omega L}{\gamma_z Q_z h_v v} = \frac{\gamma_1 - \gamma}{\gamma_z} \frac{\omega}{vS} \frac{Q_s}{Q_z} \qquad (2.1.4-3)$$

the measure of sediment-transporting capacity is essentially obtained.

Since the rates at which the solid particles and the sediment water mixture are transported are Q_s and Q_z, respectively, the ratio of the two represents the volumetric sediment concentration C_T. Introducing thus the volumetric concentration as

$$\frac{Q_s}{Q_z} = C_T \qquad (2.1.4-4)$$

the sediment-transporting capacity becomes

$$\eta = \frac{\gamma_1 - \gamma}{\gamma_z} \frac{\omega}{v} \frac{C_T}{S} \qquad (2.1.4-5)$$

The specific gravity γ_z of the sediment water mixture may be assumed approximately to equal the specific gravity of clear water, bearing in mind the relatively low sediment concentrations in alluvial streams. The sediment-transporting capacity is then

$$\eta = \frac{\gamma_1 - \gamma}{\gamma} \frac{\omega}{v} \frac{C_T}{S} \qquad (2.1.4-6)$$

The above expression of the sediment-transporting capacity is in every respect identical with Eq. (1.3.10−9) which will be recalled to represent the portion of the total head loss needed for transporting the slurry of C_T concentration.

By introducing the concentration C (kp/m^3) generally accepted in engineering practice, and since, according to Eq. (1.3.2−7),

$$C_T = \frac{C}{\gamma_1}$$

523

the sediment-transporting capacity is obtained with the substitution $(\gamma_1 - \gamma)/\gamma = \rho'$ in the form

$$\eta = \rho' \frac{\omega}{v} \frac{C}{\gamma_1 S} = \rho' \frac{\omega C/\gamma_1}{vS} \qquad (2.1.4-7)$$

In the light of knowledge gained so far it is possible to give a physical interpretation to Eqs (2.1.4--6) and (2.1.4-7).

The term vS is a measure of the total energy loss suffered by the fluid of unit weight in unit time.

The term ωC represents the weight of sediment settling in unit time under the action of gravity over a horizontal plane of unit area. Consequently, the term $\omega C/\gamma_1$ is proportionate to the work needed in unit time for keeping in suspension, against the gravity force, the sediment volume contained in unit weight of fluid (assuming $\gamma_z \cong \gamma$).

The ratio of $\omega C/\gamma_1$ and vS is thus actually a measure of the sediment-transporting capacity.

S. Bruk and V. Miloradov have demonstrated that with simplifying assumptions permissible in the case of high Re numbers, the term under Eq. (2.1.4-6) may be considered as identical with the Richardson number Ri.

In his theoretical studies on suspended sediment transport Barenblatt has demonstrated the dimensionless expression of K, given by Eq. (1.3.6-50), to be analogous with the Richardson number. Starting from the fundamental equations of Barenblatt, S. Bruk and V. Miloradov have derived in detail the analogy of the two numbers.

Another potential approach to determining the sediment-transporting capacity is based on the fundamental equations involved in the gravitational theory of Velikanov. If the work needed in unit time for keeping the sediment in suspension — Eq. (1.3.5-29) — is divided by the work performed by the fluid phase due to slope S — Eq. (1.3.5-19) —, then

$$\eta = \frac{(\rho_1 - \rho) g\omega C_v(1 - C_v)}{\rho g S(1 - C_v)v} \qquad (2.1.4-8)$$

and, assuming that $C_v \ll 1$, which is generally permissible in alluvial streams,

$$\eta_V = \frac{(\rho_1 - \rho) g}{\rho g} \frac{\omega}{v} \frac{C_v}{S} \qquad (2.1.4-9)$$

which is essentially identical with Eq. (2.1.4-6).

Reviewing the considerations made in the foregoing in connection with the sediment-transporting capacity, it should become evident that a similar ratio is conceivable in each of the theories on the movement of suspended sediment.

524

With the slope S obtained from the Chézy formula Bruk has derived the formula

$$\eta = \rho' \frac{\omega C/\gamma_1}{v(v^2/c^2 R)} = \frac{\rho' c^2}{\gamma_1} \frac{\omega C R}{v^3} \qquad (2.1.4-10)$$

for the sediment-transporting capacity

From this expression of the sediment-transporting capacity concentration can be written as

$$C = \eta \frac{\gamma_1}{\rho' c^2} \frac{v^3}{R\omega} \qquad (2.1.4-11)$$

or with the notation $\eta(\gamma_1/\rho'c^2) = \eta_1$,

$$C = \eta_1 \frac{v^3}{R\omega} \qquad (2.1.4-12)$$

where η_1 is naturally not a dimensionless quantity. As will be perceived from the expression, the dimension of η_1 is kp sec^2/m^4, i.e. identical with the dimension of density.

With the notation $K_1 = (\rho'c^2 C/\gamma_1)$ Eq. (2.1.4−11) yields the relation

$$\eta = K_1 \frac{R\omega}{v^3} \qquad (2.1.4-13)$$

which is frequently applied in the empirical relations associated with suspended sediment transport.

K_1 involved in Eq. (2.1.4−13) is not a dimensionless quantity either. In fact, if η is the dimensionless ratio characteristic of sediment-transporting capacity, then the dimension of K_1 is m/sec^2, i.e., identical with the dimension of acceleration.

Since the specific gravities of both sediment and water in natural streams may be taken as constant with a fair degree of approximation, moreover since the changes in the velocity coefficient c of a sediment of given particle size are not substantial either, K_1 is often regarded as a measure of sediment concentration C (kp/m^3).

Although dimensional consistency is frequently neglected in empirical relations, or dimensional consistency is ensured by assigning tentatively appropriate dimensions to the constants, in Eqs (2.1.4−12) and (2.1.4−13) the dimensional character of η_1 and K_1, respectively is of a disturbing effect.

For this very reason it is believed appropriate to clarify the dimensions of individual physical quantities, just as in the case of Eqs (2.1.4−6), (2.1.4−7) and (2.1.4−11).

In *Subsection 1.1.4−2* a method suitable for introducing theoretical relations has been described in connection with the potential dynamic velocities. Remembering the principles outlined there it becomes possible to develop the following theoretical relation for determining the sediment-transporting capacity.

Assuming the specific gravity γ of water to be known, the particle size, shape and specific gravity of a particular sediment material should be characterized by the fall velocity ω and the ratio $\rho' = (\gamma_1 - \gamma)/\gamma$. The flow of water in the field of gravity g should be determined with the help of velocity v and depth D of flow, assuming that for a given set of material properties of water and sediment these represent, to a certain extent, turbulent mixing in the stream as well.

It is assumed consequently that the flow of water carrying suspended sediment of concentraton C (kp/m^3) is governed by the physical quantities

$$g, v, \omega, D, \rho' \qquad (2.1.4-14)$$

The four dimensional quantities and the single dimensionless quantity are preferably combined into the following potential dynamic velocities

$$v, \omega, \sqrt{gD},$$
$$v\rho', \omega\rho', \sqrt{gD\rho'} \qquad (2.1.4-15)$$

From the six potential dynamic velocities given by Eq. (2.1.4−15) it is possible to form −as will be remembered− several independent four-term groups of velocities. Let us select arbitrarily the independent four-term group of velocities

$$v, \omega, \sqrt{gD}, \omega\rho' \qquad (2.1.4-16)$$

from which the three independent dimensionless numbers

$$\frac{v}{\omega}, \frac{1}{\rho'}, \frac{v}{\sqrt{gD}} \qquad (2.1.4-17)$$

are obtained. The phenomenon, namely the movement of suspended sediment C, is uniquely described by these in accordance with the initial conditions.

In a stream transporting sediment of concentration C the weight of sediment transported in unit cross-sectional area and unit time will be Cv (kp/m^2 sec). With the submerged weight thereof the ratio $Cv/(\gamma_1 - \gamma)$ (m/sec) will already become the resultant velocity measuring sediment transport. Dividing this index number by one of the potential dynamic velocities, for instance, by forming the ratio

$$\frac{Cv}{(\gamma_1 - \gamma)} : v = \frac{C}{(\gamma_1 - \gamma)} \qquad (2.1.4-18)$$

the resultant dimensionless parameter is obtained as a measure of sediment transport.

From the foregoing, suspended sediment transport will be seen to be described by the theoretical relation

$$\frac{C}{(\gamma_1 - \gamma)} = F\left(\frac{v}{\omega}, \frac{1}{\rho'}, \frac{v^2}{gD}\right) \qquad (2.1.4-19)$$

526

According to Eq. (2.1.4−19) the sediment concentration C is controlled, apart from the relative difference in specific gravities, by the settling number $B = v/\omega$ as well as by $Fr = v^2/gD$.

The theoretical relation is thus − as expected−in full agreement with Eq. (1.3.10−14) developed in *Section 1.3.10* after Bruk for estimating slurry concentration.

As indicated by the results of experiments made for determining the concentration of slurry in pipes and suspended sediment in alluvial streams, the parameter in Eq. (2.1.4−18) is a function of the product of the three dimensionless numbers mentioned above. Thus

$$\frac{C}{(\gamma_1 - \gamma)} = F\left(\frac{v}{\omega} \cdot \frac{1}{\rho'} \cdot \frac{v^2}{gD}\right) = F\left(\frac{1}{g\rho'} \cdot \frac{v^3}{\omega D}\right) \qquad (2.1.4-20)$$

or multiplying the function F by $(\gamma_1 - \gamma)$

$$C = F_1\left(\gamma \frac{v^3}{g\omega D}\right) \qquad (2.1.4-21)$$

The value of γ having been assumed to be constant, the sediment concentration C will be some function F_1 of the parameter $v^3/g\omega D$.

Experiments made for determining the theoretical relation have yielded the results

$$C\frac{g\omega D}{v^3} = \eta_c \qquad (2.1.4-22)$$

or

$$\frac{C}{\eta_c} = \frac{v^3}{g\omega D} \qquad (2.1.4-23)$$

implying that the concentration C of sediment characterized by the fall velocity incorporating both particle size and specific gravity and transported by flow of velocity v and depth D is proportionate to the parameter $v^3/g\omega D$. The factor of proportionality is η_C (kp/m³), a coefficient having the dimension of concentration.

All empirical relations including the sediment-transporting capacity are based on Eqs (2.1.4−6), (2.1.4−7), (2.1.4−12), (2.1.4−13) and (2.1.4−22), although they incorporate different simplifying assumptions and are written into different forms.

A relation often encountered in the literature is that given by Eq. (2.1.4−12)

$$C = \eta_1 \frac{v^3}{D\omega}$$

where η_1 is often assigned a practically constant value for a particular water course.

527

Fig. 2.1.4—1. Suspended-sediment transport in the Danube, Tisza and Velika Morava rivers, according to the expression of Rossinsky. After Bruk and V. Miloradov

From the results of sediment measurements made under saturation conditions on a number of rivers (Eufrates, Amudarya, Yangtse, Hoangho, etc.) K. I. Rossinsky and I. V. Kuzmin found $\eta_1 = 0.024$.

Having examined the sediment transport relations suggested by several Soviet authors, F. S. Salakhov found that $\eta_1 = 0.0135$ which, in comparison with the value 0.024, implies that the sediment transported in alluvial streams is in general less than that pertaining to saturation concentration.

The boundary condition in sediment transport at which channel erosion is initiated has also been studied by Rossinsky. In this condition which may be regarded as the critical, additional sediment is scoured from the channel owing to the excess energy of flow. For this condition Rossinsky found $\eta_1 = 0.0005$.

From measurements made on the Yugoslav section of the Danube and Tisza, the Velika Morava river and tributaries S. Bruk and V. Miloradov conclude that sediment transport in these rivers is always less than under saturation conditions but is higher than the concentration at which scouring starts. The magnitude of η_1 will be seen from *Fig. 2.1.4—1* to vary between rather wide limits.

Bruk et al. have examined the parameter $\eta_1 = (CD\omega)/v^3$ also as a function of U_*. Besides the variation of η_1 the rather wide difference between the measurements on the Tisza and Danube and those on the Morava and Drina rivers is clearly reflected in *Fig. 2.1.4—2.*

528

Fig. 2.1.4—2. Rossinsky's parameter η_1 vs. the shear velocity. After Bruk

Since the dimension of η_1 is that of density, according to Eq. (2.1.4−11) it may be regarded as the resultant density of sediment of concentration C transported by water flowing at velocity v, depth D and having a specific gravity γ. The properties of sediment are represented by the fall velocity ω and the specific gravity γ_1 incorporated in η_1.

It will be realized that the resultant density γ_1 of the sediment water mixture is necessarily variable even along a particular river owing to the fact that in alluvial streams the sediment concentration C is also variable. This circumstance is clearly reflected by the studies of S. Bruk and V. Miloradov mentioned before. Since, however, the sediment concentration C and in turn the resultant density η_1 depend greatly on the hydrological properties of the water course, the trend and magnitude in variation of both will be comparable along the same water course.

The dimensional coefficient η_1 involved in *Figs 2.1.4−1 and 2.1.4−2* is related, as pointed out before, to the dimensionless η and the coefficient η_C having the dimension of concentration by the expressions

$$\eta_1 = \eta \, \frac{\gamma_1}{\rho' c^2}, \quad \text{or} \quad \eta = \eta_1 \, \frac{\rho' c^2}{\gamma_1} \qquad (2.1.4-24)$$

$$\eta_1 = \frac{\eta_C}{g}, \quad \text{or} \quad \eta_C = \eta_1 g \qquad (2.1.4-25)$$

34

529

Fig. 2.1.4—3. The η vs. U_*/v relationship with v^2/gD as parameter for the Morava river. After Bruk and V. Miloradov

As will be seen from Eqs (2.1.4—24 and 2.1.4—25) both η and η_C are parameters proportionate to the resultant density η_1 of the sediment water mixture and thus their magnitude varies in the same manner as that of the latter.

Of considerable interest is the attempt of Bruk in which the dimensionless η involved in Eqs (2.1.4—6) and (2.1.4—7) has been plotted against U_*/v and v^2/gD. In *Fig. 2.1.4—3* certain ranges of v^2/gD are rather clearly distinguishable. From measurements on the Morava river the energy consumed for transporting the suspended sediment was found to attain occasionally as much as 15% of the total energy. At identical U_*/v values, i.e. under identical roughness conditions, the ratio of energy consumption increases with decreasing Froude numbers. In other words, as flow approaches shooting conditions, the work necessary for transporting the suspended sediment decreases.

The close relationship existing between the parameters characterizing suspended-sediment transport is reflected by *Fig. 2.1.4—4* where concentration C is plotted after Bruk et al. against thes ettling number ω/v for different values of the shear velocity Froude number, U_*^2/gD. The relation plotted in the figure lends itself for estimating sediment concentration C only in the case of very fine particles, i.e. at very low flow velocities.

Using the results of measurements made in the Dunaalmás cross-section on the Danube river, the sediment-transporting capacity η has been plotted against

Fig. 2.1.4—4. Sediment concentration C vs. settling number ω/v with U_*^2/gD as parameter, on the basis of measurements on the Morava river. After Bruk and V. Miloradov

J_*/v in *Fig. 2.1.4—5*, in terms of the parameter v^2/gD. The relationship existing between the three variables is seen to be rather close but, in contrast with *Fig. 2.1.4.—3*, at Dunaalmás an increase in v^2/gD is seen to be accompanied by an increase in the value of η. The conclusion arrived at in connection with the Morava river, namely that the share of energy consumption increases with decreasing Froude numbers, is thus not supported by this figure. Moreover, from the figure will also be perceived that energy consumption in the Dunaalmás cross-section of the Danube river attains or somewhat exceeds 0.15% only.

Besides η and U_*/v, the stages on the Dunaalmás gage have been entered as the third parameter in *Fig. 2.1.4—6*. In agreement with the results of field observations the rate of sediment transport is seen in the figure to increase with rising stages. It will be perceived further that, although higher stages are accompanied by higher rates of sediment transport, there is a definite decreasing trend the magnitude of the parameter U_*/v representing friction conditions. As to be

y-axis label: $\eta \cdot 10^4 = \left(\dfrac{\partial_1 - \partial}{\partial} \cdot \dfrac{C_T}{S} \cdot \dfrac{v}{3}\right) \cdot 10^4$

Danube at DUNAALMÁS

$(2.3 \cdot 10^{-2})$

$(2.3 \cdot 10^{-2})$

Figures in brackets denote $\dfrac{v^2}{gD}$ values

$(3.1 \cdot 10^{-2})$

$(1.9 \cdot 10^{-2})$

$(1.8 \cdot 10^{-2})$

$(3.1 \cdot 10^{-2})$

$(1.39 \cdot 10^{-2})$

$(1.42 \cdot 10^{-2})$

$(1.38 \cdot 10^{-2})$

$(0.95 \cdot 10^{-2})$

x-axis label: $\dfrac{U_*}{v} \cdot 10^2$

Fig. 2.1.4−5. The η vs. U_*/v relation with v^2/gD as parameter for the Dunaalmás gaging station on the Danube

inferred from *Fig. 2.1.4−6* there is a possibility for determining approximately the rate of suspended sediment transport in terms of the stages h.

This anticipation is confirmed by *Fig. 2.1.4−7* where η has been plotted against U_*/v in terms of stages for the Nagybajcs gaging section on the Danube river.

It is of interest to note that in the Nagybajcs cross-section v^2/gD remains essentially constant regardless of variations in stage, so that no figure similar to *Fig. 2.1.4−5* applying to Dunaalmás could be constructed here.

In *Fig. 2.1.4−8* the sediment-transporting capacity η vs. concentration parameter $v^3/g\omega D$ relation has been plotted in terms of river stage for the Nagybajcs cross-section on the Danube. Owing to the considerable scatter of measurement data it was impossible to determine a positive relationship. Nevertheless, the figure clearly shows that an increase in the sediment-transporting capacity is accompanied by an increase in the parameter measuring sediment concentration

Fig. 2.1.4—6. The η vs. U_*/v relation with stage as parameter for the Dunaalmás gaging station on the Danube

Besides the independent variables selected for characterizing suspended-sediment transport, the mean velocity v actually observed is also involved in *Figs 2.1.4—2 to 2.1.4—8*. Being a resultant quantity the mean velocity v includes the influence of some of the physical quantities neglected in the starting assumptions. Remembering the statements made in connection with Eqs (1.2.6—72) to (1.2.6—74) it appears thus logical to regard v as an essentially "fictitious" independent variable.

Fig. 2.1.4—7. The η vs. U_*/v relation with stage as parameter for the Nagybajcs gaging station on the Danube

The investigations described thus far in connection with suspended-sediment transport in alluvial streams have revealed several inconsistencies. These are believed to be due to the influence of hydrological factors prevailing on the individual rivers and even in different cross-sections of the same river.

Relying on the measurement data of Simons and his co-workers, of Vanoni, Nomicos and Ismail, sediment concentration C has been plotted against $U_*/\sqrt{gd}$ by J. Larras. According to *Fig. 2.1.4—9*

$$C = 200 \left(\frac{U_*}{\sqrt{gd}} \right)^{10} \; [p/m^3] \qquad (2.1.4-26)$$

Larras has derived this relation on the basis of laboratory measurements so that its use in connection with alluvial streams appears to be unwarranted.

Ning Chien has checked the magnitude of $z = \omega/\kappa U_*$ involved in his Eq. (1.3.4—50) expressing the variation of sediment concentration with depth against the results of both laboratory and field measurements. As will be perceived from

534

Fig. 2.1.4—8. The η vs. $v^3/g\omega D$ relation with stage as parameter for the Nagybajcs gaging station on the Danube

Fig. 2.1.4 — 10 the magnitude of the exponent z_1 obtained from the measurement results is in agreement with the theoretical z values only as long as these values are very small. According to the data actually observed lower z_1 values pertain to high theoretical values of z, indicating that the actual distribution of sediment concentration over depth is more uniform than that assumed in the theory.

Concerning further studies into the exponent z_1 reference is made to the papers listed in the attached bibliography.

S. Bruk and V. Miloradov have attempted to relate the value of $C\omega$ (p/m² sec) i.e. the weight of suspended sediment settling under the action of gravity in unit time over unit horizontal area to the mean velocity of flow v in the cross-section. From *Fig. 2.1.4 — 11* the measurement data obtained on the Velika Morava river will be seen to define a rather close relationship. The data relating to the Yuzhna Morava river appear, however, to define a different relationship indicating again

Fig. 2.1.4−9. Sediment concentration C vs. $U_*/\sqrt{gd}$ according to diverse experimental data. After Larras

Fig. 2.1.4—10. $z = \omega/\kappa U_*$ vs. z_1 values actually observed, according to Ning Chien

Fig. 2.1.4—11. Mean velocity v vs. ωC according to measurements on the Morava river. After V. Miloradov

Fig. 2.1.4—12. Sediment concentration vs. discharge for gaging stations on the Danube

the advisability of determining relations of similar character for each water course individually.

Figs 2.1.4 —6 and *2.1.4—7* should be regarded as positive demonstrations of the fact that suspended-sediment transport should be investigated individually for each particular river and even in different cross-sections on the same river and of the advisability of relating it to stages or to discharges or flow velocities, these being in close hydraulic relationship with stages in the river. This approach has been adopted for studying the movement of suspended sediment in the rivers of Hungary.

The relationships between sediment concentration and stage, discharge and mean velocity, derived for various gaging sections on Hungarian rivers will be discussed extensively in *Section 3.1.2.*

Interesting conclusion on sediment transport in alluvial streams can be drawn by extending investigations, beyond the study of relations of individual cross-sections, to the comparison of relations applying to different gaging sections on the same river. Similar comparative studies have been made on the Danube, Tisza, Hernád, and Rába rivers. The rivers and gaging stations included in the study are shown in *Fig. 3.1.2—3.*

The relations established for gaging sections on the Danube will be compared first.

However desirable it would appear to compare the relations based on river stages, a comparison of this kind is made impossible by differences in stage variations in the individual cross-sections, as pointed out already in connection

538

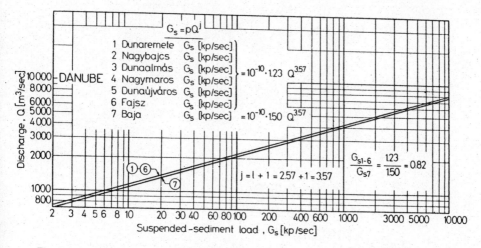

Fig. 2.1.4—13. Suspended-sediment transport vs. discharge for gaging stations on the Danube

with the study of bed load transport along the rivers. For this reason no attempt has been made to compare relations based on river stages.

Considering river regimes and hydraulic factors it should be evident that most reliable results are to be expected by comparing the relations based on discharge Q, this being unaffected by local variations in the cross-section. The comparison of relations based on the mean velocity v_k is less informative. This is due primarily to the fact that in the majority of cases C_k is intimately related to sediment supply, this being more closely related to discharge than to the mean velocity. Moreover the mean velocity in individual cross-sections depends, besides discharge, also on the shape and other properties of the cross-section. Nevertheless the comparison of relations based on mean velocity will also prove of interest.

The relations $C_k = dQ^l$ and $G_s = pQ^j$ relating discharge to sediment concentration and to the weight of sediment transported in suspension, respectively, have been determined *on the Danube river* for the gaging stations

> Dunaremete,
> Nagybajcs,
> Dunaalmás,
> Nagymaros,
> Dunaújváros,
> Fajsz and
> Baja.

The comparison of sediment concentration vs. discharge relations for the afore-mentioned seven gaging stations on the Danube will reveal the relation $C_k = F(Q)$ (kp/m³) to be identical for six of the stations proceeding downstream.

$$C_k = \gamma v_k^6$$

1 Dunaremete	$C_k\,[\text{kp/m}^3] = 0.00064$	$v_k^{8.70}$	$\dfrac{C_{k3}}{C_{k7}} = \dfrac{0.082}{0.132} = 0.62$
2 Nagybajcs	$C_k\,[\text{kp/m}^3] = 0.0080$	$v_k^{5.41}$	
3 Dunaalmás	$C_k\,[\text{kp/m}^3] = 0.082$	$v_k^{3.85}$	$\dfrac{C_{k4}}{C_{k7}} = \dfrac{0.082}{0.132} = 0.33$
DANUBE 4 Nagymaros	$C_k\,[\text{kp/m}^3] = 0.0445$	$v_k^{3.85}$	$\dfrac{C_{k5}}{C_{k7}} = \dfrac{0.082}{0.132} = 0.48$
5 Dunaújváros	$C_k\,[\text{kp/m}^3] = 0.0630$	$v_k^{3.85}$	
6 Fajsz	$C_k\,[\text{kp/m}^3] = 0.0660$	$v_k^{3.85}$	$\dfrac{C_{k6}}{C_{k7}} = \dfrac{0.082}{0.132} = 0.50$
7 Baja	$C_k\,[\text{kp/m}^3] = 0.1320$	$v_k^{3.85}$	

Fig. 2.1.4−14. Sediment concentration vs. mean velocity for gaging stations on the Danube

Even the relation applying to the Baja station differs only by a constant from the former. As indicated by *Fig. 2.1.4−12* the rate of change in mean concentration with Q is the same for all stations, while at six stations the same sediment concentration C_k pertains to the same discharge Q. Related to the other six stations, the sediment concentration at Baja pertaining to the same discharge is $1.50/1.23 = 1.22$ times as high.

Of course, the sediment load transported in unit time in suspension is related to discharge in a manner similar to the relations of sediment concentration and discharge. Since $G_s = C_k Q$, concerning the two kinds of relations, the exponents must necessarily satisfy the condition $j = (l + 1)$. From *Fig. 2.1.4−13* it will be seen that $j = 3.57$ so that it should be clear that the scattered points at individual stations have been correlated correctly and no error has been introduced into the computations.

Considering *Fig. 2.1.4−13* it will be seen that, similarly to sediment concentrations, the weight of suspended sediment G_s varies with discharge at the same rate for all stations on the Danube, moreover that at six stations the same weight of suspended sediment pertains to the same discharge. In view of $G_s = C_k Q$, the ratio of sediment weights is the same as the ratio of concentrations. Consequently, at Baja the weight of sediment G_s transported by the same discharge is 1.22 times as great as that at the other six stations.

The circumstance that, concerning the entire Hungarian section of the Danube, the concentration and suspended-sediment load pertaining to the same discharge

$$G_s = \alpha \, v_k^\beta$$

1 Dunaremete	$G_s \, [\text{kp/sec}] = 0.56 \, v_k^{9.1}$		
2 Nagybajcs	$G_s \, \text{kp/sec} = 8.2 \, v_k^{7.6}$	$\dfrac{G_{s3}}{G_{s7}} = 0.42$	$\dfrac{G_{s4}}{G_{s7}} = 0.19$
3 Dunaalmás	$G_s \, \text{kp/sec} = 237 \, v_k^{6.25}$		
DANUBE 4 Nagymaros	$G_s \, \text{kp/sec} = 108 \, v_k^{6.25}$	$\dfrac{G_{s5}}{G_{s7}} = 0.28$	$\dfrac{G_{s5}}{G_{s7}} = 0.35$
5 Dunaújváros	$G_s \, \text{kp/sec} = 160 \, v_k^{6.25}$		
6 Fajsz	$G_s \, \text{kp/sec} = 200 \, v_k^{6.25}$		
7 Baja	$G_s \, \text{kp/sec} = 570 \, v_k^{6.25}$		

Fig. 2.1.4—15. Suspended-sediment transport vs. mean velocity for gaging stations on the Danube

at Baja is greater than at the other stations is probably due to the influence of the Sió canal. The catchment area drained by the Sió canal is, in fact, different in character from the catchment of the upper Danube and so a different type of sediment is introduced into the Danube.

From the relationships existing between sediment concentrations and sediment load, on the one hand, and the discharge, on the other, it appears now safe to conclude that both C_k and G_s change at the same rate at all stations along the Hungarian reach of the Danube. Neglecting, moreover, the coefficient 1.22 as one which does not differ essentially from unity, it may even be stated that over the full length of the Hungarian section of the Danube the same sediment concentration and, of course, the same weight of suspended sediment pertains to the same discharge Q.

Owing to the tributaries Dráva, Tisza and Száva or to the catchment areas drained by these rivers, the relations between sediment concentration, sediment load and discharge may be expected to undergo changes downstream of the Dráva river in comparison to those applying to the Hungarian section.

Consider hereafter the relation of sediment concentration and sediment load to mean flow velocity over the Hungarian section of the Danube. The relations determined from results observed at the individual gaging stations have been plotted in *Figs 2.1.4—14* and *2.1.4—15.*

$$\frac{C_{k1}}{C_{k6}} = \frac{4.86}{2.24} = 2.17 \qquad \frac{C_{k1}^*}{C_{k6}^*} = \sim \frac{2.42}{1.06} = 2.30$$

$$\frac{C_{k2}}{C_{k6}} = \frac{3.10}{2.24} = 1.38 \qquad \frac{C_{k2}^*}{C_{k6}^*} = \frac{1.55}{1.06} = 1.46$$

$$\frac{C_{k3}}{C_{k6}} = \frac{3.04}{2.24} = 1.36 \qquad \frac{C_{k3}^*}{C_{k6}^*} = \frac{1.35}{1.06} = 1.27$$

$$\frac{C_{k4}}{C_{k6}} = \frac{2.64}{2.24} = 1.18 \qquad \frac{C_{k4}^*}{C_{k6}^*} = \sim \frac{1.18}{1.06} = 1.12$$

$$\frac{C_{k5}}{C_{k6}} = \frac{2.60}{2.24} = 1.16 \qquad \frac{C_{k5}^*}{C_{k6}^*} = \sim \frac{1.15}{1.06} = 1.09$$

$$C_k = dQ^l$$

Before impoundment at Tiszalök | After impoundment at Tiszalök

1 Záhony $C_k [kp/m^3] = 10^{-5} \cdot 4.86 \, Q^{144}$
2 Tiszalök $C_k [kp/m^3] = 10^{-5} \cdot 3.10 \, Q^{144}$ 2* $C_k^* = 10^{-5} \cdot 1.55 \, Q^{144}$
3 Polgár $C_k [kp/m^3] = 10^{-5} \cdot 3.04 \, Q^{144}$ 3* $C_k^* = 10^{-5} \cdot 1.35 \, Q^{144}$
4 Tiszabö $C_k [kp/m^3] = 10^{-5} \cdot 2.64 \, Q^{144}$
5 Tápé $C_k [kp/m^3] = 10^{-5} \cdot 2.60 \, Q^{144}$
6 Szeged $C_k [kp/m^3] = 10^{-5} \cdot 2.24 \, Q^{144}$ 6* $C_k^* = 10^{-5} \cdot 1.06 \, Q^{144}$

TISZA

Fig. 2.1.4—16. Sediment concentration vs. discharge for gaging stations on the Tisza river

As to be seen from *Fig. 2.1.4 – 14*, except for Dunaremete and Nagybajcs, sediment concentration at the remaining five stations changes at the same rate with mean velocity since in the equation $C_k = \gamma v_k^\delta$ the exponent is of the same magnitude. At Dunaremete and at Nagybajcs the rate at which concentration changes with flow velocity differs drastically from the former. Examining the relations applying to the individual stations, it will be appreciated that up to the highest mean velocity of 2 to 2.5 m/sec occurring in the Danube the same sediment concentration is carried at gradually lower mean velocities proceeding downstream along the river. The Dunaalmás station appears to be an exception to this rule, where the mean velocity pertaining to the same concentration is lower than at Dunaremete and Nagybajcs and even lower than that at Nagymaros, Dunaújváros and Fajsz.

542

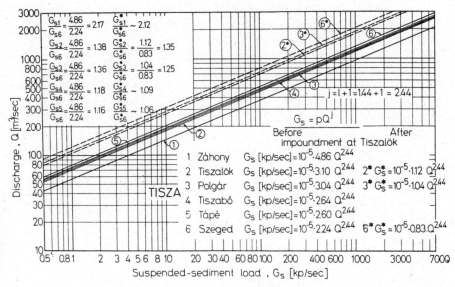

Fig. 2.1.4.—17. Suspended-sediment transport vs. discharge for gaging stations on the Tisza river

The relationship between the suspended-sediment load and mean velocity is shown in *Fig. 2.1.4 — 15* for the seven stations on the Danube. Here again, with the exception of the stations Dunaremete and Nagybajcs, the weight of sediment transported in suspension at the remaining five stations varies at the same rate with mean velocity, indicating that in the relations $G_s = \alpha v_k^\beta$ the exponent of mean velocity is identical at the five station. In the relations applying to Dunaremete and Nagybajcs the exponent assumes values other than in the other relations, though the difference is appreciably smaller than in the case of concentration.

As in the case of sediment concentration, it is of interest to note here again that proceeding downstream the same sediment load is carried by successively lower mean velocities. Of course, an outstanding value is observed here again at Dunaalmás, where the mean velocity necessary for transporting a particular weight of sediment is lower than the mean velocities at Dunaremete and Nagybajcs and even lower than those at Nagymaros, Dunaújváros and Fajsz. It would be very difficult to offer an explanation for this phenomenon.

From the general relationship that proceeding downstream successively lower mean velocities pertain to the same C_k or G_s values, important conclusions have been derived in *Section 2.1.2.* The most important of these was that suspended sediment transport in the Danube is not controlled by the hydraulic factors of the river, and that sediment concentration and the sediment load transported in suspension increases in general according to a symptomatic relation with discharge and flow velocity.

543

On the Danube the measurements after 1953 have revealed no changes over earlier periods, so that the relations given here are identical with those constructed on the basis of observations made before 1954.

On the Tisza river sediment conditions underwent considerable changes after the completion of the Tiszalök Barrage. Inasmuch as sediment observations in the period following the construction of the barrage were made at three stations only, namely Tiszalök (formerly Rázonpuszta), Polgár and Szeged, the changes in suspended-sediment transport are preferably studied on the basis of measurements prior to 1954.

Following an approach similar to that adopted on the Danube, the relationships between sediment concentration and suspended-sediment load, on the one hand, and discharges, on the other, have been compared for the Tisza river at the

Záhony
Tiszalök
Polgár
Tiszabő
Tápé and
Szeged

stations. The relations obtained will be seen to be less uniform than on the Danube, although both sediment concentration and load vary with discharge at the same rate at all stations, implying that the exponents are identical at all stations. In the function representing sediment load the exponent of Q being $j = 2.44$ and in the equation applying to sediment concentrations $l = 1.44$, the criterion $j = (l + 1)$ is again satisfied. As revealed by *Figs 2.1.4 – 16* and *2.1.4 – 17*, successively lower concentrations and weights of sediment pertain to the same discharge Q at stations situated downstream of each other on the Tisza river. On the Danube, it will be recalled, the same C_k and G_s values pertain at all stations except for Baja to the same value of Q. At Baja, on the other hand, higher concentrations and sediment load pertain to the same Q value than at the six upstream stations. This circumstance alone is insufficient to conclude whether sediment concentration and sediment load actually decrease downstream along the river. A comparison of this type will be shown to be possible exclusively for discharges of identical duration.

On the Tisza river the exponent of discharge Q in the expression of sediment concentration is $l = 1.44$, which is essentially smaller than on the Danube, where this value is $l = 2.57$. In other words, on the Tisza river sediment concentration increases with discharge at an appreciably lower rate than on the Danube and of course, the same applies also to the sediment load carried in suspension. In an attempt to explain this phenomenon it is suggested that the relationship between the concentration and sediment load and discharge – as a symptomatic relation – depends primarily on the regime of individual water courses, depending on the properties of the catchment area drained by them. Consequently the differences in the regimes of the two rivers, as well as in the properties of their respective catchment areas may be offered as an explanation.

544

It is interesting to observe that at Tiszalök and Polgár, as well as at Tiszabő and Tápé concentration and sediment load increase approximately at the same rate with increasing discharges. The rates found at Szeged and especially at Záhony differ drastically from the former and represent the extremes of these relations. The differences observable at the individual stations are believed to reflect primarily the influence of tributaries. Similar influences are observable at the Bodrog and Sajó rivers, but especially downstream of the Maros river. The explanation lies again in the different character of catchment areas drained by the individual tributaries.

The ratio of concentrations and suspended-sediment load transported by a particular discharge Q at stations is determined for the Tisza river as well.

Both concentrations and sediment load will be related to the values applying to the station farthest downstream, namely to the Szeged station.

The ratio of sediment concentrations pertaining to the same discharge at Záhony and at Szeged is $4.86/2.24 = 2.17$, meaning that at the same Q the sediment concentration at Záhony is 2.17 times that at Szeged.

Since the ratio of sediment weights is identical with the ratio of sediment concentrations, it is sufficient to calculate a single set of ratio numbers.

The sequence of ratios obtained is as follows:

Záhony : Szeged	2.17
Tiszalök : Szeged	1.38
Polgár : Szeged	1.36
Tiszabő : Szeged	1.18
Tápé : Szeged	1.16

The ratios which decrease gradually from Záhony to Tápé are rather high and lead to the false conclusion that at Záhony, for instance, the weight of sus-pended sediment transported is more than twice that at Szeged. Any mistake is readily avoided by considering that these ratios apply to the same discharges.

Concerning the relation of mean velocity to sediment concentration and sedi-ment load on the Danube it was found that except for Dunaalmás v_k values gradually decreasing downstream pertain to the same C_k and G_s values. The differences become especially great when related to the Dunaremete and Nagy-bajcs stations. It has been pointed out also that except for Dunaremete and Nagy-bajcs sediment concentration and sediment load vary at all stations on the Dan-ube at the same rate with mean velocity, which is an indication of relatively uniform channel development on the Danube.

Considering all stations on the Tisza river, no similar uniformity is observable in the relationships between mean velocity and sediment concentration as well as sediment load.

Considering sediment concentration with reference to *Fig. 2.1.4 – 18*, the ex-ponents of mean velocity will be seen to be identical at Tiszabő and at Tápé, but to depart from the exponents determined for the remaining stations. Considering

$$C_k = \delta V_k^{\delta}$$

		Before impoundment	After at Tiszalök
1	Záhony	$C_k [kp/m^3] = 1.5 \ V_k^{4.07}$	
2	Tiszalök	$C_k [kp/m^3] = 1.36 \ V_k^{4.07}$	
3	Polgár	$C_k [kp/m^3] = 4.35 \ V_k^{4.07}$	$3^* \ C_k^* = 0.49 \ V_k^{4.07}$
4	Tiszabó	$C_k [kp/m^3] = 0.37 \ V_k^{2.30}$	
5	Tápé	$C_k [kp/m^3] = 0.57 \ V_k^{2.30}$	
6	Szeged	$C_k [kp/m^3] = 0.91 \ V_k^{4.07}$	

$$\frac{C_{k1}}{C_{k6}} = 1.65 \qquad \frac{C_{k2}}{C_{k6}} = 1.49 \qquad \frac{C_{k3}}{C_{k6}} = 4.79 \qquad \frac{C_{k4}}{C_{k5}} = 0.65$$

Fig. 2.1.4—18. Sediment concentration vs. mean velocity for gaging stations on the Tisza river

sediment weights *(Fig. 2.1.4—19)* the variaton in the exponent of mean velocity is even greater. In the trend of these differences the influence of tributaries is strongly felt. The influence of river regime and the shape of cross-section at the individual stations is also important. In fact, at any particular discharge Q the mean velocity v_k is controlled by the shape of the cross-section.

It is eventually concluded for the Tisza river as well that suspended-sediment transport depends to a highly variable extent on the mean velocity of flow. The circumstance that an increase in v_k is accompanied by an increase in C_k and G_s alike, just as in the case of the Danube, can be attributed to the existence of symptomatic relations.

As mentioned before, in the period following the construction of the Tiszalök Barrage, measurements were made at Tiszalök, Polgár and Szeged only. From the results of these measurements conclusions can be drawn on the changes in sediment transport caused by the operation of the barrage. The new relations (marked by an asterisk) are entered with a dashed line in *Figs 2.1.4—16* and *2.1.4—17.* At each station the C_k and G_s values pertaining to the same discharge are seen to have decreased as expected under the influence of the barrage. In other words, the amount of suspended sediment transported in the Tisza river has diminished since the construction of the barrage. The ratios of the coefficients d and p characteristic of conditions after impoundment have been determined

546

Fig. 2.1.4—19. Suspended-sediment transport vs. mean velocity for gaging stations on the Tisza river

for Záhony, Tiszabő and Tápé under the approximate assumption that at these stations the ratios of the coefficients involved in the original relations (determined before 1954) apply also to the new d and p values.

It should be noted that the measurements performed after the construction of the barrage revealed no difference in the relationships between mean velocity and sediment concentration and sediment load at Tiszalök and Szeged, a departure being observable at Polgár only. The new relation obtained for Polgár has been entered into *Figs 2.1.4—18* and *2.1.4—19* with a dashed line. Extensive hydrological studies would be required to explain why a difference in the C_k and G_s versus v_k relations is observable at Polgár only.

The results of observations at three stations on the Hernád river after 1953 show no changes to have occurred in the sediment versus discharge relations determined before 1954. At Hidasnémeti, on the other hand, frequent changes in the channel and the formation of sand bars have affected considerably the relations based on velocities and even stages.

Subsequent investigations will be founded on results obtained before 1954.

On the Hernád river sediment concentration and sediment load versus discharge relations have been determined for the

Hidasnémeti,
Pere and
Gesztely

stations. A comparison of these will show the relations applying to the individual station to be largely the same. As to be seen from *Figs 2.1.4—20* and *2.1.4—21* the rate of change in both sediment concentration and sediment load at each of

35*

Fig. 2.1.4—20. Sediment concentration vs. discharge for gaging stations on the Hernád river

Fig. 2.1.4—21. Suspended-sediment transport vs. discharge for gaging stations on the Hernád river

the three stations is identical with discharge, indicating that the exponents are the same at all stations. The criterion $j = (l + 1) = 1.63 + 1 = 2.63$ applies of course to all three stations on the Hernád as well. As in the case of the Danube, sediment concentration and the weight of sediment in suspension carried at the same discharge decrease gradually downstream along the Hernád river. In this respect the changes in suspended-sediment transport in the Hernád river follow the same trend as along the Danube.

548

Fig. 2.1.4—22. Sediment concentration vs. mean velocity for gaging stations on the Hernád river

Fig. 2.1.4—23. Suspended-sediment transport vs. mean velocity for gaging stations on the Hernád river

Sediment concentrations and loads of suspended sediment at the same discharge in the individual stations have been related to the corresponding values at the Gesztely station and plotted in *Figs 2.1.4—20* and *2.1.4—21*, respectively. The sediment concentration and sediment load versus discharge relations display a remarkable uniformity along the river. In this connection it should be recalled that the individual stations along the Hernád river, on which several dams exist, show very wide differences in bed load transport. It appears safe to conclude therefrom that on alluvial streams influenced by dams, changes in regime conditions often entail but slight changes in suspended-sediment transport.

$$C_k = dQ^l$$

1	Szentgotthárd	$C_k\,[kp/m^3] = 10^{-4}\cdot 1.5$	$Q^{1.84}$
2	Körmend	$C_k\,[kp/m^3] = 10^{-5}\cdot 2.14$	$Q^{2.18}$
3	Sárvár	$C_k\,[kp/m^3] = 10^{-4}\cdot 3.8$	$Q^{1.42}$
4	Árpás	$C_k\,[kp/m^3] = 10^{-3}\cdot 5.2$	$Q^{0.72}$
5	Győr	$C_k\,[kp/m^3] = 10^{-4}\cdot 8.15$	$Q^{1.11}$

Fig. 2.1.4 — 24. Sediment concentration vs. discharge for gaging stations on the Rába river

On the Hernád river the concentration and load versus mean velocity relations show considerable variability, as reflected in *Figs 2.14 — 22* and *2.1.4 — 23*. The variations in the relations based on mean velocities along the water course resemble, in certain respects, those observable on the Tisza river. As pointed out already the differences in the relations based on mean velocities would be extremely difficult to explain. This applies especially to the Hernád river where river canalization has caused the velocities to vary between very wide limits so that the situation is even more involved.

On the Rába river observation data are available for the period before 1954 at the Szentgotthárd, Körmend and Sárvár stations. These results proved insufficient, however, to examine changes in sediment transport along the river. In 1954 observations were started at the Árpás and Győr stations and have been continued since together with those at the three stations mentioned before. The variations in sediment concentration and suspended-sediment load will be examined accordingly at the Szentgotthárd, Körmend, Sárvár, Árpás and Győr stations on the Rába river.

The sediment concentration versus discharge relations at the different stations have been plotted in *Fig. 2.1.4 — 24* and the variations therein are seen to be extremely wide as compared to the relations applying to the Danube, Tisza and Hernád rivers discussed before. Consequently the sediment load versus discharge relations at the individual stations display a similar variability, as reflected by

Fig. 2.1.4—25. Suspended-sediment transport vs. discharge for gaging stations on the Rába river

Fig. 2.1.4—25. The sediment concentration and sediment load versus mean velocity relations at the individual stations show considerable differences comparable to those experienced on the Tisza and Hernád rivers. It is interesting to note that according to *Fig. 2.1.4—26* the sediment concentration C_k versus mean velocity v_k relations at Körmend, Sárvár and Árpás can be described by the same expression. Consequently at these three stations and even at Szentgotthárd the G_s versus v_k relations are similar *(Fig. 2.1.4—27)*.

The relation of sediment concentration and suspended sediment load versus mean velocity at Győr is considerably different from the relations applying to the other stations. This is due obviously to the fact that under the influence of the recipient, namely the Danube, there is a considerably change in velocity conditions. The circumstance that the relation with discharges applying to the Győr station is similar to that at other stations is again in support of the earlier conclusion, namely that regularities in the variation of suspended-sediment transport along a river are preferably examined in relation to discharges.

For determining the relationship existing between the weight of sediment in suspension and the mean velocity of flow extensive studies have been made by G. V. Zheleznyakov, who observed a reduction in sediment transport on water

Fig. 2.1.4—26. Sediment concentration vs. mean velocity for gaging stations on the Rába river

Fig. 2.1.4—27. Suspended-sediment transport vs. mean velocity for gaging stations on the Rába river

courses accompanied by wide flood plains. He attributed this reduction in sediment transport to greater roughness in the flood plains.

Nevertheless, according to the results of these investigations, even sediment transport in the flood plains may be assumed at least, as a first approximation, to be proportionate to the mean velocity. It is noted, however, that before applying the $G_s = G_s(v)$ relation the properties of the flood plain should also be taken into consideration.

The results of considerations on the variation in sediment transport along the Danube, Tisza, Hernád and Rába rivers can be summarized as follows:

The fact that in the individual cross-sections the same sediment concentrations and sediment weights are occasionally observed at the same discharge should not

552

be misunderstood to imply that sediment transport is uniform in each cross-section under the same condition of the river. In order to obtain a better understanding of the variations in suspended sediment transport along a river, the concentrations and weights of sediment pertaining to discharges of identical duration must be introduced. On the Danube, for instance at Dunaremete, the discharge of 1500 m³/sec is of shorter duration than at Baja. The differences are especially significant on the Tisza river the regime of which is substantially more flashy than that of the Danube. The discharge of 500 m³/sec at Záhony is appreciably shorter in duration than at Szeged. The same combination of depth and distribution of precipitation, as well as of various other factors affecting discharge and sediment yield that results at Záhony in a discharge of $Q = 495$ m³/sec corresponding to 25% duration will give rise at Szeged to a discharge of 1118 m³/sec since at Szeged this is the discharge of 25% duration.

In order to illustrate the above statement the concentrations and weights of sediment corresponding to discharges of 25, 50 and 75% duration have been compiled for all stations on the Danube, Tisza, Hernád and Rába rivers, in *Tables 2.1.4 — 1, 2.1.4 — 2, 2.1.4 — 3* and *2.1.4 — 4*, respectively. For the sake of completeness in all four tables the concentrations and sediment load pertaining to stages of 25, 50 and 75% duration have also been entered. The concentrations and sediment load determined according to discharges and stages will be seen to show major differences which should be logical, remembering earlier considerations on the relations between suspended-sediment transport and the hydraulic properties of the water course. These differences are most preferably eliminated by forming the mean of values determined according to stages and discharges. Variations along the water course in t' e mean value of concentrations and sediment load determined on the basis of discharges and stages of 25, 50 and 75% duration have been compiled in *Figs 2.1.4 — 28, 2.1.4 — 29, 2.1.4 — 30* and *2.1.4 — 31* for the Danube, the Tisza, the Hernád and the Rába rivers, respectively. At the Győr station on the Rába the determination of stages and discharges of the same duration have proved impossible owing to backwater effect from the Danube.

From *Fig. 2.1.4 — 28* the sediment concentration pertaining to stages and discharges of the same duration on the Danube will be seen to increase slightly downstream along the river. The increase is somewhat more pronounced when considering the weight of suspended sediment. The rate at which the concentration and sediment load increase downstream generally decreases as the duration figures become higher. The figure reveals a characteristic change in slope at Dunaalmás and at Fajsz. The sudden change at Dunaalmás is due obviously to differences in the character of the Danube sections upstream and downstream from Gönyű. The change at Fajsz is believed to reflect the influence of the Sió canal. In all probability the points where these sudden changes occur should be shifted to the vicinity of Gönyű and the mouth of the Sió canal, respectively. Since no measurement data are available at these points, the actual results have been connected in keeping with general engineering practice.

Sediment concentrations and rates of suspended-sediment transport at stages and discharges
tions valid for the periods

Gaging station	Distance from mouth [km]	Duration, %	Stage, h [cm]	Discharge, Q [m³/sec]	Concentration, C_k [kp/m³] in terms of		
					stage		discharge
					by the relation $C_k = F(h)$ valid		$C_k = F(Q)$
					before 1954	after 1953	
1.	2.	3.	4.	5.	6.	7.	8.
Dunaremete	1,825.5	25	389	1,900	0.052	0.020	0.035
		50	348	1,530	0.028	0.009	0.022
		75	306	1,280	0.013	0.004	0.0098
Nagybajcs	1,801.0	25	366	2,650	0.082	0.043	0.056
		50	286	1,920	0.038	0.020	0.027
		75	223	1,420	0.0175	0.008	0.013
Dunaalmás	1,751.8	25	335	2,900	0.110	—	1.102
		50	273	2,200	0.060	—	0.051
		75	217	1,620	0.029	—	0.026
Nagymaros	1,694.6	25	294	2,940	0.135	0.090	0.092
		50	228	2,200	0.067	0.041	0.045
		75	172	1,620	0.031	0.018	0.021
Dunaújváros	1,580.6	25	365	3,200	0.150	—	0.130
		50	295	2,450	0.079	—	0.067
		75	227	1,800	0.036	—	0.033
Fajsz	1,506.7	25	453	3,360	0.152	—	0.132
		50	349	2,705	0.087	—	0.078
		75	251	2,085	0.048	—	0.041
Baja	1,479.4	25	538	3,460	0.175	—	0.155
		50	435	2,720	0.097	—	0.088
		75	341	2,100	0.053	—	0.048

The surface slope at mean river stage has also been entered into the figure. A remarkable fact is that the pronounced increase in suspended-sediment transport occurs around the change in surface slope at Szap. From this it is also concluded that suspended-sediment transport is controlled primarily by the sediment supply to the river, rather than by the hydraulic conditions prevailing therein.

554

of 25, 50 and 75% duration at several gaging stations on the Danube according to the rela-
before 1954 and after 1953

Rate of suspended-sediment transport, G_s [kp/sec] in terms of			Mean sediment concentration, C_k [kp/m³]		Mean suspended-sediment transport, G_s [kp/sec]	
stage		discharge	by the relations valid			
by the relation $G_s = F(h)$ valid		$G_s = F(Q)$	before 1954	after 1953	before 1954	after 1953
before 1954	after 1953					
9.	10.	11.	12.	13.	14.	15.
90	40	64	0.0435	0.0275	77	52
34	13	29	0.0250	0.0155	31.5	21
12	5	15	0.0114	0.0070	13.5	10
220	80	180	0.0690	0.0495	200	130
73	26	60	0.0325	0.0235	66.5	43
24	9	21	0.0152	0.0127	22.5	15
325	—	285	0.1060	—	305	—
140	—	105	0.555	—	122.5	—
50	—	35	0.0275	—	42.5	—
395	226	298	0.1135	0.0910	346.5	262
135	70	102	0.0560	0.0430	118.5	86
47	28	35	0.0260	0.0195	41.0	31.5
450	—	390	0.1400	—	420	—
175	—	150	0.0730	—	162.5	—
56	—	50	0.0345	—	53.0	—
420	—	420	0.1420	—	420	—
190	—	190	0.0825	—	190	—
78	—	74	0.0445	—	76	—
540	—	530	0.1650	—	535	—
240	—	230	0.0925	—	235	—
105	—	96	0.0505	—	100.5	—

On the Tisza river sediment concentration will be seen from *Fig. 2.1.4—29*
to remain remarkably constant at different durations. The points of changes
reflect also on the Tisza river the influence of the tributaries, namely the Bodrog
and Sajó, but primarily that of the Maros river. Sediment concentration is seen
to be decreased by the Bodrog, whereas to be increased by the Sajó and Maros

Table 2.1.4—2

Sediment concentrations and rates of suspended-sediment transport at stages and discharges of 25, 50 and 75% duration at several gages on the Tisza River

| Gaging station | Distance from mouth [km] | Duration, % | Stage, h [cm] | Discharge, Q [m³/sec] | Sediment concentration [kp/m³] in terms of | | Suspended-sediment transport [kp/sec] in terms of | | Mean sediment concentration [kp/m³] $\frac{6.+7.}{2}$ | Mean suspended-sediment transport [kp/sec] $\frac{8.+9.}{2}$ |
| | | | | | stage, $C_k = F(h)$ | discharge, $C_k = F(Q)$ | stage, $G_s = F(h)$ | discharge, $G_s = F(Q)$ | | |
1.	2.	3.	4.	5.	6.	7.	8.	9.	10.	11.
Záhony	636.721	25	9	495	0.510	0.390	195	191	0.450	193
		50	−106	313	0.237	0.205	60	63	0.221	61.5
		75	−172	198	0.118	0.105	20	20.5	0.1115	20
Tiszalök	523.920	25	106	538	0.305	0.278	165	150	0.2915	157.5
		50	−56	270	0.088	0.105	25	28	0.0965	26.5
		75	−170	120	0.0185	0.0325	2.4	3.8	0.255	3.1
Polgár	491.250	25	168	615	0.435	0.330	230	208	0.3825	219
		50	22	323	0.170	0.135	46	43	0.1525	44.5
		75	−49	193	0.090	0.063	15	12	0.0765	13.5
Tiszabő	369.200	25	320	745	0.420	0.385	252	273	0.4025	262.5
		50	105	420	0.192	0.170	80	70	0.181	75
		75	−17	272	0.096	0.090	28	25	0.093	26.5
Tápé	176.300	25	316	795	0.440	0.400	430	320	0.420	375
		50	116	440	0.190	0.170	97	78	0.180	87.5
		75	0	280	0.094	0.090	28	26	0.092	27
Szeged	170.405	25	316	1,118	0.730	0.560	720	630	0.645	675
		50	116	657	0.305	0.260	180	170	0.2825	175
		75	0	417	0.145	0.138	56	57	0.1415	56.5

Table 2.1.4—3

Sediment concentrations and rates of suspended-sediment transport at stages and discharges of 25, 50 and 75% duration at several gages on the Hernád River

Gaging station	Distance from mouth [km]	Duration, %	Stage, h [cm]	Discharge, Q [m³/sec]	Sediment concentration [kp/m³] in terms of		Suspended-sediment transport [kp/sec] in terms of		Mean sediment concentration [kp/m³] $\frac{6.+7.}{2}$	Mean suspended-sediment transport [kp/sec] $\frac{8.+9.}{2}$
					stage, $C_k = F(h)$	discharge, $C_k = F(Q)$	stage, $G_s = F(h)$	discharge, $G_s = F(Q)$		
1.	2.	3.	4.	5.	6.	7.	8.	9.	10.	11.
Hidasnémeti	83.6	25	37.0	20.0	0.052	0.055	1.20	1.15	0.0535	1.17
		50	6.0	9.5	0.0145	0.0165	0.19	0.16	0.0155	0.17
		75	−8.0	6.5	0.0074	0.0088	0.067	0.06	0.0081	0.063
Pere	61	25	60	26	0.100	0.095	3.6	2.4	0.0975	3.0
		50	34	14	0.032	0.034	0.62	0.5	0.033	0.56
		75	16	8.5	0.010	0.014	0.10	0.13	0.012	0.11
Gesztely	22.4	25	80	31	0.120	0.145	3.5	5.0	0.1325	4.25
		50	50	16	0.056	0.050	1.0	0.85	0.053	0.92
		75	31	9.2	0.030	0.020	0.4	0.22	0.025	0.31

Table 2.1.4—4

Sediment concentrations and rates of suspended-sediment transport at stages and discharges of 25, 50 and 75% duration at several gages on the Rába River

Gaging station	Distance from mouth [km]	Duration, %	Stage, h [cm]	Discharge, Q [m³/sec]	Sediment concentration [kp/m³] in terms of		Suspended-sediment transport [kp/sec] in terms of		Mean sediment concentration [kp/m³] $\frac{6.+7.}{2}$	Mean suspended-sediment transport [kp/sec] $\frac{8.+9.}{2}$
					stage, $C_k = F(h)$	discharge, $C_k = F(Q)$	stage, $G_s = F(h)$	discharge, $G_s = F(Q)$		
1.	2.	3.	4.	5.	6.	7.	8.	9.	10.	11.
Szentgotthárd	181.7	25	10	34	0.110	0.092	3.70	3.50	0.101	3.60
		50	− 12	27	0.057	0.059	1.60	1.80	0.058	1.70
		75	− 29	22	0.032	0.041	0.69	1.07	0.037	0.87
Körmend	147.9	25	60	39	0.160	0.065	5.40	2.20	0.112	3.80
		50	32	28	0.056	0.031	1.20	0.80	0.043	1.00
		75	12	20	0.011	0.015	0.12	0.28	0.013	0.20
Sárvár	84.0	25	− 2	51	0.131	0.095	6.30	5.20	0.113	5.75
		50	− 25	38	0.077	0.064	3.00	2.50	0.070	2.75
		75	− 39	29	0.050	0.043	1.70	1.28	0.046	1.49
Árpás	28.9	25	134	42	0.100	0.075	3.70	3.10	0.088	3.40
		50	101	27	0.065	0.054	1.80	1.40	0.059	1.60
		75	75	15	0.040	0.035	0.75	0.53	0.037	0.64

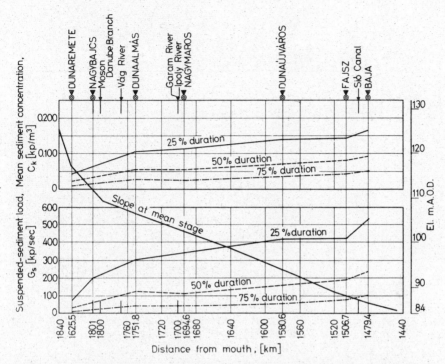

Fig. 2.1.4—28. Variations of mean values of concentration and suspended-sediment transport determined on the basis of 25, 50 and 75% duration stages and discharges on the Danube

rivers. With allowance to the influence of tributaries it would seem more appropriate to shift the points of changes in *Fig. 2.1.4—29* directly to the confluence of tributaries. This solution is indicated in the graph by the thin dashed line.

From *Fig. 2.1.4—29* the sediment load transported in suspension is seen to increase slightly downstream, a more pronounced increase occurring only over the section downstream of the mouth of the Maros river. Sediment concentration and the weight of suspended sediment is apparently unaffected by the gradually diminishing slope of the Tisza.

On the Hernád the concentration of sediment pertaining to stages and discharges of identical duration will be seen to increase in the downstream direction as is the case in the Danube. In *Fig. 2.1.4 —30* the downstream increase is remarkably constant in rate. Changes in concentration are apparently not influenced by the minor water courses feeding the Hernád. Sediment weights vary in a manner almost identical with sediment concentration.

As illustrated in *Fig. 2.1.4—31*, the sediment concentration values pertaining to stages and discharges of the same durations on the Rába river vary irregularly. At durations from 50 to 75% the mean sediment concentration decreases between

559

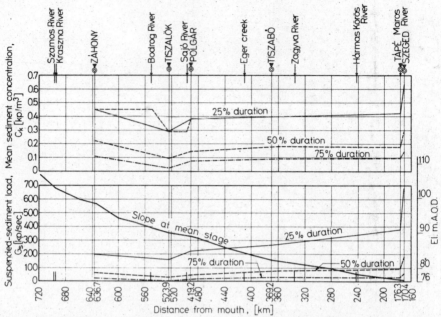

Fig. 2.1.4—29. Variations of mean values of concentration and suspended-sediment transport determined on the basis of 25, 50 and 75% duration stages and discharges on the Tisza river

Szentgotthárd and Körmend, then increases down to Sárvár decreasing again slightly to Árpás. Variations in the weight of suspended sediment resemble those in concentration.

From the studies on the variations in suspended-sediment transport along streams, performed on the Danube, Tisza, Hernád and Rába rivers, the following conclusions of general validity can be arrived at.

In major low-land streams suspended sediment transport is controlled first of all by the rate at which sediment is supplied to the stream. Sediment supply, in turn, is governed by the geology, topography, vegetation cover, as well as by the magnitude and distribution of precipitation in the catchment. Even under identical precipitation conditions, sediment supply is subject to seasonal variations. Suspended-sediment transport has been demonstrated in the foregoing to be influenced also by the tributaries.

The hydraulic propoerties of the stream, which are known to be interrelated, are of but slight influence on suspended-sediment transport. This influence is reflected primarily in the scouring and silting of the channel and the banks. On the Danube the sediment scoured from the river bed contributes little to suspended-sediment transport, so that there is only a slight relationship between suspended-sediment transport and the hydraulic factors. On the Tisza river, on the other hand, which is a well embedded stream this influence is greater but still insignificant in comparison with the total sediment transport.

560

Fig. 2.1.4—30. Variations of mean values of concentration and suspended-sediment transport determined on the basis of 25, 50, 75% duration stages and discharges on the Hernád river

The relationships existing between suspended-sediment transport and the hydraulic factors (stages, discharges and flow velocities) in the river are in general symptomatic in character. In fact, suspended-sediment transport and the hydraulic factors alike depend on the magnitude and distribution of precipitation over the catchment area, on the season, etc.

The existing relations include, of course, direct, deterministic relationships as well between sediment transport and the hydraulic factors. These have been shown, however, to be extremely loose, so that the character of relations is governed by the symptomatic trend. Of course, the quality of relations and the relative importance of the two types of relationships (direct and symptomatic) may vary appreciably for individual rivers. For this reason — as in most alluvial streams — it is best to refrain from drawing any general conclusion on suspended-sediment transport.

For the sake of completeness it should be noted that the weight of sediment transported in suspension can be expressed in certain cases also with the help of slope. These relations are, however, perhaps even less reliable than those based

36

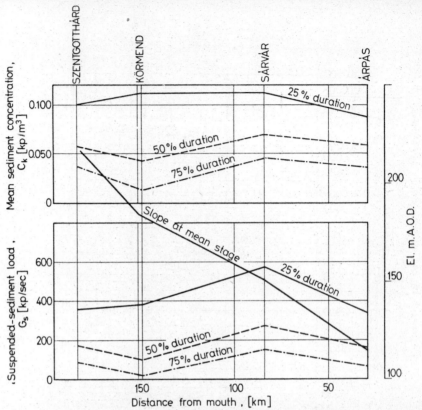

Fig. 2.1.4—31. Variations of mean values of concentration and suspended-sediment transport determined on the basis of 25, 50 and 75% duration stages and discharges on the Rába river

on the velocity of flow. The correctness of this statement will be appreciated by remembering that the mean velocity in a stream is by no means the most important hydraulic factor in suspended-sediment transport and thus the slope is even less significant. The inclusion of mean velocities into considerations may be explained first of all by the circumstance that data on the instantaneous actual velocity and the pulsation components thereof are rarely available, whereas the mean velocity in a stream is found even from the most general hydrographic observations.

Examining the average slope and the weight of the suspended sediment transported daily on the average Lane and Shulits found for different alluvial streams that

$$G_s = 21S^3 \text{ [Mp/day]} \qquad (2.1.4-27)$$

Here the average slope should be introduced in cm/km units.

As indicated by *Fig. 2.1.4—32* the data applying to individual streams scatter over a very wide range about the line representing the equation.

562

Fig. 2.1.4—32. Daily suspended-sediment transport vs. average slope for different streams a computed for 510 m³/sec discharge. After Lane and Shulits

36*

563

In *Fig. 2.1.4−32* the daily figures on suspended sediment load have been related on all streams to 510 m³/sec average discharge. The points numbered from 1 to 15 in the figure represent the original data of Lane and Shulits. The pairs of values numbered 16 to 31 have been entered after Pardé who in his paper quotes the annual average silt transport (in Mp units), the slope (in cm/km units) and the annual mean discharge (in m³/sec units) as corresponding values. Of course, in *Fig. 2.1.4−32* the data of Pardé have also been related to 510 m³/sec average discharge and expressed in Mp/day units. His data (denoted by empty circles in the figure) scatter in a wider range indicating that these are not results of actual sediment observations.

The name and location of water courses corresponding to the numbers in *Fig. 2.1.4−32* are indicated in *Table 2.1.4−5*. An attempt has been made to determine a relationship between the suspended sediment load and the average slope from the results of observations in Hungary and to gain a general expression. However, owing to the considerable scatter of corresponding pairs of values, this effort has remained unsuccessful. For completeness the results of observations in Hungary are shown together with the original data of Lane and Shulits in *Fig. 2.1.4−33*, where the data of Pardé have been omitted. By relating, instead of the sediment load transported daily, the average value of sediment concentration to slope, the reduction to the 510 m³/sec discharge becomes evidently superfluous. By determining from Eq. (2.1.4−27) the relation on sediment concentration, the expression

$$C_k = \frac{21\,000}{86\,400 \cdot 510}\, S^3 = 10^{-3}.\ 0.476 S^3\ [\text{kp/m}^3] \qquad (2.1.4-28)$$

is obtained. Consequently *Fig. 2.1.4−33* is a plot of Eq. (2.1.4−28). The points numbered 1 to 15 represent the streams examined by Lane and Shulits and shown in *Table 2.1.4−5* while the points 16 to 26, indicated by black triangles represent data on the following streams and stations in Hungary:

16.	Danube	Dunaújváros
17.	Danube	Fajsz
18.	Danube	Baja
19.	Tisza	Záhony
20.	Tisza	Tiszalök
21.	Tisza	Polgár
22.	Tisza	Tiszabő
23.	Tisza	Tápé
24.	Tisza	Szeged
25.	Sajó	Kazincbarcika
26.	Hernád	Hidasnémeti

According to *Fig. 2.1.4−33*, the original relation is in close agreement with the data on sediment transport in the Danube and the Tisza. On the other hand, the observation results on the Sajó and Hernád depart widely from Eq. (2.1.4−28).

Table 2.1.4–5

Name and country of water courses mentioned in the relation between daily rates of suspended-sediment transport and average slope

Data of E. W. Lane and S. Shulits

1. *Colorado*	Laguna Dam. Ariz., U.S.A.	9. *Red*	Alexandrea, La., U.S.A.
2. *Tigris*	Amara, Mesopotamia	10. *Rio Grande*	San Marcial, N. Mex., U.S.A.
3. *Missouri*	Kansas City, Mo., U.S.A.	11. *Yangtze*	Hangkow, China
4. *Arkansas*	Ozark, Ark., U.S.A.	12. *Fenho*	Taijuan, China
5. *Mississippi*	Grafton, Ill., U.S.A.	13. *Hwang-ho*	Chikchiava, China
6. *Mississippi*	St. Louis, Mo., U.S.A.	14. *Colorado*	Topock, Ariz., U.S.A.
7. *Mississippi*	Fulton, Tenn., U.S.A.	15. *Yung-tin-ho*	Lukoukian, China
8. *Missouri*	St. Charles, Mo., U.S.A.		

Data of M. Pardé

16. *Isère*	France	23. *Danube*	Budapest, Hungary
17. *Rhone*	Lyon, France	24. *Tisza*	Hungary
18. *Rhone*	Beaucaire, France	25. *Volga*	Kuibyshev, Soviet Union
19. *Garonne*	Toulouse, France	26. *Tigris*	Baghdad, Iraq
20. *Seine*	Paris, France	27. *Irrawady*	India
21. *Rhine*	Germany	28. *Missouri*	U.S.A.
22. *Po*	Piacenza, Italy	29. *Ohio*	U.S.A.
		30. *Upper-Mississippi*	U.S.A.
		31. *Lower-Mississippi*	U.S.A.

565

Fig. 2.1.4—33. Mean sediment concentration vs. slope for different streams

These investigations have thus demonstrated the impossibility of deriving a relationship of general validity between average sediment weights or concentrations and the slope of the stream.

2.1.5. THE RATIO OF SUSPENDED SEDIMENT AND BED LOAD

In the chapters on bed load and suspended-sediment transport alike the relative amount of sediment transported in the two different ways is shown to differ appreciably on the individual streams, yet even on different sections of the same stream.

When relating the relative weights of bed load and suspended sediment on the basis of observation data, widely different ratios are obtained. These ratios are extremely variable even within the same cross-section of a particular river. An observation commonly made on streams is that, whereas on one occasion the ratio of suspended sediment and bed load weights observed is hardly in excess of hundred, on other occasions observations at other stages and discharges in the same cross-section show ratios up to several thousands. In this way the ratios determined from field observation data are unsuited for describing the relative magnitudes of suspended-sediment and bed load transport.

Remembering that the quantities G_B, G_s and C_k describing both bed load and suspended-sediment transport can be expressed, according to experience gained so far, as exponential functions of stages, discharges and flow velocity, it should be evident that the ratio G_s/G_B at particular stations varies with stages, discharges and velocity. The most relevant information on the relative rates of suspended and bed load transport is obtained by relating to each other the fundamental expressions on both bed load and suspended-sediment weights based on stages, discharges or, occasionally, flow velocities. The advantage in this method is that the errors of observations and the deviations due to the inexactitude of functional relations have already been corrected or eliminated in the determination of the fundamental relation permitting the ratios to be determined on the basis of average values.

The equations $G_B = p_1 Q^{j_1}$ and $G_s = pQ^j$ relating the weights of bed load and suspended sediment to discharge, as well as $G_B = \alpha_1 v_k^{\beta_1}$ and $G_s = \alpha v_k^{\beta}$ relating the same to mean velocity have been introduced in *Sections 2.1.3* and *2.1.4*.

The relations based on stage yield also exponential expressions

$$G_B = u_1 h^{g_1}, \text{ or } G_s = uh^g$$

Relating the pairs of corresponding equations to each other, the ratio of sediment weights carried in suspension and of bed load is obtained with the help of the fundamental relations based on stage, discharge and flow velocity, from

Table 2.1.5—1

Values of the coefficients and exponents involved in computing the ratio of suspended-sediment to bed load transport for different gaging stations

River	Gaging station	$\dfrac{u}{u_1}$		$(g - g_1)$		$\dfrac{p}{p_1}$	$(J - J_1)$	$\dfrac{\alpha}{\alpha_1}$	$(\beta - \beta_1)$
Danube	Dunaremete	0.077	0.034*	3.61	3.96*	$3.62 \cdot 10^{-4}$	1.325	32.2	2.43
	Nagybajcs	30,000	16,000*	−2.75	−2.80*	$6.48 \cdot 10^{12}$	−3.100	3,910	−7.80
	Dunaalmás	300		−0.56		$1.76 \cdot 10^{3}$	−0.596	526	−0.42
	Nagymaros	198	110*	0.65	0.60*	$1.76 \cdot 10^{3}$	−0.597	240	−0.42
	Dunaújváros	67.3		1.39		$9.32 \cdot 10^{-3}$	1.325	320	−0.42
	Fajsz[1]	3.12		2.22		$4.66 \cdot 10^{-3}$	1.325	111	−0.42
	Baja[2]	8.80		1.70		$5.23 \cdot 10^{-3}$	1.325	95	−0.42
Rába	Szentgotthárd	650		0.15		$2.00 \cdot 10^{2}$	0.120	1,048	1.01
	Körmend	357		1.24		$1.27 \cdot 10^{2}$	0.600	1,590	1.27
Zala	Zalaapáti	662		1.01		$3.27 \cdot 10$	0.116	70.3	−0.55
Tisza	Polgár[3]	1,236	2,720**	0.004	−1.12**	$8.00 \cdot 10^{3}$	−0.300	1,963	0.68
	Tiszabő[3]	1,905		−0.78		$5.87 \cdot 10^{3}$	−0.300	773	−0.74
	Tápé[3]	7,070		−0.71		$3.25 \cdot 10^{4}$	−0.300	2,800	0.06
	Szeged[3]	646	1,022**	0.29	−0.71**	$1.63 \cdot 10^{4}$	−0.300	2,808	1.58
Sajó	Kazincbarcika	174		1.68		$3.40 \cdot 10$	−0.200	67.2	−0.99
	Miskolc[1]	464		1.18		$9.42 \cdot 10$	−0.060	645	−0.35
Hernád	Hidasnémeti[1]	364		−0.70		$2.47 \cdot 10^{2}$	−0.030	232	−0.27
	Pere	715		0.05		$5.11 \cdot 10^{2}$	−0.030	6.48	0.15
	Gesztely[1]	143		−0.40		$9.26 \cdot 10$	−0.030	0.68	−0.62

River	Gaging station	$\dfrac{u}{u_1}$	$(g - g_1)$	$\dfrac{p}{p_1}$	$(j - j_1)$	$\dfrac{\alpha}{\alpha_1}$	$(\beta - \beta_1)$
Fekete-Körös	Remete[1]	1,690	−1.63	$5.95 \cdot 10$	−0.250	193	−0.70
Sebes-Körös	Körösszakál	14.7	1.81	$1.00 \cdot 10^2$	−0.665	44.4	0.33
Berettyó	Berettyóújfalu	—	—	$2.55 \cdot 10$	0.890	115	−0.48
Maros	Deszk[5]	14.5	0.83	—	—	—	—

Note: At the gages denoted 1 to 4 the stage h_1 is indicated instead of the actual value.

[1] $\left.\begin{array}{l} \\ \\ \\ \end{array}\right\}$ h_1 = actual stage
[2] + 1 m
[3] + 2 m
[4] + 3 m
   + 0.2 m
[5] h_1 = stage at Makó   + 1 m

* With the relations valid after 1953.
** With the relations valid after closing the dam at Tiszalök. The rivers and gages listed in the table are shown in *Fig. 3.1.2–3*.

the following three equations:

$$\frac{G_s}{G_B} = \frac{u}{u_1} h^{(g-g_1)} \tag{2.1.5-1}$$

$$\frac{G_s}{G_B} = \frac{p}{p_1} Q^{(j-j_1)} \tag{2.1.5-2}$$

$$\frac{G_s}{G_B} = \frac{\alpha}{\alpha_1} v_k^{(\beta-\beta_1)} \tag{2.1.5-3}$$

The variation of bed load and suspended-sediment weight with stages, discharge and flow velocity at several stations along rivers in Hungary will be discussed in *Section 3.1.2*. The values of coefficients and exponents necessary for evaluating the ratios given by Eqs (2.1.5−1, 2.1.5−2) and (2.1.5−3) are compiled in *Table 2.1.5−1*.

In connection with *Table 2.1.5−1* it should be noted that the reliable determination of relations based on discharge and flow velocity has proved impossible for some of the stations, and − in contrast to the other stations − at Berettyó-újfalu and Deszk not even the relations based on stage could be determined. Accordingly, *Table 2.1.5−1* is incomplete.

Using the data in *Table 2.1.5−1* the ratios by weight of suspended sediment and bed load can be found for any station at any arbitrary stage, discharge or flow velocity.

Nevertheless, it is possible to arrive at certain general conclusions concerning the ratio of suspended-sediment and bed load transport, even without resorting to computations based on particular stages, discharges and flow velocities. In this respect the ratio of coefficients is of minor importance, these being representative only of the magnitude of the difference between the weights of suspended and bed load at particular stations. On the other hand the magnitude, as well the sign of the difference in exponents are indicative of the changes in the ratio of suspended and bed load weights with increasing or decreasing stages, discharges and flow velocities.

Where the difference in exponents, i.e. the value of $(g - g_1)$, $(j - j_1)$, or $(\beta - \beta_1)$ is *a positive number*, an increase in stage, in discharge or in flow velocity entails invariably an increase in the ratio G_s/G_b. However, depending on whether the positive difference of exponents is greater or smaller than unity, the increase in the ratio G_s/G_b will occur at different rates.

In cases where the difference of exponents is *a positive number greater than unity*, the ratio G_s/G_b increases with increasing stages, discharges or flow velocities at a rate higher than linearly, i.e. suspended-sediment transport increases at a much faster rate than bed load transport. This is the case, for instance, at Dunaremete where suspended-sediment transport increases drastically together with stages, discharges and flow velocities. At Dunaremete this circumstance is attributable to the fact that, whereas bed load transport is considerable even at lower stages, discharges and flow velocities, suspended-sediment transport assumes important proportions at relatively high stages only.

In cases where the difference of exponents is *positive but smaller than unity*, the rate at which the ratio G_s/G_B increases together with the hydraulic factors, (stage, discharge and velocity) is lower than that corresponding to linear proportionality. This is the case, for instance, at Szeged if the ratio of suspended and bed load transport is examined in the light of relations based on stages. Thus at Szeged rising stages are accompanied by an increase in this ratio, but the rate thereof will be lower than simple proportion.

In cases where the difference of exponents is *negative*, the ratio G_s/G_B always decreases with increasing stages, discharges or flow velocities. However, depending on whether the negative difference of exponents is greater or smaller than unity, the ratio G_s/G_B will vary at different rates.

In cases where the difference of exponents is *a negative number greater than unity*, the ratio G_s/G_B decreases with an increase in the hydraulic factors at a rate higher than simple linear proportion, i.e. bed load transport increases at a much faster rate than suspended-sediment transport. Such a negative difference greater than unity is observed at Nagybajcs, implying that at this particular station an increase in the hydraulic factors is accompanied by a reduction of the ratio at a faster rate than linear proportion or that bed load transport increases much steeper than suspended-sediment transport.

In cases where the difference of exponents is *negative and smaller than unity*, the ratio G_s/G_B will decrease with increasing hydraulic factors at a lower rate than the hydraulic factors, i.e. bed load transport will increase at a rate lower than linear proportionality over suspended sediment transport.

A simple glance at *Table 2.1.5 – 1* will already reveal that the differences of exponents applying to stages, discharges and velocities assume different signs at several stations. This circumstance appears to be conflicting since a change in sign in the difference of exponents applying to stages and discharges would imply that the change caused by an increase in stage is opposite in direction to that caused by an increase in discharge. This, however, would be in contrast with the laws of hyraulics since rising stages entail increasing discharges. In connection with similar changes in sign occurring in *Table 2.1.5 – 1* it should be remembered that changes in the ratio of suspended and bed load weights reflects the properties most particular to a cross-section. The properties of the cross-section govern, in turn, not only sediment transport but also variations in stage and discharge. It should be noted, moreover, that, especially at small values of the exponents, simplifying assumptions in the inexact functional relations or occasionally errors of observation may be responsible for changes in sign.

As far as the changes in the difference of exponents along the water course as regards both sign and magnitude are concerned it should be evident that these reflect also the influence of tributaries along with the properties particular to the individual cross-sections.

If it is desired to compare the ratio of suspended and bed load weights for a particular stream it should be clear that values of identical percentage duration must be introduced for stages, discharges and flow velocities alike. A comparison of this kind would be difficult on the basis of velocity. For this reason the variation in this ratio is examined preferably on the basis of stages and discharges of the same percentage duration.

The computation of ratios pertaining to stages and discharges of the same percentage duration on the basis of coefficients and exponents indicated in *Table 2.1.5 − 1* would be very convenient. A few attempts in this direction will already reveal that this approach leads to very wide discrepancies and, in many cases, even to contradictions. This will be understood by remembering that the exponential relations have been determined graphically, resulting in very uncertain values for the coefficient. An error of about 10% may be introduced by a 1% distortion of the tracing paper. The value of the graphical relations is hardly affected by this circumstance since, within the range of observations, even very large variations in the coefficient entail only insignificant changes in the slope of the relations. As an example it is noted that, owing to the combination of different errors, the ratio G_s/G_B corresponding to the discharge of 50% duration (about 2,250 m³ per sec) at Nagymaros was obtained as 17.7 when computed with the p and p_s values obtained graphically, whereas using the G_s and G_B values obtained from the charts representing the sediment weight versus discharge relations the ratio was found to be 269.

In view of the foregoing considerations the ratios G_s/G_B obtained on the basis of stages and discharges of identical percentage durations are introduced into the computations with the values found from the graphical relations.

In *Tables 2.1.3 − 1* to *2.1.3 − 4*, as well as *2.1.4 − 1* to *2.1.4 − 4* the weights of bed load and suspended sediment pertaining to stages and discharges on 25 50 and 75% duration have been entered for the stations along the Danube, Tisza Hernád and Rába rivers. Using the tabulated values the G_s/G_B ratios corresponding to stages and discharges of 25, 50 and 75% duration have been computed from the relations based on discharges and stages alike and, since these naturally differ from one another, their mean values have also been formed. The values thus obtained are indicated in *Table 2.1.5 − 2*, for the the Danube, in *Table 2.1.5 − 3* for the Tisza, in *Table 2.1.5 − 4* for the Hernád and in *Table 2.1.5 − * for the Rába river.

It will be perceived from *Table 2.1.5 − 2* that for the stations along the Danube − except Dunaremete − the ratio G_s/G_B ranges from about 200 to 1,900 and tha at the stations upstream of Nagymaros the G_s/G_B ratio is higher at low stage: than at higher stages. At the stations downstream of Nagymaros, the situation is reversed since at Dunaújváros, Fajsz and at Baja the ratio of suspended and bed load transport becomes higher at high stages i.e. at great discharges. Variations in the G_s/G_B ratio along the river is shown in *Fig. 2.1.5 − 1*, representing the data determined for the stations on the Danube.

According to *Table 2.1.5 − 3*, the G_s/G_B ratio on the Tisza river equals round

Table 2.1.5−2

The ratio of suspended to bed load transport at stages and durations of 25, 50 and 75% at several gages on the Danube, according to *Tables 2.1.3−1* and *2.1.4−1*

Gaging station	Duration, %	$\frac{G_s}{G_B}$ in terms of stage		$\frac{G_s}{G_B}$ in terms of discharge	Mean value	
Dunaremete	25	11.1	7.17*	10	10.6	8.56*
	50	7.07	4.82*	7.42	7.24	6.12*
	75	4.61	3.82*	5.66	5.14	4.75*
Nagybajcs	25	440	220*	265	352	242*
	50	972	555*	750	861	652*
	75	1,846	832*	1.910	1,878	1,371*
Dunaalmás	25	203		178	190	
	50	246		210	228	
	75	303		260	282	
Nagymaros	25	395	233*	238	316	235*
	50	307	210*	269	288	240*
	75	268	221*	318	293	270*
Dunaújváros	25	384		390	387	
	50	282		267	274	
	75	207		185	196	
Fajsz	25	215		200	208	
	50	141		144	142	
	75	92		106	99	
Baja	25	300		271	286	
	50	222		205	214	
	75	178		155	167	

Note: Values denoted by an * reflect the ratio of relations valid after 1953.

1000 at Polgár and at Szeged. At Tiszabő and at Tápé this ratio ranges between 500 and 750, and from 2400 to 3500, respectively. The variation in the ratio G_s/G_B has been plotted in *Fig. 2.1.5−2* showing that low stages or small discharges on the Tisza river are accompanied by higher ratios than those pertaining to higher stage or discharge values for all stations along the river.

As indicated in *Table 2.1.5−4* the G_s/G_B ratio varies from 100 to 600 or between rather narrow limits on the Hernád river. It is of interest to note that in *Fig. 2.1.5−3* in the Pere station on the Hernád river there is a but moderate increase in the ratio with increasing stages and discharges.

In *Table 2.1.5−5* the G_s/G_B ratio on the Rába river can be seen to range from about 300 to 1100. It is remarkable that this ratio is unaffected by duration at Szentgotthárd. Since data are available only for two stations on the Rába, the ratios have not been plotted graphically.

573

Table 2.1.5−3

The ratio of suspended to bed load transport at stages and discharges of 25, 50 and 75% duration at several gages on the Tisza river according to the values in *Tables 2.1.3−2* and *2.1.4−2*

Gaging station	Duration, %	$\frac{G_s}{G_B}$ in terms of stage	$\frac{G_s}{G_B}$ in terms of discharge	Mean value
Polgár	25	1,350	830	1,090
	50	1,312	955	1,134
	75	1,305	1,042	1,174
Tiszabő	25	484	478	481
	50	640	582	611
	75	847	676	762
Tápé	25	1,910	2,960	2,435
	50	2,480	3,540	3,010
	75	3,250	3,880	3,565
Szeged	25	1,110	985	1,048
	50	1,030	1,150	1,090
	75	982	1,240	1,111

Table 2.1.5−4

The ratio of suspended to bed load transport at stages and discharges of 25, 50 and 75% duration at several gages on the Hernád river, according to the values in *Tables 2.1.3−3* and *2.1.4−3*

Gaging station	Duration, %	$\frac{G_s}{G_B}$ in terms of stage	$\frac{G_s}{G_B}$ in terms of discharge	Mean value
Hidasnémeti	25	343	230	286
	50	366	229	298
	75	394	250	322
Pere	25	692	480	586
	50	620	500	560
	75	587	482	534
Gesztely	25	117	104	110
	50	127	94.5	111
	75	138	110	124

The ratio of suspended to bed load transport at stages and discharges of 25, 50 and 75% duration at gages on the Rába river according to the values in *Tables 2.1.3−4* and *2.1.4−4*

Gaging station	Duration, %	$\frac{G_s}{G_B}$ in terms of stage	$\frac{G_s}{G_B}$ in terms of discharge	Mean value
Szentgotthárd	25	629	522	575
	50	573	487	530
	75	628	487	558
Körmend	25	1,864	328	1,096
	50	923	615	769
	75	300	280	290

Summarizing our investigations concerning the magnitude of the G_s/G_B ratio it is concluded that the variations in this ratio depend greatly on the characteristic particular to a water course. A general rule on the variations in this ratio would be extremely difficult to define since the number of factors affecting the magnitude thereof is extremely large.

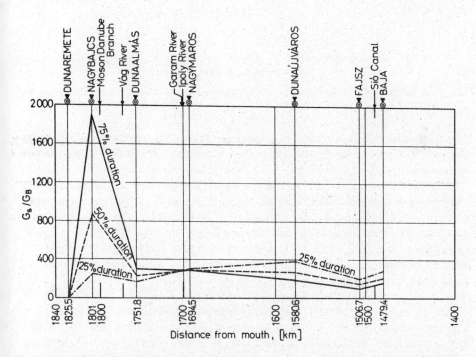

Fig. 2.1.5−1. Variations in the ratio of suspended-sediment to bed load transport determined on the basis of 25, 50 and 75% duration stages and discharges on the Danube

Fig. 2.1.5–2. Variations in the ratio of suspended sediment to bed load transport determined on the basis of 25, 50 and 75 % duration stages and discharges on the Tisza river

For the sake of completeness it should be noted that, similarly to the water courses in Hungary, considerable differences between the rate of bed load transport and suspended-sediment transport have been observed elsewhere, too. Variations in the value of this ratio on rivers in the Soviet Union have been studied extensively by G. I. Shamov. According to him the rate of bed load transport is in general 5 to 10 % of suspended sediment and the ratio G_s/G_B ranges accordingly from 20 to 10. From the data published on streams in the United States of America it is inferred that 80 % of the total sediment weight is transported in suspension and 20 % as bed load. According to Yakushov the bed load transported in the Volga river is not more than about 1 % of the suspended sediment and occasionally this value is as low as 0.08 %. From the foregoing the data of Yakushov will be seen to agree most closely with those obtained in Hungary.

In engineering practice the total weight of sediment transported by streams may be of interest. Total sediment transport G is obtained as the sum of suspended sediment and bed load, i.e.

$$G = G_s + G_B \qquad (2.1.5-4)$$

Fig. 2.1.5—3. Variations in the ratio of suspended sediment to bed load transport determined on the basis of 25, 50 and 75% duration stages and discharges on the Hernád river

Expressing the weights of sediment transported in suspension or as bed load in terms of stages, discharges or flow velocities, the total weight of sediment is found from one of the following expressions:

$$G = uh^g + \frac{u_1}{1000} h^{g_1} \; [\text{kp/sec}] \qquad (2.1.5-5)$$

$$G = pQ^j + \frac{p_1}{1000} Q^{j_1} \; [\text{kp/sec}] \qquad (2.1.5-6)$$

$$G = \alpha v_k^\beta + \frac{\alpha_1}{1000} v_k^{\beta_1} \; [\text{kp/sec}] \qquad (2.1.5-7)$$

For estimating the total weight of sediment or the total sediment transport an approach similar to that followed in estimating the ratio of suspended and bed load is adopted, i.e. the rate of total sediment transport is determined preferably with the help of relations based on stages or discharges.

2.1.6. SILTING ALONG BACKWATER REACHES

2.1.6.1. The influence of river canalization on sediment transport. River canalization is a method frequently used in recent times in river regulation. This method is of advantage in many respects for solving regulation problems. By the construction of barrages adequate depth is ensured for navigation and by eliminating extreme stage fluctuations the danger of bank erosion and channel deterioration

37

is also diminished. Besides solving regulation problems, a number of ancillary benefits also acrue from river canalization, since barrages usually permit the development of hydroelectric power and diversion by gravity, a wide variety of water uses. In many instances the basic objectives of river canalization are water power development and the diversion of water by gravity.

In river canalization a sequence of barrages is constructed by which the equilibrium existing among the hydraulic factors of the stream are necessarily modified and consequently the balance of sediment conditions is also disturbed. River canalization represents a radical and special interference with the life of alluvial streams. At the barrages erected across the streams slope conditions are altered to an extent depending on the magnitude of the head created, and the sudden artificial drop entails fundamental changes in both depth and distribution of the velocity of flow. As a consequence of these changes further modifications ensue so that the harmony of hydraulic factors is disrupted. The river reaches both upstream and downstream of a barrage are effected by these changes.

The changes occurring over certain distances both upstream and downstream are evidently of practical interest only.

The changes occurring over the sections upstream and downstream of the barrage will be evidently different in character. Upstream of the barrage the slope becomes flatter and velocities are diminished, as a consequence of which some of the sediment is deposited. Therefore silting along the backwater reach upstream of the barrage may be expected. The determination of silting is of interest not only for estimating the reduction in storage and thus for predicting the useful life of the barrage, but also for navigation. Excessive silting may affect the depth available for vessels and thus present obstacles to navigation.

As a consequence of sedimentation over the backwater reach the water released to the tail water is clearer and carries less sediment. The excess energy of water that is partly relieved of its sediment load will be consumed obviously in the direction of least resistance implying that it will deepen the channel or scour the fine fractions of the bed material corresponding to its transporting capacity. Consequently degradation of the channel may be expected to occur downstream of barrages, and this may even result in deterioration of the bed. For studying the changes resulting in sediment transport, the sections upstream and downstream of the barrages are preferably separated.

Before embarking upon a detailed discussion of changes occurring upstream and downstream of barrages it is deemed desirable to review the properties of reservoirs created by barrages and the different types thereof.

As a consequence of barrages constructed in the channel of streams, a storage reservoir with dimensions exceeding those of the original bed is created upstream of the barrage. Depending on the properties of streams, the storage reservoirs may be of a wide variety of types. The type of reservoirs will be controlled among other things by the slope of the stream and by the head created at the barrage.

Reservoirs may be classified according to a number of criteria. A criterion of classification commonly adopted is the ratio of reservoir volume to the discharge

578

in the river. Where the ratio of storage volume to river discharge is very high, as in reservoir dams, a lake of a practically horizontal surface is created above the dam differring substantially in character from impoundments where the volume to discharge ratio is smaller so that, in spite of the backwater created, the water surface upstream of the structure has still an appreciable slope. The first case is referred to as basin reservoir or dam storage, whereas the latter, as channel reservoir or river storage.

It should be noted that besides the above grouping of reservoirs, other classifications have also been suggested in the literature.

Reservoirs are classified by Shamov into two main groups and each of these into two subgroups. One of the main groups comprises lake type reservoirs which may be 1) of the shallow-basin type and 2) of the deep-basin type. The second main group includes the river type reservoirs, which, in turn, may be classified into 1) channel impoundments and 2) plain basin reservoirs.

In the classification suggested by Shamov the first main group corresponds to basin reservoirs, whereas the second main group partly to channel reservoir and partly to dam storage.

The changes in sediment conditions will depend, in both extent and type, on the kind of reservoir created. In a basin reservoir the calm lake with horizontal surface permits the entire arriving sediment load to settle. Consequently the water released through the dam is usually perfectly clear. The rate of sedimentation can be estimated if the rate of sediment transport in the stream is known.

In a channel reservoir only part of the arriving sediment is deposited. The rest is carried downstream together with the water released. The sediment entering the downstream section is especially great in volume at times of floods, since often the full flood discharge is released. For this reason the rate of silting in channel reservoirs is substantially more difficult to estimate than in the case of basin reservoirs. Information on the original rate of sediment transport is here insufficient, and the volume of sediment released must also be determined.

From the foregoing it should be clear that in a channel reservoir the method in which the dam is operated plays also an important role and the relationship between release, the head created and the arriving discharge is of paramount interest.

Comparing the percentage of annual storage volume losses due to silting in basin and channel reservoirs, they will be seen to be higher in channel reservoirs than in basin reservoirs. This fact is attributed to the relatively smaller volume of channel impoundments, the influence of which is too great to be offset by the sediment volume released together with water through the barrage.

On the other hand, the rate of silting related to unit catchment area is higher in the case of basin reservoirs since, assuming identical rates of soil erosion and sediment formation, in this type of storage the entire sediment volume is usually deposited, so that silting is caused by the entire sediment volume arriving.

The storage volume per unit catchment area is in general smaller in a channel reservoir than in a basin reservoir, which is readily undestandable since reservoir dams are commonly constructed where the largest possible storage space can be realized.

The typical data related to a basin reservoir and a channel reservoir are as follows:

	Basin reservoir	Channel reservoir
Volume to discharge ratio	high	low
Storage per unit catchment area	large	small
Volume percentage lost annually by silting	low	high
Rate of silting per unit catchment area	high	low
Observation data available	ample	sparse

2.1.6.2. Silting above barrages. Suspended sediment and bed load continuously arrive from upstream reaches. In problems associated with the silting of reservoirs the sum of sediment weight transported in suspension (G_s) and as bed load (G_B) in an average year, i.e., the sediment quantity $G = G_s + G_B$ is commonly introduced into the computation. In exceptional cases the suspended sediment and the bed load are estimated separately.

Denoting the volume of the reservoir by V, the catchment area above the dam site by F and the amount of sediment entering the reservoir annually by G, the silting process is characterized by the following parameters:

If the amount of sediment deposited annually from the arriving sediment load G is denoted by G_0, the percentage of sediment deposited is given as

$$\frac{G_0}{G} \, 100 \qquad (2.1.6-1)$$

The ratio

$$g_0 = \frac{G_0}{F} \qquad (2.1.6-2)$$

represents the annual rate of silting related to unit catchment area.

A quantity highly characteristic of silting in reservoirs is also the ratio of the annual average silting G_0 and the discharge Q_0 of water entering the reservoir in an average year.

The annual rate of silting can be expressed also as a percentage of storage volume as

$$\frac{G_0}{V} \, 100 \qquad (2.1.6-3)$$

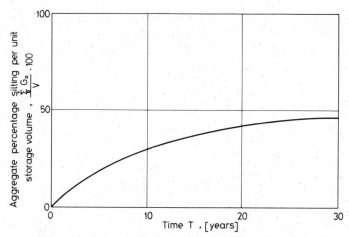

Fig. 2.1.6—1. Variations in the silting up of reservoirs with time

The storage depth s, in mm units, is obtained if the entire storage volume is distributed uniformly over the catchment area, or

$$s = \frac{V}{1000F} \qquad (2.1.6-4)$$

where V should be introduced in m^3 and F in km^2 units.

Besides the quantity s the storage volume per km^2 catchment area, i.e., the ratio

$$\frac{V}{F} \qquad (2.1.6-5)$$

can also be used.

Silting of reservoirs is often described in terms of the ratio of deposited and arriving total sediment transport, i.e. by the percentage of sediment retained.

For the silting of reservoirs the most relevant parameter is the ratio G_0/V or if, as is commonly the case, G_0 is not known in advance, the ratio G/V, as well as the percentage of sediment retained.

Ample observation data are available on both the history of silting in reservoirs and the deposition of sediment within the storage space. The first and most important experience is that silting of reservoirs occurs at extremely high rates during the first years after the construction of the barrage. Within a short period, usually not more than two or three years, the annual rate of silting is considerably attenuated. What is more, after a certain period the river tends to establish a new condition of equilibrium whereafter any additional silting becomes small enough to be neglected.

The variation of reservoir silting with time is illustrated in *Fig. 2.1.6−1*. The changes with time of the cumulated percentage silting related to unit storage volume, i.e., of the value

$$\frac{\sum\limits_{0}^{T} G_0}{V} \, 100$$

are plotted in the figure. During the first 15 years about 35% of the storage volume is lost by silting, according to this diagram. During the subsequent 15 years the increment loss in storage volume is as low as about 10%. In the case of the reservoir illustrated in the figure the new equilibrium condition developed in about 30 years, since the increment losses after this time are practically negligible.

The sediment transported by the stream into the storage space consists partly of coarse bed load, and partly of fine silt fractions carried in suspension by water. Experience has shown the coarse bed load to be deposited at the upstream end of the storage space and even farther upstream, forming deposits comparable to the delta deposits in river estuaries. These deposits are relatively small in area but of considerable height.

The bed load deposited around the backwater limit results usually in a considerable rise in water level and, on navigable water ways, is mostly serious obstacles to navigation. For this reason special measures are often necessary over such reaches to ensure the required navigation depth. The coarse bed load deposits advance gradually in time and approach the barrage continuously.

In contrast to bed load, fine sediment is deposited more uniformly over the entire reservoir area. The larger fractions of suspended sediment are, of course, deposited like bed load over the reach immediately downstream of the backwater limit. According to observations made by Shamov, only particles finer than 0.01 mm settled immediately upstream of the barrage, whereas the coarses fractions consisting of particles greater than 0.25 mm in diameter are deposited at considerable distances upstream of the barrage. In the Austin reservoir fine silt was deposited over a distance of 19 km upstream of the barrage while sand occurred in the settled material upstream of this point only.

The grain size distribution of the material deposited is greatly influenced by velocities within the reservoir. Proceeding downstream from the backwater limit the slope and the velocity of flow are gradually reduced and, accordingly, the particles deposited become gradually finer so that the finest silt fractions are usually encountered immediately upstream of the barrage.

The procedure of reservoir settling is indicated schematically in *Fig. 2.1.6−2* (for instances 1, 2, 3 and 4). The coarse bed load deposited around the backwater limit advances, forming a delta deposit. This "topset deposit" gradually approaches the barrage. The fine sediment is transported along the reservoir bottom as density current to the barrage where it forms a stratified deposit gradually increasing in height.

The advancement of the top set deposit or delta deposit of coarse sediment toward the barrage is illustrated in *Fig. 2.1.6−3;* the advancement at instances

Fig. 2.1.6—2. Different kinds of deposits in reservoirs. After Lane

1, 2 and 3 is accompanied by the displacement of the backwater limit upstream and by a gradual rise in water level around this limit.

A phenomenon frequently observed in connection with reservoir silting is the occurrence of density currents in water saturated with very fine sediment.

Stratification of water in reservoirs is a common phenomenon. It is most often due to differences in temperature but, where the stream feeding the reservoir carries large amounts of fine sediment in suspension, the sediment-laden water of relatively higher density proceeds in most cases as density current. In most reservoirs, especially in those of high volume and great depth, stratification may occur under the combined influence of differences in temperature and sediment concentration. In general the density current is understood as a gravitational flow, where one of two fluids with concentrations of an approximately identical order of magnitude but numerically different moves across, above or under the

Fig. 2.1.6—3. Progression of the "delta" deposit formed from coarse materials in reservoirs. After Harrison

Fig. 2.1.6 — 4. The silting of Lake Mead. After Howard

other fluid. In reservoir silting, the density current, i.e., the sediment-laden water of higher concentration invariably flows under the relatively clear water stored in the reservoir.

Density currents in reservoirs are of considerable interest to engineers, since a thorough understanding of the extent and nature thereof may, under certain circumstances, offer the possibility of considerably delaying the silting of reservoir space. In particular cases the density current arriving at the barrage may be utilized to pass some of the sediment into the tailwater, reducing thus the losses in storage space.

Ample literature is available on the hydraulic characteristics of density currents. For details reference is made to these papers.

No perfect engineering solutions have been found as yet for releasing sediment through the bottom outlets by density current. Experience has shown the amount of sediment that can be removed in this way from the storage space to be relatively small. Nevertheless, owing to its great significance, further studies and investigations into this problem are required.

Concerning density currents and silting in reservoirs, model tests have recently been made by N. P. Kulesh at the River Laboratory of the Leningrad Polytechnical Institute.

It should be noted that valuable observations on density currents have been made on the Colorado river in the course of studies on silting in Lake Mead above the Hoover dam. The process of silting in Lake Mead is illustrated after C. S. Howard in *Fig. 2.1.6 — 4*.

It has been observed that silting in the parts of flood plains enclosed by levees occurs at a substantially faster rate than in the channel itself. It has been demonstrated by Taylor that the flood plain of the Yort channel reservoir has completely been silted in places during thirteen years, whereas insignificant deposits occurred in the main channel during the same period.

584

Fig. 2.1.6—5. Integrating curves of deposited sediment in Faal reservoir. After Shamov

The process of silting upstream of the Faal barrage on the Dráva river has been described by Shamov. Greatest deposits have been observed to occur during the first two years whereafter the rate of silting decreased gradually and the deposits were more evenly distributed over the entire lake area. From the data observed and processed it was concluded that silting in the upstream part of the reservoir had attained equilibrium conditions after ten to fifteen years as a consequence of which sediment was transported farther towards the barrage so that almost the entire suspended-sediment load advanced into the downstream part of the lake. The cumulative curves representing the process of silting in the Faal reservoir are shown in *Fig. 2.1.6—5.*

Another observation made in the Faal reservoir was that the masses of bed load advancing towards the barrage do not simply settle on the suspended sediment deposited earlier but displace some of it in advancing. It was inferred that in advanced stages of silting some of the sediment deposited is exchanged for increasingly coarser fractions. The same phenomenon has been observed on the Danube by Z. Károlyi in connection with the Kachlet hydroelectric station.

The process of silting is influenced also by floods. A considerable part of the annual sediment load is carried into the reservoir by individual major flood waves. Where at times of floods the water is released at a reduced head or occasionally at fully opened gates through the barrage, the bulk of suspended sediment is transported without obstruction to the downstream reaches. The majority of bed load is even then deposited over the backwater reach. Where the barrage is operated at a full head even during floods, the large sediment volumes carried by the flood waves may result in considerable deposition within a very short period.

The factors influencing the process of silting above barrages are extremely manifold in character. Apart from the sediment volume transported annually by the river, silting will be influenced evidently by all factors affecting the retardance of bed load over the reach of reduced slope and flow velocity, as well as the settling of suspended sediment there.

In this respect one of the major factors controlling silting in reservoirs is the relative magnitude of storage volume. Reference to this factor has already been made in the foregoing by pointing out that in large storage reservoirs, in the case of basin reservoirs practically the entire sediment volume is deposited. Processing data on a number of reservoirs Orth has found the rate of silting per unit catchment area to increase with reservoir volume.

The rate of silting appears to be unaffected by the shape of the reservoirs, provided the ratio V/F is high. However, if the storage volume per unit catchment area is relatively small, silting may be affected by the reservoir shape on account of the settling of suspended sediment. In such cases silting in short and deep reservoirs will follow a different trend than in long and shallow basins.

The position of the reservoir along the stream may also play a role in silting in that the granulometric composition of sediment is different over the headwater, middle or lower reaches. It should be obvious that reservoirs on the headwater reaches of rivers may be silted at an appreciably faster rate by large volumes of coarse bed load than on reaches farther downstream where the amount of sediment transported as bed load and retained entirely in the reservoir is already insignificant.

From the results of laboratory experiments and field observations V. A. Melentiev at the Leningrad All-Union Hydraulic Research Institute (VNIIG) concludes that deposits vary exponentially along the length of reservoirs.

Silting may finally be influenced considerably by the manner in which the barrage is operated. In this respect it is of primary importance, especially in the case of barrages built in the river channel, whether or not flood discharges are permitted to pass without obstruction. In the first case the sediment volumes carried by flood waves, which are responsible for the bulk of sediment transported annually, are flushed almost entirely past the barrage. On the other hand, where a head is constantly maintained or where free release is exceptional, no such flushing action may be expected to occur.

The most difficult sedimentation problem associated with river canalization projects consists of predicting the anticipated rate of silting. This problem is complicated by the circumstance that no uniform and positive opinion has been

586

evolved on the observation and measurement of reservoir silting. As a consequence, the available data collected during studies on the silting of different reservoirs are rather inconsistent and often reflect the personal opinion of the investigator. In most recent times a certain improvement in this field seems to be observable. Even if no general practice can be spoken of, in the countries mostly affected the first steps have already been made towards the standardization of methods to be applied in the observation and measurements of reservoir silting. In view of the fact that no solution to the problem of predicting the rate of silting in reservoirs can be expected, unless sufficient information on silting in existing reservoirs is collected, the development of uniform and effective observation and measuring methods seems to be extremely important.

Observations and measurements on the silting of reservoirs are, of course, important not only for the above reason. The benefits accruing from observations on silting in particular reservoirs are as follows:

a) Determination of future silting in the particular reservoir, and thus the estimation of damages resulting therefrom.

b) Determination of changes in the depth to volume relation of the particular reservoir.

c) In combination with sediment observations on the stream under consideration an opportunity is presented for estimating the rate of sediment formation in the catchment area and for studying the influence of the catchment area and climatic factors on sediment formation.

d) Data are collected for solving sediment problems arising in connection with other hydraulic projects in the same catchment.

In measurements and observations on the silting of operating reservoirs the most important problem is to determine the volume of accumulated deposit, although the knowledge of the original storage volume is also of interest.

The methods used for determining the volume of sediment deposited in reservoirs have been described in Item 4, *Subsection 1.1.5.2.*

Information on the potential rate of settling is desirable already in the early design stages of reservoir projects. Although observations on the process of silting in existing reservoirs are essential for the reasons listed before, they are no more than a record of past events concerning the particular reservoir. The probable rate of silting is of interest in the design stage, this being a controlling factor in planning reservoir operation and in designing structural components. In a number of instances early warning on probable high silting rates would have discouraged the construction of reservoirs. This applies especially to many reservoirs constructed earlier and completely silted up by now.

No reliable method is so far available for accurately estimating the silting of reservoirs. Nevertheless the progress made in this field in recent years is substantial.

The methods available for estimating future silting in reservoirs will be listed subsequently.

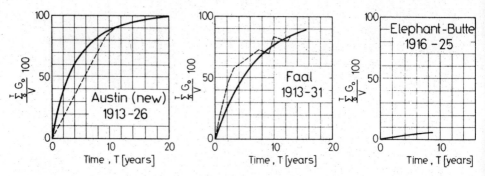

Fig. 2.1.6—6. The silting of reservoirs Austin, Faal and Elephant Butte. After Shamov

For a number of storage projects estimations have been made on the variation of percentage silting per unit storage volume, i.e. of the ratio $(G_0/V)100$. These values have been plotted against time by Shamov for several reservoirs.

The functions

$$\frac{\sum\limits_{0}^{T} G_0}{V} 100 = F(T)$$

clearly indicate the manner in which individual reservoirs are silted. Unfortunately these relations are highly specific to each particular reservoir so that no general conclusions can be drawn from them. The silting curves for the reservoirs Austin, Faal and Elephant-Butte are shown in *Fig. 2.1.6—6* after Shamov. The process of silting will be seen therefrom to follow radically different trends. Similar curves are therefore useless for predicting the loss in storage volume in a contemplated reservoir.

The plot of deposited volumes against time is a clear indication of the fact that the sediment-retaining capacity of reservoirs decreases with increasing volume of sediment deposited. This is due to the circumstance that increasing deposits in the reservoir give rise to higher velocities, and much of the suspended sediment is thus transported to the downstream sections.

The plot of percentage silting per unit storage volume against time is, however, extremely valuable, irrespective of the foregoing considerations since it may indicate whether or not the rate of silting is detrimental to the useful life of the structure. This is the main merit of these diagrams.

Another approach consists of plotting the loss in storage volume against the total storage volume, both related to unit catchment area, i.e., of determining the relation

$$\frac{G_0}{F} = F\left(\frac{V}{F}\right) \tag{2.1.6—6}$$

588

Fig. 2.1.6—7. The annual silting per unit catchment are vs. retention level. After Orth and Shamov

Relying on field observation Orth represents the above relation as a family of curves by separating the corresponding pairs of values $G_0/F = F(V/F \ 1000)$ according to different reservoirs and connecting them by separate curves.

The investigations of Orth have been extended by Shamov who completed Orth's curve with data of additional reservoirs and classified these into six types, instead of the original five categories. Shamov's diagram is shown in *Fig. 2.1.6—7*, where curve *a* indicates reservoirs on headwater reaches of rivers, where high-intensity storms and severe soil erosion are common; curve *b* is representative of reservoirs on rivers having a flashy regime, where the annual precipitation is in excess of 1000 mm; curve *c* resembles the previous category and applies to reservoirs with catchments covered by more vegetation; curve *d* is characteristic of reservoirs in hilly country with less precipitation where considerable parts of the catchment are covered with forests and cultivated fields; curve *e* applies to reservoirs in the zone of mountains of medium height, where the catchments are covered by meadows, pastures and in part by forests, while curve *f* relates to reservoirs in foothills with dense forests and in plains. These relations of Shamov may be utilized in particular cases for estimating the annual rate G_0 of silting, but still no information is obtained on the decrease of G_0 with time.

Another common approach consists of plotting the volume lost by silting per unit storage against the storage volume per unit sediment quantity.

The resulting function

$$\frac{G_0}{V} 100 = F\left(\frac{V}{G}\right)$$

$$(2.1.6-7)$$

Fig. 2.1.6—8. Ratio of the annual sediment load to reservoir volume vs. silting per unit reservoir volume. After Shamov

can be represented approximately by a hyperbola provided G_0 does not differ greatly from G. The relation constructed by assuming $G_0 = G$ is, of course, represented by a regular hyperbola. This relation is, however, unsuited for determining the rate of silting even if the weight G of sediment transported annually by the river is known. Nevertheless it is found advisable to plot this relation for it provides highly visual information on the rapid increase of silting per unit storage with decreasing storage per unit sediment volume.

The function determined by Shamov

$$\frac{G_0}{V} 100 = F\left(\frac{V}{G}\right)$$

is represented in *Fig. 2.1.6—8.*

Investigations on the silting of reservoirs have shown the rate of silting or loss in storage volume to depend also on the arriving discharge. From results of observations made on a number of reservoirs the relation of annual silting loss per unit catchment area against the ratio of the original storage volume to the entire annual in flow is shown in *Fig. 2.1.6.—9.* From the figure it will be seen that, as long as the ratio of the original storage volume to the annual inflow is smaller than about 0.8, the annual silting loss per unit catchment area increases rapidly. Once the above ratio attains the value 1.4, the annual rate of silting per unit catchment area remains practically unchanged.

The rate of silting is governed by the properties of the catchment above the barrage. In general where the runoff from the catchment is smaller but subject to frequent variations or where the shape and length of the reservoir is conducive to longer retention times, and where the sediment is coarse or susceptible to flocculation, higher rates of settling are observed. All these questions need careful

590

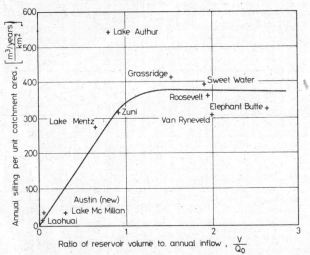

Fig. 2.1.6—9. Annual silting per unit catchment area related to the ratio of the original storage volume and the total annual inflow. After United Nations ECAFE, No. 5

consideration before a particular storage project is realized. In many instances economic advantages will accrue from constructing a barrage of lower height in the first stage and raising it subsequently to the final elevation rather than developing the greatest potential storage capacity in a single stage. The same procedure will be found advantageous also in cases where considerable evaporation losses are to be expected.

For estimating the rate of silting use can be made also of other information concerning sediment deposition in particular reservoirs. In this respect it is believed of interest to mention the observation made at the Conchas reservoir on the South Canadian river, according to which the water released through the lowest sediment sluices carries at most 5% by weight sediment. At low stages i.e. in low-water periods the amount of sediment passing the barrage was found insignificant. At the same reservoir in order to promote the release of sediment, the sediment sluices are opened as soon as sediment-laden flood waters arrive to the lake and are kept open as long as the flood discharge carries water with a sediment concentration higher than usual into the reservoir. At low and medium discharges the sediment sluices are opened once each month and kept open as long as the water is observed to carry sediment. Measurements have shown 97% of the sediment released through the sluices to belong to the 0.02 to 0.005 mm fraction. Since only an insignificant part of the sediment entering the reservoir belongs to the above fraction, the operation of the sediment-flushing sluices was found to be of no particular significance. These experiences appear to indicate that no sediment coarser than 0.02 mm can be released through the sluices. This circumstance may be utilized in estimating the silting of reservoirs. In fact if the

591

Fig. 2.1.6—10. Sediment-retarding capacity of reservoirs related to the ratio of storage volume and catchment area. After Gottschalk

amount and grain size distribution of the arriving sediment is known, the percentage by weight of the fraction finer than 0.02 mm can be determined and, deducting this from the total sediment transport, the rest may be regarded to be deposited in the reservoir. It should be noted that in connection with the canalization of the Tisza river this method was also used for computing the rate of silting. At the first glance this procedure may appear to be oversimplified and perhaps even unjustified. Remembering, however, that allowance is made thereby for the circumstance that – owing to reduced slopes and flow velocities upstream of the barrage – the stream is uncapable of transporting coarser fractions, the results may still be accepted for preliminary estimates.

For estimating the rate of reservoir silting a relation has been suggested also by L. C. Gottschalk. Having examined the silting process in a number of reservoirs he came to the conclusion that the amount of sediment deposited in the storage space was related somehow to the storage volume per unit catchment area or, using his terminology, to the storage capacity. The plot of these data (see *Fig. 2.1.6 – 10)* can thus be used for predicting, in terms of the storage volume per unit catchment area, the percentage of arriving sediment likely to be deposited in the reservoir. Gottschalk's relation is suited for directly estimating the volume of sediment settling in the reservoir. It should be understood, however, that the results obtained by using this relation are also of an approximate character because the relation has been developed by combining data on different types of reservoir. It should be noted further that Gottschalk's curves provide information only on sediment deposits likely to occur during the first years of reservoir operation but none at all on the reduction in silting rates with time. Gottschalk's relation has also been used in estimating the expected silting rates in the backwater reaches above barrages on the Tisza river.

Fig. 2.1.6−11. Sediment-retarding capacity of reservoirs related to the ratio of storage volume and catchment area. After Brune and Allen

The sediment-retaining potential of reservoirs has been expressed also by Brune and Allen in terms of the storage volume per unit catchment area. The relation illustrated in *Fig. 2.1.6 − 11* is similar to that of Gottschalk. From this figure, too, the sediment-retaining potential of reservoirs will be seen to decrease rapidly as the silting of the reservoir advances or as the storage capacity per unit catchment area diminishes. No sediment is retained at all in a completely silted reservoir.

The percentage of sediment retained has been expressed by Brune with the ratio of the storage volume V and the annual average in flow Q_a as parameter. Neglecting points applying to two intermittently operated reservoirs and to a sediment retention basin the relation applying to average conditions with a rather narrow spreading of points has been plotted in *Fig. 2.1.6 − 12*, indicating also the envelop curves yielding maximum and minimum values.

Deposition of sediment in reservoirs is obviously affected by the extent to which flow velocities over the backwater reach are reduced. This factor not only affects the settling of suspended sediment, but also sets a limit below which no bed load is transported. This consideration may also be adopted as a logical basis for estimating or predicting approximately the probable magnitude of sediment deposits.

From measurements made on the Velika Morava river above its confluence with the Danube, S. Bruk and V. Miloradov have concluded that, proceeding downstream, the mean concentration C_1 decreases with decreasing mean velocity v_1. The values of v_1 and C_1 have been related to the velocity v_0 and concentration

3 8

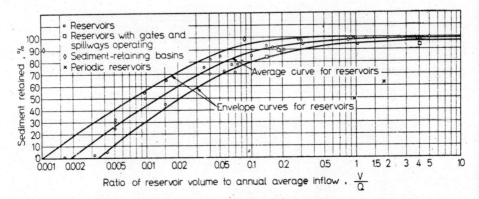

Fig. 2.1.6—12. Sediment-retarding capacity of reservoirs related to the ratio of storage volume and annual awerage inflow. After Brune

C_0 in a cross-section about 5 km upstream of the mouth. As to be seen in *Fig. 2.1.6—13* the reduction in the velocity ratio is closely related to the reduction in the concentration ratio. The reduction in concentration is attributed to silting which is a phenomenon similar to that upstream of barrages. Providing that the grain size distribution of the arriving sediment is known, the probable extent of silting can be estimated from the changes in hydraulic conditions caused by the barrage.

Besides the relation illustrated in *Fig. 2.1.6—13*, a number of approaches have been used by Bruk et al. for estimating the silting process upstream of the Iron Gate barrage under construction, including the two- and three-variable relations on sediment-transporting capacity discussed in *Section 2.1.4* in connection with *Figs 2.1.4—2, 2.1.4—3* and *2.1.4—4*.

A further simple method of estimating the rate of silting would consist of determining the minimum cross-section at which the stream is capable of transporting the arriving sediment volume and of computing the additional volume of channel storage created by the barrage as potential silting.

It should be noted finally that the estimation of reservoir silting can also be attempted on the basis of channel stability.

The construction of the barrage results in a change of slope S' and of the hydraulic radius R' as a consequence of which the mean particle diameter d_g is also bound to change, i.e. to decrease. This, however, is impossible, unless deposits occur over the reach where the slope diminishes and the hydraulic radius increases. The parameter can be used for computing the value of d'_g corresponding to the changed conditions. Since the grain size distribution curve of the bed material pertaining to the mean particle diameter d_g as well as of the arriving sediment G is known, it is possible to construct the grain size distribution curve pertaining to the new d'_g value. Once this is available the size fractions necessarily deposited for attaining the new channel stability are obtained by simple proportionality.

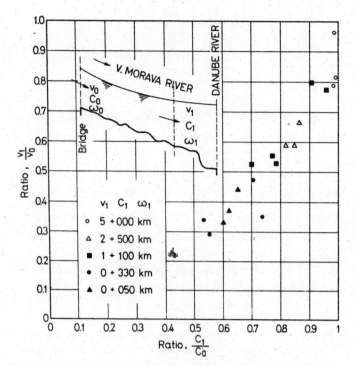

Fig. 2.1.6—13. Relative decrease of sediment concentration vs. the relative decrease of mean velocities. After Bruk and V. Miloradov

The amount deposited is estimated directly from the weight percentages of these fractions. This method is expected to yield satisfactory results in the case of channel reservoir.

This review of the methods of potential interest for estimating the rate of silting in reservoirs shows that no accurate method yielding reliable results is available. It is therefore deemed advisable to estimate silting by several methods in each particular case and to compare these for their relative merits before a decision is made. The charts of Orth and Shamov, as well as the functions of Gottschalk and Brune appear to lend themselves best for practical use. The experience gained at the Conchas reservoir may be used for checking the results obtained. The methods in which the amount of settling sediment is estimated in terms of flow velocities seem to be most promising. Involved in this problem is the theory of turbulent sediment transport, adapted of course to conditions other than those of equilibrium. It should be noted, further, that by introducing certain considerations these methods may also yield data on the advancement of silting with time.

Another difficult problem arising in connection with river canalization consists of predicting the period of silting and the variations of silting with time. It has been noted in the foregoing that the high rates of silting during the first years

Fig. 2.1.6 – 14. Variations in the silting of reservoirs with time. After Orth

after the construction of a barrage tend to decrease gradually. The experiences reported thus far also indicate that practically no silting occurs after a certain period of time. These conclusions are demonstrated clearly by Shamov's curves showing the variation in silting rates per unit storage volume. *(Fig. 2.1.6 – 6)* It should be realized at the same time that the curves

$$\frac{G}{V} \, 100 = F(T)$$

differ widely for different reservoirs, implying that great care must be exercised when drawing on past experience in estimating silting rates in new reservoirs.

The depth decreasing as a consequence of silting has been considered by Taylor. With D denoting the original depth, and x the thickness of the layer deposited annually, the depth h remaining after T years is obtained as

$$h = D(1 - x)^T \tag{2.1.6–8}$$

In considering the silting of reservoirs Orth assumes (see *Fig. 2.1.6 – 14*) that not more than V' of the storage volume V can be lost by silting and that $V' < V$. After time T the available volume V_T related to volume V' is given as

$$V_T = V'a^T \tag{2.1.6–9}$$

indicating that the available storage volume V_T is an exponential function of time T. The quantity a is representative of reservoir silting and assumes, according to Taylor, values from 0 to 1. Naturally, for obtaining a reliable estimate on the process of silting, the value of a must be determined correctly also with the method of Orth. The value of a has been found by Orth and Shamov to vary commonly from 0.75 to 1.0.

By refining the foregoing method Shamov has constructed a family of curves for estimating the time required for any particular percentage silting loss to occur. This method offers a simple means for determining the extent of silting pertaining to a given length of reservoir operation. However, to be of practical use, the value of a characteristic of reservoir silting or the amount of sediment G_0 deposited from the arriving sediment load must be known.

596

It is very difficult to make a numerical estimate on the length of time during which a particular reservoir becomes silted. The most promising approach seems to consist of estimating the number of years after which a new equilibrium condition in the river may be expected to set in. This period can, obviously, not be estimated readily, but the correct value can be approached by careful judgement. Once the length of this period is available, the reduction in annual silting can be assumed without introducing any grave error by relying on experience gained at other reservoirs. The figures obtained may be checked against the volume V' obtained by the method of minimum cross-section or by some other method.

2.1.6.3. Control of silting in reservoirs. In the majority of cases the silting of reservoirs gives rise to serious financial losses. It is therefore necessary to take efficient measure for preventing or at least retarding the process of silting.

The most logical remedy appears to consist of reducing the volumes of sediment by aforestation, gully control or by the construction of sediment-retarding dams in the catchment where sediment is produced. Yet in doing so care should be exercised to reduce sediment volumes gradually for otherwise unwanted scouring in the channel may cause other damage.

Several attempts have been made to intercept sediment upstream of the reservoir by a checking dam and to bypass the sediment thus accumulated through a diversion canal to the tailwater section.

The practice most commonly adopted for reducing the sediment volumes deposited involves the flushing of silt from the reservoir. Flushing will be in general the more effective, the lower the head at the time of flushing, the greater the discharge used for flushing, the wider the flushing gate, the deeper it is located and the longer the period of flushing. Also, flushing will be more effective on sections having originally a steep bottom. Moreover the effectiveness of flushing will increase with advancing stages of silting in the storage space. Flushing will prove more effective in straight and short reservoirs than in long and sinuous ones. Deposits of fine-grained, recently settled material can be expected to be flushed more readily from the reservoir.

As to the head at flushing, it should be noted that the release of sediment through the flushing gates will only be effective if no head is maintained at all. In fact flushing under a differential head is confined to very short distances. The length and frequency of full-gate conditions are, naturally, controlled by the normal operation requirements of the barrage.

The width of sediment-flushing gates (sluices) assumes special importance on flat streams. In such cases the discharge needed for flushing may become considerable in magnitude.

In practice a variety of measures are adopted for enhancing the flushing effect. Any successful application thereof is confined, however, to small reservoirs used for periodical, e.g. daily storage. Proposals have been advanced with the objective of enhancing the flushing effect in major reservoirs as well. An example for these is the suggestion of Bonnet according to whom a pipe network should be installed in the reservoir in order to concentrate and to increase the velocity of flushing water and to increase thus the scouring potential.

The process of silting in more than twenty reservoirs has been studied by L. G. Gvelesiani and N. P. Shmal'tzel who found flushing to offer the most successful means of silting control. These investigations resulted in suggestions concerning the time of flushing, the discharge of flushing and the most effective method of this operation.

In some important reservoirs it may be found necessary to remove the accumulated sediment by dredging. This method will be found usually too expensive, unless some use can be found for the material dredged.

Several attempts have been made to compensate for the storage volume lost on account of silting by raising the height of barrage. This measure is usually confined to reservoirs in mountainous and hilly areas.

In anticipation of silting it is highly advisable to compile a programme of releases from the reservoirs in which a certain part of the storage volume is neglected in advance. The provision of such dead storage is likely to extend the useful life of reservoirs.

2.1.6.4. Tailwater scouring. The water released from the reservoir is relatively clear and carries less sediment. Consequently it is liable to cause scouring downstream of the barrage. Some relation may be expected to exist between the section of silting and that of scouring upstream and downstream of the barrage, respectively. It should be obvious that scouring over the tailwater reach will depend on the quality of sediment and bed material downstream of the barrage, as well as on the quantity and quality of the sediment deposited upstream of the structure. The point is that the coarser fractions of the sediment will settle over the backwater reach, consequently, a finer sediment material will be transported to the downstream reaches. Downstream of the barrage the finest fractions of the material lining the channel will be scoured and transported first up to a size limit depending on the transporting capacity. The bed material in the tailwater reach is thus likely to become coarser after the construction of the barrage.

Ample data have been published in the literature on scouring downstream of barrages. The scours reported attain in general a depth of the order of metres and extend to considerable distances. The depth increases rapidly during the first years following the construction of the barrage but later at a considerably slower rate. The process of scouring is illustrated in *Fig. 2.1.6 − 15*. The points indicate the volume of scours observed during the period of a month in different years over the section between the Hoover and Davis dams on the Colorado river. Late in 1937, following the closure of the dam a volume of round 1590×10^3 m^3 will be seen to have been scoured in a month, whereas in January 1946 scouring attained not more than about 100×10^3 m^3 over the same section.

Although a great number of observation data are available, no method of general validity is available as yet for predicting the rate of scouring.

Fig. 2.1.6—15. Variations in degradation with time on the Colorado river, on the stretch between Hoover and Davis dams. After Lane

In order to develop a method permitting numerical estimates to be made on potential scouring, experiences gained thus far must be evaluated by a uniform approach.

Attempts have been made in recent times to estimate the extent of scouring by theoretical methods. Most of these are founded on the continuity of the sum of sediment transport and degradation.

In a rectangular channel of width B the continuity of degradation and sediment transport has been expressed by S. Komura with the help of the differential equation

$$\frac{\partial z}{\partial t} + \frac{1}{B(1 - \lambda)} \frac{\partial(q_t B)}{\partial x} = 0 \qquad (2.1.6-10)$$

where z is the height of the bottom above an arbitrary datum level, x is the main direction of flow, q_t is the total sediment transport, λ is the porosity of sediment and t is time.

Considering the transport relation of Kalinske – Brown, Komura gives a relation for the critical shear velocity U_{*c} and for the slope of the energy grade line.

Continuity over two cross-sections at dx distance during the short time interval dt has been expressed by S. Aksoy in the form

$$- dzdx = \frac{1}{B(1 - \lambda)} d(q_t B)dt \qquad (2.1.6-11)$$

of Eq. (2.1.6—10) since, according to him, the width B of the channel, the height z of the bottom as well as the rate of transport q_t depend on time t and on the position x of the cross-section alike. Expressed in an analytical form:

$$dB = \frac{\partial B}{\partial t}\,dt + \frac{\partial B}{\partial x}\,dx$$

$$dz = \frac{\partial z}{\partial t}\,dt + \frac{\partial z}{\partial x}\,dx \quad \text{and} \qquad (2.1.6-12)$$

$$dq_t = \frac{\partial q_t}{\partial t}\,dt + \frac{\partial q_t}{\partial x}\,dx$$

With due regard to the expressions under Eq. (2.1.6–12) the general form of the continuity equation becomes

$$\frac{\partial z}{\partial t} + \frac{\partial z}{\partial x}\frac{dx}{dt} = -\frac{1}{(1-\lambda)}\left(\frac{\partial q_t}{\partial x} + \frac{\partial q_t}{\partial x}\frac{dx}{dt}\right) =$$

$$-\frac{q_t}{B(1-\lambda)}\left(\frac{\partial B}{\partial x} + \frac{\partial B}{\partial t}\frac{dt}{dx}\right) \qquad (2.1.6-13)$$

In the general equation z, B and q_t are unknown variables depending on both t and x, whereas t and x are regarded as independent variables.

After determining the relations,

$$B = F(t, x) \quad \text{and} \quad q_t = F(t, x) \qquad (2.1.6-14)$$

the relation

$$z = F(t, x)$$

is also obtained.

As noted by Aksoy himself, the relations in Eq. (2.1.6–14) cannot be determined exactly as yet. He suggests a method of successive approximation using finite differences.

2.2. SEDIMENT AND THE HYDRAULIC FACTORS OF STREAMS

2.2.1. ALLUVIAL STREAMS

The hydraulic laws governing the flow of water in alluvial streams are closely related in several respects to the sediment and the movement thereof. For this very reason, in determining certain relationships in fluvial hydraulics, it was found necessary to abandon the results of research on solid beds and to replace them by experience gained from investigations into channels lined with a loose granular material, namely, the sediment.

The fundamental energy and continuity relations of flow apply in general to alluvial streams as well. However, the influence of the alluvial channel and the movement of sediment on the velocity of flow, on the distribution of velocities and on roughness conditions is no longer negligible. This is why a brief discussion on the velocity conditions in alluvial, sediment-laden streams having a mobile bed, as well as on the influence of bed forms and sediment on roughness is believed to be warranted.

2.2.1.1. The velocity of flow in alluvial channels. Depending on the bed forms and even on the moving sediment, the velocity coefficients or the factors representing the influence of roughness used in the past in alluvial streams may undergo variations sufficiently large to make their application impermissible.

Some of the more important results of studies made with the objective of determining the mean velocity and the distribution of velocities will be reviewed subsequently.

In 1958 H. K. Liu and S. Y. Hwang, having collected results of observations made in laboratory flumes and in alluvial channels, suggested, for estimating the mean flow velocity in alluvial stream, the relation

$$v = C_a R_b^x S^y \qquad (2.2.1-1)$$

where C_a is the velocity coefficient applying to alluvial channels, R_b (m) is the hydraulic radius related to the channel bottom, S (−) is the slope in steady flow, while x and y are dimensionless exponents. After lengthy theoretical considerations they succeeded in determining the magnitudes of x, y and C_a graphically as a function of the diameter d of sediment lining the channel. The variations of x, y and C_a (m$^{(1-x)}$/sec) with d are illustrated in *Figs 2.2.1−1, 2.2.1−2* and *2.2.1−3*, respectively, distinguishing the condition of smooth bed from that of an alluvial bottom covered with dunes.

The values applying to smooth bed are seen to be higher, implying that under otherwise identical hydraulic conditions the velocity of flow over a smooth bed covered by a fine-grained sediment material is higher. As soon as the particle size exceeds about 10 mm, the velocity of flow is no longer affected by the bed forms. The comparison of theoretical and actually observed data for the conditions of smooth bed and dunes is shown in *Figs 2.2.1−4* and *2.2.1−5*. Most data are within the 10% accuracy limit.

Stable channels form a special group of alluvial streams. According to the definition given by E. W. Lane to be discussed in *Chapter 2.3*, these are unlined earth canals conveying water, in which neither silting nor scouring occurs.

For computing the mean velocity of flow in such channels, relations have been suggested by B. D. Simons and L. M. Albertson. In their opinion the mean velocity can be written in the general form

$$v = b(R^2 S)^a \qquad (2.2.1-2)$$

Fig. 2.2.1–1. Variations of exponent *x* of hydraulic radius R_b according to particle diameter *d*. After Liu and Hwang

Fig. 2.2.1–2. Variations in exponent *y* of slope *S* according to particle diameter *d*. After Liu and Hwang

602

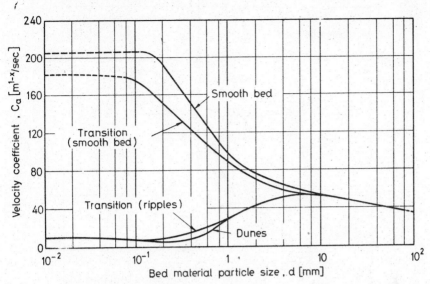

Fig. 2.2.1—3. Variations of velocity coefficient C_a according to particle diameter d. After Liu and Hwang

where the constants a and b depend on the bed material. The magnitude of these constants is determined in *Fig. 2.2.1—6* from the results of observations made in a number of canals. The magnitude of a and b varies with bed material as follows:

In coarse-grained, cohesionless bed material

$$v = 10.766(R^2 S)^{0.286} \ [\text{m/sec}] \tag{2.2.1—3}$$

In canals with a sandy bottom and side slopes of cohesive material

$$v = 10.773(R^2 S)^{1/3} \ [\text{m/sec}] \tag{2.2.1—4}$$

In canals with sandy bed and banks

$$v = 9.332(R^2 S)^{1/3} \ [\text{m/sec}] \tag{2.2.1—5}$$

In each of the above expressions the hydraulic radius R should be substituted in m units, whereas slope S is dimensionless.

In *Fig. 2.2.1—6* the dashed line applies to the Imperial canals which convey large volumes of sediment.

A number of similar relations have been developed for estimating the mean velocity. One of the most important formulae is the one suggested by Lacey:

$$v = 10.773 R^{2/3} S^{1/3} \ [\text{m/sec}] \tag{2.2.1—6}$$

which is in close agreement with the expression given by Simons—Albertson for channels having a sandy bottom and side slopes of cohesive material. In the Lacey formula no adequate allowance is made for the bed material so that diffi-

603

Fig. 2.2.1—4. Comparison of computed and measured mean velocities for smooth bed. After Liu and Hwang

culties have been encountered in its use. In many instances considerable differences were observed between the theoretical data and those actually observed.

For determining the distribution of flow velocities the logarithmic equation of Karman—Prandtl can be used, according to which

$$v = v_k + \frac{1}{\kappa} \sqrt{gDS} \left(1 + 2.3 \ \lg \frac{y}{D} \right) \qquad (2.2.1-7)$$

where v = the velocity of flow at height y above the bottom

v_k = the mean velocity

D, S, g = familiar quantities (depth, slope, acceleration by gravity)

κ = the universal constant of Karman, the value of which in clear water and for roughness of the Nikuradze type is 0.4.

The magnitude of the coefficient κ is influenced by the quantity of suspended sediment and by roughness. Many efforts have been devoted to the determination of its accurate value.

Fig. 2.2.1—5. Comparison of computed and measured mean velocities for dunes-covered bed.
After Liu and Hwang

W. W. Sayre and L. M. Albertson have studied the influence of roughness on velocity distribution by varying the density (spacing) and magnitude of roughness elements in a laboratory flume. From the results obtained the distribution of velocity has been expressed in a dimensionless form and plotted in *Fig. 2.2.1—7*. The points indicated there represent weighted averages of values observed at the same depth but in different verticals. The values were weighted according to the relative position of the vertical to the roughness elements.

The influence of the roughness elements and their arrangements, especially their spacing, on the type of velocity distribution will clearly be seen. The spacing of the roughness elements was closest in the first series of experiments (runs 1 to 7) and the loosest in the last. The distribution of velocities is described as

$$\frac{v}{\sqrt{\tau_0/\rho}} = 6.06 \lg \frac{y}{X} + 2.6 \qquad (2.2.1-8)$$

605

Fig. 2.2.1—6. Mean velocity v vs. R^2S for different bed materials. After Simons and Albertson

where X = a roughness parameter having the dimension of length representing the magnitude, spacing and shape of the roughness elements, and whose magnitude must be determined accordingly,

τ_0 = the tractive force prevailing at the bottom,

ρ = the density of the fluid.

The magnitude of these constants has been established from experimental data. For comparison the Karman–Prandtl equation

$$\frac{v}{\sqrt{\tau_0/\rho}} = 5.75 \lg \frac{y}{k_s} + 8.5 \qquad (2.2.1-9)$$

applying to the velocity distribution in turbulent flow along a rough boundary surface has also been entered into the figure with a dashed line.

The following non-linear relation has been found to exist between Nikuradze's sand roughness k_s and X

$$k_s = \frac{12.2 X^{1.053}}{y_n^{0.053}} \qquad (2.2.1-10)$$

Within the range of experimental data the ratio $k_s/X = 11$ approximately prevails. The wider spread of points representing the results of measurements made under the two widest spacings of the roughness elements may be attributed to the non-uniformity of roughness and to the effect of turbulence between the widely spaced elements.

The table within the figure:

No. of run	x [m]	k_s [m]
1 – 7	0.057	0.646
8 – 11	0.0366	0.415
12 – 15	0.0142	0.156
16 – 19	0.0265	0.294
20 – 23	0.0195	0.213
24 – 27	0.00605	0.063

Equations in the figure:

$$\frac{v}{\sqrt{\tau_0/\varrho}} = 5.75 \lg \frac{y}{k_s} + 8.5$$

$$\frac{v}{\sqrt{\tau_0/\varrho}} = 6.06 \lg \frac{y}{x} + 2.6$$

Fig. 2.2.1—7. Velocity distribution. After Sayre and Albertson

The influence of sediment transport on velocity distribution has been investigated by V. A. Vanoni, too. The velocity profiles obtained by him under two identical sets of hydraulic conditions (depth, slope, flume width) for clear water and for water carrying sediment of 0.1 mm particle size at concentration 15.8 p/lit are shown in *Fig. 2.2.1—8/a*. The friction coefficient in sediment-laden flow of higher velocity is seen to be lower. From *Fig. 2.2.1—8/b*, in which the relative distance above the bottom has been plotted to a logarithmic scale, the velocity distribution is seen to follow Karman's logarithmic law. Diminishing influence of suspended sediment on the coefficient κ, which is also shown in the figure, is of general validity and observable under laboratory conditions and in the field alike.

The velocity distribution has been studied by Vanoni and Brooks at different bed conditions. The particle size of the sediment (sand) was $d_g = 0.091$ mm, the water temperature 25 deg. C. The results obtained are shown in *Fig. 2.2.1—9* from

607

Fig. 2.2.1—8. Velocity distribution for clear water and for 15.8 p/litre sediment concentration. After Vanoni and Brooks

Fig. 2.2.1—9. Velocity distribution for different bed·configurations. After Vanoni and Brooks

608

Fig. 2.2.1—10. Velocity distribution for different bed configurations, for solid and loose bed.
After Raudkivi

which the distribution is seen to follow a logarithmic law in each of the three
bed conditions considered. At depth $D = 0.0866$ m indicated in the figure dunes
developed while at $D = 0.0744$ m dunes were observed at the walls. At depth
$D = 0.0783$ m and $D = 0.0778$ m the bed was in general smooth. The slope of
the individual curves is controlled by the magnitude of m.

The distribution of velocities in flow over sand ripples has been studied by
A. J. Raudkivi, whose data are plotted in *Fig. 2.2.1 – 10*. The velocity distribution
was found to follow the logarithmic law as long as the bed was smooth, regardless of whether the bed was solid or mobile. In flow over sand ripples, however,
certain changes were observed to occur in both solid and loose beds. The points
seem to indicate a change in slope at one-quarter of depth.

2.2.1.2. Roughness conditions in alluvial channels. As pointed out in the foregoing sections, the movement of water and sediment in alluvial channels is strongly
influenced by the bed forms developing in them. The effect thereof is commonly
included in bed roughness the magnitude of which is variable rather than constant in alluvial channels.

For describing the roughness of alluvial channels the dimensionless roughness
or friction coefficient f of Darcy—Weisbach may be accepted which, by definition, is given as

$$f = \frac{8gRS}{v^2} \qquad (2.2.1-11)$$

With due regard to the velocity coefficient c in the Chézy formula, the two coefficients are related as

$$c = \sqrt{\frac{8g}{f}}$$

or rewritten

$$\frac{c}{\sqrt{g}} = \sqrt{\frac{8}{f}} = \frac{v}{U_*} \qquad (2.2.1-12)$$

whence

$$f = 8 \left(\frac{U_*}{v}\right)^2 \qquad (2.2.1-13)$$

The magnitude of the coefficient f is affected by a number of circumstances, of which the bed form, the relative roughness (D/d), the quality, the particle size of bed material and the quantity of sediment transported may be mentioned as the most important ones.

Einstein and Barbarossa assume the tractive force τ_0 in alluvial channels to be composed of two parts, namely τ_0' and τ_0'', i.e.

$$\tau_0 = \tau_0' + \tau_0'' \qquad (2.2.1-14)$$

were τ_0' = the tractive force due to particle resistance in a smooth bed, and
τ_0'' = a supplementary tractive force due to irregularities in the channel and the banks, i.e. to the bed form.

In analogy to the tractive force, the hydraulic radius R may also be regarded as the sum of R' and R'':

$$\tau_0 = \gamma RS = \gamma S(R' + R'') \qquad (2.2.1-15)$$

and thus the shear velocity is also

$$U_* = \sqrt{gRS} = \sqrt{gR'S} + \sqrt{gRS''} = U_*' + U_*'' \qquad (2.2.1-16)$$

R' is the hydraulic radius pertaining to flow at a particular velocity and slope in the absence of shape resistance. Velocity v and R' are related to each other by Keulegan's velocity law

$$\frac{v}{U_*'} = 5.75 \lg \left(12.27 \frac{R'}{k_s} x\right) \qquad (2.2.1-17)$$

where $k_s = d_{65}$ the sand roughness of the channel, while x is a correction factor applied to hydraulically smooth beds. The magnitude thereof is given by the function

$$x = F\left(\frac{k_s}{\delta'}\right) = F\left(\frac{k_s U_*'}{11.6v}\right) \qquad (2.2.1-18)$$

If the ratio of the sand roughness k_s and the thickness δ' of the laminar sublayer is greater than 5, then $x = 1$ for practical purposes.

With the help of the foregoing equations the magnitude of R' and U_*' can be determined experimentally.

610

The assumption expressed by Eq. (2.2.1−14) implies essentially that resistances are estimated from two components. For this reason it is possible to resolve also the slope into two parts instead of the hydraulic radius. A simplified solution of this type has been introduced by Meyer-Peter − Müller:

$$\tau'_0 = \gamma S' R \tag{2.2.1−19}$$

$$\tau''_0 = \gamma S'' R \tag{2.2.1−20}$$

where S' is the slope (energy) necessary for maintaining flow at a particular velocity and depth, in the absence of shape resistance, whereas S'' is the excess slope necessary to overcome shape resistances. Since according to Eq. (2.2.1−11) the roughness coefficient f depends on slope, from the expression

$$f = \frac{8gR}{v^2}(S' + S'') \tag{2.2.1−21}$$

it follows that

$$f' = \frac{8gRS'}{v^2} \tag{2.2.1−22}$$

$$f'' = \frac{8gRS''}{v^2} \tag{2.2.1−23}$$

indicating that also the roughness coefficient is composed of two parts, with f' representing the particle roughness of the bed material and f'' representing the roughness due to bed forms.

In experiments made in laboratory flumes Vanoni and Brooks observed that under certain conditions f'' might attain values seven times as high as f'. This observation in itself should call attention to the importance of bed forms in alluvial streams.

The roughness coefficient f of Darcy − Weissbach is often introduced by a correction for the roughness of the side slopes as f_b, which applies thus to the roughness of the bottom only. The roughness f_b of the bottom may also be resolved into two components, namely the particle roughness f'_b of the bottom and f''_b denoting the form roughness thereof.

Bed roughness has been studied by Vanoni and Brooks in laboratory experiment. Variations in bed roughness f_b have been determined in terms of the mean velocity v at approximately constant D/d relative roughness and at different depths of flow. The results obtained for fractions $d_g = 0.145$ to 0.137 mm approximately and at depths $D = 7$ to 7.5 cm are shown in *Fig. 2.2.1 − 11*. The magnitude of bed roughness f_b is seen to vary radically with bed forms. It is also seen in the figure, that the surface slope and the shear velocity related to the bed are similarly affected by the bed forms. Increasing depth to 16 to 17 cm, the magnitude of f_b failed to attain 0.09 and its variation followed a law other than in the

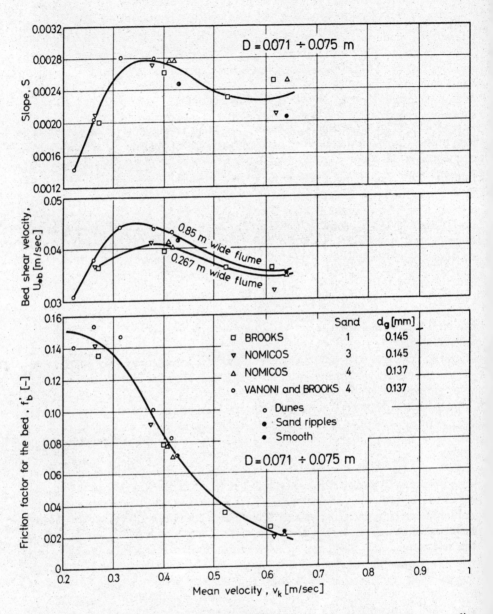

Fig. 2.2.1—11. Variations in slope, in bed shear velocity and in roughness coefficient according to mean velocity for different bed configurations. After Vanoni and Brooks

foregoing case. Vanoni and Brooks could offer no explanation for these differences.

The results of Brooks were received with much criticism for the details of which reference is made to the literature.

Brooks found the relationship existing between the rate of transport, depth and slope of flow to be highly complex. Some explanations for this circumstance have been given in *Sections 1.2.6, 1.2.7 and 1.2.8*. However, the combined role of slope and depth of flow in sediment transport in alluvial streams is even more strikingly reflected by the laws of variable critical tractive forces and variable critical velocities, where it has been demonstrated that the depth and slope of flow should always be regarded as corresponding, coupled pairs of value.

Starting from theoretical considerations Vanoni and Hwang have concluded that the form roughness f_b'' of the bed is influenced by the height h of the bed forms, by the hydraulic radius R_b of the bed and by the exposure parameter $e = A_s/A$ and, since under similar conditions the bed is hydraulically rough, it is not related to the Reynold's number. Coefficient e represents the area density of bed forms, since A_s is the horizontal projection of the lee-side of sand ripples or dunes, whereas A is the total area for which A_s is determined. Accordingly

$$f_b'' = F\left(\frac{R_b}{h}, \frac{A_s}{A}\right)$$ (2.2.1–24)

or, introducing the equivalent sand roughness k_s which is proportionate to h and A_s/A:

$$f_b'' = F\left(\frac{R_b}{k_s}\right)$$ (2.2.1–25)

According to Rouse, on the other hand, if the area density of roughness elements is small, then k_s is proportionate to the product of h and e, so that

$$f_b'' = F\left(\frac{R_b}{\dfrac{A_s}{A} \cdot h}\right)$$ (2.2.2–26)

For the experimental determination of Eq. (2.2.1−26) Vanoni and Hwang have introduced the average height $\bar{H}$ of the dunes and sand ripples, deriving the relation

$$\frac{1}{\sqrt{f_b''}} = 3.5 \lg\left(\frac{R_b}{e\bar{H}}\right) - 2.3$$ (2.2.1–27)

From the experimental results it was thus found that the bed roughness f_b'' due to the bed forms is described more exactly by the characteristic roughness dimension $e\bar{H}$ of the dunes and sand ripples, than by the equivalent sand roughness k_s. The term $R_b/e\bar{H}$ may be named the modified relative roughness.

613

Fig. 2.2.1—12. The shape roughness f_b'' of the bed according to the modified relative roughness $R_b/e\bar{H}$. After Vanoni and Brooks

The problems related to the developing and travelling of sand ripples have been studied by Raudkivi whose investigations covered the determination of pressure distribution in flowing water at solid and loose sand ripples, as well as the scouring of particles. He found the sand ripples to travel at a velocity of nearly 3 cm per hour.

Attention to the statistical analysis of dune shapes has been devoted, among others, by F. C. Nordin and E. V. Richardson, who determined the average height and length of the dunes. On the basis of the distribution parameters thereof they concluded that the height of dunes on the bottom followed a Gauss type distribution, whereas the amplitudes related to a medium datum plane followed an exponential distribution.

Simons and Albertson have found even the rate of sediment transport to be influenced by bed forms. On the basis of laboratory and field experiments they demonstrated that for a bed material of an average particle size greater than 0.2 mm and comprising different-size fractions the relationship existing between sediment transport and bed forms could be described as follows:

Flow conditions, bed forms	Sediment concentration p/lit
Subcritical flow	
sand ripples	0— 90
dunes	90—1000
transition of dunes in high-velocity flow	1000—3000
smooth bed, moving bed material	2000—5000
Supercritical flow	
standing waves	usually higher than
antidunes	4000

Variations in the roughness coefficient f have been studied also by Liu and Hwang who described the variations in f in terms of the Reynolds number

$$Re = \frac{4Rv}{v}$$

For a smooth bed they found the variations in the roughness coefficient to resemble the variations in the corresponding coefficient in pipe flow. The appearence of sand ripples on the bed is marked by a sudden increase in the roughness coefficient. Consequently the approach of Nikuradze is inapplicable to alluvial channels.

The value of shape roughness ranges from 0.02 to 0.2; for smooth bed conditions a value of 0.02 to 0.04 may be assumed.

Changes in the coefficient f in relation to sand roughness has been studied extensively with the help of roughness elements installed in laboratory flumes. The influence of roughness elements is described in general by the expression

$$\frac{1}{\sqrt{f}} = A \lg \frac{y}{k\lambda} + B \qquad (2.2.1-28)$$

where A = constant
B = constant depending on the shape of the roughness elements
y = depth of flow
k = height of the roughness elements and
λ = coefficient representing the spacing of roughness elements and the shape of the flume.

615

Fig. 2.2.1—13. Resistance coefficient $c\sqrt{g}$ related to parameter $Re = vy_n/v$ in hydraulically smooth and rough zones. After Sayre and Albertson

For a variety of element shapes (cubes, spheres, cones) the magnitude of k varies from 0 to 0.4, but above 0.4 the resistance varies in an unpredictable manner.

Using the foregoing expression and brick shapes as roughness elements Sayre and Albertson found the following numerical form:

$$\frac{c}{\sqrt{g}} = \sqrt{\frac{8}{f}} = 6.06 \lg \frac{y_n}{X} \qquad (2.2.1-29)$$

where y_n = normal depth of flow (the depth in the case where the bottom, the energy grade line and the surface are parallel)

X = roughness coefficient (having the dimension of length), representing the size, spacing and shape of the roughness elements.

These results have confirmed the opinion that the roughness coefficient is related to relative roughness by a logarithmic law.

The roughness coefficient is plotted against the Reynolds number $Re = vy_n/v$ in *Fig. 2.2.1—13.*

In this figure the experimental points are distinguished according to the ratio of the longitudinal spacing x of the roughness elements (cubes) and the height a of the cubes, as well as according to the ratio of the lateral spacing e and the height a of the cubes. From the figure the following expressions are seen to apply to the individual ranges:

In laminar flow:

$$\frac{c}{\sqrt{g}} = 0.577 Re^{1/2} \qquad (2.2.1-30)$$

Fig. 2.2.1—14. U_*/v related to parameter $v^3/g\omega D$ according to stages for the gaging section Nagybajcs on the Danube

In the hydraulically smooth ranges

$$\frac{c}{\sqrt{g}} = 5.99 \ Re^{1/8} \qquad\qquad (2.2.1-31)$$

or

$$\frac{c}{\sqrt{g}} = 6.06 \ \lg \frac{Re}{c/\sqrt{g}} + 1.2 \qquad\qquad (2.2.1-32)$$

The hydraulically rough range starts at the value

$$\frac{Re\sqrt{f}}{y_n/x} = 33 \qquad\qquad (2.2.1-33)$$

and roughness is to be computed from Eq. (2.2.1−29).

Changes in the roughness coefficient have been studied repeatedly in alluvial channels as well. As an example the relationship between the parameter

$$\frac{U_*}{v} = \frac{\sqrt{g}}{c} = \sqrt{\frac{f}{8}}$$

and $v^3/g\omega D$ is illustrated in terms of stages for the Nagybajcs gaging station on the Danube in *Fig. 2.2.1 − 14*. Roughness is seen to decrease, although slightly with rising stages. Since, as mentioned before, $v^3/g\omega D = C/\eta_c$, roughness decreases also with an increase in sediment concentration C. This logically follows from the foregoing statement, since rising stages are usually accompanied by an increase in C. This conclusion is otherwise in agreement with the results of Vanoni and Brook.

A remarkable effect of the roughness characteristic of alluvial channels is observable at times of floods. The depth of flow and, in turn, the relative roughness varies even at the same sediment material with the different conditions of bed movement. This implies that a change in the depth of flow alone entails a change in resistance. In alluvial streams the changes in depth and stage are almost continuous phenomena. It follows that a continuous change may be expected in roughness and resistances, and consequently also in the velocities. For this reason velocity cannot be determined in a particular case unless the changes in stage and the corresponding conditions of bed movement are taken into consideration.

During the passage of a flood wave the condition of bed movement may undergo repeated variations, and this results always in a change of bed roughness. For example the sand ripples may be washed away by an increase in discharge so that the bottom becomes smooth, accompanied by a reduction in roughness. As a consequence, the increase in depth due to an increase in discharge is smaller in such alluvial channels than in a solid bed. This indicates that alluvial channels are capable of adjusting themselves to individual flood waves and convey these in a manner producing only slight changes in depth under certain conditions.

The bed roughness in alluvial channels is, of course, influenced also by the shape of the bed, by bends and changes in the bottom. These influences are, however, beyond the scope of the present treatment and are not dealt with here.

2.2.2. THE HYDRAULIC GEOMETRY OF STREAMS

The development, properties and history of alluvial streams have been studied extensively in geophysics and geography making valuable contributions to hydrographic observations. These are concerned primarily with the morphological properties of streams and are thus necessarily of a qualitative character.

It would naturally be of considerable interest to complete the qualitative description by factors to which a numerical value can be assigned. The development of channels was described in 1953 on the basis of hydrographic observations by

618

L. B. Leopold and T. Maddock. These investigations were concerned with the relations existing between the hydrological and hydraulic factors, and the geometry of the channel. For this reason these relations were referred to by the pertinent collective term *"hydraulic geometry"*.

The main conclusions are summarized briefly in the following.

In alluvial streams a variety of hydraulic factors, such as surface width B, mean depth D and mean velocity v_k have been found to vary as a simple exponential function of discharge Q. It has been shown that suspended sediment transport can be expressed in a similar manner. Consequently a relationship should be expected to exist between suspended sediment transport, surface width and the mean depth of flow. If the relations

$$B = aQ^b \qquad (2.2.2-1)$$

$$D = cQ^f \qquad (2.2.2-2)$$

$$v_k = kQ^m \qquad (2.2.2-3)$$

are determined for different streams, then the identity

$$Q = BDv_k = ackQ^{(b+f+m)} \qquad (2.2.2-4)$$

should make it clear that, disregarding the discrepancies introduced in the determination of Eqs (2.2.2−1) to (2.2.2−3) as well as errors of measurement and computations, the equations

$$b + f + m = 1 \qquad (2.2.2-5)$$

and

$$ack = 1 \qquad (2.2.2-6)$$

are necessarily valid.

The relations expressed by Eqs (2.2.2−1) to (2.2.2−3) are similar for different streams and especially for different cross-sections on the same stream.

From the investigations mentioned in the foregoing it was concluded that an increase in the annual mean discharge is accompanied by an increase in the values of B, D and v_k downstream. This conclusion must not be generalized unless it is related to discharges of the same frequency along the river. The downstream increase in the flow velocity v_k is attributed, under the foregoing conditions, to the fact that D increases at a faster rate than would be required by the reduction in slope S. Concerning sediment concentration it was stated that a slight decrease occurs therein downstream along some rivers.

Remembering the relationships existing between the suspended sediment load and the hydraulic properties of the stream, the following inferences of general validity have been made:

At a constant discharge Q

619

– if the channel width B is constant, an increase in the mean velocity v_k involves an increase in the weight G_s of suspended sediment transported and, since $Q = DBv_k = $ constant, a decrease in the mean depth D of flow,

– if the mean velocity v_k is constant, the surface width B increases and G_s decreases, since $Q = $ constant, D also decreases.

Finally, at constant Q, G_s increases

a) if B decreases and v_k is constant, or

b) if v_k increases and B is constant.

In connection with these conclusions it should be remembered that these hold true only if the discharge is of the same frequency in various cross-sections of the stream.

For the case of varying discharges Leopold and Maddock have found for all values of b (i.e., according to Eq. [2.2.2−1] for all rates of increase in B with discharge) that the value of j (according to $G_s = pG^j$ the rate of increase in G_s with discharge) depends on m, namely on the rate at which the velocity of flow increases with Q, as indicated by Eq. (2.2.2−3). Since, however, $(b + f + m) = 1$, the value of f is determined by the magnitude of b and m. The results of these investigations are shown in *Fig. 2.2.2−1*, in which j is plotted against m/f for different values of b.

The relation represented in *Fig. 2.2.2.−1* is of considerable interest. In fact, if the ratio m/f and b are determined for any particular cross-section of a stream, the value of j can also be found with the result that the suspended load versus discharge relation becomes also available.

All conclusions of Leopold and Maddock apply to streams under arid climates. It should be noted, moreover, that the number of observation data was too small in the majority of cases to indicate more than the trend of these relations. Consequently when applied to particular streams, the foregoing relations may yield results contrasting with those actually observed.

For the stations Nagymaros and Dunaújváros on the Danube, the station Tápé on the Tisza and the station Hidasnémeti on the Hernád river (see *Section 3.1.2*), the following values of m/f, b and j have been determined:

	m/f	b	j
Nagymaros	$\dfrac{0.59}{0.325} = 1.815$	0.086	3.57
Dunaújváros	$\dfrac{0.48}{0.47} = 1.02$	0.053	3.57
Tápé	$\dfrac{0.62}{0.3} = 2.07$	0.08	2.44
Hidasnémeti	$\dfrac{0.55}{0.32} = 1.72$	0.13	2.63

Fig. 2.2.2—1. The growth of bed width, of mean depth, of mean velocity and of suspended-sediment transport related to increases of discharge based on *b*, *m/f* and *j* values. After Leopold and Maddock

On the basis of the corresponding m/f and b values, according to *Fig. 2.2.2—1*, the exponent j assumes the following values:

— at Nagymaros 3.14, with an acceptable difference over the value actually observed,

— at Tápé 4.08, at Hidasnémeti 3.65, indicating that the relation represented in the figure does not apply to the Tisza and Hernád rivers.

Although the relation plotted in *Fig. 2.2.2—1* has been developed by Leopold and Maddock for average transport rates and hydraulic factors of streams,

Fig. 2.2.2—2. Specific discharge q vs. water depth D according to slope S for different bed configurations. After Vanoni and Brooks

further investigations have shown these to yield acceptable results for individual flood waves as well. Consequently, by taking into consideration the changes in discharge Q and the channel parameters at particular flood waves, the **change** in the suspended load can also be found from the figure. The extension of the validity of the figure to individual flood waves implies thus that the changes in the channel induced by the passages of flood waves result necessarily also in a change in sediment concentration. As pointed out by the authors, the relations could be improved by including the bed load besides the suspended load.

In connection with the relations of "hydraulic geometry" the role of bed roughness and slope has also been studied by Leopold and Maddock.

It should be remembered that, at a constant discharge with B constant, G_s increases and D decreases with an increase in v_k. Using the Manning formula

$$v_k = \frac{1}{n} D^{2/3} S^{1/2}$$

for expressing the flow velocity, it should become clear that if v_k increases and D decreases, the value of $S^{1/2}/n$ must increase, i.e. either slope S becomes steeper or friction coefficient n becomes lower.

Roughness conditions are influenced primarily by three factors, namely the particle size of the bottom material, the morphology of the channel and the weight of sediment transported.

It is concluded from the foregoing that any change in the velocity to depth relation is of influence on sediment transport as well.

622

A number of other relations have been published in connection with hydraulic geometry. Among these mention should be made of the investigations by Vanoni and Brooks into the relationship existing between specific discharge q, slope S and depth D. In *Fig. 2.2.2−2* constructed after the measurements of Barton and Liu the relation is shown for smooth bed and dunes. At the same discharge in a smooth bed the depth is seen to be smaller and the slope to be steeper while, conversely, in a bed covered with dunes the depth is greater and the slope flatter.

2.2.3. THE INFLUENCE OF HYDRAULIC FACTORS ON BED LOAD TRANSPORT

The weight of bed load transported along the bottom is related, in a highly complex manner, to the hydraulic characteristics of the stream and even to those of the catchment area. Regardless of this it is possible in many cases to express — as demonstrated in *Section 2.1.3* − the weight of bed load with the help of a single hydraulic factor of the water course. It should be appreciated that, owing to the factors neglected, these relations are essentially stochastic in character. Stochastic relations must not be regarded as functional relations unless the difference between the values obtained from the approximate and the actually valid functional relations remains within a permissible limit and unless it is remembered that the results obtained originate from approximate relations.

For practical purposes it is desirable to introduce functional relations wherever possible. These are indeed much easier to handle than their stochastic counterparts.

When introducing approximate functional relations we should naturally be aware of the simplifying assumptions made during the computations. It is therefore found desirable to examine the criteria providing a quantitative estimate on the magnitude of errors resulting from the introduction of functional relations.

From the results of bed load measurements the rate of bed load transport is found in most cases to be described by simple exponential functions of stage h, discharge Q and the mean velocity v_k. The general form of these exponential functions is

$$G_B = u_1 h^{g_1} \qquad (2.2.3-1)$$

$$G_B = p_1 Q^{j_1} \qquad (2.2.3-2)$$

$$G_B = \alpha_1 v_k^{\beta_1} \qquad (2.2.3-3)$$

Clearly, along with the foregoing bed load transport relations, consideration must be given also to the hydraulic relationships existing between stages, discharges and mean velocities. On major streams these relations can also be described approximately with the help of exponential functions.

The hydraulic relationship between stage, discharge and velocity provides thus three additional basic equations:

$$Q = eh^r \qquad (2.2.3-4)$$

$$v_k = \lambda Q^\sigma \qquad (2.2.3-5)$$

$$v_k = \phi h^\psi \qquad (2.2.3-6)$$

The fundamental equations (2.2.3−1) to (2.2.3−6) are, of course, but approximately functional relations. For this very reason it would be misleading to expect the relations determined from the results of bed load measurements and hydrographic observations to comply with full mathematical exactness with the criteria derived from the interrelations of the six fundamental equations.

For the sake of completeness it should be noted that the afore-mentioned approximate functional relations are often impossible to determine. For instance, in streams embedded in loose alluvial deposits, if the scours and deposits are extensive, it should not be anticipated that a means can be found for describing bed load transport with the help of stages, discharges or flow velocities unequivocally. Moreover, where the material lining the bed is of a composition permitting the development of a protective layer it may also be found impossible to determine approximate functional relations.

Since the relationships may but approximately be regarded as functional relations, the Eqs (2.2.3−1) to (2.2.3−6) determined for any given cross-section of a particular stream from observation data will clearly fail to satisfy exactly the criteria that can be derived from the relationships existing mutually between the equations. Of the six fundamental equations not more than three may be regarded as independent, implying that the relations determined independently from one another are required to meet certain criteria.

The question arises what criteria are to be satisfied if the fundamental Eqs (2.2.3−1) to (2.2.3−6) are regarded as functional relations in the mathematical sense.

Combining Eqs (2.2.3−2) and (2.2.3−4) we get

$$G_B = p_1 e^{j_1} h^{r j_1}$$

whence, remembering Eq. (2.2.3−1), the following two condition equations result

$$u_1 = p_1 e^{j_1} \qquad (2.2.3-7)$$

$$g_1 = r j_1 \qquad (2.2.3-8)$$

The collation of Eqs (2.2.3−3) and (2.2.3−6) yields

$$G_B = \alpha_1 \phi^{\beta_1} h^{\beta_1 \psi}$$

whence again two condition equations are obtained

$$u_1 = \alpha_1 \phi^{\beta_1}$$ (2.2.3−9)

$$g_1 = \beta_1 \psi$$ (2.2.3−10)

Considering finally Eqs (2.2.3−3) and (2.2.3−5), the rate of bed load transport is found also from the equation

$$G_B = \alpha_1 \lambda^{\beta_1} Q^{\beta_1 \sigma}$$

from which the last two condition equations are obtained

$$p_1 = \alpha_1 \lambda^{\beta_1}$$ (2.2.3−11)

$$j_1 = \beta_1 \sigma$$ (2.2.3−12)

Since the six condition equations under Eqs (2.2.3−7) to (2.2.3−12) represent the mathematical relationships existing between quantities derived from observation data on bed load transport, discharge, stage and flow velocity, they may be regarded truly as condition equations for compensating computations. Their number is six and is thus less than the number of unknown quantities involved in Eqs (2.2.3−1) to (2.2.3−6) and consequently the number of roots is very large. The number of unknown quantities is twelve, namely the coefficients u_1, p_1 α_1, e, λ and ϕ, further the exponents g_1, j_1, β_1, r, σ and ψ.

Realizing that the fundamental relations cannot be regarded mathematically as functional relations, there appears no point in performing compensating computations on the basis of observation results for determining relations on bed load transport.

Although the six condition equations result from mathematically not fully exact functional relations, they impose certain limitations on the determination of the six fundamental relationships. In fact, if three independent equations are selected arbitrarily from the fundamental relations given by Eqs (2.2.3−1) to (2.2.3−6) and these are determined in advance by the approximate correlation of observation data, i.e. if the values of three exponents and three coefficients are determined graphically, then the three remaining equations are also determined essentially on the basis of the condition equations.

Considering bed load transport, it should be obvious that the relationships existing between the rate of transport G_B and stages, discharges and mean velocities are found expediently from observation data. It is not recommended, however, to determine either the stage or the discharge with the help of the condition equations based on the relations of bed load transport. Using a similar procedure the discrepancies inherent in the hydraulic relations of the water course would be increased by the simplifying assumptions necessarily introduced in deriving the relations on bed load transport.

In particular cases it may be found desirable to determine three independent relations from Eqs (2.2.3−1) to (2.2.3−6) on the basis of observation data and to estimate therefrom approximately the remaining expressions on bed load transport using these in combination with the condition equations. In the case of streams where only a few bed load observation data are available, more reliable information on the magnitude on bed load transport is obtained in this manner.

The determination of each of the six fundamental equations is practically justified in cases where, besides hydrographic observation data on the stream, all measurement results are available on bed load transport. Determining Eqs (2.2.3−1) to (2.2.3−6) from observation data it becomes possible to examine to what extent the coefficients and exponents determined in this manner satisfy the condition equations given by Eqs (2.2.3−7) to (2.2.3−12). As pointed out already, differences over the condition equations will necessarily result. The relative magnitude of these differences is, however, an indication whether or not the introduction of approximate functional relations is justified at all.

For several water courses in Hungary the relationships derived from observation data have been compared with the condition equations for several gaging cross-sections. It should be noted that as far as bed load transport is concerned, wide discrepancies over the condition equations have been determined. In view of the shortcomings of bed load samplers, and of the poor reliability of observation methods, these discrepancies are not surprising. Regardless of these inconsistencies the approximate functional relations have been found to provide valuable information on bed load transport in several Hungarian rivers so that their use is justified until more accurate methods of computation or observation are developed.

In *Section 3.1.1*, the above statements will be illustrated by examples in connection with the processing of observation data.

2.2.4. THE INFLUENCE OF HYDRAULIC FACTORS ON SUSPENDED-SEDIMENT TRANSPORT

As demonstrated in *Section 2.1.4*, it is often found possible to determine the weight G_s of the suspended sediment transported in unit time past a particular cross-section of streams with the help of certain hydraulic factors of the stream. Since sediment concentration C_k particular to the the mean cross-section can be estimated directly, once the sediment transport rate G_s and the discharge Q are known, the sediment concentration can also be expressed in terms of one of the hydraulic factors of the stream.

The rate of transport and sediment concentration being in general affected by several hydraulic factors of the stream, it should be obvious that the relations involving a particular hydraulic factor are essentially stochastic in character. When regarding similar stochastic relationships as mathematical functions it should always be remembered that in the mathematical sense these are just approximate functional relations.

626

Experience has shown that sediment concentration C_k and transport rate G_s can be described by the following functional relations:

$$C_k = dQ^l \qquad (2.2.4-1)$$

$$G_s = pQ^j \qquad (2.2.4-2)$$

$$C_k = th^n \qquad (2.2.4-3)$$

$$G_s = uh^g \qquad (2.2.4-4)$$

$$C_k = \gamma v_k^\delta \qquad (2.2.4-5)$$

$$G_s = \alpha v_k^\beta \qquad (2.2.4-6)$$

The relations expressed by Eqs (2.2.3−4) to (2.2.3−6) for stages, discharges and flow velocities apply, of course, to suspended-sediment transport as well. Consequently

$$Q = eh^r \qquad (2.2.4-7)$$

$$v_k = \lambda Q^\sigma \qquad (2.2.4-8)$$

$$v_k = \phi h^\psi \qquad (2.2.4-9)$$

Considering the approximate functional relations describing suspended-sediment transport in terms of the hydraulic factors, an additional function, namely the actual function relating the weight of suspended sediment to sediment concentration and discharge should also be taken into consideration:

$$G_s = C_k Q \qquad (2.2.4-10)$$

In connection with Eq. (2.2.4−10) it should be noted that it represents a mathematically exact functional relation, which follows from the definition of mean concentration.

Of the ten fundamental equations only four are independent, implying that the relations determined independently from one another must satisfy certain conditions.

For the sake of completeness it should be noted that the approximate functions given by Eqs (2.2.4−1) to (2.2.4−9) are impossible to determine in certain cases. For instance where the suspended sediment is very fine, Eqs (2.2.4−1) and (2.2.4−2) are often impossible to determine. On the other hand, where the shape of the cross-section is highly variable, not even an approximate determination of the functions under Eqs (2.2.4−7) to (2.2.4−9) is possible.

When deriving Eqs (2.2.4−1) to (2.2.4−9) from observation data for a given cross-section of a particular stream, it should be obvious that the criteria obtained by the interrelations between the individual equations will be satisfied but approximately.

Examine hereafter the criteria to be satisfied in order to regard not only Eq. (2.2.4−10) but also Eqs (2.2.4−1) to (2.2.4−9) as mathematical functions.

Combining Eqs (2.2.4−1) and (2.2.4−2) and remembering also Eq. (2.2.4−10) we have

$$d = p \qquad (2.2.4-11)$$

$$j = l + 1 \qquad (2.2.4-12)$$

Since $G_s = C_k Q$ is a true function, the condition equations, $d = p$ and $j = l + 1$ must be satisfied with mathematical exactness, disregarding inaccuracies of constructions and computations.

From the combination of the functions under Eqs (2.2.4−1) and (2.2.4−7), considering also the expressions $G_s = C_k Q$, as well as $C_k = th^n$ it follows that

$$te = pe^j \qquad (2.2.4-13)$$

$$n + r = rj \qquad (2.2.4-14)$$

From the conditions in Eqs (2.2.4−13) and (2.2.4−14)

$$G_s = pe^j h^{rj} = teh^{n+r}$$

which, in combination with Eq. (2.2.4−4), yields the condition equations

$$te = u \qquad (2.2.4-15)$$

$$n + r = g \qquad (2.2.4-16)$$

From the relations under Eqs (2.2.4−6) and (2.2.4−8) it follows that

$$G_s = \alpha \, \lambda^\beta Q^{\beta\sigma}$$

which, in combination with Eq. (2.2.4−2), yields the following two condition equations

$$p = \alpha\lambda^\beta \qquad (2.2.4-17)$$

$$j = \beta\sigma \qquad (2.2.4-18)$$

Eliminating from Eqs (2.2.4−6) and (2.2.4−9) the velocity v_k:

$$G_s = \alpha\phi^\beta h^{\beta\psi}$$

which, in combination with Eq. (2.2.4−4), yields the equations

$$u = \alpha\phi^\beta \qquad (2.2.4-19)$$

$$g = \beta\psi \qquad (2.2.4-20)$$

628

Two additional condition equations are obtained by combining Eqs (2.2.4 – 5), (2.2.4 – 6) and (2.2.4 – 8). In fact

$$av_k^\beta = \gamma v_k^\delta \sqrt[\sigma]{\frac{v_k}{\lambda}} = \gamma \left(\frac{1}{\lambda}\right)^{1/\sigma} v_k^{\left(\delta + \frac{1}{\sigma}\right)}$$

whence

$$\alpha = \gamma \left(\frac{1}{\lambda}\right)^{1/\sigma} \qquad\qquad (2.2.4-21)$$

$$\beta = \delta + \frac{1}{\sigma} \qquad\qquad (2.2.4-22)$$

Since the twelve equations (2.2.4 – 11) to (2.2.4 – 22) represent mathematical relations between the quantities derived from observation data on sediment concentration and rate of sediment transport, as well as on discharges, flow velocities and stages, they may be regarded as condition equations for compensating computation. Their number is twelve, i.e. less than the number of unknown quantities involved in Eqs (2.2.4 – 1) to (2.2.4 – 10) so that a great number of roots is obtained. The unknown quantities number eighteen, namely the cofficient d, t, u, γ, α, e, λ and ϕ as well as the exponent l, j, n, g, δ, β, r, σ and ψ.

Compensating computations based on observation data are, of course, superfluous in this case as well, since the fundamental relations are known not to be true functions.

The twelve condition equations under Eqs (2.2.4 – 11) to (2.2.4 – 22), though originating from mathematically not fully exact functions, impose certain limitations on the determination of the ten fundamental relations. In fact if three independent equations are selected arbitrarily from Eqs (2.2.4 – 1) to (2.2.4 – 9) and these are determined in advance by correlating approximate observation data, i.e. if the values of three coefficients and three exponents are determined for instance by a graphical method, then in principle the remaining six equations are also defined on the basis of the condition equations. In adopting a similar approach it would be desirable to determine, from observation data, the relationship existing between sediment transport G_s and stage or discharge, as well as between sediment concentration C_k and the velocity of flow. The determination of the remaining six relations from these and from the condition equations would be unadvisable since by doing so the errors resulting inevitably from the simplifications introduced in deriving the six relations would be increased by the simplifying assumptions involved necessarily in the relationships existing between sediment transport and stages or discharges as well as between sediment concentration and stages. Nevertheless, the condition equations may still prove useful for the approximate description of suspended-sediment transport in streams. In fact, by determining e.g. the approximate functions under Eqs (2.2.4 – 3), (2.2.4 – 8) and (2.2.4 – 9) by correlating observation data on the basis of hydrographic measurements, the twelve condition equations afford more informative data on suspended-sediment transport in streams.

The characteristic relations between suspended-sediment transport and the hydraulic properties of a stream are thus of great interest in any particular case.

The determination of each of the nine fundamental equations is practically justified in cases where, besides hydrographic observation data on the stream, all measurements on suspended-sediment transport are also available. Determining Eqs $(2.2.4-1)$ to $(2.2.4-9)$ from observation data, it becomes possible to examine to what extent the coefficients and exponents determined in this manner satisfy the condition equations under Eqs $(2.2.4-11)$ to $(2.2.4-22)$. As pointed out earlier, differences will necessarily result in the condition equations. The relative magnitude of these differences is, however, an indication whether or not the introduction of approximate functional relations is justified at all.

For several water courses in Hungary the relationships derived from observation data have been compared with the condition equations for several gaging cross-sections. Regardless of the fact that in several instances differences of considerable magnitude have been observed, the introduction of approximate functional relations has been found permissible at least for the rivers in the Hungarian plains.

In *Section 3.1.1* several examples will be quoted to illustrate the relations between suspended-sediment transport and the hydraulic factors of streams.

2.3. THE REGIME THEORY

2.3.1. REVIEW OF HISTORICAL DEVELOPMENT

2.3.1.1. The concept of the stable channel. The original term used in the theory of stable channels was "non-silting and non-scouring channel". This was followed by the term "regime theory". The terms "regime" and "stable" are truly pertinent and denote actually a condition of equilibrium of the bed.

It has been frequently stated in the literature that non-silting and non-scouring canals can be designed either with the help of the regime theory or by using the method of tractive forces. No objection could be made to a similar classification if this were to imply not more than the hydraulic factors on which the design is based. From this classification, however, the existence of not only two different methods, but of almost independent two theories could be inferred. The relations referred to collectively as the hydraulic geometry of streams have been mentioned repeatedly as an independent theory. In addition to the individual theories a number of empirical formulae, derived from direct observations, have been suggested.

630

The different methods and assumptions introduced in solving particular problems have appeared in later investigations as independent procedures and even theories, in spite of the unquestionably commendable efforts of the authors. The resulting confusion has greatly contributed to the difficulty of describing accurately the complex phenomenon of sediment transport, rendering the general application and practical use of earlier valuable and interesting results difficult and sometimes even impossible.

The only remedy to this confusion consists in regarding sediment transport and all related problems as a physical phenomenon governed by clearly defined laws. Sediment transport is indeed a physical phenomenon regardless of how accurately the laws governing it are known or understood. Any theory relies necessarily on certain basic assumptions in describing a particular phenomenon. The laws of physics are expressed also by empirical relations in an approximate form taking advantage of the favourable circumstance that in certain cases the variables taken into consideration are related closely enough to render the influence of the neglected variables negligible for practical purposes.

Considering the theories of the stable channel or the regime theory under this approach, it should be realized that it would be misleading to regard it as an independent theory as far as either results or methods are concerned. Concurring with the opinion of P. Ackers the term "regime concept" would appear more correct.

The theory of the stable channel results essentially from the statistical processing of a large volume of observation and measurement data. All investigations aimed at the theoretical interpretation of the empirical relationships concerning the stable channel have led inevitably to the general relations involved in the different problems of sediment transport. This is clearly reflected by the relevant results of Lacey, Lane, Blench, Simons, Albertson, Herbertson and others.

The above remarks are by no means intended to question the value of formulae suggested for the stable channel. In fact, the author believes them to be of great interest and includes them in the present treatment along with the empirical relations on sediment transport, with the symptomatic relations of hydrological factors and the hydraulic geometry of streams.

The theory of the stable channel has been developed in India and Pakistan where extensive irrigation projects were brought to life late in the last century. The mostly artificial canals excavated for conveying irrigation water proved difficult and expensive to maintain in the early stages of development. In order to make irrigation farming economically feasible it was found necessary to minimize the maintenance costs of irrigation canals. These efforts prompted the investigations based on practical observations, the objective of which was to establish design criteria for non-silting and non-scouring canals. The concept of non-silting and non-scouring canals was introduced in 1894—95 by R. G. Kennedy. Several definitions of the stable channel have since been suggested. Highly pertinent is the definition given by E. W. Lane according to whom unlined earth canals with neither the bottom nor the side slopes scoured by flowing water and with no appreciable silt deposits are considered stable. C. Inglis considered canals to be stable if no changes occurred in the bed from one year to the other.

Stable channels thus retain their shape, the same discharge is conveyed at the same velocities and at the same slope and even the distribution of velocity within the cross-section remains unchanged.

Channels conveying clear water free of sediment and not subject to scouring may be regarded stable. In such cases the material of the canal is of prime importance since the velocity of flow must be controlled to remain everywhere below the limit allowed for the particular material. Another factor of importance is the shape of the cross-section, mainly for ensuring a proper distribution of velocities. The side slopes are exposed to the action of gravity and to scouring at lower velocities than is the bottom. With due allowance for various hydraulic factors (slope, depth, etc.) the shape of the cross-section should be so selected as to prevent the sides from being scoured. The problem of dimensioning canals for the highest allowable velocity either with a less expensive narrow bed or with the steepest possible slope is controlled by local circumstances. At high velocities and steep slopes wide and relatively shallow canals, at which the ratio of width B to depth D is relatively high, will be found usually desirable. Where other considerations call for narrow and deep canals, excessive velocities must be avoided by reducing the bottom slope in order to prevent scouring of the banks.

In the canals of practical interest some sediment is always transported. In such cases the control of degradation and scouring is alone insufficient; care must be taken to prevent the sediment from settling. The theory of the stable channel is closely related also in this respect to the theory of sediment transport.

It is of interest to note that, unrelated to the theory of stable channel but almost parallel thereto, the concept of bed stability has been introduced in river regulation to describe bed conditions.

Although the terms stable channel and bed stability apply to practically identical conditions of water courses, the two concepts remained unrelated to each other in the course of their development. This is believed to be due principally to the fact that in the early stages investigators of stable channels and bed stability failed to realize the importance of sediment transport. The circumstance that in early studies on the stable channel no changes at all were allowed for in the bed contributed to the unrelated development of the two concepts. It should be realized that the bed of alluvial stream is necessarily subject to minor changes. Stages and discharges fluctuate in accordance with circumstances that, in turn, depend on the season, etc. The changes in slope, velocity, discharge and stage with rising and falling water levels should be remembered in this context. Quite obviously these changes should be disregarded when considering channel stability. It is, of course, fully justified to question the potential occurrence of such changes in alluvial streams once the channel is considered stable. This question has been raised indeed in the development of the stable-channel theory. It was stated as early as in 1935 by C. R. Pettis that theoretically no cross-section was conceivable even in the case of artificial canals in which the bed would be stable over the entire

632

range of discharges. If stability is identified with rigorous permanence of the bed, then a particular canal would be stable at a single well-defined discharge only. However, if the fluctuating changes of the bed are included under the term of the stable channel, it becomes theoretically possible to relate the concepts of bed stability and stable channel to each other.

The identity of the two concepts was recognized in 1942 by the author and prompted him to extend the concept of the stable channel to alluvial streams as well or to explain bed stability in alluvial streams in accordance with the theory of the stable channel. This idea has since been put forward repeatedly. The stable-channel theory was extended in 1951 by Blench to alluvial streams. The attendant problems will be dealt with in subsequent sections.

2.3.1.2. Historical development. The development of the stable-channel theory started with the early investigations of Kennedy. The principal effort in the course of development was to establish empirical relationships between the characteristic data of canals observed to be stable. Owing to local conditions and to economic reasons, these early investigations were concerned only with canals, i.e. artificial water courses. The following data were usually adopted as characteristic of the channel width B, the slope S, the mean velocity v, the discharge Q, the hydraulic radius R and the wetted perimeter P. These variables are, of course, interrelated so that in general three independent regime equations can be written for a particular cross-section or reach of the canal under consideration. The general form of these equations is

$$D = F_1(Q) \qquad (2.3.1-1)$$

$$B = F_2(Q) \qquad (2.3.1-2)$$

$$S = F_3(Q) \qquad (2.3.1-3)$$

The first "regime equation" was introduced by R. G. Kennedy in 1895 on the basis of observations performed in the Bari Doab canal network in Punjab, India.

Kennedy stated a relationship to exist for non-silting and non-scouring channels between the allowable critical mean velocity v_c and the depths of flow D:

$$v_c = cD^n \qquad (2.3.1-4)$$

implying that the allowable critical velocity increases with the depth of flow. Beyond certain depth, however, the resulting velocities become high enough to result unavoidably in the scouring of the side slopes. The obvious objection to Kennedy's relation is that the critical velocity is not related to the width and shape of the channel cross-section.

In metric units Eq. $(2.3.1-4)$ becomes:

$$v_c = 0.56D^{0.64} \qquad (2.3.1-5)$$

where D is introduced in metres to obtain the critical velocity in m/sec units.

Subsequent investigations induced Kennedy to modify the exponent involved in his formula:

$$v = 0.56D^{0.50} \qquad (2.3.1-6)$$

At the time of its publication Kennedy's formula was received with great interest and it was believed to provide the universal answer to all problems arising in the design of stable channels. In the year following the publication of Kennedy's paper not less than 26 depth-to-velocity relations were introduced for designing canals of irrigation developments in India, Pakistan, Egypt, etc.

Initially the Kennedy formula was assumed to be applicable to narrow and deep as well as to wide and shallow channels alike.

Relying also on observations made in connection with canals in India a depth-to-width ratio has been suggested by F. Woods who in subsequent papers published the following stable channel formulae:

$$D = B^n \qquad (2.3.1-7)$$

$$v_c = \lg(BD) = (1 + n)\lg B \qquad (2.3.1-8)$$

$$\frac{1}{S} = 1000 \lg Q^2 \qquad (2.3.1-9)$$

Woods is thus seen to have included, beside the depth of flow, also the width of the channel, the discharge and the slope for describing stable channels.

From his investigations made in India E. S. Lindley stated in 1919 that apart from the velocity and depth of flow, channel stability is affected also by the width B_B of the bottom. In his paper reference is made to the role of discharge and the material lining the bed, although the effect thereof has not been included separately.

For stable channels Lindley suggested the following three relations between critical velocity, the depth of flow and bottom width:

$$v_c = 1.55D^{0.57} \; [\text{m/sec}] \qquad (2.3.1-10)$$

$$v_c = 1.23B_B^{0.355} \; [\text{m/sec}] \qquad (2.3.1-11)$$

$$B_B = 0.565D^{1.61} \; [\text{m}] \qquad (2.3.1-12)$$

Depth D and bottom width B_B are to be introduced into the above expressions in m units.

Of the above expressions only two are independent and apply to canals in which the sediment particle size ranges from 0.002 to 0.02 mm.

Starting from observations made on irrigation canals in Egypt Molesworth and Yenidunia have related the sediment particle diameter d, slope S and bottom width B_B of the canal to one another by the expression:

$$d = (c_1S + a_1)\sqrt{B_B} \qquad (2.3.1-13)$$

where c_1 and a_1 are constants.

W. T. Bottomley has questioned the validity of Kennedy's assumption that the sediment transported is not related to depth. In his opinion the rate of sediment transport is proportionate to slope and unrelated to the shape of the cross-section. Irrigation canals will therefore be stable if their slope is comparable to that of the main canal or river from which the supply is diverted.

In his paper published in 1930 G. Lacey improved the conclusions drawn from stable channels. Into the formula of Kennedy, given by Eq. (2.3.1−4), he introduced the hydraulic radius instead of the depth of flow D, while he found the exponent n to be constant and of a 0.5 value.

Consequently $v_c = c_1 \sqrt{R}$. The quality of sediment in different canals is represented by the sediment factor f, the magnitude of which in the Upper-Bari Doab canal network was unity. The general form of Lacey's first equation is thus

$$v_c = c_1 \sqrt{fR} \qquad (2.3.1-14)$$

The sediment factor f is related to the diameter of sediment particles as

$$d = \frac{f^2}{a} \qquad (2.3.1-15)$$

where a is constant.

According to Lacey's second equation

$$Af^2 = kv_c^5 \qquad (2.3.1-16a)$$

or

$$Qf^2 = kv_c^6 \qquad (2.3.1-16b)$$

where A is cross-sectional area, k is constant and Q is the discharge. Lacey's Eq. (2.3.1−16b) applies to all geometrically similar canals in which v_c is identical, regardless of the sediment factor.

For stable channels Lacey has found the wetted perimeter P to be in direct proportion with the square root of discharge Q. This is expressed by Lacey's third equation:

$$P = b \sqrt{Q} \qquad (2.3.1-17)$$

where b is constant.

Since in alluvial streams the wetted perimeter may be set equal for practical purposes to the width of the bed, the foregoing equation was used by Lacey to check the bed width at several bridges in India. At the bridges considered Lacey reported the width of the bed to be in full agreement with his formula.

These studies afford a good example for extending the statements made in connection with irrigation canals to alluvial streams as well.

From the above relationships existing between velocity, hydraulic radius and discharge, the slope of stable channels can also be found

$$S = \frac{mf^{3/2}}{Q^{1/9}} \qquad (2.3.1-18)$$

635

Subsequently Lacey modified the slope formula

$$S = \frac{m_1 f^{5/3}}{Q^{1/6}}$$ (2.3.1−19)

where m and m_1 are constants.

From Lacey's foregoing expressions the hydraulic radius can also be expressed in terms of discharge:

$$R = s \frac{Q^{1/3}}{f^{1/3}}$$ (2.3.1−20)

where s constant.

In this manner also the ratio of the wetted perimeter P and the hydraulic radius R is expressed in terms of discharge:

$$\frac{P}{R} = \frac{bQ^{1/2}}{\frac{sQ^{1/3}}{f^{1/3}}} = b_1 Q^{1/6} f^{1/3}$$ (2.3.1−21a)

$b_1 \equiv b/s = $ constant.

The formula relating the ratio P/R to the velocity of flow is

$$\frac{P}{R} = l v_c$$ (2.3.1−21b)

In Eqs (2.3.1−20) and (2.3.1−21) s, b, b_1 and l denote constants.

Once the discharge Q and the particle diameter d of sediment in the canal are known, the quantities v_c, A and R can be computed from Eqs (2.3.1−14) to (2.3.1−16) needed for dimensioning a stable channel.

The cross-section of stable channels is, according to Lacey, approximately elliptical where the ratio of the longer principal axis (channel width) to the shorter principal axis (depth of flow) is governed by the quality of sediment. For coarser sediment this ratio is higher than for finer ones.

Lacey has contributed significantly to our understanding of stable channels. He has introduced a coefficient representing the quality of sediment and has considered the characteristics of the cross-section as well. The main reason preventing his relations from becoming of general validity is that he neglected the rate of sediment transport.

Lacey expected an improvement of the stable-channel theory from dimensional analysis.

For a long period up to recent times theoretical as well as practical studies on stable channels were founded on Lacey's equations described in the foregoing.

The merits of Lacey are undeniable in improving the stable-channel theory. Of special interest are his first relations regardless of the fact that he improved them later repeatedly in the light of additional experiences and data.

The importance of the sediment transport rate and velocity for changes in the canal cross-section was first pointed out by E. W. Lane who conducted his studies in connection with the designs for the All American Canal under construction in the Imperial Valley and published his results in 1935. In these studies allowance was made for all available data on stable channels, the performance of which was subject to a comparative evaluation. The relations derived from observations in irrigation networks in India and Egypt proved unsuited for general use. As an explanation he suggested that the factors to be taken into consideration in the case of stable channels range between much wider limits than believed initially. All the factors listed in connection with sediment transport in streams were found to be involved here as well. These factors are not of uniform importance. For example it should be clear that the particle size of sediment plays a much more important role than the shape of particles. Lane believed that much research into the effect of secondary factors was superfluous.

Relying on information available in 1935 Lane believed it was no use studying the relationships existing between the hydraulic factors, namely slope, roughness, the hydraulic radius and mean velocities, these having been determine with sufficient accuracy by the familiar velocity formulae.

The main merit of Lane's work is to have pointed out that, besides information on the bed material, the design of stable channels is almost exclusively a problem of sediment transport. This problem is, however, too complex to permit any generalization even in the case of streams under apparently identical conditions.

The theoretical development concerning stable channels has benefited greatly from the discussions following the publication of Lane's approach.

In the course of this discussion Lacey emphasized the important role of the parameter v_c^2/R which is proportionate to the sediment factor. He believed this parameter to be related, for various sediment materials, to the extent of turbulence in the stream and thus to the rate of transport.

The importance of the ratio v_c^2/R as a measure of the type of flow has also been emphasized by Lacey.

If S is the slope of the energy grade line, v_c is the velocity of flow, g is acceleration due to gravity and R is the hydraulic radius, then the dimensionless resistance coefficient

$$\frac{gRS}{v_c^2} = \frac{U_*^2}{v_c^2} = C \qquad (2.3.1-22)$$

may be compared, according to Lacey, to the Chézy number.

The Chézy number C has been defined by Lacey as the power product of the Reynolds and Froude numbers:

$$C = \frac{gRS}{v_c^2} = K' \left(\frac{v_c R}{v}\right)^m \left(\frac{v_c^2}{gR}\right)^p \qquad (2.3.1-23)$$

637

Lacey has demonstrated that with $m = -1/3$ and $p = 2/3$ his empirical relations satisfy the equation of the C number

$$\frac{gRS}{v_c^2} = K'' \left(\frac{v_c R}{v}\right)^{-1/3} \left(\frac{v_c^2}{gR}\right)^{2/3} \qquad (2.3.1-24)$$

Lacey's sediment factor being proportionate to the ratio v_c^2/R, the Lacey formulae expressed in terms of discharge actually satisfy Eq. (2.3.1−24).

Rearranging the foregoing expressions and introducing the wetted perimeter P we obtain actually that

$$P \propto Q^{1/2} \text{ and } \frac{P}{R} \propto v_c \qquad (2.3.1-25)$$

In his reply Lane states that the relation of the parameter P/R and velocity v_c is an ambiguous one, as indicated by observations made in the Colorado Valley. Neither is the ratio v_c^2/R considered by Lane to be sufficiently descriptive of turbulent sediment transport. Assuming steady uniform flow, the energy loss suffered in unit time by unit weight filling unit volume is proportionate to the product of slope and the mean velocity. From this interpretation of the product Sv_c it follows that in water streaming at constant velocity the energy consumed in unit time by the unit volume necessarily equals the work resulting from the drop of water during the same time, this, in turn, being equal to the product of slope and velocity.

Considering, according to Lane, Manning's equation

$$v_c = \frac{1}{n} R^{2/3} S^{1/2}$$

we have

$$Sv_c = n^2 \frac{v_c^3}{R^{4/3}} = n^2 \left(\frac{v_c^2}{R^{8/9}}\right)^{3/2} \qquad (2.3.1-26)$$

Since $R^{8/9}$ does not differ greatly from R, Lane was inclined to believe this to be the reason for the good agreement with the ratio v_c^2/R in Lacey's investigations.

It should be noted that in his recent studies Lacey found the introduction of the product Sv_c suggested by Lane to be very useful.

In an attempt to demonstrate the validity of Lacey's formulae for dune-covered canals with slopes of cohesive material experiments were conducted in 1943 by C. King. The equations introduced by him are the first to indicate the analogy existing between the regime equations of open canals and the friction loss formulae of Blasius suggested for smooth pipes. Attention is called by King to the importance of considering not only the suspended but also the bed load when writing these equations. This can be achieved by separating Lacey's sediment

638

factor into two components. The two sediment factors are with King's notation

$$F_B = v^2 D^{-1} \qquad (2.3.1-27)$$

for the bottom and

$$F_r = v^3 D^{-1} \qquad (2.3.1-28)$$

for the side slopes.

King's equations are

$$B = [QF_B/F_r]^{1/2} \qquad (2.3.1-29)$$

$$D = [QF_r/F_B^2]^{1/3} \qquad (2.3.1-30)$$

$$S = F_B^{5/6} F_r^{1/12} Q^{-1/6} v^{1/4}/\alpha g \qquad (2.3.1-31)$$

where $\alpha = 3.63$ (in the foot-pound system).

2.3.2. EQUATIONS APPLYING TO NON-SILTING AND NON-SCOURING CANALS

This review of the historical development of the stable-channel theory shows that a growing number of variables have been introduced with advancing investigations. When applied to practical problems, the individual relations were found to apply only to the canal networks from the data of which they had been derived. Endeavours to make the relations suited for general use have only resulted in the introduction of additional variables.

For this reason a new chapter was started in the development of the stable-channel theory after the investigations by Lacey and Lane. These more recent efforts take into consideration the sediment transported in the canals and extend the stable-channel theory to applications on natural streams.

Following the approach of C. N. White, C. Inglis introduced the sediment concentration $C = G_s/Q$, i.e., the rate of transport corresponding to unit discharge, as well as the fall velocity of the sediment material. Experiments made at Poona have shown for the cases in which concentration C varied inversely as the rate of silting to remain constant as long as the product $C\omega$ remained constant. The above relation applies to sediment consisting of quartz sand graded from 0.15 to 0.5 mm, in size. The experiments made by Inglis at Poona have shown further the stable-channel equations to be unaffected by changes in sediment concentration C as long as the sediment material remained the same.

With C denoting the concentration of sediment, ω the fall velocity and d the particle diameter thereof, further Q denoting discharge, B the width of the channel, D the depth, S the slope of flow, g acceleration due to gravity and v the kinematic viscosity, Inglis suggests the following expressions:

$$v_c = \alpha_3 \frac{g^{7/18}}{v^{1/36}} Q^{1/6} (dC\omega)^{1/12} \qquad (2.3.2-1)$$

$$\frac{B}{D} = \alpha_7 \frac{Q^{1/6}(C\omega)^{7/12}}{g^{5/18}v^{7/36}d^{5/12}} \qquad (2.3.2-2)$$

$$\frac{1}{S} = \alpha_5 \frac{g^{1/18}v^{5/36}Q^{1/6}}{(dC\omega)^{5/12}} \qquad (2.3.2-3)$$

In Eqs (2.3.2−1) to (2.3.2−3) α_3, α_7 and α_5 are constants for which, however, no numerical value is mentioned by Inglis.

Comparing the above expressions with Lacey's equations

$$v_c = k_1 Q^{1/6} f^{1/3} \qquad (2.3.2-4)$$

$$\frac{P}{R} = b_1 Q^{1/6} f^{1/3} \qquad (2.3.2-5)$$

$$\frac{1}{S} = \frac{Q^{1/6}}{m_1 f^{5/3}} \qquad (2.3.2-6)$$

it will be seen that with Lacey v_c differs only as far as the exponent is concerned in the relations with Q and f. On the other hand, according to the equation of Inglis, the concentration C is of little influence on velocity v_c, but of major effect on the ratio B/D and on P/R. Moreover, the slope is also greatly influenced — according to Eq. (2.3.2−3) — by the sediment concentration C. This is why the neglect of sediment concentration in stable channels may lead to appreciable differences.

In the course of theoretical studies on stable channels Soviet investigators have introduced *the concept of non-silting velocity* v_{ni}.

For the non-silting velocity N. E. Zhukovsky suggests the expression

$$v_{ni} = 0.24 + b_1 D \qquad (2.3\ 2-7)$$

where D = the depth of flow
   b_1 = a factor depending on the hydraulic characteristics of sediment particles.

Relying on numerous observations and experiments on sediment movement E. Zamarin derived for the non-silting velocity the expression

$$v_{ni} = \frac{C\omega_0 \sqrt{\omega}}{0.022 \sqrt{RS}} \qquad (2.3.2-8)$$

640

where C = average concentration
R = hydraulic radius
S = surface slope
ω = the fall velocity and

$$\omega_0 = \omega, \quad \text{for} \quad \omega \leq 0.002 \ [\text{m/sec}]$$

$$\omega_0 = 0.002, \quad \text{for} \quad \omega < 0.002 \ [\text{m/sec}]$$

Using a theoretical approach Levi computes the velocity critical for suspended sediment movement, i.e., the velocity allowable in stable channels from the expression

$$v_c = \frac{c_1 \omega \sqrt[4]{C}}{\sqrt{d}} \sqrt{D} \qquad (2.3.2-9)$$

derived from the experiments made by V. S. Knoroz on flow of slurry (solid liquid mixtures) in pipes.

The stability of stream beds embedded into an alluvial deposit comparable to the sediment transported has been studied by T. Blench who extends the regime concept to alluvial streams. His approach to the regime concept is essentially the same as that outlined in 1942 by the author in describing bed stability.

The most characteristic feature of streams in alluvial plains is that their bed is formed in sediment material carried either by themselves or by rivers that existed before they developed. In its details the process is a highly complex one but, with an appropriate time scale, well defined results can be obtained.

According to Blench in any cross-section of a stream that has reached equilibrium conditions, the bed material is composed of the sediment that is or can be transported by the stream. A particular reach of a stream is said to be in equilibrium (or in regime), if, during a certain period of time, its most characteristic measurable and observable factors do not differ appreciably from the average values before and after this period.

The approach of Blench to the regime concept of streams will be illustrated by the following considerations:

a) Select any particular discharge on a stream, e.g. the discharge of 1500 m³/sec on the Danube, as a starting basis and find, from a 20 year record, the stages at which the discharge was just 1500 m³/sec. The plot of these stages against time will usually show an irregular curve indicating periodic changes. If no definite trend in these changes can be detected, then the particular reach of the Danube may be regarded in equilibrium, whereas if a definite trend is found to exist in the changes in stage, the reach under consideration is not stable.

A time scale is bound to be associated with the concept of a stable bed. This is clearly illustrated by the above example, since data covering a few weeks are evidently inconclusive as regards changes in the stage-discharge relation on the Danube. An excessively long period of study would, however, in all probability exclude any river reach or canal from the condition of equilibrium. In the case of streams the time scale appears to be the technologically reasonable period, during which hydraulic structures are required to remain effective.

b) If a stream is assumed to have reached equilibrium, and measurements performed at several cross-sections in every month for several years yield practically unchanged results, the assumption is incorrect since the bed of the stream under consideration cannot be regarded stable. Such channels are likely to be lined by consolidated clay or sand. The bed of streams in equilibrium usually undergoes periodic changes about the equilibrium condition. Beds excavated in consolidated cohesive materials and in which neither scouring nor silting is possible are not to be classified as stable. Channels in rock are never in equilibrium, even though no silting occurs. Stable channels are, however, conceivable even in cohesive materials if a suitable sediment material is carried in suspension which, under certain conditions, could form deposits.

c) Assume a longer reach of a stream to be surveyed annually for 30 years, determining the average length of meanders each year. If the average meander length averaged over the first 15 years is found to be 1 km with a mean square deviation of $\pm 20\%$, whereas the average for the second 15 years is 1.2 km $\pm$ 15%, then the changes in meander length are consistent and, as regards meander development, the stream bed is stable. Blench admitted this procedure not to be an exact application of mathematical statistics, yet to be relevant to the problem.

d) Assume the coarse gravel bed material of a torrential stream to be set into motion at times of floods only, while at low stages to be covered by a layer of fine sand. Blench has classified such streams as stable.

In the development of alluvial streams certain simple rules can be established even without recourse to the regime theory. According to Blench five of these rules appear acceptable without further proof.

a) O. Reynolds has observed that in stable channels rather large depths related to width pertain to small discharges. This led him to the conclusion that in small canals the distortion of slope is identical with that of the depth-width ratio. This conclusion resulted from tests on river models where the bed material was observed to start moving at a sufficiently large vertical distortion only.

b) Large streams have usually flat slopes regardless of the bed material, and their bed is very wide compared to depth.

c) At the same discharge coarse bed material is accompanied by steeper slopes and higher width-to-depth ratios.

d) On large streams the meanders are wide, while on small ones they are correspondingly smaller.

e) The changes observable in the development of meanders on great streams can also be detected on small streams.

The regime theory on stable channels has been verified on the basis of observations made mainly in artificial canals. A number of observation data were, however, available also on alluvial streams believed to be in equilibrium at the time of observation. In most cases the sediment material was graded from 0.1 to 0.5 mm.

No observations on coarse sediment material were included in the studies, though the extension of results to such sediment is believed to be possible by Blench.

Several studies have been made in the past 20 years in which Blench attempted to make Lacey's equations—modified already by King and Inglis—more exact. He suggested the equations:

$$B = [(F_B/F_r)Q]^{1/2} \tag{2.3.2-10}$$

$$D = [(F_r/F_B^2)Q]^{1/3} \tag{2.3.2-11}$$

$$S = \frac{F_B^{5/6}F_r^{1/12}Q^{-1/6}\nu^{1/4}}{\alpha g} \tag{2.3.2-12}$$

where F_B = the bottom factor
F_r = the slope factor and

$$\alpha = 3.63(1 + aC) \tag{2.3.2-13}$$

In the expression a is a constant and C is sediment concentration in 10^{-3} percentages by weight in the foot-pound system of units.

Except for α the expressions of Blench are seen to be identical with those of King. By the introduction of α allowance is made, however, for sediment concentration, so the difference is nevertheless an appreciable one.

Concerning sediment transport Blench has classified streams into two categories. The transport rate is high in streams where $C > 2.0$ and low, where $C < 2.0$.

The bottom factor is written in the form v^2/D stating that in canal systems which are in equilibrium and in which the ratio of sediment transport and discharge is constant, experience has shown v^2/D to be also constant. F_B is found from the following expressions:
for $C < 2.0$
sandy bottom material:

$$F_B = 1.9d_{mean}^{1/2} \tag{2.3.2-14}$$

gravel bottom material:

$$F_B = d_{mean}^{1/3} \tag{2.3.2-15}$$

for $C > 2.0$
sandy or gravel bottom material:

$$F_B = 1.9d_{mean}^{1/2}(1 + 0.12C) \tag{2.3.2-16}$$

In supercritical flow:

$$F_B = 32.2 + 0.06(C - C_{crit}) \tag{2.3.2-17}$$

where d_{mean} [mm] = the particle diameter
C_{crit} = the critical concentration.

The slope factor $F_r = v^3/B$ is, according to Blench, unrelated to sediment transport. For silty and silty-clay soils of different cohesion it assumes values from 0.1 to 0.3. The magnitude of F_r increases with the slope inclination and with the resistance of the material, but in order to allow for time effects it seems safe to assume the value 0.3 in most cases.

Even less information is available on the coefficient a. For sand of uniform grain size $a = 1/400$, while for sandy gravel soils graded between very wide limits $a \cong 1/233$.

The generalized theory of stable channels is thus seen to be *applicable to both alluvial streams and artificial canals*. It should be recalled, however, that minor changes are considered acceptable in both without affecting their classification as stable channels.

A number of reports have been published in the literature on the practical application of the regime theory. The generalized regime theory is noted by Blench to have been applied successfully to the solution of many a practical problem, including

a) the determination of width between parallel confining dykes,

b) the prediction of scouring between bridge piers and downstreams from them,

c) the estimation of silting upstream of dams,

d) the estimation of scouring downstream of dams, and

e) selection of the appropriate scale ratios in model tests, where the theory was used to advantage in certain cases.

On streams tending to form meanders the regime equations were supplemented by two additional ones. With M_B denoting the width and M_l the length of the meander, according to Blench

$$M_B = C_B Q^{1/2} \qquad (2.3.2-18)$$

$$M_l = C_l Q^{1/2} \qquad (2.3.2-19)$$

where Q is a typical discharge, usually the greatest flood discharge. The coefficients C_B and C_l are functions of the bottom factor F_B, the slope factor F_r, and even of the flow regime of the stream.

The generalized regime theory of Blench is a clear indication of the fact that equilibrium conditions in artificial canals and natural streams alike are affected and controlled by the same factors.

Lane published his latest studies on the regime theory in 1953. During the investigations conducted at the U.S. Bureau of Reclamation attention was shifted to problems related to the tractive force. Since the influence of velocities and, in turn, of turbulence was very difficult to determine in the vicinity of the boundaries, the inclusion of the tractive force was considered preferable.

In his computations Lane used the velocities published in the literature for determining the tractive force. The velocities, as will be remembered, are influ-

644

Table 2.3.2—1

Permissible velocities in cohesionless material,
according to Soviet data

Bed material	Particle diameter [mm]	Mean velocity [m/sec]
Silt	0.005	0.15
Fine sand	0.05	0.20
Medium sand	0.25	0.30
Coarse sand	1.00	0.55
Fine gravel	2.50	0.65
Gravel	5.00	0.80
Coarse gravel	10	1.00
Rock	15	1.2
Rock	25	1.4
Rock	40	1.8
Rock	75	2.4
Rock	100	2.7
Rock	150	3.3
Rock	200	3.9

enced also by the depth of flow since, with increasing depth, the critical velocity also tends to increase.

When using velocities and tractive forces in conjunction with the regime theory, it should be realized that what matters is not their critical value. In fact, the critical values determined mostly from laboratory experiments differ from the velocities and tractive forces allowable in the prototype.

Recalling the laws of variable critical tractive forces and critical velocities, the difference between the actually critical and the allowable values will be still greater. For this reason stable channels are always designed on the basis of allowable velocities or allowable tractive forces which are usually higher than the critical values. The allowable velocity is given in handbooks in tabulated form, an example for which is known as the Telford table. More recently, Soviet investigators have tabulated allowable velocities in cohesionless bed materials of different granulometry. The mean velocities considered allowable for the channel to remain stable are given in *Table 2.3.2—1* for materials starting with silt up to the coarsest gravel. Since the mean velocity varies with depth, the values indicated in *Table 2.3.2—1* for 1.0 m depth of flow must be multiplied by the correction factors given in *Table 2.3.2—2* for other depths.

Lane used the values compiled in *Tables 2.3.2—1* and *2.3.2—2* to compute allowable tractive forces and found for the width-to-depth ratios commonly adopted by other investigators these to be in fair agreement with tractive forces mentioned as allowable in other publications.

In connection with the distribution of the tractive force along the bottom and the sides of the channel it should be noted that this force is specified as the shear

Table 2.3.2—2

Correction factors for computing the permissible velocities at depths other than 1 m, according to Soviet data

				Average depth			
Metre	0.30	0.60	1.00	1.50	2.00	2.50	3.00
Correction factor	0.8	0.9	1.00	1.1	1.15	1.20	1.25

stress acting on a certain area of the bottom and the sides rather than on individua¹ grains. No reliable method has been found for determining the distribution of tractive forces from the distribution of velocities. A mathematical approach and experiments based on membrane analogy have therefore been adopted. The results of these experiments have shown the actual tractive force at the bottom to approximate the value γDS, whereas at the sides, assuming a trapezoidal channel, the tractive force was about 0.76 γDS.

In order to complete the sparse data available, Lane intended to perform experiments but some of these are not yet concluded, while others have failed to yield the desired results. In his investigations Lane has adopted the particle size at 75% by weight passing.

From the results of observations made on canals having a stable bed, Lane has determined values for the allowable tractive force in coarse as well as in fine, cohesionless bed materials.

For coarse, cohesionless material Lane has found the numerical value of the allowable critical tractive force, expressed in kp/m² units, to equal the particle diameter d_{75}, expressed in cm units. No margin of safety being included in the values thus obtained, for coarse, cohesionless materials Lane has suggested the formula

$$\tau_m = 0.8\, d_{25} \ [\text{kp/m}^2] \qquad (2.3.2-20)$$

for computing the allowable tractive force τ_m. Here d_{25} denotes the particle size corresponding to 75% by weight of the total material passing.

For fine cohesionless materials a wide variety of values of the allowable tractive force have been suggested. Besides a graphical representation Lane has compiled also the average allowable tractive force in a tabular form in terms of the mean particle diameter.

The allowable tractive forces pertaining to different particle sizes are shown in *Table 2.3.2—3* after Lane, separately for clear water and for the cases of low and high concentration values. It has been noted by Lane in his paper that in streams where sediment concentration attains twice or three times the value of 2.3 kp/m³ in an average year the data pertaining to high concentrations should be used. Lane regards sediment concentration to be low where it attains no more than 0.57 kp/m³ twice or three times in an average year.

646

Table 2.3.2—3

Permissible tractive force in cohesionless material, clear water,
at low and high sediment concentrations, after Lane

Mean particle diameter [mm]	Permissible tractive force [kp/m²]		
	clear water	low	high
		sediment concentration	
0.1	0.122	0.244	0.366
0.2	0.127	0.254	0.381
0.5	0.146	0.269	0.406
1.0	0.195	0.293	0.435
2.0	0.293	0.391	0.538
5.0	0.684	0.806	0.904

Stable channels conveying large volumes of sediment, especially as bed load should be dimensioned with due consideration also to the laws of sediment transport.

More recent studies into the regime theory were conducted by D. B. Simons and M. L. Albertson. The objective of these studies was systematically to arrange the wealth of information obtained during the 60 years elapsed since the introduction of the theory, for artificial canals operating under a wide variety of geographical and meteorological conditions, and to compare the different relations derived from these.

It is established in advance that in alluvial channels the width of the bed, the depth and slope of flow are always variable, so that at least three equations are necessary.

The shortcomings of the regime theory have been compiled by Simons and Albertson as follows:

a) Development in the past was restricted to particular instances, making the theory unsuited for designing canal systems of different character.

b) No allowance is made for the sediment transported in the canals, the role of which may be significant in stable channels.

c) A number of empirical coefficients representing particular properties of the canals studied are involved in the relations suggested. For this reason the relations must not be applied to other canal systems, unless the original system is subject to a careful study.

Their investigation rely on data from the following countries (or canal systems):
India (Punjab and Sind)
The United States (Imperial Valley, San Luis Valley, as well as canals in Wyoming, Colorado and Nebraska).
Data relating altogether to 24 canal systems have been included in these investigations.

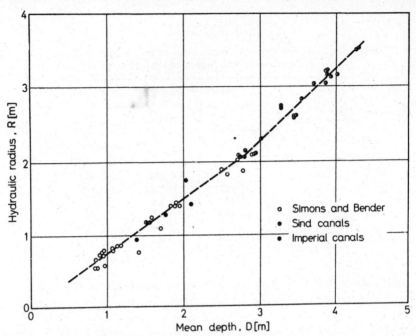

Fig. 2.3.2—1. Hydraulic radius R vs. water depth D. After Simons and Albertson

In appreciation of the decisive influence of sediment transport, Simons and Albertson state that in canals having a mobile bed, roughness conditions depend, besides the bed material, on the quantity of sediment transported and on the dynamic condition of flow. At tranquil and shooting flow the channel can be stable while assuming different bed forms.

The quantity of sediment is closely related to bed forms. Thus for instance a fine-grained sediment which occurs in slight quantities in the bed material may greatly reduce channel resistance at high sediment concentrations and affect thus considerably the evolution of channel geometry.

These investigations have shown that for channels having a stable bed in sand or finer materials the Froude number $v/\sqrt{gd} < 0.3$.

During the detailed processing of observation data the corresponding values relating to canals were plotted graphically by Simons and Albertson who determined also the mathematical form of relations for canals resembling in character.

The hydraulic radius R versus the mean depth of flow D relation is shown in *Fig. 2.3.2—1*, whereas the average width B versus wetted perimeter P relation is illustrated in *Fig. 2.3.2—2*. The relations plotted in these figures are seen to have a positive, linear trend.

From the foregoing the wetted perimeter, the hydraulic radius and the cross-sectional area can be expected to be related also to the discharge.

In *Fig. 2.3.2—3* the wetted perimeter is plotted against discharge. For channels

648

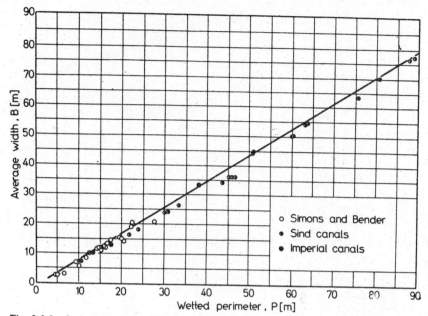

Fig. 2.3.2—2. Average bed width *B* vs. wetted perimeter *P*. After Simons and Albertson

Fig. 2.3.2—3. Wetted perimeter *P* vs. discharge *Q* for different canals. After Simons and Albertson

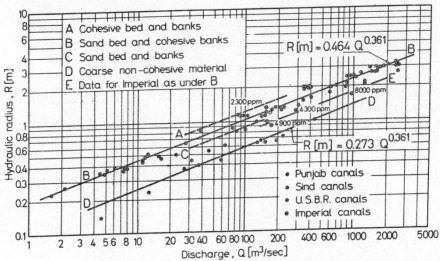

Fig. 2.3.2—4. Hydraulic radius R vs. discharge Q for different canals. After Simons and Albertson

with a bottom of sand and sides of cohesive material the wetted perimeter versus discharge relations is expressed as

$$P = 4.744 \, Q^{0.512} \; [\text{m}] \tag{2.3.2—21}$$

Relations applying to canals with their bottom and sides of sand (A), with bottom and sides of cohesive material (C), of coarse cohesionless material (D) and to the canals in the Imperial Valley (E) have also been entered into the figure. Since the canals in the Imperial Valley convey usually large volumes of fine-grained sediment, it will be seen that the same discharge is accompanied by a lower P value if the sediment concentration is high.

The hydraulic radius versus discharge relation has been reproduced in *Fig. 2.3.2—4.* The relationship existing between the hydraulic radius and the discharge was mentioned first by Lindley. In analogy to the discharge versus wetted perimeter relation Simons and Albertson have determined these relations for canals of five different bed materials (A—E). The hydraulic radius versus discharge relations is expressed for canals having a sandy bottom and cohesive sides as

$$R = 0.464 Q^{0.361} \; [\text{m}] \tag{2.3.2—22}$$

whereas for coarse, cohesionless bed material as

$$R = 0.273 Q^{0.361} \; [\text{m}] \tag{2.3.2—23}$$

In these expressions the coefficient of discharge is seen to be influenced by the bed material, while the exponent remains constant for each of the five types. From

650

Fig. 2.3.2—5. Cross-sectional area *A* vs. discharge *Q* for different canals. After Simons and Albertson

the data relating to the canal system (E) in the Imperial Valley it will again be perceived that at high sediment concentrations a smaller hydraulic radius pertains to the same discharge.

In *Fig. 2.3.2—5* the cross-sectional area *A* has been plotted against discharge *Q*.

The expression describing this relation for canals with their bottom and sides of fine sand, and for those with sides of cohesive material is

$$A = 2.245 Q^{0.873} \ [\text{m}^2] \qquad\qquad (2.3.2-24)$$

whereas in coarse loose bed materials it is

$$A = 0.939 Q^{0.873} \ [\text{m}^2] \qquad\qquad (2.3.2-25)$$

From this figure it will again be seen that the high sediment concentration in the canals of the Imperial Valley results in comparison with the other canals in a smaller flow cross-section at the same discharge.

The relations on mean velocity in stable channels have already been described extensively in *Section 2.2.1* relying also on the investigations by Simons and

Albertson. For the afore-mentioned canal systems Simons and Albertson have established numerical relations by which the mean velocity is found in different bed materials. The original data used in their studies have been plotted in *Fig. 2.2.1−6*.

The studies into the roughness of alluvial channels mentioned also in *Section 2.2.1*, although not related explicitly to stable channels, offer information on roughness conditions in stable alluvial channels as well.

Completing the above considerations attention is called to *Fig. 2.2.1−11* mentioned in connection with alluvial channels, in which the mean velocity versus slope relation has been plotted for a given depth of flow.

Although the figure is based on laboratory data and is thus not well applicable to artificial canals, the condition of the bed is seen to be of considerable influence on surface slope and shear velocity alike.

It has been established further by Simons and Albertson that stable channels are incapable of transporting more than 0.5 kp/m^3 of a sediment resembling the bed material. On the other hand, in the case of very-fine-grained wash load sediment concentration may attain values as high as 3 kp/m^3 without affecting the stability of the channel.

The quality of the bed material and the fall velocity thereof have been suggested by Simons and Albertson as factors to be investigated more closely in future research.

In conclusion it appears safe to establish that the relations concerning stable channels can be used for dimensioning only canals in which the conditions are similar to those on which the formulae are founded.

The important role of sediment transport has been established beyond doubt, although the data available so far are too few in number to permit any exact mathematical formulation.

2.3.3. NEW TRENDS IN THE REGIME THEORY

Recent studies related to the regime theory are founded practically without exception on physical considerations.

As stated in *Subsection 2.3.1.1*, the regime theory cannot be separated from the theory of sediment transport. In this new trend of research endeavours are made to establish the relations needed for designing stable channels in harmony with the theory of sediment transport. These studies have not yet resulted in the development of a comprehensive approach of practical interest and will therefore be reviewed in brief only.

Using the method of synthesis developed by Barr and Herbertson and to be described subsequently in *Section 2.5.4*, these authors have introduced theoretical relations for stable channels and suggested the application of expressions determined on this basis. They, too, emphasize that the results of observations made in the field, of laboratory experiments and of measurements made on alluvial streams having stable beds are closely interrelated and cannot be separated. They claim that the regime theory is applicable to all alluvial streams and canals in which sediment is transported at a steady rate and where the cross-section lined with a cohesionless material is of any arbitrary shape.

Considering the three fundamental equations described in the foregoing Barr and Herbertson have found the theoretical foundations thereof to be insufficient.

Of the studies into the regime theory, mention must be made of a paper by J. Zeller in which the regime equations are subject to an extensive critical review starting from their early development up to 1965. Mention is made here of the three-dimensional laboratory experiments of P. Ackers, the results of which were in complete agreement with those of Simons and Albertson, provided that the model sediment was the same.

Assuming that the work performed by the water course is necessarily minimal, W. B. Langbein used the probability theory in deriving the most important regime equations.

Any exhaustive treatment of the details of these investigations would exceed the scope of this book and the reader is referred to the contributions listed in the attached bibliography.

Finally T. Blench's most recent paper is considered important enough to be reflected upon here.

This study is also founded on the theoretical relationships existing between the physical variables dominating the phenomenon.

Suggestions made by Blench concerning future research objectives are worthy of being mentioned separately. These suggestions have been summarized in twelve points of which those believed most important by the author are as follows:

a) Research efforts by investigators making field observations, conducting laboratory experiments and performing theoretical investigations are of equal importance, and no advance is imaginable unless close correlations are maintained.

b) In each observation the granulometry of the bed material, the mean velocity and the distribution of velocities must be determined both before and after any experiment.

c) Quantitative observation data gained in alluvial channels and canals should be considered equivalent to laboratory experiments and theoretical research, expecially if related to changes in the regime of the water course due to natural factors or to human interference.

d) International co-operation, the exchange of experience is considered necessary along with the processing of data, using the same units of measurement.

In conclusion it should be emphasized that the results of the regime theory remain incomplete unless supported by the general laws of sediment transport.

2.4. SEDIMENT TRANSPORT AND RIVER REGULATION

2.4.1. PRINCIPLES AND METHODS IN CONTEMPORARY RIVER REGULATION

As an introduction to the principles and methods in contemporary river regulation it should be stated in general that the need for the deliberate development and management of water resources has increased and extended considerably the demands and requirements to be met by river regulation. These questions have been discussed in detail by J. Csoma. For details reference is made to the papers listed in the bibliography.

The principles and methods of river regulation should be selected so as to be founded on sediment transport in the streams, since the evolution of the channel and any change in the bed of streams are due to the sediment-transporting capacity of the water course.

When considering the hydrological, hydraulic and morphological aspects related to the principles and methods of river regulation it is essential to establish first the general objectives thereof. A visual demonstration of these general objectives is presented by the multipurpose regulation of rivers where no interference into the development of the channel should be decided upon until comprehensive allowance is made for natural conditions, such as the catchment area, the quantity and distribution of precipitation, erosion conditions, further for various agricultural, industrial and communal water uses.

Any water course should be regarded as a system tending to establish balanced conditions, where changes in any particular factor necessarily entail changes in the other factors. River regulation as a human interference upsets this balance, whereafter the water course tends to re-establish a state corresponding to the particular character of the river, either eliminating the structures and results of human interference in this process or achieving a new condition of equilibrium. *The primary objective in river regulation is to establish and maintain the dynamic equilibrium and stability of the channel.* The relationships existing between the hydraulic properties of the stream, the rate of sediment transport and the geometry of the channel are highly complex and tend invariably to establish some condition of equilibrium. In alluvial streams, however, equilibrium conditions exist but rarely and for rather short periods only. In this context it should be remembered that even in the absence of human interference considerable changes may result from natural influences, for instance in the hydraulic factors characteristic of the water course. *River regulation is justified when and where the river is uncapable of establishing balanced conditions.*

In modern times the growing number of water uses has entailed a sudden increase in human interference under the influence of which one or several of the factors controlling the dynamic stability of the channel undergo more or less extensive changes. Under the influence of human interference the factors controlling dynamic stability are liable to change at much faster rates than by a natural

654

process, and regulation must accordingly be performed during much shorter periods and with much greater reliability than before.

In the solution of practical river regulation problems increasing reliance on theoretical foundations is indispensable. It should be realized that no theoretical method has been developed as yet for taking into consideration the unquestionably close relationship existing between river regulation methods and phenomena of sediment transport. This applies, to an even greater extent, to the practical utilization of such relations. A number of theoretically well founded approaches have already been developed concerning both the methods of river regulation and the theory of sediment transport. The isolated application thereof is, however, impossible since river regulation presents a complex particular problem involving the combination of all hydrological, hydraulic, geographic and geologic properties of the water course.

It should be appreciated, therefore, that science at the present is not advanced far enough to provide complete answer to all of the relevant problems. It is, however, also obvious that, especially during the last two or three decades, enormous development has taken place in this field, in the course of which the exclusively empirical or exclusively theoretical and experimentally unsupported methods have been revised, adjusted, improved and combined theoretical approach now available for solving the problems encountered in river regulation and the attendent problem of sediment transport.

No details of river regulation will be discussed here but it is felt desirable to clear some of the fundamental questions.

The applications of parameters characterizing the stability of river channels may well be classified among the fundamental principles. Starting with Lokhtin several such index numbers characterizing channel stability have been suggested and are used commonly in designing stable channels. The channel stability factors will be discussed in detail in *Section 2.4.2*.

In river regulation the correct alignment of the water course is of paramount importance. A number of theories have been put forward concerning the alignment of channels. According to one of the apparently logical approaches, the determination of channel alignment should be based on characteristics resulting from the interrelation of the two basic media, namely river bed material and water.

One of the fundamental facts governing the determination of channel alignment is that alluvial channels consist of a succession of opposite bends connected by straight sections neither of which may be regarded permanent. Under this approach the primary problem in river regulation is to find the alignment which, under the particular conditions of hydrology, hydraulics and morphology, and aided by the training structures, is capable of meeting the requirements primarily of navigation, as well as of a wide variety of diversions and inlets.

The development of river bends and meanders is obviously not the result of a random combination of natural factors. In alluvial streams local irregularities and obstacles induce the river to alter its course. Basically however these are not the true causes of meander development. It has been suggested that in meander

655

development the squared sum of changes in direction of alignment must be minimum, which is at the same time in agreement with the theorem that the total work performed in meandering must be at a minimum. This property of meander development is clearly illustrated by the shape which a thin steel wire assumes between fixed points at a given length without restriction. The steel wire will tend naturally to accommodate changes in direction by uniform curvatures without any corner points. As a consequence thereof the wire assumes configurations at which the total work is minimum, since over each elementary length work will be proportionate to the square of the change in direction occurring at that point. Various shapes are sinusoidal curves in fair agreement with river meanders.

The shape of cross-section is also of considerable interest in river regulation. Cross-sectional shape is preferably described by the ratio of surface width and of the depth of flow. An adequate depth is required usually for navigation.

A method frequently applied in current river regulation practice, namely river canalization has been considered in detail in *Section 2.1.6.*

River regulation methods to be effective should be selected with due regard to sediment conditions in the particular stream.

The regulation of major navigable rivers invariably presents highly complex problems. Regulation is especially difficult over sections through which large volumes of sediment are transported and where considerable sand bars travel in a loose alluvial channel. Over such reaches the continuous variation of degrading and aggrading sections, as well as the formation of shallow sand bars make the required navigation depth and width difficult to maintain. Fluvial engineering work on the Hungarian upper reach of the Danube and the low-water regulation thereof can be traced over the past hundred years, permitting valuable experience to be collected.

It should be pointed out here that investigations and research of this kind are still insufficient although the comparison of regulation measures and results obtained would appear to offer valuable assistance in selecting the most efficient regulation methods.

Besides the establishment of general principles the correct solution of various minor problems is also essential in designing river regulation measures. One example for these is the selection of the efficient spacing and crest height of spur dykes. Economic solutions usually require, especially on major streams, to keep the number of expensive spur dykes as low as possible. According to recent investigations the spacing of spur dykes can be increased in many instances without impairing their regulating effect. The same applies to the crest height of spur dykes which should be selected preferably somewhere between the mean low stages and the annual mean stage.

As can be seen from the foregoing, any attempt at selecting the most effective regulation method is bound to fail unless adequate information on sediment conditions is available. This circumstance involves the necessity of performing research meeting the needs of the designer. It should be realized moreover that in addition to sediment conditions a number of other questions are also to be studied. Studies on the particular hydrological conditions afford the necessary understanding on river regime, whereas the studies on channel development are essential before a particular regulation method is selected. In addition to these, consideration must be given to flood control problems and even to the biological aspect arising in connection with supplying fresh water to severed bends and to abandoned beds resulting from regulation measures. It should be obvious that a variety of problems await to be clarified in connection with construction work of regulation projects.

In order to attain the desired objectives the methods of river regulation should always be selected with due regard to sediment conditions in any particular stream.

2.4.2. THE INFLUENCE OF SEDIMENT CONDITIONS IN SELECTING REGULATION METHODS

Channel development to be achieved by river regulation must be planned invariably by comparing the actual sediment transport and the sediment-transporting capacity of a particular stream. The sediment balance equation may also be included in this process. The relations describing sediment transport itself may eventually also be resorted to.

Whichever approach is adopted, consideration must be given to the condition of the channel, i.e. whether it may be regarded stable or it displays an aggrading or degrading trend. The basic object of regulation is to adjust the sediment-transporting capacity of the regulated channel to the actual rate of transport. The result to be attained eventually is the determination of the width and depth of the regulated channel, as well as of the most suitable ratio thereof.

In contemporary river regulation problems, the suspended sediment assumes a role comparable in importance to that of bed load.

In early river regulation efforts, allowance for sediment conditions was made by introducing *the channel stability factors*. This leads to the concept of channel stability which, as pointed out in *Section 2.3.1*, is equivalent in alluvial streams to the regime theory in artificial canals.

Channel stability is preferably expressed with the help of relationships between the hydraulic elements of the stream, the characteristics of the channel and sediment by observing their mutual influence in some equilibrium condition. Of course, a wide variety of ways are available for expressing the relationships between the hydraulic elements of the stream, the channel and the sediment. Most of these relationships are presented by the visual appearance of the water course itself, examplified for instance by the occurrence of coarse bed material over steep sections and of fine bed material over flat ones. It is obviously most expedient to adopt and determine those of such readily recognizable relations as are most relevant to the phenomena affecting channel development.

The first of these relationships relating the hydraulic elements of the stream, the channel and the sediment is the channel stability factor of Lokhtin. For a quantitative description of channel stability Lokhtin related in 1897 the resistance of the material lining the bed to removal to the tractive force itself and called the ratio thus obtained the channel stability factor.

After certain simplifying assumptions the factor introduced by Lokhtin for describing channel stability assumes the form

$$a = \alpha \frac{d}{S} \qquad (2.4.2-1)$$

or by substituting the kinetic energy $v^2/2g = h_v$ of a fluid element of unit weight for the slope S

$$a = \alpha_1 \frac{d}{h_v} \qquad (2.4.2-2)$$

As mentioned repeatedly, the author introduced in 1941−43 a channel stability factor of the form

$$b = \frac{d}{RS} \qquad (2.4.2-3)$$

or, if the specific gravity γ_1 of the sediment is variable,

$$b = \frac{d}{RS} \frac{\gamma_1 - \gamma}{\gamma} \qquad (2.4.2-4)$$

By extending the validity of the resistance coefficient f_c introduced by Shields for the critical condition to all conditions (including stationary) of sediment transport and denoting it by f_0, it should be realized that $b = 1/f_0$.

In 1941, then again in 1950, Einstein introduced the intensity Ψ of the stream which is also identical with the inverse value of f_0.

All these relations have been discussed in the foregoing. For this reason no more than the hydraulic assumptions made during the derivation of b will be treated here, these being relevant to the relationships existing between the bed material and the hydraulic factors of the water course.

At a particular cross-section of the stream the bed material should be characterized by the mean particle diameter d_g.

With L denoting the length of the stream say from the headwaters to a particular cross-section, the mean particle diameter d_g under stable channel conditions will vary as a function thereof, so that

$$d_g = F_1(L) \qquad (2.4.2-5)$$

The function $d_g = F_1(L)$ is easy to plot and sometimes to express in a mathematical form. At the confluence of tributaries or abrupt changes in the geology of the river valley the continuity of the function may be interrupted. However, since no claim is made at deriving a relation valid for the entire length of the stream the afore-mentioned circumstances result in no difficulties.

658

The critical mean velocity v_c is known to be approximately proportionate to the square root of the mean particle diameter d_g of the corresponding sediment, so that in general

$$v_c = a_1 \sqrt{d_g} \qquad (2.4.2-6)$$

According to the law of variable critical velocities a_1 is not constant but depends also on the hydraulic factors of the stream and on the particle diameter of the sediment. Nevertheless Eq. (2.4.2−6) is approximately valid for any particular stream section.

The mean velocity v prevailing in a stable stream channel will not be necessarily identical with, but at least proportionate to, the critical mean velocity pertaining to this d_g value, since the limit particle diameter d_g in the cross section under consideration has evolved under the influence of just this mean velocity v. Consequently

$$v = a_2 v_c = a_1 a_2 \sqrt{d_g}$$

or

$$v = a_3 \sqrt{d_g} \qquad (2.4.2-7)$$

where a_3 is in general variable but may be considered constant for a particular stream section, provided that the depths and velocities of flow are approximately identical.

The mean velocity can be expressed also in terms of the hydraulic factors of the stream, e.g. with the help of the Chézy formula:

$$v = c \sqrt{RS} \qquad (2.4.2-8)$$

Combining the above two expressions for the mean velocity

$$a_3 \sqrt{d_g} = c \sqrt{RS}$$

or

$$\frac{d_g}{RS} = a_3^{-2} c^2 S$$

and a combination of the constants yields

$$\frac{d_g}{RS} = b \qquad (2.4.2-9)$$

Unlike earlier expectations, the factor b alone has proved unsuited for characterizing channel stability. More recent nvestigations, on the other hand, have demonstrated the factor $b = 1/f_0 = \Psi$ to be the most relevant and most significant parameter in sediment transport.

The concept of channel stability later evolved without regard to sediment transport, the role of which was recognized but gradually. The final conclusion is that *the most important factor is the movement of sediment in channel stability and in the regime theory alike.* This circumstance also supports the conclusion that river regulation methods must be adopted with due regard to sediment conditions.

42*

2.5. HYDRAULIC SIMILARITY IN SEDIMENT TRANSPORT

2.5.1. HYDRAULIC SIMILARITY
IN MODEL TESTS OF SEDIMENT-CARRYING STREAMS

2.5.1.1. The problem of similarity. The problems arising in model testing are concerned primarily with the similarity of the model and the prototype. It seems therefore advisable to present a general discussion of some theorems of *mechanical similarity.*

Hydraulic model tests are founded usually on the concept of mechanical similarity. Since complete similarity cannot be attained, the restrictions gradually introduced in hydraulics endeavour to ensure the hydraulic similarity of quantities dominating the phenomenon.

Under this interpretation of similarity, two phenomena are said to be similar if the numerical value of dimensionless numbers derived from the relevant differential equations and unambiguity conditions are identical for both. As a consequence of similarity, positive relationships exist between the similarity criteria and the dimensionless dependent variables.

Under this approach to similarity, two phenomena may be similar even though involving different physical variables. The only essential condition is that the equations written with the help of dimensionless numbers combined from the variables and the unambiguity conditions should be identical.

Even in the above interpretation of similarity theory, complete similarity and approximate similarity may be distinguished depending on whether the equations describing the phenomena and the unambiguity conditions are satisfied completely or with certain simplifications only.

The conflict between mechanical similarity applied in hydraulics and the similarity theory mentioned here is, of course, an apparent one only since no attempt is made in hydraulics to attain complete mechanical similarity. Nevertheless it was felt necessary to mention the above two approaches to avoid the false impression of striving at unattainable identity when applying the theorems of mechanical similarity as practiced in hydraulics.

In model testing, it will be remembered, the prototype is reproduced at a reduced scale and the phenomenon is studied under ideal conditions with unlimited opportunity for repetition. Observations are performed in the model and from these conclusions are drawn concerning the prototype. Any exact conclusion concerning the behaviour of the prototype would imply that prototype values can be computed exactly from the quantities observed in the model. Exact conversion must be expected in mechanically similar systems only. In two mechanically similar systems — or in general in the prototype and in the model which is a mechanically similar replica of the former — corresponding physical quantities are proportionate to one another. The factor of proportionality λ is referred to as the scale factor known also as similarity transformation factor.* These scale factors are indications of the fact that in similar systems the distribution functions of the same physical quantities are proportionate to one another, corresponding mutually and positively. This alone is, however, insufficient for it is equivalent to the trivial statement that the behaviour of similar systems is similar. A similarity method is required moreover to permit the exact definition of the conditions under which two systems are similar. The only thing to recall here is that definite laws of nature prevail within any "system", and the distributions of individual physical quantities depend on the conditions under which these laws prevail. In general *two systems will be similar if similar laws of nature and similar conditions apply to both.*

The laws of nature are described by differential equations expressing the relations inherent to the phenomenon. The conditions are established by the unambiguity conditions pertaining to the differential equations. In the mathematical sense the distribution functions of individual physical variables are the solution of the differential equations describing the phenomenon under the particular un-ambiguity conditions. If two systems are similar, then the solutions are in a proportion determined by the scale ratio.

In other words, the necessary and adequate condition of similarity is that the differential equations and unambiguity conditions describing the two phenomena should be convertible mutually and positively into each other. One of the simplest (but by no means exclusive!) method of conversion is the *linear transformation* expressed by scale ratios.

The conversion of mathematical relationships describing one of the systems into a form corresponding to the mathematical relationships describing the other (prototype to the model) is called a *similarity transformation.* No proof is deemed necessary for the fact that during a transformation of this kind a certain relationship (the set of condition equations) is bound to exist between the scale ratios. These relationships permit the dimensionless numbers characteristic of the phenomenon to be determined. These numbers are required to have identical values. The term "invariant" used for them stems from this requirement. The term should, however, be used with caution since, although in mechanically similar systems all dimensionless numbers are required to have the same value, in engineering practice not each dimensionless quantity is called invariant.

It is essential, however, to make a distinction between dimensionless numbers obtained from the differential equations and those derived from the unambiguity conditions. In fact the former are invariants the identical numerical value of which is *a consequence* of similarity. In a general sense these may be called dimensionless dependent variables.

With the dimensionless numbers derived from the unambiguity conditions the situation is different. Once the laws of nature prevailing in the model are established to resemble those dominating the prototype, the similarity of the distribution

---

* Scale factors are denoted by λ, with the subscript indicating the physical quantity under consideration.

661

functions (the distribution of the dimensionless dependent variables) depends exclusively on whether the similarity of unambiguity conditions is ensured or not. Consequently *the criterion of similarity is the identical value of dimensionless numbers expressing the similarity of the unambiguity conditions.* For this reason these dimensionless numbers are named similarity criteria (in general: dimensionless independent variables). It should be emphasized that only such dimensionless numbers can be used as similarity criteria in which all physical quantities involved have the value given by the unambiguity conditions.*

Any formulation of similarity relations in sediment transport should be based essentially on the set of equations expressed by Eqs (1.3.3−37) to (1.3.3−42), these describing the general relations of the phenomenon. Although the similarity criteria obtained in this manner are of no direct practical interest owing to the absence of exact relations between the physical variables involved in the unambiguity conditions, their introduction may still prove of benefit. The necessary condition for two different phenomena related to sediment transport to be similar is that the equations describing this phenomenon should be mutually convertible into one another.

Accordingly, considering for simplicity the sediment as monodisperse and omitting thus Eqs (1.3.3−39) and (1.3.3−40), in the case of linear transformation the following eleven scale ratios must be taken into consideration:

$$\lambda_{\bar{\rho}}, \lambda_t, \lambda_x, \lambda_{\bar{v}}, \lambda_{\overline{v'v'}}, \lambda_g, \lambda_{\gamma_1}, \lambda_\omega, \lambda_{\overline{v_h}}, \lambda_{\overline{v'_h v'_h}}, \lambda_\varepsilon$$

which indicate the ratio of corresponding variables in the two phenomena.

It should be noted that in general the scale ratios applying to the geometry λ_x, velocity λ_v and λ_{v_h}, correlation $\lambda_{\overline{v'v'}}$ and $\lambda_{\overline{v'_h v'_h}}$, the external field of force (gravity, inertia etc.) λ_g, further to conductivity tensor λ_ε may be different along the individual co-ordinates. One single numerical value cannot be given to them unless the two systems are similar also geometrically. Otherwise, for instance, in two-dimensional flow, scale ratios in the y direction must also be introduced. In such cases the condition equations (I − VIII) to be derived subsequently will naturally increase in number.

Multiplying by the scale ratios with the corresponding variables involved in the equations applying to one system (the model), the equations applying to the other system (the prototype) are obtained. Introducing the scale ratios into Eqs (1.3.3−37), (1.3.3−38), (1.3.3−41) and (1.3.3−42) and assuming these to describe the phenomenon in the model, the following equations are obtained for the

---

* The exact formulation of similarity has been published in E. Szücs's *Ähnlichkeitstheorie* (Bertelsman Verlag and Publishing House of the Hungarian Academy of Sciences, 1972).

prototype:

$$\left(\frac{\lambda_{\bar{\rho}}}{\lambda_t}\right)\frac{\partial\bar{\rho}}{\partial t}+\left(\frac{\lambda_{\bar{\rho}}\lambda_{\bar{v}}}{\lambda_x}\right)\operatorname{div}\overline{\rho\mathbf{v}}=0 \tag{H-1}$$

$$\left(\frac{\lambda_{\bar{\rho}}\lambda_{\bar{v}}}{\lambda_t}\right)\frac{\partial\overline{\rho\mathbf{v}}}{\partial t}+\left(\frac{\lambda_{\bar{\rho}}\lambda_{\bar{v}}^2}{\lambda_x}\right)\operatorname{Div}[\overline{\rho\mathbf{v}}\circ\bar{\mathbf{v}}]+\left(\frac{\lambda_{\bar{\rho}}\lambda_{\overline{v'v'}}}{\lambda_x}\right)\operatorname{Div}[\overline{\rho\mathbf{v}'\circ\mathbf{v}'}]=$$

$$=(\lambda_{\bar{\rho}}\lambda_g)\,\bar{\rho}\mathbf{g}+\left(\frac{\lambda_{\gamma_1}}{\lambda_\omega}\,\lambda_{\bar{v}h}\right)\frac{\gamma_1}{\omega}\,\bar{\mathbf{v}}_h-\left(\frac{\lambda_{\gamma_1}}{\lambda_\omega}\,\lambda_{\bar{v}}\right)\frac{\gamma_1}{\omega}\,\bar{\mathbf{v}} \tag{H-2}$$

$$\left(\frac{\lambda_{\rho_1}}{\lambda_t}\right)\frac{\partial\rho_1}{\partial t}+\left(\frac{\lambda_{\rho_1}\lambda_{\bar{v}h}}{\lambda_x}\right)\operatorname{div}[\rho_1\bar{\mathbf{v}}_h]-\left(\frac{\lambda_\varepsilon\lambda_{\rho_1}}{\lambda_x^2}\right)\operatorname{div}[\varepsilon\operatorname{grad}\rho_1]=0 \tag{H-3}$$

$$\left(\frac{\lambda_{\rho_1}\lambda_{\bar{v}h}}{\lambda_t}\right)\frac{\partial\rho_1\bar{\mathbf{v}}_h}{\lambda_x}+\left(\frac{\lambda_{\rho_1}\lambda_{\bar{v}h}^2}{\lambda_x}\right)\operatorname{Div}[\rho_1\bar{\mathbf{v}}_h\circ\bar{\mathbf{v}}_h]+$$

$$+\left(\frac{\lambda_{\rho_1}\lambda_{\overline{v'_hv'_h}}}{\lambda_x}\right)\operatorname{Div}[\rho_1\overline{\mathbf{v}'_h\circ\mathbf{v}'_h}]=(\lambda_{\rho_1}\lambda_g)\,\rho_1\mathbf{g}-$$

$$-\left(\frac{\lambda_{\gamma_1}}{\lambda_\omega}\lambda_{\bar{v}h}\right)\frac{\gamma_1}{\omega}\,\bar{\mathbf{v}}_h+\left(\frac{\lambda_{\gamma_1}}{\lambda_\omega}\,\lambda_{\bar{v}}\right)\frac{\gamma_1}{\omega}\,\bar{\mathbf{v}} \tag{H-4}$$

When converting the dominant equations into each other, the relations expressing the criterion of invariance are called condition equations. In converting Eqs (1.3.3−37), (1.33−38), (1.33−41) and (1.33−42) according to Eqs (H−1), (H−2), (H−3) and (H−4) invariance is guaranteed obviously if the expressions of the scale ratios in round brackets in each of the last mentioned four equations are equal to each other within individual equations. Accordingly the following condition equations are written.

From Eq. (H−1):

$$\frac{\lambda_{\bar{\rho}}}{\lambda_t}=\frac{\lambda_{\bar{\rho}}\lambda_{\bar{v}}}{\lambda_x}\,,\quad\text{or}\quad\frac{\lambda_t\lambda_{\bar{v}}}{\lambda_x}=1$$

whence the first condition equations is

$$\frac{\bar{\mathbf{x}}\,t}{\mathbf{x}^2}=\text{idem} \tag{I}$$

and, since x is the direction of flow, this indicates the invariance of kinematic time.
From Eq. (H−2):

$$\frac{\lambda_{\bar{\rho}}\lambda_{\bar{v}}}{\lambda_t}=\frac{\lambda_{\bar{\rho}}\lambda_{\bar{v}}^2}{\lambda_x}=\frac{\lambda_{\bar{\rho}}\lambda_{\overline{v'v'}}}{\lambda_x}=\lambda_{\bar{\rho}}\lambda_g=\frac{\lambda_{\gamma_1}}{\lambda_\omega}\,\lambda_{\bar{v}h}=\frac{\lambda_{\gamma_1}}{\lambda_\omega}\,\lambda_{\bar{v}}$$

or dividing the equation by the second term:

$$\frac{\lambda_x}{\lambda_t \lambda_{\bar{v}}} = 1 = \frac{\lambda_{\overline{v'v'}}}{\lambda_{\bar{v}}^2} = \frac{\lambda_g \lambda_x}{\lambda_{\bar{v}}^2} = \frac{\lambda_{\gamma_1} \lambda_x \lambda_{\bar{v}h}}{\lambda_{\bar{\rho}} \lambda_{\bar{v}} \lambda_\omega} = \frac{\lambda_{\gamma_1} \lambda_x}{\lambda_{\bar{\rho}} \lambda_{\bar{v}} \lambda_\omega}$$

whence the following additional four condition equations (II, III, IV and V) are obtained:

$$\frac{\overline{v' \circ v'}}{\overline{v}^2} = \text{idem} \tag{IIa}$$

the criterion of Kármán, which may be replaced if the conductive momentum current $(\overline{\rho v' \circ v'})$ is expressed with the help of the expression $(\mu \, \text{Grad} \, \overline{v})$ by

$$\frac{\overline{v}x}{\nu} = Re = \text{idem} \tag{IIb}$$

i.e. the Reynolds number.

Of course, no more than one of Eqs (IIa) and (IIb) can be used simultaneously as condition equation.

From the equation

$$\frac{\lambda_g \lambda_x}{\lambda_{\bar{v}}^2} = 1$$

the invariance of the Froude number

$$\frac{\overline{v}^2}{gx} = Fr = \text{idem} \tag{III}$$

is obtained as condition equation.

In the last two terms $\lambda_{\gamma_1} = \lambda_g \lambda_{\rho_1}$ may be written. Thus it is found first that

$$\frac{\lambda_g \lambda_{\rho_1} \lambda_x \lambda_{\bar{v}h}}{\lambda_{\bar{\rho}} \lambda_{\bar{v}}^2 \lambda_\omega} = \left(\frac{\lambda_g \lambda_x}{\lambda_{\bar{v}}^2}\right) \frac{\lambda_{\bar{v}h} \lambda_{\rho_1}}{\lambda_\omega \lambda_{\bar{\rho}}} = 1$$

or, since $\lambda_g \lambda_x / \lambda_{\bar{v}}^2 = 1$, it follows that

$$\frac{\lambda_{\bar{v}h} \lambda_{\rho_1}}{\lambda_\omega \lambda_{\bar{\rho}}} = 1$$

whence

$$\frac{\overline{v}_h \rho_1}{\omega \overline{\rho}} = \text{idem} \tag{IV}$$

or, adopting in both systems, the same fluid and a monodisperse sediment, the ratio ρ_1/ρ is already constant:

$$\frac{\overline{v}_h}{\omega} = \text{idem}$$

or the invariance concerning the ratio of the main and fall velocities of the sediment is obtained as condition equation.

For the last term it may be written further that

$$\frac{\lambda_g \lambda_{\rho_1} \lambda_x}{\lambda_{\bar\rho} \lambda_{\bar v} \lambda_\omega} = \left(\frac{\lambda_g \lambda_x}{\lambda_{\bar v}^2}\right) \frac{\lambda_{\bar v} \lambda_{\rho_1}}{\lambda_\omega \lambda_{\bar\rho}} = 1$$

and since, as will be remembered, $\lambda_g \lambda_x / \lambda_{\bar v}^2 = 1$, it follows that $\lambda_{\bar v} \lambda_{\rho_1} / \lambda_\omega \lambda_{\bar\rho} = 1$ whence

$$\frac{\bar v \, \rho_1}{\omega \rho} = \text{idem} \qquad\qquad (V)$$

For $\rho_1/\rho = \text{constant}$ the condition equation

$$\frac{\bar v}{\omega} = \text{idem}$$

is obtained expressing the invariance of the ratio of the flow velocity to the fall velocity.

From Eq. (H−3)

$$\frac{\lambda_{\rho_1}}{\lambda_t} = \frac{\lambda_{\rho_1} \lambda_{\bar vh}}{\lambda_x} = \frac{\lambda_\varepsilon \lambda_{\rho_1}}{\lambda_x^2}$$

or

$$\frac{\lambda_{\bar vh} \lambda_t}{\lambda_x} = \frac{\lambda_\varepsilon \lambda_t}{\lambda_x^2} = \frac{\lambda_\varepsilon}{\lambda_{\bar vh} \lambda_x} = 1$$

whence two additional condition equations result:

$$\frac{\bar{x} \bar v_h t}{x^2} = \text{idem} \qquad\qquad (VI)$$

indicating the invariance of kinematic time of sediment transport, and

$$\frac{\epsilon}{\bar v_h x} = \text{idem} \qquad\qquad (VII)$$

which is the condition of identity of the "diffusion" Reynolds number of sediment.

From Eq. (H−4)

$$\frac{\lambda_{\rho_1} \lambda_{\bar vh}}{\lambda_t} = \frac{\lambda_{\rho_1} \lambda_{\bar vh}^2}{\lambda_x} = \frac{\lambda_{\rho_1} \lambda_{\overline{v_h' v_h'}}}{\lambda_x} = \lambda_{\rho_1} \lambda_g = \frac{\lambda_{\gamma_1} \lambda_{\bar vh}}{\lambda_\omega} = \frac{\lambda_{\gamma_1} \lambda_{\bar v}}{\lambda_\omega}$$

or dividing the expression by the second term and with the substitution $\lambda_{\gamma_1} = \lambda_{\rho_1} \lambda_g$:

$$\frac{\lambda_x}{\lambda_t \lambda_{\bar vh}} = 1 = \frac{\lambda_{\overline{v_h' v_h'}}}{\lambda_{\bar vh}^2} = \frac{\lambda_g \lambda_x}{\lambda_{\bar vh}^2} = \left(\frac{\lambda_g \lambda_x}{\lambda_{\bar vh}^2}\right) \frac{\lambda_{\bar vh}}{\lambda_\omega} = \left(\frac{\lambda_g \lambda_x}{\lambda_{\bar vh}^2}\right) \frac{\lambda_{\bar v}}{\lambda_\omega}$$

665

resulting in only one additional condition equation

$$\frac{\overline{\mathbf{v}_h' \circ \mathbf{v}_h'}}{\overline{\mathbf{v}_h^2}} = \text{idem} \qquad\qquad \text{(VIIIa)}$$

in the Kármán criterion for sediment, which can be replaced if the conductive momentum current $(\rho_1 \mathbf{v}_h' \circ \mathbf{v}_h')$ of sediment is expressed as $(\mu_h \, \text{Grad} \, \overline{\mathbf{v}}_h)$ by the sediment velocity Reynolds number

$$\frac{\overline{\mathbf{v}_h} \mathbf{x}}{\nu_h} = \text{idem} \qquad\qquad \text{(VIIIb)}$$

Only one of Eqs (VIIIa) and (VIIIb) may be introduced simultaneously.

With the assumption $\nu_h = \nu$ only three of the altogether four criteria given by Eqs (IIb), (VIIIb), (IV) and (V) would be independent.

Summarizing, the similarity of two phenomena related to sediment transport is ensured by the following eight condition equations:

$$\frac{\lambda_s \lambda_{\overline{v}}}{\lambda_x} = 1, \qquad \text{i.e.} \quad \frac{\mathbf{x}\overline{\mathbf{v}}t}{\mathbf{x}^2} = \text{idem} \qquad\qquad \text{(I)}$$

or

$$\frac{\lambda_{\overline{v'v'}}}{\lambda_{\overline{v}^2}} = 1, \qquad \text{i.e.} \quad \frac{\overline{\mathbf{v}' \circ \mathbf{v}'}}{\overline{\mathbf{v}}^2} = \text{idem} \qquad\qquad \text{(IIa)}$$

$$\frac{\lambda_{\overline{v}}^2 \lambda_x}{\lambda_\nu \lambda_{\overline{v}}} = \frac{\lambda_{\overline{v}} \lambda_x}{\lambda_\nu} = 1, \qquad \text{i.e.} \quad \frac{\overline{\mathbf{v}}\mathbf{x}}{\nu} = Re = \text{idem} \qquad\qquad \text{(IIb)}$$

$$\frac{\lambda_g \lambda_x}{\lambda_{\overline{v}}^2} = 1, \qquad \text{i.e.} \quad \frac{\overline{\mathbf{v}}^2}{g\mathbf{x}} = Fr = \text{idem} \qquad\qquad \text{(III)}$$

$$\frac{\lambda_{\overline{v}_h} \lambda_{\rho_1}}{\lambda_\omega \lambda_{\overline{\rho}}} = 1, \qquad \text{i.e.} \quad \frac{\overline{\mathbf{v}}_h \rho_1}{\omega \rho} = \text{idem} \qquad\qquad \text{(IV)}$$

$$\frac{\lambda_{\overline{v}} \lambda_{\rho_1}}{\lambda_\omega \lambda_{\overline{\rho}}} = 1, \qquad \text{i.e.} \quad \frac{\overline{\mathbf{v}} \rho_1}{\omega \rho} = \text{idem} \qquad\qquad \text{(V)}$$

$$\frac{\lambda_{\overline{v}_h} \lambda_t}{\lambda_x} = 1, \qquad \text{i.e.} \quad \frac{\mathbf{x}\overline{\mathbf{v}}_h t}{\mathbf{x}^2} = \text{idem} \qquad\qquad \text{(VI)}$$

$$\frac{\lambda_{\overline{v}_h} \lambda_x}{\lambda_\varepsilon} = 1, \qquad \text{i.e.} \quad \frac{\epsilon}{\overline{\mathbf{v}}_h \mathbf{x}} = \text{idem} \qquad\qquad \text{(VII)}$$

$$\frac{\lambda_{\overline{v_h' v_h'}}}{\lambda_{\overline{v}}^2} = 1, \qquad \text{i.e.} \quad \frac{\overline{\mathbf{v}_h' \circ \mathbf{v}_h'}}{\overline{\mathbf{v}}^2} = \text{idem} \qquad\qquad \text{(VIIIa)}$$

666

or

$$\frac{\lambda_{\bar{v}h}^2 \lambda_x}{\lambda_{vh} \lambda_{\bar{v}h}} = \frac{\lambda_{\bar{v}h} \lambda_x}{\lambda_{vh}} = 1, \qquad \text{i.e.} \quad \frac{\bar{v}_h x}{v_h} = \text{idem} \qquad\qquad \text{(VIIIb)}$$

In the unambiguity conditions pertaining to the set of equations (I) to (VIII) the range of interpretation for *the flow of water is defined by* the slope S, the depth of flow D, the particle diameter d, the roughness coefficient n, the acceleration by gravity g, as well as by the material properties of the fluid, namely the kinematic viscosity v, the density $\bar{\rho}$, etc. The flow velocity $\bar{v}$ is a function of these:

$$\bar{v} = F(S, D, d, n, g, v, \bar{p} \text{ etc.})$$

Consequently from the invariants given by Eqs (I), (IIb), (III), (V) and (VII) similarity criteria could be formed by introducing for $\bar{v}$ the above functional relation.

Similarly concerning the movement of sediment: the invariants given by Eqs (IV), (V), (VI), (VII) and (VIIIb) may be regarded similarity criteria if in the unambiguity conditions the magnitude of the sediment velocity v_h, the fall velocity ω (or the particle diameter d), the kinematic viscosity of "sediment" v_h and of the turbulent diffusion coefficient ε, or their relations with the physical variables would be available.

However, since these functional relations are unavailable, and since we do not know exactly what variables to include beside those listed above, certain simplifying assumptions must be introduced.

Whenever dealing with the hydraulic similarity of sediment-carrying alluvial streams, this approach is adopted.

Before introducing hydraulic similarity the following remarks are to be made.

The number (i) of independent invariants is controlled in each particular problem by the number (n) of the independent physical quantities and by the number (m) of the fundamental dimensions:

$$i = n - m$$

Depending on the fundamental units adopted different combinations of invariants are obtained. Of these only such independent invariants are of actual interest as have or can be given a physical interpretation. In the case of fluids this physical interpretation implies that, for instance, in the flow of a fluid of density ρ and viscosity μ at velocity v and with depth D the above dimensional quantities are connected by one and only one relation which remains constant regardless of the manner in which the fundamental units of measurement are varied. The general form of this relation solved for v is

$$v = F(D, \rho, \mu) \qquad\qquad (2.5.1-1)$$

Eq. (2.5.1−1) results, as will be recalled, in the Reynolds number.

The expression

$$v = F(g, D) \qquad\qquad (2.5.1-2)$$

describes an absolute relation and yields the Froude number.

Similarly, if H is the surface tension per unit length, then

$$v = F(H, \rho, D) \qquad\qquad (2.5.1-3)$$

is the only possible relation between the above quantities and means essentially the Weber number.

Finally with E denoting the modulus of elasticity of the fluid, the relation

$$v = F(E, \rho) \qquad\qquad (2.5.1-4)$$

yields the Rayleigh–Cauchy number.

Under the interpretation given in the foregoing the invariant characteristic numbers Re, Fr, We and Ca can be derived by using a more direct approach as well by taking the acting forces into consideration. The general similarity criterion of Newton applies to the similarity of inertia forces. Combining the inertia force with the frictional, gravity, capillary and elastic forces, respectively, the special similarity criteria mentioned above are obtained.

In the case of fluids the five forces listed above are the only ones to be taken into consideration, there being usually no influence other than inertia, friction, gravity, capillarity and elasticity to affect appreciably the flow of fluids.

Each of the five forces included generally in the study of fluid flow is coupled to one of the material properties of the fluid, in that its magnitude depends on one of these material properties. The inertia force will be remembered to apply to the inert mass of the fluid. Although the inert mass is not identical with the weighty mass yet, since the inertia of bodies is proportionate to the mass measured in terms of weight, the gravitational mass or, in the case of fluids, the density ρ thereof is eventually introduced. Consequently, in considerations on hydraulics it is fluid density that is related to the inertia force. The friction force, on the other hand, is associated with the dynamic viscosity μ, the gravity force, with density ρ, the capillary force, with molecular composition while the elastic force, with elasticity of the fluid.

From the foregoing description of the special model laws given by the Re, Fr, We and Ca numbers it will become clear that the identity of each of them ensures the similarity, besides the inertia force, of another, additional force, i.e. altogether of two forces. Moreover, two material properties of the fluid are incorporated in the invariants Re, We and Ca, whereas only one, namely density, is involved in the Fr number.

Whichever of the four invariants is adopted as the single criterion of similarity, the reproduction of three forces is necessarily neglected. On the other hand, since the number of conditions in such cases is one only, a high degree of freedom is available for ensuring (partial) similarity and for selecting the scale ratios. The most important consequence thereof is that no restrictions are imposed on the material properties of the model fluid involved in the invariant under consideration. Inasmuch as the prototype fluid is usually water, the same fluid is commonly applied in the model. It should be noted in this context already that several additional criteria must be observed even in such simple cases, entailing, of course, certain restrictions.

Certain limitations, often almost impossible to meet, are encountered when two of the afore-mentioned invariants are adopted as similarity criteria. The observation or two invariants would amount to the reproduction of three forces. Different criteria will result depending on whether the three forces are related to three, or exceptionally to two material properties of the fluid. This latter condition arises when both the inertia and the gravity forces are included among the three forces. This is because each of the two forces is related to the material property density ρ of the fluid.

A certain latitude is in general allowed by the criteria in selecting the model characteristics. If the number of physical characteristics involved in the unambiguity conditions is t and that of similarity criteria relating to them is l, the number of characteristics which can be adopted freely is

$$\xi = t - l$$

In cases where ξ is greater than 1, no special difficulties are encountered in designing the model. However if $\zeta = 1$, the particular values of all other characteristics are positively determined once a single model characteristic is adopted. Special difficulties arise if $\zeta = 0$. In such cases model tests are apparently impossible to perform. The phenomenon to be investigated must be analysed, specifying the conditions under which an approximate solution is still practicable.

Consider first the relatively simple case where the inertia force and the gravity force are included among the three forces. In studies related to the dynamic phenomena of the fluid it is best to include the friction force as the third force and thus the dynamic viscosity μ associated therewith. Similarity in such cases is ensured by the identity of the invariants

$$Re = \frac{vl\rho}{\mu} \quad \text{and} \quad Fr = \frac{v^2}{gl}$$

Similarity of the three forces selected is ensured if the ratio of the dynamic viscosities of the prototype fluid and of the model fluid or, in brief, the scale ratios of dynamic viscosity is computed from the expression

$$\lambda_\mu = \lambda_l^{3/2} \lambda_g^{1/2} \lambda_\rho \tag{2.5.1-5}$$

If the model tests are performed at the same geographical location as that of the prototype, λ_g equals unity, so that

$$\lambda_\mu = \lambda_l^{3/2} \lambda_\rho \tag{2.5.1-6}$$

Introducing kinematic viscosity, the similarity of the three forces adopted is ensured by satisfying the equation

$$\lambda_v = \frac{\lambda_\mu}{\lambda_\rho} = \lambda_l^{3/2} \qquad (2.5.1-7)$$

It will be seen from the foregoing that although one of the two material properties of the model fluid can be selected freely, the other is already defined by the foregoing equation. Consequently, where it is desired to ensure the similarity of three forces, a model fluid having dynamic viscosity or density related to the prototype fluid by Eq. (2.5.1−6) must be used even if no more than two material properties of the fluid are involved. Model fluids meeting these requirements can be made available.

Consider now the case when each of the three forces to be reproduced is related to different material properties of the fluid. This occurs, for instance, in the case of seepage through granular soils. The velocities and especially the changes in velocity being small, experience has shown inertia effects to be negligible without introducing any major error. On the other hand, at the surface of the seeping fluid the influence of capillary forces may be considerable so that the third force introduced besides gravity and friction is the capillary force. The three material properties related to the three forces are fluid density ρ, the dynamic viscosity μ and the surface tension H of the fluid, respectively.

The scale ratios π of forces are given by the following familiar equations:
For gravity force

$$\pi = \lambda_\rho \lambda_l^3 \lambda_g = 1 \qquad (2.5.1-8)$$

For friction force

$$\pi = \lambda_l^2 \lambda_\mu \lambda_t^{-1} = 1 \qquad (2.5.1-9)$$

For capillary force

$$\pi = \lambda_l \lambda_H = 1 \qquad (2.5.1-10)$$

The identity of the scale factors of the three forces π, i.e. the identity of Eqs (2.5.1−8), (2.5.1−9) and (2.5.1−10) yields two conditions equations. Assuming the same geographical location, i.e. $\lambda_g = 1$, these are:

$$\lambda_\rho \lambda_l = \lambda_\mu \lambda_t^{-1} \qquad (2.5.1-11)$$

$$\lambda_\rho \lambda_l^2 = \lambda_H \qquad (2.5.1-12)$$

Altogether five unknown scale factors are involved in Eqs (2.5.1−11) and (2.5.1−12) so that, provided that no other conditions are observed, in principle the value of three scale ratios can be adopted without restriction. One of these is

670

obviously the scale ratio of linear dimensions λ_l. The scale ratio of one of the material properties of the fluid (density, dynamic viscosity or surface tension) may be another. The third scale ratio to be freely adopted could be the scale ratio of time λ_t, but here certain kinematic relations impose limitations, the phenomenon under consideration being fluid flow. In the particular case of seepage the Darcy law may be regarded as one of these relations. Even if difficulties arising in the selection of λ_t are disregarded or eliminated somehow, it is almost unconceivable that, for instance at any given density, the dynamic viscosity and surface tension of the fluid should assume exactly the value resulting from Eqs (2.5.1 − 11) and (2.5.1 − 12). The unique solution of the condition equations (2.5.1 − 11) and (2.5.1 − 12) yields unity for all scale ratios, so that a model of the same dimensions as those of the prototype would be required. Consequently for ensuring the similarity of three forces that are related to three material properties of the fluid cannot be ensured unless the model is identical with the prototype in all respects.

In the foregoing example of the similarity of three forces an undistorted model has implicitly been assumed. In the case of seepage models this solution is practically unfeasible. In fact if the scale ratios of length, depth and capillary passages are given different values and if a fluid (e.g. oil) differing in all three material properties from the prototype fluid (water) is used, then different combinations of scale ratios can be adopted to ensure simultaneously the similarity of gravity, friction and capillary forces. In this connection several solutions have been developed by Z. Hankó for the details of which the reader is referred to the relevant literature.

From the foregoing it follows that similarity of more than three forces can only be ensured in a model which is identical with the prototype.

Since all material properties of the fluid are realized in both the prototype and the model and since all forces related to these material properties become involved, complete mechanical similarity is impossible to attain unless the model is identical in all respects with the prototype. In such models all criteria are, of course, satisfied.

Disregarding exceptional cases in hydraulic model tests water is commonly used as the model fluid. For this reason exact mechanical similarity is in principle never achieved in models differing in dimensions from the prototype. This is generally acknowledged even if the special criteria involved in any particular phenomenon studied are satisfied. It follows that in hydromechanics exact mechanical similarity is in general out of question.

Research on model testing and the mechanics of fluids has shown a particular phenomenon associated with the movement of water to be described with special clearness by other forms of the invariant numbers mentioned before. Although these special forms of the invariants must not be mistaken for new invariants, their introduction as similarity criteria in distorted models entail conditions differing from the original invariant numbers. Typical examples are the introduction of the fall velocity ω and the particle diameter d of sediment as characteristic velocity and length, respectively, in the Re and Fr numbers describing the settling of sediment, or the use of the shear velocity U_* as characteristic velocity.

The above statements are illustrated by the following example:

671

Using the shear velocity U_* in any arbitrary similarity criterion for the characteristic velocity, instead of the mean velocity v, the equation

$$\lambda_{U_*} = \lambda_v \qquad (2.5.1-13)$$

necessarily applies. Since

$$U_* = \sqrt{gDS}$$

consequently

$$\lambda_{U_*} = \lambda_D^{1/2}\lambda_S^{1/2} = \lambda_D^{1/2}\frac{\lambda_D^{1/2}}{\lambda_l^{1/2}} = \lambda_D\lambda_l^{-1/2} = \lambda_v \qquad (2.5.1-14)$$

assuming that the prototype and the model are at the same geographical location.

Where the inertia force is combined with gravity force as the forces dominating the phenomenon under consideration, the criterion of Froude must be satisfied. Consequently

$$\lambda_v = \lambda_D^{1/2} \qquad (2.5.1-15)$$

Examining Eqs (2.5.1−14) and (2.5.1−15) it will be perceived that the criteria expressed by them cannot be met unless both length and depth are reproduced to the same scale in the model.

Where it is required to satisfy the Reynolds criterion,

$$\lambda_v = \lambda_l^{-1} \qquad (2.5.1-16)$$

The conditions expressed by Eqs (2.5.1−14) and (2.5.1−16) cannot be met unless

$$\lambda_D = \lambda_l^{-1/2} \qquad (2.5.1-17)$$

which is, in the majority of cases, impossible to realize.

As can be seen from the foregoing, the introduction of special invariant characteristics entails usually additional restrictions.

Fortunately however in engineering practice the observation of exact mechanical similarity need not be adhered to strictly. In most of the phenomena to be investigated certain material properties of the fluid are found to play a secondary role only. In such cases the criteria of mechanical similarity may be regarded as approximately satisfied.

The above considerations show that, in the historical development of model testing, endeavours have increasingly been directed to meet at least the dominating conditions for particular phenomena studied. This type of similarity may be called *approximate hydraulic similarity*. The requirements involved are always less severe than in the case of exact similarity but are in general sufficient for studying the particular phenomenon. A number of terms have been suggested in the literature; in some instances dynamic similarity is mentioned, involving the danger of being easily misunderstood for mechanical similarity. These and similar terms are often misleading because they involve the possibility of supposing unintentionally exact similarity in individual detail studies.

2.5.1.2. Evolution of model-testing of sediment-carrying water courses. The general statements made on model testing apply also to sediment models. Besides the hydraulic factors in the strict sense of the word, in such models it is required to reproduce the type of sediment (its particle size d, specific gravity γ_1, granulometric composition), the quantity of sediment (the total transport q_t, bed load transport q_B), and the manner in which sediment is transported. Occasionally the type of movement must also be reproduced truly. The difficulties associated with such studies are obviously increasing, as shown by the historical evolution of the methods; the early efforts for solving the similarity problems arising with such models have remained practically unsuccessful.

In the earliest attempts at studying sediment problems with the help of models attention was focused on the choise of a model sediment suitable for experimental purposes or, in the case of a given sediment material, on the determination of the slope corresponding thereto.

H. Krey for instance suggests that the movement of sediment in the model is ensured if the depth of flow D'' is selected within the range*

$$\frac{d''}{20\,S''} \leqq D'' \leqq \frac{d''}{8S''} \qquad (2.5.1-18)$$

The lower limit of slopes in the model is thus

$$S'' = \frac{d''}{8D''} \quad \text{or} \quad S'' \geqq \frac{d''}{8D''}$$

The other limit slope is determined by the condition that subcritical flow in the prototype should be reproduced as subcritical flow in the model. The upper limit is thus defined by the condition

$$S'' \leq \frac{g''}{c''^2} \qquad (2.5.1-19)$$

where g'' is the acceleration due to gravity at the geographical location of the model, while c'' is the velocity coefficient of the model channel.

Krey's statement has been supplemented by S. Rohringer requiring the model slope to be in the same proportion to the limits given before, as in the prototype.

In the course of subsequent development the fundamental relations of sediment transport have been adopted as the basis of similarity criteria. In a number of instances the tractive force τ_0 has been reproduced with the equation $\tau_0 = \gamma DS$ which, assuming $\lambda_\gamma = 1$, means that $\lambda_D = \lambda^{1/2}$.

Besides the reproduction of critical velocity many investigators have, especially in recent times, adopted some form of the channel stability factor for ensuring similarity. The author himself has started from the channel stability factor d/DS

---

* The quantities applying to the prototype are denoted by ', whereas those applying to the model, by "

introduced by him in 1942 on the basis of earlier investigations. The introduction of the term d/DS implies for instance that

$$\lambda_d = \frac{\lambda_D^2}{\lambda_l}$$

Since the channel stability factor is already a concept associated with the domain of the stable channel it appeared perfectly logical to adopt the stable-channel relations as similarity criteria in model tests on alluvial streams. An example for these is the relation of T. Blench who suggests the following ratios for the scale ratios applying to width B, depth D, slope S and discharge Q in stable channels:

$$\lambda_B : \lambda_D : \lambda_S = \lambda_Q^{1/2} : \lambda_Q^{1/3} : \lambda_Q^{-1/6} \qquad (2.5.1-20)$$

The scale ratio of water depth is obtained eventually from Eq. (2.5.1 − 20) as

$$\lambda_D = \lambda_B^{2/3} \qquad (2.5.1-21)$$

In model tests on alluvial streams several investigators have attempted to ensure similarity on the basis of morphological characteristics. The approach is perfectly correct, the only difficulty being encountered in assigning numerical values to morphological properties.

At the Research Institute for Water Resources Development, Budapest, a method has been developed by the author for designing models of alluvial streams, using the channel stability factor introduced by him. Research work related to the method was performed in 1955 in the course of which the invariant Φ_* introduced by Einstein for describing the intensity of sediment transport was applied to ensure similarity of bed load transport.

In this method the particle diameter of sediment is denoted by d, the scale ratio of sediment particle sizes λ_d is assumed in advance, or the ratio thereof to the scale ratio of length λ_l is specified. This may be regarded as the first condition equation in this method.

The second condition equation is afforded by the channel stability factor

$$b = \frac{d}{RS} = \frac{d}{DS}$$

introduced by the author in 1942 as an invariant characteristic. Here R is the hydraulic radius, S is the slope, while D is the depth of flow that can be replaced for the hydraulic radius.

The third condition equation is defined by the intensity of sediment transport, i.e. by Einstein's invariant Φ_*. The relationship existing between the rate of bed load transport, the submerged specific gravity of sediment material and the particle diameter is expressed thereby.

The fourth condition equation is determined by the relation of time t, of length l and of the flow velocity v.

674

The fifth condition equation can be derived from the relation of the tractive force to the particle diameter d or to the flow velocity v.

The last, sixth condition equation is a simple expression of the fact that the scale ratio of slopes is given as the ratio of the scale ratios of vertical and horizontal dimensions.

This method has been intended rather as an initial approach showing some promise in model studies of alluvial streams.

The limitation common to all attempts mentioned in the foregoing is the endeavour to ensure similarity by considering only a few characteristics of sediment transport. No efforts have been made at meeting other criteria though it should be admitted this has not been possible either.

In models of this type some distortion is inevitable, and in most cases the depth, indeed, is distorted entailing the distortion of slope. Scale ratios are in general determined by the Froude criterion resulting in a number of inconsistences, as well as in departures of the model from the prototype. Of these, the inconsistencies violating the similarity of the particular phenomenon under study must be eliminated. This is done through "verification" consisting essentially of introducing additional distortions with the objective of counter-balancing the effects of the first distortion. We shall not elaborate on the rules and process of verification but shall confine ourselves to the statement that verification consists essentially of a trial-and-error procedure under rather adverse conditions since certain quantities (e.g. λ_l, λ_D, λ_S) are given definite values in advance, making thus a correct solution even more difficult. Another drawback is that modifications are not determined with the help of exact mathematical methods and computations but usually on the basis of relationships between a few quantities disregarding in general other relations. Regardless thereof the method of verification is still commonly used and should be regarded as the exclusive method, in many instance, because ample empirical experience is available and can be used to benefit in model testing in this field. In the course of verification many modifications are possible. Some of the common arbitrary modifications affect the scale ratio of discharge λ_Q, the roughness conditions, the distortion of slope resulting from vertical distortion, etc.

Recent methods derived from similarity theory, which are believed to ensure the most suitable reproduction, are essentially also some kind of verification but, instead of subsequent trials, computations are performed in advance, and a similarity transformation of the mathematical model is introduced, permitting the magnitude of each scale ratio to be selected without restriction, the differences to be controlled and, even more important, the influence and place of appearance of these differences to be predicted.

The deviations obviously cause the least problems if they crop up at places or in quantities of least importance for the phenomenon.

Since the number of conditions to be observed in models of alluvial streams is very large, simple verification is bound to remain unsuccessful with such models. The method of verification which has proved adequate in simple studies on surface profiles or flow conditions may fail in the case of models of alluvial streams.

The determinations of similarity criteria by dimensional analysis will now be discussed briefly.

Dimensional analysis will be recalled to contain no statement on the variables dominating the phenomenon, nor on the concept of similarity. Physical variables are selected arbitrarily, while the concept of similar phenomena is defined only through equation analysis. Isolated attempts at defining the concept of similarity exclusively on the basis of dimensional analysis are bound to remain unsuccessful. A theory founded on physical variables alone and disregarding the relationships existing between these variables is unrelated to similarity, since the same physical variables may be involved, in principle, in an infinite number of fundamentally different phenomena.

The similarity of two phenomena must be decided in advance, before observations are performed. Failing to do so would make the model test itself meaningless, since in such cases the similarity of the model to the prototype could only be ascertained after performing the model test; and we would thus run the risk of reproducing an entirely unrelated phenomenon in the model. No justification can be found for assuming the a priori existence of similarity relying exclusively on some "engineering instinct" or "engineering practice".

Dimensional analysis alone is thus uncapable of defining similarity or of determining the conditions of its observation. The domain of validity of similarity relations can only be outlined on the basis of the similarity theory. The concept of similarity, its necessary and adequate conditions are defined positively by similarity theory relying on equation analysis in doing so.

An additional essential difference between equation analysis and dimensional analysis should be emphasized by stating that the mathematical model of any phenomenon is confined – by definition – to its own sphere of validity.

The variables involved in any particular phenomenon are in themselves inadequate to decide the cases in which any particular variable becomes essential and in which (and for what reason) it becomes negligible. Mathematical formulation provides the means for performing computations reflecting also quantitative conditions accurately. One method of such "computations" is model testing based on similarity theory. Experimentally derived functional relations between the similarity criteria and the dependent invariants obtained by equation analysis yield the solution of the problem within the validity limits of the mathematical model of the phenomenon. Dimensional analysis, on the other hand, provides corr ect results only for the range covered by the individual variables during observations, even if these variables have been selected correctly. The invariants of dimensional analysis lend themselves positively to a more visual presentation of experimental data only, their application to other phenomena being impermissible unless checked by special experiments.

The computation method of dimensional analysis and that of equation analysis are frequently mistaken for each other. In the interest of distinction it would appear more appropriate to deal with dimensionless numbers in the former (the formulation thereof being its fundamental purpose) and to restrict the concepts of invariance and similarity criteria to equation analysis.

A comparison of dimensional analysis and similarity method will reveal that only the latter yields substantially reliable results. In cases, however, where the fundamental equations describing the phenomenon are not available, dimensional analysis must be resorted to. The uncertainty of the process should always be remembered and no result is to be accepted as positive until supported by experimental or theoretical evidence obtained by a different approach.

* * *

The above considerations will be illustrated by an example of the model of an alluvial stream.

Assume the physical properties governing the phenomenon of sediment transport to be determined or characterized

for water (the fluid) by the density ρ and the kinematic viscosity v,

for the sediment by the submerged specific gravity $(\gamma_1 - \gamma)$ and the particle diameter d,

for the water course (its dynamic condition) by the shear velocity U_*.

From the above five parameters two dimensionless groups can be composed which are positively of the form

$$\frac{U_* d}{v} = Re_* \tag{2.5.1-22}$$

and

$$\frac{U_*^2}{gd} \frac{\gamma}{\gamma_1 - \gamma} = Fr_* \frac{\gamma}{\gamma_1 - \gamma} \tag{2.5.1-23}$$

or are raised to some power, occasionally combined into products.

It should be noted in this context that the development of Eqs (2.5.1−22) and (2.5.1−23) with the help of dimensional analysis in a relatively simple manner was impossible before lengthy and tiresome research revealing U_* to be the most important factor in sediment transport, since it is much more representative of sediment movement than either the mean velocity or the product of depth and slope.

From the above considerations it follows that the equations

$$Re_*' = Re_*'' \tag{2.5.1-24}$$

and

$$\left(\frac{\gamma}{\gamma_1 - \gamma} Fr_*\right)' = \left(\frac{\gamma}{\gamma_1 - \gamma} Fr_*\right)'' \tag{2.5.1-25}$$

must be regarded as the similarity criteria in modelling sediment problems. If water is used as the model fluid to reproduce the flow of water in the prototype, so that $\lambda_g = \lambda_v = \lambda_y = 1$ and the geographical location is the same, so that $\lambda_g = 1$, then Eqs (2.5.1 − 24) and (2.5.1 − 25) yield the following two condition equations

$$\lambda_d = \frac{1}{\lambda_{U_*}} \qquad (2.5.1-26)$$

$$\lambda_d = \frac{\lambda_{U_*}^2}{\lambda_{(\gamma_1 - \gamma)}} \qquad (2.5.1-27)$$

Since, as will be recalled, from Eq. (2.5.1 − 14)

$$\lambda_{U_*} = \lambda_D^{1/2} \lambda_S^{1/2}$$

the condition equations (2.5.1 − 16) and (2.5.1 − 27) yield the expression

$$\lambda_{(\gamma_1 - \gamma)} = \lambda_{U_*}^2 = \lambda_D^{3/2} \lambda_S^{3/2} \qquad (2.5.1-28)$$

Consider first the case in which no distortion is introduced to the quantities having the dimensions of length, so that

$$\lambda_l = \lambda_D = \lambda_d$$

in which case $\lambda_S = 1$.

With these values

$$\lambda_{(\gamma_1 - \gamma)} = \lambda_l^{3/2}, \text{ s igy } \lambda_{U_*}^3 = \lambda_l^{3/2}$$

so that

$$\lambda_{U_*} = \lambda_l^{1/2}$$

From Eq. (2.5.1 − 16), on the other hand,

$$\lambda_d = \lambda_l = \frac{1}{\lambda_{U_*}} = \frac{1}{\lambda_l^{1/2}}$$

whence $\lambda_l = 1$. This implies further that all scale ratios equal unity so that, without distorting the quantities having the dimension of length, the conditions Re_* and Fr_* are satisfied by the protype only.

Consider hereafter the case where distortion is possible, i.e.

$$\lambda_l \neq \lambda_D \neq \lambda_d \text{ és } \lambda_S = \frac{\lambda_D}{\lambda_l}$$

In this case

$$\lambda_{(\gamma_1 - \gamma)} = \lambda_D^{1/2} \frac{\lambda_D^{3/2}}{\lambda_l^{3/2}} = \lambda_D^3 \lambda_l^{-3/2}$$

The scale ratio of shear velocity becomes thus

$$\lambda_{U_*} = \lambda_D^{1/2} \frac{\lambda_D^{1/2}}{\lambda_l^{1/2}} = \lambda_D \lambda_l^{-1/2} \qquad (5.2.1-29)$$

678

Further, from Eq. (2.5.1 – 26)

$$\lambda_d = \lambda_D^{-1}\lambda_l^{1/2} \qquad\qquad (2.5.1-30)$$

On the other hand it will be remembered that in open-channel flow the Fr criterion must also be satisfied. Thus, considering also Eq. (2.5.1 – 29), we have

$$\lambda_v = \lambda_D^{1/2} = \lambda_{U_*} = \lambda_D\lambda_l^{-1/2} \qquad\qquad (2.5.1-31)$$

In the foregoing it has already been demonstrated that in cases where the Fr criterion is satisfied the equation $\lambda_v = \lambda_{U*}$ cannot apply unless the model is geometrically undistorted. In fact, from Eq. (2.5.1 – 31)

$$\lambda_D^{-1/2} = \lambda_l^{-1/2}$$

so that $\lambda_D = \lambda_l$ and of course $\lambda_S = 1$.

In this way, according to Eq. (2.5.1 – 29),

$$\lambda_{U_*} = \lambda_l^{1/2} \qquad\qquad (2.5.1-32)$$

From Eq. (2.5.1 – 30), on the other hand,

$$\lambda_d = \lambda_l^{-1/2} \qquad\qquad (2.5.1-33)$$

moreover

$$\lambda_{(\gamma_1-\gamma)} = \lambda_l^{3/2} \qquad\qquad (2.5.1-34)$$

The conditions for the simultaneous observation of the criteria

$$Fr_* \frac{\gamma}{\gamma_1 - \gamma}$$

Re_* and Fr are thus as follows:
 a) no geometrical distortion must be introduced in the model,
 b) the particle size of the sediment must be distorted, so that instead of

$$\lambda_d = \lambda_l$$

the relation

$$\lambda_d = \lambda_l^{-1/2} \qquad\qquad (2.5.1-35)$$

should be applied,
 c) the submerged specific gravity of sediment must also differ from that of the prototype, i.e. the scale ratio

$$\lambda_{(\gamma_1-\gamma)} = \lambda_l^{3/2} \qquad\qquad (2.5.1-36)$$

should be applied.

Unfortunately, the scale ratios computed according to Eqs (2.5.1 – 34) and (2.5.1 – 35) are useless for practical purposes. For instance at $\lambda_l = 100$ the re-

679

sulting model sediment would have a particle diameter ten times as large, and a specific gravity thousand times less than that moving in the prototype.

If either $\lambda_d = \lambda_l$, or $\lambda_d = 1$, further if, irrespective of these, $\lambda_{(\gamma_1 - \gamma)} = \lambda_l$, or $\lambda_{(\gamma_1 - \gamma)} = 1$, all scale ratios will become unity, consequently these conditions are satisfied only in the prototype.

Therefore, the idea of determining the scale ratios for sediment-carrying models according to the conditions expressed by Eqs (2.5.1 – 24) and (2.5.1 – 25) is to be abandoned. Instead, as mentioned before, a trial-and-error method with appropriate condition equations is preferable.

It should be noted here that the nine condition equations involved in the method of H. Einstein include also the criteria

$$Fr_* \frac{\gamma}{\gamma_1 - \gamma}$$

Re_* and Fr. In the modified method suggested by the author the Fr condition is retained, while, instead of Fr_* and Re_*, a parameter meeting both simultaneously is introduced as similarity criteria into the set of equations on which computations are based.

The foregoing example has been quoted to call attention to the fact that the results obtained by dimensional analysis are to be examined carefully and, in general, other circumstances controlling the phenomenon under study are also to be taken into consideration.

It has, for instance, been found that the criteria Re_* and

$$Fr_* \cdot \frac{\gamma}{\gamma_1 - \gamma}$$

can only be statisfied by introducing an extent of distortion that is practically impossible to achieve. It will be seen eventually that, when using a model sediment of the same size and specific gravity as in the prototype, essentially no model test can be performed.

From the foregoing it follows logically that hydraulic similarity in models of sediment-carrying streams is determined preferably by verification, permitting
  – necessary modifications to be determined in advance,
  – a solution by systematical computation, and
  – discrepancies to occur in quantities that are of little influence on the particular phenomenon.

In models of sediment-carrying streams some distortion has been found inevitable. Distortion implies always that different values are assigned to scale ratios of two or more quantities having the same dimensions but different physical characteristics. Consequently by introducing two different scale ratios for no more than two quantities of the same dimension, one of the dimensions is already distorted. It should be realized that once a certain distortion is introduced, it

680

becomes inevitable to distort quantities of other dimensions as well, this being the only way in which the influence of the distortion first introduced can be at least partially counterbalanced. It should be appreciated moreover that the introduction of distortions counterbalancing each other mutually amounts to a compromise in observing the definite relationships existing between the hydraulic factors of water courses. Care should always be taken, however, to keep the violation of theoretical relations within a limit, resulting in acceptable errors concerning the phenomenon involved in the problem to be solved.

In view of the wide variety of phenomena and the problems arising in connection therewith it should be clear that no unique and positive solution is possible. The great number of often radically different methods described in the literature is attributable to this circumstance.

For studying the behaviour of sediment-carrying streams it is thus necessary to construct a distorted model for which the scale ratios are determined in combination with each other, by taking into consideration the effect of each distortion in the computation of each λ value. This involves essentially a trial-and-error method, in which all relations are observed in seeking the relatively optimum solution, i.e. the one resulting in the relatively smallest error. As mentioned before, the principle advantage of such methods is the possibility of controlling the magnitude and point of occurrence of the errors. This advantage is of considerable importance as it enables us to ensure the highest relative accuracy in the details controlling the phenomenon studied.

2.5.2. THE EINSTEIN—NING CHIEN METHOD

In 1956 H. A. Einstein and Ning Chien, then in 1957 Ning Chien developed a comprehensive method for computing distorted models of alluvial streams, which is based in part on the invariants expressing channel stability and the intensity of sediment transport. Naturally, in this method relations concerning time, distance and velocity are also involved, so that three of the nine condition equations are identical with the conditions involved in the approximate method suggested by the author in 1955.

In the method suggested by them six additional condition equations are introduced to make allowance for roughness conditions; the Froude number, the laminar boundary layer, for the ratio of total and bed load, for the duration of flow and, finally, for the ratio of the actual slope and that computed with the help of the vertical and horizontal scale ratios.

The method of Einstein and Ning Chien has proved suitable for practical computations. As noted by them, certain conditions could be derived from other relations without, however, obtaining other, improved results, the difference in the expressions obtained being only a formal one. In this context it is of interest to note that in his laboratory experiments J. L. Chauvin took into consideration friction conditions using again the relation

$$\frac{v}{\sqrt{gDS}} = \frac{v}{U_*} = c\left(\frac{D}{d}\right)^m$$

suggested by Einstein – Ning-Chien – and on the basis of Eq. (2.5.2. – 1a) – detailed subsequently.

On the other hand, P. Jensen and J. C. Lebreton have determined the relation of the dimensionless parameters of Eq. (2.2.1 – 12)

$$\frac{v}{U_*} = \sqrt{\frac{8}{f}}$$

and

$$\frac{\tau_0}{(\gamma_1 - \gamma)/d} = \frac{1}{\Psi}$$

using the roughness coefficient f of Darcy – Weissbach. According to their experiments

$$\sqrt{\frac{8}{f}} = 5.62\left(\frac{1}{\Psi}\right)^{0.32}$$

A brief discussion on Einstein – Ning Chien method will be presented below.

The ten independent scale ratios are related to one another by nine condition equations. The relations inherent to the nine condition equations or the condition equations determining the scale ratios on the basis of these relationships are derived as follows:

a) In deriving *the similarity criterion for friction conditions* Einstein and Ning Chien started from the general Manning formula, according to which flow velocity v, depth D, slope S and particle diameter d are related by the expression

$$v = \frac{c\sqrt{g}}{d^m} S^{1/2} D^{(1/2+m)} \tag{2.5.2–1a}$$

For $m = 1/6$, the familiar Manning formula is obtained

$$v = \frac{c\sqrt{g}}{d^{1/6}} S^{1/2} D^{2/3} \tag{2.5.2–1b}$$

where, as will be recalled, $1/n = c\sqrt{g}/d^{1/6}$ since $n \propto d^{1/6}$.

Considering the scale ratios from Eq. (2.5.2 – 1a) the first condition equation is

$$\lambda_v^2 \lambda_d^{2m} \lambda_c^{-2} \lambda_S^{-1} \lambda_D^{(-1-2m)} = \Delta_v \tag{2.5.2–I}$$

where the exact solution of the equations yields naturally $\Delta_v = 1$, but for certain practical purposes Δ_v may slightly differ from unity. One of the possible reasons

682

for this is, for instance, that, instead of the one allowed scale ratio, several scale ratios are given arbitrary values.

In the above expression c is a dimensionless constant in Manning's generalized equation and is proportionate to Chézy's c. The magnitude of $\lambda_c = c'/c''$, that is, of the scale ratio characterizing velocities in the prototype and the model, is found by auxiliary computations rather than from the condition equations (2.5.2−1) to (2.5.2−IX). A similar quantity is m which should be determined in such a way that this exponent should be the same in the prototype and the model.

It should be noted that the scale ratio of depth is the same as that of the hydraulic radius, so that $\lambda_R = \lambda_D$.

As to their basic roles there is no difference between the scale ratios of depth and of hydraulic radius, as long as the model is undistorted. The situation is different when it is desired or necessary to separate the resistance due to sediment particles at the bottom from that due to bed form. It is not intended to enlarge upon these details here and even the differences resulting from distortion will be neglected.

b) *The Froude condition*

$$Fr = \frac{v^2}{gD} \qquad (2.5.2-2)$$

and, if the geographical location is the same, i.e. $\lambda_g = g'/g'' = 1$, the second condition equations becomes

$$\lambda_v^2 \lambda_D^{-1} = \Delta_{Fr}^2 \qquad (2.5.2-\text{II})$$

In an exact solution $\Delta_{Fr} = 1$, but in particular cases a certain tolerance is allowable.

c) *The similarity of sediment transport* is realized if Einstein's parameter Φ_* is the same. If the ratio of various size fractions is the same in the prototype and the model, then with q_B denoting the rate of bed load transport in p/sec m units, ρ and ρ_1 the density of water and the sediment, respectively, g the gravitational acceleration and d the particle diameter of the sediment, the invariant representing the intensity of transport is

$$\Phi_* = \frac{q_B}{g(\rho_1 - \rho)} \left(\frac{\rho}{\rho_1 - \rho}\right)^{1/2} \left(\frac{1}{gd^3}\right)^{1/2} \qquad (2.5.2-3)$$

Assuming again that $\lambda_g = 1$ and the model fluid is water, so that $\lambda_\rho = 1$, the third condition equation is written with the help of scale ratios as

$$\lambda_{qB}^2 \lambda_{(\rho_1 - \rho)}^{-3} \lambda_d^{-3} = 1 \qquad (2.5.2-\text{III})$$

d) *The condition of channel stability* is expressed by the parameter

$$\Psi = \frac{\rho_1 - \rho}{\rho} \cdot \frac{d}{DS} \qquad (2.5.2-4a)$$

683

introduced by Einstein in 1941 and 1950 and mentioned as the intensity of stream flow.

As already mentioned the parameter Ψ representing the intensity of stream flow is essentially identical with the channel stability factor

$$b = \frac{d}{DS} \tag{2.5.2-4b}$$

introduced by the author in 1942.

With $\lambda_\rho = 1$, the condition of channel stability is expressed according to Eintsein and Ning Chien by the equation

$$\lambda_{(\rho_1 - \rho)}\lambda_d\lambda_D^{-1}\lambda_S^{-1} = 1 \tag{2.5.2-IV}$$

e) *The condition of the laminar boundary layer.* As will be recalled, the thickness of the laminar sublayer δ' is given as

$$\delta' = 11.6\,\frac{v}{U_*} = 11.6\,\frac{v}{\sqrt{gDS}} \tag{2.5.2-5a}$$

where v is the coefficient of kinematic viscosity and $U_* = \sqrt{gDS}$ is the shear velocity. With d denoting the particle diameter, the ratio of the latter and the thickness of the laminar sublayer is

$$\frac{d}{\delta'} = \frac{d\sqrt{gDS}}{11.6v} \tag{2.5.2-5b}$$

The term d/δ' is characteristic of the smoothness or roughness of the bed. According to M. L. Albertson, D. B. Simons and E. V. Richardson, Eq. (2.5.2–5b) can also be written in the form

$$11.6\,\frac{d}{\delta'} = \frac{U_*d}{v} = Re_{*s} \tag{}$$

implying that Re_{*s}, the sediment shear velocity Reynolds number, is approximately twelve times as great as the ratio d/δ'. Assuming that the particle diameter d of sediment is approximately identical with the linear roughness k defined by Nikuradze for pipes, the condition of sediment transport in the bed is obviously related from the viewpoint of fluid mechanics to the transition from the smooth into the rough boundary layer.

It is possible to demonstrate that the scale ratios $\lambda_{\delta'}$ and λ_d of the laminar boundary layers and particle diameters, respectively, are necessarily identical. Consequently, from Eq. (2.5.2–5b) assuming that $\lambda_v = 1$, the condition equation (2.5.2–V) in a squared form becomes

$$\lambda_D\lambda_S\lambda_d^2 = \Delta_{\delta'}^2 \tag{2.5.2-V}$$

In an exact solution $\Delta_{\delta'} = 1$ but, owing to irregularities in roughness, its value may differ slightly from unity.

f) *The condition relating the scale ratios of total transport λ_{qt} and bed load transport λ_{qB}.* The quantity B defining the ratio of total and bed load transport must be found from auxiliary computations. In general, it is advisably assumed as the mean value of ratios determined at several characteristic stages. Since

$$\frac{\lambda_{qt}}{\lambda_{qB}} = B \qquad (2.5.2-6)$$

for the scale ratios of total transport

$$\frac{q_t'}{q_t''} = \lambda_{qt}$$

and bed load transport

$$\frac{q_B'}{q_B''} = \lambda_{qB}$$

the following condition equation is obtained

$$\lambda_{qB}\lambda_{qt}^{-1} B = 1 \qquad (2.5.2-VI)$$

g) *The condition for computing the hydraulic time t_1* is obtained from the relationship existing between the velocity v of the individual particles, the distance L travelled by them and the time t_1 of travel, i.e. from the equation

$$v = \frac{L}{t_1} \qquad (2.5.2-7)$$

Consequently the seventh condition equation becomes

$$\lambda_v \lambda_{t_1} \lambda_l^{-1} = 1 \qquad (2.5.2-VII)$$

where λ_{t_1} is the scale ratio of hydraulic time.

h) Concerning *the duration of flow,* time is computed under the condition that the rate of transport should indicate the corresponding weight or the corresponding volume during a given time. The total transport q_t in unit width during a given time t_2 is defined as the sediment having the submerged weight $LD(\rho_1 - \rho)g$, where D is the depth of flow and L the distance travelled. In other words

$$q_t t_2 = LD(\rho_1 - \rho)g \qquad (2.5.2-8)$$

In terms of scale ratios, if the time scale of flow duration is λ_{t_2}, the condition equation assumes the form

$$\lambda_{qt}\lambda_{t_2}\lambda_l^{-1}\lambda_D^{-1}\lambda_{(\rho_1-\rho)}^{-1} = 1 \qquad (2.5.2-VIII)$$

i) *The condition of slope distortion* is expressed, on the basis of the relation

$$S = \frac{D}{L} \tag{2.5.2-9a}$$

by the equation $\lambda_S = \lambda_D \lambda_l^{-1}$. The vertical distortion is

$$MT = \frac{\lambda_l}{\lambda_D}$$

hence

$$MT = \lambda_S^{-1} \tag{2.5.2-9b}$$

Occasionally it is found necessary to distort the slope beyond the vertical distortion. In some instances even a slope distortion smaller than the vertical distortion may be desirable. In such cases the slope distortion is expressed by the condition equation

$$\lambda_S \lambda_l \lambda_D^{-1} = \Delta_S \tag{2.5.2-IX}$$

where Δ_S may differ slightly from unity.

The condition equations (2.5.2−I) to (2.5.2−IX) involve altogether ten independent scale ratios since λ_c is not regarded as such. The magnitude of one of the scale ratios can be chosen arbitrarily.

As mentioned before, the magnitude of λ_c, m and B must be determined in advance by auxiliary computations and may be assumed to be known as far as the solution of the nine equations is concerned. In the exact solution of the equations, Δ_v, Δ_{Fr}, $\Delta_{\delta'}$ and Δ_S equal unity. For certain practical reasons, however, the Δ values are allowed to differ slightly from unity, which permits us to select, for instance, an additional scale ratio freely.

In the method of Einstein and Ning Chien certain restrictions are encountered if the model sediment is of the same specific gravity or particle size as in the prototype. The situation is the same if the rate of the bed load transport in the model and the prototype is identical, and the same restrictions arise if the scale ratio λ_{qt} of total transport is identical with the ratio B of the scale ratios of total and bed load transport.

Sediment material obtained from the water course considered is often used in model studies. In such cases, regardless whether the identity of particle sizes is required or not, the scale ratio of submerged sediment densities is $\lambda_{(\rho_1 - \rho)} = 1$. On the basis of condition equations (2.5.2−I) to (2.5.2−IX) let us examine hereafter the effect of adopting $\lambda_{(\rho_1 - \rho)} = 1$ as the freely selected scale ratio.

In this case we have $\lambda_d = \lambda_D \lambda_S$ from Eq. (2.5.2−IV) and $\lambda_d^{-2} = \lambda_D \lambda_S$ from Eq. (2.5.2−V), meaning that $\lambda_d = 1$.

If $\lambda_{(\rho_1 - \rho)} = 1$ and $\lambda_d = 1$, then from Eq. (2.5.2−III), $\lambda_{qB} = 1$.

Finally if $\lambda_{qB} = 1$, then from Eq. (2.5.2−VI) $\lambda_{qt} = B$.

Table 2.5.2—1

Einstein—Ning Chien's method, if the value of λ_D is known

	λ_D	λ_c	B	Δ_v	Δ_{Fr}	$\Delta_{\delta'}$	Δ_s'
λ_l	$\dfrac{4m+1}{m+1}$	$\dfrac{2}{m+1}$	—	$\dfrac{1}{m+1}$	$\dfrac{-2}{m+1}$	$\dfrac{-2m}{m+1}$	1
λ_v	$\dfrac{1}{2}$	—	—	—	1	—	—
λ_S	$\dfrac{-3m}{m+1}$	$\dfrac{-2}{m+1}$	—	$\dfrac{-1}{m+1}$	$\dfrac{2}{m+1}$	$\dfrac{2m}{m+1}$	—
λ_d	$\dfrac{2m-1}{2(m+1)}$	$\dfrac{1}{m+1}$	—	$\dfrac{1}{2(m+1)}$	$\dfrac{-1}{m+1}$	$\dfrac{1}{m+1}$	
$\lambda_{(\rho_1-\rho)}$	$\dfrac{3(2m-1)}{2(m+1)}$	$\dfrac{-3}{m+1}$	—	$\dfrac{-3}{2(m+1)}$	$\dfrac{3}{m+1}$	$\dfrac{2m-1}{m+1}$	—
λ_{qB}	$\dfrac{3(2m-1)}{2(m+1)}$	$\dfrac{-3}{m+1}$	—	$\dfrac{-3}{2(m+1)}$	$\dfrac{3}{m+1}$	$\dfrac{3m}{m+1}$	—
λ_{qt}	$\dfrac{3(2m-1)}{2(m+1)}$	$\dfrac{-3}{m+1}$	1	$\dfrac{-3}{2(m+1)}$	$\dfrac{3}{m+1}$	$\dfrac{3m}{m+1}$	—
λ_{t_1}	$\dfrac{7(m+1)}{2(m+1)}$	$\dfrac{2}{m+1}$	—	$\dfrac{1}{m+1}$	$\dfrac{-(m+3)}{m+1}$	$\dfrac{-2m}{m+1}$	1
λ_{t_2}	$\dfrac{5m+2}{m+1}$	$\dfrac{2}{m+1}$	-1	$\dfrac{1}{m+1}$	$\dfrac{-2}{m+1}$	$\dfrac{-(3m+1)}{m+1}$	1

Consequently, if the scale ratio of sediment densities measured under water $\lambda_{(\rho_1-\rho)} = 1$, then the Einstein—Ning Chien condition equations yield unity for the scale ratios of sediment particle diameters λ_d and of bed load transport λ_{qB}, whereas the scale ratio of total transport λ_{qt} becomes equal to the ratio B.

It should be clear that the above scale ratios assume the same values regardless whether $\lambda_d = 1$ or $\lambda_{qB} = 1$, and even $\lambda_{qt} = B$ is adopted as the freely selected scale ratio.

Of the above restrictions, encountered in connection with condition equations (2.5.2—I) to (2.5.2—IX), those introduced by $\lambda_{qt} = B$ and $\lambda_{qB} = 1$ and, in many cases, even by the value $\lambda_d = 1$ do not usually result in major difficulties. On the other hand, the necessity of applying the same rate of bed load transport is often difficult to meet. This restriction is unquestionably a drawback of this method.

Table 2.5.2—2

Einstein—Ning Chien's method, if the value of λ_l is known

	λ_l	λ_c	B	Δ_v	Δ_{Fr}	Δ_{δ}'	Δ_s
λ_D	$\dfrac{m+1}{4m+1}$	$\dfrac{-2}{4m+1}$	—	$\dfrac{-1}{4m+1}$	$\dfrac{2}{4m+1}$	$\dfrac{2n}{4m+1}$	$\dfrac{-(m+1)}{4m+1}$
λ_v	$\dfrac{m+1}{2(4m+1)}$	$\dfrac{-1}{4m+1}$	—	$\dfrac{-1}{2(4m+1)}$	$\dfrac{2(2m+1)}{4m+1}$	$\dfrac{m}{4m+1}$	$\dfrac{-(m+1)}{2(4m+1)}$
λ_S	$\dfrac{-3m}{4m+1}$	$\dfrac{-2}{4m+1}$	—	$\dfrac{-1}{4m+1}$	$\dfrac{2}{4m+1}$	$\dfrac{2m}{4m+1}$	$\dfrac{3m}{4m+1}$
λ_d	$\dfrac{2m-1}{2(4m+1)}$	$\dfrac{2}{4m+1}$	—	$\dfrac{1}{4m+1}$	$\dfrac{-2}{4m+1}$	$\dfrac{2m+1}{4m+1}$	$\dfrac{1-2m}{2(4m+1)}$
$\lambda_{(\rho_1-\rho)}$	$\dfrac{3(1-2m)}{2(4m+1)}$	$\dfrac{-6}{4m+1}$	—	$\dfrac{-3}{4m+1}$	$\dfrac{6}{4m+1}$	$\dfrac{2m-1}{4m+1}$	$\dfrac{3(3m-1)}{2(4m+1)}$
λ_{qB}	$\dfrac{3(1-2m)}{2(4m+1)}$	$\dfrac{-6}{4m+1}$	—	$\dfrac{-3}{4m+1}$	$\dfrac{6}{4m+1}$	$\dfrac{6m}{4m+1}$	$\dfrac{3(2m-1)}{2(4m+1)}$
λ_{qt}	$\dfrac{3(1-2m)}{2(4m+1)}$	$\dfrac{-6}{4m+1}$	1	$\dfrac{-3}{4m+1}$	$\dfrac{6}{4m+1}$	$\dfrac{6m}{4m+1}$	$\dfrac{3(2m-1)}{2(4m+1)}$
λ_{t_1}	$\dfrac{7m+1}{2(4m+1)}$	$\dfrac{1}{4m+1}$	—	$\dfrac{1}{2(4m+1)}$	$\dfrac{-2(2m+1)}{4m+1}$	$\dfrac{-m}{4m+1}$	$\dfrac{m+1}{2(4m+1)}$
λ_{t_2}	$\dfrac{5m+2}{4m+1}$	$\dfrac{-2}{4m+1}$	-1	$\dfrac{-1}{4m+1}$	$\dfrac{2}{4m+1}$	$\dfrac{-(2m+1)}{4m+1}$	$\dfrac{-(m+1)}{4m+1}$

It should be noted further that in the above cases $\lambda_D = \lambda_l^{1/2}$, saying that the scale ratio of depth is the square root of the scale ratio of length. This requirement imposes the necessity of introducing a considerable vertical distortion.

Einstein and Ning Chien suggest solutions for their condition equations for the three cases where the scale ratio of depth λ_D or length λ_l or of relative density $\lambda_{(\rho_1-\rho)}$ is freely selected.

Solutions for the nine condition equations in the afore-mentioned three cases are indicated in *Tables (2.5.2—1), (2.5.2—2)* and *(2.5.2—3)*

Using these tables the values of the nine unknown scale ratios are obtained as power products of the scale ratio fixed in advance, of the B and λ_c values found in advance from auxiliary computations, as well as of the four differences Δ. The tables indicate the exponents of the fixed scale ratios, the B and λ_c values from auxiliary computations, as well as of the four differences Δ, in terms of m computed in advance.

688

Table 2.5.2—3

Einstein—Ningh Chien's method, if the value of $\lambda_{(\rho1-\rho)}$ is known

	$\lambda_{(\rho_1-\rho)}$	λ_c	B	Δ_v	Δ_{Fr}	$\Delta_{\delta'}$	Δ_s
λ_l	$\dfrac{-2(4m+1)}{3(2m-1)}$	$\dfrac{-4}{2m-1}$	—	$\dfrac{-2}{2m-1}$	$\dfrac{4}{2m-1}$	$\dfrac{2}{3}$	1
λ_D	$\dfrac{-2(m+1)}{3(2m-1)}$	$\dfrac{-2}{2m-1}$	—	$\dfrac{-1}{2m-1}$	$\dfrac{2}{2m-1}$	$\dfrac{2}{3}$	—
λ_v	$\dfrac{-(m+1)}{3(2m-1)}$	$\dfrac{-1}{2m-1}$	—	$\dfrac{-1}{3(2m-1)}$	$\dfrac{2m}{2m-1}$	$\dfrac{1}{3}$	—
λ_S	$\dfrac{2m}{2m-1}$	$\dfrac{2}{2m-1}$	—	$\dfrac{1}{2m-1}$	$\dfrac{-2}{2m-1}$	—	—
λ_d	$\dfrac{-1}{3}$	—	—	—	—	$\dfrac{2}{3}$	—
λ_{aB}	1	—	—	—	—	1	—
λ_{at}	1	—	1	—	—	1	—
λ_{t_1}	$\dfrac{-(7m+1)}{3(2m-1)}$	$\dfrac{-3}{2m-1}$	—	$\dfrac{-3}{2(2m-1)}$	$\dfrac{2(2-m)}{2m-1}$	$\dfrac{1}{3}$	1
λ_{t_2}	$\dfrac{-2(5m+2)}{3(2m-1)}$	$\dfrac{-6}{2m-1}$	-1	$\dfrac{-3}{2m-1}$	$\dfrac{6}{2m-1}$	$\dfrac{1}{3}$	1

The data of a model computed by the Einstein—Ning Chien method will be described in the subsequent section, in connection with the method modified by the author.

2.5.3. THE EINSTEIN—NING CHIEN METHOD MODIFIED BY THE AUTHOR

The results of recent research into sediment transport performed since the introduction of the Einstein—Ning Chien method have permitted certain simplifications to be introduced which, at the same time, have improved the accuracy of reproducing the different boundary conditions of sediment transport in the models of alluvial streams.

44

For the numerical determination of sediment transport boundary conditions in 1957–58, the author introduced, according to Eq. (1.2.3–8), the parameter

$$\beta = \frac{gd}{U_*^2} \frac{1}{d^N} = \frac{1}{Fr_*} \frac{1}{d^N} \qquad (2.5.3-1)$$

which, since $N = 0.882$ was found to be constant, is alone capable of determining the condition of movement. Since the experimental results apply to a sediment specific gravity $\gamma_1 = 2.65$ p/cm^3 (and, in general, to water of 20 deg. C temperature), for other specific gravities, according to Eq. (1.2.3–14), the expression

$$\beta = \frac{1}{Fr_*} \frac{1}{d^N} \frac{1}{1.65} \frac{\rho_1 - \rho}{\rho} \qquad (2.5.3-2)$$

is suggested.

In 1958–59 the author used the above parameter also for modifying the method of modelling sediment-carrying streams having mobile beds.

In the modelling method developed in 1959 the identity of the foregoing dimensional β value in both the prototype and the model was adopted as a starting basis. In the physical sense the identity of the dimensional β value is unsuited as a similarity criterion. Nevertheless, experimental evidence has in all respects justified the application of this criterion, implying that the different conditions of transport are described by the quantity β, irrespective of the physical quantities involved in the phenomenon and having in general different values. This, however, is impossible unless β is proportionate to a dimensionless parameter β_1 giving a physically correct description of the conditions of transport and unless the proportionality factor is constant, i.e. depends on physical quantities (variables) that are constant or at least approximately so.

Under this approach the dimensionless parameter β_1 has already been determined in *Section 1.2.3*. The proportionality factor is seen to depend exclusively on the acceleration due to gravity g and on the kinematic viscosity v that may actually be regarded constant with a fair degree of approximation, although it depends on water temperature. According to Eq. (1.2.3–27) the dimensionless parameter β_1 is

$$\frac{gd}{U_*^2} \frac{\rho_1 - \rho}{\rho} = \beta_1 \left(\frac{d}{v^{2/3} g^{-1/3}} \right)^N \qquad (2.5.3-3)$$

or, considering that in the experiments a sediment of $\gamma_1 = 2.65$ (p/cm^3) specific gravity was used,

$$\frac{gd}{U_*^2} \frac{1}{1.65} \frac{(\rho_1 - \rho)}{\rho} = \beta_1 \left(\frac{d}{v^{2/3} g^{-1/3}} \right)^N \qquad (2.5.3-4)$$

the condition of movement of sediment having a particle size d and density ρ_1 is thus defined in terms of $U_* = \sqrt{gDS}$.

According to Eqs (2.5.3−2) and (2.5.3−4)

$$\beta = \frac{\beta_1}{(v^{2/3}g^{-1/3})^N}$$

(2.5.3−5)

so that $[\beta] = cm^{-N}$ or since $[\beta_1] = 1$

$$\beta_1 = \beta(v^{2/3}g^{-1/3})^N$$

(2.5.3−6)

Since in studies on alluvial channels with a mobile bed water is usually adopted as the model fluid and the same geographical location is assumed, $\lambda_v = \lambda_g = 1$ and thus for identical β or β_1 values

$$\frac{\beta_1'}{\beta_1''} = \lambda_{\beta_1} = \frac{\beta'}{\beta''} = \lambda_\beta = 1$$

(2.5.3−7)

On the basis of Eq. (2.5.3−7) it will be thus appreciated that the original modified method is unaffected by assuming the identity of a physically correct parameter β_1.

It should be noted in this context that, since water of the same temperature is supposed in the prototype and the model alike, the kinematic viscosity v and density ρ (given by the condition equation of water) do not enter as independent variables.

With the foregoing in mind the modified method is derived as follows:

Parameter β_1 is considered to include all parameters commonly adopted for describing channel stability and can be used consequently for replacing the factor b, introduced by the author, as well as the parameter Ψ suggested by Einstein, i.e. to replace the condition equation (2.5.2−IV).

Moreover the condition equation written on the basis of parameter β_1 is believed to eliminate the condition equation (2.5.2−V) as well, since the value of d/δ' is defined simultaneously by the magnitude of β_1.

Supposing that the particle diameter d of the sediment material is approximately comparable to the linear roughness k defined by Nikuradze for pipes, the ratio d/δ' is representative of roughness conditions in solid beds. Thus, for instance, the data of Nikuradze in combination with the chart of the Colebrook − White equation will show the solid boundary to be perfectly rough hydraulically beyond $d/\delta' \geqq 7$. In this case, at the transition between the smooth bottom and the hydraulically perfectly rough bed, the protective laminar sublayer is disrupted and no ripples can form any more. The purpose of condition equation (2.5.2−V) derived on the basis of d/δ' is to ensure that the transition between the hydraulically smooth and rough conditions of the bed should occur under identical conditions in the prototype and the model alike. As noted by Ning Chien himself, condition equation (2.5.2−V) becomes superfluous as soon as the bed is perfectly rough hydraulically.

It should be realized that condition equation (2.5.2−V) based on the ratio d/δ' has been included separately among the conditions of Einstein and Ning

Chien because of the fact that the value of d/δ' is not defined unambiguously by the condition equation (2.5.2−IV) written on the basis of the invariant Ψ

It has been noted already that the value of d/δ is defined by the parameter β_1 for smooth and perfectly rough bottom conditions alike and even at the transition between the two. In fact according to Eq. (1.2.3.−3)

$$\frac{d}{\delta'} = \frac{U_* d}{11.6 \nu} = \frac{Re_{*s}}{11.6} \qquad (2.5.3-8)$$

On the other hand

$$Re_{*s} = Fr_* \frac{d^2 g}{U_* \nu}$$

and thus

$$\frac{d}{\delta'} = \frac{1}{11.6} Fr_* \frac{d^2 g}{U_* \nu} \qquad (2.5.3-9)$$

or expressing Fr_* from Eq. (2.5.3−4) with the help of β_1

$$\frac{d}{\delta'} = \frac{1}{11.6\beta_1 \left(\dfrac{d}{\nu^{2/3} g^{-1/3}}\right)^N} \frac{1}{1.65} \frac{(\rho_1 - \rho)}{\rho} \frac{d^2 g}{U_* \nu} =$$

$$= \frac{(\nu^{2/3} g^{-1/3})^N}{11.6\beta_1} \frac{1}{1.65} \frac{d^{(2-N)}}{U_* \nu} \frac{(\rho_1 - \rho)}{\rho} \qquad (2.5.3-10)$$

Since for any given particle size the absolute magnitude of β_1 determines the magnitude of d/δ' if the slope and depth are known, the use of a condition equation written on the basis of parameter β_1 eliminates the need of applying condition equation (2.5.2−V).

According to the modification introduced by the author the condition equation

$$\lambda_d^{(1-N)} \lambda_D^{-1} \lambda_S^{-1} \lambda_{(\rho_1 - \rho)} = \Delta_{\beta_1} \qquad (2.5.3-IVa)$$

obtained from Eq. (2.5.3−4) should be used instead of condition equation (2.5.2−IV) obviating simultaneously the use of condition equation (2.5.2−V).

In exact computations Δ_{β_1} must equal unity. It will be demonstrated, however, that considering the β_1 values characterizing boundary conditions separating the individual conditions of movement, the difference may differ appreciably from unity, depending on the absolute magnitude of β_1.

With the foregoing modifications and transformations in mind the hydraulic similarity of models of alluvial streams is most expediently determined as follows:

The number of independent variables is eleven, that of the fundamental dimensions is three and thus altogether eight condition equations are obtained.

Since $\lambda_g = 1$ is included among the eleven scale ratios, the number of those to be determined reduces to ten:

$$\lambda_l, \ \lambda_S, \ \lambda_{qB}, \ \lambda_{t_1},$$

$$\lambda_D, \ \lambda_d, \ \lambda_{qt}, \ \lambda_{t_2},$$

$$\lambda_v, \ \lambda_{(\rho_1 - \rho)}$$

For computing the magnitude of the ten scale ratios altogether eight condition equations are available, so that the magnitude of two can be assumed without restriction. The eight condition equations are as follows:

$$\lambda_v^2 \lambda_d^{2m} \lambda_c^{-2} \lambda_S^{-1} \lambda_D^{(-1-2m)} = \Delta_v \tag{2.5.3-Ia}$$

$$\lambda_v^2 \lambda_D^{-1} = \Delta_{Fr}^2 \tag{2.5.3-IIa}$$

$$\lambda_{qB}^2 \lambda_{(\rho_1-\rho)}^{-3} \lambda_d^{-3} = 1 \tag{2.5.3-IIIa}$$

$$\lambda_d^{(1-N)} \lambda_D^{-1} \lambda_S^{-1} \lambda_{(\rho_1-\rho)} = \Delta_{\beta_1} \tag{2.5.3-IVa}$$

$$\lambda_{qB} \lambda_{qt}^{-1} B = 1 \tag{2.5.3-Va}$$

$$\lambda_v \lambda_{t_1} \lambda_l^{-1} = 1 \tag{2.5.3-VIa}$$

$$\lambda_{qt} \lambda_{t_2} \lambda_l^{-1} \lambda_D^{-1} \lambda_{(\rho_1-\rho)}^{-1} = 1 \tag{2.5.3-VIIa}$$

$$\lambda_S \lambda_l \lambda_D^{-1} = \Delta_S \tag{2.5.3-VIIIa}$$

Remembering that $N = 0.882$ and $(1 - N) = 0.118 \simeq 2/17$, Eq. (2.5.3–IVa) is rewritten into the form

$$\lambda_d^2 \lambda_D^{-17} \lambda_S^{-17} \lambda_{(\rho_1-\rho)}^{-17} = \Delta_{\beta_1}^{17}$$

Besides the ten scale ratios the ratio B, the exponent m and the scale ratio λ_c are involved in condition equations (2.5.3 – Ia) to (2.5.3 – VIIIa). Their magnitudes are found as described in connection with the Einstein – Ning Chien method, by auxiliary computations.

Four Δ values are also included in the equations. Of these Δ_v, Δ_{Fr}, Δ_S must equal, in exact computations, unity just as in the Einstein – Ning Chien method but, by tolerating a certain departure from unity, some practical requirements (occasionally the unrestricted assumption of an additional scale ratio) can be satisfied.

The magnitude of Δ_{β_1} must also equal unity in exact computations, but in particular cases considerable departures from unity may be acceptable.

In the new method the magnitude of β_1 for the prototype water course is found according to Eq. (2.5.3–4) from the expression

$$\beta_1' = \frac{d'^{(1-N)}}{D'S'} \frac{1}{1.65} \frac{(\rho_1 - \rho)'}{\rho} (v^{2/3} g^{-1/3})^N \tag{2.5.3-11}$$

693

or for water of 20 deg. C temperature, since

$$(v^{2/3}g^{-1/3})^{0.882} = (4.691 \cdot 10^{-3})^N$$

$$\beta_1' = \frac{d'^{(1-N)}}{D'S'} \frac{1}{1.65} \frac{(\rho_1 - \rho)'}{\rho} (4.691 \cdot 10^{-3})^N \qquad (2.5.3-12)$$

in order to obtain, with allowance to occasional differences in specific gravity, a value applying to sediment of any arbitrary specific gravity, but to water of 20 deg. C temperature.

A similar approach is adopted for computing the β_1'' value

$$\beta_1'' = \frac{d''^{(1-N)}}{D''S''} \frac{1}{1.65} \frac{(\rho_1 - \rho)''}{\rho} (4.691 \cdot 10^{-3})^N \qquad (2.5.3-13)$$

applying to the model, again for water of 20 deg. C, but without any restriction on specific gravity.

From the plot of Eq. (2.5.3−4) in *Fig. 2.5.3−1* it will be perceived that, as long as $\beta_1' = 4.858$, the criterion for no sediment movement in the model is $\beta_1'' \geqq 4.858$. In principle $\lambda_{\beta_1} = \beta_1'/\beta_1'' = 1$ would be desirable but, since the sediment remains stationary for all values of β_1 greater than 4.858, the value of $\lambda_{\beta1}$ is indeterminate, indicating that the scale ratio may be greater, but also smaller than unity. This, of course, does not affect the strict criterion that once $\beta_1' \geqq$ $\geqq 4.858$, it is required that also $\beta_1'' \geqq 4.858$.

If $2.844 \leqq \beta_1' \leqq 4.858$ in the prototype, then the same $(2.844 \leqq \beta_1'' \leqq 4.858)$ should prevail in the model as well, for this is the only way to ensure sediment transport free of ripples and dunes in both the prototype and the model. Besides the afore-mentioned strict condition, the scale ratio of the β_1 values is theoretically bound to lie between the following two limits:

$$0.585 \leqq \lambda_{\beta_1} \leqq 1.71$$

With the development of ripples $0.5829 \leqq \beta_1' \leqq 2.844$ and this should prevail also in the model $(0.5829 \leqq \beta_1'' \leqq 2.844)$. Besides this strict condition the limits of the scale ratio of the β_1 values are

$$0.205 \leqq \lambda_{\beta_1} \leqq 4.88$$

With the development of dunes in the prototype $0.2102 \leqq \beta_1' \leqq 0.5829$, consequently this is required also in the model $(0.2102 \leqq \beta_1'' \leqq 0.5829)$. The limit values of the scale ratio are then $0.36 \leqq \lambda_{\beta_1} \leqq 2.78$.

The transition from dunes to antidunes occurs in the prototype at $0.08523 \leqq$ $\leqq \beta_1' \leqq 0.2102$. The criterion for the bed of the model to be in the same condition is $0.08523 \leqq \beta_1'' \leqq 0.2102$ and the limit values of the scale ratio are

$$0.406 \leqq \lambda_{\beta_1} \leqq 2.46.$$

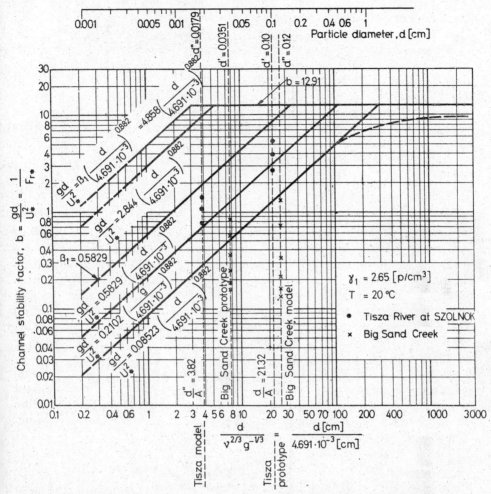

Fig. 2.5.3—1. Relation of parameter gd/U_*^2 and β_1 for different boundary conditions of sediment movement (including the scale model data of the Szolnok stretch of the Tisza river)

Antidunes appear finally in the prototype bed at $\beta_1' \leqq 0.08523$, so that necessarily $\beta_1'' \leqq 0.08523$ also in the model channel. Since here again any β_1 value smaller than 0.08523 refers to the same bed form, just as in the case of a smooth bed where sediment motion does not occur, the limit values of λ_{β_1} are likewise indeterminate, i.e., λ_{β_1} may assume values both greater and smaller than unity.

The limit values mentioned above for λ_{β_1} at different bed forms (which depend on the absolute magnitude of β_1) indicate at the same time the theoretical limits of Δ_{β_1}. Evidently, efforts must be made to keep λ_{β_1} as close to unity as possible. The questions whether or not the very wide limits mentioned above for λ_{β_1} are

695

actually acceptable can only be answered, in the opinion of the author, on the basis of experiments.

Without intending to discuss every aspect of the role played by the parameter β_1 in the phenomenon of sediment transport, we shall briefly mention a few additional regularities to be satisfied in the prototype and the model alike. From *Fig. 2.5.3 − 1*, for a sediment of $\gamma_1 = 2.65$ p/cm³ specific gravity and water of $t =$ = 20 deg. C temperature, these regularities are as follows:

a) Sediment of any particular size remains stationary at the bottom, as long as

$$\frac{gd}{U_*^2} \geqq 12.91$$

b) If

$$\frac{d}{v^{2/3}g^{-1/3}} = \frac{d}{A}$$

is greater than 0.22 but smaller than 3 (i.e., the particle is larger than about 0.05 but smaller than 0.15 mm), under certain conditions the sediment may still remain stationary, if

$$\frac{gd}{U_*^2} < 12.91$$

c) If d/A is greater than 5 (i.e., the sediment particle size is greater than about 0.25 − 0.30 mm), sediment transport is possible only parallel to the appearance of ripples, dunes, transition or antidunes.

d) If d/A is greater than 33 (i.e., the sediment particles are larger than 2.0 mm), the formation of sand ripples is impossible.

e) If d/A is greater than 100 (i.e., the particles are larger than 5 to 6 mm), the formation of dunes is impossible.

f) If d/A is greater than 280 (i.e., the particles are larger than 15 mm), no transition is possible, implying that the movement of similarly coarse particles is always accompanied by the formation of antidunes.

For values other than 20 deg. C and 2.65 p/cm³ the limit values under *a* to *f* are found according to Eq. (2.5.3 − 4).

For solving the condition equations (2.5.3 − Ia) to (2.5.3 − VIIIa), arbitrary values can be assigned, as mentioned before, to two of the scale ratios. It remains to be examined whether in the method suggested by us the choice of certain scale ratio values must be avoided owing to some restrictive considerations.

The examination of condition equations (2.5.3 − Ia) to (2.5.3 − VIIIa) yields the following conclusions:

$\lambda_{(\rho_1 - \rho)} = 1$ is a possible choice and does not necessarily make the other scale ratios equal unity.

The assumption of $\lambda_d = 1$ is also possible since the other scale ratios may then again assume values other than unity.

696

It is also possible to assume simultaneously the values $\lambda_{(\rho_1-\rho)} = 1$ and $\lambda_d = 1$ and, in this case, the values $\lambda_{qB} = 1$ and $\lambda_D = \lambda_l^{1/2}$ further $\lambda_v = \lambda_l^{1/4}$ are obtained.

The choice of $\lambda_v = 1$ should be avoided since, according to Eq. (2.5.3−IIa), this implies that $\lambda_D = 1$ so that the vertical distortion would be impermissibly great. However, beyond the excessive vertical distortion, a condition almost impossible to satisfy would be imposed by the extremely low value of the scale ratio $\lambda_{(\rho_1-\rho)}$. In fact, according to Eq. (2.5.3−IVa), remembering that $\lambda_D = 1$ and thus we have $\lambda_S \lambda_l = 1$ from Eq. (2.5.3−VIIIa), the scale ratio of submerged densities would be

$$\lambda_{(\rho_1-\rho)} = \lambda_d^{(N-1)} \lambda_S$$

which, since $N = 0.882$, would imply − for instance, with the scale ratios $\lambda_l = 100$ and $\lambda_D = 1$ and with $\lambda_S = 1/\lambda_l$ − that

$$\lambda_{(\rho_1-\rho)} = 0.01$$

saying that a material having a submerged specific gravity hundred times greater than in the prototype would be required in the model.

Consequently, the major advantage of the method suggested here is that a sediment material having the same specific gravity or particle size as in the prototype can be applied without restriction in the model. The savings made possible thereby are readily apparent.

As mentioned before, two of the ten unknown scale ratios can be adopted without restriction. In principle any two scale ratios could be chosen but, taking into consideration the possibilities available for performing model tests, the scale ratios associated with horizontal and vertical dimensions, as well as with the specific gravity and particle size of the sediment material are preferably selected.

In the majority of cases the magnitude of the scale ratio λ_l is controlled within certain limits by the space available for the tests. Likewise it will be found most economical to produce the sediment material required in the model by sieving the material stored at the laboratory. For this reason it will be found expedient in most cases to adopt in advance the values of the scale ratios λ_l and $\lambda_{(\rho_1-\rho)}$ in accordance with the particular conditions.

The magnitude of the available discharge is sometimes also a factor affecting the model test. This is why as a second alternative the scale ratios λ_l and λ_D are adopted in advance as the two unrestricted scale ratios.

In certain cases it may be found necessary to adjust the test to the particle size and specific gravity of the material available for testing. Consequently, in this third alternative the two scale ratios adopted in advance are λ_d and $\lambda_{(\rho_1-\rho)}$.

The solutions of condition equations (2.5.3−Ia) to (2.5.3−VIIIa) corresponding to the afore-mentioned three alternatives are indicated in *Tables 2.5.3−1, 2.5.3−2* and *2.5.3−3*, respectively.

The values of the eight unknown scale ratios are computed from power products involving the two scale ratios adopted in advance, the quantities B and λ_c deter-

697

Table 2.5.3—1

Bogárdi's modified method; the values of λ_t and $\lambda_{(\rho1-\rho)}$ are known

	λ_t	$\lambda_{(\rho_1-\rho)}$	B	λ_c	Δ_v	Δ_{Fv}	Δ_{β_1}	Δ_s
λ_D	$\dfrac{1-2m-N}{1-2m-N-2mN}$	$\dfrac{-2m}{1-2m-N-2mN}$	0	$\dfrac{-2+2N}{1-2m-N-2mN}$	$\dfrac{-1+N}{1-2m-N-2mN}$	$\dfrac{2-2N}{1-2m-N-2mN}$	$\dfrac{2m}{1-2m-N-2mN}$	$\dfrac{-1+N+2m}{1-2m-N-2mN}$
λ_S	$\dfrac{2mN}{1-2m-N-2mN}$	$\dfrac{-2m}{1-2m-N-2mN}$	0	$\dfrac{-2+2N}{1-2m-N-2mN}$	$\dfrac{-1+N}{1-2m-N-2mN}$	$\dfrac{2-2N}{1-2m-N-2mN}$	$\dfrac{2m}{1-2m-N-2mN}$	$\dfrac{-2mN}{1-2m-N-2mN}$
λ_d	$\dfrac{1-2m}{1-2m-N-2mN}$	$\dfrac{-1-2m}{1-2m-N-2mN}$	0	$\dfrac{-4}{1-2m-N-2mN}$	$\dfrac{-2}{1-2m-N-2mN}$	$\dfrac{4}{1-2m-N-2mN}$	$\dfrac{1+2m}{1-2m-N-2mN}$	$\dfrac{-1+2m}{1-2m-N-2mN}$
λ_v	$\dfrac{1/2-m-N/2}{1-2m-N-2mN}$	$\dfrac{-m}{1-2m-N-2mN}$	0	$\dfrac{-1+N}{1-2m-N-2mN}$	$\dfrac{-1/2+N/2}{1-2m-N-2mN}$	$\dfrac{2-2N-2m-2mN}{1-2m-N-2mN}$	$\dfrac{m}{1-2m-N-2mN}$	$\dfrac{-1/2+N/2+m}{1-2m-N-2mN}$
λ_{eB}	$\dfrac{3/2-3m}{1-2m-N-2mN}$	$\dfrac{-6m-3/2N-3mN}{1-2m-N-2mN}$	0	$\dfrac{-6}{1-2m-N-2mN}$	$\dfrac{-3}{1-2m-N-2mN}$	$\dfrac{6}{1-2m-N-2mN}$	$\dfrac{3/2+3m}{1-2m-N-2mN}$	$\dfrac{-3/2+3m}{1-2m-N-2mN}$
λ_{et}	$\dfrac{3/2-3m}{1-2m-N-2mN}$	$\dfrac{-6-3/2N-3mN}{1-2m-N-2mN}$	1	$\dfrac{-6}{1-2m-N-2mN}$	$\dfrac{-3}{1-2m-N-2mN}$	$\dfrac{6}{1-2m-N-2mN}$	$\dfrac{3/2+3m}{1-2m-N-2mN}$	$\dfrac{-3/2+3m}{1-2m-N-2mN}$
λ_{t_1}	$\dfrac{1/2-m-N/2-2mN}{1-2m-N-2mN}$	$\dfrac{m}{1-2m-N-2mN}$	0	$\dfrac{1-N}{1-2m-N-2mN}$	$\dfrac{1/2-N/2}{1-2m-N-2mN}$	$\dfrac{-2+2N+2m+2mN}{1-2m-N-2mN}$	$\dfrac{-m}{1-2m-N-2mN}$	$\dfrac{1/2-N/2-m}{1-2m-N-2mN}$
λ_{t_2}	$\dfrac{1/2-m-2N-2mN}{1-2m-N-2mN}$	$\dfrac{1+2m+N/2+mN}{1-2m-N-2mN}$	-1	$\dfrac{4+2N}{1-2m-N-2mN}$	$\dfrac{2+N}{1-2m-N-2mN}$	$\dfrac{-4-2N}{1-2m-N-2mN}$	$\dfrac{-3/2-m}{1-2m-N-2mN}$	$\dfrac{1/2+N-m}{1-2m-N-2mN}$

Table 2.5.3—2

Bogárdi's modified method; the values of λ_D and λ_l are known

	λ_D	λ_l	B	λ_c	Δ_v	Δ_{Fr}	Δ_{β_1}	Δ_s
λ_S	1	-1	0	0	0	0	0	1
λ_d	$\dfrac{1+2m}{2m}$	$\dfrac{-1}{2m}$	0	$\dfrac{2}{2m}$	$\dfrac{1}{2m}$	$\dfrac{-2}{2m}$	0	$\dfrac{1}{2m}$
λ_v	$\dfrac{1}{2}$	0	0	0	0	1	0	0
λ_{qB}	$\dfrac{6m+3/2N+3mN}{2m}$	$\dfrac{-3/2N-3m}{2m}$	0	$\dfrac{3N}{2m}$	$\dfrac{3/2N}{2m}$	$\dfrac{-3N}{2m}$	$\dfrac{3}{2}$	$\dfrac{3/2N+3m}{2m}$
λ_{qt}	$\dfrac{6m+3/2N+3mN}{2m}$	$\dfrac{-3/2N-3m}{2m}$	1	$\dfrac{3N}{2m}$	$\dfrac{3/2N}{2m}$	$\dfrac{-3N}{2m}$	$\dfrac{3}{2}$	$\dfrac{3/2N+3m}{2m}$
λ_{t_1}	$-\dfrac{1}{2}$	1	0	0	0	-1	0	0
λ_{t_2}	$\dfrac{-1-2m-N/2-mN}{2m}$	$\dfrac{1+3m+N/2}{2m}$	-1	$\dfrac{-2-N}{2m}$	$\dfrac{-1-N/2}{2m}$	$\dfrac{2+N}{2m}$	$-\dfrac{1}{2}$	$\dfrac{-1-N/2-m}{2m}$
$\lambda_{\rho_1-\rho^3}$	$\dfrac{2m-1+N+2mN}{2m}$	$\dfrac{1-N-2m}{2m}$	0	$\dfrac{-2+2N}{2m}$	$\dfrac{-1+N}{2m}$	$\dfrac{2-2N}{2m}$	1	$\dfrac{-1+N+2m}{2m}$

Table 2.5.3—3

Bogárdi's modified method; the values of λ_d and $\lambda_{(p1-p)}$ are known

	λ_d	$\lambda_{(p1-p)}$	B	λ_c	Δ_v	Δ_{Fr}	Δ_{β_1}	Δ_s
λ_D	$\dfrac{2m-1+N}{2m-1}$	$\dfrac{-1}{2m-1}$	0	$\dfrac{-2}{2m-1}$	$\dfrac{-1}{2m-1}$	$\dfrac{2}{2m-1}$	$\dfrac{1}{2m-1}$	0
λ_S	$\dfrac{-2mN}{2m-1}$	$\dfrac{2m}{2m-1}$	0	$\dfrac{2}{2m-1}$	$\dfrac{1}{2m-1}$	$\dfrac{-2}{2m-1}$	$\dfrac{-2m}{2m-1}$	0
λ_l	$\dfrac{2m-1+N+2mN}{2m-1}$	$\dfrac{-2m-1}{2m-1}$	0	$\dfrac{-4}{2m-1}$	$\dfrac{-2}{2m-1}$	$\dfrac{-4}{2m-1}$	$\dfrac{1+2m}{2m-1}$	1
λ_v	$\dfrac{m-1/2+N/2}{2m-1}$	$\dfrac{-1/2}{2m-1}$	0	$\dfrac{-1}{2m-1}$	$\dfrac{-1/2}{2m-1}$	$\dfrac{2m}{2m-1}$	$\dfrac{1/2}{2m-1}$	0
λ_{aB}	$\dfrac{3}{2}$	$\dfrac{3}{2}$	0	0	0	0	0	0
λ_{at}	$\dfrac{3}{2}$	$\dfrac{3}{2}$	1	0	0	0	0	0
λ_{t_1}	$\dfrac{m-1/2+N/2+2mN}{2m-1}$	$\dfrac{-2m-1/2}{2m-1}$	0	$\dfrac{-3}{2m-1}$	$\dfrac{-3/2}{2m-1}$	$\dfrac{4-2m}{2m-1}$	$\dfrac{1/2+2m}{2m-1}$	1
λ_{t_2}	$\dfrac{m-1/2+2N+2mN}{2m-1}$	$\dfrac{-3/2-3m}{2m-1}$	-1	$\dfrac{-6}{2m-1}$	$\dfrac{-3}{2m-1}$	$\dfrac{6}{2m-1}$	$\dfrac{2+2m}{2m-1}$	1

700

Table 2.5.3—4

Prototype
(Tisza river, Szolnok)

No.	H [cm]	Q [m³/sec]	$F \cdot 10^{-3}$ [cm²]	R' [cm]	$S' \cdot 10^5$	v' [cm/sec]	d' [cm]	$U'_* = \sqrt{gR'S'}$ [cm/sec]	$\dfrac{v'}{U_*}$	$\dfrac{R'}{d'}$	γ_1 [p/cm³]	$b' = d'/R'S'$	$\beta'_1 = \dfrac{8.791 \cdot 10^{-3} \cdot b'}{d'^{0.882}}$	$\dfrac{d'}{v'^{2/3}g^{-1/3}}$
	1.	2.	3.	4.	5.	6.	7.	8.	9.	10.	11.	12.	13.	14.
1	640	1,610	1,390	838	4.20	116	0.1	5.85	19.8	8,380	2.65	2.84	0.191	21.32
2	307	755	896	623	4.00	84	0.1	4.95	17.0	6,230	2.65	4.02	0.27	21.32
3	−53	228	406	335	550	56	0.1	4.25	13.2	3,350	2.65	5.43	0.364	21.32

701

Fig. 2.5.3—2. Relation of v/U_* and R/d based on the scale model of the Szolnok stretch of the Tisza river

mined in advance from auxiliary computations, as well as the four deviations Δ. The two scale ratios adopted in advance, the values B and λ_c found by auxiliary computations, as well as the power products of the four Δ values have been compiled in the tables in terms of the values $N = 0.882$ and m found by preliminary computation.

The foregoing method is illustrated by the computation of the scale ratios for a sediment-carrying model of a section of the Tisza river around Szolnok.

This particular section of the Tisza river is characterized by the data entered in columns 1 to 7 of *Table 2.5.3—4*, determined by cross-section surveys and velocity measurements. The computation of model data is based on corresponding combinations of data observed at three different stages. Of these the first set of data applies to high water, the second, to mean stage, whereas the third set, to low river stages.

In the first step Eq. (2.5.2—1a) is applied to compute the scale ratio $c'/c'' = \lambda_c$ of the velocity coefficient on the basis of velocity, of the hydraulic radius, of the slope and the bed material, as well as to obtain the value of the exponent m that applies to the prototype and the model alike.

For this purpose the corresponding pairs of values v'/U_* and R'/d' are computed for each of the three stages in columns 8, 9 and 10 in *Table 2.5.3—4*. Plotting these values in the log-log chart of *Fig. 2.5.3—2* the slope of the straight line connecting the three points will be found to be 0.42, while the velocity coefficient in the prototype is $c' = 0.44$. In other words the relation

$$\frac{v'}{U'_*} = c' \left(\frac{R'}{d'}\right)^m$$

becomes for the prototype

$$\frac{v'}{U'_*} = 0.44 \left(\frac{R'}{d'}\right)^{0.42}$$

The relationship between v''/U'' and R''/d'' in the model must be found by trial and error. For the scale ratio of velocity coefficients a number smaller than unity is adopted, indicating that in *Fig. 2.5.3−2* the straight line of $m = 0.42$ slope drawn by a dashed line represents the relation in the model of the two aforementioned parameters. The value corresponding to the dashed straight line adopted is $c'' = 0.63$, so that computations are started with the values $\lambda_c = = 0.44/0.63 = 0.698$ and $m = 0.42$.

For the numerical example let us consider the case in which the scale ratios λ_l and λ_D of length and depth, respectively, are adopted in advance. Taking into account the space and discharge available at the laboratory, let $\lambda_l = 160$ and $\lambda_D = 40$. In this case the scale ratios are found according to *Table 2.5.3−2.* It should be noted that for the time being all $\varDelta$ values are assumed to equal unity. Thus

$$\lambda_S = \lambda_D \lambda_l^{-1} = 40 \cdot 160^{-1} = 0.25$$

$$\lambda_d = \lambda_D^{\frac{1+2m}{2m}} \; \lambda_l^{-\frac{1}{2m}} \; \lambda_c^{\frac{2}{2m}}$$

$$\lambda_d = 40^{2.19} \cdot 160^{-1.19} \cdot 0.698^{2.381} = 3.295$$

The slopes and particle diameter in the model are found from the foregoing values of λ_S and λ_d so that, for instance, in the set of values No. 1

$$S'' = \frac{S'}{\lambda_S} = \frac{4.2 \cdot 10^{-5}}{0.25} = 16.8 \cdot 10^{-5}$$

$$d'' = \frac{0.1}{3.295} = 0.0304 \text{ cm}$$

The values R'' have been determined graphically because of the vertical distortion after tracing the cross-sections. The velocities in the model have been computed with the help of λ_v using the values in column 6 of *Table 2.5.3−4.* According to *Table 2.5.3−2,*

$$\lambda_v = \lambda_D^{1/2} = 40^{1/2} = 6.33$$

In the set of values No. 1, for instance,

$$v'' = \frac{116}{6.33} = 18. \; \text{cm/sec}$$

the shear velocities having been computed from the expression

$$U''_* = \sqrt{gR''S''}$$

Table 2.5.3—5

Model
(Tisza river, Szolnok)

No.	R'' [cm]	$S'' \cdot 10^5$	d'' [cm]	$\dfrac{R''}{d''}$	v'' [cm/sec]	$U''_* = \sqrt{gR''S''}$ [cm/sec]	$\dfrac{v''}{U''}$
	1.	2.	3.	4.	5.	6.	7.
1	16.6	16.8	0.0304	546	18.30	1.655	11.1
2	12.1	16.0	0.0304	398	13.20	1.38	9.6
3	6.94	22.0	0.0304	228	8.84	1.225	7.2

The data applying to the model, together with the values v''/U''_* and R''/d'' are compiled in *Table 2.5.3 — 5*.

Plotting the values entered in columns four and seven of Table 2.5.3 — 5 in *Fig. 2.5.3 — 2* three points are obtained, the line of best fit through which (traced with a thin line) has a slope approximately the same as the straight line inclined at $m = 0.42$ determined for the prototype relation. Nevertheless, it is displaced somewhat upward and to the left in comparison with the line assumed and controlling the relations applying to the model by λ_c. Points fitting into the dashed line assumed in advance would indicate that the m and λ_c values were correct and no further trials would be necessary. In the present case no variation in the values of λ_c and m could eliminate the resulting difference, since the value of λ_D has been assumed in advance. Consequently regardless of the values assigned to these two quantities, owing to the restriction imposed on λ_D, some difference is bound to result in the computation of additional points. For this reason it will be found expedient to establish agreement between the prototype and the model by selecting the value of some Δ quantity appropriately.

In the case of points denoted by crosses in *Fig. 2.5.3 — 2*, it would be necessary to modify, to reduce in the present case, the values v'' by one of the Δ quantities since, owing to the choice of λ and λ_D, the value of U''_* is constant. Since the relations of v''/U''_* and R''/d'' are involved, the value of $\Delta_v = 1$ in condition equation (2.5.3 — 1a) must be increased sufficiently to obtain in the model a velocity v'' computed with the help of λ_v which is in agreement with the velocity computed from the actual relation existing between the hydraulic radius, the slope, the particle diameter and the velocity coefficient. For the three points denoted by crosses the ratio of the v''/U''_* values is $11.1/8.82 = 1.35$, $9.6/7.7 = 1.25$ and $7.2/6.1 = 1.18$. Consequently, regarding their mean value the three points marked by crosses would be in agreement with the actual relation if the velocities v'' were multiplied by 1.25.

Eqs (2.5.2 — 1a) or (2.5.3 — Ia) are for the prototype

$$v'^2 d'^{2m} c'^{-2} S'^{-1} D'^{(-1-2m)} = g \qquad (2.5.3 - 14)$$

704

Table 2.5.3—6

Model, corrected
(Tisza river, Szolnok)

No.	R'' [cm]	$S'' \cdot 10^5$	d'' [cm]	$\dfrac{R''}{d''}$	$\dfrac{v''}{U}$	γ_1'' [p/cm³]	$b'' = \dfrac{d''}{R''S''}$	$\beta_1'' = \dfrac{8.791 \cdot 10^3 \cdot b''}{d''^{0,882}}$	$\dfrac{d''}{v^{2/3}g^{-1/3}}$
	1.	2.	3.	4.	5.	6.	7.	8.	9.
1	16.6	16.8	0.0179	928	11.1	1.20	0.776	0.237	3.82
2	12.1	16.0	0.0179	677	9.6	1.20	1.12	0.343	3.82
3	6.94	22	0.0179	387	7.2	1.20	1.42	0.434	3.82

and for the model

$$v''^2 d''^{2m} c''^{-2} S''^{-1} D''^{(-1-2m)} = g \qquad (2.5.3-15a)$$

The latter relation for the actual situation is represented by the points indicated by crosses. The relation assumed in advance is thus described with due regard to the foregoing, by the expression

$$(v'' \cdot 1.25)^2 d''^{2m} c''^{-2} S''^{-1} D''^{(-1-2m)} = g \qquad (2.5.3-15b)$$

The relation of the scale ratios is thus computed from the ratio of Eqs (2.5.3 − 14) and (2.5.3 − 15b) thus

$$\frac{v'^2}{(v'' \cdot 1.25)^2} \frac{d'^{2m}}{d''^{2m}} \frac{c'^{-2}}{c''^{-2}} \frac{S'^{-1}}{S''^{-1}} \frac{D'^{(-1-2m)}}{D''^{(-1-2m)}} = 1$$

whence

$$\lambda_v^2 \lambda_d^{2m} \lambda_c^{-2} \lambda_S^{-1} \lambda_D^{(-1-2m)} = \Delta_v = 1.25^2 = 1.565$$

Consequently

$$\Delta_v = 1.25^2 = 1.565$$

is the value to be used in further computations.

As to be seen from Table 2.5.3−2 the value Δ_v is not involved in the formulae of λ_S and λ_v. On the other hand, the value of λ_d must be computed again or, since the value of λ_D, λ_l and λ_c remain unchanged, the value $\lambda_d = 3.295$ must be multiplied by $\Delta_v^{1/2m}$ according to Table 2.5.3−2. In other words, the new scale ratio of sediment particle diameter is

$$\lambda_d = 3.295 \cdot 1.565^{1.19} = 5.61$$

45

taking into account that, in order to eliminate differences, Δ_v has a value other than unity. The new value of λ_d entails a new value for d'', consequently

$$d'' = \frac{0.1}{5.61} = 0.0179 \text{ cm}$$

The figures in *Table 2.5.3−5* are modified accordingly. The groups of values computed with the new d'' value are indicated in *Table 2.5.3−5*. Columns 1,2 and 5 of the Table undergo no changes since λ_d is not involved in the scale ratios listed therein. Column 4 of Table 2.5.3−6, on the other hand, must be computed with the new d'' value and, if the corresponding values of v''/U_*'' and R''/d'' computed in this manner are plotted in a graph, then according to *Fig. 2.5.3−2* these points denoted by triangles fit actually into the dashed line representing the relation in the model.

Hereafter the remaining scale ratios are computed. The scale ratio of submerged densities is, according to *Table 2.5.3−2*,

$$\lambda_{(\rho_1-\rho)} = \lambda_D^{\frac{2m-1+N+2mN}{2m}} \lambda_l^{\frac{1-N-2m}{2m}} \lambda_c^{\frac{-2+2N}{2m}} \Delta_v^{\frac{-1+N}{2m}}$$

Accordingly

$$\lambda_{(\rho_1-\rho)} = 40^{1.74} \cdot 160^{-0.86} \cdot 0.698^{-0.281} \cdot 1.565^{-0.141} = 8.16$$

$$(\gamma_1'' - \gamma) = \frac{(\gamma_1' - \gamma)}{\lambda_{(\rho_1-\rho)}} = \frac{2.65 - 1}{8.16} = \frac{1.65}{8.16} = 0.2$$

so that the specific gravity of the model sediment becomes

$$\gamma_1'' = 1.2 \ [\text{p/cm}^3]$$

The scale ratios of bed load and total load transport rates, as well as of the hydraulic and duration times remain to be computed. From *Table 2.5.3−2*

$$\lambda_{qB} = \lambda_D^{\frac{6m+(3/2)N+3mN}{2m}} \lambda_l^{\frac{-(3/2)N-3m}{2m}} \lambda_c^{\frac{3N}{2m}} \Delta_v^{\frac{(3/2)N}{2m}}$$

$$\lambda_{qB} = 40^{5.9} \cdot 160^{-3.07} \cdot 0.698^{3.15} \cdot 1.565^{1.575} = 313$$

$$\lambda_{qt} = \lambda_{qB} \cdot B = 313B$$

$$\lambda_{t_1} = \lambda_D^{-1/2} \lambda_l = 40^{-1/2} \cdot 160 = 25.3$$

$$\lambda_{t_2} = \lambda_D^{\frac{-1-2m-(N/2)-mN}{2m}} \cdot \lambda_l^{\frac{1+3m+(N/2)}{2m}} \cdot B^{-1} \cdot \lambda_c^{\frac{-1-(N/2)}{2m}} \cdot \Delta_v^{\frac{-1-(N/2)}{2m}}$$

$$\lambda_{t_2} = 40^{-3.15} \cdot 160^{3.22} \cdot B^{-1} \cdot 0.698^{-1.715} \cdot 1.565^{-1.715} = 178 \ B^{-1}$$

Since the scale ratios λ_{qt} and λ_{t_2} depend on the ratio B the magnitude of which varies in turn, usually with stage, these two scale ratios assume different values at different stages.

It has been mentioned that the bed form at which sediment is transported depends on the magnitude of the parameter β_1. It should be clear that the $\beta_1'' =$

values in the model must be the same as the β_1' values in the prototype. Of course, the numerical agreement of the channel stability factor b is not required. In columns 12 and 13 of *Table 2.5.3–4* the values of the parameter β_1' and b' have been computed for each of the three groups of values. Similarly in columns 7 and 8 of *Table 2.5.3–6* the values of b'' and of the parameter β_1'' applying to the model have been entered. In computing b'' and the parameter β_1'' allowance was made for the fact that the specific gravity of the model sediment is only 1.2 instead of 2.65. Computing, for instance, β_1'' for the first group of values

$$\beta_1'' = \frac{d''^{0.118}}{R''S''} \cdot (4.691 \cdot 10^{-3})^{0.882} = \frac{d''^{0.118}}{R''S''} \cdot 8.791 \cdot 10^{-3} =$$

$$= \frac{0.0179^{0.118}}{16.6 \cdot 16.8 \cdot 10^{-5}} \cdot 8.791 \cdot 10^{-3} = 1.96$$

the result obtained must still be multiplied by 0.121 since, according to Eq. (2.5.3–4),

$$\frac{(\gamma_1'' - \gamma)}{1.65} = \frac{0.2}{1.65} = 0.121$$

The value eventually obtained for the parameter β_1'' from the first group of values is thus

$$\beta_1'' = 1.96 \cdot 0.121 = 0.237$$

The factor of proportionality resulting from the difference in specific gravities must be taken into account also when computing the channel stability factor b''. Thus, for instance, at the first group of values

$$b'' = \frac{0.0179}{16.8 \cdot 16.6 \cdot 10^{-5}} \cdot 0.121 = 0.776$$

Comparing β_1' indicated in *Table 2.5.3–4* with the β_1'' values shown in *Table 1.5.3–6*, the difference will be seen to be negligible, implying that the condition of movement in the model will be the same as in the prototype.

For the sake of clarity consider again *Fig. 2.5.3–1* representing the relation between $b = 1/Fr_*$ and the parameter d/A at the different boundary conditions of sediment movement. Entering in this figure the parameters β_1 applying to the model and to the prototype (points denoted by full circles), it will be seen that we have succeeded in realizing in the model, with very good approximation, the condition of movement prevailing in the prototype. Actually over the Szolnok reach of the Tisza river measurement data have revealed this to be in the range of dunes development.

It is interesting to note that computing parameters b and β_1 with the help of data applying to the numerical example published in the paper of Einstein and Ning Chien, and plotting the results (inclined crosses) in *Fig. 2.5.3–1*, the identity of bed forms is seen to be realized also in the model built according to the nine condition equations suggested by them. Nevertheless the difference is greater than in the example of the Tisza river. The numerical example published by Einstein indicates that in the case of transport at sand ripples or at smooth bed or perhaps under condition of no movement the prototype is less readily reproduced in models. In fact the differences which remain insignificant in the range of antidunes may result in substantial differences with bed forms mentioned above. From this comparison it may again be concluded that the method suggested by the author for computing models of alluvial streams with the help of parameter β_1 represents a certain improvement in methodology and in accuracy.

In the method developed by the author the similarity of sediment transport is guaranteed by the invariance of relations given by Eq. (2.5.3−4) and represented for different bed forms in *Fig. 2.5.3−1* showing this general relation. However, Eq. (2.5.3−4) is based on the law of constant tractive forces. Moreover, it has been demonstrated in *Section 1.2.4* that these constant laws are invalid. This means that, depending on the conditions of observation (e.g. relative roughness or slope), different bed forms may pertain to the same β_1 value at a particular combination of d and γ_1 values. This is why, theoretically, the application of the law of variable critical tractive forces ought to be considered. However, the use of variable laws as condition equations has not been solved as yet. This is due in part to the fact that the variable laws were developed but recently, and the time has been too short for examining their potential applications. It should be recognized further that the introduction of these variable laws presents extremely complex problems whose solution can only be expected on the basis of extensive investigations.

Nevertheless, when using the modified method it appears advisable to check the bed forms in the light of the variable laws. Any resulting differences may be eliminated or at least reduced by successive approximations in which some of the quantities are varied.

2.5.4. FURTHER METHODS RELATED
TO THE HYDRAULIC SIMILARITY OF ALLUVIAL STREAMS

2.5.4.1 Yalin's method. Model techniques related to alluvial streams have been dealt with by S. Yalin in several papers. According to him exact dynamic similarity could only be realized by assigning different values to the scale ratios for each particular discharge. This is practically impossible. In order to overcome this difficulty, he has elaborated the method of "the straight line of similar conditions" which will be described in brief.

Yalin has advanced the opinion that the condition of dynamic similarity is geometric similarity, primarily the similarity in the geometry of sediment particles, i.e. of particle shapes and of the granulometric curves. All subsequent considerations are founded on this assumption. The independent variables introduced by him are

a) The density ρ and the dynamic viscosity μ controlling the physical properties of the fluid;

b) The specific gravity γ_1 and the particle diameter d controlling the physical properties of sediment;

c) The tractive force τ_0 or the shear velocity $U_* = \sqrt{\tau_0/\rho} = \sqrt{gDS}$ describing the dynamic condition of flow.

By dimensional analysis he has obtained the dimensionless numbers

$$X_1 = \frac{1}{Re_*}$$

(2.5.4−1)

and

$$X_2 = \frac{1}{Fr_*\gamma/\gamma_1}$$

(2.5.4−2)

The introduction of tractive force τ_0 as an independent variable implies that, in the expression $\tau_0 = \gamma DS = \rho g DS$ the phenomenon is governed by the magnitude of the product DS rather than by the values of D and S separately. According to the law of variable tractive forces, this assumption is invalid. Nevertheless, in model tests on alluvial streams this is the approximation to be accepted since for the time being we are not in a position to take the variable laws into consideration.

The independent variables must, however, include gravitational acceleration g, consequently, even with the variables introduced by Yalin, the number of dimensionless expressions necessarily obtained is $6 - 3 = 3$. These are

$$Re_* = \frac{U_* d\rho}{\mu}$$

(2.5.4−3)

$$Fr_* = \frac{U_*^2}{gd}$$

(2.5.4−4)

$$G = \frac{\rho g}{\gamma_1} = \frac{\gamma}{\gamma_1}$$

(2.5.4−5)

The two dimensionless numbers under Eqs (2.5.4−4) and (2.5.4−5) have been combined by Yalin who examined each dependent variable X_0 of the phenomenon as a function of X_1 and X_2:

$$X_0 = F(X_1, X_2)$$

(2.5.4−6)

Slope, for instance, is given as a function of

$$S = Fr \cdot F_1\left(Re, \frac{d}{D}\right)$$

(2.5.4−7)

709

where

$$F_1\left(Re, \frac{d}{D}\right) = \frac{1}{c_1^2}\left(\frac{d}{D}\right)^n \qquad (2.5.4-8)$$

so that the form eventually obtained is

$$\frac{S}{Fr} = \frac{1}{c_1^2}\left(\frac{D}{d}\right)^{-n} \qquad (2.5.4-9)$$

Yalin's Eq. (2.5.4−9) is identical with the first condition equation of Einstein − Ning Chien, and with that of the author given by Eq. (2.5.2−1a). In fact

$$Fr = \frac{v^2}{gD}$$

so that

$$\frac{gSD}{v^2} = \frac{U_*^2}{v^2} = \frac{1}{c_1^2}\left(\frac{D}{d}\right)^{-n} \qquad (2.5.4-10)$$

or

$$\frac{v^2}{U_*^2} = c_1^2\left(\frac{D}{d}\right)^n \qquad (2.5.4-11)$$

which upon substitution of $c = c_1$ and $n = 2m$ is the similarity criterion of friction conditions introduced earlier.

The logarithmic form of Eq. (2.5.4−9)

$$\lg\frac{S}{Fr} = \lg\left(\frac{gDS}{v^2}\right) = \lg\left(\frac{U_*^2}{v^2}\right) = \lg\frac{1}{c_1^2} - n\lg\left(\frac{D}{d}\right)$$

is plotted by a straight line. This straight line contains the geometric loci of all points that indicate similar conditions in the S/Fr, D/d system of co-ordinates. (It is for this reason that the term "straight line of similar conditions" has been introduced.)

In the $\lg S/Fr - \lg D/d$ system of co-ordinates successive points P_1', P_2', . . ., P_m' of the curve Γ' correspond to increasing actual discharges. In the model the points corresponding thereto on the Γ'' curve are defined by the straight line of slope n (see Fig. 2.5.4−1). The magnitude of n depends on the Reynolds number, on the shape of the flow cross-section and on roughness conditions.

Since, at any corresponding discharges in the prototype and in the model, c_1 and n assume identical values in both systems, while the corresponding S/Fr and D/d values are different, exact dynamic similarity is impossible to attain according to Yalin. From this he derives the necessity of adopting the discharge considered critical with regard to the objective of the model study.

Yalin claims to have improved thereby the accuracy of the "trial-end-error" procedure suggested by Einstein − Bogárdi.

710

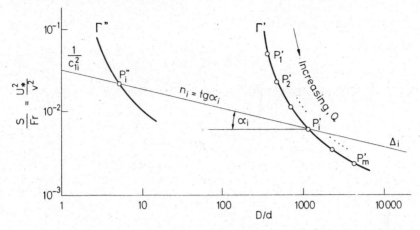

Fig. 2.5.4—1. Relation of S/Fr and D/d obtained from Yalin's scale model tests

2.5.4.2. *The investigations of Komura.* Starting from the differential equations of flow and continuity, as well as from the transport equation of Kalinske and Brown for sediment movement, S. Komura in 1960 derived expressions for the hydraulic similarity of sediment-transporting streams.

For the equivalent sand roughness k_s he uses the expressions

$$\frac{k_s}{d} = K \left[\frac{\tau_0/\rho}{(\rho_1/\rho - 1)gd} \right]^m \qquad (2.5.4-12a)$$

or

$$\frac{k_s}{d} = K \left[\frac{\tau_0}{(\gamma_1 - \gamma)d} \right]^m \qquad (2.5.4-12b)$$

The value of the constant K and the exponent m are to be determined by experiments. For instance, according to Y. Iwagaki, $K = 10$, $m = 0.769$ while, according to J. Matsunashi, $m = 3$. In general $0 \leq m \leq 3$. Komura used the value $m = 0$ in his computations.

In the equation of flow Komura introduces the friction loss by the expression

$$S - \frac{\tau_0}{\rho g R} = S - \frac{v^2 k_s^{2q}}{gE^2 R^{(2q+1)}} \qquad (2.5.4-13)$$

where the magnitude of E and q is defined by the relation

$$\frac{v}{U_*} = E \left(\frac{R}{k_s} \right)^q \qquad (2.5.4-14)$$

711

With x denoting the main direction, the bottom slope is

$$S = \frac{D}{x} \qquad (2.5.4-15)$$

The Froude criterion and the hydraulic time are given by the expressions

$$Fr = \frac{v^2}{gD} \qquad (2.5.4-16)$$

and

$$v = \frac{x}{t} \qquad (2.5.4-17)$$

respectively.

The friction slope S_f is

$$S_f = \frac{\tau_0/\rho}{gR} \qquad (2.5.4-18)$$

Komura expresses E in terms of Manning's n and of the sand roughness k_s as

$$E = \frac{k_s^q}{ng^{1/2}} \qquad (2.5.4-19)$$

In cases where the scale ratio of length differs from that of depth, i.e. $\lambda_x/\lambda_D \neq 1$, the extent of distortion is expressed as

$$\alpha = \frac{\lambda_x}{\lambda_D} \qquad (2.5.4-20)$$

The total sediment transport q_t is obtained from the Kalinske–Brown formula

$$\frac{q_t}{\sqrt{\dfrac{\tau_0}{\rho}} \cdot d} = a_s \left[\frac{\tau_s/\rho}{(\rho_1/\rho - 1)gd} \right]^p \qquad (2.5.4-21)$$

where τ_s = the tractive force expended for transporting sediment,
a_s and p = constants.

With t_s denoting the duration time, B the width of the channel, D_s the height of the bottom above a datum level and λ the pore volume of the bed material, the continuity of sediment transport is expressed by the differential equation

$$\frac{\partial D_s}{\partial t_s} + \frac{1}{B(1-\lambda)} \frac{\partial (q_t B)}{\partial x_s} = 0 \qquad (2.5.4-22)$$

This differential equation is of course essentially identical with Eq. (2.1.6−10) derived by Komura for scouring downstream of dams and for the continuity of sediment transport.

712

From Eqs (2.5.4−12b), (2.5.4−13), (2.5.4−15) to (2.5.4−19), further (2.5.4−21) and (2.5.4−22) Komura derives the following nine equations for the scale ratios:

$$\lambda_{ks}\lambda_{(\gamma_1-\gamma)}^m \lambda_d^{(m-1)}\lambda_K^{-1}\lambda_{\tau_0}^m = 1 \qquad (2.5.4-23)$$

$$\lambda_v^2\lambda_{ks}^{2q}\lambda_E^{-2}\lambda_R^{-(2q+1)}\lambda_S^{-1} = 1 \qquad (2.5.4-24)$$

$$\lambda_S\lambda_x\lambda_D^{-1} = 1 \qquad (2.5.4-25)$$

$$\lambda_v^2\lambda_D^{-1} = 1 \qquad (2,5.4-26)$$

$$\lambda_r\lambda_t\lambda_x^{-1} = 1 \qquad (2.5.4-27)$$

$$\lambda_{\tau_0}\lambda_R^{-1}\lambda_{S_f}^{-1} = 1 \qquad (2.5.4-28)$$

$$\lambda_n\lambda_E\lambda_{ks}^{-q} = 1 \qquad (2.5.4-29)$$

$$\lambda_{q_t}\lambda_{as}^{-1}\lambda_{\tau_s}^{-(p+1)}\lambda_d^{(p-1)}\lambda_{(\gamma_1-\gamma)}^p = 1 \qquad (2.5.4-30)$$

$$\lambda_{x_s}\lambda_{D_s}\lambda_{t_s}^{-1}\lambda_{q_t}^{-1}\lambda_{(1-\lambda)} = 1 \qquad (2.5.4-31)$$

In Eqs (2.5.4−23) to (2.5.4−31) altogether 21 scale ratios are involved. Of these $\lambda_{\tau_0} = \lambda_{\tau_s}$ must be satisfied for dynamic similarity. Komura assumes further that

$$\lambda_x = \lambda_{x_s}, \ \lambda_D = \lambda_{D_s}, \ \lambda_S = \lambda_{S_f} \ \text{and} \ \lambda_R = \beta\lambda_D$$

In this way the number of independent scale ratios is reduced to 16. On the other hand, by introducing the ratio β, the number of unknown quantities becomes 17.

In solving the foregoing set of equations Komura assumes the ratio β, further the scale ratios λ_E, λ_K, λ_{as}, $\lambda_{(\gamma_1-\gamma)}$, $\lambda_{(1-\lambda)}$ to be available from preliminary studies and experiments. In this way nine equations are available and, once two scale ratios are adopted, the magnitude of the remaining nine can be computed.

Using the nine condition equations Komura derives the relations between the scale ratios for two cases. In the first λ_x and λ_D, in the second λ_x and λ_d are the two scale ratios that can be selected in advance.

2.5.4.3 *The method of Zwamborn.* As in the modified procedure introduced by the author the identity of bed forms is similarly ensured by Zwamborn. In doing so he relies on the graphical relations (see *Fig. 1.2.3−2)* introduced by Albertson and his co-workers for the different boundary conditions of sediment transport between the parameters U_*/ω and $Re_{*s} = U_*d/\nu$. Since Eq. (2.5.3−4) and *Fig. (2.5.3−1)* introduced by the author for the numerical description of different boundary conditions are founded on the U_*/ω and Re_{*s} graphical relation, the condition equation introduced by Zwamborn is substantially similar to the author's parameter β_1.

Neglecting the similarity criteria of sediment transport Zwamborn takes the following criteria into account:

a) for turbulent flow in the model $Re > 600$,

b) the Froude numbers must be identical,

c) U_*/ω must be identical in the prototype and in the model,

d) the scale ratio of sand roughness must be the square root of the inverse of the scale ratio of slope and

e) the bed forms or the regime of sediment transport must satisfy the $U_*/\omega - Re_{*s}$ relation.

According to J. G. Herbertson, the above criteria are expressed by the relation

$$F\left(\frac{\sqrt{gRS}}{v/d}, \frac{v}{\sqrt{gD}}, \frac{d}{v^{2/3}g^{-1/3}}, \frac{gRS}{\omega}, \frac{D}{R}, \frac{D}{d}\right) = 0 \qquad (2.5.4-32)$$

in his "method of synthesis". The last two of these parameters have been neglected by Zwamborn although he emphasizes the importance of relative roughness D/d in his later publications.

2.5.4.4. *The method of Herbertson.* In the "method of synthesis" suggested by Herbertson the similarity criteria of sediment transport are obtained from the theoretical relation

$$F\left(\frac{Q_t}{Q}, \frac{Qg^{1/3}}{v^{5/3}}, \frac{d}{v^{2/3}g^{-1/3}}, \frac{D}{d}, \frac{D}{R}, \rho'\right) = 0 \qquad (2.5.4-33)$$

He believes a trial-and-error approach to be suitable for selecting a sediment material of a specific gravity and particle size ensuring the proper depth corresponding to the discharge and to the Fr number in the prototype.

He expects the rates of sediment transport to impose certain limitations and the necessity of taking into account also the similarity of bed forms. For this purpose he intends to use a method similar to that of Zwamborn or to that of the author.

The importance of relative roughness D/d has also been mentioned by Herbertson. It is interesting to note that, as indicated by Eq. (2.5.4–33), he considers the two kinds of time conversion superfluous in this particular case.

The method suggested by Herbertson has not yet been applied to actual model tests.

The hydraulic similarity of alluvial streams has been considered by a number of other authors. For the relevant details the reader is referred to the bibliography.

Model tests of alluvial streams present highly complex problems to which no unique solution has been found as yet. The author is of the opinion that future research should be based on the balance equations (1.3.3–37) to (1.3.3–42), and the relations between various scale ratios could then be determined in analogy with Eqs (I) to (VIII) introduced as an example in *Subsection 2.5.1.1*. Advances in hydraulics are expected to permit a more exact understanding of the relevant hydraulic phenomena.

PART THREE
PRACTICAL INTERPRETATION OF
SEDIMENT OBSERVATIONS

3.1. DATA PROCESSING AND METHODOLOGY

3.1.1. EXAMPLES FOR PROCESSING SEDIMENT OBSERVATION DATA

3.1.1.1. Observation data on sediment transport. At gaging stations greater reliability can be achieved in determining the rate of suspended-sediment transport, since bed load measurements involve, as mentioned before, a large number of difficulties. These difficulties arise again in processing observation data. *It is therefore emphasized again that the results of bed load observations should be accepted as approximate data only.*

Routine sediment observations are generally performed everywhere by identical procedures, the differences being restricted mostly to the instruments and equipment used.

In observation work the weight of sediment transported is determined in selected verticals by taking samples from the water and the bed material alike. Simultaneously the velocity is measured.

Once the processed data appear to yield adequate information on the rate of sediment transport at a particular gaging station, the observations are temporarily suspended. Observations at these gaging stations are resumed under exceptional circumstances, for instance, at very high stages only.

At each observation the mean concentration of the measuring verticals is determined and the total weight G_s [kp/sec] of suspended sediment is thus computed by using the appropriate discharge figures. The mean concentration in the cross-section is found from the relation $C_k = G_s/Q$, where Q is the discharge.

At the time of observation the stage is read, the slope, the wetted cross-section, the surface width, the mean velocity, the discharge and the mean depth of flow are computed. The mean particle diameter of suspended sediment, of bed load, and of the bed material is determined for each vertical. A mechanical analysis is run on all material samples, and the grain size distribution curves are plotted. The factors characterizing the uniformity and fineness of granulometry are computed. The average particle diameters in various verticals are averaged for the entire cross-section to find the mean particle size.

The mean particle diameters characteristic of the river section under consideration are determined by including all observation data.

The rate of bed load transport is computed by taking the width of the band of movement into consideration.

The mean concentration C_k, the weights of sediment transported in suspension and as bed load G_s and G_B, respectively, found at each observation are invariably related to stage. Wherever possible, their relations to discharges and flow velocities are established. In fact, these can be computed without performing additional

717

observations yet, concerning the characteristics of sediment transport, they supplement well hydraulically the relations based on stages.

In order to meet practical demands as far as possible, the mean concentration as well as the weight of suspended sediment and bed load are plotted against stages at each gaging station.

3.1.1.2 Methodology. Sediment transport relations for alluvial streams are obtained by processing the observation data according to different theories and using different methods. It should be noted, however, that the processing of data is also subject to certain limitations.

In view of the extremely large number of relations mentioned in the present book, it is deemed necessary to review in brief the procedure of data processing together with the methods and procedures adopted for deriving these relationships.*

It has been common practice to determine the relations of the rate of sediment transport to stage, to discharge and to velocity by a graphical method, by tracing the line of best fit. These relations being essentially stochastic in character, it would seem logical to determine them by correlation computation. In the era of mechanical computation this would actually present no undue difficulties although the relations thus obtained could not be adjusted subsequently to the conditions emerging from the hydraulic properties of the streams. Also, it is important to decide whether the difference between the graphical method and the numerical one is big enough to warrant the application of the latter in every case.

In some instances power functions would drastically distort the two-variable relationship. The method adopted assumes great importance in such cases.

An essential practical requirement in any relation is the possibility of determining therefrom the maximum value which the rate of transport or the concentration of sediment may attain. For any particular water course and especially for closely spaced gaging stations these extreme values must necessarily be comparable in magnitude. The determination of maxima is thus not only a simple problem of data processing but involves the necessity of taking into account also the properties of the particular stream.

For describing rates of sediment transport three-variable relations are sometimes necessary. These may be introduced by using different approaches.

In some instances it is found necessary to determine the rate of transport in different seasons; even transport rates at rising, falling or peaking stages may be desirable.

Aside from the relations related to rates of transport and sediment concentration, the determination of annual average values may also be important for practical purposes. For estimating these the frequency of stages or discharges must also be introduced.

The introduction of two-variable relations always involves the neglect of several hydraulically important factors. The relations adopted should therefore yield

---

* The streams and gaging stations mentioned in the examples are shown in *Fig. 3.1.2—3.*

Fig. 3.1.1—1. Sediment concentration vs. stages at Dunaalmás

results in reasonable agreement with those obtained on the basis of the hydraulic conditions discussed in *Sections 2.2.3* and *2.2.4*.

A review of the methods applied for determining the distribution of sediment concentration and flow velocity, as well as of the variation of suspended-sediment concentration over depth is finally deemed necessary.

1. *Correlation by graphical and analytical methods.* The rates of suspended-sediment and bed load transport and of sediment concentration are plotted against stages in *Figs 3.1.1—1, 3.1.1—2* and *3.1.1—3* for the Dunaalmás gaging section on the Danube river. Each of the three relations has been assumed to follow approximately an exponential function, and the relation most closely fitting the scattered points in the diagram has been traced by a heavy dashed line. The three relations determined thus by the graphical method are as follows:

$$C_k = 4.3 \cdot 10^{-3} \cdot h^{2.84} \ [\text{kp/m}^3] \qquad (3.1.1-1)$$

$$G = 4.0 \cdot h^{3.64} \ [\text{kp/sec}] \qquad (3.1.1-2)$$

$$G = 3.1 \cdot 10^{-3} \cdot h^{5.13} \ [\text{kp/sec}] \qquad (3.1.1-3)$$

where the stages h should be entered in metre units.

The observed data of sediment concentration, rates of suspended-sediment and bed load transport, together with the corresponding stages form interrelated groups of values and thus lend themselves to the analytical determination of simple two-variable relations.

Omitting the details of correlation computation, a mechanical programme has yielded the following relations for the Dunaalmás section:

For the sediment concentration to stage relation

$$C_k = 6.74 \cdot 10^{-3} \cdot h^{1.954} \ [\text{kp/m}^3] \qquad (3.1.1-4)$$

$$h = 6.674 \cdot C_k^{0.307} \ [\text{m}] \qquad (3.1.1-5)$$

719

Fig. 3.1.1—2. Suspended-sediment transport vs. stages at Dunaalmás

Fig. 3.1.1—3. Bed load transport vs. stages at Dunaalmás

for the weight of suspended sediment to stage relation

$$G_s = 4.907 \cdot h^{3.083} \ [\text{kp/sec}] \tag{3.1.1-6}$$

$$h = 8.33 \cdot 10^{-1} \cdot G_s^{0.248} \ [\text{m}] \tag{3.1.1-7}$$

for the weight of bed load to stage relation

$$G_B = 4.93 \cdot 10^{-3} \cdot h^{4.367} \ [\text{kp/sec}] \tag{3.1.1-8}$$

$$h = 3.178 \cdot G_B^{0.181} \ [\text{m}] \tag{3.1.1-9}$$

In *Figs 3.1.1—1, 3.1.1—2* and *3.1.1—3* these relations are shown by thin continuous lines. It will be realized that the relations of practical interest are those in which stage h is the independent variable, these being suitable for estimating the expected, most probable value of C_k, G_s and G_B.

From the theory of correlation computation it will be recalled that, in the case of a true functional relationship, the two intersecting straight lines would be represented by a single straight line situated necessarily between the two thin lines representing the stochastic relation. Consequently, if we wish to determine the relations by taking into account the result of correlation computation, it is preferable to adopt the full continuous line traced to halve the sector between the two intersecting straight lines, since what we want is to replace two stochastic relations by a non-existing functional relation. The relations represented by the full continuous line are described by the following expressions:

$$C_k = 3.80 \cdot 10^{-3} \cdot h^{2.61} \ [\text{kp/m}^3] \tag{3.1.1—10}$$

$$G_s = 3.10 \cdot h^{3.58} \ [\text{kp/sec}] \tag{3.1.1—11}$$

$$G_B = 3.40 \cdot 10^{-3} \cdot h^{5.00} \ [\text{kp/sec}] \tag{3.1.1—12}$$

As demonstrated by the example of the Dunaalmás gage, the approximate functional relations determined by graphical and analytical correlation are almost identical.

The repeated use of the method described above for several gages permits the conclusion that graphical correlation is alone capable of yielding satisfactory results, obviating the need for correlation computations.

In view of the spreading use of computers the significance of this conclusion must not be overestimated since otherwise lengthy and tiresome numerical computations present no difficulties for computers.

Since most relations quoted in this book originate from observations performed before 1954, graphical correlation has been used for determining most of them.

2. *Graphical correlation when power functions are grossly misleading.* In considering sediment transport it is sometimes impossible to express sediment concentration or the weight of suspended sediment and of bed load by a power function of stage.

Conditions of this type occurred at the Miskolc gaging section on the Sajó river where, as indicated in *Figs 3.1 1—4, 3 1.1—5*, no straight line could be fitted to the observation data entered into a log-log plot. The line of best fit would take the form of some curve.

In order to retain the advantages of graphical correlation by a straight line, it was necessary to find—instead of the original independent variable, in this case, of the stage h at Miskolc,—a new variable h_1 which differs in magnitude by a constant z from the value h.

The magnitude of z must evidently always be determined by computations.

Let us assume the curve best fitting the scattered points, representing corresponding pairs of concentration and stage values, to take the form shown in

46

Fig. 3.1.1—4. Sediment concentration vs. stages at Miskolc

Fig. 3.1.1—6 in this particular case. It is in general possible to find a z = constant value for which the points situated along the curve in *Fig. 3.1.1—6* —when plotted in the log-log system $h_1 = h + z$ and C_k —are concentrated along a single straight line so that the relation is expressed in the form

$$h_1 = h + z = bC_k^n \qquad (3.1.1-13)$$

The problem is thus to find a value z = constant at which Eq. (3.1.1—13) is satisfied.

The procedure of computation is as follows:

Two points for each pair are selected in *Fig. 3.1.1—6* the abscissae of which meet the condition $\lg C_2 - \lg C_1 = \lg C_4 - \lg C_3$, or

$$\frac{C_2}{C_1} = \frac{C_4}{C_3} \qquad (3.1.1-14)$$

Once the above condition is satisfied, the secants defined by the two pairs of points can be made to form a single straight line by increasing the value of h by a z value for which

$$\lg (h_2 + z) - \lg (h_1 + z) = \lg (h_4 + z) - \lg (h_3 + z)$$

or

$$\frac{h_2 + z}{h_1 + z} = \frac{h_4 + z}{h_3 + z} \qquad (3.1.1-15)$$

The magnitude of z is thus given by the expression

$$z = \frac{h_2 h_3 - h_1 h_4}{(h_1 + h_4) - (h_2 + h_3)} \qquad (3.1.1-16)$$

It should be noted that two limits occur at $z = 0$ and $z = \infty$.

722

Fig. 3.1.1—5. Suspended-sediment and bed load transport vs. stages at Miskolc

Fig. 3.1.1—6. Sketch for the method determining the $z =$ constant values

In fact if $z = 0$, then $h_2/h_1 = h_4/h_3$. Since $C_2/C_1 = C_4/C_3$, this implies that the curve traced in the original system of co-ordinates is essentially a straight line.

If $z = \infty$, then $h_2 - h_1 = h_4 - h_3 = 0$ which, in view of the original assumption $C_2/C_1 = C_4/C_3$, indicates a horizontal straight line.

As shown by the limit case $z = \infty$, the value adopted for z should be as small as possible. It should be noted that small z values are advisable also in the interest of obtaining accurate readings for h. It should be clear, moreover, that the higher the value of z, the narrower the range of scatter becomes so that in the new system the points show practically no scatter. This, of course, is due only to the distorting affect of the logarithmic scale since the original scatter of the points with respect to h is impossible to reduce actually.

The relation is insensitive to slight variations of z. On the strength of this circumstance it is possible to adopt an integer for z reasonably close to the computed value.

The curves ensuring the best fit have been determined with the method described above and entered in *Figs 3.1.1−4* and *3.1.1−5* by a dash-dot line. With these curves the magnitude of z was found to be around 1 m.

Using the $z = 1$ m value the new variable is introduced as $h_1 = h + 1$, and the foregoing relations are determined by the approximate power functions plotted in *Fig. 3.1.1−7*. The expressions

$$C_k = 6.80 \cdot 10^{-3} \cdot h_1^{3.66} \ [\text{kp/m}^3] \tag{3.1.1−17}$$

$$G_s = 1.25 \cdot 10^{-?} \cdot h_1^{6.90} \ [\text{kp/sec}] \tag{3.1.1−18}$$

$$G_B = 2.70 \cdot 10^{-5} \cdot h_1^{5.72} \ [\text{kp/sec}] \tag{3.1.1−19}$$

are in full agreement with the curves traced by full dash-dot lines in *Figs 3.1.1−4* and *3.1.1−5*. The closeness of fitting to the scattered points will be seen to be superior to that provided by the straight line.

Where it is desired to determine the sediment concentration or the weight of suspended sediment and bed load pertaining to any particular stage, it is essential to use *Figs 3.1.1−4* and *3.1.1−5* in which the stages can be red more accurately. To visualize the magnitude of errors due to inaccurate stage reading it should be noted that at stages around 50 cm an error of 10 cm in stage reading results in an error of 20 to 30%, whereas at stages around 500 cm the same 10 cm error results in a difference of 4 to 5%, for instance, in sediment concentration. Since in *Fig. 3.1.1−7* the readings have become inaccurate in the domain of low stages, the foregoing suggestion to use the curves in *Figs 3.1.1−4* and *3.1.1−5* whenever possible is fully justified.

3. *Determination of the highest transport rate expected.* Opportunities to observe the rate of transport at highest stages are very rare. This is why great difficulties are often encountered in trying to extend the relations most closely fitting the points actually observed.

Fig. 3.1.1—7. Sediment concentration, suspended-sediment and bed load transport vs. stages at Miskolc

The method applied in estimating the highest expected rate of transport is described again with reference to the Miskolc section of the Sajó river. According to *Fig. 3.1.1—4,* the highest stage at which sediment observation has been performed was 305 cm. The highest stage on record for the Miskolc gage is 533 cm. In order to use, for instance, the sediment concentration to stage relation for higher stages, it is necessary to extend the curve determined as described previously up to 533 cm in *Fig. 3.1.1—4.* Concerning visual correlation the curve traced in the figure fits the observation points apparently well. More detailed investigations have shown the extended curve to fit the observation points not only apparently, but actually as well. However, the selection of the appropriate curve in any particular case presents considerable difficulties.

The relation between sediment concentration and stages in the Miskolc gaging section has been traced to an arithmetic scale in *Fig. 3.1.1—8.* The observation points indicating low stages and the corresponding low concentration values are seen to be scattered irregularly in the plot. The relations determined in *Figs 3.1.1—4* and *3.1.1—7* have been traced in *Fig. 3.1.1—8* with a full and a dash-dotted line, respectively. In order to reduce the sizes of the plot the intermediate range of the relations has been omitted.

For lack of observations at higher stages the validity of the relations represented in *Fig. 3.1.1—8* may appear to be questionable. In fact, the relations indicated by the thin continuous line and even by the thin dashed line may also correspond to the observation points. Although three points pertaining to about 0.3 kp/m³

Fig. 3.1.1—8. Method for establishing the maximum sediment concentration in function of stages at the Miskolc section

and about 0.5 to 1.0 m stages are omitted in the former case and so are three points in the concentration ranges 0.05 to 0.03 kp/m³ and in those corresponding to stages between 1.8 and 2.5 m in the latter case, neither of these seems impossible in the arithmetic representation in the absence of observations at higher stages. If these two relations are traced again with thin continuous and thin dashed lines in *Fig. 3.1.1—4*, it will become even more apparent that, up to a concentration of about 0.4 kp/m³, these two relations may also be accepted as curves fitting the scattered observation points.

The example of the Miskolc gage shows that, in the absence of observations at higher stages, it is extremely difficult to determine the relation thoroughly tallying with the observation data if the observations performed at low and medium stages fail positively to define the character of the relation.

In determining extreme rates of sediment transport a higher degree of reliability can be attained by taking into account also the sediment transport characteristics of the particular water course. These characteristics are an additional source of information that can be exploited in estimating extreme values.

Fig. 3.1.1—9. Sediment concentration and suspended-sediment transport at Deszk related to stages at Szeged

At the Kazincbarcika gaging station situated further upstream on the Sajó river the highest concentration observed was round 24 kp/m³, as indicated in Table 3.1.2—8. It is thus logical to assume that the concentration at Miskolc must not be too far from this value. According to the relation indicated by the thin continuous line, the highest concentration would be 0.79 kp/m³ whereas according to the thin dashed line, it would be even higher than 1.000 kp/m³. The probable highest value expected at Miskolc is necessarily somewhere between these two values, and appreciably higher than the first, while appreciably lower than the second. Limiting in this way the probably highest value, the 5.5 kp/m³ concentration indicated by the dash-dotted line appears to be the most likely concentration. Naturally this value is again a tentative approximation only.

It should be noted that in most sediment-observing stations in Hungary the determination of highest concentration values is easier. In a number of cases observations are available at higher stages as well and in most cases the extreme values of neighbouring stations provide reliable data for determining the desired maximum values.

4. *Sediment transport related to stages on other gages. Three-variable relations.*
At the Deszk gaging station on the Maros river sediment transport is preferably related to stages on the Szeged gage on the Tisza river, since the stages at Deszk are greatly influenced by the stages in the recipient Tisza river. Relations of the sediment concentration and suspended-sediment weight to stages on the Szeged gage are shown in *Fig. 3.1.1—9* whereas the relation of the weight of bed load to stages at Szeged is illustrated in *Fig. 3.1.1—10*.

Fig. 3.1.1—10. Bed load transport at Deszk related to stages at Szeged

The slope of the Maros river is rather steep and thus the values related to the stages at Szeged scatter widely in both figures. Nevertheless the relations have been determine in both figures using the variable $h_1 = h + 3$ m. According to the figures the highest expected sediment concentration is 4.5 kp/m³, while the greatest weights of suspended and bed load are 6.000 kp/sec and 50 kp/sec respectively. The three extreme values are extraordinarily high in relation to the rates of sediment transport in the Tisza river.

An attempt to relate the rates of sediment transport at Deszk to the stages on the Deszk gage remained unsuccessful. In another attempt the sediment transport at Deszk was related to the stages on the Makó gage situated 20.5 km upstream. *Figs 3.1.1—11* and *3.1.1—12* show the sediment concentration and the weight of suspended sediment related to the stages on the Makó gage, to which round 1 m has been added. To each point indicating corresponding values of

Fig. 3.1.1—11. Sediment concentration at Deszk in function of stages at Makó, according to simultaneous stages at Szeged

Fig. 3.1.1—12. Suspended-sediment transport at Deszk in function of stages at Makó, according to simultaneous stages at Szeged

sediment transport at Deszk and stage at Makó the simultaneous stage on the Szeged gage has also been entered on both graphs. As will be perceived from the graphs, the relations are unaffected by the stage at Szeged. This is why in these graphs the relations between concentration and sediment weight at Deszk and the stages at Makó have been determined by neglecting the stages at Szeged.

Fig. 3.1.1—13 shows the weight of bed load at Deszk plotted against stages at Makó. In this case it was found possible to represent the relation with a set of curves by taking into account also the stages at Szeged. In the log-log plot

Fig. 3.1.1—13. Bed load transport at Deszk in function of stages at Makó, according to simultaneous stages at Szeged

729

Fig. 3.1.1—14. Relation of sediment concentration to winter, summer and average stages at Tiszabő

the curves are represented by straight lines, for which the constant *a* and the exponent *n* have been related also to the stages at Szeged. These relations are illustrated in *Fig. 3.1.1—13.*

The difficulties in determining extreme concentration and sediment weight values become even more apparent when considering the relations determined with the help of stages at Makó. As will be seen in *Figs 3.1.1—11* and *3.1.1—12,* the maximum sediment concentration is about 10 kp/m³, while the greatest suspended-sediment weight is about 12,500 kp/sec at the highest stage observed on the Makó gage. Except for the highest values on the Szamos, the Sajó and the Hernád rivers, both values are extraordinarily high compared to the extreme values determined for other water courses in Hungary. Therefore, considering the relations with the stages at Szeged, the only statement that could be made in connection with extreme rates of suspended-sediment transport is that the highest sediment concentration at Deszk is likely to range from 4.5 to 10 kp/m³, the corresponding limits for greatest suspended-sediment weights being 6,000 and 12,500 kp/sec.

The extreme rates of sediment transport mentioned in the foregoing for the Deszk gaging station are, however, not likely to occur in reality. In fact, a brief hydrological study will suffice to reveal that high stages at Makó are, as a rule, accompanied by high stages at Szeged in the Tisza river. This implies, however, that the draw-down at which the afore-mentioned highest sediment concentrations

730

Fig. 3.1.1—15. Relation of suspended-sediment transport and bed load transport to winter, summer and average stages at Tiszabő

and weights of suspended sediment at Deszk would occur is incapable of developing.

The set of curves shown in *Fig. 3.1.1—13* would, of course, yield misleading values on the highest bed load transport rate if a simple extension of the curves were adopted. The maximum would result, obviously, from extending the curve related to the lowest stage at Szeged to the highest stages at Makó. However, the occurrence of highest stages at Makó at times of low stages in the Tisza river is physically impossible. The highest rate of bed load transport must therefore be determined for certain periods only, taking the pertinent stages at Makó and Szeged into consideration. Even the value determined in this way is in many cases of but theoretical interest, since the character of stages (rising or falling) is not taken into account in the set of curves shown in *Fig. 3.1.1—13*. Yet it should be obvious that the influence of slope and related flow velocity is of considerable importance for the highest rate of bed load transport. It was found for instance that during the decade from 1931 to 1940 the highest rate of bed load transport occurred with a value of 185 kp/sec in 1939, with the stage at Makó ranging from 290 to 299 cm and with that at Szeged from 150 to 249 cm. Even this value is believed to be extremely high. For this reason and in view of the above difficulties not even an approximate value of highest bed load weight at Deszk has been estimated.

The average rate of sediment transport has been determined eventually on the basis of relations based on stages at Makó, these relations having been accepted as reliable.

It should be clear, however, that the method to be described in item 6 is unsuited for estimating the average weight of bed load transported. For this

731

Fig. 3.1.1—16. Sediment concentration vs. Tiszabő stages for summer and winter periods

purpose it was necessary to use the G_B values obtained for each of the 3653 stages at Makó observed during the ten-year period, in combination with the curve corresponding to the simultaneous stages at Szeged. For the sake of completeness the extremely lengthy calculations involved have also been performed. The results have shown the average weight of bed load transported to be no more than 0.9 kp/sec, i.e. substantially smaller than the values obtained with the help of the curves related either to the stages at Szeged or to those at Makó on the basis of commonly accepted stage frequencies.

732

Fig. 3.1.1—17. Suspended-sediment transport vs. Tiszabő stages for summer and winter periods

5. Sediment transport related to seasons and to the character of stages. Where the relation between sediment transport and stages is found to scatter between abnormally wide limits, it may be advisable to improve the relations by taking seasonal changes and the character of stage variations into consideration.

The gaging section Tiszabő on the Tisza river is a striking example. The sediment concentration and the weight of both suspended and bottom sediment have been plotted against stages at Tiszabő in *Figs 3.1.1—14* and *3.1.1—15*, respectively. The relations represented by the full lines fitting best the scattered points have been determined but these indicate the trend of variation rather than the actual relation. The looseness of these relations is presumably due not exclusively to random causes and it appeared justified to discriminate these relations according to seasons and to the character of stages.

Extensive investigations have shown the advisability of distinguishing a summer season extending from the middle of June to the end of October and a winter season lasting from the first of November to the middle of June. The sediment concentration vs. stage relation for the summer and winter seasons defined in this way is shown in *Fig. 3.1.1—16*, whereas the weights of suspended sediment and bed load are plotted against stages in *Figs 3.1.1—17* and *3.1.1—18*, respectively. Although the relations distinguished according to summer and winter seasons will be seen to scatter considerably in the three figures, especially in the case of sediment concentration, these relations still describe sediment transport

733

Fig. 3.1.1—18. Bed load transport vs. Tiszabő stages for summer and winter periods

in the Tiszabő section in a much more reliable way. By entering the seasonal relations with dashed lines in *Figs 3.1.1—14* and *3.1.1—15* it will be observed that the average relation indicated by the full line is located half-way between the seasonal relations. From *Figs 3.1.1—14* and *3.1.1—15* it will be concluded that sediment concentration and the weight of the suspended sediment, at the same stage, are appreciably higher in summer than in winter. In summer sediment concentration at high stages is higher by 90 to 120% than in winter, whereas at low stages it may be up to 400% higher.

The seasonal relations applying to bed load transport are largely identical. It is of interest to note that in the case of bed load transport the percentage difference of the summer relation is greater at high stages than at low ones.

The differences observed between sediment transport in the summer and winter seasons are due naturally to the characteristics of the catchment area. A considerable part of the catchment above the Tiszabő section is cultivated area. This is why sediment formation in the catchment is retarded even in June by the protecting plant cover, in much the same way as by frost and the snow cover in winter; and this is what justifies the assumption of the winter season to last from the first of November to June 15. Harvesting of agricultural crops is started gradually from the end of June, as a consequence of which the plant cover is removed, permitting higher rates of sediment formation.

Rising, peaking and falling stages are distinguished in *Figs 3.1.1—16 to 18*. As indicated by the plots, the character of stages is of no influence on sediment transport. The circumstance that sediment transport at Tiszabő is essentially unaffected by the character of stages is an indication of the fact that sediment

734

transport in the Tisza river around Tiszabő is controlled primarily by the quantity of sediment entering the river rather than by changes in its sediment-transporting capacity.

In this context it should be noted that the increasing rate of sediment transport accompanying rising stages is not in contrast with the above statements. In fact, rising stages are a consequence of increasing discharges which, in turn, are preceded by rains of longer duration and higher intensity. On the other hand, the rate of sediment formation in the catchment increases in direct proportion with the magnitude and intensity of precipitation falling on the catchment. Consequently stages are symptomatically related to sediment concentrations and to sediment weights, since both are in causal relation with the magnitude of runoff draining from the catchment.

6. *Determination of the annual mean sediment transport.* It has been demonstrated in the foregoing that sediment concentration, as well as the weight of suspended sediment and bed load are related approximately to stages by power functions. It follows therefrom that the mean sediment transport over a particular period of time is not identical with the value corresponding to the mean stage over the period studied. The mean values are found preferably by considering the frequency of stages recorded in the gaging section.

The data on annual mean sediment transport are most relevant. Since, however, the values determined on the basis of data related to a single year depend obviously on the characteristics of the year selected, the annual mean values are determined preferably with data of a 10 year period. In selecting the 10 year period care should be taken that the ratio of wet, average and dry years should truly reflect average conditions in the catchment of the stream under consideration. In Hungary these criteria are satisfied by the decade from 1931 to 1940, so that calculations are always based on the data for this period.

The calculations related to annual mean sediment concentration, as well as weights of suspended and bed load have been based on the stage frequency data of the years 1931 to 1940 and are shown for the Dunaalmás section on the Danube in *Table 3.1.1 — 1.*

Information on certain local conditions may be utilized for calculating the annual mean and total sediment transport with less computation work than necessary in the foregoing method. In calculating the annual total suspended-sediment transport K. V. Razmukhina, for instance, adopted Karaushev's formula and divided the year into four periods, namely those of winter mean stages, spring floods, spring recession and summer-autumn mean stages.

7. *Checks on sediment transport relations by means of hydraulic conditions.* In *Sections 2.2.3* and *2.2.4* approximate functional relations have been introduced for describing sediment concentration, as well as suspended and bed load transport in terms of discharges, stages and mean velocities. The relations between stage and discharge, further between flow velocity and discharge or stage have also been discussed.

735

Table 3.1.1—1

Annual frequency of stages at Dunaalmás on the average for the years 1931 to 1940 and the corresponding sediment concentrations and transport rates based on the final relations

Stage at Dunaalmás, h [cm]	Frequency, n [days]	Concentration, C_k [kp/m³]	Suspended transport, G_s [kp/sec]	Bed load transport, G_B [kp/sec]	Concentration × frequency, 2. × 3.	Suspended transport × frequency, 2. × 4.	Bed load transport × frequency, 2. × 5.
1.	2.	3.	4.	5.	6.	7.	8.
640—649	0.2	0.500	2,350	34	0.1000	470	6.8
630—639	0.1	0.480	2,250	31	0.0480	225	3.1
620—629	0.3	0.460	2,150	29	0.0138	645	8.7
610—619	0.2	0.440	2,050	27	0.0880	410	5.4
600—609	0.2	0.420	1,950	24	0.0840	390	4.8
590—599	0.2	0.390	1,850	22	0.0780	370	4.4
580—589	0.2	0.372	1,750	20.5	0.0744	350	4.1
570—579	0.2	0.355	1,650	19	0.0710	330	3.8
560—569	0.0	0.337	1,550	18	—	—	—
550—559	0.5	0.320	1,450	16	0.1600	725	8.0
540—549	0.0	0.308	1,440	15	—	—	—
530—539	0.2	0.296	4,330	13.5	0.0592	266	2.7
520—529	0.1	0.284	1,220	12.5	0.0284	122	1.25
510—519	0.4	0.272	1,110	11	0.1090	444	4.4
500—509	0.4	0.260	1,000	10	0.1040	400	4.0
490—499	0.5	0.250	940	9.2	0.1250	470	4.6
480—489	1.1	0.235	875	8.4	0.2590	965	9.24
470—479	1.5	0.220	810	7.2	0.3300	1,215	10.8
460—469	1.8	0.205	750	7.0	0.3700	1,350	12.6
450—459	2.2	0.190	685	6.2	0.4180	1,510	13.64
440—449	1.9	0.180	620	5.4	0.3420	1,175	10.26
430—439	2.2	0.170	575	4.9	0.3740	1,620	10.78
420—429	2.7	0.160	530	4.5	0.4320	1,430	12.15
410—419	3.5	0.150	485	4.0	0.5250	1,700	14.0
400—409	6.7	0.140	440	3.6	0.9380	2,950	24.12
390—399	5.7	0.135	400	3.1	0.7700	2,280	17.67
380—389	7.4	0.127	370	2.8	0.9600	2,740	20.72
370—379	9.0	0.118	340	2.5	1.0600	3,060	22.5
360—369	11.6	0.109	310	2.2	1.2620	3,600	25.52
350—359	12.2	0.100	280	2.0	1.2200	3,420	24.4
340—349	11.8	0.094	260	1.8	1.1100	3,070	21.24
330—339	13.6	0.088	240	1.5	1.2000	3,270	20.4
320—329	10.6	0.082	215	1.3	0.8690	2,280	13,78
310—319	13.0	0.076	190	1.1	0.9870	2,470	14.1
300—309	17.5	0.070	165	0.96	1.1900	2,890	16.8
290—299	16.3	0.065	150	0.82	1.0600	2,450	13.366
280—289	14.6	0.060	135	0.7	0.8760	1,970	10.22
270—279	17.2	0.054	120	0.6	0.9290	2,060	10.32

Table 3.1.1—1 (Continued)

Stage at Duna-almás, h [cm]	Frequency, n [days]	Concentration, C_k [kp/m³]	Suspended transport, G_s [kp/sec]	Bed load transport, G_B [kp/sec]	Concentration × frequency, 2. × 3.	Suspended transport × frequency, 2. × 4.	Bed load transport × frequency, 2. × 5.
1.	2.	3.	4.	5.	6.	7.	8.
260—269	14.7	0.048	105	0.5	0.7060	1,540	7.35
250—259	14.5	0.042	90	0.4	0.6090	1,308	5.8
240—249	15.3	0.039	80	0.35	0.5970	1,224	5.355
230—239	16.6	0.036	70	0.28	0.5970	1,162	4.648
220—229	13.9	0.032	60	0.22	0.4450	834	3.058
210—219	13.0	0.028	49	0.18	0.3640	638	2.34
200—209	12.1	0.024	38	0.15	0.2900	460	1.815
190—199	12.9	0.021	34	0.12	0.2710	439	1.548
180—189	10.5	0.0188	30	0.096	0.1975	315	1.008
170—179	9.6	0.0167	25	0.072	0.1603	240	0.6912
160—169	11.6	0.0146	20	0.054	0.1687	232	0.6264
150—159	8.8	0.0125	15	0.04	0.1100	132	0.352
140—149	4.9	0.0110	13	0.03	0.0538	64	0.147
130—139	4.4	0.0093	11	0.022	0.0409	48	0.0968
120—129	3.2	0.0076	8.5	0.015	0.0243	27	0.048
110—119	3.5	0.0059	6	0.01	0.0207	21	0.035
100—109	1.7	0.0042	3.8	0.01	0.0071	6	0.017
90— 99	2.5	0.0032	2.6	0.01	0.0080	6	0.025
80— 89	2.3	0.0025	1.8	0.01	0.0057	4	0.023
70— 79	0.7	0.0018	1.1	0.01	0.0013	1	0.007
60— 69	0.0	0.0012	0.6	0.01	—	—	—
50— 59	0.1	0.0006	0.1	0.01	0.0001	—	0.001
40— 49	0.2	0.0001	0.1	0.01	0.0002	—	0.002
30— 39	0.2	0.0001	0.1	0.01	0.0002	—	0.002
20— 29	0.1	0.0001	0.1	0.01	0.0001	—	0.001
15— 19	0.2	0.0001	0.1	0.01	0.0002	—	0.002
	365.3				23.3019	63,433	449.6744

Average concentration $\qquad C_k = \dfrac{23.3019}{365.3} = 0.0639 \text{ kp/m}^3 \approx 0.064 \text{ kp/m}^3$

Average suspended-sediment transport $G_s = \dfrac{63,433}{365.3} = 173.8 \text{ kp/sec} \approx 174 \text{ kp/sec}$

Average bed load transport $\qquad G_B = \dfrac{449.6744}{365.3} = 1.23 \text{ kg/sec} \approx 1.2 \text{ kp/sec}$

$G_s = 5,492,000$ Mp/year $\approx 3,050,000$ m³/year

$G_B = \quad 38,500$ Mp/year $\approx \quad 21,600$ m³/year

47

Fig. 3.1.1—19. Discharge vs. Dunaalmás stages

Fig. 3.1.1—20. Relation of mean velocity to discharge and stages at the Dunaújváros section

By determining all the above relations on the basis of observation data, it will become possible to establish *condition equations* from the interrelations existing between them in view of the fact that not each of these is independent. It would be mistaken to expect the condition equations to be fully satisfied since the relations established can but approximately be looked upon as functional relations. Nevertheless the differences observed when solving the condition equations will indicate whether or not the introduction of approximate functional relations was justified.

Using the condition equations mentioned above similar checks have been performed for various stations on several rivers in Hungary. As examples for these the calculations related to a gage on each of the Danube, Tisza, Sajó and Hernád rivers will be shown subsequently.

a) *For the Dunaújváros section on the Danube* the stage-to-discharge, the flow-velocity-to-discharge and flow-velocity-to-stage relations have been plotted in *Figs 3.1.1—19* and *3.1.1—20*. On the other hand, the relations of sediment concentration, as well as suspended and bed load transport to stages, discharges and velocities have been described in *Section 3.1.2* (see *Tables 3.1.2—2* and *3.1.2—3*).

Using these data *suspended sediment transport* will be considered first.

The fundamental relations expressed in Eqs (2.2.4—1) to (2.2.4—9) are available:

$$C_k = dQ^i = 10^{-10} \cdot 1.23 \cdot Q^{2.57}$$

$$G_s = pQ^j = 10^{-10} \cdot 1.23 \cdot Q^{3.57}$$

$$C_k = th^n = 0.0032 \cdot h^{3.03}$$

$$G_s = uh^g = 1.50 \cdot h^{4.45}$$

$$C_k = \gamma v_k^\delta = 0.063 \cdot v_k^{3.85}$$

$$G_s = \alpha v_k^\beta = 160 \cdot v_k^{6.25}$$

$$Q = eh^r = 650 \cdot h^{1.24}$$

$$v_k = \lambda Q^\sigma = 0.0245 \cdot Q^{0.48}$$

$$v_k = \phi h^\psi = 0.53 \cdot h^{0.6}$$

Since the nine coefficients and nine exponents involved in the fundamental equations are now available, the condition equations, Eqs (2.2.4—11) to (2.2.4—22), numbered from 1 to 12 are as follows:

1. $$d = p = 10^{-10} \cdot 1.23$$

2. $$j = l + 1 = 2.57 + 1 = 3.57$$

3. $$te = 10^{-3} \cdot 3.20 \cdot 650 = 2.08$$

$$pe^j = 10^{-10} \cdot 1.23 \cdot 650^{3.57} = 1.38$$

4. $$n + r = 3\ 03 + 1.24 = 4.27$$

$$r \cdot j = 1.24 \cdot 3,57 = 4.42$$

5.
$$te = 2.08$$
$$u = 1.50$$

6.
$$n + r = 4.27$$
$$g = 4.45$$

7.
$$\alpha\lambda^\beta = 160 \cdot 0.0245^{6.25} = 10^{-8} \cdot 1.395$$
$$p = 10^{-10} \cdot 1.23$$

8.
$$\beta\sigma = 6.25 \cdot 0.48 = 3.00$$
$$j = 3.57$$

9.
$$\alpha\phi^\beta = 160 \cdot 0.53^{6.25} = 3.05$$
$$u = 1.50$$

10.
$$\beta\phi = 6.25 \cdot 0.6 = 3.75$$
$$g = 4.45$$

11.
$$\gamma\left(\frac{1}{\lambda}\right)^{\frac{1}{\sigma}} = 0.063 \left(\frac{1}{0.0245}\right)^{\frac{1}{0.48}} = 144$$
$$\alpha = 160$$

12.
$$\delta + \frac{1}{\sigma} = 3.85 + \frac{1}{0.48} = 5.93$$
$$\beta = 6.25$$

The examination of the condition equations will reveal that although the observation data used for establishing the relations show an appreciable scattering, it is still permissible to introduce approximate functional relations for describing suspended-sediment transport in the Dunaújváros gaging section on the Danube.

Concerning the differences observed in the condition equations it should be noted that in the graphical determination of the fundamental relations the magnitudes of p and d are extremely sensitive to the slightest variation in slope. The great difference observed at condition equation 7, i.e. $p = \alpha\lambda^\beta$ is, in general, due to this fact.

Introducing into Eqs (2.2.3 − 1) to (2.2.3 − 3) *on bed load transport* the values given in *Section 3.1.2.* and remembering that the last three of the fundamental relations listed in connection with suspended sediment transport apply here as well, the following six fundamental relations are written.

740

$$G_B = u_1 h^{g_1} = 10^3 \cdot 21 \cdot h^{3.055}$$

$$G_B = p_1 Q^{j_1} = 10^{-8} \cdot 1.32 \cdot Q^{2.245}$$

$$G_B = \alpha_1 v_k^{\beta_1} = 0.5 \cdot v_k^{6.667}$$

$$Q = eh^r = 650 \cdot h^{1.24}$$

$$v_k = \lambda Q^\sigma = 0.0245 \cdot Q^{0.48}$$

$$v_k = \phi h^\psi = 0.53 \cdot h^{0.6}$$

Since the six coefficients and six exponents involved in the fundamental equations, Eqs (2.2.3−7) to (2.2.3−12) are now available, the condition equations numbered from 1 to 6 are as follows:

1.
$$p_1 \cdot e^{j_1} = 10^{-8} \cdot 1.32 \cdot 650^{2.245} = 0.0279$$
$$u_1 = 0.021$$

2.
$$r \cdot j_1 = 1.24 \cdot 2.245 = 2.782$$
$$g_1 = 3.055$$

3.
$$\alpha_1 \phi^{\beta_1} = 0.5 \cdot 0.53^{6.667} = 0.0072$$
$$u_1 = 21 \cdot 10^{-3} = 0.021$$

4.
$$\beta_1 \phi = 6.667 \cdot 0.6 = 4.0$$
$$g_1 = 3.055$$

5.
$$\alpha_1 \lambda^{\beta_1} = 0.5 \cdot 0.0245^{6.667} = 10^{-10} \cdot 1.55$$
$$p_1 = 10^{-8} \cdot 1.32$$

6.
$$\beta_1 \sigma = 6.667 \cdot 0.48 = 3.2$$
$$j_1 = 2.245$$

Fig. 3.1.1−21. Discharge at Tápé vs. Szeged stages

Fig. 3.1.1−22. Mean velocity at the Tápé section related to stages at Szeged and to discharge at Tápé

The condition equations indicating the significance of hydraulic relations for bed load transport are, consequently, much less satisfied than those applying to suspended-sediment transport. In view of the difficulties encountered in bed load observations and consequently of the appreciably wider scattering of the observation points this is entirely logical. In the absence of more accurate devices and methods of observation, on the basis of the condition equations it is again assumed that bed load transport can be described, though less accurately, by functional relations.

b) The stage-to-discharge, the velocity-to-discharge and the velocity-to-stage relations for the *Tápé gaging section on the Tisza river* are plotted in *Figs 3.1.1 − 21* and *3.1.1 − 22*. The relations of sediment concentration, suspended and bed load transport to stages, discharges and flow velocities, have been established in *Section 3.1.2* (see *Tables 3.1.2 − 4* and *3.1.2 − 5*).

It should be noted that the results of sediment observations at Tápé have been related to stages on the Szeged gage, so that the stages mentioned are always those on the Szeged gage.

As in the example quoted for the Danube, with reference to the relations derived in *Section 3.1.2 for suspended sediment* transport at Tápé, the following nine fundamental relations are written:

$$C_k = 10^{-5} \cdot 2.6 \cdot Q^{1.44}$$

$$G_s = 10^{-5} \cdot 2.6 \cdot Q^{2.44}$$

$$C_k = 0.0088 \cdot h_1^{2.18}$$

$$G_s = 0.46 \cdot h_1^{3.8}$$

$$C_k = 0.57 \cdot v_k^{2.3}$$

$$G_s = 980 \cdot v_k^{4.65}$$

$$Q = 72 \cdot h_1^{1.32}$$

$$v_k = 0.012 \cdot Q^{0.62}$$

$$v_k = 0.157 \cdot h_1^{0.8}$$

Since the nine coefficients and nine exponents involved in the fundamental equations are now available, the condition equations, Eqs (2.2.4−11) to (2.2.4−22), numbered from 1 to 12 are as follows:

1. $\qquad d = p = 10^{-5} \cdot 2.6$

2. $\qquad j = l + 1 = 1.44 + 1 = 2.44$

3. $\qquad te = 0.088 \cdot 72 = 0.634$

   $\qquad pe^j = 10^{-5} \cdot 2.6 \cdot 72^{2.44} = 0.871$

4. $\qquad n + r = 2.18 + 1.32 = 3.50$

   $\qquad rj = 1.32 \cdot 2.44 = 3.22$

5. $\qquad te = 0.634$

   $\qquad u = 0.46$

6. $\qquad n + r = 3.50$

   $\qquad g = 3.80$

7. $\qquad \alpha \lambda^\beta = 980 \cdot 0.012^{4.65} = 10^{-6} \cdot 1.15$

   $\qquad p = 10^{-5} \cdot 2.6$

8. $\qquad \beta \sigma = 4.65 \cdot 0.62 = 2.97$

   $\qquad j = 2.44$

9.
$$\alpha\phi^\beta = 980 \cdot 0.157^{4.65} = 0.355$$

$$u = 0.46$$

10.
$$\beta\psi = 4.65 \cdot 0.8 = 3.72$$

$$g = 3.80$$

11.
$$\gamma\left(\frac{1}{\lambda}\right)^{\frac{1}{\sigma}} = 0.57\left(\frac{1}{0.012}\right)^{\frac{1}{0.62}} = 687$$

$$\alpha = 980$$

12.
$$\delta + \frac{1}{\sigma} = 2.3 + \frac{1}{0.62} = 3.97$$

$$\beta = 4.65$$

The condition equations show rather small differences. The condition $p = \alpha\lambda^\beta$ forms again an exception but here a major difference is almost unavoidable in the determination of relations.

Introducing the values given in *Section 3.1.2* into Eqs (2.2.3−1) to (2.2.3−3) on bed load transport and remembering that the last three of the fundamental relations listed in connection with suspended-sediment transport apply here too, the following six fundamental relations are written:

$$G_B = 10^{-3} \cdot 1.3 \cdot h^{3.42}$$

$$G_B = 10^{-10} \cdot 8 \cdot Q^{2.74}$$

$$G_B = 0.35 \cdot v_k^{4.59}$$

$$Q = 72 \cdot h_1^{1.32}$$

$$v_k = 0.012 \cdot Q^{0.62}$$

$$v_k = 0.157 \cdot h_1^{0.8}$$

Since the six coefficients and six exponents involved in the fundamental equations are now available, the condition equations, Eqs (2.2.3−7) to (2.2.3−12) numbered from 1 to 6 are as follows:

1.
$$p_1 e^{j_1} = 10^{-10} \cdot 8 \cdot 72^{2.74} = 0.0001$$

$$u_1 = 0.0013$$

2.
$$r \cdot j_1 = 1.32 \cdot 2.74 = 3.62$$

$$g_1 = 3.42$$

744

Fig. 3.1.1−23. Discharge vs. stages at Kazincbarcika

3.
$$\alpha_1\phi^{\beta_1} = 0.35 \cdot 0.157^{4.59} = 0.000077$$

$$u_1 = 0.0013$$

4.
$$\beta_1\psi = 4.59 \cdot 0.8 = 3.67$$

$$g_1 = 3.42$$

5.
$$\alpha_1\lambda^{\beta_1} = 0.35 \cdot 0.012^{4.59} = 10^{-10} \cdot 5.3$$

$$p_1 = 10^{-10} \cdot 8$$

6.
$$\beta_1\sigma = 4.59 \cdot 0.62 = 2.845$$

$$j_1 = 2.74$$

Except for $\alpha_1\phi^{\beta} = u_1$ and $p_1e^{j_1} = u_1$, the degree of approximation indicated by the six condition equations may be regarded as rather good.

As in the case of Dunaújváros, the example of the Tápé gage on the Tisza also shows that the condition equations representing the significance of the hydraulic relations are much less satisfied in the case of bed load transport than in the case of suspended sediment. The use of approximate functional relations is neve rtheless considered permissible for the Tápé gage although the approximation is rather a crude one.

c) The stage-to-discharge, the velocity-to-discharge and velocity-to-stage relations for *the Kazincbarcika gaging section on the Sajó river* have been plotted in *Figs 3.1.1−23* and *3.1.1−24*. The relations of sediment concentration, suspended and bed load transport to stages, discharges and flow velocities have been established in *Section 3.1.2.* (see *Tables 3.1.2−6* and *3.1.2−7*).

Using these values the relations *on suspended sediment transport* will be examined first.

Fig. 3.1.1−24. Mean velocity related to discharge and stages at the Kazincbarcika section

The fundamental equations, Eqs (2.2.4−1) to (2.2.4−9) are available:

$$C_k = 10^{-4} \cdot 1.5 \cdot Q^{2.33}$$

$$G_s = 10^{-4} \cdot 1.5 \cdot Q^{3.33}$$

$$C_k = 0.12 \cdot h^{4.02}$$

$$G_s = 1.0 \cdot h^{6.66}$$

$$C_k = 0.18 \cdot v_k^{2.07}$$

$$G_s = 11.5 \cdot v_k^{4.55}$$

$$Q = 16 \cdot h^{2.22}$$

$$v_k = 0.086 \cdot Q^{0.64}$$

$$v_k = 0.56 \cdot h^{1.48}$$

Since the nine coefficients and nine exponents involved in the fundamenta equations are now available, the condition equations, Eqs (2.2.4−11) to (2.2.4−22), numbered from 1 to 12 are as follows:

1. $$d = p = 1.5 \cdot 10^{-4}$$

2. $$j = l + 1 = 2.33 + 1 = 3.33$$

3. $$te = 0.12 \cdot 16 = 1.92$$

$$pe^j = 1.5 \cdot 10^{-4} \cdot 16^{3.33} = 1.53$$

746

4.
$$n + r = 4.02 + 2.22 = 6.24$$

$$r \cdot j = 2.22 \cdot 3.33 = 7.39$$

5.
$$te = 0.12 \cdot 16 = 1.92$$

$$u = 1.0$$

6.
$$n + r = 4.02 + 2.22 = 6.24$$

$$g = 6.66$$

7.
$$\alpha\lambda^\beta = 11.5 \cdot 0.86^{4.55} = 10^{-4} \cdot 1.63$$

$$p = 1.5 \cdot 10^{-4}$$

8.
$$\beta\sigma = 4.55 \cdot 0.64 = 2.91$$

$$j = 3.33$$

9.
$$\alpha\phi^\beta = 11.5 \cdot 0.56^{4.55} = 0.82$$

$$u = 1.0$$

10.
$$\beta\psi = 4.55 \cdot 1.48 = 6.73$$

$$g = 6.66$$

11.
$$\gamma\left(\frac{1}{\lambda}\right)^{\frac{1}{\sigma}} = 0.18\left(\frac{1}{0.086}\right)^{\frac{1}{0.64}} = 8.31$$

$$\alpha = 11.5$$

12.
$$\delta + \frac{1}{\sigma} = 2.07 + \frac{1}{0.64} = 3.63$$

$$\beta = 4.55$$

An examination of the values obtained from the condition equations will show that the differences in the Kazincbarcika section are smaller than those in the Dunaújváros and Tápé sections on the Danube and the Tisza, respectively. No explanation can be offered for this fact since hydraulic relations are expected to show a better agreement on major streams.

Introducing the values given in *Section 3.1.2* into Eqs (2.2.3−1) to (2.2.3−3) *on bed load transport* and remembering that the last three of the fundamental relations listed in connection with suspended-sediment transport apply here, too, the following six fundamental relations are written:

$$G_B = 10^{-3} \cdot 5.2 \cdot h^{5.0}$$

$$G_B = 10^{-7} \cdot 5.2 \cdot Q^{3.28}$$

$$G_B = 0.25 \cdot v_k^{6.25}$$

$$Q = 16 \cdot h^{2.22}$$

$$v_k = 0.086 \cdot Q^{0.64}$$

$$v_k = 0.56 \cdot h^{1.48}$$

Since the six coefficients and six exponents involved in the fundamental equations are now available, the condition equations, Eqs (2.2.3−7) to (2.2.3−12), numbered from one to six are as follows

1. $$p_1 e^{j_1} = 5.2 \cdot 10^{-7} \cdot 16^{3.28} = 10^{-3} \cdot 4.63$$

$$u_1 = 10^{-3} \cdot 5.2$$

2. $$r \cdot j_1 = 2.22 \cdot 3.28 = 7.28$$

$$g_1 = 5.0$$

3. $$\alpha_1 \phi^{\beta_1} = 0.25 \cdot 0.56^{6.25} = 10^{-3} \cdot 6.67$$

$$u_1 = 10^{-3} \cdot 5.2$$

4. $$\beta_1 \psi = 6.25 \cdot 1.48 = 9.25$$

$$g_1 = 5.0$$

5. $$\alpha_1 \lambda^{\beta_1} = 0.25 \cdot 0.086^{6.25} = 5.47 \cdot 10^{-8}$$

$$p_1 = 5.2 \cdot 10^{-7}$$

6. $$\beta_1 \sigma = 6.24 \cdot 0.64 = 4.0$$

$$j_1 = 3.28$$

The differences observable in condition equations 2 and 4 are especially conspicuous. The difference in condition equation 5 is even greater but, as mentioned before, its significance is slight, since the magnitude of p_1 is highly sensitive to small changes in slope.

d) The stage-to-discharge, the velocity-to-discharge and velocity-to-stage relations *for the Hidasnémeti section on the Hernád* river have been plotted in *Figs 3.1.1 −25, 3.1.1−26* and *3.1.1−27*, respectively. Moreover, the relations of sediment concentration, suspended and bed load transport to discharges and flow velocities have been established in *Section 3.1.2* (see *Tables 3.1.2−6* and *3.1.2−7*).

748

Fig. 3.1.1−25. Discharge vs. stages at Hidasnémeti

Using these values the relations *on suspended sediment transport* will be examined first.

The fundamental equations, Eqs (2.2.4−1) to (2.2.4−9) are available:

$$C_k = 10^{-4} \cdot 4.2 \cdot Q^{1.63}$$

$$G_s = 10^{-4} \cdot 4.2 \cdot Q^{2.63}$$

$$C_k = 0.011 \cdot h_1^{4.85}$$

$$G_s = 0.120 \cdot h_1^{7.1}$$

$$C_k = 1.11 \cdot v_k^{3.82}$$

$$G_s = 86 \cdot v_k^{5.08}$$

$$Q = 8 \cdot h_1^{2.85}$$

$$v_k = 0.085 \cdot Q^{0.55}$$

$$v_k = 0.26 \cdot h_1^{1.53}$$

Since the nine coefficients and nine exponents involved in the fundamental equations are now available, the condition equations, Eqs (2.2.4−11) to (2.2.4−22) are as follows:

1. $\qquad d = p = 10^{-4} \cdot 4.2$

2. $\qquad j = l + 1 = 1.63 + 1 = 2.63$

3. $\qquad te = 0.011 \cdot 8 = 0.088$

$$pe^j = 10^{-4} \cdot 4.2 \cdot 8^{2.63} = 0.125$$

749

Fig. 3.1.1—26. Mean velocity vs. stages at Hidasnémeti

4. $$n + r = 4.85 + 2.85 = 7.7$$
$$r \cdot j = 2.85 \cdot 2.63 = 7.5$$

5. $$te = 0.088$$
$$u = 0.12$$

6. $$n + r = 7.7$$
$$g = 7.1$$

7. $$\alpha\lambda^{\beta} = 86 \cdot 0.085^{5.08} = 10^{-4} \cdot 3.1$$
$$p = 10^{-4} \cdot 4.2$$

8. $$\beta\sigma = 5.08 \cdot 0.55 = 2.08$$
$$j = 2.63$$

9. $$\alpha\phi^{\beta} = 86 \cdot 0.26^{5.08} = 0.091$$
$$u = 0.12$$

10. $$\beta\psi = 5.08 \cdot 1.53 = 7.77$$
$$g = 7.1$$

11. $$\gamma\left(\frac{1}{\lambda}\right)^{\frac{1}{\sigma}} = 1.11 \left(\frac{1}{0.085}\right)^{\frac{1}{0.55}} = 99.3$$

12. $$\delta + \frac{1}{\sigma} = 3.82 + \frac{1}{0.55} = 5.64$$
$$\beta = 5.08$$

750

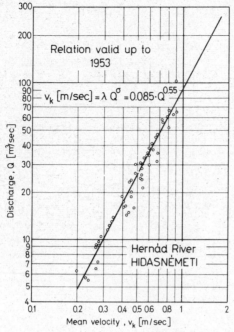

Fig. 3.1.1—27. Mean velocity vs. discharge at Hidasnémeti

It is of interest to note that, in contrast to the examples mentioned for the Danube, for the Tisza and the Sajó rivers, the differences obtained for the Hidasnémeti section are substantially smaller.

Introducing the values given in *Section 3.1.2* into Eqs (2.2.3−1) to (2.2.3−3) *on bed load transport* and remembering that the last three of the fundamental relations listed in connection with suspended-sediment transport apply here, too, the following six fundamental relations are written:

$$G_B = 10^{-4} \cdot 3.3 \cdot h_1^{7.82}$$

$$G_B = 10^{-6} \cdot 1.7 \cdot Q^{2.66}$$

$$G_B = 0.37 \, v_k^{5.35}$$

$$Q = 8 \cdot h_1^{2.85}$$

$$v_k = 0.085 \cdot Q^{0.55}$$

$$v_k = 0.26 \cdot h_1^{1.53}$$

Since the six coefficients and six exponents involved in the fundamental equations are now available, the condition equations, Eqs (2.2.3−7) to (2.2.3−12), numbered from 1 to 6 are as follows:

1. $$p_1 e^{j_1} = 10^{-6} \cdot 1.7 \cdot 8^{2.66} = 10^{-4} \cdot 4.3$$
$$u_1 = 10^{-4} \cdot 3.3$$

2. $$r \cdot j_1 = 2.85 \cdot 2.66 = 7.58$$
$$g_1 = 7.82$$

3. $$\alpha_1 \phi^{\beta_1} = 0.37 \cdot 0.26^{5.35} = 10^{-4} \cdot 5.6$$
$$u_1 = 10^{-4} \cdot 3.3$$

4. $$\beta_1 \psi = 5.35 \cdot 1.53 = 8.18$$
$$g_1 = 7.82$$

5. $$\alpha_1 \lambda^{\beta_1} = 0.37 \cdot 0.085^{5.35} = 10^{-7} \cdot 6.9$$
$$p_1 = 10^{-6} \cdot 1.7$$

6. $$\beta_1 \sigma = 5.35 \cdot 0.55 = 2.94$$
$$j_1 = 2.66$$

Except for the condition $p_1 = \alpha_1 \lambda^{\beta_1}$, the condition equations will be seen to be satisfied with conspicuously small differences, in contrast to the gaging stations of Dunaújváros, Tápé and Kazincbarcika.

As demonstrated by the examples quoted here the introduction of two-variable approximate functional relations is justified on the water courses in Hungary for calculating both suspended and bed load transport.

8. *Variations in sediment concentration and flow velocity with depth and cross-section.* For a better understanding of the movement of sediment in water coursel it is found desirable to obtain information on the distribution of sediment cons centration over depth and over the cross-section. For this purpose in the individua-verticals within a cross-section it is often necessary to obtain, instead of depth-integrated samples instantaneous point samples from different depths. Using the results of point samples and current meter measurements performed at the same time in these points the distribution of concentration and flow velocity can be represented in a graphical form.

The results of observations made on the 29th July, 1942 in the Záhony cross-section of the Tisza are shown in *Fig. 3.1.1 – 28.* From the vertical distribution of concentration the mean concentrations in the individual verticals were determined, and it was concluded that in the Záhony cross-section the concentration value equal to the mean concentration occurs in general at 55 to 72 per cent of depth below the surface. The observations at Záhony have corroborated thus the generally accepted rule, according to which the mean concentration occurs at six-tenths of depth.

The lines connecting identical velocities and concentrations in the Záhony cross-section are shown in *Fig. 3.1.1—29.* Velocities and concentrations alike show an irregular pattern. In the course of sediment investigations similar patterns have been plotted for a number of observations, but no regularity could be detected.

Observations similar to those at Záhony were made on the 22th July, 1942 at Rázompuszta (Tiszalök) with the results shown in *Figs 3.1.1—30* and *3.1.1—31.* No regularities could be detected here either. Mean concentration values occurred at 58 to 65% of depth in even better agreement with the rule of thumb on the six-tenths of depth. It should be noted however that, considering several observations, the results are far less consistent.

9. *Formulae describing the variation in sediment concentration with depth.* The variation in sediment concentration with depth has been determined on the basis of observations made on the 25th March, 1949, at Szeged. The variation in concentration with depth has been examined in vertical V of the cross-section shown in *Fig. 3.1.1—32.*

In vertical V the total depth was $D = 6.64$ m. Denoting by y the distance above the bottom, the following velocities are obtained from the data sheet:

$(D - y) =$	$v =$
$= 0$	$= 0.90$ m/sec
$= 0.30$ m	$= 0.92$ m/sec
$= 0.80$ m	$= 0.91$ m/sec
$= 2.00$ m	$= 0.91$ m/sec
$= 4.00$ m	$= 0.83$ m/sec
$= 5.20$ m	$= 0.74$ m/sec
$= 6.20$ m	$= 0.53$ m/sec
$= 6.40$ m	$= 0.47$ m/sec
$= 6.64$ m	bottom.

In vertical V sediment concentration was measured at four different depths:

$(D - y) =$	$C =$
$= 0.80$ m	$= 788$ p/m^3
$= 2.60$ m	$= 800$ p/m^3
$= 4.40$ m	$= 823$ p/m^3
$= 6.24$ m	$= 954$ p/m^3

The value $a = 0.40$ m has been adopted and thus $C_a = 954$ p/m^3 $= 0.954$ kp per m^3.

Each instantaneous sediment sample has been analysed for size distribution, and even the average diameter of the sediment material representative of the entire vertical has been determined. This was found to be $d_g = 0.035$ mm.

48

ZÁHONY (Survey Section No. 55)

Date of measurement: 29. 7. 1942   Stage: −192 cm

Verticals of measurement

I   II   III   IV   V   VI VII

Distance from
left-side section stone 100   150   200   m

Level at survey

Concentration and velocity curves

Fig. 3.1.1−28. Vertical distribution of velocities and sediment concentrations at the Záhony
section of the Tisza river, according to data measured on 29 July 1942

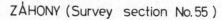

ZÁHONY (Survey section No. 55)

Date of measurement: 29. 7. 1942	Discharge	132 m³/sec
Stage [cm]	192	Mean velocity in the section	0.36 m/sec
Slope [m/km]	0.0894	Mean concenration in the section	0.098 kp/m³

Velocity distribution

Distance from left-hand section stone

Mean velocity, V_k = 0.24 0.34 0.38 0.28 0.48 0.42 0.38 0.26 [m/sec]

Concentration distribution

Mean concentration, C_k = 0.091 0.096 0.112 0.096 0.106 0.100 0.111 [kp/m³]

Fig. 3.1.1—29. Distribution of velocities and sediment concentrations at the Záhony section, according to the data measured on 29 July 1942

As a first step an attempt will be made to calculate the variation in total concentration characterizing the vertical on the basis of the average particle diameter $d_g = 0.035$ mm.

The velocities observed at different depths are used in plotting the velocity profile shown in *Fig. 3.1.1—32a.* In doing so a very slight difference results from assuming the highest velocity to occur at the surface, i.e. that the velocity gradient becomes zero at the surface. From the velocity profile the magnitude of the velocity gradient at different depths is determined graphically and the mixing coefficient ε'_h is calculated according to Eq. (1.3.4—45). The variation in ε'_h with depth is shown in *Fig. 3.1.1—32b.* Once the variation with depth of the sediment mixing coefficient is available, the variation of $1/\varepsilon'_h$ is plotted (in *Fig. 3.1.1—32c).* The value of the integral in Eq. (1.3.4—29) at any arbitrary depth is given by the area shown on the graph in *Fig. 3.1.1—32c* between depth a and the depth under consideration. Eq. (1.3.4—29) is used for calculating concentration at several depths, and the concentration profile related to the average diameter is plotted with a dashed line as in *Fig. 3.1.1—32d.*

By connecting the empty circles indicating instantaneous concentration values, the observed concentration profile shown by the continuous line is obtained.

48*

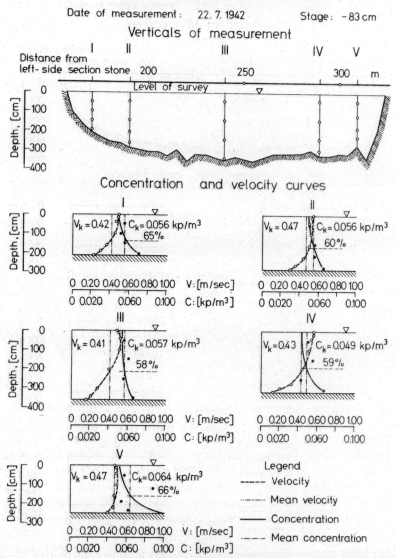

TISZALÖK (Survey Section No. 97)

Date of measurement: 22. 7. 1942   Stage: −83 cm

Fig. 3.1.1−30. Vertical distribution of velocities and sediment concentrations at the Tiszalök section, according to data measured on 22 July 1942

If the sediment mixing coefficient is assumed to be constant over the entire depth, then $1/\varepsilon_h'$ involved in Eq. (2.3.4−44) is constant with 0.342 m^2/kp sec, as obtained graphically from *Fig. 3.1.1−32c*, and the concentration profile can again be calculated. The concentration profile obtained using Eq. (1.3.4−44) is plotted with a dash-dotted line in *Fig. 3.1.1−32d*.

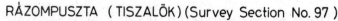

RÁZOMPUSZTA (TISZALÖK)(Survey Section No. 97)

Date of measurement 22. 7. 1942   Discharge   218 m³/sec
Stage , [cm]   - 83   Mean velocity   0.44 m/sec
Slope, [m/km]   0.0234   Mean concentration   0.055 kp/m³

Velocity , v [m/sec]

Mean velocity, V_k=0.39 0.42   0.47   0.48   0.41   0.48   0.43   0.47 0.28 [m/sec]

Concentration , C [kp/m³]

Mean concentration, C_k=0.056 0.055   0.057   0.049   0.064 [kp/m³]

Fig. 3.1.1—31. Distribuution of velocities and sediment concenιrations at the Tiszalök section, according to data measured on 29 July 1942

The difference between the two theoretical curves is seen to be insignificant. On the other hand, the theoretical curves differ by 2 to 6% from the observed concentration profile. Since these differences are within the accuracy of measurement, it is concluded that, as mentioned in the theoretical treatment, in the case of fine suspended sediment material, the concentration profile can indeed be calculated in terms of the average diameter of the entire sediment material.

The difference between the theoretical and observed concentration profiles will, obviously, be less if considerations are restricted to the variation of concentration related to a certain size fraction.

The concentration profiles have been determined for particles greater than 0.03, but smaller than 0.04 mm. As indicated by *Fig. 3.1.1—32e,* the differences are actually much smaller. It should be noted that concentrations apply in this case to the fraction between the two limits adopted. The origin of the concentration profiles was in this case the concentration $C_a = 76.3$ p/m³ $= 0.0763$ kp/m³.

Fig. 3.1.1—32. Concentration curves in the fifth vertical of the Szeged section of the Tisza river, according to data measured on 25 March 1949

For the sake of clarity the concentration profiles shown in *Fig. 3.1.1—32e* for the size fraction between 0.03 and 0.04 mm, i.e. having an average diameter of 0.035 mm, have been reproduced to a larger scale in *Fig. 3.1.1—33*.

The concentration profile corresponding to the observation data is again indicated by the continuous line whereas the concentration profiles calculated according to Eqs (1.3.4—29) and (1.3.4—44) have been entered by dashed and dash-dotted lines, respectively.

In combination with *Fig. 1.3.4—4* Vanoni's method has also been used in calculating the concentration profile for this size fraction. Since according to Vanoni the origin of the concentration profile is at $a_1 = 0.05 D = 0.332$ m, the concentration values serving as the basis of calculation have been obtained at this depth from the observed concentration profile. The concentration $C_a = 0.0778$ kp per m³ has been obtained in this manner. The concentration profile obtained after Vanoni is shown by the dotted line in *Fig. 3.1.1—33*.

The variation in concentration with depth is finally calculated with Eq. (1.3. 4—57) suggested by the Collaborating Agencies. For this calculation the concentration profile has been extended beyond the last observation point at $a = 0.40$ m above the bottom down to the bottom itself and the concentration

758

Fig. 3.1.1—33. Vertical distribution of concentration of 0.03 to 0.04 mm fraction in the fifth vertical of the Szeged section of the Tisza river, according to data measured on 25 March 1949

value $C_0 = 0.08$ kp/m^3 has been adopted in the calculations as the bottom concentration. The concentration profile obtained with Eq. (1.3.4—57) is represented in *Fig. 3.1.1—33* by the dash-dot-dot curve.

By comparing the different theoretical concentration profiles with one another and with the profile actually observed the curves traced for discrete size fractions show even smaller differences than that between the profiles for total concentration and average particle size in *Fig. 3.1.1—32d*. Logically, even in the case of concentration profiles traced in this way for individual fractions, fair agreement should be expected at fine fractions only.

In *Fig. 3.1.1—34* the concentration profiles are determined for material graded from 0.06 to 0.07 mm, i.e. having an average particle diameter of 0.065 mm. The notation used in *Fig. 3.1.1—33* has been adopted for representing the concentration profiles determined by the different theories or methods. The starting concentration values for this fraction are also from the concentration profile plotted on the basis of observation results. For this coarser fraction the differences will be seen to have become greater.

Fig. 3.1.1—35 shows the concentration profiles for the material graded from 0.1 to 0.2 mm, i.e. of an average particle diameter of 0.15 mm. The differences between the concentration profiles calculated for this size fraction by different methods are substantially greater than in the case of the two finer fractions con-

759

Fig. 3.1.1—34. Vertical distribution of concentration of 0.06 to 0.07 mm fraction in the fifth vertical of the Szeged section of the Tisza river, according to data measured on 25 March 1949

sidered before. From this it seems safe to conclude that, regardless of the method of calculation, an appreciably poorer accuracy is to be expected for coarse fractions of suspended sediment.

For the three size fractions mentioned before, i.e. for average diameters 0.035, 0.065 and 0.15 mm, the mean concentration in the vertical has also been determined. For this purpose a graphical method based on the observed concentration profile, as well as *Fig. 1.3.8—1* based on Eq. (1.3.8—2) have been used. The straight lines corresponding to the two mean concentrations are entered in *Figs 3.1.1—33, 3.1.1—34* and *3.1.1—35*. As will be seen from the three figures, the finer the sediment material, the closer the agreement between the mean concentrations obtained on the basis of observations and theoretical calculations.

The accuracy attainable in computing the concentration profile depends on the reliability with which the hydraulic factors are measured. In fact, a closer scrutiny of the methods used for the theoretical calculation of concentration profiles will show several hydraulic factors of the cross-section under consideration to be involved in the calculations. Of the hydraulic factors affecting suspended-sediment transport the slope S, the fall velocities ω, and the depth D are of special interest, and the magnitude of the acceptable error in the measurement thereof is of considerable importance. The magnitude of the error considered acceptable

760

Variation in the concentration of 0.15 mm
particles with depth

Fig. 3.1.1—35. Vertical distribution of concentration of 0.1 to 0.2 mm fraction in the fifth vertical of the Szeged section of the Tisza river, according to data measured on 25 March 1949

in measuring slopes, fall velocities and depths with a certain required accuracy can be examined preferably with the help of Velikanov's method. According to several similar studies the permissible errors in measuring slopes, fall velocity and depths are 6%, 7% and 17%, respectively, if it is desired to estimate sediment concentration with a maximum error of $\pm 3\%$. The measurement of depths with an accuracy of 17% should present no difficulties. The same applies to fall velocities since, at the small particle sizes comprising the suspended sediment material, differences greater than 8% are unlikely to occur. With slopes, however, the situation is different. The error of slope measurements in the field are known to attain often 50% or more. This is why the methods in which the actual slope plays an important role are least reliable for estimating concentration.

From the studies on the distribution of concentration with depth it is concluded that results in closest agreement with field observations can be obtained with Eq. (1.3.4—57) for fine fractions and with Eq. (1.3.4—44) for coarse ones.

3.1.2. SEDIMENT TRANSPORT IN WATER COURSES IN HUNGARY

The water courses in Hungary belong, without exception, to the Danube river system. As will be seen from *Fig. 3.1.2−1* showing the catchment areas of the major streams in Europe, the Danube catchment from the headwater reach down to the mouth at the Black Sea is highly variable, some parts consisting of the high mountains of the Alps and the Carpathian range, other parts including plains of low-land character.

The countries sharing the Danube basin and the major tributaries are shown in detail in *Fig. 3.1.2−2*. The Hungarian reach of the Danube, together with the other water courses of Hungary, can be seen to flow through a plain surrounded by the Carpathian range where only a minor part is covered by hills of moderate height and mild contour.

Sediment transport in the rivers of Hungary does not display extreme values unlike some major rivers in other countries. The two largest rivers in Hungary, namely the Danube and the Tisza, usually carry sediment volumes smaller than the average. It should be noted here that the section of the Danube upstream

Fig. 3.1.2−1. Catchment areas of major European streams

of Gönyü is exceptional in certain respects, when compared with the section downstream. In fact, over the section upstream of Gönyü the volume of bed load may attain very high values. According to the results of observations carried out thus far, the water course carrying the highest sediment load in Hungary is the Hernád river, followed by the Sajó and Szamos which transport considerable amounts of sediment at times of floods.*

As pointed out in both the "Author's Preface" and the "Introduction", a few data on sediment transport in Hungarian rivers are believed to be of interest.

The water courses in Hungary and the network of sediment observation stations are shown in *Fig. 3.1.2 − 3*, while the results of sediment observations on Hungarian rivers up to the end of 1968 are compiled in *Table 3.1.2 − 1*.

As will be seen from the Table, 5084 observations were made before the end of 1968 on fifteen rivers. Except for a few observations on the Tisza and Sajó, most observations fall into the period following 1949. Sediment observations are among the responsibilities of the Research Institute for Water Resources Development, Budapest, where the author had opportunity to participate actively in their organization and performance.

It should be added that the data from altogether 30 stations on ten rivers out of the 15 water courses and 67 observing stations figuring in *Table 3.1.2 − 1* could be processed in detail up to 1968.

One of the main reasons for this is that the number of observations made before the end of 1968 at 13 stations on the Danube, five stations on the Tisza, two on the Rába, five on the Ipoly, one station on each of the Zala and Kapos rivers, two stations on the Mura, one on the Szamos, three on the Sajó and one station on each of the Fekete-Körös, Fehér-Körös, Berettyó and Maros rivers proved inadequate for the detailed exploration of sediment conditions.

In *Sections 2.1.3, 2.1.4* and *3.1.1* a few relations have been introduced by which sediment concentration, the rates of bed load and suspended-sediment transport can be expressed in terms of discharge or mean velocity. The afore-mentioned relations are presented not only in a numerical but also in a graphical form.

The details related to the determination of these relations, their graphic representation and any more detailed examination will be omitted subsequently, and the relations concerning sediment transport in the afore-mentioned ten Hungarian rivers will be given in a tabulated form.

Table 3.1.2 − 2 shows the values of the coefficients and exponents involved in the expressions describing suspended-sediment transport in the Danube. The relations of the sediment concentration and suspended sediment transport to stages, discharges and mean velocities are all given in the Table.

---

* For detailed information on sediment transport in the rivers of Hungary the reader is referred to the author's book *Vízfolyások hordalékszállítása* (Sediment transport in rivers) published in Hungarian by the Publishing House of the Academy, Budapest in 1971.

Fig. 3.1.2 − 2. The catchment area of the Danube

Legend:
- State boundaries
- Boundary of the Danube Basin
- Water courses of the Danube Basin
- Major cities

Fig. 3.1.2 – 3. Network of sediment-gaging stations in Hungary in 1968

In *Table 3.1.2 – 3* the values of the coefficients and exponents involved in the expressions describing bed load transport in the Danube have been compiled again in terms of stages, discharges and mean velocities.

The values of the exponents and coefficients involved in the suspended-sediment relations for the Tisza river are shown in *Table 3.1.2 – 4*, whereas the same values of the bed load transport relations are compiled in *Table 3.1.2 – 5*.

Suspended-sediment transport in eight minor streams in Hungary is characterized by the data compiled in *Table 3.1.2 – 6* whereas the values applying to bed load transport in the same streams are given in *Table 3.1.2 – 7*.

For ease of comparison with sediment transport in other water courses the characteristic mean values of sediment transport in Hungarian water courses have been listed in *Table 3.1.2 – 8*, grouped according to observing stations along the streams. From the last two columns of the Table it will be appreciated that the specific sediment yield per unit area of the catchment and, in turn, the average soil erosion rate calculated therefrom are both rather low in magnitude.

In studies on sediment transport, the grain size of the sediment is clearly of importance: the average minimum, most frequent and maximum particle diameters are compiled in *Table 3.1.2 – 9* for both suspended sediment and bed load, grouped according to streams and observing stations.

Sediment transport in water courses has been demonstrated to be closely related to the hydrological properties of the particular river. The most relevant hydrological properties of the Hungarian water courses mentioned before are to be seen in *Table 3.1.2 — 10*.

In the absence of data some of the water courses are omitted from *Table 3.1. 2 — 10*. The data included indicate the distance of the observing station from the mouth, the magnitude of the catchment area above the station, its average elevation above see level, the range of stage fluctuations, i.e. the difference between the highest and lowest stages, the average width of the river bed, its depth and slope, the discharges at flood, mean and low stages, the average ratio of flood and low water discharges, the runoff volume in an average year and finally the depth of annual average precipitation on the catchment area.

Table 3.1.2—1

Sediment measurements conducted until the end of 1968
on Hungarian rivers

River	Number of observation sections	Number of measurements
1. *Danube*	20	914
2. *Tisza*	11	1,248
3. *Rába*	7	344
4. *Ipoly*	5	360
5. *Zala*	4	472
6. *Kapos*	1	35
7. *Mura*	2	25
8. *Szamos*	2	158
9. *Sajó*	5	353
10. *Hernád*	3	763
11. *Sebes-Körös*	1	85
12. *Fekete-Körös*	2	76
13. *Fehér-Körös*	1	10
14. *Berettyó*	1	143
15. *Maros*	2	98
Total:	67	5,084

Coefficients and exponents involved in the relations

River	Gaging station	Concentration C_k [kp/m³]					
		$C_k = th^n$		$C_k = dQ^l$		$C_k = \gamma v_k^\delta$	
		t	n	d	l	γ	δ
Danube	*Dunaremete*	$10^{-5} \cdot 1.45$ $10^{-6} \cdot 1.96$*	6.14 7.00*	$10^{-10} \cdot 1.23$	2.57	0.00064	8.70
	Nagybajcs	$10^{-3} \cdot 1.34$ $10^{-4} \cdot 4.77$*	3.13 3.50*	$10^{-10} \cdot 1.23$	2.57	0.0080	5.41
	Dunaalmás	$10^{-3} \cdot 2.68$	2.90	$10^{-10} \cdot 1.23$	2.57	0.0082	3.85
	Nahymaros	$10^{-3} \cdot 7.70$ $10^{-3} \cdot 3.90$*	2.68 2.95*	$10^{-10} \cdot 1.23$	2.57	0.0445	3.85
	Dunaújváros	$10^{-3} \cdot 3.20$	3.03	$10^{-10} \cdot 1.23$	2.57	0.0630	3.85
	Fajsz[1]	$10^{-4} \cdot 5.17$	3.03	$10^{-10} \cdot 1.23$	2.57	0.0660	3.85
	Baja[2]	$10^{-5} \cdot 6.52$	3.92	$10^{-10} \cdot 1.50$	2.57	0.1320	3.85

[1] h_1 = actual stage + 1 m
[2] h_1 = actual stage + 2 m
* With the relations valid after 1953
h (h_1) [m]
Q [m³/sec]
v^η [m/sec]

expressing suspended-sediment transport in the Danube

		Suspended transport G_s [kp/sec]			
$G_s = uh^g$		$G_s = pQ^j$		$G_s = \alpha v_k^\beta$	
u	g	p	j	α	β
$10^{-3} \cdot 1.06$ $10^{-4} \cdot 4.5^*$	8.35 8.70*	$10^{-10} \cdot 1.23$	3.57	0.56	9.1
$10^{-1} \cdot 5.54$ $10^{-1} \cdot 2.95^*$	4.55 4.50*	$10^{-10} \cdot 1.23$ •	3.57	8.2	7.6
1.31	4.20	$10^{-10} \cdot 1.23$	3.57	237	6.25
5.90 3.27*	3.92 3.87*	$10^{-10} \cdot 1.23$	3.57	108	6.25
1.50	4.45	$10^{-10} \cdot 1.23$	3.57	160	6.25
$10^{-2} \cdot 7.74$	4.55	$10^{-10} \cdot 1.23$	3.57	200	6.25
$10^{-3} \cdot 9.50$	5.41	$10^{-10} \cdot 1.30$	3.57	570	6.25

Table 3.1.2 — 3

Coefficients and exponents involved in the relations expressing bed load transport in the Danube

River	Gaging station	Bed load transport $G_B =$ [kp/sec]					
		$G_B = u_1 h^{g_1}$		$G_B = p_1 Q^{j_1}$		$G_B = \alpha_1 v_k^{\beta_1}$	
		u_1	g_1	p_1	j_1	α_1	β_1
Danube	Dunaremete	$10^{-2} \cdot 1.32$	4.74	$10^{-7} \cdot 3.4$	2.245	0.0174	6.67
	Nagybajcs	$10^{-5} \cdot 1.85$	7.30	$10^{-23} \cdot 1.9$	6.67	0.0021	15.4
	Dunaalmás	$10^{-3} \cdot 4.39$	4.74	$10^{-14} \cdot 7.0$	4.167	0.45	6.67
	Nagymaros	$10^{-2} \cdot 2.98$	3.27	$10^{-14} \cdot 7.0$	4.167	0.45	6.67
	Dunaújváros	$10^{-2} \cdot 2.10$	3.055	$10^{-8} \cdot 1.32$	2.245	0.5	6.67
	Fajsz[1]	$10^{-2} \cdot 2.48$	2.33	$10^{-8} \cdot 2.64$	2.245	1.8	6.67
	Baja[2]	$10^{-3} \cdot 1.08$	3.71	$10^{-8} \cdot 2.35$	2.245	6.0	6.67

[1] $h_1 =$ actual stage $+ 1$ m
[2] $h_1 =$ actual stage $+ 2$ m
h (h_1) [m]
Q [m³/sec]
v_k [m/sec]

Coefficients and exponents involved in the relation

River	Gaging station	$C_k = th^n$		$C_k = dQ^l$		$C_k = \gamma v_k^{\delta}$	
		Concentration C_k [kp/m³]					
		t	n	d	l	γ	δ
Tisza	Záhony[1]	$10^{-2} \cdot 7.94$	1.67	$10^{-5} \cdot 4.86$	1.44	1.5	4.07
	Tiszalök[1]	$10^{-1} \cdot 8.80$	3.79	$10^{-5} \cdot 3.10$	1.44	1.36	4.07
		3.95**	2.26**	$10^{-5} \cdot 1.55$**	1.44**		
	Polgár[1]	$10^{-3} \cdot 7.83$	2.60	$10^{-5} \cdot 3.04$	1.44	4.35	4.07
		$10^{-3} \cdot 5.88$**	2.07**	$10^{-5} \cdot 1.35$**	1.44**	0.49**	4.07**
	Tiszabő[1]	$10^{-3} \cdot 3.6$*	1.55*	$10^{-5} \cdot 2.64$	1.44	0.37	2.30
		$10^{-3} \cdot 7.4$*	1.97*				
	Tápé[1]	$10^{-3} \cdot 8.53$	2.18	$10^{-5} \cdot 2.60$	1.44	0.57	2.30
	Szeged[1]	$10^{-2} \cdot 1.16$	2.28	$10^{-5} \cdot 2.24$	1.44	0.91	4.07
		$10^{-2} \cdot 1.02$**	1.62**	$10^{-5} \cdot 1.06$**	1.44**		

[1] h_1 = actual stage + 3 m
* Summer—winter relation
** Relation valid after impoundment at Tiszalök
  $h (h_1)$ [m]
  Q [m³/sec]
  v_k [m/sec]

expressing suspended-sediment transport in the Tisza river

$G_s = uh^g$		$G_s = pQ^j$		$G_s = \alpha v_k^\beta$	
Suspended transport G_s [kp/sec]					
u	g	p	j	α	β
10.7	2.58	$10^{-4} \cdot 4.86$	2.44	900	5.27
$10^{-2} \cdot 1.0$	2.44	$10^{-5} \cdot 3.10$	2.44	1,000	5.27
$10^{-2} \cdot 1.0$**	2.03**	$10^{-5} \cdot 1.12$**	2.44**		
$10^{-1} \cdot 2.36$	4.45	$10^{-5} \cdot 3.04$	2.44	2,100	5.27
$10^{-1} \cdot 5.13$**	3.29**	$10^{-5} \cdot 1.04$**	2.44**	415**	5.27**
2.98*	8.56*	$10^{-5} \cdot 2.64$	2.44	375	3.85
$10^{-1} \cdot 6.9$*	3.06*				
$10^{-1} \cdot 4.45$	3.80	$10^{-5} \cdot 2.60$	2.44	980	4.65
$10^{-1} \cdot 8.40$	3.71	$10^{-5} \cdot 2.24$	2.44	1,510	6.17
1.33**	2.71**	$10^{-5} \cdot 0.83$**	2.44**		

Table 3.1.2—5

Coefficients and exponents involved in the relations expressing bed load transport in the Tisza river

River	Gaging station	$G_B = u_1 h^{g_1}$		$G_B = p_1 Q^{j_1}$		$G_B = \alpha_1 v_k^{\beta_1}$	
		Bed load transport G_B [kp/sec]					
		u_1	g_1	p_1	j_1	α_1	β_1
Tisza	Záhony[1]	—	—	—	—	—	—
	Tiszalök[1]	—	—	—	—	—	—
	Polgár[1]	$10^{-4} \cdot 1.89$	4.41	$10^{-10} \cdot 30$	2.74	1.070	4.59
	Tiszabő[1]	$10^{-4} \cdot 7.85$* $10^{-4} \cdot 4.9$	3.86* 3.77*	$10^{-10} \cdot 45$	2.74	0.485	4.59
	Tápé[1]	$10^{-5} \cdot 6.30$	4.51	$10^{-10} \cdot 8$	2.74	0.350	4.59
	Szeged[1]	$10^{-3} \cdot 1.30$	3.42	$10^{-10} \cdot 15$	2.74	0.540	4.59

[1] h_1 = actual stage + 3 m
* Summer—winter relationship

h (h_1) [m]
v_k [m/sec]

Q [m³/sec]

Coefficients and exponents involved in the relations expressing

| River | Gaging station | Concentration C_k [kp/m³] | | | | | |
| | | $C_k = th^n$ | | $C_k = dQ^l$ | | $C_k = \gamma v_k^\delta$ | |
		t	n	d	l	γ	δ
Rába	Szentgotthárd[1]	$10^{-2} \cdot 8.3$	2.80	$10^{-4} \cdot 1.5$	1.84	0.70	4.09
	Körmend	$10^{-1} \cdot 3.8$	1.72	$10^{-5} \cdot 2.14$	2.18	0.19	3.19
	Sárvár[1]	$10^{-1} \cdot 1.37$	2.05	$10^{-4} \cdot 3.8$	1.42	0.19	3.19
	Árpás	$10^{-2} \cdot 6.40$	1.61	$10^{-2} \cdot 5.2$	0.72	0.19	3.19
	Győr	—	—	$10^{-4} \cdot 8.15$	1.11	0.29	1.73
Zala	Zalaapáti	$10^{-1} \cdot 1.09$	2.07	—	—	—	—
	Balatonhidvég[4]	—	—	—	—	1.16	2.62
	Fenékpuszta[5]	—	—	—	—	—	—
Szamos	Csenger[1]	$10^{-1} \cdot 2.40$	2.13	$10^{-5} \cdot 3.60$	2.07	1.75	5.41
Sajó	Kazincbarcika	$10^{-1} \cdot 1.20$	4.01	$10^{-4} \cdot 1.5$	2.33	0.18	2.07
	Miskolc[1]	$10^{-3} \cdot 6.8$	3.66	—	—	—	—
Hernád	Hidasnémeti[1]	$10^{-2} \cdot 1.11$	4.85	$10^{-4} \cdot 4.2$	1.63	1.11	3.82
	Pere[2]	$10^{-2} \cdot 2.00$	3.07	$10^{-4} \cdot 4.6$	1.63	4.65	3.45
	Gesztely[1]	$10^{-3} \cdot 9.80$	4.21	$10^{-4} \cdot 5.0$	1.63	2.25	6.46
Sebes-Körös	Körösszakál[1]	$10^{-2} \cdot 3.80$	3.15	—	—	—	—
Fekete-Körös	Remete[1]	$10^{-3} \cdot 7.80$	2.28	—	—	—	—
Maros	Deszk[3]	$10^{-1} \cdot 1.6$	2.19	$10^{-2} \cdot 8.8$	1.44	—	—

[1] h_1 = actual stage + 1 m
[2] h_1 = actual stage + 0.2 m
[3] h_1 = stage at Makó + 1 m
[4] At the Balatonhidvég gaging station $Q_1 = Q + 0.5$ m³/sec and $v_{k1} = v_k + 0.1$ m/sec
[5] At the Fenékpuszta gaging station $v_{k1} = v_k + 0.03$ m/sec

suspended-sediment transport in the minor rivers in Hungary

Suspended transport G_s [kp/sec]					
$G_s = uh^g$		$G_s = pQ^j$		$G_s = \alpha v_k^\beta$	
u	g	p	j	α	β
2.60	3.80	$10^{-4} \cdot 2.0$	2.84	$10 \cdot 5.0$	5.56
1.86	2.44	$10^{-5} \cdot 2.74$	3.18	$10 \cdot 2.65$	5.56
6.60	2.75	$10^{-4} \cdot 2.4$	2.42	$10 \cdot 1.45$	5.56
1.70	2.78	$10^{-3} \cdot 5.2$	1.72	$10 \cdot 1.8$	8.00
—	—	$10^{-4} \cdot 8.15$	2.11	$10 \cdot 4.0$	3.04
$10^{-1} \cdot 7.55$	4.26	—	—	—	—
—	—	$10^{-3} \cdot 5.9$	1.98	6.40	3.61
—	—	—	—	6.30	2.36
17.0	3.37	$10^{-5} \cdot 3.60$	3.17	$10^{-2} \cdot 8.0$	10.0
$10^{-1} \cdot 9.3$	6.68	$10^{-4} \cdot 1.5$	3.33	11.5	4.55
$10^{-2} \cdot 1.25$	6.90	—	—	—	—
$10^{-1} \cdot 1.20$	7.10	$10^{-4} \cdot 4.2$	2.63	86	5.08
10	4.55	$10^{-4} \cdot 4.6$	2.63	0.94	4.22
$10^{-2} \cdot 5.41$	6.85	$10^{-6} \cdot 5.0$	2.63	2.30	7.58
$10^{-1} \cdot 5.65$	4.96	—	—	—	—
$10^{-2} \cdot 4.05$	4.32	—	—	—	—
1.25	3.65	$10^{-3} \cdot 3.0$	2.44	—	—

Table 3.1.2—7 on page 782.

Typical average sediment transport

River	Sediment gaging stations	Average figures for the decade 1931—1940						
		Con-centra-tion	Suspended-sediment transport			Bed load transport		
		[kp/m³]	[kp/sec]	[Mp/year]	[m³/year]	[kp/sec]	[Mp/year]	[m³/year]
Danube	Dunaremete	0.040	76	2,397,000	1,387,000	5.9	186,000	103,000
	Nagybajcs	0.060	180	5,680,000	3,210,000	0.7	22,000	12,000
	Dunaalmás	0.064	174	5,492,000	3,050,000	1.2	38,500	21,600
	Nagymaros	0.100	320	10,100,000	5,620,000	0.8	25,200	14,000
	Dunaújváros	0.115	370	11,700,000	6,500,000	0.9	28,400	15,800
	Fajsz	0.110	340	10,722,000	5,957,000	1.6	50,000	28,000
	Baja	0.130	580	18,291,000	10,162,000	1.4	44,000	24,000
Tisza	Záhony	0.425	210	6,650,000	3,680,000	—	—	—
	Tiszalök	0.295[1]	290	9,150,000	5,100,000	0.3[2]	—	—
	Polgár	0.380	310	9,780,000	5,400,000	0.22	7,000	3,900
	Tiszabő	0.300	190	6,000,000	3,330,000	0.5	16,000	8,800
	Tápé	0.340	430	10,700,000	5,900,000	0.3	9,000	5,000
	Szeged	0.560	700	22,075,000	12,260,000	0.6	19,000	11,000
Rába	Szent-gotthárd	0.134	9.0	282,200	156,800	0.0130	4,103	2,280
	Körmend	0.160	13.5	426,000	236,000	0.0027	86	48
	Sárvár	0.129	8.1	252,000	140,000	—	—	—
	Nick	—	—	—	—	—	—	—
	Vág	—	—	—	—	—	—	—
	Árpás	0.085	4.5	141,500	78,700	—	—	—
	Győr	—	—	—	—	—	—	—
Ipoly	Nógrád-szakál	—	—	—	—	—	—	—
	Balassa-gyarmat	—	—	—	—	—	—	—
	Vámos-mikola	—	—	—	—	—	—	—
	Letkés	—	—	—	—	—	—	—
	Szob	—	—	—	—	—	—	—
Zala	Zala-egerszeg	—	—	—	—	—	—	—
	Zalaapáti	0.066[3]	0.74	23,000	13,000	0.0008	25	14
	Balaton-hidvég	—	—	—	—	—	—	—
	Fenékpuszta	—	—	—	—	—	—	—

figures by rivers and gaging stations

before 1954			after 1953			Annual average	
						Maxima corresponding to the HHW	
C_k	G_s	G_B	C_k	G_s	G_B	specific sediment yield	soil erosion
[kp/m³]	[kp/sec]	[kp/sec]	[kp/m³]	[kp/sec]	[kp/sec]	[Mp/km²]	[mm]
1.52	10,800	123	1.1	6,500	—	19.6	0.010
0.85	6,500	105	0.64	3,100	—	42.0	0.021
0.70	3,800	60	—	—	—	44.3	0.022
1.30	9,800	15.9	1.000	5,500	—	55.3	0.028
1.38	11,000	10.0	—	—	—	62.0	0.031
0.80	5,000	7.0	—	—	—	56.2	0.028
1.18	675	11.1	—	—	—	87.8	0.044
4.00	4,700	—	—	—	—	202	0.101
3.30	6,100	6²	1.15	790	—	186	0.093
3.34	7,000	5	0.60	1,100	—	156	0.078
1.50	1,600	5	—	—	—	89.4	0.045
2.00	6,000	5	—	—	—	98.6	0.049
3.50	9,200	7	0.58	1,160	—	159.5	0.080
			10.0	1,500	2.70	93.3	0.047
			5.9	1,000	0.33	90.1	0.045
			4.9	800	—	45.3	0.023
			—	—	—	—	—
			1.1	235	—	21.3	0.011
			—	—	—	—	—
			—	—	—	—	—
			—	—	—	—	—
			—	—	—	—	—
			—	—	—	—	—
			—	—	—	—	—
			2.0	270	0.1	7.6	0.008
			—	—	—	—	—
			—	—	—	—	—

Table 3.1.2—8

River	Sediment gaging stations	Con-centra-tion [kp/m³]	Suspended-sediment transport [kp/sec]	[Mp/year]	[m³/year]	Bed load transport [kp/sec]	[Mp/year]	[m³/year]
Kapos	*Pincehely*	—	—	—	—	—	—	—
Mura	*Letenye*	—	—	—	—	—	—	—
	Mura-keresztúr	—	—	—	—	—	—	—
Szamos	*Csenger*	0.0764	216	6,820,000	3,780,000	—	—	—
Sajó	*Bánréve*	—	—	—	—	—	—	—
	Kazinc-barcika	1.06	110	3,470,000	1,927,000	0.1	3,000	1,600
	Berente	—	—	—	—	—	—	—
	Miskolc	0.31	46	1,490,000	828,000	0.017	350	290
	Felsőzsolca	—	—	—	—	—	—	—
Hernád	*Hidasnémeti*	0.22	26	820,000	450,000	0.2	6,000	3,300
	Pere	—	—	—	—	—	—	—
	Gesztely	0.12	15	473,000	263,000	0.2	6,000	3,300
Sebes-Körös	*Körösszakál*	0.116	8	259,000	144,000	0.074	2,340	1,300
Fekete-Körös	*Remete*	—	—	—	—	—	—	—
	Sarkad	—	—	—	—	—	—	—
Fehér-Körös	*Gyula*	—	—	—	—	—	—	—
Berettyó	*Berettyó-újfalu*	—	—	—	—	—	—	—
Maros	*Makó*	—	—	—	—	—	—	—
	Deszk	0.5	265	8,300,000	4,620,000	0.9	28,060	16,000

Average figures for the decade 1931—1940

(Continued)

Maxima corresponding to the HHW						Annual average	
before 1954			after 1953			specific sediment yield	soil erosion
C_k	G_s	G_B	C_k	G_s	G_B		
[kp/m³]	[kp/sec]	[kp/sec]	[kp/m³]	[kp/sec]	[kp/sec]	[Mp/km²]	[mm]
			—	—	—	—	—
			—	—	—	—	—
			—	—	—	—	—
			22.0	23,000	—	447	0.223
			—	—	—	—	—
			24.0	8,000	4	858	0.429
			—	—	—	—	—
			5.5	3,600	0.74	285	0.176
			—	—	—	—	—
			29.0	12,000	100	182.5	0.091
			20.0	8,000	8	—	—
			10.0	4,500	60	93.5	0.047
			9.0	3,000	8	105.6	0.053
			1.0	4,000	6	—	—
			—	—	—	—	—
			—	—	—	—	—
			—	—	—	—	—
			—	—	—	—	—
			4.5—10.0	6—10,000	—	280	.0.140

[1] Related to stage frequency in 1942—1952
[2] Estimated value
[3] Related to stage frequency in 1951—1952

777

Table 3.1.2 − 9

Typical grain sizes at different sediment gaging stations

River	Gaging station	Average sediment diameter in mm					
		suspended-sediment			bed load		
		min.	most frequent	max.	min.	most frequent	max.
Danube	Rajka	0.030	0.040	0.050	—	—	—
	Körtvélyes	0.033	—	0.040	17.0	—	22.1
	Doborgaz	0.032	0.036	0.041	13.5	24.0	34.9
	Dunaremete	0.030	0.050	0.070	4.15	14.0	30.3
	Ásványráró	0.035	0.040	0.085	17.0	—	24.4
	Szap	0.034	0.040	0.071	11.4	—	23.5
	Medve	0.033	0.040	0.065	14.4	—	22.1
	Nagybajcs	0.032	0.040	0.107	0.20	7.50	14.7
	Vének	0.032	0.036	0.048	9.93	—	11.6
	Ács	0.038	—	0.042	—	—	—
	Dunaalmás	0.036	0.050	0.248	0.12	0.30	4.80
	Esztergom	0.036	—	0.039	3.28	—	6.74
	Nagymaros	0.031	0.080	0.365	0.12	0.20	2.34
	Budapest	0.035	0.040	0.055	—	—	—
	Százhalombatta	0.038	—	0.051	—	—	—
	Dunaújváros	0.034	0.040	0.058	—	0.20	—
	Paks	0.035	0.038	0.052	0.21	—	2.06
	Fajsz	—	0.080	—	—	—	—
	Raja	0.032	0.060	0.128	0.16	0.25	0.61
	Mohács	0.026	0.040	0.054	0.15	—	0.53
Tisza	Tivadar	0.032	0.050	0.203	0.150	0.250	0.588
	Vásárosnamény	0.014	0.040	0.088	0.060	0.030	0.420
	Záhony	0.036	0.050	0.058	0.224	0.300	0.357
	Tuzsér	0.033	0.045	0.174	—	—	—
	Tiszalök	0.031	0.040	0.089	—	—	—
	Polgár	0.030	0.060	0.175	0.067	0.120	0.510
	Tiszabő	0.023	0.050	0.158	0.034	0.120	0.180
	Szolnok	0.036	0.040	0.088	—	—	—
	Algyő	0.031	0.040	0.054	—	—	—
	Szeged	0.012	0.035	0.087	0.064	0.130	0.322
Rába	Szentgotthárd	0.037	0.08	0.201	0.156	0.4	4.09
	Körmend	0.036	0.08	0.284	0.062	0.3	2.68
	Sárvár	0.042	0.05	0.142	0.263	2.0	6.84
	Nick	0.034	0.04	0.170	0.285	0.3	0.337
	Vág	0.052	0.06	0.181	0.342	1.7	4.52
	Árpás	0.031	0.04	0.068	—	—	—
	Győr	0.033	0.04	0.142	—	—	—
Ipoly	Nógrádszakál	0.027	0.05	0.112	—	—	—
	Balassagyarmat	0.035	0.04	0.156	—	—	—

(Continued)

| River | Gaging station | Average sediment diameter in mm | | | | | |
| | | suspended-sediment | | | bed load | | |
		min.	most frequency	max.	min.	most frequent	max.
	Vámosmikola	0.030	0.04	0.053	—	—	—
	Letkés	0.031	0.035	0.055	—	—	—
	Szob	0.031	0.035	0.060	—	—	—
Zala	*Zalaegerszeg*	0.033	0.04	0.067	—	—	—
	Zalaapáti	0.031	0.04	0.243	0.046	0.30	1.480
	Balatonhídvég	0.029	0.04	0.195	0.049	0.30	1.010
	Fenékpuszta	0.030	0.04	0.178	—	—	—
Kapos	*Pincehely*	0.033	0.04	0.079	0.108	0.15	0.278
Mura	*Letenye*	0.056	0.07	0.078	—	—	—
	Murakeresztúr	0.048	0.06	0.144	—	—	—
Szamos	*Csenger*	0.011	0.05	0.362	—	—	—
	Olcsvaapáti	0.035	0.05	0.078	0.196	0.25	0.322
Sajó	*Bánréve*	0.031	0.05	0.15	—	—	—
	Kazincbarcika	—	—	—	—	—	—
	Berente	—	—	—	—	—	—
	Miskolc	—	—	—	—	—	—
	Felsőzsolca	0.032	0.04	0.258	—	—	—
Hernád	*Hidasnémeti*	0.029	0.05	0.325	0.059	1.0	5.40
	Pere	—	—	—	—	—	—
	Gesztely	0.026	0.05	1.27	0.071	1.5	5.97
Sebes-Körös	*Körösszakál*	0.036	0.05	0.099	—	—	—
Fekete-Körös	*Remete*	—	—	—	—	—	—
	Sarkad	0.035	0.4	—	—	—	—
Fehér-Körös	*Gyula*	0.030	0.035	0.051	—	—	—
Berettyó	*Berettyóújfalu*	—	—	—	—	—	—
Maros	*Makó*	0.035	0.034	0.041	—	—	—
	Deszk	—	—	—	—	—	—

779

No.	River	Gaging station		Catchment area		Stage fluctuation [cm]
		Name	Distance from mouth	Size [km²]	Average elevation above sea level [mA]	
1.	Danube	Dunaremete	1,825.0	131,901	—	536
2.		Budapest	1,646.0	184,767	—	754
3.		Mohács	1,450.0	208,822	—	842
4.	Rába	Sárvár	84.0	5,566	523	610
5.	Zala	Zalaapáti	23.7	1,528	202	282
6.	Kapos	Kurd	43.7	2,119	185	491
7.	Dráva	Drávaszabolcs	68.0	35,510	780	542
8.	Mura	Letenye	24.4	13,026	845	433
9.	Ipoly	Balassagyarmat	122.0	2,765	365	300
10.	Tisza	Tiszabecs	757.0	9,707	819	640
11.		Tokaj	549.0	49,449	530	1,056
12.		Szolnok	334.0	73,113	455	1,141
13.		Szeged	172.0	138,408	431	1,173
14.	Szamos	Csenger	46.4	15,282	553	839
15.	Bodrog	Felsőberecki	47.1	12,386	409	651
16.	Sajó	Felsőzsolca	50.1	6,440	423	486
17.	Zagyva	Pásztó	133.4	488	356	478
18.	Tarna	Verpelét	55.9	574	312	515
19.	Sebes-Körös	Körösszakál	55.3	2,489	616	563
20.	Berettyó	Berettyóujfalu	45.0	3,712	200	668
21.	Hármas-Körös	mouth	0	27,537	229	1,181
22.	Maros	Makó	23.7	30,149	642	658

in Hungary

Average channel			Flood	Mean	Dry-weather	Ratio of extreme discharges	Annual runoff volume 10⁶ [m³/year]	Annual average pre-cipita-tion [mm]	Note
width [m]	depth [m]	slope [cm/km]	discharge [m³/sec]						
at mean stage									
300	4.0	28	9,600	2,025	570.00	16.8	63,860	—	
550	5.0	7	8,600	2,376	615.00	14.0	74,930	—	
550	5.0	7	7,850	2,400	618.00	12.8	75,686	—	
30	3.0	74	560	36	6.50	86.0	1,148	859	
40	2.0	20	137	6	0.25	548.0	183	755	
20	2.0	36	130	5	0.22	591.0	161	683	
150	2.5	21	2,100	600	200.00	10.5	18,920	975	
80	2.0	48	1,050	150	50.00	21.0	4,730	951	
20	2.0	30	360	15	0.20	1,800.0	511	672	
100	3.0	20	3,360	190	29.00	116.0	5,992	1,073	
150	6.0	3	4,000	464	52.80	76.0	14,633	805	
200	7.0	4	3,820	546	64.80	59.0	17,218	746	
200	7.0	4	4,700	810	95.00	49.0	25,544	709	
100	2.5	10	1,350	120	15.00	90.0	3,784	756	
50	3.0	3	1,300	120	4.00	325.0	3,784	761	
60	2.0	51	520	32	2.40	217.0	1,022	693	
25	2.5	65	150	1	0.04	3,750.0	44	591	
10	1.5	200	860	3	0.015	57,300.0	82	593	
48	3.2	30	600	25	1.90	31.5	788	793	
40	2.0	18	270	8	0.20	1,350.0	249	620	
70	3.0	4	1,330	67	4.2	316	2,140	653	
90	3.5	26	180	160	22.00	81.8	5,045	707	

Table 3.1.2—7

Coefficients and exponents involved in the relations expressing bed load transport in minor rivers in Hungary

| River | Gaging station | Bed load transport $G_B[kp/sec]$ | | | | | |
| | | $G_B = u_1 h^{g_1}$ | | $G_B = p_1 Q^{j_1}$ | | $G_B = \alpha_1 v_\beta^{k_1}$ | |
		u_1	g_1	p_1	j_1	α_1	β_1
Rába	Szentgotthárd	$10^{-3} \cdot 4.0$	3.65	$10^{-6} \cdot 1.0$	2.76	0.0475	4.55
	Körmend	$10^{-5} \cdot 5.2$	1.19	$10^{-7} \cdot 2.15$	2.58	0.0165	4.29
	Sárvár[1]	—	—	—	—	—	—
	Árpás	—	—	—	—	—	—
	Győr	—	—	—	—	—	—
Zala	Zalaapáti	$10^{-3} \cdot 1.14$	3.25	—	—	—	—
	Balatonhidvég	—	—	—	—	—	—
	Fenékpuszta	—	—	—	—	—	—
Szamos	Csenger[1]	—	—	—	—		—
Sajó	Kazincbarcika	$10^{-3} \cdot 5.35$	5.00	$10^{-7} \cdot 5.2$	3.28	0.25	6.25
	Miskolc[1]	$10^{-5} \cdot 2.7$	5.72	—	—	—	—
Hernád	Hidasnémeti[1]	$10^{-4} \cdot 3.30$	7.82	$10^{-6} \cdot 1.70$	2.66	0.37	5.35
	Pere[2]	$10^{-3} \cdot 1.40$	4.50	$10^{-6} \cdot 0.9$	2.66	0.145	4.07
	Gesztely[1]	$10^{-4} \cdot 3.79$	7.25	$10^{-6} \cdot 5.4$	2.66	3.40	8.2
Sebes-Körös	Körösszakál	—	—	—	—	—	—
Fekete-Körös	Remete[1]	$10^{-5} \cdot 2.40$	5.95	—	—	—	—
Maros	Deszk[3]	***	***	—	—	2.75	6.67

[1] h_1 = actual stage + 1 m
[2] h_1 = actual stage + 0.2 m
[3] h_1 = stage at Makó + 1 m
*** The relation includes three variables h (h_1) [m]; Q [m³/sec]; v_k [m/sec]

782

LIST OF SYMBOLS

L	Length
T	Time
M	Mass
Θ	Temperature
E	Energy, work $(ML^2T^{-2} = FL)$
F	Force, gravity force (MLT^{-2})
a	The longest of three mutually perpendicular diameters of a particle (L); coefficient; constant; channel stability factor; relative difference in density; exponent
a_1	Length of half-axis of sediment particle (L)
a_r	Factor
A	Annual average soil loss (Mp/ha. year); surface area, area of sediment particle in plan (L^2); parameter (L)
A_*	Constant
A'	Factor expressing rate of bed load transport
A''	Parameter
A_s	The work performed by the pulsation of molecular tension in the turbulent flow field (E); horizontal projection of the lee-side of sand waves (L^2)
A_v, A_c	Factors
b	The intermediate in length of the three mutually perpendicular axes of a partice (L); coefficient; constant; channel stability factor; pulsation energy related to unit mass of non-uniform fluid (EM^{-1}); exponent
b_1	Length of half-axis of sediment particle (L)
B	Mathematical description of boundary surface; width of channel (canal), of water surface, average width of catchment area (L); settling number; mean energy of pulsation (E)
B_*	Constant
B''	Parameter
B_B	Bottom width (L)
c	The shortest of the three mutually perpendicular axes of a particle (L); sediment concentration as percentage by weight; wear per unit weight; velocity coefficient $(L^{1/2} T^{-1})$; coefficient
$\bar{c}$	Parameter expressing the ratio of discharge and sediment transport as percentage by weight

c_1	Length of half-axis of sediment particle (L)
c_1, c_2, c_3, c_4, c_5, c_6	Coefficients
C	Factor representing crop pattern; sediment concentration (FL^{-3}); velocity coefficient; function; coefficient
$\bar{C}$	Mean value of concentration (FL^{-3})
C'	Pulsating part of concentration (FL^{-3})
Ca	Cauchy number
C_a	Velocity coefficient in alluvial channels ($L^{(1-x)} T^{-1}$); sediment concentration at height a above the bottom (FL^{-3})
C_{crit}	Critical concentration (FL^{-3})
C_d	Drag coefficient of particles
$C\phi$	Average drag coefficient of spherical particles
C_f	Concentration of bottom material (FL^{-3})
C_k	Dimensionless ratio; actual mean concentration in a vertical or in a section (FL^{-3})
C_l	Concentration of suspended sediment (FL^{-3}); coefficient
C_s	Sediment coefficient ($L^{3/2} T^{-1} F^{-2}$); sediment concentration as percentage by weight
C_v, $\bar{C}_v$	Velikanov's volume concentration of slurry and its mean value in time
C_x	Resistance coefficient due to friction
C_0	Concentration at the bottom (FL^{-3})
$\bar{C}_A$	Mean concentration (FL^{-3})
C_B	Coefficient ($L^3 F^{-1} T^{-1}$)
C_D	Dimensionless resistance coefficient; friction coefficient
C_G	Goryunov's "Standard" concentration of slurry
C_L	Constant; coefficient
C_T, C_{T_1}	Volume concentration; slurry concentration
d	Symbol of differentiation
d	Diameter of circle enveloping projection on plane of sediment particle in most stable position, particle diameter (L); coefficient
d_{av}	Average particle diameter of granular material (L)
d_g	Mean particle diameter (L)
d_m	Mean particle diameter (L)
$d_{\max}$	Greatest particle diameter (L)
d_s	Fictitious particle diameter (L)
D	Depth of flow, pipe diameter (L)
D_c	Critical depth of flow (L)
D_0	Diameter (L)
D_*	Dimensionless number; parameter
e	Base of Neperian logarithm
e	Energy density (EL^{-3}); parameter of exposure; coefficient
E	Soil loss (acre − inch); flow resistance (F); kinetic energy, energy (E); Young's modulus of elasticity (FL^{-2})
$\mathbf{E}_{ik}$	Momentum source density ($ML^{-2} T^{-2}$, or FL^{-3})

E^0	Kinetic energy of unit volume of inhomogeneous fluid (EL^{-3})
f	Surface coefficient; friction coefficient, roughness coefficient; exponent; sediment coefficient; function symbol
f_b	Roughness of channel bottom
f_b'	Particle roughness of channel bottom
f_b''	Form roughness of channel bottom
f_c	Dimensionless resistance coefficient; Shields's parameter
f_{ci}	Resistance coefficient of the ith fraction
f_i	Component along x_i of interaction force between sediment and fluid
f_0	Resistance coefficient
$\mathbf{f}$	Oriented surface (L^2)
F	Area, surface, cross-sectional area of pipe, catchment area above dam cross-section (L^2); time factor
$F\ (F_1,\ F_2)$	Function symbol
$F_a,\ F_b$	Area (L^2)
F_*	Sediment transport parameter
F_r	Sediment factor on slope
F_B	Sediment factor on bottom
F_1	Coefficient
Fr	Froude number
Fr_s	Fall velocity Froude number
Fr_*	Sediment shear velocity Froude number
g	Function symbol
g	Gravitational acceleration (LT^{-2}); exponent
$g(B)$	Rate of sediment transport from the scouring space in terms of boundary surface and location
$g(S)$	Rate of sediment recharge to scouring space
g_i	Gravitational acceleration along x_i (LT^{-2})
g_1	Exponent
G	Sediment transport parameter; grain parameter; weight of sediment particle (F); discharge expressed as weight, total rate of annual transport (FT^{-1})
G'	Downward force on settling particle, weight of sediment particle (F)
G_0	Sediment settling annually in a reservoir (FT^{-1})
G_0'	Initial weight of sediment particle (F)
G_n	Weight of bed load (F)
G_s	Weight of total suspended sediment, average suspended sediment arriving annually into a reservoire (FT^{-1})
G_t	Total sediment transport (FT^{-1})
G_*	Sediment transport parameter
G_B	Bed load transport, bed load arriving annually into a reservoir (FT^{-1})
h	Stage (L)

h_v	Differential level, pressure head, kinetic energy of unit fluid weight (L)
H	Surface tension (FL^{-1}); impact force (F); differential elevation (L)
i	Index of flatness; independent invariants; direction of coordinate axis
I	Coefficient of soil erosion potential (inch); radiation intensity ($EL^{-2}T^{-1}$)
I_i	Outflow, current (mass: MT^{-1}, energy: ET^{-1}, momentum: F, ...)
I_0	Incident intensity of monochromatic radiation ($EL^{-2}T^{-1}$)
j, j_i	Exponent; direction of co-ordinate axis
J_i	Surface current density (mass: $ML^{-2}T^{-1}$, energy: $EL^{-2}T^{-1}$, momentum: FL^{-2}, ...)
J_{cond}	Conductive current (mass: MT^{-1}, energy: ET^{-1}, momentum: F, ...)
J_{conv}	Convective current (mass: MT^{-1}, energy: ET^{-1}, momentum: F, ...)
k	Volume constant; coefficient; wearing coefficient; size fraction
k', k''	Coefficient
k_e	Coefficient of hyralic roughness
k_i	Current density of turbulent energy of fluid particles ($EL^{-2}T^{-1}$)
k_{is}	Current density of turbulent energy of solid particles ($EL^{-2}T^{-1}$)
k_r	Part of k_s due to roughness of sediment particles
k_s	Strickler's coefficient of bottom roughness, Nikuradze's sand roughness, equivalent sand roughness
K	Coefficient of soil erosion potential; extent of wearing; coefficient; amount of tracer supply (F)
K_0'	Coefficient depending on volume density of slurry
K_1	Coefficient (LT^{-2})
K_1, K_2	Coefficients
K_x	Empirical coefficient
l	Length (L); exponent; coefficient; number of correlating similarity criteria
lg	Symbol denoting logarithm to base 10
ln	Symbol of natural logarithm
L	Length of slope (ft); conductivity or transfer coefficient; pipe length, distance of gaging section from source area (L)
L, L_{il}	Conductivity coefficient of conductive current density (mass: L^2T^{-1}, energy: $EL^{-1}T^{-1}\Theta^{-1}$, momentum: $FL^{-2}T$, ...)
L, L_k, L_{ik}	Proportionality coefficients; conductivity coefficient of momentum current density ($ML^{-3}T^{-1}$, or $FL^{-4}T$)
m	Exponent; thickness of the moving layer (L); mass (M); constant; number of basic dimensions
m_i	Constant
M	Uniformity coefficient
M_1	Length of meander (L)

786

M_0, (M_r)	Moment (FL)
M_B	Width of meander (L)
n	Roughness coefficient (TL^{-1}); Manning's roughness coefficient; exponent; empirical coefficient; independent physical quantities
N	Exponent; total number of particles
N_0	Quantity of radioactive substance at time $t = 0$ (F); actual power output per unit surface area ($EL^{-2}T^{-1}$)
N_c	Critical power output per unit surface area ($EL^{-2}T^{-1}$)
N_k	Number of particles in the kth fraction
N_t	Quantity of radioactive substance at time $t = t$ (F)
p	Total sediment transport in unit time (L^3T^{-1}); percentage by weight; pressure, mechanical stress, total hydrodynamic pressure of the disperse system (FL^{-2}); probability; symbol of fraction; coefficient
Δp	Differential pressure (FL^{-2})
p''	Egiazaroff's bed load transport parameter
p_{ik}	Component of the molecular stress tensor of disperse medium (FL^{-2})
p_1, p_2	Pressure (FL^{-2}); coefficient
P	Coefficient of cultivation method; wetted perimeter of the cross-section (L); parameter
P_{30}	Rainfall depth in 30 minutes, occurring once every second year
q	Discharge in unit width, discharge of sediment-carrying water (L^2T^{-1}); universal constant
q_1, q_2	Universal constant
q_c	Critical discharge in unit width (L^2T^{-1})
q_i	Source density (mass: $ML^{-3}T^{-1}$, energy: $EL^{-3}T^{-1}$, momentum: FL^{-3}, ...)
q_j	Tracer material introduced in width B (FT^{-1})
q_s	Suspended-sediment transport in unit width, unit sediment transport ($FT^{-1}L^{-1}$)
q_t	Total sediment transport in unit width (L^2T^{-1})
q_{th}	Weight of sediment expressed as rate of sediment transport per unit width (L^2T^{-1})
q_B	Weight of bed load in unit width ($FL^{-1}T^{-1}$)
q_B'	Submerged weight of bed load transport ($FL^{-1}T^{-1}$)
q_B^*	Sediment transport parameter of Garde – Albertson
Q	Discharge, total discharge (volume current) (L^3T^{-1})
Q_0	Discharge causing sediment transport (L^3T^{-1})
Q_c	Critical discharge (L^3T^{-1})
Q_i	Source (mass: MT^{-1}, energy: ET^{-1}, momentum: F, ...)
Q_{hw}	Greatest design discharge (L^3T^{-1})
Q_{lw}	Smallest design discharge (L^3T^{-1})
Q_s	Suspended-sediment transport in the entire cross-section, expressed as volume (L^3T^{-1})
Q_t	Total sediment transport (L^3T^{-1})

Q_z	Discharge of sediment-carrying water $(L^3 T^{-1})$
Q_B	Sediment transport (volume current) $(L^3 T^{-1})$
r	Ratio of the longest and shortest dimension of mineral component particles; surface ratio; exponent; radius of spherical solid particles of equal size, radius of pipe (L)
r_1, r_2, r_3, r_4	Partial correlation coefficients
r_r	Settling percentage
R	Coefficient of plant cover; precipitation coefficient; hydraulic radius (L)
$\mathbf{R}$	Interaction force between the fluid and the sediment (FL^{-3})
Re	Reynolds number
Re_s	Fall velocity Reynolds number
Re_*	Shear velocity Reynolds number
Re_{*s}	Sediment shear velocity Reynolds number
R_s	Fictitious Reynolds number; hydraulic radius related to bottom resistance (L)
R_b	Hydraulic radius related to the channel bottom (L)
R_i	Component of interaction force between the fluid and the particles (FL^{-3})
s	Sediment coefficient of Schoklitsch; portion of pressure acting on the fluid phase; distance travelled by sediment, storage height (L)
sec	Second
S	Slope of terrain; slope of water surface; slope of energy grade line
SF	Shape factor
S_c	Critical gradient
S_{cr}	Gradient at critical slurry velocity
S_e	Slope of the energy grade line
S_{en}	Entrance hydraulic gradient
S_{ex}	Exit hydraulic gradient
S_f	Bottom slope
S_t	Slope of energy grade line in smooth pipe
S_z	Gradient in slurry transport; loss per unit length in slurry transport
S_R	Slope of the energy grade line related to bottom resistance
t	Time (T); temperature (Θ); sediment transport parameter; coefficient
t_c, t_{c_1}, t_{c_2}	Parameters
T	Area (L^2); temperature (Θ); diffusion coefficient per unit path length (LT^{-1}); time of reservoir filling (T)
T^x	Extent of velocity fluctuation (L)
T_{ij}	Conductive momentum current density (FL^{-2})
u	Velocity at distance y above the bottom, vertical velocity component (LT^{-1}); coefficient
u'	Pulsation velocity (LT^{-1})
u_h	Vertical velocity component of solid particle (LT^{-1})
u_i	Coefficient

788

$u_i,\ u_j$	Components along x_i, x_j of fluid flow velocity (LT^{-1})
u_0	Mean velocity of bottom layer (LT^{-1})
U	Electrostatic potential
$\mathbf{U}$	Unit tensor
U_*	Shear velocity (LT^{-1})
$U_*',\ U_*''$	Components of shear velocity (LT^{-1})
v	Main flow velocity (LT^{-1})
v	Mean velocity over time in a particular point (LT^{-1})
$\mathbf{v}'$	Pulsation velocity (LT^{-1})
$\mathbf{v}$	Convective flow velocity, fluid flow velocity (LT^{-1})
v_c	Critical mean velocity (LT^{-1})
v_c	Mean value over time of critical velocity (LT^{-1})
v_{ce}	Critical edge velocity (LT^{-1})
v_{cf}	Critical bottom velocity (LT^{-1})
v_{cr}	Critical velocity (LT^{-1})
v_{cr}'	Critical velocity of mixed size fractions (LT^{-1})
v_f	Bottom velocity (LT^{-1})
v_{fsz}	Surface velocity (LT^{-1})
v_h	Sediment velocity, main velocity of sediment (LT^{-1})
$\mathbf{v}_h$	Average velocity of particles (LT^{-1})
v_{hv}	Virtual velocity of bed load particles (LT^{-1})
v_i	Potential dynamic velocities (LT^{-1})
v_k	Mean velocity (LT^{-1})
v_{ni}	Non-silting velocity (LT^{-1})
v_0	Characteristic constant velocity (LT^{-1})
v_p	Velocity of parallel flow (LT^{-1})
v_s	Travelling velocity of sediment (LT^{-1})
v_y	Velocity along the main direction acting at the center of gravity of particle (LT^{-1})
V	Volume, fluid volume, reservoir capacity (L^3)
V'	Reservoir volume potentially lost by silting (L^3)
V_*	Constant (LT^{-1})
V_e	Volume of ellipsoid of revolution (L^3)
$V_i,\ V_j$	Flow velocity along i and j of mass center of medium of unit volume (LT^{-1})
V_t	Actual volume of sediment particle (L^3)
$w,\ \hat{w}$	Complex potential; mean flow velocity according to kinetic energy on fluid (LT^{-1})
$w',\ w_s'$	Pulsation velocity (LT^{-1})
w_s	Mean flow velocity of solid particles (LT^{-1})
We	Weber number
W_i	Submerged weight of sediment particle (F)
x	Variable along the direction of flow; layer thickness (L); exponent; correction factor

789

x_i	Dimension; extensive quantity (mass: M, energy: E, momentum: FT, ...)
X	Roughness parameter (L)
$\mathbf{X}$	Density of external force field (FL^{-3})
X_{is}, X_i	External force components (FL^{-3})
X_1, X_2, X_3, X_4	Independent variables; dimensionless numbers
y	Vertical distance (L); exponent
y_i	Logarithm of dimension x_i
y_n	Normal depth (L)
y_0	Initial height of prismatic sediment particle (L)
Y	Correction factor
$\overline{Y}$	Arithmetic mean of dependent variable
Y_1, Y_2, Y_3, Y_4	Dependent variables
z	Variable; bottom above given reference level (L)
z_1, z_2	System of units of measurement
α	Angle of sliding, angle of inclination (degrees); coefficient; slope of channel bottom; coefficient
α_1, α_2, ... α_n	Coefficients expressing distortion; exponents; constants
β	Parameter expressing the condition of movement $(L^{-0.882})$; the ratio of sediment transports; coefficient; parameter
β_1	Parameter expressing the condition of movement; exponent
β_x	Correction factor
γ	Specific gravity, specific gravity of water (FL^{-3}); coefficient
γ_t	Bulk density of sediment (FL^{-3})
γ_z	Bulk density of sediment-carrying water, bulk density of slurry (FL^{-3})
γ_{zm}	Specific gravity of moving slurry (FL^{-3})
γ_1	Specific gravity of sediment (FL^{-3})
δ	Correction factor; exponent
δ'	Thickness of laminar boundary layer (L)
Δ	Roughness coefficient
Δ_0	Non-uniformity coefficient
ε	Parameter $(L^{0.941}T^{-1})$; coefficient; eddy viscosity coefficient (L^2T^{-1}); relative roughness
ε'	Coefficient; dynamic eddy viscosity coefficient $(FL^{-2}T)$
$\boldsymbol{\epsilon}$	Conductivity tensor (L^2T^{-1})
ε_h	Sediment mixing coefficient (L^2T^{-1})
ε_h'	Dynamic sediment mixing coefficients $(FL^{-2}T)$
ε_x, ε_y	Tensor components (L^2T^{-1})
ζ	Coefficient of pipe friction
η	Coefficient depending on depth of flow $(L^{-1/2})$; relative depth of flow; ratio; factor expressing sediment transporting capacity
η_0	Coefficient
η_1	Coefficient $(FT^2L_-^4)$

Θ	Natural underwater slope of sediment material; correction factor; function
κ	Karman's universal constant; universal constant; thickness of annual deposit in reservoirs (L)
λ	Resistance coefficient; resistance coefficient of Darcy—Weissbach; coefficient; scale factor; proportionality coefficient (subscript indicates the physical quantity considered); coefficient representing the density of roughness elements; porosity of sediment material
λ_z	Resistance coefficient in slurry transport
μ	Coefficient of absolute viscosity ($FL^{-2}T$); coefficient of linear radiation absorption; chemical potential (EM^{-1}); coefficient of conductivity
μ_h	Fictitious dynamic viscosity coefficient of sediment ($FL^{-2}T$)
μ_t	Viscosity at temperature t deg. C ($FL^{-2}T$)
v	Coefficient of kinematic viscosity (L^2T^{-1})
v_h	Fictitious kinematic viscosity coefficient of sediment (L^2T^{-1})
ξ	Correction factor
π	Ludolf number; scale ratio of forces
$\boldsymbol{\pi}$	Stress tensor (FL^{-2})
π_{ij}	Component ij of convective momentum current density (FL^{-2})
π_{ik}	Component of turbulent stress tensor due to the pulsation current of fluid particles (FL^{-2})
π_{iks}	Component of turbulent stress tensor due to the pulsation current of solid particles (FL^{-2})
ρ	Fluid density (ML^{-3}, or FT^2L^{-4})
ρ'	Relative density
$\bar{\rho}$	Resultant density of dispersion (ML^{-3})
ρ_1	Density of particle, sediment grain, density of sediment (ML^{-3})
ρ_z	Slurry density (ML^{-3})
σ	Standard deviation; exponent
σ_g	Geometric standard deviation
τ	Shear stress, tractive force (FL^{-2})
τ^*	Parameter of Garde—Albertson
τ_{av}	Average tractive force (FL^{-2})
τ_c	Critical tractive force (FL^{-2})
$\tau_{ij}^{(1)}$	Component ji of tensor of viscous fluid stress (FL^{-2})
$\tau_{ij}^{(2)}$	Component ji of stress tensor due to particle interaction (FL^{-2})
τ_m	Tractive force in continuous movement, allowable tractive force (FL^{-2})
τ_0	Friction force, shear stress, actual tractive force, tractive force on channel bottom (FL^{-2})
τ_0'	Unused tractive force (part not consumed by resistances), tractive force due to particle resistance in smooth bed (FL^{-2})
τ_0''	Supplementary tractive force depending on bed form (FL^{-2})

791

τ_r	Tractive force at sediment oscillation (FL^{-2})
ϕ	Shape factor; coefficient
Φ	Sediment transport parameter
Φ'	Intensity of sediment transport
Φ_*	Sediment transport intensity in case of mixed size fractions
Φ_A	Sediment transport parameter
Φ_B	Sediment transport parameter
Φ_{B_1} (Φ_{B_2}, Φ_{B_3}, Φ_{B_4})	Dimensionless parameter measuring sediment transport
Φ_E	Sediment transport parameter of Egiazaroff
Φ_K	Sediment transport parameter of Kalinske
Φ_L	Sediment transport parameter of Laursen
Φ_P	Sediment transport parameter of Pedroli
Φ_S	Sediment transport parameter of Shields
Φ_{S-K-A}	Sediment transport parameter of Sato
ψ	Sediment characteristic; coefficient depending on granulometry or on sediment concentration; exponent
Ψ	Intensity of stream
Ψ_*	The intensity of stream for mixed sediment fractions
Ψ_A	Intensity of stream
ω	Fall velocity (LT^{-1})
$\bar{\omega}$	Resultant fall velocity of sediment (LT^{-1})
$\omega_{(C)}$	Fall velocity decreased by sediment concentration C (LT^{-1})
ω_D	Fall velocity in cylinder of diameter D (LT_-^{1})
ω_s	Fictitious fall velocity (LT^{-1})
ω_t	Fall velocity at temperature t deg. C, actuall fall velocity (LT^{-1})
ω_1	Decrease of fall velocity (LT^{-1})
Ω_A	Volume (L^3)

UNITS

Length:	metre	m			
	centimetre	cm;	1 cm	$=$	10^{-2} m
	millimetre	mm;	1 mm	$=$	10^{-3} m
	micron	μ;	1 μ	$=$	10^{-6} m
	kilometre	km;	1 km	$=$	10^3 m
Time:	second	sec			
Force, gravity force:					
	kilopond	kp			
	pond	p;	1 p	$=$	10^{-3} kp
	Megapond	Mp;	1 Mp	$=$	10^3 kp

Conversion table:

$$1 \text{ m} = 39.37 \text{ inches} = 3.28 \text{ foot}$$
$$1 \text{ foot} = 0.3048 \text{ m}$$
$$1 \text{ m}^2 = 0.133 \text{ ft}^2$$
$$1 \text{ ft}^2 = 0.0929 \text{ m}^2$$
$$1 \text{ m}^3 = 35.314 \text{ ft}^3$$
$$1 \text{ ft}^3 = 0.0283 \text{ m}^3$$
$$1 \text{ kp} = 2.2046 \text{ lb}$$
$$1 \text{ lb} = 0.4536 \text{ kp}$$

SI units:

$$1 \text{ kp} = 9.81 \text{ N}$$
$$1 \text{ N} = 0.102 \text{ kp}$$

LITERATURE

Abdel-Rahman, N. M.: The effect of flowing water on cohesive beds. The Swiss Federal Institue of Technology, Zürich 1963.

Ackers, P.: Experiment on small streams in alluvium. ASCE Hydraulics Division, HY 4, July 1964.

Airy, W.: Min. Proc. of the Inst. of Civ. Eng. 82, 1885.

Aksoy, S.: River-bed degradation downstream of dams. XIVth Congress of IAHR, Vol. 3. Paper C 33, Paris, 1971, pp. 275—281.

Albertson, M. L.—Simons, D. B.—Richardson, E. V.: Discussion: "Mechanics of sediment-ripple formation" by Hsiu-Kuan Liu. ASCE Hydraulics Division HY 1, Vol. 84, 1958.

Allen, J.: Scale models in hydraulic engineering. London—New York—Toronto 1946.

Ammer, A.: Neue Wege und Mittel des Flussbaues bei der Regulierung der Donau in Nieder-österreich. Die Wasserwirtschaft Nr. 9. 1928.

— Neue Wege und Mittel des Flussbaues bei der Regulierung der Donau in Niederösterreich. Die Wasserwirtschaft Nr. 12. 1928 (Fortsetzung von Heft 11, S. 183)

Ananyan, A. K.: Determination de la formation du lit riviéres, crée par suite de l'abaissement de la côte leurs bases d'erosion. AIHR. Comptes-rendus de la Neuvième Assemblée Générale (Dubrovnik) 1961, IV/10—1.

— Dvizhenie zhidkosti na povorote vodovoda (Movement of fluid in river bend). Izd. A. N. Arm. SSR, Yerevan 1957.

Anderson, A. G.: The characteristics of sediment waves formed by flow in open channels. Proc. Third Midwestern Conf. on Fluid Mechanics, Univ. of Minesota, Minneapolis, Minn., 1953.

Anderson, A. G.—Davenport, J. T.: The use of submerged groins for the regulation of alluvial streams. Symposium, Current Problems in River Training and Sediment Movement, 1/a, Budapest, 1968.

Apmann, R. P.—Rumer, R. R.: Diffusion of sediment in developing flow. ASCE Hydraulics Division, HY 1, January 1970.

Appel, D. W.: An instrument for rapid size-frequency analysis of sediment. Fifth Hydraulics Conference Bull. 34. Iowa 1953.

Bagnolds, R. A.: The flow of cohesionless grains in fluids. Philosphical Transactions, Royal Soc., London, Vol. 249, No. 964, 1956.

— Some flume experiments on large grains. Proc. Inst. Civ. Engineers, London, April 1955.

— The movement of desert sand. Proc. Roy. Soc. London, ser. A, No. 892, Vol. 157., December, 1936.

Balassa, M.: Korszerű hidromechanizáció (Current practice in slurry transport). Vízügyi szakmai irodalmi beszámolók, 1965.

Balló, M.: A Duna-folyam vegyi viszonyairól Buda-Pest mellett (The chemistry of Danube water over the Budapest section). Math. és Természettud. Közl. XI. 1873.

Barenblatt, G. I.: O dvizhenii vzveshennykh chastits v turbulentnom potoke (On the movement of suspended sediment in turbulent flow). Prikladnaya Matematika i Mekhanika, XVII, 1953, p. 261.

Barr, D. I. H.: Discriminating formulation of n term nondimensional functional equations from $(n + 1)$ term dimensionally homogeneous equations, with particular reference to incompressible viscous flow. Proc. Inst. Civil Engineers. Vol. 39. 1968.

- Method of synthesis - Basic procedures for the new approach to similitude. Water Power-Spray, May-April 1969.
- Density currents and public health engineering. Water and Water Engineering. Vol. 70. No. 850. 1966.

Barr, D. I. H.-Herbertson, J. G.: Bed-load transport at high shear stress. ASCE Hydraulics Division HY 5, September 1967.

Barr, D. I. H.-Herbertson, J. G.: Similitude theory applied to correlation of flume sediment transport data. Water Resources Research. Vol. 4. No 2. 1968.

Barr, D. I. H.-Herbertson, J. G.: A similitude framework of regime theory. Proc. ICE. Vol. 41, 1968.

Barr, D. I. H.-Shaikh, A. H.: Model simulation of surface profiles in tidal and non-tidal watercourses. The Engineer, Vol. 222. No. 5779, 1966.

Barr, D. I. H.-Smith, A. A.: Application of similitude theory to correlation of uniform flow data. The Institution of Civil Engineers, London 1967.

Barr, D. I. H.-Smith, A. A.-Frazer, W.: A hydraulic model study of heat dissipation at Longannet Power Station. The Institute of Civil Engineers, London 1968.

Bata, G.-Knezevich, B.: Some observations on density current in the laboratory and in the field. Minnesota International Hydraulics Convention, September 1-4. 1953.

Bauer, L.-Tille, W.: Untersuchungen zur regionalen Differenzierung des Sinkstofftransports in Thüringen und seiner Beziehungen zur Bodenerosion. Symposium. Budapest 1968.

Blau, E.: Beschreibung des von der Forschungsanstalt für Schiffahrt, Wasser- und Grundbau entwickelten Geschiebefängers mit Sedimentabsaugung. Symposium on Current Problems in River Training and Sediment Movement, 1/b, Budapest 1968.

Blench, T.: Coordination in mobile-bed hydraulics. ASCE Hydraulics Division, HY 6, 1969.
- Regime formulas for bed-load transport. University of Alberta, Canada.
- Regime theory for self-formed sediment bearing channels. ASCE Hydraulics Division 77, 1951.

Bogárdi, J.: A Duna mederanyagának összetétele (Composition of the bed material of the Danube). Study submitted to the Common Hungarian-Czechoslovakian Technical Committee, 1949, Manuscript.
- A hordalékmozgató erő (The tractive force). Technica 3, 1943.
- A hordalékmozgás elmélete (The theory of sediment transport). Akadémiai Kiadó, Budapest, 1955.
- A hordalékmozgás jelentősége a folyószabályozásban (The significance of sediment transport in river regulation). Advanced river regulation. OVH, 1969.
- A hordalék szerepe a folyószabályozásban (The role of sediment in river regulation). Mérnök-Továbbképző Intézet, 2373, Budapest 1954.
- A hasonlóság kérdése, különös tekintettel a hordalékos vízfolyások kismintavizsgálatára. (The problem of similarity with special regard to model experiments on sediment-carrying streams). Hidrológiai Közlöny, No. 3. 1963.
- A görgetett hordalék jellemzőinek folyóhossz szerinti változása (Variations in bed load parameters along rivers). Beszámoló a VITUKI 1954. évi munkásságról, 1955.
- A kismintavizsgálatok fejlődése és szerepe a vízgazdálkodásban (The development and role of model experiments in water management). MTA Műszaki Tud. Oszt. Közl. 33. 1964.
- A Sajó hordalékszállítása és a hordalékos víz ülepítése (Sediment transport in the Sajó river and settling of the sediment). Hidrológiai Közlöny 11-12. 1949. and 1-2. 1950.
- A lebegtetett hordalék (Suspended sediment). Mérnöki Továbbképző Intézet. M 18. Budapest, 1952.
- A lebegtetett hordalék töménysége (The concentration of suspended sediment). Hidrológiai Közlöny, Vol. 27. No. 9-12. 1947.

796

— A folyócsatornázással kapcsolatos hordalékproblémák (Sediment problems related to river canalization). MTA Műszaki Tud. Oszt. Közleményei, 2. 1—4. 1952.

— Folyócsatornázással kapcsolatos hordalékvizsgálatok (Sediment studies related to river canalization). Mérnök-Továbbképző Intézet M 33. Budapest, 1952.

— Hordalékmérési kísérletek a Felső-Dunán (Sediment measurement experiments on the Upper Danube). Vízügyi Közlemények, No. 1. 1939.

— Hordalékméréseink eddigi eredményei (Results attained thus far in sediment measurements). Vízügyi Közlemények, No. 2. 1954.

— Hordalékmozgás a folyószabályozásban (Sediment transport in river regulation). Vízügyi Közlemények, No. 3—4. 1942.

— Hordalékmozgás folyókban (Sediment transport in streams). Mérnöki Továbbképző Int. 38. 1942.

— Hordalékos folyóvizek ülepítésének néhány gyakorlati kérdése (Practical problems in settling sediment-laden stream water). Vízügyi Közlemények, No. II. 1951.

— Dimenzióanalízis és hasonlóság (Dimensional analysis and similarity). Utah State University C.E. 260. Lectures delivered in 1964, in Logan, Utah, USA.

— Kapcsolatok elméleti vizsgálata a vízfolyások hordalékszállításánál (Theoretical study of relationships on sediment transport in rivers). Hidrológiai Közlöny, No. 4. 1967.

— Kevés víz — víz — sok víz (Lack of water — water — surplus water). Akadémiai Kiadó, Budapest, 1967.

— Lebegtetett hordalékmozgás a Tisza záhony—rázompusztai szakaszán (The movement of suspended sediment between Záhony and Rázompuszta in the Tisza river). Vízügyi Közlemények, No. 3—4. 1949.

— Mozgó medrű folyók hidraulikai hasonlósága és a hordalékmozgás törvényszerűségei (Hydraulic similarity of movable-bed rivers and the laws governing sediment transport). VITUKI beszámoló 1957, Műszaki Könyvkiadó, Budapest 1959.

— Korrelációszámítás és alkalmazása a hidrológiában (Correlation computations and their application in hydrology). Akadémiai Kiadó 1952.

— Néhány újabb törvényszerűség a hordalékmozgás elméletében (Some new relationships in the theory of sediment transport). Hidrológiai Közlöny, No. 4 1958.

— Paraméterek és invariánsszámok szerepe a hordalékmozgást jellemző törvényszerűségekben (The role of parameters and invariants in the relationships applying to sediment transport). ÉKME Közl. No. 1—2. 1959.

— Vízfolyások hordalékmérése (Sediment measurements in water courses). Hidrológiai Közlöny, No. 7—12. 1942.

— Vízfolyások hordalékszállítása (Sediment transport in rivers). Akadémiai Kiadó, Budapest, 1971.

— Vízfolyások hordalékszállító képességének meghatározása (Determination of the sediment-transporting capacity of water courses). Hidrológiai Közlöny, No. 4. 1962.

— Jellegzetes összefüggések a görgetett hordalék szállítása és a vízfolyások hidraulikai jellemzői között (Characteristic relationships between bed load transport and the hydraulic characteristics of water courses). Hidrológiai Közlöny, Vol. 36. No. 2. 1956.

— A mederállandóságra és a hordalékmozgásra vonatkozó vizsgálatok (Studies on channel stability and sediment transport). MTA Műszaki Tud. Oszt. Közleményei, 19. No. 4. 1956; Acta Technica 17. No. 1—2. 1957.

— Kapcsolatok hordalékot szállító vízfolyások fizikai jellemzői között (Relations between the physical parameters of sediment-carrying water courses). Hidraulikai Konferencia, Budapest, 1960.

— Összefoglaló a "Folyami hidraulika, hordalék" kérdéscsoporthoz (Summary on the subject "River hydraulics, sediment"). Hidraulikai Konferencia, Budapest, 1. 1960.

— Bestimmung der Grenzzusände bei der Geschiebebewegung. Die Wasserwirtschaft, No. 7. 1968.

- Channel stability and sediment movement. VI Convegno Italiano di Idraulica e Costru zioni Idrauliche, Padova 1959.
- Current problems in river training and sediment movement. Vízügyi Közlemények, Special Number 1—1969. Budapest.
- Discussion: "A similitude framework of regime theory" by D. I. H. Barr—J. G. Herbertson. Proc. Instn. Civ. Engrs. 1968, 41 (December) pp. 761—781. Discussion: 1970, 45 (February) pp. 285—328.
- Discussion: "European concepts of sediment transportation" by J. Bogárdi. ASCE Hydraulics Division HY 6, Vol. 93. 1967. Closure.
- Discussion: "Mechanics of sediment-ripple formation" by Hsin-Kuan Liu. ASCE Hydraulics Division HY 5, 1958.
- Discussion: "The sediment load of streams" by E. M. Laursen. ASCE, Hydraulics Division HY 6, Vol. 84, 1958.
- Discussion: "Mechanics of sediment ripple formation" by J. Bogárdi, corrections. ASCE Hydraulics Division HY 7. Vol. 84. 1958.
- Discussion: "Discharge formula for straight channels" by K. H. Liu—S. Y. Hwang. ASCE Hydraulics Division HY 7, 1960.
- European concepts of sediment transportation. ASCE Hydraulics Division HY 1, January 1965.
- Fluvial sediment transportation. Reprinted from: Advances in Hydroscience, Vol. 8. 1972. pp. 183—259. Academic Press, Inc. New York and London.
- Hydraulic similarity of river models with movable bed. Acta Technica XXIV. 3—4. 1959.
- Incipient sediment motion in terms of the critical mean velocity. Acta Technica 62. 1968.
- Kennzeichnung des Beginnes der Geschiebebewegung durch die kritische mittlere Geschwindigkeit. Hidrológiai Közlöny, 9. 1968.
- Mesure du débit solide des rivières en Hongrie. La Huille Blanche No. 2. 1951.
- Sediment problems in relation to the Danube—Tisza—Danube Canal System in the Vojvodina. Food and Agriculture Organisation of the United Nations. Rome 1961.
- Sediment transportation. International Post-Graduate Course in Hydrology, UNESCO, Padova 1969.
- Sediment transportation in alluvial streams. International post-graduate course. Budapest 1968.
- Some concepts of model investigations on sediment transporting watercourses. Acta Technica, 50. 1965.
- Some aspects of the application of the theory of sediment transportation to engineering problems. Journal of Geophysical Research, Vol. 66. No. 10. 1961.
- Some characteristic relations concerning suspended sediment transportations. The Port Engineer, No. 4. Calcutta 1955.
- Summary of the measurements in Hungary of sediment transportation, with special reference to their quantitative bearing on erosion. Extrait des comptes rendus et rapports assemblée générale de Toronto 1957. Tome I. Gentbrugge 1958.
- The critical mean velocity as a criterion for incipient sediment motion. A folyószabályozás és hordalékmozgás időszerű kérdései. Symposium. Budapest 1968.
- Theoretische Untersuchung der Beziehungen der Feststofffrachten. Die Wasserwirtschaft, 59. Jahrgang, H. 12. 1969.
- Über die Zu- und Abnahme des Schwebestoffgehalts in den Flüssen mit der Änderung des Abflusses. Die Wasserwirtschaft, 47. Jg. H. 3. 1956.
- Validity of theoretical foundations of the relationships. International Post-Graduate Course. Padova 1967.
- Zeitgemässe Konzeption für die Untersuchung der Feststofführung der Gewässer. Österreichische Wasserwirtschaft, Jahrg. 18. H. 7/8. 1966.

Bogárdi, J.—Yen, C. H.: Traction of pebbles by flowing water. Iowa City 1938.

Bogárdi, J.—Szűcs, E.: Balance equations of suspended sediment transportation. Acta Technica 69. No. 1—2, 1970.

Bogdánfy, Ö.: A természetes vízfolyások hidraulikája (Hydraulics of natural water courses). Budapest 1906.

Bottomley, W. F.: A new theory of silt and scour. Engineering 125. 1928.

Breitschneider, H.: Einige Ähnlichkeitsbetrachtungen zur Geschiebformel von Meyer-Peter und Müller. Die Wasserwirtschaft, 58. Jahrgang, Heft 9, September 1968.

Brooks, N. H.: Mechanics of streams with movable beds of fine sand. ASCE Transactions, Vol. 123. 1958.

Bruk, S.: Observations on some assumptions in suspended sediment transport kinetics Saopštenja Instituta Vodoprivedu "Jaroslav Černi", Vol. XIV. No. 40.

— Hidraulika (I., II., III.). Rudarsko Geološki Fakultet, Beograd, Beograd 1967

Bruk, S.—Miloradov, V.: Calculation of sedimentation in backwater-affected rivers with particular attention to the Danube upstream of the Djerdap high dam. Symposium on Current Problems in River Training and Sediment Movement, 2/b, Budapest, 1968.

Brune, G. M.: Rates of sediment production in midwestern United States. U.S. Dept. Agr., Soil Conserv. Serv., SCS-TP-65, Milwaukee, Wis., August 1948.

— Trap efficiency of reservoirs: Trans. Am. Geophys. Union, Vol. 34, No. 3, June 1953.

Buckingham, E.: On physically similar systems; Illustration of use of dimensional equations. Physical Review IV. 2. 1914.

Cabelka, J.—Novák, P.: Hydraulic research. Vol. 1. Model research. SNTL, Prague 1964. (In Czech)

Camp, T. R.: The effect of turbulence in retarding settling. Proceedings of the Second Hydraulics Conference. Bull. 27.

— Sedimentation and the design of settling tanks. Transactions ASCE 1946.

Canali, L.—Allodi, G.: Contribution à l'étude sur le transport solide en suspension dans les cours d'eau et sur la dégradation du sol dans le bassin du Po. International Commission for Scientific Hydrology. Bull. n. 4. 1962.

Carey, W. C.: Formation of flood plain lands. ASCE Hydraulics Division HY 3, May 1969.

Carter, C. E.—Dendy, F. E.: Runoff and soil loss from pastured loess soils in North Mississippi Water Resources Conference, Jackson, Mississippi 1966.

Casey, H. J.: Über Geschiebebewegung. Berlin 1935.

Cavazza, S.: Sul trasporto torbido in fase di piena dei corsi d'acqua naturali. Atti dell'VIII Convegno italiano di Idraulica e Costruzioni idrauliche. Pisa 1963.

Cecen, K.—Bayazit, M.: Deposition and scour downstreams from semipermeable structures. International Association for Hydraulic Research. XIIth Congress No. 2. 1967.

Cecen, K.—Bayazit, M.: Free fall of cylinders through water in a vertical pipe and standard penetration test in water. Commission International des Grands Barrages. Istambul 1967.

Chabert, J.—Chauvin, J. L.: Formation des dunes et des rides dans les modèles fluviaux. Bulletin du centre de Recherches et d'Essais de Chatou, No. 4. 1963.

Chang, Y. L.: Laboratory investigation of flume traction and transportation. ASCE Hydraulics Division, nov. 1947.

Chapter, V.: Sediment control methods introduced and watershed area. ASCE Hydraulics Division HY 2, March 1969.

Chauvin, J. L.: Similitude des modèles de cours d'eau à fond mobile. Similitude in movable-bed river models. Bulletin du centre de Recherches et d'Essais de Chatou, No. 1. 1962. T. P. 240.

Chorley, R. J.: Geomorphology and general systems theory. U.S. Government Printing Office, Washington 1962.

Christiansen, J. E.: Distribution of silt in open channels. Transactions AGU Sixteenth Annual Meeting 1935.

Colby, B. R.: Scour and fill in sand-bed streams. U.S. Government Printing Office, Washington 1964.

799

Coleman, N. L.: A new examination of sediment suspension in open channels. Journal of Hydraulic Research, No. 1. 1969.

Collaborating Agencies: Analytical study of methods of sampling suspended sediment. Report No. 3. Iowa City 1941.

— Equipment used for sampling bed-load and bed material. Report No. 2. Iowa City 1940.

— Methods of analysing sediment samples. Report No. 4. Iowa City 1941.

Conti, L.: Trasporto solido nei corsi d'acqua. Anali dei Lavori Pubblici. 1930, No. 4.

Courtois, G.—Sauzay, G.: Les méthodes de bilan des taux de comtage de traceurs radioactifs appliquées à la mesure des débits massiques de charriage. La Houille Blanche, No. 3. 1966.

Csoma, J.: A dunai vízerőműrendszer hatása a hordalékviszonyok alakulására (Effect of hydroelectric development on sediment conditions in the Danube). VITUKI 8.04.03.02.02.

— A Felső-Dunára vonatkozó tanulmányok értékelése, az egységes főmeder kialakítását célzó vizsgálatok (Analysis of studies on the Upper Danube, studies aimed at the development of a main channel). 3.7 témaszám: 6.2.2.

— A felső-dunai mellékágrendszerek mederváltozása (Channel changes in the branch system along the Upper Danube). Földrajzi Értesítő XVII. 3. 1968.

— A Keleti Főcsatorna torkolati szakaszának feltöltődése (Silting over the downstream end section of the Eastern Main Canal). VITUKI Beszámoló 5.8, 1964.

— A mederanyag-mintavétel és a minta megbízhatóságának vizsgálata (Study on the reliability of bed material sampling and of the samples obtained). Hidrológiai Közlöny, No. 3. 1964.

— A hordalékosság vizsgálata a duzzasztott térben (Studies on sediment in the backwater reach). VITUKI témaszám: 8.04.05.02.02/c/2.

— A lebegtetett hordalék vizsgálata a duzzasztott térben a kismintakísérletek eredményeinek felhasználásával (Studies on suspended sediment in the backwater reach relying on the results of model experiments). VITUKI témaszám: 8.04.03.02.02/c/1. 1966.

— A vízfolyások által szállított görgetett hordalék mennyiségének meghatározása (Estimation of bed load transported in water courses). Hidrológiai Közlöny, No. 2. 1966.

Csoma, J.—Dohnalik, J.: A tiszalöki duzzasztott folyószakasz hordalék- és mederanyagviszonyainak hatása a mederalakulásra (Influence of sediment and bed material conditions on channel development over the backwater reach upstream of Tiszalök). VITUKI Beszámoló 1960.

Csoma, J.—Zboray, K.—Szilágyi, J.: A tiszalöki duzzasztott tér víz-, hordalék- és jéglevonulási viszonyai (Flow, sediment and ice travel conditions over the Tiszalök backwater reach). Vízügyi Közlemények, No. 2. 1967.

Csuka, J.: A hordaléknyilvántartás megbízhatóságának vizsgálata (Reliability study on bed load surveys). VITUKI témaszám: 1.2.4.e.

— 1960. évig működő hordalékmérési állomások adatainak értékelése (Evaluation of data from the sediment-measuring stations operated up to 1960). VITUKI Beszámoló 1961.

— Siócsatornázással összefüggő hordalékvizsgálatok (Sediment studies related to the canalization of the Sió Canal). VITUKI Beszámoló 1963.

Dementiev, M. A.: Obshchie uravneniya i dinamicheskoe podobie vzvecencushchkikh potokov (General equations and dynamic similarities of sediment-transporting streams). Izv. VNIIG 73.

Dendy, F. E.: Sedimentation in the Nation's Reservoirs. Journal of Soil and Water Conservation, Vol. 23. N. 4. 1968.

Dendy, F. E.—Spraberry, J. A.—Champion, W. A.: Sediment deposition in reservoirs in the United States. ARS 41—137. December 1967.

Dobbins, W. E.: Effect of turbulence on sedimentation. ASCE Hydraulics Division 109, 1943.

Dohnalik, J.: A görgetett hordalékmérés és feldolgozás alkalmazott módszereinek és műszereinek leírása és azok kritikai elemzése (Description and critical analysis of methods and devices for obtaining and processing bed load data). VITUKI Budapest, 1968.

— A lebegtetett hordalék mintavételekre szolgáló műszerek leírása és az ezekkel szerzett tapasztalatok (Description of devices for taking suspended-sediment samples and the experiences gained with them). VITUKI Budapest 1966.

Dohnalik, J.—Csoma, J.: A tiszalöki duzzasztott folyószakasz feliszapolódásának vizsgálata (Studies on silting over the Tiszalök backwater reach). Hidraulikai Konferencia, Budapest 1960.

Donat, J.: Über Sohlenangriff und Geschiebebetrieb. Die Wasserwirtschaft, Nr. 26, 27. 1929.

Du Boys, P.: Le Rhone et les rivières à lit affouillable. Annales des Ponts et Chaussées 1879.

Du Buat, L. G.: Principles d'Hydraulique. Paris 1786.

Durand, R.: Basic relationships of the transportation of solids in pipes. Experimental research. Proceedings Minnesota International Hydraulics Convention. Minneapolis 1953.

— Transport hydraulique du graver et galets en conduite. La Houille Blanche, No. B. 609. 1951.

Durand, R.—Cohen de Lara, G.: Vitesse de chute des grain de sable dans les fluides en milieu infini. La Huille Blanche, Mai 1953.

Düll, F.: Das Gesetz des Geschiebeabriebes. Berlin 1930.

— Ermittlung der Schwemmstofführung in natürlichen Gewässern. Die Bautechnik 35—38. 1929.

Dyakov, P. P.: Gidromekhanizatsiya zemlyanykh rabot na zheleznodorozhnom transporte (Slurry transport in railroad construction). Moscow 1950.

Eakin, H. M.: Silting of reservoirs. U.S. Dept. of Agriculture, Technical Bull. No. 524. July 1936.

Egiazaroff, I. V.: Polyphase currents with non-uniform sediments and the physics of river flow. 13th Congress IAHR. 1969.

— Torrential sediment flows and the possibility of their calculation and laboratory research on models. Symposium, Budapest 1968.

Ehrenberger, R.: Direkte Geschiebemessungen an der Donau bei Wien und bisherige Ergebnisse. Die Wasserwirtschaft, Wien 1931.

— Geschiebemessungen an Flüssen mittels Auffanggeräten und Modellversuche mit letzteren. Wasserwirtschaft 33—36. 1932.

— Geschiebetrieb und Geschiebefracht der Donau in Wien auf Grund direkter Messungen. Wasserkraft und Wasserwirtschaft, Jahrg. 36. Heft 12. 1942.

— Zur Frage der Kennzeichnung von Flussgeschieben. Die Wasserkraft und Wasserwirtschaft, Heft 17/18. 1931.

Einstein, H. A.: Der Geschiebebetrieb als Wahrscheinlichkeitsproblem. Mitt. Versuchsanst. für Wasserbau an der Eidg. Techn. Hochschule, Zürich 1937.

— Die Eichung des in Rhein verwendeten Geschiebefängers. Schweizerische Bauzeitung 11/14. 1937.

— Flow on movable bed. Proc. of the 2nd Hydraulic Conference. University of Iowa Studies in Engineering. Bul. 27. 1943.

— Formulae for the transportation of bed-load. ASCE 107. 1942.

— Geschiebebetrieb. SBZ Zürich 1934.

— The bed-load function for sediment transportation in open channel flows. U.S. Department of Agriculture, Technical Bulletin No. 1026. 1950.

— River sedimentation. Ven Te Chow: Handbook of applied hydrology. McGrav-Hill Company. London 1964.

Einstein, H. A.—Ning Chien: Similarity of distorted river models with movable bed. Trans. Am. soc. Civil Engrs. Vol. 121. 1956.

Eisner, F.: Offene Gerinne. Handbuch der Experimentalphysik. Vol. IV.

Elzerman, J. J.—Frijlink, H. C.: Present state of the investigations bed-load movement in Holland, IXth Assembly of the IUGG, Brussels, No. 1—4. 1951.

51

Entz, B.: A Balaton feltöltődése (Silting of Lake Balaton). Vízgazdálkodás, No. 2. 1962.

Erdélyszky, Zs.—Stelczer, K.: Investigation into the movement of fluvial bed-load with radioisotopes. "Isotopes in Hydrology" IAEA. Wienna 1967.

Erkek, C.: Beitrag zur Berechnung des Geschiebetriebes in offenen Gerinnen mit beweglicher Sohle unter besonderer Berücksichtigung der Flachlandflüsse. Mitteilungen aus dem Leichtweiss-Institut für Wasserbau und Grundbau der Technischen Hochschule Braunschweig. Heft 17. 1967.

Engels, H.: Versuche über den Reibungswiderstand zwischen Wasser und Bettsohle. Zeitschrift f. Bauwesen, 1912.

Fargue, L.: La forme du lit des rivières à fond mobile. Paris 1908.

Faris, O. A.: The silt load of Texas streams. U.S. Dep. of Agricul. Tech. Bulletin, No. 382. 1933

Fáy, Gy.—Zselev, B.: Die mathematischen Grundlagen der Kornungsanalyse von gemahlenen Körnmengen. Acta Techn. 44. 1963.

Fáy, Gy.—Zselev, B.: Grundlagen der Zerkleinerungstheorie I—II. Energietechnik 12. 1962.

Fényes, I.: Termosztatika és termodinamika (Thermostatics and thermodynamics). Műszaki Könyvkiadó, Bucapest 1969.

Filep, L.: Feltöltés iszapolással és az iszap folyatása nyílt csatornákban (Fill construction by hydraulic method and the conveyance of silt in open canals). Vízügyi Közlemények, No. 1. 1930.

Forcheimer, Ph.: Geschiebebewegung in Flüssen. Zeitschrift für Bauwesen, 1923.

— Hydraulik. Leipzig—Berlin 1930.

Frankl,.F. I.: The theory of sediment transportation (in Russian). DAN SSR, Vol. 72, 1953.

— Energy equations of suspended-sediment transportation (in Russian). DAN SSR, Vol. 102, 1955.

Freeman, I. R.: Hydraulic laboratory practice. 1929.

Friedkin, J. F.: A laboratory study of the meandering of alluvial rivers. U.S. Waterways Experiment Station, Wicksburg 1945.

Frosini, P.: Contributi italiani allo studio del transporto solido dei corsi d'acqua. International Commission for Scientific Hydrology. Bull. n. 21. 1936.

Führböter, A.: Über die Förderung von Sand-Wasser Gemischen in Rohrleitungen. Mitteil. des Franzius-Inst. Heft 19, Hannover 1961.

Garde, R. J.—Albertson, M. L.: Bed-load transport in alluvial channels. La Huille Blanche, N. 3, Mai—June 1961.

Garde, R. J.—Bogárdi, J.: Discussion: "Discharge formula for straight alluvial channels" by H. K. Liu and S. Y. Hwang. ASCE Hydraulics Division HY 7 July 1960.

Garde, R. J.—Ranga Raju, K. G.: Resistance relationships for alluvial channel flow. ASCE Hydraulics Division, HY 4, July 1966.

Garde, R. J.—Ranga Raju, K. G.: Regime criteria for alluvial streams. ASCE Hydraulics Division, H9 6, November 1963.

Gherardelli, L.: Sul trasporto solido per sospensione. Atti del V Convegno Italiano di Idraulica Torino 1957.

Giandotti, M.: Studi sulle portate solide del Po e sulle variazioni fisiche del suo alveo. International Commission for Scientific Hydrology. Bull. n. 15. 1930.

— Contributo allo studio del trasciamento del materiale nell'alveo dei torrenti. Annali dei Lavori Pubblici. 1929. n. 8.

Gilbert, G. K.: Transportation of debris by running water. U.S. Geological Survey Professional Paper. 86. 1914.

Gilbert, M.—Durand, R.—Condolics, E.: Etude experimentale du refoulement des materiaux en conduites, en particulier des produits de dragage et des schlammes. Transport hydraulique et decantation des materiaux solides. Grenoble 1952.

Goncharov, V. I.: Dvizhenie nanosov v ravnomernom potoka (Movement of sediment in steady flow). ONTI Leningrad—Moscow 1938.
— Dinamika ruslovykh potokov (Stream flow dynamics). Gidrometeoizdat, Leningrad 1962
Goryunov, S. I.: Sposob priblizhennogo rascheta gidrotransporta (Estimating slurry transport in pipelines). Trudy VNIIG, 1959.
Gottschalk, L. C.: Analysis and use of reservoir sedimentation data. Bureau of Reclamation, Sedimentation Conference 1948.
— Measurement of sedimentation in small reservoirs. ASCE Hydraulics Division Vol. 77. Separate No. 55. January 1951.
— Reservoir sedimentation. Ven Te Chow: Handbook of applied hydrology. McGraw-Hill Company. London 1964.
Graf, W. H.: Hydraulics of sediment transport. McGraw-Hill Book Company, New York 1971.
Gruner, H. E.: Studien in der Schweiz über Geschiebebewegungen in Gewässern. Die Wasserwirtschaft, Nr. 15. 1929.
Guglielmini, D.: Opera omnia. 1697.
Guy, H. P.: An analysis of some storm-period variables affecting stream sediment transport. U.S. Government Printing Office, Washington 1964.
Guy, H. P.—Simons, D. B.: Dissimilarity between spatial and weighted velocity. U.S. Geol. Survey Prof. Art. 149. Fort Collins, Colo 1964.
Gvelesiani, L. G.—Shmal'tzel, N. P.: Studies of storage work silting of hydroelectric power plants on mountain rivers and silt depositing fighting. XIVth Congress of the IAHR, Vol. 5. Paper 105. Paris 1971, pp. 17—20.
Hankó, Z.: A hasonlóság kielégítése szivárgási jelenségek kismintavizsgálatában (The problem of similarity in seepage model studies). MTA Osztályközlemények 35. No. 1—4. 1965.
— A vízfolyások hordalékszállító képességéről (On sediment-transporting capacity of streams). Vízügyi Közlemények, Vol. XVIII. No. 4. 1966.
— Nyílt felszínű vízfolyások hordalékszállító képessége (On the sediment-transporting capacity of open channels). Hidrológiai Közlöny, No. 7. 1964.
— Természetes vízfolyások kismintavizsgálatai (Model studies on alluvial streams). MTA Osztályközlemények 33, 1—4, 1964.
— Über die das Geschiebe in Bewegung setzende kritische mittlere Geschwindigkeit. Symposium, Budapest 1968.
— Über die Geschiebebefrachtungsfähigkeit der Wasserläufe. Vysokého Učeni Techn. v Brne. Ročnik 1967, čislo 1—2.
Hamamori, A.: A theoretical investigation on the fluctuation of bed-load transport. Hydraulics Laboratories Delft, May 1962.
Harleman, D. R. F.—Elder, R. A.: Withdrawal from two-layer stratified flows. ASCE Hydraulics Division. HY 4, July 1965.
Hartke, H.—Mauersberger, P.: Messung der Sedimentbewegung in Flüssen, in Seen und im Marinen Küstenbereich mit Hilfe von magnetischen Indikatoren. Symposium, Budapest 1968.
Hartung, F.: Hydraulische und mathematische Modelle an Flüssen. Die Wasserwirtschaft, 60. Jahrgang, Heft 1/2. 1970.
Haszpra, O.: Hordalékos vízfolyás vízhozamnyilvántartási szelvényének kismintavizsgálata (Model studies on permanent gaging sections in alluvial water courses). Vízügyi Közlemények, No. 3. 1963.
— Hozzászólás Csoma János: A vízfolyások által szállított görgetett hordalék mennyiségének meghatározása c. tanulmányához (Discussion on the paper "Determination of bed load transport by alluvial streams" by Csoma, J.). Hidrológiai Közlöny, No. 7. 1966.
Herbertson, J. G.: Data correlations for sediment transport in flumes. Reprints of Bull. of the IASH. XIII. No. 2. 1968.
— Scaling procedures for mobile bed hydraulic models in terms of similitude theory. IAHR. Vol. 7. No. 3. 1969.

Herbich, J. B.: Large-scale roughness in open-channel flow. ASCE Hydraulics Division, HY 6, 1964.
Heywood, H.: Measurement of the fineness of powered materials. Inst. of Mech. Eng. Proc. 140. 1938.
Hino, M.: Turbulent flow with suspended particles. Journal of the Hydraulics Division, HY 4. 1963.
Ho, P. Y.: Abhängigkeit der Geschiebebewegung von der Kornform und der Temperatur. Berlin 1939.
Holeman, J. N.: The sediment yield of major rivers of the world. U.S. Department of Agriculture, Hyattsville 1968.
Hooker, E. H.: The suspension of solids in flowing water. ASCE Hydraulics Division 791.1896.
Horusitzky, H.: Nyitramegyei Tornóc és Ürmény környéke (The environment of Tornóc and Ürmény in Nyitra County). M. Kir. Földtani Int. Évi Jelentés 1903.
Horváth, F.—Szűcs, E.: Similarity of dust-fluid flow. Acta Technica 66. 1—3. 1969.
Howard, C. S.: Density current in lake Mead. Proceedings Minnesota International Hydraulics Convention. Minneapolis 1953.
— Suspended matter in Colorado river. 1925—1928. U.S. Water Supply Paper No. 636-B.
Humphreys, A. A.—Abbot, H. J.: The physics and hydraulics of the Mississippi river. 1861.
Hurst, H. E.: The suspension of sand in water. Proc. Royal Soc. London, 124. 1929.
IAHR: Proceedings Minnesota International Hydraulics Convention. Minneapolis, Minnesota 1953.
— Report of the Fourth Meeting IAHR. Bombay 2—5 I. 1951.
Ibad-Zade, Yu. A.: Obobshchennyi metod rascheta raskhoda donnykh nanosov (Generalized method of computing bed load transport). On pages 58—58 of the book: Dvizhenie nanosov v otkrytykh ruslakh (Sediment transport in open channels). Institut Vodnykh Problem. Izd. "Nauka", Moscow 1970.
Ibad-Zade, Yu. A.—Kiyasbeili, T. K.: Formirovanie rusel rek (Morphology of river beds). Izd. AN. Azerb. SSR, Baku 1966. Izv. AN. SSSR 2, 6, 8, 9, 11, 12. 1952.
Indri, E.: Il problema del trasporto solido ed i risultati di recenti ricerche. Societa Editrice Riviste Industrie Elettriche 1941.
— Sulla forza di trascinamento delle correnti liquide. L'Energia Elettrica XI. 1934.
Inglis, C. C.: Historical note on empirical equations, developed by engineers in India for flow of water and sand in alluvial channels. IAHR Second Meeting, Stockholm 1948.
— The effect of variations in charge and grade on the slopes and shapes of channels. Proceedings IAHR 1949.
Ippen, A. T.—Verma, R. P.: The motion of discrete particles along the bed of a turbulent stream. Proc. Minnesota International Hydraulics Convention, Sept. 1—4. 1953.
Ismail, H. M.: Turbulent transfer mechanism and suspended sediment in closed channels. ASCE Hydraulics Division, Vol. 77. Separate No. 56. February 1951.
Ivicsics, L.: A görgetett hordalék zörejének mérése (Measurement of bed load noise). Mérés és Automatik, No. 5. 1953.
— A görgetett hordalék zörejének megfigyelése (Observation of noise generated by bed load movement). Hidrológiai Közlöny 36. No. 4. 1956.
— A Keleti Főcsatorna felső szakaszának feltöltődése (Silting over the entrance section of the Eastern Main Canal). Beszámoló a VITUKI 1957. évi munkájáról. 5. 1959.
— Hosszanti átfolyású ülepítő medencék áramlástani vizsgálata (Hydraulic study on flow-through horizontal settling basins). Kandidátusi disszertáció, Budapest 1954.
— Ülepítőmedencék hidraulikai méretezése és az ülepedési sebesség meghatározása (Hydraulic dimensioning of settling basins and determination of the settling velocity). Vízügyi Közlemények, No. 1/2, 1957.
Jeffreys, H.: On the transport of sediment in streams. Proceedings Cambridge Phil. Soc. 25.1929.
Jensen, P.—Lebreton, J. C.: Quelques résultats experimentaux concernant les caracteristiques des dunes et leur representation sur les modèles à fonds mobiles. Bulletin de la Direction

des Etudes et Recherches — Série A. Nucléaire, Hydraulique, Thermique, No. 4. 1969. pp. 15—34.

Johnson, J. W.: Discussion: "Laboratory investigations of flume traction and transportation" by L. Y. Chang. Transactions of ASCE 104, 1939.

Johnson, P.—Muir, T. C.: Acoustic detection of sediment movement. Journal of Hydraulic Research, Vol. 7. 1969. No. 9.

Kalinske, A. A.: Investigations of liquid turbulence and suspended material transportation. University of Pennsylvania Bicentennial Conference.

— Relation of the statistical theory of turbulence to hydraulic. American Society of Civil Engineers, New York 1940.

— Criteria for determining sand-transport by surface-creep and salation. Transactions of 1942 of the American Geophysical Union.

— Suspended-material transportation under non-equilibrium conditions. Transactions of 1940 of the American Geophysical Union.

Kalinske, A. A.—Hsia, C. H.: Study of transportation of fine sediment by flowing water. University of Iowa Studies in Engineering, Bulletin No. 29.

Kalinske, A. A.—Pien, C. L.: Experiments of eddy-diffusion and suspended-material transportation in open channels. TAGU 1943.

Kalinske, A.A.—Van Driest, E. R.: Application of statistical theory of turbulence to hydraulic problems. Proc. 5th International Congress of Applied Mechanics. 1938.

Kalmár, Gy.: A hordalékmozgás kísérleti tanulmányozása (Experimental studies on sediment transport). A II. sz. Vízépítéstani Tanszék kísérletei. Budapest 1952. (Manuscript)

Karaushev, A. V.: Gidravlika rek i vodokhranilishch (River and reservoir hydraulics). Izd. "Rechnoi Transport", 1955.

— Rechnaya gidravlika (Fluvial hydraulics). Gidromet. Izd. Leningrad 1969.

Klimentov, A.: O raskhodakh i deistvitel'nykh udel'nykh vesakh pul'py (On costs and specific weight in slurry transport). Gidrotekhn. Stroit. 1953. 6.

Knoroz, V S.: Nerazmyvayushchie skorosti dlya melkozernistykh gruntov (Non-scouring velocities for fine-grained soils). Gidrotekhn. Stroit. 1953, 8.

Karádi, G.: A lebegtetett hordalékmozgás kérdéséről (On problems in suspended-sediment transport). Hidrológiai Közlöny, No. 11—12. 1953.

— Mozgó medrű kismintakísérletek a morfológiai viszonyok figyelembevételével (Movable-bed river models taking morphology into consideration). Vízügyi Közlemények, No. II. 1953.

Kármán, T.: Turbulence. Journal of the Aeronautical Society, December 1937.

Károlyi, Z.: A felsődunai hordaléktanulmányok eddigi eredményei (Results attained thus far in sediment studies on the Upper Danube). Vízügyi Közlemények, 31. No. 1. 1951.

— A dunai hordalékvizsgálatok eredményeiből leszűrhető morfológiai következtetések (Conclusions on morphology derived from the results of sediment studies on the Upper Danube). Földrajzi Értesítő 7, No. 3. 1958.

— A hordalékmozgató erők meghatározása természetes vízfolyásoknál (Determination of the tractive force in alluvial channels). Vízügyi Közlemények 31. No. 1—2. 1949.

— Hordalékmérés és hordalékhozam (Sediment observations and sediment transport). Mérnöki Továbbképző Intézet, 1952.

— A folyami hordalék mennyiségi csökkenése kopás következtében (Reduction in the quantity of river sediment due to wearing). Vízügyi Közlemények, 35. No. 2. 1953.

— Kísérletek hordalékfogóval (Bed load trap experiments). Vízügyi Közlemények, 29. No 1—4. 1947.

— A Felső-Duna feltöltődő szakaszán észlelhető kavicslerakódás mennyiségének meghatározása (Estimation of gravel quantities deposited on the aggradation section of the Upper Danube). Vízügyi Közlemények, 39. No. 3. 1957.

— A hordalékmozgás jellegzetességei folyók medrében (Characteristics of sediment transport in alluvial channels). Földrajzi Értesítő, No. 1. 1960.

— Feladataink a görgetett hordalékvizsgálatok fejlesztése terén (Problems in the development of bed load studies). Vízügyi Közlemények, No. 1. 1962.

— Hordaléklerakódás az eringi Inn-erőmű duzzasztóterében (Sediment deposition in the backwater reach of the power plant Fring on the Inn river). Vízügyi Közl. No. 2. 1962

— Sarkantyúkkal való folyószabályozás (River regulation with spurdikes). ÉKME No. 1—2 1960.

— Mesures se rapportant au debit solide du haut-Danube Hongrois. Association Internationale de Recherches pour Travaux Hydrauliques. Grenoble 1949.

— Folgerungen aus den Ergebnissen der Geschiebemessungen an der Donau. Österreichische Wasserwirtschaft, Wien. No. 10. 1957.

Kellerhals, R.: Stable channels with gravel-paved beds. ASCE Hydraulics Division HY Vol. 1967.

Kennedy, J. F.: The mechanics of dunes and antidunes in erodible-bed channels. W. M. Keck Laboratory of Hydraulics and Water Resources. Pasadena 1963.

Kennedy, R. G.: Hydraulic diagram for canals in earth. Minutes of Proceedings Inst. C. E. 119. 1895.

— On the prevention of silting in irrigation channels. Minutes of Proceedings Inst. C.E. 1895.

Keulegan, G. H.: Laws of turbulent flow in open channels. Nat. Bureau of Standards Jour. Res. 21. 1938.

Kéz, A.: Hogyan mozog a kavics a vízfolyás medrében? (How is gravel transported in alluvial channels?). Földrajzi Értesítő, 7. No. 3. 1958.

Komura, S.: Bulk properties of river-bed sediment and its applications to sediment hydraulics. Proc. 11th Japan National Congress for Appl. Mech. 1961.

— Similarity and design methods of river models with movable bed. Trans. of JSCE No. 80. April 1962.

— Prediction of river-bed degradation below dams. XIVth Congress of IAHR, Vol. 3. Paper C 31. Paris 1971. pp. 257—264.

Kovács, Gy.: Folyószabályozási kísérletek végrehajtása (Performance of river model tests). Mérnöki Továbbképző Intézet, 1954.

— Irányelvek mozgó medrű kisminták számításához (Principles of computing movable-bed river models). Hidrológiai Közlöny, No. 11—12. 1952.

Kozák, M.: A zagy koncentrációjának és hozamának mérési módszerei (Methods of measuring the concentration and transport rate of slurry). Bányászati Lapok, No. 5. 1963.

— Inhomogén talajt szállító zagyvezeték hidraulikai ellenállásának közelítő számítása (Approximate estimation of the hydraulic resistance in slurry lines transporting non-uniform soil). Hidrológiai Közlöny, No. 2. 1961.

Kramer, H.: Modellgeschiebe und Schleppkraft. Berlin 1932.

— Sand mixtures and sand movement in fluvial models. Transactions ASCE 1935.

Kreps, H.: Das Problem der Ermittlung einer Jahresgeschiebefracht aus einer beschränkten Zahl von Messungen. Österreichische Wasserwirtschaft 1961.

Kresser, W.: Gedanken zur Geschiebe und Schwebschtofführung der Gewässer. Österreichische Wasserwirtschaft, Jahrgang 16, Heft 1/2.

Kreuter, F.: Beitrag zur Theorie der Geschiebeführung. Zeitschrift für Gewässerkunde, 1898.

Krey, H.: Grenzen der Übertragbarkeit der Versuchsergebnisse und Modellähnlichkeit bei praktischen Flussbauversuchen. Zeitschr. f. angewandte Math. u. Mechanik.

— Widerstand von Sandkörnern und Kugeln bei der Bewegung im Wasser als Grundlage der Schwemmstoffbewegung in unseren Flüssen. Mitteilung VWS H. 1.

Kulesh, N. P.: Experimental study of reservoirs with density currents formed during the flood, calculation principles for silting of such reservoirs. XIVth Congress of IAHR, Vol. 5. Paper 104. Paris 1971, pp. 13—16.

Kuo-chang Ling—Chi-fen Pan—Yuan-lin Lin: Sediment problems and watershed management in Taiwan. For the International Hydrological Decade. Taiwan Power Company. Taipei, Taiwan 1969.

Kurzmann, S.: Beobachtungen über Geschiebeführung. München 1919.
— Neue Forschungen über Geschiebeführung. Wasserkraft und Wasserwirtschaft. 1927.
Labaye, G.—Károlyi, Z.: A folyóvizek hordaléka. Note sur la débit des cours d'eau. La Houille Blanche A/1948. Rev.: Vízügyi Közlemények, No. 3—4. 1950.
Lacey, G.: Sediment transport and the regime concept. College of Engineering Utah State University, Logan, Utah 1964.
— Stable channels in alluvium. Minutes of Proc. Inst. C.E. 129. 1930.
Lane, W.: Collection of data of the solids load of flowing streams. Journal of the Association of Chinese and American Engineers, XIX, No. 3. 1938.
— Charge as a factor in stable irrigation canals. Irrigation and Power Journal, Vol. XII. No. 2. 1955.
— Design of stable channels. ASCE Trans. Vol. 120. p. 1234. 1955.
— Notes on limit of sediment concentration. Journal of Sedimentary Petrology. Vol. 10. No. 2. 1940.
— Predicting stages for the Lower Mississippi. Civil Engineering, Februar 1937.
— The behavior of soil materials in water retaining structures. Soil Science Society of America, Proc. Vol. 1. 1937.
— The effect of cutting off bends in rivers. Third Hydraulics Conference. Bull. 31. Iowa 1947.
— Some aspects of reservoir sedimentation. Irrigation and Power Journal, Vol. X. 1953.
— Progress report on studies on the design of stable channels by Bureau of Reclamation. ASCE Hydraulics Division, September 1953.
— Stable channels in erodible material. Transactions ASCE 102, 1937.
Lane, E. W.—Kalinske, A. A.: Engineering calculations of suspended sediment. Reprinted in USA from Transactions of 1941 of the American Geophysical Union.
Lane, E. W.—Kalinske, A. A.: The relation of suspended to bed material in rivers. Reprinted in USA from Transactions of 1941 of the American Geophysical Union.
Larras, J.: Energy gradient of uniform linear flows on movable bottoms. Comptes-Rendus de l'Académie des Sciences, Paris 29 Mars, 1965.
— Pertes de charge dans les écoulements uniformes, sur fonds mobiles recouverts de dunes. C. R. Sc. Paris, t. 257, 28 Octobre 1963, Groupe 2.
— Average concentration of suspended matters in a uniform linear flow. Comptes-Rendus de l'Académie des Sciences, Paris, Octobre 1965.
Lászlóffy, W.: A szabad felszínnel folyó víz sebességének számítása (Computation of the velocity of open-channel flow). Vízügyi Közlemények, No. 1—2. 1950.
Laursen, E. M.: The total sediment load of streams. Journal of the Hydraulics Division HY 1, 1958.
— Observations on the nature of scour. Proc. of the Fifth Hydraulics Conference. Bull. 34. 1953.
Laursen, E. M.—Carstens, M. R.—Ismail, M. H.: Discussion of turbulent transfer mechanism and suspended sediment in closed channels. Proceedings ASCE 78. Separate No. D-56.
Laursen, E. M.—Matthews, G. H.—Blench, T.: Discussion of regime theory for self-formed sediment bearing channels. Proceedings ASCE 78, 1951.
Lazzari, F.: Determinazione esperimentale del coefficiente di resistenza di ellissoidi di rotazione mediante caduta libera in acqua. XI. Convegno di Idraulica, Genova 1968.
Leopold, L. B.—Langbein, B. L.: The concept of entropy in landscape evolution. U.S. Department of the interior U.S. Government Printing Office. Washington 1962.
Leopold, L. B.—Maddock, T.: Relation of suspended sediment concentration to channel scour and fill. Proceedings of the Fifth Hydraulics Conference. No. 426. 1952.
Leopold, L. B.—Maddock, Jr., T.: The hydraulic geometry of stream channels and some physiographic implications. U.S. Government Printing Office. Washington 1953.
Leppik, E.: Studium der Geschiebe und Sinkstoffbewegung in Flussläufen unter besonderer Betrachtung derselben in der Narowa. II. Baltischen hydrologischen und hydrometrischen Konferenz. Tallin 1928.

807

— Untersuchungsmethoden der Sinkstoffe und des Geschiebes und deren Vereinheitlichung. Wasserwirtschaft, Nr. 7. 1937.

Levi, I. I.: Dinamika ruslovykh potokov (Stream flow dynamics). Gosenergoizdat, Moscow 1948.

Levin, L.: Nouveau dispositif de dessablement des canaux. Génie civile 1937.

Liggett, J. A.: Mathematical flow determination in open channels. ASCE Mechanics Division EM 4, 1968.

Lindley, E. S.: Regime channels. Proc. Punjab Engineering Congress 7, 1919.

Linsley, R. K.—Kohler, M. A.—Paulhus, J. L. H.: Applied hydrology: New York—Toronto— London 1949.

Liu, Hsin-Kuan: Mechanics of sediment-ripple formation. ASCE Hydraulics Division, HY 2, Paper 1197.

Liu, Hsin-Kuan—Hwang, Shoi-Yan: A discharge formula for flow in straight alluvial channels ASCE in Portland. Oregon, June 1958.

Liu, Hsin-Kuan—Hwang, Shoi-Yan: Discharge formula for straight alluvial channels. ASCE Hydraulics Division, HY 11, 1959.

Lokhtin, V. M.: O mekhanizme rechnogo rusla (On the mechanismof river beds). Kazan 1897.

Lopatin, G. V.: Nanocy rek SSSR (obrazovanie i perevoz) (River sediments in the USSR. Origin and transport). Geografgiz. Moscow 1952.

Losievsky, A. I.—Letnev, S. V.: Ruslovye laboratornye issledovaniya (Laboratory studies on rivers). Rechizdat. Moscow 1953.

Lovera, F.—Kennedy, J. F.: Friction-factors for flat-bed flows in sand channels. ASCE Hydraulics Division, HY 4, July 1969.

Ludin, A.: Über den Begriff des bettbildenden Wasserstandes. Die Wasserwirtschaft, Nf. 36, 1932.

Lugn, A. L.: Methods of collecting sediment samples from the Mississippi river. University of Iowa Studies in Natural History XI/8.

Maddock, T.: Discussion on "Similitude theory applied to correlation on flume sediment transport data" by D. I. H. Barr and J. G. Herbertson. Water Resources Reserach, Vol. 4, No. 5, October 1968.

Márton, J.—V. Nagy, I.: Vízöblítéses földmunkák (Earthwork by hydraulic methods). OVF Budapest 1966.

Martos, F.: Hidraulikus széntermelés (Hydraulic coal mining). Műszaki Élet, 18, 1956.

Marzolo, F.: Sull'affinamento dei materiali di trasporto. Atti del V Convegno Italiano di Idraulica. Torino 1957.

Maurer, Gy.: Vízöblítéses földmunkák (Earthwork by hydraulic methods). Közlekedésügyi Min. Budapest 1953.

Mavis, F. T.—Chitty, Ho—Yung-Cheng, Tu: The transportation of detritus by flowing water, I. University of Iowa Studies, No. 294. Bull. 5. 1935.

Mavis, F. T.—Liu, T. Y.—Soucek, E.: The transportation of detritus by flowing water, II. University of Iowa Studies, Bull. 11.

Mayrhoffer, A.: Normalprofil und Ausgleichsgefälle geschiebführender Flüsse. Österreichische Wasserwirtschaft, 7—8. 1964.

McDowell, J. C.—Stephens, J. C.—Stewart, E. H.: Radiocarbon chronology of the Florida Everglades Peat. Soil Science Society of America, Proceedings. Vol. 33. N. 5. 1969.

McDowell, L. L.: Sediment movement as defined by radioactive tracers: A preliminary report. Symposium 2. Sediment in streams. Paper No. 60.

McDowell, L. L.—Bolton, G. C.—Ryan. M. E.: Sediment production from a Lafayette county Mississippi gully. Mississippi Water Resources Conference. Jackson, Mississippi 1967.

McHenry, J. R.: Field test of an X-ray sediment-concentration gage. ASCE Hydraulics Division HY 2, 1968.

— Performance of nuclear-sediment concentration gauges. International Atomic Energy Agency, Vienna 1967.

– Measurement of sediment density with gamma probes. Symposium 4. Sedimentation in Reservoirs, Paper No. 90. Oxford.

McHenry, J. R.—Coleman, N. L.—Willis, J. C.—Murphree, C. E.—Bolton, G. C.—Sanson, O. W.—Gill, A. C.: Performance of nuclear sediment-concentration gauges. In "Isotopes in Hydrology". International Atomic Energy Agency, Vienna 1967, pp. 207—225.

McHenry, J. R.—Gill, A. C.: Consolidation of sediments in a small reservoir in North Mississippi measured *in situ* with a Gamma probe. Proc. Mississippi Water Resources Conference 1969.

McHenry, J. R.—Hawks, P. H.: Sedimentation survey of lake Guayabel, Puerto Rico. Mississippi Water Resources Conference. Jackson. Mississippi 1966.

McNown, J. S.—Pin-Nam Lin: Sediment concentration and fall velocity. Second Midwestern Conference on Fluid Mechanics. The Ohio State University 1952.

McNown, J. S.—Malaika, J.: Effect of particle shape on settling velocity at low Reynolds-numbers. TAGU 31/1, 1950.

Measurement and analysis of sediment loads in streams. Report. No. 7. A study of new methods for size analysis of suspended sediment samples. Iowa City, Iowa 1943.

– Report No. 9. Density of sediments deposited in reservoirs. Iowa City, Iowa 1943.

– Report No. 10. Accuracy of sediment size analyses made by the bottom withdrawal tube method. Minneaplis 1953.

– Report No. 11. The development and calibration of the visual-accumulation tube. Minneapolis 1957.

Melentiev, V. A.: Variations in the solid discharge along the length of the sedimentation zone during silting of reservoirs. XIVth Congress of the IAHR, Vol. 5. Paper 103, Paris 1971, pp. 9—12.

Meyer-Peter, E.—Favre: Neuere Versuchsresultate über den Geschiebetrieb. SBZ, Zürich 1934.

Mezősi, J.—Donáth, É.: A Tisza és a Maros oldott és lebegtetett anyagának vizsgálata (Investigation of dissolved and suspended materials in the Tisza and Maros rivers). Hidrológiai Közlöny, 34, No. 3—4, 1954.

Mikhailova, N. A.: Perenos tverdykh chastits turbulentnymi potokami vody (Transport of solid particles in turbulent flow). Gidrometeorologicheskoe Izd. Leningrad 1966.

Miller, C. R.: Advances in sedimentation relevant to watershed problems. ASCE Hydraulics Division Vol. 8, No. 1. 1965.

Miller, C. R.—Bowie, A. J.: Sediment sampling instrumentation and techniques. The Transactions of the ASAE (vol. 8. no. 2.) Saint Joseph, Michigan 1965.

Miloradov, M.: Some elements for calculating bed deformation in self-cutting alluvial water courses. Saopštenja Instituta za Vodoprivedu "Jaroslav Černi", Vol. XIV. No. 40.

– River bed deformation calculations based on field investigations. Symposium on Current Problems in River Training and Sediment Movement, 2/b. Budapest 1968.

Miloradov, V.: Investigations into the suspended sediments of the Danube and its tributaries. Symposium on Current Problems in River Training and Sediment Movement, 3. Budapest, 1968.

– Some results of measuring sedimentation on the river Velika Morava. Saopštenia instituta za Vodoprivedu "Jaroslav Černi", Vol. XIV. No. 40.

Molesworth—Yenidunia: Irrigation practice in Egypt. 1922.

Montefusco, L.: Sull'inizio del moto di sedimenti incoerenti eterogenei. Ist. di Idraulica dell'Università di Bologna, 1969.

Mosonyi, E.—Kovács, Gy.: Kismintatörvények a nehézségi és súrlódó erő együttes figyelembevételére (Model laws for taking gravity and friction forces simultaneously into consideration). Hidrológiai Közlöny, No. 7—8. 1952.

Muir, T. C.: Sampling and analysis of coarse riverbed sediments. Proc. Mississippi. Water Resources Conference 1969.

Murphree, C. E.—Bolton, G. C.—McHenry, J. R.—Parson, D. A.: Field test of an X-ray sediment concentration gage. Proc. ASCE, Hydraulics Division, HY 2, 1968. pp. 515—528.

809

Mühlhofer, L.: Untersuchungen über die Schwebestoff- und Geschiebeführung des Inn nächst Kirchbichl. Die Wasserwirtschaft Nr. 1—6, 1933.

Neil, C. R.: Stability of course bed-material in open channel flow. Edmonton 1967.

Nelson, M. E.—Benedict, P. C.: Study of methods used in measurement and analysis of sediment loads in streams. American Society of Civil Engineers. Annual Convention Spokane, Washington 1946.

Németh, E.: Hidrológia és hidrometria (Hydrology and hydrometry). Budapest 1954.

— Hidromechanika (Hydromechanics). Budapest 1954.

— Invariáns számok szerepe a kismintakísérleteknél (The role of invariant numbers in model experiments). MTA Osztályközlemények, X. 3—4. 1953.

Nesper: Ergebnisse der Geschiebemessungen. Schweizerische Bauzeitung No. 12. 1937.

Nikuradze, A: Untersuchungen über die Geschwindigkeitsverteilung in turbulenten Strömungen. VDI-Verlag 1926.

Ning Chien: The present status of research on sediment transport. ASCE Hydraulic Division Vol. 121. 1956.

Nordin, C. F.: Study of channel erosion and sediment transport. ASCE, Hydraulics Division HY 4, July 1969.

Nordin, C. F.—Algert, H. J.: Spectral analysis of sand waves. Proc. ASCE, Hydraulics, Division HY 5, 1966. pp. 95—114.

Nordin, C. F.—Dempster, G. R.: Vertical distribution of velocity and suspended sediment Middle Rio Grande New Mexico. U.S. Government Printing Office, Washington 1963.

Nordin, C. F.—Richardson, E. V.: Statistical description of sand wave from streambed profiles. U.S. Geol. Survey, Ft. Collins, Colo.

Novák, P.: Bed-load meters-development of a new type and determination of their efficiency with the aid of scale models. IAHR Seventh General Meeting. Lisboa 1957.

— Erfahrungen über Anwendung der Ähnlichkeitsgesetze im wasserbaulichen Versuchswesen. Wissenschaftliche Zeitschrift der Techn. Universität, Dresden 1963.

O'Brien, M. P.: Review of theory of turbulent flow and its relation to sediment transportation. AGU 1933.

O'Loughlin, E. M.: Resistance to flow over boundaries with small roughness concentrations. Ph. D. Dissertation, University of Iowa 1965.

O'Loughlin, E. M.—Shastri Annambhotta, V. S.: Flow phenomena near rough boundaries. Journal of Hydraulic Research.

Orth, F.: Die Verlandung von Staubecken. Die Bautechnik H. 26. 1934.

Owens, J. S.: The settlement and transport of sand in water. Engineering 1912.

Pákozdy, V.—Ungár, T.—Váradi, P.: A Maros homokjának ásvány-kőzettani vizsgálata (Mineralogical-petrographic study of Maros river sand). Hidrológiai Közlöny, No. 3—4. 1949.

Pardé, M.: Cours de potamologie. École des Ingenieurs Hydrauliciens. Grenoble. Vol. 2. 1943.

Parson, D. A.: Sedimentation laboratory expansion. The ole Miss Engineer, January 1970.

— Vegetative control of streambank erosion. Miscellaneous publication 970, USDA.

Pasteiner, D.: A Tisza folyó lebegő hordaléka (Suspended sediment of the Tisza river). Vízrajzi Évkönyv, XIII.

Pásztor, D.—Szivák, A.: A hidraulikus szállítás (Hydraulic material transport). Vízügyi Közlemények, No. 4. 1961.

Pedroli, R.: Trasporto di materiale solido in canali a fondo fisso e liscio. Communicazione dell'Ufficio federale dell'economia delle acque. No. 43. 1963.

Penck, A.: Die Donau. Wien 1890.

Per Bruun: Engineering aspects of sediment transport. Reviews in Eng. Geology, I. 1962.

Pernecker, L.—Vollmers, H.: Neue Betrachtungsmöglichkeiten des Feststofftransportes in offenen Gerinnen. Die Wasserwirtschaft, 55. Jahrgang, Heft 12, Dezember 1965.

Piest, R. F.: The role of the large strom as a sediment contributor. Miscellaneous publication 970, USDA.

Pólya, G.: Zur Kinematik der Geschiebebewegung. 1937.

Polyakov, B. V.: Metodika issledovanii rechnykh nanosov i perekatov (Methodology for studying river sediment and sand bars). Leningrad, Moscow 1940.

Popov, I. V.: Deformatsii rechnykh rusel i gidrotekhnicheskoe stroitel'stvo (gidrologomorfologicheskaya teoriya ruslovogo protsessa i ee primenenie). (Deterioration of river beds and hydrotechnical construction (Hydrologo-morphologic theory of channel processes and their application)). Gidrometeoizdat, Leningrad 1965.

Posey, C. J.: Routing of floods through reservoirs with especial attention to determination of spilway capacity for small reservoirs. Iowa 1938.

— Anchorages for reinforcing bars. Associated State Engineering Societies, Iowa 1933.

Posey, C. J.—Hsing, P. S.: Hydraulic jump in trapezoidal channels. Iowa 1938.

Prandtl, L.: Neue Ergebnisse der Turbulenzforschung. Zeitschrift des VDI, No. 4. 1933.

Proceedings of the Federal Inter-Agency Sedimentation Conference. Washington, January 1948.

Raichlen, F.: Some turbulence measurement in water. ASCE Mechanics Division, EM 2, 1967.

Rákóczi, L.: A Balaton iszap- és homokvándorlásának vizsgálata jelzőanyagokkal (Tracer study on silt drift and sand drift in Lake Balaton). VITUKI Project No. 8.01.03.03.01.

— A görgetett hordalék mozgásának vizsgálata radioaktív izotópok segítségével (Radioactive isotopes used for studying bed load transport). Hidrológiai Közlöny, 1961, No. 6.

— Hordalékkeverékek mozgásának vizsgálata luminescens nyomjelzők segítségével (Studies on the movement of mixed-size bed load with the help of luminescent tracers). VITUKI Beszámoló. 1965.

— Újabb irányzatok a hordalékmozgás laboratóriumi kutatásában (Recent trends in the laboratory study of sediment transport). Hidrológiai Közlöny, No. 12. 1967.

— Experiments for the quantitative determination of bed-load transport by tracers. Symposium, Budapest 1968.

Raudkivi, A. J.: Study of sediment ripple formation. ASCE Hydraulics Division, HY 6, 1963.

Razmukhina, K. V.: Primenenie formuly transportiruyushchei sposobnosti potoka dlya rascheta godovogo stoka vzveshennykh nanosov (Computing the annual suspended-sediment transport based on transporting capacity). Trudy, Vypusk 175. Glavnoe Upravlenie gidrometeorologicheskoi sluzhby pri Sovete Ministrov SSSR, Gidrometeoizdat, Leningrad 1969.

Rehbock, Th.: Bettausbildung. Abfluss und Geschiebebewegung bei Wasserläufen. Zeitschrift der Deutschen Geologischen Gesellschaft, 81. 1929.

Reitz, W.: Über Geschiebebewegung. Wasserwirtschaft und Technik. Nr. 28—30. 1936.

Rémy-Berzencovich, E.: Analyse des Feststofftriebes in Flussläufen. Die Wasserwirtschaft, 1959

— Eine neue Methode zur Ermittlung des Feststofftriebes in Flussläufen. Österreichische Wasserwirtschaft, 1959/3.

— Feststofftrieb und Hydraulik: Eine Klarstellung der Zusammenhänge mit Hilfe der mathematischen Statistik. Österreichische Wasserwirtschaft, 13. Jg. Heft 1. Wien 1961.

Richardson, E. G.: Suspension of solids in a turbulent stream. Proc. Royal Society of London 162. 1937.

Roer, G. N.: Gidravlicheskie raschety napornogo gidrotransporta grunta (Hydraulic calculations of slurry transport in closed pipes). Moscow 1952.

Rohringer, A.: Beitrag zur Frage: Studium der hydrotechnischen Fragen mit Hilfe von Laboratoriumsversuchen an Modellen in verkleinertem Massstab. — I. Abteilung, 3. Mitteilung XV. Internationaler Schiffahrtskongress, Venedig 1931.

— Modellversuche über die Regulierung des Bogyiszlóer Donaudurchstiches in Ungarn. Deutsche Wasserwirtschaft, Nr. 8. 1930.

— Regulierung eingedeichter freifliessender Flüsse und Ströme. XVI. Internationaler Schiffahrtskongress, Brüssel 1935.

— Töltésezett folyók szabályozása (Regulation of rivers between levees). Vízügyi Közlemények, No. I. 1936.

811

Rossetti, M.: Indagini e studi sul trasporto solido. Annali Idrologici dell'Ufficio Idrografico del Po, Parma 1956.

Rossinsky, K. I.: (editor) Dvizhenie nanosov v otkrytykh potokakh (Sediment transport in open channels). Institut Vodnykh Problem. Izd. "Nauka", Moscow 1970.

Rossinsky, K. I.—Kuzmin, I. A.: Rechnoe ruslo (River bed). Gidrologicheskie osnovy rechnoi gidrotekhniki (Hydrologic foundations of fluvial engineering). Izd. AN SSSR, Moscow 1950.

Rouse, H.: An analysis of sediment transportation in the light of fluid turbulence. U.S. Department of Agriculture, Soil Conservation Service, T.P. 25. 1939.

— Experiments on the mechanics of sediment suspension. Proc. 5th International Congress of Applied Mechanics 1939.

— Modern conceptions of the mechanics of fluid turbulence. Proceedings ASCE 1937.

— Evaluation of boundary roughness. Second Hydraulics Conference. Bull. 27. University of Iowa Studies in Engineering 1934.

— Suspension of sediment in upward flow. Reprinted from University of Iowa Studies in Engineering, Bull. 26. 1939—40.

Rubatta, A.: Modelli fluviali independenti dal numero di Froude. VIII. Convegno di Idraulica. Pisa 1963.

— Inizio del modellamento indotto dal moto ondoso su fondo incoerente a grossa granulometria. IX. Convegno di Idraulica. Trieste 1965.

Rubey, W. W.: Settling velocities of gravel, sand and silt. Amer. Jour. Sci. 25. 1933.

— The force required to move particles on a stream bed. USA Geological Survey. Professional Paper 189-E.

Rzhanitsyn, N. A.: Modelirovanie estestvennykh ruslovykh potokov na razmyvaemykh modelyakh (Modelling flow in natural channels by movable-bed models). Sbornik "Ruslovye protsessy", Izd. AN SSSR, Moscow 1958.

Sabathiel, J.: A hordalékviszonyok hatása a folyószabályozási módszerek kialakításánál (The impact of sediment conditions on the development of river regulation methods). Symposium Budapest 1968.

Salamin, P.: Mezőgazdasági vízgazdálkodás (Water management in agriculture). Tankönyvkiadó, Budapest 1966.

Sanoyan, V. G.: Theoretical determination of the sediment transporting capacity of watercourses . . ., Symposium on Current Problems in River training and sediment movement. 3. Budapest 1968.

Sárosi, L.— Kaposi, L.: Kvázi-stacionárius áramlásnál a fenékhordalék mozgásának vizsgálata sebességingadozások mérése alapján (Study on bed load transport in quasi-steady flow by measuring velocity fluctuations). Symposium, Budapest 1968.

Sauermann, H. B.: Hydraulic model study of St. Lucia Estuary. Transactions of the S. A. Inst. of Civil Eng. Vol. 8. No. 6. 1967.

Sayre, W. W.: Dispersion of silt particles in open channel flow. ASCE Hydraulics Division HY 3. 1969.

Sayre, W. W.—Albertson, L.: Roughness spacing in rigid open channels. ASCE Trans. Vol. 128. 1963.

Sayre, W. W.— Guy, H. P.— Chamberlain, A. R.: Uptake and transport of radionucleides by streams sediments. U.S. Government Printing Office, Washington 1963.

Scarpi, G.: Influenza della forma del materiale di fondo sull'inizio del movimento. L'Energia Elettrica, No. 4. Vol. XLV, 1968.

Schaffernak, F.: Der Einfluss der Koppelung von Flusssystemen auf das Geschieberegime. Die Wasserwirtschaft, Nr. 18—19. 1930.

— Hydrographie. Wien 1935.

— Neue Grundlagen für die Berechnung der Geschiebeführung in Flussläufen. Leipzig— Wien 1922.

Schlag, A.: Les partes de charge en conduites transportant des materiaux solides. CEDEBEAU 111. 1960.

Schmidt, W.: Der Massenaustausch in freier Luft und verwandte Erscheinungen. Probleme der Kosm. Phis., Hamburg VI.. 1925.

Schober, T.: Versuche über den Reibungswiderstand zwischen dem Wasser und benetztem Umfange. Dresden 1916.

Schoklitsch, A.: Der Geschiebebetrieb und die Geschiebefracht. Wasserkraft und Wasserwirtschaft, No. 4. 1934.
— Der Wasserbau. Wien 1930.
— Geschiebebewegung in Flüssen und an Stauwerken. Wien 1926.
— Über die Verkleinerung der Geschiebe der Flussläufen. Sitzungsbericht Akad. Wiss. Wien 1933.
— Über die Verlandung von Stauräumen. Wasserkraft und Wasserwirtschaft, 20. 1937.
— Über Schleppkraft und Geschiebebewegung. Leipzig— Berlin 1914.

Schields, A.: Anwendung der Ähnlichkeitsmechanik und der Turbulenzforschung auf die Geschiebebewegung. Mitteilungen der preussischen Versuchsanstalt für Wasserbau und Schiffbau. H. 26. Berlin 1936.

Sedimentation Manual Committee on Sedimentation, Sediment transportation mechanics: Introduction and properties of sediment. ASCE Hydraulics Division HY 4, July 1962.
— Density currents. ASCE Hydraulics Division, HY5, September 1963.
— Suspension of sediment. ASCE Hydraulics Division HY 5, September 1963.
— Wind erosion and transportation. ASCE Hydraulics Division HY 5, March 1965.
— Nature of sedimentation problems. ASCE Hydraulics Division HY 2, March 1965.
— Erosion of sediment. ASCE Hydraulics Division HY 4, July 1962.
— Initiation of motion. ASCE Hydraulics Division HY 2, March 1966.

Seiichi Sato— Hideo Kikkawa— Kazuo Ashida: Research on the bed-load transportation (I.) Journal of Research of PWRI, Vol. 2. Tokyo 1958.

Sensidoni, F.: Rilievi e determinazioni sul trasporto solido del fiume Reno a Malalbergo. Annali dei Lavori Pubblici, 1938, n. 1.

Shamov, G. I.: Zailenie vodokhranilishch (Silting in reservoirs). Leningrad— Moscow 1939.
— Stok vzveshennykh nanosov rek SSSR (Sediment load of rivers in the Soviet Union). Trudy GGI 20. (47), Leningrad 1949.

Shulits, S.: Rational equation of river-bed profile. Transactions American Geophysical Union 1941.

Shulits, S.— Corfitz n, W. E.: Bed-load transportation and the stable-channel problem. Transactions of the American Geophysical Union 1937.

Shulits, S.— Hill, R. D.: Bed-load formulas. USDA, December 1968.

Simons, D. B.— Albertson, M. L.: Uniform water conveyance channel in alluvial material. ASCE Transactions, Vol. 128. 1963.

Simons, D. B.— Vice, P. B.: Elements of open channel flow and sediment transport. U.S. Geological Survey, Fort Collins.

Siniscalchi, C.: Alcune caratteristiche del movimento di materiale solido nel moto ondoso e nel moto uniforme. IX Convegno di Idraulica e Costruzioni Idrauliche, Trieste, Maggio 1965.

Sokolov, C. Ya.: Otstoinye basseiny dlya irrigatsii i gidrostantsii (Sediment retention for irrigation and power development). Moscow 1945.

Somogyi, S.: Adatok a folyómedrek szakaszjellegének és hordalékszállításának összefüggéséhez (Contribution to the relationship between character and sediment transport of alluvial channels). Symposium Budapest 1968.

Soucek, E.— Mavis, F. T.— Howe, H. E.: Satro weir investigations furnish discharge coefficients. Engineering News-Record Nov. 12. 1936.

Spraberry, J. A.— Bowie, A. J.: Predicting sediment yields from complex watersheds. Trans. of the ASAE, Vol. 12. No. 24. 1967.

Stafford, C. H.: Valley sedimentation in North-central Mississippi. Mississipppi Water Resources Conference, Jackson, Mississippi 1968.
Starosolszky, Ö.: The influence of sedimentation and silting in watercourses. Symposium Budapest 1968.
Stelczer, K.: A folyami hordalék kopása (Wearing of river sediment). Vízügyi Közlemények, No. 2. 1967.
— Investigation of bed-load movement. Symposium, Budapest 1968.
— Der Geschiebeabschliff. Wasserwirtschaft No. 9. 1968.
— La determination de l'usure de débit solide charrié dans des cours d'eau naturels. IUGG Symposium on River Morphology, Bern 1967.
— Problems relating to bed-morphology with special regard to permissible velocities. XI. Kongr. IAHR. Leningrad 1965.
— Report on the research project "Study into bed-load movement using radioactive tracers". VITUKI Budapest 1969.
Stepanova, A. I.: Raspredelenie srednei mutnosti rek po territorii poluostrova Kamchatki i svyaz' ee s prirodnymi faktoram (Distribution of mean sediment concentration of the rivers of the Kamchatka peninsula related to natural factors). Trudy, Vypusk 175. Glavnoe Upravlenie gidrometeorologicheskoi sluzhby pri Sovete Ministrov SSSR, Gidrometeoizdat. Leningrad 1969.
Sternberg, H.: Untersuchungen über Längen- und Querprofile geschiebführender Flüsse. Zeitschrift für Bauwesen 1875.
Straub, L. G.: Effect of channel-contraction works upon regiment of movable bed streams. TAGU 1934.
— Hydraulic and sedimentary characteristics of rivers. TAGU Thirteens Annual Meeting 1932.
— Transportation of sediment in suspension. Civil Engineering, May 1936.
— Report of the Committee on Dynamics of Streams, 1934—35. American Geophysical Union, Sixteenth Annual Meeting 1935.
Straub, L. G.—Anderson, A. G.: Experiments on selfaerated flow in open channels. ASCE Hydraulics Division HY 7, December 1958.
Subcommittee on Sedimentation, ICWR: A summary of the work of the Federal Inter-Agency Sedimentation Project. Jackson, Mississippi 1963.
Supino, G.: Le reti idrauliche. Seconda edizione, Casa Editrice Prof. R. Pátron, Bologna 1965.
Sutherland, A. J.: Entrainment of fine sediments by turbulent flows. California Institute of Technology Pasadena, No. KH-R-13. 1966.
— Proposed mechanism for sediment entrainment by turbulent flows. Journal of Geophysical Research, Vol. 72. No. 24. 1967.
Szesztay, K.: A keszthelyi öböl feliszapolódása (Silting in the Bay of Keszthely). VITUKI 1961.
— A Balaton medrének feltöltődéséről (On the silting up of Lake Balaton). Hidrológiai Tájékoztató 1961.
Szilágyi, Gy.: Mozgó medrű folyók modellkísérlete (Model experiments on movable-bed rivers). MTA Műszaki Tud. Osztály Közleményei, No. 3—4. 1953.
Szolgay, J.—Náther, B.: Niektoré poznatky zo studia splaveninového rezimu Dunaja (Some data on the suspended-sediment regime of the Danube). Vodohospodársky casopis. Rocnik II.c.1. Bratislava 1954.
Szűcs, E.: A hasonlóságelmélet alapjai (The fundamentals of similarity theory). Műszaki Könyvkiadó, Budapest 1967.
— A hasonlóságelmélet alkalmazása. Modellkísérletek (Applications of similarity theory. Scale models). Műszaki Könyvkiadó, Budapest 1969.
— Dialógusok a műszaki tudományokról (Dialogues on technical sciences). Műszaki Könyvkiadó, Budapest 1971.
— Ähnlichkeitstheorie. Bertelsman Verlag—Ung. Akademie Verlag, Budapest 1972.
Takáts, T.: A Duna lebegő hordaléka Budapesten (Suspended sediment in the Danube at Budapest). Hidrológiai Közlöny, No. X. 1930.

Taylor, E.—Mckenzie: Punjab practice in silt observations. Punjab Irrigation Research Institute, Lahore Research Publication II/15. 1936.

Taylor, G. I.: Statistical theory of turbulence. Proc. of Royal Society of London, 151A, 1935.

Tester, A. C.: The measurement of the shapes of rock particles. Jour. of Sedimentary Petrology I/1.

Tőry, K.: A Duna és szabályozása (The Danube and its regulation). Budapest 1953.

— A Felső-Duna mederemelkedése (Bed aggradation over the Upper Danube). Vízgazdálkodás No. 1. 1961.

Twenhofel, H.: Treatise on sedimentation. 1926.

United Nations: The sediment problem. Bangkok 1953.

Ursic, S. J.: Sediment yields from small watershed under various landuses and forest covers. Miscellaneous publication 970. USDA.

U.S.A. Waterway Experiment Station: Studies of river bed materials and their movement etc. Paper 17. January 1935.

Valembois, J.: Étude sur modèle du transport littoral, conditions de similitude. Extrat de "Proceedings of the Seventh Conference on Coastal Engineering". La Haye, Aout 1960.

Vanoni, V. A.: Transportation of suspended sediment by water. Trans. ASCE 111, 1946.

— Review of research activities in sedimentation. VIII. Convegno di Idraulica. Pisa 1963.

— Some effects of suspended sediment of flow characteristics. Proceedings of the Fifth Hydraulics Conference, Bull. 34. Iowa 1953.

√ Vanoni, V. A.—Brooks, N. H.: Laboratory studies of the roughness and suspended load of alluvial streams. M.R.D. Sediment Series No. 11. 1957.

√ Vanoni, V. A.—Hwang, Li-San: Relations between bed forms and friction in streams. ASCE Hydraulics Division HY 3. 1967.

Vanoni, V. A.—Nomicos, G. W.: Resistance properties of sediment-laden streams. ASCE Trans. Vol. 125. 1960.

Velikanov, M. A.: Perenos vzveshennykh nanosov turbulentnym potokom (Transport of suspended sediment in turbulent flow). Izd. AN SSSR, OTN No. 3. 1944.

— Dvizhenie nanosov (Movement of sediment). Izd. Minrechflota SSSR, Moscow 1948.

— Dinamika ruslovykh potokov. I. Struktura potoka (1954). II. Nanosy i ruslo (1955). (Stream flow dynamics. I. Flow structure [1954]. II. Sediment and rivers [1955]). Gostekhizdat. Moscow.

— Tri tipa dvizheniya rechnykh nanosov (Three types of river sediment movement). Izd. AN SSSR OTN. Energiy i Transport, No. 1. 1963.

VITUKI (Research Institute for Water Resources Development, Budapest): A fajlagos görgetett hordalékszállítás meghatározása a Meyer-Peter-féle egyenlet alapján (Estimation of the specific rate of bed load transport by the Meyer-Peter formula). Budapest.

— A görgetett hordalékmérés és feldolgozás alkalmazott módszereinek és műszereinek leírása és azok kritikai jellemzése (Description and critical evaluation of the methods and instruments used in bed load observations and in processing the data obtained). Budapest 1966.

— A lebegtetett hordalék-mintavételekre szolgáló műszerek leírása és az ezekkel szerzett tapasztalatok (Description of suspended-sediment samplers and the experiences gained therewith). Budapest 1966.

— A hordalékszállítás alapjelenségeinek és összefüggéseinek meghatározása (Determination of the fundamental phenomena and laws in sediment transport). 8.01.03.02.06./1965.

— Hidromechanizációs anyagszállítás és földmunkaszállítás fejlesztése (Development of hydraulic material and soil transport). Tsz.: 7782/6-207. 1968.

— Módszertani kutatások a hordalékszállítás alapjelenségeinek és összefüggéseinek meghatározására (Methodological research for determining the fundamental phenomena and relations in sediment transport). Tsz.: 8.01.03.02.04/a. 1966.

V. Nagy, I.: A lebegtetett hordalék eloszlása turbulens vízmozgásban (Distribution of suspended-sediment materials in turbulent flow). 5.2. VITUKI.

— Öntözőcsatornák hordalékszállítása (Sediment transport in irrigation canals). Hidrológiai Közlöny, No. 5. 1961.
— The applicability of Frankl's equations for the investigation of suspended sediments. IAHR Eleventh Congress. Leningrad 1965.
— The theory of suspended sediment transportation. VIII. Convegno di Idraulica, Pisa 1963.
— Über einige Fragen der Diffusionstheorie der Geschiebebewegungen. Hidraulikai Konferencia, Budapest 1960.
V. Nagy, I.— Karádi, G.: A görgetett hordalék mozgásával kapcsolatos vizsgálatok újabb eredményei (Results of recent investigations into bed load movement). Hidrológiai Közlöny, No. 3. 1960.
de Vries, M.: Transients in bed-load transport (basic considerations). Hydraulics Laboratory Delft. August 1959.
White, C. M.: The influence of transported solids upon rivers. Section of Potamology International Union of Geodesy and Geophysics, Washington D.C. 1939.
Willi, W.: Zur Frage der Sohlenerosionen bei grossen Gefällen. Dissertation ETH Zürich 1965.
Willis, J. C.: Comments on "Similitude theory applied to correlation of flume sediment transport data" by D. I. H. Barr and J. G. Herbertson. Water Resources Research, Vol. 5. No. 4. 1969.
— Discussion: "Sediment transportation mechanics: Initiation of motion". ASCE Hydraulics Division HY 1, January 1967.
Willis, J. C.—Bowie, A. J.—Parsons, D. A.: Sediment transport rates for Coles creek and Buffalo river near Natchez, Mississippi. Progress Report Proc. Mississippi Water Resources Conference 1969.
Wittmann, H.: Der Einfluss der Korrektion des Rheins zwischen Basel und Mannheim auf die Geschiebebewegung des Rheins. Deutsche Wasserwirtschaft 10, 11, 12, 1927.
Wittmann, H.— Böss, P.: Wasser und Geschiebebewegung in gekrümmten Flussstrecken. Berlin 1938.
Wolfsbauer: Die chemische Zusammensetzung der Donau vor Wien im Jahre 1878. Sitzungsbericht der Akademie der Wissenschaften, II. Wien 1878.
Woods, F. W.: Normal data of design for Kennedy channels. Punjab, July 1917.
Yalin, M. S.: Similarity in sediment transport by currents. Hydraulics research, Paper No. 6. Her Majesty's Stationery Office, London 1965.
— A theoretical study of stable alluvial systems. Golden Jubilee Symposium. Central Water and Power Research Station. Poona 1966.
— Über die Naturähnlichkeit der Geschiebebewegungen bei Modellversuchen. Die Bautechnik 36. Jahrgang H. 3. 1959. März
Yufin, A. P.: Utochnenie metodiki rascheta gidrotransporta odnorodnogo grunta po stal'nym gorizontal'nym trubam (Improved methods of calculating transport of uniform material in horizontal steel pipes). Sbornik "Gidravlika sooruzhenii i dinamika rechnyk rusel". AN SSSR, Moscow 1959.
— Dvizhenie neodnorodnoi zhidkosti po gorizontal'nym stal'nym nezailennym trubam (Movement of non-uniform fluid in horizontal steel pipes free of deposits). Izv. Otd. Tekhn. Nauk AN SSSR 8, 1949.
Zamarin, E.: Transportnaya sposobnost' otkrytykh rusel (Transporting capacity of open channels). Moscow 1948.
Zeller, J.: Einführung in den Sedimenttransport offener Gerinne. Schweizerische Bauzeitung, 81. Jahrgang, 34, 35, 36. Heft. 1963.
— Die "Regime-Theorie", eine Methode zur Bemessung stabiler Flussgerinne. Schweizerische Bauzeitung, 83. Jahrgang, Heft 5. 1965.
Zheleznyakov, G. V.: Relation deficit of mean velocity of unstable river flow, kinematic effect in river beds with flood plains. IAHR, XI. Congress. Vol. III. Leningrad 1965.
Zhukovsky, N. E.: O snezhnykh zanosakh i zailenii rek (On snow drifts and river silting). Sobr. Soch. tom 3, Gostekhnizdat 1949.

AUTHOR INDEX

819

820

824

stopper bottle 141
storage capacity 593
— volume 593—594
stratification of deposits 583
surface current density 354
surface tension 124
suspended sediment 34, 346—481
— — concentration, *see* sediment concentration
— — transport 346—481
suspension of sediment 103
symmetrical tensor 430
symptomatic relations 109

tailwater scouring 598
"topset deposit" 582
tracers 128, 133—136
artificial — 136
luminescent — 134—135
magnetic — 138
radibactive — 135—138
tractive force 80, 96, 106, 137, 160, 367, 610, 673
average — — 81
resultant — — 168
triaxial dimensions 38, 40
turbulent mixing 103
— sediment-transport theory 103, 366—384

uniformity coefficient 44
USDA Sediment Laboratory, Oxford 140, 142

USWES, US Water Experiment Station 85

variable critical velocities 211
law of — — — 211—242, 659
variable tractive forces
theory of — — — 175
theory of critical — — — 178, 186
velocity coefficient "c" 378, 609
— distribution 604—609
mean — 545—547
"verification" 675
virtual bed load velocity 354
—· velocity 337—338
viscosity 438
VNIIG, Research Institute for Hydrotechnique, Leningrad 131
volumetric concentration 350
VITUKI, Research Institute for Water Resources Development, Budapest 329, 336, 468

wash load 32, 35, 652
water sampler, automatic 142
— sampling 104, 139—140
— temperature 169—170, 187, 194, 239
wearing of bed load 328—345 (*see also* abrasion)
weathering 328
Weber number 110

Young's modulus 124